A NEW EDITION OF

THE PULITZER

PRIZE PLAYS

EDITED BY Kathryn Coe & William H. Cordell

INTRODUCTION BY William Lyon Phelps

RANDOM HOUSE · NEW YORK · *Publishers*

PRINTED IN THE UNITED STATES OF AMERICA

CONTENTS

CONTENTS

INTRODUCTION

BY WILLIAM LYON PHELPS

Joseph Pulitzer died October 29, 1911. The bequests in his will, their individual variety and common purpose, have probably attracted more widespread attention in America than any bequests since the last testament of Cecil Rhodes.

Several million dollars were left for the School of Journalism at Columbia University, other moneys for resident and traveling fellowships; then came the list of annual prizes—the best newspaper editorial, the best example of a reporter's work, the best American novel, the best book of the year on United States history, the best American biography; and finally, the matter with which we are concerned in this volume, the best American stage-play.

Here is the original statement in the will:

8th. *Annually, for the original American play, performed in New York, which shall best represent the educational value and power of the stage in raising the standard of good morals, good taste and good manners, One thousand dollars ($1000).*

Under the powers of the Advisory Board of the School of Journalism at Columbia, this provision was in 1928 changed to read as follows:

For the original American play, performed in New York, which shall best represent the educational value and power of the stage, One thousand dollars.

A second change was made in 1934, so that the provision now reads:

For the original American play, performed in New York, which shall best represent the educational value and power of the stage, preferably one dealing with American life, One thousand dollars.

These two changes were salutary; the elision in 1928 of the phrase about good morals, etc. got rid of a metaphysical distinction and a hobble.

The second change in 1934 was equally wise; it simply gave the Committee and then the final Court assistance in deciding between (let us say) two plays that might be of about equal artistic merit.

A Committee of three men has been annually appointed by Columbia; this committee reports in the Spring to the Advisory Board of the School of Journalism, recommending, either unanimously or by a majority vote, the play most deserving of the award. The award of course is made by the Trustees of Columbia University on the recommendation of the Advisory Board of the School of Journalism.

The three members of the committee on the Pulitzer Prize Play who make the original recommendation act only on their own personal responsibility and in their work as jurors have no possible relation with the American Academy, with the National Institute, or with any organization of any kind.

In the year 1934 a slight change was made in the method of the Committee's report; the change being simply to put in writing what has always been desirable. Instead of recommending one play only, the Committee is asked to make out a brief list of plays in the order of its preference. For example, in the year 1935 the Committee handed in a list of four plays, in the order of merit.

If Joseph Pulitzer could return to the scenes of his earthly activity, he would heartily rejoice over the immense success of his plans, and of the fulfillment of his purposes.

The annual excitement over the awards is keen and widespread; and there is more excitement and (often) more bitter controversy over the Prize Play than over any other item.

All this is exactly as it should be; to see so many Americans engaged in hot arguments over what is exclusively a question of Art, is a very good thing indeed. F. P. A. has suggested that a week every year be set apart, called "Finding Fault with Pulitzer Prize Week."

Here follows the list from the first year of the award until now:

1. *Why Marry?* by Jesse Lynch Williams (deceased)—1917-1918.
   No award—1918-1919.
2. *Beyond the Horizon* by Eugene O'Neill—1919-1920.
3. *Miss Lulu Bett* by Zona Gale—1920-1921.
4. *"Anna Christie"* by Eugene O'Neill—1921-1922.
5. *Icebound* by Owen Davis—1922-1923.
6. *Hell-bent fer Heaven* by Hatcher Hughes—1923-1924.
7. *They Knew What They Wanted* by Sidney Howard—1924-1925.
8. *Craig's Wife* by George Kelly—1925-1926.
9. *In Abraham's Bosom* by Paul Green—1926-1927.
10. *Strange Interlude* by Eugene O'Neill—1927-1928.
11. *Street Scene* by Elmer Rice—1928-1929.
12. *The Green Pastures* by Marc Connelly—1929-1930.
13. *Alison's House* by Susan Glaspell—1930-1931.
14. *Of Thee I Sing* by George S. Kaufman and Morrie Ryskind, music and lyrics by George and Ira Gershwin—1931-1932.
15. *Both Your Houses* by Maxwell Anderson—1932-1933.

16. *Men in White* by Sidney Kingsley—1933-1934.

*17. *The Old Maid* by Zoe Akins—1934-1935.

18. *Idiot's Delight* by Robert E. Sherwood—1935-1936.

19. *You Can't Take it With You* by Kaufman and Hart—1936-1937.

20. *Our Town* by Thornton Wilder—1937-1938.

21. *Abe Lincoln in Illinois* by Robert E. Sherwood—1938-1939.

In 1923-24 the choice of the Committee was *The Show-Off* by George Kelly; and in 1933-34 the choice was *Mary of Scotland* by Maxwell Anderson.

No form of art has shown more striking or more rapid development in America than the art of the playwright; at the turn of the century the foremost American dramatist alive or dead was Clyde Fitch; and his place was challenged only by Augustus Thomas.

How significant is the Pulitzer award in the development of contemporary American drama I am not prepared to say; but I think its influence has been and is noticeable. A glance at the chronological order of the prize awards is certainly interesting. In the first year, 1917-1918, the award was given to *Why Marry?* That was surely a creditable performance in its day, but during the last ten years, it would not even have been considered. It is significant also that in the year following the first award, that is to say, 1918-1919, the Committee could find no play worthy of a prize.

In the year 1914, Eugene O'Neill, then twenty-six years old, began to devote himself to play-writing; and in five years, 1919, he won the Pulitzer Prize with *Beyond the Horizon*. I should like to see that drama revived, for while it might seem to its author only tentative, I believe it is theatrically effective. With the advent of Mr. O'Neill, the American stage advanced; and it is worth remembering that the three awards of the Pulitzer Prize to him (in 1921-1922 for *"Anna Christie"* and in 1927-1928 for *Strange Interlude*) were more largely and more enthusiastically ratified by public opinion than almost any others. Perhaps it is worth remarking in passing, however, that the award to *"Anna Christie"* came only after a heated discussion in the committee, and finally only by a majority of two to one instead of by unanimous vote. I was on the committee that year, and I fought vigorously for *"Anna Christie;"* one of the other two members refused to agree and held out to the end; taking as his ground the phrase then in the conditions of award about good morals, good taste and good manners.

Looking over the list of playwrights who have received the award is like

* The publishers of the 1935 Pulitzer Prize Play, *The Old Maid*, refused under any circumstances to grant permission for its inclusion in this volume, despite the request of the author.

watching the development of contemporary American drama—to mention only Eugene O'Neill, Sidney Howard, George Kelly, Elmer Rice, Marc Connelly, George S. Kaufman, Maxwell Anderson, Sidney Kingsley, Thornton Wilder, and Robert E. Sherwood.

These men worthily represent the modern American drama and they are all comparatively young. O'Neill was born in 1888, the late Sidney Howard in 1891, Elmer Rice in 1892, Marc Connelly in 1890, George S. Kaufman in 1889, Maxwell Anderson in 1888, Robert E. Sherwood in 1896, and Thornton Wilder in 1897.

In addition to the plays for which they were awarded the Pulitzer Prize, consider this list: *Ah, Wilderness!, Mourning Becomes Electra, Lazarus Laughed, Days Without End, Emperor Jones, The Hairy Ape,* by Eugene O'Neill; *The Silver Cord, Yellowjack, Dodsworth,* by Sidney Howard; *The Adding Machine, Counsellor-at-Law, The Left Bank,* by Elmer Rice; *The Wisdom Tooth,* by Marc Connelly; the long list of successful plays in which George Kaufman has been co-author; *Elizabeth the Queen, Mary of Scotland, Valley Forge, Saturday's Children, Key Largo, What Price Glory?* (with Laurence Stallings), by Maxwell Anderson; and the plays of Clifford Odets, S. N. Behrman, Lillian Hellman, and Irwin Shaw.

Now, when we remember that every one of the plays I have mentioned was written after the World War, it will be apparent what tremendous strides the American theatre has made in the last twenty years. Since the death of Shakespeare, the greatest period in British drama was from 1895 to 1925; but during the last fifteen years, 1925-1940, it is certain that more really important plays have been written and produced by Americans than by the British. In 1910 such a situation would have been inconceivable.

Furthermore, the growth of the Theatre Guild, the Group Theatre, the Playwrights' Company, and the immense number of Little Theatres is a significant sign of the times.

The last four awards have proved how high the standard of American drama has actually risen; no country in the world today has a more promising future in the theatre than the United States. In 1936 and in 1939 Mr. Robert E. Sherwood won the Pulitzer Prize in Drama with *Idiot's Delight* and *Abe Lincoln in Illinois.* The former is a powerful play which combines first-rate "theatre" with terrific satire against war—not propaganda, not a tract, but a work of art with inescapable implications. One or two critics have suggested that in the case of *Abe Lincoln in Illinois* it was the greatness of the hero rather than that of the playwright that made the piece successful. But such a criticism works both ways; for it may be reasonably suggested that it is more difficult to write a successful play on so familiar a theme than to introduce a new or obscure character. Certain it is that the spectators were so taken by the reality of this biographical drama that they forgot it was "only a play."

Thornton Wilder has been awarded the Pulitzer Prize in two different fields of art—the novel and the drama. In 1928 he received the award for *The Bridge of San Luis Rey;* and exactly ten years later, in 1938, for his play *Our Town.* This is one of the best plays in the history of the Pulitzer Prize, combining faithful realism with an almost overwhelming reach of the imagination; a fourth-dimension play. In 1937 the award was given, with an equally unanimous popular ratification, to Messrs. Hart and Kaufman, for their irresistible comedy *You Can't Take It With You,* one of the most diverting pieces that has ever been seen on the American stage. It fulfills, in the opinion of Dr. Johnson, the chief aim of comedy which is to keep the audience continually merry. I have never seen audiences more happy with laughter. And its humor is original, full of surprises. Enormously funny as it is, it is based on a text in the *New Testament:* "For we brought nothing into this world, and it is certain we can carry nothing out." I Tim.vi:7.

In short, this volume is an amazingly varied and rich collection, and I congratulate its editors and publishers for what I believe is a real service to American drama.

Yale University, January, 1940.

ACKNOWLEDGMENTS

WHY MARRY? by Jesse Lynch Williams
Copyright and published, 1914, 1918, by Charles Scribner's Sons.
Reprinted by permission of Charles Scribner's Sons.

BEYOND THE HORIZON by Eugene O'Neill
Copyright and published, 1920, 1925, by Horace Liveright, Inc., New York.
Reprinted by permission of Random House.

MISS LULU BETT by Zona Gale
Copyright and published, 1921, by D. Appleton and Company.
Reprinted by arrangement with the publishers, D. Appleton-Century Company, New York, N. Y.

"ANNA CHRISTIE" by Eugene O'Neill
Copyright and published, 1922, 1925, by Horace Liveright, Inc., New York.
Reprinted by permission of Random House.

ICEBOUND by Owen Davis
Copyright, 1922, 1923, by Owen Davis. Published by Little, Brown and Co.
Reprinted by permission of Little, Brown and Co., Boston, Massachusetts.

HELL-BENT FER HEAVEN by Hatcher Hughes
Copyright, 1923, 1924, by Hatcher Hughes. Published by Harper and Bros.
Reprinted by permission of Mr. Hughes and Harper and Bros.

THEY KNEW WHAT THEY WANTED by Sidney Howard
Copyright, 1924, by Sidney Howard.
Copyright and published, 1925, by Doubleday, Page and Co., New York.
Reprinted by permission of The Theatre Guild, Inc. and Samuel French, Inc.

CRAIG'S WIFE by George Kelly
Copyright, 1925, 1926, by George Kelly. Published by Little, Brown and Co.
Reprinted by permission of Little, Brown and Co., Boston, Massachusetts.

IN ABRAHAM'S BOSOM by Paul Green
Copyright, 1926, by Paul Green.
Copyright and published, 1927, by Robert M. McBride and Company, New York.
Reprinted by permission of Mr. Green and Robert M. McBride and Company.

STRANGE INTERLUDE by Eugene O'Neill
Copyright and published, 1928, by Horace Liveright, Inc., New York.
Reprinted by permission of Random House.

STREET SCENE by Elmer Rice
Copyright, 1928, 1929, by Elmer Rice.
Published, 1929, by Samuel French, Inc., New York.
Reprinted by permission of Mr. Rice and Samuel French, Inc.

Why Marry?

BY JESSE LYNCH WILLIAMS

TO

HARRIET AND JAMES LEES LAIDLAW

JESSE LYNCH WILLIAMS

Jesse Lynch Williams was born at Sterling, Illinois, in 1871. He was graduated from Princeton University with the A.B. degree in 1892, A.M. in 1895, and Litt.D. in 1919. Mr. Williams's first book was *Princeton Stories* (1895); with John DeWitt as co-author, he wrote a *History of Princeton University*. He was married to Alice Laidlaw in 1898. Having gained brief but varied newspaper experience in New York, he published, in 1899, a volume of newspaper tales, the most notable of which was *The Stolen Story*. A dramatization by Mr. Williams of *The Stolen Story* was produced more than two hundred times on the New York stage and elsewhere; later he shortened the same drama into a one-act play. When *The Day-Dreamer* appeared in 1906, the original short story was re-discovered in the guise of a full-length novel.

Adventures of a Freshman, New York Sketches, My Lost Duchess, The Girl and the Game, Mr. Cleveland, a Personal Impression, The Married Life of the Frederic Carrolls and *Remating Time* are among his other works. At one time a fellow in creative arts at the University of Michigan, he was also a member of the National Institute of Arts and Letters and of the Authors' League of America, which he served as president in 1921. He died in the fall of 1929.

First produced by Selwyn and Company at the Astor Theatre, New York, December 25, 1917, *Why Marry?* received the Pulitzer award for 1917-1918.

THE PEOPLE AT THE HOUSE

(As You Meet Them)

JEAN, the host's younger sister, who has been brought up to be married and nothing else.

REX, an unmarried neighbor, who has not been brought up to be anything but rich.

LUCY, the hostess, who is trying her best to be "just an old-fashioned wife" in a new-fashioned home.

UNCLE EVERETT, a Judge, who belongs to the older generation and yet understands the new—and believes in divorce.

COUSIN THEODORE, a clergyman and yet a human being, who believes in everything—except divorce.

JOHN, who owns the house and almost every one in it—and does not believe in divorce.

HELEN, the host's other sister, whom every one wants to marry, but who doesn't want to marry any one.

ERNEST, a scientist, who believes in neither divorce nor marriage but makes a great discovery.

THE BUTLER.

THE FOOTMAN.

SCENE

The scene is a week-end at a country house not far away; the time, Saturday afternoon, Sunday morning, and Sunday evening.

WHY MARRY?

ACT ONE

Up from the fragrant garden comes a girl, running. She takes the broad terrace steps two at a stride, laughing, breathless, fleet as a fawn, sweet as a rose. She is hotly pursued by a boy, handsome, ardent, attractively selfish, and just now blindly determined to catch the pretty creature before she gains the protecting shelter of home. She is determined to let him but not to let him know it. . . . There, she might have darted in through the open door, but it is such a cold, formal entrance; she pretends to be exhausted, dodges behind a stone tea-table, and, turning, faces him, each panting and laughing excitedly; she alluring and defiant, he merry and dominant.

She is twenty-five and he is a year or two older, but they are both children; in other words, unmarried.

REX. Think I'll let you say that to me?

JEAN (*making a face at him*). Think I'm afraid of you!

REX. Take it back, I tell you.

JEAN. I won't.

REX. I'll make you.

JEAN (*with a dance step*). Think so, do you?

REX. I warn you.

JEAN. Booh-woo!
(*He makes a feint to the right, then dashes to the left and catches her.*)

REX (*triumphantly*). Now! . . . You would, would you?

JEAN (*struggling*). Let me go.

REX. I couldn't think of it.

JEAN (*seizes his hands to free herself— can't*). You're so strong—it isn't fair.

REX. You're so sweet—it isn't fair.
(*Smiling down at her struggles, rejoicing in his strength, her weakness, he gently draws her near.*)

JEAN (*knows what is coming*). No, Rex.

REX. Yes.

JEAN. You mustn't.

REX. But I will.
(*He laughs and kisses her lightly on the cheek. Therefore she struggles furiously. Therefore he does it again. And again. Suddenly he enfolds her completely and kisses her passionately — cheeks, mouth, eyes—until she gasps in alarm. Laughter has gone from them now.*)

JEAN. Oh, please! . . . some one will come.

REX (*with the intoxication of such moments*). I don't care who comes—I love you.

JEAN. No . . . let me go.

REX. Not till you kiss me, Jean. (JEAN *hesitates, brushes his cheek lightly with her lips, and in pretty confusion tries to escape.*) Not till you say you love me, Jean. (*Eyes hidden in his coat, she bobs her head. He laughs and loves it.*) Say it!

JEAN. I—er—do.

REX. Do *what*? . . . Say it! . . .
(*She cannot. He swings her about, bringing her face close to his.*)

JEAN. I love you, Rex. Are you sure you love me?

REX. Am I sure! You irresistible little—
(*Begins to kiss her. Masculine triumph.*)

JEAN. And want to marry me, Rex?

REX (*stops—startled—had not thought of that*). Why — er — of course. What did you suppose! (*Drops his eyes, sobered.*)

5

JEAN (*feminine triumph*). And me "a penniless orphing"?

REX (*fascinated by the way she says it, he laughs. Then, his honor touched*). Why, what kind of a man do you take me for! (*And wants her lips again.*)

JEAN (*giving herself to him, head sinks upon his shoulder*). Then, oh, Rex, love me and be nice to me and—and take me away from all this!
(*She covers her face with her hands and sobs. He pats her tenderly, with a manly look on his face.*)

LUCY *comes up from the garden. She is dressed in white with a garden hat, a garden basket filled with flowers in one hand, long scissors in the other. She is* JOHN's *wife, the mistress of the house, sister-in-law to* JEAN; *conspicuously a "sweet" woman, affectedly so, a contrast with* JEAN's *more modern, less delicate charm.* JEAN *is frank and brave,* LUCY *indirect and timid, pretty but fading, forty but fighting it.*

JEAN (*laughing*). It's all right, Lucy— we're engaged!

LUCY. Well, I should hope so! (*Shoots a look at* JEAN, *"So?"*)

REX (*recovering himself*). I have often tried to thank you and good old John for letting me come over here so much, but now! How can I *ever* thank you? See-what-I-mean?

LUCY. I'll tell you how. Behave yourself after you are married to John's little sister.

JEAN. Rex, have you had a fearful past? How fascinating!

REX. I'm going to have a glorious future, all right.

JEAN. Not unless you do as I tell you. Going to obey me, Rex?

REX. You bet I am.

JEAN. Then begin now. Go! . . . Get out! (*She pushes* REX, *laughing and protesting, toward the garden.*) I want to tell Lucy how nice you are. Run along over to the golf club, and by and by—if you *are* a good boy—you can take me out in your new car. (*REX kisses the hand on his arm and leaves,*

laughing.) My dear, he has five cars! Thank you so much.
(*Alone, they throw off the mask worn before men.*)

LUCY. Now, deary, tell me all about it. How did it happen?

JEAN. Oh, I simply followed your advice.

LUCY. Picked a quarrel with him?

JEAN (*laughing*). Yes, I pretended to believe in woman suffrage!

LUCY. Good! They hate that.

JEAN. I told him all men were bullying brutes!

LUCY. They are! And then you ran away?

JEAN. Of course.

LUCY. And he after you?

JEAN. Of course.

LUCY. And you let him catch you?

JEAN. Of cour—well . . . he caught me. (*They both laugh.*)

LUCY. I can guess the rest.

JEAN. Why, it didn't take five minutes.

LUCY. And now it's to last through all eternity. . . . Isn't love wonderful?

JEAN. Um-hum. Wonderful. (*They begin to cull out the flowers.*)

LUCY. But you do love him, dear, don't you?

JEAN (*arranging flowers*). I did then. I don't now. Why is that, Lucy?

LUCY. Oh, but you will learn to love him. (*JEAN shrugs, drops flowers, and turns away.*) Now, now! no worrying—it brings wrinkles! (*Patting* JEAN's *shoulder.*) Rex is just the sort to give the woman he adores everything in the world.

JEAN (*wriggling out of* LUCY's *embrace*). I am not the woman he adores.

LUCY. Why, Jean! He's engaged to you.

JEAN. But he's in love with my sister. You know that as well as I do.

LUCY (*uncomfortably*). Oh, well, he was once, but not now. Men admire these independent women, but they don't marry them. Nobody wants to marry a sexless freak with a scientific degree.

JEAN. Oh, what's the use, Lucy? He's still wild about Helen, and she still laughs at him. So you and John have trotted out the little sister. Why not be honest about it?

LUCY. Well, I may be old-fashioned, but I don't think it's nice to talk this way when you're just engaged.

JEAN. Here comes your "sexless freak"— not with a degree, either.

LUCY (*following* JEAN's *gaze*). With a man!

JEAN (*smiling*). With *my* man.
(HELEN, *with* REX *bending toward her eagerly, appears. She is a beautiful woman of twenty-nine, tall, strong, glorious— plenty of old-fashioned charm, despite her new-fashioned ideas. She is dressed in a tennis costume and is swinging a racquet.*)

REX. But they told me you were going to stay abroad all winter.

HELEN. My work, Rex—I had to get back to work.

REX. Work! . . . You are too good to work.

JEAN (*amused, not jealous*). Is this your high-powered car, Rex? Have you learned to run it yet?

REX (*startled*). But . . . well . . . you see, I met Helen on the way. See-what-I-mean?

JEAN (*laughing*). Oh, we see.

REX. But I hadn't seen her for so long. I thought—(*Looks from* HELEN *to* JEAN.) . . . wait, I'll get the car. (*He hurries off.*)

LUCY (*to* JEAN). Why couldn't she have stayed abroad!

JEAN. Helen, don't talk about your work before Lucy—it shocks her.

HELEN. Oh, very well; make it my "career"!

JEAN (*arm around* HELEN). Ssh—that's worse.

LUCY. Helen, dear, I deem it my duty to tell you that you are being talked about.

HELEN. Lucy, dear, do you always find your true happiness in duty?

LUCY. Well, if you think you are going back to that horrid place again . . . after what happened that night? John won't hear of it.

HELEN. If the Baker Institute of Medical Experiment is not a respectable place you should make John resign as trustee. (*She laughs it off.*)

LUCY. John is trustee of—oh, nearly everything. That makes it all the worse. It isn't as if you had to work.

HELEN. Oh, but John is so rich now, his credit can stand it. And you oughtn't to mind! Why, some of our most fashionable families now contain freaks like me. It's becoming quite smart, just as in former days one of the sons would go into the Church or the navy.

LUCY. Well, of course, I am old-fashioned, but going down-town every day with the men,—it seems so unwomanly.

HELEN. But wasn't I womanly for years? Instead of going down-town and working with highbrows, I stayed up-town and played with lowbrows—until I was bored to death.

LUCY (*sighs*). Yes, that's what comes of going to college, leaving the home, getting these new ideas. All the same, Helen, the men, really nice men, don't like it.

HELEN. Well, you see, I don't like really nice men, so that makes it agreeable all around.

LUCY. If it were only art or music or something feminine, but that awful laboratory! How can a lady poison poor, innocent little monkeys?

HELEN. If I were a lady I'd *dine* with monkeys. . . . Do you know what the word means, Lucy? In Anglo-Saxon times "lady" meant "one who gives loaves"; now, one who *takes* a loaf.

LUCY. Very clever, my dear, but some day you'll be sorry. No man, Helen, likes a woman to have independent views.

JEAN. Helen can afford to have independent views; she has an independent income —she earns it.

LUCY. Independent income! Her salary wouldn't pay for your hats.

JEAN. All the same, I wish I had gone to college; I wish I had learned a profession.

LUCY. What have these New Women accomplished? Just one thing: they are destroying chivalry!

HELEN. Not entirely, Lucy, not entirely. For instance, I am the best assistant Ernest Hamilton has, but the worst paid; the others are all men. Hurray for chivalry!

LUCY. Well, I'm just an old-fashioned wife. Woman's sphere is the home. My husband says so.

HELEN. But suppose you haven't any husband! What can a spinster do in the home?

LUCY. *Stay* in it—till she gets one! That's what the old-fashioned spinster used to do.

HELEN. The old-fashioned spinster used to spin.

LUCY. At any rate, the old-fashioned spinster did not stay out of her home all night and get herself compromised, talked about, sent abroad! Or, if she did, she knew enough to remain abroad until the gossip blew over. (LUCY *turns to leave.*)

HELEN (*mischievously*). Ah, that wonderful night! (LUCY *turns back, amazed.*) The night we discovered the Hamilton antitoxin, the night that made the Baker Institute famous! And, just think, I had a hand in it, Lucy, a hand in the unwomanly work of saving children's lives! But, of course, an old-fashioned spinster would have blushed and said: "Excuse me, Doctor Hamilton, but we must now let a year's work go to waste because you are a man and I am a woman, and it's dark outdoors!" . . . That's the way to preserve true chivalry.

LUCY. You think we can't see through all this? Science—fiddlesticks! The good-looking young scientist—that's why you couldn't stay abroad. We see it, John sees it, and now every one will see it. Then how will you feel?

HELEN. Ernest *is* rather good-looking, isn't he?

LUCY. Do you think your brother will let you marry a mere scientist! . . . Oh, well, Doctor Hamilton is in love with his work —fortunately. . . . Besides, he's a thoroughbred; he wouldn't even look at a girl who throws herself at his head.

HELEN. So I needn't try any longer? Too bad.

LUCY (*losing her temper and going*). Oh, you New Women are quite superior, aren't you? . . . Thank heavens, little Jean didn't elbow *her* way into men's affairs; she had no unwomanly ambitions for a career! But she is engaged to Rex Baker!

HELEN. Jean, is this true?

LUCY (*triumphantly*). *Marriage* is woman's only true career.

HELEN. Jean! You can't, you won't, you mustn't marry Rex!

LUCY (*flouncing out*). "She who will not when she may," my dear!

JEAN (*avoiding* HELEN'S *eyes*). Lucy hears John coming—he'd take her head off if she weren't there to meet him. (HELEN *only looks at her.*) He bullies and browbeats her worse than ever. I can't stand it here much longer. It's getting on my nerves.

HELEN. Jean! You care for Rex no more than I do.

JEAN (*still evasive*). John's bringing out Uncle Everett and Cousin Theodore. My dear, the whole family is up in the air about you.

HELEN. Oh, I can take care of myself, but you! . . . Jean, you're not the sort to marry Rex or any other man, unless you simply can't live without him.

JEAN (*after a little pause*). Well . . . how can I live without him—without some man? You can support yourself. I can't.

HELEN. But you wouldn't live on a man you didn't really love!

JEAN. Why not? Lucy does; most wives live on men they don't really love. To stop doing so and get divorced is wrong, you know.

HELEN. Jean, Jean, poor little Jean!

JEAN. Well, I'd rather have domestic unhappiness of my own than watch other people's all my life.

HELEN. I don't like to hurt you, dear, but — (*Takes* JEAN's *face and raises it.*) How about that nice boy at the Harvard Law School?

JEAN. Don't! (*Controls herself, then, in a low voice.*) Bob is still at the Law School, Helen.

HELEN. Can't you wait, dear?

JEAN. He never asked me to, Helen.

HELEN. He would, if you let him.

JEAN. It wouldn't be fair. It takes so long to get started. Everything costs so much. Why, nowadays, men in the professions, unless they have private means, can't marry until nearly *forty*. When Bob is forty I'll be forty, Helen.

HELEN. Ah, but when a girl really cares!

JEAN. Helen, do *you* know?

HELEN. Never mind about me—you!

JEAN. Oh, we'll get over it, I suppose. . . . People do! Some day, perhaps, he'll smile and say: "Just think, I once loved *that* fat old thing!" (*Suddenly changes to sobbing.*) Helen! when Rex caught me and kissed me I shut my eyes and tried to think it was Bob.

HELEN (*takes* JEAN *in her arms*). You can't keep on thinking so, dear.

JEAN. But that isn't the worst! When he held me fast and I couldn't get away, I began . . . to forget Bob . . . to forget everything . . . (*Breaks off, overcome with shame.*) But not now, not now! It's not the same thing at all. (*Buries face in* HELEN's *breast and sobs it out.*) Oh, I feel like the devil, dear. . . . And all this time he doesn't really want me—he wants you, you! I trapped him into it; I trapped him!

HELEN. And I know Rex—he's a good sport; he'll stick to it, if you do, dear— only you won't! You've caught him by playing on his worst—don't hold him by playing on his best!

JEAN. But what shall I do? I'm nearly twenty-six. I've got to escape from home in some way.

HELEN. But what a way!

(REX *returns.*)

REX. Ready, Jean? (*To* HELEN.) Lucy and John and your Cousin Theodore are in there having a fine, old-fashioned family fight with the judge.

HELEN. With Uncle Everett? What about?

REX. They shut up when they saw me. All I heard was the parson—"Marriage is a social institution." Grand old row, though. (*A* BUTLER *and* FOOTMAN *appear, wheeling a tea-wagon.*) Looks as if they were coming out here.

HELEN. Then I am going in. (*Detaining* JEAN.) You will follow my advice?

JEAN (*apart to* HELEN). Oh, I don't know. Soon or late I must follow the only profession I have learned.

(JEAN *leaves with* REX. HELEN *watches them, sighs, and goes in. The* SERVANTS *arrange the tea-table and go into the house.* LUCY *comes out, followed by her husband,* JOHN, *and the* JUDGE, *who is* UNCLE EVERETT, *and* COUSIN THEODORE.
JOHN, *the masterful type of successful American business man; well set up, close-cropped mustache, inclined to baldness; keen eye, vibrant voice, quick movements, quick decisions, quick temper.*
UNCLE EVERETT *is a genial satirist with a cynical tolerance of the ways of the world, which he understands, laughs at, and rather likes.*
COUSIN THEODORE, *a care-worn rector, who, though he buttons his collar behind, likes those who don't; a noble soul, self-sacrificing and sanctified, but he does not obtrude his profession upon others—never talks shop unless asked to do so, and prides himself upon not being a bigot.*
They are continuing an earnest discussion,*

with the intimate manner of friendly members of the same family. JOHN, LUCY, *and* THEODORE *deeply concerned;* UNCLE EVERETT *detached and amused.*)

THEODORE. But, Uncle Everett, hasn't Aunt Julia always been a good wife to you?

JUDGE. Quite so, quite so, a good wife, Theodore, a good wife.

LUCY. And a devoted mother to your children, Uncle Everett?

JUDGE. Devoted, Lucy, devoted.

JOHN. She has always obeyed you, Uncle Everett.

JUDGE. Yes, John—a true, old-fashioned woman.

THEODORE. She has been a great help to me in the parish work, Uncle Everett.

JUDGE. An earnest worker in the vineyard, Theodore—in fact, I might say, a model female.

ALL. Then why, *why* do you want a divorce?

JUDGE. Because, damn it, I don't like her!

LUCY. But think of poor Aunt Julia!

JUDGE. But, damn it, she doesn't like *me.*

THEODORE (*wagging head sadly*). Ah, yes, I suppose there has been fault on both sides.

JUDGE. Not at all! No fault on either side. . . . Both patterns of Christian fortitude to the end! We still are. Just listen to this telegram.

LUCY (*puzzled*). From Aunt Julia?

JUDGE. Yes, from Aunt Julia in Reno. Not used to travelling without me; knew I'd worry. Thoughtful of her, wasn't it? (*Puts on glasses.*) A night letter. Much cheaper; your Aunt Julia was always a frugal wife. Besides, she never could keep within ten words. (*Reads.*) "Arrived safely. Charming rooms with plenty of air and sunlight. Our case docketed for March 15th. Wish you were here to see the women in Divorcee Row—overdressed and underbred." Rather neat, eh? "Overdressed and underbred." "I should love to hear *your* comments on the various types." Now, isn't that sweet of her? Well, you know, I always *could* make her laugh—except when I made her cry. "Write soon. With love, Julia." Now (*folds telegram*), isn't that a nice message? From a wife suing for divorce? You happily married people couldn't beat that. (*Pats telegram and pockets it tenderly.*)

JOHN (*like a practical business man*). But if there's no other woman, no other man— what's it all about?

JUDGE. She likes her beefsteak well done; I like mine underdone. She likes one window open—about so much (*indicates four inches*); I like all the windows open wide! She likes to stay at home; I like to travel. She loves the opera and hates the theatre; I love the theatre and hate the opera.

THEODORE. Stop! aren't you willing to make a few little sacrifices for each other? Haven't you character enough for that?

JUDGE. We've been making sacrifices for twenty-five years, a quarter of a century! Character enough to last us now . . . Why, I remember the first dinner we had together after we were pronounced man and wife, with a full choral service and a great many expensive flowers — quite a smart wedding, Lucy, for those simple days. "Darling," I asked my blushing bride, "do you like tutti-frutti ice-cream?" "I adore it, dearest," she murmured. I hated it, but nobly sacrificed myself and gave her tutti-frutti and gained character every evening of our honeymoon! Then when we got back and began our "new life" together in our "little home," my darling gave *me* tutti-frutti and indigestion *once a week* until I nearly died!

LUCY. But why didn't you tell her?

JUDGE. I did; I did. Got chronic dyspepsia and struck! "*You* may adore this stuff, *darling,*" I said, "but I hate it." "So do I, dearest," says she. "Then why in thunder have you had it all these years, *sweetheart?*" "For your sake, *beloved!*" And that tells the whole story of our married life. We have nothing in common but a love of divorce and a mutual abhorrence of tutti-frutti. "Two souls with but a single thought, two hearts that beat as one!" It has been the dream of our lives to get apart, and each has nobly refrained for the other's sake. And all in vain!

JOHN. Bah! All a cloak to hide his real motive. And he knows it!

JUDGE (*after a painful pause*). I may as well confess. (*Looks around to see if overheard. Whispers.*) For over twenty years I—I have broken my marriage vow! (LUCY *drops her eyes.* THEODORE *aghast.* JOHN *wags head.*) So has your Aunt Julia!

THEODORE. No! not that!

JUDGE. Well, we solemnly promised to love each other until death did us part. We have broken that sacred vow! I don't love *her;* she doesn't love *me* — not in the least!

JOHN. Rot! A matured, middle-aged man, a distinguished member of the bar — break up his home for that? Damned rot!

JUDGE. Right again, John. That's not why I'm breaking up my home. I prefer my club. What does the modern home amount to? Merely a place to leave your wife.

LUCY. Of course, it doesn't matter about the poor little wife left at home.

JUDGE. Wrong, Lucy, it does matter. That's why I *stayed* at home and was bored to death with her prattle about clothes and the opera, instead of dining at the club with my intellectual equals, picking up business there, getting rich like John, supplying her with *more* clothes and a whole *box* at the opera, like yours, Lucy.

LUCY (*shoots a glance at her husband*). Oh, that's the way you men *always* talk. It never occurs to you that business, business, *business* is *just* as much of a bore to us!

JUDGE. Wrong again! It did occur to *me* — hence the divorce! She couldn't stand seeing *me* bored; I couldn't stand seeing *her* bored. Once we could deceive each other; but now — too well acquainted; our happy home — a hollow mockery!

THEODORE. You ought to be ashamed! I love my home!

JOHN. So do I. (*He glances sternly at* LUCY.)

LUCY (*nervously*). So do I.

JUDGE. All right. Stick to it, if you love it. Only, don't claim credit for doing what you enjoy. I stuck to my home for a quarter of a century and disliked it the whole time. At last I'm free to say so. Just think of it, Lucy, free to utter those things about marriage we all know are true but don't dare say! Free to be honest, John! No longer a hypocrite, no longer a liar! A soul set free, Theodore — two souls, in fact. "Two souls with but a single thought — "

THEODORE. Stop! You have *children* to consider, not merely your own selfish happiness!

LUCY. Yes, think of Tom and little Julia!

JUDGE. We did . . . for a quarter of a century — sacrificed everything to them, even our self-respect; but now — what's the use? We are childless now. Tom and Julia have both left us for "little homes" of their own to love.

THEODORE. Ah, but don't you want them to have the old home to come back to?

JUDGE. "No place like home" for children, eh? You're right — can't have too much of it. Most children only have *one* home. Ours will have *two!* When they get bored with one they can try the other.

THEODORE. But, seriously, Uncle Everett — "Whom God hath joined together!"

LUCY (*clasping* JOHN'S *arm*). Yes, Uncle Everett, marriages are made in heaven.

JUDGE. I see; quite so; but your Aunt Julia and I were joined together by a pink parasol made in Paris.

JOHN. What rot! Stop your fooling and speak the truth, man.

JUDGE. Just what I'm doing — that's why you think I'm fooling. A very pretty parasol — but it wasn't made in heaven. You see, God made poor, dear Julia pale, but on that fatal day, twenty-five years ago, the pink parasol, not God, made her rosy and irresistible. I did the rest — with the aid of a clergyman, whom I tipped even more liberally than the waiter who served us tutti-frutti. Blame *me* for it, blame her, the parasol, the parson, but do not, my dear Theodore, blame the Deity for our own mistakes. It's so blasphemous. (*A pause.* LUCY *takes place at the tea-table to serve tea.*)

LUCY. And to think we invited *you,* of all people, here to-day of all days! (*To* JOHN.) We mustn't let Rex know. The Bakers don't believe in divorce.

JOHN. What's this? You don't mean that Jean—?

LUCY. Yes! Just in time — before he knew Helen was back.

JOHN (*jumps up*). She's landed him! She's landed him! We're marrying into the Baker family! The Baker family! (*Shaking hands right and left.*) Why, she'll have more money than any of us! . . . Well, well! We'll all have to stand around before little Jean now! . . . My, my! Lucy, you're a wonder! Those pearls — I'll buy them; they're yours! Hurry for Lucy! (*Kisses* LUCY.)

LUCY (*feeling her importance*). Now, if I could only get *Helen* out of this awful mess and safely married to some nice man!

JUDGE (*sipping his tea*). Meaning one having money?

THEODORE. The Hamiltons are an older family than the Bakers, Lucy, older than our own.

JUDGE. Meaning they *once* had money.

JOHN (*still pacing to and fro*). Waste a beauty on a bacteriologist? A crime!

THEODORE. See here, John, Ernest Hamilton is the biggest thing you've got in the Baker Institute! One of the loveliest fellows in the world, too, and if you expect me — why did you ask us here, anyway?

JUDGE. Far as I can make out, we're here to help one of John's sisters marry a man she doesn't love and prevent the other from marrying the man she does.

JOHN. Oh, look here: I've nothing against young Hamilton. . . . I *like* him — proud of all he's done for the institute. Why, Mr. Baker is tickled to death about the Hamilton antitoxin. But, Theodore, this is a prac-

tical world. Your scientific friend gets just two thousand dollars a year! . . . Lucy, send for Helen. (LUCY *goes obediently.*)

JUDGE. Well, why not give the young man a raise?

JOHN. Oh, that's not a bad salary for scientists, college professors, and that sort of thing. Why, even the head of the institute himself gets less than the superintendent of my mills. No future in science.

JUDGE. Perfectly practical, Theodore. The superintendent of John's mills saves the company thousands of dollars. These bacteriologists merely save the nation thousands of babies. All our laws, written and unwritten, value private property above human life. I'm a distinguished jurist and I always render my decisions accordingly. I'd be reversed by the United States Supreme Court if I didn't. We're all rewarded in inverse ratio to our usefulness to society, Theodore. That's why "practical men" think changes are "dangerous."

JOHN. Muck-raker!

JUDGE. It's all on a sliding scale, John. For keeping up the cost of living you and old man Baker get . . . (*Stretches arms out full length.*) Heaven only knows how much. For saving the Constitution I get . . . a good deal. (*Hands three feet apart.*) For saving in wages and operating expenses your superintendent gets so much. (*Hands two feet apart.*) For saving human life Ernest Hamilton gets that. (*Hands six inches apart.*) For saving immortal souls Theodore gets—(*Holds up two forefingers an inch apart.*) Now, if any one came along and saved the world—

THEODORE (*interrupts*). They crucified Him.

JOHN. Muck-raker, muck-raker.

LUCY (*returning*). Tried my best, John, but Helen says she prefers to talk with you alone some time.

JOHN (*furious*). She "prefers"? See here! Am I master in my own house or not?

JUDGE. But Helen is a guest in it now. No longer under your control, John. She's the New Woman.

THEODORE. John, *you* can't stop that girl's marrying Ernest, if she wants to; he's head over heels in love with her.

LUCY. What! We thought he was in love with his work!

THEODORE. He thinks there's no hope for him, poor boy.

LUCY (*to* JOHN). And she is mad about him!

JOHN (*to* LUCY). And he is on the way out here now!

THEODORE. What! He's coming to see her?

JOHN. No, no, thinks she's still in Paris — so she was when I invited him, damn it — but something had to be done and done delicately. That's why I invited you two.

JUDGE (*bursts out laughing*). Beautiful! These lovers haven't met for a month, and to-night there's a moon!

THEODORE (*also laughs*). You may as well give in, John. It's the simplest solution.

LUCY (*timidly*). Yes, John, she's nearly thirty, and think how she treats all the *nice* men.

JOHN. Who's doing this? You go tell Helen . . . that her Uncle Everett wants to see her! (LUCY *shrugs, starts reluctantly, and lingers listening.*)

THEODORE. Now, uncle, you have more influence over her than any of us—don't let her know about . . . Aunt Julia. Helen thinks the world of you.

JUDGE. Of course not, never let the rising generation suspect the truth about marriage — if you want 'em to marry.

THEODORE. There are other truths than unpleasant truths, Uncle Everett, other marriages than unhappy marriages.

JUDGE. Want me to tell her the truth about your marriage?

LUCY (*at the door*). Why, uncle! Even *you* must admit that Theodore and Mary are happy. (JOHN *is too much surprised to notice* LUCY'*s presence.*)

JUDGE. Happy? What's that got to do with it? Marriage is a social institution. Theodore said so. . . . Every time a boy kisses a girl she should first inquire: "A sacrifice for society?" And if he says, "I want to gain character, sweetheart," then—"Darling, do your duty!" and he'll do it.

LUCY. Well, Theodore has certainly done *his* duty by society -- six children!

JUDGE. Then society hasn't done its duty by Theodore — only one salary!

JOHN. The more credit to him! He and Mary have sacrificed everything to their children and the Church — even health!

THEODORE. We don't need your pity! We don't want your praise! Poverty, suffering, even separation, have only drawn us closer together. We love each other through it all! Why, in the last letter the doctor let her write she said, she said — (*Suddenly overcome with emotion, turns abruptly.*) If you'll excuse me, Lucy . . . Sanitarium . . . the telephone. (THEODORE *goes into the house.*)

JUDGE. Not praise or pity but something more substantial and, by George, I'll get it for them! (*Turns to* JOHN, *who interrupts.*)

JOHN. See the example *he* sets to society— I honor him for it.

JUDGE. Fine! but that doesn't seem to restore Mary's radiant health, Theodore's brilliant youth.

LUCY. Ah, but they have their *children* — think how they adore those beautiful children!

JUDGE. No, don't think how they adore them, think how they *rear* those beautiful children—in the streets; one little daughter dead from contagion; one son going to the devil from other things picked up in the street! If marriage is a social institution, look at it socially. Why, a marriage like mine is worth a dozen like theirs — to Society. Look at my well-launched children; look at my useful career, as a jackal to Big Business; look at my now perfectly contented spouse!

LUCY. But if you are divorced!

JUDGE. Is the object of marriage merely to stay married?

LUCY. But character, think of the character they have gained.

JUDGE. Oh, is it to gain character at the expense of helpless offspring? Society doesn't gain by that — it loses, Lucy, it loses. . . . But simply because, God bless 'em, "they love each other through it all," you sentimental standpatters believe in lying about it, do you?

JOHN (*bored, whips out pocket check-book and fountain pen*). Oh, talk, talk, talk! Money talks for *me*. . . .. But they're both so confoundedly proud!

JUDGE. Go on, write that check! (JOHN *writes.*) They must sacrifice their pride, John. Nothing else left to sacrifice, I'm afraid.

JOHN. Well, you get this to them somehow. (*Hands check to* JUDGE.)

JUDGE. Aha! Talk did it. . . . Five thousand? Generous John!

JOHN (*impatiently*). Never mind about me. *That* problem is all settled; now about Helen. . . . Lucy! I thought I told you — (LUCY, *in a guilty hurry, escapes into the house.*)

JUDGE. John, charity never settles problems; it perpetuates them. You can't cure social defects by individual treatment.

JOHN (*more impatiently*). Does talk settle anything?

JUDGE. Everything. We may even settle the marriage problem if we talk honestly. (THEODORE *returns from telephoning to the sanitarium.*) Theodore, it's all right! John honestly believes in setting an example to society! Crazy to have his sisters go and do likewise!

THEODORE. Splendid, John! I knew you'd see it — an ideal match.

JUDGE (*overriding* JOHN). Right, Theodore, ideal. This scientific suitor will shower everything upon her John honors and admires: A host of servants — I mean sacrifices; carriages and motors — I mean character and morals; just what her brother advocates in Sunday-school — for others. An ideal marriage.

JOHN (*hands in pockets*). You think you're awfully funny, don't you? Humph! I do more for the Church, for education, art, science than all the rest of the family combined. Incidentally, I'm not divorced. . . . But this is a practical world, Theodore, I've got to protect my own.

LUCY (*returning*). Helen will be here in a minute.

JOHN (*suddenly getting an idea*). Ah! I have it! I know how to keep them apart!

THEODORE. Be careful, John — these two love each other.

JUDGE. Yes, young people still fall in love. Whether we make it hard or easy for them — they *will* do it. But, mark my words, unless we *reform marriage,* there is going to be a sympathetic *strike* against it — as there is already against having children. Instead of making it harder to get apart, we've got to make it easier to stay together. Otherwise the ancient bluff will soon be called!

LUCY. Sssh! Here she comes.

THEODORE. *Please* don't talk this way before her.

JUDGE. All right, I'm not divorced yet, . . . still in the conspiracy of silence. (HELEN *appears at the door. A sudden silence.*)

HELEN (*kissing* THEODORE *and* JUDGE *affectionately*). I'm *so* sorry to hear about dear Mary. (*To* JUDGE.) But why didn't Aunt Julia come? Is she ill, too? (*Slight panic in the family party.*)

JUDGE. She's gone to Re-Re-Rio Janeiro — I mean to Santa Barbara — wants a complete change — The Rest Cure. (*To* THEODORE *apart.*) Lie number one. (*Another silence.* LUCY *makes tea for* HELEN.)

HELEN (*taking the cup*). Well, go on!

THEODORE. Go on with what?

HELEN (*stirring tea*). Your discussion of marriage.

LUCY. How did you know?

HELEN. Oh, it's in the air. Everybody's talking about it nowadays. (*She sips tea, and the others look conscious.*)

THEODORE. My dear, marriage is woman's only true career.

HELEN (*raising her shield of flippancy*). So Lucy tells me, Cousin Theodore. But a woman cannot pursue her career, she must be pursued by it; otherwise she is unwomanly.

JUDGE. Ahem. As we passed through the library a while ago, I think I saw your little sister being pursued by her career.

HELEN. Yes, uncle, but Jean is a true woman. I'm only a New Woman.

JUDGE. All the same, you'll be an old woman some day — if you don't watch out.

HELEN. Ah, yes, my life's a failure. I haven't trapped a man into a contract to support me.

LUCY (*picks up knitting bag and does her best to look like "just an old-fashioned wife"*). You ought to be ashamed! Making marriage so mercenary. Helen, dear, haven't you New Women any sentiment?

HELEN. Enough sentiment not to make a mercenary marriage, Lucy, dear.

JUDGE. Ahem! And what kind of a marriage do you expect to make?

HELEN. Not any, thank you, uncle.

JUDGE. What! You don't believe in holy matrimony?

HELEN. Only as a last extremity, uncle, like unholy divorce.

JUDGE (*jumps*). What do *you* know about that?

HELEN. I know all about it! (*Others jump.*) I have been reading up on the subject. (*All relax, relieved, but now gather about the young woman.*)

(*Together*) {

THEODORE. Come now, simply because many young people rush into marriage without thinking—

LUCY. Simply because these New Women —

JOHN. Simply because one marriage in a thousand ends in divorce —

}

HELEN. Wait! . . . One in a thousand? Dear me, what an idealist you are, John! In America, one marriage in every eleven now ends in divorce. And yet you wonder why I hesitate.

JOHN. One in eleven — rot! (*To* JUDGE.) All this muck-raking should be suppressed by the Government. "One in eleven!" Bah!

HELEN (*demurely*). The Government's own statistics, John. (*They all turn to the* JUDGE *for denial, but he nods confirmation, with a complacent smile, murmuring: "Two souls with but a single thought."*)

LUCY (*sweetly knitting*). Well, I may be old-fashioned, but it seems to *me* that nice girls shouldn't *think* of such things. . . . Their husbands will tell them all they ought to know about marriage — after they're married.

HELEN. Ah, I see. Nice girls mustn't think until after they rush in, but they mustn't rush in until after they think. You married people make it all so simple for us.

JUDGE. Right! The way to cure all evil is for nice people to close their minds and mouths to it. It's "unpleasant" for a pure mind, and it "leaves a bad taste in the mouth." So there you are, my dear.

JOHN (*coming in strong*). Oh, talk, talk, talk! I've had enough. See here, young lady, I offered to pay all your expenses abroad for a year. You didn't seem to appreciate it—well, the trustees of the institute are now to give Doctor Hamilton a year abroad. How do you like that? (*All turn and look at* HELEN.)

HELEN. Splendid! Just what he needs! Doctor Metchnikoff told me in Paris that

America always kills its big men with routine. When do we start? (*She tries to look very businesslike.*)

JOHN (*springing to his feet*). "We!" Do you think *you* are going?

HELEN. Of course! I'm his assistant—quite indispensable to him . . . (*To all.*) Oh, well, if you don't believe me, ask him!

JOHN (*pacing to and fro*). What next! Paris! Alone, with a man!—Here's where I call a halt!

HELEN. But if my work calls me, I don't really see what you have to say about it, John.

JOHN. Better not defy me, Helen. (*He scowls.*)

HELEN. Better not bully me, John. (*She smiles.*)

JOHN. I am your brother.

HELEN. But not my owner! (*Then, instead of defiance, she turns with animated interest to the others.*) You know, all women used to be owned by men. Formerly they ruled us by physical force—now by financial force. . . . But at last they are to lose even *that* hold upon us—poor dears! (*Pats* JOHN's *shoulder playfully.*)

JOHN (*amused, but serious*). That's all right in theory, but this is a practical world. My pull got you into the institute; my pull can get you out. You give up this wild idea or give up your job!

HELEN (*delighted*). What did I tell you? Financial force! They still try it, you see. (*To* JOHN.) What if I refused to give up either, John?

JOHN (*emphatic*). Then as a trustee of the institute I ask for your resignation—right here and now! (*Turns away.*) I guess *that* will hold her at home a while.

HELEN. I simply *must* go to Paris now. I've nothing else to do!

JOHN (*with a confident smile*). You will, eh? Who'll pay your expenses this time?

HELEN (*matter of fact*). Doctor Hamilton.

LUCY. Helen! please! You oughtn't to say such things even in joke.

HELEN. He'll take me along as his private secretary, if I ask him. (*A pause. The others look at one another helplessly.*)

JUDGE. John, she's got you. You might as well quit.

JOHN. Nonsense. I have just begun. You'll see.

THEODORE. If you're so independent, my dear, why don't you marry your scientist and be done with it?

HELEN (*resents the intrusion but hides her feelings*). Can you keep a secret? (*They all seem to think they can and gather near.*) He has never asked me! (*The family seems annoyed.*)

LUCY (*with match-making ardor*). No wonder, dear, he has never seen you except in that awful apron. But those stunning dinner gowns John bought you in Paris! My dear, in evening dress you are quite irresistible!

JUDGE (*apart to* THEODORE). Irresistible? Pink parasols. What a system!

HELEN. But you see, I don't *want* him to ask me. I've had all I could do to keep him from it. (*The family seems perplexed.*)

JOHN. She's got *some* sense left.

LUCY. But suppose he did ask you, dear?

HELEN. Why, I'd simply refer the matter to John, of course. If John said, "Love him," I'd love him; if John said, "Don't love him," I'd turn it off like electric light. (*The family is becoming exasperated.*)

LUCY (*insinuating*). Oh, you can't deceive us. We know how much you admire him, Helen.

HELEN. Oh, no you don't! (*The family is amazed.*) Not even he does. Did you ever hear how he risked his life in battle down in Cuba? Why, he's a perfect hero of romance!

JOHN (*mutters*). Never even saw a war—mollycoddle germ killer!

HELEN. Not in the war with Spain—the war against yellow fever, John. . . . No drums to make him brave, no correspondents to make him famous—he merely rolled up his sleeve and let an innocent-looking mosquito bite him. Then took notes on his symptoms till he became delirious. . . . He happened to be among those who recovered. (*The family is impressed.*)

THEODORE. Old-fashioned maidens used to marry their heroes, Helen.

HELEN (*arising, briskly*). But this new-fashioned hero gets only two thousand dollars a year, Theodore. (*She turns to escape.*)

JOHN (*nodding*). I told you she had sense.

THEODORE. Helen! You selfish, too? Why, Mary and I married on half that, didn't we, John? (*He looks around. The family looks away.*)

HELEN (*with unintended emphasis*). Doctor Hamilton needs every cent of that enormous salary—books, travel, scientific conferences—all the advantages he simply must have if he's to keep at the top and do his best work for the world. The most selfish thing a girl can do is to marry a poor man. (*With that she hurries up the steps.*)

THEODORE (*following her*). All the same, deep down under it all, she has a true woman's yearning for a home to care for and a mate to love. (*She is silently crying.*) Why, Helen, dear, what's the matter?

HELEN (*hiding her emotion*). Oh, why can't they let me *alone!* They make what ought to be the holiest and most beautiful thing in life the most horrible and dishonest. They make me hate marriage—hate it! (*Unseen by* HELEN, *the* BUTLER *steps out.*)

THEODORE (*patting her shoulder*). Just you wait till the right one comes along.

BUTLER (*to* LUCY). Doctor Hamilton has come, ma'am.

HELEN (*with an old-fashioned gasp*). Good heavens! (*And runs to the family.*)

LUCY. Show Doctor Hamilton out. (*The* BUTLER *goes.*)

HELEN. A plot to entrap him! (*Running to and fro wildly.*) But it's no use! I'm going . . . until he's gone! (HELEN *runs into the garden.*)

JUDGE. Fighting hard, poor child.

THEODORE. But what'll we do?

JUDGE. Don't worry—she can't stay away—the sweet thing!

JOHN. Now listen, we must all jolly him up—he'll be shy in these surroundings.

JUDGE. Going to surrender, John?

JOHN. What I am going to do requires finesse.

LUCY (*in a flutter, seeing* HAMILTON *approach*). Oh, dear! how does one talk to highbrows?

JUDGE. Talk to him about himself! Highbrows, lowbrows, all men love it.

(ERNEST HAMILTON, *discoverer of the Hamilton antitoxin, is a fine-looking fellow of about thirty-five, without the spectacles or absent-mindedness somehow expected of scientific genius. He talks little but very rapidly and sees everything. It does not occur to him to be shy or embarrassed "in these surroundings"—not because he is habituated to so much luxury, on three thousand a year, nor because he despises it; he likes it; but he likes other things even more. That is why he works for two thousand a year, instead of working for fat, fashionable fees in private practice.*
JOHN *meets his distinguished guest at the door—effusively, yet with that smiling condescension which wealthy trustees sometimes show to "scientists, college professors, and that sort of thing."*)

JOHN. Ah, Doctor Hamilton! Delighted to see you on my little farm at last. Out here I'm just a plain, old-fashioned farmer.

(ERNEST *glances about at the magnificence and smiles imperceptibly. He makes no audible replies to the glad welcome, but bows urbanely, master of himself and the situation.*)

LUCY. Doctor Hamilton! So good of you to come.

THEODORE. How are you, Ernest? Glad to see you.

LUCY. I don't think you've met our uncle, Judge Grey.

JUDGE (*humorously adopting their manner*). Charmed! I've heard so much about you!—from my niece.

LUCY (*to* ERNEST'S *rescue, like a tactful hostess*). A cup of tea, Doctor Hamilton?

ERNEST (*unperturbed by the reference to* HELEN). Thanks.

JOHN (*while* LUCY *makes tea. Trustee manner*). I have often desired to express my admiration of your heroism in the war against yellow fever in er—ah—*Cuba,* when you let an innocent-looking mosquito bite you—

LUCY (*nodding and poising sugar-tongs*). And then took notes on your symptoms till you became delirious!

ERNEST. No sugar, thanks. (*He looks from one to another with considerable interest.*)

JUDGE. No drums to make you famous, no war correspondents to make you brave—I mean the other way round.

ERNEST (*to* LUCY *poising cream pitcher*). No cream, please.

JOHN. Senator Root says this one triumph alone saves *twenty million dollars a year* to the business interests of the United States! I call that true patriotism.

ERNEST (*with a nod of assent to* LUCY). Lemon.

THEODORE (*with sincerity*). General Wood says it saves more *human lives* a year than were lost in the whole Spanish War! I call it service.

JUDGE. Colonel Goethals says the Panama Canal could not have been built if it hadn't been for you self-sacrificing scientists. Not only that, but you have abolished forever from the United States a scourge which for more than a century had through periodic outbreaks spread terror, devastation, and death. (*A pause.*)

ERNEST (*bored, but trying to hide it*). The ones who deserve your praise are the four who died to prove that theory. . . . (*He smiles.*) Of course, you all know their names. . . . (*He looks at* JOHN, *who looks at* JUDGE, *who looks at* LUCY, *who looks at* THEODORE. *He takes up his cup.*) Delicious tea.

THEODORE. Ah, but they didn't do it for fame, for money—that's the beauty of the sacrifice.

ERNEST (*with a smile*). Quite so. . . . That's what Congress told us when we suggested a pension for the widow of the first victim.

ALL. What! Did Congress refuse the pension?

ERNEST (*finishes his tea*). They finally voted the sum of seventeen dollars a month for the widow and no less than two dollars a month extra for each of his children. . . .

LUCY. Is that all?

ERNEST. No. . . . We pestered Congress to death until, a few years ago, they replaced the pension with an annuity of one hundred and twenty-five dollars a month—though some of them said it was a very bad precedent to establish. (*Returns cup to* LUCY.) No more, thanks, delicious. (*And turns to admire the wide-sweeping view of the farm, hands in pockets.*)

JOHN (*after a pause*). Well, I think our scientists might well be called philanthropists.

ERNEST. Hardly! You see, every one *knows* the names of philanthropists. . . . Better let it go at "scientists."

JUDGE. He's right. Philanthropists don't give their lives, they give their names—they have 'em carved in stone over their institutes and libraries. (JOHN *approaches and joins his guest.*)

ERNEST. Charming little farm you have here.

JOHN. Doctor Hamilton, America kills its big men with routine. You are too valuable to the nation to lose—the trustees think you need a year abroad.

ERNEST. That's strange, I came out here to suggest that very thing. . . . Somebody has been saying kind things about me in Paris. Just had a letter from the great Metchnikoff —wants me to come over and work in the Pasteur! Chance of a lifetime! . . . You didn't have to jolly me up to consent to that!

JOHN (*pacing terrace with his guest, arm in arm*). By the by, my sister is rather keen on science.

ERNEST. Best assistant I ever had. You can pile an awful lot of routine on a woman. The female of the species is more faithful than the male. . . . She's over there already. We can get right to work.

JOHN. She'll be back before you start.

ERNEST (*stops short*). I didn't know that. . . . Well, what is it? (JOHN *hesitates, turns to the family, all watching with breathless interest.*)

THEODORE. Don't you see, old chap, under the circumstances it would hardly do for her to go back to Paris with you.

ERNEST. Why not?

LUCY. You're a man.

ERNEST (*smiling*). You mean I'm dangerous?

LUCY. But she's a woman.

JUDGE. They mean *she's* dangerous.

JOHN. My dear fellow, we are going to ask you quite frankly to decline to take her.

ERNEST (*looks about at the circle of anxious faces. He won't let them read him*). So that's it, eh? . . . But it's the chance of a lifetime for her, too. She needs it more than I do. She's had so little chance to do original work.

JOHN. But she's a woman.

ERNEST. Just what has that to do with it?

JOHN. Everything. We have the highest respect for you, Doctor Hamilton, but also . . . one must respect the opinions of the world, you know.

ERNEST (*thinks it over*). That's right. One must. I forgot to think of that. . . . It's curious, but when working with women of ability one learns to respect them so much that one quite loses the habit of insulting them. Too bad how new conditions spoil fine old customs. . . . Suppose you let her go and let me stay. I can find plenty to do here, I fancy.

JOHN. I fear it would offend our generous benefactor, Mr. Baker. He has set his heart on your going abroad, meeting other big men, getting new ideas for our great humanitarian work. (*The family exchange glances while* JOHN *lies on.*) Besides, my sister would only go to accommodate you. She particularly desires to stay here this winter. That's why she is returning so soon, you see.

ERNEST (*believes it*). Oh, I see. . . . I'm sure I have no desire to *drag* her over with me. . . . (*Smiles at himself.*) I rather thought the opportunity to continue our experiments together . . . but that's all right.

JOHN. Then it's all settled—you agree to go alone?

ERNEST (*a slight pause*). Yes, alone. It's quite settled.

JOHN. How soon could you start?

ERNEST (*absently*). How soon? Why, just as soon as I get some one to run my department.

JOHN. Could my sister run it?

ERNEST (*smiles*). Could she run it? It can't run without her! She's as systematic as (*to* LUCY)—as a good housekeeper.

JOHN (*with a satisfied look at the others*). Then *that's* all fixed! She'll stay when I tell her that you want her to. Could you arrange to start at once?

ERNEST (*hesitates*). By leaving here tonight, I could.

JOHN (*with a triumphant look at the family*). Then I'll telephone for your passage —I have a pull with all the steamship lines. (*Going.*) Of course I hate to cut short your week-end, but I don't want to spoil any scientific careers.

(JOHN *hurries in to telephone.* ERNEST *starts too, as if to stop him but restrains the impulse. He stands alone by the door gazing out over the landscape while* LUCY, THEODORE, *and the* JUDGE *discuss him in low tones by the tea-table.*)

LUCY. Can't you see, you stupid men! He's crazy about her—but thinks there's no hope.

THEODORE. When she finds he's leaving for a year . . . she'll change her mind about marriage! (ERNEST *comes back to earth and to the house-party.*)

JUDGE (*to* ERNEST, *joining them*). Ahem! We were just discussing the marriage danger—I mean the marriage problem.

ERNEST (*with a smile*). Go right on—don't mind me.

THEODORE (*old-friend manner*). See here. When are *you* ever going to marry?

ERNEST (*modern bachelor's laugh*). When am I ever going to get more than two thousand a year?

THEODORE. Bah! what has money got to do with it! Just you wait till the right one comes along.

(HELEN *comes along, stealing up the steps from the garden on tiptoe with the grave, absorbed look of a hunter stalking game. She catches sight of the man she wants and stops short, as motionless as if frozen. But not so! Her lovely hands were poised; one of them now goes to her bosom and presses there. There is nothing icy about this New Woman now.*)

ERNEST (*as unconscious of danger as a mountain-lion on an inaccessible height, smiles easily at his sentimental old friend* THEODORE). How do you know "the right one" hasn't come aleady?

(THEODORE *catches sight of* HELEN. *She shakes her head in silent pleading, taps a finger on her lips, and in a panic flees noiselessly across toward the door.*)

THEODORE (*suppressing a laugh*). Then don't let her go by!
(HELEN *stops at the door and makes a face at* THEODORE.)

ERNEST (*affecting indifference*). Oh, I couldn't stop her, even if I wanted to.

THEODORE (*turning to wink at* HELEN). How do you know? Did you ever ask her?

ERNEST. To marry me? Oh, no! She hasn't any money.

THEODORE (HELEN *is dumbfounded*). Money! You wouldn't marry for money! (HELEN *draws near to hear the answer.*)

ERNEST. You don't suppose I'd marry a woman who hadn't any? Most selfish thing a poor man can do. (HELEN *is interested.*)

THEODORE. Oh, fiddlesticks! You modern young people—

ERNEST (*interrupts*). Make her a sort of superior servant in an inferior home—not that girl! (HELEN *is pleased.*)

THEODORE. Feministic nonsense! The old-fashioned womanly woman—

ERNEST. Sentimental twaddle! What makes it more "womanly" to do menial work *for* men than intellectual work *with* them? (HELEN *delighted, applauds noiselessly.*)

THEODORE. All the same, I'll bet you wouldn't let a little thing like that stand in your way if you really cared for a woman enough to marry her.

ERNEST (*benign and secure*). But, as it happens, I don't. Nothing could induce me to marry. (HELEN *raises her chin, her eyes glitter dangerously.*)

THEODORE. So you are going to run away to Europe like a coward?

ERNEST (*smiles patronizingly*). Theodore, you are such a incorrigible idealist! I have nothing to be afraid of—I simply do not care to *marry!*

HELEN. That's just what *I* said! (*All turn and behold* HELEN.)

ERNEST. My heavens! (*He steps back like a coward.*)

HELEN. But I agree with you perfectly. (*She holds out her hand to him.*) I was so afraid you believed in marriage. (*He rushes to her eagerly.*)

JUDGE (*as the lovers shake hands*). You wronged him. Apologize.

ERNEST. Why—why—all this time, I thought *you* had the usual attitude.

JUDGE. Wronged *her*. Both apologize.

HELEN. Why didn't you ever tell me you had such enlightened views?

ERNEST. Why didn't you ever tell me?

JUDGE. Each understands the other now. Everything lovely!

HELEN. Think of the discussions we might have had!

JUDGE. Not too late yet. Julia and I had discussions for a quarter of a century.

HELEN. Don't think I had any hand in this. (*Laughs.*) I was going to warn you, but now—it is unnecessary now.

ERNEST. Warn me? What do you mean?

HELEN. Can't you see? It was all a plot! (LUCY *draws near noiselessly.*) A plot to entrap you in marriage! They had about given me up as a bad job. *You* were my last hope. They were going to throw me at your head. (*Louder, but without turning.*) Weren't you, Lucy dear?

LUCY (*caught listening, turns abruptly to the others*). These New Women are utterly shameless.

HELEN (*to* ERNEST). These old-fashioned women are utterly shameless. After a decent interval, they will all with one accord make excuses to leave us here alone, so that I can—(*she comes nearer*) ensnare you! (ERNEST *laughs nervously.*) Lucy is going to say—(*imitates* LUCY's *sweet tones*): "If you'll excuse me, I always take forty winks before dressing." Dressing is the hardest work Lucy has to do. Cousin Theodore will find that he *must* write to his wife, and Uncle Everett will feel a yearning for the billiard room. (ERNEST *is nodding and chuckling.*) They're hanging on longer than usual to-day, and I simply must have a talk with you.

ERNEST. Our shop-talk would scandalize 'em!

HELEN. Wait, I'll get rid of them! (*She sits and begins to make tea.*)

ERNEST. I've had my tea, thanks.

HELEN. Stupid! Sit down. (*Indicates a chair close to hers. He takes it cautiously.*) We'll have a little fun with them in a minute. (*She is busy now making tea.*)

THEODORE (*to* LUCY *and the* JUDGE *apart*). You may be right, Uncle Everett, but upon my word it is the strangest courtship I ever witnessed.

LUCY. They ought to be spanked.

JUDGE. Don't worry, old Mother Nature will attend to that.

LUCY. Well, I may be old-fashioned, but—

JUDGE (*interrupting*). But this is merely a new fashion, my dear Lucy. Nature her ancient custom holds, let science say what it will.

HELEN (*handing cup to* ERNEST *with a glance at the others*). Now, then, be attentive to me. (*He leans toward her rather shyly, abashed by her nearness. She makes eyes at him reproachfully.*) Oh, can't you be more attentive than *that*? (*She acts like a coquette and he looks into her beautiful eyes and while he is doing so she says with a fascinating drawl*) Now tell me a-all about anterior poliomyelitis!

ERNEST (*suddenly taken aback, he laughs*). Nothing doing since you left. (*And bends close to explain.*)

LUCY. If you'll excuse me, Doctor Hamilton, I always take forty winks before dressing. We dine at eight. (*Going, she signals to the others.* ERNEST *and* HELEN *exchange smiles.*)

THEODORE (*laughing, to* LUCY). Ss't! Don't tell John what's going on! Keep him busy telephoning. (LUCY *nods excitedly and almost runs to obey the Church.*) Helen, if you and Ernest will excuse me, I really must write to Mary.

(*Their shoulders are close together and they seem too absorbed to reply.* THEODORE *smiles down upon them and signals the* JUDGE *to come along. The* JUDGE, *however, shakes his head but waves* THEODORE *into the house. Uncle Everett looks at the lovers with quizzical interest. He draws near and eavesdrops shamelessly.*)

HELEN. You oughtn't to have dropped the polio experiments.

ERNEST. You oughtn't to have dropped me —right in the *midst* of the experiments. Those agar plates you were incubating dried up and spoiled. You played the very devil with my data.

JUDGE. God bless my soul! what are we coming to?

HELEN (*without turning*). It's perfectly proper for your little ears, uncle, only you can't understand a word of it. Won't *any* one play billiards with you?

JUDGE. But I'm fascinated. It's so idyllic. Makes me feel young again.

HELEN (*to* ERNEST). Oh, you have plenty of men assistants who can estimate antitoxin units.

ERNEST. Men assistants lose interest. They are all so confoundedly ambitious to do original work. Why is it women can stand day after day of monotonous detail better than men?

HELEN. Because men always made them tend the home!

JUDGE. Ah, nothing like a good old-fashioned love scene—in the scientific spirit.

HELEN. Uncle, dear! *Can't* you see that he is paying me wonderful compliments? Haven't you any tact? Go and play Canfield in the library.

JUDGE (*lighting cigar*). Very well, I'll leave you to your own devices—and may God, *your* God, have mercy on your scientific souls.

HELEN (*with sudden animation and camaraderie, thinking they are alone*). Now I must tell you what Doctor Metchnikoff said about you and your future!

JUDGE. Sst! (HELEN *and* ERNEST *turn.*) My children—(*Pause—raises his hand.*) Don't forget the scientific spirit! (*The* JUDGE *saunters off into the garden, smoking.*)

ERNEST. How did you ever meet Metchnikoff?

HELEN (*chaffing*). I had worked under Hamilton! They *all* wanted to meet me.

ERNEST (*with an unmistakable look*). U'm . . . was that why? (*Fleeing danger.*) Didn't you let them know your part in that discovery? Why, if it hadn't been for you, I should never have stumbled upon the thing at all.

HELEN. Oh, I know my place too well for that! Talk about *artistic* temperament, you scientists are worse than prima donnas.

ERNEST (*takes printers' proofs out of pocket, hands them to her in silence*). Some proofs of a monograph I was correcting on the train. Mind hammering those loose sentences of mine into decent English? You can write—I can't.

HELEN (*reading innocently*). "Recent Experiments in Anterior Poliomyelitis by Ernest Hamilton, M.D., Ph.D., and Helen" —what! why, you've put *my* name with yours! (*Much excited and delighted.*)

ERNEST. Well, if you object—like a prima donna— (*Takes out pencil to mark on proof.*)

HELEN (*snatching proofs away*). Object? Why, this makes my reputation in the scientific world.

ERNEST. Well, didn't you make mine?

HELEN (*still glowing with pride, but touched by his unexpected generosity*). You can't imagine what this means to me. It's so hard for a woman to get any recognition. Most men have but one use for us. If we get interested in anything but *them* it is "unwomanly"—they call it "a fad." But they've *got* to take me seriously now. My name with Ernest Hamilton's! (*Points to her name and swaggers back and forth.*)

ERNEST (*bantering*). But then, you see, you are a very exceptional woman. Why, you have a mind like a man.

HELEN. Like a man? (*Coming close to him, tempting him.*) If you had a mind like a woman you would know better than to say that to me!

(*Re-enter* JUDGE *from garden. He smiles and glances at them. The lovers keep quiet as he crosses to the door. Then they look at each other and smile.* JUDGE *has gone into the house. It is nearly dark. The moon is rising.*)

ERNEST (*raises eyebrows*). They all take for granted that I want to make love to you. (*Smiles but avoids her eyes.*)

HELEN (*avoids his*). Well, you took for granted that I wanted you to! . . . You are about the most conceited man I ever knew.

ERNEST. How can I help it when you admire me so?

HELEN. I? Admire you?

ERNEST. You're always telling me what great things I'm going to do—stimulating me, pushing me along. Why, after you left, everything went slump. Tell me, why did you leave? Was I rude to you? Did I hurt your feelings?

HELEN. Not in the least. It was entirely out of respect for *your* feelings.

ERNEST. *My* feelings? (*Laughing.*) Oh, I see. You got it into your head that *I* wanted to marry *you!*

HELEN. Men sometimes do.

ERNEST (*looks away*). I suppose they do.

HELEN. It's been known to happen.

ERNEST. Talk about conceit! Well, you needn't be afraid! I'll never ask you to marry *me.*

HELEN (*turns and looks at him a moment*). You can't imagine what a weight this takes off my mind. (*She looks away and sighs.*)

ERNEST (*enthusiastically*). Yes! I feel as if a veil between us had been lifted.
(*He looks away and sighs too. Some one begins "Tristan and Isolde" on the piano within. The moon is up.*)

HELEN (*after a pause*). Suppose we talk about—our work.

ERNEST. Yes! Our work. Let's drop the other subject. Look at the moon! (*Music and the moonlight flooding them.*)

HELEN. Seriously, you promise never to mention the subject again? (*She keeps her eyes averted.*)

ERNEST. I promise. (*He keeps his eyes averted.*)

HELEN (*turning to him with a sudden change to girlish enthusiasm*). Then I'll go to Paris with you!

ERNEST (*recoils*). What's that?

HELEN. Why, Doctor Metchnikoff—he promised me he would invite you.

ERNEST. Yes, but—

HELEN. Don't miss the chance of a lifetime!

ERNEST. No, but you—*you* can't come!

HELEN (*simply*). If you need me I can, and you just said—

ERNEST. But you mustn't come to Paris with me!

HELEN. Don't you want me with you?

ERNEST. You are to stay at home and run the department for me.

HELEN (*stepping back*). Don't you want me with you?

ERNEST (*stepping forward, with his heart in voice*). Do I *want* you! (*Stops.*) But I am a man—you are a woman.

HELEN. What of it? Are you one of those small men who care what people say? No! That's not your reason! (*She sees that it is not.*) What is it? You must tell me.

ERNEST (*hesitates*). It's only for your sake.

HELEN (*with feeling*). Think of all I've done for *your* sake. You wouldn't be going yourself but for me! I was the one to see you needed it, I proposed it to Metchnikoff —I urged him—*made* him ask you—for *your sake!* And now am I to be left at home like a child because you don't care to be embarrassed with me?

ERNEST. Oh, please! This is so unfair. But I simply can't take you now.

HELEN (*with growing scorn*). Oh! You are all alike. You pile work upon me until I nearly drop, you play upon my interest, my sympathy—you get all you can out of me—my youth, my strength, my best! And then, just as I, too, have a chance to arrive in my profession, you, of all men, throw me over! I hate men. I hate you!

ERNEST. And I love you!
(*They stare at each other in silence, the moonlight flooding* HELEN's *face, the music coming clear.*)

HELEN (*in an awed whisper, stepping back slowly*). I've done it! I've done it! I *knew* I'd do it!

ERNEST. No. I did it. Forgive me. I had to do it.

HELEN. Oh, and this spoils everything!

ERNEST (*comes closer*). No! It glorifies everything! (*He breaks loose.*) I have loved you from the first day you came and looked up at me for orders. I didn't want you there; I didn't want any woman there. I tried to tire you out with overwork but couldn't. I tried to drive you out by rudeness, but you stayed. And that made me love you more. Oh, I love you! I love you! I love you!

HELEN. Don't; oh, don't love me!

ERNEST (*still closer*). Why, I never knew there could be women like you. I thought women were merely something to be wanted and worshipped, petted and patronized. But now—why, I love everything about you: your wonderful, brave eyes that face the naked facts of life and are not ashamed; those beautiful hands that toiled so long, so well, so close to mine and not afraid, not afraid!

HELEN. You mustn't! I *am* afraid now! I made you say it. (*Smiling and crying.*) I have always wanted to make you say it. I have always sworn you shouldn't.

ERNEST (*pained*). Because you cannot care enough?

HELEN. Enough? . . . Too much.

ERNEST (*overwhelmed*). You—love—me! (*He takes her in his arms, a silent embrace with only the bland blasé moon looking on.*)

HELEN. It is because I love you that I didn't want you to say it—only I did. It is because I love you that I went abroad—to stay, only I couldn't! I couldn't stay away! (*She holds his face in her hands.*) Oh, do you know how I love you? No! . . . you're only a *man*!

ERNEST (*kissing her rapturously*). Every day there in the laboratory, when you in your apron—that dear apron which I stole from your locker when you left me—when you asked for orders—did you know that I wanted to say: "Love me"! Every day when you took up your work, did you never guess that I wanted to take you up in my arms?

HELEN (*smiling up into his face*). Why didn't you?

ERNEST. Thank God I didn't! For while we worked there together I came to know you as few men ever know the women they desire. Woman can be more than sex, as man is more than sex. And all this makes man and woman not less but more *overwhelmingly* desirable and necessary to each other, and makes both things last—not for a few years, but forever!

(*Sound of voices approaching from the garden. The lovers separate. It is* JEAN *and* REX, REX *laughing,* JEAN *dodging until caught and kissed.*)

JEAN. No, no—it's time to dress. . . . Be good, Rex—don't!

(*Without seeing* HELEN *and* ERNEST, *they disappear into the house.* HELEN *is suddenly changed, as if awakened from a spell of enchantment.*)

HELEN. What have we done! This is all moonlight and madness. To-morrow comes the clear light of day.

ERNEST. Ah, but we'll love each other to-morrow!

HELEN. But we cannot marry—then or any other to-morrow.

ERNEST. Can't? What nonsense!

HELEN (*shaking her head and restraining him*). I have slaved for you all these months—not because I wanted to win you from your work but to help you in it. And now—after all—shall I destroy you? No! No!

ERNEST. I *love* you—you love *me*—nothing else matters.

HELEN. Everything else matters. I'm not a little débutante to be persuaded that I am needed because I am wanted! I haven't *played* with you; I have *worked* with you, and I *know!* Think of Theodore! Think of Lucy! And now poor little Jean. Marry you? Never!

ERNEST. You mean your career?

HELEN (*with supreme scorn*). My career? No! yours—always yours!

ERNEST (*with the same scorn and a snap of the fingers*). Then *that* for my career. I'll go back into private practice and make a million.

HELEN. That's just what I said you'd do. Just what you must not do! Your work is needed by the world.

ERNEST (*wooing*). You are my world and I need you. . . . But there is no love without

marriage, no marriage without money. . . . We can take it or leave it. Can we leave it? No! I can't—you can't! Come! (*She steps back slowly.*) Why should we sacrifice the best! Come!

HELEN. So *this* is what marriage means! Then I *cannot* marry you, Ernest!

ERNEST. You cannot do without me, Helen! (*Holds out his arms.*) Come! You have been in my arms once. You and I can never forget that now. We can never go back now. It's all—or nothing now. Come! (*She is struggling against her passion. He stands still, with arms held out.*) I shall not woo you against your will, but you are coming to me! Because, by all the powers of earth and heaven, you are mine and I am yours! Come!

(*Like a homing pigeon she darts into his arms with a gasp of joy. A rapturous embrace in silence with the moonlight streaming down upon them. The music has stopped.*)

(JOHN, *dressed for dinner, strolls out upon the terrace. He stops abruptly upon discovering them. The lovers are too absorbed to be aware of his presence.*)

ACT TWO

It is the next morning, Sunday.

It appears that at JOHN's *country place they have breakfast at small tables out upon the broad, shaded terrace overlooking the glorious view of his little farm.*

ERNEST *and* THEODORE, *the scientist and the clergyman, are breakfasting together. The others are either breakfasting in their rooms or are not yet down, it being Sunday.*

The man of God is enjoying his material blessings heartily. Also he seems to be enjoying his view of the man of science, who eats little and says less.

THEODORE (*with coffee-cup poised*). What's the matter with your appetite this morning, Ernest? (ERNEST, *gazing up at one of the second-story windows, does not hear. The door opens. He starts. Then, seeing it's only a servant with food, he sighs.*) Expecting something? The codfish balls? Well, here they are. (ERNEST *refuses the proffered codfish balls, scowls, brings out cigar case,*

lights cigar, looks at watch, and fidgets.*) Oh, I know—you're crazy to go with me —to church! (ERNEST *doesn't hear. Creates a cloud of smoke.*) Their regular rector is ill. So I agreed to take the service this morning. . . . Always the way when off for a rest . . . isn't it? (*No answer.* THEODORE *gets up, walks around the table, and shouts in* ERNEST's *face.*) Isn't it?

ERNEST (*startled*). I beg your pardon?

THEODORE (*laughs*, ERNEST *wondering what's the joke*). Oh, you're hopeless! (*Going.*) I can't stand people who talk so much at breakfast.

ERNEST (*suddenly wakes up*). Wait a minute. Sit down. Have a cigar. Let's talk about God. (THEODORE *stops smiling.*) But I mean it. I'd like to have a religion myself.

THEODORE. I had an idea you took no stock in religion. (*Takes the cigar.* ERNEST *holds a match for him.*)

ERNEST (*enthusiastically*). Just what I thought, until . . . well, I've made a discovery, a great discovery!

THEODORE. A scientific discovery?

ERNEST (*with a wave of the hand*). It makes all science look like a . . . mere machine.

THEODORE. Well, if you feel so strongly about it . . . better come to church after all!

ERNEST. I'm not talking about the Church —I'm talking about *religion*.

THEODORE. You're not talking about religion; you're talking about—love.

ERNEST (*quietly*). Certainly; the same thing, isn't it? I'm talking about the divine fire that glorifies life and perpetuates it— the one eternal thing we mortals share with God. . . . If *that* isn't religious, what is? (THEODORE *smiles indulgently.*) Tell me, Theodore—you know I wasn't allowed to go to church when young, and since then I've always worked on the holy Sabbath day, like yourself—does the Church still let innocent human beings think there's something inherently wrong about sex? (THEODORE *drops his eyes.* ERNEST *disgusted with him.*) I see! Good people should drop their eyes even at the mention of the word.

THEODORE. Sex is a necessary evil, I admit, but—

ERNEST (*laughs*). Evil! The God-given impulse which accounts for you sitting there, for me sitting here? The splendid instinct which writes our poetry, builds our civilizations, founds our churches—the very heart and soul of life is evil. Really, Theodore, I don't know much about religion, but that strikes me as blasphemy against the Creator.

THEODORE. Very scientific, my boy, very modern; but the Church believed in marriage before Science was born.

ERNEST. As a compromise with evil?

THEODORE. As a sacrament of religion—and so do you!

ERNEST. Good! Then why practise and preach marriage as a sacrament of property? "Who giveth this woman to be married to this man—" Women are still goods and chattels to be given or sold, are they?

THEODORE. Oh, nonsense!

ERNEST. Then why keep on making them promise to "serve and obey"? Why marry them with a ring—the link of the ancient chain? (*He smiles.*) In the days of physical force it was made of iron—now of gold. But it's still a chain, isn't it?

THEODORE. Symbols, my dear fellow, not to be taken in a literal sense—time-honored and beautiful symbols.

ERNEST. But why insult a woman you respect—even symbolically?

THEODORE (*with a laugh*). Oh, you scientists!

ERNEST (*joining in the laugh*). We try to find the truth—and you try to hide it, eh? Well, there's one thing we have in common, anyway—one faith I'll never doubt again; I believe in Heaven now. I always shall.

THEODORE. Do you mind telling me why, my boy?

ERNEST. Not in the least. I've been there. (JOHN *comes out to breakfast. He is scowling.*) Good morning; could you spare me five minutes?

JOHN (*ringing bell*). Haven't had breakfast yet.

ERNEST. After breakfast?

JOHN. I've an appointment with young Baker.

ERNEST (*smiles*). I'll wait my turn.

JOHN. Going to be pretty busy to-day—you, too, I suppose, if you're sailing to-morrow.

ERNEST. I can postpone sailing. This is more important.

JOHN. I should hate to see *anything* interfere with your career.

(LUCY *also arrives for breakfast. She "always pours her husband's coffee."*)

ERNEST. I appreciate your interest, but I'll look out for my "career." (*To* LUCY.) Could you tell me when your sister will be down?

JOHN (*overriding* LUCY). My sister is ill and won't be down at all . . . until *after* you *leave.*

(LUCY *pretends not to hear.* THEODORE *walks away.*)

ERNEST (*aroused, but calm*). I don't believe you quite understand. It is a matter of indifference to me whether we have a talk or not. Entirely out of courtesy to you that I suggest it.

JOHN. Don't inconvenience yourself on my account.

ERNEST (*shrugs shoulders and turns to* THEODORE). Wait, I think I'll sit in church till train time.

THEODORE (*smoothing it over*). Come along. I'm going to preach about marriage! (THEODORE *starts off.*)

ERNEST (*going, turns to* LUCY). Thanks for your kindness. Will you ask the valet to pack my things, please? I'll call for them on the way to the station. (*To* JOHN.) Do you understand? I have no favors to ask of you. You don't own your sister—she owns herself. (*The scientist goes to church.*)

JOHN (*with a loud laugh, turns to* LUCY). Rather impertinent for a two-thousand-dollar man, I think. (*Resumes breakfast, picks up newspaper.* LUCY *says nothing, attending to his wants solicitously.*) Bah! what does this highbrow know about the power men of my sort can use . . . when we have to? (LUCY *cringes dutifully in*

silence. JOHN, *paper in one hand, brusquely passes cup to* LUCY *with other.*) Helen got her own way about college, about work, about living in her own apartment—but if she thinks she can put *this* across! Humph! These modern women must learn their place. (LUCY, *smiling timidly, returns cup.* JOHN *takes it without thanks, busied in newspapers. A look of resentment creeps over* LUCY's *pretty face, now that he can't see her.*) Ah! I've got something up my sleeve for that young woman. (LUCY *says nothing, looks of contempt while he reads.*) Well, why don't you say something?

LUCY (*startled*). I thought you didn't like me to talk at breakfast, dear.

JOHN. Think I like you to sit there like a mummy? (*No reply.*) Haven't you *any*-thing to say? (*Apparently not.*) You never have any more, nothing interesting. . . . Does it ever occur to you that I'd like to be diverted? . . . No!

LUCY. Yes. . . . Would you mind very much if . . . if I left you, John?

JOHN. Left me? When—where—how long?

LUCY (*gathering courage*). Now—any place—entirely.

JOHN (*bursts out laughing*). What suddenly put *this* notion in your head?

LUCY. I'm sorry—John, but I've had it—oh, for years. I never dared ask you till now.

JOHN (*still glancing over paper*). Like to leave me, would you? . . . You have no grounds for divorce, my dear.

LUCY. But *you* will have—after I leave you.

JOHN (*yawns*). You have no lover to leave with.

LUCY (*daintily*). But couldn't I just desert you—without anything horrid?

JOHN (*reads*). No money to desert with.

LUCY (*springs up—at bay*). You won't let me escape decently when I tell you I don't want to stay? When I tell you I can't stand being under your roof any longer? When I tell you I'm sick of this life?

JOHN (*gets up calmly*). But, you see, I can stand it. I want you to stay. I'm not sick of it. You belong to me.

LUCY (*shrinking away as he approaches*). Don't touch me! Every time you come near me I have to nerve myself to stand it.

JOHN. What's got into you? Don't I give you everything money can buy? My God, if I only gave you something to worry about; if I ran after other women like old man Baker—

LUCY. If you only would!—Then you'd let *me* alone. To me you are repulsive.

JOHN (*taking hold of her*). Lucy! You are my wife.

LUCY (*looking him straight in the eye*). But you don't respect me, and I—I hate you—oh, how I hate you!

JOHN (*holds her fast*). I am your husband, your lawful husband.

LUCY (*stops struggling*). Yes, this is lawful—but, oh, what laws you men have made for women!

(*The* JUDGE *comes out, carrying a telegram.*)

JUDGE. Rather early in the day for conjugal embraces, if you should ask me. (JOHN *and* LUCY *separate.*) Makes me quite sentimental and homesick. (JUDGE *raises telegram and kisses it.*)

LUCY (*calming herself*). From Aunt Julia again? Do you get telegrams every day from Reno?

JUDGE. No, but she caught cold. Went to the theatre last night and caught a cold. So she wired me—naturally; got the habit of telling me her troubles, can't break it, even in Reno.

JOHN. I thought she hated the theatre!

JUDGE. So she does, but I'm fond of it; she went for my sake. She's got the habit of sacrificing herself for me. Just as hard to break good habits as bad.

JOHN. True women enjoy sacrificing themselves.

JUDGE. Yes, that's what we tell them. Well, we ought to know. We make 'em do it. (*Brings out a fountain pen and sits abruptly.*) That's what I'll tell her. I can hear her laugh. You know her laugh.

LUCY (*rings for a servant*). A telegraph blank?

JUDGE (*with a humorous expression he brings a whole pad of telegraph blanks out of another pocket*). Carry them with me nowadays. (*Begins to write.*) Wish I hadn't sold my Western Union, John.

JOHN. I don't believe you want that divorce very much.

JUDGE. It doesn't matter what *I* want—what she wants is the point. You must give the woman you marry tutti-frutti, divorces—everything. . . . Why, I've got the habit myself, and God knows I don't enjoy sacrifice—I'm a man! The superior sex!

JOHN. I don't believe you appreciate that wife of yours.

JUDGE (*between the words he's writing*). Don't I? It isn't every wife that'd travel away out to Reno—you know how she hates travelling—and go to a theatre—and catch a cold—and get a divorce—all for the sake of an uncongenial husband. (*Suddenly getting an idea, strikes table.*) I know what gave her a cold. She raised all the windows in her bedroom—for *my* sake!—I always kept them down for *her* sake. I'll have to scold her. (*Bends to his writing again.*) Poor little thing! She doesn't know how to take care of herself without me. I doubt if she ever will. (*Looks over telegram. A* SERVANT *comes, takes telegram, and goes.*)

JOHN. Uncle Everett, I want your advice.

JUDGE. John! do *you* want a divorce?

JOHN. No, we are not that sort, are we, Lucy? (*No answer.*) *Are* we, dear?

LUCY (*after a pause*). No, we are not that sort!

JOHN. We believe in the sanctity of the home, the holiness of marriage.

LUCY. Yes, we believe in—"the holiness of marriage"! (*Turns away, covering her face with her hands and shuddering.*)

JOHN. Lucy, tell Helen and Jean to come here. (LUCY *goes.*) Well, young Baker spoke to me about Jean last night. I told him I'd think it over and give him my decision this morning.

JUDGE. That's right. Mustn't seem too anxious, John. When the properly qualified male offers one of our dependent females a chance at woman's only true career, of course it's up to us to look disappointed.

JOHN. But I didn't bring up the little matter you spoke of.

JUDGE. About that chorus girl? . . . Afraid of scaring him off?

JOHN. Not at all, but—well, it's all over and it's all fixed. No scandal, no blackmail.

JUDGE. Hum! By the way, got anything on Hamilton?

JOHN. I don't believe in saints myself.

JUDGE. I see. . . . Good thing, for Jean Rex isn't a saint. I suppose you'd break off the match.

(REX, *in riding clothes, comes out.* JOHN *salutes him warmly. The* JUDGE *is reading the paper.*)

REX (*not eagerly*). Well?

JOHN. Well, of course, you realize that you're asking a great deal of me, Rex, but —(*Offers hand to* REX *warmly.*) Be good to her, my boy, be good to her.

REX (*shaking hands, forced warmth*). Thanks awfully. See-what-I-mean? (*To* JUDGE.) Congratulate me, Judge; I'm the happiest of men.

JUDGE (*looking up from newspaper*). So I see. Don't let it worry you.

(JEAN, *in riding costume, comes from the house.*)

JOHN (*signalling* JUDGE *to leave*). If Helen asks for me, I'm in the garden.

JUDGE. If any telegrams come for me, I'm writing to *my wife!*

(JEAN *and* REX *alone, they look at each other, not very loverlike.*)

JEAN (*impulsively*). You weren't in love with me yesterday. You aren't now. You would get out of it if you honorably could. But you honorably *can't!* So you have spoken to John; you are going to see it through, because you're a good sport. . . . I admire you for that, Rex, too much to hold you to it. You are released.

REX (*amazed*). Why—why—you—you suppose I want to be released?

JEAN. Well, I do! . . . Yesterday I let you propose to me when I cared for some one else. That's not fair to you, to me, to him!

REX (*in a sudden fury*). Who is he? What do you mean by this? Why didn't you tell me?

JEAN. I'm telling you now. What have you ever told me about yourself?

REX (*blinking*). You had no right to play fast and loose with me.

JEAN. I'm making the only amends I can. You are free, I tell you.

REX. I don't want to be free! He can't have you! You are mine! If you think you can make me stop loving you—

JEAN (*interrupting*). Love, Rex? Only jealousy. You've never been in love with me —you've always been in love with Helen. But you couldn't get her, so you took me. Isn't that true, Rex?

REX (*after an uncomfortable pause*). I'll be honest with you, too. Yesterday I wasn't really very serious. I felt like a brute afterward. You tried your best to prevent what happened and ran away from me. But now—

JEAN. Don't you know why I ran away? To make you follow. I made you catch me. I made you kiss me. Then you realized that we had been thrown together constantly— deliberately thrown together, if you care to know it—and, well, that's how many marriages are made. But I shan't marry on such terms. It's indecent!

REX (*another pause*). I never thought a *woman* could be capable of such honesty! . . . Oh, what a bully sport you are! You aren't like the rest that have been shoved at me. Why, I can respect you. You are the one for me. (*He tries to take her.*)

JEAN (*restraining him with dignity*). I am sorry, Rex, but I am not for you.

REX. Jean! without you . . . don't you see —I'll go straight to the devil!

JEAN. That old, cowardly dodge? Any man who has no more backbone than that— why, I wouldn't marry you if you were the last man in the world.

REX (*frantic to possess what he cannot have*). You won't, eh? We'll see about that. I want you now as I never wanted anything in my life, and I'll win you from him yet. You'll see!

(HELEN *now appears.*)

HELEN. Oh, I beg your pardon. Lucy said John was out here.

JEAN. I'll call him. (*She runs down into the garden.*)

REX. I'll call him. (*He runs after* JEAN. HELEN *helplessly watches them go, sighs, standing by the garden steps until* JOHN *ascends. He looks at* HELEN *a moment, wondering how to begin. She looks so capable and unafraid of him.*)

JOHN. If you hadn't gone to college, you could have done what Jean is doing.

HELEN (*with a shrug and a smile*). But how proud you must be, John, to have a sister who isn't compelled to marry one man while in love with another. *Now*, aren't you glad I went to college? (*She laughs good-naturedly at him.*)

JOHN. Humph! If you think I'd let a sister of mine marry one of old man Baker's two-thousand-dollar employees—

HELEN. Why, John, didn't Ernest tell you? Doctor Hawksbee has offered him a partnership. Just think of that!

JOHN. What! Going back into private practice?

HELEN. But it's such a fashionable practice. Hawksbee's made a million at it.

JOHN. But the institute needs Hamilton.

HELEN. Ah, but we need the money!

JOHN (*disconcerted*). So you are going to spoil a noble career, are you? That's selfish. I didn't think it of you. There are thousands of successful physicians, but there is only one Ernest Hamilton.

HELEN (*laughs*). Oh, don't worry, John, he has promised me to keep his two-thousand-dollar job.

JOHN. Ah, I'm glad. You must let nothing interfere with his great humanitarian work. Think what it means to the lives of little children! Think what it means to the future of the race! Why, every one says his greatest usefulness has hardly begun!

HELEN. Oh, I know all that, I've thought of all that.

JOHN. Now, such men should be kept free from cares and anxiety. What was it you said yesterday? "He needs every cent of his salary for books, travel, all the advantages he simply must have for efficiency." To marry a poor man—most selfish thing a girl could do!

HELEN. Yes, John, that's what I said yesterday.

JOHN (*scoring*). But that was before he asked you! (HELEN *smiles. He sneers.*) Rather pleased with yourself now, aren't you? "Just a woman after all"—heroine of cheap magazine story! Sacrifices career for love! . . . All very pretty and romantic, my dear—but how about the man you love! Want to sacrifice his career, too?

HELEN. But I'm not going to sacrifice what you are pleased to call my career. . . . Therefore he won't have to sacrifice his.

JOHN. What! going to keep on working? Will he let the woman he loves work!

HELEN (*demure*). Well, you see, he says I'm "too good" to loaf.

JOHN. Humph! who'll take care of your home when you're at work? Who'll take care of your work when you're at home? Look at it practically. To maintain such a home as he needs on such a salary as he has —why, it would take all your time, all your energy. To keep him in his class you'll have to drop out of your own, become a household drudge, a servant.

HELEN. And if I am willing?

JOHN. Then where's your intellectual companionship? How'll you help his work? Expense for him, disillusionment for both. If you're the woman you pretend to be, you won't marry that man!

HELEN (*strong*). The world needs his work, but he needs mine, and we both need each other.

JOHN (*stronger*). And marriage would only handicap his work, ruin yours, and put you apart. You know that's true. You've seen it happen with others. You have told me so yourself!

HELEN. Then that settles it! We must not, cannot, shall not marry. We have no right to marry. I agree with all you say—it would not join us together; it would put us asunder.

JOHN. And you'll give him up? Good! Good!

HELEN. Give him up? Never! The right to work, the right to love—those rights are inalienable. No, we'll give up marriage but not each other.

JOHN. But—but—I don't understand.

HELEN (*straight in his eyes*). We need each other—in our work and in our life—and we're to have each other—until life is ended and our work is done. Now, do you understand?

JOHN (*recoiling*). Are you in your right mind? Think what you're saying.

HELEN. I have thought all night, John. You have shown me how to say it.

JOHN. But, but—why, this is utterly unbelievable! Why, I'm not even shocked. Do you notice? I'm not even shocked? Because everything you have said, everything you have done—it all proves that you are a good woman.

HELEN. If I were a bad woman, I'd inveigle him into marriage, John.

JOHN. Inveigle! Marriage! Are you crazy? . . . Oh, this is all one of your highbrow jokes!

HELEN. John, weren't you serious when you said marriage would destroy him?

JOHN. But this would destroy *you*!

HELEN. Well, even if that were so, which is more important to the world? Which is more important to your "great humanitarian work"?

JOHN. Ah, very clever! A bluff to gain my consent to marrying him—a trick to get his salary raised.

HELEN (*with force*). John, nothing you can do, nothing you can say, will ever gain my consent to marrying him. I've not told you half my reasons.

JOHN. My God! my own sister! And did you, for one moment, dream that I would consent to that!

HELEN. Not for one moment. I'm not asking your consent. I'm just telling you.

JOHN (*after scrutinizing her*). Ridiculous! If you really meant to run away with this fellow, would you come and tell *me*, your own brother?

HELEN. Do you suppose I'd *run* away without telling, even my own brother?

JOHN (*looks at her a moment; she returns his gaze*). Bah!—all pose and poppycock! (*He abruptly touches bell.*) I'll soon put a stop to this nonsense. (*Muttering.*) Damnedest thing I ever heard of.

HELEN. John, I understand exactly what I'm doing. You never will. But nothing you can do can stop me now.

JOHN. We'll see about that. (*The* BUTLER *appears.*) Ask the others to step out here at once; all except Miss Jean and Mr. Baker, I don't want them. Is Doctor Hamilton about?

BUTLER. No, sir, he went to church.

JOHN. All right. (*The* BUTLER *disappears.*) To church! My God!

(HELEN *pays no attention. She gazes straight out into the future, head high, eyes clear and wide open.*)

JOHN. First of all, when the others come out, I'm going to ask them to look you in the face. Then you can make this statement to them, if you wish, and—look them in the face.

HELEN (*with quiet scorn*). If I were being forced into such a marriage as poor little Jean's, I would kill myself. But in the eyes of God, who made love, no matter how I may appear in the eyes of man, who made marriage, I know that I am doing right.

(LUCY *comes out, followed by the* JUDGE.)

JOHN (*not seeing them. He is loud*). Say that to Uncle Everett and Cousin Theodore! Say that to my wife, stand up and say that to the world, if you dare.

LUCY (*to* JUDGE). She has told him!

JOHN (*wheeling about*). What! did she tell you? Why didn't you come to me at once?

LUCY (*tremulous*). She said she wanted to tell you herself. I didn't think she'd dare!

(*They all turn to look at* HELEN. THEODORE *comes back from church alone.*)

HELEN. It had to be announced, of course.

THEODORE (*advancing, beaming*). Announced? What is announced?

(*All turn to him in a panic.*)

LUCY (*hurriedly*). Their engagement, Theodore!

JUDGE (*overriding* HELEN). Yes, John has given his consent at last—example to society. (*Prods* JOHN.)

JOHN (*also overrides* HELEN). Of course! One of the finest fellows in the world.

THEODORE (*delighted*). And withal he has a deep religious nature. Congratulations. My dear, he'll make an ideal husband. (*Takes both* HELEN'S *hands, about to kiss her.*)

HELEN (*can't help smiling*). Thank you, cousin, but I don't want a husband. (*A sudden silence.*)

THEODORE (*looks from one to the other*). A lover's quarrel?—already!

JUDGE (*enjoying it*). No, Theodore. these lovers are in perfect accord. They both have conscientious scruples against marriage.

JOHN. Conscientious!

JUDGE. So they are simply going to set up housekeeping without the mere formality of a wedding ceremony.

(THEODORE *drops* HELEN'S *hands.*)

HELEN (*quietly*). We are going to do nothing of the sort.

THEODORE. Uncle Everett! (*Takes her hands again.*)

HELEN. We are not going to set up housekeeping at all. He will keep his present quarters and I mine.

JOHN. But they are going to belong to each other.

THEODORE (*drops* HELEN'S *hands—aghast*). I don't believe it.

JUDGE (*apart to* THEODORE). The strike against marriage. It was bound to come.

THEODORE (*to* JUDGE). But Church and State—(*indicates self and* JUDGE) must break this strike.

HELEN. John is a practical man. He will prove to you that such a home as we could afford would only be a stumbling-block to Ernest's usefulness, a hollow sphere for mine. You can't fill it with mere happiness, Lucy, not for long, not for long.

JUDGE (*restrains* THEODORE *about to reply*). Oh, let her get it all nicely talked out, then she'll take a nap and wake up feeling better. (*Whispering.*) We've driven her to this ourselves, but she really doesn't mean a word of it. Come, dear child, tell us all about this nightmare.

HELEN (*smiles at the* JUDGE). Why, think what would happen to an eager intellect like Ernest Hamilton's if he had to come back to a narrow-minded apartment or a dreary suburb every evening and eat morbid meals opposite a housewife regaling him with the social ambitions of the other commuters. Ugh! It has ruined enough brilliant men already. (JUDGE *restrains* THEODORE *and others who want to interrupt.*) Now at the University Club he dines, at slight expense compared with keeping up a home, upon the best food in the city with some of the best scientists in the country. . . . Marriage would divorce him from all that, would transplant him from an atmosphere of ideas into an atmosphere of worries. We should be forced into the same deadly ruts as the rest of you, uncle. Do you want me to destroy a great career, Theodore?

THEODORE. Do you want to be a blot upon that career?

HELEN (*lightly*). I'd rather be a blot than a blight, and that's what I'd be if I became his bride. Ask John.

LUCY. Do you want to be disgraced, despised, ostracized!

HELEN (*smiles at* LUCY). A choice of evils, dear; of course, none of those costly well-kept wives on your visiting list will call upon me. But instead of one day at home, instead of making a tired husband work for me, I'll have all my days free to work with him, like the old-fashioned woman you admire! Instead of being an expense, I'll be a help to him; instead of being separated by marriage and divergent interests, we'll be united by love and common peril. . . . Isn't that the orthodox way to gain character, Theodore?

JOHN. Oh, this is all damned nonsense! Look here, you've either got to marry this fellow now or else go away and never see him again; never, never!

HELEN. Just what I thought, John. I intended never to see him again. That was why I let you send me abroad. But I'll never, never do it again. (*Smiling like an engaged girl.*) It was perfectly dreadful! Ernest couldn't get along without me at all, poor old thing. And I, why, I nearly died.

JOHN. Then you'll have to be married, that's all.

THE OTHERS. Why, of course you'll have to, that's all.

HELEN (*nodding*). Oh, I know just how you feel about it. I thought so, too, at first, but I can't marry Ernest Hamilton. I love him.

THEODORE. But if you love him truly— marriage, my dear, brings together those who love each other truly.

HELEN. But those who love each other truly don't need anything to bring them together. The difficulty is to keep apart. (*A reminiscent shudder.*)

JOHN. That's all romantic rot! Every one feels that way at first.

HELEN. At first! Then the practical object of marriage is not to bring together those who love each other, but to keep together those who do not? (*To* LUCY.) What a dreadful thing marriage must be.

(JUDGE *chokes down a chuckle.*)

JUDGE. Ah, so you wish to be free to separate. Now we have it.

HELEN. To separate? What an idea! On the contrary, we wish to be free to keep together! In the old days when they had interests in common marriage used to make man and woman one, but now it puts them apart. Can't you see it all about you? He goes down-town and works; she stays up-town and plays. He belongs to the laboring class; she belongs to the leisure class. At best, they seldom work at the same or similar trades. Legally it may be a union, but socially it's a mésalliance—in the eyes of God it's often worse. . . . No wonder that one in eleven ends in divorce. The only way to avoid spiritual separation is to shun legal union like a contagious disease. Modern marriage *is* divorce. (*She turns to go, defiantly.*) I've found my work, I've found my mate, and so has he! What more can any human being ask?

(*The* BUTLER *appears.*)

BUTLER (*to* JOHN). Doctor Hamilton is outside in a taxicab, sir.

JOHN. Show him here at once!

BUTLER. He says he does not care to come in, sir, unless you are ready to talk to him now.

JOHN. Well, of all the nerve! You bet I'm ready! (*Starts off.* HELEN *starts, too.*)

JUDGE (*intercepting them calmly*). Wait a minute—wait a minute. (*To* SERVANT.) Ask Doctor Hamilton kindly to wait in the library. (*The* BUTLER *goes.*) Now, we're all a bit overwrought. (*Soothes* HELEN, *pats her hand, puts arm about her, gradually leads her back.*) I still believe in you, Helen, I still believe in him. (*To all.*) It's simply that he's so deeply absorbed in his great work for mankind that he doesn't realize what he is asking Helen to do.

HELEN (*quietly*). So I told him . . . when he asked me to marry him.

ALL. What! He *asked* you to *marry* him?

HELEN. Of course! *Implored* me to marry him. (*She adds, smiling.*) So absorbed— not in mankind, but in me—that he "didn't realize what he was asking me to do."

LUCY (*utterly amazed*). And you refused him! The man who loves you honorably?

HELEN (*demurely*). Of course! You don't suppose I'd take advantage of the poor fellow's weakness. Women often do, I admit —even when not in love, sometimes. . . . Not because they're depraved but dependent.

JOHN (*to all*). And then he proposed this wicked substitute! Poisoned her innocent mind—the bounder!

HELEN. But he did nothing of the sort.

JOHN. Oh, your own idea, was it?

HELEN. Of course!

JOHN (*to all*). And he is willing to take advantage of the poor child's ignorance— the cad! (*To* THEODORE.) "Deep religious nature," eh?

THEODORE. I can't believe it of him.

HELEN. He knows nothing about it yet. I haven't even seen him since I made my decision.

(*All exchange bewildered glances.*)

JOHN (*apart to* JUDGE). We've got to get him off to Paris. It's our only hope.

JUDGE (*apart to* JOHN). You can't stop her following. She's on the edge of the precipice —do you want to shove her over? You are dealing with big people here and a big passion.

(*The* BUTLER *returns.*)

BUTLER. Doctor Hamilton asks to see Miss Helen while waiting.

JUDGE (*calmly to* BUTLER). Tell Doctor Hamilton that Miss Helen will see him here.

(*The* BUTLER *leaves.*)

JOHN. Are you crazy! We've got to keep 'em apart—our one chance to save her.

JUDGE. No, bring them together. *That* is our one chance. Come, we'll go down into the garden and they'll have a nice little talk. Nothing like talk, John, honest talk, to clear these marriage problems. (*Going.*)

JOHN. And let them elope? In that taxicab? —not on your life! (*Runs to and fro.*)

JUDGE. Come, John, girls never notify the family in advance when they plan elopements. It's not done.

THEODORE (*going*). Uncle Everett is right. Ernest will bring her to her senses. He *has* a deep religious nature.

(*JUDGE leads* JOHN *away to the garden.*)

LUCY (*lingering—to* HELEN). If you offer yourself on such terms to the man who loves you honorably, he'll never look at you again.

THEODORE (*leading* LUCY *off to garden*). Don't worry! She won't.

(*ERNEST rushes out to* HELEN.)

HELEN. Ernest!

ERNEST. At last! (*He takes her in his arms; she clings to him and gazes into his eyes; a long embrace.*) Tell me that you're all right again.

HELEN (*smiling with love and trust*). Except that you deserted me, dear, just when I needed you most. Ernest, Ernest! never leave me again.

ERNEST. Deserted you? Why, your brother said you were ill.

HELEN. Ah, I see . . . he was mistaken.

ERNEST (*jubilant and boyish*). But never mind now, I've got you at last, and I'll never, never let you go. You've got to sail with me to-morrow. Together! Oh, think! Together. (*Another embrace.*)

HELEN. Are you *sure* you love me?

ERNEST (*laughs from sheer joy of her nearness*). Am I sure? Ten million times more to-day than yesterday.

HELEN. Even so . . . it is not, and can never be, as I love you.

ERNEST (*with her hands in his, gayly*). Then you can apologize.

HELEN. Apologize?

ERNEST. For saying, years and years ago—in other words, last night—that you didn't think you'd marry me after all. (*She starts.*) Why, what's the matter? You're trembling like a leaf. You *are* ill!

HELEN. No; oh, no.

ERNEST (*tenderly*). Still a few lingering doubts? I had hoped a good night's rest would put those little prejudices to sleep forever.

HELEN. Sleep? (*She shakes her head, gazing at him soberly.*)

ERNEST. So you could not sleep? Neither could I; I was too happy to sleep. I was afraid I'd miss some wondrous throbbing thought of your loveliness. (*Takes her passive hand, puts a kiss in it, and closes it reverently while she looks into his eyes without moving.*) Do you know, I'm disappointed in love. I always thought it meant soft sighs and pretty speeches. It means an agony of longing, delicious agony, but, oh, terrific. (*She says nothing.*) Dear, dear girl, it may be easy for you, but I can't stand much more of this.

HELEN. Nor I.

ERNEST. You must come to Paris with me or I'll stay home. All through the night I had waking visions of our being parted. Just when we had found each other at last. Some terrible impersonal monster stepped in between us and said: "No. Now that you have had your glimpse of heaven—away! Ye twain shall not enter here. . . ." Silly, wasn't it? But I couldn't get the horror of it out of my head.

HELEN (*nodding*). Do you know why, Ernest? Because it was in mine. It came from my thought to yours. You and I are attuned like wireless instruments. Even in the old blind days, there in the laboratory I used to read your mind. Shall I tell you the name of the monster that would put us asunder? . . . Its name is Marriage.

ERNEST. But I need you. You know that. And you need me. It's too late. We are helpless now—in the clutch of forces more potent than our little selves—forces that brought us into the world—forces that have made the world. Whether you will or no, this beautiful binding power is sweeping you and me together. And you must yield.

HELEN (*reaching for his hand*). Ah, my dear, could anything make it more beautiful, more binding than it is now?

ERNEST. It is perfect. The one divine thing we share with God. The Church is right in that respect. I used to look upon marriage as a mere contract. It's a religious sacrament.

HELEN. Does the wedding ceremony make it sacred?

ERNEST. That mediæval incantation! No, love, which is given by God, not the artificial form made by man.

HELEN. I knew it! I knew you'd see it—the mistake of all the ages. They've tried to make love fit marriage. It can't be done. Marriage must be changed to fit love. (*Impulsively.*) Yes, I'll go to Paris with you.

ERNEST (*about to take her in his arms*). You darling!

HELEN (*steps back*). But not as your wife.

ERNEST (*stops—perplexed*). You mean . . . without marriage?

HELEN. I mean without marriage.

(*They look into each other's eyes.*)

ERNEST. A moment ago I thought I loved you as much as man could love woman. I was mistaken in you—I was mistaken in myself. For now I love you as man never loved before. You superb, you wonderful woman!

HELEN (*holds out her hand to be shaken, not caressed*). Then you agree?

ERNEST (*kneels, kisses her hand, and arises*). Of course not! You blessed girl, don't you suppose I understand? It's all for my sake. Therefore for your sake—no.

HELEN. Then for my sake—for the sake of everything our love stands for!

ERNEST (*laughing fondly*). Do you think I'd let you do anything for anybody's sake you're sure, later, to regret?

HELEN. Then don't ask me to marry you, Ernest. We'd both regret that later. It would destroy the two things that have brought us together, love and work.

ERNEST. Nonsense. Nothing could do that. . . . And besides, think of our poor horrified families! Think of the world's view!

HELEN. Aren't we sacrificing enough for the world—money, comforts, even children? Must we also sacrifice each other to the world? Must we be hypocrites because others are? Must we, too, be cowards and take on the protective coloring of our species?

ERNEST. Our ideas may be higher than society's, but society rewards and punishes its members according to its own ideas, not ours.

HELEN. Do you want society's rewards? Do you fear society's punishment?

ERNEST (*jubilantly enfolding her*). With you in my arms, I want nothing from heaven, I fear nothing from hell; but, my dear (*shrugs and comes down to earth with a smile and releases her*), consider the price, consider the price.

HELEN. Aren't you willing to pay the price?

ERNEST. I? Yes! But it's the woman, always the woman, who pays.

HELEN. I am willing to pay.

ERNEST. I am not willing to let you.

HELEN. You'll have to be, dear. I shall go with you on my terms or not at all.

ERNEST (*with decision*). You will come with me as my wife or stay at home.

HELEN (*gasping*). Now? After all I've said, all I've done? Ernest: I've told the family! I relied upon you. I took for granted— Ernest, you wouldn't—you couldn't leave me behind now.

ERNEST. Thanks to you and what you've made of me, I must and will.

HELEN. Ernest! (*Opens her arms to him to take her.*)

ERNEST (*about to enfold her—resists*). No! If you love me enough for that (*points to her pleading hands*)—I love you enough for this. (*He turns to go.*) Come when you're ready to marry me.

HELEN (*shrill, excited, angered*). Do you think this has been easy for me? Do you think I'll offer myself again on any terms? Never!

ERNEST. You must marry me—and you will.

HELEN. You don't know me. Good-by!

ERNEST. Very well! (ERNEST, *afraid to stay, goes at once. She waits motionless until she hears the automobile carrying him away. She immediately turns from stone to tears, with a low wail. In utter despair, hands outstretched she sinks down upon a bench and buries her face in her hands.*)

HELEN. Oh, Ernest! . . . How could you?

(LUCY, THEODORE, JUDGE *and* JOHN *all hurry back, all excited.*)

THEODORE. Did you see his horrified look?

LUCY. Fairly running away—revolted. Ah! (*Points at* HELEN. HELEN *arises, defiant, confident, calm.*)

JOHN (*to* HELEN). What did I tell you!

LUCY. You have thrown away the love of an honorable man.

THEODORE. Trampled upon the finest feelings of a deep nature.

JOHN. Let this be a lesson to you. You've lost your chance to marry, your chance to work, and now, by heavens! you will cut out "independence" and stay at home, *where women belong,* and live down this disgrace . . . if you can.

LUCY. With one excuse or another—he'll stay away. He'll never come back.

HELEN (*clear and confident as if clairvoyant*). He will! He is coming now. . . . He is crossing the hall. . . . He is passing through the library. . . . He's here! (*But she doesn't turn.* ERNEST *reappears at the door and takes in the situation at a glance.*)

JOHN (*still turned toward* HELEN). He'll never look at you again, and I don't blame him! I'm a man; I know. We don't respect women who sell out so cheap.

ERNEST. You lie! (*All turn, astounded.* HELEN *runs toward* ERNEST *with a cry of joy.* JOHN *starts to block her. To* JOHN.) Stop! You're not fit to touch her. No man is.

JOHN (*with a sarcastic laugh*). Humph! I suppose that's why you ran away.

ERNEST. Yes. To protect her from myself.

JOHN. Then why come back?

ERNEST. To protect her from you! You cowards, you hypocrites! (*He rushes down to* HELEN, *puts his strong arm about her shoulder and whispers rapidly.*) Just as I started, something stopped me. In a flash I saw . . . all this.

HELEN (*clasping his arm with both hands*). I made you come! I made you see!

JOHN (*advances menacingly*). By what right are you here in my home? By what right do you take my sister in your arms?

ERNEST. By a right more ancient than man-made law! I have come to the cry of my mate. I'm here to fight for the woman I love! (*Arm about* HELEN, *defies the world. To all.*) My trip to Paris is postponed. One week from to-day gather all your family here, and in your home we'll make our declaration to the world.

JOHN. In my home! Ha! Not if I know it.

JUDGE (*restraining* JOHN). Play for time, John—he'll bring her around.

JOHN (*to* ERNEST). Do you mean to marry her or not? Speak my language!

(ERNEST *releases* HELEN *and steps across to* JOHN.)

ERNEST. *She* decides that—not you.

(*All turn to* HELEN.)

HELEN. Never!

JOHN (*shaking off* JUDGE. *To* HELEN). You'll go with this damned fanatic only over my dead body.

HELEN (*high*). And that will only cry aloud the thing you wish to hide from the world you fear.

(*Just now* JEAN *is seen slowly returning from the garden without* REX. *Her pretty head is bent and, busy with her own sad thoughts, she is startled by the following:*)

ERNEST. There are laws to prevent marriage in some cases but none to enforce marriage on women—unless they will it.

JOHN (*beside himself with rage*). Enforce! Do you think I'll ever *allow* a sister of mine to marry a libertine?

JEAN (*thinks they are discussing her, and is outraged*). But I'm not going to marry him! My engagement is broken.

(*General consternation. Sobbing,* JEAN *runs into house.*)

JOHN. My God, what next? Lucy, don't let Rex get away! You know what he'll do— and when he sobers up, it may be too late. (*To* ERNEST.) As for you, you snake, you get right out of here.

JUDGE (*in the sudden silence*). Now you've done it, John.

ERNEST. Oh, very well, this is your property.

HELEN. But *I* am not! I go, too! (*She runs to* ERNEST.)

THEODORE. Don't commit this sin!

JOHN. Let her go! She's no sister of mine.

JUDGE (*the only calm one*). If she leaves this house now, it's all up.

JOHN. A woman who will give herself to a man without marriage is no sister of mine.

HELEN (*about to go, turns, leaning on* ERNEST. *To all*). Give! . . . But if I *sold* myself, as you are forcing poor little Jean to do, to a libertine she does not love, who does not love her—that is not sin! That is respectability! To urge and aid her to entrap a man into marriage by playing the shameless tricks of the only trade men want women to learn—that is holy matrimony. But to give yourself of your own free will to the man you love and trust and can help, the man who loves and needs and has won the right to have you—oh, if this is sin, then let me live and die a sinner! (*She turns to* ERNEST, *gives him a look of complete love and trust, then bursts into tears upon his shoulder, his arms enfolding her protectingly.*)

ACT THREE

It is well along in the afternoon of the same busy day of rest. Most unaccountably— until the JUDGE *accounts for it later—the terrace has been decked out with festoons and flowers since the excitement of the morning. Japanese lanterns have been hung, though it is not yet time to light them and though it is Sunday in a pious household.*

Most incongruously and lugubriously, LUCY *is pacing to and fro in silent concern.*

THEODORE *now comes out of the house, also looking harassed.* LUCY *turns to him inquiringly. He shakes his head sadly.*

LUCY. No word from Uncle Everett?

THEODORE. No word. He must have reached town long ago, unless he had tire trouble. . . . It's a bad sign, Lucy, a bad sign. He would surely telephone us.

LUCY. Oh, if he *only* hadn't missed their train!

THEODORE (*hopelessly*). Uncle Everett is the only one who could have brought them to their senses.

LUCY. It may not be too late. He took our fastest car, our best chauffeur.

THEODORE. Detectives are to watch all the steamers to-morrow. John telephoned at once.

LUCY. But to-morrow will be too late! And, oh! when it all comes out in the newspapers! The ghastly head-lines—"well-known scientist, beautiful daughter of a prominent family!" Oh! What will people say?

(JOHN, *hurried and worried, rushes out shouting for* LUCY.)

JOHN. Any news? Any news? (THEODORE *and* LUCY *give him gestures of despair.*) Then it's too late. (*He, too, paces to and fro in fury. Then bracing up.*) Well, I found Rex, over at the Golf Club. Terribly cut up. But listen; not a drink, not one! . . . Where's Jean? Got to see her at once.

THEODORE. Locked herself up in her room, John, crying her little heart out!

JOHN. Rex is a changed man, I tell you. We've got to patch it up, and we've got to do it *quick!*

LUCY. But, John! When the Bakers hear about Helen . . . Rex marry into our family? Never! We're disgraced, John, disgraced!

JOHN (*impatiently*). But they're not *going* to hear about Helen. No one knows, and no one *will*. Helen has simply returned to Paris to complete her scientific research. My press-agent—he's attending to all that.

THEODORE. But questions, gossip, rumor—it's bound to come out in time!

JOHN. In time; but meanwhile, if Jean marries Rex, the Bakers will *have* to stand for it. What's more, they'll make *other* people stand for it. Backed by the Bakers, no one will *dare* turn us down. . . . Our position in the world, my business relations with the old man—*everything hangs on little Jean* now. Tell her I've simply got to see her. (LUCY *hesitates*.) Hurry! Rex is coming over later. (*He catches sight of the table, festoons, etc.*) Heavens! What's all this tomfoolery?

LUCY (*going*). Uncle Everett's orders—he wouldn't stop to explain. He left word to summon the whole family for dinner. (LUCY *goes*.)

JOHN (*shrilly*). The whole family! . . . To-day of all days!

THEODORE. John! You must not, shall not, force Jean to marry this man.

JOHN (*unappreciated*). Haven't I done everything for my sister? Can't they even *marry* for *me*?

THEODORE. The man she loves or none at all.

JOHN. That cub at the law school? No money to keep a wife, no prospects of any. His father's a college professor.

THEODORE (*shaking head sadly*). "No love without marriage, no marriage without—money!" Ernest Hamilton's words this morning, when we walked to church.

JOHN (*watching house expectantly*). Survival of the fittest, Theodore, survival of the fittest.

THEODORE. The fittest for what?—for making money! the only kind of fitness encouraged to survive, to reproduce its species.

JOHN. If the ability to make money is not the test of fitness, what is?

THEODORE. Then you are more fit than a hundred Hamiltons, are you? And Rex? How fit is he? Rex never made a cent in his life.

JOHN. He's got it, all the same. . . . See here! Haven't I enough to worry me without your butting in? Jean's got to marry *some*body, *some*time, hasn't she?

THEODORE. But not Rex, not if I can prevent it.

JOHN. But you can't—you have nothing to do with it . . . except to perform the ceremony and get a big, fat fee for it.

THEODORE. I—marry Jean and Rex? Never!

(JEAN *comes out. She is frightened and turns timidly to* THEODORE *for protection.*)

JOHN. Jean, don't detain Theodore. He has an important business letter to write. (THEODORE *turns to* JOHN *indignantly*.) Your wife's sanatorium bills—better settle up before they dun you again.

THEODORE. With your money?
(*Takes* JOHN's *check out of pocket, about to tear it.*)

JOHN (*catching* THEODORE's *hand*). For Mary's sake, for the children's—don't give way to selfish pride. . . . Want to kill your wife? Then take her out of the sanatorium. Want to ruin your children? Then take them out of school! . . . Cash your check, I tell you, and pay your debts!

(THEODORE *glances at* JEAN, *at check. A struggle. At bay, he finally pockets check and dejectedly goes into the house.*)

JEAN (*with a wet handkerchief in hand.*) Well? If I refuse to marry Rex? . . . Cut off my allowance or merely bully me to death?

JOHN (*kindly*). Oh, come! You've filled your romantic little head full of novels. I never force *anybody* to do *anything*. (*Suddenly breaks out.*) My heavens! what's the matter with all of you? I only want to give you and Lucy and Helen and Theodore and the whole family the best of everything in life! And what do I get for it? I'm a brutal husband, a bullying brother, and a malefactor of wealth. Lord! I guess I have some rights, even if I have got money!

JEAN. Rex has money, too. Should that give him the right to women? I, too, have some rights—even though I *am* a woman.

JOHN. Any woman who can't care enough for a Baker to marry him—Rex is the sort who would do everything in the world for the woman he loves, everything. All the Bakers are like that.

JEAN. But what would he do for the woman he no longer loves?

JOHN. He wasn't fool enough to tell you about that?

JEAN. About what?

JOHN (*halting*). Nothing—I thought—I tell you, Rex has reformed.

JEAN. You thought I meant his "past." I meant his future . . . and my own.

JOHN. Well, if you expect to find a saint, you'll never get married at all.

JEAN. And if I never married at all?

JOHN. *Then* what will you do?

JEAN (*with a wail of despair*). That's it— then what *should* I do—what *could* I do? Oh, it's so unfair, so unfair to train girls only for this! What chance, what choice have I? To live on the bounty of a disapproving brother or a man I do not love! Oh, how I envy Helen! If I only had a chance, a decent chance!

JOHN. Any sensible girl would envy your chance. You'll never have another like it. You'll never have another at all! Grab it, I tell you, grab it. (REX *comes quietly, a determined look on his face,* JOHN *sees him.*) Now, think, before too late, think hard. Think what it means to be an old maid. (*And leaves them abruptly.*)

(JEAN *stands alone, looking very pretty in girlish distress.* REX *gazes at her a moment and then with sudden passion he silently rushes over, seizes her in his arms, kisses her furiously.*)

JEAN (*indignant, struggles, frees herself, and rubs her cheek*). Ugh! How could you!

REX. Because I love you!

JEAN. Love! It isn't even respect now.

REX. Has that fellow ever kissed you?

JEAN. I have begged you never to refer to him again.

REX. He has! He has held you in his arms. He has kissed your lips, your cheeks, your eyes!

JEAN. How many women have you held in your arms? Have I ever tried to find out?

REX. Ah! you don't deny it, you can't.

JEAN. I can! *He* respects me. I don't deserve it, but he does.

REX. Thank heavens! Oh, you don't know how this has tormented me, little Jean. The thought of any other man's coming near you—why I couldn't have felt the same toward you again, I just couldn't.

JEAN (*bites her lips—then deliberately*). Well, then . . . other men have come near me . . . other men have kissed me, Rex.

REX (*getting wild again*). What! When? Where?

JEAN (*laughing cynically*). Oh, in conservatories in town, John's camp in the North Woods, motor rides in the country—once or twice out here on this very terrace, when I've felt sentimental in the moonlight.

REX (*recoiling*). Oh! Jean! I never supposed *you* were that sort!

JEAN (*with distaste*). Oh, I don't make a habit of it! I'm not *that* sort. But . . . well, this isn't all I could tell you about myself, Rex.

REX. Don't! . . . Oh, what do you mean— quick.

JEAN. Oh, I've merely been handled, not hurt. Slightly shop-worn but as good as new.

REX (*after a pause, quietly*). Jean, what makes you say such horribly honest things to me?

JEAN. Yesterday I did you a great unkindness, Rex. I deserve to suffer for it. . . . You don't suppose I enjoy talking this way about myself?

REX. I never heard a girl—a nice girl— talk like this before.

JEAN. Naturally not. Usually "nice" girls hide it. It's an instinct in women—to keep up their value. . . . Often I've had thoughts and feelings which "nice" girls of your artificial ideal are supposed never to have at all. Perfectly natural, too, especially girls of my sort. We have so little to occupy our minds, except men! To have a useful, absorbing occupation—it rubs off the bloom, lowers our price in the market, you see.

REX. Oh, stop! . . . If you're not going to marry me, say so, but——

JEAN. But I am! . . . I am not going to be a dependent old maid. (REX, *bewildered, only gazes at her*.) But, first, I want you to know exactly what you're getting for your money. That seems only businesslike.

REX (*recoils*). Would you only marry me for that?

JEAN. I told you I loved another man. Do you want me?

REX (*with jealousy returning*). Do I want you! He shan't have you. (*He comes close*.)

JEAN. Then take me.

REX (*seizes her passionately*). I'll make you love *me!* (*Kisses her triumphantly*.) I'll bring a different light into those cold eyes of yours. Wait until you're married! Wait until you're awakened. I'll make you forget that man, all other men. You are to be mine—all mine, all mine! (*During this embrace* JEAN *is quite passive, holds up her cheek to be kissed, and when he seeks her lips she shuts her eyes and gives him her lips. He suddenly stops, chilled; holding her at arm's length*.) But I don't care to marry an iceberg. Can't you love me a little? Haven't you any sentiment in your cynical little soul . . . you irresistible darling!

JEAN. In my soul? Yes! It's only my body I'm selling, you know.
(*Then deliberately—clearly without passion—throws her arms about his neck, clinging close and kissing him repeatedly until* REX *responds*.)

REX. Look out, here comes the parson.
(THEODORE *comes out of the house*.)

JEAN. Oh, Theodore! Rex and I have come to an understanding. . . . Will you solemnize our blessed union?

THEODORE. Not unless you truly love each other. Marriage is sacred.

JEAN (*rapidly*). A large church wedding —that will make it sacred. A full choral service—many expensive flowers—all the smartest people invited—that always makes the union of two souls sacred.

THEODORE. Those who truly love—their friends should witness the solemn rite, but——

JEAN (*interrupts. To* REX). And my wedding gown will be white satin with a point-lace veil caught up with orange-blossoms and a diamond tiara—"the gift of the groom"—that ought to make it solemn.

THEODORE. The white veil is the symbol of purity, Jean.

JEAN (*rattling on wildly*). Of purity, Rex, do you hear? Whenever you see a bride in the white symbol of purity she is pure— that proves it. That makes it all so beautiful! so sacred! so holy! holy! holy!
(*Hysterically turns and runs into the house as* JOHN *comes out*.)

THEODORE (*following*). Jean, you must not, you shall not—(JOHN *blocks* THEODORE. REX *runs in after* JEAN. *To* JOHN.) John, I warn you! I'll prevent this marriage. I'll tell every clergyman in the diocese. I'll inform the bishop himself. This marriage would be a sacrilege.

JOHN. You dare threaten me—after all I've done for you!

THEODORE. Your five thousand was a loan —not a bribe—every cent of it will be returned.

JOHN. You can't return it. I wouldn't let you if you could. Come, it's all in the family. (THEODORE *shakes his head*.) You know that beautiful Gothic chapel old man Baker is building on his estate? He likes you. I'll tell him you're just the man he's looking for—safe and sane—no socialistic tendencies.

THEODORE. Don't trouble yourself—he offered me the place this morning.

JOHN. You didn't refuse it!

THEODORE. I did—this morning. But since my last talk with you I've reconsidered, I've telephoned my acceptance.

JOHN (*genuinely glad*). Bully! Great! Why, now you're fixed for life. "Only one kind of fitness encouraged," eh? . . . Right always triumphs in the end. Never lose your faith again, Theodore.

THEODORE. Right? That whited sepulchre! his mill hands dying like flies, his private life a public scandal!

JOHN (*with a cynical grin*). Then why accept his tainted money?

THEODORE (*from his soul*). To keep my wife alive. To keep my children out of the streets. To keep myself out of deeper debt to you. That's why I accept it—that's why many a man sells his soul to the devil. . . . If I had only myself to consider—why, to me a little thing like death would be a blessed luxury. But I, why, John, I cannot afford—even to die. I must compromise and live—live for those dependent on me. . . . Your five thousand will be returned with interest, but your little sister will not be married to a man she does not want.

JOHN. But Rex wants *her* and money talks in this world, louder than the Church. Refuse to marry Baker's son and how long will you keep Baker's chapel? . . . Think it over, Theodore, think it over.
(*Suddenly the* JUDGE *in motor garments covered with dust comes out panting, followed by* LUCY *calling.*)

LUCY. Uncle Everett! Uncle Everett!

JUDGE. John! Oh, John!

JOHN. Where is she!

THEODORE. You were too late!

JUDGE. Wait! Give me time to get my breath.
(*Fans himself with his cap and mops brow.*)

JOHN. My detective—didn't he meet their train?

(JUDGE *nods yes.*)

LUCY. But they saw him first?

(JUDGE *shakes head no.*)

THEODORE. Didn't he follow them?

(JUDGE *nods yes.*)

JOHN. Where'd they go? Where are they? Speak, man, speak!

JUDGE (*raises cap and handkerchief*). Now, just give me a chance and I'll tell the whole story. . . . The detective was waiting at the station. He saw them step out of the train. He followed them to the cab-stand. He watched them get into a taxi—jumped into another himself—and away they went, pursued by the detective and blissfully ignorant of his existence. . . . Even now they don't know they were being watched—or else . . . well, they might have taken another course.

LUCY. Quick! Tell us the worst.

JUDGE (*hesitates*). Well . . . they drove straight to Helen's apartment.

LUCY. And you were too late. I thought so.

JOHN. But my detective?

JUDGE. He followed and reported to me when I reached town.

LUCY. Reported what? Tell us all.

JUDGE. First he saw Ernest help Helen out of the taxi—very tenderly, like this. Little they realized then how every detail was to be reported to you now!

JOHN. Go on! go on!

JUDGE. Then the detective saw Ernest deliberately——

LUCY. Yes, go on.

JUDGE. Deliberately lift his hat like this, say "good afternoon" just like that, and drive on to his own apartment a mile away.
(*There is a sudden silence; the others waiting, the* JUDGE *now sits down.*)

LUCY. Oh, is that all?

THEODORE. Why, it's exactly as if they were engaged!

JUDGE. No, Theodore, not *exactly* as if engaged.

JOHN. You're keeping something back from us! Speak!

JUDGE, (*gets up from chair*). Must I tell you? It's rather delicate. . . . Well, he didn't

even step into the vestibule to kiss her good-by.
(*All look at each other.*)

JOHN. But where are they now? Quick!

LUCY. They met later! I knew it.

JUDGE. Yes, it's true. They are alone together at this very moment.

ALL. Where! where?

JUDGE (*pointing to house*). There.

JOHN. What! What are they doing here?

JUDGE (*resumes fanning*). Discussing the marriage problem. (*General rejoicing and relief.*) Sssh! Not so loud, you might interrupt them.

JOHN (*nodding knowingly*). Cold feet! Knew he'd lose his job.

LUCY. The disgrace. She couldn't face it.

THEODORE. No, conscience. A deep religious nature.
(*They all think it over a moment, each sure of his own diagnosis.*)

JOHN (*turning to* JUDGE *with amusement*). So! Decided the soul-mate theory wouldn't work in practice, eh?

THEODORE *and* LUCY. And they agree to marry?

JUDGE (*stops fanning*). Marry? My, no! Nothing like that. They think less of marriage than ever now! Helen is using woman's sweet indirect influence on Ernest in there at this moment!
(*All start toward the house impulsively, but on second thoughts they all stop.*)

JOHN. Then how on earth did you get them back!

JUDGE (*lighting cigar*). Oh, perfectly simple, I promised Helen you'd apologize to Ernest; promised Ernest you'd apologize to Helen. (*To* LUCY.) Promised both you'd arrange a nice little family party for 'em. They bear no grudge. They're too happy.

LUCY (*horrified. Indicates table*). The family party—for *them*? Horrors!

JUDGE (*tossing away match*). Yes, here in your happy home. (*The others turn on the* JUDGE *indignantly.*) Well, don't jump on *me*. I tell you they positively decline to elope until after they tell the whole damn family. Considerate of them, I say. You don't deserve it, if you ask me.

JOHN (*incredulous*). Tell the whole... see here, are they crazy? Are *you* crazy? Do you think *I'm* crazy?
(*Impetuously turns toward the house, a man of action.*)

JUDGE (*stopping* JOHN). Wait! ... You've already done your best to destroy your sister—but you've utterly failed. They have done nothing wrong—*as yet*. Why, they are the finest, truest, noblest pair of lovers I ever met! Now, aren't they, Theodore?

THEODORE. I can't say that I call Helen's ideas of marriage "noble," exactly!

JUDGE (*grandiloquent*). She is willing to sacrifice even marriage for his career. Isn't that noble? And he! willing to sacrifice even his career for marriage. Both noble, if you ask me.

JOHN (*loud*). Noble tommy-rot—a pair of pig-headed, highbrow fools! They don't have to sacrifice anything for anybody. Can't they work together just as well married as unmarried?

JUDGE (*slyly*). That's what I said to her, but you had already convinced her that it was impractical. Work and marriage— "combine the two, and you'll fail at both" —your own warning, John.

JOHN (*angry*). B'r'r—you think you're very funny, don't you! But that's my sister in there, planning to be that fellow's mistress—right here in my own house! Anything funny about that!

JUDGE (*stepping aside*). All right, go put a stop to it then! (JOHN *starts toward house.*) It's your own house—turn her out again. (JOHN *stops short.*) What are you going to do about it, John? (JOHN *has no answer.*) Drive little Jean into marriage with a man she does not love—she is an old-fashioned girl. But your other sister—you can't make her marry even the man she does love, unless she sees fit. She is the New Woman! Society can no longer force females into wedlock—so it is forcing them out . . . by the thousands! Approve of it? Of course not. But what good will our disapproval do? They will only laugh at you. The strike is on. Few of the strikers will let you see it. Few of the strikers have Helen's courage. But, believe it or not, the strike will spread. It cannot be crushed by law or force. Unless society wakes up and reforms its rules and regulations of marriage, marriage is doomed. . . . What are you going to do about it? (*Silence.*) I thought so—nothing. Call them bad women and let it go at that. Blame it all on human nature, made by God, and leave untouched our human institutions, made by man. You poor little pessimists! human nature to-day is better than it ever was, but our most important institution is worse—the most sacred relationship in life has become a jest in the market-place. . . . You funny little cowards, you're afraid of life, afraid of love, afraid of truth. You worship lies, and call it God!

JOHN (*interrupts*). All right, all right—but we can't change marriage overnight just to suit Helen. What are *you* going to do about it?

JUDGE. There's just one thing to do. Will you back me up in everything I say?

JOHN (*acknowledging his own defeat*). Anything—everything.

JUDGE. Then tell Helen she doesn't have to marry, that, with the best intentions, the Church has made a muddle of monogamy.

THEODORE. Uncle Everett, I protest.

JUDGE. That we all admire their consecrated courage and advise their trying this conscientious experiment.

JOHN. Not if I have anything to say about it!

JUDGE. But you haven't. Do please get that through your head. . . . Theodore, they've talked enough, ask them to step out here and receive John's blessing. (*Impatiently.*) Go on—I'll fix John. (THEODORE *goes.*) (*To* JOHN, *who is about to burst forth.*) Oh, see here, did you ever pull a dog into the house against his will? . . . Let him

alone and he'll follow you in, wag his tail, and lick your hand.

JOHN. You mean, they'll come in, be respectable?

JUDGE. Admit that marriage has numerous drawbacks—and they'll see its advantages. Deny it—and they'll see nothing but each other. Marriage *is* in a bad way, but it's the less of two evils. Marriage *must* adjust itself to the New Woman—*but* the New Woman must meanwhile adjust herself to marriage. (*Briskly to* LUCY.) Now, then, did you send out that hurry call for the family this evening?

LUCY. Yes, they're on their way here now, but Uncle Everett, Doctor Hamilton said, next week.

JUDGE. Yes, I know—it'll be a little surprise party for Helen. . . . Did you order some music?

LUCY. Yes, the musicians are to be stationed in the library.

JUDGE. Excellent, excellent. (*Indicates tables and festoons.*) All that junk will help, too. A good Sunday supper this evening, Lucy; your best champagne, John—gay spirits, family affection, warm approval, toasts to the future. Why, all we'll have to do is— (*Breaks off.*) Here they come. Now follow my lead. They've done a lot of thinking since you saw them last, but— make one misstep and it's all off.

LUCY. Be nice to her, John. It was just a girlish impulse.
(JOHN *opens arms to receive* HELEN.)

JOHN. My sister! All is forgiven.

HELEN (*stops short, her lip curls*). You forgive *me*?
(*Before* JOHN *can reply*, THEODORE *and* ERNEST *follow, talking.*)

ERNEST. But I tell you he had a perfect right to put me off his property. The thing I can't overlook— (*Sees* JOHN *and* LUCY. *Points finger at them accusingly.*) Theodore has told me what you thought. . . . Please don't judge us by yourselves again —you licentious-minded married people! (*He shrugs his shoulders with fastidious disgust and turns his back upon them.*)

JOHN (*gasping*). Well, I'll be damned.

JUDGE (*whispers*). Stand for it—he's right.

THEODORE. But Ernest . . . I'm bound to say when two people run away together——

ERNEST. Ah, Theodore! you, too? Are all married people alike? Did we want to "run away" as you call it? Did we not ask for a week to think it over? Did we not stipulate that in any case we must frankly face the family first? But this person—what did he do? He ordered us off his property, like trespassers! What could we do? Sit down in the road and wait a week? Bah! we went home—you suspicious married people, you hypocritical, unspeakable married people! (JUDGE *has difficulty in restraining* JOHN.) Why, I believe our good friend the Judge here is the only decent-minded, properly married person on your property.

JOHN (*bursting out*). Decent-minded— why, he's div——
(LUCY *stops him.*)

JUDGE (*steps in*). Dev-oted to his wife. Lucy is jealous of what I'm doing for my wife. (*Controls laughter.*) Now come, we must all just let bygones be bygones. We know your intentions are honorable, your courage admirable; and for whatever was amiss in word, or deed, or thought, we all humbly apologize—don't we, John? (JOHN *bows uncomfortably.*) Lucy? Theodore? And now I want you all to tell Ernest and Helen what you told me—that their arguments against marriage are unanswerable, their logic unimpeachable, and we no longer have the slightest intention or desire to get them divorced by matrimony. (JOHN, THEODORE, *and* LUCY *look dubious.* JUDGE *crosses over and pinches them.* HELEN *and* ERNEST *are utterly bewildered.*) Why, we wouldn't let a little thing like marriage come between them for the world, would we, John? would we, Lucy? would we, Theodore?

JOHN (*with an effort*). I agree with Uncle Everett entirely.

JUDGE. And you, Theodore?

THEODORE (*in a low voice*). Perfectly.

JUDGE. And you, Lucy?

LUCY (*with a nervous glance at* JOHN). Absolutely.

JUDGE (*to the lovers*). There. You see? (ERNEST *looks from one to the other in amazement.*)

HELEN (*laughingly*). I don't believe a word of it!

JUDGE. Why not? why not?

HELEN. Very well, then invite the whole family here next Sunday!

JUDGE. They'll be here in an hour. (*Points to tables.*)

HELEN *and* ERNEST (*recoiling*). In an hour!

JUDGE. Yes, you are to begin your new life together this evening! Isn't it lovely?

HELEN (*gasping*). But that's so sudden. Why, we—we aren't ready.

THEODORE. Just as ready as you'll ever be.

JUDGE. Ernest's vacation begins to-morrow —your honeymoon.

HELEN. But, don't you see—

LUCY. Those new Paris clothes John gave you—your trousseau.

ERNEST. Well, but——

JUDGE. And this family gathering this evening, your—in a manner of speaking— wedding party. (*Waving aside all the lovers' objections.*) Now, it's all fixed, let's go and dress for the—as it were—ceremony.

ERNEST (*blocks the way. Serious*). Wait! Did I ever say I would not marry this woman?
(*All stop, turn, exchange glances.*)

JUDGE (*apart*). Ah! a broad-minded chap.

JOHN (*with a wink at* JUDGE). Ah! so you think you'd like to marry my sister after all?

ERNEST. Oh, you're an ass! What have I been doing for the past twenty-four hours? Begging her to marry me. What have you been doing? Preventing it. Why did I postpone sailing for a week? Why did I insist upon the family party? (*Comes nearer to* JOHN.) You're an idiot.

JUDGE (*pinching* JOHN). Stand for it, John. You've got to stand for it. Tell him you love him like a brother . . . in-law.

JOHN (*controls himself*). Well, I . . . I—you have my consent, Doctor Hamilton, I'm sure.

ERNEST. *Your* consent! What's that got to do with it? (*They all turn toward* HELEN. ERNEST *steps between them*.) Now wait! . . . This morning you tried bullying. Did it work? This afternoon bluffing. Think *that* will work? (*Hand on* HELEN's *shoulder.*) You can't frighten her into marriage. I've tried that myself. We've got to appeal to some higher motive than self-interest or superstition with *this* woman, racial motives, unselfish motives. (*With force.*) But don't talk to me about her being "immoral." I won't stand for it. If you want her to marry, prove the morality of marriage

THEODORE. The "morality of marriage"! What next?

ERNEST (*to* THEODORE). That's what I said —the morality of *marriage!* This woman is not on trial before you. Marriage is on trial before her, and thus far I'm bound to say you've not made out a good case for it. But simply *justify* her marrying me, and —I give you my word—you can perform the ceremony this very evening. No license is required in this State, you know. (*This creates a sensation.*)

JUDGE. Now, what could be fairer than that! (*To* HELEN.) Do you agree to this?

HELEN (*she nods*). We agree in everything.

JUDGE. *Both* broad-minded!

HELEN (*quietly*). I never said I did not believe in a legal wedding—(*others surprised*) for those who can afford the luxury of children. . . . But for those who have to take it out in working for other people's children all their lives—a ceremony seems like a subterfuge. Without children I don't see how any marriage is ever consummated —socially.

THEODORE. Ah, but this relationship—it's a sacred thing in itself.

HELEN (*sincerely*). I know it. I want to do right, Theodore, please believe that I do!

But the kind of marriage preached by the Church and practised by the world—does that cherish the real sacredness of this relationship? Of course, I can only judge from appearances, but so often marriage seems to destroy the sacredness—yes, and also the usefulness—of this relationship!

ERNEST. But, my dear girl——

HELEN (*smiles*). He thinks so, too. Only he has a quaint, mannish notion that he must "protect me." (*To* ERNEST, *patting his arm.*) Haven't you, dear? (*Again she has raised the shield of flippancy.*)

JUDGE. What did I tell you, Theodore? The old marriage doesn't fit for the New Woman. A self-supporting girl like Helen objects to obeying a mere man—like Ernest.

HELEN (*patting the* JUDGE's *arm affectionately, too*). Uncle Everett, you know nothing about it! You think you understand the new generation. The only generation you understand is the one which clamored for "Woman's Rights." (*To* ERNEST.) I obey you already—every day of my life, do I not, dear? (*Looking up into his face.*) You're my "boss," aren't you, Ernest? (*To* JUDGE.) But I do object to contracting by law for what is better done by love.

JUDGE (*laughs fondly*). But suppose the promise to obey were left out?

HELEN. But the contract to love—(*To* THEODORE.) that's so much worse, it seems to me. Obedience is a mere matter of will, is it not? But when a man promises to love until death——

THEODORE. Are you so cold, so scientific, so *unsexed,* that you cannot trust the man you love?

HELEN. Why, Theodore, if I didn't trust him I'd *marry* him! Contracts are not for those who trust—they're for those who don't.

LUCY (*takes* HELEN *apart*). Now, I may be old-fashioned, Helen, but I'm a married woman, and I know men. You never can tell, my dear, you never can tell.

HELEN. Do you think I'd live with a man who did not love me? Do you think I'd live *on* a man I did not love? (LUCY *blinks*.) Why, what kind of a woman should I be then! The name wife—would that change it? Calling it holy—would that hallow it? . . . Every woman, married or not, knows the truth about this! In her soul woman has always known. But until to-day has never dared to tell.

ERNEST (*approaching* HELEN). Oh, come now—those vows—they aren't intended in a literal sense. Ask Theodore. Why, no sane person means half of that gibberish. "With all my worldly goods I thee endow" —millions of men have said it—how many ever did it? How many clergymen ever expect them to! . . . It's all a polite fiction in beautiful, sonorous English.

HELEN. The most sacred relationship in life! Ernest, shall you and I enter it unadvisedly, lightly, and with LIES on our lips? . . . Simply because others do?

ERNEST (*a little impatient*). But the whole world stands for this. And the world won't stand for that.

HELEN. Is that reverently, soberly, and in the fear of God? No, cynically, selfishly, and in the fear of man. I don't want to be obstinate, I don't like to set myself up as "holier than thou," but, Ernest, unless we begin honestly, we'll end dishonestly. Somehow marriage seems wicked to me.

JUDGE (*nudging* THEODORE). How do you like that?

THEODORE. John is right—they've gone mad.

ERNEST. All the same, you've got to marry me—you've simply *got* to.

HELEN. You are mistaken. I do *not* have to marry *any* one. I can support myself.

ERNEST. Then I'm disappointed in you.

HELEN. And I in you.

ERNEST. I thought you were sensible.

HELEN. I thought you were honest.

ERNEST. Honest! You accuse me of dishonesty?

HELEN. You don't believe in "half of that gibberish." Yet you are willing to work the Church for our own worldly advantage! You are willing to prostitute the most sacred thing in life! . . . If that is not dishonest, what is!

ERNEST. And you are the woman I love and want to marry! In all my life I was never accused of dishonesty before.

HELEN. You never tried to marry before. No one is honest about marriage.

ERNEST. I never shall try again. I'm going to Paris to-morrow and I'm going alone.

HELEN. Then do it. Don't threaten it so often—do it.

ERNEST. I shall. And I'll never come back.

HELEN. Nobody asked you to.

ERNEST. Helen—for the last time—just for my sake—marry me.

HELEN. For the last time—no! no! NO!! I won't be a hypocrite even for your sake. (*She turns away, he starts off, then stops, rushes over to her.*)

ERNEST (*holds out arms*). I can't. You know it. Without you I'm nothing.

HELEN (*taking both his hands*). Without you. . . . Oh, my dear, my dear.

ERNEST. Forgive me, forgive me.

HELEN. It was all my fault.

ERNEST. No, I was a brute. I'm not worthy of you.

HELEN (*covering his lips with her hand*). Sssh—I can't stand it—I was perfectly horrid to you. And you were doing it all for my sake. (*Laughing and crying.*) You dear old thing—I knew it all the time. (*They seem about to embrace.*)

JUDGE (*shaking with laughter*). Was there ever in the world anything like it! . . . Well, children, see here. He's willing to lie for your sake. She's willing to die for your sake. Now, why not just split the difference and have a civil ceremony for *our* sake.

THEODORE. No, they will marry for a better reason. Think of the *sin* of it! (*To* HELEN.) Have you no sense of sin?

JUDGE. If not, think of the humor of it! Have you no sense of humor?

HELEN (*still drying eyes and smiling to* JUDGE). Not a scrap. Neither has Ernest. Have you, dear?

ERNEST. I *hope* not—judging from those who always say they have.

THEODORE (*solemnly*). Helen, look at Ernest—Ernest look at Helen. (*The lovers do so.*) Look into each other's very souls! . . . You know, you *must* know, that in the eyes of God this thing would be a sin, a heinous sin.
(*The lovers gaze deep into each other's eyes in silence.*)

ERNEST (*tremulous from the emotion he has just been through*). The glory and the gladness I see in this woman's eyes a sin? Her trust in me, my worship of her, our new-found belief in a future life, our greater usefulness together in this—bah! don't talk to me about sin! Such women cannot sin—they love.

JOHN (*tired out*). Oh, you can talk all night, but this is a practical world. How long could you keep your job in the institute? Then how'll you live! Private practice? No respectable home will let you inside the door.

ERNEST. I've seen the inside of respectable homes. I want no more. (*Taking from his pocket a piece of paper.*) This morning I came to ask for your sister's hand in marriage. Your manners did not please me. So I cabled over to Metchnikoff. (*Hands cablegram to* JOHN.) His answer. Positions await us both at the Pasteur Institute in Paris. That luxurious suite on to-morrow's steamer still waits in my name.

THEODORE. Ernest! Stop! Think! This woman's soul is in your hands.

(ERNEST *seems to hesitate.* HELEN *crosses to him.* JUDGE *seizes* JOHN, *whispers, and shoves him across.*)

JOHN. Doctor Hamilton! I apologize! . . . You're a man of the world. You know what this means—she doesn't. She is in your power—for God's sake go to Paris without her.

(JOHN *tries to lead* HELEN *away from* ERNEST. *She shudders at* JOHN'S *masterful touch and clings to her lover.*)

ERNEST. And leave her here in *your* power? Never again! You've forced her out of her work—you'd force her into legalized prostitution, if you could, like her innocent little sister. (*Snatches* HELEN *away from* JOHN.) No, married or not, she sails with me in the morning. That's final.
(*The lovers turn away together.*)

JUDGE. Where are you going?

HELEN. To ask Marie to pack my trunk.

ERNEST. To telephone for a motor.

JUDGE. But you won't start until after the family party?

ERNEST. Of course not.
(*In a sudden silence* HELEN *and* ERNEST *walk into the house, leaving the family in despair.*)

JUDGE (*after a long sigh, to* JOHN). I knew you'd bungle it, I knew it—but there's still a chance, just one more card to play.
(*The* BUTLER *comes out.*)

LUCY. Good heavens! Already?

BUTLER. Mr. and Mrs. Willoughby, Doctor and Mrs. Grey, and the Misses Grey.

LUCY (*flurried*). And we're not even dressed!

JUDGE. No matter. It's Sunday—many orthodox people . . . why, Mr. Baker won't even dine out on Sunday.

(*Enter the persons announced. Greetings.* "How warm it is for September." . . . "And how's the baby, Margaret?" *etc.* JOHN *and* JUDGE *apart are planning excitedly.* JEAN *and* REX *come out, and finally* HELEN, *followed by* ERNEST.)

BUTLER. Dinner is served, ma'am.

(*The* SECOND MAN *touches button. Japanese lanterns glow, silver shines, and all move toward the tables, a happy, united family.*)

LUCY (*going-to-dinner manner as she leads the way*). We can hardly go out formally because we're already out, you know. Aunt Susan, will you sit over there on John's right? Doctor Hamilton by me? Rex on the other side?

JOHN. Here, Helen. No, Jean, you are beside Rex, you know.

JUDGE. Until married, then you're separated.

LUCY. Cousin Charlie—that's it. (*All take their places.*) Most extraordinary weather for September, isn't it?

JUDGE (*he slaps his cheek*). Isn't it?

LUCY (*shocked and hurt*). That's the first mosquito I have ever known on our place.

JOHN (*indignantly*). We never have mosquitoes here. You must have been mistaken.
(*The servants are passing in and out of house with courses. The* BUTLER *now brings a telegram to* JUDGE.)

JUDGE. From Julia! (*Tears it open eagerly, reads, and then shouts.*) She's coming back to me, she's coming back! Look at that, look at that!
(*Jumps up and shows telegram to* JOHN. *Then taking it around to* LUCY *he sings to tune of "Merrily we roll along":*
Aunt Julia is coming back
Coming back—coming back
Aunt Julia is coming back
Coming back from Reno.

HELEN (*laughing*). From Reno? That sounds like divorce, Uncle Everett.

JUDGE. Like divorce? Does *that* sound like divorce? (*Takes telegram from* LUCY *and hands it to* HELEN.) Read it aloud.

HELEN (*reading*). "Dear boy, I can't stand it, either. Come to me or I go to you."

JUDGE (*sings during the reading*). Coming back from Reno. (*Breaks off—to* HELEN.) So you thought we wanted a divorce, did you?

HELEN. I never dreamed of such a thing.

JUDGE (*looks at her a moment, then in a burst*). Well, *I* did. The dream of my life—your Aunt Julia's, too. We thought we believed in trial marriage, but we don't—we believe in trial *separation!*

THEODORE (*uncomfortably*). They thought they didn't love each other, but they do, you see.

JUDGE. We don't, we don't, but we can't get along without each other . . . got the habit of having each other around and can't break it. . . . This morning I telegraphed: "Are you doing this just for my sake?" She replied, "Tutti-frutti." (*Sings.*) Aunt Julia's coming back. Oh, I'm too happy to eat. (*Singing, while others eat and drink.*)

Coming back, coming back,
Aunt Julia is coming back
Coming back from Reno.

And I don't care who knows it. The more the better for marriage. The truth—give me more truth, give me more—champagne. (BUTLER *fills glass as* JUDGE *raises it.*) Here's to your Aunt Julia, the best wife—I ever had. (*All rise, drink, laugh, and sit down.*) And I'll never, never get another. . . . You know I thought maybe I might. Oh, Everett, Everett, you sly dog, you old idiot you!

JOHN (*arises, clearing throat, tapping on glasses for silence*). And now, speaking of divorce, I have an engagement to announce. (*Some laughter but all quiet down. He smiles at* JEAN.) Of course, you can't guess whose. Friends, it is my privilege to announce the engagement of my good friend Rex Baker to my dear sister Jean. (*Gentle applause and congratulations. Music begins.*) And so I will now ask all to arise and drink to the health and prosperity of my little sister and my brother-in-law to be! And my best wish is that they will be as happy as my better half and me. (*All cheer and drink health standing.*) Speech, Rex!
(*Some of them playfully try to put him on his feet.*)

REX (*shaking his head and maintaining his seat*). I can't make a speech. I'm too happy for words—See-what-I-mean?

HELEN (*in a low, significant tone*). Jean, aren't you going to say something?

JEAN (*arises, all silent, she looks at* LUCY, REX, JOHN). Words cannot describe my happiness, either. (*She resumes her seat,*

and all gather round to congratulate JEAN
and REX.)

JOHN (*rapping for quiet*). One moment,
one moment. Another toast, another toast!
(*Others quiet down.*) We have with us tonight one who, in honoring whom we hon-
our ourselves, one who with capital back of
him would soon become the greatest scientist in America! (JUDGE *leads applause,*
"hear, hear!" *etc.* JOHN *raises glass.*) To the
distinguished guest whom I am proud to
welcome to my humble board, to the noble
humanitarian whom Mr. Baker delights to
honor, to the good friend whom we all admire and trust, Doctor Ernest Hamilton!
(*All applaud and about to drink health,*
JUDGE *jumps up.*)

JUDGE. And to his fair collaborator! the
brave woman who at this modern warrior's
side daily risks her life for others, handling
death and disease in those mighty but un-
sung battles for the common weal! (*Applause.*) A New Woman? No, friends,
look behind the stupid names the mob
would cast, like stones to destroy, look and
you will see your true conservative—willing to appear radical in order to conserve
woman's work in the world! willing to appear ridiculous to right ancient wrongs!
willing even to appear *wrong*—for those
she loves! Ah, the same old-fashioned woman we all adore, in a form so new we
blindly fail to understand her glorious advent before our very eyes! To Helen, the
gracious embodiment of all that is sweetest, noblest, and best in womanhood—to
Helen! Our lovely Helen!

JOHN (*up again at once*). Family approval,
social esteem, and an honored career—all
this is theirs for the asking! To-day to me
they have confessed their love—to-night to
you I now announce . . . their engagement!
Long life and happiness to Helen and Ernest!
(*Great enthusiasm—even pounding on
the table.* ERNEST *arises, looking surprised.*
JOHN *signalling to rest of family to join
in.*)

THE FAMILY (*glasses raised, drowning out
ERNEST*). Long life and happiness, long life
and happiness!

ERNEST (*raises hand*). Wait! Before you
drink this toast. . . . (*The glasses stop midway. Sudden silence.*) Your congratulations we appreciate, your kind wishes we
desire—but not on false pretences. We are
not engaged to be married.
(*In the tense silence a shudder ripples the
family joy.*)

REX (*apart to* JEAN). Gee! They had a
scrap, too?

JOHN (*up, nervously.* ERNEST *still standing*). If I may interrupt. . . . He has financial reasons—I respect him for it. But this
very day the Baker Institute in recognition
of Doctor Hamilton's distinguished services to humanity has doubled his salary—
doubled it! It's all right now—it's all right.

REX (*apart to* JEAN). Four thousand, eh?
. . . get a very decent touring car for that.

ERNEST (*to all*). That is very kind, but that
is not the point. True, our mutual needs
are such that we cannot live nor work
apart, but our convictions are such that we
cannot live and work *together*—in what
you have the humor to call "holy wedlock." Now, Helen, the motor is waiting.
(*Sensation. Gasps of amazement and horror. Some jump up from table. A chair is
upset.* ERNEST *holds* HELEN'S *wrap. General
movement and murmurs.*)

JOHN (*barring way*). You leave this house
only over my dead body.
(*Others gather around lovers.*)

JUDGE (*to all*). Stand back! . . . Let him
among you who has a purer ideal of love,
a higher conception of duty cast the first
stone.
(*All stop. Silenced.*)

THEODORE. But this man and this woman
would destroy marriage!

JUDGE (*standing beside lovers*). No! Such
as they will not destroy marriage—they
will save it! They restore the vital substance while we preserve the empty shell.
Everything they have said, everything they
have done, proves it. The promise to love—
they could not help it—they took it—I
heard them. The instinct for secrecy—they
felt it—we all do—but straightway they
told the next of kin. (*Points to* JOHN.)

Even when insulted and driven forth from the tribe, they indignantly refused to be driven into each other's arms until you of the same blood could hear them plight their troth! Believe in marriage! Why, there never was, there never will be a more perfect tribute to true marriage than from this fearless pair you now accuse of seeking to destroy it! (JOHN *tries to interrupt, but the* JUDGE *waves him down.*) They have been not only honorable but old-fashioned, save in the one orthodox detail of accepting the authority constituted by society for *its* protection and for *theirs.* (*To* HELEN *and* ERNEST.) But now, I'm sure, before starting on their wedding journey—another old-fashioned convention they believe in—that, just to please us if not themselves, they will consent to be united in the bonds of holy wedlock by Cousin Theodore who stands ready and waiting with prayer-book in hand.

(*Family subsides. Everybody happy.* THEODORE *steps up, opens prayer-book.*)

THEODORE. "Dearly beloved, we are gathered together here in the sight of God—"

HELEN (*suddenly loud and clear*). Theodore! are you going to marry Rex and Jean?

JOHN (*impatiently*). Of course, of course, Mr. Baker's chaplain.

ERNEST (*recoiling*). Theodore! You! Are you going to stand up and tell the world that God has joined those two together—GOD?

(THEODORE *looks at* JOHN *but does not deny it and says nothing.*)

HELEN. Then you will be blaspheming love—and God who made it. No, you shall not marry us.

ERNEST (*agreeing with* HELEN). Some things are too sacred to be profaned.

THEODORE (*overwhelmed*). Profaned? . . . By the Church?

JOHN. Your love too sacred for the Church? The Church has a name for such love! The world a name for such women!

ERNEST (*about to strike* JOHN, *then shrugs*). A rotten world! A kept Church! Come, let's get away from it all! Come!

(HELEN *offers her hand in farewell to* LUCY, *but* JOHN *shields her from* HELEN's *touch, then to* JEAN. REX *shields* JEAN *from contamination, but* JEAN *weeps.*)

JUDGE (*barring the way. To* ERNEST). Stop! You cannot! The very tie that binds you to this woman binds you to us and to the whole world with hooks of steel! (*The lovers are still going.* JUDGE *ascends steps, facing them.*) For the last time! before too late! Ernest! You *know* that in the eyes of God you *are* taking this woman to be your wife.

ERNEST. In the eyes of *God,* I *do* take Helen to be my wife—but—

JUDGE. You, Helen! Speak, woman, speak!

HELEN. I take Ernest to be my husband in the eyes of God, but—

JUDGE (*raises his hand augustly and in a voice of authority*). Then, since you, Ernest, and you, Helen, have made this solemn declaration before God and in the presence of witnesses, I, by the authority vested in me by the laws of this State do now pronounce you man and wife!

(MR. *and* MRS. HAMILTON *look at each other bewildered. Meanwhile the silence has been pierced, first by a little hysterical scream from* JEAN, *then the others all wake up and crowd about the happy pair, congratulating them. The women who had snubbed* HELEN *before cover her with kisses, and now she is fit for their embraces.*)

JOHN (*to* THEODORE). Saved! Saved! Respectable at last, thank God. (*Raising his glass and hammering for attention.*) Here's to the bride and groom.

(*All cheer, raise glasses, and drink.*)

ERNEST (*when the noise dies down. As the others kiss* HELEN). A moment ago you were a bad woman. Now (*to all*) behold! she is a good woman. Marriage is wonderful.

(JOHN *and* LUCY *run to* JUDGE *and shake hands.*)

JUDGE (*to* JOHN *and* LUCY, *his wife*). Yes, Respectability has triumphed this time, but let Society take warning and beware! beware! beware!

Curtain.

Beyond the Horizon

BY EUGENE O'NEILL

EUGENE O'NEILL

Eugene Gladstone O'Neill was born in New York City in 1888. During the first seven years of his life he and his mother accompanied his father, a popular and romantic actor, on road tours. For the next six years he attended two Catholic boarding schools, then spent four years at Betts Academy at Stamford, Connecticut, and studied one year at Princeton University. Employment as secretary with a small mail-order firm on lower Broadway, New York City, followed. In 1909, O'Neill set forth on a gold-prospecting trip to Honduras, finding malarial fever but no gold. Returning to the United States he became assistant manager for *The White Sister* company on a road tour. At the end of this tour, he shipped to Buenos Aires, on a Norwegian barque. In the Argentine, he found work with the Westinghouse Electric Co., Swift Packing Co. and Singer Sewing Machine Co. A voyage on a cattle ship took him to Durban, South Africa; then he signed as ordinary seaman on a British tramp steamer, and subsequently as able-bodied seaman on the American Line in the trans-Atlantic service.

His sea-faring over, O'Neill returned to the theatre, now as an actor in a condensed version of *Monte Cristo* in which his father starred in a vaudeville tour. For a period of six months O'Neill worked as a reporter for the New London, Connecticut, *Telegraph*. In December, 1912, after years of irregular living, O'Neill's health broke down. He was sent to a Connecticut sanatorium for the treatment of incipient tuberculosis. It was here that the urge to write plays instead of verse or newspaper articles had its first impetus. Soon after his complete recovery from illness in 1913, he devoted himself to the writing of one-act plays.

The publication of his first book, *Thirst and Other One-Act Plays* (1914), was financed by his father. A year of study in the famous 47 Workshop drama class at Harvard was the next step in his development as a playwright. While living in Provincetown and later in Greenwich Village, O'Neill joined forces with the newly organized Provincetown Players, who were the first to produce his one-act plays. With the production in 1920 of *Beyond the Horizon,* O'Neill became established as a major dramatist. His rise to an unchallenged position as the foremost figure in the American drama was rapid, and his plays won for him international fame. His third and only happy marital venture occurred in 1929, when he was married to Carlotta Monterey, the actress.

Shy and retiring by nature, O'Neill rarely attends the theatre. His preference is to read the plays in which he is interested. "Acting," he insists, "simply gets between me and the play." He is a member of the Authors' League of America, the Dramatists' Guild and the American Academy of Arts and Letters, and an Associate Member of the Irish Academy. As one critic has put it and as countless readers will concur: "Above all the rest stands Eugene Gladstone O'Neill, his head wreathed with the laurels of a decade's thoughtful and utterly sincere work." O'Neill is not only an extremely prolific writer but always the resourceful innovator and experimentalist. The body of his work consists of some twenty-one long plays and sixteen plays in one act. The first of his full-length plays produced in New York, *Beyond the Horizon,* which was awarded the Pulitzer prize for 1919-1920, is a realistic drama in which Robert, defeated in his desire to get away to sea, is overwhelmed and dies in his own complete futility. As the dying Robert rationalizes his defeat and expires pointing out to Ruth and Andrew his visionary ecstasy, the lyrical speeches reveal the dramatist's recurrent theme of beauty and tragedy. Human aspirations and defeat, great dreams and empty fulfillments, evanescent happiness and unrelieved tragedy are the substance and spirit of the O'Neill dramas. In *Anna Christie,* the Pulitzer Prize play for 1921-1922, O'Neill produced a work of stark realism. Anna, the prostitute, is involved in the timeless tragedy of love and a past. *All God's Chillun Got Wings* and *The Hairy Ape* are semi-expressionistic dramas with social implications; the former treats of the relations between a white woman and a Negro, and the latter deals with the search of a stoker for his place in an alien and incomprehensible world. In *The Great God Brown* and *Dynamo,* O'Neill experiments effectively with masks and symbolism. *The Emperor Jones,* with tom-toms sounding from normal to accelerated pulse beat as the action develops, is a tour-de-force of the imagination. The legend of Ponce de Leon in his search for eternal youth provides the background for the poetic romance, *The Fountain. Desire Under the Elms,* with its bleak New England setting and Freudian plot, is an unrelieved tragedy that has its origins in the soil and in the passions of those who live by it.

In *Strange Interlude,* the Pulitzer prize play for 1927-1928, O'Neill experiments with a new dramatic technique and a modern psychological plot. Here the methods of the novelist have been summoned to the stage in a sensational manner; the characters not only speak but think aloud. Aspirations and frustrations pervade this novelistic drama.

In what has been acclaimed one of his greatest works, the trilogy *Mourning Becomes Electra,* O'Neill again employs a psychological plot, but turns to a classic source for the framework of his drama. The work itself is comparable in directness, force and inevitability to the tragedies of the ancient Greeks.

To imply that O'Neill is more attentive to method than to substance would be rank injustice to his work. No modern dramatist is more concerned with human motives and ultimate values. Implicit in his plays is a quest for a rational and dignified conception of man's place in the universe. The search for a religion worthy of modern man has been one of his chief preoccupations. In his earlier plays this search is constantly suggested, but never is it so fully and definitely realized as in his latest work, *Days Without End,* in which John Loving eventually succeeds in the struggle against his baser nature, represented on the stage by a second character who wears a sneering death mask of John himself. Because they are fraught with profound meanings, his plays gain in dramatic intensity. Depth of meaning always adds force and tragic significance to his plots and characters. The comedy, *Ah, Wilderness!* provides a striking contrast by its natural and spontaneous humor to previous O'Neill plays.

O'Neill has been compared to many playwrights but to none so appropriately as to Aeschylus, for he resembles that great dramatist of ancient Greece in the tragic grandeur and terrible force of his work. St. John Ervine, the English writer, has called O'Neill the "Marlowe of America, preparing the path for its Shakespeare." This appellation is apt in at least one respect: O'Neill, like Marlowe, is at heart a poet, disappointed but not irreparably hurt by the tragic urgencies of life. In the words of John Wood Krutch, "All the striving, the protest and the passion of his nature have found a clear adequate channel in his art."

Beyond the Horizon, the Pulitzer Prize drama for 1919-1920, was first produced by John D. Williams at the Morosco Theatre, New York City, February 2, 1920.

CHARACTERS

JAMES MAYO, a farmer.

KATE MAYO, his wife.

CAPTAIN DICK SCOTT, of the bark *Sunda,* her brother.

ANDREW MAYO   sons of JAMES MAYO.
ROBERT MAYO

RUTH ATKINS.

MRS. ATKINS, her widowed mother.

MARY.

BEN, a farm hand.

DOCTOR FAWCETT.

SCENES

ACT ONE

SCENE I: The Road. Sunset of a day in Spring.

SCENE II: The Farm House. The same night.

ACT TWO

(*Three years later*)

SCENE I: The Farm House. Noon of a Summer day.

SCENE II: The top of a hill on the farm overlooking the sea. The following day.

ACT THREE

(*Five years later*)

SCENE I: The Farm House. Dawn of a day in late Fall.

SCENE II: The Road. Sunrise.

BEYOND THE HORIZON

ACT ONE

SCENE I

A section of country highway. The road runs diagonally from the left, forward, to the right, rear, and can be seen in the distance winding toward the horizon like a pale ribbon between the low, rolling hills with their freshly plowed fields clearly divided from each other, checkerboard fashion, by the lines of stone walls and rough snake fences.

The forward triangle cut off by the road is a section of a field, from the dark earth of which myriad bright-green blades of fall-sown rye are sprouting. A straggling line of piled rocks, too low to be called a wall, separates this field from the road.

To the rear of the road is a ditch with a sloping, grassy bank on the far side. From the center of this an old, gnarled apple tree, just budding into leaf, strains its twisted branches heavenwards, black against the pallor of distance. A snake fence sidles from left to right along the top of the bank, passing beneath the apple tree.

The hushed twilight of a day in May is just beginning. The horizon hills are still rimmed by a faint line of flame, and the sky above them glows with the crimson flush of the sunset. This fades gradually as the action of the scene progresses.

At the rise of the curtain, ROBERT MAYO *is discovered sitting on the fence. He is a tall, slender young man of twenty-three. There is a touch of the poet about him expressed in his high forehead and wide, dark eyes. His features are delicate and refined, leaning to weakness in the mouth and chin. He is dressed in gray corduroy trousers pushed into high laced boots, and a blue flannel shirt with a bright colored tie. He is reading a book by the fading sunset light. He shuts this, keeping a finger in to mark the place, and turns his head toward the horizon, gazing out over the fields and hills. His lips move as if he were reciting something to himself.*

His brother ANDREW *comes along the road from the right, returning from his work in the fields. He is twenty-seven years old, an opposite type to* ROBERT—*husky, sun-bronzed, handsome in a large-featured, manly fashion—a son of the soil, intelligent in a shrewd way, but with nothing of the intellectual about him. He wears overalls, leather boots, a gray flannel shirt open at the neck, and a soft, mud-stained hat pushed back on his head. He stops to talk to* ROBERT, *leaning on the hoe he carries.*

ANDREW (*seeing* ROBERT *has not noticed his presence—in a loud shout*). Hey there! (ROBERT *turns with a start. Seeing who it is, he smiles.*) Gosh, you do take the prize for day-dreaming! And I see you've toted one of the old books along with you. (*He crosses the ditch and sits on the fence near his brother.*) What is it this time—poetry, I'll bet. (*He reaches for the book.*) Let me see.

ROBERT (*handing it to him rather reluctantly*). Look out you don't get it full of dirt.

ANDREW (*glancing at his hands*). That isn't dirt—it's good clean earth. (*He turns over the pages. His eyes read something and he gives an exclamation of disgust.*) Hump! (*With a provoking grin at his brother he reads aloud in a doleful, sing-song voice.*) "I have loved wind and light and the bright sea. But holy and most sacred night, not as I love and have loved thee." (*He hands the book back.*) Here! Take it and bury it. I suppose it's that year in college gave you a liking for that kind of stuff. I'm darn glad I stopped at high school, or maybe I'd been crazy too. (*He grins and slaps* ROBERT *on the back affectionately.*) Imagine me reading poetry and plowing at the same time! The team'd run away, I'll bet.

ROBERT (*laughing*). Or picture me plowing.

ANDREW. You should have gone back to college last fall, like I know you wanted to. You're fitted for that sort of thing—just as I ain't.

ROBERT. You know why I didn't go back, Andy. Pa didn't like the idea, even if he didn't say so; and I know he wanted the money to use improving the farm. And besides, I'm not keen on being a student, just because you see me reading books all the time. What I want to do now is keep on moving so that I won't take root in any one place.

ANDREW. Well, the trip you're leaving on tomorrow will keep you moving all right. (*At this mention of the trip they both fall silent. There is a pause. Finally* ANDREW *goes on, awkwardly, attempting to speak casually.*) Uncle says you'll be gone three years.

ROBERT. About that, he figures.

ANDREW (*moodily*). That's a long time.

ROBERT. Not so long when you come to consider it. You know the *Sunda* sails around the Horn for Yokohama first, and that's a long voyage on a sailing ship; and if we go to any of the other places Uncle Dick mentions—India, or Australia, or South Africa, or South America—they'll be long voyages, too.

ANDREW. You can have all those foreign parts for all of me. (*After a pause.*) Ma's going to miss you a lot, Rob.

ROBERT. Yes—and I'll miss her.

ANDREW. And Pa ain't feeling none too happy to have you go—though he's been trying not to show it.

ROBERT. I can see how he feels.

ANDREW. And you can bet that I'm not giving any cheers about it. (*He puts one hand on the fence near* ROBERT.)

ROBERT (*putting one hand on top of* ANDREW's *with a gesture almost of shyness*). I know that, too, Andy.

ANDREW. I'll miss you as much as anybody, I guess. You see, you and I ain't like most brothers—always fighting and separated a lot of the time, while we've always been together—just the two of us. It's different with us. That's why it hits so hard, I guess.

ROBERT (*with feeling*). It's just as hard for me, Andy—believe that! I hate to leave you and the old folks—but—I feel I've got to. There's something calling me— (*He points to the horizon.*) Oh, I can't just explain it to you, Andy.

ANDREW. No need to, Rob. (*Angry at himself.*) Hell! You want to go—that's all there is to it; and I wouldn't have you miss this chance for the world.

ROBERT. It's fine of you to feel that way, Andy.

ANDREW. Huh! I'd be a nice son-of-a-gun if I didn't, wouldn't I? When I know how you need this sea trip to make a new man of you—in the body, I mean—and give you your full health back.

ROBERT (*a trifle impatiently*). All of you seem to keep harping on my health. You were so used to seeing me lying around the house in the old days that you never will get over the notion that I'm a chronic invalid. You don't realize how I've bucked up in the past few years. If I had no other excuse for going on Uncle Dick's ship but just my health, I'd stay right here and start in plowing.

ANDREW. Can't be done. Farming ain't your nature. There's all the difference shown in just the way us two feel about the farm. You—well, you like the home part of it, I expect; but as a place to work and grow things, you hate it. Ain't that right?

ROBERT. Yes, I suppose it is. For you it's different. You're a Mayo through and through. You're wedded to the soil. You're as much a product of it as an ear of corn is, or a tree. Father is the same. This farm is his life-work, and he's happy in knowing that another Mayo, inspired by the same love, will take up the work where he leaves off. I can understand your attitude, and Pa's; and I think it's wonderful and sincere. But I—well, I'm not made that way.

ANDREW. No, you ain't; but when it comes to understanding, I guess I realize that you've got your own angle of looking at things.

ROBERT (*musingly*). I wonder if you do, really.

ANDREW (*confidently*). Sure I do. You've seen a bit of the world, enough to make the farm seem small, and you've got the itch to see it all.

ROBERT. It's more than that, Andy.

ANDREW. Oh, of course. I know you're going to learn navigation, and all about a ship, so's you can be an officer. That's natural, too. There's fair pay in it, I expect, when you consider that you've always got a home and grub thrown in; and if you're set on traveling, you can go anywhere you're a mind to without paying fare.

ROBERT (*with a smile that is half sad*). It's more than that, Andy.

ANDREW. Sure it is. There's always a chance of a good thing coming your way in some of those foreign ports or other. I've heard there are great opportunities for a young fellow with his eyes open in some of those new countries that are just being opened up. (*Jovially.*) I'll bet that's what you've been turning over in your mind under all your quietness! (*He slaps his brother on the back with a laugh.*) Well, if you get to be a millionaire all of a sudden, call 'round once in a while and I'll pass the plate to you. We could use a lot of money right here on the farm without hurting it any.

ROBERT (*forced to laugh*). I've never considered that practical side of it for a minute, Andy.

ANDREW. Well, you ought to.

ROBERT. No, I oughtn't. (*Pointing to the horizon—dreamily.*) Supposing I was to tell you that it's just Beauty that's calling me, the beauty of the far off and unknown, the mystery and spell of the East which lures me in the books I've read, the need of the freedom of great wide spaces, the joy of wandering on and on—in quest of the secret which is hidden over there, beyond the horizon? Suppose I told you that was the one and only reason for my going?

ANDREW. I should say you were nutty.

ROBERT (*frowning*). Don't, Andy. I'm serious.

ANDREW. Then you might as well stay here, because we've got all you're looking for right on this farm. There's wide space enough, Lord knows; and you can have all the sea you want by walking a mile down to the beach; and there's plenty of horizon to look at, and beauty enough for anyone, except in the winter. (*He grins.*) As for the mystery and spell, I haven't met 'em yet, but they're probably lying around somewheres. I'll have you understand this is a first-class farm with all the fixings. (*He laughs.*)

ROBERT (*joining in the laughter in spite of himself*). It's no use talking to you, you chump!

ANDREW. You'd better not say anything to Uncle Dick about spells and things when you're on the ship. He'll likely chuck you overboard for a Jonah. (*He jumps down from fence.*) I'd better run along. I've got to wash up some as long as Ruth's Ma is coming over for supper.

ROBERT (*pointedly—almost bitterly*). And Ruth.

ANDREW (*confused—looking everywhere except at* ROBERT—*trying to appear unconcerned*). Yes, Ruth'll be staying too. Well, I better hustle, I guess, and— (*He steps over the ditch to the road while he is talking.*)

ROBERT (*who appears to be fighting some strong inward emotion—impulsively*). Wait a minute, Andy! (*He jumps down from the fence.*) There is something I want to— (*He stops abruptly, biting his lips, his face coloring.*)

ANDREW (*facing him; half-defiantly*). Yes?

ROBERT (*confusedly*). No—never mind— it doesn't matter, it was nothing.

ANDREW (*after a pause, during which he stares fixedly at* ROBERT'*s averted face*). Maybe I can guess— what you were going to say— but I guess you're right not to talk about it. (*He pulls* ROBERT'*s hand from his side and grips it tensely; the two brothers stand looking into each other's eyes for a minute.*) We can't help those things, Rob. (*He turns away, suddenly releasing* ROBERT'*s hand.*) You'll be coming along shortly, won't you?

ROBERT (*dully*). Yes.

ANDREW. See you later, then. (*He walks off down the road to the left.* ROBERT *stares after him for a moment; then climbs to the fence rail again, and looks out over the hills, an expression of deep grief on his face. After a moment or so,* RUTH *enters hurriedly from the left. She is a healthy, blonde, out-of-door girl of twenty, with a graceful, slender figure. Her face, though inclined to roundness, is undeniably pretty, its large eyes of a deep blue set off strikingly by the sun-bronzed complexion. Her small, regular features are marked by a certain strength—an underlying, stubborn fixity of purpose hidden in the frankly-appealing charm of her fresh youthfulness. She wears a simple white dress but no hat.*)

RUTH (*seeing him*). Hello, Rob!

ROBERT (*startled*). Hello, Ruth!

RUTH (*jumps the ditch and perches on the fence beside him*). I was looking for you.

ROBERT (*pointedly*). Andy just left here.

RUTH. I know. I met him on the road a second ago. He told me you were here. (*Tenderly playful.*) I wasn't looking for Andy, Smarty, if that's what you mean. I was looking for *you.*

ROBERT. Because I'm going away tomorrow?

RUTH. Because your mother was anxious to have you come home and asked me to look for you. I just wheeled Ma over to your house.

ROBERT (*perfunctorily*). How is your mother?

RUTH (*a shadow coming over her face*). She's about the same. She never seems to get any better or any worse. Oh, Rob, I do wish she'd try to make the best of things that can't be helped.

ROBERT. Has she been nagging at you again?

RUTH (*nods her head, and then breaks forth rebelliously*). She never stops nagging. No matter what I do for her she finds fault. If only Pa was still living— (*She stops as if ashamed of her outburst.*) I suppose I shouldn't complain this way. (*She sighs.*) Poor Ma, Lord knows it's hard enough for her. I suppose it's natural to be cross when you're not able ever to walk a step. Oh, I'd like to be going away some place—like you!

ROBERT. It's hard to stay—and equally hard to go, sometimes.

RUTH. There! If I'm not the stupid body! I swore I wasn't going to speak about your trip—until after you'd gone; and there I go, first thing!

ROBERT. Why didn't you want to speak of it?

RUTH. Because I didn't want to spoil this last night you're here. Oh, Rob, I'm going to—we're all going to miss you so awfully. Your mother is going around looking as if she'd burst out crying any minute. You ought to know how I feel. Andy and you and I—why it seems as if we'd always been together.

ROBERT (*with a wry attempt at a smile*). You and Andy will still have each other. It'll be harder for me without anyone.

RUTH. But you'll have new sights and new people to take your mind off; while we'll be here with the old, familiar place to remind us every minute of the day. It's a shame you're going—just at this time, in spring, when everything is getting so nice. (*With a sigh.*) I oughtn't to talk that way when I know going's the best thing for you. You're bound to find all sorts of opportunities to get on, your father says.

ROBERT (*heatedly*). I don't give a damn about that! I wouldn't take a voyage across the road for the best opportunity in the world of the kind Pa thinks of. (*He smiles at his own irritation.*) Excuse me, Ruth, for getting worked up over it; but Andy gave me an overdose of the practical considerations.

RUTH (*slowly, puzzled*). Well, then if it isn't— (*With sudden intensity.*) Oh, Rob, why *do* you want to go?

ROBERT (*turning to her quickly, in surprise—slowly*). Why do you ask that, Ruth?

RUTH (*dropping her eyes before his searching glance*). Because— (*Lamely.*) It seems such a shame.

ROBERT (*insistently*). Why?

RUTH. Oh, because—everything.

ROBERT. I could hardly back out now, even if I wanted to. And I'll be forgotten before you know it.

RUTH (*indignantly*). You won't! I'll never forget— (*She stops and turns away to hide her confusion.*)

ROBERT (*softly*). Will you promise me that?

RUTH (*evasively*). Of course. It's mean of you to think that any of us would forget so easily.

ROBERT (*disappointedly*). Oh!

RUTH (*with an attempt at lightness*). But you haven't told me your reason for leaving yet?

ROBERT (*moodily*). I doubt if you'll understand. It's difficult to explain, even to myself. Either you feel it, or you don't. I can remember being conscious of it first when I was only a kid—you haven't forgotten what a sickly specimen I was then, in those days, have you?

RUTH (*with a shudder*). Let's not think about them.

ROBERT. You'll have to, to understand. Well, in those days, when Ma was fixing meals, she used to get me out of the way by pushing my chair to the west window and telling me to look out and be quiet. That wasn't hard. I guess I was always quiet.

RUTH (*compassionately*). Yes, you always were—and you suffering so much, too!

ROBERT (*musingly*). So I used to stare out over the fields to the hills, out there— (*He points to the horizon.*) and somehow after a time I'd forget any pain I was in, and start dreaming. I knew the sea was over beyond those hills—the folks had told me—and I used to wonder what the sea was like, and try to form a picture of it in my mind. (*With a smile.*) There was all the mystery in the world to me then about that—far-off sea—and there still is! It called to me then just as it does now. (*After a slight pause.*) And other times my eyes would follow this road, winding off into the distance, toward the hills, as if it, too, was searching for the sea. And I'd promise myself that when I grew up and was strong, I'd follow that road, and it and I would find the sea together. (*With a smile.*) You see, my making this trip is only keeping that promise of long ago.

RUTH (*charmed by his low, musical voice telling the dreams of his childhood*). Yes, I see.

ROBERT. Those were the only happy moments of my life then, dreaming there at the window. I liked to be all alone—those times. I got to know all the different kinds of sunsets by heart. And all those sunsets took place over there— (*He points*) beyond the horizon. So gradually I came to believe that all the wonders of the world happened on the other side of those hills. There was the home of the good fairies who performed beautiful miracles. I believed in fairies then. (*With a smile.*) Perhaps I still do believe in them. Anyway, in those days they were real enough, and sometimes I could actually hear them calling to me to come out and play with them, dance with them down the road in the dusk in a game of hide-and-seek to find out where the sun was hiding himself. They sang their little songs to me, songs that told of all the wonderful things they had in their home on the other side of the hills; and they promised to show me all of them, if I'd only come, come! But I couldn't come then, and I used to cry sometimes and Ma would think I was in pain. (*He breaks off suddenly with a laugh.*) That's why I'm going now, I suppose. For I can still hear them calling. But the horizon is as far away and as luring as ever. (*He turns to her—softly.*) Do you understand now, Ruth?

RUTH (*spellbound, in a whisper*). Yes.

ROBERT. You feel it then?

RUTH. Yes, yes, I do! (*Unconsciously she snuggles close against his side. His arm steals about her as if he were not aware of the action.*) Oh, Rob, how could I help feeling it? You tell things so beautifully!

ROBERT (*suddenly realizing that his arm is around her, and that her head is resting on his shoulder, gently takes his arm away.* RUTH, *brought back to herself, is overcome with confusion*). So now you know why I'm going. It's for that reason—that and one other.

RUTH. You've another? Then you must tell me that, too.

ROBERT (*looking at her searchingly. She drops her eyes before his gaze*). I wonder if I ought to! You'll promise not to be angry—whatever it is?

RUTH (*softly, her face still averted*). Yes, I promise.

ROBERT (*simply*). I love you. That's the other reason.

RUTH (*hiding her face in her hands*). Oh, Rob!

ROBERT. I wasn't going to tell you, but I feel I have to. It can't matter now that I'm going so far away, and for so long—perhaps forever. I've loved you all these years, but the realization never came till I agreed to go away with Uncle Dick. Then I thought of leaving you, and the pain of that thought revealed to me in a flash—that I loved you, had loved you as long as I could remember. (*He gently pulls one of* RUTH's *hands away from her face.*) You mustn't mind my telling you this, Ruth. I realize how impossible it all is—and I understand; for the revelation of my own love seemed to open my eyes to the love of others. I saw Andy's love for you—and I knew that you must love him.

RUTH (*breaking out stormily*). I don't! I don't love Andy! I don't! (ROBERT *stares at her in stupid astonishment.* RUTH *weeps hysterically.*) Whatever—put such a fool

notion into—into your head? (*She suddenly throws her arms about his neck and hides her head on his shoulder.*) Oh, Rob! Don't go away! Please! You mustn't, now! You can't! I won't let you! It'd break my—my heart!

ROBERT. (*The expression of stupid bewilderment giving way to one of overwhelming joy. He presses her close to him—slowly and tenderly.*) Do you mean that—that you love me?

RUTH (*sobbing*). Yes, yes—of course I do—what d'you s'pose? (*She lifts up her head and looks into his eyes with a tremulous smile.*) You stupid thing! (*He kisses her.*) I've loved you right along.

ROBERT (*mystified*). But you and Andy were always together!

RUTH. Because you never seemed to want to go any place with me. You were always reading an old book, and not paying any attention to me. I was too proud to let you see I cared because I thought the year you had away to college had made you stuck-up, and you thought yourself too educated to waste any time on me.

ROBERT (*kissing her*). And I was thinking—(*With a laugh.*) What fools we've both been!

RUTH (*overcome by a sudden fear*). You won't go away on the trip, will you, Rob? You'll tell them you can't go on account of me, won't you? You can't go now! You can't!

ROBERT (*bewildered*). Perhaps—you can come too.

RUTH. Oh, Rob, don't be so foolish. You know I can't. Who'd take care of ma? Don't you see I couldn't go—on her account? (*She clings to him imploringly.*) Please don't go—not now. Tell them you've decided not to. They won't mind. I know your mother and father'll be glad. They'll all be. They don't want you to go so far away from them. Please, Rob! We'll be so happy here together where it's natural and we know things. Please tell me you won't go!

ROBERT (*face to face with a definite, final decision, betrays the conflict going on within him*). But—Ruth—I—Uncle Dick—

RUTH. He won't mind when he knows it's for your happiness to stay. How could he? (*As* ROBERT *remains silent she bursts into sobs again.*) Oh, Rob! And you said—you loved me!

ROBERT (*conquered by this appeal—an irrevocable decision in his voice*). I won't go, Ruth. I promise you. There! Don't cry! (*He presses her to him, stroking her hair tenderly. After a pause he speaks with happy hopefulness.*) Perhaps after all Andy was right—righter than he knew—when he said I could find all the things I was seeking for here, at home on the farm. I think love must have been the secret—the secret that called to me from over the world's rim—the secret beyond every horizon; and when I did not come, it came to me. (*He clasps* RUTH *to him fiercely.*) Oh, Ruth, our love is sweeter than any distant dream! (*He kisses her passionately and steps to the ground, lifting* RUTH *in his arms and carrying her to the road where he puts her down.*)

RUTH (*with a happy laugh*). My, but you're strong!

ROBERT. Come! We'll go and tell them at once.

RUTH (*dismayed*). Oh, no, don't, Rob, not till after I've gone. There'd be bound to be such a scene with them all together.

ROBERT (*kissing her—gayly*). As you like —little Miss Common Sense!

RUTH. Let's go, then. (*She takes his hand, and they start to go off left.* ROBERT *suddenly stops and turns as though for a last look at the hills and the dying sunset flush.*)

ROBERT (*looking upward and pointing*). See! The first star. (*He bends down and kisses her tenderly.*) Our star!

RUTH (*in a soft murmur*). Yes. Our very own star. (*They stand for a moment looking up at it, their arms around each other. Then* RUTH *takes his hand again and starts to lead him away*). Come, Rob, let's go. (*His eyes are fixed again on the horizon as he half turns to follow her.* RUTH *urges.*) We'll be late for supper, Rob.

ROBERT (*shakes his head impatiently, as though he were throwing off some disturbing thought—with a laugh*). All right. We'll run then. Come on! (*They run off laughing as*

The Curtain Falls.

SCENE II

The sitting room of the Mayo farm house about nine o'clock the same night. On the left, two windows looking out on the fields. Against the wall between the windows, an old-fashioned walnut desk. In the left corner, rear, a sideboard with a mirror. In the rear wall to the right of the sideboard, a window looking out on the road. Next to the window a door leading out into the yard. Farther right, a black horse-hair sofa, and another door opening on a bedroom. In the corner, a straight-backed chair. In the right wall, near the middle, an open doorway leading to the kitchen. Farther forward a double-heater stove with coal scuttle, etc. In the center of the newly carpeted floor, an oak dining-room table with a red cover. In the center of the table, a large oil reading lamp. Four chairs, three rockers with crocheted tidies on their backs, and one straight-backed, are placed about the table. The walls are papered a dark red with a scrolly-figured pattern.

Everything in the room is clean, well-kept, and in its exact place, yet there is no suggestion of primness about the whole. Rather the atmosphere is one of the orderly comfort of a simple, hard-earned prosperity, enjoyed and maintained by the family as a unit.

JAMES MAYO, *his wife, her brother,* CAPTAIN DICK SCOTT, *and* ANDREW *are discovered.*

MAYO *is his son* ANDREW *over again in body and face—an* ANDREW *sixty-five years old with a short, square, white beard.* MRS. MAYO *is a slight, round-faced, rather prim-looking woman of fifty-five who had once been a school teacher. The labors of a farmer's wife have bent but not broken her, and she retains a certain refinement of movement and expression foreign to the* MAYO *part of the family. Whatever of resemblance* ROBERT *has to his parents may be traced to her. Her brother, the* CAPTAIN, *is short and stocky, with a weather-beaten, jovial face and a white mustache—a typical old salt, loud of voice and given to gesture. He is fifty-eight years old.*

JAMES MAYO *sits in front of the table. He wears spectacles, and a farm journal which he has been reading lies in his lap.* THE CAPTAIN *leans forward from a chair in the rear, his hands on the table in front of him.* ANDREW *is tilted back on the straight-backed chair to the left, his chin sunk forward on his chest, staring at the carpet, preoccupied and frowning.*

As the curtain rises the CAPTAIN *is just finishing the relation of some sea episode. The others are pretending an interest which is belied by the absent-minded expressions on their faces.*

THE CAPTAIN (*chuckling*). And that mission woman, she hails me on the dock as I was acomin' ashore, and she says—with her silly face all screwed up serious as judgment—"Captain," she says, "would you be so kind as to tell me where the sea-gulls sleeps at nights?" Blow me if them warn't her exact words! (*He slaps the table with the palm of his hands and laughs loudly. The others force smiles.*) Ain't that just like a fool woman's question? And I looks at her serious as I could, "Ma'm," says I, "I couldn't rightly answer that question. I ain't never seed a sea-gull in his bunk yet. The next time I hears one snorin'," I says, "I'll make a note of where he's turned in, and write you a letter 'bout it." And then she calls me a fool real spiteful and tacks away from me quick. (*He laughs again uproariously.*) So I got rid of her that way. (*The others smile but immediately relapse into expressions of gloom again.*)

MRS. MAYO (*absent-mindedly—feeling that she has to say something*). But when it comes to that, where *do* sea-gulls sleep, Dick?

SCOTT (*slapping the table*). Ho! Ho! Listen to her, James. 'Nother one! Well, if that don't beat all hell—'scuse me for cussin', Kate.

MAYO (*with a twinkle in his eyes*). They unhitch their wings, Katey, and spreads 'em out on a wave for a bed.

SCOTT. And then they tells the fish to whistle to 'em when it's time to turn out. Ho! Ho!

MRS. MAYO (*with a forced smile*). You men folks are too smart to live, aren't you? (*She resumes her knitting.* MAYO *pretends to read his paper;* ANDREW *stares at the floor.*)

SCOTT (*looks from one to the other of them with a puzzled air. Finally he is unable to bear the thick silence a minute longer, and blurts out*): You folks look as if you was settin' up with a corpse. (*With exaggerated concern.*) God A'mighty, there ain't anyone dead, be there?

MAYO (*sharply*). Don't play the dunce, Dick! You know as well as we do there ain't no great cause to be feelin' chipper.

SCOTT (*argumentatively*). And there ain't no cause to be wearin' mourning, either, I can make out.

MRS. MAYO (*indignantly*). How can you talk that way, Dick Scott, when you're taking our Robbie away from us, in the middle of the night, you might say, just to get on that old boat of yours on time! I think you might wait until morning when he's had his breakfast.

SCOTT (*appealing to the others hopelessly*). Ain't that a woman's way o' seein' things for you? God A'mighty, Kate, I can't give orders to the tide that it's got to be high just when it suits me to have it. I ain't gettin' no fun out o' missin' sleep and leavin' here at six bells myself. (*Protestingly.*) And the *Sunda* ain't an old ship—leastways, not very old—and she's good's she ever was.

MRS. MAYO (*her lips trembling*). I wish Robbie weren't going.

MAYO (*looking at her over his glasses— consolingly*). There, Katey!

MRS. MAYO (*rebelliously*). Well, I *do* wish he wasn't!

SCOTT. You shouldn't be taking it so hard, 's far as I kin see. This vige'll make a man of him. I'll see to it he learns how to navigate, 'n' study for a mate's c'tificate right off—and it'll give him a trade for the rest of his life, if he wants to travel.

MRS. MAYO. But I don't want him to travel all his life. You've got to see he comes home when this trip is over. Then he'll be all well, and he'll want to—to marry—(AND- REW *sits forward in his chair with an abrupt movement*)—and settle down right here. (*She stares down at the knitting in her lap—after a pause.*) I never realized how hard it was going to be for me to have Robbie go—or I wouldn't have considered it a minute.

SCOTT. It ain't no good goin' on that way, Kate, now it's all settled.

MRS. MAYO (*on the verge of tears*). It's all right for *you* to talk. You've never had any children. You don't know what it means to be parted from them—and Robbie my youngest, too. (ANDREW *frowns and fidgets in his chair.*)

ANDREW (*suddenly turning to them*). There's one thing none of you seem to take into consideration—that Rob wants to go. He's dead set on it. He's been dreaming over this trip ever since it was first talked about. It wouldn't be fair to him not to have him go. (*A sudden uneasiness seems to strike him.*) At least, not if he still feels the same way about it he did when he was talking to me this evening.

MAYO (*with an air of decision*). Andy's right, Katey. That ends all argyment, you can see that. (*Looking at his big silver watch.*) Wonder what's happened to Robert? He's been gone long enough to wheel the widder to home, certain. He can't be out dreamin' at the stars his last night.

MRS. MAYO (*a bit reproachfully*). Why didn't you wheel Mrs. Atkins back tonight, Andy? You usually do when she and Ruth come over.

ANDREW (*avoiding her eyes*). I thought maybe Robert wanted to tonight. He offered to go right away when they were leaving.

MRS. MAYO. He only wanted to be polite.

ANDREW (*gets to his feet*). Well, he'll be right back, I guess. (*He turns to his father.*) Guess I'll go take a look at the black cow, Pa—see if she's ailing any.

MAYO. Yes—better had, son. (ANDREW *goes into the kitchen on the right.*)

SCOTT (*as he goes out—in a low tone*). There's the boy that would make a good, strong sea-farin' man—if he'd a mind to.

MAYO (*sharply*). Don't you put no such fool notions in Andy's head, Dick—or you 'n' me's goin' to fall out. (*Then he smiles.*) You couldn't tempt him, no ways. Andy's a Mayo bred in the bone, and he's a born farmer, and a damn good one, too. He'll live and die right here on this farm, like I expect to. (*With proud confidence.*) And he'll make this one of the slickest, best- payin' farms in the state, too, afore he gits through!

SCOTT. Seems to me it's a pretty slick place right now.

MAYO (*shaking his head*). It's too small. We need more land to make it amount to much, and we ain't got the capital to buy it.

(ANDREW *enters from the kitchen. His hat is on, and he carries a lighted lantern in his hand. He goes to the door in the rear leading out.*)

ANDREW (*opens the door and pauses*). Anything else you can think of to be done, Pa?

MAYO. No, nothin' I know of. (ANDREW *goes out, shutting the door.*)

MRS. MAYO (*after a pause*). What's come over Andy tonight, I wonder? He acts so strange.

MAYO. He does seem sort o' glum and out of sorts. It's 'count o' Robert leavin', I s'pose. (*To* SCOTT) Dick, you wouldn't believe how them boys o' mine sticks together. They ain't like most brothers. They've been thick as thieves all their lives, with nary a quarrel I kin remember.

SCOTT. No need to tell me that. I can see how they take to each other.

MRS. MAYO (*pursuing her train of thought*). Did you notice, James, how queer everyone was at supper? Robert seemed stirred up about something; and Ruth was so flustered and giggly; and Andy sat there dumb, looking as if he'd lost his best friend; and all of them only nibbled at their food.

MAYO. Guess they was all thinkin' about tomorrow, same as us.

MRS. MAYO (*shaking her head*). No. I'm afraid somethin's happened—somethin' else.

MAYO. You mean—'bout Ruth?

MRS. MAYO. Yes.

MAYO (*after a pause—frowning*). I hope her and Andy ain't had a serious fallin'-out. I always sorter hoped they'd hitch up together sooner or later. What d'you say, Dick? Don't you think them two'd pair up well?

SCOTT (*nodding his head approvingly*). A sweet, wholesome couple they'd make.

MAYO. It'd be a good thing for Andy in more ways than one. I ain't what you'd call calculatin' generally, and I b'lieve in lettin' young folks run their affairs to suit themselves; but there's advantages for both o' them in this match you can't overlook in reason. The Atkins farm is right next to ourn. Jined together they'd make a jim-dandy of a place, with plenty o' room to work in. And bein' a widder with only a daughter, and laid up all the time to boot, Mrs. Atkins can't do nothin' with the place as it ought to be done. She needs a man, a first-class farmer, to take hold o' things; and Andy's just the one.

MRS. MAYO (*abruptly*). I don't think Ruth loves Andy.

MAYO. You don't? Well, maybe a woman's eyes is sharper in such things, but—they're always together. And if she don't love him now, she'll likely come around to it in time. (*As* MRS. MAYO *shakes her head.*) You seem mighty fixed in your opinion, Katey. How d'you know?

MRS. MAYO. It's just—what I feel.

MAYO (*a light breaking over him*). You don't mean to say— (MRS. MAYO *nods.* MAYO *chuckles scornfully.*) Shucks! I'm losin' my respect for your eyesight, Katey. Why Robert ain't got no time for Ruth, 'cept as a friend!

MRS. MAYO (*warningly*). Sss-h-h! (*The door from the yard opens, and* ROBERT *enters. He is smiling happily, and humming a song to himself, but as he comes into the room an undercurrent of nervous uneasiness manifests itself in his bearing.*)

MAYO. So here you be at last! (ROBERT *comes forward and sits on* ANDY's *chair.* MAYO *smiles slyly at his wife.*) What have you been doin' all this time—countin' the stars to see if they all come out right and proper?

ROBERT. There's only one I'll ever look for any more, Pa.

MAYO (*reproachfully*). You might've even not wasted time lookin' for that one—your last night.

MRS. MAYO (*as if she were speaking to a child*). You ought to have worn your coat a sharp night like this, Robbie.

SCOTT (*disgustedly*). God A'mighty, Kate, you treat Robert as if he was one year old!

MRS. MAYO (*notices* ROBERT's *nervous uneasiness*). You look all worked up over something, Robbie. What is it?

ROBERT (*swallowing hard, looks quickly from one to the other of them—then begins determinedly*). Yes, there is something—something I must tell you—all of you. (*As he begins to talk* ANDREW *enters quietly from the rear, closing the door behind him, and setting the lighted lantern on the floor. He remains standing by the door, his arms folded, listening to* ROBERT *with a repressed expression of pain on his face.* ROBERT *is so much taken up with what he is going to say that he does not notice* ANDREW'S *presence.*) Something I discovered only this evening—very beautiful and wonderful—something I did not take into consideration previously because I hadn't dared to hope that such happiness could ever come to me. (*Appealingly.*) You must all remember that fact, won't you?

MAYO (*frowning*). Let's get to the point, son.

ROBERT (*with a trace of defiance*). Well, the point is this, Pa: I'm not going—I mean—I can't go tomorrow with Uncle Dick—or at any future time, either.

MRS. MAYO (*with a sharp sigh of joyful relief*). Oh, Robbie, I'm so glad!

MAYO (*astounded*). You ain't serious, be you, Robert? (*Severely.*) Seems to me it's a pretty late hour in the day for you to be upsettin' all your plans so sudden!

ROBERT. I asked you to remember that until this evening I didn't know myself. I had never dared to dream—

MAYO (*irritably*). What is this foolishness you're talkin' of?

ROBERT (*flushing*). Ruth told me this evening that—she loved me. It was after I'd confessed I loved her. I told her I hadn't been conscious of my love until after the trip had been arranged, and I realized it would mean—leaving her. That was the truth. I *didn't* know until then. (*As if justifying himself to the others.*) I hadn't intended telling her anything but—suddenly—I felt I must. I didn't think it would matter, because I was going away. And I thought she loved—someone else. (*Slowly—his eyes shining.*) And then she cried and said it was I she'd loved all the time, but I hadn't seen it.

MRS. MAYO (*rushes over and throws her arms about him*). I knew it! I was just telling your father when you came in—and, oh, Robbie, I'm so happy you're not going!

ROBERT (*kissing her*). I knew you'd be glad, Ma.

MAYO (*bewilderedly*). Well, I'll be damned! You do beat all for gettin' folks' minds all tangled up, Robert. And Ruth too! Whatever got into her of a sudden? Why, I was thinkin'—

MRS. MAYO (*hurriedly—in a tone of warning*). Never mind what you were thinking, James. It wouldn't be any use telling us that now. (*Meaningly.*) And what you were hoping for turns out just the same almost, doesn't it?

MAYO (*thoughtfully—beginning to see this side of the argument*). Yes; I suppose you're right, Katey. (*Scratching his head in puzzlement.*) But how it ever come about! It do beat anything ever I heard. (*Finally he gets up with a sheepish grin and walks over to* ROBERT.) We're glad you ain't goin', your Ma and I, for we'd have missed you terrible, that's certain and sure; and we're glad you've found happiness. Ruth's a fine girl and'll make a good wife to you.

ROBERT (*much moved*). Thank you, Pa. (*He grips his father's hand in his.*)

ANDREW (*his face tense and drawn comes forward and holds out his hand, forcing a smile*). I guess it's my turn to offer congratulations, isn't it?

ROBERT (*with a startled cry when his brother appears before him so suddenly*). Andy! (*Confused.*) Why—I—I didn't see you. Were you here when—

ANDREW. I heard everything you said; and here's wishing you every happiness, you and Ruth. You both deserve the best there is.

ROBERT (*taking his hand*). Thanks, Andy, it's fine of you to—(*His voice dies away as he sees the pain in* ANDREW'S *eyes.*)

ANDREW (*giving his brother's hand a final grip*). Good luck to you both! (*He turns away and goes back to the rear where he bends over the lantern, fumbling with it to hide his emotion from the others.*)

MRS. MAYO (*to the* CAPTAIN, *who has been too flabbergasted by* ROBERT'S *decision to say a word*). What's the matter, Dick? Aren't you going to congratulate Robbie?

SCOTT (*embarrassed*). Of course I be! (*He gets to his feet and shakes* ROBERT's *hand, muttering a vague*) Luck to you, boy. (*He stands beside* ROBERT *as if he wanted to say something more but doesn't know how to go about it.*)

ROBERT. Thanks, Uncle Dick.

SCOTT. So you're not acomin' on the *Sunda* with me? (*His voice indicates disbelief*).

ROBERT. I can't, Uncle—not now. I wouldn't miss it for anything else in the world under any other circumstances. (*He sighs unconsciously.*) But you see I've found—a bigger dream. (*Then with joyous high spirits.*) I want you all to understand one thing—I'm not going to be a loafer on your hands any longer. This means the beginning of a new life for me in every way. I'm going to settle right down and take a real interest in the farm, and do my share. I'll prove to you, Pa, that I'm as good a Mayo as you are—or Andy, when I want to be.

MAYO (*kindly but skeptically*). That's the right spirit, Robert. Ain't none of us doubts your willin'ness, but you ain't never learned—

ROBERT. Then I'm going to start learning right away, and you'll teach me, won't you?

MAYO (*mollifyingly*). Of course I will, boy, and be glad to, only you'd best go easy at first.

SCOTT (*who has listened to this conversation in mingled consternation and amazement*). You don't mean to tell me you're goin' to let him stay, do you, James?

MAYO. Why, things bein' as they be, Robert's free to do as he's a mind to.

MRS. MAYO. *Let him!* The very idea!

SCOTT (*more and more ruffled*). Then all I got to say is, you're a soft, weak-willed critter to be permittin' a boy—and women, too—to be layin' your course for you wherever they damn pleases.

MAYO (*slyly amused*). It's just the same with me as 'twas with you, Dick. You can't order the tides on the seas to suit you, and I ain't pretendin' I can reg'late love for young folks.

SCOTT (*scornfully*). Love! They ain't old enough to know love when they sight it! Love! I'm ashamed of you, Robert, to go lettin' a little huggin' and kissin' in the dark spoil your chances to make a man out o' yourself. It ain't common sense—no siree, it ain't—not by a hell of a sight! (*He pounds the table with his fists in exasperation.*)

MRS. MAYO (*laughing provokingly at her brother*). A fine one you are to be talking about love, Dick—an old cranky bachelor like you. Goodness sakes!

SCOTT (*exasperated by their joking*). I've never been a damn fool like most, if that's what you're steerin' at.

MRS. MAYO (*tauntingly*). Sour grapes, aren't they, Dick? (*She laughs.* ROBERT *and his father chuckle.* SCOTT *sputters with annoyance.*) Good gracious, Dick, you do act silly, flying into a temper over nothing.

SCOTT (*indignantly*). Nothin'! You talk as if I wasn't concerned nohow in this here business. Seems to me I've got a right to have my say. Ain't I made all arrangements with the owners and stocked up with some special grub all on Robert's account?

ROBERT. You've been fine, Uncle Dick; and I appreciate it. Truly.

MAYO. 'Course; we all does, Dick.

SCOTT (*unplacated*). I've been countin' sure on havin' Robert for company on this vige —to sorta talk to and show things to, and teach, kinda, and I got my mind so set on havin' him I'm goin' to be double lonesome this vige. (*He pounds on the table, attempting to cover up this confession of weakness.*) Darn all this silly lovin' business, anyway. (*Irritably.*) But all this talk ain't tellin' me what I'm to do with that sta'b'd cabin I fixed up. It's all painted white, an' a bran new mattress on the bunk, 'n' new sheets 'n' blankets 'n' things. And Chips built in a book-case so's Robert could take his books along—with a slidin' bar fixed across't it, mind, so's they couldn't fall out no matter how she rolled. (*With excited consternation.*) What d'you suppose my officers is goin' to think when there's no one comes aboard to occupy that sta'b'd cabin? And the men what did the work on it—what'll *they* think? (*He shakes his finger indignantly.*) They're liable as not to suspicion it was a *woman* I'd planned to ship along, and that she gave me the go-by at the last moment! (*He wipes his perspiring brow in anguish at this thought.*) Gawd A'mighty! They're only lookin' to have the laugh on me for something like that. They're liable to b'lieve anything, those fellers is!

MAYO (*with a wink*). Then there's nothing to it but for you to get right out and hunt up a wife somewheres for that spick 'n' span cabin. She'll have to be a pretty one, too, to match it. (*He looks at his watch with exaggerated concern.*) You ain't got much time to find her, Dick.

SCOTT (*as the others smile—sulkily*). You kin go to thunder, Jim Mayo!

ANDREW (*comes forward from where he has been standing by the door, rear, brooding. His face is set in a look of grim determination*). You needn't worry about that spare cabin, Uncle Dick, if you've a mind to take me in Robert's place.

ROBERT (*turning to him quickly*). Andy! (*He sees at once the fixed resolve in his brother's eyes, and realizes immediately the reason for it—in consternation.*) Andy, you mustn't!

ANDREW. You've made your decision, Rob, and now I've made mine. You're out of this, remember.

ROBERT (*hurt by his brother's tone*). But Andy—

ANDREW. Don't interfere, Rob—that's all I ask. (*Turning to his uncle.*) You haven't answered my question, Uncle Dick.

SCOTT (*clearing his throat, with an uneasy side glance at* JAMES MAYO *who is staring at his elder son as if he thought he had suddenly gone mad*). O' course, I'd be glad to have you, Andy.

ANDREW. It's settled then. I can pack the little I want to take in a few minutes.

MRS. MAYO. Don't be a fool, Dick. Andy's only joking you.

SCOTT (*disgruntledly*). It's hard to tell who's jokin' and who's not in this house.

ANDREW (*firmly*). I'm not joking, Uncle Dick. (*As* SCOTT *looks at him uncertainly.*) You needn't be afraid I'll go back on my word.

ROBERT (*hurt by the insinuation he feels in* ANDREW's *tone*). Andy! That isn't fair!

MAYO (*frowning*). Seems to me this ain't no subject to joke over—not for Andy.

ANDREW (*facing his father*). I agree with you, Pa, and I tell you again, once and for all, that I've made up my mind to go.

MAYO (*dumbfounded—unable to doubt the determination in* ANDREW's *voice—helplessly*). But why, son? Why?

ANDREW (*evasively*). I've always wanted to go.

ROBERT. Andy!

ANDREW (*half angrily*). You shut up, Rob! (*Turning to his father again.*) I didn't ever mention it because as long as Rob was going I knew it was no use; but now Rob's staying on here, there isn't any reason for me not to go.

MAYO (*breathing hard*). No reason? Can you stand there and say that to me, Andrew?

MRS. MAYO (*hastily—seeing the gathering storm*). He doesn't mean a word of it, James.

MAYO (*making a gesture to her to keep silence*). Let me talk, Katey. (*In a more kindly tone.*) What's come over you so sudden, Andy? You know's well as I do that it wouldn't be fair o' you to run off at a moment's notice right now when we're up to our necks in hard work.

ANDREW (*avoiding his eyes*). Rob'll hold his end up as soon as he learns.

MAYO. Robert was never cut out for a farmer, and you was.

ANDREW. You can easily get a man to do my work.

MAYO (*restraining his anger with an effort*). It sounds strange to hear you, Andy, that I always thought had good sense, talkin' crazy like that. (*Scornfully.*) Get a man to take your place! You ain't been workin' here for no hire, Andy, that you kin give me your notice to quit like you've done. The farm is yourn as well as mine. You've always worked on it with that understanding; and what you're sayin' you intend doin' is just skulkin' out o' your rightful responsibility.

ANDREW (*looking at the floor—simply*). I'm sorry, Pa. (*After a slight pause.*) It's no use talking any more about it.

MRS. MAYO (*in relief*). There! I knew Andy'd come to his senses!

ANDREW. Don't get the wrong idea, Ma. I'm not backing out.

MAYO. You mean you're goin' in spite of—everythin'?

ANDREW. Yes. I'm going. I've got to. (*He looks at his father defiantly.*) I feel I oughtn't to miss this chance to go out into the world and see things, and—I want to go.

MAYO (*with bitter scorn*). So—you want to go out into the world and see thin's! (*His voice raised and quivering with anger.*) I never thought I'd live to see the day when a son o' mine 'd look me in the face and tell a bare-faced lie! (*Bursting out.*) You're a liar, Andy Mayo, and a mean one to boot!

MRS. MAYO. James!

ROBERT. Pa!

SCOTT. Steady there, Jim!

MAYO (*waving their protests aside*). He is and he knows it.

ANDREW (*his face flushed*). I won't argue with you, Pa. You can think as badly of me as you like.

MAYO (*shaking his finger at* ANDY, *in a cold rage*). You know I'm speakin' truth—that's why you're afraid to argy! You lie when you say you want to go 'way—and see thin's! You ain't got no likin' in the world to go. I've watched you grow up, and I know your ways, and they're my ways. You're runnin' against your own nature, and you're goin' to be a 'mighty sorry for it if you do. 'S if I didn't know your real reason for runnin' away! And runnin' away's the only words to fit it. You're runnin' away 'cause you're put out and riled 'cause your own brother's got Ruth 'stead o' you, and—

ANDREW (*his face crimson—tensely*). Stop, Pa! I won't stand hearing that—not even from you!

MRS. MAYO (*rushing to* ANDY *and putting her arms about him protectingly*). Don't mind him, Andy dear. He don't mean a word he's saying! (ROBERT *stands rigidly, his hands clenched, his face contracted by pain.* SCOTT *sits dumbfounded and open-mouthed.* ANDREW *soothes his mother who is on the verge of tears.*)

MAYO (*in angry triumph*). It's the truth, Andy Mayo! And you ought to be bowed in shame to think of it!

ROBERT (*protestingly*). Pa!

MRS. MAYO (*coming from* ANDREW *to his father; puts her hands on his shoulders as though to try and push him back in the chair from which he has risen*). Won't you be still, James? Please won't you?

MAYO (*looking at* ANDREW *over his wife's shoulder—stubbornly*). The truth—God's truth!

MRS. MAYO. Sh-h-h! (*She tries to put a finger across his lips, but he twists his head away.*)

ANDREW (*who has regained control over himself*). You're wrong, Pa, it isn't truth. (*With defiant assertiveness.*) I don't love Ruth. I never loved her, and the thought of such a thing never entered my head.

MAYO (*with an angry snort of disbelief*). Hump! You're pilin' lie on lie!

ANDREW (*losing his temper—bitterly*). I suppose it'd be hard for you to explain anyone's wanting to leave this blessed farm except for some outside reason like that. But I'm sick and tired of it—whether you want to believe me or not—and that's why I'm glad to get a chance to move on.

ROBERT. Andy! Don't! You're only making it worse.

ANDREW (*sulkily*). I don't care. I've done my share of work here. I've earned my right to quit when I want to. (*Suddenly overcome with anger and grief; with rising intensity.*) I'm sick and tired of the whole damn business. I hate the farm and every inch of ground in it. I'm sick of digging in the dirt and sweating in the sun like a slave without getting a word of thanks for it. (*Tears of rage starting to his eyes—hoarsely.*) I'm through, through for good and all; and if Uncle Dick won't take me on his ship, I'll find another. I'll get away somewhere, somehow.

MRS. MAYO (*in a frightened voice*). Don't you answer him, James. He doesn't know what he's saying. Don't say a word to him 'til he's in his right senses again. Please James, don't—

MAYO (*pushes her away from him; his face is drawn and pale with the violence of his passion. He glares at* ANDREW *as if he hated him*). You dare to—you dare to speak like that to me? You talk like that 'bout this farm—the Mayo farm—where you was born—you—you—(*He clenches his fist above his head and advances threateningly on* ANDREW.) You damned whelp!

MRS. MAYO (*with a shriek*). James! (*She covers her face with her hands and sinks weakly into* MAYO's *chair.* ANDREW *remains standing motionless, his face pale and set.*)

SCOTT (*starting to his feet and stretching his arms across the table toward* MAYO). Easy there, Jim!

ROBERT (*throwing himself between father and brother*). Stop! Are you mad?

MAYO (*grabs* ROBERT's *arm and pushes him aside—then stands for a moment gasping for breath before* ANDREW. *He points to the door with a shaking finger*). Yes—go!—go!—You're no son o' mine—no son o' mine! You can go to hell if you want to! Don't let me find you here—in the mornin'—or—or—I'll *throw* you out!

ROBERT. Pa! For God's sake! (MRS. MAYO *bursts into noisy sobbing*).

MAYO (*gulps convulsively and glares at* ANDREW). You go—tomorrow mornin'—and by God—don't come back—don't dare come back—by God, not while I'm livin'—or I'll—I'll—(*He shakes over his muttered threat and strides toward the door rear, right.*)

MRS. MAYO (*rising and throwing her arms around him—hysterically*). James! James! Where are you going?

MAYO (*incoherently*). I'm goin'—to bed, Katey. It's late, Katey—it's late. (*He goes out*).

MRS. MAYO (*following him, pleading hysterically*). James! Take back what you've said to Andy. James! (*She follows him out.* ROBERT *and the* CAPTAIN *stare after them with horrified eyes.* ANDREW *stands rigidly looking straight in front of him, his fists clenched at his sides.*)

SCOTT (*the first to find his voice—with an explosive sigh*). Well, if he ain't the devil himself when he's roused! You oughtn't to have talked to him that way, Andy 'bout the damn farm, knowin' how touchy he is about it. (*With another sigh.*) Well, you won't mind what he's said in anger. He'll be sorry for it when he's calmed down a bit.

ANDREW (*in a dead voice*). You don't know him. (*Defiantly.*) What's said is said and can't be unsaid; and I've chosen.

ROBERT (*with violent protest*). Andy! You can't go! This is all so stupid—and terrible!

ANDREW (*coldly*). I'll talk to you in a minute, Rob. (*Crushed by his brother's attitude* ROBERT *sinks down into a chair, holding his head in his hands.*)

SCOTT (*comes and slaps* ANDREW *on the back*). I'm damned glad you're shippin' on, Andy. I like your spirit, and the way you spoke up to him. (*Lowering his voice to a cautious whisper.*) The sea's the place for a young feller like you that isn't half dead 'n' alive. (*He gives* ANDY *a final approving slap.*) You 'n' me 'll get along like twins, see if we don't. I'm goin' aloft to turn in.

Don't forget to pack your dunnage. And git some sleep, if you 'kin. We'll want to sneak out extra early b'fore they're up. It'll do away with more argyments. Robert can drive us down to the town, and bring back the team. (*He goes to the door in the rear, left.*) Well, good night.

ANDREW. Good night. (SCOTT *goes out. The two brothers remain silent for a moment. Then* ANDREW *comes over to his brother and puts a hand on his back. He speaks in a low voice, full of feeling.*) Buck up, Rob. It ain't any use crying over spilt milk; and it'll all turn out for the best—let's hope. It couldn't be helped—what's happened.

ROBERT (*wildly*). But it's a lie, Andy, a lie!

ANDREW. Of course it's a lie. You know it and I know it,—but that's all ought to know it.

ROBERT. Pa'll never forgive you. Oh, the whole affair is so senseless—tragic. Why did you think you must go away?

ANDREW. You know better than to ask that. You know why. (*Fiercely.*) I can wish you and Ruth all the good luck in the world, and I do, and I mean it; but you can't expect me to stay around here and watch you two together, day after day—and me alone. I couldn't stand it—not after all the plans I'd made to happen on this place thinking —(*his voice breaks*) thinking she cared for me.

ROBERT (*putting a hand on his brother's arm*). God! It's horrible! I feel so guilty— to think that I should be the cause of your suffering, after we've been such pals all our lives. If I could have foreseen what'd happen, I swear to you I'd have never said a word to Ruth. I swear I wouldn't have, Andy!

ANDREW. I know you wouldn't; and that would've been worse, for Ruth would've suffered then. (*He pats his brother's shoulder.*) It's best as it is. It had to be, and I've got to stand the gaff, that's all. Pa'll see how I felt—after a time. (*As* ROBERT *shakes his head*)—and if he don't—well, it can't be helped.

ROBERT. But think of Ma! God, Andy, you can't go! You can't!

ANDREW (*fiercely*). I've got to go—to get away! I've got to, I tell you. I'd go crazy here, bein' reminded every second of the day what a fool I'd made of myself. I've got to get away and try and forget, if I can. And I'd hate the farm if I stayed, hate it for bringin' things back. I couldn't take interest in the work any more, work with no purpose in sight. Can't you see what a hell it'd be? You love her too, Rob. Put yourself in my place, and remember I haven't stopped loving her, and couldn't if I was to stay. Would that be fair to you or to her? Put yourself in my place. (*He shakes his brother fiercely by the shoulder.*) What'd you do then? Tell me the truth! You love her. What'd you do?

ROBERT (*chokingly*). I'd—I'd go, Andy! (*He buries his face in his hands with a shuddering sob.*) God!

ANDREW (*seeming to relax suddenly all over his body—in a low, steady voice*). Then you know why I got to go; and there's nothing more to be said.

ROBERT (*in a frenzy of rebellion*). Why did this have to happen to us? It's damnable! (*He looks about him wildly, as if his vengeance were seeking the responsible fate*).

ANDREW (*soothingly—again putting his hands on his brother's shoulder*). It's no use fussing any more, Rob. It's done. (*Forcing a smile.*) I guess Ruth's got a right to have who she likes. She made a good choice —and God bless her for it!

ROBERT. Andy! Oh, I wish I could tell you half I feel of how fine you are!

ANDREW (*interrupting him quickly*). Shut up! Let's go to bed. I've got to be up long before sun-up. You, too, if you're going to drive us down.

ROBERT. Yes. Yes.

ANDREW (*turning down the lamp*). And I've got to pack yet. (*He yawns with utter weariness.*) I'm as tired as if I'd been plowing twenty-four hours at a stretch. (*Dully.*) I feel—dead. (ROBERT *covers his face again with his hands.* ANDREW *shakes his head as if to get rid of his thoughts, and continues with a poor attempt at cheery briskness.*)

I'm going to douse the light. Come on. (*He slaps his brother on the back.* ROBERT *does not move.* ANDREW *bends over and blows out the lamp. His voice comes from the darkness.*) Don't sit there mourning, Rob. It'll all come out in the wash. Come on and get some sleep. Everything'll turn out all right in the end. (ROBERT *can be heard stumbling to his feet, and the dark figures of the two brothers can be seen groping their way toward the doorway in the rear as*

The Curtain Falls.

ACT TWO

SCENE I

Same as Act One, Scene Two. Sitting room of the farm house about half past twelve in the afternoon of a hot, sun-baked day in mid-summer, three years later. All the windows are open, but no breeze stirs the soiled white curtains. A patched screen door is in the rear. Through it the yard can be seen, its small stretch of lawn divided by the dirt path leading to the door from the gate in the white picket fence which borders the road.

The room has changed, not so much in its outward appearance as in its general atmosphere. Little significant details give evidence of carelessness, of inefficiency, of an industry gone to seed. The chairs appear shabby from lack of paint; the table cover is spotted and askew; holes show in the curtains; a child's doll, with one arm gone, lies under the table; a hoe stands in a corner; a man's coat is flung on the couch in the rear; the desk is cluttered up with odds and ends; a number of books are piled carelessly on the sideboard. The noon enervation of the sultry, scorching day seems to have penetrated indoors, causing even inanimate objects to wear an aspect of despondent exhaustion.

A place is set at the end of the table, left, for someone's dinner. Through the open door to the kitchen comes the clatter of dishes being washed, interrupted at intervals by a woman's irritated voice and the peevish whining of a child.

At the rise of the curtain MRS. MAYO *and* MRS. ATKINS *are discovered sitting facing each other,* MRS. MAYO *to the rear,* MRS. ATKINS *to the right of the table.* MRS. MAYO'S *face has lost all character, disintegrated, become a weak mask wearing a helpless, doleful expression of being constantly on the verge of comfortless tears. She speaks in an uncertain voice, without assertiveness, as if all power of willing had deserted her.* MRS. ATKINS *is in her wheel chair. She is a thin, pale-faced, unintelligent-looking woman of about forty-eight, with hard, bright eyes. A victim of partial paralysis for many years, condemned to be pushed from day to day of her life in a wheel chair, she has developed the selfish, irritable nature of the chronic invalid. Both women are dressed in black.* MRS. ATKINS *knits nervously as she talks. A ball of unused yarn, with needles stuck through it, lies on the table before* MRS. MAYO.*

MRS. ATKINS (*with a disapproving glance at the place set on the table*). Robert's late for his dinner again, as usual. I don't see why Ruth puts up with it, and I've told her so. Many's the time I've said to her "It's about time you put a stop to his nonsense.

Does he suppose you're runnin' a hotel— with no one to help with things?" But she don't pay no attention. She's as bad as he is, a'most—thinks she knows better than an old, sick body like me.

MRS. MAYO (*dully*). Robbie's always late for things. He can't help it, Sarah.

MRS. ATKINS (*with a snort*). Can't help it! How you do go on, Kate, findin' excuses for him! Anybody can help anything they've a mind to—as long as they've got health, and ain't rendered helpless like me —(*She adds as a pious afterthought*)— through the will of God.

MRS. MAYO. Robbie can't.

MRS. ATKINS. Can't! It do make me mad, Kate Mayo, to see folks that God gave all the use of their limbs to potterin' round and wastin' time doin' everything the wrong way—and me powerless to help and at their mercy, you might say. And it ain't that I haven't pointed the right way to 'em. I've talked to Robert thousands of times and told him how things ought to be done. You know that, Kate Mayo. But d'you s'pose he takes any notice of what I say? Or Ruth, either—my own daughter? No, they think I'm a crazy, cranky old woman, half dead a'ready, and the sooner I'm in the grave and out o' the way the better it'd suit them.

MRS. MAYO. You mustn't talk that way, Sarah. They're not as wicked as that. And you've got years and years before you.

MRS. ATKINS. You're like the rest, Kate. You don't know how near the end I am. Well, at least I can go to my eternal rest with a clear conscience. I've done all a body could do to avert ruin from this house. On their heads be it!

MRS. MAYO (*with hopeless indifference*). Things might be worse. Robert never had any experience in farming. You can't expect him to learn in a day.

MRS. ATKINS (*snappily*). He's had three years to learn, and he's gettin' worse 'stead of better. Not on'y your place but mine too is driftin' to rack and ruin, and I can't do nothin' to prevent.

MRS. MAYO (*with a spark of assertiveness*). You can't say but Robbie works hard, Sarah.

MRS. ATKINS. What good's workin' hard if it don't accomplish anythin', I'd like to know?

MRS. MAYO. Robbie's had bad luck against him.

MRS. ATKINS. Say what you've a mind to, Kate, the proof of the puddin's in the eatin'; and you can't deny that things have been goin' from bad to worse ever since your husband died two years back.

MRS. MAYO (*wiping tears from her eyes with her handkerchief*). It was God's will that he should be taken.

MRS. ATKINS (*triumphantly*). It was God's punishment on James Mayo for the blasphemin' and denyin' of God he done all his sinful life! (MRS. MAYO *begins to weep softly*.) There, Kate, I shouldn't be remindin' you, I know. He's at peace, poor man, and forgiven, let's pray.

MRS. MAYO (*wiping her eyes—simply*). James was a good man.

MRS. ATKINS (*ignoring this remark*). What I was sayin' was that since Robert's been in charge things've been goin' down hill steady. You don't know *how* bad they are. Robert don't let on to you what's happenin'; and you'd never see it yourself if 'twas under your nose. But, thank the Lord, Ruth still comes to me once in a while for advice when she's worried near out of her senses by his goin's-on. Do you know what she told me last night? But I forgot, she said not to tell you—still I think you've got a right to know, and it's my duty not to let such things go on behind your back.

MRS. MAYO (*wearily*). You can tell me if you want to.

MRS. ATKINS (*bending over toward her— in a low voice*). Ruth was almost crazy about it. Robert told her he'd have to mortgage the farm—said he didn't know how he'd pull through till harvest without it, and he can't get money any other way. (*She straightens up—indignantly*.) Now what do you think of your Robert?

up the path and opens the screen door quietly and comes into the room. He, too, has aged. His shoulders are stooped as if under too great a burden. His eyes are dull and lifeless, his face burned by the sun and unshaven for days. Streaks of sweat have smudged the layer of dust on his cheeks. His lips drawn down at the corners, give him a hopeless, resigned expression. The three years have accentuated the weakness of his mouth and chin. He is dressed in overalls, laced boots, and a flannel shirt open at the neck.)

ROBERT (*throwing his hat over on the sofa—with a great sigh of exhaustion*). Phew! The sun's hot today! (RUTH *is startled. At first she makes an instinctive motion as if to hide the letter in her bosom. She immediately thinks better of this and sits with the letter in her hands looking at him with defiant eyes. He bends down and kisses her.*)

RUTH (*feeling of her cheek—irritably*). Why don't you shave? You look awful.

ROBERT (*indifferently*). I forgot—and it's too much trouble this weather.

MARY (*throwing aside her doll, runs to him with a happy cry*). Dada! Dada!

ROBERT (*swinging her up above his head—lovingly*). And how's this little girl of mine this hot day, eh?

MARY (*screeching happily*). Dada! Dada!

RUTH (*in annoyance*). Don't do that to her! You know it's time for her nap and you'll get her all waked up; then I'll be the one that'll have to sit beside her till she falls asleep.

ROBERT (*sitting down in the chair on the left of table and cuddling MARY on his lap*). You needn't bother. I'll put her to bed.

RUTH (*shortly*). You've got to get back to your work, I s'pose.

ROBERT (*with a sigh*). Yes, I was forgetting. (*He glances at the open letter on RUTH's lap.*) Reading Andy's letter again? I should think you'd know it by heart by this time.

RUTH (*coloring as if she's been accused of something—defiantly*). I've got a right to

read it, haven't I? He says it's meant for all of us.

ROBERT (*with a trace of irritation*). Right? Don't be so silly. There's no question of right. I was only saying that you must know all that's in it after so many readings.

RUTH. Well, I don't. (*She puts the letter on the table and gets wearily to her feet.*) I s'pose you'll be wanting your dinner now.

ROBERT (*listlessly*). I don't care. I'm not hungry.

RUTH. And here I been keeping it hot for you!

ROBERT (*irritably*). Oh, all right then. Bring it in and I'll try to eat.

RUTH. I've got to get her to bed first. (*She goes to lift MARY off his lap.*) Come, dear. It's after time and you can hardly keep your eyes open now.

MARY (*crying*). No, no! (*Appealing to her father.*) Dada! No!

RUTH (*accusingly to ROBERT*). There! Now see what you've done! I told you not to—

ROBERT (*shortly*). Let her alone, then. She's all right where she is. She'll fall asleep on my lap in a minute if you'll stop bothering her.

RUTH (*hotly*). She'll not do any such thing! She's got to learn to mind me! (*Shaking her finger at MARY.*) You naughty child! Will you come with Mama when she tells you for your own good?

MARY (*clinging to her father*). No, Dada!

RUTH (*losing her temper*). A good spanking's what you need, my young lady—and you'll get one from me if you don't mind better, d'you hear? (MARY *starts to whimper frightenedly.*)

ROBERT (*with sudden anger*). Leave her alone! How often have I told you not to threaten her with whipping? I won't have it. (*Soothing the wailing MARY.*) There! There, little girl! Baby mustn't cry. Dada won't like you if you do. Dada'll hold you and you must promise to go to sleep like a good little girl. Will you when Dada asks you?

MARY (*cuddling up to him*). Yes, Dada.

RUTH (*looking at them, her pale face set and drawn*). A fine one you are to be telling folks how to do things! (*She bites her lips. Husband and wife look into each other's eyes with something akin to hatred in their expressions; then* RUTH *turns away with a shrug of affected indifference.*) All right, take care of her then, if you think it's so easy. (*She walks away into the kitchen.*)

ROBERT (*smoothing* MARY's *hair—tenderly*). We'll show Mama you're a good little girl, won't we?

MARY (*crooning drowsily*). Dada, Dada.

ROBERT. Let's see: Does your mother take off your shoes and stockings before your nap?

MARY (*nodding with half-shut eyes*). Yes, Dada.

ROBERT (*taking off her shoes and stockings*). We'll show Mama we know how to do those things, won't we? There's one old shoe off—and there's the other old shoe—and here's one old stocking—and there's the other old stocking. There we are, all nice and cool and comfy. (*He bends down and kisses her.*) And now will you promise to go right to sleep if Dada takes you to bed? (MARY *nods sleepily.*) That's the good little girl. (*He gathers her up in his arms carefully and carries her into the bedroom. His voice can be heard faintly as he lulls the child to sleep.* RUTH *comes out of the kitchen and gets the plate from the table. She hears the voice from the room and tiptoes to the door to look in. Then she starts for the kitchen but stands for a moment thinking, a look of ill-concealed jealousy on her face. At a noise from inside she hurriedly disappears into the kitchen. A moment later* ROBERT *re-enters. He comes forward and picks up the shoes and stockings which he shoves carelessly under the table. Then, seeing no one about, he goes to the sideboard and selects a book. Coming back to his chair, he sits down and immediately becomes absorbed in reading.* RUTH *returns from the kitchen bringing his plate heaped with food, and a cup of tea. She sets those before him and sits down in her former place.* ROBERT *continues to read, oblivious to the food on the table.*)

RUTH (*after watching him irritably for a moment*). For heaven's sakes, put down that old book! Don't you see your dinner's getting cold?

ROBERT (*closing his book*). Excuse me, Ruth. I -didn't notice. (*He picks up his knife and fork and begins to eat gingerly, without appetite*).

RUTH. I should think you might have some feeling for me, Rob, and not always be late for meals. If you think it's fun sweltering in that oven of a kitchen to keep things warm for you, you're mistaken.

ROBERT. I'm sorry, Ruth, really I am. Something crops up every day to delay me. I mean to be here on time.

RUTH (*with a sigh*). Mean-tos don't count.

ROBERT (*with a conciliating smile*). Then punish me, Ruth. Let the food get cold and don't bother about me.

RUTH. I'd have to wait just the same to wash up after you.

ROBERT. But I can wash up.

RUTH. A nice mess there'd be then!

ROBERT (*with an attempt at lightness*). The food is lucky to be able to get cold this weather. (*As* RUTH *doesn't answer or smile he opens his book and resumes his reading, forcing himself to take a mouthful of food every now and then.* RUTH *stares at him in annoyance.*)

RUTH. And besides, you've got your own work that's got to be done.

ROBERT (*absent-mindedly, without taking his eyes from the book*). Yes, of course.

RUTH (*spitefully*). Work you'll never get done by reading books all the time.

ROBERT (*shutting the book with a snap*). Why do you persist in nagging at me for getting pleasure out of reading? Is it because—(*He checks himself abruptly.*)

RUTH (*coloring*). Because I'm too stupid to understand them, I s'pose you were going to say.

ROBERT (*shamefacedly*). No—no. (*In exasperation.*) Why do you goad me into saying things I don't mean? Haven't I got my share of troubles trying to work this cursed farm without you adding to them? You know how hard I've tried to keep things going in spite of bad luck—

RUTH (*scornfully*). Bad luck!

ROBERT. And my own very apparent unfitness for the job, I was going to add; but you can't deny there's been bad luck to it, too. Why don't you take things into consideration? Why can't we pull together? We used to. I know it's hard on you also. Then why can't we help each other instead of hindering?

RUTH (*sullenly*). I do the best I know how.

ROBERT (*gets up and puts his hand on her shoulder*). I know you do. But let's both of us try to do better. We can both improve. Say a word of encouragement once in a while when things go wrong, even if it is my fault. You know the odds I've been up against since Pa died. I'm not a farmer. I've never claimed to be one. But there's nothing else I can do under the circumstances, and I've got to pull things through somehow. With your help, I can do it. With you against me— (*He shrugs his shoulders. There is a pause. Then he bends down and kisses her hair—with an attempt at cheerfulness.*) So you promise that; and I'll promise to be here when the clock strikes—and anything else you tell me to. Is it a bargain?

RUTH (*dully*). I s'pose so. (*They are interrupted by the sound of a loud knock at the kitchen door.*) There's someone at the kitchen door. (*She hurries out. A moment later she reappears.*) It's Ben.

ROBERT (*frowning.*) What's the trouble now, I wonder? (*In a loud voice*) Come on in here, Ben. (*BEN slouches in from the kitchen. He is a hulking, awkward young fellow with a heavy, stupid face and shifty, cunning eyes. He is dressed in overalls, boots, etc., and wears a broad-brimmed hat of coarse straw pushed back on his head.*) Well, Ben, what's the matter?

BEN (*drawlingly*). The mowin' machine's bust.

ROBERT. Why, that can't be. The man fixed it only last week.

BEN. It's bust just the same.

ROBERT. And can't you fix it?

BEN. No. Don't know what's the matter with the goll-darned thing. 'Twon't work, anyhow.

ROBERT (*getting up and going for his hat*). Wait a minute and I'll go look it over. There can't be much the matter with it.

BEN (*impudently*). Don't make no diff'rence t' me whether there be or not. I'm quittin'.

ROBERT (*anxiously*). You don't mean you're throwing up your job here?

BEN. That's what! My month's up today and I want what's owin' t' me.

ROBERT. But why are you quitting now, Ben, when you know I've so much work on hand? I'll have a hard time getting another man at such short notice.

BEN. That's for you to figger. I'm quittin'.

ROBERT. But what's your reason? You haven't any complaint to make about the way you've been treated, have you?

BEN. No. 'Tain't that. (*Shaking his finger.*) Look-a-here. I'm sick o' being made fun at, that's what; an' I got a job up to Timms' place; an' I'm quittin' here.

ROBERT. Being made fun of? I don't understand you. Who's making fun of you?

BEN. They all do. When I drive down with the milk in the mornin' they all laughs and jokes at me—that boy up to Harris' and the new feller up to Slocum's, and Bill Evans down to Meade's, and all the rest on 'em.

ROBERT. That's a queer reason for leaving me flat. Won't they laugh at you just the same when you're working for Timms?

BEN. They wouldn't dare to. Timms is the best farm hereabouts. They was laughin' at me for workin' for *you*, that's what! "How're things up to the Mayo place?" they hollers every mornin'. "What's Robert doin' now—pasturin' the cattle in the corn-lot? Is he seasonin' his hay with rain this year, same as last?" they shouts. "Or is he inventin' some 'lectrical milkin' engine to fool them dry cows o' his into givin' hard cider?" (*Very much ruffled.*) That's like they talks; and I ain't goin' to put up with it no longer. Everyone's always knowed me as a first-class hand hereabouts, and I ain't wantin' 'em to get no different notion. So I'm quittin' you. And I wants what's comin' to me.

ROBERT (*coldly*). Oh, if that's the case, you can go to the devil. You'll get your money tomorrow when I get back from town—not before!

BEN (*turning to doorway to kitchen*). That suits me. (*As he goes out he speaks back over his shoulder.*) And see that I do get it, or there'll be trouble. (*He disappears and the slamming of the kitchen door is heard.*)

ROBERT (*as* RUTH *comes from where she has been standing by the doorway and sits down dejectedly in her old place*). The stupid damn fool! And now what about the haying? That's an example of what I'm up against. No one can say I'm responsible for that.

RUTH. He wouldn't dare act that way with anyone else! (*Spitefully, with a glance at* ANDREW'S *letter on the table.*) It's lucky Andy's coming back.

ROBERT (*without resentment*). Yes, Andy'll see the right thing to do in a jiffy. (*With an affectionate smile.*) I wonder if the old chump's changed much? He doesn't seem to from his letters, does he? (*Shaking his head.*) But just the same I doubt if he'll want to settle down to a humdrum farm life, after all he's been through.

RUTH (*resentfully*). Andy's not like you. He likes the farm.

ROBERT (*immersed in his own thoughts—enthusiastically*). Gad, the things he's seen and experienced! Think of the places he's been! All the wonderful far places I used to dream about! God, how I envy him! What a trip! (*He springs to his feet and instinctively goes to the window and stares out at the horizon.*)

RUTH (*bitterly*). I s'pose you're sorry now you didn't go?

ROBERT (*too occupied with his own thoughts to hear her—vindictively*). Oh, those cursed hills out there that I used to think promised me so much! How I've grown to hate the sight of them! They're like the walls of a narrow prison yard shutting me in from all the freedom and wonder of life! (*He turns back to the room with a gesture of loathing.*) Sometimes I think if it wasn't for you, Ruth, and—(*his voice softening*)—little Mary, I'd chuck everything up and walk down the road with just one desire in my heart—to put the whole rim of the world between me and those hills, and be able to breathe freely once more! (*He sinks down into his chair and smiles with bitter self-scorn.*) There I go dreaming again—my old fool dreams.

RUTH (*in a low, repressed voice—her eyes smoldering*). You're not the only one!

ROBERT (*buried in his own thoughts—bitterly*). And Andy, who's had the chance—what has he got out of it? His letters read like the diary of a—of a farmer! "We're in Singapore now. It's a dirty hole of a place and hotter than hell. Two of the crew are down with fever and we're short-handed on the work. I'll be damn glad when we sail again, although tacking back and forth in these blistering seas is a rotten job too!" (*Scornfully.*) That's about the way he summed up his impressions of the East.

RUTH (*her repressed voice trembling*). You needn't make fun of Andy.

ROBERT. When I think—but what's the use? You know I wasn't making fun of Andy personally, but his attitude toward things is—

RUTH (*her eyes flashing—bursting into uncontrollable rage*). You was too making fun of him! And I ain't going to stand for it! You ought to be ashamed of yourself! (ROBERT *stares at her in amazement. She continues furiously.*) A fine one to talk about anyone else—after the way you've ruined everything with your lazy loafing! —and the stupid way you do things!

ROBERT (*angrily*). Stop that kind of talk, do you hear?

RUTH. You findin' fault—with your own brother who's ten times the man you ever was or ever will be! You're jealous, that's what! Jealous because he's made a man of himself, while you're nothing but a—but a— (*She stutters incoherently, overcome by rage.*)

ROBERT. Ruth! Ruth! You'll be sorry for talking like that.

RUTH. I won't! I won't never be sorry! I'm only saying what I've been thinking for years.

ROBERT (*aghast*). Ruth! You can't mean that!

RUTH. What do you think—living with a man like you—having to suffer all the time because you've never been man enough to work and do things like other people. But no! You never own up to that. You think you're so much better than other folks, with your college education, where you never learned a thing, and always reading your stupid books instead of working. I s'pose you think I ought to be *proud* to be your wife—a poor, ignorant thing like me! (*Fiercely.*) But I'm not. I hate it! I hate the sight of you. Oh, if I'd only known! If I hadn't been such a fool to listen to your cheap, silly, poetry talk that you learned out of books! If I could have seen how you were in your true self—like you are now—I'd have killed myself before I'd have married you! I was sorry for it before we'd been together a month. I knew what you were really like—when it was too late.

ROBERT (*his voice raised loudly*). And now —I'm finding out what you're really like —what a—a creature I've been living with. (*With a harsh laugh.*) God! It wasn't that I haven't guessed how mean and small you are—but I've kept on telling myself that I must be wrong—like a fool!—like a damned fool!

RUTH. You were saying you'd go out on the road if it wasn't for me. Well, you can go, and the sooner the better! I don't care! I'll be glad to get rid of you! The farm'll be better off too. There's been a curse on it ever since you took hold. So go! Go and be a tramp like you've always wanted. It's all you're good for. I can get along without you, don't you worry. (*Exulting fiercely.*)

Andy's coming back, don't forget that! He'll attend to things like they should be. He'll show what a man can do! I don't need you. Andy's coming!

ROBERT (*they are both standing.* ROBERT *grabs her by the shoulders and glares into her eyes*). What do you mean? (*He shakes her violently.*) What are you thinking of? What's in your evil mind, you—you— (*His voice is a harsh shout.*)

RUTH (*in a defiant scream*). Yes I do mean it! I'd say it if you was to kill me! I do love Andy. I do! I do! I always loved him. (*Exultantly.*) And he loves me! He loves me! I know he does. He always did! And you know he did, too! So go! Go if you want to!

ROBERT (*throwing her away from him. She staggers back against the table—thickly*). You—you slut! (*He stands glaring at her as she leans back, supporting herself by the table, gasping for breath. A loud frightened whimper sounds from the awakened child in the bedroom. It continues. The man and woman stand looking at one another in horror, the extent of their terrible quarrel brought home to them. A pause. The noise of a horse and carriage comes from the road before the house. The two, suddenly struck by the same premonition, listen to it breathlessly, as to a sound heard in a dream. It stops. They hear* ANDY's *voice from the road shouting a long hail—"Ahoy there!"*)

RUTH (*with a strangled cry of joy*). Andy! Andy! (*She rushes and grabs the knob of the screen door, about to fling it open.*)

ROBERT (*in a voice of command that forces obedience*). Stop! (*He goes to the door and gently pushes the trembling* RUTH *away from it. The child's crying rises to a louder pitch.*) I'll meet Andy. You better go in to Mary, Ruth. (*She looks at him defiantly for a moment, but there is something in his eyes that makes her turn and walk slowly into the bedroom.*)

ANDY's VOICE (*in a louder shout*). Ahoy there, Rob!

ROBERT (*in an answering shout of forced cheeriness*). Hello, Andy! (*He opens the door and walks out as*

The Curtain Falls.

SCENE II

The top of a hill on the farm. It is about eleven o'clock the next morning. The day is hot and cloudless. In the distance the sea can be seen.

The top of the hill slopes downward slightly toward the left. A big boulder stands in the center toward the rear. Further right, a large oak tree. The faint trace of a path leading upward to it from the left foreground can be detectd through the bleached, sunscorched grass.

ROBERT *is discovered sitting on the boulder, his chin resting on his hands, staring out toward the horizon seaward. His face is pale and haggard, his expression one of utter despondency.* MARY *is sitting on the grass near him in the shade, playing with her doll, singing happily to herself. Presently she casts a curious glance at her father, and, propping her doll up against the tree, comes over and clambers to his side.*

MARY (*pulling at his hand—solicitously*). Dada sick?

ROBERT (*looking at her with a forced smile*). No, dear. Why?

MARY. Play wif Mary.

ROBERT (*gently*). No, dear, not today. Dada doesn't feel like playing today.

MARY (*protestingly*). Yes, Dada!

ROBERT. No, dear. Dada does feel sick—a little. He's got a bad headache.

MARY. Mary see. (*He bends his head. She pats his hair.*) Bad head.

ROBERT (*kissing her—with a smile*). There! It's better now, dear, thank you. (*She cuddles up close against him. There is a pause during which each of them looks out seaward. Finally* ROBERT *turns to her tenderly.*) Would you like Dada to go away?—far, far away?

MARY (*tearfully*). No! No! No, Dada, no!

ROBERT. Don't you like Uncle Andy—the man that came yesterday—not the old man with the white mustache—the other?

MARY. Mary loves Dada.

ROBERT (*with fierce determination*). He won't go away, baby. He was only joking. He couldn't leave his little Mary. (*He presses the child in his arms.*)

MARY (*with an exclamation of pain*). Oh! Hurt!

ROBERT. I'm sorry, little girl. (*He lifts her down to the grass.*) Go play with Dolly, that's a good girl; and be careful to keep in the shade. (*She reluctantly leaves him and takes up her doll again. A moment later she points down the hill to the left.*)

MARY. Mans, Dada.

ROBERT (*looking that way*). It's your Uncle Andy. (*A moment later* ANDREW *comes up from the left, whistling cheerfully. He has changed but little in appearance, except for the fact that his face has been deeply bronzed by his years in the tropics; but there is a decided change in his manner. The old easy-going good-nature seems to have been partly lost in a breezy, business-like briskness of voice and gesture. There is an authoritative note in his speech as though he were accustomed to give orders and have them obeyed as a matter of course. He is dressed in the simple blue uniform and cap of a merchant ship's officer.*)

ANDREW. Here you are, eh?

ROBERT. Hello, Andy.

ANDREW (*going over to* MARY). And who's this young lady I find you all alone with, eh? Who's this pretty young lady? (*He tickles the laughing, squirming* MARY, *then*

lifts her up at arm's length over his head.)
Upsy—daisy! (*He sets her down on the
ground again.*) And there you are! (*He
walks over and sits down on the boulder
beside* ROBERT *who moves to one side to
make room for him.*) Ruth told me I'd
probably find you up top-side here; but I'd
have guessed it, anyway. (*He digs his
brother in the ribs affectionately.*) Still up
to your old tricks, you old beggar! I can remember how you used to come up here to
mope and dream in the old days.

ROBERT (*with a smile*). I come up here now
because it's the coolest place on the farm.
I've given up dreaming.

ANDREW (*grinning*). I don't believe it. You
can't have changed that much. (*After a
pause—with boyish enthusiasm.*) Say, it
sure brings back old times to be up here
with you having a chin all by our lone-
somes again. I feel great being back home.

ROBERT. It's great for us to have you back.

ANDREW (*after a pause—meaningly*). I've
been looking over the old place with Ruth.
Things don't seem to be—

ROBERT (*his face flushing—interrupts his
brother shortly*). Never mind the damn
farm! Let's talk about something interesting. This is the first chance I've had to have
a word with you alone. Tell me about your
trip.

ANDREW. Why, I thought I told you everything in my letters.

ROBERT (*smiling*). Your letters were—
sketchy, to say the least.

ANDREW. Oh, I know I'm no author. You
needn't be afraid of hurting my feelings.
I'd rather go through a typhoon again than
write a letter.

ROBERT (*with eager interest*). Then you
were through a typhoon?

ANDREW. Yes—in the China sea. Had to
run before it under bare poles for two days.
I thought we were bound down for Davy
Jones, sure. Never dreamed waves could
get so big or the wind blow so hard. If it
hadn't been for Uncle Dick being such a
good skipper we'd have gone to the sharks,

all of us. As it was we came out minus a
main top-mast and had to beat back to
Hong-Kong for repairs. But I must have
written you all this.

ROBERT. You never mentioned it.

ANDREW. Well, there was so much dirty
work getting things ship-shape again I
must have forgotten about it.

ROBERT (*looking at* ANDREW—*marveling*).
Forget a typhoon? (*with a trace of scorn.*)
You're a strange combination, Andy. And
is what you've told me all you remember
about it?

ANDREW. Oh, I could give you your belly-
ful of details if I wanted to turn loose on
you. It was all-wool-and-a-yard-wide-Hell,
I'll tell you. You ought to have been there.
I remember thinking about you at the
worst of it, and saying to myself: "This'd
cure Rob of them ideas of his about the
beautiful sea, if he could see it." And it
would have too, you bet! (*He nods emphatically.*)

ROBERT (*dryly*). The sea doesn't seem to
have impressed you very favorably.

ANDREW. I should say it didn't! I'll never set
foot on a ship again if I can help it—except
to carry me some place I can't get to by
train.

ROBERT. But you studied to become an officer!

ANDREW. Had to do something or I'd gone
mad. The days were like years. (*He
laughs.*) And as for the East you used to
rave about—well, you ought to see it, and
smell it! One walk down one of their filthy
narrow streets with the tropic sun beating
on it would sicken you for life with the
"wonder and mystery" you used to dream
of.

ROBERT (*shrinking from his brother with a
glance of aversion*). So all you found in the
East was a stench?

ANDREW. *A* stench! Ten thousand of them!

ROBERT. But you did like some of the places,
judging from your letters—Sydney, Buenos Aires—

ANDREW. Yes, Sydney's a good town. (*Enthusiastically*.) But Buenos Aires—there's the place for you. Argentine's a country where a fellow has a chance to make good. You're right I like it. And I'll tell you, Rob, that's right where I'm going just as soon as I've seen you folks a while and can get a ship. I can get a berth as second officer, and I'll jump the ship when I get there. I'll need every cent of the wages Uncle's paid me to get a start at something in B. A.

ROBERT (*staring at his brother—slowly*). So you're not going to stay on the farm?

ANDREW. Why sure not! Did you think I was? There wouldn't be any sense. One of us is enough to run this little place.

ROBERT. I suppose it does seem small to you now.

ANDREW (*not noticing the sarcasm in ROBERT's tone*). You've no idea, Rob, what a splendid place Argentine is. I had a letter from a marine insurance chap that I'd made friends with in Hong-Kong to his brother, who's in the grain business in Buenos Aires. He took quite a fancy to me, and what's more important, he offered me a job if I'd come back there. I'd have taken it on the spot, only I couldn't leave Uncle Dick in the lurch, and I'd promised you folks to come home. But I'm going back there, you bet, and then you watch me get on! (*He slaps* ROBERT *on the back*.) But don't you think it's a big chance, Rob?

ROBERT. It's fine—for you, Andy.

ANDREW. We call this a farm—but you ought to hear about the farms down there —ten square miles where we've got an acre. It's a new country where big things are opening up—and I want to get in on something big before I die. I'm no fool when it comes to farming, and I know something about grain. I've been reading up a lot on it, too, lately. (*He notices* ROBERT's *absent-minded expression and laughs*.) Wake up, you old poetry book worm, you! I know my talking about business makes you want to choke me, doesn't it?

ROBERT (*with an embarrassed smile*). No, Andy, I—I just happened to think of something else. (*Frowning*.) There've been lots of times lately that I've wished I had some of your faculty for business.

ANDREW (*soberly*). There's something I want to talk about, Rob,—the farm. You don't mind, do you?

ROBERT. No.

ANDREW. I walked over it this morning with Ruth—and she told me about things — (*Evasively*.) I could see the place had run down; but you mustn't blame yourself. When luck's against anyone—

ROBERT. Don't, Andy! It *is* my fault. You know it as well as I do. The best I've ever done was to make ends meet.

ANDREW (*after a pause*). I've got over a thousand saved, and you can have that.

ROBERT (*firmly*). No. You need that for your start in Buenos Aires.

ANDREW. I don't. I can—

ROBERT (*determinedly*). No, Andy! Once and for all, no! I won't hear of it!

ANDREW (*protestingly*). You obstinate old son of a gun!

ROBERT. Oh, everything'll be on a sound footing after harvest. Don't worry about it.

ANDREW (*doubtfully*). Maybe. (*After a pause*.) It's too bad Pa couldn't have lived to see things through. (*With feeling*.) It cut me up a lot—hearing he was dead. He never—softened up, did he—about me, I mean?

ROBERT. He never understood, that's a kinder way of putting it. He does now.

ANDREW (*after a pause*). You've forgotten all about what—caused me to go, haven't you, Rob? (ROBERT *nods but keeps his face averted*.) I was a slushier damn fool in those days than you were. But it was an act of Providence I did go. It opened my eyes to how I'd been fooling myself. Why, I'd forgotten all about—that—before I'd been at sea six months.

ROBERT (*turns and looks into* ANDREW's *eyes searchingly*). You're speaking of— Ruth?

ANDREW (*confused*). Yes. I didn't want you to get false notions in your head, or I wouldn't say anything. (*Looking* ROBERT *squarely in the eyes.*) I'm telling you the truth when I say I'd forgotten long ago. It don't sound well for me, getting over things so easy, but I guess it never really amounted to more than a kid idea I was letting rule me. I'm certain now I never was in love—I was getting fun out of thinking I was—and being a hero to myself. (*He heaves a great sigh of relief.*) There! Gosh, I'm glad that's off my chest. I've been feeling sort of awkward ever since I've been home, thinking of what you two might think. (*A trace of appeal in his voice.*) You've got it all straight now, haven't you, Rob?

ROBERT (*in a low voice*). Yes, Andy.

ANDREW. And I'll tell Ruth, too, if I can get up the nerve. She must feel kind of funny having me round—after what used to be —and not knowing how I feel about it.

ROBERT (*slowly*). Perhaps—for her sake— you'd better not tell her.

ANDREW. For her sake? Oh, you mean she wouldn't want to be reminded of my foolishness? Still, I think it'd be worse if—

ROBERT (*breaking out—in an agonized voice*). Do as you please, Andy; but for God's sake, let's not talk about it! (*There is a pause.* ANDREW *stares at* ROBERT *in hurt stupefaction.* ROBERT *continues after a moment in a voice which he vainly attempts to keep calm.*) Excuse me, Andy. This rotten headache has my nerves shot to pieces.

ANDREW (*mumbling*). It's all right, Rob— long as you're not sore at me.

ROBERT. Where did Uncle Dick disappear to this morning?

ANDREW. He went down to the port to see to things on the *Sunda.* He said he didn't know exactly when he'd be back. I'll have to go down and tend to the ship when he comes. That's why I dressed up in these togs.

MARY (*pointing down the hill to the left*). See! Mama! Mama! (*She struggles to her feet.* RUTH *appears at left. She is dressed in white, shows she has been fixing up. She looks pretty, flushed and full of life.*)

MARY (*running to her mother*). Mama!

RUTH (*kissing her*). Hello, dear! (*She walks toward the rock and addresses* ROBERT *coldly.*) Jake wants to see you about something. He finished working where he was. He's waiting for you at the road.

ROBERT (*getting up—wearily*). I'll go down right away. (*As he looks at* RUTH, *noting her changed appearance, his face darkens with pain.*)

RUTH. And take Mary with you, please. (*To* MARY.) Go with Dada, that's a good girl. Grandma has your dinner most ready for you.

ROBERT (*shortly*). Come, Mary!

MARY (*taking his hand and dancing happily beside him*). Dada! Dada! (*They go down the hill to the left.* RUTH *looks after them for a moment, frowning—then turns to* ANDY *with a smile.*) I'm going to sit down. Come on, Andy. It'll be like old times. (*She jumps lightly to the top of the rock and sits down.*) It's so fine and cool up here after the house.

ANDREW (*half-sitting on the side of the boulder*). Yes. It's great.

RUTH. I've taken a holiday in honor of your arrival. (*Laughing excitedly.*) I feel so free I'd like to have wings and fly over the sea. You're a man. You can't know how awful and stupid it is—cooking and washing dishes all the time.

ANDREW (*making a wry face*). I can guess.

RUTH. Besides, your mother just insisted on getting your first dinner to home, she's that happy at having you back. You'd think I was planning to poison you the flurried way she shooed me out of the kitchen.

ANDREW. That's just like Ma, bless her!

RUTH. She's missed you terrible. We all have. And you can't deny the farm has, after what I showed you and told you when we was looking over the place this morning.

ANDREW (*with a frown*). Things are run down, that's a fact! It's too darn hard on poor old Rob.

RUTH (*scornfully*). It's his own fault. He never takes any interest in things.

ANDREW (*reprovingly*). You can't blame him. He wasn't born for it; but I know he's done his best for your sake and the old folks and the little girl.

RUTH (*indifferently*). Yes, I suppose he has. (*Gayly.*) But thank the Lord, all those days are over now. The "hard luck" Rob's always blaming won't last long when you take hold, Andy. All the farm's ever needed was someone with the knack of looking ahead and preparing for what's going to happen.

ANDREW. Yes, Rob hasn't got that. He's frank to own up to that himself. I'm going to try and hire a good man for him—an experienced farmer—to work the place on a salary and percentage. That'll take it off of Rob's hands, and he needn't be worrying himself to death any more. He looks all worn out, Ruth. He ought to be careful.

RUTH (*absent-mindedly*). Yes, I s'pose. (*Her mind is filled with premonitions by the first part of his statement.*) Why do you want to hire a man to oversee things? Seems as if now that you're back it wouldn't be needful.

ANDREW. Oh, of course I'll attend to everything while I'm here. I mean after I'm gone.

RUTH (*as if she couldn't believe her ears*). Gone!

ANDREW. Yes. When I leave for the Argentine again.

RUTH (*aghast*). You're going away to sea!

ANDREW. Not to sea, no; I'm through with the sea for good as a job. I'm going down to Buenos Aires to get in the grain business.

RUTH. But—that's far off—isn't it?

ANDREW (*easily*). Six thousand miles more or less. It's quite a trip. (*With enthusiasm.*) I've got a peach of a chance down there, Ruth. Ask Rob if I haven't. I've just been telling him all about it.

RUTH (*a flush of anger coming over her face*). And didn't he try to stop you from going?

ANDREW (*in surprise*). No, of course not. Why?

RUTH (*slowly and vindictively*). That's just like him—not to.

ANDREW (*resentfully*). Rob's too good a chum to try and stop me when he knows I'm set on a thing. And he could see just as soon's I told him what a good chance it was.

RUTH (*dazedly*). And you're bound on going?

ANDREW. Sure thing. Oh, I don't mean right off. I'll have to wait for a ship sailing there for quite a while, likely. Anyway, I want to stay to home and visit with you folks a spell before I go.

RUTH (*dumbly*). I s'pose. (*With sudden anguish.*) Oh, Andy, you can't go! You can't. Why we've all thought—we've all been hoping and praying you was coming home to stay, to settle down on the farm and see to things. You mustn't go! Think of how your Ma'll take on if you go—and how the farm'll be ruined if you leave it to Rob to look after. You can see that.

ANDREW (*frowning*). Rob hasn't done so bad. When I get a man to direct things the farm'll be safe enough.

RUTH (*insistently*). But your Ma—think of her.

ANDREW. She's used to me being away. She won't object when she knows it's best for her and all of us for me to go. You ask Rob. In a couple of years down there I'll make my pile, see if I don't; and then I'll come back and settle down and turn this farm into the crackiest place in the whole state. In the meantime, I can help you both from down there. (*Earnestly.*) I tell you, Ruth, I'm going to make good right from the minute I land, if working hard and a determination to get on can do it; and I *know* they can! (*Excitedly—in a rather boastful tone.*) I tell you, I feel ripe for bigger things than settling down here. The trip did that for me, anyway. It showed me the world is a larger proposition than ever I thought it was in the old days. I couldn't be content any more stuck here like a fly in molasses. It all seems trifling, somehow. You ought to be able to understand what I feel.

RUTH (*dully*). Yes—I s'pose I ought. (*After a pause—a sudden suspicion forming in her mind.*) What did Rob tell you —about me?

ANDREW. Tell? About you? Why, nothing.

RUTH (*staring at him intensely*). Are you telling me the truth, Andy Mayo? Didn't he say—I— (*She stops confusedly.*)

ANDREW (*surprised*). No, he didn't mention you, I can remember. Why? What made you think he did?

RUTH (*wringing her hands*). Oh, I wish I could tell if you're lying or not!

ANDREW (*indignantly*). What're you talking about? I didn't used to lie to you, did I? And what in the name of God is there to lie for?

RUTH (*still unconvinced*). Are you sure— will you swear—it isn't the reason— (*She lowers her eyes and half turns away from him.*) The same reason that made you go last time that's driving you away again? 'Cause if it is—I was going to say—you mustn't go—on that account. (*Her voice sinks to a tremulous, tender whisper as she finishes.*)

ANDREW (*confused—forces a laugh*). Oh, is *that* what you're driving at? Well, you needn't worry about that no more— (*Soberly.*) I don't blame you, Ruth, feeling embarrassed having me around again, after the way I played the dumb fool about going away last time.

RUTH (*her hope crushed—with a gasp of pain*). Oh, Andy!

ANDREW (*misunderstanding*). I know I oughtn't to talk about such foolishness to you. Still I figure it's better to get it out of my system so's we three can be together same's years ago, and not be worried thinking one of us might have the wrong notion.

RUTH. Andy! Please! Don't!

ANDREW. Let me finish now that I've started. It'll help clear things up. I don't want you to think once a fool always a fool, and be upset all the time I'm here on my fool account. I want you to believe I put all that silly nonsense back of me a long time ago—and now—it seems—well—as if you'd always been my sister, that's what. Ruth.

RUTH (*at the end of her endurance— laughing hysterically*). For God's sake, Andy—won't you please stop talking! (*She again hides her face in her hands, her bowed shoulders trembling.*)

ANDREW (*ruefully*). Seem's if I put my foot in it whenever I open my mouth today. Rob shut me up with almost the same words when I tried speaking to him about it.

RUTH (*fiercely*). You told him—what you've told me?

ANDREW (*astounded*). Why sure! Why not?

RUTH (*shuddering*). Oh, my God!

ANDREW (*alarmed*). Why? Shouldn't I have?

RUTH (*hysterically*). Oh, I don't care what you do! I don't care! Leave me alone! (*ANDREW gets up and walks down the hill to the left, embarrassed, hurt, and greatly puzzled by her behavior.*)

ANDREW (*after a pause—pointing down the hill*). Hello! Here they come back—and the Captain's with them. How'd he come to get back so soon, I wonder? That means I've got to hustle down to the port and get on board. Rob's got the baby with him. (*He comes back to the boulder.* RUTH *keeps her face averted from him.*) Gosh, I never saw a father so tied up in a kid as Rob is! He just watches every move she makes. And I don't blame him. You both got a right to feel proud of her. She's surely a little winner. (*He glances at* RUTH *to see if this very obvious attempt to get back in her good graces is having any effect.*) I can see the likeness to Rob standing out all over her, can't you? But there's no denying she's your young one, either. There's something about her eyes—

RUTH (*piteously*). Oh, Andy, I've a head-ache! I don't want to talk! Leave me alone, won't you please?

ANDREW (*stands staring at her for a moment—then walks away saying in a hurt tone*): Everybody hereabouts seems to be on edge today. I begin to feel as if I'm not wanted around. (*He stands near the path, left, kicking at the grass with the toe of his shoe. A moment later* CAPTAIN DICK SCOTT *enters, followed by* ROBERT *carrying* MARY. *The* CAPTAIN *seems scarcely to have changed at all from the jovial, booming person he was three years before. He wears a uniform similar to* ANDREW's. *He is puffing and breathless from his climb and mops wildly at his perspiring countenance.* ROBERT *casts a quick glance at* ANDREW, *noticing the latter's discomfited look, and then turns his eyes on* RUTH *who, at their approach, has moved so her back is toward them, her chin resting on her hands as she stares out seaward.*)

MARY. Mama! Mama! (ROBERT *puts her down and she runs to her mother.* RUTH *turns and grabs her up in her arms with a sudden fierce tenderness, quickly turning away again from the others. During the following scene she keeps* MARY *in her arms.*)

SCOTT (*wheezily*). Phew! I got great news for you, Andy. Let me get my wind first. Phew! God A'mighty, mountin' this damned hill is worser'n goin aloft to the skys'l yard in a blow. I got to lay to a while. (*He sits down on the grass, mopping his face.*)

ANDREW. I didn't look for you this soon, Uncle.

SCOTT. I didn't figger it, neither; but I run across a bit o' news down to the Seamen's Home made me 'bout ship and set all sail back here to find you.

ANDREW (*eagerly*). What is it, Uncle?

SCOTT. Passin' by the Home I thought I'd drop in an' let 'em know I'd be lackin' a mate next trip count o' your leavin'. Their man in charge o' the shippin' asked after you 'special curious. "Do you think he'd consider a berth as Second on a steamer, Captain?" he asks. I was goin' to say no when I thinks o' you wantin' to get back down south to the Plate agen; so I asks him: "What is she and where's she bound?" "She's the *El Paso*, a brand new tramp," he says, "and she's bound for Buenos Aires."

ANDREW (*his eyes lighting up—excitedly*). Gosh, that is luck! When does she sail?

SCOTT. Tomorrow mornin'. I didn't know if you'd want to ship away agen so quick an' I told him so. "Tell him I'll hold the berth open for him until late this afternoon," he says. So there you be, an' you can make your own choice.

ANDREW. I'd like to take it. There may not be another ship for Buenos Aires with a vacancy in months. (*His eyes roving from* ROBERT *to* RUTH *and back again—uncertainly.*) Still—damn it all—tomorrow morning *is* soon. I wish she wasn't leaving for a week or so. That'd give me a chance —it seems hard to go right away again when I've just got home. And yet it's a chance in a thousand— (*Appealing to* ROBERT.) What do you think, Rob? What would you do?

ROBERT (*forcing a smile*). He who hesitates, you know. (*Frowning.*) It's a piece of good luck thrown in your way—and— I think you owe it to yourself to jump at it. But don't ask me to decide for you.

RUTH (*turning to look at* ANDREW—*in a tone of fierce resentment*). Yes, go Andy! (*She turns quickly away again. There is a moment of embarrassed silence.*)

ANDREW (*thoughtfully*). Yes, I guess I will. It'll be the best thing for all of us in the end, don't you think so, Rob? (ROBERT *nods but remains silent.*)

SCOTT (*getting to his feet*). Then, that's settled.

ANDREW (*now that he has definitely made a decision his voice rings with hopeful strength and energy*). Yes, I'll take the berth. The sooner I go the sooner I'll be back, that's a certainty; and I won't come back with empty hands next time. You bet I won't!

SCOTT. You ain't got so much time, Andy. To make sure you'd best leave here soon's you kin. I got to get right back aboard. You'd best come with me.

ANDREW. I'll go to the house and repack my bag right away.

ROBERT (*quietly*). You'll both be here for dinner, won't you?

ANDREW (*worriedly*). I don't know. Will there be time? What time is it now, I wonder?

ROBERT (*reproachfully*). Ma's been getting dinner especially for you, Andy.

ANDREW (*flushing—shamefacedly*). Hell! And I was forgetting! Of course I'll stay for dinner if I missed every damned ship in the world. (*He turns to the* CAPTAIN— *briskly.*) Come on, Uncle. Walk down with me to the house and you can tell me more about this berth on the way. I've got to pack before dinner. (*He and the* CAPTAIN *start down to the left.* ANDREW *calls back over his shoulder.*) You're coming soon, aren't you, Rob?

ROBERT. Yes. I'll be right down. (ANDREW *and the* CAPTAIN *leave.* RUTH *puts* MARY *on*

the ground and hides her face in her hands. Her shoulders shake as if she were sobbing. ROBERT *stares at her with a grim, sombre expression.* MARY *walks backward toward* ROBERT, *her wondering eyes fixed on her mother.*)

MARY (*her voice vaguely frightened, taking her father's hand*). Dada, Mama's cryin', Dada.

ROBERT (*bending down and stroking her hair—in a voice he endeavors to keep from being harsh*). No, she isn't, little girl. The sun hurts her eyes, that's all. Aren't you beginning to feel hungry, Mary?

MARY (*decidedly*). Yes, Dada.

ROBERT (*meaningly*). It must be your dinner time now.

RUTH (*in a muffled voice*). I'm coming, Mary. (*She wipes her eyes quickly and, without looking at* ROBERT, *comes and takes* MARY's *hand—in a dead voice.*) Come on and I'll get your dinner for you. (*She walks out left, her eyes fixed on the ground, the skipping* MARY *tugging at her hand.* ROBERT *waits a moment for them to get ahead and then slowly follows as*

The Curtain Falls.

ACT THREE

SCENE I

Same as Act Two, Scene One—The sitting room of the farm house about six o'clock in the morning of a day toward the end of October five years later. It is not yet dawn, but as the action progresses the darkness outside the windows gradually fades to gray.

The room, seen by the light of the shadeless oil lamp with a smoky chimney which stands on the table, presents an appearance of decay, of dissolution. The curtains at the windows are torn and dirty and one of them is missing. The closed desk is gray with accumulated dust as if it had not been used in years. Blotches of dampness disfigure the wall paper. Threadbare trails, leading to the kitchen and outer doors, show in the faded carpet. The top of the coverless table is stained with the imprints of hot dishes and spilt food. The rung of one rocker has been clumsily mended with a piece of plain board. A brown coating of rust covers the unblacked stove. A pile of wood is stacked up carelessly against the wall by the stove.

The whole atmosphere of the room, contrasted with that of former years, is one of an habitual poverty too hopelessly resigned to be any longer ashamed or even conscious of itself.

At the rise of the curtain RUTH *is discovered sitting by the stove, with hands outstretched to the warmth as if the air in the room were damp and cold. A heavy shawl is wrapped about her shoulders, half-concealing her dress of deep mourning. She has aged horribly. Her pale, deeply lined face has the stony lack of expression of one to whom nothing more can ever happen, whose capacity for emotion has been exhausted. When she speaks her voice is without timbre, low and monotonous. The negligent disorder of her dress, the slovenly arrangement of her hair, now streaked with gray, her muddied shoes run down at the heel, give full evidence of the apathy in which she lives.*

Her mother is asleep in her wheel chair beside the stove toward the rear, wrapped up in a blanket.

There is a sound from the open bedroom door in the rear as if someone were getting out of bed. RUTH *turns in that direction with a look of dull annoyance. A moment later* ROBERT *appears in the doorway, leaning weakly against it for support. His hair is long and unkempt, his face and body emaciated. There are bright patches of crimson over his cheek bones and his eyes are burning with fever. He is dressed in corduroy pants, a flannel shirt, and wears worn carpet slippers on his bare feet.*

RUTH (*dully*). S-s-s-h-! Ma's asleep.

ROBERT (*speaking with an effort*). I won't wake her. (*He walks weakly to a rocker by the side of the table and sinks down in it exhausted.*)

RUTH (*staring at the stove*). You better come near the fire where it's warm.

ROBERT. No. I'm burning up now.

RUTH. That's the fever. You know the doctor told you not to get up and move round.

ROBERT (*irritably*). That old fossil! He doesn't know anything. Go to bed and stay there—that's his only prescription.

RUTH (*indifferently*). How are you feeling now?

ROBERT (*buoyantly*). Better! Much better than I've felt in ages. Really I'm fine now —only very weak. It's the turning point, I guess. From now on I'll pick up so quick I'll surprise you—and no thanks to that old fool of a country quack, either.

RUTH. He's always tended to us.

ROBERT. Always helped us to die, you mean! He "tended" to Pa and Ma and—(*his voice breaks*)—and to—Mary.

RUTH (*dully*). He did the best he knew, I s'pose. (*After a pause.*) Well, Andy's bringing a specialist with him when he comes. That ought to suit you.

ROBERT (*bitterly*). Is that why you're waiting up all night?

RUTH. Yes.

ROBERT. For Andy?

RUTH (*without a trace of feeling*). Somebody had got to. It's only right for someone to meet him after he's been gone five years.

ROBERT (*with bitter mockery*). Five years! It's a long time.

RUTH. Yes.

ROBERT (*meaningly*). To wait!

RUTH (*indifferently*). It's past now.

ROBERT. Yes, it's past. (*After a pause.*) Have you got his two telegrams with you? (RUTH *nods.*) Let me see them, will you? My head was so full of fever when they came I couldn't make head or tail to them. (*Hastily.*) But I'm feeling fine now. Let me read them again. (RUTH *takes them from the bosom of her dress and hands them to him.*)

RUTH. Here. The first one's on top.

ROBERT (*opening it*). New York. "Just landed from steamer. Have important business to wind up here. Will be home as soon as deal is completed." (*He smiles bitterly.*) Business first was always Andy's motto. (*He reads.*) "Hope you are all well. Andy." (*He repeats ironically.*) "Hope you are all well!"

RUTH (*dully*). He couldn't know you'd been took sick till I answered that and told him.

ROBERT (*contritely*). Of course he couldn't. I'm a fool. I'm touchy about nothing lately. Just what did you say in your reply?

RUTH (*inconsequentially*). I had to send it collect.

ROBERT (*irritably*). What did you say was the matter with me?

RUTH. I wrote you had lung trouble.

ROBERT (*flying into a petty temper*). You *are* a fool! How often have I explained to you that it's *pleurisy* is the matter with me. You can't seem to get it in your head that the pleura is outside the lungs, not in them!

RUTH (*callously*). I only wrote what Doctor Smith told me.

ROBERT (*angrily*). He's a damned ignoramus!

RUTH (*dully*). Makes no difference. I had to tell Andy something, didn't I?

ROBERT (*after a pause, opening the other telegram*). He sent this last evening. Let's see. (*He reads.*) "Leave for home on midnight train. Just received your wire. Am bringing specialist to see Rob. Will motor to farm from Port." (*He calculates.*) What time is it now?

RUTH. Round six, must be.

ROBERT. He ought to be here soon. I'm glad he's bringing a doctor who knows something. A specialist will tell you in a second that there's nothing the matter with my lungs.

RUTH (*stolidly*). You've been coughing an awful lot lately.

ROBERT (*irritably*). What nonsense! For God's sake, haven't you ever had a bad cold yourself? (RUTH *stares at the stove in silence.* ROBERT *fidgets in his chair. There is a pause. Finally* ROBERT's *eyes are fixed on the sleeping* MRS. ATKINS.) Your mother is lucky to be able to sleep so soundly.

RUTH. Ma's tired. She's been sitting up with me most of the night.

ROBERT (*mockingly*). Is she waiting for Andy, too? (*There is a pause.* ROBERT *sighs.*) I couldn't get to sleep to save my soul. I counted ten million sheep if I counted one. No use! I gave up trying finally and just lay there in the dark thinking. (*He pauses, then continues in a tone of tender sympathy.*) I was thinking about you, Ruth—of how hard these last years must have been for you. (*Appealingly.*) I'm sorry, Ruth.

RUTH (*in a dead voice*). I don't know. They're past now. They were hard on all of us.

ROBERT. Yes; on all of us but Andy. (*With a flash of sick jealousy.*) Andy's made a big success of himself—the kind he wanted. (*Mockingly.*) And now he's coming home to let us admire his greatness. (*Frowning —irritably.*) What am I talking about? My brain must be sick, too. (*After a pause.*) Yes, these years have been terrible for both of us. (*His voice is lowered to a trembling whisper.*) Especially the last eight months since Mary—died. (*He forces back a sob with a convulsive shudder—then breaks out in a passionate agony.*) Our last hope of happiness! I could curse God from the bottom of my soul—if there was a God! (*He is racked by a violent fit of coughing and hurriedly puts his handkerchief to his lips.*)

RUTH (*without looking at him*). Mary's better off—being dead.

ROBERT (*gloomily*). We'd all be better off for that matter. (*With a sudden exasperation.*) You tell that mother of yours she's got to stop saying that Mary's death was due to a weak constitution inherited from me. (*On the verge of tears of weakness.*) It's got to stop, I tell you!

RUTH (*sharply*). S-h-h! You'll wake her; and then she'll nag at me—not you.

ROBERT (*coughs and lies back in his chair weakly—a pause*). It's all because your mother's down on me for not begging Andy for help.

RUTH (*resentfully*). You might have. He's got plenty.

ROBERT. How can *you* of all people think of taking money from *him*?

RUTH (*dully*). I don't see the harm. He's your own brother.

ROBERT (*shrugging his shoulders*). What's the use of talking to you? Well, *I* couldn't. (*Proudly.*) And I've managed to keep things going, thank God. You can't deny that without help I've succeeded in— (*He breaks off with a bitter laugh.*) My God, what am I boasting of? Debts to this one and that, taxes, interest unpaid! I'm a fool! (*He lies back in his chair closing his eyes for a moment, then speaks in a low voice.*) I'll be frank, Ruth. I've been an utter failure, and I've dragged you with me. I couldn't blame you in all justice—for hating me.

RUTH (*without feeling*). I don't hate you. It's been my fault too, I s'pose.

ROBERT. No. You couldn't help loving— Andy.

RUTH (*dully*). I don't love anyone.

ROBERT (*waving her remark aside*). You needn't deny it. It doesn't matter. (*After a pause—with a tender smile.*) Do you know Ruth, what I've been dreaming back there in the dark? (*With a short laugh.*) I was planning our future when I get well. (*He looks at her with appealing eyes as if afraid she will sneer at him. Her expression does not change. She stares at the stove. His voice takes on a note of eagerness.*) After all, why shouldn't we have a future? We're young yet. If we can only shake off the curse of this farm! It's the farm that's ruined our lives, damn it! And now that Andy's coming back—I'm going to sink my foolish pride, Ruth! I'll borrow the money from him to give us a good start in the city. We'll go where people live instead of stagnating, and start all over again. (*Confidently.*) I won't be the failure there that I've been here, Ruth. You won't need to be ashamed of me there. I'll be a prove to you the reading I've done can be put to some use. (*Vaguely.*) I'll write, or something of that sort. I've always wanted to write. (*Pleadingly.*) You'll want to do that, won't you, Ruth?

RUTH (*dully*). There's Ma.

ROBERT. She can come with us.

RUTH. She wouldn't.

ROBERT (*angrily*). So that's your answer! (*He trembles with violent passion. His voice is so strange that* RUTH *turns to look at him in alarm.*) You're lying, Ruth! Your mother's just an excuse. You want to stay here. You think that because Andy's coming back that— (*He chokes and has an attack of coughing.*)

RUTH (*getting up—in a frightened voice*). What's the matter? (*She goes to him.*) I'll go with you, Rob. Stop that coughing for goodness' sake! It's awful bad for you. (*She soothes him in dull tones.*) I'll go with you to the city—soon's you're well again. Honest I will, Rob, I promise! (ROB *lies back and closes his eyes. She stands looking down at him anxiously.*) Do you feel better now?

ROBERT. Yes. (RUTH *goes back to her chair. After a pause he opens his eyes and sits up in his chair. His face is flushed and happy.*) Then you *will* go, Ruth?

RUTH. Yes.

ROBERT (*excitedly*). We'll make a new start, Ruth—just you and I. Life owes us some happiness after what we've been through. (*Vehemently.*) It must! Otherwise our suffering would be meaningless— and that is unthinkable.

RUTH (*worried by his excitement*). Yes, yes, of course, Rob, but you mustn't—

ROBERT. Oh, don't be afraid. I feel completely well, really I do—now that I can hope again. Oh, if you knew how glorious it feels to have something to look forward to! Can't you feel the thrill of it, too—the vision of a new life opening up after all the horrible years?

RUTH. Yes, yes, but do be—

ROBERT. Nonsense! I won't be careful. I'm getting back all my strength. (*He gets lightly to his feet.*) See! I feel light as a feather. (*He walks to her chair and bends down to kiss her smilingly.*) One kiss—the first in years, isn't it?—to greet the dawn of a new life together.

RUTH (*submitting to his kiss—worriedly*). Sit down, Rob, for goodness' sake!

ROBERT (*with tender obstinacy—stroking her hair*). I won't sit down. You're silly to worry. (*He rests one hand on the back of her chair.*) Listen. All our suffering has been a test through which we had to pass to prove ourselves worthy of a finer realization. (*Exultingly.*) And we did pass through it! It hasn't broken us! And now the dream is to come true! Don't you see?

RUTH (*looking at him with frightened eyes as if she thought he had gone mad*). Yes, Rob, I see; but won't you go back to bed now and rest?

ROBERT. No. I'm going to see the sun rise. It's an augury of good fortune. (*He goes quickly to the window in the rear left, and pushing the curtains aside, stands looking out.* RUTH *springs to her feet and comes quickly to the table, left, where she remains watching* ROBERT *in a tense, expectant attitude. As he peers out his body seems gradually to sag, to grow limp and tired. His voice is mournful as he speaks.*) No sun yet. It isn't time. All I can see is the black rim of the damned hills outlined against a creeping grayness. (*He turns around; letting the curtains fall back, stretching a hand out to the wall to support himself. His false strength of a moment has evaporated, leaving his face drawn and hollow-eyed. He makes a pitiful attempt to smile.*) That's not a very happy augury, is it? But the sun'll come—soon. (*He sways weakly.*)

RUTH (*hurrying to his side and supporting him*). Please go to bed, won't you, Rob? You don't want to be all wore out when the specialist comes, do you?

ROBERT (*quickly*). No. That's right. He mustn't think I'm sicker than I am. And I feel as if I could sleep now—(*Cheerfully*)—a good, sound, restful sleep.

RUTH (*helping him to the bedroom door*). That's what you need most. (*They go inside. A moment later she reappears calling back.*) I'll shut this door so's you'll be quiet. (*She closes the door and goes quickly to her mother and shakes her by the shoulder.*) Ma! Ma! Wake up!

MRS. ATKINS (*coming out of her sleep with a start*). Glory be! What's the matter with you?

RUTH. It was Rob. He's just been talking to me out here. I put him back to bed. (*Now that she is sure her mother is awake her fear passes and she relapses into dull indifference. She sits down in her chair and stares at the stove—dully.*) He acted—funny; and his eyes looked so—so wild like.

MRS. ATKINS (*with asperity*). And is that all you woke me out of a sound sleep for, and scared me near out of my wits?

RUTH. I was afraid. He talked so crazy. I couldn't quiet him. I didn't want to be alone with him that way. Lord knows what he might do.

MRS. ATKINS (*scornfully*). Humph! A help I'd be to you and me not able to move a step! Why didn't you run and get Jake?

RUTH (*dully*). Jake isn't here. He quit last night. He hasn't been paid in three months.

MRS. ATKINS (*indignantly*). I can't blame him. What decent person'd want to work on a place like this? (*With sudden exasperation.*) Oh, I wish you'd never married that man!

RUTH (*wearily*). You oughtn't to talk about him now when he's sick in his bed.

MRS. ATKINS (*working herself into a fit of rage*). You know very well, Ruth Mayo, if it wasn't for me helpin' you on the sly out of my savin's, you'd both been in the poor house—and all 'count of his pigheaded pride in not lettin' Andy know the state thin's were in. A nice thin' for me to have to support him out of what I'd saved for my last days—and me an invalid with no one to look to!

RUTH. Andy'll pay you back, Ma. I can tell him so's Rob'll never know.

MRS. ATKINS (*with a snort*). What'd Rob think you and him was livin' on, I'd like to know?

RUTH (*dully*). He didn't think about it, I s'pose. (*After a slight pause.*) He said he'd made up his mind to ask Andy for help when he comes. (*As a clock in the kitchen strikes six.*) Six o'clock. Andy ought to get here directly.

MRS. ATKINS. D'you think this special doctor'll do Rob any good?

RUTH (*hopelessly*). I don't know. (*The two women remain silent for a time staring dejectedly at the stove.*)

MRS. ATKINS (*shivering irritably*). For goodness' sake put some wood on that fire. I'm most freezin'!

RUTH (*pointing to the door in the rear*). Don't talk so loud. Let him sleep if he can. (*She gets wearily from the chair and puts a few pieces of wood in the stove.*) This is the last of the wood. I don't know who'll cut more now that Jake's left. (*She sighs and walks to the window in the rear, left, pulls the curtains aside, and looks out.*) It's getting gray out. (*She comes back to the stove.*) Looks like it'd be a nice day. (*She stretches out her hands to warm them.*) Must've been a heavy frost last night. We're paying for the spell of warm weather we've been having. (*The throbbing whine of a motor sounds from the distance outside.*)

MRS. ATKINS (*sharply*). S-h-h! Listen! Ain't that an auto I hear?

RUTH (*without interest*). Yes. It's Andy, I s'pose.

MRS. ATKINS (*with nervous irritation*). Don't sit there like a silly goose. Look at the state of this room! What'll this strange doctor think of us? Look at the lamp chimney all smoke! Gracious sakes, Ruth—

RUTH (*indifferently*). I've got a lamp all cleaned up in the kitchen.

MRS. ATKINS (*peremptorily*). Wheel me in there this minute. I don't want him to see me looking a sight. I'll lay down in the room the other side. You don't need me now and I'm dead for sleep. (*RUTH wheels her mother off right. The noise of the motor grows louder and finally ceases as the car stops on the road before the farmhouse. RUTH returns from the kitchen with a lighted lamp in her hand which she sets on the table beside the other. The sound of footsteps on the path is heard—then a sharp rap on the door. RUTH goes and opens it. ANDREW enters, followed by DOCTOR FAWCETT carrying a small black bag. ANDREW has changed greatly. His face seems to have grown highstrung, hardened by the look of decisiveness which comes from being constantly under a strain where judgments on the spur of the moment are compelled to be accurate. His eyes are keener and more alert. There is even a suggestion of ruthless cunning about them. At present, however, his expression is one of tense anxiety. DOCTOR FAWCETT is a short, dark, middle-aged man with a Vandyke beard. He wears glasses.*)

RUTH. Hello, Andy! I've been waiting—

ANDREW (*kissing her hastily*). I got here as soon as I could. (*He throws off his cap and heavy overcoat on the table, introducing RUTH and the DOCTOR as he does so. He is dressed in an expensive business suit and appears stouter.*) My sister-in-law, Mrs. Mayo—Doctor Fawcett. (*They bow to each other silently. ANDREW casts a quick glance about the room.*) Where's Rob?

RUTH (*pointing*). In there.

ANDREW. I'll take your coat and hat, Doctor. (*As he helps the DOCTOR with his things.*) Is he very bad, Ruth?

RUTH (*dully*). He's been getting weaker.

ANDREW. Damn! This way, Doctor. Bring the lamp, Ruth. (*He goes into the bedroom, followed by the DOCTOR and RUTH carrying the clean lamp. RUTH reappears almost immediately closing the door behind her, and goes slowly to the outside door, which she opens, and stands in the doorway looking out. The sound of* ANDREW's *and* ROBERT's *voices comes from the bedroom. A moment later* ANDREW *re-enters, closing the door softly. He comes forward and sinks down in the rocker on the right of table, leaning his head on his hand. His face is drawn in a shocked expression of great grief. He sighs heavily, staring mournfully in front of him.* RUTH *turns and stands watching him. Then she shuts the door and returns to her chair by the stove, turning it so she can face him.*)

ANDREW (*glancing up quickly—in a harsh voice*). How long has this been going on?

RUTH. You mean—how long has he been sick?

ANDREW (*shortly*). Of course! What else?

RUTH. It was last summer he had a bad spell first, but he's been ailin' ever since Mary died—eight months ago.

ANDREW (*harshly*). Why didn't you let me know—cable me? Do you want him to die, all of you? I'm damned if it doesn't look that way! (*His voice breaking.*) Poor old chap! To be sick in this out-of-the-way hole without anyone to attend to him but a country quack! It's a damned shame!

RUTH (*dully*). I wanted to send you word once, but he only got mad when I told him. He was too proud to ask anything, he said.

ANDREW. Proud? To ask *me*? (*He jumps to his feet and paces nervously back and forth.*) I can't understand the way you've acted. Didn't you see how sick he was getting? Couldn't you realize—why, I nearly dropped in my tracks when I saw him! He looks—(*He shudders*)—terrible! (*With fierce scorn.*) I suppose you're so used to the idea of his being delicate that you took his sickness as a matter of course. God, if I'd only known!

RUTH (*without emotion*). A letter takes so long to get where you were—and we couldn't afford to telegraph. We owed everyone already, and I couldn't ask Ma. She'd been giving me money out of her savings till she hadn't much left. Don't say anything to Rob about it. I never told him.

He'd only be mad at me if he knew. But I had to, because—God knows how we'd have got on if I hadn't.

ANDREW. You mean to say— (*His eyes seem to take in the poverty-stricken appearance of the room for the first time.*) You sent that telegram to me collect. Was it because— (RUTH *nods silently.* ANDREW *pounds on the table with his fist.*) Good God! And all this time I've been—why I've had everything! (*He sits down in his chair and pulls it close to* RUTH's—*impulsively.*) But—I can' get it through my head. Why? Why? What has happened? How did it ever come about? Tell me!

RUTH (*dully*). There's nothing much to tell. Things kept getting worse, that's all—and Rob didn't seem to care. He never took any interest since way back when your Ma died. After that he got men to take charge, and they nearly all cheated him—he couldn't tell—and left one after another. Then after Mary died he didn't pay no heed to anything any more—just stayed indoors and took to reading books again. So I had to ask Ma if she wouldn't help us some.

ANDREW (*surprised and horrified*). Why, damn it, this is frightful! Rob must be mad not to have let me know. Too proud to ask help of *me!* What's the matter with him, in God's name? (*A sudden, horrible suspicion entering his mind.*) Ruth! Tell me the truth. His mind hasn't gone back on him, has it?

RUTH (*dully*). I don't know. Mary's dying broke him up terrible—but he's used to her being gone by this, I s'pose.

ANDREW (*looking at her queerly*). Do you mean to say *you're* used to it?

RUTH (*in a dead voice*). There's a time comes—when you don't mind any more—anything.

ANDREW (*looks at her fixedly for a moment—with great pity*). I'm sorry, Ruth—if I seemed to blame you. I didn't realize—The sight of Rob lying in bed there, so gone to pieces—it made me furious at everyone Forgive me, Ruth.

RUTH. There's nothing to forgive. It doesn't matter.

ANDREW (*springing to his feet again and pacing up and down*). Thank God I came back before it was too late. This doctor will know exactly what to do. That's the first thing to think of. When Rob's on his feet again we can get the farm working on a sound basis once more. I'll see to that—before I leave.

RUTH. You're going away again?

ANDREW. I've got to.

RUTH. You wrote Rob you was coming back to stay this time.

ANDREW. I expected to—until I got to New York. Then I learned certain facts that make it necessary. (*With a short laugh.*) To be candid, Ruth, I'm not the rich man you've probably been led to believe by my letters—not now. I was when I wrote them. I made money hand over fist as long as I stuck to legitimate trading; but I wasn't content with that. I wanted it to come easier, so like all the rest of the idiots, I tried speculation. Oh, I won all right! Several times I've been almost a millionaire —on paper—and then come down to earth again with a bump. Finally the strain was too much. I got disgusted with myself and made up my mind to get out and come home and forget it and really live again. (*He gives a harsh laugh.*) And now comes the funny part. The day before the steamer sailed I saw what I thought was a chance to become a millionaire again. (*He snaps his fingers.*) That easy! I plunged. Then, before things broke, I left—I was so confident I couldn't be wrong. But when I landed in New York—I wired you I had business to wind up, didn't I? Well, it was the business that wound me up! (*He smiles grimly, pacing up and down, his hands in his pockets.*)

RUTH (*dully*). You found—you'd lost everything?

ANDREW (*sitting down again*). Practically. (*He takes a cigar from his pocket, bites the end off, and lights it.*) Oh, I don't mean I'm dead broke. I've saved ten thousand from the wreckage, maybe twenty. But that's a poor showing for five years' hard work. That's why I'll have to go back. (*Confidently.*) I can make it up in a year or so down there—and I don't need but a shoestring to start with. (*A weary expression comes over his face and he sighs heavily.*) I wish I didn't have to. I'm sick of it all.

RUTH. It's too bad—things seem to go wrong so.

ANDREW (*shaking off his depression—briskly*). They might be much worse. There's enough left to fix the farm O. K. before I go. I won't leave till Rob's on his feet again. In the meantime I'll make things fly around here. (*With satisfaction.*) I need a rest, and the kind of rest I need is hard work in the open—just like I used to do in the old days. (*Stopping abruptly and lowering his voice cautiously.*) Not a word to Rob about my losing money! Remember that, Ruth! You can see why. If he's grown so touchy he'd never accept a cent if he thought I was hard up; see?

RUTH. Yes, Andy. (*After a pause, during which* ANDREW *puffs at his cigar abstractedly, his mind evidently busy with plans for the future, the bedroom door is opened and* DOCTOR FAWCETT *enters, carrying a bag. He closes the door quietly behind him and comes forward, a grave expression on his face.* ANDREW *springs out of his chair.*)

ANDREW. Ah, Doctor! (*He pushes a chair between his own and* RUTH's.) Won't you have a chair?

FAWCETT (*glancing at his watch*). I must catch the nine o'clock back to the city. It's imperative. I have only a moment. (*Sitting down and clearing his throat—in a perfunctory, impersonal voice.*) The case of your brother, Mr. Mayo, is— (*He stops and glances at* RUTH *and says meaningly to* ANDREW.) Perhaps it would be better if you and I—

RUTH (*with dogged resentment*). I know what you mean, Doctor. (*Dully.*) Don't be afraid I can't stand it. I'm used to bearing trouble by this; and I can guess what you've found out. (*She hesitates for a moment—then continues in a monotonous voice.*) Rob's going to die.

ANDREW (*angrily*). Ruth!

FAWCETT (*raising his hand as if to command silence*). I am afraid my diagnosis of your brother's condition forces me to the same conclusion as Mrs. Mayo's.

ANDREW (*groaning*). But, Doctor, surely—

FAWCETT (*calmly*). Your brother hasn't long to live—perhaps a few days, perhaps only a few hours. It's a marvel that he's alive at this moment. My examination revealed that both of his lungs are terribly affected.

ANDREW (*brokenly*). Good God! (RUTH *keeps her eyes fixed on her lap in a trance-like stare.*)

FAWCETT. I am sorry I have to tell you this. If there was anything that could be done—

ANDREW. There isn't anything?

FAWCETT (*shaking his head*). It's too late. Six months ago there might have—

ANDREW (*in anguish*). But if we were to take him to the mountains—or to Arizona —or—

FAWCETT. That might have prolonged his life six months ago. (ANDREW *groans.*) But now— (*He shrugs his shoulders significantly.*)

ANDREW (*appalled by a sudden thought*). Good heavens, you haven't told him this, have you, Doctor?

FAWCETT. No. I lied to him. I said a change of climate— (*He looks at his watch again nervously.*) I must leave you. (*He gets up.*)

ANDREW (*getting to his feet—insistently*). But there must still be some chance—

FAWCETT (*as if he were reassuring a child*). There is always that last chance—the miracle. (*He puts on his hat and coat—bowing to* RUTH.) Good-by, Mrs. Mayo.

RUTH (*without raising her eyes—dully*). Good-by.

ANDREW (*mechanically*). I'll walk to the car with you, Doctor. (*They go out of the door.* RUTH *sits motionlessly. The motor is heard starting and the noise gradually re-*cedes into the distance. ANDREW *re-enters and sits down in his chair, holding his head in his hands.*) Ruth! (*She lifts her eyes to his.*) Hadn't we better go in and see him? God! I'm afraid to! I know he'll read it in my face. (*The bedroom door is noiselessly opened and* ROBERT *appears in the doorway. His cheeks are flushed with fever, and his eyes appear unusually large and brilliant.* ANDREW *continues with a groan.*) It can't be, Ruth. It can't be as hopeless as he said. There's always a fighting chance. We'll take Rob to Arizona. He's *got* to get well. There *must* be a chance!

ROBERT (*in a gentle tone*). Why must there, Andy? (RUTH *turns and stares at him with terrified eyes.*)

ANDREW (*whirling around*). Rob! (*Scoldingly.*) What are you doing out of bed? (*He gets up and goes to him.*) Get right back now and obey the Doc, or you're going to get a licking from me!

ROBERT (*ignoring these remarks*). Help me over to the chair, please, Andy.

ANDREW. Like hell I will! You're going right back to bed, that's where you're going, and stay there! (*He takes hold of* ROBERT'S *arm.*)

ROBERT (*mockingly*). Stay there till I die, eh, Andy? (*Coldly.*) Don't behave like a child. I'm sick of lying down. I'll be more rested sitting up. (*As* ANDREW *hesitates— violently.*) I swear I'll get out of bed every time you put me there. You'll have to sit on my chest, and that wouldn't help my health any. Come on, Andy. Don't play the fool. I want to talk to you, and I'm going to. (*With a grim smile.*) A dying man has some rights, hasn't he?

ANDREW (*with a shudder*). Don't talk that way, for God's sake! I'll only let you sit down if you'll promise that. Remember. (*He helps* ROBERT *to the chair between his own and* RUTH'S.) Easy now! There you are! Wait, and I'll get a pillow for you. (*He goes into the bedroom.* ROBERT *looks at* RUTH *who shrinks away from him in terror.* ROBERT *smiles bitterly.* ANDREW *comes back with the pillow which he places behind* ROBERT'S *back.*) How's that?

ROBERT (*with an affectionate smile*). Fine! Thank you! (*As* ANDREW *sits down.*) Listen, Andy. You've asked me not to talk— and I won't after I've made my position clear. (*Slowly.*) In the first place I know I'm dying. (RUTH *bows her head and covers her face with her hands. She remains like this all during the scene between the two brothers.*)

ANDREW. Rob! That isn't so!

ROBERT (*wearily*). It *is* so! Don't lie to me. After Ruth put me to bed before you came, I saw it clearly for the first time. (*Bitterly.*) I'd been making plans for our future— Ruth's and mine—so it came hard at first —the realization. Then when the doctor examined me, I knew—although he tried to lie about it. And then to make sure I listened at the door to what he told you. So don't mock me with fairy tales about Arizona, or any such rot as that. Because I'm dying is no reason you should treat me as an imbecile or a coward. Now that I'm sure what's happening I can say Kismet to it with all my heart. It was only the silly uncertainty that hurt. (*There is a pause.* ANDREW *looks around in impotent anguish, not knowing what to say.* ROBERT *regards him with an affectionate smile.*)

ANDREW (*finally blurts out*). It isn't foolish. You *have* got a chance. If you heard all the Doctor said that ought to prove it to you.

ROBERT. Oh, you mean when he spoke of the miracle? (*Dryly.*) I don't believe in miracles—in my case. Besides, I know more than any doctor on earth *could* know —because I *feel* what's coming. (*Dismissing the subject.*) But we've agreed not to talk of it. Tell me about yourself, Andy. That's what I'm interested in. Your letters were too brief and far apart to be illuminating.

ANDREW. I meant to write oftener.

ROBERT (*with a trace of irony*). I judge from them you've accomplished all you set out to do five years ago?

ANDREW. That isn't much to boast of.

ROBERT (*surprised*). Have you really, honestly reached that conclusion?

ANDREW. Well, it doesn't seem to amount to much now.

ROBERT. But you're rich, aren't you?

ANDREW (*with a quick glance at* RUTH). Yes, I s'pose so.

ROBERT. I'm glad. You can do to the farm all I've undone. But what did you do down there? Tell me. You went in the grain business with that friend of yours?

ANDREW. Yes. After two years I had a share in it. I sold out last year. (*He is answering* ROBERT'S *questions with great reluctance.*)

ROBERT. And then?

ANDREW. I went in on my own.

ROBERT. Still in grain?

ANDREW. Yes.

ROBERT. What's the matter? You look as if I were accusing you of something.

ANDREW. I'm proud enough of the first four years. It's after that I'm not boasting of. I took to speculating.

ROBERT. In wheat?

ANDREW. Yes.

ROBERT. And you made money—gambling?

ANDREW. Yes.

ROBERT (*thoughtfully*). I've been wondering what the great change was in you. (*After a pause.*) You—a farmer—to gamble in a wheat pit with scraps of paper. There's a spiritual significance in that picture, Andy. (*He smiles bitterly.*) I'm a failure, and Ruth's another—but we can both justly lay some of the blame for our stumbling on God. But you're the deepest-dyed failure of the three, Andy. You've spent eight years running away from yourself. Do you see what I mean? You used to be a creator when you loved the farm. You and life were in harmonious partnership. And now— (*He stops as if seeking vainly for words.*) My brain is muddled. But part of what I mean is that your gambling with the thing you used to love to create proves how far astray— So you'll be punished. You'll have to suffer to win back— (*His*

voice grows weaker and he sighs wearily.)
It's no use. I can't say it. (*He lies back and closes his eyes, breathing pantingly.*)

ANDREW (*slowly*). I think I know what you're driving at, Rob—and it's true, I guess. (ROBERT *smiles gratefully and stretches out his hand, which* ANDREW *takes in his.*)

ROBERT. I want you to promise me to do one thing, Andy, after—

ANDREW. I'll promise anything, as God is my Judge!

ROBERT. Remember, Andy, Ruth has suffered double her share. (*His voice faltering with weakness.*) Only through contact with suffering, Andy, will you—awaken. Listen. You must marry Ruth—afterwards.

RUTH (*with a cry*). Rob! (ROBERT *lies back, his eyes closed, gasping heavily for breath.*)

ANDREW (*making signs to her to humor him—gently*). You're tired out, Rob. You better lie down and rest a while, don't you think? We can talk later on.

ROBERT (*with a mocking smile*). Later on! You always were an optimist, Andy! (*He sighs with exhaustion.*) Yes, I'll go and rest a while. (*As* ANDREW *comes to help him.*) It must be near sunrise, isn't it?

ANDREW. It's after six.

ROBERT (*as* ANDREW *helps him into the bedroom*). Shut the door, Andy. I want to be alone. (ANDREW *reappears and shuts the door softly. He comes and sits down on his chair again, supporting his head on his hands. His face is drawn with the intensity of his dry-eyed anguish.*)

RUTH (*glancing at him—fearfully*). He's out of his mind now, isn't he?

ANDREW. He may be a little delirious. The fever would do that. (*With impotent rage.*) God, what a shame! And there's nothing we can do but sit and—wait! (*He springs from his chair and walks to the stove.*)

RUTH (*dully*). He was talking—wild—like he used to—only this time it sounded —unnatural, don't you think?

ANDREW. I don't know. The things he said to me had truth in them—even if he did talk them way up in the air, like he always sees things. Still— (*He glances down at* RUTH *keenly.*) Why do you suppose he wanted us to promise we'd— (*Confusedly.*) You know what he said.

RUTH (*dully*). His mind was wandering, I s'pose.

ANDREW (*with conviction*). No—there was something back of it.

RUTH. He wanted to make sure I'd be all right—after he'd gone, I expect.

ANDREW. No, it wasn't that. He knows very well I'd naturally look after you without— anything like that.

RUTH. He might be thinking of—something happened five years back, the time you came home from the trip.

ANDREW. What happened? What do you mean?

RUTH (*dully*). We had a fight.

ANDREW. A fight? What has that to do with me?

RUTH. It was about you—in a way.

ANDREW (*amazed*). About *me?*

RUTH. Yes, mostly. You see I'd found out I'd made a mistake about Rob soon after we were married—when it was too late.

ANDREW. Mistake? (*Slowly.*) You mean— you found out you didn't love Rob?

RUTH. Yes.

ANDREW. Good God!

RUTH. And then I thought that when Mary came it'd be different, and I'd love him; but it didn't happen that way. And I couldn't bear with his blundering and book-reading—and I grew to hate him, almost.

ANDREW. Ruth!

RUTH. I couldn't help it. No woman could. It had to be because I loved someone else, I'd found out. (*She sighs wearily.*) It can't do no harm to tell you now—when it's all past and gone—and dead. *You* were the one I really loved—only I didn't come to the knowledge of it till too late.

ANDREW (*stunned*). Ruth! Do you know what you're saying?

RUTH. It was true—then. (*With sudden fierceness.*) How could I help it? No woman could.

ANDREW. Then—you loved me—that time I came home?

RUTH (*doggedly*). I'd known your real reason for leaving home the first time—everybody knew it—and for three years I'd been thinking—

ANDREW. That I loved you?

RUTH. Yes. Then that day on the hill you laughed about what a fool you'd been for loving me once—and I knew it was all over.

ANDREW. Good God, but I never thought— (*He stops, shuddering at his remembrance.*) And did Rob—

RUTH. That was what I'd started to tell. We'd had a fight just before you came and I got crazy mad—and I told him all I've told you.

ANDREW (*gaping at her speechlessly for a moment*). You told Rob—you loved me?

RUTH. Yes.

ANDREW (*shrinking away from her in horror*). You—you—you mad fool, you! How could you do such a thing?

RUTH. I couldn't help it. I'd got to the end of bearing things—without talking.

ANDREW. Then Rob must have known every moment I stayed here! And yet he never said or showed—God, how he must have suffered! Didn't you know how much he loved you?

RUTH (*dully*). Yes. I knew he liked me.

ANDREW. Liked you! What kind of a woman are you? Couldn't you have kept silent? Did you have to torture him? No wonder he's dying! And you've lived together for five years with this between you?

RUTH. We've lived in the same house.

ANDREW. Does he still think—

RUTH. I don't know. We've never spoke a word about it since that day. Maybe, from the way he went on, he s'poses I care for you yet.

ANDREW. But you don't. It's outrageous. It's stupid! You don't love me!

RUTH (*slowly*). I wouldn't know how to feel love, even if I tried, any more.

ANDREW (*brutally*). And I don't love you, that's sure! (*He sinks into his chair, his head between his hands.*) It's damnable such a thing should be between Rob and me. Why, I love Rob better'n anybody in the world and always did. There isn't a thing on God's green earth I wouldn't have done to keep trouble away from him. And I have to be the very one—it's damnable! How am I going to face him again? What can I say to him now? (*He groans with anguished rage. After a pause.*) He asked me to promise—what am I going to do?

RUTH. You can promise—so's it'll ease his mind—and not mean anything.

ANDREW. What? Lie to him now—when he's dying? (*Determinedly.*) No! It's *you* who'll have to do the lying, since it must be done. You've got a chance now to undo some of all the suffering you've brought on Rob. Go in to him! Tell him you never loved me—it was all a mistake. Tell him you only said so because you were mad and didn't know what you were saying! Tell him something, anything, that'll bring him peace!

RUTH (*dully*). He wouldn't believe me.

ANDREW (*furiously*). You've got to make him believe you, do you hear? You've got to—now—hurry—you never know when it may be too late. (*As she hesitates—imploringly.*) For God's sake, Ruth! Don't you see you owe it to him? You'll never forgive yourself if you don't.

RUTH (*dully*). I'll go. (*She gets wearily to her feet and walks slowly toward the bedroom.*) But it won't do any good. (AN-

DREW's *eyes are fixed on her anxiously. She opens the door and steps inside the room. She remains standing there for a minute. Then she calls in a frightened voice.*) Rob! Where are you? (*Then she hurries back, trembling with fright.*) Andy! Andy! He's gone!

ANDREW (*misunderstanding her—his face pale with dread*). He's not—

RUTH (*interrupting him—hysterically*). He's gone! The bed's empty. The window's wide open. He must have crawled out into the yard!

ANDREW (*springing to his feet. He rushes into the bedroom and returns immediately with an expression of alarmed amazement on his face.*) Come! He can't have gone far! (*Grabbing his hat he takes* RUTH's *arm and shoves her toward the door.*) Come on! (*Opening the door.*) Let's hope to God — (*The door closes behind them, cutting off his words as*

The Curtain Falls.

SCENE II

Same as Act One, Scene One—A section of country highway. The sky to the east is already alight with bright color and a thin, quivering line of flame is spreading slowly along the horizon rim of the dark hills. The roadside, however, is still steeped in the grayness of the dawn, shadowy and vague. The field in the foreground has a wild uncultivated appearance, as if it had been allowed to remain fallow the preceding summer. Parts of the snake-fence in the rear have been broken down. The apple tree is leafless and seems dead.

ROBERT *staggers weakly in from the left. He stumbles into the ditch and lies there for a moment; then crawls with a great effort to the top of the bank where he can see the sun rise, and collapses weakly.* RUTH *and* ANDREW *come hurriedly along the road from the left.*

ANDREW (*stopping and looking about him*). There he is! I knew it! I knew we'd find him here.

ROBERT (*trying to raise himself to a sitting position as they hasten to his side—with a wan smile*). I thought I'd given you the slip.

ANDREW (*with kindly bullying*). Well, you didn't, you old scoundrel, and we're going to take you right back where you belong —in bed. (*He makes a motion to lift* ROBERT.)

ROBERT. Don't, Andy. Don't, I tell you!

ANDREW. You're in pain?

ROBERT (*simply*). No. I'm dying. (*He falls back weakly.* RUTH *sinks down beside him with a sob and pillows his head on her lap.* ANDREW *stands looking down at him helplessly.* ROBERT *moves his head restlessly on* RUTH's *lap.*) I couldn't stand it back there in the room. It seemed as if all my life— I'd been cooped in a room. So I thought I'd try to end as I might have—if I'd had the courage—alone—in a ditch by the open road—watching the sun rise.

ANDREW. Rob! Don't talk. You're wasting your strength. Rest a while and then we'll carry you—

ROBERT. Still hoping, Andy? Don't. I know. (*There is a pause during which he breathes heavily, straining his eyes toward the horizon.*) The sun comes so slowly. (*With an ironical smile.*) The doctor told me to go to the far-off places—and I'd be cured. He was right. That was always the cure for me. It's too late—for this life—but — (*He has a fit of coughing which racks his body.*)

ANDREW (*with a hoarse sob*). Rob! (*He clenches his fists in an impotent rage against Fate.*) God! God! (RUTH *sobs brokenly and wipes* ROBERT's *lips with her handkerchief.*)

ROBERT (*in a voice which is suddenly ringing with the happiness of hope*). You mustn't feel sorry for me. Don't you see I'm happy at last—free—free!—freed from the farm—free to wander on and on —eternally! (*He raises himself on his elbow, his face radiant, and points to the horizon.*) Look! Isn't it beautiful beyond the hills? I can hear the old voices calling me to come— (*Exultantly.*) And this time I'm going! It isn't the end. It's a free beginning—the start of my voyage! I've won to my trip—the right of release—beyond the horizon! Oh, you ought to be glad—glad —for my sake! (*He collapses weakly.*) Andy! (ANDREW *bends down to him.*) Remember Ruth—

ANDREW. I'll take care of her, I swear to you, Rob!

ROBERT. Ruth has suffered—remember, Andy—only through sacrifice—the secret beyond there— (*He suddenly raises himself with his last remaining strength and points to the horizon where the edge of the sun's disc is rising from the rim of the hills.*) The sun! (*He remains with his eyes fixed on it for a moment. A rattling noise throbs from his throat. He mumbles.*) Remember! (*And falls back and is still.* RUTH *gives a cry of horror and springs to her feet, shuddering, her hands over her eyes.* ANDREW *bends on one knee beside the body,* placing a hand over ROBERT's heart, then he kisses his brother reverently on the forehead and stands up.*)

ANDREW (*facing* RUTH, *the body between them—in a dead voice*). He's dead. (*With a sudden burst of fury.*) God damn you, you never told him!

RUTH (*piteously*). He was so happy without my lying to him.

ANDREW (*pointing to the body—trembling with the violence of his rage*). This is your doing, you damn woman, you coward, you murderess!

RUTH (*sobbing*). Don't, Andy! I couldn't help it—and he knew how I'd suffered, too. He told you—to remember.

ANDREW (*stares at her for a moment, his rage ebbing away, an expression of deep pity gradually coming over his face. Then he glances down at his brother and speaks brokenly in a compassionate voice*). Forgive me, Ruth—for his sake—and I'll remember— (RUTH *lets her hands fall from her face and looks at him uncomprehendingly. He lifts his eyes to hers and forces out falteringly.*) I—you—we've both made a mess of things! We must try to help each other—and—in time—we'll come to know what's right— (*Desperately.*) And perhaps we— (*But* RUTH, *if she is aware of his words, gives no sign. She remains silent, gazing at him dully with the sad humility of exhaustion, her mind already sinking back into that spent calm beyond the further troubling of any hope.*)

The Curtain Falls.

Miss Lulu Bett

BY ZONA GALE

TO BROCK PEMBERTON
IN DEEP APPRECIATION OF HIS CREATIVE WORK
IN PRODUCING AND STAGING THIS PLAY

ZONA GALE

Zona Gale was born in Portage, Wisconsin, in 1874. She studied at the University of Wisconsin and received the B.L. degree in 1895, M.L. in 1899, and Litt.D. in 1929. At the age of seven Miss Gale herself printed, illustrated and bound in ribbons her first book of fiction and verse. After her graduation from the university she served two years on the staffs of Milwaukee newspapers, writing in her spare time. In 1901 she joined the staff of the New York *World*. Despite the fact that she was writing continually, her first story was not accepted until 1904. In 1906 her first novel, *Romance Island,* appeared.

Among her best-known short-story volumes are *Friendship Village, Friendship Village Love Stories, Neighborhood Stories, Peace in Friendship Village, Yellow Gentians and Blue, Bridal Pond* and *Old Fashioned Tales.* Her most important novels are *Birth, Miss Lulu Bett, Faint Perfume, Preface to a Life, Borgia,* and *Papa La Fleur. When I Was a Little Girl* and *Portage, Wisconsin and Other Essays* are reminiscences and impressions by Miss Gale, while *The Secret Way* is a book of verse.

Miss Gale served six years as a member of the Board of Regents of the University of Wisconsin. She is an honorary member of Phi Beta Kappa (Western Reserve) and was a member of Wisconsin's Free Library Commission from 1921 to 1933. In 1928 she was married to William Llywelyn Breese.

Zona Gale's plays are invested with the same distinctive qualities found in her fiction; indeed, her long plays are dramatizations of her best-known novels: *Miss Lulu Bett* from the novel of the same name, *Mister Pitt* from *Birth,* and *Faint Perfume* from the novel of the same name.

Produced by Brock Pemberton at the Belmont Theatre, New York, December 27, 1920, *Miss Lulu Bett* was awarded the Pulitzer Prize for 1920-1921.

CHARACTERS

DWIGHT DEACON

INA DEACON

DIANA DEACON

MONONA DEACON

NINIAN DEACON

LULU BETT

MRS. BETT

BOBBY LARKIN

MR. CORNISH

SCENES

ACT ONE

SCENE   I: The Deacon dining-room.

SCENE   II: The same. A week later.

ACT TWO

SCENE   I: Side porch of the Deacon house. Evening, a month
after Lulu's marriage.

SCENE   II: The same.

SCENE   III: The same. Evening, a week later.

ACT THREE

The same.

MISS LULU BETT

ACT ONE

SCENE I

THE DEACON DINING-ROOM: *Plain rose paper, oak sideboard, straight chairs, a soft old brown divan, table laid for supper. Large pictures of, say, "Paul and Virginia" and Abbott Thayer's "Motherhood." A door left leads to kitchen; a door right front leads to the passage and the "other" room. Back are two windows with lace curtains, revealing shrubbery or blossoming plants; and a shelf with a clock and a photograph of Ninian Deacon. Over the table is a gas burner in a glass globe. In the center of the table is a pink tulip in a pot. The stage is empty.*

(Enter MONONA. She tiptoes to the table, tastes a dish or two, hides a cooky in her frock; begins a terrible little chant on miscellaneous notes.)

(Enter DWIGHT DEACON.)

DWIGHT. What! You don't mean you're in time for supper, baby?

MONONA. I ain't a baby.

DWIGHT. Ain't. Ain't. Ain't.

MONONA. Well, I ain't.

DWIGHT. We shall have to take you in hand, mama and I. We shall-have-to-take-you in hand.

MONONA. I ain't such a bad girl.

DWIGHT. Ain't. Ain't. Ain't.
(Enter INA, Door R. E.)

INA. Dwightie! Have I kept you waiting?

DWIGHT. It's all right, my pet. Bear and forbear. Bear and forbear.

INA. Everything's on the table. I didn't hear Lulu call us, though. She's fearfully careless. And Dwight, she looks so bad—when there's company I hate to have her around. *(They seat themselves.)*

DWIGHT. My dear Ina, your sister is very different from you.

INA. Well, Lulu certainly is a trial. Come Monona.

DWIGHT. Live and let live, my dear. We have to overlook, you know. What have we on the festive board to-night?

INA. We have creamed salmon. On toast.

MONONA. I don't want any.

DWIGHT. *What's* this? *No* salmon?

MONONA. No.

INA. Oh now, pet! You liked it before.

MONONA. I don't want any.

DWIGHT. Just a little? A very little? What is this? Progeny will not eat?

INA. She can eat if she will eat. The trouble is, she will *not* take the time.

DWIGHT. She don't put her mind on her meals.

INA. Now, pettie, you must eat or you'll get sick.

MONONA. I don't want any.

INA. Well, pettie—then how would you like a nice egg?

MONONA. No.

INA. Some bread and milk?

MONONA. No.
(Enter LULU BETT. She carries a plate of muffins.)

INA. Lulu, Monona won't eat a thing. I should think you might think of something to fix for her.

109

LULU. Can't I make her a little milk toast?

MONONA. Yes!

INA. Well now, sister. Don't toast it too much. That last was too—and it's no use, she will *not* eat it if it's burned.

LULU. I won't burn it on purpose.

INA. Well, see that you don't . . . Lulu! Which milk are you going to take?

LULU. The bottle that sets in front, won't I?

INA. But that's yesterday's milk. No, take the fresh bottle from over back. Monona must be nourished.

LULU. But then the yesterday's'll sour and I can't make a custard pie—

DWIGHT. Kindly settle these domestic matters without bringing them to my attention at meal time. (*Observes the tulip.*) Flowers! Who's been having flowers sent in?

INA. Ask Lulu.

DWIGHT. Suitors?

LULU. It was a quarter. There'll be five flowers.

DWIGHT. You bought it?

LULU. Yes. Five flowers. That's a nickel apiece.

DWIGHT. Yet we give you a home on the supposition that you have no money to spend, even for the necessities.

INA. Well, but Dwightie. Lulu isn't strong enough to work. What's the use—

DWIGHT. The justice business and the dental profession do not warrant the purchase of spring flowers in my home.

INA. Well, but Dwightie—

DWIGHT. No more. Lulu meant no harm.

INA. The back bottle, Lulu. And be as quick as you can. Remember, the back bottle. She has a terrible will, hangs on to her own ideas, and hangs on—
(*Exit Lulu.*)

DWIGHT. Forbearance my pet, forbearance. Baked potatoes. That's good—that's good.

The baked potato contains more nourishment than potatoes prepared in any other way. Roasting retains it.

INA. That's what I always think.

DWIGHT. Where's your mother? Isn't she coming to supper?

INA. No. Tantrum.

DWIGHT. Oh ho, mama has a tantrum, eh? My dear Ina, your mother is getting old. She don't have as many clear-headed days as she did.

INA. Mama's mind is just as good as it ever was, sometimes.

DWIGHT. Hadn't I better call her up?

INA. You know how mama is.
(*Enter* LULU. *She takes flowerpot from table and throws it out the window. Exit* LULU.)

DWIGHT. I'd better see. (*Goes to door and opens it.*) Mother Bett! . . . Come and have some supper. . . . Looks to me Lulu's muffins go down pretty easy! Come on—I had something funny to tell you and Ina. . . . (*Returns.*) No use. She's got a tall one on to-night, evidently. What's the matter with her?

INA. Well, I told Lulu to put the creamed salmon on the new blue platter, and mama thought I ought to use the old deep dish.

DWIGHT. You reminded her that you are mistress here in your own home. But gently, I hope?

INA. Well—I reminded her. She said if I kept on using the best dishes I wouldn't have a cup left for my own wake.

DWIGHT. And my little puss insisted?

INA. Why of course. I wanted to have the table look nice for you, didn't I?

DWIGHT. My precious pussy.

INA. So then she walked off to her room. (MONONA *sings her terrible little chant.*) Quiet, pettie, quiet!

DWIGHT. Softly, softly *softly,* SOFTLY! . . . Well, here we are, aren't we? I tell you people don't know what living is if they don't belong in a little family circle.

INA. That's what I always think.

DWIGHT. Just coming home here and sort of settling down—it's worth more than a tonic at a dollar the bottle. Look at this room. See this table. Could anything be pleasanter?

INA. Monona! Now, it's all over both ruffles. And mama does try so hard. . . .

DWIGHT. My dear. Can't you put your mind on the occasion?

INA. Well, but Monona *is* so messy.

DWIGHT. Women can*not* generalize. (*Clock strikes half hour.*) Curious how that clock loses. It must be fully quarter to. It is quarter to! I'm pretty good at guessing time.

INA. I've often noticed that.

DWIGHT. That clock is a terrible trial. Last night it was only twenty-three after when the half hour struck.

INA. Twenty-one, I thought.

DWIGHT. Twenty-three. My dear Ina, didn't I particularly notice? It was twenty-three.

MONONA (*like lightning*). I want my milk toast, I want my milk toast, I want my milk toast.

INA. Do hurry, sister. She's going to get nervous.

(MONONA *chants her chant. Enter* LULU.)

LULU. I've got the toast here.

INA. Did you burn it?

LULU. Not black.

DWIGHT. There we are. Milk toast like a kuween. Where is our young lady daughter to-night?

INA. She's at Jenny Plows, at a teaparty.

DWIGHT. Oh ho, teaparty. Is it?

LULU. We told you that this noon.

DWIGHT (*frowning at* LULU). How much is salmon the can now, Ina?

INA. How much is it, Lulu?

LULU. The large ones are forty, that used to be twenty-five. And the small ones that were ten, they're twenty-five. The butter's about all gone. Shall I wait for the butter woman or get some creamery?

DWIGHT. Not at meal time, if you please, Lulu. The conversation at my table must not deal with domestic matters.

LULU. I suppose salmon made me think of butter.

DWIGHT. There is not the remotest connection. Salmon comes from a river. Butter comes from a cow. A cow bears no relation to a river. A cow may drink from a river, she may do that, but I doubt if that was in your mind when you spoke—you're not that subtle.

LULU. No, that wasn't in my mind. (*Enter* MOTHER BETT.)

DWIGHT. Well, Mama Bett, hungry now?

MRS. BETT. No, I'm not hungry.

INA. We put a potato in the oven for you, mama.

MRS. BETT. No, I thank you.

DWIGHT. And a muffin, Mama Bett.

MRS. BETT. No, I thank you.

LULU. Mama, can't I fix you some fresh tea?

MRS. BETT. That's right, Lulie. You're a good girl. And see that you put in enough tea so as a body can taste tea part of the way down.

INA. Sit here with us, mama.

MRS. BETT. No, I thank you. I'll stand and keep my figger.

DWIGHT. You know you look like a queen when you stand up, straight back, high head, a regular wonder for your years, you are.

MRS. BETT. Sometimes I think you try to flatter me. (*Sits.*)
(*Doorbell.*)

MONONA. I'll go. I'll go. Let me go.

DWIGHT. Now what can anybody be thinking of to call just at meal time. Can't I even have a quiet supper with my family without the outside world clamoring?

LULU. Maybe that's the butter woman.

DWIGHT. Lulu, no more about the butter, please.

MONONA. Come on in. Here's Bobby to see you, papa, let's feed him.

DWIGHT. Oh ho! So I'm the favored one. Then draw up to the festive board, Robert. A baked potato?

BOBBY. No, sir. I—I wanted something else.

DWIGHT. What's this? Came to see the justice about getting married, did you? Or the dentist to have your tooth pulled—eh? Same thing—eh, Ina? Ha! ha! ha!

BOBBY. I—I wondered whether—I thought if you would give me a job. . . .

DWIGHT. So that's it.

BOBBY. I thought maybe I might cut the grass or cut—cut something.

DWIGHT. My boy, every man should cut his own grass. Every man should come home at night, throw off his coat and, in his vigor, cut his own grass.

BOBBY. Yes, sir.

DWIGHT. Exercise, exercise is next to bread—next to gluten. Hold on, though—hold on. After dental hours I want to begin presently to work my garden. I have two lots. Property is a burden. Suppose you cut the grass on the one lot through the spring.

BOBBY. Good enough, sir. Can I start right in now? It isn't dark yet.

DWIGHT. That's right, that's right. Energy—it's the driving power of the nation. (*They rise,* DWIGHT *goes toward the door with* BOBBY.) Start right in, by all means. You'll find the mower in the shed, oiled and ready. Tools always ready—that's my motto, my boy. (*Enter* DI *and* CORNISH. CORNISH *carries many favors.*) Ah ha!

DI. Where is everybody? Oh, hullo, Bobby! You came to see me?

BOBBY. Oh, hullo! No. I came to see your father.

DI. Did you? Well, there he is. Look at him.

BOBBY. You don't need to tell me where to look or what to do. Good-by. I'll find the mower, Mr. Deacon. (*Exit.*)

DWIGHT. Mama! What do you s'pose? Di thought she had a beau— How are you, Cornish?

DI. Oh, papa! Why, I just hate Bobby Larkin, and the whole school knows it. Mama, wasn't Mr. Cornish nice to help carry my favors?

INA. Ah, Mr. Cornish! You see what a popular little girl we have.

CORNISH. Yes, I suppose so. That is—isn't that remarkable, Mrs. Deacon? (*He tries to greet* LULU, *who is clearing the table.*)

DI. Oh, papa, the sweetest party—and the dearest supper and the darlingest decorations and the georgeousest— Monona, let go of me!

DWIGHT. Children, children, can't we have peace in this house?

MONONA. Ah, you'll catch it for talking so smarty.

DI. Oh, will I?

INA. Monona, don't stand listening to older people. Run around and play. (MONONA *runs a swift circle and returns to her attitude of listener.*)

CORNISH. Pardon me—this is Miss Bett, isn't it?

LULU. I—Lulu Bett, yes.

CORNISH. I had the pleasure of meeting you the night I was here for supper.

LULU. I didn't think you'd remember.

CORNISH. Don't you think I'd remember that meat pie?

LULU. Oh, yes. The meat pie. You might remember the meat pie. (*Exit, carrying plates.*)

CORNISH. What in the dickens did I say that for?

INA. Oh, Lulu likes it. She's a wonderful cook. I don't know what we should do without her.

DWIGHT. A most exemplary woman is Lulu.

INA. That's eggsemplary, Dwightie.

DWIGHT. My darling little dictionary.

DI. Mama, Mr. Cornish and I have promised to go back to help Jenny.

INA. How nice! And Mr. Cornish, do let us see you oftener.

DWIGHT. Yes, yes, Cornish. Drop in. Any time, you know.

CORNISH. I'll be glad to come. I do get pretty lonesome evenings. (*Enter* LULU, *clearing table.*) I eat out around. I guess that's why your cooking made such an impression on me, Miss Lulu.

LULU. Yes. Yes. I s'pose it would take something like that. . . .

CORNISH. Oh, no, no! I didn't mean—you mustn't think I meant— What'd I say that for?

LULU. Don't mind. They always say that to me. (*Exit with dishes.*)

DI. Come on, Mr. Cornish. Jenny'll be waiting. Monona, let *go* of me!

MONONA. *I* don't want you!

DWIGHT. Early, darling, early! Get her back here early, Mr. Cornish.

CORNISH. Oh, I'll have her back here as soon as ever she'll come—well, ah—I mean. . . .

DI. Good-by Dwight and Ina! (*Exit* DI *and* CORNISH.)

DWIGHT. Nice fellow, nice fellow. Don't know whether he'll make a go of his piano store, but he's studying law evenings.

INA. But we don't know anything about him, Dwight. A stranger so.

DWIGHT. On the contrary I know a great deal about him. I know that he has a little inheritance coming to him.

INA. An inheritance—really? I *thought* he was from a good family.

DWIGHT. My mercenary little pussy.

INA. Well, if he comes here so very much you know what we may expect.

DWIGHT. What may we expect?

INA. He'll fall in love with Di. And a young girl is awfully flattered when a good-looking older man pays her attention. Haven't you noticed that?

DWIGHT. How women generalize! My dear Ina, I have other matters to notice.

INA. Monona. Stop listening! Run about and play. (MONONA *runs her circle and returns.*) Well, look at that clock. It's almost your bedtime, anyway. (*Enter* LULU.)

MONONA. No.

INA. It certainly is.

MONONA. That clock's wrong. Papa said so.

INA. Mama says bedtime. In ten minutes.

MONONA. I won't go all night.

DWIGHT. Daughter, daughter, daughter. . . .

MONONA. I won't go for a week. (DWIGHT *sees on clock shelf a letter.*)

INA. Oh, Dwight! It came this morning. I forgot.

LULU. I forgot too. And I laid it up there.

DWIGHT. Isn't it understood that my mail can't wait like this?

LULU. I know. I'm sorry. But you hardly ever get a letter.

DWIGHT. Of course pressing matters go to my office. Still my mail should have more careful— (*He reads.*) Now! What do you think I have to tell you?

INA. Oh, Dwightie! Something nice?

DWIGHT. That depends. I'll like it. So'll Lulu. It's company.

MONONA. I hope they bring me something decent.

INA. Oh, Dwight, who?

DWIGHT. My brother, from Oregon.

INA. Ninian coming here?

DWIGHT. Some day next week. He don't know what a charmer Lulu is or he'd come quicker.

INA. Dwight, it's been years since you've seen him.

DWIGHT. Nineteen — twenty. Must be twenty.

INA. And he's never seen me.

DWIGHT. Nor Lulu.

INA. And think where he's been. South America—Mexico—Panama and all. We must put it in the paper.

MRS. BETT. Who's coming? Why don't you say who's coming? You all act so dumb.

LULU. It's Dwight's brother, mother. His brother from Oregon.

MRS. BETT. Never heard of him.

LULU (taking photograph from shelf). That one, mother. You've dusted his picture lots of times.

MRS. BETT. That? Got to have him around long?

DWIGHT. I don't know. Wait till he sees Lulu. I expect when he sees Lulu you can't drive him away. He's going to take one look at Lulu and settle down here for life. He's going to think Lulu is—

LULU. I—think the tea must be steeped now. (Exit.)

DWIGHT. He's going to think Lulu is a stunner—a stunner. . . . (The clock strikes. MONONA shrieks.) Is the progeny hurt?

INA. Bedtime. Now, Monona, be mama's nice little lady. . . . Monona, quiet, pettie, quiet. . . . (LULU enters with tea and toast.) Lulu, won't you take her to bed? You know Dwight and I are going to Study Club.

LULU. There, mother. Yes, I'll take her to bed. Come, Monona. And stop that noise instantly. (MONONA stops. As they cross DWIGHT spies the tulip on LULU's gown.)

DWIGHT. Lulu. One moment. You picked the flower on the plant.

LULU. Yes. I—picked it.

DWIGHT. She buys a hothouse plant and then ruins it!

LULU. I—I— (She draws MONONA swiftly left; exeunt; the door slams.)

DWIGHT. What a pity Lulu hasn't your manners, pettie.

MRS. BETT. What do you care? She's got yours.

DWIGHT. Mother Bett! Fare thee well.

MRS. BETT. How do you stand him? The lump!

INA. Mama dear, now drink your tea. Good-night, sweetie.

MRS. BETT. You needn't think I forgot about the platter, because I ain't. Of all the extravagant doin's, courtin' the poorhouse— (Exeunt DWIGHT and INA. MRS BETT continues to look after them, her lips moving. At door appears BOBBY.)

BOBBY. Where's Mr. Deacon?

MRS. BETT. Gone, thank the Lord!

BOBBY. I've got the grass cut.

MRS. BETT. You act like it was a trick.

BOBBY. Is—is everybody gone?

MRS. BETT. Who's this you're talkin' to?

BOBBY. Yes, well, I meant—I guess I'll go now. (Enter DI.)

DI. Well, Bobby Larkin. Are you cutting grass in the dining room?

BOBBY. No, ma'am, I was not cutting grass in the dining room.
(Enter LULU, collects her mother's dishes, folds cloth and watches.)

DI. I used to think you were pretty nice, but I don't like you any more.

BOBBY. Yes you used to! Is that why you made fun of me all the time?

DI. I had to. They all were teasing me about you.

BOBBY. They were? Teasing you about me?

DI. I had to make them stop so I teased you. I never wanted to.

BOBBY. Well, I never thought it was anything like that.

DI. Of course you didn't. I—wanted to tell you.

BOBBY. You wanted—

DI. Of course I did. You must go now—they're hearing us.

BOBBY. Say—

DI. Good-night. Go the back way, Bobby—you nice thing. (*Exit* BOBBY.) Aunt Lulu, give me the cookies, please, and the apples. Mr. Cornish is on the front porch . . . mama and papa won't be home till late, will they?

LULU. I don't think so.

DI. Well, I'll see to the hall light. Don't you bother. Good-night.

LULU. Good-night, Di. (*Exit* DI.)

MRS. BETT. My land! How she wiggles and chitters.

LULU. Mother, could you hear them? Di and Bobby Larkin?

MRS. BETT. Mother hears a-plenty.

LULU. How easy she done it . . . got him right over . . . how did she do that?

MRS. BETT. Di wiggles and chitters.

LULU. It was just the other day I taught her to sew . . . I wonder if Ina knows.

MRS. BETT. What's the use of you findin' fault with Inie? Where'd you been if she hadn't married I'd like to know? . . . What say? . . . eh? . . . I'm goin' to bed. . . . You always was jealous of Inie. (*Exit* MRS. BETT.)

(LULU *crosses to shelf, takes down photograph of* NINIAN DEACON, *holds it, looks at it.*)

Curtain.

SCENE II

SAME SET. *Late afternoon. A week later. The table is cleared of dishes, and has an oilcloth cover.* BOBBY *is discovered outside the window, on whose sill* DI *is sitting.*

BOBBY. So you despise me for cutting grass?

DI. No, I don't. But if you're going to be a great man why don't you get started at it?

BOBBY. I am started at it—inside. But it don't earn me a cent yet.

DI. Bobby, Bobby! I know you're great now, don't you ever think I don't, but I want everybody else to know.

BOBBY. Di, when you said that it sounded just like a—a you know.

DI. Like what?

BOBBY. Like a wife. Gee, what a word that is!

DI. Isn't it? It's ever so much more exciting word than husband.
(*Enter* LULU, *followed by* MONONA. LULU *carries bowl, pan of apples, paring knife.* MONONA *carries basket of apples and a towel. As* LULU *rattles dishes,* DI *turns, sees* LULU. BOBBY *disappears from window.*)

DI. There's never any privacy in this house. (*Exit* DI.)

LULU. Hurry, Monona, I must make the pies before I get dinner. Now wipe every one.

MONONA. What for?

LULU. To make the pies.

MONONA. What do you want to make pies for?

LULU. To eat.

MONONA. What do you want to eat for?

LULU. To grow strong—and even sensible.

MONONA. It's no fun asking you a string of questions. You never get mad. Mama gets good and mad. So does papa.

LULU. Then why do you ask them questions?

MONONA. Oh, I like to get them going.

LULU. Monona!

MONONA. I told mama I didn't pass, just so I could hear her.

LULU. Why, Monona!

MONONA. Then when I told her I did pass, she did it again. When she's mad she makes awful funny faces.

LULU. You love her, don't you, Monona?

MONONA. I love her best when there's company. If there was always company, I'd always love her. Isn't she sweet before Uncle Ninian though?

LULU. I—I don't know. Monona, you mustn't talk so.

MONONA. He's been here a week and mama hasn't been cross once. Want to know what he said about you?

LULU. I—did he—did he say anything about me?

MONONA. He told papa you were the best cook he'd ever ate. Said he'd et a good many.

LULU. The cooking. It's always the cooking.

MONONA. He said some more, but I can't remember.

LULU. Monona, what else did he say?

MONONA. I don't know.

LULU. Try. . . .

MONONA. Here he is now. Ask him to his face. Hullo, Uncle Ninian! Good-by. (*Exit* MONONA. *Enter* NINIAN.)

NINIAN. Hello, kitten! Ask him what! What do you want to ask him?

LULU. I—I think I was wondering what kind of pies you like best.

NINIAN. That's easy. I like your kind of pies best. The best ever. Every day since I've been here I've seen you baking, Mrs. Bett.

LULU. Yes, I bake. What did you call me then?

NINIAN. Mrs. Bett—isn't it? Every one says just Lulu, but I took it for granted. . . . Well, now—is it Mrs. or Miss Lulu Bett?

LULU. It's Miss. . . . From choice.

NINIAN. You bet! Oh, you bet! Never doubted that.

LULU. What kind of a Mr. are you?

NINIAN. Never give myself away. Say, by George, I never thought of that before. There's no telling whether a man's married or not, by his name.

LULU. It doesn't matter.

NINIAN. Why?

LULU. Not so many people want to know.

NINIAN. Say, you're pretty good, aren't you?

LULU. If I am it never took me very far.

NINIAN. Where you been mostly?

LULU. Here. I've always been here. Fifteen years with Ina. Before that we lived in the country.

NINIAN. Never been anywhere much?

LULU. Never been anywhere at all.

NINIAN. H . . . m. Well, I want to tell you something about yourself.

LULU. About me?

NINIAN. Something that I'll bet you don't even know. It's this: I think you have it pretty hard around here.

LULU. Oh, no!

NINIAN. See here. Do you have to work like this all the time? I guess you won't mind my asking.

LULU. But I ought to work. I have a home with them. Mother too.

NINIAN. But glory! You ought to have some kind of a life of your own.

LULU. How could I do that?

NINIAN. A man don't even know what he's like till he's roamed around on his own. . . . Roamed around on his own. Course a woman don't understand that.

LULU. Why don't she? Why don't she?

NINIAN. Do you? (LULU *nods.*) I've had twenty-five years of galloping about—Brazil, Mexico, Panama.

LULU. My!

NINIAN. It's the life.

LULU. Must be. I—

NINIAN. Yes, you. Why, you've never had a thing! I guess you don't know how it seems to me, coming along—a stranger so. I don't like it.

LULU. They're very good to me.

NINIAN. Do you know why you think that? Because you've never had anybody really good to you. That's why.

LULU. But they treat me good.

NINIAN. They make a slavey of you. Regular slavey. Damned shame *I* call it.

LULU. But we have our whole living—

NINIAN. And you earn it. I been watching you ever since I've been here. Don't you ever go anywhere?

LULU. Oh, no, I don't go anywhere. I—

NINIAN. Lord! Don't you want to? Of course you do.

LULU. Of course I'd like to get clear away—or I used to want to.

NINIAN. Say—you've been a blamed fine-looking woman.

LULU. You must have been a good-looking man once yourself.

NINIAN. You're pretty good. I don't see how you do it—darned if I do.

LULU. How I do what?

NINIAN. Why come back, quick like that, with what you say. You don't look it.

LULU. It must be my grand education.

NINIAN. Education: I ain't never had it and I ain't never missed it.

LULU. Most folks are happy without an education.

NINIAN. You're not very happy, though.

LULU. Oh, no.

NINIAN. Well you ought to get up and get out of here—find—find some work you *like* to do.

LULU. But, you see, I can't do any other work—that's the trouble—women like me can't do any other work.

NINIAN. But you make this whole house go round.

LULU. If I do, nobody knows it.

NINIAN. I know it. I hadn't been in the house twenty-four hours till I knew it.

LULU. You did? You thought that. . . . Yes, well if I do I hate making it go round.

NINIAN. See here—couldn't you tell me a little bit about—what you'd *like* to do? If you had your own way?

LULU. I don't know—now.

NINIAN. What did you ever think you'd like to do?

LULU. Take care of folks that needed me. I—I mean sick folks or old folks or—like that. Take *care* of them. Have them—have them want me.

NINIAN. By George! You're a wonder.

LULU. Am I? Ask Dwight.

NINIAN. Dwight. I could knock the top of his head off the way he speaks to you. I'd like to see you get out of this, I certainly would.

LULU. I can't get out. I'll never get out—now.

NINIAN. Don't keep saying "now" like that. You—you put me out of business, darned if you don't.

LULU. Oh, I don't mean to feel sorry for myself—you stop making me feel sorry for myself!

NINIAN. I know one thing—I'm going to give Dwight Deacon a chunk of my mind.

LULU. Oh, no! no! no! I wouldn't want you to do that. Thank you.

NINIAN. Well, somebody ought to do something. See here—while I'm staying around you know you've got a friend in me, don't you?

LULU. Do I?

NINIAN. You bet you do.

LULU. Not just my cooking?

NINIAN. Oh, come now—why, I liked you the first moment I saw you.

LULU. Honest?

NINIAN. Go on—go on. Did you like me?

LULU. Now you're just being polite.

NINIAN. Say, I wish there was some way—

LULU. Don't you bother about me.

NINIAN. I wish there was some way—(MO-NONA's *voice chants*.) (*Enter* MONONA.)

MONONA. You've had him long enough, Aunt Lulu—Can't you pay me some 'tention?

NINIAN. Come here. Give us a kiss. My stars, what a great big tall girl! Have to put a board on her head to stop this growing.

MONONA (*Seeing diamond*). What's that?

NINIAN. That diamond came from Santa Claus. He has a jewelry shop in heaven. I have twenty others like this one. I keep the others to wear on the Sundays when the sun comes up in the west.

MONONA. Does the sun ever come up in the west?

NINIAN. Sure—on my honor. Some day I'm going to melt a diamond and eat it. Then you sparkle all over in the dark, ever after. I'm going to plant one too, some day. Then you can grow a diamond vine. Yes, on my honor.

LULU. Don't do that— don't do that.

NINIAN. What?

LULU. To her. That's lying.

NINIAN. Oh, no. That's not lying. That's just drama. Drama. Do you like going to a good show?

LULU. I've never been to any—only those that come here.

NINIAN. Think of that now. Don't you ever go to the city?

LULU. I haven't been in six years and over.

NINIAN. Well, sir, I'll tell you what I'm going to do with you. While I'm here I'm going to take you and Ina and Dwight up to the city, to see a show.

LULU. Oh, you don't want me to go.

NINIAN. Yes, sir. I'll give you one good time. Dinner and a show.

LULU. Ina and Dwight do that sometimes. I can't imagine me.

NINIAN. Well, you're coming with me. I'll look up something good. And you tell me just what you like to eat and we'll order it—

LULU. It's been years since I've eaten anything that I haven't cooked myself.

NINIAN. It has. Say, by George! why shouldn't we go to the city *to-night*.

LULU. To-night?

NINIAN. Yes. If Dwight and Ina will. It's early yet. What do you say?

LULU. You sure you want me to go? Why —I don't know whether I've got anything I could wear.

NINIAN. Sure you have.

LULU. I—yes, I have. I could wear the waist I always thought they'd use—if I died.

NINIAN. Sure you could wear that. Just the thing. And throw some things in a bag—it'll be too late to come back to-night. Now don't you back out. . . .

LULU. Oh, the pies—

NINIAN. Forget the pies—well, no, I wouldn't say that. But hustle them up.

LULU. Oh, maybe Ina wont go. . . .

NINIAN. Leave Ina to me. (*Exit* NINIAN.)

LULU. Mother, mother! Monona, put the rest of those apples back in the basket and carry them out.

MONONA. Yes, Aunt Lulu.

LULU. I can't get ready. They'll leave me behind. Mother! Hurry, Monona. We must-n't leave such a looking house. Mother! Monona, don't you drop those apples. (MO-NONA *drops them all.*) My heavens, my pies aren't in the oven yet. (*Enter* MRS. BETT.)

MRS. BETT. Who wants their mother?

LULU. Mother, please pick up these things for me—quick.

MRS. BETT (*leisurely*). What is the rush, Lulie?

LULU. Mother, Mr. Deacon—Ninian, you know—wants Ina and Dwight and me to go to the theater to-night in the city.

MRS. BETT. Does, does he? Well, you mind me, Lulie, and go on. It'll do you good.

LULU. Yes, mother. I will. (*Exit with pies.*)

MRS. BETT. No need breaking everybody's neck off, though, as I know of. Monona, get out from under my feet.

MONONA. Grandma, compared between what I am, you are nothing.

MRS. BETT. What do you mean—little ape?

MONONA. It's no fun to get you going. You're too easy, grandma dear! (*Exit. En-ter* NINIAN.)

NINIAN. All right—Dwight and Ina are game. Oh, Mrs. Bett! Won't you come to the theater with us to-night?

MRS. BETT. No. I'm fooled enough without fooling myself on purpose. But Lulie can go.

NINIAN. You don't let her go too much, do you, Mrs. Bett?

MRS. BETT. Well, I ain't never let her go to the altar if that's what you mean.

NINIAN. Don't you think she'd be better off?

MRS. BETT. Wouldn't make much difference. Why look at me. A husband, six children, four of 'em under the sod with him. And sometimes I feel as though nothin' more had happened to me than has happened to Lulie. It's all gone. For me just the same as for her. Only she ain't had the pain. (*Yawns.*) What was I talkin' about just then?

NINIAN. Why—why—er, we were talking about going to the theater.

MRS. BETT. Going to the theater, are you? (*Enter* LULU.)

NINIAN. It's all right, Miss Lulu. They'll go—both of them. Dwight is telephoning for the seats.

LULU. I was wondering why you should be so kind to me.

NINIAN. Kind? Why, this is for my own pleasure, Miss Lulu. That's what I think of mostly.

LULU. But just see. It's so wonderful. Half an hour ago I never thought I'd be going to the city now—with you all. . . .

NINIAN. I'm an impulsive cuss you'll find, Miss Lulu.

LULU. But this is so wonderful. . . . (*Enter* INA.) Ina, isn't it beautiful that we're go-ing?

INA. Oh, are you going?

NINIAN. Of course she's going. Great snakes, why not?

INA. Only that Lulu never goes anywhere.

NINIAN. Whose fault is that?

LULU. Just habit. Pure habit.

NINIAN. Pure cussedness somewhere. Miss Lulu, now you go and get ready and Ina and I'll finish straightening up here.

LULU. Oh, I'll finish.

NINIAN. Go and get ready. I want to see that waist.

LULU. Oh, but I don't need to go yet—

NINIAN. Ina, you tell her to go—

INA. Well, but Lulu, you aren't going to bother to change your dress, are you? You can slip something on over.

LULU. If you think this would do—

NINIAN. It will not do. Not for my party! (*Shuts the door upon her.*)

INA. How in the world did you ever get Lulu to go, Ninian? *We* never did.

NINIAN. It was very simple. I invited her.

INA. Oh, you mean—

NINIAN. I invited her. (*Doorbell rings.*) Shall I answer it?

INA. Will you, please? (*Exit* NINIAN.) Mother, have you seen Di anywhere?

MRS. BETT. I ain't done nothing but see her. (*Motions to window.*)

INA (*At window*). Forevermore. That Larkin boy again. Di! Diana Deacon! Come here at once.

DI's VOICE. Yes, mama. (*At window.*) Want me?

INA. I want you to stop making a spectacle of *me* before the neighborhood.

DI. Of *you!*

INA. Certainly. What will people think of me if they see you talking with Robert Larkin the whole afternoon?

DI. We weren't thinking about you, mummy.

INA. No. You never do think about me. Nobody thinks about me. And mama does try so hard—

DI. Oh, mama, I've heard you say that fifty hundred times.

INA. And what impression does it make? None. . . . Nobody listens to me. Nobody. (*Enter* NINIAN *and* CORNISH.)

NINIAN. All right to bring him in here?

INA. Oh, Mr. Cornish! how very nice to see you.

CORNISH. Good afternoon, Mrs. Deacon. How are you, Miss Di?

NINIAN. I've just been asking Mr. Cornish if he won't join us to-night for dinner and the show.

INA. Oh, Mr. Cornish, do—we'd be so glad.

CORNISH. Why, why, if that wouldn't be—

NINIAN. You're invited, Di, you know.

DI. Me? Oh, how heavenly! Oh, but I've an engagement with Bobby—

INA. But I'm sure you'd break that to go with Uncle Ninian and Mr. Cornish.

DI. Well, I'd break it to go to the theater—

INA. Why, Di Deacon!

DI. Oh, of course to go with Uncle Ninian and Mr. Cornish.

CORNISH. This is awfully good of you. I dropped in because I got so lonesome I didn't know what else to do—that is, I mean. . . .

NINIAN. We get it. We get it.

INA. We'd love to see you any time, Mr. Cornish. Now if you'll excuse Di and me one minute.

DI. Uncle Ninian, you're a lamb. (*Exeunt* DI *and* INA.)

MRS. BETT. I'm just about the same as I was.

CORNISH. What—er—oh, Mrs. Bett, I didn't see you.

MRS. BETT. I don't complain. But it wouldn't turn my head if some of you spoke to me once in a while. Say—can you tell me what these folks are up to?

CORNISH. Up to . . . up to?

MRS. BETT. Yes. They're all stepping round here, up to something. I don't know what.

NINIAN. Why, Mrs. Bett, we're going to the city to the theater, you know.

MRS. BETT. Well, why didn't you say so? (*Enter* DWIGHT.)

DWIGHT. Ha! Everybody ready? Well, well, well, well. How are you, Cornish? You going too, Ina says.

CORNISH. Yes, I thought I might as well. I mean—

DWIGHT. That's right, that's right. Mama Bett. Look here!

MRS. BETT. What's that?

DWIGHT. *Ice* cream—it's *ice* cream. Who is it sits home and has *ice* cream put in her lap like a ku-ween?

MRS. BETT. Vanilly or chocolate?

DWIGHT. Chocolate, Mama Bett.

MRS. BETT. Vanilly sets better. . . . I'll put it in the ice chest—I *may* eat it. (*Takes spoon from sideboard. Exit.* CORNISH *goes with her.*)

DWIGHT. Where's the lovely Lulu?

NINIAN. She'll be here directly.

DWIGHT. Now what I want to know, Nin, is how you've hypnotized the lovely Lulu into this thing.

NINIAN. Into going? Dwight, I'll tell you about that. I asked her to go with us. Do you get it? I invited the woman.

DWIGHT. Ah, but with a way—with a way. She's never been anywhere like this with us. . . . Well, Nin, how does it seem to see me settled down into a respectable married citizen in my own town—eh?

NINIAN. Oh—you seem just like yourself.

DWIGHT. Yes, yes. I don't change much. Don't feel a day older than I ever did.

NINIAN. And you don't act it.

DWIGHT. Eh, you wouldn't think it to look at us, but our aunt had her hands pretty full bringing us up. Nin, we must certainly run up state and see Aunt Mollie while you're here. She isn't very well.

NINIAN. I don't know whether I'll have time or not.

DWIGHT. Nin, I love that woman. She's an angel. When I think of her I feel—I give you my word—I feel like somebody else. (*Enter* MRS. BETT *and* CORNISH.)

NINIAN. Nice old lady.

MRS. BETT. Who's a nice old lady?

DWIGHT. You, Mama Bett! Who else but you—eh? Well, now, Nin, what about you. You've been saying mighty little about yourself. What's been happening to you, anyway?—

NINIAN. That's the question.

DWIGHT. Traveling mostly—eh?

NINIAN. Yes, traveling mostly.

DWIGHT. I thought Ina and I might get over to the other side this year, but I guess not—I guess not.

MRS. BETT. Pity not to have went while the going was good.

DWIGHT. What's that, Mama Bett? (*Enter* LULU.) Ah, the lovely Lulu. She comes, she comes! My word what a costoom. And a *coiffure*.

LULU. Thank you. How do you do, Mr. Cornish?

CORNISH. How do you do, Miss Lulu? You see they're taking me along too.

LULU. That's nice. But, Mr. Deacon, I'm afraid I can't go after all. I haven't any gloves.

NINIAN. No backing out now.

DWIGHT. Can't you wear some old gloves of Ina's?

LULU. No, no. Ina's gloves are too fat for me—I mean too—mother, how does this hat look?

MRS. BETT. You'd ought to know how it looks, Lulie. You've had it on your head for ten years, hand-running.

LULU. And I haven't any theater cape. I couldn't go with my jacket and no gloves, could I?

DWIGHT. Now why need a charmer like you care about clothes!

LULU. I wouldn't want you gentlemen to be ashamed of me.

CORNISH. Why, Miss Lulu, you look real neat.

MRS. BETT. Act as good as you look, Lulie. You mind me and go on. (*Enter* INA.)

DWIGHT. Ha! All ready with our hat on! For a wonder, all ready with our hat on.

INA. That isn't really necessary, Dwight.

LULU. Ina, I wondered—I thought about your linen duster. Would it hurt if I wore that?

DWIGHT. The new one?

LULU. Oh no, no. The old one.

INA. Why take it, Lulu, yes, certainly. Get it, Dwightie, there in the hall. (DWIGHT *goes.*)

CORNISH. Miss Lulu, with all the solid virtues you've got, you don't need to think for a moment of how you look.

LULU. Now you're remembering the meat pie again, aren't you? (*Enter* DWIGHT.)

DWIGHT. Now! The festive opera cloak. Allow me! My word, what a picture! Lulu the charmer dressed for her deboo into society, eh?

NINIAN. Dwight, shut your head. I want you to understand this is Miss Lulu Bett's party—and if she says to leave you home, we'll do it.

DWIGHT. Ah, ha! An understanding between these two.

CORNISH. Well, Miss Lulu, *I* think you're just fine anyway.

LULU. Oh, thank you. Thank you. . . . (*Enter* DI.)

INA. All ready, darling?

DI. All ready—and so excited! Isn't it exciting, Mr. Cornish?

DWIGHT. Bless me if the whole family isn't assembled. Now isn't this pleasant! Ten—

let me see—twelve minutes before we need set out. Then the city and dinner—not just Lulu's cooking, but dinner! By a chef.

INA. That's sheff, Dwightie. Not cheff.

DWIGHT (*indicating* INA). Little crusty tonight. Pettie, your hat's just a little mite—no, over the other way.

INA. Was there anything to prevent your speaking of that before?

LULU. Ina, that hat's ever so much prettier than the old one.

INA. I never saw anything the matter with the old one.

DWIGHT. She'll be all right when we get started—out among the bright lights. Adventure—adventure is what the woman wants. I'm too tame for her.

INA. Idiot. (*Back at window,* BOBBY LARKIN *appears.* DI *slips across to him.*)

MRS. BETT. I s'pose you all think I like being left sitting here stark alone?

NINIAN. Why, Mrs. Bett—

INA. Why, mama—

LULU. Oh, mother, I'll stay with you.

DWIGHT. Oh, look here, if she really minds staying alone I'll stay with her.

MRS. BETT. Where you going anyway?

LULU. The theater, mama.

MRS. BETT. First I've heard of it. (MONONA *is heard chanting.*)

INA. You'll have Monona with you, mama. (MRS. BETT *utters one note of laughter, thin and high.*) (*Enter* MONONA.)

MONONA. Where you going?

INA. The city, dear. (MONONA *cries.*) Now quiet, pettie, quiet—

MONONA. You've all got to bring me something. And I'm going to sit up and eat it, too.

MRS. BETT. Come here, you poor, neglected child. (*Throughout the following scene* MRS. BETT *is absorbed with* MONONA, *and* DI *with* BOBBY.)

DWIGHT. What's Lulu the charmer so still for, eh?

LULU. I was thinking how nice it is to be going off with you all like this.

DWIGHT. Such a moment advertises to the single the joys of family life as Ina and I live it.

INA. It's curious that you've never married, Ninian.

NINIAN. Don't say it like that. Maybe I have. Or maybe I will.

DWIGHT. She wants everybody to marry but she wishes she hadn't.

INA. Do you *have* to be so foolish?

DWIGHT. Hi—better get started before she makes a scene. It's too early yet, though. Well—Lulu, you dance on the table.

INA. Why, Dwight?

DWIGHT. Got to amuse ourselves somehow. They'll begin to read the funeral service over us.

NINIAN. Why not the wedding service?

DWIGHT. Ha, ha, ha!

NINIAN. I shouldn't object. Should you, Miss Lulu?

LULU. I—I don't know it so I can't say it.

NINIAN. I can say it.

DWIGHT. Where'd you learn it?

NINIAN. Goes like this: I, Ninian, take thee, Lulu, to be my wedded wife.

DWIGHT. Lulu don't dare say that.

NINIAN. Show him, Miss Lulu.

LULU. I, Lulu, take thee, Ninian, to be my wedded husband.

NINIAN. You will?

LULU. I will. There—I guess I can join in like the rest of you.

NINIAN. And I will. There, by Jove! have we entertained the company, or haven't we?

INA. Oh, honestly—I don't think you ought to—holy things so—what's the matter, Dwightie?

DWIGHT. Say, by George, you know, a civil wedding is binding in this state.

NINIAN. A civil wedding—oh, well—

DWIGHT. But I happen to be a magistrate.

INA. Why, Dwightie—why, Dwightie. . . .

CORNISH. Mr. Deacon, this can't be possible.

DWIGHT. I tell you, what these two have said is all that they have to say according to law. And there don't have to be witnesses —say!

LULU. Don't . . . don't . . . don't let Dwight scare you.

NINIAN. Scare me! why, I think it's a good job done if you ask me. (*Their eyes meet in silence.*)

INA. Mercy, sister!

DWIGHT. Oh, well—I should say we can have it set aside up in the city and no one will be the wiser.

NINIAN. Set aside nothing. I'd like to see it stand.

INA. Ninian, are you serious?

NINIAN. Of course I'm serious.

INA. Lulu. You hear him? What are you going to say to that?

LULU. He isn't in earnest.

NINIAN. I am in earnest—hope to die.

LULU. Oh, no, no!

NINIAN. You come with me. We'll have it done over again somewhere if you say so.

LULU. Why—why—that couldn't be. . . .

NINIAN. Why couldn't it be—why couldn't it?

LULU. How could you want me?

NINIAN. Didn't I tell you I liked you from the first minute I saw you?

LULU. Yes. Yes, you did. But—no, no. I couldn't let you—

NINIAN. Never mind that. Would *you* be willing to go with me? Would you?

LULU. But you—you said you wanted—oh, maybe you're just doing this because—

NINIAN. Lulu. Never mind any of that. Would *you* be willing to go with me?

LULU. Oh, if I thought—

NINIAN. Good girl—

INA. Why, Lulu. Why, Dwight. It can't be legal.

DWIGHT. Why? Because it's your sister? I've married dozens of couples this way. Dozens.

NINIAN. Good enough—eh, Lulu?

LULU. It's—it's all right, I guess.

DWIGHT. Well, I'll be dished.

CORNISH. Well, by Jerusalem. . . .

INA. Sister!

NINIAN. I was going to make a trip south this month on my way home from here. Suppose we make sure of this thing and start right off. You'd like that, wouldn't you? Going to Savannah?

LULU. Yes, I'd like that.

NINIAN. Then that's checked off.

DWIGHT. I suppose we call off our trip to the city to-night then.

NINIAN. Call off nothing. Come along. Give us a send-off. You can shoot our trunks after us, can't you? All right, Miss Lulu—er—er, Mrs. Lulu?

LULU. If you won't be ashamed of me.

NINIAN. I can buy you some things in the city to-morrow.

LULU. Oh. . . .

INA. Oh, mama, mama! Did you hear? Di! Aunt Lulu's married.

DI. Married? Aunt Lulu?

INA. Just now. Right here. By papa.

DI. Oh, to Mr. Cornish?

CORNISH. No, Miss Di. Don't you worry.

INA. To Ninian, mama. They've just been married—Lulu and Ninian.

MRS. BETT. Who's going to do your work?

LULU. Oh, mother dearest—I don't know who will. I ought not to have done this. Well, of course, I didn't do it—

MRS. BETT. I knew well enough you were all keeping something from me.

INA. But, mama! It was so sudden—

LULU. I never planned to do it, mother—not like this—

MRS. BETT. Well, Inie, I should think Lulie might have had a little more consideration to her than this. (*At the window, behind the curtain,* DI *has just kissed* BOBBY *good-by.*)

LULU. Mother dearest, tell me it's all right.

MRS. BETT. This is what comes of going to the theater.

LULU. Mother—

DWIGHT. Come on, everybody, if we're going to make that train.

NINIAN. Yes. Let's get out of this.

CORNISH. Come, Miss Di.

INA. Oh, I'm so *flustrated!*

DWIGHT. Come, come, come all! On to the festive city!

MONONA (*dancing stiffly up and down*). I was to a wedding! I was to a wedding!

NINIAN. Good-by, Mama Bett!

LULU. Mother, mother! Don't forget the two pies!

Curtain.

ACT TWO

SCENE I

SIDE PORCH, *wicker furnished. At the back are two windows, attractively curtained and revealing shaded lamps; between the windows a door, of good lines, set in white clapboards. The porch is raised but a step or two. Low greenery, and a path leading off sharply left. It is evening, a month after* LULU's *marriage.*

(*Discover* INA, DWIGHT, MRS. BETT *and* MONONA.)

INA. Dwight dear, the screen has never been put on that back window.

DWIGHT. Now, why can't my puss remind me of that in the morning instead of the only time I have to take my ease with my family.

INA. But, Dwight, in the mornings you are so busy—

DWIGHT. What an argumentative puss you are. By Jove! look at that rambler rosebush. It's got to be sprayed.

INA. You've said that every night for a week, Dwight....

DWIGHT. Don't exaggerate like that, Ina. It's bad for Monona.

INA. Dwight, look, quick. There go our new neighbors. They have a limousine— Perhaps I have been a little slow about calling. Look at them, Dwight!

DWIGHT. My dear Ina, I see them. Do you want me to pat them on the back?

INA. Well, I think you might be interested. (MONONA *chants softly.*) Dwight, I wonder if Monona really has a musical gift.

DWIGHT. She's a most unusual child. Do you know it? (*Enter* DI, *from house.*)

INA. Oh, they both are. Where are *you* going, I'd like to know?

DI. Mama, I have to go down to the liberry.

INA. It seems to me you have to go to the library every evening. Dwight, do you think she ought to go?

DWIGHT. Diana, is it necessary that you go?

DI. Well, everybody else goes, and—

INA. I will not have you downtown in the evenings.

DI. But you let me go last night.

INA. All the better reason why you should *not* go to-night.

MONONA. Mama, let me go with her.

INA. Very well, Di, you may go and take your sister.

MONONA. Goody, goody! last time you wouldn't let me go.

INA. That's why mama's going to let you go to-night.

DWIGHT. I thought you said the child must go to bed half an hour earlier because she wouldn't eat her egg.

INA. Yes, that's so, I did. Monona, you can't go.

MONONA. But I didn't want my egg—honest I didn't.

INA. Makes no difference. You must eat or you'll get sick. Mama's going to teach you to eat. Go on, Di, to the library if it's necessary.

DWIGHT. I suppose Bobby Larkin has to go to the library to-night, eh?

INA. Dwight, I wouldn't joke her about him. Scold her about him, the way you did this morning.

DI. But papa was cross about something else this morning. And to-night he isn't. Goody-by, Dwight and Ina! (*Exit* DI.)

MONONA. I hate the whole family.

MRS. BETT. Well, I should think she would.

INA. Why, mama! Why, Pettie Deacon! (MONONA *weeps silently.*)

DWIGHT (*to* INA). Say no more, my dear. It's best to overlook. Show a sweet spirit. . .

MRS. BETT. About as much like a father and mother as a cat and dog.

DWIGHT. We've got to learn—

MRS. BETT. Performin' like a pair of weathercocks. (*Both talking at once.*)

DWIGHT. Mother Bett! Are you talking, or am I?

MRS. BETT. I am. But you don't seem to know it.

DWIGHT. Let us talk, pussy, and she'll simmer down. Ah—nothing new from the bride and groom?

INA. No, Dwight. And it's been a week since Lulu wrote. She said he'd bought her a new red dress—and a hat. Isn't it too funny—to think of Lulu—

DWIGHT. I don't understand why they plan to go straight to Oregon without coming here first.

INA. It isn't a bit fair to mama, going off that way. Leaving her own mother—why, she may never see mama again.

MRS. BETT. Oh I'm going to last on quite a while yet.

DWIGHT. Of course you are, Mama Bett. You're my best girl. That reminds me, Ina, we must run up to visit Aunt Mollie. We ought to run up there next week. She isn't well.

INA. Let's do that. Dear me, I wish Lulu was here to leave in charge. I certainly do miss Lulu—lots of ways.

MRS. BETT. 'Specially when it comes mealtime.

INA. Is that somebody coming here?

DWIGHT. Looks like it—yes, so it is. Some caller, as usual. (*Enter* LULU.) Well, if it isn't Miss Lulu Bett!

INA. Why, sister!

MRS. BETT. Lulie. Lulie. Lulie.

LULU. How did you know?

INA. Know what?

LULU. That it isn't Lulu Deacon.

DWIGHT. What's this?

INA. Isn't Lulu Deacon. What are you talking?

LULU. Didn't he write to you?

DWIGHT. Not a word. All we've had we had from you—the last from Savannah, Georgia.

LULU. Savannah, Georgia. . . .

DWIGHT. Well, but he's here with you, isn't he?

INA. Where is he? Isn't he here?

LULU. Must be most to Oregon by this time.

DWIGHT. Oregon?

LULU. You see, he had another wife.

INA. Another wife!

DWIGHT. Why, he had not!

LULU. Yes, another wife. He hasn't seen her for fifteen years and he thinks she's dead. But he isn't sure.

DWIGHT. Nonsense. Why of course she's dead if he thinks so.

LULU. I had to be sure.

INA. Monona! Go upstairs to bed at once.

MONONA. It's only quarter of.

INA. Do as mama tells you.

MONONA. But—

INA. Monona! (*She goes, kissing them all good-night and taking her time about it. Everything is suspended while she kisses them and departs, walking slowly backward.*)

MRS. BETT. Married? Lulie, was your husband married?

LULU. Yes, my husband was married, mother.

INA. Mercy, think of anything like that in our family.

DWIGHT. Well, go on—go on. Tell us about it.

LULU. We were going to Oregon. First down to New Orleans and then out to California and up the coast. . . . Well, then at Savannah, Georgia, he said he thought I better know first. So then he told me.

DWIGHT. Yes—well, what did he say?

LULU. Cora Waters. Cora Waters. She married him down in San Diego eighteen years ago. She went to South America with him.

DWIGHT. Well, he never let us know of it, if she did.

LULU. No. She married him just before he went. Then in South America, after two years, she ran away. That's all he knows.

DWIGHT. That's a pretty story.

LULU. He says if she was alive she'd be after him for a divorce. And she never has been so he thinks she must be dead. The trouble is he wasn't sure. And I had to be sure.

INA. Well, but mercy! Couldn't he find out now?

LULU. It might take a long time and I didn't want to stay and not know.

INA. Well then why didn't he say so here?

LULU. He would have. But you know how sudden everything was. He said he thought about telling us right here that afternoon when—when it happened, but of course that'd been hard, wouldn't it? And then he felt so sure she was dead.

INA. Why did he tell you at all then?

DWIGHT. Yes. Why indeed?

LULU. I thought that just at first but only just at first. Of course that wouldn't have been right. And then you see he gave me my choice.

DWIGHT. Gave you your choice?

LULU. Yes. About going on and taking the chances. He gave me my choice when he told me, there in Savannah, Georgia.

DWIGHT. What made him conclude by then that you ought to be told?

LULU. Why, he'd got to thinking about it. (*A silence.*) The only thing as long as it happened I kind of wish he hadn't told me till we got to Oregon.

INA. Lulu! Oh, you poor poor thing. . . . (MRS. BETT *suddenly joins* INA *in tears, rocking her body.*)

LULU. Don't, mother. Oh, Ina, don't. . . . He felt bad too.

DWIGHT. He! He must have.

INA. It's you. It's you. *My* sister!

LULU. I never thought of it making you both feel bad. I knew it would make Dwight feel bad. I mean, it was his brother—

INA. Thank goodness! nobody need know about it.

LULU. Oh, yes. People will have to know.

DWIGHT. I do not see the necessity.

LULU. Why, what would they think?

DWIGHT. What difference does it make what they think?

LULU. Why, I shouldn't like—you see they might—why, Dwight, I think we'll have to tell them.

DWIGHT. You do. You think the disgrace of bigamy in this family is something the whole town will have to know about.

LULU. Say. I never thought about it being that.

DWIGHT. What did you think it was? And whose disgrace is it, pray?

LULU. Mine. And Ninian's.

DWIGHT. Ninian's. Well, he's gone. But you're here. And I'm here—and my family. Folks'll feel sorry for you. But this disgrace, that would reflect on me.

LULU. But if we don't tell what'll they think?

DWIGHT. They'll think what they always think when a wife leaves her husband. They'll think you couldn't get along. That's all.

LULU. I should hate that. I wouldn't want them to think I hadn't been a good wife to Ninian.

DWIGHT. Wife? You never were his wife. That's just the point.

LULU. Oh!

DWIGHT. Don't you realize the position he's in? ... See here—do you intend—Are you going to sue Ninian?

LULU. Oh! no! no! no!

INA. Why, Lulu, any one would think you loved him.

LULU. I do love him. And he loved me. Don't you think I know? He loved me.

INA. Lulu.

LULU. I love him—I do, and I'm not ashamed to tell you.

MRS. BETT. Lulie, Lulie, was his other wife —was she *there*?

LULU. No, no, mother. She wasn't there.

MRS. BETT. Then it ain't so bad. I was afraid maybe she turned you out.

LULU. No, no. It wasn't that bad, mother.

DWIGHT. In fact I simply will not have it, Lulu. You expect, I take it, to make your home with us in the future on the old terms.

LULU. Well—

DWIGHT. I mean did Ninian give you any money?

LULU. No. He didn't give me any money —only enough to get home on. And I kept my suit and the other dress—why! I wouldn't have taken any money.

DWIGHT. That means that you will have to continue to live here on the old terms and of course I'm quite willing that you should.

Let me tell you, however, that this is on condition—on condition that this disgraceful business is kept to ourselves.

INA. Truly, Lulu, wouldn't that be best? They'll talk anyway. But this way they'll only talk about you and the other way it'll be about all of us.

LULU. But the other way would be the truth.

DWIGHT. My dear Lulu, are you sure of that?

LULU. Sure?

DWIGHT. Yes. Did he give you any proofs?

LULU. Proofs?

DWIGHT. Letters—documents of any sort? Any sort of assurance that he was speaking the truth?

LULU. Why—no. Proofs––no. He told me.

DWIGHT. He told you!

LULU. That was hard enough to have to do. It was terrible for him to have to do. What proofs—

DWIGHT. I may as well tell you that I myself have no idea that Ninian told you the truth. He was always imagining things, inventing things—you must have seen that. I know him pretty well—have been in touch with him more or less the whole time. In short I haven't the least idea he was ever married before.

LULU. I never thought of that.

DWIGHT. Look here—hadn't you and he had some little tiff when he told you?

LULU. No—no! Not once. He was very good to me. This dress—and my shoes— and my hat. And another dress, too. (*She takes off her hat.*) He liked the red wing —I wanted black—oh, Dwight! He did tell me the truth!

DWIGHT. As long as there's any doubt about it—and I feel the gravest doubts—I desire that you should keep silent and protect my family from this scandal. I have taken you into my confidence about these doubts for your own profit.

LULU. My own profit! (*Moves toward the door.*)

INA. Lulu—you see! We just couldn't have this known about Dwight's own brother, could we now?

DWIGHT. You have it in your own hands to repay me, Lulu, for anything that you feel I may have done for you in the past. You also have it in your hands to decide whether your home here continues. This is not a pleasant position for me to find myself in. In fact it is distinctly unpleasant I may say.

But you see for yourself. (*Lulu goes into the house.*)

MRS. BETT. Wasn't she married when she thought she was?

INA. Mama, do please remember Monona. Yes—Dwight thinks now she's married all right and that it was all right, all the time.

MRS. BETT. Well, I hope so, for pity sakes.

MONONA'S VOICE (*from upstairs*). Mama! Come on and hear me say my prayers, why don't you?

Darkness.

SCENE II

INA *seated.* MONONA *jumping on and off the porch, chanting.* (*Enter* DWIGHT.)

DWIGHT. Ah, this is great . . . no place like home after all, is there?

INA. Now Monona, sit down and be quiet. You've played enough for one day. (*Enter* MRS. BETT.)

MONONA. How do you know I have?

DWIGHT. Ah, Mama Bett. Coming out to enjoy the evening air?

MRS. BETT. No, I thank you.

DWIGHT. Well, well, well, let's see what's new in the great press of our country. . . . (*They are now seated in the approximate positions assumed at the opening of* SCENE I.)

INA. Dwight dear, nothing has been done about that screen for the back window.

DWIGHT. Now why couldn't my puss have reminded me of that this morning instead of waiting for the only time I have to take my ease with my family.

INA. But Dwightie, in the mornings you're so busy—

DWIGHT. You are argumentative, pussy— you certainly are. And you ought to curb it. For that matter I haven't sprayed that rambler rosebush.

INA. Every single night for a month you've spoken of spraying that rosebush.

DWIGHT. Ina, will you cease your exaggerations on Monona's account if not on mine. Exaggeration, my pet, is one of the worst of female faults. Exaggeration—

INA. Look, Dwight! our new neighbors have got a dog. Great big brute of a thing. He's going to tear up every towel I spread on our grass. . . . (*Enter* DI, *from the house.*) Now, Di, where are you going?

DI. Mama, I have to go down to the liberry.

INA. Now, Di—

DI. You let me go last night.

MONONA. Mama, I can go, can't I? Because you wouldn't let me go last night.

INA. No, Monona, you may *not* go.

MONONA. Oh, why not?

INA. Because mama says so. Isn't that enough?

MRS. BETT. Anybody'd think you was the king—layin' down the law an' layin' down the law an' layin' down—Where's Lulie?

DI. Mama, isn't Uncle Ninian coming back?

INA. Hush. . . . No. Now don't ask mama any more questions.

DI. But supposing people ask me. What'll I say?

INA. Don't say anything at all about Aunt Lulu.

DI. But, mama, what has she done?

INA. Di! Don't you think mama knows best?

DI (softly). No, I don't. . . . Well anyway Aunt Lulu's got on a perfectly beautiful dress to-night. . . .

INA. And you know, Dwight, Lulu's clothes give me the funniest feeling. As if Lulu was wearing things bought for her by some one that wasn't—that was—

DWIGHT. By her husband who has left her.

DI. Is that what it is, papa?

DWIGHT. That's what it is, my little girl.

DI. Well, I think it's a shame. And I think Uncle Ninian is a slunge.

INA. Di Deacon!

DI. I do! And I'd be ashamed to think anything else. I'd like to tell everybody.

DWIGHT. There's no need for secrecy now.

INA. Dwight, really—do you think we ought—

DWIGHT. No need whatever for secrecy. The truth is Lulu's husband has tired of her and sent her home. We may as well face it.

INA. But Dwight—how awful for Lulu. . . .

DWIGHT. Lulu has us to stand by her. (Enter LULU.)

LULU. That sounds good. That I have you to stand by me.

DWIGHT. My dear Lulu, the family bond is the strongest bond in the world. Family. Tribe. The—er—pack. Standing up for the family honor, the family reputation is the highest nobility. (Exit DI by degrees. Left.) I tell you of all history the most beautiful product is the family tie. Of it are born family consideration—

INA. Why, you don't look like yourself . . . is it your hair, Lulu? You look so strange.

LULU. Don't you like it? Ninian liked it.

DWIGHT. In that case I think you'd show more modesty if you arranged your hair in the old way.

LULU. Yes, you would think so. Dwight, I want you to give me Ninian's Oregon address.

DWIGHT. You want what?

LULU. Ninian's Oregon address. It's a funny thing but I haven't it.

DWIGHT. It would seem that you have no particular need for that particular address.

LULU. Yes I have. I want it. You have it haven't you, Dwight?

DWIGHT. Certainly I have it.

LULU. Won't you please write it down for me? (She offers him tablet.)

DWIGHT. My dear Lulu, now why revive anything? No good can come by—

LULU. But why shouldn't I have his address?

DWIGHT. If everything is over between you why should you?

LULU. But you say he's still my husband.

DWIGHT. If my brother has shown his inclination as plainly as I judge that he has it is certainly not my place to put you in touch with him again.

LULU. I don't know whose place it is. But I've got to know more—I've got to know more, Dwight. This afternoon I went to the post office to ask for his address—it seemed so strange to be doing that, after all that's been—They didn't know his address —I could see how they wondered at my asking. And I knew how the others wondered—Mis' Martin, Mis' Curtis, Mis' Grove. "Where you hiding that handsome husband of yours?" they said. All I could say was that he isn't here. Dwight! I won't live like that. I want to know the truth. You give me Ninian's address.

DWIGHT. My dear Lulu! My *dear* Lulu! You are not the one to write to him. Have you no delicacy?

LULU. So much delicacy that I want to be sure whether I'm married or not.

DWIGHT. Then I myself will take this up with my brother. I will write to him about it.

LULU. Here's everything—if you're going to write him, do it now.

DWIGHT. My dear Lulu! don't be absurd.

LULU. Ina! Help me! If this was Dwight—and they didn't know whether he had another wife or not and you wanted to ask him and you didn't know where he was—oh, don't you see? Help me.

INA. Well of course. I see it all, Lulu. And yet—why not let Dwight do it in his own way? Wouldn't that be better?

LULU. Mother!

MRS. BETT. Lulie. Set down. Set down, why don't you?

LULU. Dwight, you write that letter to Ninian. And you make him tell you so that you'll understand. I know he spoke the truth. But I want you to know.

DWIGHT. M—m. And then I suppose as soon as you have the proofs you're going to tell it all over town.

LULU. I'm going to tell it all over town just as it is—unless you write to him.

INA. Lulu! Oh, you wouldn't!

LULU. I would. I will.

DWIGHT. And get turned out of the house as you would be?

INA. Dwight. Oh, you wouldn't!

DWIGHT. I would. I will. Lulu knows it.

LULU. I shall tell what I know and then leave your house anyway unless you get Ninian's word. And you're going to write to him now.

DWIGHT. You would leave your mother? And leave Ina?

LULU. Leave everything.

INA. Oh, Dwight! We can't get along without Lulu.

DWIGHT. Isn't this like a couple of women? . . . Rather than let you in for a show of temper, Lulu, I'd do anything. (*Writes.*)

MONONA (*behind* INA). Mama, can I write Uncle Ninian a little letter, too?

INA. For pity sakes, aren't you in bed yet?

MONONA. It's only quarter of.

INA. Well you may go to bed *now* because you have sat there listening. How often must mama tell you not to listen to grown people.

MONONA. Do they always say something bad?

INA. Monona, you are to go up to bed at once. (*She makes her leisurely rounds for kisses.*)

MONONA. Papa, it's your turn to hear me say my prayers to-night.

DWIGHT. Very well, pettie. When you're ready call me. (*Exit* MONONA.) There Lulu. The deed is done. Now I hope you're satisfied. (*Places the letter in his pocket.*)

LULU. I want you to give me the letter to mail, please.

DWIGHT. Why this haste, sister mine? I'll mail it in the morning.

LULU. I'll mail it now. Now.

DWIGHT. I may take a little stroll before bedtime—I'll mail it then. There's nothing like a brisk walk to induce sound restful sleep.

LULU. I'll mail the letter now.

DWIGHT. I suppose I'll have to humor your sister, Ina. Purely on your account you understand. (*Hands the letter.*)

INA. Oh, Dwight, how good you are!

LULU. There's—there's one thing more I want to speak about. If—if you and Ina go to your Aunt Mollie's then Ninian's letter might come while you're away.

DWIGHT. Conceivably. Letters do come while a man's away.

LULU. Yes. And I thought if you wouldn't mind if I opened it—

DWIGHT. Opened it? Opened *my* letter?

LULU. Yes, you see it'll be about me mostly. You wouldn't mind if I did open it?

DWIGHT. But you say you know what will be in it, *Miss* Bett?

LULU. I did know till you—I've got to see that letter, Dwight.

DWIGHT. And so you shall. But not until I show it to you. My dear Lulu, you know how I hate having my mail interfered with. You shall see the letter all in good time when Ina and I return.

LULU. You wouldn't want to let me—just see what he says?

DWIGHT. I prefer always to open my own letters.

LULU. Very well, Dwight. (*She moves away. Right.*)

INA. And Lulu, I meant to ask you: Don't you think it might be better if you—if you kept out of sight for a few days?

LULU. Why?

INA. Why set people wondering till we have to?

LULU. They don't have to wonder as far as I'm concerned. (*Exit.*)

MRS. BETT. I'm going through the kitchen to set with Grandma Gates. She always says my visits are like a dose of medicine. (*Exit* MRS. BETT.)

INA. It certainly has changed Lulu—a man coming into her life. She never spoke to me like that before.

DWIGHT. I saw she wasn't herself. I'd do anything to avoid having a scene—you know that. . . . You do know that, don't you?

INA. But I really think you ought to have written to Ninian. It's—it's not a nice position for Lulu.

DWIGHT. Nice! But whom has she got to blame for it?

INA. Why, Ninian.

DWIGHT. Herself! To tell you the truth, I was perfectly amazed at the way she snapped him up here that afternoon.

INA. Why, but Dwight—

DWIGHT. Brazen. Oh, it was brazen.

INA. It was just fun in the first place.

DWIGHT. But no really nice woman—

INA. Dwightie—what did you say in the letter?

DWIGHT. What did I say? I said, I said: "DEAR BROTHER, I take it that the first wife story was devised to relieve you of a distasteful situation. Kindly confirm. Family well as usual. Business fair." Covers it, don't it?

INA. Oh, Dwightie—how complete that is.

DWIGHT. I'm pretty good at writing brief concise letters—that say the whole thing, eh?

INA. I've often noticed that. . . .

DWIGHT. My precious pussy. . . . Oh, how unlike Lulu you are! (*Right.* DI *and* BOBBY *appear, walking very slowly and very near.*) (DWIGHT *rises, holds out his arms.*)

INA. Poor dear foolish Lulu! oh, Dwight—what if it was Di in Lulu's place?

DWIGHT. Such a thing couldn't happen to Di. Di was born with ladylike feelings. (*They enter the house.* INA *extinguishes a lamp.* DWIGHT *turns down the hall gas. Pause.* DI *and* BOBBY *come to the veranda.*)

DI. Bobby dear! You don't kiss me as if you really wanted to kiss me to-night. . . .

Darkness

SCENE III

THE SAME. *Evening, a week later. Stage flooded with moonlight, house lighted. At the piano, just inside the window,* LULU *and* CORNISH *are finishing a song together,* LULU *accompanying.*

How sweet the happy evening's close,
'Tis the hour of sweet repose—
      Good-night.

The summer wind has sunk to rest,
The moon serenely bright
Unfolds her calm and gentle ray,
Softly now she seems to say,
      Good-night.

(*As they sing,* DI *slips into the house, unseen.*)

CORNISH. Why, Miss Lulu, you're quite a musician.

LULU. Oh, no. I've never played in front of anybody— (*They come to the porch.*) I don't know what Ina and Dwight would say if they heard me.

CORNISH. What a pretty dress that is, Miss Lulu!

LULU. I made this from one of Ina's old ones since she's been gone. I don't know what Ina and Dwight are going to say about this dress, made like this, when they get home.

CORNISH. When are they coming back?

LULU. Any time now. They've been gone most a week. Do you know I never had but one compliment before that wasn't for my cooking.

CORNISH. You haven't!

LULU. He told me I done up my hair nice. That was after I took notice how the ladies in Savannah, Georgia, done up theirs.

CORNISH. I guess you can do most anything you set your hand to, Miss Lulu: Look after Miss Di and sing and play and cook—

LULU. Yes, cook. But I can't earn anything. I'd like to earn something.

CORNISH. You would! Why, you have it fine here, I thought.

LULU. Oh, fine, yes. Dwight gives me what I have. And I do their work.

CORNISH. I see. I never thought of that. . . . (*Pause.*)

LULU. You're wondering why I didn't stay with *him!*

CORNISH. Oh, no.

LULU. Yes you are! The whole town's wondering. They're all talking about me.

CORNISH. Well, Miss Lulu, you know it don't make any difference to your friends what people say.

LULU. But they don't know the truth. You see, he had another wife.

CORNISH. Lord sakes!

LULU. Dwight thinks it isn't true. He thinks—he didn't have another wife. . . . You see, Dwight thinks he didn't want me.

CORNISH. But—your husband—I mean, why doesn't he write to Mr. Deacon and tell him the truth—

LULU. He has written. The letter's in there on the piano.

CORNISH. What'd he say?

LULU. Dwight doesn't like me to touch his mail. I'll have to wait till he comes back.

CORNISH. Lord sakes! . . . You—you—you're too nice a girl to get a deal like this. Darned if you aren't.

LULU. Oh, no.

CORNISH. Yes you are, too! And there ain't a thing I can do.

LULU. It's a good deal to have somebody to talk to. . . .

CORNISH. Sure it is.

LULU. . . . Cora Waters. Cora Waters, of San Diego, California. And she never heard of me.

CORNISH. No. She never did, did she? Ain't life the darn—
(*Enter* MRS. BETT.)

MRS. BETT. I got Monona into bed. And it's no fool of a job neither.

LULU. Did you, mother? Come and sit down.

MRS. BETT. Yes. She went to bed with a full set of doll dishes. . . . Ain't it nice with the folks all gone? . . . I don't hear any more playin' and singin'. It sounded real good.

LULU. We sung all I knew how to play, mama.

MRS. BETT. I use' to play on the melodeon.

CORNISH. Well, well, well.

MRS. BETT. That was when I was·first married. We had a little log house in a clearing in York State. I was seventeen—and he was nineteen. While he was chopping I use' to sit on a log with my sewing. Jenny was born in that house. I was alone at the time. I was alone with her when she died, too. She was sixteen—little bits of hands she had— (*Yawns. Rises, wanders toward door.*) Can't we have some more playin' and singin'?

LULU. After a little while, mama—dear.

MRS. BETT. It went kind of nice—that last tune you sung. (*Hums the air. Enters house.*)

CORNISH. I must be going along too, Miss Lulu.

LULU. I can't think why Di doesn't come. She ought not to be out like this without telling me.
(MRS. BETT *appears beside the piano, lifts and examines the letters lying there.*)

CORNISH. Well, don't you mind on my account. I've enjoyed every minute I've been here.

LULU. Mother! Those are Dwight's letters —don't you touch them.

MRS. BETT. I ain't hurting them or him either. (*Disappears, the letters in her hand.*)

CORNISH. Good-night, Miss Lulu. If there was anything I could do at any time you'd let me know, wouldn't you?

LULU. Oh, thank you.

CORNISH. I've had an awful nice time, singing, and listening to you talk—well of course—I mean the supper was just fine! And so was the music.

LULU. Oh, no.
(MRS. BETT *appears at the door with a letter.*)

MRS. BETT. Lulie. I guess you didn't notice. This one's from Ninian.

LULU. Mother—

MRS. BETT. I opened it—why of course I did. It's from Ninian. (*Holds out unfolded letter and an old newspaper clipping.*) The paper's awful old—years back, looks like. See. Says "Corie Waters, music hall singer —married last night to Ninian Deacon"— Say, Lulie, that must be her.

LULU. Yes, that's her. That's her—Cora Waters. . . . Oh, then he *was* married to her just like he said!

CORNISH. Oh, Miss Lulu! I'm so sorry!,

LULU. No, no. Because he wanted me! He didn't say that just to get rid of me!

CORNISH. Oh, that way. . . . I see. . . .

LULU. I'm so thankful it wasn't that.

MRS. BETT. Then everything's all right onct more. Ain't that nice!

LULU. I'm so thankful it wasn't that.

CORNISH. Yes, I can understand that. Well, I—I guess I ought to be going now, Miss Lulu. . . . Why, it *is* Miss Lulu Bett, isn't it?

LULU (*abstractedly, with the paper*). Yes —yes—good-night, Mr. Cornish. Good-night.

CORNISH. Good-night, Miss Lulu. . . . I wonder if you would let me tell you something.

LULU. Why—

CORNISH. I guess I don't amount to much. I'll never be a lawyer. I'm no good at business and everything I say sounds wrong to me. And yet I do believe I do know enough not to bully a woman—not to make her unhappy, maybe even—I could make her a little happy. Miss Lulu, I hate to see you looking and talking so sad. Do you think we could possibly arrange—

LULU. Oh!

CORNISH. I guess maybe you've heard something about a little something I'm supposed to inherit. Well, I got it. Of course, it's only five hundred dollars. We could get that little Warden house and furnish up the parlor with pianos—that is, if you could ever think of marrying me.

LULU. Don't say that—don't say that!

MRS. BETT. Better take him, Lulie. A girl ought to take any young man that will propose in front of her mother!

CORNISH. Of course if you loved him very much then I'd ought not to be talking this way to you.

LULU. You see Ninian was the first person who was ever kind to me. Nobody ever wanted me, nobody ever even thought of me. Then he came. It might have been somebody else. It might have been you. But it happened to be Ninian and I do love him.

CORNISH. I see. I guess you'll forgive me for what I said.

LULU. Of course.

CORNISH. Miss Lulu, if that five hundred could be of any use to you, I wish you'd take it.

LULU. Oh, thank you, thank you, I couldn't.

CORNISH. Well, I guess I'll be stepping along. If you should want me, I'm always there. I guess you know that. (*Exit.*)

MRS. BETT. Better burn that up. I wouldn't have it round.

LULU. But mother! Mother dear, try to understand. This means that Ninian told the truth. He wasn't just trying to get rid of me.

MRS. BETT. Did he want you to stay with him?

LULU. I don't know. But I think he did. Anyway, now I know the truth about him.

MRS. BETT. Well, I wouldn't want anybody else to know. Here, let me have it and burn it up.

LULU. Mama, mama! Aren't you glad for me that now I can prove Ninian wasn't just making up a story so I'd go away?

MRS. BETT (*clearly and beautifully*). Oh, Lulu! My little girl! Is that what they said about you? Mother knows it wasn't like that. Mother knows he loved you. . . . How still it is here! Where's Inie?

LULU. They've gone away, you know. . . .

MRS. BETT. Well, I guess I'll step over to Grandma Gates's a spell. See how her rheumatism is. I'll be back before long—I'll be back. . . . (*Exit. For a moment* LULU *breaks down and sobs. Rises to lay* DWIGHT's *letter through the window on piano. Slight sound. She listens. Enter* DI *from house. She is carrying a traveling bag.*)

LULU. Di! Why Di! What does this mean? Where were you going? Why, mama won't like your carrying her nice new satchel. . . .

DI. Aunt Lulu—the idea. What right have you to interfere with me like this?

LULU. Di, you must explain to me what this means. . . . Di, where can you be going with a satchel this time of the night? Di Deacon, are you running away with somebody?

DI. You have no right to ask me questions, Aunt Lulu.

LULU. Di, you're going off with Bobby Larkin. Aren't you? Aren't you?

DI. If I am it's entirely our own affair.

LULU. Why, Di. If you and Bobby want to be married why not let us get you up a nice wedding here at home—

DI. Aunt Lulu, you're a funny person to be telling *me* what to do.

LULU. I love you just as much as if I was married happy, in a home.

DI. Well, you aren't. And I'm going to do just as I think best. Bobby and I are the ones most concerned in this, Aunt Lulu.

LULU. But—but getting married is for your whole life!

DI. Yours wasn't.

LULU. Di, my dear little girl, you must wait at least till mama and papa get home.

DI. That's likely. They say I'm not to be married till I'm twenty-one.

LULU. Well, but how young that is.

DI. It is to you. It isn't young to me, remember, Aunt Lulu.

LULU. But this is wrong—it is wrong!

DI. There's nothing wrong about getting married if you stay married.

LULU. Well, then it can't be wrong to let your mother and father know.

DI. It isn't. But they'd treat me wrong. Mama'd cry and say I was disgracing *her*. And papa—first he'd scold me and then he'd joke me about it. He'd joke me about it every day for weeks, every morning at breakfast, every night here on the porch—he'd joke me.

LULU. Why, Di! Do you feel that way, too?

DI. You don't know what it is to be laughed at or paid no attention to, everything you say.

LULU. Don't I? Don't I? Is that why you're going?

DI. Well, it's one reason.

LULU. But Di, do you love Bobby Larkin?

DI. Well. . . . I could love almost anybody real nice that was nice to me.

LULU. Di . . . Di. . . .

DI. It's true. (BOBBY *enters.*) You ought to know that. . . . You did it. Mama said so.

LULU. Don't you think that I don't know. . . .

DI. Oh, Bobby, she's trying to stop us! But she can't do it—I've told her so—

BOBBY. She don't have to stop us. We're stopped.

DI. What do you mean?

BOBBY. We're minors.

DI. Well, gracious—you didn't have to tell them that.

BOBBY. No. They knew *I* was.

DI. But, silly. Why didn't you tell them you're not.

BOBBY. But I am.

DI. For pity sakes—don't you know how to do anything?

BOBBY. What would you have me do, I'd like to know?

DI. Why tell them we're both—whatever it is they want us to be. We look it. We know we're responsible—that's all they care for. Well, you are a funny. . . .

BOBBY. You wanted me to lie?

DI. Oh! don't make out you never told a fib.

BOBBY. Well, but this—why, Di—about a thing like this. . . .

DI. I never heard of a lover flatting out like that!

BOBBY. Anyhow, there's nothing to do now. The cat's out. I've told our ages. We've got to have our folks in on it.

DI. Is that all you can think of?

BOBBY. What else is there to think of?

DI. Why, let's go to Bainbridge or Holt and tell them we're of age and be married there.

LULU. Di, wherever you go I'll go with you. I won't let you out of my sight.

DI. Bobby, why don't you answer her?

BOBBY. But I'm not going to Bainbridge or Holt or any town and lie, to get you or any other girl.

DI. You're about as much like a man in a story as—as papa is.
(*Enter* DWIGHT *and* INA.)

DWIGHT. What's this? What's this about papa?

INA. Well, what's all this going on here?

LULU. Why, Ina!

DI. Oh, mama! I—I didn't know you were coming so soon. Hello, dear! Hello, papa! Here's—here's Bobby. . . .

DWIGHT. What an unexpected pleasure, *Master* Bobby.

BOBBY. Good-evening, Mrs. Deacon. Good-evening, Mr. Deacon.

DWIGHT. And Lulu. Is it Lulu? Is this lovely houri our Lulu? Is this Miss Lulu Bett? Or is this Lulu something else by now? You can't tell what Lulu'll do when you leave her alone at home. Ina—our festive ball gown!

LULU. Ina, I made it out of that old muslin of yours, you know. I thought you wouldn't care—

INA. Oh, that! I was going to use it for Di but it doesn't matter. You are welcome to it, Lulu. Little youthful for anything but home wear, isn't it?

DWIGHT. It looks like a wedding gown. Why are you wearing a wedding gown—eh, Lulu?

INA. Di Deacon, what have you got mama's new bag for?

DI. I haven't done anything to the bag, mama.

INA. Well, but what are you doing with it here?

DI. Oh, nothing! Did you—did you have a good time?

INA. Yes, we did—but I can't see. . . . Dwight, look at Di with my new black satchel.

DWIGHT. What is this, Diana?

DI. Well, I'm—I'm not going to use it for anything.

INA. I wish somebody would explain what is going on here. Lulu, can't you explain?

DWIGHT. Aha! Now, if Lulu is going to explain that's something like it. When Lulu begins to explain we get imagination going.

LULU. Di and I have a little secret. Can't we have a little secret if we want one?

DWIGHT. Upon my word, she has a beautiful secret. I don't know about your secrets, Lulu.
(*Enter* MRS. BETT.)

MRS. BETT. Hello, Inie.

INA. Oh, mother dear. . . .

DWIGHT. Well, Mother Bett. . . .

MRS. BETT. That you, Dwight? (*To* BOBBY.) . . . Don't you help me. I guess I can help myself yet awhile. (*Climbs the two steps.*) (*To* DI.) Made up your mind to come home, did you? (*Seats herself.*) I got a joke. Grandma Gates says it's all over town they wouldn't give Di and Bobby Larkin a license to get married. (*Single note of laughter, thin and high.*)

DWIGHT. What nonsense!

INA. Is it nonsense? Haven't I been trying to find out where the new black bag went? Di! Look at mama. . . .

DI. Listen to that, Bobby. Listen!

INA. That won't do, Di. You can't deceive mama, and don't you try.

BOBBY. Mrs. Deacon, I—

DWIGHT. Diana!

DI. Yes, papa.

DWIGHT. Answer your mother. Answer *me*. Is there anything in this absurd tale?

DI. No, papa.

DWIGHT. Nothing whatever?

DI. No, papa.

DWIGHT. Can you imagine how such a ridiculous story started?

DI. No, papa.

DWIGHT. Very well. Now we know where we are. If anybody hears this report repeated, send them to *me*.

INA. Well, but that satchel—

DWIGHT. One moment. Lulu will of course verify what the child has said.

LULU. If you cannot settle this with Di, you cannot settle it with me.

DWIGHT. A shifty answer. You're a bird at misrepresenting facts. . . .

LULU. Oh! . . .

DWIGHT. Lulu, the bird!

LULU. Lulu, the dove to put up with you. (*Exit.*)

INA. Bobby wanted to say something. . . .

BOBBY. No, Mrs. Deacon. I have nothing—more to say. I'll—I'll go now.

DWIGHT. Good-night, Robert.
(INA *and* DWIGHT *transfer bags and wraps to the house.*)

BOBBY. Good-night, Mr. Deacon. Good-by, Di.
(DI *follows* BOBBY. *Right.*)

DI. Bobby, come back, you hate a lie—but what else could I do?

BOBBY. What else could you do? I'd rather they never let us see each other again than to lose in the way I've lost you now.

DI. Bobby!

BOBBY. It's true. We mustn't talk about it.

DI. Bobby! I'll go back and tell them all.

BOBBY. You can't go back. Not out of a thing like that. Good-by, Di. (*Exit.*)
(*Enter* DWIGHT *and* INA.)

DI. If you have any fear that I may elope with Bobby Larkin, let it rest. I shall never marry him if he asks me fifty times a day.

INA. Really, darling?

DI. Really and truly, and he knows it, too.

DWIGHT. A-ha! The lovelorn maiden all forlorn makes up her mind not to be so lorn as she thought she was. How does it seem not to be in love with him, Di—eh?

DI. Papa, if you make fun of me any more I'll—I'll let the first train of cars I can find run over me. . . . (*Sobs as she runs to house.*)

MRS. BETT. Wait, darling! Tell grandma! Did Bobby have another wife too?
(*Exeunt* MRS. BETT *and* DI.)

INA. Di, I'd be ashamed, when papa's so good to you. Oh, my! what parents have to put up with. . . .

DWIGHT. Bear and forbear, pettie—bear and forbear. . . . By the way, Lulu, haven't I some mail somewhere about?

LULU. Yes, there's a letter there. I'll get it for you. (*She reaches through the window.*)

DWIGHT. A-ha! An epistle from my dear brother Ninian.

INA. Oh, from Ninian, Dwight?

DWIGHT. From Ninian—the husband of Miss Lulu Bett. . . . You opened the letter? . . . Your sister has been opening my mail.

INA. But, Dwight, if it's from Ninian—

DWIGHT. It is my mail.

INA. Well, what does he say?

DWIGHT. I shall read the letter in my own time. My present concern is this disregard for my wishes. What excuse have you to offer?

LULU. None.

INA. Dwight, she knows what's in it and we don't. Hurry up.

DWIGHT. She is an ungrateful woman. (*Opens the letter, with the clipping.*)

INA (*over his shoulder*). Ah! . . . Dwight, then he was . . .

DWIGHT. M—m—m—m. So after having been absent with my brother for a month you find that you were not married to him.

LULU. You see, Dwight, he told the truth. He did have another wife. He didn't just leave me.

DWIGHT. But this seems to me to make you considerably worse off than if he had.

LULU. Oh, no! No! If he hadn't—hadn't liked me, he wouldn't have told me about her. You see that, don't you?

DWIGHT. That your apology? . . . Look here, Lulu! This is a bad business. The less you say about it the better for all our sakes. You see that, don't you?

LULU. See that? Why, no. I wanted you to write to him so I could tell the truth. You said I mustn't tell the truth till I had the proofs.

DWIGHT. Tell whom?

LULU. Tell everybody. I want them to know.

DWIGHT. Then you care nothing for our feelings in this matter?

LULU. Your feelings?

DWIGHT. How this will reflect on us—it's nothing to you that we have a brother who's a bigamist?

LULU. But it's me—it's me.

DWIGHT. You! You're completely out of it. You've nothing more to say about it whatever. Just let it be as it is . . . drop it. That's all I suggest.

LULU. I want people to know the truth.

DWIGHT. But it's nobody's business but our business . . . for all our sakes let us drop this matter. . . . Now I tell you, Lulu—here are three of us. Our interests are the same in this thing—only Ninian is our relative and he's nothing to you now. Is he?

LULU. Why—

DWIGHT. Let's have a vote. Your snap judgment is to tell this disgraceful fact broadcast. Mine is, least said soonest mended. What do you say, Ina?

INA. Oh, goodness—if we get mixed up in a scandal like this we'll never get away from it. Why, I wouldn't have people know of it for worlds.

DWIGHT. Exactly. Ina has stated it exactly Lulu, I think you should be reconciled.

INA. My poor, poor sister! Oh, Dwight! when I think of it—what have I done, what have *we* done—that I should have a good kind loving husband—be so protected, so loved, when other women . . . Darling! You *know* how sorry I am—we all are—

LULU. Then give me the only thing I've got —that's my pride. My pride that he didn't want to get rid of me.

DWIGHT. What about my pride? Do you think I want everybody to know that my brother did a thing like that?

LULU. You can't help that.

DWIGHT. But I want you to help it. I want you to promise me that you won't shame us like this before all our friends.

LULU. You want me to promise what?

DWIGHT. I want you—I ask you to promise me that you will keep this with us—a family secret.

LULU. No! No! I won't do it! I won't do it} I won't do it!

DWIGHT. You refuse to do this small thing for us?

LULU. Can't you understand anything? I've lived here all my life—on your money. I've not been strong enough to work they say—well, but I've been strong enough to be a hired girl in your house—and I've been glad to pay for my keep. . . . But there wasn't a thing about it that I liked. Nothing about being here that I liked. . . . Well, then I got a little something, same as other folks. I thought I was married and I went off on the train and he bought me things and I saw different towns. And then it was all a mistake. I didn't have any of it. I came back here and went into your kitchen again—I don't know why I came back. I suppose it's because I'm most thirty-four and new things ain't so easy any more—

but what have I got or what'll I ever have? And now you want to put on to me having folks look at me and think he run off and left me and having them all wonder. I can't stand it. I can't stand it. I can't. . . .

DWIGHT. You'd rather they'd know he fooled you when he had another wife?

LULU. Yes. Because he wanted me. How do I know—maybe he wanted me only just because he was lonesome, the way I was. I don't care why. And I won't have folks think he went and left me.

DWIGHT. That is wicked vanity.

LULU. That's the truth. Well, why can't they know the truth?

DWIGHT. And bring disgrace on us all?

LULU. It's me—It's me—

DWIGHT. You—you—you—you're always thinking of yourself.

LULU. Who else thinks of me? And who do you think of—who do you think of, Dwight? I'll tell you that, because I know you better than any one else in the world knows you—better even than Ina. And I know that you'd sacrifice Ina, Di, mother, Monona, Ninian—everybody, just to your own idea of who you are. You're one of the men who can smother a whole family and not even know you're doing it.

DWIGHT. You listen to me. It's Ninian I'm thinking about.

LULU. Ninian. . . .

DWIGHT. Yes, yes . . . Ninian! . . . Of course if you don't care what happens to him, it doesn't matter.

LULU. What do you mean?

DWIGHT. If you don't love him any more. . . .

LULU. You know I love him. I'll always love him.

DWIGHT. That's likely. A woman doesn't send the man she loves to prison.

LULU. I send him to prison! Why, he's brought me the only happiness I've ever had. . . .

DWIGHT. But prison is just where he'll go and you'll be the one to send him there.

LULU. Oh! That couldn't be. . . . That couldn't be. . . .

DWIGHT. Don't you realize that bigamy is a crime? If you tell this thing he'll go to prison . . . nothing can save him.

LULU. I never thought of that. . . .

DWIGHT. It's time you did think. Now will you promise to keep this with us, a family secret?

LULU. Yes. I promise.

DWIGHT. You will? . . .

LULU. Yes . . . I will.

DWIGHT. A . . . h. You'll be happy some day to think you've done this for us, Lulu.

LULU. I s'pose so. . . .

INA. This makes up for everything. My sweet self-sacrificing sister!

LULU. Oh, stop that!

INA. Oh, the pity of it . . . the pity of it! . . .

LULU. Don't you go around pitying me! I'll have you know I'm glad the whole thing happened.

Curtain.

ACT THREE

THE SAME. Discover MRS. BETT, *tidying the porch and singing. It is the following morning.* (*Enter* LULU *with bag.*)

MRS. BETT. Where you going now, for pity sakes?

LULU. Mother. Now, mother darling, listen and try to understand.

MRS. BETT. Well, I am listening, Lulie.

LULU. Mother, I can't stay here. I can't stay here any longer. I've got to get clear away from Dwight and Ina.

MRS. BETT. You want to live somewhere else, Lulie?

LULU. I can't live here and have people think Ninian left me. I can't tell the truth and bring disgrace on Ninian. And I can't stay here in Dwight's kitchen a day longer. Oh, mother! I wish you could see—

MRS. BETT. Why, Lulie, I do see that.

LULU. You do, mother?

MRS. BETT. I've often wondered why you didn't go before.

LULU. Oh, mother, you dear—

MRS. BETT. You needn't think because I'm old I don't know a thing or two.

LULU. You want me to go?

MRS. BETT. It's all I can do for you now, Lulie. Just to want you to go. I'm old and I'm weak and I can't keep care of you like when you was little.

LULU. Oh, mother, I'm so glad!

MRS. BETT. I ain't exactly glad—

LULU. Dearest, I mean I was so afraid you wouldn't understand—

MRS. BETT. Why wouldn't I understand, I'd like to know? You speak like I didn't have a brain in my skull.

LULU. No, dear, but—

MRS. BETT. You mind me, Lulie, and go on. Go on. . . . Say, scat's sake, you can't go. You ain't got any money.

LULU. Yes, mother, I have. I've got twelve dollars.

MRS. BETT. And I ain't got much. Only enough to bury me nice.

LULU. Don't you worry, mother. I'll be all right. I'll get work.

MRS. BETT. Mother wants to help you. Here, Lulie, you take my funeral fifty. Joke on Dwight to make him bury me.

LULU. Oh, no, mother, I couldn't.

MRS. BETT. You mind me, Lulie. Do as mother tells you.

LULU. Mother, dearest! Oh, I wish I could take you with me!

MRS. BETT. You needn't to worry about me. If I get lonesome I can give Dwight the dickens.

LULU. Good-by—dear—good-by. I'll go the back way, they won't see me. (LULU *kisses her and turns away. Left.*)

MRS. BETT. Lulie. Mother loves you. You know that, don't you?

LULU. Dearest, yes—yes, I do know. (*She goes.* MRS. BETT *trembles, turns, sees her dustcloth, goes on working and begins to hum.*)
(*Enter* DWIGHT.)

DWIGHT. Ready for breakfast, Mama Bett?

MRS. BETT. No, I ain't ready.

DWIGHT. Neither is the breakfast. Lulu must be having the tantrum.

MRS. BETT. I s'pose you think that's funny.

DWIGHT. Lulu ought to think of you—old folks ought to have regular meals—

MRS. BETT. Old? Old? Me, old?

DWIGHT. Well, you're hungry. That's what makes you so cross, Mama Bett.

MRS. BETT. All you think of is food, anyhow.

DWIGHT. Who has a better right? Who provides the food we eat?

MRS. BETT. That's all you're good for.

DWIGHT. Well, I may not amount to much in this old world of ours but I flatter myself I'm a good provider.

MRS. BETT. If I was going to brag I'd brag original.

DWIGHT. You mustn't talk like that. You know you're my best girl.

MRS. BETT. Don't you best-girl me.

DWIGHT. There, there, there. . . .

MRS. BETT. Now look at you. Walking all over me like I wasn't here—like I wasn't nowhere.

DWIGHT. Now, Mama Bett, you're havin' the tantrum.

MRS. BETT. Am I? All right then I am. What you going to do about it? How you going to stop me?

DWIGHT. Now, now, now, now. . . .
(*Enter* INA.)

INA. Dwight, I can't think what's happened to Lulu. Breakfast isn't even started.

DWIGHT. Lulu must be having a rendezvous.
(*Grandma snorts.*)

INA. That's randevoo, Dwightie. Not rendezvous.

DWIGHT. You two are pretty particular, seems to me.

MRS. BETT. Oh, no! We ain't used to the best.
(DI *is at the door.*)

DI. Hello, family! What's the matter with breakfast?

MRS. BETT. There ain't any.

INA. Di, let's you and I get breakfast just to show Aunt Lulu that we can.

MRS. BETT. Say if you two are going to get breakfast, I'll go over to Grandma Gates for a snack.
(*Enter* MONONA.)

MONONA. What do you s'pose? Aunt Lulu's trunk is locked and strapped in her room.

INA. Monona, stop imagining things.

MONONA. Well, it is. And I saw her going down the walk with her satchel when I was washing me.

DWIGHT. Lulu must be completely out of her mind.

MRS. BETT. First time I've known her to show good sense in years.

INA. Why, mama!

DWIGHT. Mother Bett, do you know where Lulu is?

MRS. BETT. Mother knows a-plenty.

INA. Mama, what do you mean?

MRS. BETT. I know all about Lulie being gone. She went this morning. I told her to go.

INA. Why, mama! How can you talk so! When Dwight has been so good to you and Lulu. . . .

MRS. BETT. Good, yes, he's give us a pillow and a baked potato—

DWIGHT. So! You and Lulu presume to upset the arrangement of my household without one word to me.

MRS. BETT. Upset, upset— You cockroach! . . .

INA. Monona! Stop listening. Now run away and play. Di, you go and begin breakfast.

DI. Yes, mummy.

MONONA. Aw, let me stay.

INA. (*Exeunt* DI *and* MONONA.) Go at once, children. Mother, you ought not to use such language before young people.

MRS. BETT. Don't you think they're fooled. What do you suppose Di was going to run away with Bobby Larkin for, only to get away from you.

DWIGHT. Mother Bett!

MRS. BETT. What do you suppose Lulu married Ninian for—only to get shed of both of you.

INA. Oh please, please, somebody think a little bit of me. Dwight, do go after Lulu —go to the depot—she couldn't get away before the 8:37.

DWIGHT. My dear Ina, my dignity—

INA. Oh, please do go!

DWIGHT. Oh, my heavens! what a house full! of women—

INA. Dwight, we can't get along without Lulu.

DWIGHT. Upsetting things about my ears. ... (*Exit.*)

INA. Mama, I do think it's too bad of you— oh! now I'll try to get some breakfast. (*Exit.*)

MRS. BETT. Going to try to, he-e! (*Enter* MONONA.)

MONONA. Oh, grandma isn't it fun with so much going on!

MRS. BETT. What's that, you little ape?

MONONA. Oh, I just love it! Everybody makes such funny faces.

MRS. BETT. Some people are born with funny faces. Monona, ain't you ever going to grow up?

MONONA. Grandma, I am grown up.

MRS. BETT. You don't act like it.

MONONA. Well, grown folks don't neither.

MRS. BETT. Sh-hh-hhh, stop talking back to me.

MONONA. Everybody shushes me. If I don't talk, how'll they know I'm there?

MRS. BETT. I guess they could bear up if they didn't know you was there.

MONONA. I'd better get in, or I'll catch it. (MONONA *sings a silly song.*)

MRS. BETT (*rocking in rhythm with the song*). Scot's sake, what am I doing! Them wicked words.
(*Enter* DI.)

DI. Monona, mama wants you.

MONONA. I'd better go or I'll catch it. I'll catch it anyway— (*Exit.*)
(*Enter* NINIAN.)

DI. Uncle Ninian! Well it's just about time you showed up.

NINIAN. You're right, Di. But I came as soon as I could.

DI. You might as well know. I think you're a perfect slunge.

MRS. BETT. Land sakes!

NINIAN. Mrs. Bett.

MRS. BETT. Don't you come near me! Don't you speak to me! You whited centipede!

NINIAN. That's what I expected and that's what I deserve.

MRS. BETT. Move on! Move on!

NINIAN. Let me tell you something first, Mother Bett.

MRS. BETT. Don't you "mother" me.

NINIAN. Yes, that's just what I mean, *Mother* Bett. I've found that the woman I married died in Rio years ago. Here's a letter from the consul.

MRS. BETT. Dead? Ain't that nice! But what ailed you all the time? A man with any get-up-and-get would have known that all along.

NINIAN. I'm not excusing myself any, Mother Bett.

MRS. BETT. Well, perhaps you're as good as you know how to be. Anyway, your mother's responsible for a good deal without counting you.

NINIAN. Mother Bett, where is Lulu?

MRS. BETT. Who. Lulie? Oh, she's run away.

NINIAN. What do you say?

MRS. BETT. She's gone off on the train this morning. I told her to go.

NINIAN. Mother Bett, Mother Bett—where has she gone?

MRS. BETT. Gone to call her soul her own, I guess.

NINIAN. But Mother Bett, where did Lulu go?

MRS. BETT. She might be at the depot.

NINIAN. Can I catch her?

MRS. BETT. You can catch her if ye can run in them white—mittens.

NINIAN. Run? Watch me. (*Exit running*.)

DI. Oh! Grandma, isn't it just too romantic?

MRS. BETT. What do you mean—rheumatic?
(*Enter* MONONA.)

MONONA. Breakfast's ready, grandma.

MRS. BETT. Breakfast! I wouldn't know coffee from flapjacks.

MONONA. I've been catching it all morning and I didn't do a thing.

MRS. BETT. What's that, little ape?

MONONA. Grandma, honestly, do you see why because Aunt Lulu ran away the whole family should pick on me?

MRS. BETT. Come here, you poor neglected child!

MONONA. Mama's getting breakfast and she's burned all over and she's so cross—m-m-m. Why here she comes now!

MRS. BETT. Who?

DI. Aunt Lulu!
(*Enter* LULU.)

LULU. Mother—

MONONA. Oh, goody—now they'll pick on you instead of me.

MRS. BETT (*softly*). Monona! You run down the road as tight as you can and catch your Uncle Ninian quick— Sh-sh-sh—

MONONA. Uncle Ninian! Oh—oh! (*Exit*.)

LULU. Mother—what do you think I've heard?

MRS. BETT. Land knows! my head's whirlin'. Who found you?

LULU. Found me?

MRS. BETT. I can count up to 'leven in this house that's went after you or went after them that went after them— Oh land! . . .

LULU. Mother, the station agent said to me just now when I went to buy my ticket, he said, "You just missed your husband. He went hurrying up the street." I couldn't go till I knew.

DI. Why, Aunt Lulu, haven't you heard—

MRS. BETT. Sh-h-h— Leave it burst.
(*Enter* DWIGHT.)

DWIGHT. So . . . after making me traipse all over town for you and before breakfast. . . . What is the meaning of this, Lulu? Answer me.

MRS. BETT. Sit down, Dwight. Take off your hat why don't you?
(*Enter* INA.)

INA. Forevermore.

LULU. Were you looking for me, Dwight?

DWIGHT. What about our breakfast, may I ask?

LULU. Haven't you had your breakfast, Dwight? I had mine in the bakery.

MRS. BETT. In the bakery! On expense!

INA. Lulu, where have you been?

LULU. How good of you to miss me!

INA. Lulu, you don't act like yourself.

LULU. That's the way I heard the women talk in Savannah, Georgia. "So good of you to miss me."

DWIGHT. Lulu, let's have no more of this nonsense. . . .

LULU. Whose nonsense, Dwight? I've left your home for good and all. I'm going somewhere else to work.

INA. Why, Lulu, what will people think of Dwight and me if we let you do that?

DWIGHT. So you thought better of the promise you made to us last evening not to tell our affairs broadcast.

LULU. Your affairs? No, Dwight, you can tell them anything you like when I'm gone.

INA. How am I ever going to keep house without you? Dwight, you've simply got to make her stay. When I think of what I went through while she was away . . . everything boils over, and what I don't expect to b-b-boil b-b-burns. Sister, how can you be so cruel when Dwight and I—

DWIGHT. Patience, patience, pettie . . . Lulu, I ask you to stay here where you belong.

LULU. No, Dwight, I'm through.

DWIGHT. So, sister mine, have you found some other man willing to run away with you?

LULU. That will do, Dwight. You've pretended so long you can't be honest with yourself, any of the time. Your whole life is a lie.

MRS. BETT. Save your breath, Lulie. (*Enter* MONONA *with* NINIAN.)

DWIGHT. At least, Miss Lulu Bett, neither Ina nor I ever had to lie about our marriage.

MONONA. Here he is, grandma.

LULU. Oh. . . .

NINIAN. What's that your saying, Dwight?

INA. Forevermore!

LULU. Ninian. . . .

NINIAN. Lulu. . . . So I didn't miss you.

DWIGHT. Ha! ha! . . . The happy bridegroom comes at last. What's the meaning of this, Ninian?

NINIAN. I'll bet he's made life beautiful for you since you got back. Anything more to say, Dwight?

DWIGHT. Yes, Lulu was planning to run away. . . . I was telling her she'd better stay here at home where she'd have us to stand by her.

NINIAN. Yes, I've heard how you stood by her. You're a magnificent protector, you are!

DWIGHT. Look here, Nin, don't you feel that you have to sacrifice yourself. Lulu is well enough off here.

INA. She was quite happy until you came, Ninian.

NINIAN. You hypocrites!

MRS. BETT. Hypocrites! He-e!

INA. Children, stop listening to older people.

DI. Oh, mama! . . .

MONONA (*crying*). Oh . . . Let me stay!

INA. Children! . . . (*Exeunt* DI *and* MONONA.) Ninian, how can you say such things to us!

NINIAN. Lulu has suffered as much from you as she has from me.

MRS. BETT. That's right, Ninian. Plain talk won't hurt nobody around here.

NINIAN. Lulu, can you forgive me?

LULU. But Cora Waters . . . what of her?

DWIGHT. Yes, what about your other wife?

NINIAN. I haven't any other wife—just Lulu.

MRS. BETT. Cora Waters is dead. I knew it all along.

LULU. Ninian, is it true?

NINIAN. Yes, it's true.

MRS. BETT. He's confided in his mother. He told me all about it.

NINIAN. Will you come back to me, Lulu?

MRS. BETT. Better take him, Lulie. You can have that fifty to furnish up the parlor.

LULU. Oh, mother! I wish we could have you with us.

NINIAN. Do you forgive me?

LULU. I forgave you in Savannah, Georgia.

Curtain.

"Anna Christie"

BY EUGENE O'NEILL

CHARACTERS

"JOHNNY-THE-PRIEST."

TWO LONGSHOREMEN.

A POSTMAN.

LARRY, bartender.

CHRIS. CHRISTOPHERSON, captain of the barge *Simeon Winthrop.*

MARTHY OWEN.

ANNA CHRISTOPHERSON, Chris's daughter.

THREE MEN OF A STEAMER'S CREW.

MAT BURKE, a stoker.

JOHNSON, deckhand on the barge.

SCENES

ACT ONE

"Johnny-the-Priest's" saloon near the water front, New York City.

ACT TWO

The barge, *Simeon Winthrop,* at anchor in the harbor of Provincetown, Mass. Ten days later.

ACT THREE

Cabin of the barge, at dock in Boston. A week later.

ACT FOUR

The same. Two days later.

"ANNA CHRISTIE"

ACT ONE

SCENE. "JOHNNY-THE-PRIEST'S" *saloon near South Street, New York City. The stage is divided into two sections, showing a small back room on the right. On the left, forward, of the barroom, a large window looking out on the street. Beyond it, the main entrance—a double swinging door. Farther back, another window. The bar runs from left to right nearly the whole length of the rear wall. In back of the bar, a small showcase displaying a few bottles of case goods, for which there is evidently little call. The remainder of the rear space in front of the large mirrors is occupied by half-barrels of cheap whisky of the "nickel-a-shot" variety, from which the liquor is drawn by means of spigots. On the right is an open doorway leading to the back room. In the back room are four round wooden tables with five chairs grouped about each. In the rear, a family entrance opening on a side street.*

It is late afternoon of a day in fall.

As the curtain rises, JOHNNY *is discovered.* "JOHNNY-THE-PRIEST" *deserves his nickname. With his pale, thin, clean-shaven face, mild blue eyes and white hair, a cassock would seem more suited to him than the apron he wears. Neither his voice nor his general manner dispel this illusion which has made him a personage of the water front. They are soft and bland. But beneath all his mildness one senses the man behind the mask—cynical, callous, hard as nails. He is lounging at ease behind the bar, a pair of spectacles on his nose, reading an evening paper.*

Two longshoremen enter from the street, wearing their working aprons, the button of the union pinned conspicuously on the caps pulled sideways on their heads at an aggressive angle.

FIRST LONGSHOREMAN (*as they range themselves at the bar*). Gimme a shock. Number Two. (*He tosses a coin on the bar.*)

SECOND LONGSHOREMAN. Same here. (JOHNNY *sets two glasses of barrel whisky before them.*)

FIRST LONGSHOREMAN. Here's luck! (*The other nods. They gulp down their whisky.*)

SECOND LONGSHOREMAN (*putting money on the bar*). Give us another.

FIRST LONGSHOREMAN. Gimme a scoop this time—lager and porter. I'm dry.

SECOND LONGSHOREMAN. Same here. (JOHNNY *draws the lager and porter and sets the big, foaming schooners before them. They drink down half the contents and start to talk together hurriedly in low tones. The door on the left is swung open and* LARRY *enters. He is a boyish, red-cheeked, rather good-looking young fellow of twenty or so.*)

LARRY (*nodding to* JOHNNY—*cheerily*). Hello, boss.

JOHNNY. Hello, Larry. (*With a glance at his watch.*) Just on time. (LARRY *goes to the right behind the bar, takes off his coat, and puts on an apron.*)

FIRST LONGSHOREMAN (*abruptly*). Let's drink up and get back to it. (*They finish their drinks and go out left.* THE POSTMAN *enters as they leave. He exchanges nods with* JOHNNY *and throws a letter on the bar.*)

THE POSTMAN. Addressed care of you, Johnny. Know him?

JOHNNY (*picks up the letter, adjusting his spectacles.* LARRY *comes and peers over his shoulders.* JOHNNY *reads very slowly).* Christopher Christopherson.

THE POSTMAN (*helpfully*). Square-head name.

LARRY. Old Chris—that's who.

JOHNNY. Oh, sure. I was forgetting Chris carried a hell of a name like that. Letters come here for him sometimes before, I remember now. Long time ago, though.

THE POSTMAN. It'll get him all right then?

JOHNNY. Sure thing. He comes here whenever he's in port.

THE POSTMAN (*turning to go*). Sailor, eh?

JOHNNY (*with a grin*). Captain of a coal barge.

THE POSTMAN (*laughing*). Some job! Well, s'long.

JOHNNY. S'long. I'll see he gets it. (THE POSTMAN *goes out.* JOHNNY *scrutinizes the letter.*) You got good eyes, Larry. Where's it from?

LARRY (*after a glance*). St. Paul. That'll be in Minnesota, I'm thinkin'. Looks like a woman's writing, too, the old divil!

JOHNNY. He's got a daughter somewheres out West, I think he told me once. (*He puts the letter on the cash register.*) Come to think of it, I ain't seen old Chris in a dog's age. (*Putting his overcoat on, he comes around the end of the bar.*) Guess I'll be gettin' home. See you tomorrow.

LARRY. Good-night to ye, boss. (*As* JOHNNY *goes toward the street door, it is pushed open and* CHRISTOPHER CHRISTOPHERSON *enters. He is a short, squat, broad-shouldered man of about fifty, with a round, weather-beaten, red face from which his light blue eyes peer short-sightedly, twinkling with a simple good humor. His large mouth, overhung by a thick, drooping, yellow mustache, is childishly self-willed and weak, of an obstinate kindliness. A thick neck is jammed like a post into the heavy trunk of his body. His arms with their big, hairy, freckled hands, and his stumpy legs terminating in large flat feet, are awkwardly short and muscular. He walks with a clum-*

sy, rolling gait. His voice, when not raised in a hollow boom, is toned down to a sly, confidential half-whisper with something vaguely plaintive in its quality. He is dressed in a wrinkled, ill-fitting dark suit of shore clothes, and wears a faded cap of gray cloth over his mop of grizzled, blond hair. Just now his face beams with a too-blissful happiness, and he has evidently been drinking. He reaches his hand out to JOHNNY.)

CHRIS. Hello, Yohnny! Have drink on me. Come on, Larry. Give us drink. Have one yourself. (*Putting his hand in his pocket.*) Ay gat money—plenty money. . . .

JOHNNY (*shakes* CHRIS *by the hand*). Speak of the devil. We was just talkin' about you.

LARRY (*coming to the end of the bar*). Hello, Chris. Put it there. (*They shake hands.*)

CHRIS (*beaming*). Give us drink.

JOHNNY (*with a grin*). You got a half-snootful now. Where'd you get it?

CHRIS (*grinning*). Oder fallar on oder barge—Irish fallar—he gat bottle vhisky and we drank it, yust us two. Dot vhisky gat kick, by yingo! Ay yust come ashore. Give us drink, Larry. Ay vas little drunk, not much. Yust feel good. (*He laughs and commences to sing in a nasal, high-pitched quaver.*) "My Yosephine, come board de ship. Long time Ay vait for you. De moon, she shi-i-i-ine. She looka yust like you. Tchee-tchee, tchee-tchee, tchee-tchee, tchee-tchee." (*To the accompaniment of this last he waves his hand as if he were conducting an orchestra.*)

JOHNNY (*with a laugh*). Same old Yosie. eh Chris?

CHRIS. You don't know good song when you hear him. Italian fallar on oder barge, he learn me dat. Give us drink. (*He throws change on the bar.*)

LARRY (*with a professional air*). What's your pleasure, gentlemen?

JOHNNY. Small beer, Larry.

CHRIS. Vhisky—Number Two.

LARRY (*as he gets their drinks*). I'll take a cigar on you.

CHRIS (*lifting his glass*): Skoal! (*He drinks.*)

JOHNNY. Drink hearty.

CHRIS (*immediately*). Have oder drink.

JOHNNY. No. Some other time. Got to go home now. So you've just landed? Where are you in from this time?

CHRIS. Norfolk. Ve make slow voyage— dirty vedder—yust fog, fog, fog, all bloody time! (*There is an insistent ring from the doorbell at the family entrance in the back room.* CHRIS *gives a start—hurriedly.*) Ay go open, Larry. Ay forgat. It vas Marthy. She come with me. (*He goes into the back room.*)

LARRY (*with a chuckle*). He's still got that same cow livin' with him, the old fool!

JOHNNY (*with a grin*). A sport, Chris is. Well, I'll beat it home. S'long. (*He goes to the street door.*)

LARRY. So long, boss.

JOHNNY. Oh—don't forget to give him his letter.

LARRY. I won't. (JOHNNY *goes out. In the meantime,* CHRIS *has opened the family entrance door, admitting* MARTHY. *She might be forty or fifty. Her jowly, mottled face, with its thick red nose, is streaked with interlacing purple veins. Her thick, gray hair is piled anyhow in a greasy mop on top of her round head. Her figure is flabby and fat; her breath comes in wheezy gasps; she speaks in a loud, mannish voice, punctuated by explosions of hoarse laughter. But there still twinkles in her blood-shot blue eyes a youthful lust for life which hard usage has failed to stifle, a sense of humor mocking, but good-tempered. She wears a man's cap, double-breasted man's jacket, and a grimy, calico skirt. Her bare feet are encased in a man's brogans several sizes too large for her, which gives her a shuffling, wobbly gait.*)

MARTHY (*grumblingly*). What yuh tryin' to do, Dutchy—keep me standin' out there all day? (*She comes forward and sits at the table in the right corner, front.*)

CHRIS (*mollifyingly*). Ay'm sorry, Marthy. Ay talk to Yohnny. Ay forgat. What you goin' take for drink?

MARTHY (*appeased*). Gimme a scoop of lager an' ale.

CHRIS. Ay go bring him back. (*He returns to the bar.*) Lager and ale for Marthy, Larry. Vhisky for me. (*He throws change on the bar.*)

LARRY. Right you are. (*Then remembering, he takes the letter from in back of the bar.*) Here's a letter for you—from St. Paul, Minnesota—and a lady's writin'.' (*He grins.*)

CHRIS (*quickly—taking it*). Oh, den it come from my daughter, Anna. She live dere. (*He turns the letter over in his hands uncertainly.*) Ay don't gat letter from Anna—must be a year.

LARRY (*jokingly*). That's a fine fairy tale to be tellin'—your daughter! Sure I'll bet it's some bum.

CHRIS (*soberly*). No. Dis come from Anna. (*Engrossed by the letter in his hand—uncertainly.*) By golly, Ay tank Ay'm too drunk for read dis letter from Anna. Ay tank Ay sat down for a minute. You bring drinks in back room, Larry. (*He goes into the room on right.*)

MARTHY (*angrily*). Where's my lager an' ale, yuh big stiff?

CHRIS (*preoccupied*). Larry bring him. (*He sits down opposite her.* LARRY *brings in the drinks and sets them on the table. He and* MARTHY *exchange nods of recognition.* LARRY *stands looking at* CHRIS *curiously.* MARTHY *takes a long draught of her schooner and heaves a huge sigh of satisfaction, wiping her mouth with the back of her hand.* CHRIS *stares at the letter for a moment—slowly opens it, and, squinting his eyes, commences to read laboriously, his lips moving as he spells out the words. As he reads his face lights up with an expression of mingled joy and bewilderment.*)

LARRY. Good news?

MARTHY (*her curiosity also aroused*). What's that yuh got—a letter, fur Gawd's sake?

CHRIS (*pauses for a moment, after finishing the letter, as if to let the news sink in—then suddenly pounds his fist on the table with happy excitement*). Py yiminy! Yust tank, Anna say she's comin' here right avay! She gat sick on yob in St. Paul, she say. It's short letter, don't tal me much more'n dat. (*Beaming.*) Py golly, dat's good news all at one time for ole fallar! (*Then turning to* MARTHY, *rather shamefacedly.*) You know, Marthy, Ay've tole you Ay don't see my Anna since she vas little gel in Sveden five year ole.

MARTHY. How old'll she be now?

CHRIS. She must be—lat me see—she must be twenty year ole, py Yo!

LARRY (*surprised*). You've not seen her in fifteen years?

CHRIS (*suddenly growing somber—in a low tone*). No. Ven she vas little gel, Ay vas bo'sun on vindjammer. Ay never gat home only few time dem year. Ay'm fool sailor fallar. My voman—Anna's mother—she gat tired vait all time Sveden for me ven Ay don't never come. She come dis country, bring Anna, dey go out Minnesota, live with her cousins on farm. Den ven her mo'der die ven Ay vas on voyage, Ay tank it's better dem cousins keep Anna. Ay tank it's better Anna live on farm, den she don't know dat ole davil, sea, she don't know fa'der like me.

LARRY (*with a wink at* MARTHY). This girl, now, 'll be marryin' a sailor herself, likely. It's in the blood.

CHRIS (*suddenly springing to his feet and smashing his fist on the table in a rage*). No, py God! She don't do dat!

MARTHY (*grasping her schooner hastily—angrily*). Hey, look out, yuh nut! Wanta spill my suds for me?

LARRY (*amazed*). Oho, what's up with you? Ain't you a sailor yourself now, and always been?

CHRIS (*slowly*). Dat's yust vhy Ay say it. (*Forcing a smile.*) Sailor vas all right fallar, but not for marry gel. No. Ay know dat. Anna's mo'der, she know it, too.

LARRY (*as* CHRIS *remains sunk in gloomy reflection*). When is your daughter comin'? Soon?

CHRIS (*roused*). Py yiminy, Ay forgat. (*Reads through the letter hurriedly.*) She say she come right avay, dat's all.

LARRY. She'll maybe be comin' here to look for you, I s'pose. (*He returns to the bar, whistling. Left alone with* MARTHY, *who stares at him with a twinkle of malicious humor in her eyes,* CHRIS *suddenly becomes desperately ill-at-ease. He fidgets, then gets up hurriedly.*)

CHRIS. Ay gat speak with Larry. Ay be right back. (*Mollifyingly.*) Ay bring you oder drink.

MARTHY (*emptying her glass*). Sure. That's me. (*As he retreats with the glass she guffaws after him derisively.*)

CHRIS (*to* LARRY *in an alarmed whisper*). Py yingo, Ay gat gat Marthy shore off barge before Anna come! Anna raise hell if she find dat out. Marthy raise hell, too, for go, py golly!

LARRY (*with a chuckle*). Serve ye right, ye old divil—havin' a woman at your age!

CHRIS (*scratching his head in a quandary*). You tal me lie for tal Marthy, Larry, so's she gat off barge quick.

LARRY. She knows your daughter's comin'. Tell her to get the hell out of it.

CHRIS. No. Ay don't like make her feel bad.

LARRY. You're an old mush! Keep your girl away from the barge, then. She'll likely want to stay ashore anyway. (*Curiously.*) What does she work at, your Anna?

CHRIS. She stay on dem cousins' farm till two year ago. Dan she gat yob nurse gel in St. Paul. (*Then shaking his head resolutely.*) But Ay don't vant for her gat yob now. Ay vant for her stay with me.

LARRY (*scornfully*). On a coal barge! She'll not like that, I'm thinkin'.

MARTHY (*shouts from next room*). Don't I get that bucket o' suds, Dutchy?

CHRIS (*startled—in apprehensive confusion*). Yes, Ay come, Marthy.

LARRY (*drawing the lager and ale, hands it to* CHRIS—*laughing.*) Now you're in for it! You'd better tell her straight to get out!

CHRIS (*shaking in his boots*). Py golly. (*He takes her drink in to* MARTHY *and sits down at the table. She sips it in silence.* LARRY *moves quietly close to the partition to listen, grinning with expectation.* CHRIS *seems on the verge of speaking, hesitates, gulps down his whisky desperately as if seeking for courage. He attempts to whistle a few bars of "Yosephine" with careless bravado, but the whistle peters out futilely.* MARTHY *stares at him keenly, taking in his embarrassment with a malicious twinkle of amusement in her eye.* CHRIS *clears his throat.*) Marthy—

MARTHY (*aggressively*). Wha's that? (*Then, pretending to fly into a rage, her eyes enjoying* CHRIS' *misery.*) I'm wise to what's in back of your nut, Dutchy. Yuh want to git rid o' me, huh?—now she's comin'. Gimme the bum's rush ashore, huh? Lemme tell yuh, Dutchy, there ain't a square-head workin' on a boat man enough to git away with that. Don't start nothin' yuh can't finish!

CHRIS (*miserably*). Ay don't start nutting, Marthy.

MARTHY (*glares at him for a second—then cannot control a burst of laughter*). Ho-ho! Yuh're a scream, Square-head—an honest-ter-Gawd knockout! Ho-ho! (*She wheezes, panting for breath.*)

CHRIS (*with childish pique*). Ay don't see nutting for laugh at.

MARTHY. Take a slant in the mirror and yuh'll see. Ho-ho! (*Recovering from her mirth—chuckling, scornfully.*) A square-head tryin' to kid Marthy Owen at this late day!—after me campin' with barge men the last twenty years. I'm wise to the game, up, down, and sideways. I ain't been born and dragged up on the water front for nothin'. Think I'd make trouble, huh? Not me! I'll pack up me duds an' beat it. I'm quittin' yuh, get me? I'm tellin' yuh I'm sick of stickin' with yuh, and I'm leavin' yuh flat, see? There's plenty of other guys on other barges waitin' for me. Always was, I always found. (*She claps the aston-ished* CHRIS *on the back.*) So cheer up, Dutchy! I'll be offen the barge before she comes. You'll be rid o' me for good—and me o' you—good riddance for both of us. Ho-ho!

CHRIS (*seriously*). Ay don' tank dat. You vas good gel, Marthy.

MARTHY (*grinning*). Good girl? Aw, can the bull! Well, yuh treated me square, yuh-self. So it's fifty-fifty. Nobody's sore at nobody. We're still good frien's, huh? (*LARRY returns to bar.*)

CHRIS (*beaming now that he sees his troubles disappearing*). Yes, py golly.

MARTHY. That's the talkin'! In all my time I tried never to split with a guy with no hard feelin's. But what was yuh so scared about—that I'd kick up a row? That ain't Marthy's way. (*Scornfully.*) Think I'd break my heart to lose yuh? Commit suicide, huh? Ho-ho! Gawd! The world's full o' men if that's all I'd worry about! (*Then with a grin, after emptying her glass.*) Blow me to another scoop, huh? I'll drink your kid's health for yuh.

CHRIS (*eagerly*). Sure tang. Ay go gat him. (*He takes the two glasses into the bar.*) Oder drink. Same for both.

LARRY (*getting the drinks and putting them on the bar*). She's not such a bad lot, that one.

CHRIS (*jovially*). She's good gel, Ay tal you! Py golly, Ay calabrate now! Give me vhisky here at bar, too. (*He puts down money.* LARRY *serves him.*) You have drink, Larry.

LARRY (*virtuously*). You know I never touch it.

CHRIS. You don't know what you miss. Skoal! (*He drinks—then begins to sing loudly.*) "My Yosephine, come board de ship—" (*He picks up the drinks for* MARTHY *and himself and walks unsteadily into the back room, singing.*) "De moon, she shi-i-i-ine. She looks yust like you. Tchee-tchee, tchee-tchee, tchee-tchee, tchee-tchee."

MARTHY (*grinning, hands to ears*). Gawd!

CHRIS (*sitting down*). Ay'm good singer, yes? Ve drink, eh? Skoal! Ay calabrate! (*He drinks.*) Ay calabrate 'cause Anna's coming home. You know, Marthy, Ay never write for her to come, 'cause Ay tank Ay'm no good for her. But all time Ay hope like hell some day she vant for see me and den she come. And dat's vay it happen now, py yiminy! (*His face beaming.*) What you tank she look like, Marthy? Ay bet you she's fine, good, strong gel, pooty like hell! Living on farm made her like dat. And Ay bet you some day she marry good, steady land fallar here in East, have home all her own, have kits—and dan Ay'm ole grandfader, py golly! And Ay go visit dem every time Ay gat in port near! (*Bursting with joy.*) By yiminy crickens, Ay calabrate dat! (*Shouts.*) Bring oder drink, Larry! (*He smashes his fist on the table with a bang.*)

LARRY (*coming in from bar—irritably*). Easy there! Don't be breakin' the table, you old goat!

CHRIS (*by way of reply, grins foolishly and begins to sing*). "My Yosephine, come board de ship—"

MARTHY (*touching* CHRIS' *arm persuasively*). You're soused to the ears, Dutchy. Go out and put a feed into you. It'll sober you up. (*Then as* CHRIS *shakes his head obstinately.*) Listen, yuh old nut! Yuh don't know what time your kid's liable to show up. Yuh want to be sober when she comes, don't yuh?

CHRIS (*aroused—gets unsteadily to his feet*). Py golly, yes.

LARRY. That's good sense for you. A good beef stew'll fix you. Go round the corner.

CHRIS. All right. Ay be back soon, Marthy.

(CHRIS *goes through the bar and out the street door.*)

LARRY. He'll come round all right with some grub in him.

MARTHY. Sure. (LARRY *goes back to the bar and resumes his newspaper.* MARTHY *sips what is left of her schooner reflectively. There is the ring of the family entrance bell.* LARRY *comes to the door and opens it a trifle—then, with a puzzled expression,* pulls it wide. ANNA CHRISTOPHERSON *enters. She is a tall, blond, fully-developed girl of twenty, handsome after a large, Vikingdaughter fashion but now run down in health and plainly showing all the outward evidences of belonging to the world's oldest profession. Her youthful face is already hard and cynical beneath its layer of makeup. Her clothes are the tawdry finery of peasant stock turned prostitute. She comes and sinks wearily in a chair by the table, left front.*)

ANNA. Gimme a whisky—ginger ale on the side. (*Then, as* LARRY *turns to go, forcing a winning smile at him.*) And don't be stingy, baby.

LARRY (*sarcastically*). Shall I serve it in a pail?

ANNA (*with a hard laugh*). That suits me down to the ground. (LARRY *goes into the bar. The two women size each other up with frank stares.* LARRY *comes back with the drink which he sets before* ANNA *and returns to the bar again.* ANNA *downs her drink at a gulp. Then, after a moment, as the alcohol begins to rouse her, she turns to* MARTHY *with a friendly smile.*) Gee, I needed that bad, all right, all right!

MARTHY (*nodding her head sympathetically*). Sure—yuh look all in. Been on a bat?

ANNA. No—traveling—day and a half on the train. Had to sit up all night in the dirty coach, too. Gawd, I thought I'd never get here!

MARTHY (*with a start—looking at her intently*). Where'd yuh come from, huh?

ANNA. St. Paul—out in Minnesota.

MARTHY (*staring at her in amazement—slowly*). So—yuh're—(*She suddenly bursts out into hoarse, ironical laughter.*) Gawd!

ANNA. All the way from Minnesota, sure. (*Flaring up.*) What you laughing at? Me?

MARTHY (*hastily*). No, honest, kid. I was thinkin' of somethin' else.

ANNA (*mollified—with a smile*). Well, I wouldn't blame you, at that. Guess I do look rotten—yust out of the hospital two weeks. I'm going to have another 'ski. What d'you say? Have something on me?

MARTHY. Sure I will. T'anks. (*She calls.*) Hey, Larry! Little service! (*He comes in.*)

ANNA. Same for me.

MARTHY. Same here. (LARRY *takes their glasses and goes out.*)

ANNA. Why don't you come sit over here, be sociable? I'm a dead stranger in this burg —and I ain't spoke a word with no one since day before yesterday.

MARTHY. Sure thing. (*She shuffles over to* ANNA's *table and sits down opposite her.* LARRY *brings the drinks and* ANNA *pays him.*)

ANNA. Skoal! Here's how! (*She drinks.*)

MARTHY. Here's luck! (*She takes a gulp from her schooner.*)

ANNA (*taking a package of Sweet Caporal cigarettes from her bag*). Let you smoke in here, won't they?

MARTHY (*doubtfully*). Sure. (*Then with evident anxiety.*) On'y trow it away if yuh hear someone comin'.

ANNA (*lighting one and taking a deep inhale*). Gee, they're fussy in this dump, ain't they? (*She puffs, staring at the table top.* MARTHY *looks her over with a new penetrating interest, taking in every detail of her face.* ANNA *suddenly becomes conscious of this appraising stare—resentfully.*) Ain't nothing wrong with me, is there? You're looking hard enough.

MARTHY (*irritated by the other's tone— scornfully*). Ain't got to look much. I got your number the minute you stepped in the door.

ANNA (*her eyes narrowing*). Ain't you smart! Well, I got yours, too, without no trouble. You're me forty years from now. That's you! (*She gives a hard little laugh.*)

MARTHY (*angrily*). Is that so? Well, I'll tell you straight, kiddo, that Marthy Owen never—(*She catches herself up short—with a grin.*) What are you and me scrappin' over? Let's cut it out, huh? Me, I don't want no hard feelin's with no one. (*Extending her hand.*) Shake and forget it, huh?

ANNA (*shakes her hand gladly*). Only too glad to. I ain't looking for trouble. Let's have 'nother. What d'you say?

MARTHY (*shaking her head*). Not for mine. I'm full up. And you—Had anythin' to eat lately?

ANNA. Not since this morning on the train.

MARTHY. Then yuh better go easy on it, hadn't yuh?

ANNA (*after a moment's hesitation*). Guess you're right. I got to meet someone, too. But my nerves is on edge after that rotten trip.

MARTHY. Yuh said yuh was just outa the hospital?

ANNA. Two weeks ago. (*Leaning over to* MARTHY *confidentially.*) The joint I was in out in St. Paul got raided. That was the start. The judge give all us girls thirty days. The others didn't seem to mind being in the cooler much. Some of 'em was used to it. But me, I couldn't stand it. It got my goat right—couldn't eat or sleep or nothing. I never could stand being caged up nowheres. I got good and sick and they had to send me to the hospital. It was nice there. I was sorry to leave it, honest!

MARTHY (*after a slight pause*). Did yuh say yuh got to meet someone here?

ANNA. Yes. Oh, not what you mean. It's my Old Man I got to meet. Honest! It's funny, too. I ain't seen him since I was a kid— don't even know what he looks like—yust had a letter every now and then. This was always the only address he give me to write him back. He's yanitor of some building here now—used to be a sailor.

MARTHY (*astonished*). Janitor!

ANNA. Sure. And I was thinking maybe, seeing he ain't never done a thing for me in my life, he might be willing to stake me to a room and eats till I get rested up. (*Wearily.*) Gee, I sure need that rest! I'm knocked out. (*Then resignedly.*) But I ain't expecting much from him. Give you a kick when you're down, that's what all men do. (*With sudden passion.*) Men, I hate 'em—all of 'em! And I don't expect he'll turn out no better than the rest. (*Then with sudden interest.*) Say, do you hang out around this dump much?

MARTHY. Oh, off and on.

ANNA. Then maybe you know him—my Old Man—or at least seen him?

MARTHY. It ain't old Chris, is it?

ANNA. Old Chris?

MARTHY. Chris Christopherson, his full name is.

ANNA (*excitedly*). Yes, that's him! Anna Christopherson—that's my real name—only out there I called myself Anna Christie. So you know him, eh?

MARTHY (*evasively*). Seen him about for years.

ANNA. Say, what's he like, tell me, honest?

MARTHY. Oh, he's short and—

ANNA (*impatiently*). I don't care what he looks like. What kind is he?

MARTHY (*earnestly*). Well, yuh can bet your life, kid, he's as good an old guy as ever walked on two feet. That goes!

ANNA (*pleased*). I'm glad to hear it. Then you think's he'll stake me to that rest cure I'm after?

MARTHY (*emphatically*). Surest thing you know. (*Disgustedly.*) But where'd yuh get the idea he was a janitor?

ANNA. He wrote me he was himself.

MARTHY. Well, he was lyin'. He ain't. He's captain of a barge—five men under him.

ANNA (*disgustedly in her turn*). A barge? What kind of a barge?

MARTHY. Coal, mostly.

ANNA. A coal barge! (*with a harsh laugh.*) If that ain't a swell job to find your long-lost Old Man working at! Gee, I knew something'd be bound to turn out wrong—always does with me. That puts my idea of his giving me a rest on the bum.

MARTHY. What d'yuh mean?

ANNA. I s'pose he lives on the boat, don't he?

MARTHY. Sure. What about it? Can't you live on it, too?

ANNA (*scornfully*). Me? On a dirty coal barge! What d'you think I am?

MARTHY (*resentfully*). What d'yuh know about barges, huh? Bet yuh ain't never seen one. That's what comes of his bringing yuh up inland—away from the old devil sea—where yuh'd be safe—Gawd! (*The irony of it strikes her sense of humor and she laughs hoarsely.*)

ANNA (*angrily*). His bringing me up! Is that what he tells people! I like his nerve! He let them cousins of my Old Woman's keep me on their farm and work me to death like a dog.

MARTHY. Well, he's got queer notions on some things. I've heard him say a farm was the best place for a kid.

ANNA. Sure. That's what he'd always answer back—and a lot of crazy stuff about staying away from the sea—stuff I couldn't make head or tail to. I thought he must be nutty.

MARTHY. He is on that one point. (*Casually.*) So yuh didn't fall for life on the farm, huh?

ANNA. I should say not! The old man of the family, his wife, and four sons—I had to slave for all of 'em. I was only a poor relation, and they treated me worse than they dare treat a hired girl. (*After a moment's hesitation—somberly.*) It was one of the sons—the youngest—started me—when I was sixteen. After that, I hated 'em so I'd killed 'em all if I'd stayed. So I run away—to St. Paul.

MARTHY (*who has been listening sympathetically*). I've heard Old Chris talkin' about your bein' a nurse girl out there. Was that all a bluff yuh put up when yuh wrote him?

ANNA. Not on your life, it wasn't. It was true for two years. I didn't go wrong all at one jump. Being a nurse girl was yust what finished me. Taking care of other people's kids, always listening to their bawling and crying, caged in, when you're only a kid yourself and want to go out and see things. At last I got the chance—to get into that house. And you bet your life I took it! (*Defiantly.*) And I ain't sorry neither. (*After a pause—with bitter hatred.*) It was all men's fault—the whole business. It was men on the farm ordering and beating me —and giving me the wrong start. Then when I was a nurse, it was men again hanging around, bothering me, trying to see what they could get. (*She gives a hard laugh.*) And now it's men all the time. Gawd, I hate 'em all, every mother's son of 'em! Don't you?

MARTHY. Oh, I dunno. There's good ones and bad ones, kid. You've just had a run of bad luck with 'em, that's all. Your Old Man, now—old Chris—he's a good one.

ANNA (*sceptically*). He'll have to show me.

MARTHY. Yuh kept right on writing him yuh was a nurse girl still, even after yuh was in the house, didn't yuh?

ANNA. Sure. (*Cynically.*) Not that I think he'd care a darn.

MARTHY. Yuh're all wrong about him, kid. (*Earnestly.*) I know Old Chris well for a long time. He's talked to me 'bout you lots o' times. He thinks the world o' you, honest he does.

ANNA. Aw, quit the kiddin'!

MARTHY. Honest! Only, he's a simple old guy, see? He's got nutty notions. But he means well, honest. Listen to me, kid— (*She is interrupted by the opening and shutting of the street door in the bar and by hearing* CHRIS' *voice.*) Ssshh!

ANNA. What's up?

CHRIS (*who has entered the bar. He seems considerably sobered up*). Py golly, Larry, dat grub taste good. Marthy in back?

LARRY. Sure—and another tramp with her. (CHRIS *starts for the entrance to the back room.*)

MARTHY (*to* ANNA *in a hurried, nervous whisper*). That's him now. He's comin' in here. Brace up!

ANNA. Who? (CHRIS *opens the door.*)

MARTHY (*as if she were greeting him for the first time*). Why, hello, Old Chris. (*Then before he can speak, she shuffles hurriedly past him into the bar, beckoning him to follow her.*) Come here. I wanta tell yuh somethin'. (*He goes out to her. She speaks hurriedly in a low voice.*) Listen! I'm goin' to beat it down to the barge— pack up me duds and blow. That's her in there—your Anna—just come—waitin' for yuh. Treat her right, see? She's been sick. Well, s'long! (*She goes into the back room—to* ANNA.) S'long, kid. I gotta beat it now. See yuh later.

ANNA (*nervously*). So long. (MARTHY *goes quickly out of the family entrance.*)

LARRY (*looking at the stupefied* CHRIS *curiously*). Well, what's up now?

CHRIS (*vaguely*). Nutting—nutting. (*He stands before the door to the back room in an agony of embarrassed emotion—then he forces himself to a bold decision, pushes open the door and walks in. He stands there, casts a shy glance at Anna, whose brilliant clothes, and, to him, high-toned appearance, awe him terribly. He looks about him with pitiful nervousness as if to avoid the appraising look with which she takes in his face, his clothes, etc.—his voice seeming to plead for her forbearance.*) Anna!

ANNA (*acutely embarrassed in her turn*). Hello—father. She told me it was you. I yust got here a little while ago.

CHRIS (*goes slowly over to her chair*). It's good—for see you—after all dem years, Anna. (*He bends down over her. After an embarrassed struggle they manage to kiss each other.*)

ANNA (*a trace of genuine feeling in her voice*). It's good to see you, too.

CHRIS (*grasps her arms and looks into her face—then overcome by a wave of fierce tenderness*). Anna lilla! Anna lilla! (*Takes her in his arms.*)

ANNA (*shrinks away from him, half-frightened*). What's that—Swedish? I don't know it. (*Then as if seeking relief from the tension in a voluble chatter.*) Gee, I had an awful trip coming here. I'm all in. I had to sit up in the dirty coach all night—couldn't get no sleep, hardly—and then I had a hard job finding this place. I never been in New York before, you know, and—

CHRIS (*who has been staring down at her face admiringly, not hearing what she says—impulsively*). You know you vas awful pooty gel, Anna? Ay bet all men see you fall in love with you, py yiminy!

ANNA (*repelled—harshly*). Cut it! You talk same as they all do.

CHRIS (*hurt—humbly*). Ain't no harm for your fader talk dat vay, Anna.

ANNA (*forcing a short laugh*). No—course not. Only—it's funny to see you and not remember nothing. You're like—a stranger.

CHRIS (*sadly*). Ay s'pose. Ay never come home only a few times ven you vas kit in Sveden. You don't remember dat?

ANNA. No. (*Resentfully.*) But why didn't you never come home them days? Why didn't you never come out West to see me?

CHRIS (*slowly*). Ay tank, after your mo'der die, ven Ay vas avay on voyage, it's better for you you don't never see me! (*He sinks down in the chair opposite her dejectedly—then turns to her—sadly.*) Ay don't know, Anna, vhy Ay never come home Sveden in ole year. Ay vant come home end of every voyage. Ay vant see your mo'der, your two bro'der before dey vas drowned, you ven you was born—but—Ay—don't go. Ay sign on oder ships—go South America, go Australia, go China, go every port all over world many times—but Ay never go aboard ship sail for Sveden. Ven Ay gat money for pay passage home as passenger den—(*He bows his head guiltily.*) Ay forgat and Ay spend all money. Ven Ay tank again, it's too late. (*He sighs.*) Ay don't know why but dat's vay with most sailor fallar, Anna. Dat ole davil sea make dem crazy fools with her dirty tricks. It's so.

ANNA (*who has watched him keenly while he has been speaking—with a trace of scorn in her voice.*) Then you think the sea's to blame for everything, eh? Well, you're still workin' on it, ain't you, spite of all you used to write me about hating it. That dame was here told me you was captain of a coal barge—and you wrote me you was yanitor of a building!

CHRIS (*embarrassed but lying glibly*). Oh, Ay vork on land long time as yanitor. Yust short time ago Ay got dis yob cause Ay vas sick, need open air.

ANNA (*sceptically*). Sick? You? You'd never think it.

CHRIS. And, Anna, dis ain't real sailor yob. Dis ain't real boat on sea. She's yust ole tub—like piece of land with house on it dat float. Yob on her ain't sea yob. No. Ay don't gat yob on sea, Anna, if Ay die first. Ay swear dat ven your mo'der die. Ay keep my word, py yingo!

ANNA (*perplexed*). Well, I can't see no difference. (*Dismissing the subject.*) Speaking of being sick, I been there myself—yust out of the hospital two weeks ago.

CHRIS (*immediately all concern*). You, Anna? Py golly! (*Anxiously.*) You feel better now, dough, don't you? You look little tired, dat's all!

ANNA (*wearily*). I am. Tired to death. I need a long rest and I don't see much chance of getting it.

CHRIS. What you mean, Anna?

ANNA. Well, when I made up my mind to come to see you, I thought you was a yanitor—that you'd have a place where, maybe, if you didn't mind having me, I could visit a while and rest up—till I felt able to get back on the job again.

CHRIS (*eagerly*). But Ay gat place, Anna—nice place. You rest all you want, py yiminy! You don't never have to vork as nurse gel no more. You stay with me, py golly!

ANNA (*surprised and pleased by his eagerness—with a smile*). Then you're really glad to see me—honest?

CHRIS (*pressing one of her hands in both of his*). Anna, Ay like see you like hell, Ay tal you! And don't you talk no more about gatting yob. You stay with me. Ay don't see you for long time, you don't forgat dat. (*His voice trembles.*) Ay'm gatting ole. Ay gat no one in world but you.

ANNA (*touched—embarrassed by this unfamiliar emotion*). Thanks. It sounds good to hear someone—talk to me that way. Say, though—if you're so lonely—it's funny— why ain't you ever married again?

CHRIS (*shaking his head emphatically—after a pause*). Ay love your mo'der too much for ever do dat, Anna.

ANNA (*impressed—slowly*). I don't remember nothing about her. What was she like? Tell me.

CHRIS. Ay tal you all about everytang—and you tal me all tangs happen to you. But not here now. Dis ain't good place for young gel, anyway. Only no good sailor fallar come here for gat drunk. (*He gets to his feet quickly and picks up her bag.*) You come with me, Anna. You need lie down, gat rest.

ANNA (*half rises to her feet, then sits down again*). Where're you going?

CHRIS. Come. Ve gat on board.

ANNA (*disappointedly*). On board your barge, you mean? (*Dryly.*) Nix for mine! (*Then seeing his crestfallen look—forcing a smile.*) Do you think that's a good place for a young girl like me—a coal barge?

CHRIS (*dully*). Yes, Ay tank. (*He hesitates —then continues more and more pleadingly.*) You don't know how nice it's on barge, Anna. Tug come and ve gat towed out on voyage—yust water all round, and sun, and fresh air, and good grub for make you strong, healthy gel. You see many tangs you don't see before. You gat moonlight at night, maybe; see steamer pass; see schooner make sail—see everytang dat's pooty. You need take rest like dat. You work too hard for young gel already. You need vacation, yes!

ANNA (*who has listened to him with a growing interest—with an uncertain laugh*). It sounds good to hear you tell it. I'd sure like a trip on the water, all right. It's the barge idea has me stopped. Well, I'll

go down with you and have a look—and maybe I'll take a chance. Gee, I'd do anything once.

CHRIS (*picks up her bag again*). Ve go, eh?

ANNA. What's the rush? Wait a second. (*Forgetting the situation for a moment, she relapses into the familiar form and flashes one of her winning trade smiles at him.*) Gee, I'm thirsty.

CHRIS (*sets down her bag immediately— hastily*). Ay'm sorry, Anna. What you tank you like for drink, eh?

ANNA (*promptly*). I'll take a— (*Then suddenly reminded—confusedly.*) I don't know. What'a they got here?

CHRIS (*with a grin*). Ay don't tank dey got much fancy drink for young gel in dis place, Anna. Yinger ale—sas'prilla, maybe.

ANNA (*forcing a laugh herself*). Make it sas, then.

CHRIS (*coming up to her—with a wink*). Ay tal you, Anna, ve calabrate, yes—dis one time because ve meet after many year. (*In a half whisper, embarrassedly.*) Dey gat good port vine, Anna. It's good for you, Ay tank—little bit—for give you appetite. It ain't strong, neider. One glass don't go to your head, Ay promise.

ANNA (*with a half hysterical laugh*). All right. I'll take port.

CHRIS. Ay go gat him. (*He goes out to the bar. As soon as the door closes,* ANNA *starts to her feet.*)

ANNA (*picking up her bag—half-aloud— stammeringly*). Gawd, I can't stand this! I better beat it. (*Then she lets her bag drop, stumbles over to her chair again, and covering her face with her hands, begins to sob.*)

LARRY (*putting down his paper as* CHRIS *comes up—with a grin*). Well, who's the blond?

CHRIS (*proudly*). Dat vas Anna, Larry.

LARRY (*in amazement*). Your daughter, Anna? (CHRIS *nods.* LARRY *lets a long, low whistle escape him and turns away embarrassedly.*)

CHRIS. Don't you tank she vas pooty gel, Larry?

LARRY (*rising to the occasion*). Sure! A peach!

CHRIS. You bet you! Give me drink for take back—one port vine for Anna—she calabrate dis one time with me—and small beer for me.

LARRY (*as he gets the drinks*). Small beer for you, eh? She's reformin' you already.

CHRIS (*pleased*). You bet! (*He takes the drinks. As she hears him coming,* ANNA *hastily dries her eyes, tries to smile.* CHRIS *comes in and sets the drinks down on the table—stares at her for a second anxiously—patting her hand.*) You look tired, Anna. Vell, Ay make you take good long rest now. (*Picking up his beer.*) Come, you drink vine. It put new life in you. (*She lifts her glass—he grins.*) Skoal, Anna! You know dat Svedish word?

ANNA. Skoal! (*downing her port at a gulp like a drink of whisky—her lips trembling.*) Skoal? Guess I know that word, all right, all right!

The Curtain Falls.

ACT TWO

SCENE. *Ten days later. The stern of the deeply-laden barge,* Simeon Winthrop, *at anchor in the outer harbor of Provincetown, Mass. It is ten o'clock at night. Dense fog shrouds the barge on all sides, and she floats motionless on a calm. A lantern set up on an immense coil of thick hawser sheds a dull, filtering light on objects near it—the heavy steel bits for making fast the tow lines, etc. In the rear is the cabin, its misty windows glowing wanly with the light of a lamp inside. The chimney of the cabin stove rises a few feet above the roof. The doleful tolling of bells, on Long Point, on ships at anchor, breaks the silence at regular intervals.*

As the curtain rises, ANNA *is discovered standing near the coil of rope on which the lantern is placed. She looks healthy, transformed, the natural color has come back to her face. She has on a black oilskin coat, but wears no hat. She is staring out into the fog astern with an expression of awed wonder. The cabin door is pushed open and* CHRIS *appears. He is dressed in yellow oilskins—coat, pants, sou'wester—and wears high sea-boots.*

CHRIS (*the glare from the cabin still in his eyes, peers blinkingly astern*). Anna! (*Receiving no reply, he calls again, this time with apparent apprehension.*) Anna!

ANNA (*with a start—making a gesture with her hand as if to impose silence—in a hushed whisper*). Yes, here I am. What d'you want?

CHRIS (*walks over to her—solicitously*). Don't you come turn in, Anna? It's late—after four bells. It ain't good for you stay out here in fog, Ay tank.

ANNA. Why not? (*With a trace of strange exultation.*) I love this fog! Honest! It's so—(*She hesitates, groping for a word.*) Funny and still. I feel as if I was—out of things altogether.

CHRIS (*spitting disgustedly*). Fog's vorst one of her dirty tricks, py yingo!

ANNA (*with a short laugh*). Beefing about the sea again? I'm getting so's I love it, the little I've seen.

CHRIS (*glancing at her moodily*). Dat's foolish talk, Anna. You see her more, you don't talk dat vay. (*Then seeing her irritation, he hastily adopts a more cheerful tone.*) But Ay'm glad you like it on barge. Ay'm glad it makes you feel good again. (*With a placating grin.*) You like live like dis alone with ole fa'der, eh?

ANNA. Sure I do. Everything's been so different from anything I ever come across before. And now—this fog—Gee, I wouldn't have missed it for nothing. I never thought living on ships was so different from land. Gee, I'd yust love to work on it, honest I would, if I was a man. I don't wonder you always been a sailor.

CHRIS (*vehemently*). Ay ain't sailor, Anna. And dis ain't real sea. You only see nice part. (*Then as she doesn't answer, he continues hopefully.*) Vell, fog lift in morning, Ay tank.

ANNA (*the exultation again in her voice*). I love it! I don't give a rap if it never lifts! (CHRIS *fidgets from one foot to the other worriedly.* ANNA *continues slowly, after a pause.*) It makes me feel clean—out here —'s if I'd taken a bath.

CHRIS (*after a pause*). You better go in cabin read book. Dat put you to sleep.

ANNA. I don't want to sleep. I want to stay out here—and think about things.

CHRIS (*walks away from her toward the cabin—then comes back*). You act funny tonight, Anna.

ANNA (*her voice rising angrily*). Say, what're you trying to do—make things rotten? You been kind as kind can be to me and I certainly appreciate it—only don't spoil it all now. (*Then, seeing the hurt expression on her father's face, she forces a smile.*) Let's talk of something else. Come. Sit down here. (*She points to the coil of rope.*)

CHRIS (*sits down beside her with a sigh*). It's gatting pooty late in night, Anna. Must be near five bells.

ANNA (*interestedly*). Five bells? What time is that?

CHRIS. Half past ten.

ANNA. Funny I don't know nothing about sea talk—but those cousins was always talking crops and that stuff. Gee, wasn't I sick of it—and of them!

CHRIS. You don't like live on farm, Anna?

ANNA. I've told you a hundred times I hated it. (*Decidedly.*) I'd rather have one drop of ocean than all the farms in the world! Honest! And you wouldn't like a farm, neither. Here's where you belong. (*She makes a sweeping gesture seaward.*) But not on a coal barge. You belong on a real ship, sailing all over the world.

CHRIS (*moodily*). Ay've done dat many year, Anna, when Ay vas damn fool.

ANNA (*disgustedly*). Oh, rats! (*After a pause she speaks musingly.*) Was the men in our family always sailors—as far back as you know about?

CHRIS (*shortly*). Yes. Damn fools! All men in our village on coast, Sveden, go to sea. Ain't nutting else for dem to do. My fa'der die on board ship in Indian Ocean. He's buried at sea. Ay don't never know him only little bit. Den my tree bro'der, older'n me, dey go on ships. Den Ay go, too. Den my mo'der she's left all 'lone. She die pooty quick after dat—all 'lone. Ve vas all avay on voyage when she die. (*He pauses sadly.*) Two my bro'der dey gat lost on fishing boat same like your bro'ders vas drowned. My oder bro'der, he save money, give up sea, den he die home in bed. He's only one dat ole davil don't kill. (*Defiantly.*) But me, Ay bet you Ay die ashore in bed, too!

ANNA. Were all of 'em yust plain sailors?

CHRIS. Able body seaman, most of dem. (*With a certain pride.*) Dey vas all smart seaman, too—A one. (*Then after hesitating a moment—shyly.*) Ay vas bo'sun.

ANNA. Bo'sun?

CHRIS. Dat's kind of officer.

ANNA. Gee, that was fine. What does he do?

CHRIS (*after a second's hesitation, plunged into gloom again by his fear of her enthusiasm*). Hard vork all time. It's rotten, Ay tal you, for go to sea. (*Determined to disgust her with sea life—volubly.*) Dey're all fool fallar, dem fallar in our family. Dey all vork rotten yob on sea for nutting, don't care nutting but yust gat big pay day in pocket, gat drunk, gat robbed, ship avay again on oder voyage. Dey don't come home. Dey don't do anytang like good man do. And dat ole davil, sea, sooner, later she svallow dem up.

ANNA (*with an excited laugh*). Good sports, I'd call 'em. (*Then hastily.*) But say—listen—did all the women of the family marry sailors?

CHRIS (*eagerly—seeing a chance to drive home his point*). Yes—and it's bad on dem like hell vorst of all. Dey don't see deir men only once in long while. Dey set and vait all 'lone. And vhen deir boys grows up, go to sea, dey sit and vait some more. (*Vehemently.*) Any gel marry sailor, she's crazy fool! Your mo'der she tal you same tang if she vas alive. (*He relapses into an attitude of somber brooding.*)

ANNA (*after a pause—dreamily*). Funny! I do feel sort of—nutty, tonight. I feel old.

CHRIS (*mystified*). Ole?

ANNA. Sure—like I'd been living a long, long time—out here in the fog. (*Frowning perplexedly.*) I don't know how to tell you yust what I mean. It's like I'd come home after a long visit away some place. It all seems like I'd been here before lots of times—on boats—in this same fog. (*With a short laugh.*) You must think I'm off my base.

CHRIS (*gruffly*). Anybody feel funny dat vay in fog.

ANNA (*persistently*). But why d'you s'pose I feel so—so—like I'd found something I'd missed and been looking for—'s if this was the right place for me to fit in? And I seem to have forgot—everything that's happened—like it didn't matter no more. And I feel clean, somehow—like you feel yust after you've took a bath. And I feel happy for once—yes, honest!—happier than I ever been anywhere before! (*As CHRIS makes no comment but a heavy sigh, she continues wonderingly.*) It's nutty for me to feel that way, don't you think?

CHRIS (*a grim foreboding in his voice*). Ay tank Ay'm damn fool for bring you on voyage, Anna.

ANNA (*impressed by his tone*). You talk— nutty tonight yourself. You act 's if you was scared something was going to happen.

CHRIS. Only God know dat, Anna.

ANNA (*half-mockingly*). Then it'll be Gawd's will, like the preachers say—what does happen.

CHRIS (*starts to his feet with fierce protest*). No! Dat ole davil, sea, she ain't God! (*In the pause of silence that comes after his defiance a hail in a man's husky, exhausted voice comes faintly out of the fog to port.*) "Ahoy!" (CHRIS *gives a startled exclamation.*)

ANNA (*jumping to her feet*). What's that?

CHRIS (*who has regained his composure— sheepishly*). Py golly, dat scare me for minute. It's only some fallar hail, Anna—lose his course in fog. Must be fisherman's power boat. His engine break down, Ay guess. (*The "ahoy" comes again through the wall of fog, sounding much nearer this time.* CHRIS *goes over to the port bulwark.*) Sound from dis side. She come in from open sea. (*He holds his hands to his mouth, megaphone-fashion, and shouts back.*) Ahoy, dere! Vat's trouble?

THE VOICE (*this time sounding nearer but up forward toward the bow*). Heave a rope when we come alongside. (*Then irritably.*) Where are ye, ye scut?

CHRIS. Ay hear dem rowing. Dey come up by bow, Ay tank. (*Then shouting out again.*) Dis vay!

THE VOICE. Right ye are! (*There is a muffled sound of oars in oar-locks.*)

ANNA (*half to herself—resentfully*). Why don't that guy stay where he belongs?

CHRIS (*hurriedly*). Ay go up bow. All hands asleep 'cepting fallar on vatch. Ay gat heave line to dat fallar. (*He picks up a coil of rope and hurries off toward the bow.* ANNA *walks back toward the extreme stern as if she wanted to remain as much isolated as possible. She turns her back on the proceedings and stares out into the fog.* THE VOICE *is heard again shouting "Ahoy" and* CHRIS *answering "Dis vay." Then there is a pause—the murmur of excited voices—then the scuffling of feet.* CHRIS *appears from around the cabin to port. He is supporting the limp form of a man dressed in dungarees, holding one of the man's arms around his neck. The deckhand,* JOHNSON, *a young blond Swede, follows him, helping along another exhausted man similar fashion.* ANNA *turns to look at them.* CHRIS *stops for a second—volubly.*) Anna! You come help, vill you? You find vhisky in cabin. Dese fallars need drink for fix dem. Dey vas near dead.

ANNA (*hurrying to him*). Sure—but who are they? What's the trouble ?

CHRIS. Sailor fallars. Deir steamer gat wrecked. Dey been five days in open boat—four fallars—only one left able stand up. Come, Anna. (*She precedes him into the cabin, holding the door open while he and* JOHNSON *carry in their burdens. The door is shut, then opened again as* JOHNSON *comes out.* CHRIS' *voice shouts after him.*) Go gat oder fallar, Yohnson.

JOHNSON. Yes, sir. (*He goes. The door is closed again.* MAT BURKE *stumbles in around the port side of the cabin. He moves slowly, feeling his way uncertainly, keeping hold of the port bulwark with his right hand to steady himself. He is stripped to the waist, has on nothing but a pair of dirty dungaree pants. He is a powerful, broad-chested six-footer, his face handsome in a hard, rough, bold, defiant way. He is about thirty, in the full power of his heavy-muscled, immense strength. His dark eyes are bloodshot and wild from sleeplessness. The muscles of his arms and shoulders are lumped in knots and bunches, the veins of his fore-arms stand out like blue cords. He finds his way to the coil of hawser and sits down on it facing the cabin, his back bowed, head in his hands, in an attitude of spent weariness.*)

BURKE (*talking aloud to himself*). Row, ye divil! Row! (*Then lifting his head and looking about him.*) What's this tub? Well, we're safe anyway—with the help of God. (*He makes the sign of the cross mechanically.* JOHNSON *comes along the deck to port, supporting the fourth man, who is babbling to himself incoherently.* BURKE *glances at him disdainfully.*) Is it losing the small wits ye iver had, ye are? Deck-scrubbing scut! (*They pass him and go into the cabin, leaving the door open.* BURKE *sags forward wearily.*) I'm bate out —bate out entirely.

ANNA (*comes out of the cabin with a tumbler quarter-full of whisky in her hand. She gives a start when she sees* BURKE *so near her, the light from the open door falling full on him. Then, overcoming what is evidently a feeling of repulsion, she comes up beside him.*) Here you are. Here's a drink for you. You need it, I guess.

BURKE (*lifting his head slowly—confusedly*). Is it dreaming I am?

ANNA (*half smiling*). Drink it and you'll find it ain't no dream.

BURKE. To hell with the drink—but I'll take it just the same. (*He tosses it down.*) Ahah! I'm needin' that—and 'tis fine stuff. (*Looking up at her with frank, grinning admiration.*) But 'twasn't booze I meant when I said, was I dreaming. I thought you was some mermaid out of the sea come to torment me. (*He reaches out to feel of her arm.*) Aye, rale flesh and blood, divil a less.

ANNA (*coldly. Stepping back from him*). Cut that.

BURKE. But tell me, isn't this a barge I'm on—or isn't it?

ANNA. Sure.

BURKE. And what is a fine handsome woman the like of you doing on this scow?

ANNA (*coldly*). Never you mind. (*Then half-amused in spite of herself.*) Say, you're a great one, honest—starting right in kidding after what you been through.

BURKE (*delighted—proudly*). Ah, it was nothing—aisy for a rale man with guts to him, the like of me. (*He laughs.*) All in the day's work, darlin'. (*Then, more seriously but still in a boastful tone, confidenti-*

ally.) But I won't be denying 'twas a damn narrow squeak. We'd all ought to be with Davy Jones at the bottom of the sea, be rights. And only for me, I'm telling you, and the great strength and guts is in me, we'd be being scoffed by the fishes this minute!

ANNA (*contemptuously*). Gee, you hate yourself, don't you? (*Then turning away from him indifferently.*) Well, you'd better come in and lie down. You must want to sleep.

BURKE (*stung—rising unsteadily to his feet with chest out and head thrown back—resentfully*). Lie down and sleep, is it? Divil a wink I'm after having for two days and nights and divil a bit I'm needing now. Let you not be thinking I'm the like of them three weak scuts come in the boat with me. I could lick the three of them sitting down with one hand tied behind me. They may be bate out, but I'm not—and I've been rowing the boat with them lying in the bottom not able to raise a hand for the last two days we was in it. (*Furiously, as he sees this is making no impression on her.*) And I can lick all hands on this tub, wan be wan, tired as I am!

ANNA (*sarcastically*). Gee, ain't you a hard guy! (*Then, with a trace of sympathy, as she notices him swaying from weakness.*) But never mind that fight talk. I'll take your word for all you've said. Go on and sit down out here, anyway, if I can't get you to come inside. (*He sits down weakly.*) You're all in, you might as well own up to it.

BURKE (*fiercely*). The hell I am!

ANNA (*coldly*). Well, be stubborn then for all I care. And I must say I don't care for your language. The men I know don't pull that rough stuff when ladies are around.

BURKE (*getting unsteadily to his feet again —in a rage*). Ladies! Ho-ho! Divil mend you! Let you not be making game of me. What would ladies be doing on this bloody hulk? (*As ANNA attempts to go to the cabin, he lurches into her path.*) Aisy, now! You're not the old Square-head's woman, I suppose you'll be telling me next—living in his cabin with him, no less! (*Seeing the*

cold, hostile expression on ANNA's *face, he suddenly changes his tone to one of boisterous joviality.*) But I do be thinking, iver since the first look my eyes took at you, that it's a fool you are to be wasting yourself—a fine, handsome girl—on a stumpy runt of a man like that old Swede. There's too many strapping great lads on the sea would give their heart's blood for one kiss of you!

ANNA (*scornfully*). Lads like you, eh?

BURKE (*grinning*). Ye take the words out 'o my mouth. I'm the proper lad for you, if it's meself do be saying it. (*With a quick movement he puts his arms about her waist.*) Whisht, now, me daisy! Himself's in the cabin. It's wan of your kisses I'm needing to take the tiredness from me bones. Wan kiss, now! (*He presses her to him and attempts to kiss her.*)

ANNA (*struggling fiercely*). Leggo of me, you big mutt! (*She pushes him away with all her might. BURKE, weak and tottering, is caught off his guard. He is thrown down backward and, in falling, hits his head a hard thump against the bulwark. He lies there still, knocked out for the moment. ANNA stands for a second, looking down at him frightenedly. Then she kneels down beside him and raises his head to her knee, staring into his face anxiously for some sign of life.*)

BURKE (*stirring a bit—mutteringly*). God stiffen it!. (*He opens his eyes and blinks up at her with vague wonder.*)

ANNA (*letting his head sink back on the deck, rising to her feet with a sigh of relief*). You're coming to all right, eh? Gee, I was scared for a moment I'd killed you.

BURKE (*with difficulty rising to a sitting position—scornfully*). Killed, is it? It'd take more than a bit of a blow to crack my thick skull. (*Then looking at her with the most intense admiration.*) But, glory be, it's a power of strength is in them two fine arms of yours. There's not a man in the world can say the same as you, that he seen Mat Burke lying at his feet and him dead to the world.

ANNA (*rather remorsefully*). Forget it. I'm sorry it happened, see? (*BURKE rises and sits on bench. Then severely.*) Only you had no right to be getting fresh with me. Listen, now, and don't go getting any more wrong notions. I'm on this barge because I'm making a trip with my father. The captain's my father. Now you know.

BURKE. The old square—the old Swede, I mean?

ANNA. Yes.

BURKE (*rising—peering at her face*). Sure I might have known it, if I wasn't a bloody fool from birth. Where else'd you get that fine yellow hair is like a golden crown on your head?

ANNA (*with an amused laugh*). Say, nothing stops you, does it? (*Then attempting a severe tone again.*) But don't you think you ought to be apologizing for what you said and done yust a minute ago, instead of trying to kid me with that mush?

BURKE (*indignantly*). Mush! (*Then bending forward toward her with very intense earnestness.*) Indade and I will ask your pardon a thousand times—and on my knees, if ye like. I didn't mean a word of what I said or did. (*Resentful again for a second.*) But divil a woman in all the ports of the world has iver made a great fool of me that way before!

ANNA (*with amused sarcasm*). I see. You mean you're a lady-killer and they all fall for you.

BURKE (*offended. Passionately.*) Leave off your fooling! 'Tis that is after getting my back up at you. (*Earnestly.*) 'Tis no lie I'm telling you about the women. (*Ruefully.*) Though it's a great jackass I am to be mistaking you, even in anger, for the like of them cows on the waterfront is the only women I've met up with since I was growed to a man. (*As ANNA shrinks away from him at this, he hurries on pleadingly.*) I'm a hard, rough man and I'm not fit, I'm thinking, to be kissing the shoe-soles of a fine, dacent girl the like of yourself. 'Tis only the ignorance of your kind made me see you wrong. So you'll forgive me, for the love of God, and let us be friends from this out. (*Passionately.*) I'm thinking I'd rather be friends with you than have my wish for

anything else in the world. (*He holds out his hand to her shyly.*)

ANNA (*looking queerly at him, perplexed and worried, but moved and pleased in spite of herself—takes his hand uncertainly*). Sure.

BURKE (*with boyish delight*). God bless you! (*In his excitement he squeezes her hand tight.*)

ANNA. Ouch!

BURKE (*hastily dropping her hand—ruefully*). Your pardon, Miss. 'Tis a clumsy ape I am. (*Then simply—glancing down his arm proudly.*) It's great power I have in my hand and arm, and I do be forgetting it at times.

ANNA (*nursing her crushed hand and glancing at his arm, not without a trace of his own admiration*). Gee, you're some strong, all right.

BURKE (*delighted*). It's no lie, and why shouldn't I be, with me shoveling a million tons of coal in the stokeholes of ships since I was a lad only. (*He pats the coil of hawser invitingly.*) Let you sit down, now, Miss and I'll be telling you a bit of myself, and you'll be telling me a bit of yourself, and in an hour we'll be as old friends as if we was born in the same house. (*He pulls at her sleeve shyly.*) Sit down now, if you plaze.

ANNA (*with a half laugh*). Well— (*She sits down.*) But we won't talk about me, see? You tell me about yourself and about the wreck.

BURKE (*flattered*). I'll tell you, surely. But can I be asking you one question, Miss, has my head in a puzzle?

ANNA (*guardedly*). Well—I dunno—what is it?

BURKE. What is it you do when you're not taking a trip with the Old Man? For I'm thinking a fine girl the like of you ain't living always on this tub.

ANNA (*uneasily*). No—of course I ain't. (*She searches his face suspiciously, afraid there may be some hidden insinuation in his words. Seeing his simple frankness, she goes on confidently.*) Well, I'll tell you. I'm a governess, see? I take care of kids for people and learn them things.

BURKE (*impressed*). A governess, is it? You must be smart, surely.

ANNA. But let's not talk about me. Tell me about the wreck, like you promised me you would.

BURKE (*importantly*). 'Twas this way, Miss. Two weeks out we ran into the divil's own storm, and she sprang wan hell of a leak up for-ard. The skipper was hoping to make Boston before another blow would finish her, but ten days back we met up with another storm the like of the first, only worse. Four days we was in it with green seas raking over her from bow to stern. That was a terrible time, God help us. (*Proudly.*) And if 'twasn't for me and my great strength, I'm telling you—and it's God's truth—there'd been mutiny itself in the stokehole. 'Twas me held them to it, with a kick to wan and a clout to another, and they not caring a damn for the engineers any more, but fearing a clout of my right arm more than they'd fear the sea itself. (*He glances at her anxiously, eager for her approval.*)

ANNA (*concealing a smile—amused by this boyish boasting of his*). You did some hard work, didn't you?

BURKE (*promptly*). I did that! I'm a divil for sticking it out when them that's weak give up. But much good it did anyone! 'Twas a mad, fightin' scramble in the last seconds with each man for himself. I disremember how it come about, but there was the four of us in wan boat and when we was raised high on a great wave I took a look about and divil a sight there was of ship or men on top of the sea.

ANNA (*in a subdued voice*). Then all the others was drowned?

BURKE. They was, surely.

ANNA (*with a shudder*). What a terrible end!

BURKE (*turns to her*). A terrible end for the like of them swabs does live on land, maybe. But for the like of us does be roaming the seas, a good end, I'm telling you—quick and clane.

ANNA (*struck by the word*). Yes, clean. That's yust the word for—all of it—the way it makes me feel.

BURKE. The sea, you mean? (*Interestedly.*) I'm thinking you have a bit of it in your blood, too. Your Old Man wasn't only a barge rat—begging your pardon—all his life, by the cut of him.

ANNA. No, he was bo'sun on sailing ships for years. And all the men on both sides of the family have gone to sea as far back as he remembers, he says. All the women have married sailors, too.

BURKE (*with intense satisfaction*). Did they, now? They had spirit in them. It's only on the sea you'd find rale men with guts is fit to wed with fine, high-tempered girls (*then he adds half-boldly*) the like of yourself.

ANNA (*with a laugh*). There you go kiddin' again. (*Then seeing his hurt expression—quickly.*) But you was going to tell me about yourself. You're Irish, of course I can tell that.

BURKE (*stoutly*). Yes, thank God, though I've not seen a sight of it in fifteen years or more.

ANNA (*thoughtfully*). Sailors never do go home hardly, do they? That's what my father was saying.

BURKE. He wasn't telling no lie. (*With sudden melancholy.*) It's a hard and lonesome life, the sea is. The only women you'd meet in the ports of the world who'd be willing to speak you a kind word isn't women at all. You know the kind I mane, and they're a poor, wicked lot, God forgive them. They're looking to steal the money from you only.

ANNA (*her face averted—rising to her feet —agitatedly*). I think—I guess I'd better see what's doing inside.

BURKE (*afraid he has offended her—beseechingly*). Don't go, I'm saying! Is it I've given you offense with my talk of the like of them? Don't heed it at all! I'm clumsy in my wits when it comes to talking proper with a girl the like of you. And why wouldn't I be? Since the day I left home for to go to sea punching coal, this is the first time I've had a word with a rale, dacent woman. So don't turn your back on me now, and we beginning to be friends.

ANNA (*turning to him again—forcing a smile*). I'm not sore at you, honest.

BURKE (*gratefully*). God bless you!

ANNA (*changing the subject abruptly*). But if you honestly think the sea's such a rotten life, why don't you get out of it?

BURKE (*surprised*). Work on land, is it? (*She nods. He spits scornfully.*) Digging spuds in the muck from dawn to dark, I suppose? (*Vehemently.*) I wasn't made for it, Miss.

ANNA (*with a laugh*). I thought you'd say that.

BURKE (*argumentatively*). But there's good jobs and bad jobs at sea, like there'd be on land. I'm thinking if it's in the stokehole of a proper liner I was, I'd be able to have a little house and be home to it wan week out of four. And I'm thinking that maybe then I'd have the luck to find a fine dacent girl—the like of yourself, now—would be willing to wed with me.

ANNA (*turning away from him with a short laugh—uneasily*). Why, sure. Why not?

BURKE (*edging up close to her—exultantly*). Then you think a girl the like of yourself might maybe not mind the past at all but only seeing the good herself put in me?

ANNA (*in the same tone*). Why, sure.

BURKE (*passionately*). She'd not be sorry for it, I'd take my oath! 'Tis no more drinking and roving about I'd be doing then, but giving my pay day into her hand and staying at home with her as meek as a lamb each night of the week I'd be in port.

ANNA (*moved in spite of herself and troubled by this half-concealed proposal—with a forced laugh*). All you got to do is find the girl.

BURKE. I have found her!

ANNA (*half-frightenedly—trying to laugh it off*). You have? When? I thought you was saying—

BURKE (*boldly and forcefully*). This night. (*Hanging his head—humbly.*) If she'll be having me. (*Then raising his eyes to hers —simply.*) 'Tis you I mean.

ANNA (*is held by his eyes for a moment— then shrinks back from him with a strange, broken laugh*). Say—are you—going crazy? Are you trying to kid me? Proposing—to me!—for Gawd's sake!—on such short acquaintance? (*CHRIS comes out of the cabin and stands staring blinkingly astern. When he makes out ANNA in such intimate proximity to this strange sailor, an angry expression comes over his face.*)

BURKE (*following her—with fierce, pleading insistence*). I'm telling you there's the will of God in it that brought me safe through the storm and fog to the wan spot in the world where you was! Think of that now, and isn't it queer—

CHRIS. Anna! (*He comes toward them, raging, his fists clenched.*) Anna, you gat in cabin, you hear!

ANNA (*all her emotions immediately transformed into resentment at his bullying tone*). Who d'you think you're talking to —a slave?

CHRIS (*hurt—his voice breaking—pleadingly*). You need gat rest, Anna. You gat sleep. (*She does not move. He turns on BURKE furiously.*) What are you doing here, you sailor fallar? You ain't sick like oders. You gat in fo'c's'tle. Dey give you bunk. (*Threateningly.*) You hurry, Ay tal you!

ANNA (*impulsively*). But he is sick. Look at him. He can hardly stand up.

BURKE (*straightening and throwing out his chest—with a bold laugh*). Is it giving me orders ye are, me bucko? Let you look out, then! With wan hand, weak as I am, I can break ye in two and fling the pieces over the side—and your crew after you. (*Stopping abruptly.*) I was forgetting. You're her Old Man and I'd not raise a fist to you for the world. (*His knees sag, he wavers and seems about to fall.* ANNA *utters an exclamation of alarm and hurries to his side.*)

ANNA (*taking one of his arms over her shoulder*). Come on in the cabin. You can have my bed if there ain't no other place.

BURKE (*wth jubilant happiness—as they proceed toward the cabin*). Glory be to God, is it holding my arm about your neck you are! Anna! Anna! Sure it's a sweet name is suited to you.

ANNA (*guiding him carefully*). Sssh! Sssh!

BURKE. Whisht, is it? Indade, and I'll not. I'll be roaring it out like a fog horn over the sea! You're the girl of the world and we'll be marrying soon and I don't care who knows it!

ANNA (*as she guides him through the cabin door*). Ssshh! Never mind that talk. You go to sleep. (*They go out of sight in the cabin.* CHRIS, *who has been listening to* BURKE'S *last words with open-mouthed amazement stands looking after them despe-rately.*)

CHRIS (*turns suddenly and shakes his fist out at the sea—with bitter hatred*). Dat's your dirty trick, damn ole davil, you! (*Then in a frenzy of rage.*) But, py God, you don't do dat! Not while Ay'm living! No, py God, you don't!

The Curtain Falls.

ACT THREE

SCENE. *The interior of the cabin on the barge,* Simeon Winthrop (*at dock in Boston*)— *a narrow, low-ceilinged compartment the walls of which are painted a light brown with white trimmings. In the rear on the left, a door leading to the sleeping quarters. In the far left corner, a large locker-closet, painted white, on the door of which a mirror hangs on a nail. In the rear wall, two small square windows and a door opening out on the deck toward the stern. In the right wall, two more windows looking out on the port deck. White curtains, clean and stiff, are at the windows. A table with two cane-bottomed chairs stands in the center of the cabin. A dilapidated, wicker rocker, painted brown, is also by the table.*

It is afternoon of a sunny day about a week later. From the harbor and docks outside, muffled by the closed door and windows, comes the sound of steamers' whistles and the puffing snort of the donkey engines of some ship unloading nearby.

As the curtain rises, CHRIS *and* ANNA *are discovered.* ANNA *is seated in the rocking-chair by the table, with a newspaper in her hands. She is not reading but staring straight in front of her. She looks unhappy, troubled, frowningly concentrated on her thoughts.* CHRIS *wanders about the room, casting quick, uneasy side glances at her face, then stopping to peer absent-mindedly out of the window. His attitude betrays an overwhelming, gloomy anxiety which has him on tenterhooks. He pretends to be engaged in setting things ship-shape, but this occupation is confined to picking up some object, staring at it stupidly for a second, then aimlessly putting it down again. He clears his throat and starts to sing to himself in a low, doleful voice: "My Yosephine, come board de ship. Long time Ay vait for you."*

ANNA (*turning on him, sarcastically*). I'm glad someone's feeling good. (*Wearily.*) Gee, I sure wish we was out of this dump and back in New York.

CHRIS (*with a sigh*). Ay'm glad vhen ve sail again, too. (*Then, as she makes no comment, he goes on with a ponderous attempt at sarcasm.*) Ay don't see vhy you don't like Boston, dough. You have good time here, Ay tank. You go ashore all time, every day and night veek ve've been here. You go to movies, see show, gat all kinds fun— (*His eyes hard with hatred.*) All with that damn Irish fallar!

ANNA (*with weary scorn*). Oh, for heaven's sake, are you off on that again? Where's the harm in his taking me around? D'you want me to sit all day and night in this cabin with you—and knit? Ain't I got a right to have as good a time as I can?

CHRIS. It ain't right kind of fun—not with that fallar, no.

ANNA. I been back on board every night by eleven, ain't I? (*Then struck by some thought—looks at him with keen suspicion—with rising anger.*) Say, look here, what d'you mean by what you yust said?

CHRIS (*hastily*). Nutting but what Ay say, Anna.

ANNA. You said "ain't right" and you said it funny. Say, listen here, you ain't trying to insinuate that there's something wrong between us, are you?

CHRIS (*horrified*). No, Anna! No, Ay svear to God, Ay never tank dat!

ANNA (*mollified by his very evident sincerity—sitting down again*). Well, don't you never think it neither if you want me ever to speak to you again. (*Angrily again.*) If I ever dreamt you thought that, I'd get the hell out of this barge so quick you couldn't see me for dust.

CHRIS (*soothingly*). Ay wouldn't never dream— (*Then after a second's pause, reprovingly.*) You vas gatting learn to svear. Dat ain't nice for young gel, you tank?

ANNA (*with a faint trace of a smile*). Excuse me. You ain't used to such language, I know. (*Mockingly.*) That's what your taking me to sea has done for me.

CHRIS (*indignantly*). No, it ain't me. It's dat damn sailor fallar learn you bad tangs.

ANNA. He ain't a sailor. He's a stoker.

CHRIS (*forcibly*). Dat vas million times vorse, Ay tal you! Dem fallars dat vork below shoveling coal vas de dirtiest, rough gang of no-good fallars in vorld!

ANNA. I'd hate to hear you say that to Mat.

CHRIS. Oh, Ay tal him same tang. You don't gat it in head Ay'm scared of him yust 'cause he vas stronger'n Ay vas. (*Menacingly.*) You don't gat for fight with fists with dem fallars. Dere's oder vay for fix him.

ANNA (*glancing at him with sudden alarm*). What d'you mean?

CHRIS (*sullenly*). Nutting.

ANNA. You'd better not. I wouldn't start no trouble with him if I was you. He might forget some time that you was old and my father—and then you'd be out of luck.

CHRIS (*with smoldering hatred*). Vell, yust let him! Ay'm ole bird maybe, but Ay bet Ay show him trick or two.

ANNA (*suddenly changing her tone—persuasively*). Aw come on, be good. What's eating you, anyway? Don't you want no one to be nice to me except yourself?

CHRIS (*placated—coming to her—eagerly*). Yes, Ay do, Anna—only not fallar on sea. But Ay like for you marry steady fallar got good yob on land. You have little home in country all your own—

ANNA (*rising to her feet—brusquely*). Oh, cut it out! (*Scornfully.*) Little home in the country! I wish you could have seen the little home in the country where you had me in jail till I was sixteen! (*With rising irritation.*) Some day you're going to get me so mad with that talk, I'm going to turn loose on you and tell you—a lot of things that'll open your eyes.

CHRIS (*alarmed*). Ay don't vant—

ANNA. I know you don't; but you keep on talking yust the same.

CHRIS. Ay don't talk no more den, Anna.

ANNA. Then promise me you'll cut out saying nasty things about Mat Burke every chance you get.

CHRIS (*evasive and suspicious*). Vhy? You like dat fallar—very much, Anna?

ANNA. Yes, I certainly do! He's a regular man, no matter what faults he's got. One of his fingers is worth all the hundreds of men I met out there—inland.

CHRIS (*his face darkening*). Maybe you tank you love him, den?

ANNA (*defiantly*). What of it if I do?

CHRIS (*scowling and forcing out the words*). Maybe—you tank you—marry him?

ANNA (*shaking her head*). No! (CHRIS' face lights up with relief. ANNA *continues slowly, a trace of sadness in her voice.*) If I'd met him four years ago—or even two years ago—I'd have jumped at the chance, I tell you that straight. And I would now—only he's such a simple guy—a big kid—and I ain't got the heart to fool him. (*She breaks off suddenly.*) But don't never say again he ain't good enough for me. It's me ain't good enough for him.

CHRIS (*snorts scornfully*). Py yiminy, you go crazy, Ay tank!

ANNA (*with a mournful laugh*). Well, I been thinking I was myself the last few days. (*She goes and takes a shawl from a hook near the door and throws it over her shoulders.*) Guess I'll take a walk down to the end of the dock for a minute and see what's doing. I love to watch the ships passing. Mat'll be along before long, I guess. Tell him where I am, will you?

CHRIS (*despondently*). All right, Ay tal him. (ANNA *goes out the doorway on rear.* CHRIS *follows her out and stands on the deck outside for a moment looking after her. Then he comes back inside and shuts the door. He stands looking out of the window—mutters—"Dirty ole davil, you." Then he goes to the table, sets the cloth straight mechanically, picks up the newspaper* ANNA *has let fall to the floor and sits down in the rocking-chair. He stares at the paper for a while, then puts it on table,* holds his head in his hands and sighs drearily. The noise of a man's heavy footsteps comes from the deck outside and there is a loud knock on the door. CHRIS *starts, makes a move as if to get up and go to the door, then thinks better of it and sits still. The knock is repeated—then as no answer comes, the door is flung open and* MAT BURKE *appears.* CHRIS *scowls at the intruder and his hand instinctively goes back to the sheath knife on his hip.* BURKE *is dressed up—wears a cheap blue suit, a striped cotton shirt with a black tie, and black shoes newly shined. His face is beaming with good humor.*)

BURKE (*as he sees* CHRIS—*in a jovial tone of mockery*). Well, God bless who's here! (*He bends down and squeezes his huge form through the narrow doorway.*) And how is the world treating you this afternoon, Anna's father?

CHRIS (*sullenly*). Pooty goot—if it ain't for some fallars.

BURKE (*with a grin*). Meaning me, do you? (*He laughs.*) Well, if you ain't the funny old crank of a man! (*Then soberly.*) Where's herself? (CHRIS *sits dumb, scowling, his eyes averted.* BURKE *is irritated by this silence.*) Where's Anna, I'm after asking you?

CHRIS (*hesitating—then grouchily*). She go down end of dock.

BURKE. I'll be going down to her, then. But first I'm thinking I'll take this chance when we're alone to have a word with you. (*He sits down opposite* CHRIS *at the table and leans over toward him.*) And that word is soon said. I'm marrying your Anna before this day is out, and you might as well make up your mind to it whether you like it or no.

CHRIS (*glaring at him with hatred and forcing a scornful laugh*). Ho-ho! Dat's easy for say!

BURKE. You mean I won't? (*Scornfully.*) Is it the like of yourself will stop me, are you thinking?

CHRIS. Yes, Ay stop it, if it come to vorst.

BURKE (*with scornful pity*). God help you!

CHRIS. But ain't no need for me do dat. Anna—

BURKE (*smiling confidently*). Is it Anna you think will prevent me?

CHRIS. Yes.

BURKE. And I'm telling you she'll not. She knows I'm loving her, and she loves me the same, and I know it.

CHRIS. Ho-ho! She only have fun. She make big fool of you, dat's all!

BURKE (*unshaken—pleasantly*). That's a lie in your throat, divil mend you!

CHRIS. No, it ain't lie. She tal me yust before she go out she never marry fallar like you.

BURKE. I'll not believe it. 'Tis a great old liar you are, and a divil to be making a power of trouble if you had your way. But 'tis not trouble I'm looking for, and me sitting down here. (*Earnestly.*) Let us be talking it out now as man to man. You're her father, and wouldn't it be a shame for us to be at each other's throats like a pair of dogs, and I married with Anna. So out with the truth, man alive. What is it you're holding against me at all?

CHRIS (*a bit placated, in spite of himself, by* BURKE's *evident sincerity—but puzzled and suspicious*). Vell—Ay don't vant for Anna gat married. Listen, you fallar. Ay'm a ole man. Ay don't see Anna for fifteen year. She vas all Ay gat in vorld. And now ven she come on first trip—you tank Ay vant her leave me 'lone again?

BURKE (*heartily*). Let you not be thinking I have no heart at all for the way you'd be feeling.

CHRIS (*astonished and encouraged—trying to plead persuasively*). Den you do right tang, eh? You ship avay again, leave Anna alone. (*Cajolingly.*) Big fallar like you dat's on sea, he don't need vife. He gat new gel in every port, you know dat.

BURKE (*angrily for a second*). God stiffen you! (*Then controlling himself—calmly.*) I'll not be giving you the lie on that. But divil take you, there's a time comes to every man, on sea or land, that isn't a born fool, when he's sick of the lot of them cows, and wearing his heart out to meet up with a fine dacent girl, and have a home to call his own and be rearing up children in it. 'Tis small use you're asking me to leave Anna. She's the wan woman of the world for me, and I can't live without her now, I'm thinking.

CHRIS. You forgat all about her in one veek out of port, Ay bet you!

BURKE. You don't know the like I am. Death itself wouldn't make me forget her. So let you not be making talk to me about leaving her. I'll not, and be damned to you! It won't be so bad for you as you'd make out at all. She'll be living here in the States, and her married to me. And you'd be seeing her often so—a sight more often than ever you saw her the fifteen years she was growing up in the West. It's quare you'd be the one to be making great trouble about her leaving you when you never laid eyes on her once in all them years.

CHRIS (*guiltily*). Ay taught it vas better Anna stay away, grow up inland where she don't ever know ole davil, sea.

BURKE (*scornfully*). Is it blaming the sea for your troubles ye are again, God help you? Well, Anna knows it now. 'Twas in her blood, anyway.

CHRIS. And Ay don't vant she ever know no-good fallar on sea—

BURKE. She knows one now.

CHRIS (*banging the table with his fist—furiously*). Dat's yust it! Dat's yust what you are—no-good, sailor fallar! You tank Ay lat her life be made sorry by you like her mo'der's vas by me! No, Ay svear! She don't marry you if Ay gat kill you first!

BURKE (*looks at him a moment, in astonishment—then laughing uproariously*). Ho-ho! Glory be to God, it's bold talk you have for a stumpy runt of a man!

CHRIS (*threateningly*). Vell—you see!

BURKE (*with grinning defiance*). I'll see, surely! I'll see myself and Anna married this day, I'm telling you. (*Then with contemptuous exasperation.*) It's quare fool's blather you have about the sea done this and the sea done that. You'd ought to be 'shamed to be saying the like, and you an old sailor yourself. I'm after hearing a lot of it from you and a lot more that Anna's told me you do be saying to her, and I'm thinking it's a poor weak thing you are, and not a man at all!

CHRIS (*darkly*). You see if Ay'm man—maybe quicker'n you tank.

BURKE (*contemptuously*). Yerra, don't be boasting. I'm thinking 'tis out of your wits you've got with fright of the sea. You'd be wishing Anna married to a farmer, she told me. That'd be a swate match, surely! Would you have a fine girl the like of Anna lying down at nights with a muddy scut stinking of pigs and dung? Or would you have her tied for life to the like of them skinny, shriveled swabs does be working in cities?

CHRIS. Dat's lie, you fool!

BURKE. 'Tis not. 'Tis your own mad notions I'm after telling. But you know the truth in your heart, if great fear of the sea has made you a liar and coward itself. (*Pounding the table.*) The sea's the only life for a man with guts in him isn't afraid of his own shadow! 'Tis only on the sea he's free, and him roving the face of the world, seeing all things, and not giving a damn for saving up money, or stealing from his friends, or any of the black tricks that a landlubber'd waste his life on. 'Twas yourself knew it once, and you a bo'sun for years.

CHRIS (*sputtering with rage*). You vas crazy fool, Ay tal you!

BURKE. You've swallowed the anchor. The sea give you a clout once, knocked you down, and you're not man enough to get up for another, but lie there for the rest of your life howling bloody murder. (*Proudly.*) Isn't it myself the sea has nearly drowned, and me battered and bate till I was that close to hell I could hear the flames roaring, and never a groan out of me till the sea gave up and it seeing the great strength and guts of a man was in me?

CHRIS (*scornfully*). Yes, you vas hell of fallar, hear you tal it!

BURKE (*angrily*). You'll be calling me a liar once too often, me old bucko! Wasn't the whole story of it and my picture itself in the newspapers of Boston a week back? (*Looking* CHRIS *up and down belittlingly.*) Sure I'd like to see you in the best of your youth do the like of what I done in the storm and after. 'Tis a mad lunatic, screeching with fear, you'd be this minute!

CHRIS. Ho-ho! You vas young fool! In ole years when Ay was on windyammer, Ay vas through hundred storms vorse'n dat! Ships vas ships den—and men dat sail on dem vas real men. And now what you gat on steamers? You gat fallars on deck don't know ship from mudscow. (*With a meaning glance at* BURKE.) And below deck you gat fallars yust know how for shovel coal—might yust as vell vork on coal vagon ashore!

BURKE (*stung—angrily*). Is it casting insults at the men in the stokehole ye are, ye old ape? God stiffen you! Wan of them is worth any ten stock-fish-swilling Squareheads ever shipped on a windbag!

CHRIS (*his face working with rage, his hand going back to the sheath-knife on his hip*). Irish svine, you!

BURKE (*tauntingly*). Don't ye like the Irish, ye old baboon? 'Tis that you're needing in your family, I'm telling you—an Irishman and a man of the stokehole—to put guts in it so that you'll not be having grandchildren would be fearful cowards and jackasses the like of yourself!

CHRIS (*half rising from his chair—in a voice choked with rage*). You look out!

BURKE (*watching him intently—a mocking smile on his lips*). And it's that you'll be having, no matter what you'll do to prevent; for Anna and me'll be married this day, and no old fool the like of you will stop us when I've made up my mind.

CHRIS (*with a hoarse cry*). You don't! (*He throws himself at* BURKE, *knife in hand, knocking his chair over backwards.* BURKE *springs to his feet quickly in time to meet the attack. He laughs with the pure love of battle. The old Swede is like a child in his hands.* BURKE *does not strike or mistreat him in any way, but simply twists his right hand behind his back and forces the knife from his fingers. He throws the knife into a far corner of the room—tauntingly.*)

BURKE. Old men is getting childish should-n't play with knives. (*Holding the struggling* CHRIS *at arm's length—with a sudden rush of anger, drawing back his fist.*) I've half a mind to hit you a great clout will put sense in your. square head. Kape off me now, I'm warning you! (*He gives* CHRIS *a push with the flat of his hand which sends the old Swede staggering back against the cabin wall, where he remains standing, panting heavily, his eyes fixed on* BURKE *with hatred, as if he were only collecting his strength to rush at him again.*)

BURKE (*warningly*). Now don't be coming at me again, I'm saying, or I'll flatten you on the floor with a blow, if 'tis Anna's father you are itself! I've no patience left for you. (*Then with an amused laugh.*) Well, 'tis a bold old man you are just the same, and I'd never think it was in you to come tackling me alone. (*A shadow crosses the cabin windows. Both men start.* ANNA *appears in the doorway.*)

ANNA (*with pleased surprise as she sees* BURKE). Hello, Mat. Are you here already? I was down— (*She stops, looking from one to the other, sensing immediately that something has happened.*) What's up? (*Then noticing the overturned chair—in alarm.*) How'd that chair get knocked over? (*Turning on* BURKE *reproachfully.*) You ain't been fighting with him, Mat— after you promised?

BURKE (*his old self again*). I've not laid a hand on him, Anna. (*He goes and picks up the chair, then turning on the still questioning* ANNA—*with a reassuring smile.*) Let you not be worried at all. 'Twas only a bit of an argument we was having to pass the time till you'd come.

ANNA. It must have been some argument when you got to throwing chairs. (*She turns to* CHRIS.) Why don't you say something? What was it about?

CHRIS (*relaxing at last—avoiding her eyes —sheepishly*). Ve vas talking about ships and fallars on sea.

ANNA (*with a relieved smile*). Oh—the old stuff, eh?

BURKE (*suddenly seeming to come to a bold decision—with a defiant grin at* CHRIS). He's not after telling you the whole of it. We was arguing about you mostly.

ANNA (*with a frown*). About me?

BURKE. And we'll be finishing it out right here and now in your presence if you're willing. (*He sits down at the left of table.*)

ANNA (*uncertainly—looking from him to her father*). Sure. Tell me what it's all about.

CHRIS (*advancing toward the table—protesting to* BURKE). No! You don't do dat, you! You tal him you don't vant for hear him talk, Anna.

ANNA. But I do. I want this cleared up.

CHRIS (*miserably afraid now*). Vell, not now, anyvay. You vas going ashore, yes? You ain't got time—

ANNA (*firmly*). Yes, right here and now. (*She turns to* BURKE.) You tell me, Mat, since he don't want to.

BURKE (*draws a deep breath—then plunges in boldly*). The whole of it's in a few words only. So's he'd make no mistake, and him hating the sight of me, I told him in his teeth I loved you. (*Passionately.*) And that's God's truth, Anna, and well you know it!

CHRIS (*scornfully—forcing a laugh*). Ho-ho! He tal same tang to gel every port he go!

ANNA (*shrinking from her father with repulsion—resentfully*). Shut up, can't you? (*Then to* BURKE—*feelingly.*) I know it's true, Mat. I don't mind what he says.

BURKE (*humbly grateful*). God bless you!

ANNA. And then what?

BURKE. And then— (*Hesitatingly.*) And then I said— (*He looks at her pleadingly.*) I said I was sure—I told him I thought you have a bit of love for me, too. (*Passionately.*) Say you do, Anna! Let you not destroy me entirely, for the love of God! (*He grasps both her hands in his two.*)

ANNA (*deeply moved and troubled—forcing a trembling laugh*). So you told him that, Mat? No wonder he was mad. (*Forcing out the words.*) Well, maybe it's true, Mat. Maybe I do. I been thinking and thinking—I didn't want to, Mat, I'll own up to that—I tried to cut it out—but— (*She laughs helplessly.*) I guess I can't help it anyhow. So I guess I do, Mat. (*Then with a sudden joyous defiance.*) Sure I do! What's the use of kidding myself different? Sure I love you, Mat!

CHRIS (*with a cry of pain*). Anna! (*He sits crushed.*)

BURKE (*with a great depth of sincerity in his humble gratitude*). God be praised!

ANNA (*assertively*). And I ain't never loved a man in my life before, you can always believe that—no matter what happens.

BURKE (*goes over to her and puts his arms around her*). Sure I do be believing ivery word you iver said or iver will say. And 'tis you and me will be having a grand, beautiful life together to the end of our days! (*He tries to kiss her. At first she turns away her head—then, overcome by a fierce impulse of passionate love, she takes his head in both her hands and holds his face close to hers, staring into his eyes. Then she kisses him full on the lips.*)

ANNA (*pushing him away from her—forcing a broken laugh*). Good-by. (*She walks to the doorway in rear—stands with her back toward them, looking out. Her shoulders quiver once or twice as if she were fighting back her sobs.*)

BURKE (*too in the seventh heaven of bliss to get any correct interpretation of her word—with a laugh*). Good-by, is it? The divil you say! I'll be coming back at you in a second for more of the same! (*To CHRIS, who has quickened to instant attention at his daughter's good-by, and has looked at her with a stirring of foolish hope in his eyes.*) Now, me old bucko, what'll you be saying? You heard the words from her own lips. Confess I've bate you. Own up like a man when you're bate fair and square. And here's my hand to you— (*Holds out his hand.*) And let you take it and we'll shake and forget what's over and done, and be friends from this out.

CHRIS (*with implacable hatred*). Ay don't shake hands with you fallar—not vhile Ay live!

BURKE (*offended*). The back of my hand to you then, if that suits you better. (*Growling.*) 'Tis a rotten bad loser you are, divil mend you!

CHRIS. Ay don't lose. (*Trying to be scornful and self-convincing.*) Anna say she like you little bit but you don't hear her say she marry you, Ay bet. (*At the sound of her name ANNA has turned round to them. Her face is composed and calm again, but it is the dead calm of despair.*)

BURKE (*scornfully*). No, and I wasn't hearing her say the sun is shining, either.

CHRIS (*doggedly*). Dat's all right. She don't say it, yust same.

ANNA (*quietly—coming forward to them*). No, I didn't say it, Mat.

CHRIS (*eagerly*). Dere! You hear!

BURKE (*misunderstanding her—with a grin*). You're waiting till you do be asked, you mane? Well, I'm asking you now. And we'll be married this day, with the help of God!

ANNA (*gently*). You heard what I said, Mat—after I kissed you?

BURKE (*alarmed by something in her manner*). No—I disremember.

ANNA. I said good-by. (*Her voice trembling.*) That kiss was for good-by, Mat.

BURKE (*terrified*). What d'you mane?

ANNA. I can't marry you, Mat—and we've said good-by. That's all.

CHRIS (*unable to hold back his exultation*). Ay know it! Ay know dat vas so!

BURKE (*jumping to his feet—unable to believe his ears*). Anna! Is it making game of me you'd be? 'Tis a quare time to joke with me, and don't be doing it, for the love of God.

ANNA (*looking him in the eyes—steadily*). D'you think I'd kid you? No, I'm not joking, Mat. I mean what I said.

BURKE. Ye don't! Ye can't! 'Tis mad you are, I'm telling you!

ANNA (*fixedly*). No, I'm not.

BURKE (*desperately*). But what's come over you so sudden? You was saying you loved me—

ANNA. I'll say that as often as you want me to. It's true.

BURKE (*bewilderedly*). Then why—what, in the divil's name— Oh, God help me, I can't make head or tail to it at all!

ANNA. Because it's the best way out I can figure, Mat. (*Her voice catching.*) I been thinking it over and thinking it over day and night all week. Don't think it ain't hard on me, too, Mat.

BURKE. For the love of God, tell me then, what is it that's preventing you wedding me when the two of us has love? (*Suddenly getting an idea and pointing at* CHRIS —*exasperatedly.*) Is it giving heed to the like of that old fool ye are, and him hating me and filling your ears full of bloody lies against me?

CHRIS (*getting to his feet—raging triumphantly before* ANNA *has a chance to get in a word*). Yes, Anna believe me, not you! She know her old fa'der don't lie like you.

ANNA (*turning on her father angrily*). You sit down, d'you hear? Where do you come in butting in and making things worse? You're like a devil, you are! (*Harshly.*) Good Lord, and I was beginning to like you, beginning to forget all I've got held up against you!

CHRIS (*crushed feebly*). You ain't got nutting for hold against me, Anna.

ANNA. Ain't I yust! Well, lemme tell you— (*She glances at* BURKE *and stops abruptly.*) Say, Mat, I'm s'prised at you. You didn't think anything he'd said—

BURKE (*glumly*). Sure, what else would it be?

ANNA. Think I've ever paid any attention to all his crazy bull? Gee, you must take me for a five-year-old kid.

BURKE (*puzzled and beginning to be irritated at her too*). I don't know how to take you, with your saying this one minute and that the next.

ANNA. Well, he has nothing to do with it.

BURKE. Then what is it has? Tell me, and don't keep me waiting and sweating blood.

ANNA (*resolutely*). I can't tell you—and I won't. I got a good reason—and that's all you need to know. I can't marry you, that's all there is to it. (*Distractedly.*) So, for Gawd's sake, let's talk of something else.

BURKE. I'll not! (*Then fearfully.*) Is it married to someone else you are—in the West maybe?

ANNA (*vehemently*). I should say not.

BURKE (*regaining his courage*). To the divil with all other reasons then. They don't matter with me at all. (*He gets to his feet confidently, assuming a masterful tone.*) I'm thinking you're the like of them women can't make up their mind till they're drove to it. Well, then, I'll make up your mind for you bloody quick. (*He takes her by the arms, grinning to soften his serious bullying.*) We've had enough of talk! Let you be going into your room now and be dressing in your best and we'll be going ashore.

CHRIS (*aroused—angrily*). No, py God, she don't do that! (*Takes hold of her arm.*)

ANNA (*who has listened to* BURKE *in astonishment. She draws away from him, instinctively repelled by his tone, but not exactly sure if he is serious or not—a trace of resentment in her voice*). Say, where do you get that stuff?

BURKE (*imperiously*). Never mind, now! Let you go get dressed, I'm saying. (*Then turning to* CHRIS.) We'll be seeing who'll win in the end—me or you.

CHRIS (*to* ANNA—*also in an authoritative tone*). You stay right here, Anna, you hear! (ANNA *stands looking from one to the other of them as if she thought they had both gone crazy. Then the expression of her face freezes into the hardened sneer of her experience.*)

BURKE (*violently*). She'll not! She'll do what I say! You've had your hold on her long enough. It's my turn now.

ANNA (*with a hard laugh*). Your turn? Say, what am I, anyway?

BURKE. 'Tis not what you are, 'tis what you're going to be this day—and that's wedded to me before night comes. Hurry up now with your dressing.

CHRIS (*commandingly*). You don't do one tang he say, Anna! (ANNA *laughs mockingly.*)

BURKE. She will, so!

CHRIS. Ay tal you she don't! Ay'm her fa'der.

BURKE. She will in spite of you. She's taking my orders from this out, not yours.

ANNA (*laughing again*). Orders is good!

BURKE (*turning to her impatiently*). Hurry up now, and shake a leg. We've no time to be wasting. (*Irritated as she doesn't move.*) Do you hear what I'm telling you?

CHRIS. You stay dere, Anna!

ANNA (*at the end of her patience—blazing out at them passionately*). You can go to hell, both of you! (*There is something in her tone that makes them forget their quarrel and turn to her in a stunned amazement.* ANNA *laughs wildly.*) You're just like the rest of them—you two! Gawd, you'd think I was a piece of furniture! I'll show you! Sit down now! (*As they hesitate—furiously.*) Sit down and let me talk for a minute. You're all wrong, see? Listen to me! I'm going to tell you something—and then I'm going to beat it. (*To* BURKE—*with a harsh laugh.*) I'm going to tell you a funny story, so pay attention. (*Pointing to* CHRIS.) I've been meaning to turn it loose on him every time he'd get my goat with his bull about keeping me safe inland. I wasn't going to tell you, but you've forced me into it. What's the dif? It's all wrong anyway, and you might as well get cured that way as any other. (*With hard mocking.*) Only don't forget what you said a minute ago about it not mattering to you what other reason I got so long as I wasn't married to no one else.

BURKE (*manfully*). That's my word, and I'll stick to it!

ANNA (*laughing bitterly*). What a chance! You make me laugh, honest! Want to bet you will? Wait 'n see! (*She stands at the table rear, looking from one to the other of the two men with her hard, mocking smile. Then she begins, fighting to control her emotion and speak calmly.*) First thing is, I want to tell you two guys something. You was going on 's if one of you had got to own me. But nobody owns me, see?—'cepting myself. I'll do what I please and no man, I don't give a hoot who he is, can tell me what to do! I ain't asking either of you for a living. I can make it myself—one way or other. I'm my own boss. So put that in your pipe and smoke it! You and your orders!

BURKE (*protestingly*). I wasn't meaning it that way at all and well you know it. You've no call to be raising this rumpus with me. (*Pointing to* CHRIS.) 'Tis him you've a right—

ANNA. I'm coming to him. But you—you did mean it that way, too. You sounded—yust like all the rest. (*Hysterically.*) But, damn it, shut up! Let me talk for a change!

BURKE. 'Tis quare, rough talk, that—for a dacent girl the like of you!

ANNA (*with a hard laugh*). Decent? Who told you I was? (CHRIS *is sitting with bowed shoulders, his head in his hands. She leans over in exasperation and shakes him violently by the shoulder.*) Don't go to sleep, Old Man! Listen here, I'm talking to you now!

CHRIS (*straightening up and looking about as if he were seeking a way to escape—with frightened foreboding in his voice.*) Ay don't vant to hear it. You vas going out of head, Ay tank, Anna.

ANNA (*violently*). Well, living with you is enough to drive anyone off their nut. Your bunk about the farm being so fine! Didn't I write you year after year how rotten it was and what a dirty slave them cousins made of me? What'd you care? Nothing! Not even enough to come out and see me! That crazy bull about wanting to keep me away from the sea don't go down with me! You yust didn't want to be bothered with me! You're like all the rest of 'em!

CHRIS (*feebly*). Anna! It ain't so—

ANNA (*not heeding his interruption—revengefully*). But one thing I never wrote you. It was one of them cousins that you think is such nice people—the youngest son—Paul—that started me wrong. (*Loudly.*) It wasn't none of my fault. I hated him worse'n hell and he knew it. But he was big and strong—(*pointing to Burke*)—like you!

BURKE (*half springing to his feet—his fists clenched*). God blarst it! (*He sinks slowly back in his chair again, the knuckles showing white on his clenched hands, his face tense with the effort to suppress his grief and rage.*)

CHRIS (*in a cry of horrified pain*). Anna!

ANNA (*to him—seeming not to have heard their interruptions*). That was why I run away from the farm. That was what made me get a yob as nurse girl in St. Paul. (*With a hard, mocking laugh.*) And you think that was a nice yob for a girl, too, don't you? (*Sarcastically.*) With all them nice inland fellers yust looking for a chance to marry me, I s'pose. Marry me? What a chance! They wasn't looking for marrying. (*As BURKE lets a groan of fury escape him—desperately.*) I'm owning up to everything fair and square. I was caged in, I tell you—yust like in yail—taking care of other people's kids—listening to 'em bawling and crying day and night—when I wanted to be out—and I was lonesome—lonesome as hell! (*With a sudden weariness in her voice.*) So I give up finally. What was the use? (*She stops and looks at the two men. Both are motionless and silent. CHRIS seems in a stupor of despair, his house of cards fallen about him. BURKE's face is livid with the rage that is eating him up, but he is too stunned and bewildered yet to find a vent for it. The condemnation she feels in their silence goads ANNA into a harsh, strident defiance.*) You don't say nothing—either of you—but I know what you're thinking. You're like all the rest! (*To CHRIS—furiously.*) And who's to

blame for it, me or you? If you'd even acted like a man—if you'd even had been a regular father and had me with you—maybe things would be different!

CHRIS (*in agony*). Don't talk dat vay, Anna! Ay go crazy! Ay von't listen! (*Puts his hands over his ears.*)

ANNA (*infuriated by his action—stridently*). You will too listen! (*She leans over and pulls his hands from his ears—with hysterical rage.*) You—keeping me safe inland—I wasn't no nurse girl the last two years—I lied when I wrote you—I was in a house, that's what!—yes, that kind of a house—the kind sailors like you and Mat goes to in port—and your nice inland men, too—and all men, God damn 'em! I hate 'em! Hate 'em! (*She breaks into hysterical sobbing, throwing herself into the chair and hiding her face in her hands on the table. The two men have sprung to their feet.*)

CHRIS (*whimpering like a child*). Anna! Anna! It's lie! It's lie! (*He stands wringing his hands together and begins to weep.*)

BURKE (*his whole great body tense like a spring—dully and gropingly*). So that's what's in it!

ANNA (*raising her head at the sound of his voice—with extreme mocking bitterness*). I s'pose you remember your promise, Mat? No other reason was to count with you so long as I wasn't married already. So I s'pose you want me to get dressed and go ashore, don't you? (*She laughs.*) Yes, you do!

BURKE (*on the verge of his outbreak—stammeringly*). God stiffen you!

ANNA (*trying to keep up her hard, bitter tone, but gradually letting a note of pitiful pleading creep in*). I s'pose if I tried to tell you I wasn't—that—no more you'd believe me, wouldn't you? Yes, you would! And if I told you that yust getting out in this barge, and being on the sea had changed me and made me feel different about things, 's if all I'd been through wasn't me and didn't count and was yust like it never happened—you'd laugh, wouldn't you? And you'd die laughing sure if I said that meeting you that funny way that night in the fog, and afterwards seeing that you was straight goods stuck on me, had got me to thinking for the first time, and I sized you up as a different kind of man—a sea man as different from the ones on land as water is from mud—and that was why I got stuck on you, too. I wanted to marry you and fool you, but I couldn't. Don't you see how I've changed? I couldn't marry you with you believing a lie—and I was shamed to tell you the truth—till the both of you forced my hand, and I seen you was the same as all the rest. And now, give me a bawling out and beat it, like I can tell you're going to. (*She stops, looking at* BURKE. *He is silent, his face averted, his features beginning to work with fury. She pleads passionately.*) Will you believe it if I tell you that loving you has made me—clean? It's the straight goods, honest! (*Then as he doesn't reply —bitterly.*) Like hell you will! You're like all the rest!

BURKE (*blazing out—turning on her in a perfect frenzy of rage—his voice trembling with passion*). The rest, is it? God's curse on you! Clane, is it? You slut, you, I'll be killing you now! (*He picks up the chair on which he has been sitting and, swinging it high over his shoulder, springs toward her.* CHRIS *rushes forward with a cry of alarm, trying to ward off the blow from his daughter.* ANNA *looks up into* BURKE's *eyes with the fearlessness of despair.* BURKE *checks himself, the chair held in the air.*)

CHRIS (*wildly*). Stop, you crazy fool! You vant to murder her!

ANNA (*pushing her father away brusquely, her eyes still holding* BURKE's). Keep out of this, you! (*To* BURKE—*dully.*) Well, ain't you got the nerve to do it? Go ahead! I'll be thankful to you, honest. I'm sick of the whole game.

BURKE (*throwing the chair away into a corner of the room—helplessly*). I can't do it, God help me, and your two eyes looking at me. (*Furiously.*) Though I do be thinking I'd have a good right to smash your skull like a rotten egg. Was there iver a woman in the world had the rottenness in her that you have, and was there iver a man the like

of me was made the fool of the world, and me thinking thoughts about you, and having great love for you, and dreaming dreams of the fine life we'd have when we'd be wedded! (*His voice high pitched in a lamentation that is like a keen.*) Yerra, God help me! I'm destroyed entirely and my heart is broken in bits! I'm asking God himself, was it for this He'd have me roaming the earth since I was a lad only, to come to black shame in the end, where I'd be giving a power of love to a woman is the same as others you'd meet in any hookershanty in port, with red gowns on them and paint on their grinning mugs, would be sleeping with any man for a dollar or two!

ANNA (*in a scream*). Don't, Mat! For Gawd's sake! (*Then raging and pounding on the table with her hands.*) Get out of here! Leave me alone! Get out of here!

BURKE (*his anger rushing back on him*). I'll be going, surely! And I'll be drinking sloos of whisky will wash that black kiss of yours off my lips; and I'll be getting dead rotten drunk so I'll not remember if 'twas iver born you was at all; and I'll be shipping away on some boat will take me to the other end of the world where I'll never see your face again! (*He turns toward the door.*)

CHRIS (*who has been standing in a stupor —suddenly grasping* BURKE *by the arm —stupidly*). No, you don't go. Ay tank maybe it's better Anna marry you now.

BURKE (*shaking* CHRIS *off—furiously*). Lave go of me, ye old ape! Marry her, is it? I'd see her roasting in hell first! I'm shipping away out of this, I'm telling you! (*Pointing to* ANNA—*passionately.*) And my curse on you and the curse of Almighty God and all the Saints! You've destroyed me this day and may you lie awake in the long nights, tormented with thoughts of Mat Burke and the great wrong you've done him!

ANNA (*in anguish*). Mat! (*But he turns without another word and strides out of the doorway.* ANNA *looks after him wildly, starts to run after him, then hides her face in her outstretched arms, sobbing.* CHRIS *stands in a stupor, staring at the floor.*)

CHRIS (*after a pause, dully*). Ay tank Ay go ashore, too.

ANNA (*looking up, wildly*). Not after him! Let him go! Don't you dare—

CHRIS (*somberly*). Ay go for gat drink.

ANNA (*with a harsh laugh*). So I'm driving you to drink, too, eh? I s'pose you want to get drunk so's you can forget—like him?

CHRIS (*bursting out angrily*). Yes, Ay vant! You tank Ay like hear dem tangs. (*Breaking down—weeping.*) Ay tank you vasn't dat kind of gel, Anna.

ANNA (*mockingly*). And I s'pose you want me to beat it, don't you? You don't want me here disgracing you, I s'pose?

CHRIS. No, you stay here! (*Goes over and pats her on the shoulder, the tears running down his face.*) Ain't your fault, Anna, Ay know dat. (*She looks up at him, softened. He bursts into rage.*) It's dat ole davil, sea, do this to me! (*He shakes his fist at the door.*) It's her dirty tricks! It vas all right on barge with yust you and me. Den she bring dat Irish fallar in fog, she make you like him, she make you fight with me all time! If dat Irish fallar don't never come, you don't never tal me dem tangs, Ay don't never know, and everytang's all right. (*He shakes his fist again.*) Dirty ole davil!

ANNA (*with spent weariness*). Oh, what's the use? Go on ashore and get drunk.

CHRIS (*goes into room on left and gets his cap. He goes to the door, silent and stupid —then turns*). You vait here, Anna?

ANNA (*dully*). Maybe—and maybe not. Maybe I'll get drunk, too. Maybe I'll—But what the hell do you care what I do? Go on and beat it. (CHRIS *turns stupidly and goes out.* ANNA *sits at the table, staring straight in front of her.*)

The Curtain Falls.

ACT FOUR

SCENE. *Same as Act Three, about nine o'clock of a foggy night two days later. The whistles of steamers in the harbor can be heard. The cabin is lighted by a small lamp on the table. A suit case stands in the middle of the floor.* ANNA *is sitting in the rocking-chair. She wears a hat, is all dressed up as in Act One. Her face is pale, looks terribly tired and worn, as if the two days just past had been ones of suffering and sleepless nights. She stares before her despondently, her chin in her hands. There is a timid knock on the door in rear.* ANNA *jumps to her feet with a startled exclamation and looks toward the door with an expression of mingled hope and fear.*

ANNA (*faintly*). Come in. (*Then summoning her courage—more resolutely.*) Come in. (*The door is opened and* CHRIS *appears in the doorway. He is in a very bleary, bedraggled condition, suffering from the after effects of his drunk. A tin pail full of foaming beer is in his hand. He comes forward, his eyes avoiding* ANNA'S. *He mutters stupidly.*) It's foggy.

ANNA (*looking him over with contempt*). So you come back at last, did you? You're a fine looking sight! (*Then jeeringly*). I thought you'd beaten it for good on ac-, count of the disgrace I'd brought on you.

CHRIS (*wincing—faintly*). Don't say dat, Anna, please! (*He sits in a chair by the table, setting down the can of beer, holding his head in his hands.*)

ANNA (*looks at him with a certain sympathy*). What's the trouble? Feeling sick?

CHRIS (*dully*). Inside my head feel sick.

ANNA. Well, what d'you expect after being soused for two days? (*Resentfully.*) It serves you right. A fine thing—you leaving me alone on this barge all that time!

CHRIS (*humbly*). Ay'm sorry, Anna.

ANNA (*scornfully*). Sorry!

CHRIS. But Ay'm not sick inside head vay you mean. Ay'm sick from tank too much about you, about me.

ANNA. And how about me? D'you suppose I ain't been thinking, too?

CHRIS. Ay'm sorry, Anna. (*He sees her bag and gives a start.*) You pack your bag, Anna? You vas going—?

ANNA (*forcibly*). Yes, I was going right back to what you think.

CHRIS. Anna!

ANNA. I went ashore to get a train for New York. I'd been waiting and waiting till I was sick of it. Then I changed my mind and decided not to go today. But I'm going first thing tomorrow, so it'll all be the same in the end.

CHRIS (*raising his head—pleadingly*). No, you never do dat, Anna!

ANNA (*with a sneer*). Why not, I'd like to know?

CHRIS. You don't never gat to do—dat vay —no more, Ay tal you. Ay fix dat up all right.

ANNA (*suspiciously*). Fix what up?

CHRIS (*not seeming to have heard her question—sadly*). You vas vaiting, you say? You vasn't vaiting for me, Ay bet.

ANNA (*callously*). You'd win.

CHRIS. For dat Irish fallar?

ANNA (*defiantly*). Yes—if you want to know! (*Then with a forlorn laugh.*) If he did come back it'd only be 'cause he wanted to beat me up or kill me, I suppose. But even if he did, I'd rather have him come than not show up at all. I wouldn't care what he did.

CHRIS. Ay guess it's true you vas in love with him all right.

ANNA. You guess!

CHRIS (*turning to her earnestly*). And Ay'm sorry for you like hell he don't come, Anna!

ANNA (*softened*). Seems to me you've changed your tune a lot.

CHRIS. Ay've been tanking, and Ay guess it vas all my fault—all bad tangs dat happen to you. (*Pleadingly.*) You try for not hate me, Anna. Ay'm crazy ole fool, dat's all.

ANNA. Who said I hated you?

CHRIS. Ay'm sorry for everytang Ay do wrong for you, Anna. Ay vant for you be happy all rest of your life for make up! It make you happy marry dat Irish fallar, Ay vant it, too.

ANNA (*dully*). Well, there ain't no chance. But I'm glad you think different about it, anyway.

CHRIS (*supplicatingly*). And you tank— maybe—you forgive me sometime?

ANNA (*with a wan smile*). I'll forgive you right now.

CHRIS (*seizing her hand and kissing it— brokenly*). Anna lilla! Anna lilla!

ANNA (*touched but a bit embarrassed*). Don't bawl about it. There ain't nothing to forgive, anyway. It ain't your fault, and it ain't mine, and it ain't his neither. We're all poor nuts, and things happen, and we yust get mixed in wrong, that's all.

CHRIS (*eagerly*). You say right tang, Anna, py golly! It ain't nobody's fault! (*Shaking his fist.*) It's dat ole davil, sea!

ANNA (*with an exasperated laugh*). Gee, won't you ever can that stuff? (CHRIS *relapses into injured silence. After a pause* ANNA *continues curiously.*) You said a minute ago you'd fixed something up—about me. What was it?

CHRIS (*after a hesitating pause*). Ay'm shipping avay on sea again, Anna.

ANNA (*astounded*). You're—what?

CHRIS. Ay sign on steamer sail tomorrow. Ay gat my ole yob—bo'sun. (ANNA *stares at him. As he goes on, a bitter smile comes over her face.*) Ay tank dat's best tang for you. Ay only bring you bad luck, Ay tank. Ay make your mo'der's life sorry. Ay don't vant make yours dat way, but Ay do yust same. Dat ole davil, sea, she makes me Yonah man ain't no good for nobody. And Ay tank now it ain't no use fight with sea. No man dat live going to beat her, py yingo!

ANNA (*with a laugh of helpless bitterness*). So that's how you've fixed me, is it?

CHRIS. Yes, Ay tank if dat ole davil gat me back she leave you alone den.

ANNA (*bitterly*). But, for Gawd's sake, don't you see you're doing the same thing you've always done? Don't you see—? (*But she sees the look of obsessed stubbornness on her father's face and gives it up helplessly.*) But what's the use of talking? You ain't right, that's what. I'll never blame you for nothing no more. But how you could figure out that was fixing me—!

CHRIS. Dat ain't all. Ay gat dem fallars in steamship office to pay you all money coming to me every month vhile Ay'm avay.

ANNA (*with a hard laugh*). Thanks. But I guess I won't be hard up for no small change.

CHRIS (*hurt—humbly*). It ain't much, Ay know, but it's plenty for keep you so you never gat go back—

ANNA (*shortly*). Shut up, will you? We'll talk about it later, see?

CHRIS (*after a pause—ingratiatingly*). You like Ay go ashore look for dat Irish fallar, Anna?

ANNA (*angrily*). Not much! Think I want to drag him back?

CHRIS (*after a pause—uncomfortably*). Py golly, dat booze don't go vell. Give me fever, Ay tank. Ay feel hot like hell. (*He takes off his coat and lets it drop on the floor. There is a loud thud.*)

ANNA (*with a start*). What you got in your pocket, for Pete's sake—a ton of lead? (*She reaches down, takes the coat and pulls out a revolver—looks from it to him in*

amazement.) A gun? What were you doing with this?

CHRIS (*sheepishly*). Ay forget. Ain't nothing. Ain't loaded, anyvay.

ANNA (*breaking it open to make sure—then closing it again—looking at him suspiciously*). That ain't telling me why you got it?

CHRIS. Ay'm ole fool. Ay got it when Ay go ashore first. Ay tank den it's all fault of dat Irish fallar.

ANNA (*with a shudder*). Say, you're crazier than I thought. I never dreamt you'd go that far.

CHRIS (*quickly*). Ay don't. Ay gat better sense right avay. Ay don't never buy bullets even. It ain't his fault, Ay know.

ANNA (*still suspicious of him*). Well, I'll take care of this for a while, loaded or not. (*She puts it in the drawer of table and closes the drawer.*)

CHRIS (*placatingly*). Throw it overboard if you vant. Ay don't care. (*Then after a pause.*) Py golly, Ay tank Ay go lie down. Ay feel sick. (ANNA *takes a magazine from the table.* CHRIS *hesitates by her chair.*) Ve talk again before Ay go, yes?

ANNA (*dully*). Where's this ship going to?

CHRIS. Cape Town. Dat's in South Africa. She's British steamer called Londonderry. (*He stands hesitatingly—finally blurts out.*) Anna—you forgive me sure?

ANNA (*wearily*). Sure I do. You ain't to blame. You're yust—what you are—like me.

CHRIS (*pleadingly*). Den—you lat me kiss you again once?

ANNA (*raising her face—forcing a wan smile*). Sure. No hard feelings.

CHRIS (*kisses her brokenly*). Anna lilla; Ay—(*He fights for words to express himself, but finds none—miserably—with a sob.*) Ay can't say it. Good-night, Anna.

ANNA. Good-night. (*He picks up the can of beer and goes slowly into the room on left, his shoulders bowed his head sunk for-*

ward dejectedly. He closes the door after him. ANNA *turns over the pages of the magazine, trying desperately to banish her thoughts by looking at the pictures. This fails to distract her, and flinging the magazine back on the table, she springs to her feet and walks about the cabin distractedly, clenching and unclenching her hands. She speaks aloud to herself in a tense, trembling voice.*) Gawd, I can't stand this much longer! What am I waiting for anyway?—like a damn fool! (*She laughs helplessly, then checks herself abruptly, as she hears the sound of heavy footsteps on the deck outside. She appears to recognize these and her face lights up with joy. She gasps.*) Mat! (*A strange terror seems suddenly to seize her. She rushes to the table, takes the revolver out of drawer and crouches down in the corner, left, behind the cupboard. A moment later the door is flung open and* MAT BURKE *appears in the doorway. He is in bad shape—his clothes torn and dirty, covered with sawdust as if he had been grovelling or sleeping on barroom floors. There is a red bruise on his forehead over one of his eyes, another over one cheekbone, his knuckles are skinned and raw—plain evidence of the fighting he has been through on his "bat." His eyes are bloodshot and heavy-lidded, his face has a bloated look. But beyond these appearances—the results of heavy drinking—there is an expression in his eyes of wild mental turmoil, of impotent animal rage baffled by its own abject misery.*)

BURKE (*peers blinkingly about the cabin —hoarsely*). Let you not be hiding from me, whoever's here—though 'tis well you know I'd have a right to come back and murder you. (*He stops to listen. Hearing no sound, he closes the door behind him and comes forward to the table. He throws himself into the rocking-chair—despondently.*) There's no one here, I'm thinking, and 'tis a great fool I am to be coming. (*With a sort of dumb, uncomprehending anguish.*) Yerra, Mat Burke, 'tis a great jackass you've become and what's got into you at all, at all? She's gone out of this long ago, I'm telling you, and you'll never see her face again. (ANNA *stands up, hesitating, struggling between joy and fear.* BURKE'S *eyes fall on* ANNA'S *bag. He leans*

over to examine it.*) What's this? (*Joyfully.*) It's hers. She's not gone! But where is she? Ashore? (*Darkly.*) What would she be doing ashore on this rotten night? (*His face suddenly convulsed with grief and rage.*) 'Tis that, is it? Oh, God's curse on her! (*Raging.*) I'll wait till she comes and choke her dirty life out. (ANNA *starts, her face grows hard. She steps into the room, the revolver in her right hand by her side.*)

ANNA (*in a cold, hard tone*). What are you doing here?

BURKE (*wheeling about with a terrified gasp*). Glory be to God! (*They remain motionless and silent for a moment, holding each other's eyes.*)

ANNA (*in the same hard voice*). Well, can't you talk?

BURKE (*trying to fall into an easy, careless tone*). You've a year's growth scared out of me, coming at me so sudden and me thinking I was alone.

ANNA. You've got your nerve butting in here without knocking or nothing. What d'you want?

BURKE (*airily*). Oh, nothing much. I was wanting to have a last word with you, that's all. (*He moves a step toward her.*)

ANNA (*sharply—raising the revolver in her hand*). Careful now! Don't try getting too close. I heard what you said you'd do to me.

BURKE (*noticing the revolver for the first time*). Is it murdering me you'd be now, God forgive you? (*Then with a contemptuous laugh.*) Or is it thinking I'd be frightened by that old tin whistle? (*He walks straight for her.*)

ANNA (*wildly*). Look out, I tell you!.

BURKE (*who has come so close that the revolver is almost touching his chest*). Let you shoot, then! (*Then with sudden wild grief.*) Let you shoot, I'm saying, and be done with it! Let you end me with a shot and I'll be thanking you, for it's a rotten dog's life I've lived the past two days since I've known what you are, till I'm after wishing I was never born at all!

ANNA. (*overcome—letting the revolver drop to the floor, as if her fingers had no strength to hold it—hysterically*). What d'you want coming here? Why don't you beat it? Go on! (*She passes him and sinks down in the rocking-chair.*)

BURKE (*following her—mournfully*). 'Tis right you'd be asking why did I come. (*Then angrily.*) 'Tis because 'tis a great weak fool of the world I am, and me tormented with the wickedness you'd told of yourself, and drinking oceans of booze that'd make me forget. Forget? Divil a word I'd forget, and your face grinning always in front of my eyes, awake or asleep, till I do be thinking a madhouse is the proper place for me.

ANNA (*glancing at his hands and face—scornfully*). You look like you ought to be put away some place. Wonder you wasn't pulled in. You been scrapping, too, ain't you?

BURKE. I have—with every scut would take off his coat to me! (*Fiercely.*) And each time I'd be hitting one a clout in the mug, it wasn't his face I'd be seeing at all, but yours, and me wanting to drive you a blow would knock you out of this world where I wouldn't be seeing or thinking more of you.

ANNA (*her lips trembling pitifully*). Thanks!

BURKE (*walking up and down—distractedly*). That's right, make game of me! Oh, I'm a great coward surely, to be coming back to speak with you at all. You've a right to laugh at me.

ANNA. I ain't laughing at you, Mat.

BURKE (*unheeding*). You to be what you are, and me to be Mat Burke, and me to be drove back to look at you again! 'Tis black shame is on me!

ANNA (*resentfully*). Then get out. No one's holding you!

BURKE (*bewilderedly*). And me to listen to that talk from a woman like you and be frightened to close her mouth with a slap! Oh, God help me, I'm a yellow coward for all men to spit at! (*Then furiously.*) But

I'll not be getting out of this 'till I've had me word. (*Raising his fist threateningly.*) And let you look out how you'd drive me! (*Letting his fist fall helplessly.*) Don't be angry now! I'm raving like a real lunatic, I'm thinking, and the sorrow you put on me has my brains drownded in grief. (*Suddenly bending down to her and grasping her arm intensely.*) Tell me it's a lie, I'm saying! That's what I'm after coming to hear you say.

ANNA (*dully*). A lie? What?

BURKE (*with passionate entreaty*). All the badness you told me two days back. Sure it must be a lie! You was only making game of me, wasn't you? Tell me 'twas a lie, Anna, and I'll be saying prayers of thanks on my two knees to the Almighty God!

ANNA (*terribly shaken—faintly*). I can't, Mat. (*As he turns away—imploringly.*) Oh, Mat, won't you see that no matter what I was I ain't that any more? Why, listen! I packed up my bag this afternoon and went ashore. I'd been waiting here all alone for two days, thinking maybe you'd come back—thinking maybe you'd think over all I'd said—and maybe—oh, I don't know what I was hoping! But I was afraid to even go out of the cabin for a second, honest—afraid you might come and not find me here. Then I gave up hope when you didn't show up and I went to the railroad station. I was going to New York. I was going back—

BURKE (*hoarsely*). God's curse on you!

ANNA. Listen, Mat! You hadn't come, and I'd gave up hope. But—in the station—I couldn't go. I'd bought my ticket and everything. (*She takes the ticket from her dress and tries to hold it before his eyes.*) But I got to thinking about you—and I couldn't take the train—I couldn't! So I come back here—to wait some more. Oh, Mat, don't you see I've changed? Can't you forgive what's dead and gone—and forget it?

BURKE (*turning on her—overcome by rage again*). Forget, is it? I'll not forget till my dying day, I'm telling you, and me tormented with thoughts. (*In a frenzy.*) Oh,

I'm wishing I had wan of then fornenst me this minute and I'd beat him with my fists till he'd be a bloody corpse! I'm wishing the whole lot of them will roast in hell till the Judgment Day—and yourself along with them, for you're as bad as they are.

ANNA (*shuddering*). Mat! (*Then after a pause—in a voice of dead, stony calm.*) Well, you've had your say. Now you better beat it.

BURKE (*starts slowly for the door—hesitates—then after a pause*). And what'll you be doing?

ANNA. What difference does it make to you?

BURKE. I'm asking you!

ANNA (*in the same tone*). My bag's packed and I got my ticket. I'll go to New York tomorrow.

BURKE (*helplessly*). You mean—you'll be doing the same again?

ANNA (*stonily*). Yes.

BURKE (*in anguish*). You'll not! Don't torment me with that talk! 'Tis a she-divil you are sent to drive me mad entirely!

ANNA (*her voice breaking*). Oh, for Gawd's sake, Mat, leave me alone! Go away! Don't you see I'm licked? Why d'you want to keep on kicking me?

BURKE (*indignantly*). And don't you deserve the worst I'd say, God forgive you?

ANNA. All right. Maybe I do. But don't rub it in. Why ain't you done what you said you was going to? Why ain't you got that ship was going to take you to the other side of the earth where you'd never see me again?

BURKE. I have.

ANNA (*startled*). What—then you're going —honest?

BURKE. I signed on today at noon, drunk as I was—and she's sailing tomorrow.

ANNA. And where's she going to?

BURKE. Cape Town.

ANNA (*the memory of having heard that name a little while before coming to her—with a start, confusedly*). Cape Town? Where's that? Far away?

BURKE. 'Tis at the end of Africa. That's far for you.

ANNA (*forcing a laugh*). You're keeping your word all right, ain't you? (*After a slight pause—curiously.*) What's the boat's name?

BURKE. The Londonderry.

ANNA (*it suddenly comes to her that this is the same ship her father is sailing on*). The Londonderry! It's the same—Oh, this is too much! (*With wild, ironical laughter.*) Ha-ha-ha!

BURKE. What's up with you now?

ANNA. Ha-ha-ha! It's funny, funny! I'll die laughing!

BURKE (*irritated*). Laughing at what?

ANNA. It's a secret. You'll know soon enough. It's funny. (*Controlling herself— after a pause—cynically.*) What kind of a place is this Cape Town? Plenty of dames there, I suppose?

BURKE. To hell with them! That I may never see another woman to my dying hour!

ANNA. That's what you say now, but I'll bet by the time you get there you'll have forgot all about me and start in talking the same old bull you talked to me to the first one you meet.

BURKE (*offended*). I'll not, then! God mend you, is it making me out to be the like of yourself you are, and you taking up with this one and that all the years of your life?

ANNA (*angrily assertive*). Yes, that's yust what I do mean! You been doing the same thing all your life, picking up a new girl in every port. How're you any better than I was?

BURKE (*thoroughly exasperated*). Is it no shame you have at all? I'm a fool to be wasting talk on you and you hardened in badness. I'll go out of this and lave you alone forever. (*He starts for the door—then stops to turn on her furiously.*) And I suppose 'tis the same lies you told them all before that you told to me?

ANNA (*indignantly*). That's a lie! I never did!

BURKE (*miserably*). You'd be saying that, anyway.

ANNA (*forcibly, with growing intensity*). Are you trying to accuse me—of being in love—really in love—with them?

BURKE. I'm thinking you were, surely.

ANNA (*furiously, as if this were the last insult—advancing on him threateningly.*) You mutt, you! I've stood enough from you. Don't you dare. (*With scornful bitterness.*) Love 'em! Oh, my Gawd! You damn thick-head! Love 'em? (*Savagely.*) I hated 'em, I tell you! Hated 'em, hated 'em, hated 'em! And may Gawd strike me dead this minute and my mother, too, if she was alive, if I ain't telling you the honest truth!

BURKE (*immensely pleased by her vehemence—a light beginning to break over his face—but still uncertain, torn between doubt and the desire to believe—helplessly*). If I could only be believing you now!

ANNA (*distractedly*). Oh, what's the use? What's the use of me talking? What's the use of anything? (*Pleadingly.*) Oh, Mat, you mustn't think that for a second! You mustn't! Think all the other bad about me you want to, and I won't kick, 'cause you've a right to. But don't think that! (*On the point of tears.*) I couldn't bear it! It'd be yust too much to know you was going away where I'd never see you again—thinking that about me!

BURKE (*after an inward struggle—tensely—forcing out the words with difficulty*). If I was believing—that you'd never had love for any other man in the world but me—I could be forgetting the rest, maybe.

ANNA (*with a cry of joy*). Mat!

BURKE (*slowly*). If 'tis truth you're after telling, I'd have a right, maybe, to believe you'd changed—and that I'd changed you

myself till the thing you'd been all your life wouldn't be you any more at all.

ANNA (*hanging on his words—breathlessly*). Oh, Mat! That's what I been trying to tell you all along!

BURKE (*simply*). For I've a power of strength in me to lead men the way I want, and women, too, maybe, and I'm thinking I'd change you to a new woman entirely, so I'd never know, or you either, what kind of woman you'd been in the past at all.

ANNA. Yes, you could, Mat! I know you could!

BURKE. And I'm thinking 'twasn't your fault, maybe, but having that old ape for a father that left you to grow up alone, made you what you was. And if I could be believing 'tis only me you—

ANNA (*distractedly*). You got to believe it, Mat! What can I do? I'll do anything, anything you want to prove I'm not lying!

BURKE (*suddenly seems to have a solution. He feels in the pocket of his coat and grasps something—solemnly*). Would you be willing to swear an oath, now—a terrible, fearful oath would send your soul to the divils in hell if you was lying?

ANNA (*eagerly*). Sure, I'll swear, Mat—on anything!

BURKE (*takes a small, cheap old crucifix from his pocket and holds it up for her to see*). Will you swear on this?

ANNA (*reaching out for it*). Yes. Sure I will. Give it to me.

BURKE (*holding it away*). 'Tis a cross was given me by my mother, God rest her soul. (*He makes the sign of the cross mechanically.*) I was a lad only, and she told me to keep it by me if I'd be waking or sleeping and never lose it, and it'd bring me luck. She died soon after. But I'm after keeping it with me from that day to this, and I'm telling you there's great power in it, and 'tis great bad luck it's saved me from and me roaming the seas, and I having it tied round my neck when my last ship sunk, and it bringing me safe to land when the others went to their death. (*Very earnest-*

ly.) And I'm warning you now, if you'd swear an oath on this, 'tis my old woman herself will be looking down from Hivin above, and praying Almighty God and the Saints to put a great curse on you if she'd hear you swearing a lie!

ANNA (*awed by his manner—superstitiously*). I wouldn't have the nerve—honest— if it was a lie. But it's the truth and I ain't scared to swear. Give it to me.

BURKE (*handing it to her—almost frightenedly, as if he feared for her safety*). Be careful what you'd swear, I'm saying.

ANNA (*holding the cross gingerly*). Well— what do you want me to swear? You say it.

BURKE. Swear I'm the only man in the world ivir you felt love for.

ANNA (*looking into his eyes steadily*). I swear it.

BURKE. And that you'll be forgetting from this day all the badness you've done and never do the like of it again.

ANNA (*forcibly*). I swear it! I swear it by God!

BURKE. And may the blackest curse of God strike you if you're lying. Say it now!

ANNA. And may the blackest curse of God strike me if I'm lying!

BURKE (*with a stupendous sigh*). Oh, glory be to God, I'm after believing you now! (*He takes the cross from her hand, his face beaming with joy, and puts it back in his pocket. He puts his arm about her waist and is about to kiss her when he stops, appalled by some terrible doubt.*)

ANNA (*alarmed*). What's the matter with you?

BURKE (*with sudden fierce questioning*). Is it Catholic ye are?

ANNA (*confused*). No. Why?

BURKE (*filled with a sort of bewildered foreboding*). Oh, God, help me! (*With a dark glance of suspicion at her.*) There's some divil's trickery in it, to be swearing an oath on a Catholic cross and you wan of the others.

ANNA (*distractedly*). Oh, Mat, don't you believe me?

BURKE (*miserably*). If it isn't a Catholic you are—

ANNA. I ain't nothing. What's the difference? Didn't you hear me swear?

BURKE (*passionately*). Oh, I'd a right to stay away from you—but I couldn't! I was loving you in spite of it all and wanting to be with you, God forgive me, no matter what you are. I'd go mad if I'd not have you! I'd be killing the world— (*He seizes her in his arms and kisses her fiercely.*)

ANNA (*with a gasp of joy*). Mat!

BURKE (*suddenly holding her away from him and staring into her eyes as if to probe into her soul—slowly*). If your oath is no proper oath at all, I'll have to be taking your naked word for it and have you anyway, I'm thinking—I'm needing you that bad!

ANNA (*hurt—reproachfully*). Mat! I swore, didn't I?

BURKE (*defiantly, as if challenging fate*). Oath or no oath, 'tis no matter. We'll be wedded in the morning, with the help of God. (*Still more defiantly.*) We'll be happy now, the two of us, in spite of the divil! (*He crushes her to him and kisses her again. The door on the left is pushed open and* CHRIS *appears in the doorway. He stands blinking at them. At first the old expression of hatred of* BURKE *comes into his eyes instinctively. Then a look of resignation and relief takes its place. His face lights up with a sudden happy thought. He turns back into the bedroom—reappears immediately with the tin can of beer in his hand—grinning.*)

CHRIS. Ve have drink on this, py golly! (*They break away from each other with startled exclamations.*)

BURKE (*explosively*). God stiffen it! (*He takes a step toward* CHRIS *threateningly.*)

ANNA (*happily—to her father*). That's the way to talk! (*With a laugh.*) And say, it's about time for you and Mat to kiss and make up. You're going to be shipmates on the Londonderry, did you know it?

BURKE (*astounded*). Shipmates—Has himself—

CHRIS (*equally astounded*). Ay vas bo'sun on her.

BURKE. The divil! (*Then angrily.*) You'd be going back to sea and leaving her alone, would you?

ANNA (*quickly*). It's all right, Mat. That's where he belongs, and I want him to go. You got to go, too; we'll need the money. (*With a laugh, as she gets the glasses.*) And as for me being alone, that runs in the family, and I'll get used to it. (*Pouring out their glasses.*) I'll get a little house somewhere and I'll make a regular place for you two to come back to—wait and see. And now you drink up and be friends.

BURKE (*happily—but still a bit resentful against the old man*). Sure! (*Clinking his glass against* CHRIS') Here's luck to you! (*He drinks.*)

CHRIS (*subdued—his face melancholy*). Skoal. (*He drinks.*)

BURKE (*to* ANNA, *with a wink*). You'll not be lonesome long. I'll see to that, with the help of God. 'Tis himself here will be having a grandchild to ride on his foot, I'm telling you!

ANNA (*turning away in embarrassment*). Quit the kidding now. (*She picks up her bag and goes into the room on left. As soon as she is gone* BURKE *relapses into an attitude of gloomy thought.* CHRIS *stares at his beer absent-mindedly. Finally* BURKE *turns on him.*)

BURKE. Is it any religion at all you have, you and your Anna?

CHRIS (*surprised*). Vhy yes. Ve vas Lutheran in ole country.

BURKE (*horrified*). Luthers, is it? (*Then with a grim resignation, slowly, aloud to himself.*) Well, I'm damned then surely. Yerra, what's the difference? 'Tis the will of God, anyway.

CHRIS (*moodily preoccupied with his own thoughts—speaks with somber premonition as* ANNA *re-enters from the left*). It's funny. It's queer, yes—you and me shipping on same boat dat vay. It ain't right. Ay don't know—it's dat funny vay ole davil sea do her vorst dirty tricks, yes. It's so. (*He gets up and goes back and, opening the door, stares out into the darkness.*)

BURKE (*nodding his head in gloomy acquiescence—with a great sigh*). I'm fearing maybe you have the right of it for once, divil take you.

ANNA (*forcing a laugh*). Gee, Mat, you ain't agreeing with him, are you? (*She comes forward and puts her arm about his shoulder—with a determined gayety.*) Aw say, what's the matter? Cut out the gloom. We're all fixed now, ain't we, me and you? (*Pours out more beer into his glass and fills one for herself—slaps him on the back.*) Come on! Here's to the sea, no matter what! Be a game sport and drink to that! Come on! (*She gulps down her glass.* BURKE *banishes his superstitious premonitions with a defiant jerk of his head, grins up at her, and drinks to her toast.*)

CHRIS (*looking out into the night—lost in his somber preoccupation—shakes his head and mutters*). Fog, fog, fog, all bloody time. You can't see vhere you vas going, no. Only dat ole davil, sea—she knows! (*The two stare at him. From the harbor comes the muffled, mournful wail of steamers' whistles.*)

The Curtain Falls.

Icebound

BY OWEN DAVIS

OWEN DAVIS

Owen Davis, America's most prolific writer of plays, was born in Portland, Maine, in 1874. A student at the University of Tennessee one year, he studied the next three years at Harvard in preparation for the profession of civil engineering. The four years following his graduation from Harvard, however, were spent in acting with a stock company and assisting in the revision and strengthening of the popular-priced melodramas presented. He managed to secure the production of his first play in 1898. In 1902 he married Elizabeth Breyer, by whom he has two sons, Donald and Owen.

Mr. Davis believes that "beauty in the modern play is in the thought, not the dialogue. A play consists of 100,000 words, 20,000 on paper and 80,000 in the waste basket." In 1931 a highly amusing volume of Mr. Davis' memoirs as a playwright was published under the title *I'd Like To Do It Again*. He is a member of the National Institute of Arts and Letters, of the American Dramatists, and of the Authors' League of America.

Owen Davis is the author of some four hundred plays. In 1900 he created a vogue for melodramas with such plays as *Nellie the Beautiful Cloak Model, Chinatown Charlie,* and *My Lady Nell,* admittedly designed to satisfy the most lurid and undiscriminating tastes. A tendency toward realism was manifested in later plays, such as *An Everyday Man, Sinners,* and *Opportunity.*

A rare resilience has been shown by Mr. Davis in his ability to turn from melodrama to serious plays without losing the naturalness of dialogue, the facility of treatment, and the sense of ironic comedy. *The Detour* (1921) has been ranked by Heywood Broun among the five or six best plays ever written by Americans. During the past few years Mr. Davis has achieved success in the cinema and radio, although he has in no degree forsaken writing for the stage.

Produced by Harris, Lewis and Gordon at the Harris Theatre, New York, in February, 1923, *Icebound* won the Pulitzer Prize for 1922-1923.

CHARACTERS

HENRY JORDAN.

EMMA, his wife.

NETTIE, her daughter by a former marriage.

SADIE FELLOWS, once Sadie Jordan, a widow.

ORIN, her son.

ELLA JORDAN, the unmarried sister.

DOCTOR CURTIS.

JANE CROSBY, a second cousin of the Jordans.

JUDGE BRADFORD.

BEN JORDAN.

HANNAH.

JIM JAY.

SCENES

ACT ONE

The parlor of the Jordan homestead, 4 p. m., October, 1922.

ACT TWO

The sitting room of the Jordan homestead, two months later.
Afternoon.

ACT THREE

Same as Act One, late in the following March.

ICEBOUND

ACT ONE

SCENE: *The parlor of the Jordan Homestead at Veazie, Maine.*

It is late October, and through the two windows at the back one may see a bleak countryside, the grass brown and lifeless, and the bare limbs of the trees silhouetted against a gray sky. Here, in the room that for a hundred years has been the rallying point of the Jordan family, a group of relatives are gathered to await the death of the old woman who is the head of their clan. The room in which they wait is as dull and as drab as the lives of those who have lived within its walls. Here we have the cleanliness that is next to godliness, but no sign of either comfort or beauty, both of which are looked upon with suspicion as being signposts on the road to perdition.

In this group are the following characters: HENRY JORDAN, *a heavy-set man of fifty, worn by his business cares into a dull sort of hopeless resignation;* EMMA, *his wife, a stout and rather formidable woman of forty, with a look of chronic displeasure;* NETTIE, *her daughter by a former marriage, a vain and shallow little rustic beauty;* SADIE, *a thin, tight-lipped woman of forty, a widow and a gossip;* ORIN, *her son, a pasty-faced boy of ten with large spectacles;* ELLA, *a "Maiden lady" of thirty-six, restless and dissatisfied.*

ELLA *and* SADIE, *true Jordans by birth, are a degree above* EMMA *in social standing, at least they were until* HENRY'S *marriage to* EMMA *made her a somewhat resentful member of the family. In* EMMA'S *dialogue and in her reactions, I have attempted a rather nice distinction between the two grades of rural middle-class folk; the younger characters here, as in most other communities, have advanced one step.*

Rise: At rise there is a long silence; the occupants of the room are ill at ease. EMMA *is grim and frowning.* NETTIE *sits with a simper of youthful vanity, looking stealthily at herself from time to time in a small mirror set in the top of her cheap vanity case.* ELLA *and* SADIE *have been crying and dab at their eyes a bit ostentatiously. Henry makes a thoughtful note with a pencil, then returns his notebook to his pocket and warms his hands at the stove.*

There is a low whistle of a cold autumn wind as some dead leaves are blown past the window. Orin, who has a cold in his head, sniffs viciously; the others, with the exception of his mother, look at him in remonstrance. An eight-day clock in sight, through the door to the hall, strikes four.

EMMA (*sternly*). Four o'clock.

HENRY (*looks at watch*). Five minutes of. That clock's been fast for more'n thirty years.

NETTIE (*looks at wrist watch*). My watch says two minutes after.

HENRY. Well, it's wrong!

EMMA (*acidly*). You gave it to her yourself, didn't you?

SADIE (*sighs*). Good Land! What does it matter?

NETTIE (*offended*). Oh! Doesn't it? Oh!

ELLA. Maybe it does to you. She ain't your blood relation.

EMMA. Nettie loves her grandma, don't you dear?

NETTIE. Some folks not so far off may get fooled before long about how much grandma and I was to each other.

EMMA (*sternly*). You hush!
(*Again there is a pause, and again it is broken by a loud sniff from Orin, as the women look at him in disgust. Sadie speaks up in his defense.*)

SADIE. He's got kind of a cold in his head.

HENRY. The question is, ain't he got a handkerchief?

SADIE. Here, Orin!
(*She hands him her handkerchief.*)

ELLA. The idea! No handkerchief when you've come expectin' some one to die!

ORIN. I had one, but I used it up.
(*He blows his nose.*)

HENRY. After four. Well, I expect they'll have to close the store without me.

ELLA. I left everything just as soon as Jane sent me word!

SADIE. Why should Jane be with her instead of you or me, her own daughters?

HENRY. You girls always made her nervous, and I guess she's pretty low. (*He looks at his watch again.*) I said I'd be back before closin' time. I don't know as I dare to trust those boys.

EMMA. You can't tell about things, when Sadie's husband died we sat there most all night.

SADIE (*angrily*). Yes, and you grudged it to him, I knew it then and it isn't likely I'm going to forget it.

ELLA. Will was a good man, but even you can't say he was ever very dependable.

EMMA. My first husband died sudden— (*she turns to* NETTIE)—you can't remember it, dear.

ELLA. *You* didn't remember it very long, it wa'n't much more'n a year before you married Henry.

HENRY (*sighs*). Well, he was as dead then as he's ever got to be. (*He turns and glances nervously out window.*) I don't know but what I could just run down to the store for a minute, then hurry right back.

SADIE. You're the oldest of her children, a body would think you'd be ashamed.

HENRY. Oh, I'll stay. (*There is a silence.* ORIN *sniffs.* ELLA *glares at him.*)

ELLA. Of course he *could* sit somewhere else.
(SADIE *puts her arm about* ORIN *and looks spitefully at* ELLA. DOCTOR CURTIS, *an elderly country physician, comes down the stairs and enters the room, all turn to look at him.*)

DOCTOR. No change at all. I'm sendin' Jane to the drug store.

ELLA (*rises eagerly*). I'll just run up and sit with mother. (SADIE *jumps up and starts for door.*)

SADIE. It might be better if I went.

ELLA. Why might it?
(*They stand glaring at each other before either attempts to pass the* DOCTOR, *whose ample form almost blocks the doorway.*)

SADIE. *I've* been a wife and a mother.

DOCTOR. Hannah's with her, you know. I told you I didn't want anybody up there but Jane and Hannah.

ELLA. But we're her own daughters.

DOCTOR. You don't have to tell me, I brought both of you into the world. The right nursing might pull her through, even now; nothing else can, and I've got the two women I want. (*He crosses to* HENRY *at stove.*) Why don't you put a little wood on the fire?

HENRY. Why—I thought 'twas warm enough.

ELLA. Because you was standin' in front of it gettin' all the heat.
(HENRY *fills the stove from wood basket.* JANE CROSBY *enters on stairs and crosses into the room.* JANE *is twenty-four, a plainly dressed girl of quiet manner. She has been "driven into herself" as one of our characters would describe it, by her lack of sympathy and affection and as a natural result she is not especially articulate; she speaks, as a rule, in short sentences, and has cultivated an outward coldness that in the*

course of time has become almost aggressive.)

JANE. I'll go now, Doctor; you'd better go back to her. Hannah's frightened.

DOCTOR. Get it as quick as you can, Jane; I don't know as it's any use, but we've got to keep on tryin'.

JANE. Yes. (*She exits;* DOCTOR *warms his hands.*)

DOCTOR. Jane's been up with her three nights. I don't know when I've seen a more dependable girl.

ELLA. She ought to be.

HENRY. If there's any gratitude in the world.

DOCTOR. Oh, I guess there is; maybe there'd be more if there was more reason for it. It's awful cold up there, but I guess I'll be gettin' back. (*He crosses toward door.*)

HENRY. Doctor! (*He looks at his watch.*)

DOCTOR (*stops in doorway*). Well?

HENRY. It's quite a bit past four, I don't suppose—I don't suppose you can tell—

DOCTOR. No, I can't tell. (*He turns and exits up the stairs.*)

ELLA. There's no fool like an old fool.

SADIE. Did you hear him? "Didn't know when he'd seen a more dependable girl than her!"

EMMA. Makes a lot of difference who's goin' to depend on her. I ain't, for one.

NETTIE. If I set out to tell how she's treated me lots of times, when I've come over here to see grandma, nobody would believe a word of it.

SADIE. Mother took her in out of charity.

ELLA. And kept her out of spite.

HENRY. I don't know as you ought to say that, Ella.

ELLA. It's my place she took, in my own mother's house. I'd been here now, but for her. I ain't goin' to forget that. No! Me, all these years payin' board and slavin' my life out, makin' hats, like a nigger.

NETTIE (*smartly*). Oh! So *that's* what they're like. I've often wondered!

ELLA (*rises*). You'll keep that common little thing of your wife's from insultin' me, Henry Jordan, or I won't stay here another minute.

EMMA (*angry*). Common!

NETTIE. Mother!

HENRY (*sternly*). Hush up! All of yer!

SADIE. It's Jane we ought to be talkin' about.

EMMA. Just as soon as you're the head of the family, Henry, you've got to tell her she ain't wanted here!

HENRY. Well—I don't know as I'd want to do anything that wasn't right. She's been here quite a spell.

SADIE. Eight years!

ELLA. And just a step-cousin, once removed.

HENRY. I guess mother's made her earn her keep. I don't know as ever there was much love lost between 'em.

EMMA. As soon as your mother's dead, you'll send her packing.

HENRY. We'll see. I don't like countin' on mother's going; that way.

SADIE (*hopefully*). Grandmother lived to eighty-four.

HENRY. All our folks was long lived; nothin' lasts like it used to,—Poor mother!

ELLA. Of course she'll divide equal, between us three?

HENRY (*doubtfully*). Well, I don't know!

SADIE. Orin is her only grandchild; she won't forget that.

HENRY. Nettie, there, is just the same as my own. I adopted her legal, when I married Emma.

EMMA. Of course you did. Your mother's too—just a woman to make distinctions!

NETTIE. Yes, and the funny part of it is grandma may leave me a whole lot, for all any of *you* know.

ELLA. Nonsense! She'll divide equally between us three; won't she, Henry?

HENRY (*sadly*). She'll do as she pleases, I guess we all know that.

ELLA. She's a religious woman, she's *got* to be fair!

HENRY. Well, I guess it would be fair enough if she was to remember the trouble I've had with my business. I don't know what she's worth, she's as tight-mouthed as a bear trap, but I could use more'n a third of quite a little sum.

ELLA. Well, you won't get it. Not if I go to law.

EMMA. It's disgusting. Talking about money at a time like this.

HENRY. I like to see folks reasonable. I don't know what you'd want of a third of all mother's got, Ella.

SADIE (*to* ELLA). You, all alone in the world!

ELLA. Maybe I won't be, when I get that money.

SADIE. You don't mean you'd get married?

EMMA. At your age!

ELLA. I mean I never had anything in all my life; now I'm going to. I'm the youngest of all of you, except Ben, and he never was a real Jordan. I've never had a chance; I've been stuck here till I'm most forty, worse than if I was dead, fifty times worse! Now I'm going to buy things—everything I want—I don't care what—I'll buy it, even if it's a man! Anything I want!

NETTIE. A *man!* (NETTIE *looks at* ELLA *in cruel amazement and all but* ORIN *burst into a laugh*—ELLA *turns up and hides her face against the window as* ORIN *pulls at his mother's skirt.*)

ORIN. Mum! Mum! I thought you told me not to laugh, not once, while we was here!

HENRY. You're right, nephew, and we're wrong, all of us. I'm sorry, Ella, we're all sorry.

ELLA (*wipes her eyes*). Laugh if you want to—maybe it won't be so long before I do some of it myself.

HENRY (*thoughtfully*). Equally between us three? Well, poor mother knows best of course. (*He sighs.*)

SADIE. She wouldn't leave *him* any, would she,—Ben?

ELLA (*shocked*). Ben!

HENRY (*in cold anger*). She's a woman of her word; no!

SADIE. If he was here he'd get around her; he always did!

HENRY. Not again!

SADIE. If she ever spoiled anybody it was him, and she's had to pay for it. Sometimes it looks like it was a sort of a judgment.

HENRY. There hasn't been a Jordan, before Ben, who's disgraced the name in more'n a hundred years; he stands indicted before the Grand Jury for some of his drunken devilment. If he hadn't run away, like the criminal he is, he'd be in the State's Prison now, down to Thomaston. Don't talk *Ben* to me, after the way he broke mother's heart, and hurt my credit!

NETTIE. I don't remember him very well. Mother thought it better I shouldn't come around last time he was here; but he looked real nice in his uniform.

SADIE. It was his bein' born so long after us that made him seem like an outsider; father and mother hadn't had any children for years and years! Of course I never want to sit in judgment on my own parents, but I never approved of it; it never seemed quite —what I call proper.

NETTIE (*to* EMMA). Mother, don't you think I'd better leave the room?

SADIE (*angrily*). Not if half the stories I've heard about you are true, I don't.

HENRY. Come, come, no rows! Is this a time or place for spite? We've always been a united family, we've always got to be,— leavin' Ben out, of course. You can't make a silk purse out of a sow's ear.

ORIN. Mum! Say, Mum! (*He pulls at* SADIE'S *dress.*) Why should anybody want to make a silk purse out of a sow's ear?

ELLA. Can't you stop that boy askin' such fool questions?

SADIE. Well, as far as that goes, why should they? It never sounded reasonable to me.

HENRY (*sternly*). Decent folks don't reason about religion; they just accept it.

ORIN. You could make a skin purse out of a sow's ear, but I'll be darned if you could make a silk purse out of one. I'll bet God couldn't.

HENRY. Are you going to let him talk about God like that, like he was a real person?

ELLA. I don't know as a body could expect any better; his father was a Baptist!

SADIE (*angrily*). His father was a good man, and if he talked about God different from what you do, it was because he knew more about him. And as for my being here at all—(*she rises with her arms about* ORIN)—I wouldn't do it, not for anything less than my own mother's deathbed.

HENRY. This family don't ever agree on nothin' but just to differ.

EMMA. As far as I see, the only time you ever get together is when one of you is dead.

ELLA. Maybe that's the reason I got such a feelin' against funerals.
(*The outside door opens and* JANE *enters, a druggist's bottle in her hand; she is followed by* JOHN BRADFORD, *a man of about thirty-five. He is better dressed than any of the others and is a man of a more cosmopolitan type,—a New Englander, but a university man, the local judge and the leading lawyer of the town.*)

JANE. I met Judge Bradford on the way.

JUDGE (JOHN BRADFORD). Court set late. I couldn't get here before. Jane tells me that she's very low.

HENRY. Yes.

JUDGE. I can't realize it; she has always been so strong, so dominant.

ELLA. In the midst of life we are in death.

ORIN. Say, Mum, that's in the Bible too!

SADIE. Hush!

ORIN. Well, ain't it?

SADIE. Will you hush?

HENRY. It's our duty to hope so long as we can.

JUDGE. Yes, of course.

JANE. I'll take this right up. (*She exits up the stairs.*)

JUDGE (*removes his coat*). I'll wait.

SADIE. She can't see you; she ain't really what a body could call in her right mind.

JUDGE. So Jane said. (*He crosses to stove and warms his hands.*)

ELLA (*sighs*). It's a sad time for us, Judge!

JUDGE. She was always such a wonderful woman.

HENRY. An awful time for us. Did you come up Main Street, Judge?

JUDGE. Yes.

HENRY. Did you happen to notice if my store was open?

JUDGE. No.

HENRY. Not that it matters—

SADIE. Nothing matters now.

HENRY. No—Mother wasn't ever the kind to neglect things; if the worst does come she'll find herself prepared. Won't she? Won't she, Judge?

JUDGE. Her affairs are, as usual, in perfect order.

HENRY. In every way?

JUDGE (*looks at him coldly*). Her will is drawn and is on deposit in my office, if that is what you mean.

HENRY. Well—that *is* what I mean—I'm no hypocrite.

EMMA. He's the oldest of the family. He's got a right to ask, hasn't he?

JUDGE. Yes.

HENRY (*honestly*). If I could make her well by givin' up everything I've got in the world, or ever expect to git, I'd do it!

SADIE. All of us would.

HENRY. If it's in my mind at all, as I stand here, that she's a rich woman, it's because my mind's so worried, the way business has been, that I'm drove most frantic; it's because, well—because I'm human; because I can't help it.

ELLA (*bitterly*). You're a man! What do you think it's been for me!

SADIE (*with arm about* ORIN). His father didn't leave much, you all know that, and it's been scrimp and save till I'm all worn to skin and bone.

ELLA. Just to the three of us, that would be fair.

HENRY. Judge! My brother's name ain't in her will, is it? Tell me that? Ben's name ain't there!

JUDGE. I'd rather not talk about it, Henry.

ELLA. She'd cut him off, she said, the last time he disgraced us, and she's a woman of her word.

SADIE (*eagerly, to* JUDGE). And the very next day she sent for you because I was here when she telephoned; and you came to her that very afternoon because I saw you from my front window cross right up to this door.

JUDGE. Possibly. I frequently drop in to discuss business matters with your mother for a moment on my way home.

SADIE. It was five minutes to four when you went in that day, and six minutes to five when you came out, by the clock on my mantel.

JUDGE. Your brother has been gone for al most two years; your memory is very clear.

ELLA. So's her window.

NETTIE. I know folks in this town that are scared to go past it.

SADIE (*to her*). I know others that ought to be.

HENRY (*discouraged*). Every time you folks meet there's trouble.
(JANE *enters down the stairs and into the room.*)

JUDGE (*looks at her*). Well, Jane?

JANE. No change. It's—it's pitiful, to see her like that.
(SADIE *sobs and covers her face.*)

HENRY. It's best we should try to bear this without any fuss, she'd 'a' wanted it that way.

SADIE. She didn't even want me to cry when poor Will died, but I did; and somehow I don't know but it made things easier.

HENRY. When father died she didn't shed a tear; she's been a strong woman, always.
(*The early fall twilight has come on and the stage is rather dim, the hall at Right is in deep shadow, at the end of* HENRY's *speech the outside door supposedly out at Right is opened, then shut rather violently.*)

ELLA (*startled*). Someone's come in.

SADIE. Nobody's got any right— (*She rises as some one is heard coming along the hall.*)

HENRY (*sternly*). Who's that out there? Who is it?

ORIN. Mum! Who is it! (*He clings to his mother afraid, as all turn to the door, and* BEN JORDAN *steps into the room and faces them with a smile of reckless contempt.* BEN *is the black sheep of the Jordan family, years younger than any of the others, a wild, selfish, arrogant fellow, handsome but sulky and defiant. His clothes are cheap and dirty and he is rather pale and looks dissipated. He doesn't speak but stands openly sneering at their look of astonishment.*)

JANE (*quietly*). I'm glad you've come, Ben.

BEN (*contemptuously*). You are?

JANE. Yes, your mother's awful sick.

BEN. She's alive?

JANE. Yes.

BEN. Well— (*He looks contemptuously about.*) Nobody missin'. The Jordans are gathered again, handkerchiefs and all.

HENRY. You'll be arrested soon as folks know you've come.

BEN (*scornfully*). And I suppose you wouldn't bail me out, would you, Henry?

HENRY (*simply*). No, I wouldn't.

BEN. God! You're still the same, all of you. You stink of the Ark, the whole tribe. It takes more than a few Edisons to change the Jordans!

ELLA. How'd you get here? How'd you know about mother?

BEN (*nods at* JANE). She sent me word, to Bangor.

SADIE (*to* JANE). How'd you get to know where he was?

JANE (*quietly*). I knew.

HENRY. How'd you come; you don't look like you had much money?

BEN. She sent it. (*He nods toward* JANE.) God knows, it wasn't much.

ELLA (*to* JANE). Did mother tell you to—?

BEN. Of course she did!

JANE (*quietly*). No, she didn't.

HENRY. You sent your own money?

JANE. Yes, as he said it wasn't much, but I didn't have much.

BEN (*astonished*). Why did you do it?

JANE. I knew she was going to die; twice I asked her if she wanted to see you, and she said no—

HENRY. And yet you sent for him?

JANE. Yes.

HENRY. Why?

JANE. He was the one she really wanted. I thought she'd die happier seeing him.

ELLA. You took a lot on yourself, didn't you?

JANE. Yes, she's been a lonely old woman. I hated to think of her there, in the church-yard, hungry for him.

BEN. I'll go to her.

JANE. It's too late; she wouldn't know you.

BEN. I'll go.

JANE. The doctor will call us when he thinks we ought to come.

BEN (*fiercely*). I'm going now.

HENRY (*steps forward*). No, you ain't.

BEN. Do you think I came here, standin' a chance of bein' sent to jail, to let *you* tell me what to do?

HENRY. If she's dyin' up there, it's more'n half from what you've made her suffer; you'll wait here till we go to her together.

EMMA. Henry's right.

SADIE. Of course he is.

ELLA. Nobody but Ben would have the impudence to show his face here, after what he's done.

BEN. I'm going just the same!

HENRY. No, you ain't.
(*Their voices become loud.*)

EMMA. Henry! Don't let him go!

SADIE. Stop him.

ELLA (*grows shrill*). He's a disgrace to us. He always was.

HENRY. You'll stay right where you are. (*He puts his hand heavily on* BEN's *shoulder*—BEN *throws him off fiercely.*)

BEN. Damn you! Keep your hands off me! (HENRY *staggers back and strikes against a table that falls to the floor with a crash.* NETTIE *screams.*)

JANE. Stop it—stop! You must!

JUDGE. Are you crazy? Have you no sense of decency?
(DOCTOR CURTIS *comes quickly downstairs.*)

DOCTOR. What's this noise? I forbid it. Your mother has heard you.

HENRY (*ashamed*). I'm sorry.

BEN (*sulkily*). I didn't mean to make a row.

HENRY. It's him. (*He looks bitterly at* BEN.) He brings out all the worst in us. He brought trouble into the world with him when he came, and ever since.

(HANNAH, *a middle-aged servant, comes hastily halfway downstairs and calls out sharply.*)

HANNAH. Doctor! Come, Doctor! (*She exits up the stairs, as the* DOCTOR *crosses through the hall and follows her.*)

ORIN (*afraid*). Is she dead, Mum? Does Hannah mean she's dead!

(SADIE *hides her head on his shoulder and weeps.*)

JANE. I'll go to her. (*She exits.*)

ELLA (*violently*). She'll go. There ain't scarcely a drop of Jordan blood in her veins, and *she's* the one that goes to mother.

EMMA (*coldly*). Light the lamp, Nettie; it's gettin' dark.

NETTIE. Yes, mother. (*She starts to light lamp.*)

HENRY. I'm ashamed of my part in it, makin' a row, with her on her deathbed.

BEN. You had it right, I guess. I've made trouble ever since I came into the world.

NETTIE. There! (*She lights lamp; footlights go up.*)

JUDGE (*sternly*). You shouldn't have come here; you know that, Ben.

BEN. I've always known that, any place I've been, exceptin' only those two years in the Army. That's the only time I ever was in right.

JUDGE (*sternly*). I would find it easier to pity you if you had any one to blame besides yourself.

BEN. Pity? Do you think I want your pity? (*There is a pause.* JANE *is seen on stairs, they all turn to her nervously as she comes down and crosses into room. She stops at the door looking at them.*)

HENRY (*slowly*). Mother—mother's—gone!

JANE. Yes.

(*There is a moment's silence broken by the low sobs of the women who for a moment forget their selfishness in the presence of death.*)

HENRY. The Jordans won't ever be the same; she was the last of the old stock, mother was—No, the Jordans won't ever be the same.

(DOCTOR CURTIS *comes downstairs and into the room.*)

DOCTOR. It's no use tryin' to tell you what I feel. I've known her since I was a boy. I did the best I could.

HENRY. The best anybody could, Doctor, we know that.

DOCTOR. I've got a call I'd better make— (*He looks at watch*)—should have been there hours ago, but I hadn't the heart to leave her. Who's in charge here?

HENRY. I am, of course.

DOCTOR. I've made arrangements with Hannah; she'll tell you. I'll say good night now.

HENRY. Good night, Doctor.

JANE. And thank you.

DOCTOR. We did our best, Jane. (*He exits.*)

SADIE. He's gettin' old. When Orin had the stomach trouble a month ago, I sent for Doctor Morris. I felt sort of guilty doin' it, but I thought it was my duty.

JUDGE. You will let me help you, Jane?

JANE. Hannah and I can attend to everything. Henry! (*She turns to him.*) You might come over for a minute this evening and we can talk things over. I'll make the bed up in your old room, Ben, if you want to stay.

EMMA (*rises and looks at* JANE *coldly*). Now, Henry Jordan, if she's all through givin' orders, maybe you'll begin.

ELLA. Well, I should say so. Let's have an understandin'.

SADIE. You tell her the truth, Henry, or else one of us will do it for you.

HENRY (*hesitates*). Maybe it might be best if I should wait until after the funeral.

ELLA. You tell her now, or I will.

JANE. Tell me what?

HENRY. We was thinkin' now that mother's dead, that there wasn't much use in your stayin' on here.

JANE. Yes? (*She looks at him intently.*)

HENRY. We don't aim to be hard, and we don't want it said we was mean about it; you can stay on here, if you want to, until after the funeral, maybe a little longer, and I don't know but what between us, we'd be willing to help you till you found a place somewheres.

JANE. You can't help me, any of you. Of course now she's dead, I'll go. I'll be glad to go.

ELLA. Glad!

JANE (*turns on them*). I hate you, the whole raft of you. I'll be glad to get away from you. She was the only one of you worth loving, and she didn't want it.

EMMA. If that's how you feel, I say the sooner you went the better.

HENRY. Not till after the funeral. I don't want it said we was hard to her.

JUDGE (*quietly*). Jane isn't going at all, Henry.

HENRY. What's that?

ELLA. Of course she's going.

JUDGE. No, she belongs here in this house.

HENRY. Not after I say she don't.

JUDGE. Even then, because it's hers.

SADIE. Hers?

JUDGE. From the moment of your mother's death, everything here belonged to Jane.

HENRY. Not everything.

JUDGE. Yes, everything—your mother's whole estate.

BEN. Ha! Ha! Ha! (*He sits at right, laughing bitterly.*)

JANE. That can't be, Judge, you must be wrong. It's a mistake.

JUDGE. No.

HENRY. My mother did this?

JUDGE. Yes.

HENRY. Why? You've got to tell me why!

JUDGE. That isn't a part of my duties.

HENRY. She couldn't have done a thing like that without sayin' why. She said something, didn't she?

JUDGE. I don't know that I care to repeat it.

HENRY (*fiercely*). You must repeat it!

JUDGE. Very well. The day that will was drawn she said to me, "The Jordans are all waiting for me to die, like carrion crows around a sick cow in a pasture, watchin' till the last twitch of life is out of me before they pounce. I'm going to fool them," she said, "I'm going to surprise them; they are all fools but Jane—Jane's no fool."

BEN (*bitterly*). No—Ha! Ha! Ha! Jane's no fool!

JUDGE. And she went on—(*He turns to* JANE.) You'll forgive me Jane; she said, "Jane is stubborn, and set, and wilful, but she's no fool. She'll do better by the Jordan money than any of them."

ELLA. We'll go to law, that's what we'll do!

SADIE. That's it, we'll go to law.

HENRY (*to* JUDGE). We can break that will; you know we can!

JUDGE. It's possible.

HENRY. Possible! You *know*, don't yer! You're supposed to be a good lawyer.

JUDGE. Of course if I *am* a good lawyer you can't break that will, because you see I drew it.

ELLA. And we get nothing, not a dollar, after waitin' all these years?

JUDGE. There are small bequests left to each of you.

SADIE. How much?

JUDGE. One hundred dollars each.

ELLA (*shrilly*). One hundred dollars.

JUDGE. I said that they were small.

BEN. You said a mouthful!

ELLA. Ha! Ha! Ha! Ha! Ha! (*She laughs wildly.*)

HENRY (*sternly*). Stop your noise, Ella.

ELLA. I— Ha! Ha! Ha!— I told you I was going to have my laugh, didn't I? Ha! Ha! Ha!

ORIN (*pulls* SADIE's *dress*). Mum! What's she laughin' for?

SADIE. You hush!

EMMA (*faces them all in evil triumph*). If anybody asked me, I'd say it was a judgment on all of yer. You Jordans was always stuck up, always thought you was better'n anybody else. I guess I ought to know, I married into yer!—You a rich family?— You the salt of the Earth—You Jordans! You paupers—Ha! Ha! Ha!

ORIN (*pulls* SADIE's *skirt*). Ain't she still dead, Mum! Ain't grandma still dead?

SADIE (*angrily*). Of course she is.

ORIN. But I thought we was all goin' to cry!

SADIE. Cry then, you awful little brat. (*She slaps his face and he roars loudly; she takes him by the arm and yanks him out of the room, followed by* HENRY, EMMA, NETTIE *and* ELLA—*through his roars, they all speak together as they go.*)

EMMA (*to* HENRY). One hundred dollars! After all your blowin'.

HENRY. It's you, and that child of yourn; you turned her against me.

NETTIE. Well, I just won't spend my hundred dollars for mournin'. I'll wear my old black dress!

ELLA. And me makin' hats all the rest of my life—just makin' hats!
(*The front door is heard to shut behind them.* JANE, BEN *and* JUDGE *are alone.* JUDGE *stands by stove.* JANE *is up by window, looking out at the deepening twilight.* BEN *sits at right.*)

BEN. Ha! Ha! Ha! "Crow buzzards" mother called us—the last of the Jordans—crow buzzards—and that's what we are.

JUDGE. You can't stay here, Ben; you know that as well as I do. I signed the warrant for your arrest myself. It's been over a year since the Grand Jury indicted you for arson.

BEN. You mean you'll give me up?

JANE. You won't do that, Judge; you're here as her friend.

JUDGE. No, but if it's known he's here, I couldn't save him, and it's bound to be known.

JANE (*to* BEN). Were you careful coming?

BEN. Yes.

JUDGE. It's bound to be known.

BEN. He means they'll tell on me. (*He nods his head toward door.*) My brother, or my sisters.

JUDGE. No, I don't think they'd do that.

BEN. Let 'em! What do I care. I'm sick of hiding out, half starved! Let 'em do what they please. All I know is one thing,— when they put her into her grave her sons and daughters are goin' to be standin' there, like the Jordans always do.

JANE (*quietly*). Hannah will have your room ready by now. There are some clean shirts and things that was your father's; I'll bring them to you.

BEN (*uneasily*). Can I go up there, just a minute?

JANE. To your mother?

BEN. Yes.

JANE. If you want to.

BEN. I do.

JANE. Yes, you can go.
(BEN *turns and exits up the stairs.* JANE *crosses and sits by stove, sinking wearily into the chair.*)

JUDGE. And she left him nothing, just that hundred dollars, and only that because I told her it was the safest way to do it. I thought he was her one weakness, but it seems she didn't have any.

JANE. No.

JUDGE. She was a grim old woman, Jane.

JANE. I think I could have loved her, but she didn't want it.

JUDGE. And yet she left you everything.

JANE. I don't understand.

JUDGE. She left a sealed letter for you. It's in my strong box; you may learn from it that she cared more about you than you think.

JANE. No.

JUDGE. There was more kindness in her heart than most people gave her credit for.

JANE. For her own, for Uncle Ned, who never did for her, for Ned, for the Jordan name. I don't understand, and I don't think I care so very much; it's been a hard week, Judge. (*She rests her head against the back of the chair.*)

JUDGE. I know, and you're all worn out.

JANE. Yes.

JUDGE. It's a lot of money, Jane.

JANE. I suppose so.

JUDGE. And so you're a rich woman. I am curious to know how you feel?

JANE. Just tired. (*She shuts her eyes. For a moment he looks at her with a smile, then turns and quietly fills the stove with wood as* BEN *comes slowly downstairs and into the room.*)

BEN. If there was only something I could do for her.

JUDGE. Jane's asleep, Ben.

BEN. Did she look like that, unhappy, all the time?

JUDGE. Yes.

BEN. Crow buzzards! God damn the Jordans!
(*Front door bell rings sharply,* BEN *is startled.*)

JUDGE. Steady there! It's just one of the neighbors, I guess. (*Bell rings again as* HANNAH *crosses downstairs and to hall.*) Hannah knows enough not to let any one in.

BEN (*slowly*). When I got back, time before this, from France, I tried to go straight, but it wasn't any good, I just don't belong—
(HANNAH *enters frightened.*)

HANNAH. It's Jim Jay!

BEN (*to* JUDGE). And you didn't think my own blood would sell me?
(JIM JAY, *a large, kindly man of middle age, enters.*)

JIM. I'm sorry, Ben, I've come for you!
(JANE *wakes, startled, and springs up.*)

JANE. What is it?

JIM. I got to take him, Jane.

BEN (*turns fiercely*). Have you!

JIM (*quietly*). I'm armed, Ben—better not be foolish!

JANE. He'll go with you, Mr. Jay. He won't resist.

JIM (*quietly*). He mustn't. You got a bad name, Ben, and I ain't a-goin' to take any chances.

BEN. I thought I'd get to go to her funeral, anyway, before they got me.

JIM. Well, you could, maybe, if you was to fix a bail bond. You'd take bail for him, wouldn't you, Judge?

JUDGE. It's a felony; I'd have to have good security.

JANE. I'm a rich woman, you said just now. Could I give bail for him?

JUDGE. Yes.

BEN (*to her*). So the money ain't enough. You want all us Jordans fawnin' on you for favors. Well, all of 'em but me will; by mornin' the buzzards will be flocking round you thick! You're going to hear a lot about how much folks love you, but you ain't goin' to hear it from me.

JANE (*turns to him quietly*). Why did you come here, Ben, when I wrote you she was dying?

BEN. Why did I come?

JANE. Was it because you loved her, because you wanted to ask her to forgive you, before she died—or was it because you wanted to get something for yourself?

BEN (*hesitates*). How does a feller know why he does what he does?

JANE. I'm just curious. You've got so much contempt for the rest, I was just wondering? You were wild, Ben, and hard, but you were honest—what brought you here?

BEN (*sulkily*). The money.

JANE. I thought so. Then when you saw her you were sorry, but even then the money was in your mind—well—it's mine now. And you've got to take your choice, —you can do what I tell you, or you'll go with Mr. Jay.

BEN. Is that so? Well I guess there ain't much doubt about what I'll do. Come on, Jim!

JIM. All right. (*He takes a pair of handcuffs from his pocket.*) You'll have to slip these on, Ben.

BEN (*steps back*). No—wait—(*He turns desperately to* JANE.) What is it you want?

JANE. I want you to do as I say.

BEN (*after a look at* JIM *and the handcuffs*). I'll do it.

JANE. I thought so. (*She turns to* JUDGE.) Can you fix the bond up here?

JUDGE. Yes. (*He sits at table and takes pen, ink and paper from a drawer.*) I can hold court right here long enough for that.

JIM. This is my prisoner, Judge, and here's the warrant. (*He puts warrant on table.*)

JANE. First he's got to swear, before you, to my conditions.

BEN. What conditions?

JANE. When will his trial be, Judge?

JUDGE. Not before the spring term, I should think—say early April.

JANE. You'll stay here till then, Ben; you won't leave town! You'll work the farm,—there's plenty to be done.

BEN (*sulkily*). I don't know how to work a farm.

JANE. I do. You'll just do what I tell you.

BEN. Be your slave? That's what you mean, ain't it?

JANE. I've been about that here for eight years.

BEN. And now it's your turn to get square on a Jordan!

JANE. You'll work for once, and work every day. The first day you don't I'll surrender you to the judge, and he'll jail you. The rest of the Jordans will live as I tell them to live, or for the first time in any of their lives, they'll live on what they earn. Don't forget, Ben, that right now I'm the head of the family.

JUDGE (*to* BEN). You heard the conditions? Shall I make out the bond?

BEN (*reluctantly*). Yes. (*He sits moodily at right, looking down at the floor.* JANE *looks at him for a moment, then turns up to window.*)

JANE. It's snowing!

JIM. Thought I smelled it. (*He buttons his coat.*) Well, nothin' to keep me. is there, Judge?

JUDGE. No. (*He starts to write out the bond with a rusty pen.*) This pen is rusty!

JIM. I was sorry to hear about the old lady. It's too bad, but that's the way of things.

JUDGE (*writes*). Yes.

JIM. Well—It's early for snow, not but what it's a good thing for the winter wheat. (*He exits.*)

Curtain.

ACT TWO

SCENE: *Sitting room of the Jordan homestead some two months later.*

This room also shows some traces of a family's daily life, and to that extent is less desolate than the "parlor" of the first act, although the stern faith of the Puritan makes no concession to the thing we have learned to call "good taste." The old-fashioned simplicity seen in such a room as this has resulted from poverty, both of mind and of purse, and has nothing akin to the simplicity of the artist; as a matter of fact, your true descendants of the settlers of 1605 would be the first to resent such an implication; to them the arts are directly connected with heathen practices, and any incense burned before the altars of the Graces still smells to them of brimstone.

At back center folding doors, now partly open, lead to dining room. In this room may be seen the dining table, back of the table a window looking out on to the farm yard, now deep in midwinter snow. At right is an open fireplace with a log fire. Below fireplace a door to hall. Up left door to small vestibule in which is the outside door. Down left a window overlooking a snowbound countryside. The clock above the fireplace is set for quarter past four. Several straight-backed chairs and a woodbox by fireplace. A sewing table and lamp at center. A sewing machine near window at left. A wall cupboard on the wall right of the doors to the dining room. An old sofa down left, two chairs at right. When the door at left, in vestibule, is opened, one may see a path up to the door, between two walls of snow.

Discovered: ELLA *sits right at sewing machine, hemming some rough towels.* ORIN *and* NETTIE *are by fireplace.* SADIE *sits right of center.* SADIE *and* ORIN *are dressed for outdoors.* NETTIE's *coat, hat and overshoes are on a hat-rack by door at left.* ORIN, *as the curtain goes up, is putting a log on the fire.*

SADIE (*acidly to* ELLA). Why shouldn't he put wood on the fire if he wants to?

ELLA (*at sewing machine*). Because it ain't your wood.

SADIE. No, it's *hers!* Everything is hers!

ELLA. And maybe she just don't know it.

NETTIE (*at fireplace*). Ah! (*She bends closer to the fire as the log blazes up.*) I do love a good fire! Oh, it's nice to be warm!

SADIE. There's somethin' sensual about it.

NETTIE. Mother told me that the next time you started talkin' indecent I was to leave the room.

SADIE. Tell your mother I don't wonder she's sort of worried about you. I'd be if you was *my* daughter.

ELLA. I don't see why you can't let Nettie alone!

NETTIE. She's always picking on me, Aunt Ella! To hear her talk anybody would think I was terrible.

SADIE. I know more about what's going on than some folks think I do.

NETTIE. Then you know a lot. I heard Horace Bevins say a week ago that he didn't know as it was any use tryin' to have a Masonic Lodge in the same town as you.

SADIE. They never was a Bevins yet didn't have his tongue hung from the middle; the day his mother was married she answered both the responses.

ORIN. Mum! Mum! Shall I take my coat off; are we going to stay, Mum?

SADIE. No, we ain't going to stay. I just want to see Cousin Jane for a minute.

ELLA. She's in the kitchen with Hannah.

SADIE. Watchin' her, I bet! I wonder Hannah puts up with it.

ELLA. If you was to live with Jane for a spell, I guess you'd find you had a plenty to put up with.

SADIE. It's enough to make the Jordans turn in their graves, all of 'em at once.

ELLA. I guess all she'd say would be, "Let 'em if it seemed to make 'em any more comfortable."
(JANE *enters. She has an apron on and some towels over her arm.*)

JANE. Are those towels finished?

ELLA. Some is! Maybe I'd done all of 'em if I'd been a centipede.

JANE. Oh! I didn't see you, Sadie.

SADIE. Oh! Ha, ha! Well, I ain't surprised.

JANE (*with* ELLA, *selecting finished towels*). Well, Orin, does the tooth still hurt you?

ORIN. Naw, it don't hurt me none now. I got it in a bottle. (*He takes small bottle from pocket.*)

NETTIE. Oh, you nasty thing. You get away!

SADIE (*angrily*). What did I tell you about showin' that tooth to folks!

JANE. Never mind, Orin, just run out to the barn and tell your Uncle Ben we've got to have a path cleared under the clothes line.

ORIN. All right. (*He crosses toward door.*)

JANE. Hannah's going to wash to-morrow, tell him. I'll expect a good wide path.

ORIN. I'll tell him. (*He exits.*)

SADIE. I must say you keep Ben right at it, don't you?

JANE. Yes. (*She takes the last finished towel and speaks to* ELLA.) I'll come back for more.

SADIE (*as* JANE *crosses*). First I thought he'd go to jail before he'd work, but he didn't, did he?

JANE. No. (*She exits right.*)

SADIE. Yes. No! Yes. No! Folks that ain't got no more gift of gab ain't got much gift of intellect. I s'pose Hannah's out there.

ELLA. Yes, she keeps all of us just everlastingly at it.

SADIE. When Jane comes back, I wish you and Nettie would leave me alone with her, just for a minute.

ELLA (*as she works over sewing machine*). It won't do you much good; she won't lend any more money.

SADIE. Mother always helped me. I've got a right to expect it.

ELLA (*as she bites off a thread*). Expectin' ain't gettin'.

SADIE. I don't know what I'll do.

ELLA. You had money out of her; so has Henry.

SADIE (*shocked*). You don't mean to say your father's been borrowin' from her. (*This to* NETTIE.)

NETTIE. He's always borrowin'. Didn't he borrow the hundred dollars grandma left me? I'm not going to stand it much longer.

ELLA. Henry's havin' trouble with his business.

SADIE. We're fools to put up with it. Everybody says so. We ought to contest the will.

ELLA. Everybody says so but the lawyers; they won't none of 'em touch the case without they get money in advance.

SADIE. How much money? Didn't your father find out, Nettie?

NETTIE. The least was five hundred dollars.

ELLA. Can you see us raisin' that?

SADIE. If we was short, we might borrow it from Jane.

ELLA. We'd have to be smarter'n I see any signs of; she's through lendin'.

SADIE. How do you know?

ELLA. I tried it myself.

SADIE. What do you want money for? Ain't she takin' you in to live with her?

ELLA. I don't call myself beholden for that. She had to have some one, with Ben here, and her unmarried, and next to no relation to him.

NETTIE. Everybody's callin' you the chaperon! (*She laughs.*) Not but what they ought to be one with *him* around; he's awful good-lookin'.

SADIE. You keep away from him. He's no blood kin of yours, and he's a bad man, if he is a Jordan. Always makes up to everything he sees in petticoats, and always did.

NETTIE. Thanks for the compliment, but I'm not looking for any jailbirds.

ELLA. It will be awful, Ben in State's Prison, —and I guess he'll have to go, soon as he stands his trial.

SADIE. He got drunk and had a fight with the two Kimbal boys, and they licked him, and that night he burned down their barn; everybody knows it.

ELLA. He's bad, all through, Ben is.

NETTIE. He'll get about five years, father says. I guess that will take some of the spunk out of him.
(*A sound in the hall at right.*)

ELLA. Hush! I think he's coming.
(BEN *enters at right with a big armful of firewood and crosses and drops it heavily into woodbox, then turns and looks at them in silence.*)

SADIE. Seems kind of funny, your luggin' in the wood.

BEN (*bitterly*). Does it?

SADIE. Did you see Orin out there?

BEN. Yes, he went along home.

SADIE. How do you like workin'?

BEN. How do you think I like it? Workin' a big farm in winter, tendin' the stock and milking ten cows. How do I like it? (*As he stands by fire* NETTIE *looks up at him.*)

NETTIE. I think it's just a shame!

SADIE (*turns to* ELLA). Are you going to make towels all the afternoon?

ELLA. I am till they're done, then I expect she'll find somethin' else for me to do.

NETTIE (*to* BEN). Do you know I'm sorry for you, awful sorry? (*She speaks low.* ELLA *and* SADIE *are at the other side of room.*)

BEN. Then you're the only one.

NETTIE. Maybe I am, but I'm like that.

BEN. Another month of it, then State's Prison, I guess. I don't know as I'll be sorry when the time comes.

NETTIE. Oh, Uncle Ben! No, I'm not goin' to call you *that*. After all, you're not really any relation, are you? I mean to me?

BEN. No.

NETTIE (*softly*). I'm just going to call you Ben!

BEN. You're a good kid, Nettie.

NETTIE. Oh, it isn't that, Ben, but it does just seem too awful.
(*As she looks up at him, the outside door opens and* HENRY *and* EMMA *enter. They see* NETTIE *and* BEN *together by the fire.*)

EMMA (*sternly*). Nettie!

NETTIE (*sweetly*). Yes, mother?

EMMA. You come away from him.

BEN (*angrily*). What do you mean by that?

EMMA. You tell him, Henry.

HENRY. I don't know as it's any use to—

EMMA (*sternly*). Tell him what I mean.

HENRY (*to* BEN). Emma thinks, considerin' everything, that it's best Nettie shouldn't talk to you.

BEN. Why don't you keep her at home then? You don't suppose I want to talk to her.

EMMA. Oh, we ain't wanted here, I guess. We know that, not by you, or by *her*;— and Henry's the oldest of the Jordans. All this would be his, if there was any justice in the world.

NETTIE. Father wouldn't have taken that hundred dollars grandma left me if there had been any justice in the world. That's what I came here for, not to talk to him. To tell Cousin Jane what father did, and to tell her about Nellie Namlin's Christmas party, and that I've got to have a new dress. I've just got to!

SADIE. A new dress, and my rent ain't paid. She's got to pay it. My Orin's got to have a roof over his head.

HENRY. I don't know as you've got any call to be pestering Jane all the time.

ELLA. She's always wantin' something.

SADIE. What about you? Didn't you tell me yourself you tried to borrow from her?

ELLA. I got a chance to set up in business, so as I can be independent. I can go in with Mary Stanton, dressmakin'. I can do it for two hundred dollars, and she's got to give it to me.

HENRY. You ought to be ashamed, all three of you, worryin' Jane all day long. It's more'n flesh and blood can stand!

NETTIE (to him). Didn't you say at breakfast you was coming here to-day to make Cousin Jane endorse a note for you? Didn't you?

EMMA (fiercely). You hush!

BEN (at back by window). Ha! Ha! Ha! Crow buzzards.

HENRY. Endorsing a note ain't lending money, is it? It's a matter of business. I guess my note's good.

BEN. Take it to the bank without her name on it and see how good it is.

EMMA. You don't think we want to ask her favors, but Henry's in bad trouble and she'll just have to help us this time.

BEN. There's one way out of your troubles. One thing you could all do, for a change, instead of making Jane pay all your bills. I wonder you haven't any of you thought of it.

HENRY. What could we do?

BEN. Go to work and earn something for yourselves.

SADIE. Like you do, I suppose.

EMMA. The laughing-stock of all Veazie!

ELLA. Everybody's talkin' about it, anywhere you go.

NETTIE. Jane Crosby's White Slave, that's what they call you. Jane Crosby's White Slave.

BEN (fiercely). They call me that, do they?

ELLA (to NETTIE). Why can't you ever hold your tongue?

BEN (in cold anger). I've been a damned fool. I'm through.
(HANNAH enters.)

HANNAH. She wants you.

BEN. Jane?

HANNAH. Yes.

BEN. I won't come.

HANNAH. There'll be another row.

BEN. Tell her I said I wouldn't come. (He sits.)

HANNAH. She's awful set, you know, when she wants anything.

BEN. You tell her I won't come.

HANNAH. Well, I don't say I hanker none to tell her, but I'd rather be in my shoes than yourn. (She exits.)

SADIE. Well, I must say I don't blame you a mite.

EMMA. If the Jordans is a lot of slaves, I guess it's pretty near time we knew it.

HENRY (worried). She'll turn you over to Judge Bradford, Ben; he'll lock you up. It ain't goin' to help me none with the bank, a brother of mine bein' in jail.

BEN. So they're laughing at me, are they, damn them!

NETTIE (at door right). She's coming!
(There is a moment's pause and JANE en-

ters door right. HANNAH follows to door and looks on eagerly.)

JANE. I sent for you, Ben.

BEN. I won't budge.

JANE (wearily). Must we go through all this again?

BEN. I ain't going to move out of this chair to-day. You do what you damned please.

JANE. I am sorry, but you must.

BEN. Send for Jim Jay, have me locked up, do as you please. Oh, I've said it before, but this time I mean it.

JANE. And you won't come?

BEN. No.

JANE. Then I'll do the best I can alone. (She crosses up to wall closet and opens it and selects a large bottle, and turns. Ben rises quickly.)

BEN. What do you want of that?

JANE. It's one of the horses. I don't know what's the matter with her. She's down in her stall, just breathing. She won't pay any attention to me.

BEN. Old Nellie?

JANE. Yes.

BEN. What you got? (He steps to her and takes the bottle from her and looks at it.) That stuff's no good. Here! (He steps to cabinet and selects another bottle.) If you hadn't spent five minutes stalling around, I might have had a better chance. (He exits quickly at left.)

HANNAH. I allers said 'twas easier to catch flies with honey than 'twas with vinegar.

HENRY. What's Ben know about horses?

JANE. A lot.

HENRY. I didn't know that.

JANE. Neither did Ben, six weeks ago. (She exits.)

HENRY. Mother was like that, about animals. I guess Ben sort of takes after her.

EMMA (shocked). Ben! Like your mother!

HANNAH. Of course he is. He's the "spit and image of her." (She exits.)

NETTIE. She made him go! It wouldn't surprise me a mite if she'd pushed that old horse over herself.
(JANE enters.)

JANE. He wouldn't let me in the barn. (For the first time in the play, she laughs lightly.) Well—(She looks about at them) we have quite a family gathering here this afternoon. I am wondering if there is any—special reason for it.

HENRY. I wanted to talk with yer for just a minute, Jane.

SADIE. So do I.

JANE. Anybody else? (She looks about.)

ELLA. I do.

NETTIE. So do I.

JANE. I've a lot to do; suppose I answer you all at once. I'm sorry, but I won't lend you any money.

HENRY. Of course, I didn't think they'd call that note of mine; it's only five hundred, and you could just endorse it.

JANE. No!

SADIE. I was going to ask you—

JANE. No!

ELLA. I got a chance to be independent, Jane, and—

JANE. No. I haven't any money. I won't have before the first of the month.

EMMA. No money!

HENRY. I bet you're worth as much to-day as you was the day mother died.

JANE. To a penny. I've lived, and run this house, and half supported all of you on what I've made the place earn. Yesterday I spent the first dollar that I didn't have to spend. I mean, on myself. But that's no business of yours. I am worth just as much as the day I took the property, and I'm not going to run behind, so you see, after all, I'm a real Jordan.

EMMA. Seems so. I never know one of 'em yet who didn't seem to think he could take it with him.

HENRY. Well, Jane, I don't know as it's any use tryin' to get you to change your mind?

JANE. I'm sorry.

EMMA. You can leave that for us to be. I guess it's about the only thing we've got a right to. Get your things on, Nettie!

NETTIE. I'm going to stay a while with Aunt Ella; I won't be late.

HENRY. I don't know what I'm goin' to do about that note. I s'pose I'll find some way out of it.

JANE. I hope so.

EMMA. Thank yer. Of course we know there's always the poorhouse. Come, Henry. (*She exits at left, leaving the outside door open.*)

HENRY. Emma is a little upset. I hope you won't mind her talk. I guess her part of it ain't any too easy. (*He exits, shutting the door.*)

ELLA (*to* JANE). Poor Henry! Of course I s'pose you're right not to lend it to him. But I don't know as *I* could do it, but I'm sensitive.

JANE. Perhaps it's harder to say no than you think.
(HANNAH *enters.*)

HANNAH. I got everything ready for tomorrow's wash, but the sheets off your bed, Miss Ella.

ELLA. Good Land! I forgot 'em. Nettie will bring 'em right down.

NETTIE (*to* JANE). After that, I'm going to stay and help Aunt Ella. I was wondering if you'd be here all the afternoon.

JANE. Yes.

NETTIE (*charmingly*). Nothing special, you know. I'd just like to have a little visit with you. (*She exits at left with* ELLA.)

HANNAH (*looks after her*). Every time I listen to that girl I get fur on my tongue.

JANE. Fur?

HANNAH. Like when my dyspepsia's coming. There's two things I can't abide, her and cucumbers. (*She crosses to door left.*)

JANE. Hannah!

HANNAH (*stops*). Well?

JANE (*rather shyly*). We are going to have rather a special supper to-night.

HANNAH (*doubtfully*). We are?

JANE. Yes. That's why I had you roast that turkey yesterday.

HANNAH (*firmly*). That's for Sunday!

JANE. No, it's for to-night.

HANNAH (*angrily*). Why is it?

JANE. It's my birthday.

HANNAH. I didn't know that.

JANE. No, it isn't exactly a national holiday, but we'll have the turkey, and I'll get some preserves up, and I want you to bake a cake, a round one. We'll have candles on it. I got some at the store this morning.

HANNAH (*shocked*). Candles?

JANE. Yes.

HANNAH. Who's going to be to this party?

JANE (*a little self-conscious*). Why—just —just ourselves.

HANNAH. Just you and Mr. Ben and Miss Ella?

JANE. Yes.

HANNAH. You don't want candles on that cake, you want crape on it. (*She exits door left.*)
(JANE *crosses up and starts to clear the dining-room table of its red table cover, as Ben enters door left.*)

BEN (*cheerfully*). Well, I fixed Old Nellie up. (*He puts his bottle back in its place in the wall cabinet.*) Just got her in time. Thought she was gone for a minute, but she's going to be all right.

JANE. That's good. (*She folds the tablecloth up and puts it away.*)

BEN (*in front of fire*). She knew what I was doin' for her too; you could tell by the way she looked at me! She'll be all right, poor old critter. I remember her when she was a colt, year before I went to high school.

(JANE *crosses into room, shutting the dining-room door after her.*)

JANE. You like animals, don't you, Ben?

BEN (*surprised*). I don't know. I don't like to see 'em suffer.

JANE. Why?

BEN. I guess it's mostly because they ain't to blame for it. I mean what comes to 'em ain't their fault. If a woman thinks she's sick, till she gets sick, that's her business. If a man gets drunk, or eats like a hog, he's got to pay for it, and he ought to. Animals live cleaner than we do anyhow—and when you do anything for 'em they've got gratitude. Folks haven't.

JANE. Hand me that sewing basket, Ben. (*She has seated herself at left center by table.* BEN *at left of table, hands her the basket as she picks up some sewing.*)

BEN. It's funny, but except for a dog or two, I don't remember carin' nothin' for any of the live things, when I lived here I mean.

JANE. I guess that's because you didn't do much for them.

BEN. I guess so—Sometimes I kind of think I'd like to be here when spring comes—and see all the young critters coming into the world—I should think there'd be a lot a feller could do, to make it easier for 'em.

JANE. Yes.

BEN. Everybody's always makin' a fuss over women and their babies. I guess animals have got some feelings, too.

JANE (*sewing*). Yes.

BEN. I *know* it—Yes, sometimes, I sort of wish I could be here, in the spring.

JANE. You'll be a big help.

BEN. I'll be in prison. (*He looks at her. She drops her head and goes on sewing.*) You forgot that, didn't yer?

JANE. Yes.

BEN. What's the difference? A prison ain't just a place; it's bein' somewheres you don't want to be, and that's where I've always been.

JANE. You liked the army?

BEN. I s'pose so.

JANE. Why?

BEN. I don't know, there was things to do, and you did 'em.

JANE. And some one to tell you what to do?

BEN. Maybe that's it, somebody that knew better'n I did. It galled me at first, but pretty soon we got over in France, an' I saw we was really doin' something, then I didn't mind. I just got to doin' what I was told, and it worked out all right.

JANE. You liked France, too?

BEN. Yes.

JANE. I'd like to hear you tell about it.

BEN. Maybe I'll go back there some time. I don't know as I'd mind farming a place over there. Most of their farms are awful little, but I don't know but what I'd like it.

JANE. Farming is farming. Why not try it here?

BEN. Look out there! (*He points out of the window at the drifted snow.*) It's like that half the year, froze up, everything, most of all the people. Just a family by itself, maybe. Just a few folks, good an' bad, month after month, with nothin' to think about but just the mean little things, that really don't amount to nothin', but get to be bigger than all the world outside.

JANE (*sewing*). Somebody must do the farming, Ben.

BEN. Somebody like the Jordans, that's been doin' it generation after generation. Well, look at us. I heard a feller, in a Y.M.C.A. hut, tellin' how nature brought animals into the world, able to face what they had to face—

JANE. Yes, Ben?

BEN. That's what nature's done for us Jordans,—brought us into the world half froze before we was born. Brought us into the world mean, and hard, so's we could live the hard, mean life we have to live.

JANE. I don't know, Ben, but what you could live it different.

BEN. They *laugh* over there, and sing, and God knows when I was there they didn't have much to sing about. I was at a rest camp, near Nancy, after I got wounded. I told you about the French lady with all those children that I got billeted with.

JANE. Yes.

BEN. They used to *sing,* right at the table, and laugh! God! It brought a lump in my throat mor'n once, lookin' at them, and rememberin' the Jordans!

JANE. I guess there wasn't much laughing at your family table.

BEN. Summers nobody had much time for it, and winters,—well, I guess you know.

JANE. Yes.

BEN. Just a few folks together, day after day, and every little thing you don't like about the other raspin' on your nerves 'til it almost drives you crazy! Most folks quiet, because they've said all the things they've got to say a hundred times; other folks talkin', talkin', talkin' about nothing. Sometimes somebody sort of laughs, and it scares you; seems like laughter needs the sun, same as flowers do. Icebound, that's what we are all of us, inside and out. (*He stands looking grimly out window.*)

JANE. Not all. I laughed a lot before I came here to live.

BEN (*turns and looks at her*). I remember, you were just a little girl.

JANE. I was fourteen. See if there's a spool of black sewing cotton in that drawer.

BEN (*looking in drawer*). You mean thread?

JANE. Yes.

BEN. This it? (*He holds up a spool of white thread.*)

JANE. Would you call that black?

BEN (*looks it over*). No—it ain't black. (*He searches and finds black thread.*) Maybe this is it!

JANE. Maybe it is! (*She takes it.*) You were with that French family quite a while, weren't you?

BEN. Most a month; they was well off, you know; I mean, they was, before the war. It was a nice house.

JANE (*sewing*). How nice?

BEN (*hesitates*). I don't know, things—well—useful, you know, but nice, not like this. (*He looks about.*)

JANE (*looks around with a sigh*). It's not very pretty, but it could be. I could make it.

BEN. If you did, folks would be sayin' you wasn't respectable.

JANE. Tell me about the dinner they gave you the night before you went back to your company.

BEN. I told you.

JANE. Tell me again.

BEN (*smiles to himself at the remembrance*). They was all dressed up, the whole family, and there I was with just my dirty old uniform.

JANE. Yes.

BEN (*lost in his recollections*). It was a fine dinner, but it wasn't that. It was their doin' so much for me, folks like that—I've sort of pictured 'em lots of times since then.

JANE. Go on.

BEN. All of the young ones laughing and happy, and the mother too, laughing and tryin' to talk to me, and neither one of us knowing much about what the other one was sayin'. (*He and* JANE *both laugh.*)

JANE. And the oldest daughter? The one that was most grown up?

BEN. She was scared of me somehow, but I don't know as ever I've seen a girl like her, before or since.

JANE. Maybe 'twas that dress you told me about; seems to me you don't remember much else about her; not so much as what color her hair was, only just that that dress was blue.

BEN (*thoughtfully*). Yes.

JANE (*sewing*). Sometimes you say dark blue! (*She is watching him closely through half-shut eyes.*)

BEN (*absently*). I guess so.

JANE. And then I say, dark as something I point out to you, that isn't dark at all, and you say, "No, lighter than that!"

BEN (*absently*). Just—sort of blue.

JANE. Yes, sort of blue. It had lace on it, too, didn't it?

BEN. Lace? Maybe—yes, lace.

JANE. There's more than one blue dress in the world.

BEN. Like enough. Maybe there's mor'n one family like that lady's, but I'll be damned if they live in Veazie. (*He crosses and opens cupboard and selects a bottle.*) I might as well run out and see how the old mare is getting on. (*He selects bottle from shelf.*)

JANE. And you've got to shovel those paths for the clothes lines yet.

BEN. I know.

JANE. Well, don't forget.

BEN. It ain't likely you'll let me. (*He exits at door right.* JANE *laughs softly to herself, and runs to closet and takes out a large cardboard box and putting it on the table, she cuts the string and removes the wrapping paper, then lifts the cover of the box and draws out a dainty light-blue gown with soft lace on the neck and sleeves. She holds it up joyfully, then, covering her own dress with it, she looks at herself in a mirror on wall. As she stands smiling at her reflection, there is a sharp knock on the outside door.* JANE *hastily returns dress to box and as the knock is repeated, she puts the box under the sofa at left and crosses and opens the outside door.* JUDGE BRADFORD *enters.*)

JANE. Oh, it's you, Judge! Come in.

JUDGE. I thought I'd stop on my way home and see how you were getting on, Jane.

JANE. I'll take your coat.

JUDGE. I'll just put it here. (*He puts coat on chair.*) Have you time to sit down a minute?

JANE. Of course. (*They sit.*)

JUDGE (*looks at her*). That isn't a smile on your lips, is it, Jane?

JANE. Maybe—

JUDGE (*laughingly*). I'm glad I came!

JANE. It's my birthday.

JUDGE. Why, Jane! (*He crosses to her and holds out his hand. She takes it.*) Many happy returns!

JANE (*thoughtfully*). Many—happy returns—that's a lot to ask for.

JUDGE. You're about twenty-two, or twenty-three, aren't you?

JANE. Twenty-three.

JUDGE. Time enough ahead of you. (*His eye falls on the box, imperfectly hidden under the sofa; out of it a bit of the blue dress is sticking.*) Hello! What's all that?

JANE. My birthday present.

JUDGE. Who gave it to you?

JANE. I did.

JUDGE. Good! It's about time you started to blossom out.

JANE. I ordered a lot of things from Boston; they'll be here to-morrow.

JUDGE. I suppose that one's a dress?

JANE. Yes.

JUDGE (*bends over to look*). Light blue, isn't it?

JANE (*smiles*). Just sort of blue—with lace on it.

JUDGE. Oh, you're going to wear it, I suppose, in honor of your birthday?

JANE (*startled*). To-night—oh, no—soon maybe, but not to-night.

JUDGE (*smiles*). How soon?

JANE. Soon as I dare to; not just yet.

JUDGE. You have plenty of money; you ought to have every comfort in the world, and some of the luxuries.

JANE (*gravely*). Judge! I want you to do something for me.

JUDGE. And of course I'll do it.

JANE. I want you to get Ben off. I want you to fix it so he won't go to State's Prison.

JUDGE. But if he's guilty, Jane?

JANE. I want you to go to old Mr. Kimbal for me and offer to pay him for that barn of his that Ben burned down. Then I want you to fix it so he won't push the case, so's Ben gets off.

JUDGE. Do you know what you are asking of me?

JANE. To get Ben off.

JUDGE. To compound a felony.

JANE. Those are just words, Judge, and words don't matter much to me. I might say I wasn't asking you to compound a felony, I was askin' you to save a sinner, but those would be just words too. There's nobody else; you've *got* to help me.

JUDGE (*thoughtfully*). I've always thought a lot could be done for Ben, by a good lawyer.

JANE. It doesn't matter how, so long as it's done.

JUDGE. He was drinking, with a crowd of young men; the two Kimbal boys jumped on him and beat him up rather badly. That's about all we know, aside from the fact that Ben was drunk, and that that night the Kimbals' barn was set on fire.

JANE. Just so long as you can get him off, Judge.

JUDGE. I think a case of assault could be made against the Kimbal boys, and I think it would stand.

JANE. What of it?

JUDGE. It is quite possible that the old man, if he knew that action was to be taken against his sons, and if he could be tactfully assured of payment for his barn, say by Ben, in a year's time, might be persuaded to petition to have the indictment against Ben withdrawn. In that event, I think the chances would be very much in Ben's favor.

JANE. I don't care what names you call it, so long as it's done. Will you fix it?

JUDGE. Well, it's not exactly a proper proceeding for a Judge of the Circuit Court.

JANE. I knew you'd do it.

JUDGE. Yes, and I think you knew why, didn't you?

JANE. Ever since she's died, you've helped me about everything. Before she died you were just as good to me, and nobody else was.

JUDGE. I am glad you said that, because it clears me from the charge of being what poor Ben calls "one of the crow buzzards," and I don't want you to think me that.

JANE. No, you're not that.

JUDGE. I love you, Jane.

JANE. No!

JUDGE. Yes—I've done that for a long while. Don't you think you could get used to the thought of being my wife?

JANE (*gently*). No.

JUDGE. I think I could make you happy.

JANE. No.

JUDGE. I am afraid being happy is something you don't know very much about.

JANE. No.

JUDGE. It isn't a thing that I am going to hurry you over, my dear, but neither is it a thing that I am going to give up hoping for.

JANE. When you told me, that day, that Mrs. Jordan had left me all her money, I couldn't understand; then, afterwards, you gave me the letter she left for me. I want you to read it.

JUDGE. What has her letter to do with us?

JANE. Maybe, reading it, you'll get to know something you've got a right to know, better than I could tell it to you.

JUDGE. Very well.

JANE. It's here. (*She opens drawer, and selects a letter in a woman's old-fashioned handwriting, from a large envelope of papers.*) She was a cold woman, Judge. She never let me get close to her, although I tried. She didn't love me. I was as sure of it then as I am now. (*She holds out the letter.*) Read it.

JUDGE. If it's about the thing I've been speaking of, I'd rather hear it in your voice.

JANE (*reads*). "My dear Jane, the doctor tells me I haven't long to live, and so I'm doing this, the meanest thing I think I've ever done to you. I'm leaving you the Jordan money. Since my husband died, there has been just one person I could get to care about; that's Ben, who was my baby so long after all the others had forgotten how to love me. And Ben's a bad son, and a bad man. I can't leave him the money; he'd squander it, and the Jordans' money came hard."

JUDGE. Poor woman! It was a bitter thing for her to have to write like that.

JANE (*reads on*). "If squandering the money would bring him happiness, I'd face all the Jordans in the other world and laugh at them, but I know there's only just one chance to save my boy,—through a woman who will hold out her heart to him and let him trample on it, as he has on mine."

JUDGE (*in sudden fear*). Jane!

JANE (*reads on*). "Who'd work, and pray, and live for him, until as age comes on, and maybe he gets a little tired, he'll turn to her. And you're that woman, Jane; you've loved him ever since you came to us. Although he doesn't even know it. The Jordan name is his, the money's yours, and maybe there'll be another life for you to

guard. God knows it isn't much I'm leaving you, but you can't refuse it, because you love him, and when he knows the money is yours, he will want to marry you. I'm a wicked old woman. Maybe you'll learn to forgive me as time goes on—It takes a long time to make a Jordan." (*JANE drops her hand to her side.*) Then she just signed her name.

JUDGE. Is the damnable thing she says there true?

JANE. Yes, Judge.

JUDGE. And you're going to do this thing for her?

JANE. No, for him.

JUDGE (*bitterly*). He isn't worth it.

JANE. I guess you don't understand.

JUDGE. No. (*He crosses and picks up his coat.*)

JANE. You can't go like that, angry. You have to pay a price for being a good man, Judge—I need your help.

JUDGE. You mean *he* needs my help?

JANE. Yes, and you'll have to give it to him, if what you said a little while ago was true.

JUDGE (*after a pause*). It *was* true, Jane. I'll help him. (*He picks up his hat.*)

JANE. I've an errand at the store. I'll go with you. (*She takes hat and coat from rack and puts them on.*)

JUDGE. Is it anything I could have sent up for you?

JANE (*putting on coat*). I guess not. You see, I've got to match a color.

JUDGE. Another new dress?

JANE (*they start toward door*) Just a ribbon, for my hair.

JUDGE. I didn't know women still wore ribbons in their hair.

JANE. It seems they do—in France. (*They exit together at left to the outside door and off.*)

(NETTIE *and* ELLA *enter quickly, after a slight pause,* NETTIE *running in from right, followed more sedately by* ELLA.)

NETTIE. You see! I was right! She went with him. (*She has run to window left and is looking out.*)

ELLA. That's what money does. If mother hadn't left her everything, he wouldn't have touched her with a ten-foot pole.

NETTIE. Well, if she's fool enough to stay in this place, I guess he's about the best there is.

ELLA. Then trust her for gettin' him; by the time she gets through in Veazie, this town will be barer than Mother Hubbard's cupboard by the time the dog got there. (*Her eye falls on* JANE's *box, partly under sofa.*) What's that? (*She bends over, looking at it.*)

NETTIE. What?

ELLA. I never saw it before. (*She draws it out.*) Looks like a dress. See! Blue silk!

NETTIE. Open it.

ELLA (*hesitates*). Must be hers! Maybe she wouldn't like it.

NETTIE. Maybe she wouldn't know it.

ELLA. A cat can look at a king! (*She opens the box and holds up the blue dress.*)

NETTIE. Oh! Oh!

ELLA (*really moved*). Some folks would say a dress like that wasn't decent, but I wouldn't care, not if it was mine, and it might have been mine—but for. her.

NETTIE. Yours! Grandma wouldn't have left her money to you. She hated old people. Everybody does. She'd have left it to me, but for Jane Crosby!

ELLA (*looks at dress*). I always wanted a dress like this, when I was young. I used to dream about one, but mother only laughed. For years I counted on gettin' me what I wanted, when she died; now I never will.

NETTIE (*fiercely*). I will—somehow!

ELLA. Maybe, but not me. Oh, if I could have the feelin' of a dress like that on me, if I could wear it once, where folks could see me—Just once! Oh, I know how they'd laugh—I wouldn't care—

NETTIE (*almost in tears*). I can't stand it if she's going to wear things like that.

ELLA. I'll put it back. (*She starts to do so.*)

NETTIE (*catches her hand*). Not yet.

ELLA. I guess the less we look at it, the better off we'll be. (*There is a ring at the front door.*)

NETTIE. Who's that?

ELLA. Here! (*She hands the box to* NET-TIE.) Shove it back under the sofa. I'll go and see. (*She turns and crosses to door left and out to the vestibule.* NETTIE, *with the box in her arms, hesitates for a moment then turns and exits at right, taking the box with her.* ELLA *opens the outside door at left, showing* ORIN *on the doorstep.* ELLA *looks at him angrily.*) For time's sake, what are *you* ringing the bell for?

ORIN. Mum says for me not to act like I belonged here.

ELLA. Well, I'm goin' to shut the door. Git in or git out!

ORIN. I got a note. (*He enters room as* ELLA *shuts door.*) It's for her.

ELLA (*holds out hand*). Let me see it.

ORIN. Mum said not to let on I had nothin' if you came nosin' around.
(JANE *enters from left.*)

JANE. I just ran across to the store. I haven't been five minutes. (*She takes coat off.*)

ELLA. He's got a note for you, from Sadie.

JANE. Oh, let me see it, Orin.

ORIN (*gives her note*). She said, if you said is they an answer, I was to say yes, they is.

JANE. Just a minute. (*She opens note and reads it.*)

ELLA. I must say she didn't lose much time.

JANE (*after reading note*). Poor Sadie! Wait, Orin! (*She sits at table and takes checkbook from the drawer and writes.*) Just take this to your mother.

ELLA. You don't mean you're goin' to—

JANE. Be quiet, Ella. Here, Orin. (*She hands him check.*) Don't lose it, and run along.

ORIN. All right. Mum said we was goin' to have dinner early, and go to a movie! Good night.

JANE (*again writing in checkbook*). Good night. (ORIN *exits.*)

ELLA. So you sent her her rent money, after all?

JANE. Here! (*She rises and hands a check to* ELLA.)

ELLA. What's that?

JANE. Two hundred dollars. You can try that dressmaking business if you want to, Ella.

ELLA (*looks at check*). Two hundred dollars!

JANE. You needn't thank me.

ELLA. That ain't it. I was just wonderin' what's come over you all of a sudden. (BEN *enters.*)

JANE. It's my birthday, that's all. Did you know it was my birthday, Ben?

BEN (*carelessly*). Is it? I shoveled them damned paths! (*He crosses and sits by fire.*)

JANE. Ella's going into the dressmaking business, Ben.

BEN (*moodily*). What of it?

ELLA. That's what I say. It ain't much of a business. (*She exits at right; outside it grows to dusk.*)

JANE. Are you tired?

BEN. Maybe. (*He stretches his feet out toward fire.*)

JANE. You've done a lot of work to-day.

BEN. And every day.

JANE. I don't suppose you know how much good it's done you, how well you look!

BEN. Beauty's only skin deep.

JANE. Folks change, even in a few weeks, outside and in. Hard work don't hurt anybody.

BEN. I got chilblains on my feet. The damned shoes are stiffer than they ever was.

JANE. Icebound, you said. Maybe it don't have to be like that. Sometimes, just lately, it's seemed to me that if folks would try, things needn't be so bad. All of 'em try, I mean, for themselves, and for everybody else.

BEN. If I was you, I'd go somewheres and hire a hall.

JANE. If you'd put some pork fat on those shoes to-night, your feet wouldn't hurt so bad.

BEN. Maybe. (*He sits looking moodily into the fire. After a moment's hesitation,* JANE *crosses and sits in the chair beside his. The evening shadows deepen around them but the glow from the fire lights their faces.*)

JANE. I'm lonesome to-night. We always made a lot of birthdays when I was a girl.

BEN. Some do.

JANE. Your mother didn't. She found me once trying, the day I was fifteen. I remember how she laughed at me.

BEN. All the Jordans have got a sense of humor.

JANE. She wasn't a Jordan, not until she married your father.

BEN. When a woman marries into a family, she mostly shuts her eyes and jumps in all over.

JANE. Your mother was the best of the whole lot of you. Anyway, I think so.

BEN. I *know* it. I always thought a lot of her, in spite of our being relations.

JANE. She loved you, Ben.

BEN. She left me without a dollar, knowin' I was going to State's Prison, and what I'd be by the time I get out.

JANE. Maybe some day you'll understand why she did it.

BEN. Because she thought you'd take better care of the money than any of the rest of us.

JANE. And you hate me because of that, the way all the rest of the Jordans do?

BEN. Sometimes.

JANE (*sadly*). I suppose it's natural.

BEN. But I ain't such a fool as Henry, and the woman folks. They think you took advantage and fooled her into what she did. I thought so at first, now I don't.

JANE. What do you think now, Ben?

BEN. She'd watched you; she knew you were worth mor'n all of us in a lump. I know it, too, but some way it riles me worse than if you wasn't.

JANE. That's silly!

BEN (*with growing resentment*). Don't you suppose I know what you've been doin' to me? Tryin' to make a man of me. Tryin' to help me. Standing up to me and fightin' me every day, tryin' to teach me to be decent. Workin' over me like I was a baby, or somethin', and you was tryin' to teach me how to walk. Gettin' me so upset that every time I don't do what I ought to do, I get all het up inside; I never was so damned uncomfortable in all my life.

JANE. And I never was so happy.

BEN. I s'pose God knew what he was about when he made women.

JANE. Of course he did.

BEN. Anyhow, he gave 'em the best of it, all right.

JANE. You don't mean that! You *can't!*

BEN. I do. Let a man get miserable, and he *is* miserable. A woman ain't really happy no other way.

JANE. Maybe you think I'm having an easier time right now than you are.

BEN. I know it.

JANE. They all hate me, and they all want something, all the time. I can't say yes, and it's hard to always say no. Then there's the farm, big, and poor, and all worked out. The Jordans have been taking their living out of this soil for more than a hundred years, and never putting anything back.

BEN. Just themselves, that's all.

JANE. Worked right, like they do out West, this place could be what it ought to be. How can I do that? It needs a man.

BEN. I been thinkin' lately things could be done a whole lot different.

JANE. By a man, if he loved the old place —You Jordans robbed this soil always. Suppose one of you tried to pay it back—it would mean work and money, for a couple of years maybe, then I guess you'd see what gratitude meant.

BEN. It could be done; it ought to be.

JANE. By you, Ben!

BEN. No—I guess I ain't got the judgment.

JANE. You've got it, if you'd learn to use it.

BEN. Anyhow, I've got just a month, that's all.

JANE. Maybe you'll have more.

BEN. I'm as good as convicted as I sit here. I've only got a month.

JANE. Then help me for that month. We could plan how to start out in the spring. I've got books that will help us, and I can get more. We could do a lot!

BEN. I don't know but what we could!

JANE (*bends toward him*). Will you shake hands on it? (*She offers her hand.*)

BEN (*surprised*). What for?

JANE. Oh, just because we never have.

BEN. We ain't goin' to change *everything,* are we?

JANE. One thing. We're going to be friends.

BEN (*takes her hand awkwardly*). You're a good sport, game as a man, gamer maybe.

JANE. And now for the surprise.

BEN. The what!

JANE (*draws her hand away and rises*). You'll see. I want you to sit right here, until I open those doors. (*She points to doors to dining room.*)

BEN. I wasn't thinkin' of movin'.

JANE. Just sit right there.

BEN. And do what?

JANE. Think.

BEN. What of?

JANE. Oh, anything—so long as it's pleasant—of the spring that's coming—

BEN. In the prison down at Thomaston.

JANE. Of France then, of the family that was so good to you—of the beautiful lady—of the daughter, if you want to, the one that was most grown up—and of the wonderful blue dress. Just shut your eyes and think, till I come back! (*She exits through doors to dining room and closes the doors after her.* BEN *sits in glow from the fire, his eyes closed. In a moment the door at right is thrown open and* NETTIE *stands in the doorway, the light from the hall falling on her. She has on* JANE's *blue dress and is radiant with youth and excitement.*)

NETTIE. Ben! Look at me! Look, Ben!

BEN. What?

NETTIE. Look, Ben! (*He looks at her and for a moment sits in stupid wonder, then rises slowly to his feet.*)

BEN. It's—It's Nettie!

NETTIE. Did you ever see anything so lovely, did you?

BEN. You're—you're a woman, Nettie!

NETTIE. Of course I am, you stupid!

BEN (*crosses down to her*). God! How I've starved for somethin' pretty to look at! God! How I've starved for it!

NETTIE. That's why I came down, I wanted you to see! I waited there in the hall till she went out.

BEN. And you've been here all the time, and I haven't so much as looked at you!

NETTIE (*softly*). You've been in trouble, Ben!

BEN. I'll get out of that somehow! I'm going to make a fight. I ain't goin' to let 'em take me now.

NETTIE. Honest, Ben?

BEN. Not now. Oh, you pretty kid! You pretty little thing! (*He catches her fiercely in his arms.*)

NETTIE. You mustn't, Ben!

BEN (*triumphant*). Mustn't! You don't know me!

NETTIE. Just one then! (*She holds up her lips, and as he kisses her ardently, the dining-room doors back of them open and* JANE *stands in the doorway, looking at them. She has removed her apron and has made some poor attempt at dressing up. Back of her we see the table bravely spread for the festive birthday party. There is a large turkey and other special dishes, and a round cake on which blaze twenty-three tiny candles. They turn their heads, startled, as* JANE *looks at them, and* BEN *tightens his arms defiantly about* NETTIE.) Let me go!

BEN (*holding her and looking past her to* JANE). No! (*Then to* JANE.) Why are you looking at me like that?

NETTIE. Let me go.

BEN (*to* JANE). To hell with your dream of grubbing in the dirt. Now I know what I want, and I'm going to get it.

NETTIE. Let go, dear. (*She draws away.*) I'm ashamed about wearin' your dress, Cousin Jane. I'll take it right off.

JANE. You needn't. I guess I don't want it any more. (*For the first time her eyes leave* BEN's *face. She turns and steps past them to the door at right and calls.*) Supper's ready, Ella!

(HANNAH *enters at back in dining room with a plate of hot biscuits.*)

Curtain.

ACT THREE

Scene: *Same as Act One. Parlor at the Jordans', two months later.*

At rise the characters are grouped exactly as they were at the opening of the play. The white slip covers, however, have been removed from the chairs, and the backing through the window shows partly melted snow drifts. HENRY *sighs; the clock strikes two.* HENRY *looks at his watch.*

There is a pause. The outside door slams and BEN *enters and looks about.*

BEN. Well—here we all are again.

SADIE (*sadly*). Yes.

HENRY. I ain't been in this room before since the funeral.

SADIE. And I ain't, and the last time before that was when father died.

EMMA. I sat right here, in the same chair I'm settin' in now, but to your grandfather's funeral, right after I married Henry, I was treated like one of the poor relations! I had to stand up.

HENRY. I remember; it made considerable trouble.

ELLA. I don't know as it was ever what I called a cheerful room.

HENRY (*severely*). A parlor's where a person's supposed to sit and think of God, and you couldn't expect it to be cheerful!

ELLA (*looks about*). Seems like we'd had trouble and disgrace enough in this family without her takin' all the slip covers off of the chairs and sofa!

EMMA. It ain't *right!*

SADIE. That Boston woman that's building the house over on Elm Street ain't so much as goin' to have a parlor. I stopped her right on the street and asked her what she was plannin' to do soon as the first of 'em died.

EMMA. What did she say?

SADIE. Said she tried not to think about such things.

HENRY (*sternly*). We got Atheists enough in this town right now.

BEN. Well, if Jane's coming I wish she'd come; this ain't exactly my idea of pleasant company.

ELLA. She says we're all to wait in here for Judge Bradford.

SADIE. What did she send for us for?

ELLA. I don't know.

EMMA. Why didn't you ask her?

ELLA. I did, and she most bit my head off.

BEN. She most bites mine off every time I see her. I must say she's changed, Jane has; she ain't the same girl at all she was a few weeks ago.

NETTIE. She's actin' just awful, especially to me!

SADIE. Of course, I'd be the last one to say anything against her, but—

BEN. But nothin'! There ain't one of you here fit to tie her shoes!

SADIE. *We* ain't?

BEN. And I ain't! The only difference between us is I ain't worth much and I know it, and you ain't worth nothin' and you don't.

EMMA. I guess you'd better be careful how you talk!

NETTIE. If anybody says anything about Jane lately, that's the way he always talks!

The worse she treats him the better he seems to like it.

SADIE. Well, I don't know as I'm surprised more about his insultin' the rest of us, but it's sort of comical his talkin' that way about you, Nettie.

EMMA. Nettie! What's Nettie got to do with him?

SADIE. Oh! Excuse me! I didn't know 'twas supposed to be a secret.

EMMA. What is?

SADIE. About the way those two have been carryin' on together!

HENRY. What!

ELLA. Ben and Nettie!

NETTIE (*afraid*). Stop her, Ben, can't you?

BEN. If I knew a way to stop women like her I'd patent it and get rich!

EMMA (*sternly*). Him and Nettie?

SADIE. They passed my house together *once* a week ago Wednesday, *once* the Tuesday before that, and *twice* the Sunday after New Year's.

HENRY. Together!

SADIE. And Eben Tilden's boy told Abbie Palsey that Tilly Hickson heard Aaron Hamlin say he'd seen 'em together at the picture show!

HENRY (*to* BEN). Is it true?

EMMA. You've been with him after all I told you!

BEN. It ain't going to hurt her none just to talk to me, is it?

EMMA. Them that touches pitch gets defiled!

HENRY (*to* NETTIE). I want you to tell me everything that's took place between you two.

SADIE. Wait!

HENRY. What?

SADIE. Orin! Leave the room!

NETTIE. He don't have to leave the room. I don't care who knows what happened!

HENRY. Go on then.

NETTIE. Well—Ben and I—We—Just for a few days—anyway, it was all his fault.

BEN. She threw me down because I was going to prison.

NETTIE. He said he'd get out of it somehow, but he can't, and I just won't have folks laughing at me!

BEN. It's all right, it never meant nothin' to her, and I guess it didn't mean much to me. It's just as well it's over.

NETTIE. It's a whole lot better.

HENRY. Well—what's passed is passed. Folks that plant the wind reap the whirlwind! There's no use cryin' over spilled milk.

ORIN. Say, Mum! What do you s'pose Uncle Henry thinks he means when he says things?

HENRY. Somehow I can't help wishin' you was my son for just about five minutes. (HANNAH *and* JUDGE BRADFORD *enter*.)

HANNAH. They're all in here, Judge.

JUDGE. Good afternoon.

HENRY. How are you, Judge?

SADIE. It's a mild day; winter's most over. Stop scratching yourself. (*This last to* ORIN *who seems to be uneasy and frequently scratches himself.*)

HANNAH (*at door*). I'll tell her you're here, Judge. She'll be right down. (HANNAH *exits.*)

ELLA. Won't you sit?

JUDGE. Thanks. (*He sits by table.*)

BEN. What's it about? Why did she say we was to all be here at two o'clock?

JUDGE. She will probably be able to answer that question herself, Ben.

SADIE (*to* ORIN). Don't.

ORIN. What?

SADIE. Scratch!

ORIN. Oh.
(JANE *enters. The* JUDGE *rises.*)

JUDGE. Well, Jane?

JANE. Don't get up, Judge.

JUDGE. Will you sit here? (JUDGE *turns to get a chair for* JANE. ORIN *scratches himself.* ELLA *rises.*)

ELLA. What is the matter with this brat?

ORIN. I itch!

SADIE. It's warm, and he's got on his heavy flannels! He's as clean as you are!
(JANE *and* JUDGE *sit.*)

BEN. You said to heat this room up and wait here for you and the Judge. Why? I got my stock to tend.

HENRY. It's a bad time for me to get away from the store. What was it you wanted of us?

JANE. I'm afraid it isn't going to be easy to tell you.

JUDGE. Won't you let me do it, Jane?

JANE. No. I've come to know that your mother didn't really want that I should have the Jordan money.

SADIE. What's that?

JANE. I put it as simply as I could.

BEN. You mean a later will's been found?

JUDGE. No.

JANE. In a way, Judge, it's like there had. Your mother left me a letter dated later than the will.

ELLA. Leavin' the money different?

JANE. Tellin' what she really wanted.

BEN. Well, what did she want?

JANE. It was like she left me all her money in trust, so I could keep it safe until the time she was hopin' for come, and in a way it did come, not quite like she wanted it, but near enough so I can give up a burden I haven't strength enough to carry any more. (*She stops.*)

JUDGE. Let me finish, Jane. Jane has asked me to draw a deed of gift, making the Jordan property over to Ben.

BEN. Why?

JANE. She wanted you to have it.

BEN. Why didn't she will it to me, then?

JANE. She was afraid to trust you.

BEN. Well?

JANE. You've learned to work; you'll keep on working.

HENRY. You mean to say my mother wanted him to have it all?

JANE. Yes.

HENRY. I am a religious man, but there was a time when even Job gave up! So—all our money goes to Ben—and he can't even buy himself out of prison!

JANE (*after a pause*). Ben isn't going to prison.

BEN. Why? Who's to stop it?

JUDGE (*after a look from* JANE). Kimbal agreed not to press the charge against you. It seems that there were certain extenuating circumstances. A motion has been made for the dismissal of the indictment, and it won't be opposed.

BEN. Why did he? Who fixed this thing.

JANE. Judge Bradford did. (*She looks at* JUDGE.)

BEN (*slowly*). It means a lot to me. There's things I'd like to do. I haven't dared to think about 'em lately—now I'll do 'em. (*There is a pause.*)

HENRY. Well, Ben, so you've got the money! I guess maybe it's better than her havin' it; after all blood's thicker than water! We'll help you any way we can and—er —of course you'll help us.

BEN. Why will I?

HENRY. We're brothers, Ben! We're old Jordans!

BEN. What was we when I got back from France? There was a band met us boys at the station. I was your brother all right that day, only somehow, in just a little while you forgot about it. I was a Jordan when I was hidin' out from the police, and all that kept me from starvin' was the money Jane sent me! I was your brother the night mother died, and you said you wouldn't go my bail.

ELLA. You ain't going to be hard, Ben!

BEN. I'm the head of the family now, ain't I, and you can bet all you've got I'm going to be a real Jordan.

HENRY. I think, Ben—

BEN. From now on, there ain't nobody got any right to think in this house but just me! So run along home, the whole pack of you, and after this, when you feel like you must come here—come separate.

ELLA. Turn us out, Ben?

BEN. Sure, why not?

NETTIE (*crosses to him. Sweetly*). There ain't any reason why *we* can't be friends, is there?

BEN. Well, I don't know. There's only one way I could ever get to trust you.

NETTIE. What way, Ben?

BEN. I'd have to go to jail for five years and see if you'd wait for me!

EMMA. It's an awful thing for a mother to have a fool for a child.

ELLA (*goes upstage with* NETTIE). Well, I must say you made a nice mess of things!

NETTIE (*exits with* ELLA). Well, I don't care! I don't see how anybody would expect me to be a mind reader!

SADIE. Come, Orin—say good-by to your Uncle Ben.

ORIN. What will I do that for?

SADIE. Because I tell you to!

ORIN. Yesterday you told me he wasn't worth speakin' to!

SADIE. Are you going to move, you stupid little idiot? (*She drags him out.*)

ORIN (*as they go*). What did I say? You let me alone!

HENRY. I was wonderin', Ben, how you'd feel about endorsing that note of mine.

BEN. You was?

HENRY. Yes, I don't know what I'm going to do about it.

BEN. As far as I care, you can go nail it on a door. (HENRY *and* EMMA *start to exit*.) No, hold on, I'll pay it.

HENRY. You will!

BEN. Yes, I don't know as it would do me much good at the bank, havin' a brother of mine in the poorhouse. (BEN *laughs as* HENRY *and* EMMA *exit*.)

JUDGE. Well, Ben? "Uneasy lies the head that wears a crown."

BEN (*down to stove*). Depends on the head. Mine's thick, I guess. Anyhow, none of them is going to bother it. I'm boss here now.

JUDGE. You'll find a copy here of the inventory of the estate, and other legal papers. Everything is in order.

JANE. And my accounts, Ben; you'll find the exact amount your mother left. I spent some money about six weeks ago, on myself, but I've been careful ever since and I've made up for it.

BEN. You said, Judge, she didn't have to go by that letter of my mother's, if she didn't want to? She didn't have to give anything back at all?

JUDGE. No, she didn't.

BEN. Then if I was you— (*to* JANE) I wouldn't talk so much about the little you spent on yourself. I guess to look at you it wasn't much.

JANE. Yes, it was.

BEN. Well, we'll fix things so you can keep on spendin'. Only let's see somethin' come of it. I never was so damned sick of anything in my life as I am of that old black dress of yours! (*Crosses stage up and over right.*)

JANE. I've got plenty of clothes upstairs. I'm sorry now I ever bought them, but I'll take them with me when I go.

BEN. Go? Go where?

JANE. To Old Town. I've got a place there, clerking in the Pulp Mill.

BEN. You!

JANE. Yes.

BEN. But what about me?

JUDGE. Don't you think Jane has done about enough for you?

BEN. She's done a lot, she's given up the money. I don't know as I like that; 'course I like gettin' it, but not if she's going away.

JANE. I couldn't stay now, and I wouldn't want to.

BEN. I don't suppose you remember about plannin' what you and me was to do with this old farm?

JANE. I remember.

BEN. Well—then what are you going away for?

JANE. Because I couldn't be happy here, Ben—It's been harder than anything I ever thought could come to anybody, the last few weeks here—and so I'm going. (*She turns to* JUDGE.) I'll go upstairs and get my things. I'll stop at your office, Judge, on the way to the station.

JUDGE. Thank you, Jane.

BEN. You're goin' to-day? Before I order my new farm machinery or anything? You're goin' to leave me with all this work on my hands?

JANE. Yes, Ben. (*She exits.*)

BEN. Well—that's a lesson to me! Oh, she's a good woman! I ain't denyin' that—but she's fickle!

JUDGE. You're a fool, Ben!

BEN. I been doin' kitchen police around this town for quite a spell now, Judge, but from this day on I ain't goin' to take that sort of talk from anybody.

JUDGE. I assure you that you won't have to take any sort of talk at all from me. (*He starts for the door.*)

BEN. I didn't mean that. I don't want you to think I ain't grateful for all you've done for me.

JUDGE (*coldly*). I have done nothing for you.

BEN. If it wasn't for you, I'd want to die; that's what I did want. I was afraid of that prison, just a coward about it. Now I'm a free man, with a big life openin' out ahead of me—I got everything in the world right here in my two hands, everything—and I owe it to you!

JUDGE. I am very glad to say that you don't owe me anything. I don't like you, I haven't forgiven you for what you did to your mother's life. Nor for a worse thing, one you haven't brains enough to even know you've done. Don't be grateful to me, Ben, please. I think nothing could distress me more than that.

BEN. You've been a good friend to me.

JUDGE. I haven't meant to be, as I said I don't like you. I haven't any faith in you. I don't believe in this new life of yours. You made a mess of the old one, and I think you will of the new.

BEN. No matter what you say, you can't get away from me. I'll be grateful till I die. But for you I'd have gone to that damned prison!

JUDGE. But for Jane.

BEN. How Jane?

JUDGE. How Jane? Jane went your bond the day your mother died. Jane took you in and taught you how to work, made you work, taught you through the one decent spot in you something of a thing you'd never know, self-respect. Worked over you, petted you, coaxed you—held you up— Then you hurt her—but she kept on—She went herself to Kimbal, after he had refused me, and got his help to keep you out of prison—then, against my will, against the best that I could do to stop her, she turns over all this to you—and goes out with nothing—and you ask "How Jane?"

BEN. Why? Why has she done this all this, for me?

(*The* JUDGE *looks at* BEN *with contempt and turns and exits.* BEN *is left in deep thought.* JANE *comes downstairs dressed for a journey with a hand bag, etc. She enters*).

JANE. Goody-by, Ben. (*She crosses to him, her hand out.*) Good-by. Won't you say good-by?

BEN. First, there's some things I got to know about.

JANE (*smiles*). I guess there's not much left for us to say, Ben.

BEN (*she crosses to door, but he gets ahead of her*). There's things I got to know. (*She looks at him but does not speak.*) The Judge tells me 'twas you got Kimbal to let me go free. (*He looks at her—she half turns away.*) Answer me. (*Pause.*) The Judge tells me you gave up what was yours —to me—without no other reason than because you wanted me to have it. That's true, ain't it? (*Pause.*) You sent me every cent you had, when you knew mother was dying, then you went bail for me, like he said—and did all them other things. I don't know as any woman ever did any more—. I want to know why!

JANE. Why do you think?

BEN. I don't know—I sort of thought— sort of hoped—

JANE (*bravely*). It was because I loved her, Ben—

BEN. Oh. (*He turns away disappointed.*)

JANE. You're forgetting, I guess, how long we was alone here—when you was in France—then the months we didn't know where you was, when the police was looking for you—She used to make me promise if ever I could I'd help you.

BEN. Well—all I've got to say is you're no liar.

JANE. Good-by. (*She turns to go.*)

BEN. Wait. (*Closes door.*) Let's see that letter you said she left for you.

JANE. No. I won't do that. I've done enough; you're free, you've got the money and the farm.

BEN (*crosses in front of table and sits left of table*). They ain't worth a damn with you gone—I didn't know that till just now, but they ain't.

JANE. It's sort of sudden, the way you found that out.

BEN. Oh, it don't take long for a man to get hungry—it only takes just a minute for a man to die; you can burn down a barn quick enough, or do a murder; it's just living and getting old that takes a lot of time —Can't you stay here, Jane?

JANE. There's Nettie.

BEN. Nettie—that couldn't stand the gaff —that run out on me when I was in trouble.

JANE. It doesn't matter what folks do, if you love 'em enough.

BEN. What do you know about it? I suppose you've been in love a lot of times?

JANE. No.

BEN. Then you be quiet and let an expert talk. I was lonesome and I wanted a woman; she was pretty and I wanted to kiss her —that ain't what I call love.

JANE. You. You don't even know the meaning of the word.

BEN. That don't worry me none—I guess the feller that wrote the dictionary was a whole lot older'n I am before he got down to the L's.

JANE. You've got good in you, Ben, deep down, if you'd only try. (BEN *turns.*) I know, it's always been that way! You've never tried for long; you've never had a real ambition.

BEN. When I was a kid I wanted to spit farther than anybody.

JANE. Good-by. (*She starts up to door.*)

BEN. And so you're going to break your word? (JANE *turns, hurt.*)

BEN. I don't know what't was you promised mother, but you've broke your word. No man ever needed a woman more'n I need you, and you're leaving me.

JANE. That isn't fair.

BEN. It's true, ain't it; truth ain't always fair—You ain't helped me none, you've hurt me—worse than being broke, worse than bein' in jail.

JANE. It don't seem like I could stand to have you talk like that.

BEN. What you done you done for her. I didn't count, I never have, not with you.

JANE. When you've been trying to do a thing as long as I have, it gets to be a part of you.

BEN. You done it all for her—well—she's dead—you'd better go.

JANE. Maybe I had, but if I do it will be with the truth between us. Here's the letter she left for me, Ben—I got a feeling somehow like she was here with us now, like she wanted you to read it. (*She holds it out.*) It's like she was guiding us from the grave—read it. (*Crosses up to window.*)

BEN (*reads*). "My dear Jane: The doctor tells me I haven't long to live and so I am doing this, the meanest thing I think I've ever done to you. I'm leaving you the Jordan money. Since my husband died there has been just one person I could get to care about, that's Ben, who was my baby so long after all the others had forgotten how to love me. (*He mumbles the letter to himself, then brings out the words.*) Hold out her heart and let him trample on it, as he has on mine." (*Slowly he breaks down. sobbing bitterly.*)

JANE. Don't, Ben—

BEN. Look what I done to her. Look what I done.

JANE (*hand on his shoulder*). Oh, my dear —my dear!

BEN. I did love her, mor'n she thought, mor'n I ever knew how to tell her!

JANE (*kneels beside him*). It wasn't all your fault—you were a lonely boy—she never said much—she was like you, Ben, ashamed to show the best that's in you.

BEN (*bitterly*). The best in me. I ain't fit that you should touch me, Jane—you'd better go.

JANE. Not if you need me, Ben, and I think you do.

BEN. I love you—mor'n I ever thought I could—tenderer—truer—but I'm no good —You couldn't trust me—I couldn't trust myself.

JANE. Spring's coming, Ben, everywhere, to you and me, if you would only try.

BEN. Can a feller change—just 'cause he wants to?

JANE. I don't want you changed. I want you what you are, the best of you—just a man that loves me—if you do love me, Ben.

BEN. Can't you help me to be fit?

JANE. I'm going to do the thing I always meant to do—good times and bad, Ben, I'm going to share with you.

BEN. God knows I—

JANE. Hush, Ben—I don't want another promise.

BEN. What do you want?

JANE. You said I was a good sport once— You shook hands on what we'd do to bring this old place back—there's plenty to be done. I'll stay and help you if you want me.

BEN. A good sport? (*He takes her hand.*) I'll say you're all of that.
(HANNAH *enters.*)

HANNAH. If you ain't careful you'll miss that train.

JANE. That's just what I want to do.

HANNAH. You ain't going?

JANE. I'm never going, Hannah.

HANNAH. You going to marry him?

BEN. You bet your life she is!

HANNAH. I guess you'll be mighty happy— marriage changes folks—and any change in him will be a big improvement. (*She picks up* JANE's *bag and exits*—JANE *and* BEN *laugh.*)

Curtain.

Hell-Bent fer Heaven

BY HATCHER HUGHES

HATCHER HUGHES

Hatcher Hughes was born on a farm near Polkville, North Carolina, in 1884. He studied at the University of North Carolina and received the A.B. degree in 1907, A.M. in 1909. During his undergraduate years he wrote a number of short stories for newspaper publication. While doing graduate study at the University of North Carolina he also served as an instructor in the department of English. Two years of additional graduate study were spent at Columbia University. In 1912 he became a lecturer in the Department of English at Columbia, and organized the courses in playwriting.

During the World War Mr. Hughes was a Captain in the United States Army. Since 1923 he has been Assistant Professor of English at Columbia. His principal courses are in playwriting. In 1930 he married Janet Ranney Cool. He is a member of the National Institute of Arts and Letters and of the Century Association.

Produced by Marc Klaw, Inc., at the Klaw Theatre, New York, January 4, 1924, *Hell-Bent fer Heaven* received the Pulitzer award for 1923-1924.

CHARACTERS

(In the order of their appearance)

DAVID HUNT.

MEG HUNT.

SID HUNT.

RUFE PRYOR.

MATT HUNT.

ANDY LOWRY.

JUDE LOWRY.

SCENE

The Hunt home in the Carolina mountains. The action takes place between four o'clock in the afternoon and nine o'clock at night on a midsummer day.

HELL-BENT FER HEAVEN

ACT ONE

Interior of MATT HUNT'S *home in the Carolina mountains. The walls and ceiling are of rough boards, smoked and stained with age. The furniture is old and hand-made.*

The place is neat and home-like in the old-fashioned way. At the left, toward the rear, is a rough staircase with crude balustrade. Under the staircase, facing the right wall, is a small door opening into the cellar. To the right of this there is another door leading into the kitchen.

The outside door is in the rear wall and opens directly on a porch covered with flowering shrubs. A "Red Rambler" rose hangs over the doorway on a trellis. There are windows on each side of the door, through which you catch a glimpse of a river valley with mountains in the background. To the left of the door is a gun rack with ancient and modern firearms.

It is late afternoon and the bright sunlight, visible through the doors and windows, is tempered by the lengthening shadows. A bluish vapor hangs over the river, half concealing the distant peaks of the mountains.

Old DAVID HUNT *enters from without. He is a rugged, well-preserved man of eighty. His snow-white hair and beard contrast vividly with the ruddy glow of his face. The peculiar radiance of countenance that comes with serene old age is heightened in him by the brilliant sunlight, which brings into full relief a personality that is rich, humorous, and mellow without a touch of sentimentality. He carries an old muzzle-loading rifle, which he places in the gun rack after removing the percussion cap.*

A moment later his daughter-in-law, MEG HUNT, *a strong, active woman of forty-odd, enters from the kitchen, carrying an earthenware bowl full of garden peas.*

MEG. Whew! I declar—it's hot enough in that kitchen to brile bacon 'thout a fire! (*She sits down and begins to shell peas.*)

DAVID (*mops his face*). It's hot 'nough everwhar to-day.

MEG. I reckon it'll storm ag'in afore night.

DAVID. If it don't it'll miss a good chance.

MEG. Whar you been?

DAVID. Up along the river. I thought I might run across that hawk that's been arter your young turkeys.

MEG. Did you see it?

DAVID (*seats himself and helps her shell peas*). Not close enough to speak to him. But I didn't foller him fur. I thought I'd kinder like to be around when Sid gits home.

MEG (*glances toward the door uneasily*). Seems quair they hain't come yit. With Matt a-leavin' here at daybreak they'd ought ha' been home two hours ago.

DAVID. Well, it takes time on a day like this. Matt ain't a-goin' to push them colts up the mountain this weather. An' Sid, apt as not, didn't git thar on time. He never wus a lad to be governed by clocks (*chuckles softly*) ner nothin' else under the sun 'at I ever hyeard of!

MEG. I wonder what he'll be like now! Mebby the war's changed him!

DAVID. Mebby so.

MEG. When it fust started I mind they wus lots in the papers about our soldiers a-goin' into battle a-prayin' an' readin' their Bibles. Sid allus wus good about readin' his Bible.

DAVID (*chuckles slyly*). Yeh, 'specially the fightin' parts. (*She starts slightly and a shadow crosses her face.*) But don't you worry about Sid. He'll settle down. They's plenty o' time fer that. (*Beaming with unconscious pride.*) I use to be jist like him when I was a lad, an' now look at me. You don't see me a-tearin' around the country on hossback a-cussin' an' raisin' Ole Ned.

MEG. No; but I wouldn't put it past you if you had the strength.

DAVID. Hey?

MEG. It's your flesh that's got religion, not your sperit.

DAVID (*laughs good-naturedly*). I ain't denyin' it, though I reckon you'd like it better if I'us ashamed o' havin' been young an' strong. You're jist like all women, Meg. When they find a man's got a little sap in him they think he's headed straight fer the devil.
(*Horses are heard in the distance.* MEG *springs up excitedly.*)

MEG. Thar! I *know* tha‍t's them!

DAVID. It sounds like it—from here. (*Shading his eyes with his hand, he looks up the river, while she peeps over his shoulder.*) It's Matt, all right, but I don't see Sid.

MEG (*turns away querulously*). Well, it's no more'n I expected! I've had a feelin' ever sence they took him across that ocean that I'd never see him ag'in!
(SID, *dressed in civilian clothes, with khaki shirt and hat, enters from the kitchen, eating a large piece of pie. He is a handsome and vigorous young fellow, with the unmistakable slouch of the mountaineer.*)

SID. Hello, Mam!

MEG. Sid! (*She hugs him, with tears in her eyes. He laughs and pats her on the back, taking another bite of pie.*) What'd you sneak in through the kitchen an' skeer me like this fer? I thought you hadn't come!

SID. I didn't sneak. I jist nachelly come around to the place whar the cookin's done. (*Shaking hands with* DAVID.) H'lo, Gran'-pap! How air you?

DAVID. I can still lick any eighty-year-old man my size in the mountains if I can ketch him.

SID (*laughs and turns his attention to* MEG *again*). Well, Mam, it seems right nachel to see you ag'in. How you been makin' out?

MEG. I've been jist about as common. I worried lots about you. An' you ain't a-lookin' none too fat. I'll bet you hain't had nothin' fit to eat sence you left home.

SID. Shucks! I'm all right! Better'n when I went away.

DAVID. You 'pear to me to be about as sassy as ever. I reckon you knowed you 'us a hero?

SID. Yeh, I read about it in the papers.

DAVID (*makes a face and spits*). The things they've printed about you's enough to make a healthy man spew! I'll bet if the truth 'us knowed you didn't do half as hard fightin' as I done in the Confederate war!

SID (*grins mischievously*). You didn't have as many notches on your gun when you got back.

DAVID. Mebby I wusn't as big a liar afore I went.

SID. You didn't have to be; you wusn't a-goin' to as big a war.

DAVID. Size ain't everything in a war! They was bigger men in the one I went to!

SID. Well, I dunno. We had Pershin' an' Fotch.

DAVID (*contemptuously*). Pershin' an' Fotch! Chiggers an' seed-ticks! Knee-high to a gnat 'longside o' Stonewall Jackson an' Robert E. Lee!

MEG. Lord! Sid hain't no more'n stepped in the house, an' you start fightin' your ole wars all over ag'in!

DAVID (*chuckles wisely*). She's dis'p'inted in you, Sid. You're too robustious to suit her. She's been hopin' you'd come back sorter peakin' an' pinin' so she could mammy you an' fatten you up.

MEG (*looks at him quickly with a startled expression*). What ever put that notion in your head?

DAVID. Well, I've noticed that you allus pay more attention to the runts among the pigs an' chickens than you do to the healthy uns.
(RUFE *appears at the top of the stairs, unobserved by the others. He is thirty, of medium height, with pale face and shifty, uncertain manner.*)

MEG. They need more—jist like humans. When the Saviour was on earth he ministered to the halt an' blind an' didn't bother about t'others. What's the use in doin' fer folks like you an' Matt? You've neither of you ever been sick a day in your life.

DAVID. I ain't complainin'. A man cain't have everything in this world. An' as a constancy I'd rather have a good stomach an' sound sleep as affection from women.

RUFE (*comes downstairs, smiling at DAVID with an expression of great compassion and humility*). I reckon that's a hint that I'm bein' treated too well here.

DAVID. No; I didn't even know you was in hearin' distance, Rufe. I thought you 'us out thar 'tendin' the store.

RUFE. Well, whether you meant it er not, I want you to know 'at I agree with you. I know I don't deserve the blessin's of a home like this an' a woman in it that's as good to me as my own mammy that died when I 'us little! If she'd ha' lived I might ha' been more deservin'.

MEG. Sid, you rickollect Rufe, don't you, that use' to work fer Joe Bedford down on Sandy Fork?

SID. Shore I do. You're the feller that's been a-helpin' Pa while I 'us away. (*He shakes hands cordially. There is a suggestion of constraint in RUFE's manner.*) How's your health?

RUFE. I cain't brag on myself much.

SID. What's the trouble? You're lookin' all right.

RUFE. Yeh, I am, on the outside. The thing's in here (*taps himself on the stomach*), whatever it is. I tried to git in the army arter you left, but they wouldn't have me.

DAVID. Fust I ever hyeard of it, Rufe.

MEG (*with a show of annoyance*). Well, it's not the fust I've hyeard of it. Rufe don't tell his business to everybody.

DAVID. What post did you go to to git edzamined—if 'tain't no secret?

RUFE. I wusn't edzamined by no army doctor. I wus a-goin' to be, but a man down at Pineville looked me over an' said it wusn't no use.

DAVID. Wus he a doctor?

RUFE (*evasively*). Not edzackly; but he had worked fer one an' knowed how to edzamine folks.

DAVID (*chuckles*). Oh, I see! Like the man by playin' the fiddle: he'd seed it done! Well, them army doctors wouldn't ha' been so pertickler, jedgin' by some o' the samples I seen that got by 'em.

RUFE. I hyeard they let the bars down toward the end. But I'd jist as soon stay out of a fight if I cain't git in tell it's over.

SID. That's the best time to git in.

RUFE (*looks at him in surprise*). Didn't you like fightin'? One o' the papers here said as how you took to it like a fish to water.

SID (*laughs ironically*). Shore I did! It 'us pie to me!

DAVID. That's another lie, Sid!
(SID *laughs.*)

RUFE. Well, I reckon a man can have too much o' anything. But I b'lieve I'd like war if I had the health to stand up under it. (DAVID *grunts incredulously.*) I dunno why, but my mind seems to run nachelly to fightin'.

DAVID. That's because your legs'ld run nachelly t'other way.

MEG (*annoyed*). You've never seed 'em run, have you?

DAVID. No; but he comes of a peaceful family. I mind his gran'daddy durin' the Confederate war. He wus so peaceful that he knocked his front teeth out tell he couldn't bite the ends offen the paper cater'ges we used then, so he wouldn't have to go.

RUFE. He didn't b'lieve in fightin' about niggers! He'd ha' fit all right if he'd had as much to fight fer as Sid had!

DAVID. What did Sid fight fer? I'll bet *he* don't know.

SID. Then you got another bet comin'. I fit to lick t'other side!

DAVID. Well, you're the fust un I've seed that knowed, an' I've axed lots of 'em. An' I reckon our men wusn't the only ones. That gang o' Germans that you got a medal fer ketchin' must ha' been kinder hazy in their minds about the needcessity o' fightin'. (*He pats himself significantly on the stomach.*) I'll bet they had some sort o' inside trouble—like Rufe.

SID (*laughing*). I know dern well they did!

RUFE. How'd you find it out, Sid? You couldn't talk their talk, could you?

SID. No, but I could tell by the way they acted. Soon as each seed t'other we both started to run. But I looked back first. When I seed they wus a-runnin' away, too, I tuk after 'em a-hollerin' an' shootin' like hell had broke loose, an' the whole bunch surrendered!

RUFE. An' they give you a medal fer it! Why, I could ha' done that!

DAVID. You might, Rufe, if you'd ha' thought to look back. (*He turns to* SID.) I reckon their army had found out they wus peaceful folks an' put 'em out thar to git ketched. The dam Yankees use' to do that. An' from what I've hyeard o' these here Germans they're jist a bastard breed o' Yankees.

MEG. Whar is your medal, Sid?

SID. I cain't show it to you now. I busted the last button offen my drawers while ago an' I got 'em pinned up with it.

(MATT HUNT, *a vigorous mountaineer of forty-five, appears on the doorstep and be-gins stamping the mud off his boots. He carries a lap robe and a "slicker" across his arm.*)

SID. But here comes Pap. He's got sompen I can show you. (*To* MATT.) Ha' you got that package fer Mam?

MATT (*fumbling under the lap robe*). Yeh, it's here som'ers.

MEG. What is it?

MATT (*throwing the package into her lap*). You'll have to ax Sid. He fetched it.

SID. It's some sort o' female sompen that a French gal asked me to bring you. I dunno what you'd call it.

MEG (*turning the package over doubtfully*). Umn! If all I've hyeard about them gals over thar's so, I dunno's I want it.

DAVID (*starts to take it*). Le' me see it.

MEG (*taking it away from him*). Yeh, I'll bet you'd take it! (*She opens the package gingerly and takes out a beautiful lace brassière.*) La! Did she knit this herself?

SID. I reckon so. She 'us allus a-piddlin' at sompen like that.

MEG (*holds it up to the light admiringly*). Umn-umph! It's purty enough, but I hain't the least notion what it's fer!

DAVID. Ahem! Does she look anything like her knittin', Sid?

SID. Yeh, some.

MEG. Well, hope you cain't see through her as easy. (SID *laughs*.) You didn't let her fool you up with her good looks, did you?

SID. Well, I didn't fetch her back with me, like some of 'em done.

DAVID. If you had, I know a gal here that'ld ha' scratched her eyes out.

(RUFE *rises nervously and crosses the room.* MEG *glances at him sympathetically.*)

MATT. Whar you goin', Rufe?

RUFE. Nowhere. I jist got tired o' settin' in one place.

DAVID (*laughs knowingly*). Rufe allus gits tired o' the place whar he's a-settin' when you start talkin' about Jude Lowry.

MEG. I don't blame him. You talk so much about gals they ain't nothin' new left to say about 'em.

RUFE. I reckon they air jist about alike the world over. Wus the French uns after you all the time, Sid, same as them here?

SID. I cain't say 'at I 'us bothered by 'em much.

DAVID. I'll bet you wusn't lonesome. An' you won't be here. They're lots bolder'n they wus when you left. They's times now when I don't feel safe myself. If I 'us your age I'd marry Jude Lowry er some other gal fer pertection. Give me a woman every time to fight a woman.
(*At mention of* JUDE LOWRY, RUFE *gets up again and moves toward the door aimlessly.*)

MATT. Air you jist changin' your settin' place ag'in, Rufe, er air you goin' out to the store?

MEG (*with a sudden flare of temper*). What difference does it make to you which he's a-doin'?

MATT. None in pertickler. Only I thought if he 'us a-goin' out thar he could fetch Sid's pack in when he comes back.

RUFE (*with an expression of martyrdom*). All right, Matt, I'll fetch it. O' course what you hired me fer wus to tend the store. But I'll be a nigger fer Sid—er anything else you ax me!

MATT (*rises angrily*). What's that you're a-bellyachin' about now?

RUFE. I aint a—

MATT (*storming impatiently*). Air you a-goin' to git that pack er not?

RUFE. Why, I jist told you I wus!

MEG. Didn't you hear him say it? They ain't no need in bawlin' at him like that! He's got feelin's, like the rest of us!

SID. Hold on, Paw. I don't want to be the cause o' no fracas. I've toted that ole pack all over the world an' 'tain't a-goin' to hurt me to fetch it this much further.

MATT. No, you stay whar you air! He's got out of enough work here!

RUFE. I ain't a-tryin' to git out o' nothin'! I'm a-tryin' hard to do anything you ax me, no matter what it is! (*He goes out.*)

MATT. I never knowed nobody to git me r'iled up like he does. (*To* SID.) That's the kind o' help I've had while you 'us away.

SID. Yeh, I've seed folks like him—kinder tetchy.

MEG. It's enough to make him tetchy, with your paw an' grandpaw a-pickin' on him all the time jist 'cause he ain't as big an' strong as they air.

DAVID. You don't ketch me an' Matt a-pickin' on chil'en jist 'cause they ain't as big an' strong as we air. I've noticed when folks gits picked on it's gene'ly 'cause they deserve it.

MEG. You could git along 'ith Rufe if you tried.

MATT. Yeh, I expect we could if we laid awake nights figgerin' how to keep from hurtin' his feelin's—like you do. 'Tain't only he's tetchy—though God knows I'm sick o' hearin' him bellyache—but he's lazy er born tired, I dunno which. Why, he ain't wuth his salt!

DAVID. 'Specially sence he got that camp-meetin' brand o' religion. I've never seed a man so hell-bent fer heaven as he is!

RUFE (*enters with the pack and sets it down*). Thar 'tis, Sid.

SID. Much obliged, Rufe. (*He takes the pack and opens it.*)

RUFE. No 'casion. I'm glad to do anything I can to please Matt.

MATT. Well, I got jist one thing more fer you to do. I want you to pack up your duds an' make tracks away from here.

(RUFE *is dumfounded. He looks at* MEG *appealingly.*)

MEG. Matt! You ain't a-goin' to turn him off at this time o' year?

MATT. Course I am. I didn't adopt him fer life when I hired him. I told him he could stay tell Sid come back.

MEG. But he cain't git another clerkin' job. An' it's too late to start a crap now.

MATT. He'd orter thought o' that before. He's knowed fer a month that Sid wus comin' home.

RUFE. He's right, Meg. I might ha' knowed this 'ld happen. (*He goes toward* MATT *with a malicious expression.*) But I'm a-goin' to tell you sompen fer your own good, Matt. God so loved the world that he give His only begotten Son to die so 'at everybody 'at wanted to might be saved. But you've never took advantage o' His offer. I cain't understand that in a close trader like you, Matt. If the offer o' free salvation 'us a box o' free terbacker fer the store you'd never let it git by. (MATT *makes an angry move.* RUFE *backs away.*) Understand, I'm a-sayin' this in a true Christian sperit—fer your own good. The Scripture says to love our enemies an' do good to them that despitefully uses us.

MATT. Dadburn you, I don't want you a-lovin' me, ner doin' good to me, nuther!

RUFE. I know you don't, Matt. But I cain't help it—an' you cain't, neither! That's one thing you ain't the boss of!

MATT (*menacingly*). Go on up an' pack your duds an' git out o' here!

RUFE (*backing away toward the stairs*). All right, Matt. You're the boss o' that. You can hector me an' bully me about the things o' this world, but you cain't keep me from lovin' your immortal soul. An' you cain't take away my reward which is in heaven. An' you cain't escape yourn— which ain't! (*He disappears upstairs.* MATT *glares after him, his right arm trembling significantly.*)

MEG. It's the truth that hurts, Matt. Your reward *ain't* in heaven.

MATT (*raging inwardly*). I wish he'd go thar er *som'ers* an' git hisn!

DAVID. I cain't make him out. If he 'us jist a plain hypocrite I'd know how to take him. But he 'pears to honestly b'lieve everybody's got to be like him afore they're saved.

MEG. Mebby they *has* got to be different from you an' Matt.

SID. Pap, if you don't want him in the store, does it happen to be so's you could let him finish out the summer at the sawmill?

DAVID. Shucks, Sid! Don't waste no worry on him. They ain't money enough in the county to hire him to stay at a sawmill a week.

MATT. No, it's too much like work. If he wants a job let him go to them city folks that's a-puttin' in that dam out here. They'll take anything that comes along. An' he'd mix in fine with them furriners.

MEG. You know he ain't strong enough fer that sort o' work.

SID. This is your business, Paw, an' I reckon you can 'tend to it 'thout any help from me. But I wisht you could see your way ta keep him awhile longer.

MATT. What fer?

SID. Well, I got some private affairs to look after.

MEG. An' you'd orter have a chance to rest up, too.

SID. Yeh, I *would* kinder like to spree around a little fer a change.

MATT. Well, if you want some time to yourself, I've stood Rufe two years. I reckon I can' stand him another month. But I dunno what sort o' private affairs you've got to look after.

SID. If I told you they wouldn't be private. (*He glances at* DAVID *with a humorous twinkle.*) Fer one thing, I need time to think up some tales to tell about how I won the war.

DAVID. I reckon you've got enough thought up already.

SID. I admit I got the makin's o' some good-sized uns. But I want to try 'em out on you an' git 'em to runnin' slick afore I swear to 'em. (*He takes a large bottle from the pack and gives it to* DAVID.) Here, Gran'pap! Any time you git in a fight an' want to ketch t'other feller, jist take a swaller o' that.

MEG (*disapprovingly*). What is it—licker?

SID. It's one breed of it. The French call it cone-yack.

DAVID (*sniffs the cork*). It smells like it might be that.

MEG. Wus licker the best thing you could think of to bring your gran'pa?

DAVID (*laughing*). She's afeard you're a-startin' me on my downward career, son. An' you may be. I knowed a man once that started when he wus about my age—an' he drunk hisself to death when he 'us a hundred an' two!

MEG. Well, jist the same, he might ha' thought o' sompen better to bring you. (*Looking through the things in the pack.*) Whar's the Bible I give you? Didn't you find room to fetch that?

SID. Somebody stole it.

MEG. Not your Bible?

SID. Yeh. They'll steal anything, in the army.

MEG. Why, I never hyeard o' sich a thing! An' you went through the whole war like a heathen, 'thout so much as a Testyment?

DAVID. The Baptis' preacher here said they 'us men over thar a-givin' 'em away to any-body 'at wanted 'em.

SID. Yeh, but they never got up whar we wus till after the fightin' 'us over. An' I didn't need one so bad then.

VOICE (*outside in the distance*). Hello!

MEG. That's Andy 'ith the mail!

SID (*goes to the door and waves to him*). H'lo, Andy!

ANDY. Well, I'll be derned! Is that you, Sid?

SID. A piece of me. Whyn't you come on in an' swop lies?

ANDY. I'm skeered you'll want too much boot jedgin' by the size o' them they've been printin' about you.

SID. Don't let that worry you none.
(ANDY, *a healthy young fellow, comes in. His face is slightly flushed with whisky, but he is not drunk.*)

ANDY (*shakes hands cordially*). You look healthy as a hell-cat!

SID. Yeh, I can still eat—an' drink some too when I can git it.

ANDY. Don't let not gittin' it bother you. That's all talk. I reckon you're derned glad you went over?

SID. I am now. But they 'us once er twice while I 'us thar I'd jist as soon ha' been back.

ANDY. You're lucky. They hain't been no time I wusn't sorry I didn't go.

SID. What 'us the trouble? Wouldn't they have you?

ANDY. Have me, hell! They'd ha' jumped at me! But Mam an' Paw wheedled me into claimin' edzemption so's I could help cut that patch o' timber up the river fer the gov'ment. An' now I'm totin' the mail.

SID. Well, don't be so down-hearted. Some-body's got to tote it.

ANDY. But, dam' it all, I want a job that gives me more elbow room! Every time I look at that piddlin' mail sack an' think o' what you've been through, I git so goddern mad at myself an' everybody else 'at I feel like startin' a war o' my own right here in the mountains!
(*While* ANDY *is talking,* RUFE *comes down-stairs with a small bag in his hand. At* ANDY's *suggestion of starting a war of his own he stops suddenly and stands as if rooted to the spot.* MEG *also moves uneasily and exchanges significant glances ·with* MATT *and* DAVID.)

DAVID. Why don't you? Rufe here says he's sp'ilin' fer a fight!

ANDY. Rufe! Good Lord! If he 'us in hell he wouldn't fight fire!

RUFE. Thank God, I'm not headed to'ard hell, like some folks!

ANDY. I know you claimed edzemption when you j'ined the church. Well, every man to his likin'. But hereafter I'm a-goin' to take what's comin' to me in this world *an'* the next! An' that 'minds me, afore I fergit it: have you got any forty-five ammynition in the store?

RUFE. Ax Matt. I ain't a-workin' here no longer.

ANDY. What's the matter? Lost your job?

SID. That's all fixed up, Rufe. I won't be workin' much fer a while an' Paw says you can stay another month.

MATT (*looks at* RUFE *questioningly*). That is, if he wants to stay bad 'nough to tend to his business?

RUFE. They ain't no use axin' me if I want to stay. I got nowhere else to go. As fer 'tendin' to my business, I'll do what I've allus tried to do, render unto Cæsar the things that are Cæsar's an' unto God the things that are God's!

SID. Then that's settled. I dunno whose department the ammynition belongs to. But go ahead an' git them caterdges fer Andy an' I'll come out an' beat you both shootin' 'ith this popgun here. (*He takes a German pistol out of the pack.*)

ANDY (*looks at the pistol*). You don't call that thing a gun, do you?

SID. No, it's a Dutch peace-pipe.

DAVID. I don't believe I ever seed any like that. How does it work?

SID (*hands him the pistol*). It's automatic. You pull the trigger and it goes right on spittin' like a man chawin' terbacker.

DAVID (*passing the pistol on to* MATT). Huh! I wouldn't be ketched dead in the woods with it.

SID. Why not?

DAVID. Because it's a insult to shootin'-men, that's why! It's built on the notion that you're a-goin' to miss all your fust shots!

ANDY. How'd you git aholt of it, Sid?

SID. I smoked a Dutchman outen it by provin' to him that I 'us a peacefuler man 'n he was.

ANDY. Does it shoot any better 'n ourn?

SID. That's what I want to find out.

ANDY. Hell! Hain't you tried it yit?

SID. Not from the hind end. The feller I got it from missed me the first shot.

MEG (*eagerly, with a slight catch in her voice*). Did he surrender, Sid—an' give it to you—after he'd shot at you?

SID. N—no, not edzactly. (*Quietly.*) But he didn't have no further use fer it, so I stuck it in my pocket an' fetched it along.

MEG (*with a sudden revulsion of feeling*). Thou shalt not kill!

ANDY. Ner git killed if you can help it! (*He starts toward the door.*) Come on, Sid! We'll soon find out whether this thing hits whar you hold her er not!

MEG (*with intense emotion*). No! Sid ain't a-goin'!

SID (*looks at her, puzzled*). Why, Mam! What sort of a graveyard rabbit has crossed your path? Me an' Andy use' to have shootin' matches 'thout you makin' no fuss about it!

MEG. I don't keer! I've seed enough shootin' an' fightin' in my time! An' I've hyeard enough talk about war!

SID. 'Tain't a-goin' to do no harm fer us to shoot at a spot on a tree!

MEG. 'Tain't a-goin' to do no good! (*With a sudden flare of passion.*) An' I wisht you'd throw that pistol in the river! The man it belonged to had a mammy, too! Think how she feels—wherever she is!

ANDY. If he had been to as many shootin' matches as Sid, mebby you'd be the one that's a-feelin' that way!

RUFE. It wusn't the shootin' matches that saved Sid. It 'us the will o' God.

SID. Mebby so, Rufe. But I've noticed, other things bein' ekal, God generally sides 'ith the feller that shoots the straightest.

MEG. Oh! Cain't you talk o' nothin' but shootin' an' killin'? I wish I could go some place where I'd never hear guns mentioned ag'in as long as I live!

RUFE. You can! We can all go thar if we live right! (*He hesitates and looks at* MATT *out of the corner of his eye.*) An' that 'minds me, boys: if I 'us you I wouldn't have no more shootin' matches. It 'us at a shootin' match that the feud fust started 'twixt your two gran'daddies. (*In an instant the faces of the men become tense with amazement.* RUFE *is conscious of this, but continues with a show of innocence.*) An' they 'us both fetched home on stretchers, 'long 'ith lots more o' your kin on both sides, afore it 'us patched up. I know 'tain't none o' my business—

MATT (*his right fist trembling dangerously*). Then why the hell don't you keep your mouth shut!

RUFE (*cowering in fear*). I 'us only warnin' 'em fer their own good! They're frien'-ly now an' I want 'em to stay that way!

MATT. You've got a dam' poor way o' showin' it! You know that's sompen we don't talk about here! If I didn't know you 'us a born fool I'd—

MEG. He meant everything fer the best, Matt!

MATT. That's what you allus say.

RUFE. All right, if you don't want me to do you a good turn, I won't. Hereafter they can shoot er do what they please, I won't open my mouth!

SID. You needn't pester your mind about me an' Andy, Rufe. We've knowed all about the war 'twixt our fam'lies sence we 'us knee-high. An' it's never made our trigger fingers itch none. Has it, Andy?

ANDY. Not a durned bit! We nachelly hain't talked about it, but I reckon we could if we had to.

SID. I don't reckon nothin' about it; I know it! Me an' you could talk about anything 'thout fightin'—'cept religion!

ANDY. Ha, ha, ha! I'd even take a crack at that with you, fer I expect we've got about the same sort!

SID. Well, my mouth ain't no prayer-book an' I don't try to make it sound like one.

ANDY. Me nother! You cain't make a sheep outen a wild cat by tyin' a bunch o' wool to its tail.

DAVID. You two young jackasses think you're mighty smart a-runnin' down religion! But I want to tell you sompen: I've lived in this ole world longer 'n both of you put together, an' they ain't nothin' to be ashamed of in bein' a Christian!

RUFE. I'm glad to know you feel that way about it!

DAVID. Hey! What's that you said?

ANDY (*slyly, with an amused twinkle*). You hyeard what he said. He's a-hintin' that he didn't know, from the way you behaved, that you *wus* a Christian.
(DAVID *grips his stick and glares at* RUFE.)

DAVID. He won't *say* that, not to my face! If he does, dad-burn him, I'll show him whether I'm a Christian or not!

SID (*laughs*). What'll you do, turn t'other cheek?

DAVID. I might—once! Consoun you, I b'lieve you agree with him! You an' Andy are so puffed up 'ith pride an' wind that you think nobody but women an' runts ever gits religion! But I'm here to tell you that I seed a preacher onee right down thar in the Baptis' church that could pick you both up by the scruff o' the neck an' shake you down to your nachel size!

MATT. An' he didn't 'pologize fer havin' religion, nuther!

DAVID. No, sir-ee, not by a jugful! The fust day big meetin' started he picked out the wust sinner they wus in the congregation an' p'inted his finger at his nose an' told him right out in meetin' that he 'us a-goin' jist as straight to hell as if he 'us shot out of his own gun!

SID. An' d'you mean to say, Gran-pap, that you set thar an' took it all 'thout a word?

DAVID. Who told you it 'us me?

SID (*laughing*). Nobody, but I 'lowed it wus.

DAVID. Well, you 'lowed right! But I didn't set thar an' take it. No, I 'us jist as much of a jackass as you an' Andy. I riz up an' walked out on the platform where he 'us a-standin' an' sez to him, sez I, "You're a mighty big preacher! I can see that by lookin' at you. But what I want to find out is whether your religion's in proportion to your size!" An' 'ith that I hauled away 'ith the flat o' my hand an' smacked him like all possessed on the right cheek! (*He pauses dramatically.*)

ANDY. Well, wus his religion fool-proof?

DAVID. I'm a-comin' to that. I seed him grit his teeth an' trimble from top to toe jist like a steam engine in britches! But he ketched hisself in time an' turned t'other cheek! (*He pauses again.*)

SID. An' what'd you do then?

DAVID. I done jist what you er any other young jackass 'ld ha' done 'ith Satan aggin' him on: I smit him ag'in!

SID. Ha, ha, ha! I reckon he turned ag'in?

DAVID. I jedge not, fer when I come to they wus two men a-rubbin' me, an' he 'us a-goin' right on preachin' an' explainin' Scripture as cool as if nothin' had happened! He said the Saviour never told us what to do after we'd turned t'other cheek once, for he took it fer granted any durn fool 'ld know! (RUFE *shifts uneasily and starts to say something, but* DAVID *glares at him and he subsides.*) An' 'ith that fer a text he whirled in an' preached the best sermon I ever hyeard on the person o' Christ! He said the reason so many folks thought Christ 'us a weak an' womanish sort of a man 'us because they 'us runts theirselves an' wanted Him to keep 'em in countenance. Then he took the Scripture, passage an' verse, an' proved jist the sort o' man Christ wus! Now I'll bet every one of you here thinks he used speritual power when he drove the thieves out o' the temple! (*He looks around at them triumphantly.*) But, 'ey ganny, he didn't!

RUFE. How do *you* know he didn't?

DAVID. B'cause he didn't have to, that's how! I never seed a man yit appeal fer speritual power when he could do it his self!

RUFE. An' did he turn the water into wine the same way?

DAVID. No, that 'us a merricle. But if he'd ha' been a weak, water-drinkin' man it stands to reason he wouldn't ha' turned water into wine! You'd know that if you'd read your Bible the way you'd orter, 'stid nosin' aroun' in it fer the texts that suit you.

RUFE. I've read it from kiver to kiver! I know it back'ards.

DAVID. That's the only way you do know it! You'd have to have the right sort o' religion to read it for'ards!

RUFE. They's only one right sort! That's the sort Jesus had! An', thanks to Him, I got that!

DAVID. Shucks! Jesus wouldn't know your religion if he met it in the road! *He* didn't wait till the war broke out an' skeered Him afore He got His! He wa'n't that sort! I did have hopes that Sid might start preachin' the real Jesus religion when he got back, but's fur as I can make out he's like these here piddlin' 'Piscopalians that run that mission school over thar. He ain't got no sort at all! An' as fer the sort o' religion most folks has got around here, it's a stench in the nostrils o' God!

RUFE. You needn't look so straight at me! I know who you're a-hittin' at!

DAVID. I wusn't a-hittin' at nobody in pertickler! But I've allus hyeard you could tell who's hit by who hollers.

RUFE. I'm satisfied 'ith my religion!

DAVID. That's a shore sign God ain't.

MEG. La! I'd jist as soon hear you talk about war as religion!

DAVID. It allus has been a peacefuler subjec'.

MEG. Cain't you think o' nothing else? David, I thought you said you 'us a-goin' to rob a bee-gum fer Sid afore supper.

DAVID. That's so! I'd 'most fergot. I'll see if I can git 'nough fer him to mess up his mouth with. It's rained so much the past month the bees ain't had no time to work. Matt, want to hold the smudge fer me?

MATT. Yeh. (*Rises and crosses to the outer door.*) Hold on! Some one else 'll have to help you, Paw. I better round up that hay. Looks like a shower afore long. (*He goes out.*)

DAVID. Yeh, kinder feels like it. Come along, Meg; you can hold the smudge.

MEG (*looks at* SID *and* ANDY *significantly*). I'd orter be startin' supper. I reckon Sid can help you.

DAVID. Sid! He ain't no hand 'ith bees, an' you know it! Look here, Meg, if he covered hisself up from head to toe he wouldn't be as safe as he is right here 'ith Andy. So come on an' stop your frettin'! (*He goes out through the kitchen, followed by* MEG.)

ANDY (*getting ready to go*). I reckon I'd better be tappin' the sand. Sid, awhile ago you seemed to be worried 'bout where you'd git your next drink.

SID. I ain't losin' no sleep over it.

ANDY. Well, I got a bottle o' blockade out here in the mail pouch, if you—

RUFE (*eagerly*). Where'd you git it, Andy?

ANDY. That's my business.

RUFE. I've hyeard that new stuff they're makin' now's so fiery that it'll burn your insides out. (*He looks around and lowers his voice confidentially.*) You ought to see some I got.

ANDY. You! I thought you'd gone prohybition!

RUFE. This is some I had afore I j'ined the church. It's over twenty year old.

ANDY. Oh, hell!

RUFE. I swear it on a stack o' Bibles!

SID. If you had it afore you j'ined the church, how'd it ever live to be twenty year old?

ANDY. That's what I'd like to know!

RUFE. Well, I allus did have a weak stummick, you know that. An' it's been lots wuss the past few years. Any sort o' licker's apt to gag me!

ANDY. That don't count fer no twenty years!

RUFE. I ain't claimin' I had it in my possession all that time. D'you mind that tale 'bout the revenue raid way back yonder, when Bob Fortenbury buried all his licker in the bed o' Buck Spring Creek an' never could find it 'cause it come a rain an' washed his marks away?

ANDY. Yeh?

RUFE. Well, me an' Bill Hedgpeth unkivered a ten-gallon keg one day 'bout three year ago when we 'us dynamitin' fish. (*Enthusiastically.*) An' it's the best stuff you ever stuck your tongue into! So thick an' sirupy it clings to the sides o' the bottle jist like 'lasses!

ANDY (*interrupting him*). Stop! Is they any left?

RUFE. Some. Why?

ANDY. Why! Ha, ha! Did you hear that, Sid? He wants to know why? 'Course you don't want to sell it?

RUFE. Well, my advice to everybody is to let licker alone. But if folks is bound they're a-goin' to drink the stuff, I s'pose tain't no more 'n right to help 'em git sompen good.

ANDY (*slaps him on the back*). Spoke like a true Christian!

RUFE. That's what I try to be, Andy. An' ef that licker o' mine'll help you out I don't want to make nuthin' on it. The only thing is—I bought Bill Hedgpeth's share, an' if I'm a-goin' to be out of a job soon I *would* kinder like to git back jist what I paid fer it.

ANDY. Well, you won't have no trouble a-squarin' yourself if it tastes anything like you say.

RUFE. You don't have to take my word for it. I got a sample bottle. (*He makes a move toward the stairs.*) Come on up an' try it!

ANDY (*hesitating*). I've had about all I can tote. But I reckon one more drink like that won't load me down. (*As he turns to follow* RUFE *he hears a noise outside and looks off in the direction of the store.*) Oh, hell! Thar's Sis—out at the store!

SID. What's the trouble?

ANDY. Trouble! Jude's got religion sence you left—like Rufe! An' she has a jeeminy fit every time she smells licker on me! But drive on, Rufe! Dam' it all, I'm free, white, an' twenty-one! (*He goes upstairs.* RUFE *hangs back.* SID *goes to the door and looks out.*)

RUFE (*insinuatingly*). I meant fer you to sample it too, Sid!

SID (*intent on the door*). Much obliged. You an' Andy go ahead. I'll go out an' see what Jude wants.

RUFE (*with venom behind the jest*). I know what's the matter 'ith you! Now 'at you know Jude's got religion, you want her to think you're sproutin' wings!

SID (*surprised, turns and looks at him*). Have you staked out any grounds fer objectin' to what she thinks about me?

RUFE. Why, Sid, you didn't take me serious, did you? She's all free country as fur as I'm concerned! I wus only jokin'!

SID. Oh, I see! Well, whichever way it is, you got some business o' your *own* upstairs an' you better go along an' 'tend to it—without me.
(RUFE *makes a move as if to reply, but changes his mind and goes upstairs, throwing a malignant glance over his shoulder at* SID. JUDE, *a handsome mountain girl, is seen approaching.* SID *smiles mischievously and steps back into the corner behind the door.* JUDE *enters and looks about her.*)

JUDE (*calls through the open door into the kitchen*). Miz Hunt!

SID (*steps out, smiling*). Ahem!

JUDE (*startled, looks at him in amazement*). Sid! (*She takes a step toward him.* SID *presses his lips together firmly and assumes a pose of martyrdom.*) What's the matter? (*She comes nearer, eagerly.*)

Cain't you talk? (SID *stands rigidly at attention and shakes his head solemnly.*) Oh! You hain't been shell-shocked ner tetched in the head? (SID *shakes his head again solemnly as before.*) Then why don't you say sompen? (*She takes hold of his arms, with increasing alarm.*) You know me, don't you? (SID *seizes her suddenly and kisses her. After a moment she frees herself and looks at him again with amazement. He clicks his heels together and assumes his martyr's pose, but his mouth twitches with the ghost of a smile.*) Sid, if you don't tell me why you're actin' this way I'm a-goin' to scream!

SID. I ain't actin'! This is nachel!

JUDE. Nachel?

SID. Yeh. Don't you mind the last time you seen me you told me never to speak to you ag'in as long as I lived?

JUDE. Oh! So that's it!

SID (*laughs guiltily*). Yeh! You know I allus did try to please you!

JUDE (*backs away from him angrily*). If you didn't aim to speak to me, what'd you go an' kiss me fer?

SID. You didn't say nothin' about not kissin' you.

JUDE. I never kick afore I'm spurred! You knowed all the time I didn't mean it when I told you never to speak to me no more. An', anyhow, you could ha' writ!

SID. I thought o' writin'. But I ain't much of a hand at settin' things down on paper. I 'lowed I could argy with you better when I got you where I could sorter surround you!

JUDE. That's another thing! You'd ought to kep' your hands offen me! (*With a suggestion of coquetry.*) I still ain't a-goin' to marry you!

SID. Oh! (*He turns away teasingly.*) Well, nobody axed you.

JUDE (*her eyes blazing dangerously*). You needn't throw that up to me!

SID. Oh, come on, Jude, le's be sensible. (*He tries to take her hands.*) I'll quarrel with you an' court you all you want me to after we're married.

JUDE. You act like you had a morgidge on me!
(*During the preceding two speeches* ANDY *and* RUFE *are seen coming downstairs.* ANDY *is in the state of exhilaration that precedes complete intoxication. At* SID's *suggestion of marriage,* RUFE *halts on the stairs and looks at him with a malignant expression.*)

ANDY (*thickly, with a drunken flourish*). Hello, Sis!

JUDE. Andy! You're drunk ag'in!

ANDY. Well! What're you a-goin' to do about it, little Sis? Pray? (*She hangs her head in shame and doesn't answer. He continues, belligerently.*) I'm free, white, an' twenty-one! An' it's a free country! Come on, Rufe! (*To* SID, *confidentially.*) Me an' Rufe's got some tradin' to do! (*He winks elaborately.*) Ss-sh! (*He starts out,* JUDE *makes a move to follow him.*) Wait! Steady! Where *you* goin'?

JUDE. To the store. I got some tradin' to do, too!

ANDY. Aw right. Then let Sid wait on you! Me an' Rufe 'll stay right here till you come back! Our business is private!

RUFE (*eagerly*). I expect you'd better let me go with her, Andy. I know where the things are better 'n Sid.

ANDY. No! I object! You stay right dam' where you are! (*To* JUDE.) Now—go ahead! An' Sid, don't fergit my caterdges!

SID. I reckon we'll have to call that shootin' match off, Andy. Mam's kickin' up sich a row about it.

ANDY. Ha, ha, ha! She's afeard we'll start another war! All right, it's off! But bring me a box o' caterdges jist the same as if it wusn't.

SID (*in a lower tone to* JUDE). Come on! Don't cross him! (*Then to* ANDY.) What sort o' caterdges, Andy?

ANDY. The sort that raises the most hell!

SID. Ha, ha! All right. But that don't tell me much. You can grow a purty good crop o' hell 'ith any sort if you'll water 'em 'ith enough licker! (*He and* JUDE *go out front.*)

ANDY (*looks after him drunkenly*). Does *he* think I'm drunk, too?

RUFE. I dunno what he thinks! (*Insinuatingly.*) But did you hear what he 'us a-sayin' to Jude jist now?

ANDY. To Jude? (*He draws himself up stiffly.*) Wus it anything outen th' way?

RUFE. *I'd* think so. He wus a-talkin' about marryin' her. (ANDY *relaxes, with an expression of boredom.*) But mebby you don't object to the Hunts an' Lowries a-swoppin' blood *that* way instid o' the way they use' to!

ANDY (*starts violently and lays his hand on his pistol*). Swoppin' blood! Wus Sid a-talkin' about the Hunts an' Lowries a-swoppin' blood like they use' to?

RUFE. 'Tain't like you to be skeered of him, Andy!

ANDY. Umn? Wha's 'at? (*He lurches toward* RUFE *drunkenly and seizes him by the collar.*) Any man 'at says I'm afraid o' Sid Hunt's a God-dam' liar!

RUFE. I didn't say it! (ANDY *relaxes his grip and grunts interrogatively.* RUFE *continues, glancing suggestively in the direction that* SID *has gone.*) But I know the man that did.

ANDY. Umn? You know the man 'at said I—Who is he?

RUFE. I ain't tellin' no tales, but he don't live more'n a thousand miles from here!

ANDY. Wus it Sid hisself?

RUFE. I ain't a-sayin' who it wus. But as your friend, Andy, I'm a-goin' to warn you o' one thing: don't you start nothin' 'ith Sid that you ain't prepared to end! Rickollect the last time the Hunts an' Lowries fit they 'us three more Lowries killed 'n they was Hunts!

ANDY (*with the superhuman calm of the drunken man*). Did Sid brag about that?

RUFE. I ain't a-sayin' what Sid done! I'm a-talkin' to you now as a friend fer your own good!

ANDY. Three more Lowries 'n Hunts! (*Weeping with rage.*) The God-dam' bastard! Where is he? Where is he? (*He starts outside.* RUFE *restrains him.*)

RUFE. Ca'm yourself, Andy! He'll be back here any minute!

ANDY. Rufe, are you fer me er ag'in' me?

RUFE. I'll stick by a friend, Andy, till Jedgment Day!

ANDY. Then gimme your hand! Fer jist as shore as sunrise I'm a-goin' to ekalize things!

RUFE. I'm sorry to hear you talk this way, Andy!

ANDY (*opens his pistol and examines it*). You be-lieve in Provydence, don't you, Rufe?

RUFE. I don't believe nothin' 'bout it. I know it!

ANDY. Look! (*He shows him the pistol.*) It's a-goin' to take six Hunts to make things ekal an' I got jist six caterdges left! That's Provydence!

RUFE (*not understanding him*). My advice to you, Andy, is to drop this! The Hunts are dangerous folks! Sid in pertickler, now 'at he's been through the war! You'd a heap better pocket your pride an' live in peace with him if you can, fer if he gits started he won't stop at *nothin'!* I know him!

ANDY. But you don't know me, Rufe! You think I'm skeered! Well, jist wait! This is a free country an' everybody in it ought to be ekal! Three more Lowries 'n Hunts— that ain't ekal! (*He breaks down and weeps with rage as the curtain falls.*)

ACT TWO

The same scene, a few minutes later. ANDY *sits staring blankly at the door with an expression of tragic determination.* RUFE *goes to the window and looks eagerly in the direction of the store.*

ANDY (*sits up stiffly*). Is he comin'?

RUFE (*comes over fearfully and lays his hand on* ANDY's *shoulder*). Andy, is they still evil in your heart in spite o' what I've said to you?

ANDY (*between a sob and a laugh*). Ha! ha! Brother, let us pray! (*He clasps his hands over his pistol and prays in the fashion of a minister with a hymn-book.*) O Lord, look down on this poor sinner an' make him love his enemies an' do good to 'em! (*He bursts into unholy laughter.*) Ha, ha, ha! I'll do good to him, all right!

RUFE. You ain't a-goin' to kill him *now!*

ANDY. Every man has to die when his time comes! (SID *and* JUDE *are seen coming to-*

ward the house. ANDY *watches them with the unnatural calm of the drunken man.* RUFE, *frightened, slinks away toward the kitchen door as they enter.*)

JUDE (*tactfully*). Andy, I'm ready to go home now if you are.

ANDY. You know the way, an' the road's open!

JUDE. But I don't want to go by myself.

ANDY. I got some business to settle 'ith Sid!

JUDE. Well, I can wait fer you. I want to see Miz Hunt, anyhow. (*She goes into the kitchen.*)

SID. Here's your caterdges, Andy.

ANDY (*fumbles in his pocket for his purse*). An' here's your money!

SID. That's all right. I charged 'em.

ANDY. 'Tain't all right! Not by a dam' sight!

SID (*humoring him*). Well, Andy, jist as you say. (*He takes the money and gives him the cartridges.*) I'll scratch 'em off the book the next time I go out there.

ANDY. Rufe'll scratch 'em off! Don't fergit that, Rufe! (*He looks at* SID *with deadly calm.*) I don't want no Hunt—in hell ner out—to say 'at I killed him on a credit!

SID (*turns on him squarely, uncertain whether he is joking or not*). The Hunts hain't never accused you o' not payin' your debts, Andy!

ANDY. They've had room to! I've owed 'em a passel o' lead ever sence I 'us born! An' I'm a-goin' to pay it now!

SID. What's the trouble with him, Rufe? He seems to have sompen on his mind.

RUFE. I don't know! He's been a-talkin' plumb wild! I tried to ca'm him, but I couldn't!

ANDY. You keep out o' this, Rufe! (*To* SID, *with the same deadly calm.*) Sid Hunt, this is a free country, ain't it?

SID. That's what they call it, Andy!

ANDY. If it's a free country, then everybody in it ought to be ekal!

SID. Well, ain't they? Some's had more to drink 'n others, but that's nothin' to quarrel about.

ANDY. I admit it, but that ain't the p'int. When the Hunts an' Lowries fought the last time the Hunts killed three more Lowries 'n the Lowries killed Hunts! Do you call that ekal?

SID. That's all over now, Andy!

ANDY. But it ain't ekal—is it?

SID. Why, Andy, that happened so long ago—afore me an' you 'us born!

ANDY. That ain't the p'int. It ain't ekal!

SID. All right, then, it ain't. But what do you want me to do to equalize things?

ANDY. I don't want you to do a dam' thing but holler! I'll do the ekalizin'! An' they's only one way! The Hunts killed three more Lowries 'n the Lowries killed Hunts! I'm a-goin' to kill three more Hunts 'n the Hunts killed Lowries!

SID (*trying to appear calm*). Three more. That sounds reasonable enough. Now lemme see, how many Hunts 'ill that make in all?

ANDY. Only six! An' I got jist six caterdges in my pistol! That's provydential!

SID. It does look like it. The only question is which six Hunts it's a-goin' to be. (*Coaxingly.*) Now I'll tell you, Andy, I've got lots o' no-'count kin—

ANDY. No! You cain't come that on me! I got no-'count kin, too! They ain't worth killin'.

SID. I expect you're right about that, Andy.

ANDY. I know dam' well I'm right!

SID. Now look here, Andy, I want this thing done like it ought to be. (*Persuasively.*) Now I'll tell you what I'll do. You go home an' study 'bout this overnight an' come back to-morrow mornin'. If you still want to kill six of us then, I'll let you take your pick.

ANDY. Ha, ha! You think I'm a dam' fool, don't you? Well, I am; but I ain't that sort!

SID. All right, Andy, jist as you say! If you'd druther begin on what you got here now, I'll send fer 'em. Only, they ain't enough to make out your six. (*Significantly to* RUFE.) Rufe, step out thar an' tell Pap an' Gran'pap that Andy 'ld like to see 'em here on pertickler business.

ANDY. No! (*To* RUFE.) You grow to the place where you're a-standin'! (*Turns to* SID.) Don't neither of you move a peg ner bat a eye!

SID. All right, Andy. Whatever you say's gospel as fur as I'm concerned!

ANDY. I know dam' well it is! Rufe, git your banjer! (RUFE *obeys, taking the banjo from a peg on the wall.*) Can you pick "Turkey in the Straw"?

RUFE. I use' to could. But I hain't practiced no jig tunes lately.

ANDY. You're a-goin' to practice one now! Set down thar an' let 'er go! (RUFE *hesitates.*) Set down, I tell you. This ain't no time to stand up fer Jesus! (RUFE *seats himself and strikes the first note.* ANDY *turns on* SID *with an expression of maudlin determination.*) Sid Hunt, the Scripture says they's a time fer everything!

SID. That's right, Andy!

ANDY. I know dam' well it's right! (*He pauses to recall what he was going to say.*) When the Hunts an' Lowries fought the last time, the Hunts made my grandaddy dance afore they shot him! (*He cocks his pistol.*) This is the time to dance!

SID. Well, you're the boss! Whatever you say goes 'ith me!

ANDY. Then cut your patchin'! (RUFE *strikes up "Turkey in the Straw" and* SID *starts to dance.* ANDY *follows him, keeping time with his pistol.* SID *moves gradually toward the outside door, but* ANDY *heads him off.*) Sash-i-ate! (SID *dances back toward the center of the room.* ANDY *follows him, calling the figures with increasing tempo.*) For'ard an' back! Corners turn an' sash-i-ate! Hit the floor! Swing an' circle! Ladies change an' gents the same! Right an' left! The shoo-fly swing! Sash-i-ate! (SID *sashays toward the kitchen door.* ANDY *rushes after him.*)

RUFE (*seeing the muzzle of the pistol pointed in his direction, screams with terror*). Oh! Don't—!

ANDY (*raises the pistol and covers* SID). Wait! Swing your partner! (SID *turns and looks into the muzzle of the pistol.*) That's right! Face the music!

(SID *wipes the perspiration from his forehead, but gives no other sign of fear.* JUDE *appears from the kitchen.*)

JUDE. Andy! What are you—

ANDY. Git to hell out o' here if you don't want a bullet in you!

(JUDE *rushes forward with a piercing scream.* SID *springs under* ANDY's *arm, thrusting it upward with a twist. The pistol falls to the floor.* SID *releases* ANDY *and seizes the pistol.*)

RUFE. Thank the Lord!

JUDE (*rushing between* ANDY *and* SID). Don't kill him!

SID. I ain't a-goin' to.

ANDY. That's a lie—you air a-goin' to. Come on! You got me. Why don't you shoot?

SID. I dunno's killing you 'ld equalize things any, Andy.

JUDE. What's the matter with him, Sid? (MEG *and* DAVID *enter hurriedly from the kitchen.*)

SID. You'll have to ax somebody 'at knows. He's a-settin' out to kill as many more Hunts as the Hunts killed Lowries in a feud fifty years ago!

MEG (*with a shudder of horror*). Oh! It's all beginnin' over ag'in!

DAVID. This is your work, Rufe!

SID. Now don't go packin' it on Rufe! He done all he could to ca'm Andy!

DAVID. Mebby so! (*He looks at* RUFE, *who stands with an expression of martyrdom.*) I b'lieve in givin' the devil his dues! But he knowed Andy 'us a-drinkin' when he started that talk about the feud!

SID. My experience has been that a man don't take fire at a notion like that when he's drunk 'less he's been thinkin' some 'bout it when he's sober! (*He puts the pistol in his pocket and takes hold of* ANDY's *arm.*) Come on, Andy! I'm a-goin' to put you on your horse now an' send you home, where you ought to be!

JUDE (*steps toward him with an apologetic air*). I'll take keer of him, Sid!

SID. He's sober enough to go home by hisself. You stay here. I want to talk to you 'bout this. (*He leads* ANDY *out.*)

MEG (*to David*). Go on out thar with 'em an' see 'at they don't start fightin' ag'in! (DAVID *follows them.* MEG *lifts her apron to her eyes and sobs despairingly.*) It's all a-startin' over jist like it did the first time! I'll never see another minute's peace now as long as I live!

JUDE. I never thought my brother 'ld act like that!

MEG. 'Taint your fault! They cain't none of us help what our folks do! (*She goes into the kitchen, weeping.*)

RUFE. They ain't no use grievin' about it. I'd druther see everybody live together in peace. But fer all we know, this may ha' been so ordered. If it wus it'll all work out fer the best in the end.

JUDE. How'd Andy ever git started quarrelin' 'ith Sid?

RUFE. Trouble don't generally start all on one side. But I'm a friend to both of 'em an' I'm a-goin' to keep my mouth shet.

JUDE. I know Sid wouldn't ha' crossed him a-purpose when he's a-drinkin'.

RUFE. Well, as I said afore, I ain't a-takin' sides neither way. But Sid can be mighty overbearin' when he's a mind to.

JUDE. What'd he say to Andy?

RUFE. Some folks don't have to say things; they can look 'em. (*He cuts his eye at her significantly.*) But you'll understand what I mean when you marry Sid.

JUDE. I hain't said yit I 'us a-goin' to marry him!

RUFE (*eagerly*). You hain't said you wasn't?

JUDE (*with simple dignity*). No; an' I dunno's I have any call to say it now. I don't know what's a-goin' to happen now!

RUFE. If you do marry him you'll find out lots o' things about him that you didn't know before. I know you think I'm a-sayin' this fer selfish reasons! But I ain't! Sence I first told you I loved you, Jude, I've learned to sing "less o' self an' more o' Thee"! It's not my own good I'm after now, but your good—only yourn! An' I tell you, Jude, ef you marry Sid I know you're a-goin' to rue it the longest day you live!

JUDE. Well, suppose you an' Sid found out you both knowed the same thing about me?

RUFE. The question is, which is right an' which is wrong.

JUDE. An' who's a-goin' to settle that?

RUFE. Him—up yonder!

JUDE. Do you think He bothers his head much about who's a-goin' to marry who?

RUFE. I know He does! I'll tell you why!

JUDE. I'd ruther not hear it now! I got too much else to think about—with killin' in the air!

RUFE. But I want to explain afore it's too late. I want you to know that my love fer you wus ordained from above. The first time I ever thought o' marryin' you, Jude, 'us when I seen you in church the day I got religion!

JUDE. Mebby you wouldn't ha' thought of it then if you'd been a-studyin' 'bout your religion like you'd ought ha' been.

RUFE. I wus, Jude! That's jist the p'int! The whole thing 'us spiritual! I mind it jist as well as if it 'us yistidy! Preachin' 'us over an' they 'us singin' "None but Christ." When they come to the verse,

"I sighed fer rest an' happiness,
    I yearned fer them, not Thee;
But while I passed my Saviour by,
    His love laid hold o' me,"

I looked across the aisle an' seen you a-settin' thar a-singin'! An' sompen hot swep' over me jist like fire! At first I thought it 'us Satan a-temptin' me, an' I tried to look t'other way. I don't never look at the women's side in the meetin'-house. Anybody 'at knows me'll tell you that. But I couldn't look no other way then. Some power greater an' stronger 'n me seemed to have holt o' my neck, a-twistin' it around toward you. I 'us absolutely helpless, jist as helpless as a child! But I didn't know what it wus till they got to the last verse. You know how it goes:

"The pleasures lost I sadly mourned,
  But never wept fer Thee,
Tell grace my sightless eyes received,
  Thy lov-li-ness to see."

It 'us then that the scales dropped from my eyes! An' I seen the truth! An' when I did, everything in the whole world 'us changed fer me! I loved everybody an' everything! An' I 'us so happy I felt jist like I 'us a-floatin' away on a ocean o' joy!

JUDE. If you felt like that you'd better let well enough alone. I couldn't make you no happier by marryin' you.

RUFE. Yes, you could, Jude! (*With a mystical suggestion.*) The half has never been told!

JUDE. The half o' what?

RUFE (*looks at her significantly - and chants*).

"I've hyeard of a beautiful city,
  Fur away in the Kingdom o' God;
I've hyeard how its walls are o' jasper,
  How its streets are golden an' broad!
In the midst o' the street is life's river,
  Clear as crystal an' pyor to behold.

(*Rolling his eyes mystically.*)

Not half o' the joys that await 'em
  To mortals has ever been told!
Not half has ever been told!
  Not half o' the joys that await 'em
To mortals has ever been told!"

You know how the rest of it goes!

JUDE. Yeh, but that's heaven. An' they ain't no marryin' ner givin' in marriage thar!

RUFE. Yes, they is, Jude! They's spiritual marriage! That's what I mean!

JUDE. No, that ain't the sort you're a-thinkin' about.

RUFE. You're wrong thar! That's the only sort I ever think about! I can say truthfully, Jude, that I've never had a thought about you ner no other woman that I'd be ashamed to tell to the angels in heaven!

SID (*enters at the front, laughing*). Angels in heaven, eh?

JUDE. Sid! Did Andy git off home all right?

SID. Not yit. I left him out thar behind the store.

JUDE. Is he sick?

SID. Yeh—but he'll soon be over it. He was throwin' it off purty fast when I left.

JUDE. You didn't give him back his pistol, did you?

SID. No. They ain't nuthin' to worry about, Jude. He'll be all right when he's sober. Besides, Grandpap's out there with him. So I thought I'd come in an' have a little talk 'ith you; that is, if I ain't a-cuttin' short a preachment by Rufe. When I come in he was sayin' sompen 'bout angels in heaven.

JUDE. He says he can tell 'em all his thoughts about women. An' that's more 'n you can do, I expect!

SID. Ha, ha! Well, I hadn't thought about tryin' jist yit!

RUFE. 'Tain't nothin' to laugh about! A man hain't got no right to look at a woman, much less marry 'er, tell he can think right thoughts about her!

SID. How's he a-goin' to know what sort o' thoughts he can think about her tell he looks at her?

RUFE. All my thoughts about 'em are right thoughts. (*Maliciously, with his eyes on JUDE.*) But o' course I hain't never seen them French gals you 'us a-tellin' about while ago!

JUDE. What 'us he a-sayin' about French gals?

RUFE. Don't ax *me*. I ain't a-carryin' no tales.

SID. You've said enough already. (*He makes a move toward him half angrily, then stops with a puzzled expression.*) I cain't quite make you out, Rufe. I dunno whether you're a trouble breeder or whether you're jist teched in the head with religion. But whichever it is, I want you to git this much straight: Me an' Jude's a-goin' to be married, an' anything I want her to know about them French gals I'll tell her myself.

JUDE. I've never said I 'us a-goin' to marry you!

SID. Well, if you've got any doubts on the subject I'll clear 'em up (*he glances at* RUFE *significantly*) as soon as I have a chance to talk to you by yourself!

RUFE. You needn't knock me down with it. I'm perfectly willin' to give you your chance with Jude. I guess she can jedge whether she could be happy yoked up to a unbeliever. (*He puts on his hat and goes out stiffly.*)

SID (*laughing*). Religion certainly does take a quair turn 'ith some folks!

JUDE. It don't seem to be a-troublin' you none. Sid, how'd Andy ever come to think o' shootin' you?

SID. You got me! He'd been mixin' his licker, I reckon.

JUDE. That don't 'count fer it! What'd you mean while ago when you said a man didn't act like Andy when he's drunk 'less he's been studyin' some about it when he's sober?

SID. Jist what I said. He don't generally.

JUDE. Then you think Andy's been holdin' a grudge ag'in' you?

SID. I cain't account fer him flarin' up like he did no other way. Has he ever said anything to you about evenin' up the score between the Hunts an' Lowries? (*She starts and takes a step away from him with instinctive distrust.*) You needn't be afraid to tell me!

JUDE. I ain't afraid to tell nobody the truth! (*With suppressed emotion.*) It's a lie I'd be afraid to tell—er to act! (*She sees from his expression that he doesn't understand her.*) I b'lieve you know more about what started Andy's tantrum 'n you purtend to!

SID. Jude, you don't think I picked a fuss 'ith Andy!

JUDE. I dunno what I think! But I know Andy didn't bear no grudge ag'in' you!

SID. The chances are he wouldn't ha' told you if he had!

JUDE. An' I wouldn't tell *you*—if you did ask me!

SID. Why wouldn't you?

JUDE. 'Cause Andy's my brother! That's reason enough, ain't it?

SID. But I'm the man that's a-goin' to marry you!

JUDE. That's what you've been a-sayin'.

SID. Well, you are a-goin' ter marry me, ain't you?

JUDE. I wus mebbe—before. But now—I dunno.

SID. Now see here, Jude! If this trouble with Andy is a-standin' between us we might as well settle it right now.

JUDE (*with a flare of passion*). You got no right to make me take sides ag'in' my own flesh an' blood!

SID. I ain't a-goin' to try to make you. That's sompen you'll have to decide fer yourself. The Bible says a man an' woman ought to leave their daddy an' mammy an' all the rest o' their kin an' stick together in spite o' the devil—at least, that's the sense of it. I don't purtend to pattern after Scripture like Rufe, but that part allus hit me as bein' jist about right. An' if you don't feel the same way, I want to know it now.

JUDE. But I—(*She looks at him dumbly.*)

SID. They ain't no room fer "buts" here, Jude. If you've got any doubt about whose side you'd be on in a fight between me an' your folks, you'd better give yourself the benefit of 'em.

JUDE. I couldn't never go back on my own kin!

SID. Then that's settled. (*He turns away.*) We don't belong together.

JUDE. You don't actially think our folks are a-goin' to start fightin' ag'in', do you, Sid?

SID. Not if I can keep 'em from it. But that ain't the p'int; if they do start, I don't want no weak sister fer a wife. If a woman ain't fur a man she's purty apt to be ag'in' him. They don't come a-settin' on the fence.

JUDE. You mean I got to—take sides ag'in' my own folks?

SID. I mean you've got to stand by me if you marry me. (*She looks at him helplessly. He meets her gaze firmly, without flinching.*)

JUDE (*breaks down, sobbing*). But it ain't right! You know it ain't right to go ag'in' my own blood!

SID. Well, nobody ain't a-makin' you marry me.

JUDE (*turns on him angrily*). What do you keep on a-sayin' that fer when it ain't so! You know I cain't do nothin' else! (*She sobs incoherently and puts her arms about him.*)

SID (*embracing her tenderly*). I sorter hoped you couldn't, Jude. But I wanted you to find out fer yourself.

JUDE (*still sobbing*). I'm a-goin' to do what's right, but it's terrible hard. Andy's my own brother! 'Tain't in human nacher to—

SID. Don't you worry about that! They ain't a-goin' to be no trouble. I jist wanted to find out whar you stood in case they wus. But you jist leave all that to me. Nuthin' ain't a-goin' to happen to Andy ner nobody else.

(MATT *and* DAVID *are seen coming toward the front door.* SID *and* JUDE *separate.* JUDE *turns away toward the kitchen to hide her tears.*)

DAVID. Sid, me and Matt—(*Sees* JUDE *and hesitates.*) Step out here a minute, Sid.

SID. Is it about Andy?

DAVID. Yeh.

SID. Well, you can talk afore Jude. Me an' her's decided to git married.

DAVID. Well, I'm glad o' that!

MATT. Mebbe it'll help to keep the peace.

SID. It 'd orter. Go right ahead an say what you're a-mind to. Jude knows all about the row with Andy, and they ain't no doubt where she stands.

DAVID. Well, Matt and me's been a-talkin' it over an' we think you'd better ride up an' ax Andy's daddy to come down here.

JUDE. What do you want 'ith Paw?

DAVID. We want to talk to him 'bout Andy.

SID. Whyn't you wait tell Andy's hisself ag'in an' let me an' him talk this over? I never knowed no good to come o' one o' these fam'ly talkin'-matches yit. Me an' Andy can patch things up if you'll jist let us alone.

DAVID. This ain't no time fer patchwork. I want to git Jim Lowry right here on the ground, face to face 'ith you an' Andy, an' tell him edzactly what happened afore the tale has a chance to grow. I've allus found him reasonable enough.
(RUFE *enters at the front.*)

RUFE. Jude, Andy said tell you he 'us ready to start home now an' to ax you if you 'us a-goin' with him.

JUDE (*to* DAVID). Do you want him to wait tell you send fer Paw? If you do I'll tell him.

DAVID. That's my advice, but I don't want to be pig-headed about it.

SID. I don't neither. Mebby your way's the best. But if Andy's reached the state o' 'countability ag'in, I'd like to know how he stands on it afore we send fer his daddy. I know if I 'us Andy it 'ld jist make me mad.

JUDE. I'll talk to him an' see what he says. (*She goes out.*)

SID. How is he now, Rufe—sober enough to ride his horse home?

RUFE. Yeh, I reckon so. I never seed licker go to nobody's head like it did to hisn. When a man talks as wild as he did while ago, I believe it 'ld be better fer everybody concerned—hisself included—to put him behind bars. If I 'us in your place I'd certainly have him bound by law to keep the peace.

DAVID. Folks that *can* be bound by law to keep the peace don't have to be. They're blood kin to them that looks around fer somebody to hold 'em when a fight starts. Andy belongs to t'other breed. (*Goes to window, turns to* MATT *and* SID.) They must ha' been a reg'lar toad-strangler up the river last night. She's a-b'ilin' like a kittle o' fish!

MATT. I noticed it 'us risin' purty sharp as me an' Sid crossed the bridge.

SID. 'Tain't out o' banks yit, is it?

DAVID. Nowhere 'cept in the low places. She soon will be, though, if she keeps on! I never seed the ole sow a-gittin' her bristles up so fast!

RUFE. They'd be a camp-meetin' time if that big dam busted, an' they's one wing of it that ain't finished yit.

DAVID. You needn't lose no sleep over that. I 'us up thar t'other day, an' they ain't water enough this side o' Jordan to shake that wall. Nothin' short of a box o' dynamite 'ld ever make a dent on it.

RUFE. It wouldn't surprise me much if some o' the folks that fit so hard to keep 'em from puttin' it in tried blastin' to git it out. They's one of 'em that's been a-sendin' to town by me fer a mighty heap o' dynamite to dig wells with.

DAVID. In my opinion, Rufe, you've been usin' a good part o' that dynamite yourself.

RUFE. Me! I'd like to know what I'd be usin' it fer!

DAVID. To kill fish. I've seed you come back several times lately 'ith a fine string o' trout. An' I never noticed no hook marks in their mouths.

RUFE. I allus fish 'ith a tiny little pin-hook, to keep from tearin' their mouths! I'm thankful to say I can ketch 'em 'cordin' to law. I don't have to blast 'em out 'ith dynamite! (*He goes out.*)

MATT (*glances in the direction that he has gone*). Somebody's been a-blastin' 'em lately. I've seed lots o' little uns a-floatin' downstream dead.

ANDY (*in the distance*). I'm all right—you don't need to help me.
(JUDE *is seen coming toward the door with him. He is much sobered, but still slightly unsteady on his legs. There is a moment of constrained silence as he enters and looks about him.*)

SID. Here, Andy, have a cheer!

ANDY (*hangs his head shamefacedly*). No. Much obliged. I can stand all right. Jude said you axed her to marry you.

SID. Yeh, that's right, Andy.

ANDY. Well, I reckon they ain't no use in tellin' you that I made a fool o' myself while ago. You 'us all here an' seed it. But she wanted me to say it, and— (*He stops, unable to find suitable words.*)

SID. Fergit it, Andy. That's what I'm a-goin' to do. Somebody done some purty tall talkin', I admit. But I expect it 'us the licker you drunk, instid o' you.

ANDY. I dunno 'bout that. But I know it 'us me that drunk the licker!

DAVID. 'Tain't none o' my business, Andy, but if I found out they 'us truck I couldn't put inside o' me 'thout addlin' my brains, I'll be derned if I wouldn't keep it out er bust!

ANDY. I'm a-goin' to keep it out hereafter if I know myself!

SID. Then here's sompen you can take home with you when you start. (*He takes* ANDY's *pistol out of his pocket and offers it to him.*)

ANDY (*starts to take it and stops*). No! I'll git it some other time!

SID (*puzzled*). Why don't you want to take it now?

ANDY. I dunno whether I'm sober enough yit!

SID. Ha, ha! If that's all 'at's worryin' you, I'll run the resk! (*He drops the pistol in* ANDY's *holster.*)

JUDE (*nervously*). We'd better be goin', Andy!

SID. Wait till I saddle a horse an' I'll go a piece with you. I want to see how it feels to have my feet in stirrups ag'in after walkin' all over the world.

DAVID (*who has been looking at the weather signs*). I don't want to hurry nobody off, but from the way the clouds air a-b'il-in' over the mountain thar it wouldn't s'r-prise me if we had fallin' weather ag'in afore night.

(MATT *goes out to look at the clouds.*)

SID. Well, I ain't skeered of a little water. (*He goes out.*)

DAVID. I ain't, nuther. But I'm like all Baptists; I abominate havin' it sprinkled on me.

JUDE (*looks into the kitchen, then turns to* DAVID). Where'd Miz Hunt go?

DAVID. I expect she's out thar a-roundin' up her young turkeys. 'Bout half of 'em got draggled in the rain yistidy, an' they're droopin' an' dyin' like good children.

(JUDE *goes out through the kitchen.* DA-VID *follows her.* ANDY *sits gloomily, his face in his hands.* RUFE *enters at the front and looks at him furtively.*)

RUFE (*comes forward*). Well, Andy, I jist hyeard Matt say everythin' is all smoothed over an' they ain't a-goin' to be no more trouble.

ANDY (*grunts, without looking at him*). Yeh, that's right.

RUFE. I certainly hope it is.

ANDY. I ain't a-goin' ter rake up the past, if Sid don't! An' I guess he won't, now that he's a-goin' to marry Jude.

RUFE (*starts*). Oh, is he a-goin' ter marry her?

ANDY. Yeh, they got it all fixed up.

RUFE. That'd orter help some. (*Then with a nervous laugh.*) I see you got your pistol back. (*Comes toward* ANDY, *lowering his voice guardedly.*) Andy, if I tell you som-pen as a friend, will you swear on the Bible never to breathe it to a soul?

ANDY. My word's as good as my oath!

RUFE. I know it is! An' that's all I want!

ANDY. Then consider 'at you've got it!

RUFE (*comes still closer to him*). You value your life, don't you, Andy?

ANDY. I reckon I do. I've had plenty o' chances to throw it away, an' I hain't took none of 'em yit.

RUFE. Well, you got another now! (*Significantly.*) If I 'us in your place I'd make myself as scarce as hen teeth around here!

ANDY. What are you drivin' at? Have they got a bullet salted fer me?

RUFE (*gives him an eloquent look*). If they have they hain't told me!

ANDY. I don't want to know what they've told you! I want to know what you know!

RUFE. As man to man?

ANDY. Yeh, as man to man!

RUFE. I'm a-takin' a big chance to tell you! But you've allus been my friend, Andy! An' I'll stick by a friend tell Jedgment. They're all I got left in the world!

ANDY (*impatiently*). Well, come on! What are they up to?

RUFE. Jist now—afore you come in—

ANDY. Yeh?

RUFE. Sid an' his daddy an' the ole rooster 'us a-holdin' a inquest over you!

ANDY. A inquest!

RUFE. That's what *I'd* call it!

ANDY. What 'us the verdick—death from nachel causes?

RUFE. They didn't edzackly *say* that.

ANDY. But you know what they meant?

RUFE. We never *know* nothin' in this world. But my advice to you is not to let Sid ketch you by yourself in a lonesome spot in the woods 'less you want to wear a wooden overcoat.

ANDY. If that's his game, why didn't he let daylight through me when he had a good excuse? (*Lays his hand on his pistol.*) An' what'd he gimme back my pistol fer?

RUFE. You don't know Sid like I do. He's deeper 'n he looks. If he'd ha' killed you while ago when he had a chance, Jude 'ld never ha' married him. But he's made hisself solid 'ith her now by lettin' you off. He can afford to wait to put you to sleep tell they ain't nobody a-lookin', though that ain't a-pesterin' his mind much, fer he knows the law cain't tetch him.

ANDY. Why cain't it?

RUFE. 'Cause you threatened his life in the presence o' witnesses.

ANDY. Has he got all that figgered out aforehand?

RUFE. That an' more. (*He hears footsteps outside and glances toward the door.*) Here he comes now. You watch him! He'll be so smooth with you that butter won't melt in his mouth! (SID *enters briskly.*)

SID. I'm ready, Andy, if you are. Where's Jude?

ANDY. I dunno! She went out thar to look fer your mammy!

SID. Jist set still. I'll call her. I hope your head ain't a-feelin' top heavy, fer I expect we're a-goin' to have to do some hard ridin' to keep ahead o' that cloud. It looks like it might rain tadpoles. (*He goes out through the kitchen.*)

RUFE. Thar! What'd I tell you!

ANDY. Well, I've done all I could! I admitted to 'im 'at I 'us wrong to breach that ole fight ag'in!

RUFE. I know you did, Andy. An' 'tain't a-goin' to do you no good to eat more dirt fer 'em 'less you're prepared to eat six feet of it. Fer I hyeard Sid tell his daddy that you wusn't the sort o' man as could be bound by his word to keep the peace.

ANDY. That's sompen I can't understand, Rufe! If I had it in my heart to kill a man, I couldn't act toward him like I 'us his friend!

RUFE. Me nuther. I b'lieve in speakin' my mind an' lettin' whatever comes up come

out. But you have to fight fire with fire; you can't afford to take no chances when your life's at stake.

ANDY. What 'ld you do if you 'us in my place?

RUFE. I ain't a-sayin' what I *would* do, but I know one thing I *wouldn't:* I wouldn't wait fer him to git the drop on me! I'd be the early **bird!**

ANDY. No! I won't shoot first, 'less he starts it! But I'm a-goin' to keep my eyes glued on him, an' the first suspicious move he makes (*he pats the handle of his pistol caressingly*) one or t'other of us'll be buzzard's meat!

RUFE (*insinuatingly*). That's all right—if he don't take a crack at you from the bushes!
(*It has grown suddenly darker. A gust of wind strikes the house, followed by thunder and lightning.* SID, JUDE, DAVID *and* MEG *enter from kitchen.*)

SID. Andy, looks like it's a-tunin' up fer a reg'lar harrycane! What do you say to havin' your horse put up an' stayin' a while longer?

ANDY. No, I guess I'll be movin' along.

SID. You might jist as well stay.

DAVID. Yeh, why not?

ANDY. I got to go!

SID. Andy, I hope you ain't got a notion 'at they's any hard feelin's (*claps him on the shoulder*), 'cause they ain't.

DAVID. 'Course not!

SID. Jude'll stay. Won't you, Jude?

JUDE. I reckon I'd better. They won't expect me back in a storm. They won't expect Andy, neither.

ANDY. I've told you 'at I'm a-goin', storm er no storm!

SID. Well, you know your own business. Ef you're sot on goin', let's git started. (*Starts out.*)

MEG (*stopping him*). Sid, they ain't no need o' your goin'!

SID. Yes, they is. Whatever Andy's reason fer goin' is, I reckon I got a better one. I don't intend to waste no time a-gittin' things settled with Jude's paw. An' I couldn't ha' picked a better time. If he makes any objection, I'll have the ups on him while she's waterbound!

JUDE. I dunno's water 'ld help you keep me here ef I didn't want to stay!

SID (*laughs*). Well, anyway, I'll tell your folks not to expect you tell you git thar. Are you ready, Andy?

ANDY. You bet your boots I am! I'm ready fer anything—hell er high water!

SID (*glances at the sky*). It looks like we might have a little o' both afore long! (*Calls back.*) I'll be back fer supper if nothin' happens! (*He goes out with* ANDY. MEG *follows them to the door and looks after them anxiously. Pause.*)

RUFE (*goes to the door and stands by* MEG). I wouldn't worry! If any harm's a-goin' to come to 'em, worryin' won't stop it!

MEG. I wusn't thinkin' 'bout that so much as this everlastin' rain! I'd think it 'ld git out o' water some time an' stop! We hain't had three hours o' sunshine on a stretch in over a month!

DAVID. Well, I wouldn't lose heart jist because you've had a few turkeys drabbled! Think what a time old Noah's wife had a-roundin' up her menagery! (MEG *goes to the fireplace and begins fumbling with the kindling.*) What in the nation are you a-buildin' a fire fer? You ain't cold?

MEG. No, but the air feels damp. An' everything in the house molds so if I don't dry it out once an' a while!

DAVID. Then lemme start it fer you! (*He takes the kindling and proceeds to lay the fire.*) I never seed a woman yit that could build a fire 'thout gittin' it catawampused!

JUDE. I've noticed that all the things that men want to do are a man's job; an' them they don't, like washin' dishes an' milkin', are a woman's.

DAVID. Then how do you count fer it that when I tried milkin' fer you a long time ago the ole cow kicked so I couldn't? She seemed to know it wusn't a man's job!

MEG. She had room to kick. You pinched her teats to make her!

DAVID. Lord forgive you, Meg! How'd you ever come to think a thing like that?

MEG. I didn't think it. I hyeard you a-braggin' about it to Sid one day when you thought I wusn't a-listenin'.

DAVID. That's the trouble 'ith women these days: they've been a-listenin' to men's talk till they've got too smart fer comfort! If they keep on, I dunno how men are a-goin' to live 'ith the next generation of 'em!

JUDE. I dunno's I'd live 'ith one that pinched my cow to keep from milkin' her.

DAVID. Then you'd better warn Sid as soon as you marry him, fer it 'ld be jist like him to try it!

MEG. 'Course it would, now 'at you've put him up to it!

DAVID. Well, as long as the women tell the gals all they know, it's nothin' but right that men should give their kind the benefit o' their experience. If they didn't, the women 'ld soon be on top!

RUFE. I dunno's that 'ld be sich a calamity. If women had their way they'd be less fightin' an' drinkin' an' more folks a-workin' fer the comin' o' the Kingdom o' Heaven on earth!

MEG. At least they'd be fewer a-pinchin' pore dumb brutes to git out o' doin' any sort o' work. Men ain't perfect. I can think o' lots o' ways o' improvin' the breed.

DAVID. It's a quair thing to me that woman, ever sence the Lord made her out o' man's crookedest part, has allus considered it her main job to keep him straight!

MEG. If that's her main job, she's made a purty pore job of it!

DAVID. Well, a man's got to stay on top, somehow.

RUFE. Yeh! By hook er by crook!

DAVID. Edzactly! The strong uns do it by hook an' the weak uns by crook! That's the only difference! (*A shot is heard in the distance, followed almost instantly by a second. They all start and look at one another in alarm, as if afraid to put their fear in words.* DAVID *continues with pretended indifference.*) Wus that somebody a-shootin'?

MEG. Yes! (*She rushes to the door and listens.*)

DAVID. Which way was it?

MEG (*with a half-dazed expression, her eyes in the distance*). Up the road!

DAVID. Oh, I reckon it's Andy a-lettin' off steam!

RUFE. Yeh, that must ha' been what it wus.

MEG. It couldn't ha' been Andy! He hain't got his pistol!

JUDE. Oh! (*She sinks into a chair.*)

MEG (*pityingly*). Now they ain't no use in that, Jude! I know what you're thinkin'; but if Sid had wanted to harm Andy he'd ha' done it here while ago!

JUDE. That ain't what I'm skeered of!

MEG (*with sudden change of expression as the idea dawns on her*). Did Sid give Andy back his pistol?

JUDE (*almost inaudibly, nodding her head*). Yes!

MEG (*looks first at* JUDE *and then at* DAVID *with blazing eyes*). What'd he do it fer?

DAVID. Why, Meg, I b'lieve you're plum tarryfied! They ain't no sense in makin' things no wuss 'n they are! (*A horse is heard approaching at a gallop.*)

MEG (*turns eagerly in the direction of the sound*). What's that?

DAVID. It's Sid a-comin' back. I reckon he must ha' forgot sompen. It beats me the way you can make a bear outen a bush!

RUFE (*sympathetically*). She cain't help her thoughts!

MEG (*who has stepped outside on the doorstep, utters a piercing cry*). Oh, God! (RUFE *runs to the door and looks out.* MEG *turns and staggers blindly into the house, her face covered with her apron.* DAVID *and* JUDE *catch her as she is about to sink to the floor.*)

DAVID. Dern it all, Meg, what's the matter with you? (*As they place her in a chair.*) I declare I never seed a growed-up woman as chicken-hearted as she is!

RUFE (*shakes his head ominously*). That *does* look bad!

DAVID. What looks bad, you dad-burned fool!

RUFE. Nothin'—only that 'us Sid's horse 'ith the empty saddle that she seed a-turnin' in at the barn gate!

DAVID. Well, what if it wus?

RUFE. Nothin'! I jist don't like the looks of it! That's all!

DAVID. Well, I hope it's all from you!

MEG (*rocks back and forth, sobbing*). They ain't no use in foolin' ourselves! It's happened! He's dead! Andy's killed him!

DAVID. Now stop your ravin', Meg! They's a thousand ways that horse might ha' got loose! It might ha' throwed him! (MATT *enters at the front, grim and determined.*)

MATT. No, it didn't! It's not a buckin' horse! You know that as well as I do! An' I've never seed it skeer at nothin' sence I got it! (*He takes the shotgun from the rack and starts out.*)

DAVID (*takes the rifle*). Wait! I'm a-goin' with you an' see what's happened!

MEG. Matt! Don't take the guns! If Sid's dead, fightin' won't bring him back!

MATT. I never said it would. If he's dead, my business is 'ith the man that killed him!

RUFE. Vengeance is mine, saith the Lord! I will repay!

DAVID. He has to have a instrument to work through! Even God cain't smite evildoers 'thout a fist! (*He goes out with* MATT. MEG *sways back and forth despairingly.*)

MEG. If they is a God an' He's almighty like they say, I cain't see why He don't stop things like this!

RUFE. Mebby He don't want to stop 'em!

MEG. Then He ain't a just God!

RUFE (*moves away from her instinctively*). I wouldn't say things like that, Meg! All His jedgments are just an' righteous altogether!

JUDE. Do you call it right fer Sid to go through the war an' then be struck down by Andy the minute he gits home?

RUFE. That ain't fer us to say. (*Piously.*) He knows what Sid done while he 'us away in the war. We don't.

JUDE. Andy ain't a God-fearin' man, neither!
(*A vivid flash of lightning illumines the scene.*)

RUFE. I know he ain't. An' vengeance is on his track, too. It's writ that the heathen shall rage an' the wicked destroy one another. That's a part o' God's plan.

JUDE. That don't make it right!

RUFE. God don't have to jestify his ways to man. Let Him be right if you have to make out everybody else wrong's what I say, an' they's good Scripture fer it.

JUDE. They's Scripture fer everything! Job's wife told him to cuss God an' die!
(*A loud clap of thunder shakes the house.* RUFE *shrinks away toward the stairs.*)

RUFE. If you're a-goin' to talk blasphemy, 'ith a thundercloud a-comin' up, I'll have to leave you! (*He goes halfway up the stairs and stops.* MEG *puts on her bonnet and throws a shawl about her shoulders.*)

JUDE. Are you a-goin' out?

MEG. Yes! I cain't set here! (*JUDE prepares to follow her.*)

JUDE. I cain't neither. I'll go with you and see if they've found him. Ef Sid's dead, I'll kill the man 'at killed him—if it's my own brother!

MEG. That won't bring Sid back, but it 'ld leave the Hunts' hands clean. An' mebby it might keep the war from startin' ag'in. (*Hopelessly.*) But you won't do it. You'll find blood's thicker 'n water.

JUDE (*with resolution*). I will—I'll kill him 'ith my own hands!
(*They go out together.* RUFE *creeps down the stairs in a state of intense excitement.*)

RUFE. It 'ld be awful if she killed her own brother! I couldn't marry a woman that had done that! (*He goes to the door and makes a move as if to call to* JUDE, *but stops.*) She won't do it. She couldn't. It wouldn't be nachel. They'll see him first, anyhow. O God! Don't let her commit a sin that she could never git fergiveness fer! (*The kitchen door opens and* SID *enters.* RUFE *recoils with a cry of terror.*) A-a-a-ah! (SID *looks at him in amazement.*) Is that you, Sid?

SID. I sorter thought mebby it wus! What the hell's the matter with you? Are you havin' a fit?

RUFE. No, I'm all right! You come in kinder ghost-like an' I thought mebbe you might ha' been killed!

SID. You thought right. I might ha' been.

RUFE. What's happened to Andy?

SID. I dunno. Where's all the folks?

RUFE. I hain't seen 'em. I jist now come downstairs.

SID. They ain't all out o' the house in this storm?

RUFE. They must be out at the barn, lookin' arter the critters.

SID. Yeh, I reckon that's it.

RUFE. Sid, you didn't do nuthin' to rile Andy, did you?

SID. Not to my knowledge I didn't. My saddle geart wus loose an' I got off my horse to fix it. He seed me reach in my back pocket fer my knife, an' afore you could say scat he jerked out his pistol an' put a bullet through my hat!

RUFE. I shore am glad it 'us your hat, Sid, an' not you!

SID. Well, I ain't sorry, myself. (*He pokes his finger through the bullet hole in his hat.*) It's a good hat, but a air-hole er two won't hurt nothin' this sort o' weather.

RUFE. What 'd he do arter he shot at you?

SID. I didn't stay to see. When I found out he meant business I turned my horse loose an' cut fer the bushes. I'd like to know what's got into Andy.

RUFE. 'Tis quair the way he's actin'!

SID (*comes toward* RUFE *thoughtfully*). What 'd he say to you up thar while ago when you give him that licker—afore it all started?

RUFE (*starts violently*). Nothin'! He didn't say nothin', I tell you—not a word! (SID *looks at him suspiciously. He flares up in a fit of anger.*) You needn't try to accuse me! I never put him up to it! (*Sobbing.*) O God! I wish I 'us dead! Every time anything goes wrong it's me! I'm to blame!

SID. I ain't accusin' you o' puttin' him up to it! What I want to know is how his mind got to runnin' so strong on that old war 'twixt the Hunts an' the Lowries!

RUFE. You hyeard what I said about it here! That's all I know!

SID. Then what are you a-gittin' so excited about?

RUFE. It's enough to excite anybody, to have a thing like that throwed up to him! An' you needn't ax me no more questions, fer I ain't a-goin' to answer 'em!

SID. All right! I'll ask Andy when I see him!

RUFE. If you do he'll only tell you a mess o' lies! You cain't believe him!

SID. Oh, so you're afraid he'll tell lies on you?

RUFE. Any man 'll lie to save his own skin, ef you git 'im in a tight corner.

SID. Well, I'm a-goin' to ax him, 'cause I'm curious to know jist what them lies air that you're afraid he's a-goin' to tell. (*Going to window.*) You say the folks is at the barn? They ain't no light thar. Did my hoss come back?

RUFE. I dunno!

SID. Have they gone after Andy?

RUFE. I told you I don't know!

SID (*glances at gun rack*). The guns are gone! Jist what I thought! (*Starts to rush out.*)

RUFE (*stopping him*). Hold on, Sid; you cain't do nothin' 'bout it now! They must ha' left afore you come in, and they'd natchelly go the short way and be halfway over the mountain by this time! It's too late to stop 'em now!

SID. By God, you don't want me to stop 'em. I believe you knowed all along where they wus, only you 'us afraid o' what Andy could tell.

RUFE. That's right! Blame it on me! I don't wish him no harm! I don't wish nobody no harm!

SID. Does that telephone wire along the river run from the dam to the settlement over thar?

RUFE. Why? Are you a-thinkin' o' phonin' from the dam to head off Matt an' your gran'daddy?

SID. That's my business. As I mind it, the phone's in that tool house on a ledge right down under the dam!

RUFE. You'd never git to that house now! You'd have to walk out to it on boards across that sluice o' water! It's dangerous when the river ain't up! You might jist as well commit suicide as try it now! I wouldn't do it to save my own brother, let alone a man 'at had tried to kill me! An' all you'll git out o' Andy is a passel o' lies about me! Natchelly he'll say I agged him on—

SID (*seizing him by the throat*). An', damn you, I believe that's jist what you did do!

RUFE (*screams hysterically*). No, I didn't, Sid! I swear to God I didn't! All I said wus that you 'us a dangerous man an' not to cross you! That if you got started—

SID (*tightening his grip*). So! I'm right! You *wus* at the bottom of it. Did you do it apurpose?

RUFE. God forgive you, Sid, fer sich a thought!

SID. An' God damn you! (*He hurls* RUFE *into a corner of the room and rushes out at the front. A blinding flash of lightning envelops him.* RUFE *lies on his elbow, cowering in fear, till the thunder crashes and reverberates. Then suddenly he rises to his knees and clasps his hands in prayer.*)

RUFE. Did you hear what he said, God? I can put up 'ith his insults to me, but when it comes to blasphemin' Thy holy name it does look like it's time to call a halt. But You know what You're a-doin', God, an' I don't. I'm only a ignerunt sinner. You know more in a minute 'n I could ever know in a million years. It bothers me, though, Lord, that You let the wicked prosper more 'n the righteous. They git the best o' everything in this world now. It wusn't so in Bible times, Lord. Then You cut the wicked down afore the congregation o' Israel. An' the dread o' You an 'the fear o' You wus on all people. But now Your name is a byword among sinners. You hyeard that Yourself jist now. (*His voice has been gradually increasing in volume till it culminates in an emotional climax. He rises and goes to the door, trembling in every limb.*) I ain't presumin' to give You advice, Lord! You know Your own business. But if You'd make an edzample o' this blasphemer—if You'd strike him down in the abomination of his wickedness by a bolt o' lightnin', it 'ld serve as a warnin' to all like him. An' they'd be sich another revival o' 'ole-time religion in these mountains as You've never seed since the earthquake. (*He pauses again as if struck by a new thought. His knees gradually give way beneath him and he sinks to the floor.*) In Your Holy Word, Lord, I know You commanded your servants to slay all blasphemers. Mebby You think that's enough. An' mebby it ought to be. (*He pleads with great fervor.*) But I'd druther You'd do it Yourself, Lord. You can do it better 'n I can. An' it 'ld have more effect. But I want You to understand, God, that I ain't no coward. If it don't suit You to do it Yourself—I'll do it fer You—I don't keer if they hang me. You died fer me once, an' I'm willin' to die fer You if You want me to. They wus a time, Lord, when my proud heart said, "All o' self an' none o' Thee." Then You come a-knockin' at the door o' my sinful soul an' I whispered, "Some o' self an' some o' Thee." But that's all changed now, Lord. I'm Yourn an' You are mine. An' the burden o' my song now is, "None o' self an' all o' Thee." You can do with me what You please, Lord. If it's Your will that this blasphemer shall die, I've got a whole box o' dynamite out in the store, with a time fuse long enough so I can git back here afore it explodes. I can blow up the dam while he's under thar a-telephonin', an' the waters o' Your wrath 'll sweep over him like they did over Pharaoh an' his hosts in olden times! An' the fear o' You an' the dread o' You 'll be on all nations ag'in! (*A heavy gust of wind strikes the house, followed by terrific thunder and lightning.* RUFE *rises to a standing position, his knees trembling. As the noise of the thunder dies away his fear is transformed into joy. He stands firmly on his feet and looks toward heaven, his voice ringing out triumphantly.*) I hear You, Lord! An', like Joshua o' old, I go to do Your will! (*He rushes out.*)

Curtain.

ACT THREE

The same scene, a quarter of an hour later. It is now totally dark outside. The only light within is a warm glow from the fireplace. The storm has settled into a steady downpour of rain. There are still occasional flashes of lightning mingled with the distant rumbling of thunder.

MATT appears at the front door, driving ANDY before him at the point of a gun. DAVID follows them into the house, shaking the water from his hat at the door. ANDY seats himself, laughing defiantly in a mood of reckless despair.

MATT (*glances about the room, then calls upstairs*). H'llo! H'llo, Sid! (*Looks at ANDY.*) Hm!

DAVID. 'Parently they ain't *nobody* here.

MATT (*goes to the kitchen door and calls*). Sid! H'llo! (*Comes back, his eyes on ANDY*). Jist as I expected!

ANDY (*tauntingly, in a spirit of bravado*). Well, I must ha' been a better shot 'n I thought I wus!

MATT (*with a growl of rage*). Yeh, an' now 'at that p'int is settled— (*He brings his gun to bear on ANDY significantly.*)

DAVID (*seizes the barrel of the gun and thrusts it upward*). Hold on, Matt! I've seed more fightin' 'n you ever did. An' we ain't a-goin' to start another row 'ith the Lowries lessen we have to. Sid might ha' come back, an' then set out ag'in arter us. We could ha' missed him easy enough if he 'us on hossback when we took that short cut across the mountain.

MATT (*reluctantly*). All right! I'll see if his hoss is still at the barn. (*He goes out through the kitchen.*)

DAVID. Andy, if I 'us as near hell as you air, I wouldn't try to hurry matters none.

ANDY (*chants derisively*). If I git thar afore you do I'll tell 'em you're a-comin' too!

DAVID (*looks at him understandingly*). Hmn! (*He seats himself, his gun across his knees, ready for quick action.*)

ANDY (*gazes at DAVID defiantly till the silence begins to get on his nerves*). Well, ole Rooster! Whyn't you say sompen? How's your whiskers?

DAVID. They're 'bout as common, Andy. How's everything 'ith you?

ANDY. Fine as a fiddle. I never felt better in my life.

DAVID. You're a-lookin' well.

ANDY. That's more 'n I can say fer you. (*Laughs.*) Do you know what you look like, a-settin' thar 'ith that ole lock, stock an' bar'l that you call a gun?

DAVID. I expect I look a right smart like Johnny-on-the-spot to some folks I could name.

ANDY. Not to me, you don't! You look ed-zackly like a crow sign in a watermillon patch! You ought to hire yourself out fer one! It 'ld give you sompen to do an' wouldn't skeer the crows none!

DAVID. I've skeered bigger game 'n crows in my time.

ANDY. You've never skeered me—if that's what you're a-drivin' at!

DAVID. You cain't fool me, Andy. A· man don't work as hard as you're a-workin' now to prove he ain't skeered unless he is.
(*RUFE rushes up to the door, panting from exhaustion. He sees DAVID and stops suddenly in the doorway.*)

DAVID. You seem to be in a hurry, Rufe.

RUFE (*confused*). Yeh—I—I wanted to git in out o' the rain. It's got so I have sore throat every time I git wet.

DAVID. Where's Meg an' Jude?

RUFE. They stepped up the road a little piece to see if they could find out anything about Sid.

DAVID. Then he didn't come back here?

RUFE (*hesitates, confusedly*). Who—Sid? If he did I didn't see him! An' I've been out o' the house fer jist a minute. I jist stepped out to the spring an' back to see if the milk box 'us flooded. (*Eagerly.*) Didn't *you* see ner hear nothin' of him?

DAVID (*glances at* ANDY). Nothin' we could count on.

RUFE. Well, he couldn't ha' come home 'thout me— (*He sees* ANDY *and starts guiltily.*) Oh! Air you here, Andy?

ANDY. Yeh, I'm here. I got a invitation I jist couldn't refuse.

RUFE (*tentatively, to* DAVID). Couldn't Andy tell you nothin' 'bout Sid?

ANDY (*significantly*). I could, Rufe, but didn't! All I told 'em wus that I shot at him, an' as fur as I could see I missed him. (RUFE *breathes more easily.* ANDY *continues in the same spirit of bravado, glancing at* DAVID.) But they wouldn't ha' been no doubt about it if I hadn't drunk so much pop-skull that my hand 'us shaky!

RUFE. You ought to thank the Lord you didn't hit him, Andy!

ANDY. No! If I didn't hit him it 'us the licker saved him this time, not the Lord! (MATT *enters through the kitchen door, carrying a lighted lantern.* RUFE *shrinks back into the corner near the bed.*)

MATT. He ain't at the barn, an' the hoss is in the stall! Does that satisfy you? (*He makes a menacing move toward* ANDY.)

DAVID (*stopping him*). Not edzackly. Arter all, Sid might ha' been crippled so he couldn't git home. Afore you start shootin' you'd better take the lantern an' search that patch o' woods. I'll 'tend to Andy.

MATT. In that case we'd orter tie him up. If you ever take your eyes offen him it 'ld be jist like him to snatch that ole gun an' blow your brains out.

DAVID. I'll take my chance o' that. But we can tie him if it 'll ease your mind any. I'll git a hame-string. (*He goes into the kitchen. There is a brief silence.* MATT *places the lantern on the floor, keeping his eyes on* ANDY *and his gun ready.*)

RUFE (*to break the silence*). I certainly do hope 'at nothin' ain't happened to Sid! (*A loud explosion is heard in the distance.* RUFE *starts with an expression of intense excitement.*)

MATT. What the devil was that?

RUFE (*slinks toward the door*). It must ha' been thunder! That's all it wus! It couldn't ha' been nothin' else! (*He slips out and is seen rushing away past the window.*)

MATT (*as if to himself*). Sounded to me like blastin'.

ANDY. Mebby it 'us the stopper blowed out o' hell!

MATT. You'll be able to tell more about that a little later when you git thar! (*He glares at* ANDY *menacingly.* JUDE *enters from the kitchen, followed by* MEG *with a lantern, which she places on the table.*)

ANDY. Well, Sis, have you come fer the funeral.
(*She turns away from him to conceal her emotion.*)

MATT (*to* MEG). You didn't see ner hear nothin' o' Sid?

MEG. No! What happened to him?

MATT. That's what I'm a-tryin' to find out.

MEG (*looks at* ANDY). Don't *he* know?

MATT. 'Course he knows, but he ain't a-goin' to tell us tell he has to!
(MEG *looks at* ANDY *with an expression of dumb hopelessness. He avoids her eyes.*)

JUDE (*comes between* MATT *and* ANDY *in a burst of rage*). Why don't you tell what you done with him?

ANDY. Why don't a mewly cow have horns?

MEG (*despairingly to* MATT). Couldn't you git nothin' out of him?

MATT. Nothin' but a passel o' words!

ANDY (*apologetically, his eyes on* MEG). I told you I shot at him an' missed him!

JUDE. If you missed him, whar is he? Why don't he come home? (*He looks at her enigmatically and whistles a jig. She flies into a rage.*) Stop that an' answer me er I'll— (*She seizes* MATT's *gun as if to take it from him.*)

ANDY. Aw right, Sis, blaze away! But I'd ruther you'd let Matt do it. He's a better shot 'n you are. (*She releases the gun.*) As fer Sid—at the rate he 'us a-goin', the last time I seen him he'd ought to be in Chiny by now, if he hain't run hisself to death.

MATT. That's a lie on the face of it!

ANDY. Well then, I killed him an' buried him in the sand. How's that fer the truth? (MEG *and* JUDE *turn away with a gesture of revulsion.*)

MATT. You'd be closer to it, in my opinion, if you said you killed him an' throwed him over the cliff into the river!

ANDY. That *would* ha' been less trouble 'n buryin' him if I'd ha' hit him.

MATT (*sarcastically*). You missed him apurpose, I reckon!

ANDY. No, Matt! Don't git no wrong notions about me! I missed him because I couldn't hit him!

MATT. It's jist as well you ain't axin' fer mercy, fer all you're a-goin' to git is jestice —an' plenty of it!

ANDY. You don't have to tell me that. I know you're a-goin' to send me to hell the short way. But I don't want you to make no mistake about one thing: when I go I'll go a-standin' up on my hind legs. I won't go a-crawlin' ner a-whinin' fer mercy. (*Glancing at* MEG *and* JUDE *again.*) To the best o' my knowledge an' belief, I didn't kill Sid. That's the truth. (*He turns to*

MATT *belligerently.*) But I tried my damnedest to kill him! An' that's the truth, too!

JUDE (*accusingly*). What 'd you have ag'in' him?

ANDY (*enigmatically, after a brief silence*). He turned his toes out too fur when he walked.
(MEG *and* JUDE *turn away angrily.*)

MATT (*restraining himself with difficulty*). Is that the best reason you can think of?

ANDY. It's good enough, ain't it?

MATT (*brings the gun to bear on him*). What do you want us to tell your folks?

ANDY. Jist say I got drunk an' turned my toes *up* too fur!

DAVID (*enters with the hame-strings and hands one to* MATT). Here! You tie his feet. (MATT *lays his gun down and begins tying* ANDY's *feet to the chair.*) I'll 'tend to his arms. (*Stretching one of the hame-strings out as he seizes* ANDY's *arms.*) I reckon these air long enough.

MATT. You've been long enough a-gittin' 'em.

ANDY. Yeh. A little more an' Matt 'ld ha' fixed things so's you wouldn't ha' needed 'em.

MATT. It wouldn't ha' been no mistake, nuther. If he didn't kill Sid, he tried to!

ANDY. Yeh, I told you it wusn't my fault I didn't.
(MATT, *who has finished tying him, grabs his gun, with a growl of rage.*)

DAVID (*cuffs* ANDY). Keep your mouth shet! (*To* MATT.) Go on! They'll be plenty o' time to settle 'ith him when you git back! (MATT *takes the lantern and goes out, closing the door. There is a brief pause. The roar of rushing water is vaguely perceptible in the distance.*)

JUDE (*listens*). D' you hear that?

DAVID (*with a puzzled expression*). Yeh. It must be another cloud a-comin' up.

JUDE. I never hyeard a cloud roar like that.

DAVID. 'Tis quair. Sounds like wind er hail.

MEG. It don't sound like that to me. I dunno what it is.
(RUFE *is seen rushing past the window. He flings the door open and stands with his hands above his head, pointing toward heaven, his eyes rolling in a fine frenzy of excitement.*)

RUFE. It's come! It's come!

DAVID. What's come?

RUFE. The day o' His Wrath—when the saints an' the sinners shall be parted right an' left! (*He shakes his finger at* ANDY.) Brother, will you be able to stan' on that day? That's the question every man here's got to answer—an' every woman, too!

DAVID. You speak as one havin' authority, Rufe.

RUFE. I speak what I know!

DAVID. Have you been up to heaven to git the latest news?

RUFE. No, I hain't been to heaven yit! But I've been about my Master's business!

DAVID. Well, I hope fer His sake that you 'tended to it better 'n you do to ourn.

RUFE. I know I done what He told me! That's all I know—an' all I want to know —on this earth!

MEG (*despairingly*). I reckon that's enough fer any of us. But I *would* like to know what happened to Sid. I don't feel that I can ever close my eyes in sleep er death tell I find out.

RUFE (*starts violently*). If he's in that patch o' woods where Andy left him, it's too late to find him! The river's all over everything! Look! (*He opens the door and points toward it.*)

MEG. Oh! Is that what's a-makin' the noise?

RUFE. Yeh, it's a-sweepin' everything afore it!
(MEG, DAVID, *and* JUDE *go outside and stand gazing in wonder at the flood.*)

ANDY (*calls excitedly, under his breath*). Rufe! Come here! (RUFE *turns and looks at him.*) Quick! Take my knife—it's in my right-hand pocket—an' cut these things! (RUFE *moves toward the door, pretending not to hear.*) Did you hear what I said?

RUFE. Yeh, I hyeard you, Andy.

ANDY. Then hurry up!

RUFE. They'd know I done it, Andy!

ANDY. No, they won't! I'll take keer o' you! I've stuck by you so fur an' hain't told 'em nothin'! An' this may be your only chance to help me. If the river's over that patch o' woods Matt 'll be back here in a minute. Come on! We can go down the cellar stairs an' git out! They won't be watchin' fer us thar! The outside cellar door ain't locked, is it?

RUFE. I dunno, Andy! But Matt 'ld be shore to ketch me! I'll do anything in my power, Andy! (*Starts to kneel.*) I'll pray fer you!

ANDY (*shouts recklessly, unable to conceal his contempt*). No! You needn't do no prayin' fer me! But they's one little turn you can do!

RUFE (*eagerly*). All right, Andy! I'll do anything you say!

ANDY. Then step down to hell an' tell the devil to have the place good an' hot afore *we* git thar! Fer you're a-goin' with me!

RUFE (*alarmed by* ANDY's *manner*). You ain't a-goin' to tell 'em what I told you?

ANDY. I'm a-goin' to tell 'em all I know— an' a little bit more—if you don't turn me loose dam' quick!

RUFE. But you put yourself on oath, Andy!

ANDY. It's a poor fool 'at can put hisself on oath an' cain't take hisself off!

RUFE. Andy, don't say things like that! You may not have much longer to live! An' if you break your oath an' tell 'em, you'll lose all chance o' gittin' to heaven!

ANDY. Heaven be damned! I ain't like you, Rufe! We're both a-goin' to hell, but I'm a-goin' thar by choice!

(MATT *enters through the kitchen with the lantern and puts his gun in the rack.* MEG, JUDE, *and* DAVID, *seeing him, return from the porch.*)

MEG. Couldn't you go no further?

MATT. No, they's been a cloudbust up the river. A wall o' water swep' down past me ten foot high. I jist managed to git out o' the way, when it struck the foot o' the cliffs and shook 'em like a earthquake. (*He starts toward the kitchen door.*)

MEG. Whar 're you a-goin' now?

MATT. Out to the barn to pen up the cattle afore they git washed away. (*He goes out.*)

JUDE (*sobbing*). Oh! It jist seems like I cain't never stand it to set here—an' the river a-coverin' up everything out thar!

DAVID. Don't fret 'bout the river! The wust it ever does is to come high enough to flood the cellar a little. We're allus safe here.

JUDE. 'Tain't us I'm a-thinkin' about!

RUFE. It certainly is a quair time—everything a-comin' at once!

ANDY. Yeh, it's Jedgment Day! (*He sings mockingly, his eyes on* RUFE.)

Are you ready, are you ready fer the comin' o' the Lord?
Are you livin' as he bids you in His Word —in His Word?
Are you walkin' in the light? Is your hope o' heaven bright?
Could you welcome Him to-night? Not by a dam' sight!

RUFE. Andy, I want you to stop that sort o' thing!

ANDY. Oh! I 'us afeard I 'us a-trampin' on your toes!

RUFE. If it 'us jist mine you 'us a-trampin' on I wouldn't say a word! But it ain't! It's His—up yonder!

ANDY. Ha! ha! I didn't know you 'us a-standin' in His shoes, Rufe!

RUFE. You'd a heap better 'umble your proud heart an' quit mockin' an' revilin', Andy! The Good Book says that them that reviles God's handiwork shall die! (*With a convulsive gesture.*) An' they shall, too!

ANDY. Yeh, when their time comes—like you an' me an' everybody else.

RUFE (*in a sort of prophetic ecstasy*). That time has come! This is the beginnin' of a new world! To-morrow 'll be the dawn of a new day!

ANDY. It allus has been!

MEG (*provoked beyond endurance*). That ain't what he means, an' you know it!

RUFE. Have patience with him, Meg. We may snatch him like a brand from the burnin' yit. On that day, Andy, the wicked 'll be scattered like chaff afore a mighty wind, an' there 'll be weepin' an' gnashin' o' teeth! Selah!

ANDY. Toot! Toot! Hurrah fer hell!

MEG. You blasphemer! David, why don't you make him shet his mouth?

DAVID. I know the lad too well to think could break his sperit short o' killin' him. An' I ain't a-goin' to do that tell I find out fer shore, no matter how hard he tries to make me. (*He seats himself in the armchair, his gun across his knee.*) Arter all, Meg, the Lord's will's too big a thing fer any one man to git a strangle hold on it. Rufe's dead certain that God allus sees eye to eye 'ith him on every question. Fer all we know, God hisself may consider *that* more blasphemous 'n what Andy's a-doin'.

RUFE (*his face distorted with malignant rage, shakes his finger at* DAVID). Woe unto thee, Chorazin! Woe unto thee, Bethsady! Fer—

DAVID (*springs up menacingly*). Woe unto you if you don't quit bawlin' Scripture in my years! (RUFE *recoils, taking refuge behind* MEG. DAVID *seats himself again.*) You don't know what you're a-talkin' about, nohow! If your brains 'us turned to dynamite, they wouldn't be enough of 'em to blow the hat offen your head! (*To* ANDY, *with a puzzled expression.*) Sompen outen the ordinary's happened to him!

ANDY (*his eyes on* RUFE). Yeh, an' he don't seem to want to tell about it!

MEG. If you'd ever experienced real religion yourselves, you'd know what's the matter with him!

DAVID. Humph! What makes you think what he's got's real religion?

MEG. By their fruits ye shall know 'em. When I mourned fer Sid you an' Matt didn't bring me no comfort. All you thought of wus vengeance. But I feel comforted some now (*she pats* RUFE's *hands protectingly*) an' Rufe done it.

DAVID. Shucks! If comfort in time o' trouble 'us religion, most folks could git more of it outen a bottle o' licker 'n they could outen the Bible! (*He looks straight at* RUFE *as he says this.*)

RUFE (*angrily*). Are you accusin' me o' bein' loaded?

DAVID. Right up to the gills, Rufe. You're drunk on sompen. I dunno whether it's licker er religion.

ANDY. What difference does it make? One's jist as dangerous as t'other when it gits into a cracked head.

JUDE. The time 'll come, Andy, when you'll wish you'd prayed 'stid o' scoffin'!

MEG. Yeh, you'll be beggin' Rufe yit fer a drop o' water to cool your tongue in Torment!

RUFE. Let 'em revile me! I don't keer! Let 'em persecute me, lie about me, crucify me! I don't keer what they do! Fer verily I say unto you it 'll be better fer Sodom an' Gomorrow on the day o' Jedgment than fer them! (*He looks at* ANDY *and* DAVID *significantly.*) An' that day ain't fur off as it has been! If I 'us a mind to I could tell you things that 'ld curdle your blood an' dry up the marrer in your bones!

MEG (*credulously*). Have you seen a vision, Rufe?

RUFE (*rolls his eyes mystically toward* ANDY). What I've seen I've seen! He that hath years to hear let him hear! (*He pauses and gazes about him impressively in the fashion of one "possessed of the Spirit."*) An', lo, there wus a great earthquake! An' the sun become black as sackcloth o' hair an' the moon become as blood! An' the stars o' heaven fell into the earth, even as a fig tree casteth her untimely figs when she is a-shaken of a mighty wind! An' the heavens parted as a scroll when it is rolled together! An' every mountain an' island were moved out o' their places! An' the kings o' the earth, an' the great men, an' the rich men, an' the chief captains, an' the mighty men hid theirselves in the dens an' in the rocks o' the mountains; an' said to the rocks an' the mountains, fall on us an' hide us from the face of Him— (*He has gradually worked himself up to an emotional singsong like that of the old-fashioned mountain preacher.* MEG *and* JUDE *have been swaying rhythmically in tune with his voice. They now join in shouting* "Halleluyah!" "Amen!" "Blessed be His Name!" *etc. Inspired by this, he continues with increasing fervor, losing all control of himself*)—that sitteth on the throne—ah! An' from the wrath o' the Lamb—ah! Fer the gr-r-r-eat day o' His wrath has come—ah—!

ANDY. Whoa, ole hoss, er you'll bust your bellyband! When I tell my religious experience I won't have to stop to suck wind! I'll spit it out quick!

RUFE (*shakes his finger at* ANDY *impressively*). If you'd seen what I've seen an' hyeard what I've hyeard your tongue 'ld cleave to the roof o' your mouth! Woe unto the covenant breaker, fer—

ANDY. No, Rufe! You cain't come that on me! Oath er no oath, my tongue won't cleave wuth a dam! It's loose at both ends an' it's a-gittin' looser every minute! If you don't spill the truth, I'm a-goin' to! An' that mighty—

RUFE (*frantically, to* MEG *and* JUDE). Don't listen to him! His mouth is foul 'ith blasphemy!

ANDY. Bretherin an' sisterin, listen!—

RUFE (*begins to sing and drowns* ANDY's *voice*).
"I am bound fer the Promised Land! (*He swings his arms camp-meeting fashion. The women join in and sing with great fervor.*)

I am bound fer the Promised Land!
Oh, who will come an' go with me?
I am bound fer the Promised Land!"

ANDY (*with mingled admiration and contempt*). I dunno what the devil 'll do 'ith you, Rufe! One thing's certain, they ain't no place in hell hot enough fer you!

MEG. David, I've stood all that I'm a-goin' to! If you won't do nothin' about it, I will!

DAVID (*rising*). Well, what do you want me to do?

MEG. I don't keer—jist so you git him out o' my sight!

RUFE. Whyn't you put him in the cellar? (*He catches* ANDY'S *eye and gives him a significant look.* ANDY, *who is about to speak, interprets this to mean that* RUFE *has decided to help him escape, and remains silent.*)

MEG. We can. That's more like the place whar he'd ought ha' been put in the first place.

DAVID (*starts untying* ANDY). All right, Meg, I'll 'tend to him. But you'd better git me the key to the outside door, so I can lock him in, case he breaks loose. (*She goes into the kitchen.*)

ANDY (*looks at* RUFE *significantly*). Well, Rufe, in partin' lemme wish you a long life (*menacingly*) an' plenty o' time to save yourself from the hell fire you're so skeered of.

RUFE (*with a look of understanding*). Don't you worry about that, Andy. I'll pray fer you—an' do anything else I can. (*MEG returns from the kitchen.*)

DAVID. Did you git that key?

MEG. Yeh, here 'tis. (*Vindictively to* ANDY.) An' I hope you lock him in tight!

ANDY (*sings as* DAVID *starts toward the cellar with him*).

Wonderful love! Oh, wonderful love!
I'll sing of its fullness forever!
I've found the way that leadeth above!
It's the way down into the cellar!

(*He disappears into the cellar with* DAVID. MEG *goes ahead of them with the lantern and lights the way.* DAVID *closes the door behind him.*)

MEG (*in the cellar*). Lord! The water's risin' in here! That ain't from the river?

DAVID. No, I reckon it's jist a wet-weather spring!
(*RUFE goes to the door and looks out. He is evidently pleased by what he sees.* JUDE, *puzzled by his manner, goes to the door and turns back, startled and alarmed.*)

JUDE. Look! The river! Did you see it?

RUFE. Yeh, I seed it!

JUDE. It's 'most up to the porch steps!

RUFE. Well, 'tain't nothin' to git excited about. We're safe. An' Andy's all right, too. It 'ld have to come lots higher afore it could harm him.
(*The outside cellar door is heard to slam.* JUDE *steps out on the porch and looks in the direction of the noise.*)

JUDE (*calls*). Whar you a-goin', Meg—out to the barn?

MEG. Yeh.

JUDE. Wait a minute an' I'll help you.

DAVID. No, Jude, you stay under shelter!
(*JUDE stands on the porch, gazing out into the darkness.* RUFE *glances at her, then goes over to the cellar door and opens it cautiously, keeping an eye on* JUDE.)

RUFE (*calls softly*). Andy! Is the water comin' in?

ANDY (*guardedly, from the cellar*). Yeh, it's jist startin'. You'd better hurry an' turn me loose afore they git back!

RUFE. I cain't right now. I think I hear Matt comin'. Don't worry 'bout drowndin'. It's jist a little rain water a-seepin' in.

ANDY (*roars angrily*). That's a lie, you son of a sheep-killin' bitch!
(*RUFE slams the door to quickly and looks at* JUDE *to see if she has heard.*)

JUDE (*comes inside*). What 'us that Andy 'us a-hollerin' about?

RUFE. Nothin'—Jist more cussin'. Don't grieve about him, Jude. Everybody cain't be saved. Some are born fer glory an' some fer shame. Andy seems to be one o' them that 'us born fer shame.

JUDE (*sinks on the bed and sobs despairingly*). 'Tain't Andy I'm a-grievin' about!

RUFE. Then it's him—Sid?

JUDE (*nods brokenly*). Yeh!

RUFE (*closes the outside door, then seats himself on the bed beside her*). Don't grieve 'bout him, Jude. He wusn't born fer glory, neither. You ought to build your hopes on a firmer foundation. They's still treasure in heaven if you'll seek it the right way.

JUDE (*half sobbing*). That's what I'm a-tryin' to do, Rufe! But all my faith—everything—seems gone now!

RUFE (*moving closer, gradually*). That's a good sign. The darkest hour o' the sperit is allus jist afore dawn. Think, Jude, what a friend we have in Him! Oh, what peace we often forfeit—oh, what needless pain we bear—all because we do not carry everything to Him in prayer!

JUDE. I want to carry it to Him, but I cain't! Seems like I'm froze up inside!

RUFE (*working himself into an emotional singsong again*). I know what's the matter 'ith you, Jude, you ain't a-trustin' Him! (*He touches her on the shoulder, gradually stealing his arm around her.*) All you got to do is to trust Him—fully trust Him —sweetly trust Him—

JUDE (*swaying with the same emotional ecstasy as before*). I see! Halleluyah!

RUFE. That's right! He'll save you! (*She sways with the rhythm of his words, whispering, "Halleluyah" ecstatically.*) You're on the right track. Go right on trustin' Him. He'll comfort you!

JUDE (*louder*). Halleluyah! Bless His name! Halleluyah! Halleluyah!

RUFE. That's it! You're a-gittin' right now! Jist imagine you're a-leanin' on the everlastin' arms! (*She lays her head on his shoulder in a state of half consciousness.*) That's the way! He'll comfort you! (*He has gradually inclined his face toward hers as if fascinated by the singsong of his own voice. Suddenly he kisses her passionately on the lips. She awakes from her stupor and stands gazing at him with an expression of intense surprise.*)

RUFE. Don't look at me like that, Jude! It's perfectly all right! (*Dropping into the emotional cadence again.*) The Scripture says fer the brethren an' sisteren to greet one another with a holy kiss! That's all it wus, Jude—jist a holy kiss! Go right on trustin' Him—fully trustin'—sweetly trustin'—

JUDE (*yielding to her former mood*). Halleluyah! Halleluyah!

RUFE. Let them that's subjec' to the law live by it. Me an' you ain't subjec' to it. We've been redeemed!

JUDE. Glory! Halleluyah!

RUFE (*slipping his arm around her again*). It's all right, Jude! 'Tain't no harm fer the Lord's lambs to play together! Go right on trustin'!

JUDE. Glory! Glory! Halleluyah!
(*Some one is heard entering the kitchen. He releases* JUDE *and stands by the door innocently.*)

MEG (*enters from the kitchen*). Jude, if you want sompen to do you can come out an' help me move my young turkeys. The water's might' nigh up to the coops! An' David an' Matt are busy wrastlin' 'ith them calves.

JUDE. All right, Meg.

MEG. An' while I'm here David said fer us to fix Andy so he could keep above water if the river keeps on a-comin' up like it is now.

RUFE. You an' Jude go ahead. I'll fix Andy.

MEG. Can you do it by yourself 'thout lettin' him git loose?

RUFE. Yeh, I can manage him. I won't untie his hands. You go on an' 'tend to your turkeys while you can.

(MEG *and* JUDE *go out taking the lantern. The only light in the room is the glow from the fireplace.*)

RUFE (*hesitates, then goes to the cellar door and calls softly*). Andy! (*Getting no reply, he lifts his voice slightly.*) Andy, you ain't drownded, are you?

ANDY (*roars with suppressed rage*). No, you ring-tailed runt! An' I ain't a-goin' to drown tell I've told 'em the truth about that shootin'! You'd better git your second verse ready! You're a-goin' to need it!

RUFE (*closes the door in a panic of fear, hesitates a moment, then opens it and calls down insinuatingly*). All I wanted, Andy, wus to tell you that if you'll gimme your solemn word not to tell, I might mebby could help you now!

ANDY (*defiantly*). Not by a dam' sight! I'm a-goin' to hell a-straddle o' your neck!
(RUFE *closes the door and backs away, paralyzed with fear. He thinks a moment, then rushes to the gun rack, takes down the shotgun, and goes over to the light of the fire to see if it is loaded. It is, and he moves toward the cellar door with it. But he stops halfway and comes back as if he had forgotten something.*)

RUFE (*drops on his knees, still holding the gun*). O Lord, Thy will be done, not mine! I won't kill him lessen You want me to!
(SID *enters at the front. His clothes are torn and his face and arms are bruised and smeared with mud. He stops on seeing* RUFE *and is about to make his presence known, but changes his mind and steps back toward the door.*)

RUFE. If it's your will that he shall die too—

SID (*in a deep voice*). Mene, mene, tekel upharsin!

RUFE (*not daring to look around*). Is that you, God?

SID. I'm the ghost o' Sid Hunt!

RUFE (*turns fearfully and sees* SID). Who are you a-lookin fer? (SID *looks straight at him without speaking.* RUFE, *still on his knees, shrinks back in the corner near the bed.*) What are you a-doin' here? You don't need to be a-walkin'!

SID. I've got to ha'nt somebody. You know I didn't die a natchel death.

RUFE. All death is natchel—if you look at it right!

SID. An' all ha'ntin's natchel, too, if you look at it right.

RUFE (*shrinks back still further in a paroxysm of fear*). You'd better go back whar you come from!

SID. I've got orders to find out who murdered me.

RUFE. Them orders may ha' come from below! You don't have to pay no 'tention to 'em!

SID. They come from above.

RUFE (*cowering*). Who is it you got orders to ha'nt?

SID. You!

RUFE (*recoiling hysterically*). I didn't do it! I swear on the Bible I didn't!

SID (*takes a step toward him*). If you didn't, who did? I'm a-goin' to ha'nt you till I find out.

RUFE (*beside himself with fear*). Then I'll tell you who done it! It 'us Him—up yonder!

SID. God?

RUFE (*nods his head in speechless awe*).

SID. How d' you know?

RUFE. I 'us thar when it happened!

SID. Will you swear that to His face afore the bar o' jedgment?

RUFE. I'll swear the truth to anybody's face anywhere any time!

SID. Then come on. (*He beckons to* RUFE *and moves toward the door.*)

RUFE. Whar 're you a-goin'?

SID. Up thar whar He is, afore the bar o' jedgment.

RUFE (*draws back in terror*). No, Sid! I cain't! I cain't go up thar!

SID. What's the reason you cain't?

RUFE. I—I ain't dead yit!

SID. Oh, that's all right. I'll fix you up when we git outside.

RUFE. What do you want me to go up thar fer now—like this—when I ain't ready?

SID. Fer a witness ag'inst Him.

RUFE. Him—up yonder! You cain't try Him! He's Almighty!

SID. He's almighty tired o' bein' the scapegoat fer folks that do all the meanness they can think of an' call it religion!

RUFE (*whispers in awed tones*). Have you seen Him, Sid? (SID *looks at him with Sphinx-like expression.*) Did He say I killed you?

SID. I'll tell you what He said when I git you face to face with Him.

RUFE (*draws back*). No! If He says I done it, that settles it! Let Him be true, though every man a liar! I've allus said that an' I say it still! But what He meant, Sid, wus that I 'us his instrument!

SID (*grimly*). I see! You done it, but you done it all fer His sake! (*He goes toward him menacingly.*)

RUFE (*backs away, shrieking with terror*). Don't kill me! I tell you it 'us the power o' the Lord a-workin' in me!

ANDY (*shouts from the cellar in the same tone as* RUFE's). Pray, brethren, pray! The day is breakin'!

SID (*stops, surprised*). Is that Andy?

ANDY (*sings, mockingly*).

Roll, Jordan, roll! Roll, Jordan, roll!
You'd orter be in the cellar now
Jist to hear ole Jordan roll!

SID. What's Andy a-doin' in the cellar?

RUFE. Your folks put him thar!

SID. What fer?

RUFE. They thought mebby it 'us him that murdered you!

SID. Then you didn't tell 'em it 'us Him up yonder that done it?

RUFE. I hain't —yit!

SID. No, an' I reckon you hain't found time to tell 'em 'bout seein' me alive after the shootin', neither?

RUFE. Andy meant to kill you, Sid! An' that's the same thing! They wus murder in his heart!

SID. Yeh, an' I'm a-goin' to find out why! (*He opens the cellar door and disappears inside.*)

RUFE (*rushes forward hysterically*). He won't tell you the truth! They ain't no use ha'ntin' him!
(SID *closes the door in his face. He stands trembling a moment, undecided what to do. His eye falls on the bag which he had left by the table in the afternoon. He seizes this and rushes out at the front door. As he reaches the porch and sees that the water is up to the door, he recoils and comes back frantically and throws himself face downward on the bed.*)

DAVID (*enters from the kitchen, speaking to* MEG *and* JUDE, *who are just behind him*). I've never seed the water up to the kitchen doorstep afore. At this rate— (*Seeing* RUFE.) Well, Rufe, you seem to be improvin' each shinin' hour.
(MEG, JUDE, *and* MATT *enter with the two lanterns, which they place on the table.*)

RUFE (*rises from the bed, trembling in every limb*). I've seen Sid!

MEG. Sid! (*They all stop and look at him, for an explanation.*)

RUFE. His ghost! Right here in this room! I jist been talkin' to him!

MEG. Glory be! Then he's walkin'!

JUDE. What'd he say, Rufe?

RUFE (*starts*). I don't mind it all now!

MEG (*swaying back and forth in a frenzy of excitement*). Did he look natchel, Rufe? An' whar'd he go?

DAVID. Shucks, Meg! Don't let him git you all worked up over nothin'! He's lost what little mind he ever had!

MEG. Other folks has seen ghosts an' talked to 'em—folks 'ith jist as good sense as you've got!

DAVID. But only folks that believe in 'em. It's quair they don't come after the ole doubtin' Thomases like me once an' a while.

MEG. How'd he appear to you, Rufe?

RUFE. I dunno! (*The cellar door opens.* RUFE *recoils in horror.*) Here he comes now!
(ANDY *comes out of the cellar amid general consternation.*)

ANDY (*starts for* RUFE). Hark, brother, hark! The dead are wakin'!
(RUFE *retreats to the farthest corner of the room.*)

MATT (*steps in front of* ANDY). Here! Who turned you loose?

ANDY. Ax the ha'nt o' the man I murdered! (*Calls back into the cellar.*) Come on out, old ghost! Nobody ain't a-goin' to hurt you! I left all my silver bullets at home!

SID (*enters from the cellar*). You couldn't hit me if you had 'em, jedgin' by the samples o' your shootin' I've seen.

JUDE. Sid! (*She takes a step toward him and stops.*) Is it you er your ghost?

SID. It's me, all right. (*He holds out his arms toward her.*) Here, tetch me an' see! (*She touches him cautiously, then throws her arms about him.*)

MEG. An' we all thought you 'us dead! (*She begins to weep hysterically on his shoulder.*)

SID. Now, Mam, don't you an' Jude spill no more water on me! I'm wet enough as 'tis!

MEG (*trying to control herself*). Ain't you hurt *nowhar?*

SID. No! Andy couldn't hit a barn door! (ANDY *looks at the floor sheepishly.*)

MEG (*flaring up at the thought*). Well, it wusn't his fault he didn't kill you!

MATT. Yeh, he said so hisself! (*He glares at* ANDY *menacingly.*)

SID (*goes over to* ANDY *and places his hand on his shoulder*). Now, folks, don't go pickin' on Andy. A man o' his marksmanship deserves a lot o' sympathy. (*He glances at* RUFE.) Besides, we've been swoppin' experiences down thar in the cellar, an' we've 'bout decided it wusn't edzackly *his* fault that he shot at me.

MATT (*takes a step toward* .RUFE). Wus Rufe mixed up in that?

ANDY. Yeh, an' that ain't the worst o' his troubles! (*He goes toward* RUFE, *rolling back his sleeves significantly.*) Pray, brother, pray! The day is breaking!
(*With a suppressed cry of terror* RUFE *runs over to* MEG *for protection.*)

MEG. You keep your hands offen him!

JUDE. Yeh, you needn't go packin' it on Rufe jist to save your own skin!

SID. Now, Jude! Wait a minute! Mebby you'll change your tune when Rufe gits through explainin' jist how I come to get drownded.

JUDE. Drownded!

SID. Yeh. This wet ain't all rain. I been in swimmin' sence I seen you last.

MEG. La! What in the world, Sid?

SID. It all happened when that new dam give way.

DAVID. Did that new dam bust?

SID. It didn't edzackly bust. (*He looks straight at* RUFE.) It wus blowed up with dynamite! (*They all turn and look at* RUFE.)

MATT. Dynamite!

RUFE (*appeals to* MEG). I didn't do it! I swear on a stack o' Bibles I didn't!

MEG (*lays her hand on him protectingly*). 'Course you didn't! Don't you worry! They shan't tetch you!

RUFE. It 'us Him up yonder! He done it! (*He turns to the men.*) I know *you* won't believe me, O ye o' little faith! But if it's the last word I ever utter on earth, He appeared to me in the storm an' I hyeard His voice!

MATT, ANDY (*together*). Shucks! Aw, hell! (DAVID *stands staring at* RUFE.)

MEG. Don't pay no 'tention to them Pharisees, Rufe! Go right on an' tell what happened!

RUFE. It 'us while you 'us out a-lookin' fer Sid. He come in an' accused me o' aggin' Andy on to shoot him! He cussed an' reviled an' took God's name in vain!

MEG. Sid, you ought to be ashamed o' yourself!

RUFE. Then he went out to the dam to telephone an' head off Matt! I knowed the blame 'us all a-goin' to fall on me, an' I knelt thar to pray! (*Pointing.*) Right thar in that very spot! (*He looks around him and lowers his voice impressively.*) An' all of a sudden God appeared to me in thunder an' lightnin'!—

MEG (*clasps her hands in an attitude of worship*). Glory to—

RUFE (*continues without pausing*). An' He spoke to me in a still small voice, but loud aplenty fer me to hear!

JUDE (*sways rhythmically*). Halleluyah! Bless His name!

MEG. What'd He say?

RUFE (*with a convulsive movement of the muscles of his face*). "Gird up your loins," He says, "an' take that box o' dynamite you got out thar in the store an' go forth an' blow up the dam while he's under thar a-telephonin'!"
(MATT *and* DAVID *make an unconscious move toward him and stop, unable to believe their ears.* ANDY *stands rigid, his eyes fixed grimly on* RUFE.)

JUDE (*recoiling with horror*). Oh!

MEG (*her whole nature transformed to venomous rage*). Then you *did* do it! You tried to murder him!

RUFE (*backs away in terror*). I know it seems quair now, Meg! But He works in a mysterious way! I 'us only—

MEG (*makes a move toward him with clenched hands.*). Take him out o' here an' kill him! If you don't I'll—

DAVID (*stopping her*). Now ca'm yourself, Meg!

RUFE. I didn't do it, I tell you! I 'us only His instrument!

MATT (*reaching for his gun*). Yeh, an' so am I!

ANDY. No, Matt! This is my job! Sid's done promised me I could do it! An' I don't want no weepons—(*holding up his hands*)—jist these two instruments! (*He makes a dash for* RUFE, *who runs into the cellar and slams the door behind him, holding it from the inside.* ANDY *shakes the door, trying to open it.*)

RUFE (*behind the door*). O Lord, if You're ever a-goin' to help me, help me now! (*He sings frantically, without regard to the tune.*)

　　I am bound fer the promised land!
　　I am bound fer the promised land!

ANDY (*still tugging at the door*). The son of a biscuit eater! He's actially tryin' to play the same trick on God that he played on me!

MATT. What's the matter? Is he holdin' the latch?

ANDY. Yeh. It's your door, but I'll give you ten dollars to let me yank it offen its hinges!

MEG. The door don't make no difference! Go on an' git him!

MATT. Yeh, I'll stand the damage!

DAVID. Now hold on, boys!

MEG. David Hunt, are you a-stickin' up fer that reptile?

DAVID. No, Meg. But I hain't lost my belief in the Lord on Rufe's account. Fact is, I ain't so shore but what I believe in Him more 'n ever.

ANDY. Holy Moses! He's gone hell-bent fer glory, too!

MATT (*moves toward the door*). Well, he ain't a-goin' to stop us by shoutin', "Lord!"

ANDY. Yeh, the Lord had His chance to punish Rufe an' didn't do it!

DAVID. That's jist the p'int. (ANDY *starts to break in the door.* DAVID *seizes his arm, and holds* MATT *back also.*) He didn't punish him. But He may do it yit if you give Him a chance. (*Quickly, as they show signs of impatience.*) An' arter what's happened here to-night we'd orter be willin' to foller the Lord uphill back'ards 'ith our eyes shet!

ANDY. Arter what's happened here to-night!

DAVID. Edzackly! Take it right straight through from beginnin' to end an' the Lord's been on our side every pop—even to blowin' up that dadburned dam that had never orter been put in!

MATT. That's so! I hadn't thought o' that!

ANDY. Aw! I've seen all I want o' that love-your-enemy truck to-night! I'm a-goin' through that door!

SID (*who has gone to the door to look at the river, comes toward* ANDY). Well, don't be so brash about it, Andy. I expect Gran'-pap's right—

ANDY. Well, I'll be—! Have you gone crazy, too?

SID. No, but I believe in givin' everybody a chance—includin' the Lord. This is a job I expect He understands better 'n we do. An' we're all in His hands jist now. You see the river ain't through risin' yit. It'll be over the top o' this house afore mornin' unless a merricle happens. (*They are all sobered by this and turn toward* SID *anxiously.*)

DAVID. What makes you think that?

SID. While I 'us down thar under the dam a-telephonin', a message come through that all the dams between here an' Asheville had busted an' the river 'us a-sweepin' everything afore it. It 'us twenty-five feet above highwater at Eagle Bluff. An' they said if this new dam didn't hold it 'ld be lots wuss down here afore mornin'.

DAVID. Then we're all a-goin' to have to swim fer our lives!

MEG. Has the water s'rrounded the house?

MATT. Yeh. It's six feet deep twixt here an' the nearest hill!

MEG. Then they ain't nothin' left fer me an' Jude to do but pray, fer we cain't swim!

SID (*smiles and pats her on the back*). Cheer up, Mam! Things ain't as bad as that yit. As I 'us a-comin' down the river in that turmoil o' water I hooked on to a loose boat and fetched it ashore with me. It's tied out thar now. An' we'd better not lose much time a-gittin' in it, fer that dam'll bust up in sections. An' they's liable to be another wave like the first un.

MEG. Is they room in the boat to take anything with us, Sid?

SID. No, nothin' but ourselves.

DAVID (*takes his rifle from the rack*). Well, I'm a-goin' to take this ole gun if I have to swim!
(MEG *begins snatching a few small things from the table and mantel.* MATT *takes the shotgun.*)

SID (*goes toward the door*). Come on, Andy. I want you to handle a oar.

RUFE (*shouts from the cellar*). You ain't a-goin' to leave me here to drownd? I cain't swim, neither!

ANDY. What makes you think you're a-goin' to drownd? Keep right on trustin' Him up yonder! He'll save you if you've done as much fer Him as you say you have! (*He goes out at the front with* SID. RUFE *is heard praying as* MEG, JUDE, MATT, *and* DAVID *finish gathering up their things and follow* SID *and* ANDY.)

RUFE. O God, save me! You can save me if You will! I dunno how, but I know You can! I've got faith in You! I never have doubted You, an' I ain't a-goin' to doubt You now jist because I'm in a tight place! But everybody ain't like me, God! They's lots o' folks that has to have proof! An' if You save the others an' don't save me, like the fool, they're a-goin' to say in their hearts they ain't no God! (*There is a moment's silence. He opens the cellar door and peeps out cautiously. Seeing that the room is empty, he rushes to the front door and looks out, then shrinks back, terrified by what he sees.*) They're right! (*His voice drops to a hoarse whisper.*) They ain't no God! (*A malignant expression sweeps over his face.*) If they is He hain't got no use fer folks like me! He's fer them that's on top! That's what He is! (*He suddenly rises on his toes, as if impelled by some power outside himself, and hurls defiance toward heaven.*) Damn you, God! (*He gradually collapses, muttering brokenly in a fit of terror.*) Now I've done it! I've committed the unpardonable sin! (*Then he screams hysterically as the curtain falls.*) Help! Help! Come here, everybody, come here!

They Knew What They Wanted

BY SIDNEY HOWARD

SIDNEY HOWARD

Sidney Coe Howard was born at Oakland, California, in 1891. He was graduated from the University of California in 1915. The following year he began special dramatic work in the 47 Workshop class at Harvard, but left to serve with the American Ambulance force on the Western front and in the Balkans during the early part of the World War. After the declaration of war by the United States he became a captain of the United States Army Aviation Service. In 1919 he was a member of the editorial staff of *Life,* becoming literary editor three years later. In 1922 he married Clare Jenness Eames, an actress, now deceased. At one time Mr. Howard served as special investigator and feature writer for the *New Republic* and for *Hearst's International Magazine.* He is a member of the American Dramatists, the National Institute of Arts and Letters, and the Authors' League of America. His second marriage occurred in 1931 to Leopoldine Blaine Damrosch.

Mr. Howard is the author of *Labor Spy,* based on reporting done for the *New Republic,* and *Three Flights Up,* a group of four stories.

They Knew What They Wanted was written in Venice in 1923. As a boy Mr. Howard knew the Napa Valley in California and the Italian-Swiss wine growers of that district, which is the scene of the play.

Following the production of *They Knew What They Wanted* Mr. Howard was hailed by dramatic critics as a force to reckon with in the American drama.

Produced by the Theatre Guild at the Garrick Theatre, New York, November 24, 1924, *They Knew What They Wanted* was awarded the Pulitzer Prize for 1924-1925.

CHARACTERS

AMY.

TONY.

JOE.

FATHER McKEE.

THE DOCTOR.

THE R. F. D.

AH GEE.

TWO ITALIAN FARMHANDS.

ITALIAN WEDDING GUESTS, including a tenor, a soloist on the accordion, a mandolin and a guitar player, men, women, and children.

SCENE

Tony's farmhouse in the Napa Valley, California.

ACT ONE

Morning, in early summer.

ACT TWO

Evening. Same day.

ACT THREE

Three months later.

THEY KNEW WHAT THEY WANTED

SCENE

The scene of the play is the home of an Italian winegrower in the Napa Valley in California. All of the action takes place in the main downstairs room which serves as general living and dining room.

It is necessary to understand that the house is not in the least Spanish in its architecture. As a matter of fact, it would serve any respectable Middle-Western farmer as a fitting and inconspicuous residence. It was built in the 'nineties of wood, is painted white on its exterior, and has only one story.

A door at the back, the main one to the outer world, gives on the porch. Another door, to the right of the audience, gives on the kitchen. The kitchen is three steps above the level of the room and so placed that the audience can see into it. It is completely furnished. A third door, to the left of the audience, gives on a flight of steps which leads to the cellar of the house. A fourth door, also on the left and farther down stage, gives on the bedroom.

The back wall should also be broken by windows; on the right of the central door, a bay window, on the left, a double flat window.

The view from the house is over a valley and toward brown Californian hills. The landscape is checkered with cultivation. Some of the checkers are orchards. Most of them are vineyards. The foreground is all vines. Vines twine about the pillars of the porch. In the beginning of the play—it begins in summer—the grapes on the porch vines are small and green. In the last act—three months having elapsed—they are large and purple.

The back stage must be so arranged that people who approach the house from the highroad appear to mount the porch steps from a much lower level. At other times, however, it is required that the characters be able to go and come on the level of the house itself where the farmyard is.

Inside the room the wall paper and the carpet are new and garish. The cheapest variety of lace curtains hangs in the windows. The furniture is new and includes a golden-oak dining table with chairs to match, a morris chair, another easy chair, a chest of drawers, a sideboard, a hat rack.

On one wall hangs a picture of Garibaldi. A picture of George Washington hangs over the central door. Other mural decorations include a poster of the Navigazione Generale Italiana, a still-life chromo, a religious chromo, and a small mirror.

On the hat rack hangs a double-barrelled shotgun draped with a loaded cartridge belt.

The whole impression must be one of gaiety and simple good living.

ACT ONE

The red, white, and green of Italy combine with the red, white, and blue of these United States in bunting, garlands of fluted paper, pompons, and plumes of shredded tissue, to make up a scheme of decoration which is, to say the least, violent. The picture of Garibaldi is draped with an American flag. The picture of Washington with an Italian flag. The full glare of the early morning sun streams in through door and windows.

The room is fairly littered with boxes. Atop one of these, from which it has just been extracted, stands a handsome wedding cake, surmounted by statuary representing the ideal bride and groom in full regalia under a bell. The boxes are all addressed to

Tony Patucci,
R. F. D., Napa, Calif.

AH GEE *stands on a ladder on the porch outside the open entrance door, hanging Chinese lanterns. He is a silent, spare Chinaman, of age maturely indeterminate. He wears blue overalls and a black chambray shirt.*

JOE—*dark, sloppy, beautiful, and young—is busy opening a packing case in the center of the stage. His back is turned upon the door.*

JOE (*as he works, he half sings, half mutters to himself the words of "Remember," an I. W. W. song, to the tune of "Hold the Fort"*).

"We speak to you from jail to-day,
　Two hundred union men,
We're here because the bosses' laws
　Bring slavery again."

(*Through this the curtain rises and* FATHER MCKEE *is seen climbing the porch steps. He wears the sober garb of a Catholic priest, not over clean, what with dust, spots, and all. He nods to* AH GEE *and comes into the doorway. He stands a moment to mop his large, pale face with a red bandana. Then he lowers lugubrious disapproval upon everything in sight. Then he yawns.*

He is one of those clerics who can never mention anything except to denounce it. And his technique of denunciation is quite special to himself. It consists in a long, throaty abstention from inflection of any kind which culminates in a vocal explosion when he reaches the accented syllable of a word upon which his emphasis depends. This word always seems to wake him up for an instant. Once it is spoken, however, he relapses into semi-somnolence for the remainder of his remarks. At heart, he is genial and kindly enough, quite the American counterpart of the French village curé.*)

FATHER MCKEE. Hello, Joe.

JOE. Hello there, Padre. What do you think?

FATHER MCKEE. Looks to me like a bawdy house.

JOE. It's goin' to be *some* festa. . . . Lily Cups! What do you know about that for style?

FATHER MCKEE. Where's Tony?

JOE (*nods toward the door of the bedroom*). In there gettin' dolled up. . . . Hey, there, bridegroom! The Padre's out here.

FATHER MCKEE. I come up to have a serious talk with Tony.

JOE. Well, for God's sake, don't get him upset no more'n what he is already. He's been stallin' around all mornin', afraid to go down and meet the bride. You better leave him alone.

FATHER MCKEE. I'm always glad to have your advice, Joe. I didn't look to find you still hangin' 'round.

JOE. Oh, didn't you, Padre?

FATHER MCKEE. Tony told me you'd decided to go away.

JOE. Well, Padre, I'll tell you how it is. (*He grins impudently.*) I don't believe in stayin' any one place too long. 'Tain't fair for me not to give the rest of California a chance at my society. But I ain't goin' before I seen all the fun, got Tony safely married, an' kissed the bride. (*He turns to the door and* AH GEE.) That's fine, Ah Gee. Better take these here Lily Cups in the kitchen when you get through.
(*Magnificently* TONY *enters from the bedroom. He is stout, floridly bronzed, sixty years old, vigorous, jovial, simple, and excitable. His great gift is for gesture. Today we meet him in his Sunday best, a very brilliant purple suit with a more than oriental waistcoat which serves to display a stupendous gold watch chain. He wears a boiled shirt, an emerald-green tie, and a derby hat. He carries his new patent-leather shoes in his hand. He seems to be perspiring rather freely.*)

TONY. Looka me! I'm da most stylish fella in da world.

FATHER MCKEE. I come up to talk to you, Tony.

TONY. I'm glad you come, Padre. How you like my clothes, eh? Costa playnta good money! (*Attention is called to the shoes.*) For da feet. . . .

JOE (*a motion to the wedding cake*). How's it strike you, Tony.

TONY. Madonna! (*He throws his shoes into the morris chair. His hat assumes a terrific angle. He cannot keep his hands off that cake.*) Look, Padre! From Frisco! Special! Twelve dollar' an' two bits! Look! (*The miniature bride and groom particularly please him.*) Ees Tony an' his Amy!

JOE. Them lanterns is Ah Gee's personal donation.

TONY. Thank you, Ah Gee! Ees verra fine. Ah Gee, you go an' bring vino, now, for Padre, eh? (AH GEE *obeys the order, taking the Lily Cups with him into his kitchen.*)

JOE. Show some speed now, Tony. It's past nine. 'Tain't hardly pretty to keep the bride waitin'.

TONY (*as he sits down to the struggle with his shoes*). I'm goin' verra quick.

FATHER MCKEE. I got to have a word with you, Tony, before you go to the station.

JOE. The Padre's been tryin' to tell me you're scared to have me around where I can kiss the bride. (*He picks up a couple of flags and goes outside.*)

TONY (*in undisguised terror*). You ain't goin' be kissin' no bride, Joe. You hear dat?

JOE (*off stage he is heard singing*).

"We laugh and sing, we have no fear
    Our hearts are always light,
We know that every Wobbly true
    Will carry on the fight."

TONY. He's too goddam fresh, dat fella, with kissin' my Amy an' all dose goddam Wobbly songs. Don' you think so, Padre?

FATHER MCKEE. I didn't come up here to talk about Joe, Tony. I come up to talk about this here weddin'.

TONY. I'm glad you come, Padre. I'm verra bad scare'.

FATHER MCKEE. You got good reason for bein' scared, if you want to know what *I* think.

TONY. I got verra special reason.

FATHER MCKEE. What reason?

TONY. Don' you never mind! Da's my secret dat I don' tell nobody. You tell Joe he go away quick, Padre. Den, maybe, ees all right.

FATHER MCKEE. So that's it! Well, I don't blame you for that.

TONY (*deeply indignant at the implication*). Oh! . . . No, by God! . . . You don' ondrastan', Padre. Joe is like my own son to me! Ees som'thing verra different. Madonna mia! Ees som'thing I been doin' myself! Ees som'thing Tony's been doin' w'at's goin' mak' verra bad trouble for Tony.

FATHER MCKEE. I'll tell Joe nothin'. You've made your own bed and if you won't get off it while there's time, you got to lie on it. But I want you to understand that I don't like nothin' 'bout this here weddin'. It ain't got my approval.

TONY (*the first shoe slips on and he sits up in amazement*). You don' like weddin', Padre?

FATHER MCKEE. No, I don't. An' that's just what I come up here to tell you. I don't like nothin' about it, an' if you persist in goin' ahead in spite of my advice, I don't want you sayin' afterwards that you wasn't warned.

TONY. Dio mio! (*He amplifies this with the sign of the cross. Then his confidence rather returns to him.*) Aw . . . tak' a pinch-a snuff! You mak' me tire', Padre! You think festa is no good for people. You padre fellas don' know nothing. Work! Work! Work evra day! Den, by-an'-by, is comin' festa. After festa workin' is more easy. (*He resumes the shoe problem.*)

FATHER MCKEE. Tony, you know perfectly well that I ain't got no more objection to no festa than I have to any other pomp of the flesh. But I'm your spirichool advisor an' I been mullin' this weddin' over in my mind an' I come to the conclusion that I'm agin it. I don't like it at all. I got my reasons for what I say.

TONY (*does the Padre guess his secret?*). W'at reason you got?

FATHER MCKEE. In the first place, you ain't got no business marryin' no woman who ain't a good Cath'lic.

TONY (*immeasurable relief*). Ees no matter.

FATHER MCKEE. A mixed marriage ain't no better'n plain livin' in sin.

TONY. Ain' we got you for keep' sin away, Padre?

FATHER MCKEE. Why ain't you marryin' a woman out of your own parish instead of trapesin' all the way to Frisco to pick out a heretic?

TONY. Is no good womans in dees parish.

FATHER MCKEE. What's wrong with 'em?

TONY. Joe is sleepin' with evra one.

FATHER MCKEE. That ain't the point.

TONY (*enlisting the shoe to help his gesticulation*). Oh, ees point all right, Padre. Joe is told me 'bout evrathing. I been lookin' all 'round here at all da womans in dees parish. I been lookin' evra place for twent' mile. Ees no good womans for wife here. Joe is told me 'bout evra one. Den I'm gone to Napa for look all 'round dere an' in Napa ees no better . . . ees just da same like here. So den I go down all da way to Frisco for look after wife an' I find my Amy. She is like a rose, all wilt'. You puttin' water on her an' she come out most beautiful. I'm goin' marry with my Amy, Padre, an' I don' marry with nobody else. She's been tellin' me she is no Cath'lic. I say, w'at I care? By an' by, maybe, if we bein' patient, we bringin' her in da church, an' showin' her da candles and da Madonna, all fix up good with flowers and da big tin heart, an' evrathing smellin' so prett' an' you preachin' verra loud an' da music an' evrathing, maybe . . . by an' by . . . (*He turns again to his shoe.*) But now ees no matter. W'at I care?

FATHER MCKEE. It don't look good to me.

TONY. Ees all right. . . . If you don' want my Amy an' me gettin' married with good Cath'lic priest like you, den, by God—

FATHER MCKEE. I ain't said I wouldn't marry you.

TONY. Eh bene!

FATHER MCKEE. I'm only tryin' to tell you. . .

TONY. Ahi! Dio mio. . . . (*The shoe goes on, producing intense pain.*) He look much better as he feel!

FATHER MCKEE. There ain't no good in no old man marryin' with no young woman.

TONY. You think anybody marry with old woman? Tak' a pinch-a snuff!

FATHER MCKEE. I know one old man who married a young woman an' she carried on with a stage driver!

TONY. Dio mio!

FATHER MCKEE. He had knowed her all her life, too, an' you ain't knowed your Amy more'n 'bout five minutes.

TONY. Ees no matter.

FATHER MCKEE. An' I know another fellow who married one of them city girls like your Amy without bein' properly acquainted an' she turned out to be a scarlet woman.

TONY. My Amy don' do dat.
(AH GEE *enters from kitchen with two glasses and a bottle of wine.*)

FATHER MCKEE. Ain't you just now been tellin' me you're scared of her seein' Joe?

TONY. No, by God!

FATHER MCKEE. Joe ain't the only young fellow around, either!

TONY. Young fellas is no matter. Only Joe. An' I ain' scare' over Joe excep' for special reason. You tell Joe, Padre . . . (*He is returning to his old subject, but the wine distracts him.*) Ah-h-h!

FATHER MCKEE. Why didn't you get married forty years ago?

TONY. I think you know verra good w'y. Ees because I'm no dam' fool. . . . W'en I'm young, I got nothing. I'm broke all da time, you remember? I got no money for havin' wife. I don' want no wife for mak' her work all da time. Da's no good, dat. Da's mak' her no more young, no more prett'. Evrabody say Tony is crazy for no' havin' wife. I say Tony is no dam' fool. W'at is happen? Pro'ibish' is com'. Salute! (*A glass of wine.* AH GEE *has returned to his kitchen.*) An' w'at I say? I say, "Ees dam' fool law. Ees dam' fool fellas for bein' scare' an' pullin' up da grape' for tryin' growin' som'thing different." W'at I'm doin'? I'm keep the grape, eh? I say, "I come in dees country for growin' da grape!

God mak' dees country for growin' da grape! Ees not for pro'ibish' God mak' dees country. Ees for growin' da grape!" Ees true? Sure ees true! (*Another glass of wine.*) An' w'at happen? Before pro'ibish' I sell my grape' for ten, maybe twelve dollar' da ton. Now I sell my grape' some'time one hundra dollar' da ton. Pro'ibish' is mak' me verra rich. (*Another glass of wine.*) I got my fine house. I got Joe for bein' foreman. I got two men for helpin' Joe. I got one Chink for cook. I got one Ford car. I got all I want, evrathing, excep' only wife. Now I'm goin' have wife. Verra nice an' young an' fat. Not for work. No! For sit an' holdin' da hands and havin' kids. Three kids. (*He demonstrates the altitude of each.*) Antonio . . . Giuseppe . . . Anna . . . Da's like trees an' cows an' all good people. Da's fine for God an' evrabody! I tell you, Padre, Tony know w'at he want!

FATHER MCKEE. Whatever made you think a man of your age could have children? (*This staggers* TONY.) I tell you, Tony, it ain't possible.

TONY. Eh? Tony is too old for havin' kids? I tell you, Tony can have twent' kids if he want! I tell you Tony can have kids w en he is one hundra year' old. Dio mio! From da sole of his feet to da top of his hat, Tony is big, strong man! I think I ondrastan' you verra good, Padre. Tony is not too old for havin' kids. He's too rich, eh? (*This rather strikes home.*) Yah! Tony is rich an', if he don' have no kids, den da church is gettin' all Tony's money an da Padre is gettin' Tony's fine house all fix' up good for livin' in, eh?

FATHER MCKEE (*a very severe shepherd*). Tony!

TONY (*the horns of the devil with his fingers*). Don' you go for puttin' no evil eye on Tony an' his Amy!

FATHER MCKEE. You're givin' way to ignorant superstition, which ain't right in no good Cath'lic.

TONY (*on his feet in a panic*). Dio mio! My Amy is comin' on dat train an' here you keep me, sittin', talkin'. . . .

FATHER MCKEE. You irreverent old lunatic, you, if you're bent on marryin', I'll marry you. (JOE *reappears in the doorway.*) But I don't want you comin' around afterwards squawkin' about it.

TONY. Eh, Joe! Da Padre don' want me gettin' marry with my Amy because he's scare' da church don' never get my money!

JOE. For cripe's sake, Tony, ain't you heard that whistle?

TONY. I go! I go!

JOE. Train's in now.

TONY. Porco Dio! Ah Gee!

JOE. Fix your tie.

TONY. I fix. . . . (AH GEE *comes from the kitchen for his master's order.*) Un altro fiasco. (AH GEE *returns to the kitchen.*)

JOE. You won't make no hit if you're drunk, Tony.

TONY. Not drunk, Joe. Only scare'. Verra bad scare'.

JOE. Bridegrooms is always scared.

TONY. Jes' Chris', maybe I'm sick!

JOE. No!

TONY. Santa Maria, I *am* sick!

JOE. What's wrong with you?

TONY. I don' know! I'm sick! I'm sick! I'm sick!
(AH GEE *returns with the wine bottle refilled.* TONY *seeks prompt solace.* AH GEE *goes back to his kitchen.*)

JOE. You'll be a helluva sight sicker if you don't lay off that stuff.

TONY. I canno' go for get my Amy, Joe. I canno' go. . . .

JOE. All right. I'll go . . .

TONY. Oh, by God! No! NO!

JOE. Tony, it you drive the Ford down the hill in this state of mind you'll break your dam' neck.

TONY (*more solace*). I feel good now. I drive fine. I don' want nobody for go for my Amy but only me. . . . (*Then he weakens again.*) Joe, I'm scare', I'm scare', I'm scare'!

JOE. What you scared of, Tony?

TONY. Maybe my Amy. . .

JOE. Come on, beat it!

TONY. I feel good now an' I don' want nobody for go for my Amy but only me. You bet! (*He starts.*)

JOE. That's the boy!

TONY (*another relapse*). Joe, you don' get mad if I ask you som'thing? I got verra good reason, Joe . . . Joe . . . how soon you goin' away, Joe?

JOE. You don't *want* me to go, do you?

TONY. I think ees much better.

JOE. What's the idea, Tony?

TONY. Joe . . . som'thing is happen', da's all. . . . You go, Joe. I been tryin' for three days for ask you dees, Joe, an' I been scare' you get mad. I pay you double extra for goin' to-day, for goin' now, eh? Joe? Verra quick?

JOE. An' miss the festa? Like hell!

TONY. Joe, you don' ondrastan'. . . .

JOE. Forget it, Tony.

TONY. Joe. . .

JOE. If you keep her waitin', she'll go back to Frisco.

TONY. Dio mio! (*He goes to the door and turns yet once again.*) Joe . . .? (*He catches* FATHER MCKEE's *eye.*) Som'thing verra bad is goin' happen with Tony. . . . Clean evrathing clean before my Amy come. (*He is really gone.* JOE *follows him out and stands on the porch looking after him. A Ford motor roars and dies away into high speed.*)

FATHER MCKEE (*at the window*). Look at him!

JOE. He could drive that Ford in his sleep.

FATHER MCKEE. I don't hold with no old man gallivantin'.

JOE. Don't you fret, Padre. Didn't I tell you not to get him all worked up? (*This ruffles the good priest who makes to follow* TONY. JOE *intercepts him and forces him back into the room.*)

FATHER MCKEE. Well?

JOE. Sit down a minute. You been tellin' Tony what you think. Now I got some tellin' to do.

FATHER MCKEE. Have you, indeed? Well, I don't see no good—

JOE. Maybe *I* don't see much good, but what the hell!

FATHER MCKEE. Young man! That's the pernicious doctrine of Lacey Fairey.

JOE. What's that?

FATHER MCKEE. A French expression meanin' "Sufficient unto the day."

JOE. What of it? If folks is bent on makin' mistakes, an' you can't stop 'em, let 'em go ahead, that's what I say. I don't want nobody hatin' my guts for bein' too dam' right all the time, see? Not bein' a priest, I aim to get along with folks. That way, when they're in wrong, I can be some use.

FATHER MCKEE. That ain't in accord with the teachin's of Jesus.

JOE. A helluva lot you an' me know about the teachin's of Jesus!

FATHER MCKEE. Joe, if you ain't goin' to be rev'rent . . .

JOE. I'm talkin' now.

FATHER MCKEE. Oh, are you?

JOE. Yeah. I wouldn't have no harm come to Tony, not for anything in the world, see? An' I been agitatin' against this weddin' a lot longer'n you have an' I know what it's all about, see? I'm here goin' on five months, now, an' that's longer'n I ever stayed any one place.

FATHER MCKEE. Is it?

JOE. Excep' once in jail, it is. An' I been lookin' after Tony all the time since I come here. I come in to bum a meal an' I stayed five months. Five months I been workin' for Tony an' lookin' after him and he's treated me dam' good an' that's God's truth. I wouldn't have worked that long for him if he hadn't treated me dam' good, either. I ain't none too strong for stayin' put, you know. I like to move an' now I'm goin' to move. I'm what the papers call a "unskilled migratory" an' I got to migrate, see? Tony wants me to go an' I want to go. But, what I want to know is: who's goin' to look after Tony when I'm gone?

FATHER MCKEE. Ain't that his wife's place?

JOE. Sure it's his wife's place. But suppose this weddin' don't turn out so good? Are you goin' to look out for him?

FATHER MCKEE. Ain't Tony my spirachool charge an' responsibility?

JOE. All *right!* An' I ain't so sure you're goin' to have much trouble, either. Amy looks to me like a fair to middlin' smart kid an' she knows what she's in for, too.

FATHER MCKEE. You seem to be well informed, Joe! Do you happen to know the lady?

JOE. I ain't never laid eyes on her. (*Then the implication percolates.*) Oh, I may go chasin' women plenty, but I don't chase Tony's wife, see? An' I ain't fixin' to, neither. Just get that straight.

FATHER MCKEE. I'm glad to hear it, Joe.

JOE. But I happen to know about her. Didn't I have to write all Tony's letters for him? You wouldn't expect Tony to be writin' to no lady with *his* education, would you?

FATHER MCKEE. No, I can't say that I would.

JOE. Why, I even had to read him the letters she wrote back. That's how I got my dope. An' what I say is: she's got plenty of sense. Don't you fool yourself she hasn't. I'll show you. (*He goes to the chest of drawers for some letters and photographs. He brings them back to the* PADRE.) You can see for yourself. (*And he submits Exhibit A—a letter.*) Tony goes to Frisco lookin' for a wife, see? The nut! An' he finds Amy waitin' on table in a spaghetti joint. Joint's called "Il Trovatore." Can you beat it? He ain't even got the nerve to speak to her. He don't even go back to see her again. He just falls for her, gets her name from the boss an' comes home an' makes me write her a letter proposin' marriage. That's her answer.

FATHER MCKEE. It's good clear writin'. It's a good letter. It looks like she's got more character'n what I thought. But, just the same, it ain't no way to conduct a courtship.

JOE. There's worse ways.

FATHER MCKEE. She says she likes the letter you wrote.

JOE. The second time I wrote, I told her all about the farm an' just how she was goin' to be fixed. Oh, I was careful not to say nothin' about Tony's money. Only the Ford. I thought she ought to know about the Ford. (*He hands the second letter over.*) An' she wrote this one back.

FATHER MCKEE. She likes the country, does she? She wants Tony's photo.

JOE. Say, you ought to have seen Tony gettin' his face shot! By God! It took me a whole week to talk him into it. An' when I did get him down there—you know that place across from the depot? —dam' if he wasn't scared right out of his pants!

FATHER MCKEE. By what?

JOE. By the camera! Would you believe it? We had to clamp him into the chair, both of us, the photographer an' me! You ought to have seen that wop sweat! And when we try to point the machine at him, he gives a yell you could hear a block an' runs right out in the street!

FATHER MCKEE. No!

JOE. I couldn't get him back, only I promised to let the guy shoot me first. They was some pictures! Tony's (*he hands a specimen to the* PADRE) sure looks like him, but she must have seen somethin' in it, because she sent hers right back. (*He studies* AMY's *photograph for a moment before submitting it.*) Here. Not bad, huh?

FATHER MCKEE (*a long and very pleased contemplation*). There ain't no explainin' women! (*He returns the photograph.*) Do you think she's straight, Joe?

JOE. What the hell! If she ain't, she wants to be. That's the main thing.

FATHER MCKEE. Maybe it won't turn out so bad, after all. There's always this about life: no man don't never get everything he sets out to get, but half the time he don't never find out he ain't got it.

JOE. Oh, if you're goin' off on that tack!

FATHER MCKEE. It's the tack life travels on, with the help of Almighty God.

JOE. What the hell! Life ain't so bad.

FATHER MCKEE. I'm delighted to hear you say so!

JOE (*he has returned the exhibits to the drawer*). I never put over anything half so good myself!

FATHER MCKEE. Do you think Tony's goin' to put it over?

JOE. Wait and see.

FATHER MCKEE. Well, I don't know how I can approve of this weddin', but I'm willin' to give it the benefit of my sanction an' to do all I can to help it along an' look out for Tony. Does that satisfy you? . . . Just the same, I don't believe in unnecessary chances, Joe. Pull along out of here like Tony asked you to.

JOE. Say, you make me sore! Why, anybody 'ud think, to hear you talk, that I'm all set to . . .

(*The* R. F. D. *has appeared on the porch. He carries a dusty coat on his arm, and wipes the sweat from his brow with his blue handkerchief. He wears a gray flannel shirt, old trousers hitched to suspenders that are none too secure. His badge is his only sign of office. He is an eager, tobacco-chewing old countryman.*)

THE R. F. D. Hey, Tony! Tony! (*As he reaches the door.*) Where's Tony? 'Mornin', Padre.

JOE. Tony's gone to town. You're early.

THE R. F. D. That's more'n Tony is. I got to get his signature on a piece of registered mail.

JOE. What is it?

THE R. F. D. It's his wife. (JOE *and the* PRIEST *rise astonished.*) Sure! I got her outside in the buckboard an' she's madder'n hell because Tony didn't meet her. She's some girl, too. I never heard the beat! Lands a girl like that an' don't even take the trouble to— (*The other two are already at the windows.*)

JOE. Where'd *you* find her?

THE R. F. D. I finds her pacin' up and down the platform an' I gives her a lift. I sure do hate to see a good-lookin' girl cry—an' she sure was cryin'. I reckoned Tony couldn't get the Ford started so—

FATHER MCKEE. He went down all right. I wonder what happened to him?

JOE. He must have took the short cut.

FATHER MCKEE. Didn't you pass him?

JOE. I knew I ought to have went instead.

FATHER MCKEE. He wasn't in no condition.

THE R. F. D. I'll have a look on my way back.

JOE. What are *we* goin' to do with her?

THE R. F. D. Ask her in.

JOE. Ah Gee! (*He goes out, calling.*) Giorgio! Angelo! (THE R. F. D. *follows him.* AH GEE *comes from his kitchen and evinces some confusion, but does not hold back from the summons.* FATHER MCKEE *arranges his costume and goes out last. The stage remains empty for a moment. A babble of voices is heard, voices that speak both English and Italian.* JOE *is heard shouting.*) Lend a hand with that trunk!

AMY'S VOICE. How do you do? I'm pleased to meet you. I certainly had some time getting here. I certainly expected somebody would meet me at the station.

FATHER MCKEE'S VOICE. The old man left all right.

JOE'S VOICE. He started a little too late.

THE R. F. D.'S VOICE. I'll have a look for him. (*The rest is lost in a babble of Italian as* AMY *comes on to the porch and the others follow her, not the least among them being the two Italian hands,* GIORGIO *and* ANGELO *whose volubility subsides only as* AMY *enters the room. As for* AMY, *she is all that* TONY *said of her and much more. She wears a pretty dress, new, ready-made, and inexpensive, and a charming and equally cheap hat. Her shoes are bright coloured and her handbag matches them. But her own loveliness is quite beyond belief. She is small and plump and vivid and her golden hair shimmers about her face like morning sunshine. She herself shines with an inner, constitutional energy. Her look is, to be sure, just a little tired. She probably is not more than twenty-two or -three, but she seems older. Her great quality is definiteness. It lends pathos to her whole personality. At the moment, her vanity is piqued by* TONY'S *remissness and she carries matters with a hand a little too high to be entirely convincing. She is embarrassed, of course, but she won't admit it.*)

AMY (*as she enters*). I must say it ain't my idea of the way a gentleman ought to welcome his blooming bride. I don't get it. I don't get it at all. What was the matter?

JOE. Why, nothin'.

FATHER MCKEE. He was scared.

AMY. Scared of me? Why didn't you come yourself?

JOE. I wanted to, but . . .

AMY (*the decorations have caught her eye.*) Say, did you folks go and do all this for the wedding?

JOE. Sure we did.

AMY. Well, if that ain't the cutest ever! A regular wop wedding! Excuse me. I meant Italian. (*The "I" is long.*)

JOE. That's all right.

AMY. And here's the priest, too, all set and ready. Say! I can see right now I'm going to like it here.

JOE. I don't guess nobody's goin' to kick at that.

AMY. All right, then, I'll forgive you. That's the way I am. Forgive and forget! I always believe in letting bygones be bygones. And down at the station I was thinking: Well, if they ain't got enough sense of politeness to come after the bride, I'm going to hop the very next train back to Frisco. I'd have done it, too, only— would you believe it?—I didn't have the price of a ticket! I spent the last cent I had on this hat. Say, when I remembered that, maybe I didn't cry! That's what I was crying over when you come up. (*This last to the* R. F. D.; *otherwise her eyes have scarcely left* JOE's *face.*)

THE R. F. D. Pleased to have been of service, ma'am.

AMY. Well, you certainly was of service. But here I am alive and well, as they say, so I guess we don't need to fuss about that any more. I guess I'll sit down. (*She does so.*)

JOE. Here's the cook an' the hands to pay their respects.

ANGELO (*a deep obeisance to* AMY). Eh, la nostra padrona! Tanti auguri, cara Signora, e buona festa! Come sta? Ha fatto buon viaggio? (*Here* GIORGIO *adds his voice.*)

ANGELO (*together*)	GIORGIO
Siamo tanto contenti di vedevla. Speriamo che si troverà sempre bene e felice nella casa ospitale del nostro generoso padrone.	Sia la benvenuta, egregia Signora, Auguriamo la buona fortuna a lei, e al suo stimatissimo sposo. Che la Santa Madonna le dia la sua benedizione e che tutti i santi l'accompagnino nel matrimonio!

JOE. Hey, that's enough!

AMY. Now, that was very nice of them. I liked every word they said. I guess I better study up on the lingo. All I know is words like spaghetti and raviole. . . .

ANGELO *and* GIORGIO (*sotto voce*). Ah! La Signora parla Italiano!

AMY. . . . I guess you got plenty of that around. Well, you can't make me mad. I just love it. (*Then she sees* AH GEE's *ceremonious obeisance.*) How do you do? Are you the cook?

AH GEE. Yes, missy. Velly good cook!

AMY. Say! I didn't know I drew a chef. You didn't tell me. (AH GEE *takes himself off.*) Say, my baggage is out there.

JOE. All right boys, lend a hand. (ANGELO *and* GIORGIO *go down the steps.*)

AMY. If you don't mind I'll just keep an eye on them. My wedding dress is in that trunk. I bet you didn't expect me to bring a wedding dress. Well, I didn't expect to, myself. And I don't know why I did. But I did! I just blew myself. I said: "You only get married once" and—I got a veil, too. I got the whole works. (*She hears her trunk en route.*) Go easy there! (*She is out on the porch.*)

THE R. F. D. Well, that's her.

JOE (*as he goes to help*). She ain't bad.

FATHER MCKEE. No, she ain't half bad.

AMY (*calling down*). Not upside down! Be careful, can't you?

THE R. F. D. I don't hold much with city girls myself, but—

JOE (*calling down*). Careful boys! Look out for that vine! Gimme the grip.

FATHER MCKEE. Oh, she's above the average.

THE R. F. D. (*nudging him*). Do you think she . . . ?

FATHER MCKEE. I wouldn't hardly like to say off-hand, but . . .

THE R. F. D. I wouldn't think so.

FATHER MCKEE. Joe, do you think she . . . ?

JOE. No. Not her. Not on your life. (*He puts grip down inside the bedroom door. At the same time* ANGELO *and* GIORGIO *carry in* AMY's *pathetic little trunk, which they take into the bedroom.*)

THE R. F. D. Well, I got my deliveries.

FATHER MCKEE. I'll come along with you. You stay here an' keep things conversational, Joe.

JOE. No! I'll come, too.

THE R. F. D. Till the groom turns up, Joe. You don't want her to get all upset again, do you?

FATHER MCKEE (*as* AMY *comes along the porch to the door*). Shh! Don't get her worryin'.

AMY (*in the doorway, finishing the feminine touch of powder to the nose*). I thought a little of this wouldn't make me any harder to look at.

THE R. F. D. We'll have to be movin' on, ma'am.

FATHER MCKEE. Yes.

AMY (*shaking hands with him*). I'm pleased to have made your acquaintance.

THE R. F. D. I hope to have the pleasure soon again.

AMY. Why, ain't you coming to the wedding?

THE R. F. D. Sure I am, if I'm invited.

AMY. I'll never forgive you, if you don't. And I certainly want to thank you for the lift. (*A handshake to him.*) Thank you. . . . Good-bye. . . . Good-bye. . . .

THE R. F. D. Good-bye, ma'am. (*He shuffles out.* JOE *starts to follow.*)

AMY. You ain't going, too?

JOE. Well, I—

THE R. F. D. (*through the window*). Just the Padre an' me.

FATHER MCKEE (*as he goes, to* JOE). We'll send him right up.

THE R. F. D. (*as they disappear*). Good-bye, ma'am.

AMY. Good-bye. See you later. (*Awkward silence.*) I ain't sorry they went. I think they ought to have done it sooner and left us to get acquainted. They got me all fussed up staring that way. I just couldn't think of what to say next. A girl gets kind of fussed, coming off like this to marry a man she ain't never seen. I was a mile up in the air. I—I guess I must have sounded kind of fresh. I wouldn't want you to think I was fresh.

JOE. I didn't.

AMY. I'm glad you didn't. You know, I like it up here already. You got it fixed up so cute and—(*She discovers the cake.*) *and that.* . . . It was awful nice of you to think of that. And the view! Is them all vines?

JOE. Yeah. . . . (*An awkward pause.*)

AMY. It certainly is a pretty sight. Coming up I could taste the wind way down inside me. It made me think of where I used to live.

JOE. Where was that?

AMY. In the Santa Clara. You know, I wrote you.

JOE. Oh, yeah. In the Santa Clara. I forgot.

AMY. We had a big place in the Santa Clara. Prunes and apricots. Ninety acres in prunes and fifty in apricots. . . . (*Again an awkward silence.*) I guess I'll sit down. (*She does so.*) There ought to have been good money in prunes and apricots. But the prunes didn't do so good and the apricots got the leaf curl.

JOE. You're quite a farmer.

AMY. My old man was, but he got to drinking.

JOE. That's bad.

AMY. So we lost it after my mother died. But I used to love it there. In the spring, when the blossoms was out, I used to climb up on the windmill at night, when there was a moon. You never saw such a pretty sight as them blossoms in the moonlight. You could see for miles and miles all round—for miles and miles.

JOE. It must have been pretty. (*Awkward pause.*)

AMY. Ever been in the Santa Clara?

JOE. Sure. I worked there before I come here.

AMY. Where did you work?

JOE. Near Mountain View. I forget the guy's name.

AMY. I went to school in Mountain View. Our place was near there. Ever know Father O'Donnell?

JOE. No.

AMY. Thought you might have, being a Catholic and all.

JOE. I was organizer for the Wobblies.

AMY. The Wobblies?

JOE. I. W. W.

AMY. Say! You ain't one of them?

JOE. I used to be.

AMY. I sure am glad you gave that up. You don't talk one bit like an Italian.

JOE. I ain't. Only by descent. I was born in Frisco.

AMY. Oh, in Frisco? I see. . . . I'm Swiss by descent myself. My father was born in Switzerland and my grandfather, on my mother's side, he was born there, too. I don't know what that makes me—Swiss cheese, I guess. . . . (*She laughs.* JOE *does not. This crushes her and there is another awkward gap.*) Our old house in the Santa Clara was bigger than this one, but it wasn't near so pretty. I must say you keep this house nice and clean for having no woman around. Our house got awful dirty toward the end. You see, my mother got to drinking, too. Hard stuff, you know. I got nothing against beer or vino, but the hard stuff don't do nobody any good. . . . That how you stand on prohibition?

JOE. Sure, I guess so.

AMY. I'm glad to hear that. I sure am. I don't want no more experience with the hard stuff. . . . That certainly is some view. Got the Santa Clara beat a mile. The Santa Clara's so flat. You couldn't get no view at all unless you climbed up on that windmill like I told you about. . . . Our old house had a cellar. Has this house got a cellar?

JOE. Sure, it has. Underneath the whole house. (*She goes to the cellar door to see.*)

AMY. I used to hide in our cellar when things got too rough upstairs. You could hear the feet running around over your head, but they never come down in the cellar after me because there was a ladder, and when you're that way you don't care much for ladders. . . . They always took it out on me.

JOE. Did they?

AMY. Yeah. I always had the cellar though. I used to play down there hot days. It smelt like apricots.

JOE. Our cellar smells like hell. It's full of vino.

AMY. That's a nice clean smell. It's sour, but it's healthy.

JOE. You're a regular wop, ain't you?

AMY. Well, after two years in a spaghetti joint! I like Italians. They always left me alone. I guess it wouldn't have done 'em much good getting fresh with me, at that. . . . Say, I'm getting pretty confidential.

JOE. Go right ahead.

AMY. All right. . . . I guess I ain't got much reason for being shy with you, at that. I wouldn't never have said I was going to marry an Italian, though. But I guess I just jumped at the chance. I got so tired of things. Oh, everything! I used to think I just couldn't keep on any longer.

JOE. Poor kid!

AMY. Oh, I usually know which side my bread's buttered on. I just said to myself: "He looks all right and I like the country and anyway it can't be no worse than this." And I said: "Why shouldn't I take a chance? He's taking just as much of a chance on me as I am on him."

JOE. That's fair enough.

AMY. Sure it is. And—maybe I hadn't ought to say it—but when I come in here and seen all you done, fixing things up for the wedding and all, and looked out the window, and smelt that wind, I said to myself, I said: "Amy, old kid, you're in gravy." Now, what do you think of that for an admission?

JOE. You're dead right. That's just what I said when I come here. I only intended to stay a few days. I'm that way, see? I been here goin' on five months now.

AMY. Is *that* all?

JOE. That's the longest I ever stayed any one place since I was old enough to dress myself.

AMY. You *have* been a rover!

JOE. I been all over—with the Wobblies, you see. Before I come here, that is.

AMY. What did you used to do?

JOE. Cherries an' hops—melons down in the Imperial an' oranges down South an' the railroad an' the oilfields. . . . Before I come here. When I come here I just stayed. Maybe I was gettin' tired of bummin'. Now I'm tired of this. But I don't mind.

AMY. Well, don't get too tired of it. I'm not a bit strong for moving myself. I had all I want of that in my time.

JOE. I guess you have.

AMY. I wonder what you think of me coming all the way up here like I did, all by myself, to marry a man I ain't never seen, only his photograph.

JOE. You couldn't have picked a better man.

AMY. Say! Don't get a swelled head, will you?

JOE. Who, me?

AMY. Oh, no, nobody! (AH GEE *passes along the porch.*) I hope you're right that's all. And I guess you are, at that. And believe me, if I thought this wasn't a permanent offer, I wouldn't be here. I mean business. I hope you do.

JOE. Me?

AMY. Well, I certainly ain't referring to the Chink.

JOE. Say, who do you think . . . ?

AMY (*touching his sleeve with a kind of gentle diffidence which is her first attempt at intimacy*). Don't get sore. The minute I came in I knew I was all right. I am. Why, I feel just as comfortable as if we was old friends. There don't seem to be anything strange in me being here like I am. Not now, anyhow. It just goes to show you: you never can tell how things is going to turn out. Why, if a fortune-teller had told me that I would come up here like I did, do you know what I would have said to her? I'd have said, "You're no fortune-teller." Life sure is funny, though. It's lucky for me I can say that now and laugh when I say it. I ain't always been so good at laughing. I guess we'll get used to each other in time. Don't you think we will, Tony?

JOE. Tony? Say, I ain't . . ! Oh, Jesus! (*His words are lost in the roar of a Ford motor as it approaches, and the motor, in turn, is drowned in wild cries of dismay from* GIORGIO *and* ANGELO. *The tension between the two in the room is broken by the excited entrance of* AH GEE, *who has evidently seen, from his kitchen window, the cause of disturbance.*)

FATHER MCKEE (*calling from off stage*). Joe! Joe!

JOE (*following* AH GEE *toward the door*). What is it? (*From the porch he sees what it is.*) What—Is he dead? . . . Take that bench! (*He disappears in the direction of the disturbance which continues in both English and Italian.*)

AMY. What's the matter? Is somebody hurt?

(*The* DOCTOR, *with his fedora hat and his little black satchel, appears. He is the perfect young rural medico, just out of medical school and full of learned importance.*)

THE DOCTOR. I'll get the ambulance.

JOE (*following him in*). Is he bad, Doc?

THE DOCTOR (*as he goes into the bedroom*). Both legs above the knee—compound fractures.

JOE. Why didn't you take him to the hospital?

THE R. F. D. (*as he enters*). The Ford went right off the bridge.

FATHER MCKEE (*as he enters*). Not two hundred yards from here, Joe.

THE R. F. D. Must have fell twenty feet!

FATHER MCKEE. Never seen such a wreck! (*To* AMY.) We found him lyin' in two feet of water. The car was turned right upside down.

AMY. But who is it? I don't get it. I don't know what's happened.

FATHER MCKEE. Two broken legs, that's what's happened.

THE DOCTOR (*he reappears in his shirt sleeves*). Better lend a hand, Joe!
(*He vanishes again.* GIORGIO *and* ANGELO *appear, carrying the bench and apostrophizing the deity in Italian.* TONY *is recumbent and unconscious on this improvised stretcher. Much "steady" from* JOE. *Much "There now, Tony" from the* R. F. D. *Much and prolonged groaning from* TONY.)

JOE (*as the bench is set down*). All right now, Tony.

TONY (*reviving*). AH-h-h! . . . Ees you, Joe?

JOE. Yeah. It's me. Amy's here.

TONY. Amy? Ees all right, Joe? You been makin' evrathing all right?

JOE. Sure. Everything's fine.

TONY. Where is my Amy? (*He sees her where she stands dumbfounded against the wall.*) Ah-h-h, Amy! . . . Amy, don' be standin' way off dere! Come over here for shake hands. (AMY *shakes her head.*) You ain' mad with me, Amy? . . . (AMY *shakes her head again.*) Amy ain' mad with me, Joe?

JOE. Nobody's mad. . . . Don't you worry.

TONY. Den we have da weddin' just da same? We have da weddin' just da same? (*The* DOCTOR *appears in the bedroom doorway, holding a hypodermic.*)

JOE. Sure, we will.

THE DOCTOR. All right, boys, bring him in. I want to give him another one of these and clean up his cuts.

JOE. Come on now, boys! Avanti! Careful there!

TONY. Amy! . . . Amy! . . . (*The jar of movement hurts him. He breaks down into groans and is carried into the bedroom. All others go with him except* JOE *and* AMY.)

JOE (*as he starts to go, a strangled sound from* AMY *arrests him. He turns and meets her gaze. He closes the door*). This is tough on you.

AMY (*almost voiceless with her terrible surmise*). Who—who is that old guy?

JOE. That? That's Tony. . . .

AMY. Tony?

JOE. It's too bad he never got to meet you. It's too bad he wasn't here when you come. (AMY *sways desperately a moment, then, with a choked cry, makes for the bedroom.*) You can't go in there.

AMY. I want my trunk.

JOE. Now, listen! It ain't Tony's fault he's had an accident. . . .

AMY. Of all the dirty, low-down tricks that was ever played on a girl!

JOE. An' it ain't his fault you made a little mistake.

AMY. What do you think you are—a bunch of Houdinis? (*She tears open her handbag which she put down on the table at her first entrance and produces a photograph.*) Is this your photo or isn't it?

JOE (*in amazement*). Where did you get it?

AMY. Where do you think I got it?

JOE. Good God, Tony didn't send you this, did he? For God's sake, tell me! Did Tony send you this?

AMY. Ain't I just told you?

JOE. By God, he must have been plumb crazy! By God, he was so dead gone on you he was afraid you wouldn't have nothin' to do with an old man like him. . . . He didn't have the nerve. . . . An he just went an' sent you my photo instead of his. . . . Tony's like that, Amy. He ain't nothing but a kid. He's like a puppy, Tony is. Honest, Amy, it's God's truth I'm telling you. . . . I wouldn't have had nothin' to do with no such thing. Honest I wouldn't. I did write the letters for him, but that was only because he don't write good English like I do.

AMY. That ain't no excuse.

JOE. But there wasn't one word in them letters that wasn't God's own truth. I never knew nothin' about this photo, though. Honest to God, I never! An' Tony never meant no harm neither, Amy. Honest he never. An' he's been after me to beat it, too. Every day he has. . . . Sure it was a dirty trick an' he was crazy to think he could get away with it. I ain't denyin' it's the dirtiest trick I ever heard of. . . . Only he didn't mean no harm.

AMY. Oh, didn't he? Well, how about *my* feelings? How about *me?*

JOE. I'll do everything I can to square it. I'll drive you right down to the station now, and you can hop the first train back.

AMY. Oh, *can* I? And what do you expect me to do when I get there? Ain't I thrown up my job there? Do you think jobs is easy for a girl to get? And ain't I spent every cent I had on my trousseau?

JOE. I'll make Tony square it.

AMY. Oh, my God! Oh, my God! I got to go back and wait on table! What'll all those girls say when they see me? And I ain't even got the price of my ticket!

JOE. We can fix that.

AMY. I'll get a lawyer, I will! I wish to God I hadn't never heard of no wops!

JOE. Don't start cryin'. (*He tries to comfort her.*)

AMY. You take your hands off me and get my things.

JOE. All right. . . . (*He looks at her a moment, his distress quite evident. Then he gives it up and goes into the bedroom. As he opens the door, the* DOCTOR *and* TONY *are audible. He closes the door after him.*)
(AMY *picks up the few belongings she has left about the room. She stands a moment holding them, looking about her, at the four walls, at the country outside. Then her eye falls upon* JOE's *photograph which still lies, face-up, on the table. She takes it in her hand and looks at it. Mechanically she makes as though to put it into the bosom of her dress. She changes her mind, drops it on the table and looks around her again. She seems to reach a decision. Her face sets and she pushes the photograph vigorously away from her.* JOE *returns with her satchel.*)

JOE. The doc's give him something to make him sleep. They're goin' to get an ambulance an' take him to the hospital. We can take the doc's Ford an' . . . It's a shame, but . . .

AMY. I ain't going.

JOE. What?

AMY. No. I ain't going. Why should I go? I like the country. This place suits me all right. It's just what I was looking for. I'm here and I might as well stick. I guess he ain't so bad, at that. I guess I could have done a lot worse. If he wants to marry me, I'm game. I'm game to see it through. It's nice up here. (*She pulls off her hat and sits, exhausted.* JOE *stares in mute admiration as the curtain falls.*)

ACT TWO

The scene remains unchanged. It is late evening of the same day. The lanterns out-of-doors have been burning so long that some of them have already guttered out. The room is lighted by two oil lamps.

TONY lies groaning faintly on a cot, his legs encased in a plaster cast, his eternal wine bottle by his side. The DOCTOR sits beside him.

Outside, the festa is in full swing. A desperate Italian tenor is singing "La Donna è Mobile" from "Rigoletto" as the curtain rises. His tones ring frantically out.

A short pause follows the song. The hiss of a sky rocket is audible. The light from the rocket flares through the windows and a long "Ah" rises from the crowd out-of-doors.

TONY. Fireworks!

THE DOCTOR. Lie quiet.

TONY. Someone verra sick in bed. Poveretto! Poveretto! Tony miss festa. (*Gay voices outside call to children and children answer. The* DOCTOR *rises impatiently and goes to the door.* TONY *turns his head ever so slightly.*) Eh, Doc! W'ere you go?

THE DOCTOR. It's high time those coyotes went home. (*Applause rings from the crowd. The tenor is again vigorously repeating the last phrase and cadenza of "La Donna è Mobile."*)

TONY. Dat fella is no coyot'! He is music artiste.

THE DOCTOR. It's a marvel to me the man has any lungs left. He's been howling for five hours.

TONY. You don' ondrastan' such music. Come è bella! Ees "Rigoletto!"

THE DOCTOR. Look here now, Tony! I let you out of the hospital to get married.

TONY. You bet your life! You think any goddam doc is stoppin' me from gettin' married?

THE DOCTOR. I'm talking medicine, not love.

TONY. You talkin' too goddam much. You been spoil evrathing.

THE DOCTOR. Now, be reasonable, Tony. I let them bring you in here where you could see your friends.

TONY. An' den you mak' all my friends go outside.

THE DOCTOR. You're a sick man.

TONY. Ahi! Tony is verra sick . . . verra sick!

THE DOCTOR. Enough's enough. Why, half of what you have been through to-day would have killed a white man! You wops are crazy.

TONY. I don' let nobody stop no festa in my house. You go outside an' have a good time.

THE DOCTOR. I don't sing and I don't dance and I don't talk Italian and I don't drink.

TONY. I'm surprise' how much you don' know, Doc. (*He laughs. The jar is painful. He groans. The* DOCTOR *comes over to his bedside.*) W'ere is my Amy?

THE DOCTOR. She's all right. Keep quiet.

TONY. You goin' look for my Amy, Doc? You goin' see if she is havin' fine time? (*Mandolins, a guitar, and an accordion strike up a sentimental waltz outside.*)

THE DOCTOR. If you'll be quiet. (*Humoring him, he goes to the door.*) I can see her from here and she's having a splendid time. Does that satisfy you?

TONY. Now evrabody goin' for dance!
(*A brief silence filled by the dance music to which* TONY, *the incorrigible, beats time. Then* JOE *and* AH GEE *come along the porch pushing a wheelbarrow, a little flurry of the crowd in their wake. The* DOCTOR *shoos out the crowd.* JOE *and* AH GEE *come in.*)

JOE. How you makin' out, Tony?

TONY. Verra sick, Joe. Is festa goin' good?

JOE. Festa's goin' fine, Tony. Me and Ah Gee's after more vino.

TONY. Da's good! Da's good!

JOE. Sure it's good. But it's a wonder everybody ain't drownded already.

TONY. Italian fellas don' get drownded in vino. Is my Amy havin' good fun, Joe?

JOE. Sure, she is! She's playin' with the kids.

TONY. Ah! . . . You go in da cellar with Ah Gee, Joe, and bring back playnta vino. Den you come back here and mak' little talk with Tony.

JOE. That's the idea. . . . (*He goes into the cellar, followed by* AH GEE.)

THE DOCTOR (*in the door, a fractious eye on the festa*). Those mothers ought to be reported for keeping youngsters up this time of night. (*A pause filled with voices and laughter.*)

TONY (*crescendo*). Doc! Doc! Doc! (*The* DOCTOR *turns.*) You think I am well next week, Doc?

THE DOCTOR. I sincerely hope, Tony, that you may be well in six months.

TONY. Six month'?

THE DOCTOR. You don't seem to realize what a bad smash you had. (*As he sits down to his professional manner.*) Both tibia and fibula are fractured in the right leg. The femur is crushed in the left, and the ischium damaged as well. Now, if no systemic complications develop . . .

TONY. Oh, my God!

THE DOCTOR. . . . six months. . . .

TONY (*crescendo again*). Six month'! Six month'! Six month'!

THE DOCTOR. You won't make it any shorter by exciting yourself.

TONY. Da's right, Doc. Ees no good get excit'. I ondraştan'. But six month' . . . (*A pause.*) Doc, I'm goin' ask you som'thing an' you goin' tell me just da truth, eh?

THE DOCTOR. I know what's on your mind, Tony. If you keep quiet and take care of yourself, you'll have all the kids you want.

TONY. How many?

THE DOCTOR. Ten, anyway!

TONY. Three is playnta.
(*The music is loud again as* JOE *and* AH GEE *come back from the cellar with the new barrel of wine. They load it on the wheelbarrow and* AH GEE *takes it off to the thirsty populace.* JOE *remains behind.*)

THE DOCTOR. In the meanwhile Amy's going to have her hands full, taking care of you.

TONY (*violently*). I don' marry with no woman for mak' her work. I don't want my Amy do nothing but only be happy an' fat.

JOE. There ain't nothin' too good for Tony. He marries a fine wife to play the piano for him an' he's goin' to rent a trained nurse to take care of him.
(AH GEE *is greeted with shouts of "Vino! Vino!" from the men and "Viva Antonio" from the girls.*)

TONY. You bet your life!

THE DOCTOR. Renting trained nurses is expensive, Tony.

TONY. I got playnta money.
(*The concertina and the mandolin begin playing the chorus of "Funiculi, Funicula!" The music is continued throughout the following scene.*)

JOE (*cigarette business*). You old son of a gun! Give us a light, doc.

THE DOCTOR. Not in here, Joe!
(JOE *takes his cigarette outside. He sits with a wave to the crowd, who answer, "Joe! Joe!"*)

TONY. Is my Amy havin' good fun, Joe?

JOE. Sure. She's dancin' with the postman.

TONY. Da's good! Ees verra funny weddin' for me, Joe, but my Amy must have good time.

THE DOCTOR. Tony's got it bad.

JOE. Don't blame him. She's some girl.

TONY. I got to talk verra secret with Joe, Doc. You go outside for talk with my Amy. You better get good acquaint' with my Amy, Doc.
(*Applause outside for the dancers.*)

JOE. You could do worse, an' that's a fact.

THE DOCTOR. Tony's got to go to sleep.
(*The crowd outside shouts vociferously.*)

JOE. I won't keep him up.

TONY. Just a little w'ile, Doc? Fifteen minute'?

THE DOCTOR. Well, don't make it any longer. I want some sleep myself. Anybody would think I haven't a thing to do but take care of Tony.

JOE. We know you're a busy baby, Doc.

THE DOCTOR. Busy is right. (*Very expansive.*) To-morrow, now, I've got two confinements I'm watching and an appendicitis, all up on the St. Helena road. Then, just the other side of town, I've got the most beautiful tumor you could hope to see. And the sheriff's wife! Operated her yesterday. Gallstones. Gallstones? They were cobblestones. I never saw such a case! And then, with my regular practice and my own scientific researches to keep up with things.

TONY. Corpo Dio, goddam, Doc; don' be tellin' me no more 'bout who is sick and w'at he's sick for! I'm sick playnta myself, an' I got playnta trouble here. You go outside an' leave me for talk with Joe.

THE DOCTOR. All right, but I won't have any more nonsense when I come back. (*He goes; to* JOE *on the porch.*) I cannot be responsible unless the patient enjoys complete quiet, after a shock like this to his nervous system.

JOE. Has Tony got a nervous system?

THE DOCTOR. Of course he has! (*He disappears. A shout welcomes him.*)

TONY. W'at is nervous system, Joe?

JOE. It's what makes things hurt, Tony.

TONY. I got playnta.
(JOE *comes in and stands over* TONY *for a moment with a look of half-tender amusement on his face.* TONY *hums distractedly keeping time with one hand to the music of "Funiculi, Funicula." With the end of the music he drops his hands with a sigh.*)

JOE. What's on your mind, Tony?

TONY. Oh, Joe! . . . Joe!! . . . Joe!!

JOE. What's the matter, Tony. Ain't you feelin' good?

TONY. Ees Amy! . . .
(JOE *sits in the* DOCTOR's *chair, hitching it closer to the bed.*)

JOE. What do you want for a nickel? She married you, didn't she?

TONY. I'm scare', Joe. I'm scare' verra bad. I love my Amy, but my Amy don' love me.

JOE. Give her time, can't you? She wouldn't have married you if she wasn't all set to go through on the level.

TONY. You think?

JOE. Hell, I *know*.

TONY. W'at Amy say w'en she see me dees morning?

JOE. Oh, forget it, I tell you.

TONY. I got to know, Joe. You got to tell me. She's pretty goddam mad, eh?

JOE. Well, if she was, she got over it.

TONY. W'at I'm goin' to do for mak' evrathing all right, Joe? Da's w'at I want to know.

JOE. I tell you everythin' *is* all right, Tony. Oh, I ain't sayin' you ain't got to keep things movin' along easy an' friendly an' all. But that ain't goin' to be so hard. Just be good to her and take care of her. That's what Amy needs. She's tired, poor kid!

TONY. I'm all ready for tak' care like hell.

JOE. From what Amy was tellin' me this mornin', she's been a-havin' a helluva hard life for a girl, an' if she come through straight like she did, well, there ain't no credit due nobody but just only herself, and that's a fact.

TONY. You're a goddam smart fella, Joe.

JOE. I dunno how smart I am, Tony, but you can't tell me much. Not about women, you can't. Believe me, a girl gets a lousy deal any way you look at it. (*He reflects upon this for an instant before he illustrates.*) Take a fella, now, a young fella like me, see? It's goin' to do him good to knock around an' have his troubles an' all. (*A solemn shake of the head.*) But knockin' around just raises hell with a girl. She can't stand it. She can't stand it, because it ain't in her nature to get away with the whole show like a fella can. (TONY *is much impressed and signifies approval with a grunt.*) If a fella wants a meal, he swipes it, don't he? A girl can't be swipin' things. It 'ud make her feel bad. She'd think she was doin' somethin' wrong. (*This surprises* TONY, *but he is willing to take* JOE'S *word for it.*) Gee, I sure would hate to be a woman!

TONY (*nodding agreement*). Nobody is wantin' to be woman, Joe . . . But ees playnta good womans like my Amy!

JOE. Sure, there's good ones an' bad ones. But that ain't exactly what I mean, Tony. What I mean is, as far as I can see, it don't make a helluva lot of difference what a woman is: good or bad, young or old . . .

TONY. I lik' best fat!

JOE. . . . all women is up· against it, and it's a dirty shame, too, because women ain't so bad. They ain't much use, maybe, but they ain't so bad.

TONY. My Amy is goin' have evrathing she want.

JOE. Ever heard anythin' about this dam' women's rights stuff? You know. Equality of the sexes. Woman doin' a man's work an' all that bunk?

TONY. Da's crazy idea!

JOE. The idea ain't so bad.

TONY. Ees crazy idea! Looka me! You think any woman is goin' be doin' my work? No, by God! I tell you, Joe, woman is best for sit in da house an' love da husband.

JOE. The trouble with women is, there's too goddam many of 'em. Why, I was readin' in the paper only the other day about England havin' three and a half women to every man.

TONY. W'at you mean?—half a womans!

JOE. I'm only tellin' you what the paper said.

TONY. Ees crazy idea! Half a womans! I tell you, Joe . . .

JOE. I been lookin' women over from San Diego to Seattle an' what most of 'em is after is a home. A good safe home, whether they get any rights with it or not. You take my advice an' make everythin'· nice an' comfortable for Amy an'· you won't have no trouble. Amy's satisfied here. Don't you kid yourself she ain't.
(*Outside the crowd is off again, the tenors leading them in "Maria Mari."*)

TONY. You're a good boy, Joe, you're pretty smart.

JOE. I'm just tellin' you the truth. You're dam' lucky you picked a girl like Amy.

TONY (*a moment of comfort; then despair again*). Ees no good, Joe—ees no good.

JOE. Oh, for cripe's sake, Tony!

TONY. I'm tellin' you, Joe, ees no good. I'm the most unhappy fella in the world. W'y? Because I been verra bad sinner an' God is goin' get me for sure! He's broke both my legs already an' he's not finish' with me yet! God is no cheap fella, Joe. God is lookin' out at Tony right now, and you know what he's· sayin'? He's sayin': "Tony, you been one goddam sonuvabitch for playin' goddam dirty trick on Amy!" Da's w'at· God is sayin', Joe, an' I know verra good w'at God is goin' do more. Just for playin' goddam dirty trick like dat on Amy, Tony don' never have no kids, never! W'at you think is mak' me do such a thing, Joe?

JOE. Oh, hell, you always was crazy.

TONY. Ees no good, for such a bad fella like me gettin' married. God is goin' fix me playnta, all right.

JOE. I seen God let worse guys'n you get by.

TONY. You think?

JOE. If you want to square things, you better make Amy glad you done what you done.

TONY. You think? . . . Yes. . . . (*Pause.*) Look, Joe. . . . (*He draws a plush box from under his blanket.*) Ees present for Amy. You open him.

JOE (*obeying*). Say! Them's what I call regular earrings!

TONY. You bet your life! He's cost four hundra dollar'!

JOE. Are them real diamonds?

TONY (*nodding*). I guess Amy like 'em pretty good, eh?

JOE. She'll be crazy about 'em. You're a pretty wise old wop, Tony, ain't you? (*He hands the box back to* TONY, *who laughs delightedly.* JOE *looks at him for a moment then goes to door and calls out.*) Amy!

TONY. Eh, Joe!

JOE. You're goin' to make the presentation right away now. That'll settle your worries for you. . . . Amy, come here! Tony wants to see you!

TONY. You think is good time now?

JOE. I *know*. . . . Amy!
(AMY *appears in doorway. She wears her wedding dress and veil. The dress is undeniably pretty and only wrong in one or two places. The veil has been pulled rather askew. The whole picture is at once charming and pathetic.*)

AMY. What's the idea? (*Her voice is a little tired. She does not look at* JOE.)

JOE. Tony wants you.

AMY (*she comes in stolidly and takes the chair farthest from* TONY's *cot. She sits there stiffly*). Well, here I am.

TONY (*ultra-tenderly*). My Amy is tire'!

AMY. You don't blame me, do you? I've had quite a day. Gee, them kids out there have been climbing all over me.

TONY. Da's good.

AMY. Oh, I don't mind kids if they go to bed when they ought to and know how to behave. Believe me, if I ever have any kids, they're going to behave.

TONY. You hear dat, Joe?

AMY. I said "if." (*A silence.*) I wouldn't object.

TONY (*amorously*). Amy . . . Come over here.

AMY (*rising quickly*). I guess I ain't so tired. I guess I better go back or they'll be wondering what's become of the blooming bride. Some bloom, huh? (*The fireworks hiss and flare again and* AMY, *very like a little girl, is out on the porch for the delight of seeing them. The enthusiasm of the crowd fairly rattles the windows.*) They sure do yell out there! When you get enough wops together and put enough vino in 'em, they sure can speak up! . . . I think I'll take off my veil. (*She does.*) Phew! That thing don't look like no weight at all, but it feels like a ton of bricks.

TONY. Amy, come over here.

AMY. I'm all right where I am.

TONY. Amy!

AMY. What?

TONY. You like earrings, Amy?

AMY. Earrings? I'm human, ain't I?

JOE. That's the idea.

AMY (*a real snarl*). I didn't speak to you. I was addressing Tony.

TONY. Ah, you call me Tony for da first time!

AMY. Expect me to call my husband mister? That'd sound swell, wouldn't it? Tony. Short for Antonio. Antonio and Cleopatra, huh? Can you beat it? You'll have to call me Cleo.

TONY. I like better Amy.

AMY. There ain't no short for Amy. It's French and it means beloved. Beloved! Can you beat it? The boss in the spaghetti palace told me that the night he tried to give me a twelve-dollar pearl necklace. Twelve dollars! He was some sport. When he seen I couldn't see it that way, he give it to Blanche. She was the other girl that worked there. He had a wife and three kids too. (TONY *beckons again and* AMY *takes further refuge in conversation.*) I like that name Blanche. I used to wish my name was Blanche instead of Amy. Blanche got in trouble. Poor Blanche! Gee, I was sorry for that girl!

TONY. Come over here, Amy. (*He holds out the box.*)

AMY. What's that?

TONY. Ees my present for my Amy.

AMY. What you got there, Tony?

TONY. For you.

AMY. Something for me? (*By this time, she has got over to the cot. She takes the box.*) Honest? Well, now, if that isn't sweet of you, Tony. (*She opens it.*) Oh! . . . Oh!! . . . Oh!!!

TONY. Ees for mak' Amy happy.

JOE. They're real! Real diamonds!

TONY. You bet your life! Four hundra dollar'.

AMY. I . . . I . . . (*Tears come.*) Real diamonds. . . . (*She sits in the* DOCTOR's *chair and cries and cries.*)

TONY. Don' cry, Amy! Don' cry! Ees no' for cry, earrings! Ees for festa! Ees for marryin' with Tony!

AMY. I don't know what to say! I don't know what to do!

JOE. Put 'em on. (*He gets the mirror, brings it over to where* AMY *sits, and holds it for her while she begins to put the earrings on. Her sobs gradually subside.*)

AMY. I had another pair once, so I got my ears pierced already. Ma pierced my ears herself with a needle and thread. Only these kind screw on! Say, ain't they beautiful! My others were turquoises and gold. Real turquoises and real gold. But these here cost four hundred dollars! Oh, I never dreamed of anything so gorgeous! (*She takes the mirror from* JOE.)

TONY. Amy . . . Amy . . .

AMY. Can I wear 'em whenever I want?

TONY. You can wear 'em in da bed if you want!

AMY. Oh, thank you, Tony! (*She is just about to kiss him.*)

JOE. Now, everything's fine!

AMY (*furiously*). Say what's the idea? What have you got to do with this? You're always buttin' in. Say . . . (*Suddenly she remembers the momentous photograph which still lies on the table.*) Wait a minute. (*She picks it up and hands it quite violently to* JOE.) Here's your picture.

TONY (*watching in terror*). Santa Maria!

AMY. Here! You better take it! Take it, I tell you! I don't want it.
(JOE *looks first at the photograph, then at the lady.*)

JOE. I guess you ain't far wrong, Amy. I hope there ain't no hard feelin's.

AMY. Why should there be any hard feelings?

TONY. Benissimo!

JOE. All right. Only I didn't want you to think. . . . (*A long pause.*)

AMY (*very steadily*). You ain't got much of a swelled head, have you, Mr. Joe?
(JOE's *face falls. The tension is snapped by a gesture from* TONY.)

TONY. Tear him up, Joe! Tear him up!
(JOE *obeys.*)

AMY. Now we don't ever have to think of that again.

TONY. Madonna! . . . Da's verra good.

AMY. You see, that's the only way to do. There ain't no use of keeping things around to remind you of what you want to forget. Start in all over again new and fresh. That's my way. Burn up everything you want to put behind you. No reminders and no souvenirs. I been doing that regular about once a month ever since I was a kid. No memories for me. No hard feelings. It's a great life, if you don't weaken. I guess, if I keep at it long enough, I may get somewhere, some day. (*She turns and deliberately kisses* TONY *on the brow.*)

JOE (*to* TONY). Will that hold you? I guess you don't need to worry no more after that. I guess that fixes your troubles for good. I guess you better admit I was pretty near right.

TONY. Now you know for w'y I been wantin' you go away, Joe. Dat goddam picture photograph! But evrathing is fix' now. Evrathing is fine. You don' need go away now, Joe.

JOE. You don't need me now. I guess I can migrate now. You got Amy to take care of you.

TONY. No! No! I need you here for tak' care of my vineyard. I don' let you go away now. Amy don' let you go away now.

AMY. Is he thinking of going away, Tony?

TONY. He don't go now, Dio mio! Ees no good Joe goin' away and leavin' Tony sick in da bed with nobody for runnin' vineyard!

JOE. You'll get somebody.

AMY. When's he going?

TONY. He say to-morrow. You don' let him go, Amy?

AMY. I got nothing to say about it.

TONY. You hear dat, Joe. Amy is askin' you for stay here.

AMY (*scorn*). Yes, I am!

JOE. I got to go, Tony. I just plain got to go.

AMY. If he won't stay for you, Tony, he won't stay for me. It ain't the place of a lady to be coaxing him, anyhow. . . . (*She*

again turns malevolent attention upon JOE.) Where you headed for?

JOE. The next place.

AMY. What's the idea?

JOE. I just got to be on my way, an' that's all there is to it.

TONY. Ees all dose goddam Wobblies, Amy. You tell him stay here, w'ile Tony is so sick in da bed like dees. You don' go to-morrow, Joe. You and me is talkin' more by-an'-by, in da mornin'.

JOE. Oh, what's the use? I'm goin', I tell you.

AMY (*smiling darkly*). It must be pretty swell, being free and independent and beating it around the country just however you feel like, sleeping any place the notion hits you, no ties, work a day and bum a week, here and there, you and the—what do you call 'em? Wobblies? Huh! I never could see much in it myself. Calling in at farmhouses for a plate of cold stew and a slab of last Sunday's pie. Down in the Santa Clara we used to keep a dog for those boys. I guess it's a fine life if you like it. Only I never had much use for hoboes myself.

TONY. Joe ain' no hobo, Amy!

AMY. Ain't he?

JOE (*completely discomfited*). I guess I'll say good-night.

FATHER MCKEE (*furiously shouting off stage*). You got no business callin' it sacramental, because it ain't got no sanction from the Church!
(TONY *looks at the pair of them in unbelieving horror.* JOE *starts to go.* AMY *smiles triumphantly. Then the situation is saved by a tumult of voices and the porch is suddenly packed with the guests of the festa: men, women, and children, old and young, fat and lean. They follow* THE DOCTOR *and* FATHER MCKEE, *who are engaged in a furious argument.*)

THE DOCTOR. Is the Church opposed to the law or is it not?

FATHER MCKEE. The Church is opposed to interfering with the divine gifts of Providence.

THE DOCTOR (*as he enters*). It's the greatest reform since the abolition of slavery.

FATHER MCKEE (*as he enters*). "The ruler of the feast calleth the bridegroom and sayeth unto him: 'Every man setteth on first the good wine'."

THE DOCTOR. Oh, hell!

FATHER MCKEE. You're a godless heretic, young man, or you wouldn't be talkin' such blasphemy! I ain't got no sympathy with drunkenness, but there's plenty of worse things. How about chamberin'? Ain't chamberin' a worse sin than drunkenness? You think you can put a stop to drunkenness by pullin' up all the grapes. I suppose you think you can put a stop to chamberin' by pulling up all the women!

JOE. There's an argument for you, Doc.

THE DOCTOR. Alcohol is a poison to the entire alimentary system whether you make it in a still or in a wine barrel. It's poison, and poison's no good for any man. As for the Church . . .

FATHER MCKEE (*beside himself*). It ain't poison if you don't get drunk on it, an' you don't get drunk if you're a good Cath'lic!

THE DOCTOR. I suppose that drunkenness is confined to such scientific heretics as myself?

AMY. You certainly was lappin' it up outside, Doc.

TONY. Don' fight!

FATHER MCKEE. You'll have to pardon me, Tony, but when I hear these heretics gettin' full on bootleg liquor and callin' it sacramental!
(*The rest of the argument is drowned in the pandemonium of the crowd. At first* THE DOCTOR *tries to keep them out.*)

THE GUESTS. Buona notte! Buon riposo! Evviva Antonio! Tanti auguri! Felice notte! Tante grazie!

JOE. Festa's over.

THE GUESTS. Come sta Antonio? Come va? Voglio veder la padrona! Grazie, Antonio! Buona notte! Tanti auguri! A rivederci!

THE DOCTOR (*to* JOE). Tell them to cut the row!

THE GUESTS. Grazie, Antonio! Mille grazie, Antonio! Buona notte, Antonio! Tanti auguri! A rivederci!

THE DOCTOR. Keep those wops out of here! There's been enough noise already with this bigoted old soak.

FATHER MCKEE. You heretical, blasphemin' . . .

TONY. Padre, Madonna mia, don' fight no more! (*To the crowd.*) Eh!

THE DOCTOR (*still holding the crowd back in the doorway*). No, you can't come in here!

THE GUESTS. Si, si, dottore! Si, si, dottore! Prego, dottore!

THE DOCTOR. No! Tony's too sick!

TONY. Tak' a pinch-a snuff, Doc, an' sit down. (*The guests surge in as* TONY *calls to them.*) Vieni! Vieni qui! Venite tutti! Venite tutti!

THE GUESTS. Come va? Sta bene? Sta meglio, Antonio? Ha tanto sofferto, poveretto! Poveretto!

TONY (*picking out a small boy*). Ecco il mio Giovannino! Ah, com' è grande e bello e forte! Quanto pesa?

GIOVANNINO'S MOTHER. Ah, si, è grande, non è vero? Pesa sessanta cinque libbre.

TONY. Sessanta cinque! (*To* AMY.) Amy, looka him! He weigh' sixty-five pound', an' he's only . . . (*To the mother.*) Quant' anni?

GIOVANNINO'S MOTHER. Soltanto nove.

TONY. He's only nine year' old an' he weigh sixty-five pound'!

ANOTHER MOTHER. Antonio, ecco la mia.
(*A little girl runs to throw her arms around* TONY'S *neck and kiss him. Exclamations of delight.*)

TONY (*to the mother*). Ah! Come si chia-ma?

THE SECOND MOTHER. Maria Maddalena Rosina Vittoria Emanuela.

TONY. Maria Maddalena Rosina Vit— (*To* AMY.) Looka Maria Maddalena! Ah, Maria Maddalena is goin' grow up an' be a fine, beautiful lady like my Amy.

GIOVANNINO'S MOTHER. E il mio Giovannino! (*To* MARIA'S MOTHER.) Santa Madonna! Ella non è più bella che il mio Giovannino!

MARIA'S MOTHER (*furious*). Si, è più bella! È molto più bella che un ragazzone come questo.

GIOVANNINO'S MOTHER. Non è ragazzone, senti!

MARIA'S MOTHER. Si! Ma, la mia carina.

THE MEN (*hilariously*). Giovannino! Giovannino!

THE WOMEN (*at the same time*). Maria Maddalena! Maria Maddalena!

THE DOCTOR. Come on, now, get out! We've had enough of this!

ANGELO *and* GIORGIO (*facing the howling mob*). Basta! Basta! Via! Via! Fuori! Avanti! Al diavolo!
(*Uproar and retreat.*)

AMY (*on the porch, she stops them*). No, wait a minute! I want to tell 'em all good-night. Good-night! Good-night! Thank you. I've had the very best wedding that ever was and I'm the happiest girl in the world because you've been so good to me. Come back to-morrow and see Tony and tell him all the news. Good-night and God bless you.

VOICES. Siamo molto contenti! Com' è gentile! Com' è bella! Com' è simpatica! Grazie tanto, Amy!

JOE. They say thank you and God bless you. . . . Beat it, now. Buona notte! Run along. Come back to-morrow.
(*As they go down the hill, tenor, concertina, and chorus strike into song.*)

TONY. Oh, Amy, I w'isper in your ear, Amy. You ain' goin' be mad with Tony for bein' so crazy-wild with love? You come in da house like da spring come in da winter. You come in da house like da pink flower dat sit on da window sill. W'en you come da whole world is like da inside da wine cup. You ondrastan', Amy? I canno' help talkin' dees way. I got for tell you, Amy, an' I ain' got no English language for tell you. My Amy is so good, so prett'! My Amy. . . . (*He fairly breaks down.* AMY *pats his hand.*)

JOE (*to* FATHER MCKEE). Look at the poor wop. (*He is just going.*)

THE DOCTOR. Don't go, Joe. I want a hand with Tony.

FATHER MCKEE. Listen. . . . (*He holds up his hand for them to attend to the music. He pours wine into a cup.*) Here's to the bridal couple!

JOE (*same business*). Doc?

THE DOCTOR. No, thanks.

AMY. Oh, Doctor!

TONY. Doc, you no drink Tony's health?

THE DOCTOR. Oh, all right! (*He drinks with the others.*) Nasty stuff. (*He drains his glass. They laugh, all of them:*) Off to bed with you now, Tony!

TONY. My leg is hurt too much. I canno' sleep.

THE DOCTOR. I've got something that'll make you sleep. (*He mixes a powder in water and presents it to* TONY *for consumption.*)

TONY. Jes' Chris'! I canno' drink water, Doc! (*With the* DOCTOR'S *consent he adds wine to the draught.*)

THE DOCTOR. That's right. . . . Drink up. . . . (*The potion is downed.*)

TONY. Amy, you lookin' sad!

JOE. Do you blame her? She's had some day. (*A pat on her shoulder. She shrinks angrily.*)

AMY. I ain't sad. . . . It was a swell wedding and everybody had a swell time. Hear that?

They're still singing. Ain't it pretty? And I don't want to hear no more of what the Doc was telling me outside about bringing a trained nurse up here from Napa. I'm all the nurse Tony needs, and don't nobody be afraid of my working, because there's nothing I like better. And when Tony's good and strong and don't have to be in bed all the time, we'll have Giorgio and Angelo carry him out in the sun and I'll sit beside him and read the paper out loud and we'll look at the view and feel that nice wind and we'll just enjoy ourselves. And the doc'll come up and see us. And the Padre, too, if they can keep from fighting. And if Joe goes away—why—he goes away, that's all. Don't nobody fret about little Amy. She's going to be all right.

(*The* DOCTOR *and the* PRIEST *exchange approving glances.*)

FATHER MCKEE. Amy, you're a credit to the parish.

THE DOCTOR (*at the head of the cot*). Joe, take that end!

TONY (*still spellbound*). My Amy. . . .

AMY. Yes, Tony?

TONY. I'm sleepy.

THE DOCTOR (*as* JOE *and he lift the cot*). Not too high.

TONY (*groaning, he can still reach to take his bottle along*). Wait!

JOE. Steady! You hold the door, Padre.

THE DOCTOR. Easy now! Not too fast.

AMY. Watch out for his hand!

THE DOCTOR. Take shorter steps, Joe. Every man ought to be taught how to carry a stretcher. Why, when I was in France . . . (*He backs through the door.*) Lower your end, Joe! You'll give him apoplexy.

TONY. Oh! . . .

JOE. I got him. . . . (*He follows through the door with the foot of the cot. Another groan from* TONY. AMY *takes a step toward door.*)

FATHER MCKEE. Better give 'em a minute. (*He goes into the bedroom.* AMY *is left alone. She stands quite still for a moment; then, giddily, drops into a chair.* FATHER MCKEE *returns.*)

FATHER MCKEE. You're a fine brave girl.

AMY. Thanks.

FATHER MCKEE. We have our trials, all of us.

AMY. Sure, I know that.

FATHER MCKEE. If ever you need a word of comfort, call on me, my daughter.

AMY. Thanks.

FATHER MCKEE. You may not be a Cath'lic, but I'll do my best by you. (AMY *smiles wanly.*) I had my doubts of this here marriage, but God knows who's meant for who in this world. He ain't done a bad turn by either you or Tony.

AMY. I got no kick.

(*The* DOCTOR *enters, quietly closing the bedroom door after him.*)

FATHER MCKEE. Be patient with him. He's old enough to be your father, and no man ain't got no business marryin' at his age, but he's a good fella.

AMY. I guess I better go in there now.

THE DOCTOR (*wiping his hands medically on his spotless handkerchief*). He's asleep. I've never known the like. Never in all my years of practice. It's a case that ought to be written up for the whole, entire medical profession. Both legs broken in the morning. Tibia, fibula, femur, and ischium. X-rayed and set inside of an hour after the accident. Patient married at noon and survives ten hours of whooping Dago celebration with no apparent ill effects.

AMY (*grim*). Yeah! What do you want me to do, Doctor?

THE DOCTOR. Let me send up a nurse in the morning.

AMY. No.

THE DOCTOR. A man in a cast's a handful. It's going to be a long siege.

AMY. I can manage. (*Suddenly desperate.*) God! I got to have something to do!

THE DOCTOR. Well. . . . (*He shrugs his shoulders.*) If he wakes up to-night, give him another one of those powders in a little wine. Wine won't harm the drug and water might kill the patient. Eh, Padre?

AMY. Is that all, Doctor?

THE DOCTOR. That's all. I'll come up early in the morning.

AMY. Thanks.

THE DOCTOR. Sure about the nurse? (*She nods.*) You take it pretty calmly.

AMY. Ain't much else I can do, is there?

THE DOCTOR. Good-night. Joe's fixing you up a bed. He'll be here if you want him.

FATHER MCKEE (*going with the* DOCTOR). I ain't kissed the bride.

THE DOCTOR. Come on! (*He pushes* FATHER MCKEE *in front of him and they go off. Their voices die away.*)
(AMY *goes to the table and mechanically removes her earrings.* AH GEE *enters by the outer door with a tray of glasses.* JOE *enters from the bedroom, closing the door carefully after him.*)

JOE. You turn in, Ah Gee. I'm going to sleep in here. (AH GEE *goes to his kitchen.* JOE *watches* AMY *with the same puzzled frown he has worn since she first turned upon him.*) Amy . . . (*She stiffens.*) I got you fixed up in Tony's big bed. I'm goin' to sleep in here in case you want any help.

AMY. All right.

JOE. Well, good-night. (*He goes about making himself comfortable for the night.*)

AMY. Good-night, Joe.

JOE. Keep a stiff upper lip. Everything's going to turn out O. K. Good-night.

AMY. You certainly do think you're God Almighty, don't you?

JOE. I don't get you.

AMY. Oh, well, let it go. I guess I don't feel so good.

JOE (*still busy with his bed*). Maybe it's the vino. It don't agree with some folks. (*A slight pause.*)

AMY. I guess I'm just nervous.

JOE. I'd be nervous myself if I'd just been married.

AMY. Would you?

JOE. If I was a girl, I would.

AMY. Maybe that's why I'm nervous.

JOE. Sure it is. I often think how it must be for a girl takin' a big, important step like gettin' married. Everything new an' diff'-rent an' all that.

AMY. Yeah.

JOE. But I wouldn't let it worry me if I was you.

AMY. I won't, Mister Joe. (*She takes up one of the lamps.*)

JOE. That's the idea. Good-night.

AMY. Good-night. (*She turns and looks desperately at him.*)

JOE. Say, look here, Amy . . .

AMY. I don't remember of giving you leave to use my Christian name.

JOE. Excuse me . . . only . . . there's something I just got to say to you before I go away. Because I am going. I'm going in the morning just as soon as Tony wakes up so's I can tell him good-by. But there's something I just got to ask you.

AMY. What is it?

JOE. You like Tony all right, don't you?

AMY. I married him, didn't I? And I let him give me jewelry, too, didn't I? A nice, self-respecting girl don't accept jewelry from a man she don't like. Not real jewelry.

JOE. I know that . . . only . . . it ain't just what I mean. Because, Tony—oh, he's a nut an' a wop an' all that, but he's just the best old fella I ever knew. Regular salt of the earth, Tony is. I wouldn't like to see Tony in trouble or unhappy or gettin' his feelings hurt or anything in that line. . . .

AMY (*dangerously*). Oh, wouldn't you?

JOE. No. An' it's all up to you now. . . . An' . . . well, you see what a fine old fella he is, don't you?

AMY. I ain't been complaining about him that I remember. When I start in complaining there'll be plenty of time then for outsiders to butt in and make remarks.

JOE. Don't get sore.

AMY (*fury again*). Who's sore? Say, listen to me. I know what I'm about, see? I married for a home, see? Well, I got a home, ain't I? I wanted to get away from working in the city. Well, I got away, didn't I? I'm in the country, ain't I? And I ain't working so very hard, either, that I can notice. Oh, I know what's expected of me and I ain't going to lay down on my job. Don't you fret. You be on your way, and mind your own business.

JOE. Oh, all right!

AMY. I got all I bargained for and then some. I'm fixed. I'm satisfied. I didn't come up here . . . like I did . . . looking for love . . . or . . . or anything like that.

JOE. All I got to say is it's a good thing you got so dam' much sense.

AMY. I'll thank you not to swear about me, too. . . .

JOE. You got me wrong, Amy. I apologize. Maybe I was only seein' Tony's side of the question. Some girls would have been sorer'n you was over what old Tony done to get you here. But you're a real sport, that's what you are. You're a great girl an' I'm all for you. (*He emphasizes his approval with another patronizing pat on her shoulder.*)

AMY. Oh, for God's sake, leave me alone, can't you?

JOE (*who can grow angry himself*). Sure, I can! Good-night!

AMY. Good-night! (*She stands quite still, so does he. Far, far away the irrepressible tenor resumes "Maria Mari."*)

JOE. I'm sleeping in here in case . . .

AMY. There won't be any need of your putting yourself out.

JOE. How do you know but what Tony . . .

AMY. I can take care of Tony and the further off *you* keep yourself the better I'll be pleased. (*Their eyes blaze.*)

JOE. Well, if you feel that way, I'll go back to my own shack. (*He grabs his coat and makes for the door.*) That wop'll be singing all night. (*He is out on the porch.*)

AMY. Joe!

JOE. What? (*He returns.*)

AMY. Would you mind waiting just a minute? There's something *I* got to ask *you*.

JOE. Shoot. . . .

AMY. You got to tell *me* the truth this time. You just got to tell me the truth. . . . You really and honestly didn't know nothing about his sending me that photo of you instead of his own, did you? You didn't know nothing at all about that?

JOE. Honest to God, I didn't. . . . Honest to God. . . .

AMY. On your sacred word of honor?

JOE. Honest.

AMY. I'm glad. And I want to apologize to you for what I said just now . . . and for that other thing I said about your being a common hobo and all. . . . I'm sorry, Joe. Will you forgive me?

JOE. Oh, that's all right.

AMY. I wouldn't want to have you go away to-morrow thinking what a mean character I got.

JOE. Nothing like that.

AMY. You mean it?

JOE. Shake. (*They shake hands, standing in the doorway.*) You're cryin'! . . . What's the matter, kid?

AMY. Oh, I don't know. . . . Nothing. . . . I'm all right. . . .

JOE. Come on! Don't get upset. Just make the best of things.

AMY. It ain't that.

JOE. Well, just make the best of things, anyway.

AMY. I'm trying to! I'm trying to!

JOE (*his hands on her shoulders*). You're married to a good man. I know the weddin' was kind of funny with Tony all smashed up an' all. But you just hold on a while an' everythin'll be O. K. You'll see!

AMY. I bet all those people are laughing at me.

JOE. No, they ain't.

AMY. I bet you're laughing at me.

JOE. I ain't, Amy. I'm sorry. . . .

AMY (*moving back from him*). Leave me alone, can't you?

JOE (*his voice very low*). Say, you're all right, Amy. . . . You're plumb all right.

AMY. I always was all right till I come up here. Now I wish I was dead! I wish I was dead!

JOE. Don' talk that way. You're all right. . . . (*Clumsily, he takes her arm. She stumbles. He catches her. There is a moment of silence broken only by their deep breathing as the physical being of one is communicated to the physical being of the other. Suddenly and irresistibly he clutches her to his breast and kisses her. She struggles a moment, then abandons herself.*)

TONY (*calling out in the bedroom*). Amy! (*She breaks loose, sobbing hysterically.*)

JOE (*a whisper*). Jesus! (*She stifles a little cry and turns for the bedroom door.*) No, you don't. . . . (*He catches her.*)

AMY (*struggling*). Let me go!

TONY. Amy!

(*She breaks free, terrified, and runs out of the house.* JOE *stands listening a moment, then runs after her as the curtain falls.*)

ACT THREE

The scene is unchanged, but the woman's presence has made itself felt. Handsome, though inexpensive, cretonne curtains grace the windows. A garish jardirière of porcelain holds a geranium plant and stands upon a colored oriental tabouret. The lamps have acquired art shades: one of some light-colored silk on a wire form and adorned with roses of the same material in a lighter shade, the other of parchment painted with windmills and Dutch kiddies. New pictures selected from the stock-in-trade of almost any provincial "art department" hang upon the walls; one of them, perhaps, a portrait of a well-known lady screen star. These have replaced Washington and Garibaldi and the Italian Steamship Company's poster. Painted and elaborately befringed leather sofa cushions fill the large chairs. It is hoped that one of the variety showing the head of Hiawatha can be secured for this, as they say, "touch." A brilliantly embroidered centerpiece covers the dining-room table and the flowers in the middle are palpably artificial. A white wastepaper basket is girt by a cerise ribbon which makes some corner of the room splendid. A victrola graces another corner.

Three months have passed. It is mid-afternoon.

An invalid chair has been made by laying a board between the seat of the morris chair and the top of a box. In this TONY *reclines, his crutches lying on the floor by his side.* FATHER MCKEE *nods drowsily in another chair.* JOE *sits on the porch rail outside the window perusing the scareheads of an I. W. W. paper.*

FATHER MCKEE (*continuing the discussion*). Now, Joe, don't be tryin' to tell me that things is goin' to be any better for havin' a revolution, because they ain't. Gover'ment's always gover'ment no matter what you call it, an' no particular kind of gover'ment ain't no more'n a label anyway. You don't change nothin' by givin' it a new name. Stick a "peppermint" label on a bottle of castor oil an' then drink it an' see what happens to you. Castor oil happens!

TONY. I am work' just as much like Joe an' I don' want changin' nothing.

JOE. I suppose you both come over here in the first place because you was satisfied with everythin' just like it was in the old country?

FATHER MCKEE. Human nature ain't nothin' but human nature an' the only way you ever could make a gover'ment is by obedience. Scalliwaggin' around about grievances an' labels don't accomplish nothin'. An' the only way you can make a revolution anythin' but a mess to no purpose is to change the people's ideas an' thank goodness there ain't nobody can accomplish that. It can't be done.

JOE. They're changin' already, Padre.

FATHER MCKEE. I'm talkin' to you with the cassock off, Joe. I'm lettin' you in on the secrets of the Mother Church. She knows the stock of ideas the world over an' she knows they don't never change. The Mother Church just keeps hammerin' an' hammerin' the same old nails because she knows there ain't no new ones worth hammerin'.

TONY. People come in da Unita State' because ees good place. I been comin' for mak' money.

JOE. You certainly succeeded.

TONY. You don' ondrastan', Joe. You got crazy idea. I'm comin' here for mak' money an' you want tak' my money all away.

JOE. What's your idea of progress, Padre?

FATHER MCKEE. Improvin' yourself! Now, Joe, it comes to my notice that you been 'round here talkin' pretty uppity 'bout the U. S. gover'ment. 'Tain't no good just makin' slurrin' remarks 'bout the gover'ment when you ain't got the ability nor the power to do nothin' toward improvin' it. You have got the power to do somethin' toward improvin' yourself, but I don't see you doin' it.

TONY. W'at I care for gover'ment? Peoples is tellin' me king is no good an' freedom is verra fine. W'at I care for king? W'at I care for freedom? Evrabody say dees gover'ment is bad for havin' pro'ibish'. I say pro'ibish' mak' me dam' rich. Evra man got his own idea w'at is good for evrabody else.

JOE. You're a bloomin' capitalist, that's what you are!

TONY. You mak' me tire', Joe. Evra minute talkin' 'bout Russia. . . . Russia. . . . Tak' a pinch-a snuff an' shut up!

JOE. Russia's got the right idea.

FATHER MCKEE. Now, listen to me, young man. If you had the energy an' the reverence for authority and the continence that Tony has, you wouldn't be carryin' on 'bout no revolutions in Russia. 'T'ain't sense. I've read a-plenty of your radical literature an' if you ask me, it's just plain stupid. I may be a priest an' I may be a celibate, but that don't make me no less of a man. An' no real man ain't never got no use for carryin's on. You radicals, Joe, you're always an' forever hollerin' an' carryin' on 'bout your rights. How 'bout your duties? There ain't no one to prevent your doin' your duties but you ain't never done 'em in your life.

JOE. I'm savin' my duties for the brotherhood of man.

TONY. Dio mio!

FATHER MCKEE. You're talkin' a lot of balderdash. Mind your own business an' leave the brotherhood of man to me. Brothers is *my* job.

TONY. You think evrabody's goin' be brother like dat an' don' scrap no more? Ees crazy idea! You ain' got no good sense, Joe, you an' dose goddam Wobblies.

FATHER MCKEE. I been mullin' this over in my mind, Joe, ever since Tony asked me to come up an' talk to you. An' I come to the conclusion that capital an' labor'll go on scrappin' to the end of time and they'll always be a certain number of people that'll stand up for the under dog. I been standin' up for the underdog all my life . . .

JOE (*indignant, he comes into the room*). Yes, you have! A helluva lot of standin' up you ever done for anybody but yourself!

TONY (*talking at the same time*). Now, Joe, don' you be gettin' fresh! You listen to w'at da Padre's sayin'!

FATHER MCKEE (*talking at the same time*). . . . but I learned a long time ago that the dog on top needs just as much standin' up for as the other kind and I ain't got much use for either of 'em because both of 'em's always complainin' an' carryin' on.

TONY. I been 'Merican citizen for twent' year'. I been vote evra year—some times two times. Ees fine thing, vote! I like. He mak' me feel like I am good man an' patriotic fella. But w'at I know 'bout vote? I don' know nothing. I don' care nothing. You think you know so much, eh? You want for change evrathing an' we'n you got evrathing change' like you want, some other fella is comin' for changin' you. Ees no good. (*A defiant look about him.*) You look-a me an' do like I done. You marry with good wife like my Amy an' live quiet in a fine house an' gettin' rich like me an' . . . an' . . . an' raisin' playnta kids like I am goin' do. Da's w'at is for life. Not for runnin' evra place, goddam to hell gover'-ment with goddam Wobblies!

JOE. Now you got Tony goin' on kids again. I sure am catchin' all that's comin' my way. But, just the same, I'm goin' to take my trip to Frisco an' see what's what.

FATHER MCKEE. Well, Joe, I can understand your wantin' to shake the dust of this place off'n your feet. But I got to tell you that the adventures of the spirit is a great deal more interestin' than the adventures of the flesh. No man can't do no more'n

'bout six things with his flesh. But he can have a heap of fun with his immortal soul.

TONY. Joe is dam' lucky havin' good job here. Last time he talk 'bout goin' away, he tak' my advice an' stay here for runnin' da vineyard. Dees time he better tak' my advice some more.
(FATHER MCKEE *is fingering* JOE's *papers ominously.*)

JOE. I'll just trouble you for them papers, Padre.

FATHER MCKEE. If you take my advice you'll burn 'em.

TONY. Joe don' mean no harm.

JOE. Maybe I don't mean nothin' at all. Maybe I'm just restless an' rarin' to go. I read these things an' they make me think A man ought to think if he can. Oh, not tall talk. Just what he could be doin' himself. I think how I could get into the scrap. I ought to have been in on the dock strike at San Pedro, but I wasn't. I don't want to miss another big fight like that, do I? You fellows don't understand, but that's the way it is. An' maybe you're right an' I'm wrong. I can't help that. Maybe when I get down to Frisco I'll hear the same old bull from the same old loud-mouths, just like it used to be. Maybe I'll get disgusted and beat it south for the orange pickin's, or maybe go back on the railroad, or maybe in the oilfields. But, what the hell! I been hangin' around here on the point of goin' for three months now. I might just as well pick up and clear out to-morrow or the day after. I'll come back some day, Tony. Anyway, there ain't no use of expectin' anythin' out of a guy like me. Don't get sore. What the hell!

TONY. You goin' in da jail, sure!

JOE. I could go worse places. A guy went to jail up in Quincy, in Plumas County, awhile back, for carryin' a Wobbly card—like this one, see? (*He displays the famous bit of red cardboard.*) His lawyer pleads with the judge to go easy on the sentence. "Your honor," he says, "this chap served in France an' won the Croy de Gaire an' the Distinguished Service Cross." An' right there the guy jumps up an' says: "Don't you pay no attention to that stuff," he says. "I don't want no credit for no services I ever performed for no gover'ment that tells me I got to go to jail to stand up for my rights."

FATHER MCKEE. Do you want to go to jail?

JOE. There's worse places, I tell you. I been there before, too. That guy in Quincy got the limit an' I'd like to shake hands with him, I would. Tony says this is a free country. Well, Tony ought to know. He's a bootlegger.

TONY (*indignantly*). Hah!

JOE. What I say is: about the only freedom we got left is the freedom to choose which one of our rights we'll go to jail for.

FATHER MCKEE (*super-sententiously*). Joe .

TONY. Shhh! Here's Amy!

AMY (*off stage*). Ah Gee!
(JOE *rises;* FATHER MCKEE *pauses in his harangue;* TONY *beams;* AMY *enters. She wears a bright dress and a red-straw hat which pushes her hair down about her face. A duster swings dashingly from her shoulders. Her market basket hangs from her arm. She has stuffed some late lupin in the top of it.*)

AMY. Scrapping again, are you? What's the matter, this time? Has Joe got another attack of the foot-itch? (*She sets the basket down on the table, doffs hat and duster, and, as she does so, sees* JOE's *papers.*) Oho! So that's it. (*Patiently* JOE *folds the papers up.*) See them, Tony? (*She exhibits the lupin and begins to stuff it into the vase with the artificial flowers.*) Ain't they sweet? They're so pretty they might be artificial.

FATHER MCKEE. We been talkin' 'bout reformin' the social system.

AMY. Well, you got a fine day for it. (*She hugs* TONY's *head and lets him pat her hand.*) Ain't the doctor come yet?

TONY. Doc don' come to-day.

AMY. Sure he does.

JOE. He comes on Thursday.

FATHER MCKEE. To-day's Wednesday.

AMY. Well, I never! Here they are reforming the world and they don't even know what day of the week it is. Ain't men the limit?

TONY. Nobody is so smart like my Amy. (*With a toss of her head she swirls off into the kitchen.*)

AMY. Don't let me stop you! Go right ahead. (*In the kitchen.*) Ah Gee . . . Oh, there you are. . . .

FATHER MCKEE. Thursday! It's my day to talk to the boys down at the parish school.

JOE. Hand 'em what you just been handin' me, Padre.

FATHER MCKEE. What I told you was confidential, Joe. I'm sorry you won't listen to it.

AMY (*she returns, carrying a dish with apples and a knife*). See them, Tony?

TONY. Apples!

AMY. Guess what for?

TONY. Apples pie?

AMY (*she sits beside* TONY *and falls to on the apples*). Well, the world may need reforming but I got no kick. The grapes is near ripe and ready for picking. The nights is getting longer, the mornings is getting colder and Tony's getting better. Down town they're putting up the posters for the circus and I hear the show's going into winter quarters just the other side of Napa. I guess that's all the remarks I got to make.

JOE. Here's the doc, now. . . .
(*A Ford motor.*)

THE DOCTOR (*off stage*). Hello!

AMY. Yoo hoo!
(*The* DOCTOR *appears, shakes hands with* AMY, *nods to* JOE *and the* PADRE, *and comes in to* TONY.)

THE DOCTOR. Well, how do the crutches go?

AMY. Just fine.

TONY. You want see me walkin', Doc?

THE DOCTOR. Perhaps, I do. Let's see. . . . (*He feels the injured legs.*) Tibia . . . Fibula . . . Feels all right.

TONY (*with a proud, anatomical gesture*). Ischium?

THE DOCTOR (*he rises and nods approvingly*). All right, Tony, show us what you can do. No jumping, mind! Lend him a hand, Joe.
(*He stands aside to watch.* JOE *assists* TONY. *Grunting,* TONY *stands on his crutches and grins proudly.*)

TONY. Ees hurtin' here. (*Indicating arm pits.*) But ees goin' fine! (*A few tottering steps.*)

THE DOCTOR. Steady! Whoa! (*Laughter as* TONY *barely makes a chair.*) You ought to be put on exhibition. If anyone had told me that day when I had you on the table that I should see you on crutches in three months! Well, all I can say is, it pays to know how to set a fracture.

AMY. I guess it makes you realize what a good doctor you are.

THE DOCTOR. He owes something to your nursing, ma'am.

FATHER MCKEE. It's like the layin' on of hands, her nursin' is.

AMY. Funny you're saying that, Padre. I once had my fortune told down in Frisco. Out of a palmistry book one of my friends had. Everything in your hand means something, you know. See those bumps? Ain't they funny? Well, the book said that those bumps mean you're a good nurse and can take care of anybody no matter how sick he is. That's why I wouldn't let you send for no trained nurse, Doc. I was afraid she wouldn't have my bumps. . . . Gee, I got funny hands! . . .

THE DOCTOR. I'm not sure that medical science pays much attention to the nursing bump, ma'am, but you have certainly got it. I'll admit that.

TONY. My Amy is da best nurse I ever see.

AMY. Oh, Tony!

THE DOCTOR. I'm going to put your patient outside in the sun. Is there a good level place?

AMY. Under the arbor! . . . Oh Tony!

TONY. After three month' in dees goddam house!

THE DOCTOR. Fix him up right with a big easy chair.

AMY. And plenty of pillows.

TONY. Amy, you ain' forgot how you promise' 'bout readin' da paper outside in da sun?

AMY. You bet I ain't forgot.

THE DOCTOR. Go on, now. I want to see you fixed.

TONY (*hobbles to the door and calls out*). Giorgio . . . Angelo . . . Eccomi!
(GIORGIO *and* ANGELO *arrive in a whirlwind of Italian.* TONY *hobbles out of sight.* AMY *follows with two pillows, looking back at the* DOCTOR *and laughing.* FATHER MCKEE *carries the board and box. The* DOCTOR *goes to the door as though he intended following them. He stands looking out and speaks without turning.*)

THE DOCTOR. Joe . . .

JOE. What is it?

THE DOCTOR. I hear you're going away.

JOE. Yeah. I'm really goin' this time.

THE DOCTOR. Where to?

JOE. Search me. Frisco first.

THE DOCTOR. Hadn't you better take Amy with you? (*He turns then and looks sternly into* JOE's *startled eyes.*)

JOE. What?

THE DOCTOR. You heard me.

JOE. I don't get you.

THE DOCTOR. Amy came to see me last week. I didn't tell her what the trouble was. I didn't have the heart. I put her off. . . . Oh, it's easy to fool a woman. But you can't fool a doctor, Joe. (*A step nearer* JOE *and eyes hard on his face.*) Tony isn't the father. . . . He couldn't be. (*A long pause.*)

JOE (*under his breath*). Oh, Christ!

THE DOCTOR. I thought so. (*Another long pause.*) I've been trying to figure out how to make things easiest for Tony. It upset me a good deal. Doctors get shocked more often than you'd think. . . . And a girl like Amy, too. . . . I didn't know what to do. I guess it's up to you.

JOE. Poor old Tony!

THE DOCTOR. You might have thought of him sooner—and of Amy, too, for that matter.

JOE. It wasn't on purpose. It was only once! But—honest to God, we wouldn't have either of us have put anything like that over on old Tony. Not for a million dollars!

THE DOCTOR. You couldn't have wasted much time about it.

JOE. It was the first night.

THE DOCTOR. Good Lord!

JOE. It just happened. There was a reason you don't know about. I'm a swell guy, ain't I? To do a thing like that to a fellow like Tony.

THE DOCTOR. Shall I tell Tony? Or Amy?

JOE. No. . . . Gimme time to think.

THE DOCTOR. There's no concealing this. Don't try anything of that sort. I won't have it.

JOE. No.

THE DOCTOR. This is going to come near killing him.
(JOE *nods fearsomely. The* DOCTOR *turns and is going when* AMY *appears, marshalling* ANGELO *and* GIORGIO.)

AMY. Just cut out the welcome to our city stuff and carry this chair down there under the arbor where the boss is. (*As they pick it up, she turns to the* DOCTOR.) Say! You'd think to hear 'em that Tony'd just been raised from the dead. (*She turns back to the two Italians.*) Put it in the shade. . . . Mind that varnish, you club-footed wops.

. . . There. . . . (*She has seen the chair safely along the porch. She returns and makes for the bedroom, saying, as she goes.*) He wants a cover and everything you can think of. . . .

THE DOCTOR (*to* JOE). Let me know if I can do anything.
(AMY *returns carrying a great, thick quilt. She cuts for the door, muttering happily to herself. On the porch she stops to call through the window to the stricken* JOE.)

AMY. Joe—just hand me them newspapers, will you?

JOE (*obeying*). Here.

AMY (*in the doorway, her arms filled with papers and comforter, she sees his face*). Gee—you look something fierce.

JOE (*in a strangled voice*). Amy . . .

AMY. What is it?

JOE. I got to see you by an' by. . . . I got to see you alone . . . (*She starts to speak. He sees that he has frightened her.*) God damn . . . oh, God damn. . . .

AMY. What's the matter with you? What you scaring me this way for?

JOE. Amy. . . . Just a minute ago . . .

AMY. Make it snappy. . . . I don't like this being alone with you. . . . It makes me think . . . I want to forget all that.

JOE. Yeah . . . An' me . . . that's what I mean.

AMY. What?

JOE (*after an awful pause*). You're goin' to have a kid. (*She stares incredulously at him without making a sound.*) Yeah. . . . It's so, Amy. . . . I'm awfully sorry. . . . The doc just told me. . . . He found out when you was sick last week. . . . He knows all about it . . .

AMY (*she stands a moment without moving at all. Suddenly she lets quilt and papers slip to the floor and her hands clasp themselves over her abdomen*). Oh, my God! (*She picks the quilt and papers up very carefully and puts them on the table. She drops weakly into one of the chairs as though her knees had failed her, her face rigid with terror.*)

JOE. I know how it is. . . . Just keep your head, now. . . .

AMY. What am I going to do?

JOE. I got to think. . . .

AMY. If you go wrong, you're sure to get it sooner or later. I got it sooner.

JOE. That kind of talk won't help any.

AMY. I'm glad of it. It serves me right. . . .

JOE. There's ways, you know . . . there's doctor. . . .

AMY (*shakes her head vigorously*). Them kind of doctors is no good.

JOE. But maybe . . .

AMY. They're no good. I'm too far gone anyway . . . I know . . . and anyway . . . doing that . . . It's worse than the other.

JOE. I'm sorry, Amy. . . .

AMY. You being sorry ain't got nothing to do with it, either. I'm thinking of Tony.

JOE. So'm I.

AMY. Tony's a white guy if he *is* a wop.

JOE. Yeah. . . .

AMY (*desperately loud*). What am I going to do? What am I going to do?

JOE. Hey! . . . Not so loud!

AMY. But I ain't got no money . . . only my earrings. . . .

JOE. I got money enough.

AMY. You?

JOE. Tony made me save it. It's in the bank. More'n two hundred bucks. That'll see you through.

AMY. Tony'll be crazy. . . . Tony'll be just crazy.

JOE. The doc said for me to take you away with me.

AMY. You?

JOE. Yeah. . . . An' believe me, Amy, I'll do anything . . .

AMY. Going away with you won't help things any.

JOE. I'll treat you right, Amy.

AMY. Poor Tony!

JOE. I'll do the right thing if it kills me.

AMY. I must have been crazy that night.

JOE. We both was . . . but there's no use sayin' that now.

AMY. No. . . . Tony'll be crazy. (*She lifts her head, recognizing the inevitable.*) I guess the doc's right. . . . I guess I'll have to go with you. . . . Somebody's got to help me out. . . . There ain't nobody but you.

JOE. That's all right. . . . I'm willing. . . .

AMY. And afterwards . . . Oh, my God! . . . And Tony'll be thinking that all the time . . . you and me . . . Oh! (*This is an exclamation of unutterable disgust.*) Poor Tony! You don't know how good he's been to me. And all the time he was so crazy for a kid. . . . Oh, I can't stick around here now! I got to go. I got to go quick.

JOE. I'm ready, if you are.

AMY. I'll just pack my grip.

JOE. Don't take it too hard, Amy. (*He tries to take her hand.*)

AMY (*shaking him off*). None of that! I don't want no sympathy.

JOE. Excuse me.

AMY. You better get your own things.

JOE. All right. . . . I'll be back in a minute.

AMY. I'll get a move on, too.
(AH GEE *comes in with the dishes for dinner and begins to lay the table. Apparently* JOE *thinks of something more to say, but is deterred by* AH GEE's *presence. He goes quickly.* AMY *hears* AH GEE *and watches him for a moment as though she were unable to understand what he is doing.*)

AH GEE (*as he puts down dishes*). Velly good dinner tonight, Missy. Beans an' roas' veal an' apple pie!

TONY (*calling from off stage*). Eh, Joe! Eh, JOE! W'ere you go like dat? Amy! W'ere are you, Amy? (*He comes up on to the porch.*) Ah! Here you are!

AH GEE. Oh, Bossy! Velly good dinner tonight. Apple pie!

TONY (*pleased*). Ah! Apples pie! (AH GEE *goes into his kitchen.* TONY *leans against door.*) Amy! W'y you no' come back?

AMY (*who has been clinging desperately to the back of a chair*). I don't know!

TONY. You leave me alone so long.

AMY. I just come in for the papers and . . .

TONY. . . . An' Joe is runnin' crazy wild an' don' say nothing w'en I'm askin' him, "Joe, w'ere you goin' like dat?"

AMY. Joe's going away.

TONY. He's no' goin' without sayin' goo'-by?

AMY. I dunno. . . . Maybe he is. . . .

TONY. That boy mak' me verra unhappy. I been lovin' Joe like he was my own son an' he's goin' away like dat. He's no good.

AMY. People who ain't no good ain't worth worrying about. The thing to do is let 'em go and forget 'em.

TONY. Da's no' so easy like you think, Amy. I been lovin' Joe like my own son.

AMY. Joe ain't no worse than other people I could mention.

TONY. I love Joe but he don' love me.

AMY. I love you, Tony! I love you!

TONY. I know, Amy, I know.

AMY. And you ain't never going to believe that I do again.

TONY. W'at you talkin' 'bout, Amy?

AMY. Something's happened, Tony!

TONY. Eh?

AMY. It's going to make you terrible mad.

TONY. Amy!

AMY (*nerving herself*). It's going to make you just crazy, but I'm going to tell you just exactly what it is, Tony, because I ain't going to have you thinking afterwards that I wasn't grateful or that I ain't been happy here . . . happier than I ever been in my whole life. . . .

TONY. Amy!

AMY. Wait a minute. . . . I got to confess, Tony. I got to tell you the whole business so's you won't be thinking I been any worse than just what I have. . . .

TONY. Amy!

AMY. Yeah. . . . And I don't want you blaming Joe no more'n what you blame me and anyway you're a-bound to find out sooner or later, an' it'll hurt you a lot less in the long run if I tell you the truth right now, and I got to tell you the truth anyway. I simply got to. Wait a minute, Tony! I'm going to tell you the truth and after I go away and you don't see me no more you can say: "Well, she wasn't no good but it wasn't my fault." Because it wasn't your fault Tony. Not one bit, it wasn't. You didn't have nothing to do with it. And I wouldn't be going away, neither, not for a million dollars I wouldn't, only for what's happened. . . .

TONY. Amy, w'at you talkin' 'bout goin' away?

AMY. That's what I'm trying to tell you, Tony, only you got to give me chance because it ain't easy to tell you no more'n it's easy to go away. And I got to go. But it ain't because I don't love you. I do. And it ain't because I don't appreciate all you done for me. I ain't never going to forget none of it, nor you, nor this place. . . .

TONY. Amy!

AMY. Listen to me, Tony! You're going to kick me out when you hear what I got to say, but I don't care if you do. I'm going to have a baby, Tony . . . and it's . . . God help me! . . . it's Joe's baby.

TONY (*raising his crutch with a great cry of anger*). Ah!

AMY. Didn't I tell you you'd kick me out?

TONY (*faltering*). Dio mio! Dio mio! No! Amy, you fool with me? Eh?

AMY. No, I'm not fooling. It's so. And that's why I'm going away, Tony.

TONY (*pursuing her as she retreats*). You been Joe's woman!

AMY. I was crazy!

TONY. You been Joe's woman!

AMY. I was crazy.

TONY. You been lovin' Joe!

AMY. No . . . I ain't . . . I ain't . . . I never loved Joe. Honest, I never. I was crazy.

TONY. You been just like da Padre say you was. . . . You been a whore. . . .

AMY. I ain't! . . . I ain't! I been straight all my life! Only that one night. . . .

TONY. W'at night?

AMY. The first night I come here.

TONY. Da night you marry with me!

AMY. I ain't even spoke to Joe alone since that night.

TONY. You lyin'!

AMY. I swear to God I ain't! Not once! Not till to-day after the doc told him what was going to happen.

TONY. You lyin' to me! You been Joe's woman!

AMY. I ain't, Tony! That's what I'm trying to tell you. It's the truth I'm trying to tell you and now I'm going away.

TONY. You goin' away with Joe?

AMY. My God, what else can I do?

TONY (*furiously he forces her back into the corner where the shotgun is hanging, spluttering all the time with slobbering, half-intelligible rage*). I don' let you go! I don' let you go! By God, I'm goin' kill dat Joe! Questo bastardo, Joe! I'm goin' kill him an' keep you here for see me kill him! Goddam you! You goddam dirty . . . (*He has got the gun down, broken it, and is loading it.*)

AMY (*speaking at the same time*). No, you won't Tony! Don't do anything like that, now, Tony! You'll be sorry if you do! You know what'll happen to you if you do that! You know what'll happen to you, Tony! That ain't no way to act! You'll see what you get! You'll see!

TONY. Goddam! . . . You wait, you dirty . . . (*He flourishes the broken gun. She covers her eyes with her hands. JOE arrives, sees what TONY is doing, gives a cry, springs on him, wrenches the gun away. The struggle upsets TONY's balance and he topples head-long off his crutches. AMY screams.*)

AMY. Oh, his leg! (*JOE drops the gun and bends over him.*)

JOE. I tried to catch him. . . . (*TONY's bellows are terrifying to hear.*) Did you hurt yourself, Tony? (*TONY's answer is un-translatable into speech.*)

AMY (*as she pulls a chair over*). For God's sake, pick him up, can't you?

JOE (*TONY fights him, trying to choke him, and sinks into the chair, howling with pain and fury*). All right now, Tony! Steady!

AMY. Tony. . . . Tony. . . . (*She kneels down by him. TONY's roars subside into moans.*) I had to tell him! Oh, my God! I just had to tell him!

JOE. He didn't hurt himself much. (*TONY's moans break into sobs.*)

AMY. This is awful.

JOE. Get your things. Let's pull out of here. We can send the Padre up to look after him.

AMY. I'm only taking my little grip, Tony. I'm leaving the earrings on the dresser. (*She goes quickly into the bedroom. TONY's sobs keep up wretchedly and terribly.*)

JOE. Tony, I . . . (*Again TONY springs madly at JOE's throat. JOE wrenches away and runs quickly to the table where he gets a glass of wine which he brings back to TONY. TONY pushes it away, spilling the wine over his shirt. JOE drops the glass.*)

TONY. Amy! Amy! Amy! Amy!

AMY (*she comes back, with her hat on and her coat over her arm. She has her yellow grip half open with clothes sticking out.* JOE *takes it from her*). Here I am, Tony. Here I am.

TONY. W'ere you goin' Amy? W'ere you goin' away from here?

AMY. I dunno. . . . Frisco, I guess. . . .

TONY (*bitter sobs*). You goin' be livin' with Joe?

AMY (*vague misery*). I dunno. . . . No, I ain't going to live with Joe. . . . No matter what happens, I ain't.

TONY. Who is goin' be lookin' after you, Amy?

JOE. I am, Tony. I'll do the right thing if it kills me.

TONY. You? . . . You? . . . Oh, Dio mio! Dio mio! No! No!

JOE. Come on, Amy, for the love of Pete!

AMY. I'm coming.

TONY (*a hand out to stop her*). You ain' got no money, Amy.

AMY. It don't matter.

TONY. Yes!

JOE. I got plenty.

TONY. No! . . . No! . . . No! . . . Joe is no good for lookin' after womans an' baby!

AMY. Don't take on, Tony. . . . Please don't take on! Let me go, and forget all about me. There ain't no use in talking any more.

TONY. You goin' have baby!

AMY. God, I know I am!

TONY. How you goin' mak' money for keep him? Before you go, you tell me dat!

AMY. God knows. . . . I don't.

TONY. Pretty quick Joe is leavin' you desert, and den w'at is goin' happen?

JOE. I swear I'll stick, Tony!

TONY. No! *No!* NO!! Ees no good! My Amy havin' baby in da street. Ees no good.

AMY. Don't say that! For God's sake, Tony, don't say that . . .

TONY. W'at is goin' happen, Amy? W'at's goin' happen with you?

AMY. Joe . . . I can't stand no more of this.

TONY (*frenzied*). No! *No!!* NO!! NO!!!

AMY. Let go, Tony! Let go of my skirt!

TONY. You ain' goin', Amy! I don't let you go! You stayin' here with Tony!

AMY. Don't talk that way, Tony! It ain't no good.

TONY. No! No! You goin' listen to w'at Tony say now. You goin' listen, Amy. You don' love Joe. You love Tony. You been good wife, Amy. . . .

AMY. Good wife!

TONY. W'at is Tony goin' do without you?

JOE. Come on!

TONY. Amy, I get excite' just now, Amy. Excuse! Excuse! I think verra good once more. You ain' goin' with Joe. You stayin' here with Tony just like nothin' is happen', an' by an' by da little fella is come. . . .

AMY. Don't talk that way, Tony!

TONY. W'y not?

AMY. Because it ain't no way to talk!

TONY. Yes . . . yes . . . ees good sense! Ees w'at is evrabody wantin' here! You an' Joe an' me! . . . Looka Joe. Joe is wantin' go with Wobblies, eh? With goddam Wobblies. All right . . . Looka Amy . . . Amy is wantin' stay here nice an' safe in dees fine house with Tony. Is not true, eh? (AMY *nods through her tears.*) Sure is true. Look Tony, Dio mio, an' ask him w'at he want? Don' he want baby?

AMY. But not this baby, Tony?

TONY. W'at I care?

AMY. But, think of what people would say!

TONY. W'at I care w'at evrabody say? We tellin' evrabody he's Tony's baby. Den evrabody say Tony is so goddam young an' strong he's break both his leg' an' havin' baby just da same! . . . Ees good, eh? You don't go with Joe now, Amy? . . . Oh, Amy! . . .

AMY (*he has swayed her, but she looks at him as at a madman*). No. . . . It wouldn't work, Tony. . . . You wouldn't mean it afterward. . . . You're crazy. . . .

TONY (*a last frantic appeal*). No! No! No! (*Leaning back in his chair and looking around the room.*) W'at's good for me havin' dees fine house? W'at's good for me havin' all dis money w'at I got? I got nobody for give my house an' my money w'en I die. Ees for dat I want dis baby, Amy. Joe don' want him. Ees Tony want him. Amy, . . . Amy, . . . for God's sake don' go away an' leave Tony!

AMY. But, Tony! Think of what I done?

TONY. What you done was mistake in da head, not in da heart. . . . Mistake in da head is no matter.

AMY. You—you ain't kiddin' me, are you? . . . You're serious, ain't you—Tony? You'll stick to this afterwards, won't you, Tony? (*She walks slowly over to him. She throws her arms around his neck and presses his head against her breast. A prolonged pause*). Well, Joe, I guess you better be going.

JOE. You mean?

AMY. I guess you'd better be going. (JOE *straightens in great relief.*)

JOE. All right. (*He picks up his knapsack which he dropped when he came in.*) I guess you're right. (*He pulls on his cap and stands a moment in the doorway, a broad grin spreading over his face.*) I guess there ain't none of us got any kick comin', at that. No real kick. (*He goes out slowly.*)

AMY (*lifting her face*). No.
(TONY *clutches her even closer as the curtain falls.*)

Craig's Wife

BY GEORGE KELLY

"People who live to themselves, Harriet, are generally left to themselves."

MISS AUSTEN

GEORGE KELLY

George Kelly was born in Philadelphia, Pennsylvania, in 1887. Following a private education he made his début in juvenile roles in New York, later touring the country with various companies and appearing in one-act vaudeville sketches of his own authorship.

An idea which had previously occurred to Mr. Kelly for a vaudeville sketch became his first long play, *The Torchbearers,* a three-act farce satirizing the Little Theatre movement. With the confidence and limited acclaim gained through his first dramatic production, Mr. Kelly began the writing of dramas in earnest. He was widely quoted following an interview in 1924: "I haven't any method . . . I don't know where my plots come from . . . I follow no particular formula . . . I don't know anything about play construction . . . I don't want to know anything about it . . . If a thing is true it can be acted and audiences will go to see it . . . There's the whole proposition in a nutshell."

Despite his avowal that he has no method or formula in writing plays, George Kelly has few peers among contemporary American dramatists. In *Craig's Wife,* he has achieved a masterpiece of simple directness with a minimum of stage artifice. The searching analysis of the wife in this play represents one of the best character delineations to be found in the whole of American drama.

Produced by Rosalie Stewart at the Morosco Theatre, New York, October 12, 1925, *Craig's Wife* received the Pulitzer award for 1925-1926.

CHARACTERS

MISS AUSTEN.

MRS. HAROLD.

MAZIE.

MRS. CRAIG.

ETHEL LANDRETH.

WALTER CRAIG.

MRS. FRAZIER.

BILLY BIRKMIRE.

JOSEPH CATELLE.

HARRY.

EUGENE FREDERICKS.

SCENE

The living room in the home of Mrs. Walter Craig.

CRAIG'S WIFE

ACT ONE

The entire action of the play transpires between five-thirty in the evening and nine o'clock the following morning, in the living room in the home of MR. WALTER CRAIG. *This room, like all the other rooms in the house, reflects the very excellent taste and fanatical orderliness of its mistress. It is a kind of frozen grandeur, in dark, highly polished wood—strewn with gorgeous, gold-colored rugs and draped in rich brocaded satins. The piano scarf and the scarf on the oblong center table are canary-colored, and the draperies on the bay window at the left, and on the curving window on the stair landing at the back, are dark green. This curving window has a beautiful built-in window seat, with lovely cushions, and there is another built-in seat at the right of the staircase, from which the balustrade curves upwards. On the right, at the back, there is a wide door hung with brown velvet portières; and the rest of the room at the right is taken up with an ornamental mantelpiece, fancy mirror and fireplace. In front of this fireplace there is a beautiful high-backed chair. There is another big chair at the left of the center table, a small fancy chair beside the piano, and a chair at either side of the room, forward. There are two fancy benches, one immediately above the center table, and one in front of the center table. There is sufficient room between the table and this forward bench to permit of the business of passing between them. Up at the left there is a glass vestibule, one door of which opens into the room and the other out on to the front porch. As* MRS. CRAIG *enters, she appears to have been dressed for this particular room. She wears an extremely fashionable fawn-colored ensemble suit, brown slippers and stockings, and a small, dark brown velvet toque. She carries a brown leather pocket-book and a brown silk umbrella.*

MISS AUSTEN *hurries down the stairs and out through the portières at the right.* MRS. HAROLD *comes in through the door up at the left, carrying the evening newspaper and some tabourette doilies, and moves down towards the center table.*

MRS. HAROLD (*stopping halfway to the table and peering out after* MISS AUSTEN). Is there something you wanted, Miss Austen?

MISS AUSTEN. No, thanks, dear, I'm just looking for that pattern that I sent for the other day: I wanted to show it to Mrs. Frazier.

MRS. HAROLD. Lift up the lid of that worktable there, Miss Austen; I think I saw a pattern of some kind in there this morning. (*Continuing to the table and putting down the newspaper and doilies.*)

MISS AUSTEN. Yes, here it is, I have it. (*There is a sound from the right.*) I knew I left it right here somewhere. (*She hur-*ries in through the portières and up the stairs.*)

MRS. HAROLD (*moving up to the door at the left*). I gave those roses she brought to Mazie to put in some water.

MISS AUSTEN. Oh, did you—thanks ever so much.

MRS. HAROLD. She's gettin' a vase for them.

MISS AUSTEN. They're lovely, aren't they?

MRS. HAROLD. Yes, they're handsome. (*She goes out on to the porch again, and* MAZIE *comes in through the portières, carrying a vase of pink roses, which she puts on the upper corner of the small grand piano at the left.*)

MAZIE (*calling out through the French windows to* MRS. HAROLD). Did the paper come yet, Mrs. Harold?

MRS. HAROLD. Yes, I just brought it in,—it's there on the table. (MAZIE *turns and comes back to the table, picks up the paper, and strolls forward, holding it up as though to allow the light from a window at the right to fall upon it.*)

MAZIE. More rain again to-morrow.

MRS. HAROLD (*answering her from the front porch*). Does it say so?

MAZIE. Unsettled to-night and Friday— probably thunder showers. Slightly cooler, with moderate winds.

MRS. HAROLD (*coming in*). I don't know where all the rain is comin' from.

MAZIE. It isn't very nice weather for Mrs. Craig, is it?

MRS. HAROLD (*moving forward to the piano*). You can't tell; it might not be rainin' in Albany. Aren't these roses beautiful?

MAZIE. Yes, they're lovely.
(MRS. HAROLD *smells the roses.*)

MRS. HAROLD (*crossing to the foot of the stairs*). I heard her telling Miss Austen she's got over two hundred rose bushes in her garden.

MAZIE (*turning and looking at* MRS. HAROLD). Is she still upstairs?

MRS. HAROLD. Yeh. I guess she's talkin' poor Miss Austen to death. (MAZIE *laughs and resumes her paper, and* MRS. HAROLD *gives an eye around the room.*) Bring that paper out with you when you're comin', Mazie; don't leave it layin' around in here.

MAZIE. All right.

MRS. HAROLD (*moving up to the door at the left and looking out*). It 'ud be just like the lady to walk in on us. (MAZIE *turns sharply and looks at her.*)

MAZIE. Mrs. Craig, do you mean?

MRS. HAROLD. She might, you can't tell.

MAZIE. I thought you said she wouldn't be back before Saturday.

MRS. HAROLD (*coming back to the table and picking up the doilies*). That's what she told me when she was goin' away. But it's just as well to keep a day or two ahead of a woman like Mrs. Craig. Mazie (*she flicks the dust from the table with the doilies*); if she gets an idea up there that there's a pin out of place around here,—she'll take the first train out of Albany. (MAZIE *makes a sound of amusement and resumes her paper and* MRS. HAROLD *starts for the door at the right.*) Oh, there's plenty like her—I've worked for three of them; you'd think their houses were God Almighty. (*She goes into other room.*)

MAZIE. Didn't you tell me, Mrs. Harold, that you worked out on Willows Avenue one time?

MRS. HAROLD (*calling from the other room*). Yes, I worked out there for two years, at Doctor Nicholson's.

MAZIE. Did you know any people out that way by the name of Passmore?

MRS. HAROLD (*appearing between the portières*). By the name of what?

MAZIE. Passmore. Capital P-a-double s-m-o-r-e. Mr. J. Fergus Passmore and wife.

MRS. HAROLD (*coming forward at the right*). No, I don't remember anybody by that name; why?

MAZIE. Nothing.—It says here they were both found dead this morning in their home on Willows Avenue.

MRS. HAROLD. Oh, Lord have mercy on them! What happened to them?

MAZIE (*reading*). Why, it sez: "Fashionable Willows Avenue Residence Scene of Double Tragedy.—Bodies of J. Fergus Passmore and Wife, Socially Prominent in This City, Found Dead in Library from Bullet Wounds—Empty Revolver Near Fireplace—Cause of Death Shrouded in Mystery—Police Working upon Identity of Gentleman Visitor Seen Leaving Premises in Automobile Shortly After Midnight." (MAZIE *looks fearfully at* MRS. HAROLD, *who shakes her head dolefully.*) "About eight o'clock this morning upon entering the library in the home of Mr. J. Fergus Passmore of 2214 Willows Avenue, Miss Selma Coates, a colored maid—"

MRS. HAROLD. Twenty-two fourteen must be out near the lake. (*The front doorbell rings incisively.*) See who that is, Mazie. (MRS. HAROLD *disappears into the other room and* MAZIE *crosses up to the door at the left, putting down the newspaper on the table as she passes.*)

MRS. CRAIG (*out on the porch*). We can leave these right here, Ethel,—Mazie'll bring them in.

MAZIE. Oh, how do you do, Mrs. Craig.

MRS. CRAIG. Hello, Mazie.

MAZIE (*going out*). You're back a little ahead of time. (MRS. HAROLD *comes in through the portières, peering out toward the front porch.*)

MRS. CRAIG. Yes, a little. Will you take these things, Mazie?

MAZIE. Yes, Ma'm. (MRS. HAROLD *sees that it is* MRS. CRAIG, *gives a quick glance around the room, snatches up the paper from the table, and, with another glance over her right shoulder toward the front door, vanishes into the other room.*)

MRS. CRAIG. And will you see that that catch is on that screen door, Mazie—

MAZIE. Yes, Ma'm.

MRS. CRAIG (*appearing in the door*). It was half open when I came in. (*She comes into the room, sweeping it with a narrow eye, and crosses to the table to put down her handbag and umbrella.* ETHEL *wanders in after her and stands at the upper corner of the piano. The screen door closes outside.*) Take your things off, dear, and sit down; you look tired. (*She moves across to the mirror over the mantelpiece at the right, and* ETHEL *puts her handbag on the piano and commences to remove her coat and hat.*) I think there's nothing in the world so exhausting as train riding. (MAZIE *comes in, carrying a lady's satchel and a suitcase.* MRS. CRAIG *turns.*) You may as well take those things right upstairs, Mazie.

MAZIE. Yes, Ma'm.

MRS. CRAIG (*crossing up and over to* ETHEL). Put that suitcase in the corner room, Mazie—Miss Landreth'll occupy that room for the next few days.

MAZIE (*going up the stairs*). Yes, Ma'm.

MRS. CRAIG (*taking* ETHEL'S *hat and coat*). I'll take them, dear.

ETHEL. Thanks.

MRS. CRAIG. I'll have Mazie take them right up to your room. (*She puts them down on the table carefully and* ETHEL *crosses down towards the mirror, settling her hair.*)

ETHEL. I suppose I look terrible, don't I?

MRS. CRAIG (*crossing and taking* ETHEL'S *bag from the piano*). No, dear, you look quite all right. Would you like a drink of something?

ETHEL. I would like a drink of water, yes, if you don't mind. (MRS. HAROLD *appears between the portières.*)

MRS. CRAIG. Hello, Mrs. Harold.

MRS. HAROLD. I see you're back again.

MRS. CRAIG. This is Mrs. Harold, Ethel.

ETHEL. How do you do. (MRS. HAROLD *bows and* ETHEL *moves back again to the roses on the piano.*)

MRS. CRAIG. Miss Landreth will be staying here with us for a week or two, Mrs. Harold, so I wish you'd see that everything is all right in that corner room.

MRS. HAROLD. All right, I will. (MAZIE *comes down the stairs.*)

MRS. CRAIG (*moving down to the mirror, removing her coat*). And will you bring a glass of water, please, Mrs. Harold.

MRS. HAROLD. Yes, Ma'm. Just one glass?

MRS. CRAIG. Yes, I don't want any. (MRS. HAROLD *goes out again.*)

ETHEL. Aren't these roses beautiful. (MRS. CRAIG *shifts her eyes from* MAZIE, *who is gathering* ETHEL'S *things up from the table, and looks steadily at the roses.*) I don't think I've ever seen such lovely roses.

MRS. CRAIG. Yes, they're very nice. Take those things upstairs, Mazie.

MAZIE (*starting up the stairs*). Yes, Ma'm.

MRS. CRAIG. And I wish you'd use that back way when you go up and down stairs, Mazie.

MAZIE (*coming down again*). I always keep forgettin' that. (ETHEL *turns and looks at* MAZIE *and* MRS. CRAIG, *laying her coat across* MAZIE'S *arm as she passes her, moves up to look at the stairs closely.* MAZIE *goes out at the right.*)

MRS. CRAIG. This stairway'll soon look the way it did before, with everybody tramping up and down it every five minutes. (*She turns to* ETHEL *with a kind of apologetic smile, and commences to remove her gloves.*) It doesn't seem ever to occur to anybody in the house, Ethel, to use the back stairway. It's the funniest thing you've ever seen in your life, really. We might just as well not have one. No matter how many times they have to go up or down stairs, they must go tramping up and down this front way. And you know what stairs look like after they've been tramped up and down a few times. (MRS. HAROLD *comes in with a glass of water on a small silver tray.*) Thanks, Mrs. Harold.

ETHEL (*picking up a framed photograph from the piano*). Isn't this Mother's picture, Aunt Harriet?
(MRS. HAROLD *goes out.*)

MRS. CRAIG (*crossing to* ETHEL). Yes, that's your mother.

ETHEL. I thought it looked something like her.

MRS. CRAIG (*taking the picture*). She had it taken at Lakewood one summer, and I always liked it. I like that dress; it never seemed to get old-fashioned.

ETHEL (*starting to cry*). It doesn't look much like her now, does it? (*She moves forward to the chair beside the piano and sits down.*)

MRS. CRAIG (*putting the picture back on the piano*). Now, Ethel dear, you mustn't start that. Your mother's been through this very same kind of thing many times before.

ETHEL. But, I should *be* there, Aunt Harriet. Supposing something should happen.

MRS. CRAIG. But, nothing is going to happen, dear child. I haven't the slightest doubt but that your mother will come through this little spell just as she's come through all the others.

ETHEL. I don't think the others have been as serious as this, though.

MRS. CRAIG. Listen, Ethel dear, I've seen your mother at least a dozen times at what I was perfectly sure was the point of death, and she's always come around all right.

ETHEL. Well, why did Doctor Wood send for me, if he didn't think it was serious?

MRS. CRAIG. Because your mother asked him to, I suppose, dear; just as she asked him to send for me. But he certainly couldn't have thought it was so serious when he suggested you come away with me.

ETHEL. It wasn't the doctor that suggested that, Aunt Harriet, it was the night nurse, —I heard her tell him so. She said it upset Mother too much to see me, and if I were there she'd want to see me.

MRS. CRAIG. Well, that's very true, dear; but you know how she cried when you came in. And there's nothing in the world so upsetting to the heart as crying.

ETHEL. But, I should be there; it seems terrible to me now to have walked away and left Mother in that condition.

MRS. CRAIG. But, what could you do if you'd stayed, dear?

ETHEL (*with a touch of desperation*). I'd at least know what was going on.

MRS. CRAIG (*handing her the glass of water, and putting her arm around her shoulder*). Now, don't upset yourself, Ethel. Here, take a sip of this water. I'm perfectly sure you're magnifying the seriousness of your mother's condition, dear. And I most certainly should never have come away myself only that I've seen this same thing over and over again. (*She turns and settles the photograph on the piano.*) Besides, there isn't a solitary thing we could do if we'd stayed; those nurses won't allow it. (*Taking the glass from* ETHEL.) And the doctor said I was upsetting your mother,—simply because I told her a few things I thought she should be told. (*She crosses to the table and sets down the glass.*)

ETHEL. There was something I wanted to tell her, too, but he said he thought I'd better wait.

MRS. CRAIG. Well, I'd have told her anyway, if I'd been you.

ETHEL. I'm rather sorry now I didn't,—I think it would have made her easier in her mind.

MRS. CRAIG (*taking her handkerchief from her bag*). Was it something important?

ETHEL. It was about Professor Fredericks, at school. Mother met him last year when she was up there at Commencement, and she liked him very much. And when we got home she said if he ever said anything to me, she'd be glad if I could like him well enough to marry him. She said she'd feel easier about me, in case anything ever happened to *her*. And I wanted to tell her.

MRS. CRAIG. You mean he *had* said something?

ETHEL. Yes, he asked me to marry him right after Easter. But I didn't write anything about it to Mother; I thought I'd wait until she'd be up there in June for my Commencement, and then I'd tell her.

MRS. CRAIG. I don't know why your mother should be so panicky about your future, Ethel; you're only nineteen.

ETHEL. She said she'd like to feel that I'd *have* somebody.

MRS. CRAIG. Why does a person need anybody, dear; if he has money enough to get along on? (*She turns and crosses to the mirror to remove her hat.*) And, as a matter of fact, you wouldn't be left absolutely desolate even if something *did* happen to

your mother. You'd always have me—I'm your mother's sister. So that, really, I think you're a very foolish girl, Ethel, if you allow your mother's apprehensions to rush you into marriage. Unless, of course, it were an advantageous marriage.

ETHEL. She didn't want to rush me into it—she simply said she thought it would be better for me to be settled.

MRS. CRAIG (*bringing her hat back to the table, and taking a powder puff from her bag*). Well, naturally, I can understand that, of course. But, after all, simply being settled isn't everything, Ethel—a girl can be a great deal worse off being settled than when she was unsettled. And, personally, I can't conceive of being very much worse off than married to a college professor—stuck away in some dreadful place like Poughkeepsie or Northampton—with not a ten-cent piece to bless yourself with—unless you used your own money. I'm constantly reading agitations in the newspapers about the poor pay of college professors. And your marrying one of them will hardly improve the situation. (*She flips the bag back on to the table, and moves forward to a small ornamental bench in front of the center table, where she kneels.*) Did you accept this man when he asked you?

ETHEL. Practically, yes. We'd rather thought of being married sometime during the summer.

MRS. CRAIG. Then, you mean you're engaged to him?

ETHEL. Yes. I knew Mother liked him, for she said so. The only thing was, she wanted me to be sure that *I* liked him.

MRS. CRAIG. Well, that's all very nice, Ethel, but simply liking a man isn't going to go very far toward keeping things going, is it?

ETHEL. Well, I have money of my own, Aunt Harriet.

MRS. CRAIG. I know that, dear child, but surely he isn't marrying you because of that?

ETHEL. No, of course not; he doesn't know anything about that.

MRS. CRAIG. Well, I hope not—he surely wouldn't expect you to use your own money to keep *his* house going. If a man marries a girl he certainly must expect to support her, at least.

ETHEL. Well, he does expect to support me, naturally.

MRS. CRAIG. How, dear—on a professor's salary?

ETHEL. Why, lots of professors are married, Aunt Harriet.

MRS. CRAIG. But their wives are not living the way you've been accustomed to living, Ethel: not the wives of young professors, at least. And I suppose this man is young, isn't he?

ETHEL. He's twenty-seven

MRS. CRAIG. Well, there you are. He's very lucky if he's getting two hundred dollars a month: unless he's some very extraordinary kind of professor; and he can scarcely be that at twenty-seven years of age.

ETHEL. He's professor of the Romance languages.

MRS. CRAIG. Naturally. And I suppose he's told you he loves you in all of them.

ETHEL. Well, I certainly shouldn't care to think about marriage at all, Aunt Harriet, unless I were at least in love with the man. (MRS. CRAIG *gives a little smile of pained amusement, and moves toward* ETHEL.)

MRS. CRAIG. That is your age, Ethel darling: we all pass through that. It's the snare of romance,—that the later experience of life shows us to have been nothing more than the most impractical sentimentality. (*She arranges the piano scarf more precisely.*) Only the majority of women are caught with the spell of it, unfortunately; and then they are obliged to revert right back to the almost primitive feminine dependence and subjection that they've been trying to emancipate themselves from for centuries. (*She crosses to the big chair at the left of the center table and straightens it.*)

ETHEL. Well, *you* married, Aunt Harriet.

MRS. CRAIG (*leaning on the back of the chair*). But not with any romantic illusions, dear. I saw to it that my marriage should be a way toward emancipation for *me*. I had no private fortune like you, Ethel; and no special equipment,—outside of a few more or less inapplicable college theories. So the only road to independence for *me,* that *I* could see, was through the man I married. I know that must sound extremely materialistic to *you,* after listening to the professor of romantic languages;—but it isn't really; because it isn't financial independence that I speak of particularly. I knew that would come—as the result of *another* kind of independence; and that is the independence of authority—*over* the man I married. And that doesn't necessarily imply any dishonesty of attitude toward that man, either. I have a full appreciation of Mr. Craig—he's a very good man; but he's a husband—a lord and master—*my* master. And I married to be independent.

ETHEL. Independent of your husband too, do you mean?

MRS. CRAIG. Independent of everybody. I lived with a stepmother, Ethel, for nearly twelve years, and with your mother after she was married for over five; I know what it is to be on some one else's floor. And I married to be on my own—in every sense of the word. I haven't entirely achieved the condition yet—but I know it can be done. (*She turns and glances up the stairs and out through the portières, to assure herself that no one is listening.*)

ETHEL. I don't understand what you mean, exactly, Aunt Harriet.

MRS. CRAIG (*turning to Ethel again*). I mean that I'm simply exacting my share of a bargain. Mr. Craig wanted a wife and a home; and he has them. And he can be perfectly sure of them, because the wife that he got happens to be one of the kind that regards her husband and home as more or less ultimate conditions. And my share of the bargain was the security and protection that those conditions imply. And I have *them.* But, unlike Mr. Craig, I can't be absolutely sure of them; because I know that, to a very great extent, they are at the mercy of the *mood* of a *man*. (*She smiles knowingly.*) And I suppose I'm too practical minded to accept that as a sufficient guarantee of their permanence. So I must secure their permanence for myself.

ETHEL. How?

MRS. CRAIG. By securing into my own hands the control of the man upon which they are founded.

ETHEL. How are you ever going to do a thing like that, Aunt Harriet?

MRS. CRAIG. Haven't you ever made Mr. Fredericks do something you wanted him to do?

ETHEL. Yes, but I always told him that I wanted him to do it.

MRS. CRAIG (*half-sitting on the arm of the big chair*). But there are certain things that men can't be told, Ethel; they don't understand them; particularly romantic men; and Mr. Craig is inveterately idealistic.

ETHEL. But, supposing he were to find out sometime?

MRS. CRAIG. Find out what?

ETHEL. What you've just been telling me —that you wanted to control him.

MRS. CRAIG. One never comprehends, dear, what it is not in one's nature to comprehend. And even if it were possible, what about it? It's such an absolutely unprovable thing; that is, I mean to say, it isn't a thing that one does or says, specifically; it's a matter of—interpretation. (*She is amused.*) And that's where women have such a tremendous advantage over men; so few men are capable of interpreting them. But, they can always interpret themselves, if they're so disposed. And if the interpretation is for the instruction of a romantic husband, a woman can always keep it safely within the exigencies of the moment. (*She laughs a little, and moves over to Ethel, resting her hand on Ethel's shoulder.*) I know you're mentally deploring my lack of nobility.

ETHEL. No, I'm not at all, Aunt Harriet.

MRS. CRAIG. Yes, you are, I see it in your face. (*She crosses to the front of the center table.*) You think I'm a very sordid woman.

ETHEL. No, I don't think anything of the kind.

MRS. CRAIG (*turning to* ETHEL). Well, what *do* you think?

ETHEL. Well, frankly, Aunt Harriet, I don't think it's quite honest.

MRS. CRAIG. But it's very much safer, dear —for everybody. Because, as I say, if a woman is the right kind of a woman, it's better that the destiny of her home should be in *her* hands—than in any man's. (MRS. HAROLD *appears between the portières.*) Did you want to see me about something, Mrs. Harold?

MRS. HAROLD. It'll do after a while, Mrs. Craig; I thought the young lady had gone upstairs.

MRS. CRAIG. No, not yet, she's going up immediately. (*Turning to* ETHEL.) That's what I want you to do, Ethel—go upstairs and lie down for an hour or so; you'll feel ever so much better. I'll call you in time for dinner. (ETHEL *rises and moves towards the stairs.*)

ETHEL. I don't think I'll be able to eat any dinner, Aunt Harriet.

MRS. CRAIG (*guiding* ETHEL *towards the stairs*). Well, now, you might feel very different after you've had a bit of a rest.

ETHEL. I'm so terribly worried, Aunt Harriet.

MRS. CRAIG. I know, dear child, it's very trying; but it's one of the things we've got to go through with, I suppose. Besides, worrying can't possibly help her, dear. (MRS. CRAIG *continues with* ETHEL *up to the landing, and* ETHEL *goes on up the stairs.*)

ETHEL. Oh, how can I help worrying?

MRS. CRAIG. You can't help it, of course, dear; that's the reason I want you to lie down for a while. I'll be up in a few minutes—just as soon as I've seen to a few things down here. It's the room straight down the hall, to the right. Mazie's very likely in there now. And don't worry, dear. (ETHEL *disappears at the head of the stairs, and* MRS. CRAIG *looks closely at the landing, to see if she can discover any fresh scratches upon it.* MRS. HAROLD *comes in at the right.*) What was it you wanted to see me about, Mrs. Harold? (*She comes down into the room again.*)

MRS. HAROLD. Why, I wanted to tell you. Mrs. Craig, that the cook left on Thursday. She went away and didn't come back.

MRS. CRAIG. Did she get her wages?

MRS. HAROLD. I paid her up till Tuesday.

MRS. CRAIG. Did she take her things with her?

MRS. HAROLD. Why, she only had a suitcase and a small graphophone; she took *them*. But I didn't think anything about it, because she took *them* every Thursday.

MRS. CRAIG. Have you been doing the cooking since, Mrs. Harold?

MRS. HAROLD. Yes, we've been managin' between us. Mazie's a pretty good cook. I called up the Camac Agency on Saturday to send somebody out, but Miss Hewlitt said she wanted to see you first. (MRS. CRAIG *looks at her.*) She sez she's sent so many, she wants to find out what's the matter before she sends any more.

MRS. CRAIG (*crossing to the piano*). She ought to have a few of them cook for her; she'd *know* what was the matter. Where did these roses come from, Mrs. Harold?

MRS. HAROLD. Why, that woman across the street brought them over to Miss Austen.

MRS. CRAIG. Mrs. Frazier, you mean?

MRS. HAROLD. Yes, Ma'm, she brought them over to the porch—Miss Austen was sitting out there sewing.

MRS. CRAIG. Well, you'd better take them out of here, Mrs. Harold: the petals'll be all over the room.
(MRS. HAROLD *moves across to the roses,*

and MRS. CRAIG *busies herself with the draperies in the bay window beyond the piano.*)

MRS. HAROLD. You didn't have to stay away as long as you thought, did you?

MRS. CRAIG. Well, I suppose I *could* have stayed away indefinitely, if I had allowed myself to become sentimental. But I'm afraid I haven't very much patience with sick people, Mrs. Harold.
(MRS. HAROLD *takes the vase of roses and starts back across towards the portières.*)

MRS. HAROLD. Well, I suppose it takes all kinds to make a world.

MRS. CRAIG. I suppose so.

MRS. HAROLD (*stopping, and turning*). Where do you want these roses put, Mrs. Craig?

MRS. CRAIG. I don't care where you put them, Mrs. Harold, as long as they're not in the rooms; I don't want to be picking up petals every two minutes.

MRS. HAROLD. Maybe Miss Austen 'ud like them in her room.

MRS. CRAIG (*moving down to examine the spot where the vase stood*). Maybe she would; you can ask her. Is she up there now?

MRS. HAROLD. Yes, Ma'm; Mrs. Frazier is showing her something about a pattern that she has.
(MRS. CRAIG *looks at her.*)

MRS. CRAIG. Do you mean to tell me that Mrs. Frazier is upstairs, Mrs. Harold?

MRS. HAROLD. Yes, Ma'm, she's up there.

MRS. CRAIG. And how did she happen to *get* up there?

MRS. HAROLD. Well, I don't know, I'm sure, Mrs. Craig, unless Miss Austen asked her.

MRS. CRAIG. All right. (*She crosses to the foot of the stairs and looks up, and* MRS. HAROLD *goes out through the portières.*) Have there been any letters or messages for me, Mrs. Harold, since I've been away?

MRS. HAROLD. Why, there were two letters, yes; I left them in your room. (*Coming into the room again.*) One came this morning, and one came Tuesday. And there was a gentleman called Mr. Craig last night about eight o'clock, but he'd gone out. So I gave him the telephone number that Mr. Craig gave me in case anybody called him.

MRS. CRAIG. Who was the gentleman? Did you get his name?

MRS. HAROLD. Yes, Ma'm, he said his name was Birkmire.

MRS. CRAIG. Do you know if he got Mr. Craig all right?

MRS. HAROLD. Yes, Ma'm, he did; because when I told Mr. Craig this morning about him calling, he said it was all right, that he'd talked to him last night. (MRS. CRAIG *nods and moves down to the center table.*) And then he called again this afternoon about half-past four. (MRS. CRAIG *turns and looks at her.*)

MRS. CRAIG. Mr. Birkmire did?

MRS. HAROLD. Yes, Ma'm; he said he wanted Mr. Craig to get in touch with him as soon as he came in.

MRS. CRAIG. What number was it Mr. Craig gave you last night, Mrs. Harold, to have Mr. Birkmire call him at?

MRS. HAROLD. Why, it was Levering three, one hundred. I wrote it down on a piece of paper, so I wouldn't forget it.

MRS. CRAIG. All right, Mrs. Harold, I'll tell him when he comes. (MRS. HAROLD *goes out.*) And will you get another vase for those roses, Mrs. Harold, before you take them up—

MRS. HAROLD. All right, I will.

MRS. CRAIG. That one belongs down here. (*She stands and thinks quietly for a second; then, with a glance up the stairs and out after* MRS. HAROLD, *she moves to the telephone and picks it up.*) Give me Information, please. (*She waits, glancing toward the other room and up the stairs.* MAZIE *comes down the stairs.*)

MAZIE. Miss Landreth sent me down for her bag.

MRS. CRAIG. It's there on the table. (MAZIE *picks up the bag from the table and starts for the stairs again.* MRS. CRAIG *looks steadily at her and is about to speak when* MAZIE *thinks of herself and turns back, crossing towards the portières.*) Take that glass out, too, Mazie.

MAZIE (*picking up the glass from the table as she goes*). Yes, Ma'm.

MRS. CRAIG (*into the telephone*). Information? Why, could you give me the address of the telephone number, Levering three, one hundred? Oh, don't you?—All right, it isn't important—thank you very much. (*She stands thinking for a second. Then the screen door outside bangs, and she sets down the telephone and moves towards the door.* MR. CRAIG *comes in briskly, wearing a Panama hat and carrying a newspaper.*)

CRAIG. Well, look who's here, bright and smiling! (*He advances, removing his hat, and she moves a step or two towards him.*)

MRS. CRAIG. You almost beat me home.

CRAIG. How did this happen? (*He kisses her affectionately.*) When did you get in, Harriet?

MRS. CRAIG (*taking his hat and the newspaper from him and putting them on the table*). A few minutes ago. I left Albany at noon.

CRAIG (*tossing his gloves on the piano*). And how is it you didn't wire or something?

MRS. CRAIG (*picking up her own gloves from the table and straightening out the fingers*). I never thought of it, to tell the truth; there was so much to be done around there—getting Ethel's things together, and one thing and another.

CRAIG. Was Ethel there?

MRS. CRAIG. Yes, Estelle insisted that she be sent for last Saturday. And for the life of me I don't know why she did such a thing; for it upset her terribly. So the doctor said he thought the best thing to do would be to get Ethel out of her sight for a few days: so I brought here back with me. She's upstairs, lying down.

CRAIG. How *is* Estelle?

MRS. CRAIG. Why, I couldn't see that there was anything the matter with her—any more than usual. But you'd think from her letter she was dying. And then I have to walk out, and leave my house for a whole week, and go racing up to Albany.

CRAIG. Has she a trained nurse?

MRS. CRAIG (*picking up his hat from the table*). My dear, she's had two of them, for over six weeks. But you know what trained nurses are.

CRAIG. Well, I'm sorry to hear Estelle is so bad.

MRS. CRAIG (*handing him his hat*). Here, take this, Walter.

CRAIG (*drawing her back into his arms*). But I'm glad to have you back again.

MRS. CRAIG (*laughing lightly*). Stop it, Walter.

CRAIG. Seems you've been away a month instead of a week. (*He kisses the side of her head.*)

MRS. CRAIG. Don't break my bones, Walter!

CRAIG. That's what I think I'd like to do sometimes.

MRS. CRAIG (*laughing*). Now, stop it. (*He releases her and she straightens up, touching her hair.*) Stop. Here, take this hat and put it out where it belongs. (*He takes the hat and crosses above her towards the portières.*) And take this paper out of here too; this room's a sight. (*He steps back and takes the paper, then goes on out into the other room.*) Your aunt's company will be scandalized.

CRAIG (*from the other room*). Has Auntie Austen got some company?

MRS. CRAIG (*moving up to arrange the pillows on the fancy seat at the right of the stairway*). So Mrs. Harold says. She's upstairs with her.

CRAIG (*reëntering, and crossing directly over to the bay window at the left*). Who is it?

MRS. CRAIG. The lady of the roses, across the street there.

CRAIG. Mrs. Frazier?

MRS. CRAIG. Yes. She's getting very sociable.

CRAIG. She certainly has some beautiful roses over there, hasn't she?

MRS. CRAIG. She ought to have; she has nothing to do but look after them.

CRAIG. Those ramblers make a pretty effect, down at the side there, don't they?

MRS. CRAIG. Wait till you see them a week from now.

CRAIG (*turning to her*). Why?

MRS. CRAIG. Why, there'll be petals all over the place over there.

CRAIG. That ought to be prettier than the way it is now.

MRS. CRAIG. Well, you might not think it was so pretty if you had to sweep them.

CRAIG (*taking some papers from his inside pocket, and moving to the chair beside the piano*). I wouldn't sweep them up. (MRS. CRAIG *makes a sound of vast amusement.*) I can't think of anything much prettier than to have rose petals scattered all over the lawn. (*He sits down.*)

MRS. CRAIG (*straightening the big chair in front of the fireplace*). You'd have a nice looking place, I must say.

CRAIG. It's a wonder she wouldn't bring a few of those roses over here to Auntie Austen.

MRS. CRAIG. I guess she has sense enough to know that if we wanted roses we could plant some. (*She starts across towards him, above the center table, glancing towards the head of the stairs.*) Listen; she's apt to be down here any minute, Walter, and if I were you I wouldn't be sitting there when she comes; for if she sees you you'll never get away till she's told you her entire history. I've just escaped it twice. (*She gathers her things together on the table.*)

CRAIG. I've talked to her a couple of times on the way up from the garage.

MRS. CRAIG. You mean she's talked to you.

CRAIG. No, she was out there fixing the roses when I came by.

MRS. CRAIG. Of course she was. That's where she is most of the time. (*Becoming confidential, and moving towards him, below the table.*) And the funny part of it is, Walter, I don't think she realizes that people know exactly why she does it. Really, it's the most transparently obvious thing I've ever seen in my life.

CRAIG. Well, why do you think she does it?

MRS. CRAIG. Why do I think she does it?

CRAIG. Yes.

(MRS. CRAIG *laughs, with a shade of amused impatience.*)

MRS. CRAIG. Well now, Walter—why do certain women go about all the time with a child by the hand, or a dog on a leash. To facilitate the—approach. (*She returns to the table and puts her gloves in her pocketbook; and* CRAIG *sits looking at her, mystified.*) Only the lady upstairs uses roses. So, really, I wouldn't be sitting there when she comes down, if I were you, Walter; you know there *is* a danger in propinquity.

CRAIG (*resuming his letters*). I guess she could have gotten plenty of men if she'd wanted them.

MRS. CRAIG. But she may not have been able to get the kind she wanted. And *you* may be the kind. (*He looks at her and laughs.*) And this little visit this afternoon, laden with flowers, may be simply the initial attack in a very highly premeditated campaign.

CRAIG. Did you say she brought some flowers over this afternoon?

MRS. CRAIG. I said, "highly premeditated." I believe you told me you'd stopped a number of times to talk to her.

CRAIG. I've stopped twice, as a matter of fact.

MRS. CRAIG. And admired her roses?

CRAIG. There was nothing much else to talk about.

MRS. CRAIG. Of course there wasn't; that's the point. And if there hadn't been any roses, there wouldn't have been anything at all to talk about. And you wouldn't have stopped, and talked. (*She looks at him directly and smiles.*) But since you did, why —it isn't at all inconceivable that she should conclude that you probably liked roses. And that you might regard it as a very charming little gesture if she were to just bring a few over sometime—to your aunt—when your wife was out of the city.

CRAIG (*leaning back against the piano and looking at his letters*). What are you trying to do, kid me, Harriet?

MRS. CRAIG. Not at all. Don't lean back against that piano that way, Walter you might scratch it.

CRAIG. My coat won't scratch it.

MRS. CRAIG (*crossing hurriedly*). Well, there might be something in your pocket that will. (*She pushes him away from the piano.*) Now, sit up. (*She gives him a little slap on the back.*) Sit over there. (*She indicates the big chair at the left of the center table, and he rises good-naturedly and crosses to it. Then she busies herself examining the spot on the piano where he leaned, and settling the piano scarf carefully.*)

CRAIG. Yes, sir, I think that's what you're trying to do, Harriet, just kid me.

MRS. CRAIG. Well now, do you think what I've been saying is at all improbable?

CRAIG. No, it isn't improbable; it's just funny.

MRS. CRAIG (*crossing back to the table and gathering all her things up*). The flowers were on the piano when I came in.

CRAIG. Well, if they were they were for Auntie Austen.

MRS. CRAIG. Maybe they were. I sent them up to her room, anyway. So Mrs. Frazier probably thinks I *thought* they were for Auntie Austen. (*She starts for the portières at the right, and he looks after her*

and laughs. She turns and looks at him.)
What are you laughing at?

CRAIG. You.

MRS. CRAIG. Really?

CRAIG. You're very amusing to-night.

MRS. CRAIG (*coming forward at the right of the table*). And I think you're just a little bit reckless, Walter—sitting there tempting the temptress.

CRAIG. You know, I think you're getting jealous of me, Harriet.

MRS. CRAIG (*amused*). Not at all, dear boy; I'm simply suspicious of rich, middle-aged divorcees, who specialize in wayside roses. (*She leans on her umbrella.*)

CRAIG. Mrs. Frazier isn't a divorcee.

MRS. CRAIG. Isn't she?

CRAIG. No, her husband was killed in an automobile accident in 1915. She told me so herself. She was in the car with him.

MRS. CRAIG. And how is it she wasn't killed?

CRAIG (*laughing a little*). Well now, does everybody have to be killed in automobile accidents?

MRS. CRAIG. No, there's always the Galveston Flood, for husbands. You're a very guileless young man, Walter; and I'm sorry your mind doesn't work just a little bit more rapidly.

CRAIG. It works pretty thoroughly, though, when it sees the point.

MRS. CRAIG. But, that's a very slight advantage, Walter, if the point is made before you see it.

CRAIG. Do you know, I'd like to be able to see just what's going on in your mind to-night.

MRS. CRAIG. Well, if you could, I daresay you'd find something very similar to what's going on in the minds of most of our neighbors these days.

CRAIG. Now, just what do you mean by that?

MRS. CRAIG. They have eyes, Walter; and they use them. And I wish you'd use yours. And I also wish you'd tell me whose telephone number Levering three, one hundred is.

CRAIG. Fergus Passmore, why?

MRS. CRAIG. Nothing, I was just wondering. Mrs. Harold told me you gave her that number last night in case anybody wanted you, and I was wondering where it was. (*She moves towards the door again.*)

CRAIG. Fergus Passmore's. I was playing cards out there last night. I ran into him yesterday in front of the First National, and he asked me to come out there last night and play a little poker.

MRS. CRAIG. What did Billy Birkmire want you for?

CRAIG. Why, a—

MRS. CRAIG. Mrs. Harold said he called you up.

CRAIG. Yes, Fergus told me to get hold of him, too, and bring him out there; so I did; but he called me up later to tell me that his father had just come in from St. Paul, and he wouldn't be able to make it. I wasn't here when he called, so I talked to him from there.

MRS. CRAIG. I hope you're not going to get into card-playing again, Walter.

CRAIG. Why, I never gave up card-playing.

MRS. CRAIG. Well, you haven't played in nearly a year.

CRAIG. Well, I suppose that's because *you* don't play. And most of the folks know that, so they don't ask *me*. I don't suppose Fergus would have asked me yesterday, only that I happened to mention that *you* were away.

MRS. CRAIG. Was his wife there?

CRAIG. She was for a while, but she didn't play, she was going out somewhere.

MRS. CRAIG. I suppose that's the reason Fergus asked you, wasn't it?

CRAIG. What do you mean?

MRS. CRAIG. Why, you know how insanely jealous of her he used to be.

CRAIG. Well, I'm sure he was never jealous of me.

MRS. CRAIG. He was jealous of everybody, from what I could see.

CRAIG. Oh, don't be silly, Harriet.

MRS. CRAIG. Well, you wouldn't know it, Walter, even if he were.

CRAIG. Well, I'm glad I wouldn't.

MRS. CRAIG. And you come to find out, I'll bet that's just the reason Billy Birkmire dodged it. I'll bet that's just what he called you up to tell you.

CRAIG. He didn't call me up to tell me anything of the kind, now, Harriet; he simply called me to tell me that his father had come in unexpectedly from—

MRS. CRAIG. I don't mean last night; I mean when he called you to-day.

CRAIG. He didn't call me to-day.

MRS. CRAIG. He did, this afternoon, around four o'clock.

CRAIG. Here?

MRS. CRAIG. So Mrs. Harold told me. Said he wanted you to get in touch with him as soon as you came in.

CRAIG (*rising, and crossing to the telephone*). Wonder why he didn't call the office.

MRS. CRAIG (*moving towards the portières*). Probably he did, and you'd gone.

CRAIG. What's Birkmire's number, do you know?

MRS. CRAIG (*turning at the door*). Park 840, isn't it? Unless they've changed it.

CRAIG. I think it is.

MRS. CRAIG (*lowering her voice*). And I'm really serious, Walter, about that woman upstairs.

CRAIG (*into the telephone*). Park 840. (*There is a laugh from* MRS. FRAZIER, *at the head of the stairs.*)

MRS. CRAIG. So if I were you I wouldn't be here when she comes down. (*He silences her with a gesture; and, with a glance towards the head of the stairs, she goes out at the right.*)

MRS. FRAZIER. I used to have considerable difficulty myself, when I first started to use them.

CRAIG. Hello—Park 840?

MISS AUSTEN (*at the head of the stairs*). Well, I think I understand it now.

CRAIG. Is Mr. Birkmire there? (MRS. FRAZIER *and* MISS AUSTEN *come down the stairs.*) Oh, that's too bad; I just missed him, didn't I?

MRS. FRAZIER. Well now, please don't hesitate to call me, Miss Austen, if there's anything you don't understand,—

CRAIG. Yes, this is Mr. Craig speaking.

MISS AUSTEN. I will, I'll let you know.

MRS. FRAZIER. Because I haven't a solitary thing to do. (*She sees* MR. CRAIG *at the telephone, and turns to* MISS AUSTEN, *laying her finger on her lips.*)

CRAIG. Then, he'll probably be here pretty soon. (MRS. FRAZIER *comes down into the room, and* MISS AUSTEN *stops on the landing, looking at* MR. CRAIG.) Thanks—that's fine. Thank you very much. (*He hangs up.*)

MISS AUSTEN. Hello, Walter.

CRAIG. Hello, Auntie. How are you?

MISS AUSTEN (*coming down from the landing*). I didn't know you were home.

CRAIG. Just got in this minute. How do you do, Mrs. Frazier.

MRS. FRAZIER. How do you do, Mr. Craig.

MISS AUSTEN. Mrs. Frazier was kind enough to come up and show me something about a new pattern that I just bought.

CRAIG. That so?

MISS AUSTEN. Mrs. Harold tells me that Harriet is home.

CRAIG. Yes, she just got in ahead of me.

MISS AUSTEN. Did she say how Mrs. Landreth was?

CRAIG. Pretty bad shape, I imagine, from what she says.

MISS AUSTEN. Where is Harriet, upstairs?

CRAIG. Yes, she's just taken her things up.

MRS. FRAZIER. Miss Austen was telling me that Mrs. Craig's sister has heart trouble.

CRAIG. Yes, she's had it a long time.

MRS. FRAZIER. Poor woman.

MISS AUSTEN. Nearly ten years.

MRS. FRAZIER. How unfortunate. I suppose Mrs. Craig is very much upset, isn't she?

CRAIG. Yes, I suppose she is.

MRS. FRAZIER. Is she her only sister?

CRAIG. Yes, there are just the two of them.

MRS. FRAZIER. Too bad. But, that's the way it seems to go as a rule, doesn't it?

CRAIG. Yes, that's true.

MISS AUSTEN. Walter, you should see all the wonderful roses Mrs. Frazier just brought me over.
(MRS. FRAZIER *gives a little deprecating laugh and moves towards the piano at the left.*)

CRAIG. Oh, yes?

MISS AUSTEN. They're perfectly beautiful.

MRS. FRAZIER. Not a very generous giving, I'm afraid, when there are so many of them.

CRAIG *and* MISS AUSTEN (*speaking together*). CRAIG: Well, I'm sure we appreciate it very much. MISS AUSTEN: I think it's very charming of you to remember us at all.

MRS. FRAZIER. Sometimes I think perhaps I am a bit foolish to have so many of them, because it *is* a lot of work.

MISS AUSTEN. It must be; I often say that to Walter.

MRS. FRAZIER. Yes, it is. But, you see, they were more or less of a hobby with my husband when he was alive; and I suppose I tend them out of sentiment, really, more than anything else.

MISS AUSTEN. How long has your husband been dead, Mrs. Frazier?

MRS. FRAZIER. He'll be dead ten years this coming November. Yes. Yes, he died the twenty-third of November, 1915. He was injured on the second, in an automobile accident at Pride's Crossing, Massachusetts: we were on our way back from Bar Harbor—I was telling Mr. Craig about it. And he lingered from that until the twenty-third. So, you see, the melancholy days have really a very literal significance for me.

MISS AUSTEN. I should say so, indeed.

MRS. FRAZIER. Yes, that is the one month I must get away. I don't care where I go, but I must go somewhere; I couldn't stand it here; I have too many memories. So every year, as soon as ever November comes around, I just pack up my things and go out to Dayton, Ohio. I have a married daughter living out there; her husband is connected with the National Cash Register Company. And, of course, she makes all manner of fun of my annual pilgrimages to Dayton. She says instead of being in England now that April's there, with me it's in Dayton now that November's there. (*She laughs faintly.*) We have great fun about it. But, of course, her husband's business is there. And I think sometimes perhaps I should spend more time with her; I think it would help us both. But the trouble is, when I go out there, it's so very difficult for me to get away again. She has the most adorable baby—just fifteen months old; and he thinks there's nobody in the world like his grandmother. And, of course, *I* think there's nobody in the world like *him*. Although, to tell the truth, I did resent him terrifically when he was born— to think that he'd made me a grandmother. But he's quite won me over; and I suppose I'm as foolish now as all the other grandmothers.

MISS AUSTEN. Is she your only daughter, Mrs. Frazier?

MRS. FRAZIER. Yes, she was my only child.

CRAIG. Then, you live alone over here, Mrs. Frazier?

MRS. FRAZIER. All alone, yes.

MISS AUSTEN. Is that so?

MRS. FRAZIER. Yes, I've lived alone now for nearly four years—ever since my daughter was married. Alone at fifty. (*She laughs lightly.*) Rather a premature desolation, isn't it? (*She laughs again, a little.*)

CRAIG. Certainly is.

MISS AUSTEN. I should say so.

MRS. FRAZIER. I remember reading a story by that name one time, a number of years ago; and I remember thinking then, how dreadful that would be—to be left alone—especially for a woman. And yet the very same thing happened to me before I was fifty.

MISS AUSTEN. Well, didn't you ever think of going out and living with your daughter, Mrs. Frazier?

MRS. FRAZIER. Well, of course, she has never given up trying to persuade me to do that; but I always say to her, "No, darling, I will live out my days in your father's house—even though he isn't there." I say, "I have my memories, at least; and nobody can take those from me." Of course, she says I'm sentimental; (*she laughs*) but I'm not, really—not the least bit. Because if I were, I should have probably married again; but I feel that—

CRAIG. I should think you would have married again, Mrs. Frazier.

MRS. FRAZIER. Well, I suppose that would have been the logical thing to do, Mr. Craig; but, I don't know—I suppose perhaps I'm one of those one-man women. There are such women, you know.

MISS AUSTEN. Yes, indeed there are.

MRS. FRAZIER. Just as there are one-woman men. And I think it's particularly unfortunate when anything happens to the attachment of a person of that kind—whether it's death, or disillusionment, or whatever it

is—because the impairment is always so absolutely irreparable. A person of that type can never care very greatly again, about anything.

MISS AUSTEN (*looking away off*). That's very true, Mrs. Frazier.

MRS. FRAZIER (*falling into a mood*). Never. (*She shakes her head slowly from side to side; then starts.*) Well, I think I'd better go, or you'll be agreeing with my daughter that I'm sentimental.
(*They follow her towards the door.*)

MISS AUSTEN *and* CRAIG (*speaking together*). MISS AUSTEN: Oh, not at all, Mrs. Frazier; I agree with you perfectly. CRAIG: I think a little bit of sentiment is a very nice thing sometimes.

MRS. FRAZIER (*turning at the door*). And I do hope you'll tell Mrs. Craig that I was inquiring about her sister.

CRAIG. I will, Mrs. Frazier, thank you very much.

MRS. FRAZIER. I hope she'll be better soon. Good afternoon, Mr. Craig. (*She goes out.*)

CRAIG. Good afternoon, Mrs. Frazier. I hope you'll come over again very soon.

MRS. FRAZIER (*calling back*). Thanks ever so much, I shall be delighted to.

MISS AUSTEN (*following her out*). And thanks again for the roses.
(CRAIG *turns away from the door and goes up the stairs.* MRS. CRAIG *appears between the portières, looking darkly towards the bay window at the left, where* MRS. FRAZIER *can be seen passing across the lawn.*)

MRS. FRAZIER. Oh, don't mention it, dear child, I should have brought you twice as many.

MISS AUSTEN. And I'll let you know if there's anything I don't understand as I go along.

MRS. FRAZIER. Please do, now, Miss Austen; don't hesitate to call me.

MISS AUSTEN. I will, I'll let you know.

MRS. FRAZIER. Good-by.

MISS AUSTEN. Good-by, Mrs. Frazier.
(*The screen door slams.* MRS. CRAIG *moves forward to the mirror over the mantelpiece at the right.*)

MRS. CRAIG. The silly creature. (*She stands looking in the mirror, touching her hair.* MISS AUSTEN *comes in.*)

MISS AUSTEN (*stopping just inside the door*). Oh, Harriet, I was just going up to your room. How did you find your sister? Mrs. Harold told me a moment ago that you were back.

MRS. CRAIG (*without turning*). Yes, I'm back. (*Turning, with a touch of challenge in her manner.*) And I think it's about time I came back, don't you?

MISS AUSTEN. Why, dear?

MRS. CRAIG. Why?

MISS AUSTEN. Yes, I don't understand what you mean.

MRS. CRAIG. Well, from the looks of things, if I'd stayed away much longer, I should have probably come back to find my house a thoroughfare for the entire neighborhood.

MISS AUSTEN. You mean Mrs. Frazier being here?

MRS. CRAIG. You know perfectly well what I mean, Auntie Austen; please don't try to appear so innocent. (*She moves up to the foot of the stairs, to assure herself that* MR. CRAIG *is not within hearing distance.* MISS AUSTEN *gives her a long, narrow look and moves forward at the right of the piano. There is a pause; then* MRS. CRAIG *comes forward to the center table in a perfect fury.*) That's exactly what that woman's been trying to do ever since we've been here; and the minute you get my back turned you let her succeed—just for the sake of a lot of small talk. How did she happen to get in here?

MISS AUSTEN. Why, I asked her in, of course; you don't suppose she walked in of her own accord.

MRS. CRAIG. I wouldn't put it past her, if she knew I was away. (MISS AUSTEN *looks*

at her.) I know Mrs. Frazier's type better than you do. (*She settles the things on the table.*) What did you do; go over after her?

MISS AUSTEN. No, I did not. I was sewing on the porch there, and she brought me some roses over, which I think was very thoughtful of her.

MRS. CRAIG. Very thoughtful.

MISS AUSTEN. And I happened to mention the dress that I was making, and that the pattern that I'd bought for it wasn't quite clear to me. And she seemed to know from my description just what pattern it was, and very kindly offered to help me.

MRS. CRAIG. Of course; and you walked right into the trap.

MISS AUSTEN (*turning to her*). Well, why do you think she should be so anxious to get in *here*, Harriet?

MRS. CRAIG. For the same reason that a lot of other women in this neighborhood want to get in here—to satisfy their vulgar curiosity; and see what they can see.

MISS AUSTEN. And, why should you care if they do see?

MRS. CRAIG. I wouldn't gratify them—I don't want a lot of idle neighbors on visiting terms. Let them tend to their houses, and they'll have plenty to do: instead of wasting their time with a lot of silly roses. (*She crosses down to the mirror again.*) Mrs. Frazier is very likely one of those housekeepers that hides the dirt in the corners with a bunch of roses.

MISS AUSTEN. You know nothing about her house, Harriet.

MRS. CRAIG. I know what her lawn looks like,—that's enough for me. (*Turning.*) And you had to bring her upstairs, too, for fear she wouldn't see enough down here.

MISS AUSTEN. I don't suppose the woman knows what you've got in your house, Harriet.

MRS. CRAIG. Oh, Auntie Austen! Really, I wish you were as guileless in certain other respects as you seem to be in the matter of visiting neighbors.

MISS AUSTEN. A good neighbor is a very good thing sometimes, Harriet.

MRS. CRAIG. Well, you may have them; I don't want them running in and out to me.

MISS AUSTEN. None of them has ever run in and out to you so far that I remember.

MRS. CRAIG. One of them has just left.

MISS AUSTEN. She wasn't here to see you.

MRS. CRAIG. She was in my house, wasn't she?

MISS AUSTEN. And in your husband's house.

MRS. CRAIG. Oh— (*She gives a little laugh of mirthless amusement.*) Well, she was hardly here to see my husband, was she? (MISS AUSTEN *holds her eye for a second.*)

MISS AUSTEN. No, she was not; although I've no doubt you'd attempt such an interpretation if you thought there was any possibility of Walter's believing it. I don't think any extremity would be too great for you, Harriet, as long as it kept people out of the Temple of the Lord. This Holy of Holies. It's a great wonder to me you haven't asked us to take off our shoes, when we walk across the carpet. (MR. CRAIG *coughs, somewhere upstairs, and* MRS. CRAIG *moves suddenly to the foot of the stairs and looks up.*) Mrs. Frazier was here to see *me*, your husband's aunt. And I made her welcome; and so did he. And asked her to come back again. And I don't think you'd find him very much in accord with your attitude, if he knew about it.

MRS. CRAIG. Well, you'll probably tell him.

MISS AUSTEN. Oh, I've got a lot of things to tell him, Harriet.

MRS. CRAIG. I've no doubt you have.

MISS AUSTEN. I've had plenty of time to think about them during the past two years, up there in my room. And they've been particularly clear to me this past week that you've been away. That's why I've decided to tell Walter; (MRS. CRAIG *turns sharply and looks at her*) because I think he should be told. Only I want you to be here when I tell him, so that you won't be able to *twist* what I say.

MRS. CRAIG (*coming forward to the table*). You have a very good opinion of me, haven't you, Auntie Austen?

MISS AUSTEN. It isn't an opinion I have of you at all, Harriet; it's *you* that I have.

MRS. CRAIG. Well, whatever it is, I'm not at all interested in hearing about it. And I want you to know that I resent intensely your having brought Mrs. Frazier in here.

MISS AUSTEN (*turning away*). Oh, be honest about it, at least, Harriet!

MRS. CRAIG. What do you mean?

MISS AUSTEN. Why particularize on Mrs. Frazier?

MRS. CRAIG. Because I don't want her here.

MISS AUSTEN. You don't want anybody here.

MRS. CRAIG. I don't want *her*. (*She strikes the table with her knuckles.*)

MISS AUSTEN (*looking directly at her*). You don't want your husband— (MRS. CRAIG *starts slightly and then stands rigid*) only that he's necessary to the upkeep here. But if you could see how that could be managed without him, his position here wouldn't be as secure as the position of one of those pillows there. (*She indicates the pillows on the seat at the right of the stairway.*)

MRS. CRAIG. Well, I must say, Miss Austen, that's a very nice thing for you to say to me.

MISS AUSTEN. It's the truth, whether you like to hear it or not. You want your house, Harriet, and that's all you do want. And that's all you'll have, at the finish, unless you change your way. People who live to themselves, Harriet, are generally left to themselves; for other people will not go on being made miserable indefinitely for the sake of your ridiculous idolatry of house furnishings.

MRS. CRAIG. You seem to have borne it rather successfully.

MISS AUSTEN. I did it for Walter's sake; because I knew he wanted to have me here;

and I didn't want to make it difficult. But I've been practically a recluse in that room of mine upstairs ever since we've been here; just to avoid scratching that holy stairway, or leaving a footprint on one of these sacred rugs. I'm not used to that kind of stupidity. I'm accustomed to *living* in rooms; (MR. CRAIG *comes quietly down the stairs and stands on the landing, looking inquiringly from one to the other.* MRS. CRAIG *sees him out of the corner of her eye, and drifts forward to the mirror at the right*) and I think too much of myself to consider their appearance where my comfort is concerned. So I've decided to make a change. Only I want my reasons to be made perfectly clear to Walter before I go—I think I owe it to him; for his own sake as well as mine. (MISS AUSTEN *becomes aware of* CRAIG'S *presence on the stairway and turns and looks at him. There is a dead pause. Then she turns away, and* CRAIG *comes down into the room and forward at the left of the table.*)

CRAIG. What's the matter?

MRS. CRAIG (*turning*). I haven't the faintest idea, I'm sure. But from what Auntie Austen has just been saying, she seems to think there are quite a few things the matter.

CRAIG. What is it, Auntie?

MRS. CRAIG. She tells me she's going to leave us.
(*He looks at his wife, then at his aunt.*)

MISS AUSTEN. It's nothing very new, Walter.

CRAIG (*to his wife*). Going to leave the house, you mean?

MRS. CRAIG. So she says.
(*He looks at* AUNTIE AUSTEN *again.*)

CRAIG. You didn't say that, did you, Auntie?

MRS. CRAIG. Haven't I just told you she said it?

MISS AUSTEN. I am leaving to-morrow, Walter.

CRAIG. But, why? What's happened?

MRS. CRAIG. She says she finds my conduct of affairs here unendurable.

MISS AUSTEN. I'll be obliged to you, Harriet, if you'll allow me to explain the reasons for my going; I know them better than you do.

MRS. CRAIG (*turning to the large chair in front of the fireplace and sitting down*). You haven't any reasons that I can see; except the usual jealous reasons that women have—of the wives of men they've brought up.

MISS AUSTEN. You'll have plenty of time to give your version of my leaving after I've gone.

MRS. CRAIG. Well, sit down, then, and let us hear *your* version of it.

MISS AUSTEN. I prefer to stand, thank you.

MRS. CRAIG. Just as you please.

MISS AUSTEN (*glancing at the chair at the left, below the piano*). I doubt if I'd know quite *how* to sit in one of these chairs.

CRAIG. Why, what do you mean, Auntie? I can't believe that you've had any difficulty with any one; and especially with Harriet —who thinks the world of you. (MISS AUSTEN *smiles dryly.*) Now, you know she does, Auntie. Harriet is just as fond of you as I am. (*Turning to his wife.*) Why, it's incredible, positively.

MRS. CRAIG. I'm glad you're here—to hear some of this.

CRAIG. I suppose there *are* little irritations come up around a house occasionally, just as there are in any other business; but I'm sure you're too sensible, Auntie, to allow them to affect you to the extent of making you want to leave the house. Why, what would we do around here without you? It wouldn't seem to me that we had any house at all. What was it you said to Auntie, Harriet?

MRS. CRAIG. I haven't said anything to her, of course; she's simply using her imagination.

CRAIG. Then, it isn't anything that Harriet has said to you, Auntie?

MISS AUSTEN. Oh, no—Harriet never *says* anything. She simply acts; and leaves you to interpret—if you're able. And it takes a long time to be able—until you find the key. And then it's all very simple—and very ridiculous, and incredibly selfish. So much so, Walter, that I rather despair of ever convincing you of my justification for leaving your house.

CRAIG. Well, what has Harriet done, Auntie?

MRS. CRAIG. I'll tell you what I did, Walter —I objected to Auntie Austen's having brought that woman across the street there in here while I was away.

CRAIG. You mean Mrs. Frazier?

MRS. CRAIG. Yes, I mean Mrs. Frazier.

CRAIG. Why, what's the matter with Mrs. Frazier?

MRS. CRAIG. She's a vulgar old busybody, that's what's the matter with her—that's been trying to get in here ever since we've been here.

CRAIG. What do you mean, she's been trying to get *in* here?

MRS. CRAIG. You wouldn't understand if I told you, Walter. It's a form of curiosity that women have about other women's houses that men can't appreciate.

MISS AUSTEN. Harriet is chiefly provoked, Walter, because she has allowed herself to be tempted off form for a moment. She would much prefer to have excluded Mrs. Frazier by the usual method—that has been employed in the exclusion of every other man and woman that has ever visited here. But since she's blundered, she must attempt to justify herself now by arraigning Mrs. Frazier as everything from a vulgarian to a busybody—and even to insinuating that her visit here this afternoon was inspired by an interest in you.

MRS. CRAIG. I insinuated nothing of the kind. I simply asked a question in answer to an insinuation of yours.

MISS AUSTEN. The details are unimportant, Harriet; I know the principle.

MRS. CRAIG. Well, tell the truth about it, at least.

MISS AUSTEN. That is exactly what I am going to do—even at the risk of Walter's disfavor.

CRAIG. I don't think you could very well incur that, Auntie.

MISS AUSTEN. You're a man, Walter; and you're in love with your wife. And I am perfectly familiar with the usual result of interference under those circumstances.

CRAIG. Well, I hope I'm open to conviction, Auntie, if you have a grievance.

MISS AUSTEN. It isn't my own cause I'm about to plead; it doesn't matter about me. I sha'n't be here. But I don't want to be witness to the undoing of a man that was by way of becoming a very important citizen, without warning him of the danger.

CRAIG. I don't understand what you mean, Auntie.

MISS AUSTEN. That is probably the greater part of the danger, Walter—that you *don't* understand. If you did it would be scarcely necessary to warn you.

CRAIG. Of what?
(*There is a pause; and* MISS AUSTEN *looks right into his eyes.*)

MISS AUSTEN. Your wife.
(MRS. CRAIG *breaks into a mirthless laugh, at the absurdity of* MISS AUSTEN'S *implication.* CRAIG *turns and looks at her.*)

CRAIG. What are you laughing at, Harriet?

MRS. CRAIG. Why, don't you think that's very amusing?

CRAIG. I don't know that I think it's so very amusing.

MRS. CRAIG. Well, wait till you've heard the rest of it; you'll probably change your mind.

MISS AUSTEN (*looking steadily at* MRS. CRAIG). Harriet isn't really laughing, Walter.

MRS. CRAIG. What *am* I doing, crying?

MISS AUSTEN. You are whistling in the dark.

MRS. CRAIG (*vastly amused, and rising*). Oh, dear! (*She touches her hair before the mirror.*)

MISS AUSTEN. You're terrified that your secret has been discovered.
(MRS. CRAIG *turns sharply and faces her.*)

MRS. CRAIG. Really? And what *is* my secret?

MISS AUSTEN. I think it's hardly necessary to tell you that, Harriet.

MRS. CRAIG. But I'm interested in hearing it.

MISS AUSTEN. Well, you can listen while I tell it to Walter.

MRS. CRAIG. Very well.

MISS AUSTEN. But I want you to know before I tell him that it didn't remain for your outburst against Mrs. Frazier here a few minutes ago to reveal it to me; I knew it almost as soon as Walter's mother knew it.
(*There is a pause: then* MRS. CRAIG *moves a few steps towards her husband.*)

MRS. CRAIG (*with a touch of mock mysteriousness*). She means that I've been trying to poison you, secretly, Walter.

MISS AUSTEN. Not so secretly, either, Harriet.
(MRS. CRAIG *laughs lightly.*)

MRS. CRAIG (*going up towards the portières*). Well, I'm sorry I must go, for I'm sure this is going to be very amusing.

MISS AUSTEN. I've asked Harriet to stay here, Walter.
(MRS. CRAIG *turns sharply at the portières.*)

MRS. CRAIG. Well, I don't intend to stay.

MISS AUSTEN. I didn't think you would.

CRAIG. Why not, Harriet?

MRS. CRAIG. Because I have something more important to do than listen to a lot of absurdities.

MISS AUSTEN. Then I shall have to regard your going as an admission of the truth of those absurdities.

MRS. CRAIG. Well, you may regard it as you please: only I hope when you've finished discussing me, you'll be as frank in letting Walter know something of what *I've* been putting up with during the past two years. (*She goes out through the portières.*)

MISS AUSTEN. Playing the martyr as usual. (CRAIG *takes a step or two towards the portières, and they stand for a second looking after her. Then he turns and looks at his aunt.*) I could have almost spoken those last words *for* her, Walter; I know her so well.

CRAIG (*coming down to the front of the table*). I wish you'd tell me what's happened here, Auntie.

MISS AUSTEN (*crossing to him*). That isn't so easy to tell to a man, Walter; it requires a bit of elucidation.

CRAIG. What is it?

MISS AUSTEN. Walter—why do you suppose your mother asked you to promise her, when she was dying, that you'd take me with you when you married?

CRAIG. Why, I think that was a perfectly natural request, Auntie, considering what you'd been to both of us during her illness.

MISS AUSTEN. But, it wasn't as though I should *need* a home—for she knew I preferred to travel,—that that's what I was preparing to do when she was first stricken. And I never told you, Walter, but she asked *me* to promise her that I should accept your invitation when you made it. You see, she knew her woman, Walter,— the woman you were going to marry.

CRAIG. You mean that Mother didn't like Harriet?

MISS AUSTEN. Nobody could like Harriet, Walter; she doesn't want them to.

CRAIG. I like her.

MISS AUSTEN. You're blinded by a pretty face, son, as many another man has been blinded.

CRAIG. Well, what has Harriet done?

MISS AUSTEN. She's left *you* practically friendless, for one thing; because the visits of your friends imply an importance to you that is at variance with her plan: so she's made it perfectly clear to them, by a thousand little gestures, that they are not welcome in her house. Because this *is* her house, you know, Walter; it isn't yours—don't make any mistake about that. This house is what Harriet married—she didn't marry you. You simply went with the house—as a more or less regrettable necessity. And you must not obtrude; for she wants the house all to herself. So she has set about reducing you to as negligible a factor as possible in the scheme of things here.

CRAIG. You don't really believe that, Auntie, do you?

MISS AUSTEN. That is her plan concerning you, Walter, I'm telling you. That is why the visits of your friends have been discouraged.

CRAIG. I can't think that Harriet would discourage my friends, Auntie.

MISS AUSTEN. Does any of them come here?

CRAIG. Why, most of them have been here at one time or another, yes.

MISS AUSTEN. Not within the last eighteen months; and you've only been married two years.

CRAIG. Well, why shouldn't Harriet want my friends here?

MISS AUSTEN. For the same reason that she doesn't want anybody else here. Because she's a supremely selfish woman; and with the arrogance of the selfish mind, she wants to exclude the whole world—because she cannot impose her narrow little order upon it. And these four walls are the symbol of that selfish exclusion.

CRAIG (*turning away, and crossing towards the right*). I can't believe that, Auntie.

MISS AUSTEN (*extending her arms towards the front door*). Can you remember when any one has darkened that door—until here to-day, when Mrs. Frazier came over? —And you see the result of that. And why do you suppose that people have so suddenly *stopped* visiting you? They always visited you at home. It can hardly be

that you've changed so radically in two years. And I daresay all those charming young men and women that used to have such pleasant times at home, thought that when you married your house would be quite a rendezvous. But they reckoned without their—hostess, Walter—just as they are beginning to reckon without you. (*He turns and looks at her.*) You never go out any more.—Nobody ever asks you.—They're afraid you might bring her; and they don't want her.—Because she's made it perfectly clear to them that she doesn't want *them*. (CRAIG *turns away again slowly.*) And just as your friends are beginning to reckon without you in their social life, so it is only a question of time till they begin to reckon without you in their *business* life. (*He looks at her again, and she moves across towards him.*) Walter—why do you suppose your appointment as one of the directors of the local bank never materialized?

CRAIG. Why, I think Littlefield had something to do with that; he's been high-hatting me a bit lately.

MISS AUSTEN. Because Harriet insulted his wife here; I saw her do it.

CRAIG. When?

MISS AUSTEN. The week after New Year's, when Mrs. Littlefield called.

CRAIG. What did Harriet do?

MISS AUSTEN. Nothing—what Harriet always does. It was a little feline subtlety—that would sound too incredible in the ears of a man. But Mrs. Littlefield appreciated it, for all her stupidity. I *saw* her appreciate it—and you were not appointed. (CRAIG *looks away.*) And I want to tell you something else that I saw the other day in the city, or rather heard. I was having luncheon at the Colonnade, and two of your old Thursday-night poker crowd came in, and sat at a table within hearing distance of me. And presently a man and his wife came in and sat down at another table. And the wife immediately proceeded to tell the man how he should have sat down; and how he should sit now that he *was* down, and so on. And I distinctly heard one of your friends say to the other, "Listen to Craig's wife over here." (CRAIG *turns his head and looks right into* MISS AUSTEN's *eyes. There is a slight pause. Then he crosses in front of her, and continues over to the piano at the left. She moves towards the left also, going up above the table.*) That is a little straw, Walter, that should show you the way the wind is blowing. Your friends resent being told where they shall sit, and how; so they are avoiding the occasion of it—just as I am going to avoid it. But you cannot avoid it, so you must deal with it.

CRAIG. How? How should I deal with it?

MISS AUSTEN (*taking hold of the back of the chair at the left of the table*). By impressing your wife with the realization that there is a *man* of the house here, as well as a woman; and that *you* are that man. And if you don't, Walter, you are going to go the way of every other man that has ever allowed himself to be dominated by a selfish woman.—Become a pallid little echo of her distorted opinions; believing finally that every friend you ever had before you met her was trying to lead you into perdition—and that she rescued you, and made a man of you. (*She makes a little sound of bitter amusement, and turns away towards the foot of the stairs.*) The irony of it. And yet they can do it.

CRAIG (*crossing back towards the right*). Harriet could never turn me against my friends.

MISS AUSTEN (*turning at the foot of the stairs, and speaking with level conviction*). Walter—they can make men believe that the mothers that nursed them—are their arch enemies. (*She comes forward suddenly and rests her left hand on the table.*) That's why I'm warning you. For you're fighting for the life of your manhood, Walter; and I cannot in conscience leave this house without at least turning on the light here, and letting you see what it is that you're fighting against. (*She starts for the stairs, and* CRAIG *turns suddenly and follows her.*)

CRAIG. Auntie, I can't see you leave this house!

MISS AUSTEN (*stopping on the second step*). But, if I'm not happy here.

CRAIG. Well, why have I been so blind that I haven't seen that you were not happy, and fixed it so that you would be!

MISS AUSTEN (*quietly*). Because you haven't *seen* your wife, Walter.

CRAIG. Oh, I can't be convinced that there isn't an enormous element of misunderstanding between you and Harriet. (MISS AUSTEN *closes her eyes and shakes her head from side to side.*) Oh, I'm not disputing that she has a peculiar disposition—she may be all that you say of her;—but I really can't see the necessity of your leaving the house; the thing must be susceptible of some sort of adjustment. (MISS AUSTEN *lays her right hand on his shoulder.*)

MISS AUSTEN. No house is big enough, Walter, for two women who are interested in the same man.

CRAIG (*crossing over to the left*). I'll never have a minute's peace if you leave here; I'll reproach myself.

MISS AUSTEN. You have nothing to reproach yourself with, Walter; you've always been very kind and very good to me.

CRAIG. What will you do if you leave here?

MISS AUSTEN. What I've always wanted to do—travel—all over the world—far and wide: so that I shan't become—little. I have such a deadly fear of that after these past two years.

CRAIG. But I promised Mother that you'd always have a home with me, and if you go, I'll feel somehow that I'm breaking that promise.

MISS AUSTEN. You haven't a home to offer me, Walter. (*He looks at her.*) You have a house—with furniture in it—that can only be used under highly specified conditions. I have the impression somehow or other, when I look at these rooms—that they are rooms that have died—and are laid out. (*She turns and starts up the stairs.*)

CRAIG. Well, whatever they are, they'll seem less if you leave them. I don't think I'd feel worse if it were Mother herself that were leaving.

(MISS AUSTEN *turns, with her hand on the balustrade.*)

MISS AUSTEN. Be glad that it isn't your mother, Walter; she would have left long ago. (*She goes on up the stairs, and he stands looking after her. There is a ring at the front door. He turns and looks out through the French windows, then moves to the middle of the room and looks out through the portières. The bell rings again; then* MAZIE *comes down the stairs.*)

CRAIG. There's a little boy at the front door, Mazie.

MAZIE. Yes, sir, I heard the bell.

CRAIG. I'm expecting a gentleman, too, Mazie, in a few minutes; I'll be upstairs.

MAZIE. All right, Mr. Craig, I'll call you when he comes. (MAZIE *goes out to answer the bell, and* CRAIG *goes up the stairs. He stops halfway up and thinks.*)

BOY'S VOICE (*at the front door*). Why, Christine, up at the corner, sez if you're goin' to the Society to-night, would you mind payin' her dues for her; she sez she can't go to-night.

(CRAIG *disappears.*)

MAZIE. Oh, sure, tell her I'll be glad to.

BOY'S VOICE. She sez the card's in the envelope there with the money.

(MRS. HAROLD *comes in through the portières and crosses towards the door, looking out keenly.*)

MAZIE. All right, dear, tell her I'll tend to it. (*The screen door slams and* MAZIE *comes in.*)

MRS. HAROLD. Did you answer that door, Mazie?

MAZIE (*crossing below the table to the mantelpiece*). Yes, it was the tailor's little boy, up at the corner, with Christine's Society money. He sez Christine can't go to-night.

MRS. HAROLD. Is to-night Society night again already?

MAZIE (*putting an envelope back of the center ornament on the mantelpiece*). It's the third Friday.

MRS. HAROLD. I can never keep track of that old Society.

MAZIE. Do you want me to pay your dues for you?

MRS. HAROLD (*moving to the foot of the stairs*). No, dear, I'm paid up to the first of July. (MAZIE *turns from the mantelpiece and moves towards her.*) Where did Mr. Craig go—upstairs?

MAZIE. I guess so, unless he's out there somewhere.

MRS. HAROLD (*glacing towards the front porch, and taking a step or two towards* MAZIE). No, he's not out there.

MAZIE. Why, what's the matter?

MRS. HAROLD (*laying her hand on* MAZIE's *arm, and lowering her voice*). I think the old lady's goin' to leave. (*She tiptoes to the portières,* MAZIE *watching her.*)

MAZIE. Miss Austen?

(MRS. HAROLD *nods; and then looks out through the adjoining rooms.*)

MRS. HAROLD (*turning to* MAZIE). The lady made a row about Mrs. Frazier being here. (*She looks out again.*)

MAZIE. Did she?

MRS. HAROLD (*coming back*). She was furious. I knew it was coming by the face on her when she told me to take the roses out of the room. So as soon as I heard Mrs. Frazier goin', I went right up to the library; you can hear every word up there, you know, over near the radiator.

MAZIE. Yes, I know you can. Was *he* here?

MRS. HAROLD. He wasn't at first, but I think he must have come down while they were at it. I heard *her* say she didn't want her house made a thoroughfare for the neighborhood.

MAZIE. Can you imagine it—as though anybody ever came *in* here.

MRS. HAROLD. That's what *I* felt like sayin'. But Miss Austen told her.

MAZIE. Did she?

MRS. HAROLD. I should say she did. It didn't take Mrs. Craig long to get out of the room once Miss Austen got started. (*A door closes upstairs, and* MAZIE *darts to the center table and settles the table scarf.* MRS. HAROLD *steps to the big chair in front of the mantelpiece and feigns to be occupied in setting it straight.* MAZIE *glances over her right shoulder up the stairs, then steps up to the foot of the stairs and glances up. Then she hurries forward to* MRS. HAROLD *again, glancing through the portières as she goes.*)

MAZIE. What did Mrs. Craig do, walk out of the room?

MRS. HAROLD. Yes. She said she had something else to do besides listenin' to a lot of silly talk. (MAZIE *raises her eyes to heaven.*) I felt like sayin' I'd like to know what it was she had to do.

MAZIE. So would I.

MRS. HAROLD. I've been here nearly a year now, and *I* have my first time to see her do anything—only a lot of snoopin'—after somebody else has finished.

MAZIE. It's too bad Miss Austen didn't tell her that while she was at it.

MRS. HAROLD (*raising her hand, with a touch of solemnity*). She told her enough. (*She goes up to the foot of the stairs and looks up.*)

MAZIE. Well, didn't *he* say anything?

MRS. HAROLD. Not very much; Miss Austen done most of the talkin'. (*She comes down to* MAZIE's *left, confidentially.*) She told him if he didn't do something very soon, his wife 'ud make him look like an echo.

MAZIE. She will, too.

MRS. HAROLD. He said she had a peculiar disposition—and that Miss Austen didn't understand her. Well, I felt like sayin' if Miss Austen don't understand her, I do. And I'd soon tell her how well I understand her, too, only that she gives me a wide berth.

MAZIE. I feel kind of sorry for him sometimes, though.

MRS. HAROLD. Yes, it's a pity for *him*. (*Lowering her voice, and speaking with great conviction.*) She could build a nest in his ear, and he'd never know it. (*She turns to the table and settles the various ornaments.*)

MAZIE. She certainly is the hardest woman to please that I've ever worked for.

MRS. HAROLD. Well, I don't know whether she's hard to please or not, Mazie, for I've never tried to please her. I do my work, and if she don't like it she has a tongue in her head; she can soon tell me, and I can go somewhere else. I've worked in too many houses to be out of a place very long. (*Straightening up and resting her left hand on the table.*) Did I tell you about her wanting me to dust the leaves off that little tree in front of the dining-room window last week?

MAZIE. Dust the leaves?

MRS. HAROLD (*looking to heaven for witness*). That's the honest God's fact. And me with the rheumatism at the time.

MAZIE. Can you imagine such a thing?

MRS. HAROLD. Well, you know how I done it, don't you?

MAZIE. What'd you say to her?

MRS. HAROLD. I told her right up; I said, "I'll dust no tree for nobody."

MAZIE. You done right.

MRS. HAROLD. She sez, "You mean you refuse to dust it?"—"Yes," I sez, "I refuse, and," I sez, "what's more, I'm goin' to stay refuse." "Well," she sez, "it needs dusting, whether you dust it or not." "Well," I sez, "let it need it," I sez. I sez, "A little dust won't poison it." I sez, "We'll be dust ourselves some day, unless we get drownded." (*She goes to the portières.*)

MAZIE. You done right.

MRS. HAROLD. Oh, I told her. (*She glances out through the rooms.*)

MAZIE. I think the worst kind of a woman a girl can work for is one that's crazy about her house.

MRS. HAROLD. I do, too; because I think they *are* crazy half the time. You know, you can go crazy over a house, Mazie, the same as you can over anything else.

MAZIE. Sure you can.

MRS. HAROLD. Doctor Nicholson's wife was one of them; although she wasn't as generous a woman as this one.

MAZIE. No, that's one thing you've got to say for Mrs. Craig; she's not stingy.

MRS. HAROLD. No, that's true, she isn't.

MAZIE. I don't think I've ever worked in a house where there was as good a table for the help.

MRS. HAROLD. That's right; you always get whatever they get.

MAZIE. And you never have to ask for your wages, neither.
(*The doorbell rings.*)

MRS. HAROLD. No, she's very good that way.

MAZIE (*going to answer the door, settling her cap and apron*). I guess that's that gentleman Mr. Craig's expectin'.

MRS. HAROLD. Come out when you come in, Mazie. (*She goes out through the portières.* MR. CRAIG *comes down the stairs.*)

BIRKMIRE (*at the front door*). Good evening. Is Mr. Craig in?

MAZIE. Yes, sir, he's in.
(*The screen door is heard to close, and* BIRKMIRE *enters.*)

CRAIG (*coming in*). Hello, Billy, how are you?

BIRKMIRE (*shaking hands earnestly*). Hello, Walt. (*He looks right into* CRAIG'S *eyes.*)

CRAIG. I called your house a little while ago; (BIRKMIRE *turns to the piano with his*

raincoat *and hat*) there was a message here for me when I got in, saying you'd called.
(MAZIE *comes in and crosses towards the portières.*)

BIRKMIRE. Yes, I've been trying to get hold of you since four o'clock.

CRAIG. Let me take those things out of your way.
(MAZIE *stops near the portières and looks back, to see if they want her to take* BIRKMIRE'S *things.*)

BIRKMIRE. No, thanks, Walter, I've got to get right back to the house.
(MAZIE *goes out; and* CRAIG *moves down towards the table.*)

CRAIG. Your father still here?

BIRKMIRE. Yes, he'll be here for a day or two yet. (*He looks keenly out through the portières, stepping up towards the back of the room.*)

CRAIG (*watching him curiously*). What's the matter? (BIRKMIRE *makes a deft gesture, signifying that* MAZIE *may be within hearing distance.*) What is it?

BIRKMIRE (*stepping down close to* CRAIG *and laying his hand on his sleeve*). What about it, Walt?

CRAIG. About what?

BIRKMIRE. About Fergus and his wife. You were out there last night, weren't you?

CRAIG. Sure. That's where I talked to *you* from.

BIRKMIRE. Well, my God, what happened out there, Walter?

CRAIG. What do you mean?

BIRKMIRE. Haven't you seen the evening papers?

CRAIG. Not yet, no. Why?

BIRKMIRE (*smothering an exclamation, and stepping to the piano to get a newspaper out of his pocket*). Jesus, how did you miss it!

CRAIG. Why, what's happened?

BIRKMIRE. Fergus and his wife are dead.

CRAIG. What!

BIRKMIRE. Found them this morning in the library.

CRAIG. Passmore, you mean?

BIRKMIRE (*handing him the paper*). Here it is on the front page of the *Telegraph*.

CRAIG (*crossing down to the right*). What are you saying, Billy?

BIRKMIRE (*stepping over towards the portières and looking out*). It's in every paper in town.

CRAIG. Where is it?

BIRKMIRE (*coming forward at* CRAIG's *left and indicating a certain headline*). Fergus Passmore and wife found dead in library.

CRAIG. My God!

BIRKMIRE. I happened to see it over a man's shoulder coming down in the elevator in the Land Title Building about four o'clock, and I damned near had heart failure. (*He turns away to the left and takes a cigarette from a case.*) I've been trying to get you on the 'phone ever since. And I saw *her* myself at the Ritz last night at twelve o'clock. I was talking to her. I took the old man over there for a bit of supper after the show, and she was there with that military gent she's been stepping it with lately. (*Suddenly laying his hand on* CRAIG's *arm.*) That's my hunch on this thing, Walter. I think she's been playing this soldier fellow a little too much lately and Fergus has heard of it and probably called it when she got in last night, and busted up the show. You know, he was always jealous as hell of her. (*He takes a step or two towards the back and glances through the portières.*)

CRAIG. There must be a catch in this thing somewhere, Billy.

BIRKMIRE (*coming forward again*). How could there be a catch in it, Walter? Do you think they'd print that kind of stuff for a joke.

CRAIG. Well, my God, I was out there last night till twelve o'clock.

BIRKMIRE (*tearing the cigarette between his fingers*). Well, evidently this thing happened after you got away from there. Did she get in before you left there last night?

CRAIG (*looking up from the paper*). What?

BIRKMIRE. I say, did Adelaide get in last night before you left out there?

CRAIG. No, but she was there when I got out there, about nine o'clock. She was going out somewhere.

BIRKMIRE. Yes, and I know who it was she was going out *with,* too; that's the third time I've run into her with that bird lately. And I want to find out what his name is right away quick, too, for he might be in on this thing.

CRAIG. Have you been out there yet?

BIRKMIRE. Out to Fergus', you mean?

CRAIG. Yes.

BIRKMIRE. Sure, I hopped right out there as soon as I read it; but you can't get near the place.

CRAIG. I think I ought to get in touch with Police Headquarters right away, Billy.

BIRKMIRE. Well, that's why I wanted to get hold of you. It says there they're looking for a man seen leaving the house after midnight.

CRAIG. Sure, that's me.

BIRKMIRE. Well, not necessarily you, Walter.

CRAIG. That's the time I got away from there.

BIRKMIRE. That doesn't mean anything. Only I think it 'ud be a good thing to let them know right away.

CRAIG (*turning suddenly and going up to the telephone*). Sure, I'll call up right away.

BIRKMIRE (*following him up*). Well, now, wait a minute, Walter, don't move too fast; you know a thing like this can take a thousand and one turns, and we don't want to make any false move. This kind of thing 'ud be pie for the newspapers, you know;

and the fact that we were invited out there to play cards wouldn't read any too well.

CRAIG. Well, *you* weren't out there.

BIRKMIRE. I know that; but I'm not sitting back in the corner in this thing, you know, Walter. It just so happened that I *wasn't* out there. But I talked to you on the telephone out there last night, from my house, and in a thing of this kind they trace telephone calls and everything else.

CRAIG (*looking at the paper again*). My God, this is a terrible thing, though, isn't it, Billy?

BIRKMIRE (*turning away to the left, and passing his hand across his brow*). I haven't got it myself yet.

CRAIG. Terrible.

BIRKMIRE. It'll be a jar to your wife when she hears it, won't it?

CRAIG. Awful.

BIRKMIRE. She'll very likely see it in the paper up there in Albany.

CRAIG. She's back from Albany.

BIRKMIRE. Is she?

CRAIG. She got in a while ago.

BIRKMIRE. Well, she doesn't know anything about this yet, does she?

CRAIG. I don't think so; unless she happened to see the paper I brought home. I suppose it's in it.

BIRKMIRE. Sure, it's in all of them.

CRAIG. I just took it from the boy and put it in my pocket.

BIRKMIRE. Where is Harriet?

CRAIG. She's upstairs.

BIRKMIRE (*lowering his voice*). Does she know you were out there last night?

CRAIG. I don't know, I guess she does. Yes, I think I mentioned it a while ago.

BIRKMIRE (*stepping to* CRAIG's *side, and laying his hand on his arm*). Well, now, listen, Walter—If she doesn't happen to

see the paper, what she doesn't know won't bother her. And this thing is apt to clear itself up over night. It might be cleared up now, for all we know; for I suppose the police have been working on it all day. But I think the wise move for us is just to hop out there and try to find out what's going on; and if they haven't found anything out yet, just get in touch with Police Headquarters and let them know where we're at.

CRAIG (*tossing the newspaper on to the seat beside the telephone table*). Yes, let's do that. Wait till I get my hat. (*He goes through portières.*)

BIRKMIRE (*crossing to the piano for his things*). I've got my car out here; we can cut across the park and be out there in ten minutes. (*He throws his raincoat across his arm, picks up his hat, and steps quickly across to get the newspaper that* CRAIG *left on the seat. He glances up the stairs and out through the portières. Then he sees* CRAIG *coming through the adjoining room, and starts for the front door.*)

CRAIG (*entering, wearing his hat, and carrying the newspaper he brought home*). I'll take this paper with me; keep it out of sight.

BIRKMIRE. I've got the other one here in my pocket. (BIRKMIRE *goes out.*)

CRAIG (*glancing about the room as he crosses to the front door*). We take the *Globe* here in the afternoon, but I don't see it anywhere around out there. (*He goes out.*)

BIRKMIRE (*outside*). I've got the car right out here.

CRAIG (*outside*). I guess across the park will be the quickest.

BIRKMIRE. Yes, we can be over there in ten minutes.
(*There is a dead pause. Then a clock somewhere out at the right strikes half-past six, with a soft gong. There is another slight pause, and then* MRS. CRAIG *sweeps through the portières, carrying an open newspaper. She sees that no one is in the room, and rushes to the forward window to see if she*

can see MR. CRAIG *anywhere about. Then she starts for the front door, but changes her mind and rushes up to the landing of the stairway.*)

MRS. CRAIG (*calling up the stairs*). Walter! —Walter!—Are you up there, Walter? (*She hurries down into the room again and over to the portières.*) Mazie!—Mazie! (*She runs across to the front door and out.* MAZIE *comes in through the portières and looks about, then starts towards the front door.* MRS. CRAIG *hurries in again.*)

MAZIE. Were you calling me, Mrs. Craig?

MRS. CRAIG. Yes, Mazie. Have you seen anything of Mr. Craig?

MAZIE. Why, he was here a few minutes ago, Mrs. Craig, with a gentleman.

MRS. CRAIG. What gentleman? Who was he?

MAZIE. I don't know who he was, Mrs. Craig; I never saw him before.

MRS. CRAIG. Didn't you catch his name?

MAZIE. No, Ma'm, I didn't. He came in an automobile.

MRS. CRAIG. Well, did Mr. Craig go away with him?

MAZIE. I don't know whether he did or not, Mrs. Craig. I didn't know he'd gone.

MRS. CRAIG (*turning* MAZIE *around quickly by the shoulder and urging her towards*

the portières). See if Mr. Craig's hat's on the rack out there.

MAZIE (*hurrying out*). Isn't he up in his room?

MRS. CRAIG. No, he isn't. (*She turns breathlessly and looks towards the bay window at the left.*) Oh, Lord! (*Turning to the portières again.*) Is it?

MAZIE (*from somewhere out at the right*). No, Ma'm, it isn't.

MRS. CRAIG. Well, listen, Mazie, run over to the garage there and see if he's there! No, no, come this way, it's quicker. (*She waits frantically until* MAZIE *rushes through the portières and across towards the front door.*) And if he's there tell him to come over here immediately; I want to see him.

MAZIE. Yes, Ma'm. (*The screen door slams after her, and she hurries past the bay window at the left.*)

MRS. CRAIG. Hurry now, Mazie. Tell him I want him right away. (*She turns in the doorway and leans against the jamb, looking straight out, wide-eyed, and holding the newspaper against her bosom.*) Oh, my God! (*She hurries across above the center table and down to the window, forward, at the right.*) Oh, my God! (*She stands looking eagerly through the window, towards the left, as though watching* MAZIE *running down the street.*)

The Curtain Descends Slowly.

ACT TWO

Ten minutes later. MRS. CRAIG *is standing at the window, forward, reading the newspaper. She stops reading, glances out the window, and then moves with a kind of controlled desperation to the bay window at the left, where she looks out again eagerly.* MRS. HAROLD *comes in from the right.*

MRS. HAROLD. Is Mazie here, Mrs. Craig? (MRS. CRAIG *turns nervously.*)

MRS. CRAIG. No, she isn't, Mrs. Harold; I've sent her on an errand; she'll be back in a minute.

MRS. HAROLD (*turning to go out again*). I told her I thought I heard you calling her. (*Telephone bell rings.*)

MRS. CRAIG. See who that is, Mrs. Harold, will you, please?

(MRS. HAROLD *comes back and picks up the telephone.*)

MRS. HAROLD. Hello? —Hello?

MRS. CRAIG. What's the matter; don't they answer?

MRS. HAROLD. No, Ma'm, they haven't answered yet. Hello!

MRS. CRAIG (*turning to the window again*). Never mind it, Mrs. Harold; it's probably a mistake.

MRS. HAROLD (*hanging up the receiver*). It does that sometimes when it's a long-distance call.
(MRS. CRAIG *turns sharply.*)

MRS. CRAIG. They didn't say it was long distance, did they?

MRS. HAROLD. No, Ma'm, they didn't say anything; nobody answered at all.

MRS. CRAIG. Well, if they want us they'll ring again.

MRS. HAROLD. Will you tell Mazie I want her when she comes in, Mrs. Craig, please?

MRS. CRAIG. Yes, I'll send her out to you as soon as she comes back. (MRS. HAROLD *goes out through the portières, and* MRS. CRAIG *crosses over and down to the window, forward, and looks out. She sees* MAZIE *hurrying back from the garage, and steps quickly up to the door at the left.* MAZIE *can be seen running past the bay window. The screen door slams, and* MAZIE *rushes in.*) Isn't he over there, Mazie?

MAZIE. No, Ma'm, he isn't.

MRS. CRAIG. Are you sure?

MAZIE. Yes, Ma'm, I looked all around.

MRS. CRAIG. Did you go round to the back?

MAZIE. Yes, Ma'm, I looked everywhere. Old Mr. Foster was standin' over there; I ast him if he'd seen anything of Mr. Craig, but he said he hadn't.

MRS. CRAIG. Is the garage locked?

MAZIE. Yes, Ma'm, I tried the door.

MRS. CRAIG. Well, could you see whether or not the car was in there?

MAZIE. Yes, Ma'm, they're both in there, the little one, too; I looked through the glass. (MRS. CRAIG *turns away to the right, with a troubled expression, and moves down towards the mirror, and* MAZIE *moves towards the door at the right.* MRS. CRAIG *glances out the window, forward.*) I guess maybe he musta went away with that gentleman that was here.

MRS. CRAIG. He probably did. You say that gentleman came in a car, Mazie?

MAZIE. Yes, Ma'm, I think it was his; it was standin' right in front of the house when I opened the door for him.

MRS. CRAIG. All right, Mazie. Mrs. Harold wants you for something.

MAZIE (*going out*). Oh, does she?
(MRS. CRAIG *leans against the mantelpiece and thinks hard. The telephone bell rings. She turns and looks at the telephone; it rings again. Then she moves to answer it.* MAZIE *comes in.*)

MRS. CRAIG. I'll answer it, Mazie.

MAZIE. Oh, all right. (*She withdraws, and* MRS. CRAIG *picks up the telephone.*)

MRS. CRAIG (*in a subdued voice*). Mazie.

MAZIE. Yes, Ma'm?

MRS. CRAIG. Come here for a minute. (MAZIE *appears between the portières.*) Go up and see that Miss Landreth's door is closed.

MAZIE (*withdrawing*). Yes, Ma'm.

MRS. CRAIG. Be very quiet about it, now, Mazie, and don't disturb her if she's asleep.

MAZIE. All right. (*Telephone bell rings again.*)

MRS. CRAIG. Hello? —Yes? —All right. (*She glances up the stairs, and then waits.*) Hello? —Yes— (*In a louder voice.*) Hello! Yes—this is Mrs. Craig at the telephone— Mr. Craig isn't here just now, if you wanted *Mr.* Craig. Oh—why-a- Miss Landreth is lying down just now. Who is this speaking, please—Oh, I see. Why—not a thing in the world, Mr. Fredericks, except that she's very tired—We've only just now gotten in from Albany, and I suggested that she go upstairs and lie down for a while. Yes—Am I going to do what? No, I didn't understand what you said, Mr. Fredericks. Why, yes, of course, I'd go back with her if anything unforeseen developed —otherwise she can go back herself. We're simply waiting now to hear something from her mother's physician up there.— Yes, of course I'm sure. Why, why should you put yourself to that trouble, Mr. Fredericks?—There wouldn't be anything you could do when you get here.—Well, I'd much rather not call her, if you don't mind, Mr. Fredericks; she's lying down— Well, can't you tell me what it is you want to tell her—and I can give her the message? Well, probably it would, Mr. Fredericks;—it's very nice of you to be so solicitous about her, but I don't care to disturb her just now. I'm very sorry. (*She hangs up abruptly, and glances towards the head of the stairs.* MAZIE *appears between the portières.*)

MAZIE. The door was closed, Mrs. Craig.

MRS. CRAIG. All right, Mazie. (MAZIE *withdraws, and* MRS. CRAIG *moves forward, thoughtfully. There is a tap at the front door bell.* MAZIE *turns and crosses to answer the door.* MRS. CRAIG *is looking sharply toward the front door.*) See what those gentlemen want, Mazie.

MAZIE. Yes, Ma'm.

CATELLE (*at the front door*). Mr. Craig in?

MAZIE. No, sir, he's not in just now; he went out about twenty minutes ago.

CATELLE. What time do you expect him back?

MAZIE. Why, I couldn't say for certain; but I guess he'll be back in time for dinner, about seven o'clock.

CATELLE. Is his wife in?

MAZIE. Yes, sir, she's in.

CATELLE. I'd like to speak to her for a minute if I could.
(MRS. CRAIG, *who has been standing very still, listening, vanishes through the portières, looking over her shoulder apprehensively towards the front door.*)

MAZIE. Yes, sir. Will you just step in? (*The screen door closes; and immediately* MAZIE *hurries into the room.*) If you'll just take a chair for a minute I'll call her.
(CATELLE *wanders in, removing his hat, followed by* HARRY, *who also removes his hat as he enters.* CATELLE *moves down to the center table, puts his hat down, and takes a small leather notebook from his inside pocket; and* HARRY *comes forward and sits in the chair beside the piano. There is a pause.*)

HARRY. They didn't get this place with a pound of tea.

CATELLE. A lot of money. Phoenix Fire Insurance people. This lad's old man used to be president of the Company. Died about twelve years ago. I guess this gent's in line for the old man's job, if he lives.
(MRS. CRAIG *enters through the portières.* HARRY *rises, and* CATELLE *turns to her.*)

MRS. CRAIG. Good evening.

HARRY. Good evening.

CATELLE. Good evening, Ma'm. I called to see Mr. Craig.

MRS. CRAIG. Mr. Craig isn't in just now, I'm sorry.

CATELLE. Are you Mrs. Craig?

MRS. CRAIG. Yes.

CATELLE. Have you any idea what time Mr. Craig'll *be* in?

MRS. CRAIG. Why, I'm expecting him any minute; he was here less than a half-hour ago, when I went upstairs; so he must be right here in the neighborhood somewhere.

CATELLE (*consulting his watch*). I see.

MRS. CRAIG. He'll certainly be back for his dinner, at seven o'clock, if you'd care to call back.

CATELLE. Well, I've got to be over the other side of town at seven o'clock,—so it may be that you could give me the information I am looking for, as well as Mr. Craig. Would you sit down for a minute?

MRS. CRAIG. Yes, certainly. (*She turns to the chair in front of the mantelpiece and sits down.* HARRY *resumes his chair beside the piano, and* CATELLE *sits on the small bench immediately above the center table.*)

CATELLE. I thought I'd like to speak to *Mr.* Craig first, but I don't suppose it makes a great deal of difference.

MRS. CRAIG. I thought he might be over at the garage—I wanted him myself a few minutes ago; but the maid says he isn't over there.

CATELLE. Well, I'll tell you what it is I wanted to see him about, Mrs. Craig. I suppose you've seen in the evening paper about this unfortunate affair out here on Willows Avenue?

MRS. CRAIG. You mean that shooting affair?

CATELLE. Yes, at the Passmore home.

MRS. CRAIG. Yes, isn't that a dreadful thing! —I've just been reading it here.

CATELLE. Yes, it's a very sad affair.

MRS. CRAIG. They're *both* dead, aren't they?

CATELLE. Yes, they're both dead.

MRS. CRAIG. Isn't that terrible! That's what I wanted to see my husband for; I wanted to ask him if he knew that man.

CATELLE. He probably did; they're pretty well-known people here in town.

MRS. CRAIG. Yes, they must be, according to the paper. I haven't had a chance to read it all yet, I've just gotten in from Albany.

CATELLE. It's a rather peculiar case.

MRS. CRAIG. Was it a robbery or something?

CATELLE. No, there wasn't anything taken. Of course, it could have been a foiled *attempt* at robbery, but that 'ud hardly explain certain other circumstances.

MRS. CRAIG. Are you gentlemen working on the case?

CATELLE. Yes, Ma'm, we're from Police Headquarters. But, that doesn't need to alarm *you*, Mrs. Craig; there's no particular connection between that and our visit *here.*

MRS. CRAIG. Well, I'm very glad to know that.

CATELLE. No, this Passmore affair looks to me pretty clearly a matter of jealousy motive. Of course, there are one or two attendant circumstances, as there usually are in cases of this kind, but they don't mean anything, as far as the actual shooting is concerned. There was a man seen leaving the house shortly after midnight in an automobile—One of the neighbors happened to see him; but it was too dark to establish any identification. Besides, that wouldn't account for the death of *Mrs.* Passmore; because she didn't get in until after three o'clock, and the man left there between twelve and one.

MRS. CRAIG. I see.

CATELLE. But, of course, as you understand, Mrs. Craig, it's part of our business to follow up any little outside clue that we happen to get hold of that might throw some additional light on a case.

MRS. CRAIG. Yes, of course.

CATELLE. And that's what I wanted to see Mr. Craig about.

MRS. CRAIG. You mean you think Mr. Craig might be the man that was seen leaving there last night.

CATELLE. No, that circumstance is really not being seriously considered; a house of that description might have had any number of visitors during the evening.

MRS. CRAIG. That's very true.

CATELLE. But, we've had a report late this afternoon, Mrs. Craig, from the Lynnebrooke Telephone Exchange, where your light comes in, that there was a call made on your telephone here at five-twenty-seven this evening, asking for the address of the telephone number Levering three, one hundred; and that happens to be the number of the telephone at Mr. Passmore's home.

MRS. CRAIG. You mean that somebody called from here? (*She indicates the telephone.*)

CATELLE. On this telephone, yes, Ma'm. Oakdale, six, two, three. That's the number of your telephone here, isn't it?

MRS. CRAIG. Yes, that's our number.

CATELLE. That's what I've got here.

MRS. CRAIG. But I can't imagine who it would be that called.

CATELLE. The report says it was a woman's voice.

MRS. CRAIG. Who was it that reported it, do you know?

CATELLE. I couldn't tell you that, Mrs. Craig.

MRS. CRAIG. I mean to say, would it be possible that the person who reported it could have made a mistake in the number?

CATELLE. No, they're usually pretty careful in an affair of this kind.

MRS. CRAIG. And the call was made at five o'clock this evening, you say?

CATELLE. Five-twenty-seven, my report says. The operator didn't give the address, of course; it's against the telephone company's rules. And the party rang off.

MRS. CRAIG. Well, that's extraordinary. Although it might have been one of the servants—probably saw it in the evening paper and was curious to know where it was. (*Rising.*) I'll ask them.

CATELLE. Well, I could understand that curiosity if the address wasn't published; but it is; and the telephone number *isn't*. And I was interested in finding out why any one 'ud have that particular 'phone number to-day and not know the address —when it's been in all the newspapers since two o'clock this afternoon. And this call wasn't made till after five.

MRS. CRAIG. It does seem strange, doesn't it?

CATELLE. I haven't been able to figure it out.

MRS. CRAIG. But, I dare say there's some very simple explanation of it.

CATELLE. Has this telephone here been used at all, to your knowledge, Mrs. Craig, since five o'clock this afternoon?

MRS. CRAIG. Why, I *answered* a call, a few minutes ago, from Northampton, Massachusetts.

CATELLE. A long-distance call, you mean?

MRS. CRAIG. Yes. It was a Mr. Fredericks, at Smith College there, calling my niece, to inquire about her mother. Her mother is ill in Albany.

CATELLE. I see.

MRS. CRAIG. That's where we've just come from.

CATELLE. You don't know whether or not anybody from the outside has been in here since five o'clock?

MRS. CRAIG. Not to my knowledge; except a neighbor from across the avenue there, Mrs. Frazier. She brought some roses over to my husband's aunt. She was here when I got in; although I scarcely think she would have used the telephone. But, I'll ask Miss Austen if you like.

CATELLE. I wish you would, please, if you don't mind.

MRS. CRAIG (*going to the stairway landing*). Not at all. She's up in her room I believe.

CATELLE. Would you mind asking her to step down here for a few minutes?

MRS. CRAIG. Yes, certainly. (*Calling.*) Miss Austen!—Miss Austen! (*There is the sound of a door opening somewhere upstairs.*)

MISS AUSTEN (*from upstairs*). Is some one calling me?

MRS. CRAIG. Yes,—it's me, Miss Austen. Would you mind coming down here for a minute or two, Miss Austen? I'd like to speak to you.

MISS AUSTEN. All right, I'll be down in a moment.

(MRS. CRAIG *turns to come down.*)

MRS. CRAIG. If you will, please. She'll be right down.

CATELLE. Thank you very much.

MRS. CRAIG (*moving towards the portières*). I suppose I'd better call the servants too, hadn't I? They'll probably know something about it.

CATELLE. Yes, I'd like to see them for a minute.

MRS. CRAIG (*going through the portières*). I'll call them right away.
(CATELLE *looks at his watch and rises.*)

CATELLE (*crossing towards the portières*). What time have you got there, Harry? (*He watches keenly through the portières.*)

MRS. CRAIG. Mazie!

HARRY. Just seven.

MAZIE (*out at the right*). Yes, Ma'm?

MRS. CRAIG. Would you come here for a minute?

CATELLE. Do you mind if I use this 'phone here, Mrs. Craig?

MRS. CRAIG. They'll be right in. (*She enters.*)

CATELLE. Do you mind if I use this 'phone here for a minute?

MRS. CRAIG (*moving forward*). Not at all, go right ahead. I didn't hear what you said.

CATELLE. I've got a call to make at seven o'clock.

MRS. CRAIG. That's quite all right.
(*He stands holding the telephone, and* MRS. CRAIG *listens keenly.*)

CATELLE (*into the telephone*). Spring 4000. —Right.
(*There is a stillness: then the clock strikes seven, with a soft gong.* MAZIE *enters, on the third gong.*)

MAZIE. Did you want me, Mrs. Craig?
(MRS. CRAIG *motions to her to be silent;* MAZIE *stands looking from one to the other in a state of positive bewilderment.*)

CATELLE. Thielens? Catelle.—That so?— I got away from there before six. Period? Righto, Chuck. What are you trying to do, break Harry's heart? (*He gives a rather dry little laugh.*) All right, Chuck, I'll be right over. (*He hangs up and crosses to the table for his hat.*) We'd better get right

out there, Harry. (HARRY *rises and moves up to the door.*) I won't have to bother you any more right now, Mrs. Craig; there's been a bit of additional information come in over at headquarters that'll hold things up temporarily.

MRS. CRAIG (*moving towards the center table*). Well, do you want me to have Mr. Craig get in touch with you when he comes in?

CATELLE. No, we'll get in touch with him if it's necessary.

MRS. CRAIG. And you don't want to question the rest of the people now, either?
(HARRY *goes out.*)

CATELLE. Not just now, Mrs. Craig, thank you very much. (*He starts for the door.*)

MRS. CRAIG. You're welcome, I'm sure. All right, Mazie.
(MAZIE *withdraws reluctantly, her eyes fastened upon* CATELLE.)

CATELLE. I'm sorry to have had to trouble you.

MRS. CRAIG (*following him to the door*). That's quite all right.

CATELLE (*turning at the door*). You can explain the circumstances to Mr. Craig, if you will.

MRS. CRAIG. Yes, I will. He'll probably know something about it.

CATELLE (*going out*). Very likely he will.

MRS. CRAIG. And if he doesn't, I'm sure one of the others will.

CATELLE. All right, thank you very much, Mrs. Craig.

MRS. CRAIG. You're very welcome, I'm sure.

CATELLE. Good evening.

MRS. CRAIG. Good evening. (*The screen door closes, and* MRS. CRAIG *turns slowly and lifts her closed hands in a quiet panic. Then she hurries forward and across to the window and watches the two detectives going down the street.* MISS AUSTEN *comes down the stairs quietly, and stands on the landing, looking at her.*)

MISS AUSTEN. Did you want to see me about something, Harriet?

(MRS. CRAIG *starts slightly and turns.*)

MRS. CRAIG (*going out through the portières*). No, not now, Miss Austen; it isn't necessary. I'm sorry to have troubled you. (MISS AUSTEN *stands for a second looking after her; then she moves forward to the window, to see what it was that had so engaged* MRS. CRAIG'S *attention. Then she moves up towards the telephone, glancing through the portières.*)

MISS AUSTEN (*into the telephone*). Will you give me Clearfield, six, two,—six, two?—Please? (*She waits, glancing towards the portières and out the window.*) Hello? Is this the Mowers Express Office? Well, how early could I have some things taken away to-morrow morning? Six hundred and eighty Belmont Manor. Yes, just a square from the Park. Well, eight o'clock would be time enough. Miss Irene Austen. That's right. Thank you. (*She hangs up, and goes up the stairs.* MRS. CRAIG *comes through the portières, glances towards the head of the stairs, and moves to the foot of the stairs to look up. Then she steps to the telephone table and settles everything precisely.* MAZIE *appears between the portières.*)

MRS. CRAIG. What is it, Mazie?

MAZIE. Why, Mrs. Harold wants to know if she'll serve the dinner now, Mrs. Craig.

MRS. CRAIG (*moving forward, thoughtfully*). Tell her not yet for a little while, till Mr. Craig gets here; I'm expecting him any minute.

MAZIE. Yes, Ma'm. (*She goes out; and* MRS. CRAIG *stands thinking hard for a second. The screen door closes sharply, and she wheels round with a rapid movement, crossing above the center table towards the door.* CRAIG *enters, removing his hat.*)

MRS. CRAIG. Walter! Where have you been?

CRAIG. Out with Billy Birkmire. Why?

MRS. CRAIG (*indicating the outer door of the glass vestibule*). Shut that door. (*He turns and shuts it, and she moves along the foot of the stairway, glancing up and out through the portières.*)

CRAIG. (*coming into the room again*). What's the matter?

(MRS. CRAIG *turns and crosses back towards him.*)

MRS. CRAIG. My God, haven't you seen the evening paper about Fergus Passmore and his wife!

CRAIG. Yes, I've seen it.

MRS. CRAIG. Well, what about it, Walter?

CRAIG (*putting his hat down on the piano*). I don't know any more about it than you do, Harriet.

MRS. CRAIG. My God, isn't that a terrible thing! I've been nearly out of my mind for the last half-hour. I happened to see it in the paper there when I came downstairs, and I couldn't find you anywhere.

CRAIG. I went out with Birkmire.

MRS. CRAIG. Was that Birkmire that was here?

CRAIG. Yes, he wanted to see me about it.

MRS. CRAIG. I didn't even know whether you knew it or not; because you hadn't said anything about it when you came in this evening.

CRAIG. I didn't *know* it when I came in this evening.

MRS. CRAIG (*pointing at the paper on the table*). It's on the very front page of the paper there.

CRAIG. I didn't see the paper this evening till Birkmire showed it to me.

MRS. CRAIG. Well, why didn't you call me then, and not go rushing out of the house?

CRAIG. I didn't want to upset you.

MRS. CRAIG (*moving forward and across in front of the center table*). Well, I certainly couldn't have been any more upset than I have been. (*Turning to him.*) Mazie said there'd been a man here, and that you'd gone away with him in an automobile—so, of course, I didn't know what to think. I thought probably you'd been arrested or something.

(*He looks at her sharply.*)

CRAIG. What would I be arrested for?

MRS. CRAIG. Why, in connection with this thing, of course. (*Taking a step towards him.*) The Police are looking for you; you know that, don't you?

CRAIG. Who says the Police are looking for me?

MRS. CRAIG. Two of them have just left here, not five minutes ago.

CRAIG. Policemen?

MRS. CRAIG. They said they were from Police Headquarters; that's all I know.

CRAIG. And what are they looking for me for?

MRS. CRAIG. Well, now, why do you suppose they're looking for you, Walter?

CRAIG. I don't know.

MRS. CRAIG. Doesn't it say in the paper there that you were seen leaving Passmore's at twelve o'clock last night?

CRAIG. It doesn't say *I* was seen leaving there.

MRS. CRAIG. It says there was a man seen leaving there, and who else could it have been but you? You were out there, weren't you?

CRAIG. Yes.

MRS. CRAIG. Well, that's enough, isn't it? (*She turns away to her left, and crosses above the table towards the portières.*)

CRAIG. But *they* don't know that.

MRS. CRAIG. Oh, don't be absurd, Walter.

CRAIG. Who saw me?

MRS. CRAIG (*coming back towards him*). Somebody always sees in a case of this kind.

CRAIG. Who could it have been?

MRS. CRAIG. The butler saw you, didn't he?

CRAIG. What if he did?—he didn't know me from Adam. He says so there in the paper, doesn't he?

MRS. CRAIG. He could identify your picture, couldn't he?

CRAIG. Who's going to give him my picture?

MRS. CRAIG. Don't talk so loud. (*She steps back towards the portières, to assure herself that neither of the servants is listening.*)

CRAIG (*moving forward at the left of the center table*). Anyway, I don't believe he'd recognize my picture if he *did* see it; he only came into the library for a couple of minutes to serve some drinks, and went right out again. And he didn't get my name, because Fergus was sitting on the lawn when I got there and took me in himself. And the butler was in bed when I left there.

MRS. CRAIG (*coming forward at the right of the table*). Didn't any of the other servants see you?

CRAIG. Not that I know of.

MRS. CRAIG (*coming very close to him and lowering her voice*). Didn't you tell me that Billy Birkmire called you on the telephone out there last night?

CRAIG. Yes, I talked to him out there.

MRS. CRAIG. Well, didn't the butler get your name then?

CRAIG. No; Fergus answered the 'phone himself, on the extension in the library.

MRS. CRAIG. Well, those men have been here, anyway.

CRAIG. Well, what did they want?

MRS. CRAIG. Haven't I just told you what they wanted? They wanted to see *you.*

CRAIG. Did they say they knew it was I that was out there last night?

MRS. CRAIG. I don't remember *what* they said, exactly; I was too upset. But they wanted to know where you were, and, of course, I couldn't tell them; because you were here when I left the room, and then you suddenly disappeared. (*Turning away to the right.*) I was never placed in such a position in my life. I'm sure those men must have thought I was evading them. (*Turning back to him again.*) But *I* didn't know what to say to them—except that you'd probably taken a little walk around the neighborhood here; because I'd sent Mazie over to the garage to look for you as soon as I saw the paper, and she said both the cars were in there.

CRAIG. I went out in Birkmire's car.

MRS. CRAIG. Where did you go with him?

CRAIG. Over to Fergus' house.

MRS. CRAIG. And what in heaven's name did you do a thing like that for, Walter!

CRAIG. Why not?

MRS. CRAIG. Supposing you'd run into somebody out there?

CRAIG. And what if I did?

MRS. CRAIG. Do you want your name to be dragged into this thing?

CRAIG. My name 'll be dragged into it anyway, won't it?

MRS. CRAIG. Why will it?

CRAIG. You say those men have been here already.

MRS. CRAIG. And what if they have? That doesn't mean anything.

CRAIG. It means that they must have associated my name with it already, doesn't it?

MRS. CRAIG. No, it doesn't mean anything of the kind; they were simply looking for information.

CRAIG. But it was to me they *came* for that information.

MRS. CRAIG. Because you were a friend of Passmore's.

CRAIG. Exactly. And they'll very likely come back here again.

MRS. CRAIG. But you don't have to go out looking for them, do you?

CRAIG (*turning away and going up towards the door at the left*). You can't be playing any game in a thing like this, Harriet.

MRS. CRAIG (*following him up*). No, and you don't have to go rushing out to meet a lot of scandalous publicity, either. I should think your own common sense would show you what it would mean to have your name even mentioned in a thing of this kind. (*Turning away and down towards the center table.*) Why, it 'ud be in every newspaper in the country.

CRAIG (*coming forward at the right of the piano*). That wouldn't bother me in the least.

MRS. CRAIG (*aghast*). It wouldn't bother you!

CRAIG. Not the least bit—My conscience is clear.

MRS. CRAIG (*stepping to his side*). Oh, don't be so absurdly romantic, Walter!

CRAIG. It isn't a question of romanticism at all.

MRS. CRAIG. No, and it isn't a question of conscience, either. It's simply a matter of discretion. If you've had nothing to do with this thing, what's the use of becoming involved?

CRAIG. What do you mean, *if* I've had nothing to do with it?

MRS. CRAIG (*with sudden temper*). Oh, now don't start picking me up on every word! I've had cross-examination enough in the last fifteen minutes! (*She turns away to the left and crosses above the center table towards the portières.* CRAIG *takes a cigarette from a case and closes the case with a snap.* MRS. CRAIG *turns and sees that he is about to smoke.*) Now, don't smoke in this room, Walter. (*He throws the cigarette across the room to the fireplace.* MRS. CRAIG *looks at it in astonishment, and then at him.*) Well, that's a nice place to throw it, I must say. (*She goes down to the fireplace and picks it up.*)

CRAIG (*sitting in the chair at the right of the piano*). Oh, what does it matter!

MRS. CRAIG. Don't you want it?

CRAIG. What good is it, if I can't smoke it?

MRS. CRAIG (*crossing above the table towards the front door, holding the cigarette away from her, between her thumb and finger*). There are plenty of other places in the house to smoke, if you want to smoke.

CRAIG. I don't know where they are.

MRS. CRAIG (*going out the door*). You can smoke in your den, can't you?

CRAIG. If I shut the door. (*He sits thinking, deeply. The screen door slams, and* MRS. CRAIG *comes in again, looking keenly towards the portières.*) Did those men say when they'd be back here?

MRS. CRAIG. I don't remember whether they did or not;—I suppose they did. They said they'd get in touch with you if it was necessary. (*Coming forward to his side, and lowering her voice.*) But, if they *do* come back here, Walter, don't give them any more information than I did.

CRAIG. Well, I certainly won't deny that I was a friend of Fergus'.

MRS. CRAIG. You don't have to deny that you were a friend of his; but you certainly don't have to submit to a lot of cross-examination by detectives, either, simply because you happened to be a friend of his. (*She turns away and moves to the front of the center table.*) Let them go and cross-examine some of his other friends; you weren't the only friend he had.

CRAIG. Why did you submit to their cross-examination?

MRS. CRAIG (*turning to him*). Because I didn't know at the time to what extent they were justified in questioning me. I thought probably they had some information about your having been out at Passmore's last night. And I was at my wit's end, trying to keep from saying something that would imply an admission of it. I told them right away that I'd just gotten in from Albany, so I suppose they assumed that I didn't know where you'd been last night.

CRAIG. How long did they stay here?

MRS. CRAIG. About fifteen minutes, I imagine; but it seemed like a year.

CRAIG. What were they talking about all that time?

MRS. CRAIG. About you, and Fergus Passmore, and where you were, and when you'd be back, and all kinds of questions. (*She goes to the piano and picks up his hat, settling the piano scarf.*)

CRAIG. Did they say they'd been to any other of Fergus' friends?

MRS. CRAIG. I don't remember, they may have. They said something about him being very well known here socially, so they probably have. (CRAIG *thinks for a second, then rises abruptly and crosses below the center table and up to the telephone.*)

CRAIG. I think I'll call Birkmire up and see if they've been to see him.

MRS. CRAIG (*with a panicky movement towards him*). Now, wait a minute, Walter! (*She puts his hat on the table as she crosses above it.*) You're not going to do anything of the kind.

CRAIG. Why not?

MRS. CRAIG (*taking the telephone from him*). Now, go away from this 'phone. (*She draws him forward by the arm, away from the telephone.*) Let me tell you something.

CRAIG. What's the matter?

MRS. CRAIG. Don't you realize that that telephone is being watched—and that they are probably watching Birkmire's too?

CRAIG. Who is?

MRS. CRAIG. Why, the Police, of course. Haven't you any realization of your position in this affair?

CRAIG. I evidently haven't the same realization that you have.

MRS. CRAIG. Well, it's time you did have.

CRAIG. It is?

MRS. CRAIG. Yes, it is.

CRAIG. And what realization have you of my position?

MRS. CRAIG. Never mind what realization I have; that doesn't matter now. I simply know that the very first thing the Police do in a case of this kind is to watch the telephone calls to and from the house.

CRAIG. Not from this house.

MRS. CRAIG. I mean from Fergus' house.

CRAIG. I wasn't going to call Fergus' house.

MRS. CRAIG. You were going to call Billy Birkmire, weren't you?

CRAIG. At his own house, yes.

MRS. CRAIG. Well, what difference does it make, Walter. Do you think those detectives can't put two and two together? Birkmire called you last night at Passmore's, didn't he?

CRAIG. Yes.

MRS. CRAIG. And there's undoubtedly a record of the call.

CRAIG. That wouldn't involve my name, would it?

MRS. CRAIG. It would if the operator listened in.

CRAIG. And do you think she has nothing to do but listen in on calls?

MRS. CRAIG. She listened in on this one, didn't she?

CRAIG. On which one?

MRS. CRAIG. What? (*She steps back from him suddenly, and touches her hair, in an effort to appear casual.*) What did you say?

CRAIG. Which call do you say the operator listened in on?

MRS. CRAIG. I don't know which one she listened in on. But some one must have listened in on something or those men wouldn't have come here, would they?

CRAIG. Did they say the operator had reported on a call from here?

MRS. CRAIG. I don't remember what they said, distinctly. One of them kept rambling something about a telephone call, but I assumed it was the one that Birkmire made to you last night out at Fergus'.

CRAIG. Didn't they say when the call was made?

MRS. CRAIG. What does it matter when it was made, Walter?

CRAIG. It matters a lot.

MRS. CRAIG. The fact remains, doesn't it, that that telephone is undoubtedly being watched *now*.

CRAIG (*whirling round and picking up the telephone again*). Well, I want to know *why* it's being watched.

MRS. CRAIG (*springing to his side and seizing the telephone*). Now, listen to me, Walter Craig; you *must* not use that telephone. (*She looks him straight in the eyes, then moves back several steps and looks at him defiantly.*) I will not allow you to drag my name into a notorious scandal.

CRAIG (*whipping the receiver off and putting it to his ear*). I've got to find out where I'm at in this thing!

MRS. CRAIG (*raising her voice threateningly*). If you speak over that telephone I'll leave this house! (*He takes the receiver from his ear and looks at her steadily. There is a pause.*) And you know what construction 'ud be put upon that, under the circumstances.
(*He slowly hangs up and sets the telephone back onto the little table, holding her eyes steadily. Then he moves slowly towards her.*)

CRAIG. What do you mean, you'll leave this house?

MRS. CRAIG (*stonily*). I mean exactly what I said. Do you think I could stay in this neighborhood twenty-four hours after my name had been associated with a thing of this kind?

CRAIG. And haven't you any appreciation of the necessity of my knowing what's happening in this case?

MRS. CRAIG. I have no appreciation of any necessity except the necessity of keeping still.

CRAIG. But supposing something developed that would reveal absolutely the fact that I had been out there last night—

MRS. CRAIG. What *can* develop, if you keep still?

CRAIG. But, supposing something did? Wouldn't it be very much better for me to have been open and aboveboard from the beginning, instead of having played a waiting game, and probably create an attitude of suspicion where there are no grounds for any?

MRS. CRAIG. There *are* grounds for suspicion, Walter; don't evade the issue.

CRAIG. What are they?

MRS. CRAIG. The fact that you were out there last night.

CRAIG. That doesn't mean a thing.

MRS. CRAIG. Evidently not, to you.

CRAIG. Does it to you?

MRS. CRAIG. What does it matter what it means to me? It isn't for me to determine the degree of your guilt or innocence. I'm not interested.

CRAIG. You're not interested!

MRS. CRAIG. I'm interested only in the impression on the popular mind,—and the respect of the community we've got to live in.

CRAIG. You mean you'd rather know I was involved in this thing and *keep* the respect of the community, than know I was a victim of circumstances, and lose it?
(MRS. HAROLD *appears between the portières.* MRS. CRAIG *sees her over* CRAIG's *shoulder, and crosses quickly below him.*)

MRS. CRAIG. What is it, Mrs. Harold?

MRS. HAROLD. I'm sorry to bother you, Mrs. Craig, but I'm afraid the dinner'll be spoiled.

MRS. CRAIG (*going down to the mirror*). All right, Mrs. Harold, put it up; I'll be right out.
(CRAIG *moves forward to the upper right-hand corner of the center table.*)

MRS. HAROLD (*withdrawing*). All right.

CRAIG. Mrs. Harold.

MRS. HAROLD (*stopping*). Yes, sir? (*She comes back a few steps towards him.*)

CRAIG. Mrs. Harold, do you know if anybody has called that number that I gave you last night here, to-day, on this telephone?

MRS. HAROLD. You mean the number you gave me to have Mr. Birkmire call you at?

CRAIG. Yes, Levering three one hundred.

MRS. HAROLD. No, sir, I don't know that anybody has. I only gave it to Mr. Birkmire over the telephone last night when he called.

CRAIG. *You* haven't had occasion to call that number to-day on this telephone, have you, Mrs. Harold?

MRS. HAROLD. No, sir, I haven't, Mr. Craig.

CRAIG. All right, Mrs. Harold, thanks very much.
(*She starts to go, then stops and turns again.*)

MRS. HAROLD. I never even thought about it to-day until Mrs. Craig asked me for it when she came in this evening.
(*There is a pause.* CRAIG *shifts his eyes to his wife, who raises her arm slowly and touches her hair before the mirror.*)

CRAIG. All right, Mrs. Harold, thank you very much. (MRS. HAROLD *withdraws, and Craig moves up slowly towards the portières and watches her out of hearing distance. Then he turns and looks at his wife. She stands very still. He moves a step or two slowly towards her.*) It was you that made that call. (*She turns and looks at him, with a touch of defiance.*) What were you doing, checking up on me?

MRS. CRAIG (*starting up towards the portières*). Don't flatter yourself, Walter.

CRAIG. That's what you were doing, wasn't it?

MRS. CRAIG. Don't flatter yourself. The man hasn't been born yet that I'd bother checking up on.

CRAIG. Why didn't you tell the truth?

MRS. CRAIG (*whirling upon him*). Because I anticipated an attack of your romantic conscience.

CRAIG. You were playing safe; that was it, wasn't it?

MRS. CRAIG. Exactly!

CRAIG. And at my expense!

MRS. CRAIG. I knew the necessity of it with you!

CRAIG (*turning away to the left, crossing in front of the center table*). God!

MRS. CRAIG (*following him up*). I knew if I told you I made that call, you'd be on the telephone in five minutes telling the Police.

CRAIG (*turning sharply*). I intended doing that anyway.

MRS. CRAIG. You silly fool!

CRAIG. That's where I went this evening, with Birkmire, when I left here—to Police Headquarters.

MRS. CRAIG (*aghast*). Oh!

CRAIG. And the only reason I didn't tell them then was that the man in charge of the case had gone to his dinner and wouldn't be back till eight o'clock. But he'll be told *then!* (*He swings up to the front door.*)

MRS. CRAIG (*leaning across the center table, and speaking threateningly*). Well, if you do, you'll explain my leaving you, too.

CRAIG. That wouldn't worry me in the least, Harriet.

MRS. CRAIG. Well, it might worry *them.* (*He turns sharply and looks at her dismayed*).

CRAIG (*coming back to the table*). Listen to me, Harriet. Why weren't you at least *honest* with me in this thing, and not try to make it appear that *I* was responsible for the visit of those detectives?

MRS. CRAIG. Because I knew exactly what you'd do if I told you. And that would mean an explanation of why I had called up; and the next thing would be an admission of the fact that you are the man the Police are looking for.

CRAIG. But it's *you* those detectives are looking for.

MRS. CRAIG. Oh, you needn't try to turn it on to me! They wouldn't be looking for either of us if you'd stayed at home last night, instead of being out card-playing with a lot of irregular people. (*She turns down to the mirror.*)

CRAIG. What was there irregular about Fergus Passmore?

MRS. CRAIG (*turning to him, in a wrath*). There must have been some irregularity, or this thing wouldn't have happened. Everybody that knew Fergus Passmore knew that he was insanely jealous of his wife; and then *you* have to go out visiting them. (*She crosses below the table to the piano.*) I felt in my bones up there in Albany that something 'ud happen while I was away; that was the reason I didn't stay up there any longer than I absolutely had to. I knew as soon as ever my back was turned you'd be out with your friends again.
(*He looks at her, under his brows; and there is a pause.*)

CRAIG. And what has your back being turned got to do with my visiting my friends?

MRS. CRAIG. Never mind what it has to do with it; only you wouldn't have *been* visiting them if I'd been here.

CRAIG. How would you have stopped me?

MRS. CRAIG. I'd have stopped you all right, one way or another.

CRAIG. What would you have done—locked the door on me?

MRS. CRAIG. It wouldn't have been necessary to lock the door on you. (*Turning and looking at him directly.*) You haven't *been* visiting them in the last eighteen months, have you?

CRAIG. No, I haven't.

MRS. CRAIG. And they haven't been visiting you, either?

CRAIG. No, they haven't.

MRS. CRAIG (*turning away*). Well—

CRAIG (*after a slight pause*). You mean you've kept them out of here?

MRS. CRAIG (*turning to him again and looking him straight in the eyes*). Well, if I did the end justified the means; you at least haven't been in the shadow of the law in the last eighteen months.
(*He holds her eye for a second, then moves forward to the front of the table.*)

CRAIG. You're certainly running true to form, Harriet.

MRS. CRAIG. Well, I'm glad of it if I am.

CRAIG. My aunt said here a while ago that you'd driven all my friends away from this house.

MRS. CRAIG (*with level significance*). There are ways of getting rid of people without driving them away from the house.
(CRAIG *makes a little sound of bitter amusement.*)

CRAIG. And I thought she was imagining things at your expense.

MRS. CRAIG. Well, you see she probably had better perception than you'd given her credit for.
(*He turns and looks at her darkly.*)

CRAIG. Probably she had; for she perceived something else, Harriet, that may be equally true.

MRS. CRAIG. Is that so?

CRAIG. She said you were trying to get rid of me too—(*She darts a look at him*) without actually driving me away from the house. (*She laughs derisively, and moves across towards the portières. He follows her up, raising his voice.*) And I believe that's true, too.

MRS. CRAIG. Keep your voice down! Do you want everybody in the house to hear you?

CRAIG. You've admitted it, by your attitude in this affair this evening.

MRS. CRAIG (*looking at him, and moving forward to the mantelpiece*). I don't know what you're talking about.

CRAIG (*coming forward and leaning on the table*). Very well, you know what I'm talking about. And you knew what my aunt was going to talk about too, here a while ago; that's the reason you left the room before she started.

MRS. CRAIG. I'm sorry I didn't stay here now.

CRAIG. No danger of your staying here, Harriet; you couldn't bear it. (*She laughs, and he moves forward to the left.*) My God, how perfectly she knows you, Harriet! She couldn't have read you any better if you'd written it out for her. And I felt rather sorry listening to her, thinking she was probably getting a little old and suspicious; particularly when she said you had excluded my friends.

MRS. CRAIG. Do you think I wanted my house turned into a tavern?

CRAIG. My friends never turned my mother's house into a tavern.

MRS. CRAIG. They didn't play poker at your mother's house till all hours of the morning.

CRAIG. Every Thursday night for ten years; till two o'clock, if they felt like it.

MRS. CRAIG. Well, evidently, your mother and I had very different ideas of a house.

CRAIG. Very different indeed, Harriet; there was more actual home in one room of my mother's house than there'd be in all of this if we lived in it a thousand years.

MRS. CRAIG. Why didn't you stay in it, then, if you found it so attractive?

CRAIG. Now you're talking, Harriet; why didn't I do *just that*. (*He turns away to the left, then turns suddenly back.*) But, don't make any mistake that I think you didn't want my friends here simply because they played cards; you wouldn't have wanted them if they'd come here to hold prayer meetings. You didn't want them because, as my aunt says, their visits implied an importance to *me* that was at variance with your little campaign—the campaign that was to reduce me to one of those wife-ridden sheep that's afraid to buy a necktie for fear his wife might not approve of it. (*He goes up towards the front door.*)

MRS. CRAIG. Oh, don't try to make yourself out a martyr; you've had your share of this bargain.

(*He turns suddenly and looks at her, then comes forward again to the front of the table.*)

CRAIG. I never regarded this thing as a bargain.

MRS. CRAIG. Did you expect me to go into a thing as important as marriage with my eyes shut?

CRAIG. I wanted you to go into it honestly, as I went into it—fifty-fifty—And you've been playing safe right from the start. (*He turns away towards the piano.*)

MRS. CRAIG. I've been doing nothing of the kind.

CRAIG. Don't tell me what you've been doing; I see your game as clearly as my aunt sees it. (*He turns and comes back towards her.*) You've been *exploiting* me, consistently, in your shifty little business of personal safety. And you'd throw me right now to the suspicion of implication in this double murder—to preserve that safety. (*He goes back towards the piano again.*)

MRS. CRAIG (*almost crying*). I've been trying to preserve my home.

CRAIG. That's all I've heard from you since the day I married you.

MRS. CRAIG. Well, what else has a woman like me *but* her home?

CRAIG (*turning to her*). Hasn't she her husband?

MRS. CRAIG. She could lose her husband, couldn't she?—As many another woman has.

CRAIG. Couldn't she lose her home too?

MRS. CRAIG. She couldn't if she knew how to secure it.

CRAIG (*raising his finger solemnly*). That's the point in a nutshell, Harriet; if she knew how to *fix* it for herself. (*He turns away and rests his hands on the piano.*)

MRS. CRAIG. Well, what if I have fixed things for myself? You haven't lost anything by it, have you? If I've fixed them for myself I've fixed them for you too. Your home is here. And maybe if I hadn't played the game so consistently it wouldn't *be* here. And I wouldn't be the first woman that's lost her home, and her husband too, through letting the control of them get out of her hands. (*She moves up towards the back of the room, in a crying temper.*) I saw what happened to my own mother, and I made up my mind it 'ud never happen to me. (*She turns and comes forward again.*) She was one of those "I will follow thee, my husband" women— that believed everything my father told her; and all the time he was mortgaging her home over her head for another woman. And when she found it out, she did the only thing that women like her *can* do, and that was to die of a broken heart— within six months; and leave the door open for the other woman to come in as stepmother over Estelle and me. (*She turns to the mantelpiece.*) And then get rid of us both as soon as Estelle was marriageable. (*Turning to him suddenly.*) But the house was never mortgaged over *her* head, I'll promise you that; for she saw to it that it was put in her name before ever she took him; and she kept it there, too, right to the finish. (*She sweeps up towards the back of the room again.*)

CRAIG. Why didn't you ask me to put this house in *your* name?

MRS. CRAIG (*whirling upon him*). Because I didn't *want* it in my name!

CRAIG. It would have been more honest.

MRS. CRAIG (*coming forward to the right end of the table*). I haven't done anything that wasn't honest!

CRAIG. How would you know, Harriet?

MRS. CRAIG. I've simply tried to be practical; but, with your usual romanticism, you want to make me appear like a criminal for it.

CRAIG. I'm not reproaching you at all.

MRS. CRAIG. Well, you shouldn't reproach me; for there's nothing to reproach me about.

CRAIG. You simply married the wrong man, Harriet.

MRS. CRAIG (*witheringly*). I married a romantic fool! (*He looks at her narrowly, and she holds his eye.*) *That's* what I married; (*she turns away and goes up to the portières to look out*) and I'm seeing it more every day I live.
(*There is a pause. Then* CRAIG *breaks into a hard little laugh.*)

CRAIG. How well we understand each other now, Harriet.

MRS. CRAIG (*coming forward to the mantelpiece again*). Well, I understand you, anyway, whether you understand me or not. (*Speaking directly to him.*) And you ought to thank your God that I do, for I don't know what 'ud become of you if I didn't. (*She turns to the mantelpiece, and suddenly sees the card that* MAZIE *left back of the center ornament. She picks up the little envelope deftly, takes the card out and reads it.* CRAIG *regards her icily; and after a pause, he speaks—in a level, rather dangerous tone.*)

CRAIG. The brass of you—and the presumption.
(*She looks at him.*)

MRS. CRAIG. What?

CRAIG. I'm just wondering how you *get* that way.

MRS. CRAIG. How I get what way?

CRAIG. So brazenly presumptuous, as to say such a thing to me.

MRS. CRAIG. What have I said? I don't know what you're talking about.

CRAIG (*moving slowly away a step or two from the piano*). What have you ever done, or a million others like you, that would warrant the assumption of such superiority over the men you're married to?

MRS. CRAIG. Nobody's assuming any superiority.

CRAIG. Doesn't your remark admit it?

MRS. CRAIG (*turning and moving up to the portières*). Don't get yourself into a temper.

CRAIG. That you don't know what 'ud become of me only that *you* understand me.

MRS. CRAIG (*glancing through the portières*). Neither I do.

CRAIG. The presumption of you.

MRS. CRAIG. What are you standing there for, Mazie?

MAZIE AND CRAIG (*speaking together*).
MAZIE: Why, Mrs. Harold sent me in to see if you were coming in to dinner. CRAIG: That you should set yourself about to control the very destiny of a man,—

MRS. CRAIG. Yes, I'm coming right away.

MRS. CRAIG AND CRAIG (*speaking together*).
MRS. CRAIG: But I want to see you for a minute first, Mazie. CRAIG: As though I were some mental incompetent.

MAZIE. Yes, Ma'm.

MRS. CRAIG (*turning and going towards* CRAIG, *lowering her voice, and trying to silence him with a gesture*). Don't make a show of yourself in front of Mazie. (MAZIE *comes through the portières, and* MRS. CRAIG *turns to her.*) Mazie, what is this card here?

MAZIE. Why, it's the Society card, Mrs. Craig, of the Mutual Benevolent.

MRS. CRAIG. And what is it doing here?

MAZIE. Why, Christine sent it down about an hour ago, with the tailor's little boy, to know if I'd pay her dues for her.

MRS. CRAIG. And couldn't you find any place for it but back of that ornament?

MAZIE. Why, I was—

MRS. CRAIG. After all the times I've told you never to put anything on that mantelpiece.

MAZIE. Yes, you *have* told me, Mrs. Craig, but when I came in—

MRS. CRAIG. Then, why do you do it? Must I keep telling you the same thing indefinitely? You know perfectly well I never allow anybody even to *dust* that mantelpiece but myself. I even bought a special little brush for those ornaments, because I wouldn't trust them to anybody else. And yet the minute you get my back turned you must use them as a catchall for everything in the house.

MAZIE. Mrs. Harold asked me something when I came in, and—

MRS. CRAIG. I am not interested in what anybody asked you; that does not excuse you. (MAZIE *takes a handkerchief from the pocket of her apron and touches it to her eyes.*) I have told you over and over again *never* to put anything back of those ornaments; and you deliberately disobey me. You simply will *not* do as you are told. And when a girl will not do as she is told, the best thing for her to do is to go some place where she will be *made* to do it. So I want you to get your things together to-night and leave this house to-morrow morning. (MAZIE *looks at her, then turns away to leave the room.*) Here's the card. And find some place for it besides back of an ornament. (MAZIE *takes the card and withdraws.*) And tell Mrs. Harold to put up the dinner, I'll be down in two minutes; (*she starts for the stairs*) I'm going up to see what my niece wants for *her* dinner. (*She goes up the stairs haughtily. Halfway up she turns, but without stopping, and addresses* CRAIG *coldly.*) You'd better go out there and get your dinner, before it's cold. (*She disappears at the head of the stairs, and* CRAIG *stands looking at the floor. His eyes wander up the stairs after her, and then down the right side of the room. They settle upon the ornament on the mantelpiece, and he looks at it hard; then crosses slowly and picks it up. He holds it in his hand, looking at it curiously: then suddenly lifts it in the air and smashes it on the bricks in front of the mantelpiece. He stands looking at the shattered pieces for a moment; then takes a cigarette from his case and strolls back across the room towards the piano. He taps the cigarette on the case, then takes out a match and lights it, tossing the burned match on to the floor. Then he leans against the piano and smokes, thoughtfully.* MRS HAROLD *hurries in through the portières.*)

MRS. HAROLD. Did something get broke in here, Mr. Craig? (*He indicates the shattered ornament with a nod, and* MRS. HAROLD *looks towards the mantelpiece. She sees the pieces of the shattered ornament, and raising her hands and eyes to Heaven, takes a step or two towards them.*) Glory be to God this day and this night, how did that happen, Mr. Craig! Did it fall off the mantelpiece?

CRAIG (*without moving*). No, I smashed it, Mrs. Harold.

MRS. HAROLD (*puzzled*). On purpose, do you mean, Mr. Craig?

CRAIG. Yes.—I didn't like it.

MRS. CRAIG. I wish you'd tell Mrs. Craig it was you that done it, Mr. Craig; if she sees it she might think it was one of us that broke it.

CRAIG. I'll tell her all about it, Mrs. Harold; don't you worry about that. (*He straightens up and starts across slowly towards the big chair in front of the mantelpiece, and* MRS. HAROLD *moves a step or two towards the portières.*)

MRS. HAROLD (*turning to him*). Will I get the dustpan and sweep that up, Mr. Craig?

CRAIG. No, don't bother about it now, Mrs. Harold; go out and get your dinner. (*She moves towards the portières, then stops again.*)

MRS. HAROLD. Ain't you comin' to your dinner, Mr. Craig?

CRAIG (*sitting down*). No, I don't want any dinner to-night, Mrs. Harold.

MRS. HAROLD. Don't you want nothing at at all?

CRAIG. Not a thing. (*She withdraws; and he sits smoking and thinking.*)

MRS. CRAIG (*from the head of the stairs*). Are you down there, Walter?

CRAIG. Yes.

MRS. CRAIG. Listen—did something *fall* down there a minute ago?

CRAIG. No.

MRS. CRAIG. Are you sure?

CRAIG. Yes, I'm sure.

MRS. CRAIG. Well, it sounded up here as though the house fell down.

CRAIG (*after a slight pause*). Maybe it did, Harriet—I'm just sitting here wondering. (*He sits smoking. His gaze wanders up, and out, and away off.*)

The Curtain Descends Slowly.

ACT THREE

SCENE: *Same as preceding act—the following morning, about eight-thirty.* CRAIG *is still sitting in the big chair before the fireplace, asleep. After a pause,* MRS. HAROLD *enters through the portières, carrying a dustpan and hand brush. She sees* CRAIG, *looks at him curiously, and also observes the pieces of the shattered ornament and the cigarette butts at his feet. She turns and puts the dustpan and brush down on the seat at the right of the stairway, and, with a glance up the stairs, crosses and unlocks the front door and goes out. The screen door slams after her and* CRAIG *wakes. He looks around, glances at his watch, gets up and settles himself before the mirror.* MRS. HAROLD *tiptoes in, bringing the morning paper.*

CRAIG. Good morning, Mrs. Harold.

MRS. HAROLD (*stopping above the center table*). Good morning, Mr. Craig.

CRAIG. I must have made a night of it sitting here.

MRS. HAROLD. Yes, I was wondering if you'd been there all night.

CRAIG. I must have fallen asleep.

MRS. HAROLD. You must feel pretty tired, don't you?

CRAIG (*turning to her*). No, I'm all right. Is that the morning paper you have there, Mrs. Harold?

MRS. HAROLD. Yes, sir, I was just bringing it in.

CRAIG. Let me see it, will you?

MRS. HAROLD. Yes, sir. (*He takes the paper; and, stepping to the window, forward, reads it eagerly.*) Would you like a cup of coffee, Mr. Craig?

CRAIG. Yes, I'll take a little coffee if you have it.

MRS. HAROLD (*starting for the portières*). It's all made;—I'll just turn on the percolator for a minute. (*She goes out; and he stands reading. There is the sound of a door opening somewhere upstairs. He glances towards the head of the stairs, then crosses quickly up to the front door and out on to the porch.* MRS. HAROLD *comes in again; and, picking up the dustpan and brush, comes forward to the mantelpiece and starts to sweep up the ornament and cigarette butts.* MRS. CRAIG *appears on the stairway.*)

MRS. CRAIG. Mrs. Harold.

MRS. HAROLD (*straightening up*). Yes, Ma'm?

MRS. CRAIG. Has the morning paper come yet?

MRS. HAROLD. Yes, Ma'm, I just gave it to Mr. Craig; he's reading it there on the front porch.

MRS. CRAIG (*puzzled, and coming down the stairs*). What is *he* doing up so early?

MRS. HAROLD. I don't think he's been in bed at all, Mrs. Craig; he was sitting in this

big chair here when I came in this morning, and he was sitting here last night when I locked up.
(MRS. CRAIG *crosses to the bay window at the left and looks out on to the porch; and* MRS. HAROLD *resumes her sweeping.* MRS. CRAIG *becomes aware of what* MRS. HAROLD *is doing, and turns to her.*)

MRS. CRAIG. What is that you're sweeping up there, Mrs. Harold?

MRS. HAROLD (*straightening up*). Why, it's that center ornament that was here, Mrs. Craig.
(MRS. CRAIG *crosses down in front of the center table, looking wide-eyed at the vacant place on the mantelpiece.*)

MRS. CRAIG. What!

MRS. HAROLD. It got broke last night.

MRS. CRAIG. Oh, my God, Mrs. Harold, don't tell me that that's that beautiful statuette!

MRS. HAROLD. Mr. Craig said that he broke it.

MRS. CRAIG (*looking at the shattered pieces in the dustpan, which* MRS. HAROLD *is holding*). Oh, my God, look at the way it's broken!—It's smashed into a thousand pieces.

MRS. HAROLD. It must have fallen on the bricks here.

MRS. CRAIG. Oh, that never simply fell, Mrs. Harold; it's absolutely shattered—look at the size of the pieces. It's out of the question even to think of having it mended.

MRS. HAROLD. No, I don't think it could ever be mended now.

MRS. CRAIG (*almost crying*). That beautiful thing—that I wouldn't even allow anybody to go near; and look at it now.

MRS. HAROLD. It certainly is too bad.

MRS. CRAIG. And, of course, I might just as well throw those others away now, for they're absolutely meaningless without this one. (*She turns away, in a pang of grief, and moves a few steps towards the left, then suddenly turns again to* MRS. HAR-

OLD.) How on earth did it ever happen, Mrs. Harold?

MRS. HAROLD. I don't know, I'm sure, Mrs. Craig.

MRS. CRAIG. I suppose Mazie broke it for spite, didn't she?—Because I reprimanded her last night for putting things back of it.

MRS. HAROLD. No, she didn't break it, Mrs. Craig, for she was out there in the kitchen with me when we heard it fall.

MRS. CRAIG (*turning away and crossing below the center table*). Well, send her in here to me now, I want to speak to her.

MRS. HAROLD. Mr. Craig said that *he* broke it; (MRS. CRAIG *turns and looks at her*) he said he didn't like that ornament.

MRS. CRAIG. Tell Mazie I want to see her.

MRS. HAROLD. She isn't here, Mrs. Craig; she's gone.

MRS. CRAIG. You mean she's left already?

MRS. HAROLD. Yes, Ma'm, she left right after she had her breakfast.

MRS. CRAIG. Of course she did, the contemptible little devil.

MRS. HAROLD. Mr. Craig said that he'd tell you all about it.

MRS. CRAIG. Where did Mazie go?

MRS. HAROLD. She said she was goin' to her married sister's for a while.

MRS. CRAIG. Did you pay her her wages?

MRS. HAROLD. Yes, Ma'm, I paid her last night.

MRS. CRAIG (*turning away towards the front door*). All right, Mrs. Harold. (MRS. HAROLD *goes out through the portières, taking the dustpan and brush with her.*) Walter, come in here for a minute, will you? (*She glances over her shoulder, to see that* MRS. HAROLD *is out of earshot, then turns and waits till* CRAIG *comes in. He enters, carrying the newspaper.*) What does the paper say this morning about the Passmore thing?

CRAIG (*handing her the newspaper*). You're quite safe. (*He comes forward and across in front of the center table to the mirror, and straightens his tie.*)

MRS. CRAIG (*stepping forward to the piano and spreading the paper out eagerly*). What does it say?

CRAIG. His brother got in last night from Pittsburgh, with a letter that Fergus had written him, intimating his intentions.

MRS. CRAIG. Then Fergus did it himself?

CRAIG. So it appears.

MRS. CRAIG. I always told you he was jealous of his wife.
(CRAIG *turns and looks at her.*)

CRAIG. He did it because she was dishonest.

MRS. CRAIG (*reading*). I suppose this telegram here from his brother about Fergus' letter was the additional information that that detective spoke about here last night. (*She straightens up and speaks directly to* CRAIG.) He called Police Headquarters from here about seven o'clock, and then he said it wouldn't be necessary to bother us any more for a while,—that there'd been some additional information come in on the case: so I suppose that's what it was; for it says here the telegram was received at Police Headquarters at six forty-five.

CRAIG (*moving with a wearied air towards the portières*). What does it matter now, Harriet?

MRS. CRAIG. It doesn't matter *now*, but it would have mattered—only that I kept my head last night, and didn't allow you to telephone, and make a show of us all. (*He laughs bitterly.*) You can laugh, as much as you like; but you can thank me that your name isn't in every paper in the city this morning. (*She resumes her reading.*)

CRAIG. Oh, I can thank you for more than that, Harriet.

MRS. CRAIG. Well, you can thank me for that, anyway.

CRAIG. I can thank you for having given me a new name last night—that fits me so perfectly that I've decided to continue its use. You called me a romantic fool.

MRS. CRAIG. Fergus must have known about this man that Adelaide's been going around with; for it says here he'd mentioned him once before in a letter to his brother.
(MRS. HAROLD *appears between the portières.*)

MRS. HAROLD. The coffee's ready, Mr. Craig.

CRAIG (*turning quietly towards the portières*). All right, Mrs. Harold.
(*She withdraws, and he follows her.* MRS. CRAIG *looks up suddenly and crosses towards him.*)

MRS. CRAIG. Listen, Walter, come here for a minute.
(*He turns.*)

CRAIG. What?

MRS. CRAIG. Listen. (*She glances over his shoulder after* MRS. HAROLD, *then lowers her voice.*) Billy Birkmire 'ull very likely want you to go out there with him to Fergus' funeral; but don't you do it. And you'd better tell him not to go around there either; for one of you is apt to say something. And if that butler out there sees *you*, he might recognize you. And there's no use starting anything now, when the thing's all over.
(*He looks at her steadily.*)

CRAIG. Is that all you wanted to tell me?

MRS. CRAIG. Well, it's the thing to do, isn't it? It certainly wouldn't help matters *now* to say anything, would it? What are you smiling at?

CRAIG. At your wanting to help matters.

MRS. CRAIG. So I *have* wanted to help them.

CRAIG. Since when?

MRS. CRAIG (*turning away to the center table*). Well, don't let's go into all that again. I've been wanting to help *you* principally, but you don't seem to have sense enough to appreciate it.

CRAIG. Is that all you want me for?

MRS. CRAIG (*turning to him again*). No, it isn't all I want you for. I want to know about that ornament there that was broken here last night.

CRAIG. What about it?

MRS. CRAIG. I don't know *what* about it; that's the reason I'm asking you. Mrs. Harold tells me here this morning that you told her last night that you'd broken it.

CRAIG. So I did.

MRS. CRAIG. Well, you ought to be proud of yourself.

CRAIG. I was for a moment.

MRS. CRAIG. What were you doing—leaning against the mantelpiece again as usual?

CRAIG. No, it wasn't an accident; I did it deliberately.

MRS. CRAIG. What do you mean, you did it deliberately?

CRAIG. I mean that I smashed it purposely.

MRS. CRAIG. What for?

CRAIG. I became suddenly heroic.

MRS. CRAIG. I don't believe you.

CRAIG (*turning away*). Very well, that's that.

MRS. CRAIG. Why would you deliberately break a beautiful, expensive ornament like that?

CRAIG (*turning back*). I didn't break it.

MRS. CRAIG. Well, you said you did.

CRAIG (*bitterly*). I said I smashed it—into a thousand little pieces, right here on these bricks here. And then I smoked one cigarette after another, till I had your sanctum sanctorum here absolutely littered with ashes and cigarette butts. I was positively a hell of a fellow around here for about an hour last night; you should have seen me.

MRS. CRAIG. What did you do, go out of your mind or something?

CRAIG. No, I was particularly clear in my mind, strange to say. You made a remark here last night, Harriet, that completely illuminated me; and illuminated you. And suddenly I saw—for the first time—everything—just as one sees an entire landscape at midnight in a flash of lightning.

But, unfortunately, the lightning struck my house—and knocked it down; and I sat here all night wondering how I might build it up again.

MRS. CRAIG. What remark are you talking about?

CRAIG. You said that a woman might lose her husband but not her home, if she knew how to secure it.

MRS. CRAIG. Well, hasn't many a woman lost her husband?

CRAIG. And many a man has lost his life too, Harriet, because his wife has never made a sufficiently illuminating remark. But you did make it. And that other remark—when you said there were ways of getting rid of people without driving them away from the house. (*He smiles bitterly.*) I saw your entire plan of life, Harriet, and its relationship to me. And my instinct of self-preservation suggested the need of immediate action—the inauguration of a new régime here: so I smashed the little ornament there—as a kind of opening gun. And I was going to smash all the other little ornaments—and gods you had set up in the temple here, and been worshipping before me. I was going to put my house in order, including my wife; and rule it with a rod of iron. (MRS. CRAIG *turns away, faintly amused.*) I don't wonder that amuses you; it amused me; particularly when I suddenly remembered the truth of what you called me last night; and in view of that, the absurdity of my trying to sustain such a rôle indefinitely. It made me laugh—But I'm rather sorry you couldn't have seen me, anyway; I think you would at least have appreciated the sincerity of my *attempt* to continue here as your husband. (*He turns slowly and moves towards the portières.*)

MRS. CRAIG. What do you mean, your attempt to continue here as my husband?

CRAIG. The rôle is not *for* me, Harriet; I can only play a romantic part.
(*She turns her head quietly and looks at him; and he holds her eye for a second, then goes out through the portières; and she stands looking after him. Then she moves slowly to the portières and stands,*)

thinking. The doorbell rings, but evidently she doesn't hear it. She moves forward slowly, still thinking narrowly. MRS. HAROLD *comes through the portières hurriedly.*)

MRS. CRAIG. There's some one at the door, Mrs. Harold.
(*The doorbell rings again.*)

MRS. HAROLD (*hurrying across to answer the door*). I guess maybe it's the man for Miss Austen's things.

MRS. CRAIG. Is Miss Austen leaving already?

MRS. HAROLD (*stopping near the door*). I think so; she said last night she was going first thing in the morning.

MRS. CRAIG. Is she up?

MRS. HAROLD. Yes, Ma'm, she asked me to call her at seven. (*She goes out, and* MRS. CRAIG *crosses after her.*)

MRS. CRAIG. Well, if that's the man for her things, Mrs. Harold, have him go round to the side door and bring her things down the back stairway; I don't want him dragging trunks down these front stairs. (*She steps to the bay window at the left and looks out at the expressman.*)

EXPRESSMAN (*at the front door*). Trunks ready?

MRS. HAROLD. Yes, they're ready. Would you mind going around to the side door; you can bring them down the back way.

EXPRESSMAN. Around this way?

MRS. HAROLD. Yes, up the steps; I'll open it for you. (*The screen door slams, and she hurries in again, crossing towards the portières.*)

MRS. CRAIG. Are Miss Austen's things ready, Mrs. Harold?

MRS. HAROLD. Yes, Ma'm, I helped her pack last night.

MRS. CRAIG. Did she say where she was going?

MRS. HAROLD (*stopping*). Yes, Ma'm; she sez she's going to the Ritz-Carlton Hotel

now, but after that she sez she's going to travel. (*Continuing to the portières.*) I must open the door for that man. (*She goes out, and* MRS. CRAIG *stands looking after her, thinking. She moves across towards the portières and stops again, looking out through the portières.* ETHEL *hurries down the stairs, with her hat and coat on.*)

MRS. CRAIG. Ethel, dear child, what are you doing up so early?

ETHEL. I haven't been asleep all night. I've been waiting to hear some one else up.

MRS. CRAIG. You're not ill, are you, dear?

ETHEL. No, but I must go home immediately, Aunt Harriet; I'm too troubled in my mind to stay here any longer.

MRS. CRAIG. But you can't go immediately, dear.

ETHEL. I must go, Aunt Harriet.

MRS. CRAIG. But there's no train, dear, until the nine-seventeen.

ETHEL. Well, it's nearly that now, isn't it? (MRS. CRAIG *looks at her watch.*)

MRS. CRAIG. It isn't a quarter of nine yet.

ETHEL. Well, it'll take that time to get to the station, won't it?

MRS. CRAIG. It doesn't take ten minutes, dear, in a taxicab; and I can have one here in five minutes.

ETHEL (*putting her bag on the table and crossing down to the mirror*). Well, will you call one, please?

MRS. CRAIG (*moving after her*). Certainly, dear; but there's no use calling it already, you'd only have to wait around the station there.

ETHEL. I'm so worried, Aunt Harriet.

MRS. CRAIG. I know, dear child; but I'm sure you're upsetting yourself unnecessarily; we certainly would have heard something if anything had happened.

ETHEL (*turning to* MRS. CRAIG). I really should call Mr. Fredericks on the long distance, Aunt Harriet; he'll be wondering what on earth is the matter. Because I rushed away as soon as ever I got Dr. Wood's wire, and simply left a note that Mother was very ill. And he's probably called me up at home by this time and found that I'm down here; and he won't know what to think of it.

MRS. CRAIG. Well, I wouldn't worry myself too much about what he'll think, dear.

ETHEL. But he'll think it's funny that I should be down here if Mother's so ill. (*There is a sound upstairs of a trunk being moved.*)

MRS. CRAIG (*dashing towards the stairs and up on to the landing*). He probably hasn't given it a thought.

ETHEL (*moving across above the table and looking out the bay window*). Oh, don't say that, Aunt Harriet, I know he has. (MRS. CRAIG *claps her hands briskly, to attract the expressman's attention.*)

MRS. CRAIG. Please be careful of that floor there, Mr. Expressman, will you?

EXPRESSMAN. This baby got away from me. I thought it was lighter than it is.

MRS. CRAIG. Well, please try to keep it away from that wall there; I don't want that wall all scratched up; I only had it painted in April. (*There is a sound of the trunk being dragged along the hallway to the back stairs, and then a heavy thud.* MRS. CRAIG *closes her eyes in an agony of suffering and leans heavily upon the banister to keep from fainting. Then she turns and comes down into the room again.*) Mr. Craig's aunt is sending some luggage away to be mended; and those expressmen are so careless they don't care if they tear down the house.

ETHEL. I haven't had a chance to speak to Miss Austen yet.

MRS. CRAIG. I suppose she's getting dressed.

ETHEL. I haven't seen Uncle Walter yet, either.

MRS. CRAIG. He's out there having some coffee, I believe. Don't you want to come out and have some too, dear?

ETHEL. I don't think I could touch a thing, Aunt Harriet.

MRS. CRAIG. You could take a sip of coffee.

ETHEL. I don't want Uncle Walter to see me looking so terrible.

MRS. CRAIG. What does it matter, darling; he understands the circumstances. And you really shouldn't start on that trip back home without something. And when you do go back, Ethel, I want you to consider seriously what I've been saying to you about Mr. Fredericks. You're not married to him yet; and if there's anything to be done, it's now that it must be done. You can't come back and undo a thing like marriage.

ETHEL. Oh, I don't know what to do, Aunt Harriet.

MRS. CRAIG. Well, there's no hurry about doing anything just now. And don't let him hurry you. Just think it over—for his sake as well as for your own. You don't want to be a burden to him, do you?

ETHEL. Certainly not.

MRS. CRAIG. Well, what else would you be to him, dear—unless you used your own money? And that isn't conducive to respect for a man. And, in any case, you'd find in time that he'd come to resent your independence of him.

MISS AUSTEN (*at the head of the stairs*). Yes, I have it here in my bag, Mrs. Harold.

MRS. CRAIG (*drawing* ETHEL *towards the portières*). So just think it over. And come on out to the breakfast room and let me get you something. (*They go out through the portières.* MISS AUSTEN *comes down the stairs, dressed for the street. She glances through the portières and picks up the telephone.*)

MISS AUSTEN (*into the telephone*). Will you give me Market, three, three, three, three, please? Please. (MRS. HAROLD *comes down the stairs, dressed for the street, and carrying a suit case and a smaller bag.*) I think you might as well take those right out on to the porch, Mrs. Harold.

MRS. HAROLD (*going out*). Yes, Ma'm.

MISS AUSTEN. Have them ready when the cab comes. (*Into the telephone.*) Hello.—

Will you please send a taxicab to six hundred and eighty Belmont Manor, right away, please? Yes. (*She sets the telephone down and* MRS. HAROLD *comes in.*) It'll be here in a few minutes, Mrs. Harold. Are you all ready?

MRS. HAROLD. Yes, Ma'm. I'm ready.

MISS AUSTEN. Hadn't you better speak to Mrs. Craig about your keys, Mrs. Harold?

MRS. HAROLD. I left them with yours up on her dressing table.

MISS AUSTEN. I think you'd better tell her, Mrs. Harold.

MRS. HAROLD. Do you want me to tell them *you're* going?

MISS AUSTEN (*going towards the door*). No, it isn't necessary, Mrs. Harold; I'll write to Mr. Craig. But, I think you'd better tell them that *you're* going.

MRS. HAROLD. I did tell Mr. Craig I was going; I told him this morning.

MISS AUSTEN. Well, I think you'd better tell Mrs. Craig, also.

MRS. HAROLD. Yes, Ma'm.

MISS AUSTEN. There might be something she'd want to ask you.

MRS. HAROLD. All right, I'll tell her.

MISS AUSTEN. I'll sit here on the porch till the taxi comes. (*She goes out, and* MRS. HAROLD *goes to the mirror and straightens her funny hat.*)

MRS. CRAIG (*coming through the adjoining room*). Are you in there, Mrs. Harold? (MRS. HAROLD *moves up to the foot of the stairs and stands facing the portières.* MRS. CRAIG *comes in.*) Oh, I've been looking for you out there, Mrs. Harold; I wanted you to give my niece a little breakfast.

MRS. HAROLD. I've left everything ready out there, Mrs. Craig.

MRS. CRAIG. Where are you going, Mrs. Harold?

MRS. HAROLD. Why, I'm going with Miss Austen, Mrs. Craig.

MRS. CRAIG. Indeed?

MRS. HAROLD. She was tellin' me last night she was goin' to leave here, and I said I thought I'd be leavin' pretty soon myself; so she said if I was goin' anyway soon, she'd like very much to have me go with her.

MRS. CRAIG. And where are you going with her?

MRS. HAROLD. Why, we are goin' to the Ritz-Carlton first, and after that she sez she's goin' to travel for a few years.

MRS. CRAIG. Well, that ought to be a very good experience for you.

MRS. HAROLD. Yes, I've never been many places outside of here and Long Branch, and I thought I'd better take the chance while I had it.

MRS. CRAIG. And do you think it's very considerate of you, Mrs. Harold, to walk away this way without giving me any notice?

MRS. HAROLD. You didn't give Mazie much notice last night, Mrs. Craig.

MRS. CRAIG. Mazie didn't deserve any notice; she was a very disobedient girl. She absolutely refused to do what I told her.

MRS. HAROLD. Well, I haven't always done exactly what you told me to do, either, Mrs. Craig,—so maybe I deserve to go as well as Mazie.

MRS. CRAIG. Well, of course, you can suit yourself about going, Mrs. Harold, but you understand I shall have to tell Miss Hewlitt about your leaving without notice.

MRS. HAROLD. Miss Hewlitt knows all about my leaving, Mrs. Craig; she's surprised that I didn't leave long ago, to tell you the truth.

MRS. CRAIG. And why didn't you leave?

MRS. HAROLD. Well—there were no children—and it's near church. But Miss Hewlitt told me when I came here that if I stayed a month I'd be the first out of seven that did.

MRS. CRAIG. Miss Hewlitt has sent some very unsatisfactory women here.

MRS. HAROLD. A lot of them have worked in some pretty fine places.

MRS. CRAIG (*turning away, and moving down to the mirror*). Well, of course, that depends upon what a person's idea of a fine place is. And I suppose the next *batch* she sends me won't be any more satisfactory than the rest.

MRS. HAROLD. I think you're very foolish to have her send any more, Mrs. Craig, if you ask me.

MRS. CRAIG. One person can't do everything.

MRS. HAROLD. I've heard you say yourself more than once that you had to do over again everything that any woman that ever worked for you did,—so why not save the money?
(MRS. CRAIG *turns from the mirror and comes towards her.*)

MRS. CRAIG. What about the keys?

MRS. HAROLD. I left them all on your dressin' table upstairs; and Miss Austen's, too.

MRS. CRAIG. Wasn't there anything else to be left?

MRS. HAROLD. Yes, Ma'm, I left the money that I had over with the week's list in an envelope with the keys.

MRS. CRAIG (*turning to the portières*). All right.—I hope you enjoy your world tour.

MRS. HAROLD (*going towards the front door*). It'll be a change, anyway.
(MRS. CRAIG *turns at the portières.*)

MRS. CRAIG. And I hope when you come back, you'll be able to find a place that'll be as easy as this one has been.

MRS. HAROLD (*stopping at the door and turning*). Don't worry about me, Mrs. Craig; nobody belongin' to me ever died in the poorhouse. (*She goes out on to the porch, and* MRS. CRAIG *looks after her stonily. The front doorbell rings incisively, and* MRS. CRAIG *steps forward at the right and looks keenly towards the front door.*)

FREDERICKS (*at the front door*). How do you do?

MRS. HAROLD. How do you do?

FREDERICKS. I should like to see Miss Landreth, if I could. My name is Fredericks.
(MRS. CRAIG *makes a rapid movement of consternation, then looks at the portières.* ETHEL *comes through the portières.*)

ETHEL *and* MRS. HAROLD (*speaking together*). ETHEL: I think I'd better get my things, Aunt Harriet; it must be nearly nine o'clock. MRS. HAROLD: Oh, come in, please. I think Miss Landreth is just having her breakfast.
(*The screen door slams.*)

ETHEL *and* FREDERICKS (*speaking together*). ETHEL: Would you mind telephoning for a taxicab? FREDERICKS: I suppose I am a bit early.
(ETHEL *hears his voice and stops at the foot of the stairs.* MRS. CRAIG *glides out through the portières.* MRS. HAROLD *comes in at the front door.*)

MRS. HAROLD. Oh, I was just comin' to call you, Miss Landreth; there's a Mr. Fredericks here to see you.
(*He comes in.*)

FREDERICKS. Hello, Ethel.
(MRS. HAROLD *passes to the door, back of him, and goes out again.*)

ETHEL. Gene, there isn't anything happened to Mother?

FREDERICKS. Not a thing in the world, dear, that I know of.

ETHEL. You're sure?

FREDERICKS. 'Pon my word, Ethel. I haven't been to your house.

ETHEL. Well, why did you come away down here, then, at this hour of the morning?

FREDERICKS (*taking a step to her*). I wanted to see *you*. (*She begins to cry, and he takes her in his arms.*) I thought maybe you were ill or something. Don't cry, darling; I give you my word there isn't a thing wrong at home. I simply telephoned you as soon as I got your note, and they told me you'd left for here: so then I called you on the long distance. But I couldn't get any satisfaction on the long distance, and I didn't know what to think. So I just jumped on the night train and got in here at eight-twenty.

ETHEL (*straightening up and touching her hair*). I'm going back right away, Gene; there's a train at nine-seventeen from the station down town.

FREDERICKS. I'll go back with you.

ETHEL. I don't know why I ever came away in the first place.

FREDERICKS (*guiding her to the chair at the right of the piano*). Sit down here for a minute, dear; you look terribly pale. (*He puts his hat on the piano.*)

ETHEL. I haven't closed my eyes since I've been here, I've been so worried.

FREDERICKS. I've been worried about *you*, too, ever since I got your note.

ETHEL. And then I told Aunt Harriet about our engagement, and that upset me more than ever.

FREDERICKS. Why?

ETHEL. Oh, she didn't seem to approve of it exactly.

FREDERICKS. Why not?

ETHEL (*rising*). Oh, for several reasons, Gene,—I'll tell you on the train. (*She starts for the foot of the stairs.*)

FREDERICKS (*taking her hand as she passes him*). I wish you'd tell me now, Ethel.

ETHEL (*turning to him*). There isn't time, dear.

FREDERICKS. But you make me uneasy.

ETHEL. It's nothing, Gene, particularly. She simply said she thought perhaps I hadn't considered the thing sufficiently.

FREDERICKS. What is there to consider, darling, in a thing of this kind—except that we love each other.

ETHEL. But she said a thing like marriage should be considered more practically.

FREDERICKS. I don't accept that argument, Ethel; I've seen too many carefully reasoned marriages turn out badly. It's simply a chance that one has to take, more or less. And I have a good way of getting along.

ETHEL. As a single man, yes.

FREDERICKS. And even as a married man.

ETHEL. You don't know that yet, Gene, whether you have or not.

FREDERICKS. But other fellows marry, darling, and get along, on a great deal less salary than I'm getting.

ETHEL. I know that, Gene; but, as Aunt Harriet says, their wives are not living the way I've been accustomed to living. Not that I'd mind that in the least, dear; only I wouldn't want you to feel that I was making any sacrifices. And she says you might feel that in your present circumstances.

FREDERICKS. But haven't you any faith in my ability to improve those circumstances?

ETHEL. Of course; but I wouldn't want to be a burden to you in the meantime.

FREDERICKS. But you're the kind of burden I need, Ethel. You know I've had three promotions since I've known you.

ETHEL. Yes, I know you have.

FREDERICKS. Well, I attribute it to nothing but the incentive that the thought of marrying you has given me. I've worked like a dog these past two years, with just that in mind; and if it were removed,—well, I just don't think beyond that, that's all. (*He turns away to the left a few steps and stands looking straight out. She crosses and lays her hand on his arm.*)

ETHEL. I hadn't thought of not marrying you, Gene; I was just thinking whether or not it would be wise to postpone it.

FREDERICKS (*turning to her*). It *wouldn't* be wise, Ethel; it isn't a good thing to postpone a thing like marriage—so many things can happen. (*He suddenly takes her in his arms.*) And I don't want anything to happen.

ETHEL. What else have I got, Gene, if anything happened to Mother? (*She buries her face in his shoulder and cries hard.*)

FREDERICKS. Nothing's going to happen to her, sweetheart. And if it did, you wouldn't feel any worse than I'd feel if anything happened to this.

(*She continues to cry for a second, then straightens up and presses her handkerchief to her eyes.*)

ETHEL. We'd better go, Gene, it must be nearly nine o'clock. (*She starts across below the table towards the mirror, and* FREDERICKS *starts across above the table towards the telephone.* CRAIG *comes through the portières.*)

FREDERICKS. I'd better call a taxi, hadn't I?

ETHEL. Oh, Uncle Walter,—this is Mr. Fredericks.
(FREDERICKS *continues over to shake hands with* CRAIG, *and* ETHEL *moves up to* FREDERICKS' *left.*)

CRAIG (*shaking hands*). I'm glad to meet you, Mr. Fredericks.

FREDERICKS. How do you do, Mr. Craig?

ETHEL. Mr. Fredericks is the young man I'm engaged to be married to.

CRAIG. Well, I *am* glad to meet you.

FREDERICKS. Pretty lucky fellow, don't you think, Mr. Craig?

CRAIG. I'd say you were. And is it all set?

FREDERICKS. I hope so; although Ethel seems to feel a little nervous about it.

CRAIG. What are you nervous about, Ethel?

ETHEL. I'm not nervous—it isn't that. But I was telling Gene that I'd been discussing it with Aunt Harriet, and she seemed to think that probably I hadn't considered it enough.
(FREDERICKS *looks at* CRAIG.)

CRAIG. What did she want you to consider?

ETHEL. Well, she said on account of my age she didn't think I appreciated the practical side of marriage enough.

CRAIG. That's the one side of marriage that should not be appreciated too much, Ethel; it's a lack of faith in each other.

FREDERICKS. That's what I tell Ethel.

CRAIG. The only thing I think you need to consider really seriously—is whether or not you are both absolutely honest with

each other. (FREDERICKS *looks at* ETHEL, *and* CRAIG *crosses below them towards the stairs.*) It doesn't seem to me that there's very much else to worry about.

ETHEL. We're going back on that nine-seventeen, Uncle Walter; do you know the number of the taxicab company?

CRAIG (*starting up the stairs*). You won't need a taxi, I'm going right down past the station.

ETHEL. Are you going now?

CRAIG. Right away, yes. I'll get my hat. You have plenty of time; I can get you down there in less than ten minutes.

ETHEL. Uncle Walter, will you bring my satchel down when you're coming?

CRAIG. Yes, I'll get it.

ETHEL. It's on the chair there, right inside my door. (*Picking up her bag from the table and crossing down to the mirror to fix herself.*) We won't have to call a taxi.
(FREDERICKS *glances out through the portières, then comes forward, lowering his voice.*)

FREDERICKS. Did your aunt tell you I called you last night?
(ETHEL *turns and looks at him.*)

ETHEL. On the long distance, you mean?

FREDERICKS. Yes, I called you from Northampton as soon as I got your note. I called you at home first, of course, and they gave me this address.

ETHEL. And you called here?

FREDERICKS. Yes, about seven o'clock. Didn't she tell you?

ETHEL. No, she didn't, Gene.

FREDERICKS. I talked to her. She said you were asleep.

ETHEL. I couldn't have been asleep, Gene.

FREDERICKS. I asked her to call you to the telephone, but she didn't seem to want to do it. She said you'd just gotten in and you were tired out.

ETHEL. Well, I *was* tired, but she could have called me; she might have known I'd want to talk to you. Because I didn't know what you'd think of my being down here, after leaving word that I was going home.

FREDERICKS. Have you seen her this morning?

ETHEL. Yes, but she didn't say anything about it. And I was talking to her here this morning about you, too. I was saying that I ought to call *you* on the long distance, that you'd be wondering what was the matter.

CRAIG (*hurrying down the stairs with* ETHEL's *satchel*). I'll run over and get the car.

FREDERICKS. Can I take that, Mr. Craig?

CRAIG. I'll leave it out here on the porch. I'll be back in two minutes. You have lots of time.

FREDERICKS (*going to the piano for his hat*). Are you ready, Ethel?

ETHEL. Yes, I'm ready, Gene. I'd better say good-by to Aunt Harriet.

FREDERICKS. Will I wait for you outside?

ETHEL. Don't you want to meet her, Gene?

FREDERICKS. I don't think she wants to meet me, Ethel.

ETHEL. Why not?

FREDERICKS. After what you've been telling me.

ETHEL. Oh, that's nothing, Gene.

FREDERICKS. She hung up on me last night.

ETHEL. Yes, I want to ask her about that call.

FREDERICKS (*going out*). I think I'd better wait for you outside.
(ETHEL *glances through the portières, then comes forward thoughtfully at the right. There is a slight pause. Then* MRS. CRAIG *glides through the portières and crosses to the bay window to look out.* ETHEL *watches her narrowly, then moves to the right end of the center table.*)

ETHEL. I'm just going, Aunt Harriet.
(MRS. CRAIG *turns, slightly startled.*)

MRS. CRAIG. Oh, I thought you'd gone. (*She comes back towards* ETHEL.) I didn't hear anybody in here, and I was wondering if you'd gone without telling me.

ETHEL. No, I'm just going.

MRS. CRAIG. Where are Mr. Craig and Mr. Fredericks?

ETHEL. Mr. Fredericks is there on the porch. (MRS. CRAIG *turns to the front door and glances out.*) Uncle Walter's gone over to get the car.

MRS. CRAIG. Oh, he's going to drive you in.

ETHEL. Yes.

MRS. CRAIG. Well, that'll be fine,—you won't have to bother calling a taxi. (*Coming forward to* ETHEL *again.*) Did Mr. Fredericks have any word about your mother?

ETHEL. No, he hadn't been home.

MRS. CRAIG. Why don't you call him in, Ethel; I should like to meet him.

ETHEL. He thought probably you wouldn't care to meet him.

MRS. CRAIG. Why, how absurd. Why not?

ETHEL. I was telling him about what you said last night, when I told you I was going to marry him.

MRS. CRAIG. Well, my dear child, I was simply talking in a general way. My remarks weren't directed against Mr. Fredericks particularly. I'm sure he'd appreciate the logic of what I said himself.

ETHEL. He doesn't, Aunt Harriet; I told him what you said, and he takes quite the opposite view.

MRS. CRAIG. Well, of course, he has considerable to gain by the transaction, Ethel, you must remember that.

ETHEL. Well, Uncle Walter has nothing to gain by it, and he agrees with him.

MRS. CRAIG. Well, you remember I told you last night that Mr. Craig was extremely romantic.

ETHEL (*becoming very stony*). Why didn't you call me last night, Aunt Harriet, when Mr. Fredericks telephoned?

MRS. CRAIG. Because you were asleep, dear.

ETHEL. I couldn't have been asleep. I haven't closed my eyes since I've been here.

MRS. CRAIG. Well, I thought you were asleep, Ethel; I sent Mazie up to your room and she said your door was closed.

ETHEL. Well, she could have rapped.

MRS. CRAIG. Well, what was the sense of upsetting you, dear?

ETHEL. Because it was important to me.

MRS. CRAIG. I asked him if it was important, and if there was any message he wanted to leave, and he said no.

ETHEL. And you hung up on him.

MRS. CRAIG. Because he insisted upon talking to you; and you were not in any condition to be talked to. (*She turns and moves towards the bay window.*)

ETHEL. Why didn't you tell me this morning that he'd called—when I said I should call him?

MRS. CRAIG (*turning coldly*). Now, please, Ethel dear—I shan't answer any more questions about Mr. Fredericks. (*She goes to the bay window to look out.*) I've had quite enough to worry me this morning without thinking about Mr. Fredericks. He's going back with you, I suppose?

ETHEL (*crossing up to the front door*). Yes.

MRS. CRAIG (*turning to her*). Well, I'm glad you won't have to make the trip alone. Good-by, dear. (*She kisses her.*) I hope you'll let me know right away how you find your mother.

ETHEL (*holding her hand*). Aunt Harriet—

MRS. CRAIG. What, dear?

ETHEL (*after a pause, and holding her eye*). Aunt Harriet, is Uncle Walter *leaving* you?

MRS. CRAIG. Why, what on earth ever put that into your head, Ethel?

ETHEL. Something he was saying when I came to the head of the stairs to come down this morning.

MRS. CRAIG. And what was he saying?

ETHEL. Something about your having made a remark that made it impossible for him to continue here as your husband.

MRS. CRAIG. I'm sure I haven't the faintest idea what you're talking about, Ethel.

ETHEL. And then a while ago here, when I told him I was going to be married to Mr. Fredericks, he said the only thing we needed to consider seriously was whether or not we were absolutely honest with each other. And I was wondering if he'd found out.

MRS. CRAIG. Found out what?

ETHEL. That that you told me last night,—when I said I didn't think it was honest. (*There is a movement on the front porch. The screen door slams, and* MRS. CRAIG *turns away quickly and looks out the bay window.*)

CRAIG (*outside*). All set?

FREDERICKS (*outside*). All set. Ethel's inside.

ETHEL (*going out*). Good-by, Aunt Harriet.

MRS. CRAIG (*turning and following her to the door*). Good-by, dear.

ETHEL. I'll write you as soon as I get home.

MRS. CRAIG. Do, dear; let me know how your mother is.

ETHEL. Yes, I shall.
(*The screen door slams.*)

CRAIG. Ready, Ethel?

ETHEL. Yes, I'm coming, Uncle Walter. (MRS. CRAIG *turns nervously and moves across and down to the mantelpiece.*)

CRAIG. Your satchel's in the car. I'll be with you in a minute. (*He comes in, taking a little leather key case from his pocket, and crosses to the portières.*)

MRS. CRAIG. Are you going to the office now?

CRAIG. Yes, it's nearly nine o'clock. (*He goes through the portières, and* MRS. CRAIG *moves up to the portières.*)

MRS. CRAIG. Mrs. Harold says you haven't been in bed all night; you won't feel much like sitting at a desk all day.

CRAIG (*from the other room*). I'll have plenty of time to rest after a bit.
(MRS. CRAIG'S *eyes narrow, in an attempt to fathom this remark. She comes forward again at the right, slowly and thoughtfully.* CRAIG *enters, fastening the little key case, and crosses towards the front door, picking up his hat from the table as he passes.*)

MRS. CRAIG. Did you find what you were looking for?

CRAIG. I wasn't looking for anything—I was just leaving the key to your car and the garage, with some other things I've left there for you. (*He turns at the door.*) If you should want me for anything during the next week or two, Harriet, I'll be at the Ritz.
(*She turns suddenly and makes a rapid movement to the center table.*)

MRS. CRAIG. Now, listen to me, Walter Craig, you're surely not serious about leaving this house.

CRAIG. Why, I should think that decision would please you very much.

MRS. CRAIG. Well, it doesn't please me at all; it's absolutely ridiculous.

CRAIG. But it's so absolutely practical.

MRS. CRAIG. Oh, don't try to be funny.

CRAIG. And you've been deploring my lack of practicality so long.

MRS. CRAIG. I'd like to know what's practical about a man walking out and leaving his wife and his home.

CRAIG. I have no wife to leave,—for you neither loved nor honored me.

MRS. CRAIG. Well, you married me, whether I did or not.

CRAIG. I never saw you before in my life, Harriet—until last night.

MRS. CRAIG. You married me, didn't you?

CRAIG. And you married a house; and if it's agreeable to you, I'll see that you have it; and that you can go on having it, just as though I were here.

MRS. CRAIG (*turning away towards the mantelpiece*). You'll be here; unless I'm very much mistaken.

CRAIG. You don't know your man, Harriet.

MRS. CRAIG. I know him well enough for that, anyway.

CRAIG. Oh, you knew me pretty well, I'll grant you that; particularly when you said my mind worked very slowly.

MRS. CRAIG. It's working pretty slowly now, when you don't appreciate the absurdity of a move of this kind.

CRAIG. But you failed to reckon with the thoroughness of my mind, Harriet, when it *does* work. And it appreciates this situation so thoroughly that it has no illusions about the impossibility of my continuance here.

MRS. CRAIG. What is there so impossible about it?

CRAIG. We've shown our hands, Harriet, and the game is up.

MRS. CRAIG. What did I do last night that was so terrible?

CRAIG. You simply showed your hand, that was all.

MRS. CRAIG. I simply kept you from making a fool of yourself; that was all I did.

CRAIG. But you also showed me how I could keep from making a fool of myself in the future.

MRS. CRAIG. Well, you're certainly not beginning very auspiciously, I can tell you that.

CRAIG. But I shall be at least a self-respecting fool; and that's something I could never be if I stayed here. There's something in a man, Harriet, that I suppose is his essential manhood; and you insulted that last night. And I should be too embarrassed here, under your eye, knowing that you had no respect for that manhood. I should remember my lover's ardors and enthusiasms for our future; and you bearing with me contemptuously, for the sake of *your* future. I couldn't stand it.

MRS. CRAIG. You're not telling the truth; I always respected you; and I never had anything but respect for your plans, either.

CRAIG. Don't try to soften the blow, Harriet; I assure you it isn't necessary. (*He turns towards the door, and she makes a move towards him.*)

MRS. CRAIG. Where are you going when you leave here?
(*He turns and looks at her.*)

CRAIG. That 'ud be rather interesting to know, Harriet—where a lot like me are going.—Out of fashion, possibly.

MRS. CRAIG. Well, what about your things? —Aren't you going to take anything with you?

CRAIG. You may send them to me if you like.

MRS. CRAIG (*turning away*). Well, I won't send them to you; for you'll very likely be back again within a week.

CRAIG. Perhaps it will be just as well if you don't send them to me, Harriet,—for I'm rather sentimental about things; and I might look back, and be turned into a romantic fool.

MRS. CRAIG. Oh, I suppose you'll never forgive me for calling you that.

CRAIG. No, there isn't a thing in the world I don't forgive you for, Harriet; that's the reason it won't be necessary for me to come back here any more; there's nothing to adjust. I guess possibly I'm just a bit of an old-fashioned man—I must be trusted— and you never trusted me.

MRS. CRAIG. I wouldn't trust any man after what I've seen.

CRAIG. I don't blame you. But I wonder that, with all your wisdom, it never occurred to you that one cannot play a dishonest game indefinitely.

MRS. CRAIG. I haven't played any dishonest game.

CRAIG. Possibly not, according to your standards; but I think you have. And I think you know you have. And that's the rock that you and I are splitting on, Harriet. If this affair at Passmores' hadn't revealed you, something else would: so my going may as well be to-day as to-morrow. Good-by, Harriet. (*He goes out; she leans on the table. The screen door slams. She moves over to the bay window and watches him get into the automobile: then she comes forward to the window at the right and watches him down the street. After he has passed beyond her vision, her gaze wanders into the room again, and she becomes conscious of two tiny pieces of the broken ornament near the mantelpiece. She stoops and picks them up, flicking away with her foot any other invisible particles that may be about. Then she looks at the two remaining ornaments on the mantelpiece and tries to come to some conclusion about their arrangement. She places them equi-distant from each other and the ends of the mantelpiece, and stands off to observe the effect. The front doorbell rings sharply. She turns and crosses to answer it.*)

BOY'S VOICE (*at the front door*). Telegram for Mrs. Walter Craig.
(*She signs for the telegram, the screen door slams and she comes in, opening the telegram. She reads the telegram, looks straight ahead for a second, thinking— looks at the wire again, and bursts into tears—sinking into the chair at the right of the piano. She cries hard for a moment, then smooths the telegram out and reads it again.* MRS. FRAZIER *appears in the door, dressed in gray, and carrying an armload of white roses. She comes forward inquiringly.*)

MRS. FRAZIER. Good morning, Mrs. Craig. (MRS. CRAIG *doesn't hear her.*) Good morning. (MRS. CRAIG *looks at her, startled, gets up nervously and moves across to the front of the center table, touching her eyes and her hair.*) I do hope you'll pardon my walking in without ringing, but I thought Miss Austen 'ud be on the front porch, and I wanted to bring her these roses. (*She hands* MRS. CRAIG *the roses*.) I was telling her yesterday I'd bring her over some; she was saying she admired white roses so much; and I have so many of them over there just now.

MRS. CRAIG. I haven't seen her yet this morning.

MRS. FRAZIER (*preparing to go*). Well, if you'll just tell her I left them.

MRS. CRAIG. Yes, I shall; thanks ever so much.

MRS. FRAZIER (*turning back*). Oh, have you had any word about your sister this morning, Mrs. Craig? Miss Austen was telling me yesterday she was quite ill.

MRS. CRAIG (*starting to cry again*). She died this morning at six o'clock.

MRS. FRAZIER. Oh, dear me, how sad.

MRS. CRAIG. I just had this wire.

MRS. FRAZIER. Dear, dear, dear, isn't that too bad!

MRS. CRAIG. I had no idea she was so ill or I should never have come back.

MRS. FRAZIER. Dear, dear, dear, I'm so sorry. I shouldn't have bothered you at all.

MRS. CRAIG. That's quite all right.

MRS. FRAZIER. I'm sure you have my sympathy.

MRS. CRAIG. Thank you.

MRS. FRAZIER. I do hope you'll let me know, Mrs. Craig, if there's any way I can be of any service to you.

MRS. CRAIG. Thank you very much; I don't think there's anything anybody can do.

MRS. FRAZIER. I suppose you'll have to go right back up there again, won't you?

MRS. CRAIG. I don't know whether I shall be able to or not, to tell you the truth, Mrs. Frazier; it's been such a strain.

MRS. FRAZIER. Yes, those long illnesses are dreadful. But I hope you won't hesitate to let me know if there's anything I can do.

MRS. CRAIG. That's very kind of you. I'll give these roses to Miss Austen when I see her.

MRS. FRAZIER. If you will, please. (*She starts for the door*.) I'm terribly sorry. I'll run over again.
(*She goes out; and* MRS. CRAIG *stands very still until she hears the screen door close. Then she steps up to the door and clicks the latch. Then she turns, comes forward a few steps into the room again, and stands, holding the roses against her bosom and looking straight out. A clock out in one of the adjoining rooms strikes nine with a mournful gong. After the fourth gong her eyes wander in the direction of the clock and she moves slowly across towards the portières. Then she comes forward at the right, wandering, and crosses below the table to the piano. Several rose petals flutter to the floor. She stands at the piano for a moment, looking out through the bay window, then retraces her steps. She looks unseeingly at the scattered petals, continues up towards the portières, looks out through the deserted rooms, and finally stops. A few more petals drift to the floor. The curtain commences to descend, very, very slowly. She turns desolately and wanders back towards the piano again, clutching the roses close, her eyes wide and despairing*.)

In Abraham's Bosom

BY PAUL GREEN

PAUL GREEN

Paul Eliot Green, America's leading folk dramatist, was born near Lillington, North Carolina, in 1894. He was graduated from Buies Creek Academy in 1914. Teaching a country school in the winter and playing semi-professional baseball in the summer, Mr. Green had in two years saved enough money to enter the University of North Carolina. Instead, in 1917 he enlisted in the United States Army, serving successively as a private, corporal, sergeant, sergeant-major, and later as second lieutenant with the Chief of Engineers at Paris. Before leaving, however, and probably with dire forebodings, Mr. Green paid a printer of Greenville, South Carolina, seventy dollars to publish thirty copies of his first book, *Trifles of Thought,* for the satisfaction of having his literary efforts published in the event that he did not return from the war.

He received his A.B. from the University of North Carolina in 1921. The following two years he did graduate study at his home University and at Cornell. In 1922 he married Elizabeth Atkinson Lay.

Since 1923 he has been associate professor of philosophy at the University of North Carolina. A volume of his short stories, *Wide Fields,* appeared in 1928, while his novel, *Laughing Pioneer,* was published in 1932.

Produced by the Provincetown Players at the Provincetown Theatre, New York, December 30, 1926, *In Abraham's Bosom* won the Pulitzer award for 1926-1927.

CHARACTERS

ABRAHAM McCRANIE, a Negro.

GOLDIE McALLISTER, his sweetheart and later his wife.

MUH MACK, his aunt.

BUD GASKINS ⎫
LIJE HUNNEYCUTT ⎬ Turpentine hands for the Colonel.
PUNY AVERY ⎭

DOUGLASS McCRANIE, Abraham's son.

EDDIE WILLIAMS ⎫
LANIE HORTON ⎬ Students to Abe.
NEILLY McNEILL ⎭

COLONEL McCRANIE, a Southern gentleman, once the owner of slaves.

LONNIE McCRANIE, his son.

SCENES

SCENE   I: The turpentine woods of eastern North Carolina, the summer of 1885.

SCENE   II: In Abraham McCranie's cabin, spring, three years later.

SCENE   III: The school house, winter of the same year.

SCENE   IV: A house in Durham, winter, fifteen years later.

SCENE   V: The same as Scene II, an autumn evening three years later.

SCENE   VI: On a road near his home in Scene II, an hour later.

SCENE   VII: The same as Scene II, about thirty minutes later than Scene VI.

IN ABRAHAM'S BOSOM

SCENE I

In the turpentine woods of Eastern North Carolina, forty years ago, near a spring at the foot of a hill. The immediate foreground is open and clear save for a spongy growth of grass and sickly ground creepers. In the rear a wide-spreading tangle of reeds, briars, and alder bushes shuts around the spring in a semi-circle. At the right front the great body of a pine, gashed and barked by the turpentine farmer's axe, lifts straight from the earth. To the left a log lies rotting in the embrace of wild ivy. Maples, bays, dogwoods and other small trees overrun by tenacious vines raise their leafy tops to shade the spot. Through interstices in the undergrowth one can see the pine forest stretching away until the eye is lost in a colonnade of trees. The newly scraped blazes on the pines show through the brush like the downward spreading beards of old men, suggestive of the ancient gnomes of the woods, mysterious and silently watchful.

At the left front four tin dinner pails hang on a limby bush. The sound of axes against the trees, accompanied by the rhythmically guttural "han—n—h! han—n—n—h!" of the cutters comes from the distance. One of the laborers breaks into a high mournful song—

> Oh, my feets wuh wet—wid de sunrise dew,
> De morning star—wuh a witness too.
> 'Way, 'way up in de Rock of Ages,
> In God's bosom gwine be my pillah.

Presently there is a loud halloo near at hand, and another voice yodels and cries, Dinner time—m-m—e! Git yo' peas, ev'ybody! *Voices are heard nearer, a loud burst of laughter, and then three full-blooded Negroes shuffle in carrying long thin-bladed axes, which they lean against the pine at the right. They are dressed in nondescript clothes, ragged and covered with the glaze of raw turpentine. As they move up to the spring they take off their battered hats, fan themselves, and wipe the streaming sweat from their brows. Two of them are well-built and burly, one stout and past middle age with some pretension to a thin scraggly mustache, the second tall and muscled, and the third wiry, nervous and bandy-legged. They punctuate their conversation with great breaths of cool air.*

YOUNG NEGRO. Monkey walking in dis woods.

OLDER NEGRO. Yah, Jaboh progueing round and 'bout um.

LITTLE NEGRO. While us res' he roos' high in pine tree.

YOUNG NEGRO. Fall on Puny's back 'bout th'ee o'clock, git um down. Hee—hee.

PUNY. Ain't no monkey kin ride me, tell you.
(*They stand fanning themselves.*)

OLDER NEGRO. Dat nigger tough, ain't you, Puny?

PUNY. Tough as whitleather, tough 'y God! (*He gets down on his belly at the spring.*) Mouf 'bout to crack, kin drink dis heah spring dry.

OLDER NEGRO (*slouching his heavy body towards the pool*). Hunh, me too. Dat axe take water same lak a saw-mill. (*He gets down flat and drinks with the other. The water can be heard gluking over the cataract of their Adam's apples. The* YOUNGER NEGRO *opens his torn and sleeveless undershirt and stands raking the sweat from his powerful chest with curved hand.*)

385

YOUNG NEGRO (*after a moment*). Heigh, **Puny**, you'n Lije pull yo' guts out'n dat mud-hole and let de engineer take a drink. (*With a sudden thought of devilment he steps quickly forward and cracks their heads together.* PUNY *starts and falls face foremost in the spring.* LIJE, *slow and stolid, saves himself, crawls slowly upon his haunches and sits smiling good-naturedly, smacking his lips and sucking the water from the slender tails of his mustache.*)

LIJE (*cleaning his muddy hands with a bunch of leaves*). Nunh—unh, not dis time, my boy.

PUNY (*scrambling to his feet, strangling and sputtering*). Damn yo' soul, why you push me, Bud Gaskins?

BUD (*a threatening note slipping into his laugh*). Hyuh, hyuh, don't you cuss at me, bo.

PUNY. Why'n't you 'pose on somebody yo' size? Bedder try Lije dere.
(BUD *gets down and begins drinking.*)

LIJE (*drawling*). Don't keer 'f 'e do. Ducking good foh you dis hot weather.

PUNY (*helplessly*). Allus picking at me. Wisht, wisht—

BUD. Heah I is lying down. Come on do whut you wisht. (PUNY *makes no reply but turns off, wiping his face on his shirt sleeve, and staring morosely at the ground.* BUD *gets to his feet.*) Yah, reckon you sail on me and I jam yo' haid in dat spring lak a fence post and drownd you.

PUNY (*his anger smouldering*). Talk is cheap, black man, cheap! (*Suddenly afraid of his boldness in replying, he turns and looks at* BUD *in a weak pleading defiance.*)

BUD (*making a frightening movement towards him*). Mess wid me a-jowing and I knock yo' teef th'ough yo' skull.

LIJE. Hyuh, Bud, you let Puny 'lone. (*He moves over to his bucket, gets it and sits down on the log at the left.*)

BUD (*turning for his bucket with a movement of disgust*). Sho' I ain't gwine hurt him—po' pitiful bow-legs.
(PUNY *clenches his hands as if stung to the* quick, *and then beaten and forlorn reaches for his bucket, the weak member of the herd. He throws off his overall jacket, revealing himself stripped to the waist, and sits down at the pine tree.*)

LIJE (*laying out his food and singing*).

'Way, 'way up in de Rock of Ages,
In God's bosom gwine be my pillah.

BUD (*looking at* PUNY's *bony bust*). Uhp, showing off dat 'oman's breas' o' yo'n, is you? Haw-haw.

PUNY (*in sheer ineffectuality answering him blandly*). Gwine cool myse'f.

LIJE. Me too, peoples. (*He loosens his belt, pulls out his shirt-tails, undoes his shirt, and pats his belly.*) Lawd, Bud, you sho' led us a race dis mawning on dem dere boxes. Musta sweat a peck er mo'.

BUD (*taking his bucket and sitting on the ground near the center*). Race? Hunh, wait till fo' o'clock dis evening, you gwine call foh de ca'f rope, sho' 'nough. (*Tickled at the tribute to his power.*) And po' Puny, de monkey have rid him to deaf.

PUNY. Ain't no monkey rid me, I tells you. Little but loud. Be raght dere when de hawn blows.

BUD. Mought, and you slubbering yo' work. I cawners my boxes lak de Colonel calls foh. You des' gi' 'em a lick and a promise. Ain't it so, Lije?

LIJE (*swallowing a hunk of bread*). Dunno, dunno. He do all right, reckon.

PUNY. Putt us in de cotton patch, and I kin kill you off de way a king snake do a lizard.

BUD. Picking cotton! Dat 'oman and chillun's job. No reg'lar man mess wid dat. (*Waving his hand at the woods behind him.*) Turpentiming's de stuff.
(*They fall to eating heartily, peas, side-meat, molasses poured in the top of the bucket-lid from a bottle, bread and collards. The axe of a fourth hand is heard still thudding in the forest.*)

LIJE (*jerking his bread-filled hand behind him*). Whyn't Abe come on? Time he eating.

BUD. Let him r~ir. 'On't hurt hisse'f a-cutting. Gitting to be de no 'countest hand I ever see.

LIJE. Useter could cut boxes lak a house afiah.

PUNY. And hack! Lawd, dat nigger could hack.

LIJE. De champeen o' de woods and de swamps.

PUNY. Bedder'n Bud, bedder'n all. Knowed him to dip eight barrels many day.

BUD. Cain't he'p whut has been. Ain't wuth my ol' hat now. Colonel Mack say so too. And I heahd Mr. Lonnie talking rough to him over at de weaving house day 'fo' yistiddy 'bout his gitting trifling heah lately.

PUNY. Been gitting no' count since two yeah' 'go. De time when de white folks hang dat Charlie Sampson on a telegram pole—him whut 'tacked a white 'oman, and dey shoot him full o' holes, ayh!

BUD. Dey did. And dat Abe gut his neck stretched hadn't been foh de Colonel. Fool went down dere in de night and cut dat nigger down and bury 'im hese'f.

LIJE (*looking around him*). 'Twon't do to mess wid white folks and dey r'iled up.

BUD. You said it, bruvver.

PUNY (*looking around him*). Won't do. Keep to yo' work, da's all.

BUD. Yeh, work, work foh 'em. Git yo' money and yo' meat, push on th'ough, axe no questions, no sass, keep to yo' work.

LIJE. Nigger keep mouf shet, let white man do talking. He safe den.

BUD. Safe! You done said. No telegram poles, no shooting, no fiah burn um.

PUNY. Safe is best.
(*They lapse into silence under the touch of worry, something undefinable, something not to be thought upon. They swallow their food heavily. Presently* LIJE *stops and looks at the ground.*)

LIJE. Abe ain't safe.

BUD. Eyh?

LIJE (*gesturing vaguely behind him*). Abe talk too much.

BUD (*nodding*). He do, talk too much to white folks.

PUNY. Cain't he'p it, I bet.

BUD. Kin too. Didn't talk much 'fore dat boy wuh hung. Worked hard den and say nothing.

LIJE. Sump'n on he mind. Sump'n deep, worry 'im, trouble—

BUD. Trouble 'bout de nigger, wanter rise him up wid eddication—fact!

PUNY. Hunh, rise him up to git a rope roun' his neck. Nigger's place down de bottom. Git buried in he own graveyard, don't mind out.

BUD. Raght on de bottom wid deir hand and legs, muscle power, backbone, down wid de rocks and de shovels and de digging, dat's de nigger. White man on top.

LIJE. You's talking gospel.

PUNY. Abe say he gwine climb. I heah him tell de Colonel dat.

BUD. Fo' God! Whut Colonel say?

PUNY. He ain't say nothing, des' look at 'im.

LIJE. Abe is bad mixed up all down inside.

BUD. White and black make bad mixtry.

LIJE. Do dat. (*Thumping on his chest.*) Nigger down heah. (*Thumping his head.*) White mens up heah. Heart say do one thing, head say 'nudder. Bad, bad.

PUNY. De white blood in him coming to de top. Dat make him want-a climb up and be sump'n. Nigger gwine hol' him down dough. Part of him take adder de Colonel, part adder his muh, 'vision and misery inside.

LIJE. Ssh!

PUNY (*staring and looking around*). Colonel Mack he daddy, everybody knows. Lak as two peas, see de favor.

BUD (*bitingly*). Talk too much! Little bird carry news to de Colonel and he fall on you and scrush you. Ain't nigger, ain't white whut ail him. Dem damn books he gut to studying last yeah or two. Cain't go to de woods widdout 'em. Look up dere on his bucket, foh Christ sake. (*He points to the remaining tin bucket in the bush. A small book is lying on the top under the handle. Snorting.*) 'Rifmatic I bet. Give a nigger a book and des' well shoot him. All de white folks tell you dat.

PUNY (*pouring molasses on his bread*). He sma't dough, in his haid. Dat nigger gut sense.

LIJE. Has dat. Gitting so he kin cipher raght up wid de Colonel.

PUNY (*looking at* BUD). Bet some day Colonel Mack put him woods boss over us.

BUD. Ain't no nigger gwine boss me, hoss-cake. Split his haid open wid my axe.

LIJE (*leaning back and emitting a halloo*). Heighp, you, Abe! Dinner! Gwine cut all day?

BUD. Gi' him de full title and he'll heah you.

LIJE (*grinning*). Aberham, Aberham Mc-Cranie!

PUNY. Yeh, you, Aberham Lincoln, whut drapped de nigger he freedom from de balloon, you better git yo' grub!
(*An answering shout comes out of the forest.*)

BUD. Trying to cut past time, mebbe us'll think he sma't.

PUNY. Don't keer whut you think, Bud, gitting so he look down on you and de rest of us.

BUD. Damn yo' runty soul, whut you know 'bout it? Ain't no nigger living kin look down on me and git by wid it. Do, and I make 'em smell o' dat. (*He clenches his heavy fist and raises it to heaven.*)

PUNY. Jesus! Dat Abe take you up in one hand and frail yo' behime to a blister.

LIJE. Whut make you two black-gyard so much?

BUD (*to* PUNY). Keep on, keep on, little man. Some dese days you gwine come missing. (*He crams a handful of corn-bread into his mouth.*)

LIJE (*drawling*). Try a little fist and skull and work de bile out'n yo' systems. (*Looking off and singing.*)
     "Dark was de night and cold de
          ground. . . ."

BUD (*spitting in scorn*). Ain't gwine bruise my fistes on his old skull. Don't 'spec' to notice him no mo'. (*He falls to eating in huge mouthfuls.*) But he bedder quit th'owing dat Abe in my face, I tells him dat.

PUNY. Don't see why dat make you mad.

BUD. It do dough. I don't lak him and his uppity ways, I don't.

PUNY. Hunh, and you was one o' de fust to brag on him foh goin' on sho't rations so de Colonel buy him books and learn 'im to teach school.

BUD. Sho't rations. Ain't no sho't rations, and dat Goldie gal bringing him pies and stuff eve'y day. Be here wid a bucket in a few minutes, I betcha. Fool love de ve'y ground he squat on! And he look down on her caze her ign'ant. And teach school! Been heahing dat school teaching business de whole yeah. He ain't gwine teach no school. Niggers 'on't send to him, dey 'on't. Niggers don't want no schooling.

PUNY. Mought. Abe tol' me dis mornin' dat de Colonel gwine fix it wid de 'missioners or something in town today. I know whut de matter wid you, Bud. Hee-hee.

BUD. Whut?

PUNY (*hesitating*). Abe come riding by in de two-hoss coach. Us'll be bowing and a-scraping. Us'll pull off'n our hats and be "Howdy, Mister Aberham." (BUD *turns and looks at him with infinite scorn, saying nothing.*) And Bud? (BUD *makes no answer.*) Bud?

BUD. Whut?

PUNY. Dat Goldie business whut worrying you, hee-hee. She love Abe and—

BUD (*bounding up and kicking* PUNY's *bucket and food into the bushes*). Damn yo' lousy soul, minner mind stomp you in de dirt! (*He towers over the terrified* PUNY, *who lies flat on his back whimpering.*)

PUNY. Don't hit me, Bud. Foh God's sake! I des' joking.

LIJE. Go at it, fight it out. (*Singing as he watches them.*)

De bones in de grave cried Ca'vary
De night King Jesus died.

BUD (*kicking dirt at* PUNY *and going back to his bucket*). Done told him now. Ain't gwine say no mo'! Next time be my fist rammed down his th'oat, and turn him wrong side out'ards.
(ABE *comes in at the right, carrying his axe. He is a young Negro, with a touch of the mulatto in him, of twenty-five or six, tall and powerfully built, dressed much like the others in cap and turpentine-glazed clothes. He puts his axe by the pine at the right, pulls off his cap and fans himself, while he pinches his sweaty shirt loose from his skin. His shaggy head, forehead and jaw are marked with will and intelligence. But his wide nostril and a slumbrous flash in his eye that now and then shows itself suggest a passionate and dangerous person when aroused. From the change in the actions of the others when he enters it is evident that they respect and even fear him.*)

ABE. What's de trouble 'tween you and Puny, Bud?

BUD (*sullenly*). Ain't no trouble.

PUNY (*crawling around on the ground and collecting his spilled food*). Ain't nothing, Abe, I des' spilled my rations.
(ABE *gets his book down and seats himself in the shade at the left. He begins working problems, using a stub of a pencil and a sheet of crumpled paper.*)

LIJE. Puny, I got some bread left you kin have. (*He pulls a harp from his pocket and begins to blow softly.*)

PUNY (*straightening out his mashed bucket and closing it.*) I don't want nothing

else, Lije. Et all I kin hold. (*After a moment.*) Putt yo' bucket up foh you. (*He gets* LIJE's *bucket and hangs it along with his own in the limby bush.* BUD *eats in silence, puts up his bucket, gets a drink from the spring, and resumes his seat, hanging his head between his knees.* PUNY *goes to the spring and drinks.*)

BUD (*Pouring snuff into his lip*). Don't fall in an' git drownded, Puny.

PUNY. Want some water Lije? (*He goes to the log, curls himself up in the shade beside it and prepares to sleep.*)

LIJE (*stirring lazily*). Believe I does. (*He goes to the spring and drinks, returns to the pine tree and sits down.*)

PUNY. Ain't you g'in' eat no dinner, Abe? (ABE *makes no reply.*)

LIJE. Call him again. (*Touching his head with his finger.*) Deep, deep up dere.

PUNY. Heigh, Abe, bedder eat yo' grub.

ABE (*starting*). You call me?

PUNY. You so deep stud'in' didn't heah me. Bedder eat yo' dinner. Git full o' ants settin' up dere.

ABE. I goin' to eat later.

BUD. Yeh, when Goldie come.

ABE. Hunh!

BUD. You heahd me.

ABE (*irritably*). Don't let me heah no mo'.

BUD. Hunh?

ABE. You heahd me. (PUNY *snickers from his log with audible delight.* LIJE *waits a moment and then lies down.* BUD *reaches out and tears a bush from the ground and casts it angrily from him.*) I'll eat my dinner when it please me, you gentlemens allowing. (*There is a touch of anger in his voice which he apparently regrets on second thought, for he goes on more kindly.*) Goldie said she goin' to fetch me sump'n t' eat to-day. I got to work dis problem. Been on it two days now. Cain't git it out'n my head. Ain't been able to sleep two nights. (BUD *sits staring and spitting straight before him. Presently* LIJE *begins to snore, then* PUNY *follows.* ABE *goes on with his figuring.* BUD *turns over on the ground and goes to sleep.* ABE *becomes more and more absorbed in the problem he is working. He mutters to himself.*) How many sheep? How many sheep? (*He clutches at his hair, gnaws his pencil, and turns to the back of his book.*) Answer say fifteen. Cain't make it come out fifteen, cain't, seem lak, to save me. Man must have answer wrong. Six go into fo'teen, three, no, two times and—two over. (*His voice dies away as he becomes lost in his work. Presently his face begins to light up. He figures faster. Suddenly he slaps his knee.*) Dere whah I been missing it all de time. I carried two 'stid o' one. Blame fool I is. (*He hits the side of his head with his knuckle. In his excitement he calls out.*) Puny, I gitting dat answer. (*But* PUNY *is snoring away. In a moment he throws down his book with beaming face.*) I got it, folkses, I got it. Fifteen! Dat white man know whut he doing, he all time git dem answer right. (*He turns expectantly towards* LIJE.) I got it Lije. (LIJE *makes no answer. He turns toward* PUNY *again, starts to speak but sees he is asleep.*) Bud! (*But* BUD *makes no answer. The heavy breathing of the sleepers falls regularly upon his ears. His face sinks into a sort of hopeless brooding.*) Yeh, sleep, sleep, sleep yo' life away. I figger foh you, foh me, foh all de black in de world to lead 'em up out'n ignorance. Dey don't listen, dey don't heah me, dey in de wilderness, don't wanta be led. Dey sleep, sleep in bondage. (*He bows his head between his knees.*) Sleep in sin. (*Presently.*) Time me to eat. (*He reaches for his bucket and is about to open it when* PUNY *springs high into the air with a squeak of terror, and begins rolling over and over in the leaves and briars.*)

PUNY. Come heah, folkses, come heah git dis thing off'n me. (*He clutches at his breeches.* LIJE *and* BUD *start up out of their sleep.*)

LIJE. Who dat run-mad man?

BUD. Dat damn Puny, sump'n in he britches!

ABE. Be still, Puny, I git it out. (*He goes up to the frightened* PUNY, *reaches down his trousers and pulls out a mouse.*) Nothing but a little bitty old field mice. (*He throws the mouse into the thicket.* LIJE *and* BUD *break into roaring laughter.* PUNY *sits down exhausted, fanning himself angrily.*)

PUNY. Laugh, laugh, all o' you. Dat thing bite same as mud turkle. Yeh, funny, funny, lak hell to you. (*He snaps his mouth closed and fans himself the more furiously. A loud shout comes from off the left.*)

ABE. Stop yo' laughing, I heah somebody hollering.
(*A second halloo comes down the hill.*)

PUNY. Dat de Colonel and Mr. Lonnie!

BUD. Sound lak 'em. Da's who 'tis.

ABE (*going off at the left*). Heah we is, Colonel Mack, at de spring eating dinner! (*He comes back.*) Col. Mack and Mr. Lonnie coming on down heah.

PUNY. Co'se. Gut to see how many boxes us cleaned up dis mawning.

ABE. He tell me 'bout de school now. (*He stirs around him in his excitement.*) Mebbe dat his main business heah in de middle o' de day.

BUD. Hunh, mebbe. Gut some special work want done. Wanter hurry us to it, dat's whut.
(*The sound of voices is heard approaching from the left, and almost immediately the* COLONEL *and his son* LONNIE *come in. The* COLONEL *carries a riding whip. He is a stout, run-down old Southerner with all the signs of moral and intellectual decadence upon him. Lechery, whiskey, and levity of living have taken their toll of him, and yet he has retained a kind of native good-naturedness. His shirt front and once pointed beard are stained with the drippings of tobacco juice. There is something in his bearing and in the contour of his face that resembles* ABE. *His son, a heavyish florid young man of twenty-three or four, walks behind him.*)

COLONEL (*in a high jerky voice*). Snoozing, hanh?

ABE. Just finishing our dinner, suh.

PUNY. Us 'bout to wuk over-time to-day, Colonel.

COLONEL. Not likely, I reckon. Say, I want you fellows, all four of you, to get over to the swamp piece on Dry Creek. Boxes there are running over, two quarts in 'em apiece, prime virgin. (*They begin to move to their feet.*) No, I don't mean to go right now. Gabe's coming by on the big road here (*jerking his whip towards the rear*) with a load of barrels and the dippers in about a half-hour. Meet him out there.

LONNIE. Yeh, we want to git the wagons off to Fayetteville to-night.

COLONEL. How you get on cornering this morning, Bud?

BUD. Purty good, suh. Us fo' done 'bout all dat pastuh piece, suh.

COLONEL. Fine, fine. That's the way. Puny and Lije stay with you?

BUD. Raght dere eve'y jump.

LIJE. Yessuh, yessuh!

PUNY. When he gi' de call we gi' 'im de 'sponse eve'y time, suh. Yes, suh, us kept 'im crowded.

COLONEL. We got to git on, Lonnie. Want to see how the scrape's coming over on Uncle Joe's Branch. Be up on the road there in half a' hour.

LONNIE (*stopping as they go out*). Got so you doing any better work lately, Abe?

ABE (*starting*). Suh!

LONNIE. You heard me.

ABE. I didn't understand you, Mr. Lonnie.

LONNIE. You understood me all right. (*Pointing to the book on the ground.*) Let them damned books worry you still?

COLONEL. Come on, Lonnie.

ABE (*stammering*). I dunno—I—

COLONEL. Still holding out on short rations, ain't you, Abe? (*There is the least hint of pride in the* COLONEL's *voice.*)

ABE (*somewhat confused*). I studying whut I kin, slow go, slow go.

COLONEL. Stick to it. You the first nigger I ever see so determined. But then you're uncommon! (*The* COLONEL *moves on.*) Come on, Lonnie.

ABE (*following somewhat timidly after him*). Colonel Mack, did di—you—what'd dey say over dere 'bout that little school business?

COLONEL. Bless my soul, 'bout to forgit it. I talked it over with the board and most of 'em think maybe we'd better not try it yet.

ABE (*his face falling*). When dey say it might be a good time? I gitting right 'long wid dat 'rithmetic and spelling and reading. I kin teach de colored boys and gals a whole heap right now, and I'll keep studying.

COLONEL (*impatiently*). Oh, I dunno. Time'll come mebbe. Mebbe time won't come. Folks is quare things y' know. (*He moves on.*)

ABE. Cain't you git 'em to let me try it awhile? Reckon—

COLONEL. I don't know, I tell you. Got my business on my mind now.

LONNIE. He's done told you two or three times, can't you hear?

ABE (*his eyes flashing and his voice shaking with sudden uncontrollable anger.*) Yeh, yeh, I hear 'im. Dem white folks don't keer—dey—

LONNIE (*stepping before him*). Look out! none of your sass. Pa's already done more for you than you deserve. He even stood up for you and they laughing at him there in town.

ABE (*trembling*). Yeh, yeh, I knows. But dem white folks don't think—I going to show 'em, I—

LONNIE (*pushing himself before him*). Dry up. Not another word.

ABE (*his voice breaking almost into a sob*). Don't talk to me lak dat, Mr. Lonnie. Stop him, Colonel Mack, 'fore I hurt him.

(*The other Negroes draw off into a knot by the pine tree, mumbling in excitement and fear.*)

COLONEL. Stop, Lonnie! Abe, don't you talk to my son like that.

LONNIE. By God, I'm going to take some of the airs off'n him right now. You've gone around here getting sorrier and more worthless every day for the last year. What you need is a good beating, and I'm gonna give it to you. (*He steps backwards and snatches the whip from his father's hand.*)

COLONEL. Stop that, Lonnie!

LONNIE. Keep out of this yourself. (*He comes towards* ABE.) I'll beat his black hide off'n him.

ABE. Keep 'im back dere, Colonel Mack. I mought kill him! Keep 'im off.

LONNIE. Kill him! All right, do it. There, damn you! (*He strikes* ABE *across the face with his whip. With a snarl* ABE *springs upon him, tears the whip from his hands and hurls him headlong into the thicket of briars and bushes. Then he stands with his hands and head hanging down, his body shaking like one with the palsy.*)

PUNY (*screaming*). You done kilt Mr. Lonnie! Oh, Lawdy, Lawdy!

COLONEL (*running to* LONNIE *who is crawling up out of the mud with his clothes and skin torn. He is sobbing and cursing*). Are you hurt? How bad are you hurt?

LONNIE. Let me git at that son of a bitch and I'll kill him dead. (*Moaning.*) Oh, I'll beat his brains out with one o' them axes.

COLONEL. If you ain't dead, you'd better keep your hands off'n him. I'll fix him. (*He reaches down and picks up the whip. Thundering.*) Git down on your knees, Abe! Git down, you slave! I'm gonna beat you.
(ABE *jerks his head up in defiance, but before the stern face of the* COLONEL *his strength goes out of him. He puts his hands up in supplication.*)

ABE. Don't beat me, Colonel Mack, don't beat me wid dat whip!

COLONEL. Git down on your knees! I've beat many a slave, and I'll show you how it feels. (*He strikes him several blows.*)

ABE (*falling on his knees*). Oh, Lawd, have muhcy upon me!
(*The* COLONEL *begins to beat him blow upon blow.* PUNY, BUD *and* LIJE *stand near the pine in breathless anxiety.*)

PUNY. De Colonel'll kill 'im!

BUD (*seizing his arm*). Shet dat mouf, nigger!

COLONEL (*as he brings the whip down*). Let this be a lesson to you to the end of your life!

ABE (*his back twitching under the whip, his voice broken*). Muhcy, Colonel Mack, muhcy!

COLONEL. You struck a white man, you struck my son.

ABE (*raising his tear-stained face*). I yo' son too, you my daddy. (*He throws himself down before him, embracing his feet. The* COLONEL *lowers the whip, then drops it behind him.*)

LONNIE (*his voice husky with rage*). You hear what he say? Hear what he called you? (*He seizes the whip and in a blind rage strikes the prostrate* ABE *again and again.*)

COLONEL (*stepping between them*). Stop it! Give me that whip. (LONNIE *nervelessly hesitates and then reluctantly hands him the whip.*) Go on back out to the road and wait for me. Trot! (LONNIE *in disgust and rage finally goes off at the left nursing his face and his arms.*) Get up, Abe. Get up, I say.
(ABE *sits up, hugging his face between his knees. The* COLONEL *wets his handkerchief in the spring, and with his hand on* ABE's *head bathes the bruises on his neck and shoulders.*)

ABE (*in a voice grown strangely dignified and quiet*). Thank 'ee, thank 'ee, Colonel Mack.

COLONEL (*breathing heavily*). Thanky nothing. I had to beat you, Abe, had to. Think no more about it. Dangerous thing, hitting a white man. But this is the end of it. Won't be no law, nothing but this. Put some tar and honey on yourself to-night and you'll be all right to-morrow. (*The bushes are suddenly parted at the rear and a tall sinuous young mulatto woman bounds through. She carries a bucket in her hand. At the sight of the* COLONEL *bathing* ABE's *head and neck she rushes forward with a low cry. The* COLONEL *turns towards her.*) Now, Goldie, ain't no use cutting up. Abe been in a little trouble. Nothing much.

GOLDIE (*moaning*). I heahd de racket and I 'fraid somebody being kilt. Is you hurt bad, Abe, honey babe? (*She bends tenderly over him, her hand running over his hair.*) Who huht you, honey, who huht you?

COLONEL (*handing* GOLDIE *his handkerchief*). Look after him, Goldie. (*He goes out at the left calling.*) Wait a minute, Lonnie!

GOLDIE. Whut dey do to you, Abe? Who huht you? (*All the time she is rubbing his neck, dabbing his shoulders with the handkerchief, and cooing over him.*) Why'n you kill dem white mens if dey hurt you? You kin do it, break 'em lak broomstraws.

ABE (*standing up*). Ain't nobody hurt me. I crazy dat's whut, crazy in de haid. Ain't nobody hurt me.

GOLDIE (*clinging to him*). You is hurt, hurt bad. Look at yo' po' neck and shoulders. Look at 'em beat wid great whales on 'em!

ABE (*growling*). Ain't nobody hurt me, I tell you.

GOLDIE. Lay yo'se'f down heah and let me smoove off yo' forehead and put some cold water on dat mark crost yo' face. Please'm, Abe.

ABE (*suddenly crying out in a loud voice*). I ain't nothing, nothing. Dat white man beat me, beat me like a dawg. (*His voice rising into a wail.*) He flail me lak a suckegg dawg! (*He rocks his head from side to side in a frenzy of wrath.*) Lemme git to him! (*He falls on his knees searching in the leaves and finds a stone.* GOLDIE *stands wringing her hands and moaning. He jumps to his feet, raising the stone high above his head.*) Lemme git to him, I scrush his God-damn head lak a egg shell! (*He moves to the left to follow the* COLONEL. GOLDIE *throws her arms around his neck.*)

GOLDIE. No, no, you ain't gwine out dere, Abe, Abe!

PUNY (*crying out*). Stop him, Bud! Lije, keep him back!

LIJE (*coming from the pine tree*). Hyuh, now you, Abe, stop dat.

BUD (*moving quickly before him and blocking his path*). Stop dat, fool. You gwine fix it to git yo'se'f hung up on a telegram pole. Body be so full o' holes, sift sand.

GOLDIE (*sobbing*). Don't do it, Abe, sugar babe. (*She throws herself upon his breast.*)

BUD (*reaching toward her*). Seem lak you take yo'se'f off'n dat man!

ABE (*pulling her arms from around him*). Lemme loose, lemme loose. (*After a moment he throws the stone down.*) I ain't going do nothing. (*He sits down on the log at the left, holding his head in his hands.*)

GOLDIE (*bringing her bucket*). Hyuh, eat sump'n, Abe, you feel better. I gut some pie and some cake in heah foh you.

PUNY (*stepping back and forth in senseless excitement*). Somebody gwine git kilt at dis mess, somebody—

ABE (*pushing* GOLDIE *away*). I ain't want nothing t' eat, ain't hongry.

LIJE. Bedder eat, Abe. Git yo' stren'th back.

ABE (*savagely*). Ain't hongry, I keep telling you.
(GOLDIE *drops on her knees beside him and laying her head in his lap clasps her arms around him.*)

GOLDIE (*sobbing softly*). Oh, boy, boy, why dey beat you up so? Whut you do to 'em?

ABE. Fool, fool I is. Crazy, dat's it.

BUD (*sharply*). He g'in Mr. Lonnie and de Colonel back talk. Cain't sass white mens and git 'way wid it. Abe orter know better.

(LIJE *wanders over to the right blowing his harp softly and forlornly.*)

PUNY (*sitting down on the ground*). Cain't be done, Abe. Cain't.

BUD (*stripping leaves from a bush and watching* GOLDIE *as she carries on over* ABE). Hyuh, o'man, stop dat rairing. (*Muttering to himself.*) Nevah see two bigger fools.

(ABE *puts his hands mechanically on* GOLDIE's *shoulders and begins stroking her.*)

ABE. Stop it, baby. Ain't no use to cry.

(PUNY *sits with his mouth open in astonishment watching them.* LIJE *lays himself back on the ground and blows his harp, apparently no longer interested.*)

BUD (*jealousy rising within him*). Heigh, Goldie, git up from dat man's lap. He ain't keer nothing foh you. (GOLDIE's *sobs die away and she is quiet.*) He say you foolish many time. He look down on you.

GOLDIE (*raising her tear-stained face*). How you know? You jealous, Bud Gaskins. He better man dan you. Wuth whole town of you. (*Catching* ABE *by the hand and picking up her bucket.*) Come on, come on, honey, le's go off dere in de woods and eat our dinner by ourse'ves!

BUD (*coming up to her*). Hyuh, you stay out'n dat woods wid him, nigger.

ABE (*standing up*). Yeh, yeh, I come wid you. (*He moves as one in a dream, and reaches out and pushes* BUD *behind him.*)

GOLDIE (*her face alight, a sort of reckless and unreal abandonment upon her*). I knows where dere's a cool place under a big tree. And dey's cool green moss dere and soft leaves. Le's go dere, boy. I gwine tend to you and feed you. (*She moves across towards the right, leading* ABE *like a child.*) We make us a bed dere, honey. (LIJE *sits up watching them.*) Us forgit de 'membrance o' all dis trouble. (*A kind of ecstasy breaking in her voice.*) Dere de

birds sing and we hear de little branch running over de rocks. Cool dere, sweet dere, you kin sleep, honey, rest dere, baby. Yo' mammy, yo' chile gwine love you, make you fohgit.

ABE (*moved out of himself*). Yeh, yeh, I come wid you. I don't keer foh nothing, not nothing no mo'. You, des' you'n me.

GOLDIE. Ain't no worl', ain't no Lije and Bud, nobody. Us gwine make us a 'biding place and a pillah under dat green tree. (*In sweet oblivion.*) Feel yo' arms around me, my lips on yo'n. We go singing up to heaben, honey, togedder—togedder. (*They go off, her voice gradually dying away like a nun's chant.*)

BUD (*breaking a sapling in his grasp*). Gwine off, gwine off in de woods togedder dere lak hawgs.

PUNY (*bounding up, his body shaking in lascivious delight*). I gwine watch 'em—hee-hee—I gwine watch 'em.

LIJE (*knocking him back*). Bedder stay out'n dat woods. Abe kill you.

PUNY (*standing up by the pine tree*). Kin see 'em, her still a-leading 'im.

LIJE (*standing up and peering off to the right*). Dere on de cool moss and de sof' green leaves.

BUD (*stripping the limbs from the top of the broken sapling*). Ain't gwine look. Dey fools, bofe fools. (*Raging out.*) Dere she go playing de hawg. Didn't know she lak dat. (*He sucks in his breath with the sound of eating something.*) Wisht to Gohd I knowed she lak dat, I de man foh her. Bud Gaskins. I tame her, Gohd damn her, I tame her down and take dat speerit out'n her. (*He crowds out his chest and walks up and down.*)

PUNY (*grasping* LIJE's *arm*). Cain't hardly see 'em no mo', kin you?

LIJE. Kin hardly.

BUD (*his anger and jealousy disappearing in physical emotion and vulgar curiosity*). Whah dey now?

LIJE (*pointing*). Dere, dere, dey crossing de branch now.

PUNY (*breathlessly*). I see 'em. I see 'em. He arm 'round her now, her head on he shoulder. (*He capers in his excitement.*) Lawd! Lawd!

BUD (*with a loud brutal laugh as he slaps* LIJE *on the back*). On de sof' green moss.

LIJE (*laughing back and dragging his harp across his mouth*). Whah de leaves is cool.

PUNY. Cain't see 'em no mo'. (*He whirls about and turns a handspring.*) Whoopee, folkses! Gwine run away wid myse'f!

BUD (*his eyes shining*). Down whah de branch water run. (*He shuffles a jig among the leaves.*)

LIJE (*blowing upon his harp*). Singing raght up to heaben! (*He plays more wildly as they all drop into a barbaric dance that gradually mounts into a dionysiac frenzy.*)

PUNY. Heaben!

BUD. Jesus, Lawd, Fadder and Son!

LIJE (*singing loudly as they dance, the music running into a quick thumping rhythm.*)

My feets wuh wet wid de sunrise dew,
De mawning stah wuh a witness too.
'Way, 'way up in de Rock of Ages,
In God's bosom gwine be my pillow.

(*They gambol, turn and twist, run on all fours, rear themselves up on their haunches, cavort like goats.*)

PUNY. In God's bosom—hanh!

BUD. In who bosom?

LIJE. In who bosom, bubber!
(*A loud halloo comes down from the hill in the rear, unnoticed by them.*)

PUNY. In Goldie's bosom. Hee-hee-hee.

BUD *and* LIJE. Haw-haw-haw! Hee-hee-hee! In God's bosom gwine be my pillah. (*The halloo is repeated.*)

LIJE. Hyuh, dere dat Gabe calling us. Better git, or de Colonel have dat stick on our back.
(*They gather up their buckets and axes.* PUNY *clambers up the pine a few feet and drops to the ground.*)

BUD. Kin see?

PUNY. See nothing. Hee-hee!

LIJE. Gut to leave 'em now. Abe ketch it 'gin don't mind. out. He not coming wid us.

BUD. He done foh now. Dat gal gut him hard and fast. (*Snorting scornfully.*) Books, books! Rise 'em up, lak hell!

LIJE. I done told you. Heart say dis, head say dat. Bad mixtry. Bad. Crazy!

PUNY (*shouting*). Heigh, you Gabe! Coming! (*They move out at the rear up the hill, singing, laughing and jostling each other.*)
'Way, 'way down by de sweet branch water
In her bosom gwine be he pillah!
Hee-hee—haw—haw—!
(*Their loud brutally mocking laughter floats back behind them.*)

SCENE II

A SPRING *day about three years later, in* ABRAHAM MCCRANIE'S *two-room cabin. The room is roughly built of framed material and unceiled. To the right front is a fireplace with a green oakwood fire going. A wood box is to the right of the chimney. To the left rear of the room is a bed, and at the left center rear a door leads out to the porch. To the right of the door a window gives a view of wide-stretched cotton fields. Below the window close to the wall is a rough home-made chest with several books on it, and hanging between* *it and the door is a sort of calendar, with the illustration of a slave leaving his chains behind and walking up a hill towards the sunrise. There is a caption at the top of the print in large letters—"*WE ARE RISING."* Several old dresses, bonnets, and coats hang on the nails in the joists in the right rear. A door in the right center leads into the kitchen. At the left front is a dilapidated old bureau, small pieces of wood taking the place of lost casters. The top drawer is open, sagging down like a wide lip, with stray bits of clothing hanging over the edge. A bucket of water and a pan are on the bureau. There are several splint-bottomed chairs and a rocker in the room.*

When the curtain rises MUH MACK *is sitting by the fire rocking a bundle in her arms. She is a chocolate-colored Negress of near sixty, dressed in a long dirty wrapper, and barefooted. Her graying hair is wrapped in pigtails and stands around her head Medusa-like. A long snuff-stick protrudes from her mouth, and now and then the fire sputters with a frying noise as she spits into it.* GOLDIE'S *long gaunt form lies stretched on the bed at the left partly covered by a sheet, her head hanging off on her arm. She is constantly raising in her languid hand a stick with a paper tied to it to shoo away the flies.* MUH MACK *rocks and sings.*

MUH MACK.

Oohm—oohm—hoonh—oohm—
    oohm—
Dis heah baby de pu'tiest baby,
Pu'tiest baby in de lan'.
He gwine grow up champeen sojer,
Mammy's honey, onlies' man.
Oohm—oohm—hoonh—oohm—
    oohm—

GOLDIE (*in a tired voice*). How he coming now?

MUH MACK (*shaking her finger and wagging her head at the bundle*). Done seem um grow. Look at me lak he know me.

GOLDIE (*with a long sigh*). I so tiahed, tiahed. Seem lak I kin sleep forever.

MUH MACK. Lie and sleep, sleep. Git yo' stren'th.

GOLDIE. I tiahed but cain't sleep. (*She lapses into silence. The old woman rocks and sings. Presently* GOLDIE *raises her head.*) Whut day to-day?

MUH MACK. Sa'd'y.

GOLDIE. Seem lak I cain't 'member nothing. Whut day he come?

MUH MACK. He comes a-Chuesday.

GOLDIE. Dat make him—le's see, how old?

MUH MACK. Fo' day now.

GOLDIE (*suddenly sitting up with a gasp*). Dem udder two die, one th'ee days, udder'n fo'.

MUH MACK. Nanh—nanh, lie back down. Dis heah baby live be a hundred. He strong, he muscled. Dem udder po' little 'uns puny, bawn to die. De mark was on 'em f'om de fust.

GOLDIE (*bending her head between her knees and weeping softly*). Dey was so pitiful and liddle. I cain't fohgit how dey feel and fumble foh me wid deir liddle hands and dey hongry.

MUH MACK (*irritably*). Bless Gohd, crying adder dem, and gut dis fine 'un heah. Lay yo'se'f down on dat bed and res'.

GOLDIE. Cain't fohgit 'em, cain't.

MUH MACK. Hunh, mought as well and dey done plowed in de ground.

GOLDIE (*her tears beginning to flow again*). Yeh, yeh, dey is! Abe didn't try to keep Mr. Lonnie f'om cutting down dem plum bushes and plowing up dat hedgerow. I' hold it a'gin him long as I live.

MUH MACK. Why foh? De dead's 'de dead. Let de earf hab 'em. Let cotton grow over 'um. No use mo'ning. Think on de living.

GOLDIE. Po' Abe, 'on't his fault dough. He proud, stand by see white mens plow over 'em, say nothin', 'on't beg foh his babies.

MUH MACK. Cain't blame 'im! He stiff neck. God break his spirit. Gi' 'im two dead 'uns to fetch 'im down. He bedder humble now. (*Talking half to herself.*) He talk proud lak, gwine raise up big son, leader 'mong men. Fust 'un come thin, liddle lak rat. He hate 'im. He die. God call 'im. Second come, Ol' Moster keep him liddle, thin. He die too. Abe gitting down to sackcloff and ashes. God see him down crying foh muhcy. He send dis 'un, strong. Israel man. He gwine flourish, he gwine wax.

GOLDIE (*stretching herself out on the bed*). Abe say dis 'un gwine die too, same lak de udders. He don't look at 'im, pay no 'tention.

MUH MACK. Hunh, he will dough when he see 'im fleshen up wid he sucking.

GOLDIE. Whah he?

MUH MACK. Went down in de new ground planting cawn. Won't make nothing dough and it de light o' de moon. He be heah directly foh he dinner.

GOLDIE. Po' Abe wuk too hard.

MUH MACK (*snorting*). Wuk too hahd de mischief! Ain't wuk whut ail him. He studyin' ol' books and mess too much. Crap shows it.

GOLDIE. He don't look well, neiver.

MUH MACK. Cain't look well and worry all time. (*A step is heard on the porch.*) Dere he now. Take dis baby. Gut to put dinner on de table. (*She takes the baby over to* GOLDIE, *lays it by her side, goes out at the right, and is heard rattling dishes and pans in the kitchen.*)

GOLDIE (*crooning over her baby*). Now you go sleep, res' yo'se'f, git strong and grow gre't big.
(ABE *comes in at the rear carrying a hoe and a file. He is barefooted and dressed in overalls, ragged shirt and weather-stained straw hat. Sitting down near the center of the room, he begins filing his hoe.*)

ABE (*without looking around*). How you come on?

GOLDIE. Better, I reckon. (*With a sharp gasp.*) Hyuh, why you fetch dat hoe in de house?

ABE (*paying no attention to her query*). Baby still living, hunh?

GOLDIE. Abe, take dat hoe out'n dis house. Mought bring bad luck on you. (*Raising herself up in bed.*) Mought bring sump'n on de baby.

ABE. Cain't swub dem new-ground bushes wid no dull hoe.

GOLDIE (*pleading*). Take it out'n de house, I say.

ABE. When I damn ready.

GOLDIE (*calling*). Muh Mack! Muh Mack!

MUH MACK (*coming to the door at the right*). Whut ails you? (*She sees* ABE *filing his hoe.*) Lawd he'p us! Throw dat thing out, throw it out! Ain't gut no sense. Goldie too weak to be worried up.

ABE. Aw right den. I finish wid it now. Set o' fools. Eve'ything got a sign 'tached to it. Ign'ant, bline! (*He throws the hoe out through the rear door and gets a book from the chest and begins reading.*)

MUH MACK. Back at dem books, Lawd, never see sich. (*She goes scornfully back to the kitchen.*)

ABE (*half growling*). Says heah niggers gut to git out'n dem 'spicions and being 'fraid. Ain't no signs wid evil and good in 'em. I read dat last night. (*Reading and halting over the words.*) "The Negro is a superstitious person. There are signs and wonders in the weather, some fraught with evil, some with good. He plants his crops according to the moon, works and labors under the eye of some evil spirit of his own imagining." (*Closing the book with a bang.*) Heah dat?

GOLDIE. I heah but don't mind it. Mean nothing. White man wrote it, and he don't know.

ABE. Dat's jest it; he do know. Nigger one don't know. Dat book wrote foh you, Muh, and all de rest of de bline.

GOLDIE. Put up dem ol' books. Seem lak you keer mo' foh 'em dan you do dis heah baby, and he a fine boy chile.

ABE (*throwing the book back on the chest*). What he nohow? Ain't 'rested in 'im. Ain't no use being. He be dead in week. God done cuss me and my household. No luck at nothing. Cain't raise chillun, cain't raise crap, nothing. Ain't dry weather, wet. Ain't wet, dry. Heah May month and cold 'nough foh freeze. (*He stretches his feet to the fire.*) De damn crows down dere on de creek pulling up my cawn faster'n I kin plant it. (*He rocks his head.*) Jesus!

GOLDIE (*pleading*). Abe, honey, don't git down. Things coming better now. Dis boy gwine make you feel better. Heah he lie now des' smiling lak he onderstand me. (*Bending over the baby.*) Yeh you is gwine grow up and take trouble off'n yo' po' daddy. Yeh, you is.

ABE (*holding his head in his arms*). Listen to dat talk, listen dere. (*Bitterly.*) 'Oman know. She know. Heah I am wid no money to buy me shoes. (*Holding up his dust-stained foot.*) Dere you is, foot, cut wid glass, full o' b'rars, wo' out stumping de roots and snags, and I cain't buy nothing to kiver you wid.

GOLDIE. De Colonel give you shoes, you ax him.

ABE. Ain't gwine ax him nothing, not nothing. (*Suddenly clenching his fist and hitting his thigh.*) Dat man beat me, beat me at de spring th'ee yeah ago, I ain't fohgit. (*He gets up and strides over to the bed and looks down at the suckling infant.*) Dere you lie drinking yo' grub in. Whut you keer? Nothing. (*He lays his hand roughly on the baby and pinches him. The child lets out a high thin wail.*)

GOLDIE (*beating his hand off*). Quit dat pinching dat baby. Quit it!

ABE (*laughing brutally as he walks up and down the floor*). Yeh, you fight over 'im now and he be plowed in de ground lak de udders in a month. Hee-hee! Ain't dis a hell of a mess! It sho' God is. And us ain't got 'nough to feed a cat. You'n Muh

cook and slay and waste fast I make it. Note at de sto' done tuck up, crap done all mortgaged up 'head o' time. Cain't make ends meet, cain't. (*Throwing his hands out hopelessly.*) I ain't no farmer.

GOLDIE (*wretchedly*). Oh, Abe, we git on somehow, us will. And Muh'n me don't waste. I be up wid you in de fields by de middle o' de week. Po' chile, you need sleep, need rest.

ABE. Make no difference. Wuk our guts out do no good. I tell you, gal, de Nigger is down, down. De white man up dere high, setting up wid God, up dere in his favor. He git eve'ything, nigger git de scraps, leavings. (*Flaring out.*) Ain't no God foh de nigger, dat's white man's God. Dat come to me down in de new ground. (*He sits down again, tapping his feet on the floor.*)

GOLDIE (*wiping her eyes*). Honey, you gut to stop talking lak dat. Cain't be bad luck allus. I'se 'feared when you talk dat wild talk. God heah it he do. (MUH MACK *comes and stands in the door.*) He mought be doing all dis to make us good, make us humble down befo' him.

ABE. Humble down, hell! Look at de udder niggers den. Dey shout and carry on in de church, pray and pay de preachers in deir blindness. Dey humble. What do God do? Starve 'em to deaf. Kill 'em off lak flies wid consumption. Dey dying 'long de river same as de chillun in de wilderness.

MUH MACK. You blaspheaming, da's whut you doing. No wonder Gohd take yo' babies 'way, no wonder he make yo' mule die, blast down yo' plans and send de crows and cold weather and root lice to destroy yo' craps. (*Her eyes flashing.*) You gut to change yo' ways. Some day he gwine re'ch down from de clouds and grab you by de scruff o' de neck and break you cross he knee. He gi'n you fine baby chile, you don't thank him. You gut to fall down, pray, git low, git humble. (*Her voice rises into a semi-chant.*) You dere, Jesus, heah my prayer. Dis heah sinner, he weeked, he blaspheam. Save him and save dis po' liddle baby.

GOLDIE (*weeping over the child*). Do, Lawd, heah our prayer.
(ABE *sits down in his chair and stares moodily into the fire.*)

MUH MACK (*crying out*). Dem dere ol' books cause it, da's whut. Burn um up, burn um wid fiah. Yo' wild talk gwine make de Upper Powers drap lightning on dis house, gwine destroy all of us. (*She wraps her arms before her, mumbling and swaying from side to side. Suddenly she raises her head and striding over to the chest shakes her fist at the books and kicks them.*) You de trouble. I hates de sight o' you, and I wish dere wa'n't nary one o' you in de worl'.

ABE (*throwing her back*). Look out 'oman! Don't you tech my books!

MUH MACK. You mash my arm! (*With a wail she goes out at the right and is heard sobbing in the kitchen.*)

GOLDIE. Oh, you struck huh! Abe—Abe— (*She sits up in the bed rocking the baby and quieting him. A heavy step sounds on the porch.* ABE *sits before the fire smoothing out the leaves of a book, as a voice calls from the outside.*)

VOICE. Heigh, you, Abe!

GOLDIE (*quickly*). Dat de Colonel out dere, Abe.

ABE (*going to the door*). Yes, suh, dat you, Colonel Mack?

COLONEL (*coming in*). Yes. How you come on, all of you? (*He looks around the room and at the bed. Three years have worked a great change in him. He is stouter, his face mottled, and he walks with difficulty, propped on a stick.*) Been wanting to see that fine baby, Abe.

ABE (*quietly*). Yes, suh, yes, suh.

MUH MACK (*coming in*). And he sho' is a fine 'un. (*Standing near the* COLONEL.) Fine and strong same lak Abe when he wuh bawn.

COLONEL. What's the matter, Goldie? Ain't been fighting, have you all? Who was that making a racket in here?

GOLDIE (*keeping her head lowered*). I all right, Colonel Mack.

MUH MACK (*wiping her eyes*). Ain't no row, Colonel. Want you to 'suade dat Abe git rid o' dem ol' books. 'Nough trouble come on us 'count of um.

COLONEL (*laughing*). The devil, let him keep his books. He's the only nigger in the whole country worth a durn. Let me see the baby. (GOLDIE *shows the baby.*) That's a fine un, Abe. He'll live. Let me feel him. (*Holding him up.*) Heavy, gracious! (MUH MACK *looks at him intently and there is the vaguest touch of malice in her voice as she speaks.*)

MUH MACK. Lawd, it all comes to me ag'in. Jest sech a day as dis thirty yeah ago you come down heah and hold Abe up dat-a-way.

COLONEL (*looking through the window a long while*). Time hurries on, it goes by in a hurry. (ABE *looks before him with an indefinable expression on his face. A constrained silence comes over them and the* COLONEL *takes a sort of refuge in gazing intently at the child. Once or twice he clears his throat.*) Yes, Callie, we're getting old.
(*For an instant all differences are passed away and they are four human beings aware of the strangeness of their lives, conscious of what queer relationships have fastened them together.*)

MUH MACK (*starting*). Yes, suh, we ain't gut much longer.
(*Then the baby begins to cry and the* COLONEL *smiles.*)

COLONEL. Here, take him, Goldie. Favors Muh Mack, don't favor you, Abe.

ABE. Yes, suh.

COLONEL (*drawing a heavy, folded paper from his pocket slowly and with weighty dignity*). I got a little surprise for you'n Goldie, Abe. (*He puts on his spectacles, opens the paper and starts to read.*) "Whereas"—(*He stops as if convulsed with pain, and presently goes on.*) "I devise to Abraham McCranie a house and tract of land containing twenty-five acres and formerly known as the 'Howington place,' to him and his heirs forever." (*Hesitating a moment and folding the paper together.*) Then follows a description of the place in course and distance, Abe, which I won't read. It's all signed up and recorded in the court-house. (*He feels around him heavily for his stick.*)

ABE (*incredulously*). Whut dat? Dat foh me?

COLONEL. Yes, for you. A deed to this house and twenty-five acres of land, yours. (*He holds out the paper to* ABE.)

ABE (*taking it with trembling hands*). Lawd, Colonel Mack, whut I gwine say?

COLONEL. Say nothing. Say thanky if you want to.

ABE (*overcome*). Thanky, suh, thanky, suh.

COLONEL. Shake hands on it, Abe.

ABE (*wiping his hand on his coat*). Thanky, suh.
(*The* COLONEL *looks at his bent head with strange intentness, and then drops* ABE'S *hand.*)

GOLDIE. Oh, Colonel Mack! (*Her eyes are shining with thankfulness.*)

MUH MACK. Abe, you's gut land, boy, you owns you a piece o' land, Glory! (*She runs up to the* COLONEL *and covers his hands with kisses.*)

COLONEL (*waving her off*). Nothing, nothing to do for him. He deserves it. (*Looking straight at* ABE.) You do, boy. I want to see you go forward now. You had a hard time the last three years.

GOLDIE. He has, po' boy. He had it hard since de day he married me.

COLONEL. Hunh. He couldn't a done better nowhere. I know. (*The* COLONEL *picks up his stick which he has laid across the bed.*) Well, I got to move on. (*He stops near the door.*) And, Abe, how's your book business coming on?

ABE. I—I studying and reading now and den. Most too tiahed every night dough to do much.

COLONEL. Don't give up like Lonnie. Sent him to school, and sent him to school, even tried him at the university, won't stay. He ain't worth a damn, that's what. (*Turning towards the door and stopping again.*) Well, I've got another little surprise for you in celebration of that fine boy. (*He looks down and taps on the floor.*)

ABE (*excitedly*). Whut is it, Colonel Mack, suh?

COLONEL. How'd you like to try your hand at teaching a little school next fall?
(MUH MACK *throws up her hands.*)

GOLDIE (*breathlessly*). Oh, me!

ABE (*in confusion*). Teach school? Yessuh, I—

COLONEL. I'm going to have that old Quillie House fixed up and put some benches in it and a blackboard. I'll get two Negroes to serve with me on the school board and we'll try you out. (*Smiling queerly.*) I been reading your books, too, Abe.

ABE (*with a great breath*). I gwine teach school—at last!

COLONEL (*going shakily out at the door*). Yes, at last. Now don't forget your crop, Abe, and study yourself to death.

ABE (*following him*). Colonel Mack, you, you—I—I—

COLONEL. Take care of that baby. Raise him up right. And, Abe, don't forget you ain't gonna have no easy time. I'll get a lot of cussing for this, well as you. Go on eat your dinner. (*He stops on the porch and calls.*) Here, Goldie, take this fifty cents and buy the boy a stick of candy. (*He steps to the door and throws the coin on the bed.*) Take care of him and don't kill him on collards and beans. (*He goes off.*)

ABE (*calling after him*). I ain't, Colonel, I gwine raise him. I gwine make a man— (*He stops and stands watching the old man going in the lane. Then he turns and stumbles into the room with shining face.*) I— I fohgives him all. I don't 'member dat beating by de spring no mo'.

GOLDIE (*reaching out from the bed and grasping his hand*). Oh, honey babe, our troubles's ended. We gwine—we gwine have 'nough t' eat and you gwine be happy. (*She turns over in the bed and begins to cry softly.*)

ABE (*patting her shoulders*). Dere, dere, don't you cry, chile. (*He wipes his eyes with his sleeve.*) I been mean man. (*In a husky voice.*) I treat my gal mean, blaspheam 'gin de Lawd. I gwine do better, I— (*A sob chokes in his throat.*)

MUH MACK (*coming up to him and clasping her arms around him*). Bless de Lawd, you gwine do bedder now. (*She sits down in a chair and bows her head in her lap.*)

GOLDIE. He good man, de Colonel. He too good to us. Raise us up, help us.

ABE (*vaguely*). Up! Lift me up! Up! Up tow'd de sun! (*He glances at the calendar.*) Dat whup don't hurt no mo'. De 'membrance is passed away. (*Thumping on his breast.*) Ain't no mo' bitter gall in heah. Peace. It come all suddent over me. (*He suddenly falls on his knees by the bed in a sobbing burst of prayer.*) O God, God of de po' and of de sinful!

MUH MACK. Yea, our God.

ABE. De black man's God, de white man's God, de one and only God, heah me, heah my prayer.

MUH MACK (*swaying and moaning*). Heah 'im, Jesus!

GOLDIE (*softly*). We dy chillun, Lawd.

ABE. Dy little chillun, and you pow'ful. You de Almighty, us de dust in dy hand. Us po' and weak, us nothing. Lak de grasshopper, lak de po' fee-lark, swept away in de storm. Man gut no stren'th in um, no muscle kin raise him 'cepting yo' power. He walk in de wind, de wind take 'im away. Let dere be fiah, and de fiah burn um. It devour 'im. Same lak de broomstraw he fall befo' it. Man cain't stand. He lost, lost. Shet in de grave, shet till de judgment.

MUH MACK. Jesus! Jesus!

GOLDIE (*piteously*). Jesus!

ABE. He fall in de winter. He lie down in de summer. De spring come and find him gone.

MUH MACK. Ha' muhcy, our Fadder.

GOLDIE (*whispering*). Jesus, fohgive 'im.

ABE (*his voice rising into a chant*). De dirt stop up his po' mouf. Peace come to him in de ground. And de friends do cry, dey wail and beat deir breas'. Dey call foh deir love' ones, and dey don't answer. Deir tongue make no mo' speech, from de graveyard, from de deep grave.

MUH MACK. Yea, Lawd!

ABE. Dey gone at de planting, gone at de harvest. De hoe dull wid rust, de harness wait on de peg, de bridle hang, de collar hang dere useless. Dey ain't no mo' hoeing, ain't no mo' plowing, no shoe track in de furrow. Man gone, same lak a whisper, hushed in de graveyard, in de deep grave.

MUH MACK. Oh, ha' muhcy 'pon us.

GOLDIE. Muhcy!

ABE (*raising his head up, his eyes closed*). Heah us, heah us, heah me dis day, heah my po' prayer. Fohgive me my sins, my blaspheamy. Wipe out de evil o' my weeked days. Purify, make clean, fohgit de 'membrance o' my transgression. Now heah I do humble down, I do cohnfess. Lift me, raise me, up, up!

MUH MACK. Hallelujah!

GOLDIE. Amen.

ABE (*bowing his head in a storm of grief*). Re'ch down yo' hand and gimme stren'th. Now I draw nigh, I feel yo' spirit. Save me, save me now! (MUH MACK *and* GOLDIE *pray and moan aloud. Presently* ABE *stands up and cries out exultantly.*) He save me, he done save me! He done fohgive me!

MUH MACK (*clapping her hands wildly*). Bless de Lawd, bless um!

GOLDIE (*faintly*). Thank Jesus, save my baby and my husban'.

ABE *is silent a moment, his face working with emotion. He turns and bends down over the bed.*)

ABE. Po' little fellow, he sleep and rest. (*He puts his arms around* GOLDIE *and she clings to him.*) Honey chile, I changed. I gwine take new holt. From dis day I begins. I sorry foh all de past. (*He loosens her arms from around his neck and stands up, a strange set look on his face.*) I gwine keep heart now, look up, rise. I gwine lead. (*Looking down at the baby.*) I gwine raise him up a light unto peoples. He be a new Moses, he bring de chillun out of bondage, out'n sin and ign'ance. (*He turns suddenly and goes to the bucket at the left, pours some water out in a pan and sets it on the bed. Then he bends down and lifts the baby in his hand.* MUH MACK *looks up, drying her eyes.*)

GOLDIE. Whut dat, Abe? Whut dat you doing?

ABE (*dipping his hand in the water and holding the child aloft, his face lighted up in a beatific smile.*) On dis day I names you Douglass. You gwine be same lak him. Yeh, better. You gwine be a light in darkness, a mighty man. (*He dips his hand into the water and sprinkles the child.*) I baptize you and consecrate you to de salvation ob my people dis day! Amen!
(*The women stare at him transfixed, caught out of themselves. He bends his head and stands with the child stretched before him as if making an offering to some god.*)

SCENE III

WINTER *of the same year. The old Quillie house, a Negro cabin of one bare room, now fitted up as a school-house. At the left center is a squat rusty cast-iron stove, the pipe of which reels up a few feet and then topples over into an elbow to run through the wall. A box of pine knots rests on the floor by it. Four or five rough pine benches, worn slick by restless students, stretch nearly the length of the room, ending towards a small blackboard nailed to the wall in the rear center. Between the benches and the blackboard is the teacher's rickety table with a splint-bottomed chair behind it. A heavy dinner bell with a wooden handle is on the table. To the right rear is a small window, giving a glimpse of brown broomsedge stretching up a gentle hill, and beyond, a ragged field of stripped cornstalks, gray now and falling down in the rot of winter rains. To the left rear is a door opening to the outside.*

The curtain rises on the empty room. Presently ABRAHAM MCCRANIE *comes in, carrying a tin lunch bucket and two or three books. He is wearing an old overcoat and a derby hat, both making some claims to a threadbare decency. He sets the bucket and books on the table and hangs his coat and hat on a nail in the wall at the right; then comes back to the stove, revealing himself dressed in baggy trousers, worn slick with too much ironing, heavy short coat, cheap shirt, and a celluloid collar with no tie. With his pocket-knife he whittles some shavings from a pine knot and starts a fire in the stove. He looks at his watch, beats his hands together from cold, and stirs about the room, his brow wrinkled in thought and apparent worry. Again and again he goes to the door and stares out expectantly. Looking at his watch the second or third time, he takes up the bell and goes out and rings it.*

ABE (*shouting towards the empty fields*). Books! Books! Come in to books! (*He returns and sits down by the stove.*) No scholars in sight. (*With a sigh.*) Oh, me! (*He goes to the board and writes laboriously across the top:* "January 21. An idle brain is the devil's workshop." (*While he is writing, three Negro students come in carrying a bucket and a book or two each —a lazy slumbrous girl of eighteen or twenty, a stout thick-lipped youth about the same age, and a little serious-faced ragged boy of ten. ABE's face brightens at the sight of them.*) Good morning, chillun. Late. Everybody a little late.

STUDENTS (*standing uncertainly around the stove*). Good morning, Mr. Mack.

ABE (*finishing his writing*). This will be our motto foh to-day. (ABE's *speech has improved somewhat. When he speaks with conscious deliberation he substitutes "this" for "dis," "that" for "dat," and so on. But when in a hurry or excited he drops back into his old methods. He addresses the little boy.*) Read it, Eddie, out loud.

EDDIE (*eagerly*). I kin read it, Mr. Mack. (*In a slow and halting voice he reads.*) "A' idle brain is the devuh's wukshop."

ABE. Good, fine. Kin you read it, Neilly?

NEILLY (*boldly*). Yeh, suh, read it raght off.

ABE. And how 'bout you, Lanie?

LANIE (*dropping her heavy-lidded eyes*). I kin too. (*She and* NEILLY *look at each other with a fleeting smile over some secret between them.* EDDIE *gazes up at them, his lips moving silently as if over something to be told which he dare not utter.*)

ABE (*pulling out his watch*). Twenty minutes to nine. Whah the other scholars? (*No one answers.* NEILLY *gives the girl a quick look and turns deftly on his heel and kicks the stove, sticking up his lips in a low whistle.*) You see the Ragland chillun on the road, Lanie?

LANIE (*enigmatically*). Yessuh, I see 'em. (ABE *goes to the door and rings his bell again.*)

ABE. Books! Books! Come in to books! (*He puts the bell on the table and stands pondering.*) How 'bout the Maffis chillun?

NEILLY. Ain't coming!

ABE. Dey say so?

NEILLY. Yessuh.

ABE (*shortly*). Take yo' seats. We'll go on wid our lessons if nobody else' don't come. (*He turns to his table.*)

EDDIE (*pulling excitedly at* LANIE's *dress*). G'won, ax him whut he gwine do.

LANIE (*snatching herself loose from him*). Shet up. Ain't my business.

ABE. Put yo' buckets up and take yo' seats and listen to the roll-call. All the late ones ketch it on the woodpile and sweeping up the school-yard. (*Eyeing them.*) I said take yo' seat. (EDDIE *hurries to his seat.*)

NEILLY. Ain't gwine have no school, is we?

ABE. Hunh?

NEILLY. Ain't gwine be no mo' school.

(LANIE *giggles.*)

ABE (*with a worried note in his voice*). Going have school same as usual. Seem lak all of 'em late dough. Take yo' seats, time foh the spelling lesson. Won't have de scripture reading dis mawning.

NEILLY. De rest of 'em done quit school. (LANIE *giggles again.*)

ABE. Stop dat giggling and go to yo' seat. (LANIE *moves to her seat sulkily.*)

EDDIE (*in a high frightened quaver*). Mr. Mack, dey all say de school ain't gwine run no mo' and dey ain't coming.

ABE. How dey hear it? I ain't heard it. (*No one answers.*) Whah'd you folks get all dis news, Neilly?

NEILLY. Dey was all talking it down de road. We wouldn't a-come eiver, but Eddie dah beg me and Lanie so hard to come wid 'im. Ain't no mo' folks coming dough.

ABE (*hitting the table with his fist*). Sump'n' up. Dey got to show me fo' I quits, dey got to show me. Putt up yo' buckets and things, we going have school. (*They reluctantly set down their buckets near the wall and stand waiting.*) Take yo' seats, I say, and listen to yo' name. (*He pulls out a cheap arm-and-hammer memorandum book and begins calling the roll.*) Lanie Horton.

LANIE. Presunt. (*She looks around at the bare seats and gives her sensational giggle.*)

ABE. Vanderbilt Jones, absent; 'Ona May Jordan, absent; Jane Matthews, absent; Sister Matthews, absent; Jennie McAhlister, absent; Neilly McNeill.

NEILLY. Present. (*He smiles at* LANIE.)

ABE. Arthur Ragland, absent. Didn't 'spect him back nohow. Dora Ragland, absent; Nora Ragland, absent; Eddie Williams.

EDDIE. Prizzunt.
(ABE *sits drumming on the table and staring before him. The students twist about on their seats in embarrassment.*)

ABE (*roughly*). Spelling lesson! (*The three move out and stand in a line before him.*) How many of you been over it at least fo' times?
(EDDIE *raises his hand.*)

EDDIE. I been over it nine times fo'w'd and six back'ards.

ABE. You, Neilly?

NEILLY. I been over it onct and part twict, Mr. Mack.

ABE. Lanie?

LANIE. I dunno hardly.

ABE. Have you studied it any?

LANIE (*pouting*). I done lost my book somewhah.

ABE. And you wuh supposed to be head today. You'n Neilly kin clean up the paper and sweep 'round the well at recess. Le's see yo' book, Eddie. (EDDIE *hands him his book.*) Eddie you got a head-mark yistiddy; so you foot to-day. (*Opening the book.*) The first word is "chew," chew, lak vittles, Lanie, "chew."

LANIE. C-c. C-u, "chew."

ABE. One mo' trial.

LANIE (*pondering a long while*). I cain't spell dat.

ABE. Yes, you kin. Try it.

LANIE. C-h-u, "chew."

ABE. Next.

NEILLY (*smiling ruefully*). Too hahd foh me. Des' well pass on.

ABE (*working his jaws up and down*). Watch me wuk my jaws. That's chew, chewing. Spell at it, Neilly, "chew."

NEILLY (*scratching his head and nervously boring the floor with the toe of his shoe*). Cain't do it, cain't fohm no letters in my head.

ABE. I'll have to pass it den.

NEILLY (*taking a hopeless shot at it*). S-s. S-u, "chew." No, dat wrong. I seed dat word on de page, but cain't remember it now. I cain't spell it. Gi' it to Eddie, he kin.

ABE. All right, Eddie.

EDDIE. C-h-e-w—"chew." (*He darts around* NEILLY *and* LANIE *and stands triumphantly at the head of the class.*)

ABE. I goin' send you back to yo' seats to study twenty minutes. Then come back heah and don't you make no such mess of it. I'll put the writing lesson up while you study. (*They go to their seats.*) Lanie, you look wid Eddie in his book. (*He turns to the board and begins to write down the copy models. As he writes, the students mumble over their words in a drone.* NEILLY *and* LANIE *begin talking to each other in low whispers.* EDDIE *is lost in his book.* LANIE *suddenly giggles out loud, and* ABE *turns quickly from his board.*) Heigh you, Lanie, stand up in dat corner over thah. School isn't out yit.

LANIE. I ain't done nothing. (*Half audibly.*) "Isn't!"

ABE. Don't talk back. Stand in de corner wid yo' face to de wall. Hyuh, Eddie, you read in dis reader and let her have yo' book.

(LANIE *creeps over to the corner and mouths over her lesson.* ABE *finishes his apothegm,* "A Wise man will rise with the sun, or before it." *He is finishing another,* "Wise children will imitate the manners of polite people," *when there is a stir at the door and* PUNY AVERY *comes in, swallowed up in a teamster's coat and carrying a long blacksnake whip in his hand.*)

PUNY. Good mawning.

ABE. Good morning, Mr. Avery.
(*At the appellation of* "Mister" PUNY *stuffs his cap against his mouth to hide a grin.*)

PUNY. How you come on, Mr. McCrainie? Kin I warm my hands a minute? Freezing col' setting on dat waggin seat. (*He moves up to the stove and stretches his hands above it.*)

ABE. Help yo'se'f. Be a snow fo' night, I believe.

PUNY. Yeh, or—look lak it. (*He warms himself, and* ABE *sits at the table watching him questioningly. Now and then his gaze drops upon the whip.*)

ABE. Hauling lumber over the river?

PUNY. Is dat. (*Looking at* LANIE *in the corner.*) Whut she do?

ABE. Misbehaved.

PUNY. Seem lak yo' school kinda thin. (ABE *says nothing.*) Been gitting thinner ev'y since Colonel died last fall, ain't it?

ABE. Been dropping off some since then.

PUNY. Whah all de rest o' de scholars?

ABE. Haven't showed up yet.

PUNY. Uhm.

ABE. Why you want to know, might I ask.

PUNY (*authoritatively*). Already know. And foh yo' own good I come by to tell you and to bring you a message.

ABE (*looking at him intently and then waving his hand at the three students*). You chillun kin go out and have recess now. Mr. Avery wants to see me on a little business. (LANIE *and* NEILLY *get their coats and walk out.* EDDIE *remains crouched in his seat, unconscious of his surroundings.*) What message you got foh me?

PUNY. You des' well quit de school business raght heah and now. Dey ain't gwine send to you no mo'.

ABE. What's the trouble?

PUNY. Trouble! You gone and done it, you has, when you beat Will Ragland's boy yistiddy. Will so mad he kin kill you.

ABE (*anger rising in his voice*). Needn't think I'm skeahed of him.

PUNY. I knows you ain't. But you wants to keep on teaching, don't you?

ABE. Yeh, and I'm going to.

PUNY. Nunh-unh, you ain't neiver. Will went 'round last night and gut everybody to say dey won't gwine send to you no mo'. Dey ain't gwine stand foh no nigger beating deir young 'uns.

ABE (*angrily*). I had a right to beat him. I couldn't make him work no other way, and 'sides he told a lie to me. Said he didn't eat up po' little Sis Maffis' dinner. Several of 'em seen him do it.

PUNY. Cain't he'p it. You beat 'im so dey had to have a doctor foh him, and Will done gone to de sher'ff to git out papers foh you.

ABE (*starting out of his chair*). Gwine have me 'rested?

PUNY. He is dat. And mo', I reckon. And my advice to you is to git f'om heah. As a member of de school boa'd I say, bedder leave.

ABE. He think he kin run me 'way?

PUNY. Don't know what he think. Know I wouldn't lak to lie in no white man's jailhouse, dat's me.

ABE. De otheh members of the boa'd know 'bout it?

PUNY. Us had a meeting last night.

ABE. What dey say?

PUNY (*fumbling in his pockets*). Dey all side wid Will, 'count o' de beating and 'count o' dat speech you made in chu'ch last Sunday.

ABE. Wuh Mr. Lonnie dere?

PUNY. He dere and he send dis heah writing to you. (*He pulls a note from his pocket and hands it to* ABE, *who opens it excitedly.*)

ABE (*clenching his fist*). Dat man say heah —God—He say de boa'd done all 'cided de school got to stop. (*He tears the note to pieces and throws it in the stove.*) He say dere he know a good job in Raleigh at public wuk he kin git me. (*Bitterly.*) Say I do better at dat dan farming or school. (*Pacing the floor, he throws his hand above his head.*) Nanh, anh—suh, I sets a oaf on high, I ain't going let 'em run me off. Dey cain't skeah me. Dey cain't run me off lak I stole sump'n'. (*He turns on* PUNY *with blazing eyes and* EDDIE *watches him terrified.*) Why you all vote dat way? Whyn't you stand up and vote foh me? You know I trying do right. You weak, coward, no backbone.

PUNY (*backing towards the door*). I ain't gut nothing 'gin you, Abe. Why you 'buse me?

ABE. Git out o' heah. All o' you down on me. Dat speech was so. It was right. Dat beating was right. (*Crying out.*) I ain't gwine give in. Dey cain't run me. You cain't run me. I fight 'em. I stay heah. Let 'em putt me in de jail, I last till de jail rot down. (*He moves menacingly towards* PUNY, *who flees through the door and slams it after him.*) I come through deir bars, deir iron won't hold me. I'll git dere, I'll come. My flesh will be as tough as deir iron! (*He goes to the table and picks up*

his books. He opens the Bible and stands thinking. Dropping into his chair, he sits with his elbow on the table and his chin in his hand, gazing into the distance. The anger and bitterness gradually pass from his face.*) Dat man's talk, proud. Cain't push through 'thout help—(*putting his hand on the Bible*) 'thout help from up there. (*He bows his head on the table.* EDDIE *begins to sob and, leaving his seat timidly, approaches* ABE's *bent form, gulping and wiping his nose and eyes with his sleeve.* ABE *looks up and puts his arm around him.*) Son, this heah's the last of this school. But we cain't stop, we got to keep on. (EDDIE *leans his head against him, his sobs increasing.*) Got to keep studying, got to keep climbing. (*After a moment he stands up and writes across the board,* "This School is stopped for a while." LANIE *and* NEILLY *come inquiringly in.*) Chillun, ain't goin' to be no mo' school till mebbe next yeah. You kin go home. LANIE *giggles and* NEILLY *looks at him with familiar condescension.*) But I wants to dismiss with a word of prayer. (*At a sign from him,* EDDIE *falls on his knees by the table. He gets down at his chair.*) Our Father, where two or three is gathered—(NEILLY *and* LANIE *look at him, pick up their buckets and scurry out giggling and laughing loudly.* ABE *springs to his feet, his face blank with astonishment. He calls after them furiously.*) Heigh, heigh, you!
(*They are heard going off, their sharp laughter softening in the distance.*)

NEILLY. 'Fo' Gohd, he down on his knees!

LANIE (*her voice growing faint*). Yeh, and he 'bout kilt Arth yistiddy.

NEILLY. Haw—haw—haw.

LANIE. Hee—hee—hee.
(*Their voices die away.*)

SCENE IV

FIFTEEN *years later. A room in the poverty-stricken Negro section of Durham, North Carolina, as it was then. When the curtain rises,* GOLDIE *is washing at a tub placed on a goods-box at the left of the room.* MUH MACK *is seated at the fireplace at the right, bent under a slat bonnet and dozing. Pots and pans are piled around the hearth and a kettle is singing on the fire. Several garments are hanging on chairs before the fire drying.*

To the left rear is a bed with a pile of rough-dried clothes on it. A door at the center rear leads into another room. To the right of the door is a low chest with books and dishes set upon it. At the right front by the chimney is a small window letting in the sickly light of a dying winter day. In the center of the room is a small eating-table covered with a greasy, spotted oil-cloth.

For several minutes neither of the women says anything. GOLDIE *washes heavily at the tub, her body bent and disfigured with the years of toil and poverty and the violence of childbirth. She wrings out a garment and takes it to the fireplace.*

GOLDIE (*lifelessly*). Move yo'se'f, Muh. Lemme hang up dis shirt.

MUH MACK (*testily us she moves her chair with her body*). Lemme 'lone. Cain't sleep, rest—nothing.
(GOLDIE *drags up a chair, hangs the shirt on it and returns to her washing. Her movements are slow, ox-like, and in her eyes now and then comes a sort of vacant look as if some deadening disease has had its way within her brain, or as if trouble and worry have hardened her beyond the possibility of enthusiasm or grief any more. Between her eyes a deep line has furrowed itself, a line often found on the foreheads of those who think a great deal or those who are forgetting how to think at all. And her mouth has long ago fastened itself into a drawn anguished questioning that has no easeful answer in the world. She washes away at the tub, the garment making a kind of flopping sound against the board. After a moment she calls* MUH MACK.)

GOLDIE. Gitting neah 'bout day-down, Muh. Time to start supper.

MUH MACK (*whom age and poverty have made meaner than before*). Yeh, yeh, it is, and I gut to git it, I reckon.

GOLDIE (*making an effort to hurry*). Yeh, Mis' Duke got to have her clothes to-morrow, I done said.

MUH MACK (*getting slowly to her feet*). Oh, me my! My leg done gone to sleep! (*She fumbles among the pans on the hearth.*) Yo' water hyuh all gwine bile 'way.

GOLDIE. Gimme hyuh! (*She takes the kettle and pours the water into the tub and then goes on scrubbing the clothes.*)

MUH MACK. Whut I gwine cook?

GOLDIE. Make some cawn bread, and dey's a little piece o' Baltimo' meat in de chist.
(MUH MACK *arranges her pan on the fire with much grumbling and growling and goes over to the chest.*)

MUH MACK (*knocking the pile of books off with a bang*). Heah dem ol' books of Abe's piled right hyuh in de way. Minner mind to burn 'em up. Allus whah dey ain't gut no business.

GOLDIE (*abstractedly*). Yeh, yeh. Always minner mind to burn 'em.
(MUH MACK *opens the chest and pulls out a small piece of white meat.*)

MUH MACK. Hunh, look at dis, will you? Ain't mo'n 'nough to fill my old hollow toof. Cain't us git sump'n' else foh supper? I et dat old meat and cawn bread till it makes me heave to look at it.

GOLDIE. Dat all dey is.

MUH MACK. Dat won't make a mou'ful foh Abe. Whut we gwine eat?

GOLDIE. Abe won't eat it nohow, and I don't want nothing. You'n Douglass kin eat it.

MUH MACK. Bofe of you gwine die if you don't eat. Dat Abe been living off'n cawfee and bread two weeks now. No wonder he look lak a shadow and cain't ha'f do his work.

GOLDIE. Cain't eat when you ain't gut it.

MUH MACK. Well, starving ain't gwine give you stren'th to git no mo'. How you gwine keep washing foh folks and you don't eat?

GOLDIE (bowing her head in weariness over the tub, her voice rising with sudden shrillness). Oh, Lawd Gohd in heaven, I don't know.

MUH MACK. Calling on Gohd ain't gwine he'p you git no supper eiver. (Throwing the meat back into the chest and slamming the lid.) Well, I ain't gwine cook dat old mess. I'll set right heah by dis fiah and starve wid you and Abe.

GOLDIE (drying her hands on her apron). I gut des' one mo' fifty-cent piece in dat pocketbook. I'll git it and run out and buy some liver den. Po' Abe gut to live somehow. (She goes out at the rear and returns immediately holding an empty ragged purse in her hand.) Whah my ha'f dollar! Whah is it?

MUH MACK (dropping into a chair by the fire). Hunh, needn't ax me. Ain't seed it.

GOLDIE (sitting down and rocking back and forth). Somebody stole it. (Turning upon MUH MACK.) You done gin it to dat Douglass.

MUH MACK. Ain't.

GOLDIE. Yeh, you has, you has.

MUH MACK (beating the floor with her foot). Ain't, I tell you.

GOLDIE (staggering to her feet). And he off somewhah's spending it foh ice-cream and mess.

MUH MACK. Don't keer 'f I did. Po' boy do widdout all de time.

GOLDIE (falling on the tub with renewed vigor). Cain't cry now!

MUH MACK. G'won down dere and git dat man to let you have sump'n' on a credit. You can pay 'im to-morrow when Mis' Duke pay you.

GOLDIE. He done said he ain't gwine let us have no mo' widdout de money.

MUH MACK. Mebbe Abe fetch sump'n' when he come.

GOLDIE. How kin he and dey won't pay 'im off till to-morrow evening?

MUH MACK (suddenly crying out with a whimper). Look lak us gwine starve spite of all. I wants to go back home. I wants to go back to home. Mr. Lonnie won't let us do widdout.

GOLDIE. I been wanting to go back foh fifteen yeah, but Abe's gwine die fo' he go back.

MUH MACK (beating her hands together in her lap). Crazy, crazy! He de biggest fool in de whole world. He gitting down lower eve'y day. Gitting sick wuss all de time. Oh, me, whut'll become of us all!

GOLDIE (hopelessly). De Lawd mebbe'll pervide.

MUH MACK (snorting). Hunh, he mought. He ain't gwine pervide nothing less'n us do sump'n'. (Her voice falling into a sort of hypocritical whine.) Heah I is all laid up wid rheumatiz and cain't see how to trabbel no mo' and 'bout to starve. Starve, heah me!

GOLDIE (dropping into her chair again). You ain't de on'y one.

MUH MACK. Reckon I knows it. But dat don't keep my stomach f'om cutting up.

GOLDIE. We doing de best we kin by you.

MUH MACK (somewhat softened). I knows it, chile, but dat Abe, dat Abe, I say! He de trouble at de bottom of it all.

GOLDIE. Needn't keep talking 'bout Abe. Why don't you say dat to his face. He doing de best he kin.

MUH MACK (*her anger rising*). I will tell him. Dere you set, Goldie McCranie, and say dat, after he done drug you f'om pillar to post foh fifteen yeah. Doing de best he kin! He ain't nothing, des' wuss'n nothing! He des' a plumb fool. But he mammy wuh a fool befo' 'im. Da's how come he in dis worl'.

GOLDIE. Stop dat. He sick, been sick a long time, po' fellow, and he keep trying.

MUH MACK. Sick! He wa'n't sick back dere when he got into co't and lost all his land trying to git dem lawyers to keep 'im out'n jail, and he beat dat Will Raglands boy ha'f to death. (GOLDIE *bows her head in her hands, swaying from side to side.*) De devil in him! Dat's what.

GOLDIE (*wretchedly*). You done sot dere by dat fiah and told me dat same tale time and ag'in, day in, day out. I don't want to heah it no mo'.

MUH MACK. Unh-unh. And I reckon you will dough. Wuh he sick, and he cutting up a rust in Raleigh and de niggers and white folks runnin' him out'n dere? It was old Scratch in him dere too. I tells you.

GOLDIE. Dey didn't treat 'im right over dere.

MUH MACK. Hunh. No, dey didn't. And dey didn't treat him raght in Greensboro, did dey? Same old tale dere, gitting in a row wid somebody and ha' to leave. He's mean, mean lak sump'n' mad at de world.

GOLDIE (*tossing her head about her*). I dunno. I dunno. He orter nevah married me and gut tied down. Seem lak things all go wrong, crosswise foh him.

MUH MACK (*staring at her*). Hunh. Things'll be crosswise wid 'im till dey straighten 'im out in de grave. Dem's my words. (*Blowing her nose in her skirt and half weeping.*) If all dat shooting and killing in Wilmington wouldn't make 'im do better, nothing in de Gohd's world kin.

GOLDIE (*moaning*). Stop dat talking. I cain't beah it.

MUH MACK. Dat's des' whut you orter stop doing, stop beahing it. Gather up yo' duds and take me'n Douglass and whop off'n leave 'im, dat's what you orter do.

GOLDIE (*beating herself with her fists*). I ain't. I ain't. I gwine stay by 'im.

MUH MACK. Co'se you gwine stay by 'im—and starve too. Foh dat's whut you'll do. Whut he don't spend on medicine he do on dem old lodges and sich and books and newspapers. And gits turned out'n eve'y one of 'em foh his speeches and wild talk, he do. (*With grim satisfaction.*) Shoveling dat coal down at de power house reckon'll hold him down foh a while. (*With an afterthought.*) Hold 'im down till somebody crack his haid wid a shovel and tu'n 'im off. (*Stirring the fire and then folding up her hands.*) I done said my say-so now. Do no good, 'caze you so wropped up in de fool.

GOLDIE (*flaring out*). No, it won't do no good. I gwine stick by him. (*Rising and turning to her work again.*) Dey ain't never done 'im right. Dey all been down on him f'om de fust.

MUH MACK (*shrilly*). And 'll be till de last. Otheh niggers makes a living foh deir fambly. Why don't he? Allus gut his eyes on sump'n' else.

GOLDIE. He gwine be a big man yit. Dem udder niggehs do de dirty work and take whut dey kin git. Dey de low-down trash. (*Her voice trembling.*) He gwine git him a big school some dese days.

MUH MACK (*laughing scornfully*). Hee-hee—hee. Listen at him. He cain't teach nothing. De niggeh school teachers round hyuh know mo'n a minute dan Abe do in a week. Dey been to college at Raleigh and Greensboro and no telling whah. And dey gut some sense 'sides deir learning. Dat li'l Eddie Williams has. He done gone th'ough dat Shaw school in Raleigh and is off doing big wuk. Why couldn't Abe do sump'n' lak dat!

GOLDIE (*her voice breaking*). Shet up, I tell you.

MUH MACK (*sulkily*). Aw right den, but dat talk don't fill yo' stomach. (*Pulling a*

walking stick from the chimney corner.)
I gwine go down to Liza's and ax her to
gi' me some supper. (*She groans and
creaks to her feet.*)

GOLDIE. You been down to Liza's till she's
tiahed o' feeding you.

MUH MACK (*waving her stick in the air*).
Well, you feed me den.

GOLDIE. Wait'll Douglass come f'om school
and I'll git him to go down to de cawner
and git some meat f'om dat man.

MUH MACK. Done past time foh Douglass
to be heah. Mought not come till late.

GOLDIE (*drying her hands again and patting her hair*). I'll go den. You putt de
kittle on foh some cawfee and set de table
and I'll be right back. (*Far off a muffled
whistle blows.*) Dere's de power-house
whistle. Abe be heah soon. Light de lamp
and putt on de table. (*She goes out.*)

MUH MACK (*somewhat mollified, calling
after her*). Aw raght. (*She puts her stick in
the corner, fills the kettle and stirs stiffly
about her, bringing plates to the table and
laying out the knives and forks. She hobbles into the room at the rear and returns
with a lamp without any chimney, which
she lights at the fireplace and places on the
table. While she is engaged in making coffee over the fire, DOUGLASS strolls in. He is
a young Negro in short trousers, fifteen or
sixteen years old, black as MUH MACK and
with something of a wild and worthless
spirit already beginning to show in his face.
He carries two ragged books under his
arm.*)

DOUGLASS (*dropping the books by the door
and kicking them near the chest*). Heigh!

MUH MACK (*jumping*). Who?—hee—hee,
you skeahed me, honey. (*She stands up
and looks at him indulgently.*) Whah you
been so late?

DOUGLASS. Oh, round and about. Stopped
by de hot dawg stand awhile, chewing de
rag wid some fellows.

MUH MACK. How many dem sa'sage things
you eat?

DOUGLASS. Dunno. Sev'al.

MUH MACK (*leaning forward, her eyes
shining with anticipation*). Whut you
fotch me to eat?

DOUGLASS. I wanted to bring you sump'n',
but—

MUH MACK. You mean you ain't bought me
nothing wid dat fifty cents?

DOUGLASS. I fool-lak matched wid some
ub'm down dere and had to set 'em up.

MUH MACK. And I so hungry I cain't see
straight!

DOUGLASS (*nonchalantly*). I cain't help it.

MUH MACK (*threateningly*). I gwine tell
yo' daddy on you.

DOUGLASS (*looking at her*). Hunh, you better not. Do and I won't play nary piece foh
you in—in two weeks mebbe.

MUH MACK (*turning to her cooking*). Yo'
muh know 'bout it.

DOUGLASS. Why you tell her?

MUH MACK. She guessed at it. She knowed
you tuck dat money soon's she found it
gone.

DOUGLASS (*alarmed*). Pap don't know, do
he?

MUH MACK. Not yit. He ain't come f'om
wuk. (*He turns back into the room at the
rear and reappears with a guitar. Sitting
down wonderfully at ease, he begins strumming.*) Lawd, Lawd, honey, gi' us a piece
'fo' yo' daddy comes. (*He falls to playing
and MUH MACK begins to pat the floor and
skip happily now and then as she moves
about the fireplace.*) Hee-hee—dat bedder'n eating.

DOUGLASS (*hugging up the "box" and
throwing back his head in abandon*). Hee-
hee—ain't it dough! (*He turns and scowls
at the books lying on the floor, and begins
singing to them.*) Dem old books—
(*Strum, strum*) lying in de corner, (*Strum,
strum.*) Dem old books—(*Strum, strum*)
lying in de corner—(*Strum, strum.*) Lie
dere, babies, lie dere! Hee-hee—Muh
Mack, I kin make music raght out'n my
haid. (*He goes on throwing his fingers
across the strings.*)

MUH MACK. You kin, honey, you sho'ly kin. (*She sits listening happily. He wraps himself over the guitar, his fingers popping up and down the neck of the instrument with marvelous dexterity. His bowed head begins to weave about him rhythmically as he bursts into snatches of song.*)

DOUGLASS (*singing*).

Look down, look down dat lonesome road,
De hacks all dead in line.
Some give a nickel, some give a dime
To bury dis po' body o' mine.

MUH MACK (*staring at him*). I declah! I declah! Listen at dat chile.

DOUGLASS. Ne'h mind, ne'h min' me. (*Modulating with amazing swiftness from key to key.*) And dere was po' Brady. Po' old Brady.

MUH MACK. Yeh, Brady, dey laid him down to die.

DOUGLASS (*singing*).

Oh, Brady, Brady, you know you done me wrong,
You come in when de game was a-goin' on!
And dey laid po' Brady down.

Wimmens in Gawgy dey heard de news
Walking 'bout in deir little red shoes,
Dey glad, dey glad po' Brady dead.

When I close my eyes to ketch a liddle sleep,
Po' old Brady about my bed do creep,
One mo', des' one mo' rounder gone.
(*While he is singing and playing,* ABE *comes suddenly in at the rear dragging a heavy wooden box in one hand and carrying a dinner-pail in the other. He is dirty and begrimed with coal dust.*)

ABE (*shouting*). Put up dat box! (DOUGLASS *bounds out of his chair as if shot and backs away from him.*) Putt down dat damn guitah, you good-for-nothing! (ABE *hangs his cap and dinner-pail on a nail by the door and comes heavily across to the fire. His face is haggard and old and his shoulders have grown humped with the going of time.* DOUGLASS *slips out with his guitar and presently creeps in and sits stealthily*

on the chest. ABE *lays the goods box on the floor and breaks it up and places pieces of it on the fire. Then he sits down and stretches out his feet and stares moodily before him.* MUH MACK *hurries around making bread, frying the hated side meat, and arranging the table.*)

MUH MACK (*tremulously*). How you feeling? You come quick adder de whistle—

ABE. Ah, feel lak I'll stifle in heah. (*He strikes his breast once and then follows it with a fury of savage blows.*) Cain't git no wind down in dat b'iler house. (*He drags his hands wearily across his brow and shakes his head as if clearing his eyes of a fog.*) Whah Goldie?

MUH MACK. Gone out to de cawner to git some meat. Time she back.

ABE. How long fo' supper?

MUH MACK. Soon's she gits back and we kin cook de meat.

ABE (*pulling off his shoes and setting them in the corner*). I' going to lie down a minute till my head clears up. Feel lak it'll blow off at de top. (*Grasping his chair, he staggers to his feet and goes across the room. At the door he stops and looks down at* DOUGLASS.) I' going to tend to you in a little bit.
(DOUGLASS *quails before him. He goes out and slams the door.*)

MUH MACK. Whut de name o' Gohd ail him now? Wus'n ever.

DOUGLASS (*whimpering*). He gwine beat me! He'll kill me.
(*The bed is heard creaking in the rear room as* ABE *lies down.*)

MUH MACK. Whut'n de world foh? (*She stands tapping her hands together helplessly.*)

DOUGLASS. He done heahed sump'n' on me. Oh, he gwine beat me to deaf.
(ABE *is heard turning in his bed again, and he immediately appears in the door.*)

ABE. Shet up dat whimpering. Git over dere and start washing on dem clothes foh yo' po' mammy. (DOUGLASS *darts over and begins rubbing at the board and sniffing.*)

Dry up, I tell you. (ABE *turns back to his bed.*)

MUH MACK (*sitting to the fire and rocking back and forth in her anxiety*). Oh, Lawd —Lawd! (*She hides her head in her skirt grumbling and moaning. Presently* GOLDIE *comes in.*)

GOLDIE (*coming over to the tub*). Look out, son, lemme git at 'em. (*She falls to washing feverishly.*)

MUH MACK (*looking up*). Whah dat meat, Goldie?

GOLDIE. Dat man look at me and laugh, dat's whut. (*Turning angrily towards* DOUGLASS.) You went and—

MUH MACK (*throwing out her hand in alarm*). Nanh, nanh, Goldie. (*Lowering her voice and nodding to the rear.*) Abe in dere. He find out 'bout dat, he kill de boy. Done say he gwine beat 'im foh sump'n' 'nother.

GOLDIE. When he come?

MUH MACK. He des' dis minute gut heah.

GOLDIE (*in alarm*). He wuss off, I bet. (*She hurries into the room and is heard talking softly and kindly to* ABE. *He answers her with indistinct growls. In a moment* GOLDIE *returns.*) Putt what you gut on de table and le's eat. (*She goes on with her washing.*) Abe ain't feeling well. Hadder eat whut he kin, I reckon.
(MUH MACK *puts the bread, coffee and meat on the table.*)

MUH MACK. Come on, you all.

GOLDIE. Come on in, Abe. (ABE *enters in his undershirt and trousers.*) G'won and eat, I don't want nothing.

ABE (*almost falling in his chair*). Come on and set whedder you can or not. (GOLDIE *takes her place at the table.*) Come on, Douglass.

DOUGLASS. I don't want nothing eiver.
(MUH MACK *draws up her chair.*)

ABE. Don't make no difference. I said come on. (DOUGLASS *gets a chair and takes his place.* ABE *surveys the fare before him.*) Dis all you got foh a working man and he sick?

GOLDIE. I didn' have no money and— (*She gulps and drops her head to hide her tears.*)

ABE (*kindly as he reaches out and touches her shoulders*). Neveh mind, honey chile. (*He closes his eyes with weariness and sits brooding. Presently he raises his head.*) Well, neveh you mind, I ain't hungry. (*Looking at her sadly.*) But you must be plumb wore out wid all dat washing and all. (*Dropping his head.*) Le's have de blessing. Oh, Lawd, we thank Thee foh what we have befo' us. Make us truly thankful foh all Thy gifts and save us at last, we humbly beg, foh Christ's sake, Amen! (*After the blessing is over* GOLDIE *still keeps her head bowed, her shoulders heaving with sobs.* MUH MACK *pours out the coffee and hands it round.* ABE *calls to* GOLDIE.) Come on eat sump'n', Goldie, you feel better, you git yo' stren'th back. Drink some this coffee. (GOLDIE *bursting into wild sobs, goes and sits by the fire.*) What's de matter, chile?

MUH MACK. She done wuked to deaf and nothing to wuk on, dat's whut.

ABE (*drinking down a cup of steaming coffee at a gulp*). Po' me some mo' of dat! (GOLDIE's *sobs gradually die away.*) Come on, honey, don't cry no mo'.
(GOLDIE *stands up and looks towards the table with anguished face.*)

GOLDIE. Abe, Abe honey babe, whut us gwine do? (*She buries her face in her hands.*)

ABE. You done heahed sump'n', ain't you?

GOLDIE. Yeh, yeh, Liza told me. Jim done come f'om de power house and told her.

ABE (*dully*). Neveh mind. Come on drink some coffee. We talk 'bout dat directly. I got sump'n' else to tell you, too.

MUH MACK (*staring at him in fear*). Whut dat happen at de power house?

ABE. I tell you when I git good and ready. Come on, Goldie, chile. (GOLDIE *wipes her eyes and returns to the table to drink her coffee.*) Befo' we gits on what happened wid me, I got a question to ax dis young gentleman. (*Looking across at* DOUGLASS.) Why don't you eat?

DOUGLASS (*falteringly*). I ain't hongry.

ABE. Try and see do you want anything.

DOUGLASS. I cain't eat nothing.

ABE. How come?

DOUGLASS. I des' don't want nothing.

ABE (*bitterly*). I reckon I know how come. Dis evening I pass on the other side of de street and see you down dere at dat drink stand setting up dem wuthless niggers wid yo' mammy's good money. (*Savagely.*) Oh, yeh, I know dat's whah you got it. I see you last night watching her putt it away.

GOLDIE. Please don't have no mo' row, Abe.

ABE. I ain't gwine beat 'im foh dat, nunh-unh. Sump'n' else he's goin' to ketch it foh. (*Raging out.*) De teacher stop me on de street and tell me you doing wuss'n ever in yo' books and she done had to putt you back in third reader. (*Swallowing his third cup of coffee down with a hunk of bread, he stands up and stares into the distance.*) Heah we done labor and sweat foh you, fix foh you to rise up and be sump'n'. Eight yeah you been going to school and you won't work, you won't learn. (*He strikes the table with his fist, and the lamp flickers and almost goes out.*) You ain't no good. Onct I thought you gwine go on, climb, rise high and lead. (*He seizes him by the collar and, lifting him from the floor, shakes him like a rag.*)

DOUGLASS (*sputtering and choking*). Pap, papa!

MUH MACK (*whining in terror*). Stop dat! You kill him!

ABE. I teach you to fool wid dem low niggers! I git you out'n dem trifling ways or I'll break yo' back in two. (*He sits down and jerks the boy across his knee and begins beating him blindly.*) I name you foh a great man, a man what stand high lak de sun, and you turn out to be de lowest of de low! Change yo' name, dat's what you better do. (*With a cuff on the cheek he hurls him across the room, where he falls sobbing and wailing on the floor.*) Shet dat fuss up! (DOUGLASS' *sobs gradually cease.*

GOLDIE *starts toward him, but* ABE *jerks her back.*) Let 'im lie dere, de skunk and coward.
(GOLDIE *turns despairingly to her washing again.* ABE *moves to the fire and sits down, pulling a wrinkled newspaper out of his pockets, while* MUH MACK *rocks and slobbers and moans.*)

MUH MACK. You need de law on you, Abe McCranie. You beat dat po' baby—

ABE. Shet up! You what gwine ruin him. He takes adder you and yo' trifling.

MUH MACK. Oh, I gwine leave heah, find me 'nudder place to stay.

ABE. We all got to git another place to stay.

GOLDIE. Le's go back home, Abe! Le's go back.

MUH MACK. Ha' we gut to leave 'caze whut you done down at de power house? (*Wringing her hands.*) Whut you do down dere? Oh, Lawd!

ABE. Ain't no use waking up de neighborhood wid yo' yelling. I didn't do nothing but stand up foh my rights. A white man sass me and I sass back at him. And a crowd of 'em run me off. Won't be able to git no other job in dis town, God damn it! (*Standing up and shaking his fist.*) God damn de people in dis town! Dem wid deir 'bacco warehouses, and cotton mills, and money in de bank, you couldn't handle wid a shovel!

MUH MACK. Le's go back home. De Colonel fix it in his will so us could have a place to come back to. Mr. Lorrie'll rent us some land.

GOLDIE (*coming over to* ABE'S *chair and dropping on her knees beside him*). Abe, Abe, le's go back. Please do. Le's go back whah we growed up. Ain't no home foh us in no town. We gut to git back to de country. Dat's whah we belong. (*She lays her head in his lap.*)

ABE (*looking down at her tenderly*). Yeh, yeh, honey. We is gwine back. Adder all dese yeahs I knows now de town ain't no place foh us. Fifteen yeah we been trying to make it and couldn't. Dat's what I was

going to tell you. All de signs been ag'in us. I orter knowed it after three or fo' yeahs. Back home de place foh us. Back in our own country. (*Staring before him and a smile suddenly sweetening the hardness of his face.*) We go back dere and take a new start. We going to build up on a new foundation. Took all dese yeahs to show me. (*His voice rising exultantly.*) Dere's whah my work is cut out to be. It come to me dis evening while I walked on de street. (*Standing up.*) Seem lak sump'n' spoke to me and said go back on de Cape Fair River. I heard it plain lak a voice talking. "Dese streets and dese peoples ain't yo' peoples. Yo'n is de kind what works and labors wid de earf and de sun. Dem who knows de earth and the fullness thereof. Dere's whah yo' harvest is to be." And den when I come face to face wid de ruining of my boy, in my anger I see de way clear. We going back, we going back. And dere at last I knows I'm going to build up and lead! And my boy going to be a man. (*Looking at* DOUGLASS *with a hint of pleadingness.*) Ain't it so?
(*But* DOUGLASS *only stares at him coldly.*)
GOLDIE (*looking up at him*). I knows you will. I feel it des' de way you do. I keep telling Muh Mack some day you gwine git dere.

ABE (*gazing down at her*). Dese yeahs all been sent foh our trial, ain't dey, honey?

GOLDIE. Yeh, yeh, we been tried all foh a purpose.

ABE. And now we ready, ain't we, honey?

GOLDIE. We ready to go back and start all over.

MUH MACK (*repeating uncertainly*). To start all over.

ABE. To build us a monument from generation unto generation.

GOLDIE (*softly, the tears pouring from her eyes*). Yeh, yeh.

ABE. And all dis sin and tribulation and sorrow will be forgot, passed away, wiped out till de judgment, won't it, chile?

GOLDIE. It will, oh, I knows it will. We done suffered our share and Old Moster gwine be good to us now.

ABE. Good! Yeh, good! (*He sits with bowed head.*)

SCENE V

Three years later. The same as Scene Two, in ABE's *cabin on the McCranie farm. The room shows some sign of improvement over its former state. There is a lambrequin of crêpe paper on the mantel, a wooden clock, and at the right a home-fashioned bookcase with books and magazines. On the rear wall is the same colored print with the caption of the rising slave.*

ABE *is seated at a table near the front writing by a lighted lamp. He is better dressed and more alert than formerly. Further back and to the left of the fireplace sits* MUH MACK *dozing and quarreling in her rocking chair. Her head and face are hid under the same slat-bonnet, and a dirty pink "fascinator" is draped over her bony shoulders. Her huge snuff brush protrudes from her lips and now and then describes a sort of waving motion when she moves her jaws in sleep. Between her knees she clasps her walking-stick.*

Through the window at the rear come bright streaks from the orange afterglow of the west. The November sun has set and the sky near the horizon is fading into a deep gloom under an approaching cloudiness. In the oaks outside the sparrows going to roost pour out a flooding medley of sharp calls resembling the heavy dripping of rain from eaves. For a moment ABE *continues his writing and then lays down his pencil and replenishes the fire. He returns to his chair and sits drumming absently on the table.*

ABE. When Goldie coming back, Muh? (*His speech is gentle and more cultivated.*)

MUH MACK (*starting out of her sleep*). Whut you say?

ABE. When Goldie coming back from Mr. Lonnie's?

MUH MACK. When she git done o' dat washing and arning, po' thing.

ABE. Seem like it's time she was back.

MUH MACK. Whut you keer 'bout her and you setting dere all day wuking at dat old speech mess.

ABE. You going to cook any supper?

MUH MACK. Supper! You ax dat and know I cain't git out'n my chaih wid de stiffness and misery. You'll hadder eat cold.

ABE. I've done looked. Ain't nothing cold.

MUH MACK. Den you'll hadder wait till she come. Po', po' thing, wid all her trouble wonder she able to cook or work or do anything. (*She turns to her snoozing and* ABE *picks up his pencil again and gnaws at it as he works on his speech. Soon he stops and begins tapping on the table.*)

ABE. What trouble she got now?

MUH MACK (*astounded*). You ax dat and you fixing to bring mo' trouble on us wid yo' schooling and mess. And wid Mr. Lonnie down on you 'bout de crap ag'in. Lawd, Lawd! And who dat won't let his po' boy putt foot in de home? Keep 'im driv' off lak a homeless dawg. (*She wipes her eyes with a dirty rag.*)

ABE. You talk, but this time they won't be no failing. The school is going through. Then I can talk to Mr. Lonnie. Six men done already promised a thousand dollars: Cain't fail this time, nosuh.

MUH MACK. You don't 'serve nothing, and won't let po' Douglass come back to see his mammy. (*Brightly.*) Dem men mebbe ain't promised. Dey talking.

ABE (*sharply*). I know. . . . You needn't say another word about it. (*Concerned with the speech.*) I won't let Douglass darken my door.

(MUH MACK *stirs from her doze and sniffles into her rag, wiping the rheumy tears from her eyes.* ABE *turns to his writing. He writes more and more rapidly as he nears the end. Presently he throws down his pencil and stretches his arms back of his head with a weary yawn. He looks towards* MUH MACK *and speaks exultantly.*)

ABE. That's the best I've ever done. They can't go against that, they can't this time.

MUH MACK (*sleepily, rubbing her eyes and speaking coldly*). Thank God you's finished yo' speech and'll soon be outen my sight and I kin git a liddle nap.

ABE (*not noticing her*). That crowd's going to listen to me to-night.

MUH MACK. Mebbe dey will, but you's talked yo' life away, and it hain't come to nothing.

ABE (*looking at the speech*). I've done my best this time. All I got from books and experience is there, and the truth's in it. (*He gathers the closely written sheets together.*) I tell 'em— (*He turns to his speech and begins to read as he rises from his chair.*) I say, ladies and gentlemen, (*he does not notice the movement of disgust* MUH MACK *makes as she turns away from him*) this night is going to mean much in the lives of each and every one of us, big and little.

MUH MACK. Hit won't ef dey treats dey chil'en lak you treats yo' one.

ABE (*hurrying on*). It marks the founding of the Cape Fair Training School, an institution that will one day be a light to other institutions around about. It is to be our aim here, with the few teachers and facilities we can provide, to offer education to the colored children amongst us and offer it cheap. (*He turns toward* MUH MACK *and speaks with more spirit, as if his audience were directly before him. But she turns her back to him and blinks in the fire.*) Looking over the country, ladies and gentlemen, we see eight million souls striving in slavery, yea, slavery, brethren, the slavery of ignorance. And ignorance means being oppressed, both by yourselves and by others—hewers of wood and drawers of water. (*He picks up his pencil and crosses out a word.*)

MUH MACK (*sarcastically*). Dey hain't nobody been in slavery since de surrenduh. Ef dey is, how come? And I reckon de hewers o' woods and de drawers o' water is 'bout free as anybody.

ABE (*continuing his speech without noticing her*). Ignorance means sin, and sin means destruction, destruction before the law and destruction in a man's own heart. The Negro will rise when his chareckter is of the nature to cause him to rise—for on that the future of the race depends, and that chareckter is mostly to be built by education, for it cannot exist in ignorance. Let me repeat again, ladies and gentlemen. We want our children and our grandchildren to march on towards full lives and noble chareckters, and that has got to come, I say, by education. We have no other way. We got to live and learn—and think, that's it. (*He strides in front of the old woman, who has dozed off again under his eloquence. She raises her head with a jerk when he thunders at her.*) A little over forty years ago the white man's power covered us like the night. Through war and destruction we was freed. But it was freedom of the body and not freedom of the mind. And what is freedom of the body without freedom of the mind? It means nothing. It don't exist. (*Throwing his arm out in a long gesture.*) What we need is thinking people, people who will not let the body rule the head. And again I cry out, education. I been accused of wanting to make the Negro the equal of the white man. Been run from pillar to post, living in poverty because of that belief. But it is false. I never preached that doctrine. I don't say that the colored ought to be made equal to the white in society, now. We are not ready for it yet. But I do say that we have equal rights to educating and free thought and living our lives. With that all the rest will come. (*Pointing to the bookcase.*) Them books there show it. (*Caught up in the dreams of his life, he pours out a roll of words and beats the air with his fists.*) Ladies and gentlemen, what's to hinder us from starting a great center of learning here, putting our time and our hope and money and labor into it and not into the much foolishness of this life. What little education I got was by

light 'ood knots, and after reading and studying all these years, I am just a little ways along. We must give the children of the future a better chance than we have had. With this one school-building we can make a good start. Then we can get more teachers later on, more equipment, and some day a library where the boys and girls can read about men that have done something for the world. And before many years pass we will be giving instruction in how to farm, how to be carpenters, how to preach, how to teach, how to do anything. (*Forgetful of his written page, he shouts.*) And what will stop us in the end from growing into a great Negro college, a university, a light on a hill, a place the pride of both black and white. (*He stands a moment, lost in thought. Turning through the leaves of his speech, he looks towards* MUH MACK, *who sits hid under her bonnet.*) Ain't that the truth, Muh Mack? Ain't it? (*Anxiously.*) They can't stand out against that, can they? Ain't that a speech equal to the best of the white, ain't it? (*He coughs.*)

MUH MACK. Lawd Jesus! You's enough to wake de daid. And you brung on yo' cough ag'in.

ABE (*fiercely*). I tell you it's going through. I believe the people here are with me this time.

MUH MACK. Sounds like de same old tale. (*Bitterly.*) You's made dem dere speeches from Wilmington and Greensboro to I don' know where. It's foolishnesses and you knows it. (ABE *arranges the leaves of his speech without listening to her.*) Time you's learning dat white is white and black is black, and Gohd made de white to allus be bedder'n de black. It was so intended from de beginning.

ABE (*staring at her and speaking half aloud*). We been taught and kept believing that for two hundred years. (*Blazing out.*) But it's a lie, a lie, and the truth ain't in it.

MUH MACK (*going on in her whining, irritating voice*). Yeh, all yo' life you's hollered Lawd and followed Devil, and look whut it's brung you to. Ef you'd a putt as much time on picking cotton lately as you has on dat speech, you wouldn't have Mr. Lonnie down on you de way he is. De truf's in dat all right.

ABE (*trying to control his nervousness and anger*). I ain't a farmer. My business is with schools. (*Hotly.*) Can't you learn nothing? You dribbling old—, here for twenty years you've heard me talk the gospel and it ain't made no impression on you. (*He turns away, realizing the vanity of his words to her. He speaks to himself and the shadows of the room.*) That speech is so! It's so, and I got to speak in that-a-way. (*He looks about him with burning eyes and pleads as if with an unseen power.*) The truth's there. Can't you see it? (*His nostrils quiver and he goes on in a kind of sob, calling to the unbeliever hiding within the dark.*) God A'mighty knows they ain't no difference at the bottom. Color hadn't ought to count. It's the man, it's the man that lasts. (*Brokenly.*) Give us the truth! Give us the truth! (*He coughs slightly, and a queer baffled look creeps over his face. For the moment he seems to sense ultimate defeat before a hidden, unreachable enemy.*)

MUH MACK (*looking at the clock and snapping*). Thought you's bound to be at de Quillie House by six o'clock. It's done near 'bout time. Git on. I wants my nap. (*She pours snuff into her lip and turns to her snoozing again. With a hurried look at the clock,* ABE *crams his speech into his pocket, gets a plug hat from the desk, and blows out the lamp. The room is filled with great leaping shadows from the darting flames of the fireplace.*)

ABE (*at the door*). You remember what I said about Douglass.

MUH MACK. Git on, git on. (*Whining sarcastically.*) Sho' you'll be a light on de hill and de pride o' de land—and you won't even let a po' old woman see her boy.

ABE (*turning back*). Damn him! If he puts his foot in this house he'd better not let me get hold of him. They ain't no man, flesh of my flesh or not, going to lie rotten with liquor and crooks around me. That's what

I been talking against for twenty years. I drove him off for it and I'd do it again. Just because a little time's passed ain't no reason I've changed.

MUH MACK. He mought a changed and want to do bedder.

ABE (*coming back into the room*). Changed enough so he like to got arrested in town yesterday and it his first day back.

MUH MACK (*pleading in a high quavering voice*). But I gut to see him. He's been gone two yeah.

ABE. Let him come if he dares. You ruint him with your tales and wuthless guitar playing and I don't want nothing more to do with him.

MUH MACK (*mumbling to herself*). I's gwine see him 'fo' he goes 'way back yander ef I has to crawl slam over de river.

ABE (*with brightening eye*). You heard me. He ain't no longer mine, and that's the end of it.

MUH MACK (*bursting into a rage*). And yo' ain't none o' mine. You's gut all de high notions of old Colonel Mack and de white folks and don't keer nothing for yo' own. Git on. (*He stands looking at the floor, hesitating over something.*) Whut you skeered of, de dark?

ABE (*shuddering and going across the room and getting an old overcoat from a nail*). Yes, I'm afraid of it. You're right, I'm none of yours, nor my own mother either. You know what I am—no, I dunno whut I am. Sometime I think that's de trouble. (*Sharply.*) No, no, de trouble out there, around me, everywhere around me. (*The despondent looks comes back to his face and he speaks more calmly.*) I'll cut across the fields the near way. And tell Goldie not to worry. I'll be back by ten with the school good as started. (*At the door he turns back again and calls to the old woman earnestly.*) Muh Mack, don't let her worry, don't. (*But the old woman is asleep.*) Let her sleep, let us all sleep. (*He goes out softly, closing the door behind him.*)

SCENE VI

An hour later the same evening. A sandy country road twists out of the gloom of scrubby oaks and bushes at the rear and divides into a fork, one branch turning sharply to the left and the other to the right. The moon has risen low in the east, casting a sickly drunken light over the landscape through the flying clouds. To the left in a field of small loblolly pines the dim outline of a barn can be seen. The tops and the branches of the larger trees move like a vast tangle of restless arms, and the small bushes and grasses hug the earth under the wind's blustering. Down the road in the distance come the sounds of running footsteps. And farther off, almost out of hearing, the halloo as of some one pursuing. The footsteps thump nearer, and presently ABE *staggers up out of the darkness and falls panting in the edge of the bushes at the right. His hat is gone and his clothes torn. The shouts sound fainter in the night and gradually die away.*

ABE *crawls to his knees and stares back at the road, his breath coming in great gasps. His learning and pitiful efforts at cultural speech have dropped away like a worn-out garment and left him a criminal.*

ABE. Reckon, reckon dey leave me 'lone now, de damn cutth'oats! (*Holding his sides with his hands and rocking his head in pain.*) Oh, my breast feel lak it'll bust. Yeh, I outrun you, you po' white trash. (*Clambering wildly to his feet and staring up the road.*) But you done fix me now. You done got all de underholt and lay me on de bottom. (*Looking up at the sky and raising his fist above his head.*) Dere dat moon looking on it all so peaceful lak. It don't know, it can't feel what they done to me. (*Bursting out with a loud oath.*) God damn 'em to hell! Dem white sons of bitches! Dey don't gi' me no chance. Dey stop every crack, nail up every do' and shet me in. Dey stomp on me, squash me, mash me in de ground lak a worm. (*His voice breaking into a sob.*) Dey ain't no place foh me. I lost, ain't no home, no 'biding place. (*He throws himself down on the ground and lays his cheek to the earth. Unseen by him, a light begins to twinkle at the barn. He sits up and looks intently at the ground.*) Seem lak dis earf feel sweet to me. It warm me lak it feel sorry. (*Laying his hand on it as if it were a being.*) Ground, you is my last and only friend. You take me in, you keep me safe from trouble. Wisht I could dig me a hole now and cover me up and sleep till de great judgment day, and nobody never know whah I gone.

(LONNIE MCCRANNIE, *stout and middle-aged, comes in at left with a lantern.*)

LONNIE. Heigh there!

ABE (*bounding up*). Keep back, whoever you is. Stay back dere, white man.

LONNIE (*peering forward*). Who's that cutting up crazy here in the night?

ABE. Ain't nobody, nobody.

LONNIE. Well, by God, Abe, what's the matter?

ABE. That you, Mr. Lonnie?

LONNIE. Yeh. What'n the world's the matter? I was out there at the barn and heard the awfulest racket. Somebody talking like they was crazy.

ABE. Trouble, Mr. Lonnie, trouble.

LONNIE. Trouble, what sort of trouble? (*Coming closer and holding up his light before* ABE.) Great goodness, you're wet as water.

ABE (*straightening up*). I all right now. Got to go on. (*He makes a drunken step on the road towards the right.* LONNIE *gets quickly before him.*)

LONNIE. Where you going?

ABE. I going to leave heah, going clean away.

LONNIE. No, you're not. Tell me what's the matter.

ABE. Dem white men run me away from the Quillie House.

LONNIE. That's what the shouting was about, was it?

ABE. Mebbe so, suh.

LONNIE. Uh-huh. You were down there 'bout your school business, anh?

ABE. I wa'n't doing no harm. I was going to talk to 'em 'bout our school foh next year, and when I got there dey was a crowd of low-down white men dere—

LONNIE. Look out, mind how you talk.

ABE. I minding all right. When I got there they done run them lazy niggers off and told me I had to go. (*Grimly.*) Dey could-n't skeer me though. I went on in de house and started my speech. And den— (*throwing out his arms wildly*) Mr. Lon-nie, help me git back at 'em. Help me git de law on 'em.

LONNIE. What'd they do?

ABE. Dey fell on me and beat me and told me I got to git out of de country. And dey run me off. But I reckon some of 'em got dey heads cracked. (*His body swaying with weakness.*) What I going to do? I don't know what?

LONNIE. Go on home and behave yourself.

ABE (*his voice almost cracking*). I ain't done nothing. I tell you.

LONNIE (*roughly*). Serves you right. I've told you time and again to quit that mes-sing about and look after your crop and keep in your place. But you won't, you won't. I reckon you'll stay quiet now awhile.

ABE (*pleading with him*). But I done right. I ain't done nothing to be beat foh.

LONNIE. The devil you ain't! I've been off to-day all around the country trying to get hands to pick out your cotton. It's falling out and rotting in the fields.

ABE. But I ain't lost no time from the cot-ton patch, 'cepting two or three days and I was sick den. I been sick all to-day.

LONNIE. You needn't talk back to me. If you're sick what are you doing out to-night and getting yourself beat half to death? Yeh, I reckon I know such tales as that. And you needn't fool with the crop no more. I done levied on it and am going to have it housed myself.

ABE (*moving towards him*). You mean you tuck my crop away from me?

LONNIE. Don't talk to me like that, I tell you. (*A fit of coughing seizes* ABE.) Call it taking away from you if you want to. I'm done of you. Next year you can hunt an-other place.

ABE (*His face working in uncontrollable rage*). Den you's a damn thief, white man.

LONNIE (*yelling*). Stop that!

ABE (*moving towards him*). Now I'm go-ing to pay somebody back. I going to git even.

LONNIE. Stop! I'll kill you with this lan-tern.

ABE (*with a loud laugh*). Yeh, yeh, hit me. Yo' time done come. (*He makes a move-ment towards* LONNIE, *who swings his lan-tern aloft and brings it crashing down on his head. The light goes out and the two rocking forms are seen gripping each other's throats under the moon.*)

LONNIE. Let go—let go—
(ABE *gradually crushes him to the ground, choking him.*)

ABE (*gnashing his teeth and snarling like a wild animal*). I choke you, I choke yo' guts out'n yo' mouf. (*He finally throws* LONNIE's *limp body from him, and then falls upon it, beating and trampling the up-turned face.*) Dere you lie now. Dead! (*His voice trails high into a croon.*) I wipe out some de suffering of dis world now! (*Standing up and drawing away from the body.*) I—I—git even, I pay 'em back.

(He begins wiping his hands feverishly upon his trousers.) Blood! Blood, de white man's blood all over me. *(Screaming out in sudden fear.)* I done kilt somebody! Oh, Lawd, Mr. Lonnie! Mr. Lonnie! *(He falls on his knees by the body.)* What's de matter? Wake up, wake up! . . . Pshaw, he's asleep, fooling. *(Springing to his feet.)* He's dead, dead. *(The wind groans through the trees like the deep note of some enormous fiddle and then dies away with a muffled boom across the open fields.* ABE *stands frozen with horror.)* Listen at dat wind, will you! Mercy, dat his spirit riding it and crying! *(He falls prone upon the earth moaning and rocking. In a moment he sits up and holds his head tightly in his hands.)* O—oh, seem lak my head done turnt to a piece o' wood, seem lak cold as ice. *(He slaps his forehead queerly with his open palms.)* De whole world done seem turnt upside down, everything going round me lak a wheel. *(As he stares wonderingly around and gropes before him like one dreaming, the branches of the trees seem to change their characteristics and become a wild seething of mocking, menacing hands stretched forth from all sides at him. He snatches up a piece of broken fence rail and snarls at them.)* Don't tech me, I kill you! *(He stands in an attitude of defense and the branches seem to regain their normal appearance. Stupefied, he lets the rail fall to the ground and then wraps his arms spasmodically across his face.)* O Lawd, I going crazy, dat's what! *(He bends over jerking and shivering. Presently from the left he sees appear a shadowy cortège of raggle-taggle country gentry, men and boys carrying muskets, sticks and stones. Their faces, illumined by the moon, are set and frozen in the distortion of hate and revenge. In the midst of them is a young Negro being dragged along with a rope around his neck.* ABE *starts back with a gasp.)* What's dis? Whah am I? *(Suddenly terrified.)* Lawd, dat's a lynching! . . . It's de night o' dat lynching. And dat

dere's Charlie—Charlie Sampson. *(Seizing the rail.)* What you white mens doing? *(Crying out.)* Dat you, Charlie! I come save you! *(The group appear to pass silently down the road at the rear, the prisoner throwing out his arms and clawing the air as he is dragged onward.* ABE *springs forward at them and swings his rail through the air. It lands on the ground with a thud. He shrieks.)* Ghosts! Dey's ha'nts! Dey ain't no peoples! *(Jerking up his head and looking queerly around him.)* Jesus, mebbe dat's me dey hanging! *(He stands rooted in his tracks as they disappear down the road. After a moment out of the underbrush at the left steal two shadowy figures dressed in the fashion of the late fifties. One is a young good-looking Negress of twenty, the other a dandified young white man about thirty. As they move across the scene at the rear, the man looks guiltily around him as if in fear of being surprised. The woman stops and points to the thicket at the right. He nods and motions her to move on.* ABE *looks up and sees them stealing away. He leaps to his feet and stares at them in stupefaction.)* Who dat 'oman and white man? *(With a joyous cry he rushes forward.)* Mammy! Mammy! Dat you! Dis heah's Abe, yo' boy! Mammy! *(The figures begin entering the thicket.)* Mammy! Dat you, Colonel Mack? Whah you going? Stay heah, help me, I— *(The man and the woman disappear in the bushes.* ABE *stands with his mouth open, staring after them.)* Whut's all dis? Must be anudder dream—a dream. Sump'n' quare. *(He moves cautiously forward and parts the bushes and starts back with a loud oath.)* God damn 'em! Dey dere lak hawgs! *(The fearful truth breaks upon him and he shrieks.)* Stop it! Stop dat, Mammy, Colonel Mack! *(Rushing towards the bushes again and stopping as if spellbound.)* Stop dat, I tell you, dat's me! Dat's me! *(He stumbles backward over the body of* LON-NIE MCCRANIE *and, shrieking, rushes down the road at the left.)*

SCENE VII

Thirty minutes later. DOUGLASS *has arrived and with* MUH MACK *before the fire is giving an account of his travels. He is now about nineteen years old, and has developed into a reckless dissipated youth, dressed in the cheap flashy clothes of a sport.*

DOUGLASS (*turning towards* MUH MACK *with a bitter smile*). Yeh, I says it and I says it ag'in. Let dem dere Norveners putt Pap in print foh what he's trying to do foh de niggers. Ef dey could see him now down a po' dirt fahmer dey'd not think he's such a sma't man. Let him read his books and git new ide's. Dey won't change de nigger in him, not by a damn sight. He's raght down working a tenant and dat's where he belongs. Git me? Ah, him off to-night making his speeches. I bet to Christ dis heah's his last 'un.

MUH MACK. Foh God's sake don' carry on so. Come on and tell me some mo' 'bout de places you been since you left heah. (*He sits looking in the fire.*) Whut—whut's de matter? You hain't been usual so ficey-lak wid yo' pap. You been drinking?

DOUGLASS (*laughing sweetly*). Yeh, I been drinking. And I gut cause to cuss de whole works out. (*Looking at her fiercely.*) Listen heah. Let dis slip in yo' yur, foh you'd heah it soon enough. You never has swung a' eight-pound hammer, steel driving day adder day in de br'iling sun, has you? And you hain't never done it wid a ball and chain on you ca'se you is marked dang'us, has you? and dat foh a whole yeah long? Well, I has.

MUH MACK (*in astonishment*). You been on de roads since you left?

DOUGLASS (*recklessly*). I has dat and wo' de convict clo'es des' ca'se in my drunkenness I 'gun to preach some o' his doctrines 'bout dere being no difference 'twixt de cullud and de white. I knowed bedder. But I was drunk and had hearn so many o' his speeches. De judge said he'd des' stop my mouf foh a month. And I gut a knife one day and stabbed a gyard to de hollow. And dey gin me twelve months foh dat.

MUH MACK (*admiring his prowess*). You allus was one whut fou't at de drap o' de hat.

DOUGLASS (*disgustedly*). Yeh, a damn fool, and I ain't fohgit how he run me off'n heah and beat me! (*Bursting out with shining eyes.*) Hain't I gut cause to hate him and want to git him down?

MUH MACK. Gittin' on de roads ain't much, Douglass.

DOUGLASS. No, it ain't much to lie in de jug, is it? You do it and you ain't never gwine have no more peace. De cops is allus watching you. You gits de look and dey knows you. Dey tried to 'rest me yistiddy over dere, and I hadn't done nothing. And de old man was knowing to it too. But I's learnt what he'll never learn and it's dis—dat we belongs down wid de pick and de sludge hammer and de tee-arn and de steam shovel, and de heavy things—at de bottom doing de dirty work foh de white man, dat's it. And he ain't gwine stand foh us to be educated out'n it nuther. He's gwine keep us dere. It pays him to. I sees it. And adder all dese yeahs Pap keeps on trying to teach dat men is men. Some white man's gwine shoot his lights out one dese days, see ef dee don't. (*With a reckless forgetfulness.*) And so I says gimme a fast time, a liddle gin to drown down all my troubles in, and den— (*He goes over to the door and gets his guitar.*) A liddle music to top it off wid. How about it, Muh Mack?

MUH MACK (*straining her eyes through the shadows*). Whut you gut dere? (*Jubildntly.*) Lawd, Lawd! Ef you ain't brung yo' box wid you! And I ain't heerd nothing but dem sporrers by de do and dat old rain crow in de hollow since you left two yeah back. Play her, boy, play her.

(By this time he has sat down by the fire strumming.)

DOUGLASS *(tuning up while* MUH MACK *sits in a quiver of excitement).* Lemme play yo' old piece. My 'oman in Rocky Mount said 'twas de onliest chune.

MUH MACK. Dat's it! Dat's it! Lawd, gimme de "Band." I useter be put in de middle every time foh dat step. Dance all day, dance all night, des' so I's home by de broad daylight. Chile, I c'd natch'ly knock de wool off'n 'em.
(As DOUGLASS *plays she chuckles and whines with delight and almost rises from her seat. He starts in a quiet manner gradually working up to a paroxysm of pantomime and song.* MUH MACK *begins doing the Jonah's Band Party step with her heels and toes while sitting.* DOUGLASS *spreads his wriggling feet apart, leans forward with closed eyes, and commences the "call," with the old woman's quavery slobbering voice giving the "sponse.")*

CALL: Sech a kicking up san'!

SPONSE: Jonah's ban'!
(This is repeated; then comes the command to change steps.)

"Hands up, sixteen, and circle to de right,
We's gwine git big eatings heah to-night.

"Sech a kicking up san'! Jonah's Ban'!
Sech a kicking up san'! Jonah's Ban!

"Raise yo' right foot, kick it up high,
Knock dat Mobile buck in de eye.

"Sech a kicking up san'! Jonah's Ban'!
Sech a kicking up san'! Jonah's Ban!

"Stan' up, flat-foot. Jump dem bars.
Karo backwards lak a train o' cyars.

"Sech a kicking up san'! Jonah's Ban'!
Sech a kicking up sah'! Jonah's Ban!

"Dance roun', 'oman, shew 'em de p'int,
Dem yudder coons don'ter how to coonj'int."

(By this time DOUGLASS *is playing a tattoo on the wood of his box and carrying on the tune at the same time.* MUH MACK *has risen from her chair. With her dress to her knees, defying her years, she cuts several of the well-remembered steps. At sight of her bare and thin dry shanks the delirious* DOUGLASS *bursts into loud mocking guffaws and only plays faster. The door opens at the right and* GOLDIE *comes timidly in. Her face is worn and haggard, and the strained vacant look in her eyes has deepened.* MUH MACK *stops and creeps guiltily to her chair.* DOUGLASS *tapers off his music and stops. For a moment* GOLDIE *stands astonished in the door, holding a bulky tow-sack in her hand. She drops the sack and hurries over to* DOUGLASS.)*

GOLDIE. Muhcy me! I knowed 'twas you soon's I heard de guitar. And sech carrying-ons!

DOUGLASS *(rising confusedly as she comes up to him).* How you, Mam?
(She puts her hand shyly on his arm and then clings convulsively to him, her shoulders heaving with restrained sobs. He lays one arm around her and stands looking tenderly and somewhat foolishly down at her. It is evident that in his way he cares for her. She suddenly raises her head, dries her eyes with her apron, and fetches wood from the box.)

GOLDIE *(punching the fire).* Whyn't you let me know Douglass'd come, Muh Mack?

MUH MACK. He des' come.

DOUGLASS *(laying his box on the bed).* Mam, you set in dis char. You must be cold.
(She sits down wearily, and he stands with his back to the fire. MUH MACK *picks up her snuff-brush and slyly begins to dip from her tin box.)*

GOLDIE *(with a sudden start of terror).* You hain't seed yo' pap, has you?

DOUGLASS. No'm, I ain't seed 'im. I found out he done gone to de Quillie House 'fo' I come. I slipped in heah and found Muh Mack asleep. Lawd, I skeahed her with a fiah coal.

GOLDIE *(suddenly reaching out and clutching his hand to her face).* Don't you and yo' pap have no trouble. Don't agg him on. He—he—ain't well and might rile easy. We—we kin see one 'nother off.

DOUGLASS. Oh, I'se gwine be partickler. Now don't worry no mo'. It's awright.

GOLDIE (*slowly getting up*). You all set while I fix you some supper. I got something good foh Abe and de rest of us. Lemme show you. (*She brings the bag, sits down in the chair and takes out a big meaty ham-bone.* MUH MACK *eyes it hungrily. Naïvely.*) Ain't dat de finest dough? And I gut a hawg haid, too, and collards and cracklings.

DOUGLASS (*angrily*). Dat's de way wid dem damn—wid dem white folks. Dey works you to death and den shoves dey old skippery meat off on you foh pay.

GOLDIE (*a worried look coming over her face*). You hadn't ort to say dat, Douglass. Mr. Lonnie gi'n me it—all of it. And he paid me cash for my work. Abe'll have a new bottle o' medicine Monday. (*She fingers the food childishly, and* DOUGLASS *turns away with a smothered oath. Putting the food back into the bag, she stands up.*) Now I'll git you some supper.

DOUGLASS. I cain't stay foh no supper. I promised to eat down de road wid Joe Day. Le's set and talk, ca'se we don't have much time and you can cook adder I'm gone.

GOLDIE (*hesitating*). Well—lemme put dese heah in de kitchen den. (*She goes out at the right.*)

DOUGLASS (*turning sharply to* MUH MACK). What's de matter wid Mam?

MUH MACK. Won't we des' a-having of a time when she broke in?

DOUGLASS. Cut out de damn jowing. What makes Mam act so quare?

MUH MACK (*surprised*). Do how? She acts awright.

DOUGLASS. She don't. She acts sort o' lost lak—wropped up in something. (*He scratches his head perplexed.*)

MUH MACK. Ef dey's anything wrong wid her it's 'count o' trouble, I reckin.

DOUGLASS. De hell-fi'ed fool! He's drug her to death wid his wildishness.

MUH MACK. And ef it's trouble dat ails her, I reckins as how you's done yo' shur in bringing it on. (*He swallows his reply as* GOLDIE *comes in. She lights the lamp, then sits down and begins staring in the fire.*)

DOUGLASS (*after turning from one side to the other*). Mammy, whut's de matter wid you?

GOLDIE (*brushing her hand across her face and looking up as she wipes the tears from her eyes*). Lawd bless you, chile, dey ain't nothing. I's des' happy to be wid you. (*She catches his hand and holds it a moment, then drops it and begins to look in the fire again.* DOUGLASS *watches her intently a moment and then turns away as if somewhat awed by her manner. There is a noise of some one's coming up on the porch.*)

MUH MACK (*crying out in fear*). Dat's him, Douglass! I knows his step. Dat's yo' pap. (GOLDIE *stands up, wringing her hands and crying silently as* DOUGLASS *gets his guitar and hurries into the kitchen. The door at the left opens and* ABE *enters.*)

GOLDIE (*leaning forward and rousing the fire*). Did everything turn out— (MUH MACK *suddenly screams.* GOLDIE *looks up and cries out.*) Oh! (ABE *comes towards the fire. His face is bruised, his clothes torn to shreds, and he sways as he walks.*)

MUH MACK (*rising from her chair*). Dey's been adder him! Dey's been adder him!

ABE (*snarling at her*). Shet up yo' damn yowling, will you? and don't be rousing de neighborhood. I'm not dying yit. (GOLDIE *stands a moment terror-stricken and then runs up to him.*)

GOLDIE. You's hurt, hurt bad, Abe, po' baby!

ABE (*pushing her back*). Ain't hurt much. No time to doctor me now. (*He stands before the fire.* MUH MACK *collapses in her chair. He is no longer the reformer and educator, but a criminal, beaten and hunted.*) I come to tell you to git away— (*panting*) to—to leave, leave!

GOLDIE (*sobbing and burying her face in her hands*). Whut's happened! Whut's happened!

MUH MACK (*swaying in her chair and crying to herself*). Lawdy-a-muhcy on us! Lawd-a-muhcy!
(*For a moment he stands before the women silent, with closed eyes.*)

ABE (*looking at the motto on the wall and repeating the words dully*). We are rising! (*Echoing.*) We are rising!—He didn't know what he said, he didn't. (*He staggers and grips the mantel and stands listening as if to far-away sounds. He turns desperately to the cowering women.*) Git your clothes and leave. You got to go, I tell you everything's finished at de end.

GOLDIE (*wailing*). What happened at de school-house?

ABE (*pushing his bruised hand across his forehead*). I cain't, cain't quite think—yeh, they was a crowd of white men at de door with dough-faces over their faces. Said wa'n't going to be no meeting. Dey beat me, run me off. And dey give me till tomorrow to git outen de country. You got to git away, foh it's worse'n dat—oh, it is! (*Calmly and without bitterness.*) Who you reckon set 'em on me? Who you think it was told 'em about de trouble I been in before? Yeh, and he made it out terribler'n it was. Douglass told 'em. . . . He done it. My own flesh and blood. No! No! he was but ain't no more! (*Gloomily.*) But I don't blame him—dey ain't no blaming nobody no longer.

GOLDIE (*fiercely*). He didn't—he wouldn't turn ag'in' his own pa.

ABE (*sternly*). Hush! He did though. But it don't matter to-night. And you got to leave. (*Half screaming and tearing at the mantel.*) Now! Now, I tell you.

GOLDIE (*between her sobs*). Did you—who hurt you?

ABE. I tell you I've done murder, and dey coming for me.
(MUH MACK *sits doubled up with fear, her head between her arms. With a sharp gasp* GOLDIE *ceases weeping and sits strangely silent.*)

MUH MACK. Murder! Oh, Lawd-a-muhcy! (*She mumbles and sobs in her rag.*)

ABE. Dey drove me away from de meeting. I come back by the road mad. (*He gasps.*) Every white man's hand ag'in' me to de last. And Mr. Lonnie come out to de road when I passed his house and begun to abuse me about de crop. He struck at me, and I went blind all of a sudden and hit him wid my fist. Den we fou't. (*His voice growing shrill.*) And I hit him and hit him. I beat his head in. I killed him dead, dead! I beat on and on until all de madness went out of me and de dark was everywhere. Den I seed a sight—(*He stops, aghast at the remembrance.*) I left him dere in de night dead on de ground. Dey done found 'im—I heah 'em crying up dere in de night. Dey's coming to git me. (*He holds out his bruised hands.*) His blood's still shining on dem hands. (*He turns his head away in fear.*)

MUH MACK (*in a high whine of terror*). My God a-mighty! You kilt yo' own flesh!

ABE (*turning wrathfully upon her*). Yeh, yeh, some bitch went a-coupling wid a white man! And I seed it—seed it! (*He drops his hands helplessly. A sort of terror comes upon him.*) Oh, Lawd God! I'm anudder Cain. I tell you I—I scrushed his head in and beat it till I put out de stars wid blood. Mercy! Mercy! (*With his hands still held before him, he stands with bowed head. After a moment he looks up and speaks calmly, almost resignedly, his dignity coming back to him.*) This is the way it was meant to be, and I'm glad it's ended. (*He stands with his fists to his temples, and then flings out his arms in a wide gesture.*) Oh, but damn 'em! Don't dey know I want to do all for de best. (*Shaking his fist at the shadows.*) I tell you, I tell you I wanted—I've tried to make it come right. (*Lowering his head.*) And now it's come to dis.
(DOUGLASS *comes in from the kitchen and stands away before him, his face filled with shame and fear.* ABE *looks at him without interest.*)

DOUGLASS. Befo' God, Pap, I—I didn t mean no sech happenings. I never thought—

ABE (*eyeing him coldly*). Who you? (*More loudly.*) A leader, a king among men! (*To the women.*) Here's Douglass and you can go wid him.

(DOUGLASS *turns back into the kitchen and instantly runs out. His eyes are staring with fear.*)

DOUGLASS (*in a throaty whisper*). Come on, Mam! (*Twisting his cap in terror.*) Dey's coming. I heerd 'em from de kitchen do'. Dey's coming. Run, Pap! God have muh-cy!

(MUH MACK *hobbles to him and tries to pull him through the door at the right. He looks back towards his mother.*)

MUH MACK. Come on! Come on!

DOUGLASS. Mam, Mam, don't stay heah!

ABE (*raising* GOLDIE *from her chair*). Go on wid him. You ain't to blame foh nothing. (*He pushes her towards* DOUGLASS. *But she turns and throws her arms around him, clinging silently to his breast.*)

MUH MACK (*pulling* DOUGLASS). I heahs 'em. Dat's dem coming.

(*With an anxious look at* GOLDIE, DOUGLASS *hurries with* MUH MACK *through the door and into the fields.* ABE *places* GOLDIE *back in her chair and stands looking at her. He catches her by the shoulders and shakes her.*)

ABE. Tell me, what is it, Goldie! What ails you, gal? (*She sits looking dumbly at him and he draws away from her. Presently there is a sound of stamping feet outside, and voices slip in like the whispering of leaves. A stone is thrown against the house, then another and another. One crashes through the window and strikes the lamp. The room is left in semi-darkness.* ABE *with a sob of overwhelming terror falls upon his knees. Twisting his great hands together, he casts up his eyes and cries in a loud voice.*) God, God, where is you now! Where is you, God! (*He begins half sobbing and chanting.*) You has helped befo', help me now. Is you up dere? Heah my voice! (*Fear takes possession of him.*) Blast me, Lawd, in yo' thunder and lightning, if it is yo' will! Ketch me away in de whirlwind, foh I'm a sinner. Yo' will, yo' will, not mine. Let fiah and brimstone

burn me to ashes and scatter me on de earf. (*Gasping.*) I've tried, I've tried to walk de path, but I'm po' and sinful. . . . Give me peace, rest—rest in yo' bosom—if it is dy will. Save me, Jesus, save me! (*He falls sobbing to the floor.*)

VOICE (*outside*). Come out of there, you dirty nigger! (*A shudder runs through him, and his sobs grow less violent.*) Come out! Come out!

(*Another stone crashes through the room. As if ashamed of his weakness,* ABE *rises from the floor. He speaks firmly to the shadows.*)

ABE. In the end it was so intended. (*Looking around him.*) And I end here where I begun. (*He bursts out in a loud voice.*) Yet they're asleep, asleep, and I can't wake 'em!

VOICES. He's in there.
I hear him talking.
He's done talking now, goddam him!
We'll show him the law all right.
He's got a gun!
Shoot him like a dog.

ABE (*wiping his brow and again speaking in the rôle of the educator trying to convince his everlastingly silent hearers*). But they'll wake up, they'll wake—a crack of thunder and deep divided from deep—a light! A light, and it will be! (GOLDIE *still sits hunched over in her chair. As he speaks he goes to the door at the left.*) We got to be free, freedom of the soul and of the mind. Ignorance means sin and sin means destruction. (*Shouting.*) Freedom! Freedom! (*Lifting up his voice.*) Yea, yea, it was writ, "Man that is born of woman is of few days and full of trouble. . . ." Lak de wind wid no home. Ayh, ayh, nigger man, nigger man—(*He opens the door.*) I go talk to 'em, I go meet 'em—

VOICE. Hell! Lookout! There he is!

ABE. Yea, guns and killings is in vain. (*He steps out on the porch.*) What we need is to—to—(*His words are cut short by a roar from several guns. He staggers and falls with his head in the doorway.*)—and we must have—have—

(*At the sound of the guns,* GOLDIE *springs*

to her feet. For an instant everything is still. Then several shots are fired into ABE's *body.*)

VOICE. Quit the shooting. He's dead as a damned door! Now everybody get away from here—no talking, no talking. Keep quiet—quiet.

(*There is the sound of shuffling footsteps and men leaping the fence. Voices come back into the room.*)

VOICES. Yeh, mum's it.
He won't raise no more disturbances!
(*The voices grow more faint.*)
What a bloody murder he done!
He's still now, by God!
It's the only way to have peace, peace.
Peace, by God!
(GOLDIE *moves towards the door where* ABE *lies. Halfway across the room she stops and screams and then drops down beside his body. The wind blows through the house setting the sparks flying.*)

Strange Interlude

BY EUGENE O'NEILL

CHARACTERS

CHARLES MARSDEN
PROFESSOR HENRY LEEDS
NINA LEEDS, his daughter
EDMUND DARRELL
SAM EVANS
MRS. AMOS EVANS, Sam's mother
GORDON EVANS
MADELINE ARNOLD

SCENES

First Part

ACT ONE
Library, the Leeds' home in a small university town of New England—an afternoon in late summer.

ACT TWO
The same. Fall of the following year. Night.

ACT THREE
Dining room of the Evans' homestead in Northern New York State—late spring of the next year. Morning.

ACT FOUR
The same as Acts One and Two. Fall of the same year. Evening.

ACT FIVE
Sitting room of small house Evans has rented in a seashore suburb near New York. The following April. Morning.

Second Part

ACT SIX
The same. A little over a year later. Evening.

ACT SEVEN
Sitting room of the Evans' apartment on Park Avenue. Nearly eleven years later. Early afternoon.

ACT EIGHT
Section of afterdeck of the Evans' cruiser anchored near the finish line at Poughkeepsie. Ten years later. Afternoon.

ACT NINE
A terrace on the Evans' estate on Long Island. Several months later. Late afternoon.

STRANGE INTERLUDE

ACT ONE

SCENE: *The library of* PROFESSOR LEEDS' *home in a small university town in New England. This room is at the front part of his house with windows opening on the strip of lawn between the house and the quiet residential street. It is a small room with a low ceiling. The furniture has been selected with a love for old New England pieces. The walls are lined almost to the ceiling with glassed-in bookshelves. These are packed with books, principally editions, many of them old and rare, of the ancient classics in the original Greek and Latin, of the later classics in French and German and Italian, of all the English authors who wrote while s was still like an f and a few since then, the most modern probably being Thackeray. The atmosphere of the room is that of a cosy, cultured retreat, sedulously built as a sanctuary where, secure with the culture of the past at his back, a fugitive from reality can view the present safely from a distance, as a superior with condescending disdain, pity, and even amusement.*

There is a fair-sized table, a heavy armchair, a rocker, and an old bench made comfortable with cushions. The table, with the Professor's armchair at its left, is arranged toward the left of the room, the rocker is at center, the bench at right.

There is one entrance, a door in the right wall, rear.

It is late afternoon of a day in August. Sunshine, cooled and dimmed in the shade of trees, fills the room with a soothing light.

The sound of a MAID'S VOICE—*a middle-aged woman*—*explaining familiarly but respectfully from the right, and* MARSDEN *enters. He is a tall thin man of thirty-five, meticulously well-dressed in tweeds of distinctly English tailoring, his appearance that of an Anglicized New England gentleman. His face is too long for its width, his nose is high and narrow, his forehead broad, his mild blue eyes those of a dreamy self-analyst, his thin lips ironical and a bit sad. There is an indefinable feminine quality about him, but it is nothing apparent in either appearance or act. His manner is cool and poised. He speaks with a careful ease as one who listens to his own conversation. He has long fragile hands, and the stoop to his shoulders of a man weak muscularly, who has never liked athletics and has always been regarded as of delicate constitution. The main point about his personality is a quiet charm, a quality of appealing, inquisitive friendliness, always willing to listen, eager to sympathize, to like and to be liked.*

MARSDEN

(Standing just inside the door, his tall, stooped figure leaning back against the books—nodding back at the MAID *and smiling kindly).* I'll wait in here, Mary. *(His eyes follow her for a second, then return to gaze around the room slowly with an appreciative relish for the familiar significance of the books. He smiles affectionately and his amused voice recites the words with a rhetorical resonance.)* Sanctum Sanctorum!

(His voice takes on a monotonous musing quality, his eyes stare idly at his drifting thoughts). How perfectly the Professor's unique haven! . . . *(He smiles.)* Primly classical . . . when New Englander meets Greek! . . . *(Looking at the books now.)* He hasn't added one book in years . . . how old was I when I first came here? . . . six . . . with my father . . . father . . . how dim his face has grown! . . . he wanted to speak to me just before he

died . . . the hospital . . . smell of iodo-form in the cool halls . . . hot summer. . . . I bent down . . . his voice had withdrawn so far away . . . I couldn't understand him . . . what son can ever understand? . . . always too near, too soon, too distant or too late! . . . (*His face has become sad with a memory of the bewildered suffering of the adolescent boy he had been at the time of his father's death. Then he shakes his head, flinging off his thoughts, and makes himself walk about the room.*) What memories on such a smiling afternoon! . . . this pleasant old town after three months . . . I won't go to Europe again . . . couldn't write a line there . . . how answer the fierce question of all those dead and maimed? . . . too big a job for me! . . . (*He sighs —then self-mockingly.*) But back here . . . it is the interlude that gently questions . . . in this town dozing . . . decorous bodies moving with circumspection through the afternoons . . . their habits affectionately chronicled . . . an excuse for weaving amusing words . . . my novels . . . not of cosmic importance, hardly . . . (*Then self-reassuringly*) but there is a public to cherish them, evidently . . . and I can write! . . . more than one can say of these modern sex-yahoos! . . . I must start work tomorrow . . . I'd like to use the Professor in a novel sometime . . . and his wife . . . seems impossible she's been dead six years . . . so aggressively his wife! . . . poor Professor! now it's Nina who bosses him . . . but that's different . . . she has bossed me, too, ever since she was a baby . . . she's a woman now . . . known love and death . . . Gordon brought down in flames . . . two days before the armistice . . . what fiendish irony! . . . his wonderful athlete's body . . . her lover . . . charred bones in a cage of twisted steel . . . no wonder she broke down . . . Mother said she's become quite queer lately . . . Mother seemed jealous of my concern . . . why have I never fallen in love with Nina? . . . could I? . . . that way . . . used to dance her on my knee . . . sit her on my lap

. . . even now she'd never think anything about it . . . but sometimes the scent of her hair and skin . . . like a dreamy drug . . . dreamy! . . . there's the rub! . . . all dreams with me! . . . my sex life among the phantoms! . . . (*He grins torturedly.*) Why? . . . oh, this digging in gets nowhere . . . to the devil with sex! . . . our impotent pose of today to beat the loud drum on fornication! . . . boasters . . . eunuchs parading with the phallus! . . . giving themselves away . . . whom do they fool? . . . not even themselves! . . . (*His face suddenly full of an intense pain and disgust.*) Ugh! . . . always that memory! . . . why can't I ever forget? . . . as sickeningly clear as if it were yesterday . . . prep school . . . Easter vacation . . . Fatty Boggs and Jack Fraser . . . that house of cheap vice . . . one dollar! . . . why did I go? . . . Jack, the dead game sport . . . how I admired him! . . . afraid of his taunts . . . he pointed to the Italian girl . . . "Take her!" . . . daring me . . . I went . . . miserably frightened . . . what a pig she was! . . . pretty vicious face under caked powder and rouge . . . surly and contemptuous . . . lumpy body . . . short legs and thick ankles . . . slums of Naples . . . "What you gawkin' about? Git a move on, kid" . . . kid! . . . I *was* only a kid! . . . sixteen . . . test of manhood . . . ashamed to face Jack again unless . . . fool! . . . I might have lied to him! . . . but I honestly thought that wench would feel humiliated if I . . . oh, stupid kid! . . . back at the hotel I waited till they were asleep . . . then sobbed . . . thinking of Mother . . . feeling I had defiled her . . . and myself . . . forever! . . . (*Mocking bitterly.*) "Nothing half so sweet in life as love's young dream," what? . . . (*He gets to his feet impatiently.*) Why does my mind always have to dwell on that? . . . too silly . . . no importance really . . . an incident such as any boy of my age . . .

(*He hears someone coming quickly from the right and turns expectantly.* PROFESSOR LEEDS *enters, a pleased relieved expression fighting the flurried worry on his face. He* is a small, slender man of fifty-five, his hair gray, the top of his head bald. His face, prepossessing in spite of its too-small, over-refined features, is that of a retiring, studious nature. He has intelligent eyes and a smile that can be ironical. Temperamentally timid, his defense is an assumption of his complacent, superior manner of the classroom toward the world at large. This defense is strengthened by a natural tendency toward a prim provincialism where practical present-day considerations are concerned (though he is most liberal—even radical—in his tolerant understanding of the manners and morals of Greece and Imperial Rome!). This classroom poise of his, however, he cannot quite carry off outside the classroom. There is an unconvincing quality about it that leaves his larger audience—and particularly the PROFESSOR himself—subtly embarrassed. As MARSDEN is one of his old students, whom, in addition, he has known from childhood, he is perfectly at ease with him.)

MARSDEN

(Holding out his hand—with unmistakable liking). Here I am again, Professor!

PROFESSOR LEEDS

(Shaking his hand and patting him on the back—with genuine affection). So glad to see you, Charlie! A surprise, too! We didn't expect you back so soon! (He sits in his chair on the left of the table while MARSDEN sits in the rocker.)
(Looking away from MARSDEN a moment, his face now full of selfish relief as he thinks.) Fortunate, his coming back . . . always calming influence on Nina . . .

MARSDEN

And I never dreamed of returning so soon. But Europe, Professor, is the big casualty they were afraid to set down on the list.

PROFESSOR LEEDS

(His face clouding). Yes, I suppose you found everything completely changed since before the war.
(He thinks resentfully). The war . . . Gordon! . . .

MARSDEN

Europe has "gone west"—(he smiles whimsically) to America, let's hope! (Then frowningly.) I couldn't stand it. There were millions sitting up with the corpse already, who had a family right to be there—(Then matter-of-factly.) I was wasting my time, too. I couldn't write a line. (Then gaily.) But where's Nina? I must see Nina!

PROFESSOR LEEDS

She'll be right in. She said she wanted to finish thinking something out—You'll find Nina changed, Charlie, greatly changed!
(He sighs—thinking with a trace of guilty alarm). The first thing she said at breakfast . . . "I dreamed of Gordon" . . . as if she wanted to taunt me! . . . how absurd! . . . her eyes positively glared! . . .
(Suddenly blurting out resentfully). She dreams about Gordon.

MARSDEN

(Looking at him with amused surprise). Well, I'd hardly call that a change, would you?

PROFESSOR LEEDS

(Thinking, oblivious to this remark). But I must constantly bear in mind that she's not herself . . . that she's a sick girl . . .

MARSDEN

(Thinking). The morning news of Gordon's death came . . . her face like gray putty . . . beauty gone . . . no face can afford intense grief . . . it's only later when sorrow . . .
(With concern). Just what do you mean by changed, Professor? Before I left she seemed to be coming out of that horrible numbed calm.

PROFESSOR LEEDS

(Slowly and carefully). Yes, she has played a lot of golf and tennis this summer, motored around with her friends, and even danced a good deal. And she eats with a ravenous appetite.
(Thinking frightenedly). Breakfast . . . "dreamed of Gordon" . . . what a look of hate for me in her eyes! . . .

MARSDEN

But that sounds splendid! When I left she wouldn't see anyone or go anywhere.

(*Thinking pityingly*). Wandering from room to room . . . her thin body and pale lost face . . . gutted, love-abandoned eyes! . . .

PROFESSOR LEEDS

Well, now she's gone to the opposite extreme! Sees everyone—bores, fools—as if she'd lost all discrimination or wish to discriminate. And she talks interminably, Charlie—intentional nonsense, one would say! Refuses to be serious! Jeers at everything!

MARSDEN

(*Consolingly*). Oh, that's all undoubtedly part of the effort she's making to forget.

PROFESSOR LEEDS

(*Absent-mindedly*). Yes.

(*Arguing with himself*). Shall I tell him? . . . no . . . it might sound silly . . . but it's terrible to be so alone in this . . . if Nina's mother had lived . . . my wife . . . dead! . . . and for a time I actually felt released! . . . wife! . . . help-meet! . . . now I need help! . . . no use! . . . she's gone! . . .

MARSDEN

(*Watching him—thinking with a condescending affection*). Good little man . . . he looks worried . . . always fussing about something . . . he must get on Nina's nerves. . . .

(*Reassuringly*). No girl could forget Gordon in a hurry, especially after the shock of his tragic death.

PROFESSOR LEEDS

(*Irritably*). I realize that.

(*Thinking resentfully*). Gordon . . . always Gordon with everyone! . . .

MARSDEN

By the way, I located the spot near Sedan where Gordon's machine fell. Nina asked me to, you know.

PROFESSOR LEEDS

(*Irritated—expostulatingly*). For heaven's sake, don't remind her! Give her a chance to forget if you want to see her well again.

After all, Charlie, life must be lived and Nina can't live with a corpse forever! (*Trying to control his irritation and talk in an objective tone.*) You see, I'm trying to see things through clearly and unsentimentally. If you'll remember, I was as broken up as anyone over Gordon's death. I'd become so reconciled to Nina's love for him—although, as you know, I was opposed at first, and for fair reasons, I think, for the boy, for all his good looks and prowess in sport and his courses, really came of common people and had no money of his own except as he made a career for himself.

MARSDEN

(*A trifle defensively*). I'm sure he would have had a brilliant career.

PROFESSOR LEEDS

(*Impatiently*). No doubt. Although you must acknowledge, Charlie, that college heroes rarely shine brilliantly in after life. Unfortunately, the tendency to spoil them in the university is a poor training—

MARSDEN

But Gordon was absolutely unspoiled, I should say.

PROFESSOR LEEDS

(*Heatedly*). Don't misunderstand me, Charlie! I'd be the first to acknowledge— (*A bit pathetically.*) It isn't Gordon, Charlie. It's his memory, his ghost, you might call it, haunting Nina, whose influence I have come to dread because of the terrible change in her attitude toward me.

(*His face twitches as if he were on the verge of tears—he thinks desperately*). I've got to tell him . . . he will see that I acted for the best . . . that I was justified. . . .

(*He hesitates—then blurts out*). It may sound incredible, but Nina has begun to act as if she hated me!

MARSDEN

(*Startled*). Oh, come now!

PROFESSOR LEEDS

(*Insistently*). Absolutely! I haven't wanted to admit it. I've refused to believe it, until it's become too appallingly obvious in her whole attitude toward me! (*His voice trembles.*)

MARSDEN

(*Moved—expostulating*). Oh, now you're becoming morbid! Why, Nina has always idolized you! What possible reason—?

PROFESSOR LEEDS

(*Quickly*). I can answer that, I think. She has a reason. But why she should blame me when she must know I acted for the best—You probably don't know, but just before he sailed for the front Gordon wanted their marriage to take place, and Nina consented. In fact, from the insinuations she lets drop now, she must have been most eager, but at the time—However, I felt it was ill-advised and I took Gordon aside and pointed out to him that such a precipitate marriage would be unfair to Nina, and scarcely honorable on his part.

MARSDEN

(*Staring at him wonderingly*). You said that to Gordon?
  (*Thinking cynically*). A shrewd move! . . . Gordon's proud spot, fairness and honor! . . . but was it honorable of you? . . .

PROFESSOR LEEDS

(*With a touch of asperity*). Yes, I said it, and I gave him my reason. There *was* the possibility he might be killed, in the flying service rather more than a possibility, which, needless to say, I did not point out, but which Gordon undoubtedly realized, poor boy! If he were killed, he would be leaving Nina a widow, perhaps with a baby, with no resources, since he was penniless, except what pension she might get from the government; and all this while she was still at an age when a girl, especially one of Nina's charm and beauty, should have all of life before her. Decidedly, I told him, in justice to Nina, they must wait until he had come back and begun to establish his position in the world. That was the square thing. And Gordon was quick to agree with me!

MARSDEN

(*Thinking*). The square thing! . . . but we must all be crooks where hap-

piness is concerned! . . . steal or starve! . . .
  (*Then rather ironically*). And so Gordon told Nina he'd suddenly realized it wouldn't be fair to her. But I gather he didn't tell her it was your scruple originally?

PROFESSOR LEEDS

No, I asked him to keep what I said strictly confidential.

MARSDEN

(*Thinking ironically*). Trusted to his honor again! . . . old fox! . . . poor Gordon! . . .
But Nina suspects now that you—?

PROFESSOR LEEDS

(*Startled*). Yes. That's exactly it. She knows in some queer way. And she acts toward me exactly as if she thought I had deliberately destroyed her happiness, that I had hoped for Gordon's death and been secretly overjoyed when the news came! (*His voice is shaking with emotion.*) And there you have it, Charlie—the whole absurd mess!
  (*Thinking with a strident accusation*). And it's true, you contemptible . . . ! (*Then miserably defending himself.*) No! . . . I acted unselfishly . . . for her sake! . . .

MARSDEN

(*Wonderingly*). You don't mean to tell me she has accused you of all this?

PROFESSOR LEEDS

Oh, no, Charlie! Only by hints—looks—innuendos. She knows she has no real grounds, but in the present state of her mind the real and the unreal become confused—

MARSDEN

(*Thinking cynically*). As always in all minds . . . or how could men live? . . .
  (*Soothingly*). That's just what you ought to bear in your mind—the state of hers—and not get so worked up over what I should say is a combination of imagination on both your parts. (*He gets to his feet as he hears voices from the right.*) Buck up! This must be Nina coming.
  (*The* PROFESSOR *gets to his feet, hastily*

composing his features into his bland, cultured expression.)

MARSDEN

(*Thinking self-mockingly but a bit worried about himself*). My heart pounding! . . . seeing Nina again! . . . how sentimental . . . how she'd laugh if she knew! . . . and quite rightly . . . absurd for me to react as if I loved . . . that way . . . her dear old Charlie . . . ha! . . . (*He smiles with bitter self-mockery.*)

PROFESSOR LEEDS

(*Thinking worriedly*). I hope she won't make a scene . . . she's seemed on the verge all day . . . thank God, Charlie's like one of the family . . . but what a life for me! . . . with the opening of the new term only a few weeks off! . . . I can't do it . . . I'll have to call in a nerve specialist . . . but the last one did her no good . . . his outrageous fee . . . he can take it to court . . . I absolutely refuse . . . but if he should bring suit? . . . what a scandal . . . no, I'll have to pay . . . somehow . . . borrow . . . he has me in a corner, the robber! . . .

NINA

(*Enters and stands just inside the doorway looking directly at her father with defiant eyes, her face set in an expression of stubborn resolve. She is twenty, tall with broad square shoulders, slim strong hips and long beautifully developed legs—a fine athletic girl of the swimmer, tennis player, golfer type. Her straw-blond hair, framing her sun-burned face, is bobbed. Her face is striking, handsome rather than pretty, the bone structure prominent, the forehead high, the lips of her rather large mouth clearly modelled above the firm jaw. Her eyes are beautiful and bewildering, extraordinarily large and a deep greenish blue. Since* GORDON's *death they have a quality of continually shuddering before some terrible enigma, of being wounded to their depths and made defiant and resentful by their pain. Her whole manner, the charged atmosphere she gives off, is totally at variance with her healthy outdoor physique. It is strained, nerve-racked, hectic, a terrible*

tension of will alone maintaining self-possession. She is dressed in smart sport clothes. Too preoccupied with her resolve to remember or see MARSDEN, *she speaks directly to her father in a voice tensely cold and calm*). I have made up my mind, Father.

PROFESSOR LEEDS

(*Thinking distractedly*). What does she mean? . . . oh, God help me! . . . (*Flustered—hastily*). Don't you see Charlie, Nina?

MARSDEN

(*Troubled—thinking*). She has changed . . . what has happened? . . . (*He comes forward toward her—a bit embarrassed but affectionately using his pet name for her*). Hello, Nina Cara Nina! Are you trying to cut me dead, young lady?

NINA

(*Turning her eyes to* MARSDEN, *holding out her hand for him to shake, in her cool, preoccupied voice*). Hello, Charlie. (*Her eyes immediately return to her father.*) Listen, Father!

MARSDEN

(*Standing near her, concealing his chagrin*). That hurts! . . . I mean nothing! . . . but she's a sick girl . . . I must make allowance . . .

PROFESSOR LEEDS

(*Thinking distractedly*). That look in her eyes! . . . hate! . . . (*With a silly giggle*). Really, Nina, you're absolutely rude! What has Charlie done?

NINA

(*In her cool tone*). Why, nothing. Nothing at all. (*She goes to him with a detached, friendly manner.*) Did I seem rude, Charlie? I didn't mean to be. (*She kisses him with a cool, friendly smile.*) Welcome home.

(*Thinking wearily*). What has Charlie done? . . . nothing . . . and never will . . . Charlie sits beside the fierce river, immaculately timid, cool and clothed, watching the burning, frozen naked swimmers drown at last. . . .

MARSDEN

(*Thinking torturedly*). Cold lips . . . the kiss of contempt! . . . for dear old Charlie! . . .
(*Forcing a good-natured laugh*). Rude? Not a bit! (*Banteringly*) As I've often reminded you, what can I expect when the first word you ever spoke in this world was an insult to me. "Dog" you said, looking right at me—at the age of one! (*He laughs. The* PROFESSOR *laughs nervously.* NINA *smiles perfunctorily.*)

NINA

(*Thinking wearily*). The fathers laugh at little daughter Nina . . . I must get away! . . . nice Charlie doggy . . . faithful . . . fetch and carry . . . bark softly in books at the deep night. . . .

PROFESSOR LEEDS

(*Thinking*). What is she thinking? . . . I can't stand living like this! . . . (*Giggle gone to a twitching grin*). You are a cool one, Nina! You'd think you'd just seen Charlie yesterday!

NINA

(*Slowly—coolly and reflectively*). Well, the war is over. Coming back safe from Europe isn't such an unusual feat now, is it?

MARSDEN

(*Thinking bitterly*). A taunt . . . I didn't fight . . . physically unfit . . . not like Gordon . . . Gordon in flames . . . how she must resent my living! . . . thinking of me, scribbling in press bureau . . . louder and louder lies . . . drown the guns and the screams . . . deafen the world with lies . . . hired choir of liars! . . .
(*Forcing a joking tone*). Little you know the deadly risks I ran, Nina! If you'd eaten some of the food they gave me on my renovated transport, you'd shower me with congratulations!
(*The* PROFESSOR *forces a snicker.*)

NINA

(*Coolly*). Well, you're here, and that's that. (*Then suddenly expanding in a sweet, genuinely affectionate smile.*) And I *am* glad,

Charlie, always glad you're here! You know that.

MARSDEN

(*Delighted and embarrassed*). I hope so, Nina!

NINA

(*Turning on her father—determinedly*). I must finish what I started to say, Father. I've thought it all out and decided that I simply must get away from here at once— or go crazy! And I'm going on the nine-forty tonight. (*She turns to* MARSDEN *with a quick smile.*) You'll have to help me pack, Charlie!
(*Thinking with weary relief*). Now that's said . . . I'm going . . . never come back . . . oh, how I loathe this room! . . .

MARSDEN

(*Thinking with alarm*). What's this? . . . going? . . . going to whom? . . .

PROFESSOR LEEDS

(*Thinking—terrified*). Going? . . . never come back to me? . . . no! . . .
(*Desperately putting on his prim severe manner toward an unruly pupil*). This is rather a sudden decision, isn't it? You haven't mentioned before that you were considering—in fact, you've led me to believe that you were quite contented here— that is, of course I mean for the time being, and I really think—

MARSDEN

(*Looking at* NINA—*thinking with alarm*). Going away to whom? . . . (*Then watching the* PROFESSOR *with a pitying shudder.*) He's on the wrong tack with his professor's manner . . . her eyes seeing cruelly through him . . . with what terrible recognition! . . . God, never bless me with children! . . .

NINA

(*Thinking with weary scorn*). The Professor of Dead Languages is talking again . . . a dead man lectures on the past of living . . . since I was born I have been in his class, loving-attentive, pupil-daughter Nina . . . my ears numb with spiritless messages

from the dead . . . dead words droning
on . . . listening because he is my cultured father . . . a little more inclined
to deafness than the rest (let me be
just) because he is my father . . . father? . . . what is father? . . .

PROFESSOR LEEDS

(*Thinking—terrified*). I must talk
her out of it! . . . find the right words!
. . . oh, I know she won't hear me! . . .
oh, wife, why did you die, you would
have talked to her, she would have
listened to you! . . .
(*Continuing in his professor's superior*
manner)—and I really think, in justice to
yourself above all, you ought to consider
this step with great care before you definitely commit yourself. First and foremost, there is your health to be taken into
consideration. You've been very ill, Nina,
how perilously so perhaps you're not completely aware, but I assure you, and Charlie can corroborate my statement, that six
months ago the doctors thought it might
be years before—and yet, by staying home
and resting and finding healthy outdoor
recreation among your old friends, and
keeping your mind occupied with the routine of managing the household—(*he
forces a prim playful smile*) and managing
me, I might add!—you have wonderfully
improved and I think it most ill-advised in
the hottest part of August, while you're
really still a convalescent—

NINA

(*Thinking*). Talking! . . . his voice
like a fatiguing dying tune droned on
a beggar's organ . . . his words arising
from the tomb of a soul in puffs of
ashes . . . (*Torturedly.*) Ashes! . . .
oh, Gordon, my dear one! . . . oh, lips
on my lips, oh, strong arms around
me, oh, spirit so brave and generous
and gay! . . . ashes dissolving into
mud! . . . mud and ashes! . . . that's
all! . . . gone! . . . gone forever from
me! . . .

PROFESSOR LEEDS

(*Thinking angrily*) Her eyes . . . I
know that look . . . tender, loving . . .
not for me . . . damn Gordon! . . . I'm
glad he's dead! . . .

(*A touch of asperity in his voice*). And at
a couple of hours' notice to leave everything in the air, as it were—(*Then judicially.*) No, Nina, frankly, I can't see it.
You know I'd gladly consent to anything
in the world to benefit you, but—surely,
you can't have reflected!

NINA

(*Thinking torturedly*). Gordon darling, I must go away where I can
think of you in silence! . . .
(*She turns on her father, her voice trembling with the effort to keep it in control—
icily*). It's no use talking, Father. I *have*
reflected and I am going!

PROFESSOR LEEDS

(*With asperity*). But I tell you it's quite
impossible! I don't like to bring up the
money consideration but I couldn't possibly afford—And how will you support
yourself, if I may ask? Two years in the
University, I am sorry to say, won't be
much use to you when applying for a job.
And even if you had completely recovered
from your nervous breakdown, which it's
obvious to anyone you haven't, then I most
decidedly think you should finish out your
science course and take your degree before
you attempt—
(*Thinking desperately*). No use! . . .
she doesn't hear . . . thinking of Gordon . . . she'll defy me . . .

NINA

(*Thinking desperately*). I must keep
calm . . . I mustn't let go or I'll tell
him everything . . . and I mustn't tell
him . . . he's my father . . .
(*With the same cold calculating finality*).
I've already had six months' training for
a nurse. I will finish my training. There's
a doctor I know at a sanitarium for crippled soldiers—a friend of Gordon's. I
wrote to him and he answered that he'll
gladly arrange it.

PROFESSOR LEEDS

(*Thinking furiously*). Gordon's friend
. . . Gordon again! . . .
(*Severely*). You seriously mean to tell me
you, in your condition, want to nurse in a
soldiers' hospital! Absurd!

MARSDEN

(*Thinking with indignant revulsion*). Quite right, Professor! . . . her beauty . . . all those men . . . in their beds . . . it's too revolting! . . .

(*With a persuasive quizzing tone*). Yes, I must say I can't see you as a peace-time Florence Nightingale, Nina!

NINA

(*Coolly, struggling to keep control, ignoring these remarks*). So you see, Father, I've thought of everything and there's not the slightest reason to worry about me. And I've been teaching Mary how to take care of you. So you won't need me at all. You can go along as if nothing had happened —and really, nothing will have happened that hasn't already happened.

PROFESSOR LEEDS

Why, even the manner in which you address me—the tone you take—proves conclusively that you're not yourself!

NINA

(*Her voice becoming a bit uncanny, her thoughts breaking through*). No, I'm not myself yet. That's just it. Not all myself. But I've been becoming myself. And I must finish!

PROFESSOR LEEDS

(*With angry significance—to* MARSDEN). You hear her, Charlie? She's a sick girl!

NINA

(*Slowly and strangely*). I'm not sick. I'm too well. But they are sick and I must give my health to help them to live on, and to live on myself. (*With a sudden intensity in her tone.*) I must pay for my cowardly treachery to Gordon! You should understand this, Father, you who— (*She swallows hard, catching her breath.*) (*Thinking desperately*). I'm beginning to tell him! . . . I mustn't! . . . he's my father! . . .

PROFESSOR LEEDS

(*In a panic of guilty fear, but defiantly*). What do you mean? I am afraid you're not responsible for what you're saying.

NINA

(*Again with the strange intensity*). I must pay! It's my plain duty! Gordon is dead! What use is my life to me or anyone? But I must make it of use—by giving it! (*Fiercely.*) I must learn to give myself, do you hear—give and give until I can make that gift of myself for a man's happiness without scruple, without fear, without joy except in his joy! When I've accomplished this I'll have found myself, I'll know how to start in living my own life again! (*Appealing to them with a desperate impatience.*) Don't you see? In the name of the commonest decency and honor, I owe it to Gordon!

PROFESSOR LEEDS

(*Sharply*). No, I can't see—nor anyone else!

(*Thinking savagely*). I hope Gordon is in hell! . . .

MARSDEN

(*Thinking*). Give herself? . . . can she mean her body? . . . beautiful body . . . to cripples? . . . for Gordon's sake? . . . damn Gordon! . . .

(*Coldly*). What do you mean, you owe it to Gordon, Nina?

PROFESSOR LEEDS

(*Bitterly*). Yes, how ridiculous! It seems to me when you gave him your love, he got more than he could ever have hoped—

NINA

(*With fierce self-contempt*). I gave him? What did I give him? It's what I didn't give! That last night before he sailed—in his arms until my body ached—kisses until my lips were numb—knowing all that night—something in me knowing he would die, that he would never kiss me again—knowing this so surely yet with my cowardly brain lying, no, he'll come back and marry you, you'll be happy ever after and feel his children at your breasts looking up with eyes so much like his, possessing eyes so happy in possessing you! (*Then violently.*) But Gordon never possessed me! I'm still Gordon's silly virgin! And Gordon is muddy ashes! And I've lost my happiness forever! All that last night I knew he wanted me. I knew it was only the honorable code-bound Gordon, who kept commanding from his brain, no, you mustn't, you must respect her, you must wait till you have a marriage license! (*She gives a mocking laugh.*)

PROFESSOR LEEDS

(*Shocked*). Nina! This is really going too far!

MARSDEN

(*Repelled. With a superior sneer*). Oh, come now, Nina! You've been reading books. Those don't sound like your thoughts.

NINA

(*Without looking at him, her eyes on her father's—intensely*). Gordon wanted me! I wanted Gordon! I should have made him take me! I knew he would die and I would have no children, that there would be no big Gordon or little Gordon left to me, that happiness was calling me, never to call again if I refused! And yet I did refuse! I didn't make him take me! I lost him forever! And now I am lonely and not pregnant with anything at all, but—but loathing! (*She hurls this last at her father—fiercely.*) Why did I refuse? What was that cowardly something in me that cried, no, you mustn't, what would your father say?

PROFESSOR LEEDS

(*Thinking—furiously*). What an animal! . . . and my daughter! . . . she doesn't get it from me! . . . was her mother like that? . . .
(*Distractedly*). Nina! I really can't listen!

NINA

(*Savagely*). And that's exactly what my father did say! Wait, he told Gordon! Wait for Nina till the war's over, and you've got a good job and can afford a marriage license!

PROFESSOR LEEDS

(*Crumbling pitifully*). Nina! I—!

MARSDEN

(*Flurriedly—going to him*). Don't take her seriously, Professor!
(*Thinking with nervous repulsion*). Nina has changed . . . all flesh now . . .

lust . . . who would dream she was so sensual? . . . I wish I were out of this! . . . I wish I hadn't come here to-day! . . .

NINA

(*Coldly and deliberately*). Don't lie any more, Father! Today I've made up my mind to face things. I know now why Gordon suddenly dropped all idea of marriage before he left, how unfair to me he suddenly decided it would be! Unfair to me! Oh, that's humorous! To think I might have had happiness, Gordon, and now Gordon's child—(*Then directly accusing him.*) You told him it'd be unfair, you put him on his honor, didn't you?

PROFESSOR LEEDS

(*Collecting himself—woodenly*). Yes. I did it for your sake, Nina.

NINA

(*In the same voice as before*). It's too late for lies!

PROFESSOR LEEDS

(*Woodenly*). Let us say then that I *persuaded* myself it was for your sake. That may be true. You are young. You think one can live with truth. Very well. It is also true I was jealous of Gordon. I was alone and I wanted to keep your love. I hated him as one hates a thief one may not accuse nor punish. I did my best to prevent your marriage. I was glad when he died. There. Is that what you wish me to say?

NINA

Yes. Now I begin to forget I've hated you. You were braver than I, at least.

PROFESSOR LEEDS

I wanted to live comforted by your love until the end. In short, I am a man who happens to be your father. (*He hides his face in his hands and weeps softly.*) Forgive that man!

MARSDEN

(*Thinking timidly*). In short, forgive us our possessing as we forgive those who possessed before us . . . Mother must be wondering what keeps me so long . . . it's time for tea . . . I must go home . . .

NINA

(*Sadly*). Oh, I forgive you. But do you understand now that I must somehow find a way to give myself to Gordon still, that I must pay my debt and learn to forgive myself?

PROFESSOR LEEDS

Yes.

NINA

Mary will look after you.

PROFESSOR LEEDS

Mary will do very well, I'm sure.

MARSDEN

(*Thinking*). Nina has changed . . . this is no place for me . . . Mother is waiting tea. . . .
(*Then venturing on an uncertain tone of pleasantry*). Quite so, you two. But isn't this all nonsense? Nina will be back with us in a month, Professor, what with the depressing heat and humidity, and the more depressing halt and the lame!

PROFESSOR LEEDS

(*Sharply*). She must stay away until she gets well. This time I do speak for her sake.

NINA

I'll take the nine-forty. (*Turning to* MARSDEN—*with a sudden girlishness.*) Come on upstairs, Charlie, and help me pack! (*She grabs him by the hand and starts to pull him away.*)

MARSDEN

(*Shrugging his shoulders—confusedly*). Well—I don't understand this!

NINA

(*With a strange smile*). But some day I'll read it all in one of your books, Charlie, and it'll be so simple and easy to understand that I won't be able to recognize it, Charlie, let alone understand it! (*She laughs teasingly.*) Dear old Charlie!

MARSDEN

(*Thinking in agony*). God damn in hell . . . dear old Charlie! . . .
(*Then with a genial grin*). I'll have to propose, Nina, if you continue to be my sever-est critic! I'm a stickler for these little literary conventions, you know!

NINA

All right. Propose while we pack. (*She leads him off, right.*)

PROFESSOR LEEDS

(*Blows his nose, wipes his eyes, sighs, clears his throat, squares his shoulders, pulls his coat down in front, sets his tie straight, and starts to take a brisk turn about the room. His face is washed blandly clean of all emotion*). Three weeks now . . . new term . . . I will have to be looking over my notes . . . (*He looks out of window, front.*) Grass parched in the middle . . . Tom forgotten the sprinkler . . . careless . . . ah, there goes Mr. Davis of the bank . . . bank . . . my salary will go farther now . . . books I really need . . . all bosh two can live as cheaply as one . . . there are worse things than being a trained nurse . . . good background of discipline . . . she needs it . . . she may meet rich fellow there . . . mature . . . only students here for her . . . and their fathers never approve if they have anything. . . . (*He sits down with a forced sigh of peace.*) I am glad we had it out . . . his ghost will be gone now . . . no more Gordon, Gordon, Gordon, love and praise and tears, all for Gordon! . . . Mary will do very well by me . . . I will have more leisure and peace of mind . . . and Nina will come back home . . . when she is well again . . . the old Nina! . . . my little Nina! . . . she knows and she forgave me . . . she said so . . . said! . . . but could she really? . . . don't you imagine? . . . deep in her heart? . . . she still must hate? . . . oh, God! . . . I feel cold! . . . alone! . . . this home is abandoned! . . . the house is empty and full of death! . . . there is a pain about my heart! . . .
(*He calls hoarsely, getting to his feet*). Nina!

NINA'S VOICE

(*Her voice, fresh and girlish, calls from upstairs*). Yes, Father. Do you want me?

PROFESSOR LEEDS

(*Struggling with himself—goes to door and calls with affectionate blandness*). No. Never mind. Just wanted to remind you to call for a taxi in good time.

NINA'S VOICE

I won't forget.

PROFESSOR LEEDS

(*Looks at his watch*). Five-thirty just . . . nine-forty, the train . . . then . . . Nina no more! . . . four hours more . . . she'll be packing . . . then good-bye . . . a kiss . . . nothing more ever to say to each other . . . and I'll die in here some day . . . alone . . . gasp, cry out for help . . . the president will speak at the fun-eral . . . Nina will be here again . . . Nina in black . . . too late! . . .

(*He calls hoarsely*). Nina!
(*There is no answer.*)

In other room . . . doesn't hear . . . just as well . . . (*He turns to the book-case and pulls out the first volume his hands come on and opens it at random and begins to read aloud sonorously like a child whistling to keep up his courage in the dark.*)
      "Stetit unus in arcem
Erectus capitis victorque ad sidera mit-tit
Sidereos oculos propiusque adspectat Olympum
Inquiritque Iovem;" . . .

Curtain.

ACT TWO

SCENE: *The same as Scene One,* PROFESSOR LEEDS' *study. It is about nine o'clock of a night in early fall, over a year later. The appearance of the room is unchanged except that all the shades, of the color of pale flesh, are drawn down, giving the windows a suggestion of lifeless closed eyes and making the room seem more withdrawn from life than before. The reading lamp on the table is lit. Everything on the table, papers, pencils, pens, etc., is arranged in meticulous order.*

MARSDEN *is seated on the chair at center. He is dressed carefully in an English-made suit of blue serge so dark as to seem black, and which, combined with the gloomy brooding expression of his face, strongly suggests one in mourning. His tall, thin body sags wearily in the chair, his head is sunk forward, the chin almost touching his chest, his eyes stare sadly at nothing.*

MARSDEN

(*His thoughts at ebb, without empha-sis, sluggish and melancholy*). Pro-phetic Professor! . . . I remember he once said . . . shortly after Nina went away . . . "some day, in here, . . . you'll find me" . . . did he foresee? . . . no . . . everything in life is so con-temptuously accidental! . . . God's sneer at our self-importance! . . . (*Smiling grimly.*) Poor Professor! he was horribly lonely . . . tried to hide it . . . always telling you how beneficial the training at the hospital would be for her . . . poor old chap! . . . (*His voice grows husky and uncertain—he controls it—straightens himself.*) What time is it? . . . (*He takes out his watch mechanically and looks at it.*) Ten after nine. . . . Nina ought to be here. . . . (*Then with sudden bitter-ness.*) Will she feel any real grief over his death, I wonder? . . . I doubt it! . . . but why am I so resentful? . . . the two times I've visited the hospital she's been pleasant enough . . . pleasantly evasive! . . . perhaps she thought her father had sent me to spy on her . . . poor Professor! . . . at least she answered his letters . . . he used to show them to me . . . pathetically overjoyed . . . newsy, loveless scripts, telling nothing whatever about herself . . . well, she won't have to compose them any more . . . she never answered mine . . . she might at least have acknowledged them. . . . Mother thinks she's behaved quite inexcusably . . . (*Then jealously.*) I suppose every single damned inmate has fallen in love with her! . . . her eyes seemed cynical . . . sick with men . . . as though I'd looked into the eyes of a prostitute . . . not that I ever have . . . except that once . . . the dollar house . . . hers were like patent-leather buttons in a saucer of blue milk! . . . (*Getting up with a movement of impatience.*) The devil! . . . what beastly incidents our memories insist on cherishing! . . . the ugly and disgusting . . . the beautiful things we have to keep diaries to remember! . . . (*He smiles with a wry amusement for a second—then bitterly.*) That last night Nina was here . . . she talked so brazenly about giving herself . . . I wish I knew the truth of what she's been doing in that house full of men . . . particularly that self-important young ass of a doctor! . . . Gordon's friend! . . . (*He frowns at himself, determinedly puts an end to his train of thought and comes and sits down again in the chair—in sneering, conversational tones as if he were this time actually addressing another person.*) Really, it's hardly a decent time, is it, for that kind of speculation . . . with her father lying dead upstairs? . . . (*A silence as if he had respectably squelched himself—then he pulls out his watch mechanically and stares at it. As he does so a noise of a car is heard approaching, stopping at the curb beyond the garden. He jumps to his feet and starts to go to door— then hesitates confusedly.*) No, let Mary go . . . I wouldn't know what to do . . . take her in my arms? . . . kiss her? . . . right now? . . . or wait until

she? . . . (*A bell rings insistently from the back of the house. From the front voices are heard, first* NINA's, *then a man's.* MARSDEN *starts, his face suddenly angry and dejected.*) Someone with her! . . . a man! . . . I thought she'd be alone! . . . (MARY *is heard shuffling to the front door which is opened. Immediately, as* MARY *sees* NINA, *she breaks down and there is the sound of her uncontrolled sobbing and choking, incoherent words drowning out* NINA's *voice, soothing her.*)

NINA

(*As* MARY's *grief subsides a trifle, her voice is heard, flat and toneless*). Isn't Mr. Marsden here, Mary? (*She calls.*) Charlie!

MARSDEN

(*Confused—huskily*). In here—I'm in the study, Nina. (*He moves uncertainly toward the door.*)

NINA

(*Comes in and stands just inside the doorway. She is dressed in a nurse's uniform with cap, a raglan coat over it. She appears older than in the previous scene; her face is pale and much thinner, her cheek bones stand out, her mouth is taut in hard lines of a cynical scorn. Her eyes try to armor her wounded spirit with a defensive stare of disillusionment. Her training has also tended to coarsen her fiber a trifle, to make her insensitive to suffering, to give her the nurse's professionally callous attitude. In her fight to regain control of her nerves she has over-striven after the cool and efficient poise, but she is really in a more highly strung disorganized state than ever, although she is now more capable of suppressing and concealing it. She remains strikingly handsome and her physical appeal is enhanced by her pallor and the mysterious suggestion about her of hidden experience. She stares at* MARSDEN *blankly and speaks in queer flat tones*). Hello, Charlie. He's dead, Mary says.

MARSDEN

(*Nodding his head several times—stupidly*). Yes.

NINA

(*In same tones*). It's too bad. I brought Doctor Darrell. I thought there might be a chance. (*She pauses and looks about the room.*)

(*Thinking confusedly*). His books . . . his chair . . . he always sat there . . . there's his table . . . little Nina was never allowed to touch anything . . . she used to sit on his lap . . . cuddle against him . . . dreaming into the dark beyond the windows . . . warm in his arms before the fireplace . . . dreams like sparks soaring up to die in the cold dark . . . warm in his love, safe-drifting into sleep . . . "Daddy's girl, aren't you?" . . . (*She looks around and then up and down.*) His home . . . my home . . . he was my father . . . he's dead . . . (*She shakes her head.*) Yes, I hear you, little Nina, but I don't understand one word of it. . . . (*She smiles with a cynical self-contempt.*) I'm sorry, Father! . . . you see you've been dead for me a long time . . . when Gordon died, all men died . . . what did you feel for me then? . . . nothing . . . and now I feel nothing . . . it's too bad . . .

MARSDEN

(*Thinking woundedly*). I hoped she would throw herself in my arms . . . weeping . . . hide her face on my shoulder . . . "Oh, Charlie, you're all I've got left in the world . . ." (*Then angrily.*) Why did she have to bring that Darrell with her?

NINA

(*Flatly*). When I said good-bye that night I had a premonition I'd never see him again.

MARSDEN

(*Glad of this opening for moral indignation*). You've never tried to see him, Nina! (*Then overcome by disgust with himself —contritely.*) Forgive me! It was rotten of me to say that!

NINA

(*Shaking her head—flatly*). I didn't want him to see what he would have thought was me. (*Ironically.*) That's the other side

of it you couldn't dissect into words from here, Charlie! (*Then suddenly asking a necessary question in her nurse's cool, efficient tones.*) Is he upstairs? (MARSDEN *nods stupidly.*) I'll take Ned up. I might as well. (*She turns and walks out briskly.*)

MARSDEN

(*Staring after her—dully*). That isn't Nina. . . . (*Indignantly.*) They've killed her soul down there! . . . (*Tears come to his eyes suddenly and he pulls out his handkerchief and wipes them, muttering huskily.*) Poor old Professor! . . . (*Then suddenly jeering at himself.*) For God's sake, stop acting! . . . it isn't the Professor! . . . dear old Charlie is crying because she didn't weep on his shoulder . . . as he had hoped! . . .
(*He laughs harshly—then suddenly sees a man outside the doorway and stares—then calls sharply*). Who's that?

EVANS

(*His voice embarrassed and hesitating comes from the hall*). It's all right. (*He appears in the doorway, grinning bashfully.*) It's me—I, I mean—Miss Leeds told me to come in here. (*He stretches out his hand awkwardly.*) Guess you don't remember me, Mr. Marsden. Miss Leeds introduced us one day at the hospital. You were leaving just as I came in. Evans is my name.

MARSDEN

(*Who has been regarding him with waning resentment, forces a cordial smile and shakes hands*). Oh, yes. At first I couldn't place you.

EVANS

(*Awkwardly*). I sort of feel I'm butting in.

MARSDEN

(*Beginning to be taken by his likable boyish quality*). Not at all. Sit down. (*He sits in the rocker at center as* EVANS *goes to the bench at right.*)
(EVANS *sits uncomfortably hunched forward, twiddling his hat in his hands. He is above the medium height, very blond, with guileless, diffident blue eyes, his figure inclined to immature lumbering outlines. His*

face is fresh and red-cheeked, handsome in a boyish fashion. His manner is bashful with women or older men, coltishly playful with his friends. There is a lack of self-confidence, a lost and strayed appealing air about him, yet with a hint of some un-awakened obstinate force beneath his apparent weakness. Although he is twenty-five and has been out of college three years, he still wears the latest in collegiate clothes and as he looks younger than he is, he is always mistaken for an undergraduate and likes to be. It keeps him placed in life for himself.)

MARSDEN

(Studying him keenly—amused). This is certainly no giant intellect . . . overgrown boy . . . likable quality though . . .

EVANS

(Uneasy under MARSDEN'S *eyes).* Giving me the once-over . . . seems like good egg . . . Nina says he is . . . suppose I ought to say something about his books, but I can't even remember a title of one . . .
(He suddenly blurts out). You've known Nina—Miss Leeds—ever since she was a kid, haven't you?

MARSDEN

(A bit shortly). Yes. How long have you known her?

EVANS

Well—really only since she's been at the hospital, although I met her once years ago at a Prom with Gordon Shaw.

MARSDEN

(Indifferently). Oh, you knew Gordon?

EVANS

(Proudly). Sure thing! I was in his class! *(With admiration amounting to hero-worship.)* He sure was a wonder, wasn't he?

MARSDEN

(Cynically). Gordon über alles and forever! . . . I begin to appreciate the Professor's viewpoint . . .
(Casually). A fine boy! Did you know him well?

EVANS

No. The crowd he went with were mostly fellows who were good at sports—and I always was a dud. *(Forcing a smile.)* I was always one of the first to get bounced off the squad in any sport. *(Then with a flash of humble pride.)* But I never quit trying, anyway!

MARSDEN

(Consolingly). Well, the sport hero usually doesn't star after college.

EVANS

Gordon did! *(Eagerly—with intense admiration).* In the war! He was an ace! And he always fought just as cleanly as he'd played football! Even the Huns respected him!

MARSDEN

(Thinking cynically). This Gordon worshipper must be the apple of Nina's eye! . . .
(Casually). Were you in the army?

EVANS

(Shamefacedly). Yes—infantry—but I never got to the front—never saw anything exciting.
(Thinking glumly). Won't tell him I tried for flying service . . . wanted to get in Gordon's outfit . . . couldn't make the physical exam. . . . never made anything I wanted . . . suppose I'll lose out with Nina, too . . . *(Then rallying himself.)* Hey, you! . . . what's the matter with you? . . . don't quit! . . .

MARSDEN

(Who has been staring at him inquisitively). How did you happen to come out here tonight?

EVANS

I was calling on Nina when your wire came. Ned thought I better come along, too—might be of some use.

MARSDEN

(Frowning). You mean Doctor Darrell? *(*EVANS *nods.)* Is he a close friend of yours?

EVANS

(Hesitatingly). Well, sort of. Roomed in the same dorm with me at college. He was

a senior when I was a freshman. Used to
help me along in lots of ways. Took pity
on me, I was so green. Then about a year
ago when I went to the hospital to visit a
fellow who'd been in my outfit I ran into
him again. (*Then with a grin.*) But I
wouldn't say Ned was close to anyone. He's
a dyed-in-the-wool doc. He's only close to
whatever's the matter with you! (*He
chuckles—then hastily.*) But don't get me
wrong about him. He's the best egg ever!
You know him, don't you?

MARSDEN

(*Stiffly*). Barely. Nina introduced us once.
(*Thinking bitterly*). He's upstairs
alone with her . . . I hoped it would
be I who . . .

EVANS

Don't want him to get the wrong idea
of Ned . . . Ned's my best friend . . .
doing all he can to help me with Nina
. . . he thinks she'll marry me in the
end . . . God, if she only would! . . . I
wouldn't expect her to love me at first
. . . be happy only to take care of her
. . . cook her breakfast . . . bring it up
to her in bed . . . tuck the pillows behind her . . . comb her hair for her
. . . I'd be happy just to kiss her
hair! . . .

MARSDEN

(*Agitated—thinking   suspiciously*).
What are Darrell's relations with
Nina? . . . close to what's the matter
with her? . . . damned thoughts! . . .
why should I care? . . . I'll ask this
Evans . . . pump him while I have a
chance . . .
(*With forced indifference*). Is your friend,
the Doctor, "close" to Miss Leeds? She's
had quite a lot the matter with her since
her breakdown, if that's what interests
him! (*He smiles casually.*)

EVANS

(*Gives a start, awakening from his
dream*). Oh—er—yes. He's always trying
to bully her into taking better care of herself, but she only laughs at him. (*Soberly.*)
It'd be much better if she'd take his advice.

MARSDEN

(*Suspiciously*). No doubt.

EVANS

(*Pronounces with boyish solemnity*). She
isn't herself, Mr. Marsden. And I think
nursing all those poor guys keeps the war
before her when she ought to forget it. She
ought to give up nursing and be nursed for
a change, that's my idea.

MARSDEN

(*Struck by this—eagerly*). Exactly my
opinion.
(*Thinking*). If she'd settle down here
. . . I could come over every day . . .
I'd nurse her . . . Mother home . . .
Nina here . . . how I could work
then! . . .

EVANS

(*Thinking*). He certainly seems all for
me . . . so far! . . . (*Then in a sudden
flurry.*) Shall I tell him? . . . he'll be
like her guardian now . . . I've got to
know how he stands . . .
(*He starts with a solemn earnestness*). Mr.
Marsden, I—there's something I ought to
tell you, I think. You see, Nina's talked a
lot about you. I know how much she
thinks of you. And now her old man—
(*he hesitates in confusion*) I mean, her
father's dead—

MARSDEN

(*In a sort of panic—thinking*).
What's this? . . . proposal? . . . in
form? . . . for her hand? . . . to me?
. . . Father Charlie now, eh? . . . ha!
. . . God, what a fool! . . . does he imagine she'd ever love him? . . . but she
might . . . not bad-looking . . . likable,
innocent . . . something to mother . . .

EVANS

(*Blundering on regardless now*). I know
it's hardly the proper time—

MARSDEN

(*Interrupting—dryly*). Perhaps I can an-
ticipate. You want to tell me you're in love
with Nina?

EVANS

Yes, sir, and I've asked her to marry me.

MARSDEN

What did she say?

EVANS

(*Sheepishly*). Nothing. She just smiled.

MARSDEN

(*With relief*). Ah. (*Then harshly.*) Well, what could you expect? Surely you must know she still loves Gordon?

EVANS

(*Manfully*). Sure I know it—and I admire her for it! Most girls forget too easily. She ought to love Gordon for a long time yet. And I know I'm an awful wash-out compared to him—but I love her as much as he did, or anyone could! And I'll work my way up for her—I know I can!—so I can give her everything she wants. And I wouldn't ask for anything in return except the right to take care of her. (*Blurts out confusedly.*) I never think of her—that way—she's too beautiful and wonderful—not that I don't hope she'd come to love me in time—

MARSDEN

(*Sharply*). And just what do you expect me to do about all this?

EVANS

(*Taken aback*). Why—er—nothing, sir. I just thought you ought to know. (*Sheepishly he glances up at ceiling, then down at floor, twiddling his hat.*)

MARSDEN

(*Thinking—at first with a grudging appreciation and envy*). He thinks he means that . . . pure love! . . . it's easy to talk . . . he doesn't know life . . . but he might be good for Nina . . . if she were married to this simpleton would she be faithful? . . . and then I? . . . what a vile thought! . . . I don't mean that! . . .
(*Then forcing a kindly tone*). You see, there's really nothing I can do about it. (*With a smile.*) If Nina will, she will—and if she won't, she won't. But I can wish you good luck.

EVANS

(*Immediately all boyish gratitude*). Thanks! That's darn fine of you, Mr. Marsden!

MARSDEN

But I think we'd better let the subject drop, don't you? We're forgetting that her father—

EVANS

(*Guiltily embarrassed*). Yes—sure—I'm a damn fool! Excuse me!
(*There is the noise of steps from the hall and* DOCTOR DARRELL *enters. He is twenty-seven, short, dark, wiry, his movements rapid and sure, his manner cool and observant, his dark eyes analytical. His head is handsome and intelligent. There is a quality about him, provoking and disturbing to women, of intense passion which he has rigidly trained himself to control and set free only for the objective satisfaction of studying his own and their reactions; and so he has come to consider himself as immune to love through his scientific understanding of its real sexual nature. He sees* EVANS *and* MARSDEN, *nods at* MARSDEN *silently, who returns it coldly, goes to the table and taking a prescription pad from his pocket, hastily scratches on it.*)

MARSDEN

(*Thinking sneeringly*). Amusing, these young doctors! . . . perspire with the effort to appear cool! . . . writing a prescription . . . cough medicine for the corpse, perhaps! . . . good-looking? . . . more or less . . . attractive to women, I dare say. . . .

DARRELL

(*Tears it off—hands it to* EVANS). Here, Sam. Run along up the street and get this filled.

EVANS

(*With relief*). Sure. Glad of the chance for a walk. (*He goes out, rear.*)

DARRELL

(*Turning to* MARSDEN). It's for Nina. She's got to get some sleep tonight.
(*He sits down abruptly in the chair at center.* MARSDEN *unconsciously takes the* PROFESSOR's *place behind the table. The two men stare at each other for a moment,* DARRELL *with a frank probing, examining look that ruffles* MARSDEN *and makes him all the more re-*

sentful toward him). This Marsden doesn't like me ... that's evident ... but he interests me ... read his books ... wanted to know his bearing on Nina's case ... his novels just well-written surface ... no depth, no digging underneath ... why? ... has the talent but doesn't dare ... afraid he'll meet himself somewhere ... one of those poor devils who spend their lives trying not to discover which sex they belong to! ...

MARSDEN

Giving me the fishy, diagnosing eye they practice at medical school ... like freshmen from Ioway cultivating broad A's at Harvard! ... what is his specialty? ... neurologist, I think ... I hope not psychoanalyst ... a lot to account for, Herr Freud! ... punishment to fit his crimes, be forced to listen eternally during breakfast while innumerable plain ones tell him dreams about snakes ... pah, what an easy cure-all! ... sex the philosopher's stone ... "O Oedipus, O my king! The world is adopting you!" ...

DARRELL

Must pitch into him about Nina ... have to have his help ... damn little time to convince him ... he's the kind you have to explode a bomb under to get them to move ... but not too big a bomb ... they blow to pieces easily ... (*Brusquely*). Nina's gone to pot again! Not that her father's death is a shock in the usual sense of grief. I wish to God it were! No, it's a shock because it's finally convinced her she can't feel anything any more. That's what she's doing upstairs now—trying to goad herself into feeling something!

MARSDEN

(*Resentfully*). I think you're mistaken. She loved her father—

DARRELL

(*Shortly and dryly*). We can't waste time being sentimental, Marsden! She'll be down any minute, and I've got a lot to talk over with you. (*As* MARSDEN *seems again about to protest.*) Nina has a real affection for

you and I imagine you have for her. Then you'll want as much as I do to get her straightened out. She's a corking girl. She ought to have every chance for a happy life. (*Then sharply driving his words in.*) But the way she's conditioned now, there's no chance. She's piled on too many destructive experiences. A few more and she'll dive for the gutter just to get the security that comes from knowing she's touched bottom and there's no farther to go!

MARSDEN

(*Revolted and angry, half-springs to his feet*). Look here, Darrell, I'll be damned if I'll listen to such a ridiculous statement!

DARRELL

(*Curtly—with authority*). How do you know it's ridiculous? What do you know of Nina since she left home? But she hadn't been nursing with us three days before I saw she really ought to be a patient; and ever since then I've studied her case. So I think it's up to you to listen.

MARSDEN

(*Freezingly*). I'm listening.
(*With apprehensive terror*). Gutter ... has she ... I wish he wouldn't tell me! ...

DARRELL

(*Thinking*). How much need I tell him? ... can't tell him the raw truth about her promiscuity ... he isn't built to face reality ... no writer is outside of his books ... have to tone it down for him ... but not too much! ...
Nina has been giving way more and more to a morbid longing for martyrdom. The reason for it is obvious. Gordon went away without—well, let's say marrying her. The war killed him. She was left suspended. Then she began to blame herself and to want to sacrifice herself and at the same time give happiness to various fellow war-victims by pretending to love them. It's a pretty idea but it hasn't worked out. Nina's a bad actress. She hasn't convinced the men of her love—or herself of her good intentions. And each experience of this kind has only left her more a prey to a guilty conscience than before and more determined to punish herself!

MARSDEN

(*Thinking*). What does he mean? . . . how far did she? . . . how many? . . . (*Coldly and sneeringly*). May I ask on what specific actions of hers this theory of yours is based?

DARRELL

(*Coldly in turn*). On her evident craving to make an exhibition of kissing, necking, petting—whatever you call it—spooning in general—with any patient in the institution who got a case on her!
(*Ironically—thinking*). Spooning! . . . rather a mild word for her affairs . . . but strong enough for this ladylike soul. . . .

MARSDEN

(*Bitterly*). He's lying! . . . what's he trying to hide? . . . was he one of them? . . . her lover? . . . I must get her away from him . . . get her to marry Evans! . . .
(*With authority*). Then she mustn't go back to your hospital, that's certain!

DARRELL

(*Quickly*). You're quite right. And that brings me to what I want you to urge her to do.

MARSDEN

(*Thinking suspiciously*). He doesn't want her back . . . I must have been wrong . . . but there might be many reasons why he'd wish to get rid of her . . .
(*Coldly*). I think you exaggerate my influence.

DARRELL

(*Eagerly*). Not a bit. You're the last link connecting her with the girl she used to be before Gordon's death. You're closely associated in her mind with that period of happy security, of health and peace of mind. I know that from the way she talks about you. You're the only person she still respects—and really loves. (*As* MARSDEN *starts guiltily and glances at him in confusion—with a laugh.*) Oh, you needn't look frightened. I mean the sort of love she'd feel for an uncle.

MARSDEN

(*Thinking in agony*). Frightened? . . . was I? . . . only person she loves . . . and then he said "love she'd feel for an uncle" . . . Uncle Charlie now! . . . God damn him! . . .

DARRELL

(*Eyeing him*). Looks damnably upset . . . wants to evade all responsibility for her, I suppose . . . he's that kind . . . all the better! . . . he'll be only too anxious to get her safely married. . . .
(*Bluntly*). And that's why I've done all this talking. You've got to help snap her out of this.

MARSDEN

(*Bitterly*). And how, if I may ask?

DARRELL

There's only one way I can see. Get her to marry Sam Evans.

MARSDEN

(*Astonished*). Evans? (*He makes a silly gesture toward the door.*)
(*Thinking confusedly*). Wrong again . . . why does he want her married to . . . it's some trick. . . .

DARRELL

Yes, Evans. He's in love with her. And it's one of those unselfish loves you read about. And she is fond of him. In a maternal way, of course—but that's just what she needs now, someone she cares about to mother and boss and keep her occupied. And still more important, this would give her a chance to have children. She's got to find normal outlets for her craving for sacrifice. She needs normal love objects for the emotional life Gordon's death blocked up in her. Now marrying Sam ought to do the trick. Ought to. Naturally, no one can say for certain. But I think his unselfish love, combined with her real liking for him, will gradually give her back a sense of security and a feeling of being worth something to life again, and once she's got that, she'll be saved! (*He has spoken with persuasive feeling. He asks anxiously.*) Doesn't that seem good sense to you?

MARSDEN

(*Suspicious—dryly non-committal*). I'm sorry but I'm in no position to say. I don't know anything about Evans, for one thing.

DARRELL

(*Emphatically*). Well, I do. He's a fine healthy boy, clean and unspoiled. You can take my word for that. And I'm convinced he's got the right stuff in him to succeed, once he grows up and buckles down to work. He's only a big kid now, but all he needs is a little self-confidence and a sense of responsibility. He's holding down a fair job, too, considering he's just started in the advertising game—enough to keep them living. (*With a slight smile.*) I'm prescribing for Sam, too, when I boost this wedding.

MARSDEN

(*His snobbery coming out*). Do you know his family—what sort of people?—

DARRELL

(*Bitingly*). I'm not acquainted with their social qualifications, if that's what you mean! They're upstate country folks—fruit growers and farmers, well off, I believe. Simple, healthy people, I'm sure of that although I've never met them.

MARSDEN

(*A bit shamefacedly—changing the subject hastily*). Have you suggested this match to Nina?

DARRELL

Yes, a good many times lately in a half-joking way. If I were serious she wouldn't listen, she'd say I was prescribing. But I think what I've said has planted it in her mind as a possibility.

MARSDEN

(*Thinking suspiciously*). Is this Doctor her lover? . . . trying to pull the wool over my eyes? . . . use me to arrange a convenient triangle for him? . . .

(*Harshly—but trying to force a joking tone*). Do you know what I'm inclined to suspect, Doctor? That you may be in love with Nina yourself!

DARRELL

(*Astonished*). The deuce you do! What in the devil makes you think that? Not that any man mightn't fall in love with Nina. Most of them do. But I didn't happen to. And what's more I never could. In my mind she always belongs to Gordon. It's probably a reflection of her own silly fixed idea about him. (*Suddenly, dryly and harshly.*) And I couldn't share a woman —even with a ghost!

(*Thinking cynically*). Not to mention the living who have had her! . . . Sam doesn't know about them . . . and I'll bet he couldn't believe it of her even if she confessed! . . .

MARSDEN

(*Thinking baffledly*). Wrong again! . . . he isn't lying . . . but I feel he's hiding something . . . why does he speak so resentfully of Gordon's memory? . . . why do I sympathize? . . .

(*In a strange mocking ironic tone*). I can quite appreciate your feeling about Gordon. I wouldn't care to share with a ghost-lover myself. That species of dead is so invulnerably alive! Even a doctor couldn't kill one, eh? (*He forces a laugh—then in a friendly confidential tone.*) Gordon is too egregious for a ghost. That was the way Nina's father felt about him, too. (*Suddenly reminded of the dead man—in penitently sad tones.*) You didn't know her father, did you? A charming old fellow!

DARRELL

(*Hearing a noise from the hall—warningly*). Sstt!

(NINA *enters slowly. She looks from one to the other with a queer, quick, inquisitive stare, but her face is a pale expressionless mask drained of all emotional response to human contacts. It is as if her eyes were acting on their own account as restless, prying, recording instruments. The two men have risen and stare at her anxiously.* DARRELL *moves back and to one side until he is standing in relatively the same place as* MARSDEN *had occupied in the previous scene while* MARSDEN *is in her father's place and she stops where she had been. There is a pause. Then just as each of the men is about to speak, she answers as if they had asked a question.*)

NINA

(*In a queer flat voice*). Yes, he's dead—my father—whose passion created me—who began me—he is ended. There is only his end living—his death. It lives now to draw nearer me, to draw me nearer, to become my end! (*Then with a strange twisted smile.*) How we poor monkeys hide from ourselves behind the sounds called words!

MARSDEN

(*Thinking frightenedly*). How terrible she is! . . . who is she? . . . not my Nina! . . .
(*As if to reassure himself—timidly*). Nina!
(DARRELL *makes an impatient gesture for him to let her go on. What she is saying interests him and he feels talking it out will do her good. She looks at* MARSDEN *for a moment startledly as if she couldn't recognize him.*)

NINA

What? (*Then placing him—with real affection that is like a galling goad to him.*) Dear old Charlie!

MARSDEN

Dear damned Charlie! . . . She loves to torture! . . .
(*Then forcing a smile—soothingly*). Yes, Nina Cara Nina! Right here!

NINA

(*Forcing a smile*). You look frightened, Charlie. Do I seem queer? It's because I've suddenly seen the lies in the sounds called words. You know—grief, sorrow, love, father—those sounds our lips make and our hands write. You ought to know what I mean. You work with them. Have you written another novel lately? But, stop to think, you're just the one who couldn't know what I mean. With you the lies have become the only truthful things. And I suppose that's the logical conclusion to the whole evasive mess, isn't it? Do you understand me, Charlie? Say lie— (*She says it, drawing it out.*) L-i-i-e! Now say life. L-i-i-f-e! You see! Life is just a long drawn out lie with a sniffling sigh at the end! (*She laughs.*)

MARSDEN

(*In strange agony*). She's hard! . . . like a whore! . . . tearing your heart with dirty finger nails! . . . my Nina! . . . cruel bitch! . . . some day I won't bear it! . . . I'll scream out the truth about every woman! . . . no kinder at heart than dollar tarts! . . . (*Then in a passion of remorse.*) Forgive me, Mother! . . . I didn't mean all! . . .

DARRELL

(*A bit worried himself now—persuasively*). Why not sit down, Nina, and let us two gentlemen sit down?

NINA

(*Smiling at him swiftly and mechanically*). Oh, all right, Ned. (*She sits at center. He comes and sits on the bench.* MARSDEN *sits by the table. She continues sarcastically.*) Are you prescribing for me again, Ned? This is my pet doctor, Charlie. He couldn't be happy in heaven unless God called him in because He'd caught something! Did you ever know a young scientist, Charlie? He believes if you pick a lie to pieces, the pieces are the truth! I like him because he's so inhuman. But once he kissed me—in a moment of carnal weakness! I was as startled as if a mummy had done it! And then he looked so disgusted with himself! I had to laugh! (*She smiles at him with a pitying scorn.*)

DARRELL

(*Good-naturedly smiling*). That's right! Rub it in!
(*Ruffled but amused in spite of it*). I'd forgotten about that kiss . . . I was sore at myself afterwards . . . she was so damned indifferent! . . .

NINA

(*Wanderingly*). Do you know what I was doing upstairs? I was trying to pray. I tried hard to pray to the modern science God. I thought of a million light years to a spiral nebula—one other universe among innumerable others. But how could that God care about our trifling misery of death-born-of-birth? I couldn't believe in Him, and I wouldn't if I could! I'd rather imitate His indifference and prove I had that one trait at least in common!

MARSDEN

(*Worriedly*). Nina, why don't you lie down?

NINA

(*Jeeringly*). Oh, let me talk, Charlie! They're only words, remember! So many many words have jammed up into thoughts in my poor head! You'd better let them overflow or they'll burst the dam! I wanted to believe in any God at any price —a heap of stones, a mud image, a drawing on a wall, a bird, a fish, a snake, a baboon—or even a good man preaching the simple platitudes of truth, those Gospel words we love the sound of but whose meaning we pass on to spooks to live by!

MARSDEN

(*Again—half-rising—frightenedly*). Nina! You ought to stop talking. You'll work yourself into— (*He glances angrily at* DARRELL *as if demanding that, as a doctor, he do something.*)

NINA

(*With bitter hopelessness*). Oh, all right!

DARRELL

(*Answering his look—thinking*). You poor fool! . . . it'll do her good to talk this out of her system . . . and then it'll be up to you to bring her around to Sam . . .
(*Starts toward the door*). Think I'll go out and stretch my legs.

MARSDEN

(*Thinking—in a panic*). I don't want to be alone with her! . . . I don't know her! . . . I'm afraid! . . .
(*Protestingly*). Well—but—hold on— I'm sure Nina would rather—

NINA

(*Dully*). Let him go. I've said everything I can say—to him. I want to talk to you, Charlie. (DARRELL *goes out noiselessly with a meaning look at* MARSDEN—*a pause.*)

MARSDEN

(*Thinking tremblingly*). Here . . . now . . . what I hoped . . . she and I alone . . . she will cry . . . I will comfort her . . . why am I so afraid? . . . whom do I fear? . . . is it she? . . . or I? . . .

NINA

(*Suddenly, with pity yet with scorn*). Why have you always been so timid, Charlie? Why are you always afraid? What are you afraid of?

MARSDEN

(*Thinking in a panic*). She sneaked into my soul to spy! . . . (*Then boldly.*) Well then, a little truth for once in a way! . . .
(*Timidly*). I'm afraid of—of life, Nina.

NINA

(*Nodding slowly*). I know. (*After a pause —queerly.*) The mistake began when God was created in a male image. Of course, women would see Him that way, but men should have been gentlemen enough, remembering their mothers, to make God a woman! But the God of Gods—the Boss —has always been a man. That makes life so perverted, and death so unnatural. We should have imagined life as created in the birth-pain of God the Mother. Then we would understand why we, Her children, have inherited pain, for we would know that our life's rhythm beats from Her great heart, torn with the agony of love and birth. And we would feel that death meant reunion with Her, a passing back into Her substance, blood of Her blood again, peace of Her peace! (MARSDEN *has been listening to her fascinatedly. She gives a strange little laugh.*) Now wouldn't that be more logical and satisfying than having God a male whose chest thunders with egotism and is too hard for tired heads and thoroughly comfortless? Wouldn't it, Charlie?

MARSDEN

(*With a strange passionate eagerness*). Yes! It would, indeed! It would, Nina!

NINA

(*Suddenly jumping to her feet and going to him—with a horrible moaning desolation*). Oh, God, Charlie, I want to believe in something! I want to believe so I can feel! I want to feel that he is dead—my father! And I can't feel anything, Charlie! I can't feel anything at all! (*She throws herself on her knees beside him and hides her face in her hands on his knees and begins to sob—stifled torn sounds.*)

MARSDEN

(*Bends down, pats her head with trembling hands, soothes her with uncertain trembling words*). There—there—don't—Nina, please—don't cry—you'll make yourself sick—come now—get up—do! (*His hands grasping her arms he half raises her to her feet, but, her face still hidden in her hands, sobbing, she slips on to his lap like a little girl and hides her face on his shoulder. His expression becomes transported with a great happiness.*)

(*In an ecstatic whisper*). As I dreamed . . . with a deeper sweetness! . . . (*He kisses her hair with a great reverence.*) There . . . this is all my desire . . . I am this kind of lover . . . this is my love . . . she is my girl . . . not woman . . . my little girl . . . and I am brave because of her little girl's pure love . . . and I am proud . . . no more afraid . . . no more ashamed of being pure! . . . (*He kisses her hair again tenderly and smiles at himself.*)

(*Then soothingly with a teasing incongruous gaiety*). This will never do, Nina Cara Nina—never, never do, you know—I can't permit it!

NINA

(*In a muffled voice, her sobbing beginning to ebb away into sighs—in a young girl's voice*). Oh, Charlie, you're so kind and comforting! I've wanted you so!

MARSDEN

(*Immediately disturbed*). Wanted? . . . wanted? . . . not that kind of wanted . . . can she mean? . . .
(*Questioning hesitatingly*). You've wanted me, Nina?

NINA

Yes,—awfully! I've been so homesick. I've wanted to run home and 'fess up, tell how bad I've been, and be punished! Oh, I've got to be punished, Charlie, out of mercy for me, so I can forgive myself! And now Father dead, there's only you. You will,

won't you—or tell me how to punish myself? You've simply got to, if you love me!

MARSDEN

(*Thinking intensely*). If I love her! . . . oh, I do love her! . . .
(*Eagerly*). Anything you wish, Nina—anything!

NINA

(*With a comforted smile, closing her eyes and cuddling up against him*). I knew you would. Dear old Charlie! (*As he gives a wincing start.*) What is it? (*She looks up into his face.*)

MARSDEN

(*Forcing a smile—ironically*). Twinge—rheumatics—getting old, Nina.
(*Thinking with wild agony*). Dear old Charlie! . . . descended again into hell! . . .
(*Then in a flat voice*). What do you want to be punished for, Nina?

NINA

(*In a strange, far-away tone, looking up not at him but at the ceiling*). For playing the silly slut, Charlie. For giving my cool clean body to men with hot hands and greedy eyes which they called love! Ugh! (*A shiver runs over her body.*)

MARSDEN

(*Thinking with sudden agony*). Then she did! . . . the little filth! . . .
(*In his flat voice*). You mean you— (*Then pleadingly.*) But not—Darrell?

NINA

(*With simple surprise*). Ned? No, how could I? The war hadn't maimed him. There would have been no point in that. But I did with others—oh, four or five or six or seven men, Charlie. I forgot—and it doesn't matter. They were all the same. Count them all as one, and that one a ghost of nothing. That is, to me. They were important to themselves, if I remember rightly. But I forget.

MARSDEN

(*Thinking in agony*). But why? . . . the dirty little trollop! . . . why? . . .
(*In his flat voice*). Why did you do this, Nina?

NINA

(*With a sad little laugh*). God knows, Charlie! Perhaps I knew at the time but I've forgotten. It's all mixed up. There was a desire to be kind. But it's horribly hard to give anything, and frightful to receive! And to give love—oneself—not in this world! And men are difficult to please, Charlie. I seemed to feel Gordon standing against a wall with eyes bandaged and these men were a firing squad whose eyes were also bandaged—and only I could see! No, I was the blindest! I would not see! I knew it was a stupid, morbid business, that I was more maimed than they were, really, that the war had blown my heart and insides out! And I knew too that I was torturing these tortured men, morbidly supersensitive already, that they loathed the cruel mockery of my gift! Yet I kept on, from one to one, like a stupid, driven animal until one night not long ago I had a dream of Gordon diving down out of the sky in flames and he looked at me with such sad burning eyes, and all my poor maimed men, too, seemed staring out of his eyes with a burning pain, and I woke up crying, my own eyes burning. Then I saw what a fool I'd been—a guilty fool! So be kind and punish me!

MARSDEN

(*Thinking with bitter confusion*). I wish she hadn't told me this . . . it has upset me terribly! . . . I positively must run home at once . . . Mother is waiting up . . . oh, how I'd love to hate this little whore! . . . then I could punish! . . . I wish her father were alive . . . "now he's dead there's only you," she said . . . "I've wanted you," . . . (*With intense bitterness.*) Dear old Father Charlie now! . . . ha! . . . that's how she wants me! . . .
(*Then suddenly in a matter-of-fact tone that is mockingly like her father's*). Then, under the circumstances, having weighed the pros and cons, so to speak, I should say that decidedly the most desirable course—

NINA

(*Drowsily—her eyes shut*). You sound so like Father, Charlie.

MARSDEN

(*In a tone like her father's*) —is for you to marry that young Evans. He is a splendid chap, clean and boyish, with real stuff in him, too, to make a career for himself if he finds a helpmeet who will inspire him to his best efforts and bring his latent ability to the surface.

NINA

(*Drowsily*). Sam is a nice boy. Yes, it would be a career for me to bring a career to his surface. I would be busy—surface life—no more depths, please God! But I don't love him, Father.

MARSDEN

(*Blandly—in the tone like her father's*). But you like him, Nina. And he loves you devotedly. And it's time you were having children—and when children come, love comes, you know.

NINA

(*Drowsily*). I want children. I must become a mother so I can give myself. I am sick of sickness.

MARSDEN

(*Briskly*). Then it's all settled?

NINA

(*Drowsily*). Yes. (*Very sleepily.*) Thank you, Father. You've been so kind. You've let me off too easily. I don't feel as if you'd punished me hardly at all. But I'll never, never do it again, I promise—never, never!—(*She falls asleep and gives a soft little snore.*)

MARSDEN

(*Still in her father's tones—very paternally—looking down*). She's had a hard day of it, poor child! I'll carry her up to her room. (*He rises to his feet with* NINA *sleeping peacefully in his arms. At this moment* SAM EVANS *enters from the right with the package of medicine in his hand.*)

EVANS

(*Grinning respectfully*). Here's the—(*As he sees* NINA.) Oh! (*Then excitedly.*) Did she faint?

MARSDEN

(*Smiling kindly at* EVANS—*still in her fath-er's tones*). Sssh! She's asleep. She cried and then she fell asleep—like a little girl. (*Then benignantly.*) But first we spoke a word about you, Evans, and I'm sure you have every reason to hope.

EVANS

(*Overcome, his eyes on his shuffling feet and twiddling cap*). Thanks—I—I really don't know how to thank—

MARSDEN

(*Going to door—in his own voice now*). I've got to go home. My mother is waiting up for me. I'll just carry Nina upstairs and put her on her bed and throw something over her.

EVANS

Can't I help you, Mr. Marsden?

MARSDEN

(*Dully*). No. I cannot help myself. (*As* EVANS *looks puzzled and startled he adds with an ironical, self-mocking geniality.*) You'd better call me just Charlie after this. (*He smiles bitterly to himself as he goes out.*)

EVANS

(*Looks after him for a moment—then can-not restrain a joyful, coltish caper—glee-fully*). Good egg! Good old Charlie! (*As if he had heard or guessed,* MARSDEN's *bit-ter laugh comes back from the end of the hallway.*)

Curtain.

ACT THREE

SCENE: *Seven months or so later—the dining room of the* EVANS' *homestead in Northern New York State—about nine o'clock in the morning of a day in late spring of the follow-ing year.*

The room is one of those big, misproportioned dining rooms that are found in the large, jigsaw country houses scattered around the country as a result of the rural taste for grandeur in the eighties. There is a cumbersome hanging lamp suspended from chains over the exact center of the ugly table with its set of straight-backed chairs set back at spaced intervals against the walls. The wall paper, a repulsive brown, is stained at the ceiling line with damp blotches of mildew, and here and there has started to peel back where the strips join. The floor is carpeted in a smeary brown with a dark red design blurred into it. In the left wall is one window with starched white curtains looking out on a covered side porch, so that no sunlight ever gets to this room and the light from the window, although it is a beautiful warm day in the flower garden beyond the porch, is cheerless and sickly. There is a door in the rear, to left of center, that leads to a hall opening on the same porch. To the right of door a heavy sideboard, a part of the set, dis-playing some "company" china and glassware. In the right wall, a door leading to the kitchen.

NINA *is seated at the foot of the table, her back to the window, writing a letter. Her whole personality seems changed, her face has a contented expression, there is an inner calm about her. And her personal appearance has changed in kind; her face and figure have filled out, she is prettier in a conventional way and less striking and unusual; noth-ing remains of the strange fascination to her face except her unchangeably mysterious eyes.*

NINA

(*Reading what she has just written over to herself*). It's a queer house, Ned. There is something wrong with its psyche, I'm sure. Therefore you'd simply adore it. It's a hideous old place, a faded gingerbread with orange fixin's and numerous lightning rods. Around it are acres and acres of apple trees in full bloom, all white and pinkish and beautiful, like brides just tripping out of church with the bridegroom, Spring, by the arm.

Which reminds me, Ned, that it's over six months since Sam and I were married and we haven't seen hide nor hair of you since the ceremony. Do you think that is any nice way to act? You might at least drop me a line. But I'm only joking. I know how busy you must be now that you've got the chance you've always wanted to do research work. Did you get our joint letter of congratulation written after we read of your appointment?

But to get back to this house. I feel it has lost its soul and grown resigned to doing without it. It isn't haunted by anything at all—and ghosts of some sort are the only normal life a house has—like our minds, you know. So although last evening when we got here at first I said "obviously haunted" to myself, now that I've spent one night in it I know that whatever spooks there may once have been have packed up their manifestations a long time ago and drifted away over the grass, wisps of mist between the apple trees, without one backward glance of regret or recollection. It's incredible to think Sam was born and spent his childhood here. I'm glad he doesn't show it! We slept last night in the room he was born in. Or rather he slept, I couldn't. I lay awake and found it difficult to breathe, as if all the life in the air had long since been exhausted in keeping the dying living a little longer. It was hard to believe anyone had ever been born alive there. I know you're saying crossly "She's still morbid" but I'm not. I've never been more normal. I feel contented and placid. (*Looking up from the letter, thinking embarrassedly.*) Should I have told him? . . . no . . . my own secret . . . tell no one . . . not even Sam . . . why haven't I told Sam? . . . it'd do him so much good . . . he'd feel so proud of himself, poor dear . . . no . . . I want to keep it just my baby . . . only mine . . . as long as I can . . . and it will be time enough to let Ned know when I go to New York . . . he can suggest a good obstetrician . . . how delighted he'll be when he hears! . . . he always said it would be the best thing for me . . . well, I do feel happy when I think . . . and I love Sam now . . . in a way . . . it will be his baby too . . . (*Then with a happy sigh, turns back to letter.*) But speaking of Sam's birth, you really must meet his mother sometime. It's amazing how little she is like him, a strange woman from the bit I saw of her last night. She has been writing Sam regularly once a week ever since she's known we were married, the most urgent invitations to visit her. They were really more like commands, or prayers. I suspect she is terribly lonely all by herself in this big house. Sam's feeling toward her puzzles me. I don't believe he ever mentioned her until her letters began coming or that he'd ever have come to see the poor woman if I hadn't insisted. His attitude rather shocked me. It was just as though he'd forgotten he had a mother. And yet as soon as he saw her he was sweet enough. She seemed dreadfully upset to see Charlie with us, until we'd explained it was thanks to his kindness and in his car we were taking this deferred honeymoon. Charlie's like a fussy old woman about his car, he's afraid to let Sam or me drive it—

MARSDEN

(*Enters from the rear. He is spruce, dressed immaculately, his face a bit tired and resigned, but smiling kindly. He has a letter in his hand*). Good morning. (*She gives a start and instinctively covers the letter with her hand.*)

NINA

Good morning.

(*Thinking amusedly*). If he knew what I'd just written . . . poor old Charlie! . . .

(*Then indicating the letter he carries*). I see you're an early correspondent, too.

MARSDEN

(*With sudden jealous suspicion*). Why did she cover it up like that? . . . whom is she writing to? . . .

(*Coming toward her*). Just a line to Mother to let her know we've not all been murdered by rum-bandits. You know how she worries.

NINA

(*Thinking with a trace of pitying contempt*). Apron strings . . . still his devotion to her is touching . . . I hope if mine is a boy he will love me as much . . . oh, I hope it is a boy . . . healthy and strong and beautiful . . . like Gordon! . . .

(*Then suddenly sensing* MARSDEN's *curiosity—perfunctorily*). I'm writing to Ned Darrell. I've owed him one for ages. (*She folds it up and puts it aside.*)

MARSDEN

(*Thinking glumly*). I thought she'd forgotten him . . . still I suppose it's just friendly . . . and it's none of my business, now she's married. . . .

(*Perfunctorily*). How did you sleep?

NINA

Not a wink. I had the strangest feeling.

MARSDEN

Sleeping in a strange bed, I suppose. (*Jokingly.*) Did you see any ghosts?

NINA

(*With a sad smile*). No. I got the feeling the ghosts had all deserted the house and left it without a soul—as the dead so often leave the living—(*she forces a little laugh*) if you get what I mean.

MARSDEN

(*Thinking worriedly*). Slipping back into that morbid tone . . . first time in a long while . . .

(*Teasingly*). Hello! Do I hear graveyards yawning from their sleep—and yet I observe it's a gorgeous morning without, the flowers are flowering, the trees are treeing with one another, and you, if I mistake not, are on your honeymoon!

NINA

(*Immediately gaily mocking*). Oh, very well, old thing! "God's in his heaven, all's right with the world!" And Pippa's cured of the pip! (*She dances up to him.*)

MARSDEN

(*Gallantly*). Pippa is certainly a pippin this morning!

NINA

(*Kisses him quickly*). You deserve one for that! All I meant was that ghosts remind me of men's smart crack about women, you can't live with them and can't live without them. (*Stands still and looks at him teasingly.*) But there you stand proving me a liar by every breath you draw! You're ghostless and womanless—and as sleek and satisfied as a pet seal! (*She sticks out her tongue at him and makes a face of superior scorn.*) Bah! That for you, 'Fraidcat Charlie, you slacker bachelor! (*She runs to the kitchen door.*) I'm going to bum some more coffee! How about you?

MARSDEN

(*With a forced smile*). No, thank you.

(*She disappears into the kitchen.*)

(*Thinking with bitter pain*). Ghostless! . . . if she only knew . . . that joking tone hides her real contempt! . . .

(*Self-mockingly.*) "But when the girls began to play 'Fraid-cat Charlie ran away!" (*Then rallying himself.*) Bosh! . . . I haven't had such thoughts . . . not since their marriage . . . happy in her happiness . . . but is she happy? . . . in the first few months she was obviously playing a part . . . kissed him too much . . . as if she'd determined to make herself a loving wife . . . and then all of a sudden she became contented . . . her face filled out . . . her eyes lazily examined peace . . . pregnant . . . yes, she must be . . . I hope so. . . . why? . . . for her sake . . . my own, too . . . when she has a child I know I can entirely accept . . . forget I have lost her . . . lost her? . . . silly ass! . . . how can you lose what you never possessed? . . . except in dreams! . . . (*Shaking his head exasperatedly.*) Round and round . . . thoughts . . . damn pests! . . . mosquitoes of the soul . . . whine, sting, suck one's blood . . . why did I invite Nina and Sam on this tour . . . it's a business trip with me, really . . . I need a new setting for my next novel . . . "Mr. Marsden departs a bit from his familiar field" . . . well, there they were stuck in the Professor's house . . . couldn't afford a vacation . . . never had a honeymoon . . . I've pretended to be done up every night so they could . . . I've gone to bed right after dinner so they could be alone and . . . I wonder if she can really like him . . . that way? . . . (*The sound of* EVANS' *voice and his mother's is heard from the garden.* MARSDEN *goes over and carefully peers out.*) Same with his mother . . . peculiar woman . . . strong . . . good character for a novel . . . no, she's too somber . . . her eyes are the saddest . . . and, at the same time, the grimmest . . . they're coming in . . . I'll drive around the country a bit . . . give them a chance for a family conference . . . discuss Nina's pregnancy, I suppose . . . does Sam know? . . . he gives no indication . . . why do wives hide it from their husbands? . . . ancient shame . . . guilty of continuing life, of bringing fresh pain into the world . . .

(*He goes out, rear. The outside door in the hall is heard being opened and* EVANS *and his mother evidently meet* MARSDEN *as he is about to go out. Their voices, his voice explaining, are heard, then the outer door being opened and shut again as* MARSDEN *departs. A moment later* EVANS *and his mother enter the dining room.* SAM *looks timorously happy, as if he could not quite believe in his good fortune and had constantly to reassure himself about it, yet he is riding the crest of the wave, he radiates love and devotion and boyish adoration. He is a charming-looking fresh boy now. He wears a sweater and linen knickers, collegiate to the last degree. His mother is a* tiny woman with a frail figure, her head and face, framed in iron-gray hair, seeming much too large for her body, so that at first glance she gives one the impression of a wonderfully made, lifelike doll. She is only about forty-five but she looks at least sixty. Her face with its delicate features must have once been of a romantic, tender, clinging-vine beauty, but what has happened to her has compressed its defenseless curves into planes, its mouth into the thin line around a locked door, its gentle chin has been forced out aggressively by a long reliance on clenched teeth. She is very pale. Her big dark eyes are grim with the prisoner-pain of a walled-in soul. Yet a sweet loving-kindness, the ghost of an old faith and trust in life's goodness, hovers girlishly, fleetingly, about the corners of her mouth and softens into deep sorrow the shadowy grimness of her eyes. Her voice jumps startlingly in tone from a caressing gentleness to a blunted flat assertiveness, as if what she said then was merely a voice on its own without human emotion to inspire it.*)

EVANS

(*As they come in—rattling on in the cocksure boastful way of a boy showing off his prowess before his mother, confident of thrilled adulation*). In a few years you won't have to worry one way or another about the darned old apple crop. I'll be able to take care of you then. Wait and see! Of course, I'm not making so much now. I couldn't expect to. I've only just started. But I'm making good, all right, all right—since I got married—and it's only a question of time when—Why, to show you, Cole—he's the manager and the best egg ever—called me into his office and told me he'd had his eye on me, that my stuff was exactly what they wanted, and he thought I had the makings of a real find. (*Proudly.*) How's that? That's certainly fair enough, isn't it?

MRS. EVANS

(*Vaguely—she has evidently not heard much of what he said*). That's fine, Sammy.

(*Thinking apprehensively*). I do hope I'm wrong! . . . but that old shiver of dread took me the minute she stepped in the door! . . . I don't think she's told Sammy but I got to make sure. . . .

EVANS

(*Seeing her preoccupation now—deeply hurt—testily*). I'll bet you didn't hear a word I said! Are you still worrying about how the darn old apples are going to turn out?

MRS. EVANS

(*With a guilty start—protestingly*). Yes, I did hear you, Sammy—every word! That's just what I was thinking about—how proud I am you're doing so wonderful well!

EVANS

(*Mollified but still grumbling*). You'd never guess it from the gloomy way you looked! (*But encouraged to go on.*) And Cole asked me if I was married—seemed to take a real personal interest—said he was glad to hear it because marriage was what put the right kind of ambition into a fellow—unselfish ambition—working for his wife and not just himself—(*Then embarrassedly.*) He even asked me if we were expecting an addition to the family.

MRS. EVANS

(*Seeing this is her chance—quickly—forcing a smile*). I've been meaning to ask you that myself, Sammy. (*Blurts out apprehensively.*) She—Nina—she isn't going to have a baby, is she?

EVANS

(*With an indefinable guilty air—as if he were reluctant to admit it*). I—why—you mean, is she now? I don't think so, Mother. (*He strolls over to the window whistling with an exaggeratedly casual air, and looks out.*)

MRS. EVANS

(*Thinking with grim relief*). He don't know . . . there's that much to be thankful for, anyway. . . .

EVANS

(*Thinking with intense longing*). If that'd only happen! . . . soon! . . . Nina's begin to love me . . . a little . . . I've felt it the last two months . . .

God, it's made me happy! . . . before that she didn't . . . only liked me . . . that was all I asked . . . never dared hope she'd come to love me . . . even a little . . . so soon . . . sometimes I feel it's too good to be true . . . don't deserve it . . . and now . . . if that'd happen . . . then I'd feel sure . . . it'd be there . . . half Nina, half me . . . living proof! . . . (*Then an apprehensive note creeping in.*) And I know she wants a baby so much . . . one reason why she married me . . . and I know she's felt right along that then she'd love me . . . really love me . . . (*Gloomily.*) I wonder why . . . ought to have happened before this . . . hope it's nothing wrong . . . with me! . . . (*He starts, flinging off this thought—then suddenly clutching at a straw, turns hopefully to his mother*). Why did you ask me that, Mother? D'you think—?

MRS. EVANS

(*Hastily*). No, indeed! I don't think she is! I wouldn't say so at all!

EVANS

(*Dejectedly*). Oh—I thought perhaps—(*Then changing the subject.*) I suppose I ought to go up and say hello to Aunt Bessie.

MRS. EVANS

(*Her face becoming defensive—in blunted tones, a trifle pleadingly*). I wouldn't, Sammy. She hasn't seen you since you were eight. She wouldn't know you. And you're on your honeymoon, and old age is always sad to young folks. Be happy while you can! (*Then pushing him toward door.*) Look here! You catch that friend, he's just getting his car out. You drive to town with him, give me a chance to get to know my daughter-in-law, and call her to account for how she's taking care of you! (*She laughs forcedly.*)

EVANS

(*Bursting out passionately*). Better than I deserve! She's an angel, Mother! I know you'll love her!

MRS. EVANS

(*Gently*). I do already, Sammy! She's so pretty and sweet!

EVANS

(*Kisses her—joyously*). I'll tell her that. I'm going out this way and kiss her good-bye. (*He runs out through the kitchen door.*)

MRS. EVANS

(*Looking after him—passionately*). He loves her! . . . he's happy! . . . that's all that counts! . . . being happy! . . . (*Thinking apprehensively.*) If only she isn't going to have a baby . . . if only she doesn't care so much about having one . . . I got to have it out with her . . . got to! . . . no other way . . . in mercy . . . in justice . . . this has got to end with my boy . . . and he's got to live happy! . . . (*At the sound of steps from the kitchen she straightens up in her chair stiffly.*)

NINA

(*Comes in from the kitchen, a cup of coffee in her hand, smiling happily*). Good morning—(*she hesitates—then shyly*) Mother. (*She comes over and kisses her—slips down and sits on the floor beside her.*)

MRS. EVANS

(*Flusteredly—hurriedly*). Good morning! It's a real fine day, isn't it? I ought to have been here and got your breakfast, but I was out gallivanting round the place with Sammy. I hope you found everything you wanted.

NINA

Indeed I did! And I ate so much I'm ashamed of myself! (*She nods at the cup of coffee and laughs.*) See. I'm still at it.

MRS. EVANS

Good for you!

NINA

I ought to apologize for coming down so late. Sam should have called me. But I wasn't able to get to sleep until after daylight somehow.

MRS. EVANS

(*Strangely*). You couldn't sleep? Why? Did you feel anything funny—about this house?

NINA

(*Struck by her tone—looks up*). No. Why?
(*Thinking*). How her face changes' . . . what sad eyes! . . .

MRS. EVANS

(*Thinking in an agony of apprehension*). Got to start in to tell her . . . got to . . .

NINA

(*Apprehensive herself now*). That sick dead feeling . . . when something is going to happen . . . I felt it before I got the cable about Gordon . . . (*Then taking a sip of coffee, and trying to be pleasantly casual*). Sam said you wanted to talk to me.

MRS. EVANS

(*Dully*). Yes. You love my boy, don't you?

NINA

(*Startled—forcing a smile, quickly*). Why, of course!
(*Reassuring herself*). No, it isn't a lie . . . I do love him . . . the father of my baby . . .

MRS. EVANS

(*Blurts out*). Are you going to have a baby, Nina?

NINA

(*She presses* MRS. EVANS' *hand. Simply*). Yes, Mother.

MRS. EVANS

(*In her blunt flat tones—with a mechanical rapidity to her words*). Don't you think it's too soon? Don't you think you better wait until Sammy's making more money? Don't you think it'll be a drag on him and you? Why don't you just go on being happy together, just you two?

NINA

(*Thinking frightenedly*). What is behind what she's saying? . . . that feeling of death again! . . .
(*Moving away from her—repulsed*). No, I don't think any of those things, Mrs. Evans. I want a baby—beyond everything! We both do!

MRS. EVANS

(*Hopelessly*). I know. (*Then grimly.*) But you can't! You've got to make up your mind you can't!

(*Thinking fiercely—even with satisfaction*). Tell her! . . . make her suffer what I was made to suffer! . . . I've been too lonely! . . .

NINA

(*Thinking with terrified foreboding*). I knew it! . . . Out of a blue sky . . . black! . . .

(*Springing to her feet—bewilderedly*). What do you mean? How can you say a thing like that?

MRS. EVANS

(*Reaching out her hand tenderly, trying to touch* NINA). It's because I want Sammy—and you, too, child—to be happy. (*Then as* NINA *shrinks away from her hand—in her blunted tones.*) You just can't.

NINA

(*Defiantly*). But I can! I have already! I mean—I am, didn't you understand me?

MRS. EVANS

(*Gently*). I know it's hard. (*Then inexorably.*) But you can't go on!

NINA

(*Violently*). I don't believe you know what you're saying! It's too terrible for you—Sam's own mother—how would you have felt if someone—when you were going to have Sam—came to you and said —?

MRS. EVANS

(*Thinking fiercely*). Now's my chance! . . .

(*Tonelessly*). They did say it! Sam's own father did—my husband! And I said it to myself! And I did all I could, all my husband could think of, so's I wouldn't—but we didn't know enough. And right to the time the pains come on, I prayed Sammy'd be born dead, and Sammy's father prayed, but Sammy was born healthy and smiling, and we just had to love him, and live in fear. He doubled the torment of fear we lived in. And that's what you'd be in for. And Sammy, he'd go the way his father

went. And your baby, you'd be bringing it into torment. (*A bit violently.*) I tell you it'd be a crime—a crime worse than murder! (*Then recovering—commiseratingly.*) So you just can't, Nina!

NINA

(*Who has been listening distractedly —thinking*). Don't listen to her! . . . feeling of death! . . . what is it? . . . she's trying to kill my baby! . . . oh, I hate her! . . .

(*Hysterically resentful*). What do you mean? Why don't you speak plainly? (*Violently.*) I think you're horrible! Praying your baby would be born dead! That's a lie! You couldn't!

MRS. EVANS

(*Thinking*). I know what she's doing now . . . just what I did . . . trying not to believe . . . (*Fiercely.*) But I'll make her! . . . she's got to suffer, too! . . . I been too lonely! . . . she's got to share and help me save my Sammy! . . .

(*With an even more blunted flat relentless tonelessness*). I thought I was plain, but I'll be plainer. Only remember it's a family secret, and now you're one of the family. It's the curse on the Evanses. My husband's mother—she was an only child—died in an asylum and her father before her. I know that for a fact. And my husband's sister, Sammy's aunt, she's out of her mind. She lives on the top floor of this house, hasn't been out of her room in years, I've taken care of her. She just sits, doesn't say a word, but she's happy, she laughs to herself a lot, she hasn't a care in the world. But I remember when she was all right, she was always unhappy, she never got married, most people around here were afraid of the Evanses in spite of their being rich for hereabouts. They knew about the craziness going back, I guess, for heaven knows how long. I didn't know about the Evanses until after I'd married my husband. He came to the town I lived in, no one there knew about the Evanses. He didn't tell me until after we were married. He asked me to forgive him, he said he loved me so much he'd have gone mad without me, said I was his only hope of salvation. So I forgave him. I loved him an awful lot. I said to myself, I'll be his salvation—and maybe I could have been if we hadn't had Sammy born. My husband kept real well up to then. We'd swore we'd never have children, we never forgot to be careful for two whole years. Then one night we'd both gone to a dance, we'd both had a little punch to drink, just enough—to forget—driving home in the moonlight—that moonlight!—such little things at the back of big things!

NINA

(*In a dull moan*). I don't believe you! I won't believe you!

MRS. EVANS

(*Drones on*). My husband, Sammy's father, in spite of all he and I fought against it, he finally gave in to it when Sammy was only eight, he couldn't keep up any more living in fear for Sammy, thinking any minute the curse might get him, every time he was sick, or had a headache, or bumped his head, or started crying, or had a nightmare and screamed, or said something queer like children do naturally. (*A bit stridently.*) Living like that with that fear is awful torment! I know that! I went through it by his side! It nearly drove me crazy, too—but I didn't have it in my blood! And that's why I'm telling you! You got to see you can't, Nina!

NINA

(*Suddenly breaking out—frenziedly*). I don't believe you! I don't believe Sam would ever have married me if he knew!

MRS. EVANS

(*Sharply*). Who said Sammy knew? He don't know a single thing about it! That's been the work of my life, keeping him from knowing. When his father gave up and went off into it I sent Sammy right off to boarding school. I told him his father was sick, and a little while after I sent word his father was dead, and from then on until his father did really die during Sammy's second year to college, I kept him away at school in winter and camp in summers and I went to see him, I never let him come home. (*With a sigh.*) It was hard, giving up Sammy, knowing I was making him forget he had a mother. I was glad

taking care of them two kept me so busy I didn't get much chance to think then. But here's what I've come to think since, Nina: I'm certain sure my husband might have kept his mind with the help of my love if I hadn't had Sammy. And if I'd never had Sammy I'd never have loved Sammy—or missed him, would I?—and I'd have kept my husband.

NINA

(*Not heeding this last—with wild mockery*). And I thought Sam was so normal—so healthy and sane—not like me! I thought he'd give me such healthy, happy children and I'd forget myself in them and learn to love him!

MRS. EVANS

(*Horrified, jumping to her feet*). Learn to? You told me you did love Sammy!

NINA

No! Maybe I almost have—lately—but only when I thought of his baby! Now I hate him! (*She begins to weep hysterically.* MRS. EVANS *goes to her and puts her arms around her.* NINA *sobs out.*) Don't touch me! I hate you, too! Why didn't you tell him he must never marry!

MRS. EVANS

What reason could I give, without telling him everything? And I never heard about you till after you were married. Then I wanted to write to you but I was scared he might read it. And I couldn't leave her upstairs to come away to see you. I kept writing Sammy to bring you here right off, although having him come frightened me to death for fear he might get to suspect something. You got to get him right away from here, Nina! I just kept hoping you wouldn't want children right away—young folks don't nowadays—until I'd seen you and told you everything. And I thought you'd love him like I did his father, and be satisfied with him alone.

NINA

(*Lifting her head—wildly*). No! I don't! I won't! I'll leave him!

MRS. EVANS

(*Shaking her, fiercely*). You can't! He'd go crazy sure then! You'd be a devil! Don't you see how he loves you?

NINA

(*Breaking away from her—harshly*).
Well, I don't love him! I only married him
because he needed me—and I needed children! And now you tell me I've got to kill
my—oh, yes, I see I've got to, you needn't
argue any more! I love it too much to make
it run that chance! And I hate it too, now,
because it's sick, it's not my baby, it's his!
(*With terrible ironic bitterness.*) And still
you can dare to tell me I can't even leave
Sam!

MRS. EVANS

(*Very sadly and bitterly*). You just said
you married him because he needed you.
Don't he need you now—more'n ever?
But I can't tell you not to leave him, not if
you don't love him. But you oughtn't to
have married him when you didn't love
him. And it'll be your fault, what'll happen.

NINA

(*Torturedly*). What will happen?—what
do you mean?—Sam will be all right—
just as he was before—and it's not my
fault anyway!—it's not my fault!
(*Then thinking conscience-stricken-
ly*). Poor Sam . . . she's right . . . it's
not his fault . . . it's mine . . . I wanted
to use him to save myself . . . I acted
the coward again . . . as I did with
Gordon . . .

MRS. EVANS

(*Grimly*). You know what'll happen to
him if you leave him—after all I've told
you! (*Then breaking into intense pleading.*) Oh, I'd get down on my knees to you,
don't make my boy run that risk! You got
to give one Evans, the last one, a chance to
live in this world! And you'll learn to love
him, if you give up enough for him! (*Then
with a grim smile.*) Why, I even love that
idiot upstairs, I've taken care of her so
many years, lived her life for her with my
life, you might say. You give your life to
Sammy, then you'll love him same as you
love yourself. You'll have to! That's sure as
death! (*She laughs a queer gentle laugh
full of amused bitterness.*)

NINA

(*With a sort of dull stupid wonderment*).
And you've found peace?—

MRS. EVANS

(*Sardonically*). There's peace in the green
fields of Eden, they say! You got to die to
find out! (*Then proudly.*) But I can say I
feel proud of having lived fair to them that
gave me love and trusted in me!

NINA

(*Struck—confusedly*). Yes—that's true,
isn't it?
(*Thinking strangely*). Lived fair . . .
pride . . . trust . . . play the game! . . .
who is speaking to me . . . Gordon!
. . . oh, Gordon, do you mean I must
give Sam the life I didn't give you? . . .
Sam loved you too . . . he said, if we
have a boy, we'll call him Gordon in
Gordon's honor . . . Gordon's honor!
. . . what must I do now in your hon-
or, Gordon . . . yes! . . . I know! . . .
(*Speaking mechanically in a dull voice*).
All right, Mother. I'll stay with Sam.
There's nothing else I can do, is there,
when it isn't his fault, poor boy! (*Then
suddenly snapping and bursting out in a
despairing cry.*) But I'll be so lonely! I'll
have lost my baby! (*She sinks down on her
knees at* MRS. EVANS' *feet—piteously.*) Oh,
Mother, how can I keep on living?

MRS. EVANS

(*Thinking miserably*). Now she
knows my suffering . . . now I got to
help her . . . she's got a right to have a
baby . . . another baby . . . sometime
. . . somehow . . . she's giving her life
to save my Sammy . . . I got to save
her! . . .
(*Stammeringly*). Maybe, Nina—

NINA

(*Dully and resentfully again now*). And
how about Sam? You want him to be happy, don't you? It's just as important for
him as it is for me that I should have a
baby! If you know anything at all about
him, you ought to see that!

MRS. EVANS

(*Sadly*). I know that. I see that in him,
Nina. (*Gropingly.*) There must be a way
—somehow. I remember when I was carrying Sam, sometimes I'd forget I was a
wife, I'd only remember the child in me.
And then I used to wish I'd gone out de-

liberate in our first year, without my husband knowing, and picked a man, a healthy male to breed by, same's we do with stock, to give the man I loved a healthy child. And if I didn't love that other man nor him me where would be the harm? Then God would whisper: "It'd be a sin, adultery, the worst sin!" But after He'd gone I'd argue back again to myself, then we'd have a healthy child, I needn't be afraid! And maybe my husband would feel without ever knowing how he felt it, that I wasn't afraid and that child wasn't cursed and so he needn't fear and I could save him. (*Then scornfully.*) But I was too afraid of God then to have ever done it! (*Then very simply.*) He loved children so, my poor husband did, and the way they took to him, you never saw anything like it, he was a natural born father. And Sammy's the same.

NINA

(*As from a distance—strangely*). Yes, Sammy's the same. But I'm not the same as you. (*Defiantly.*) I don't believe in God the Father!

MRS. EVANS

(*Strangely*). Then it'd be easy for you. (*With a grim smile.*) And I don't believe in Him, neither, not any more. I used to be a great one for worrying about what's God and what's devil, but I got richly over it living here with poor folks that was being punished for no sins of their own, and me being punished with them for no sin but loving much. (*With decision.*) Being happy, that's the nearest we can ever come to knowing what's good! Being happy, that's good! The rest is just talk! (*She pauses—then with a strange austere sternness.*) I love my boy, Sammy. I could see how much he wants you to have a baby. Sammy's got to feel sure you love him—to be

happy. Whatever you can do to make him happy is good—is good, Nina! I don't care what! You've got to have a healthy baby—sometime—so's you can both be happy! It's your rightful duty.

NINA

(*Confusedly—in a half-whisper*). Yes, Mother.

> (*Thinking longingly*). I want to be happy! . . . it's my right . . . and my duty! . . . (*Then suddenly in guilty agony.*) Oh, my baby . . . my poor baby . . . I'm forgetting you . . . desiring another after you are dead! . . . I feel you beating against my heart for mercy . . . oh! . . . (*She weeps with bitter anguish.*)

MRS. EVANS

(*Gently and with deep sympathy*). I know what you're suffering. And I wouldn't say what I just said now only I know us two mustn't see each other ever again. You and Sammy have got to forget me. (*As* NINA *makes a motion of protest—grimly and inexorably.*) Oh, yes, you will—easy. People forget everything. They got to, poor people! And I'm saying what I said about a healthy baby so's you will remember it when you need to, after you've forgotten—this one.

NINA

(*Sobbing pitifully*). Don't! Please, Mother!

MRS. EVANS

(*With sudden tenderness—gathering* NINA *up in her arms, brokenly*). You poor child! You're like the daughter of my sorrow! You're closer to me now than ever Sammy could be! I want you to be happy! (*She begins to sob, too, kissing* NINA's *bowed head.*)

Curtain.

ACT FOUR

SCENE: *An evening early in the following winter about seven months later. The* PROFES-
SOR's *study again. The books in the cases have never been touched, their austere array
shows no gaps, but the glass separating them from the world is gray with dust, giving
them a blurred ghostly quality. The table, although it is the same, is no longer the* PRO-
FESSOR's *table, just as the other furniture in the room, by its disarrangement, betrays that
the* PROFESSOR's *well-ordered mind no longer trims it to his personality. The table has become neurotic. Volumes of the Encyclopedia Britannica mixed up with popular treatises
on Mind Training for Success, etc., looking startlingly modern and disturbing against the
background of classics in the original, are slapped helter-skelter on top of each other on it.
The titles of these books face in all directions, no one volume is placed with any relation
to the one beneath it—the effect is that they have no connected meaning. The rest of the
table is littered with an ink bottle, pens, pencils, erasers, a box of typewriting paper, and a
typewriter at the center before the chair, which is pushed back, setting the rug askew.
On the floor beside the table are an overflowing wastepaper basket, a few sheets of paper
and the rubber cover for the typewriter like a collapsed tent. The rocking chair is no
longer at center but has been pulled nearer the table, directly faces it with its back to the
bench. This bench in turn has been drawn much closer, but is now placed more to the
rear and half-faces front, its back squarely to the door in the corner.*

EVANS *is seated in the* PROFESSOR's *old chair. He has evidently been typing, or is about
to type, for a sheet of paper can be seen in the machine. He smokes a pipe, which he is
always relighting whether it needs it or not, and which he bites and shifts about and pulls
in and out and puffs at nervously. His expression is dispirited, his eyes shift about, his
shoulders are collapsed submissively. He seems much thinner, his face drawn and sallow.
The collegiate clothes are no longer natty, they need pressing and look too big for him.*

EVANS

(*Turns to his typewriter and pounds out a
few words with a sort of aimless desperation—then tears the sheet out of the machine with an exclamation of disgust,
crumples it up and throws it violently on
the floor, pushing his chair back and jumping to his feet*). Hell!

(*He begins pacing up and down the
room, puffing at his pipe, thinking tormentedly*). No use . . . can't think of a
darn thing . . . well, who could dope
out a novel ad on another powdered
milk, anyway? . . . all the stuff been
used already . . . Tartars conquering
on dried mare's milk . . . Metchnikoff,
eminent scientist . . . been done to
death . . . but simply got to work out
something or . . . Cole said, what's been

the matter with you lately? . . . you
started off so well . . . I thought you
were a real find, but your work's fallen off to nothing . . . (*He sits down on
the edge of the bench nearby, his
shoulders hunched—despondently.*)
Couldn't deny it . . . been going stale
ever since we came back from that trip
home . . . no ideas . . . I'll get fired . . .
sterile . . . (*with a guilty terror*) in
more ways than one, I guess! . . . (*He
springs to his feet as if this idea were a
pin stuck in him—lighting his already lighted pipe, walks up and
down again, forcing his thoughts into
other channels.*) Bet the old man turns
over in his grave at my writing ads in
his study . . . maybe that's why I can't
. . . bum influence . . . try tomorrow in

my bedroom . . . sleeping alone . . . since Nina got sick . . . some woman's sickness . . . wouldn't tell me . . . too modest . . . still, there are some things a husband has a right to know . . . especially when we haven't . . . in five months . . . doctor told her she mustn't, she said . . . what doctor? . . . she's never said . . . what the hell's the matter with you, do you think Nina's lying? . . . no . . . but . . . (*Desperately.*) If I was only sure it was because she's really sick . . . not just sick of me! . . . (*He sinks down in the rocking chair despondently.*) Certainly been a big change in her . . . since that visit home . . . what happened between Mother and her? . . . she says nothing . . . they seemed to like each other . . . both of them cried when we left . . . still, Nina insisted on going that same day and Mother seemed anxious to get rid of us . . . can't make it out . . . next few weeks Nina couldn't be loving enough . . . I never was so happy . . . then she crashed . . . strain of waiting and hoping she'd get pregnant . . . and nothing happening . . . that's what did it . . . my fault! . . . how d'you know? . . . you can't tell that! . . . (*He jumps to his feet again—walks up and down again distractedly.*) God, if we'd only have a kid! . . . then I'd show them all what I could do! . . . Cole always used to say I had the stuff, and Ned certainly thought so. . . . (*With sudden relieved excitement.*) By gosh, I was forgetting! . . . Ned's coming out tonight . . . forgot to tell Nina . . . mustn't let her get wise I got him to come to look her over . . . she'd hate me for swallowing my pride after he's never been to see us . . . but I had to . . . this has got my goat . . . I've got to know what's wrong . . . and Ned's the only one I can trust . . . (*He flings himself on chair in front of desk and, picking up a fresh sheet of paper, jams it into the machine.*) Gosh, I ought to try and get a new start on this before it's time . . . (*He types a sentence or two, a strained frown of consternation on his face.* NINA *comes silently through the door and stands just inside it looking*

at him. She has grown thin again, her face is pale and drawn, her movements are those of extreme nervous tension.)

NINA

(*Before she can stifle her immediate reaction of contempt and dislike*). How weak he is! . . . he'll never do anything . . . never give me my desire . . . if he'd only fall in love with someone else . . . go away . . . not be here in my father's room . . . I even have to give him a home . . . if he'd disappear . . . leave me free . . . if he'd die . . . (*Checking herself—remorsefully.*) I must stop such thoughts . . . I don't mean it . . . poor Sam! . . . trying so hard . . . loving me so much . . . I give so little in return . . . he feels I'm always watching him with scorn . . . I can't tell him it's with pity . . . how can I help watching him? . . . help worrying over his worry because of what it might lead to . . . after what his mother . . . how horrible life is! . . . he's worried now . . . he doesn't sleep . . . I hear him tossing about . . . I must sleep with him again soon . . . he's only home two nights a week . . . it isn't fair of me . . . I must try . . . I must! . . . he suspects my revulsion . . . it's hurting him . . . oh, poor dead baby I dared not bear, how I might have loved your father for your sake! . . .

EVANS

(*Suddenly feeling her presence, jerks himself to his feet—with a diffident guilty air which is noticeable about him now whenever he is in her presence*). Hello, dear. I thought you were lying down. (*Guiltily.*) Did the noise of my typing bother you? I'm terribly sorry!

NINA

(*Irritated in spite of herself*). Why is he always cringing? . . . (*She comes forward to the chair at center and sits down—forcing a smile.*) But there's nothing to be terribly sorry about! (*As he stands awkward and confused, like a schoolboy who has been called on to recite and cannot and is being "bawled out" before the class, she forces a playful tone.*) Goodness, Sam, how tragic you can get about nothing at all!

EVANS

(*Still forced to justify himself—contritely*). I know it isn't pleasant for you having me drag my work out here, trying to pound out rotten ads. (*With a short laugh.*) Trying to is right! (*Blurts out.*) I wouldn't do it except that Cole gave me a warning to buck up—or get out.

NINA

(*Stares at him, more annoyed, her eyes hardening, thinking*). Yes! ... he'll always be losing one job, getting another, starting with a burst of confidence each time, then ...
(*Cutting him with a careless sneering tone*). Well, it isn't a job to worry much about losing, is it?

EVANS

(*Wincing pitiably*). No, not much money. But I used to think there was a fine chance to rise there—but of course that's my fault, I haven't made good—(*he finishes miserably*) somehow.

NINA

(*Her antagonism giving way to remorseful pity*). What makes me so cruel? ... he's so defenseless ... his mother's baby ... poor sick baby! ... poor Sam! ... (*She jumps to her feet and goes over to him.*)

EVANS

(*As she comes—with a defensive, boastful bravery*). Oh, I can get another job just as good, all right—maybe a lot better.

NINA

(*Reassuringly*). Certainly, you can! And I'm sure you're not going to lose this one. You're always anticipating trouble. (*She kisses him and sits on the arm of his chair, putting an arm around his neck and pulling his head on to her breast.*) And it isn't your fault, you big goose, you! It's mine. I know how hard it makes everything for you, being tied to a wife who's too sick to be a wife. You ought to have married a big strapping, motherly—

EVANS

(*In the seventh heaven now—passionately*). Bunk! All the other women in the world aren't worth your little finger! It's you who ought to have married someone worth while, not a poor fish like me! But no one could love you more than I do, no matter what he was!

NINA

(*Presses his head on her breast, avoiding his eyes, kisses him on the forehead*). And I love you, Sam.
(*Staring out over his head—with loving pity, thinking*). I almost do ... poor unfortunate boy! ... at these moments ... as his mother loves him ... but that isn't enough for him ... I can hear his mother saying, "Sammy's got to feel sure you love him ... to be happy." ... I must try to make him feel sure ...
(*Speaking gently*). I want you to be happy, Sam.

EVANS

(*His face transformed with happiness*). I am—a hundred times more than I deserve!

NINA

(*Presses his head down on her breast so he cannot see her eyes—gently*). Ssshh.
(*Thinking sadly*). I promised her ... but I couldn't see how hard it would be to let him love me ... after his baby ... was gone ... it was hard even to keep on living ... after that operation ... Gordon's spirit followed me from room to room ... poor reproachful ghost! ... (*With bitter mockery.*) Oh, Gordon, I'm afraid this is a deeper point of honor than any that was ever shot down in flames! ... what would your honor say now? ... "Stick to him! ... play the game!" ... oh, yes, I know ... I'm sticking ... but he isn't happy ... I'm trying to play the game ... then why do I keep myself from him? ... but I was really sick ... for a time after ... since then, I couldn't ... but ... oh, I'll try ... I'll try soon.
(*Tenderly—but having to force herself to say it*). Doesn't my boy want to sleep with me again—sometime soon?

EVANS

(*Passionately—hardly able to believe his ears*). Oh, it'd be wonderful, Nina! But are you sure you really want me to—that you'll feel well enough?

NINA

(*Repeats his words as if she were memorizing a lesson*). Yes, I want you to. Yes, I'll feel well enough. (*He seizes her hand and kisses it in a passionately grateful silence.*)
(*She thinks with resigned finality*). There, Sammy's mother and Gordon . . . I'll play the game . . . it will make him happy for a while . . . as he was in those weeks after we'd left his mother . . . when I gave myself with a mad pleasure in torturing myself for his pleasure! . . . (*Then with weary hopelessness.*) He'll be happy until he begins to feel guilty again because I'm not pregnant . . . (*With a grim bitter smile.*) Poor Sam, if he only knew the precautions . . . as if I wouldn't die rather than take the slightest chance of that happening! . . . ever again . . . what a tragic joke it was on both of us! . . . I wanted my baby so! . . . oh, God! . . . his mother said . . . "You've got to have a healthy baby . . . sometime . . . it's your rightful duty" . . . that seemed right then . . . but now . . . it seems cowardly . . . to betray poor Sam . . . and vile to give myself . . . without love or desire . . . and yet I've given myself to men before without a thought, just to give them a moment's happiness . . . can't I do that again? . . . when it's a case of Sam's happiness? . . . and my own? . . .
(*She gets up from beside him with a hunted movement*). It must be half past eight. Charlie's coming to bring his suggestions on my outline for Gordon's biography.

EVANS

(*His bliss shattered—dejectedly*). Always happens . . . just as we get close . . . something comes between . . .
(*Then confusedly*). Say, I forgot to tell you Ned's coming out tonight.

NINA

(*Astonished*). Ned Darrell?

EVANS

Sure. I happened to run into him the other day and invited him and he said Saturday evening. He couldn't tell what train. Said never mind meeting him.

NINA

(*Excitedly*). Why didn't you tell me before, you big booby! (*She kisses him.*) There, don't mind. But it's just like you. Now someone'll have to go down to the store. And I'll have to get the spare room ready. (*She hurries to the doorway. He follows her.*)

EVANS

I'll help you.

NINA

You'll do nothing of the kind! You'll stay right downstairs and bring them in here and cover up my absence. Thank heavens, Charlie won't stay long if Ned is here. (*The doorbell rings—excitedly.*) There's one of them now. I'll run upstairs. Come up and tell me if it's Ned—and get rid of Charlie. (*She kisses him playfully and hurries out.*)

EVANS

(*Looking after her—thinks*). She seems better tonight . . . happier . . . she seems to love me . . . if she'll only get all well again, then everything will . . . (*The bell rings again.*) I must give Ned a good chance to talk to her . . . (*He goes out to the outer door—returns a moment later with* MARSDEN. *The latter's manner is preoccupied and nervous. His face has an expression of anxiety which he tries to conceal. He seems a prey to some inner fear he is trying to hide even from himself and is resolutely warding off from his consciousness. His tall, thin body stoops as if part of its sustaining will had been removed.*)

EVANS

(*With a rather forced welcoming note*). Come on in, Charlie. Nina's upstairs lying down.

MARSDEN

(*With marked relief*). Then by all means don't disturb her. I just dropped in to bring back her outline with the suggestions I've made. (*He has taken some papers out of his pocket and hands them to* EVANS.) I couldn't have stayed but a minute in any event. Mother is a bit under the weather these days.

EVANS

(*Perfunctorily*). Too bad.

(*Thinking vindictively*). Serve her right, the old scandal-monger, after the way she's gossiped about Nina! . . .

MARSDEN

(*With assumed carelessness*). Just a little indigestion. Nothing serious but it annoys her terribly.

(*Thinking frightenedly*). That dull pain she complains of . . . I don't like it . . . and she won't see anyone but old Doctor Tibbetts . . . she's sixty-eight . . . I can't help fearing . . . no! . . .

EVANS

(*Bored—vaguely*). Well, I suppose you've got to be careful of every little thing when you get to her age.

MARSDEN

(*Positively bristling*). Her age? Mother isn't so old!

EVANS

(*Surprised*). Over sixty-five, isn't she?

MARSDEN

(*Indignantly*). You're quite out there! She's under sixty-five—and in health and spirits she isn't more than fifty! Everyone remarks that!

(*Annoyed at himself*). Why did I lie to him about her age? . . . I must be on edge . . . Mother is rather difficult to live with these days, getting me worried to death, when it's probably nothing . . .

EVANS

(*Annoyed in his turn—thinking*). Why all the fuss? . . . as if I gave a damn if the old girl was a million! . . . (*Indicating the papers*). I'll give these to Nina first thing in the morning.

MARSDEN

(*Mechanically*). Righto. Thank you. (*He starts to go toward door—then turns—fus-*sily.*) But you'd better take a look while I'm here and see if it's clear. I've written on the margins. See if there's anything you can't make out. (EVANS *nods helplessly and begins reading the sheets, going back beneath the lamp.*)

MARSDEN

(*Looking around him with squeamish disapproval*). What a mess they've made of this study . . . poor Professor! . . . dead and forgotten . . . and his tomb desecrated . . . does Sam write his ads here of a week-end now? . . . the last touch! . . . and Nina labors with love at Gordon's biography . . . whom the Professor hated! . . . "life is so full of a number of things!" . . . why does everyone in the world think they can write? . . . but I've only myself to blame . . . why in the devil did I ever suggest it to her? . . . because I hoped my helping her while Sam was in the city would bring us alone together? . . . but I made the suggestion before she had that abortion performed! . . . how do you know she did? . . . because I know! . . . there are psychic affinities . . . her body confessed . . . and since then, I've felt an aversion . . . as if she were a criminal . . . she is! . . . how could she? . . . why? . . . I thought she wanted a child . . . but evidently I don't know her . . . I suppose, afraid it would spoil her figure . . . her flesh . . . her power to enslave men's senses . . . mine . . . and I had hoped . . . looked forward to her becoming a mother . . . for my peace of mind. . . . (*Catching himself—violently.*) Shut up! . . . what a base creature I'm becoming! . . . to have such thoughts when Mother is sick and I ought to be thinking only of her! . . . and it's none of my damn business, anyway! . . . (*Glaring at* EVANS *resentfully as if he were to blame.*) Look at him! . . . he'll never suspect anything! . . . what a simple-simon! . . . he adored Gordon as a newsboy does a champion pugilist! . . . and Nina writes of Gordon as if he had been a demi-god! . . . when actually he came from the commonest people! . . .

(*He suddenly speaks to* EVANS *with a really savage satisfaction*). Did I tell you I once looked up Gordon's family in Beachampton? A truly deplorable lot! When I remembered Gordon and looked at his father I had either to suspect a lover in the wood pile or to believe in an Immaculate Conception . . . that is, until I saw his mother! Then a stork became the only conceivable explanation!

EVANS

(*Who has only half-heard and hasn't understood, says vaguely*). I never saw his folks. (*Indicating the papers.*) I can make this all out all right.

MARSDEN

(*Sarcastically*). I'm glad it's understandable!

EVANS

(*Blunderingly*). I'll give it to Nina—and I hope your mother is feeling better tomorrow.

MARSDEN

(*Piqued*). Oh, I'm going. Why didn't you tell me if I was interrupting—your writing!

EVANS

(*Immediately guilty*). Oh, come on, Charlie, don't get peevish, you know I didn't mean— (*The bell rings.* EVANS *stammers in confusion, trying at a nonchalant air.*) Hello! That must be Ned. You remember Darrell. He's coming out for a little visit. Excuse me. (*He blunders out of the door.*)

MARSDEN

(*Looking after him with anger mixed with alarmed suspicion and surprise*). Darrell? . . . what's he doing here? . . . have they been meeting? . . . perhaps he was the one who performed the . . . no, his idea was she ought to have a child . . . but if she came and begged him? . . . but why should Nina beg not to have a baby? . . . (*Distractedly.*) Oh, I don't know! . . . it's all a sordid mess! . . . I ought to be going home! . . . I don't want to see Darrell! . . . (*He starts for the door—then struck by a sudden thought, stops.*) Wait . . . I could ask him about Mother . . . yes . . . good idea . . . (*He comes back to*

the middle of the room, front, and is standing there when DARRELL *enters, followed by* EVANS. DARRELL *has not changed in appearance except that his expression is graver and more thoughtful. His manner is more convincingly authoritative, more mature. He takes in* MARSDEN *from head to foot with one comprehensive glance.*)

EVANS

(*Awkwardly*). Ned, you remember Charlie Marsden?

MARSDEN

(*Holding out his hand, urbanely polite*). How are you, Doctor?

DARRELL

(*Shaking his hand—briefly*). Hello.

EVANS

I'll go up and tell Nina you're here, Ned. (*He goes, casting a resentful glance at* MARSDEN.)

MARSDEN

(*Awkwardly, as* DARRELL *sits down in the chair at center, goes over and stands by the table*). I was on the point of leaving when you rang. Then I decided to stop and renew our acquaintance. (*He stoops and picks up one sheet of paper, and puts it back carefully on the table.*)

DARRELL

(*Watching him—thinking*). Neat . . . suspiciously neat . . . he's an old maid who seduces himself in his novels . . . so I suspect . . . I'd like a chance to study him more closely. . . .

MARSDEN

(*Thinking resentfully*). What a boor! . . . he might say something! . . . (*Forcing a smile*). And I wanted to ask a favor of you, a word of advice as to the best specialist, the very best, it would be possible to consult—

DARRELL

(*Sharply*). On what?

MARSDEN

(*Almost naively*). My mother has a pain in her stomach.

DARRELL

(*Amused—dryly*). Possibly she eats too much.

MARSDEN

(*As he bends and carefully picks another sheet from the floor to place it as carefully on the table*). She doesn't eat enough to keep a canary alive. It's a dull, constant pain, she says. She's terribly worried. She's terrified by the idea of cancer. But, of course, that's perfect rot, she's never been sick a day in her life and—

DARRELL

(*Sharply*). She's showing more intelligence about her pain than you are.

MARSDEN

(*Bending down for another sheet, his voice trembling with terror*). I don't understand —quite. Do you mean to say you think—?

DARRELL

(*Brutally*). It's possible. (*He has pulled out his pen and a card and is writing.*)
(*Thinking grimly*). Explode a bomb under him, as I did once before . . . only way to get him started doing anything. . . .

MARSDEN

(*Angrily*). But—that's nonsense!

DARRELL

(*With satisfaction—unruffledly*). People who are afraid to face unpleasant possibilities until it's too late commit more murders and suicides than— (*Holds out card.*) Doctor Schultz is your man. Take her to see him—tomorrow!

MARSDEN

(*Bursting out in anger and misery*). Damn it, you're condemning her without—! (*He breaks down chokingly.*) You've no damn right!— (*He bends down, trembling all over, to pick up another piece of paper.*)

DARRELL

(*Genuinely astonished and contrite*). And I thought he was so ingrown he didn't care a damn about anyone! . . his mother . . . now I begin to see him. (*He jumps from his chair and going to*

MARSDEN *puts a hand on his shoulder— kindly*). I beg your pardon, Marsden. I only wanted to drive it in that all delay is dangerous. Your mother's pain may be due to any number of harmless causes, but you owe it to her to make sure. Here. (*He hands out the card.*)

MARSDEN

(*Straightens up and takes it, his eyes grateful now—humbly*). Thank you. I'll take her to see him tomorrow. (EVANS *comes in.*)

EVANS

(*To* MARSDEN, *blunderingly*). Say, Charlie, I don't want to hurry you but Nina wants some things at the store before it closes, and if you'd give me a lift—

MARSDEN

(*Dully*). Of course. Come along. (*He shakes hands with* DARRELL.) Good night, Doctor—and thank you.

DARRELL

Good night. (MARSDEN *goes, followed by* EVANS.)

EVANS

(*Turns in the doorway and says meaningly*). Nina'll be right down. For Pete's sake, have a good heart-to-heart talk with her, Ned!

DARRELL

(*Frowning—impatiently*). Oh—all right! Run along. (EVANS *goes.*)
(DARRELL *remains standing near the table looking after them, thinking about* MARSDEN). Queer fellow, Marsden . . . mother's boy still . . . if she dies what will he do? . . . (*Then dismissing* MARSDEN *with a shrug of his shoulders.*) Oh, well, he can always escape life in a new book. . . . (*He moves around the table examining its disorder critically, then sits down in armchair—amused.*) Evidences of authorship . . . Sam's ads? . . . isn't making good, he said . . . was I wrong in thinking he had stuff in him? . . . hope not . . . always liked Sam, don't know why exactly . . . said Nina'd gotten into a bad state again . . . what's happened to their marriage?

... I felt a bit sorry for myself at their wedding . . . not that I'd ever fallen . . . but I did envy him in a way . . . she always had strong physical attraction for me . . . that time I kissed her . . . one reason I've steered clear since . . . take no chances on emotional didos . . . need all my mind on my work . . . got rid of even that slight suspicion . . . I'd forgotten all about her . . . she's a strange girl . . . interesting case . . . I should have kept in touch on that account . . . hope she'll tell me about herself . . . can't understand her not having child . . . it's so obviously the sensible thing . . . (*Cynically.*) Probably why . . . to expect common sense of people proves you're lacking in it yourself! . . .

NINA

(*Enters silently. She has fixed herself up, put on her best dress, arranged her hair, rouged, etc.—but it is principally her mood that has changed her, making her appear a younger, prettier person for the moment.* DARRELL *immediately senses her presence, and, looking up, gets to his feet with a smile of affectionate admiration. She comes quickly over to him, saying with frank pleasure*). Hello, Ned. I'm certainly glad to see you again—after all these years!

DARRELL

(*As they shake hands—smiling*). Not as long as all that, is it?
(*Thinking admiringly*). Wonderful-looking as ever . . . Sam is a lucky devil! . . .

NINA

(*Thinking*). Strong hands like Gordon's . . . take hold of you . . . not like Sam's . . . yielding fingers that let you fall back into yourself . . .
(*Teasingly*). I ought to cut you dead after the shameful way you've ignored us!

DARRELL

(*A bit embarrassedly*). I've really meant to write.
(*His eyes examining her keenly*). Been through a lot since I saw her . . . face shows it . . . nervous tension pronounced . . . hiding behind her smile.

NINA

(*Uneasy under his glance*). I hate that professional look in his eyes . . . watching symptoms . . . without seeing me. (*With resentful mockery*). Well, what do you suspect is wrong with the patient now, Doctor? (*She laughs nervously.*) Sit down, Ned. I suppose you can't help your diagnosing stare. (*She turns from him and sits down in the rocker at center.*)

DARRELL

(*Quickly averting his eyes—sits down—jokingly*). Same old unjust accusation! You were always reading diagnosis into me, when what I was really thinking was what fine eyes you had, or what a becoming gown, or—

NINA

(*Smiling*). Or what a becoming alibi you could cook up! Oh, I know you! (*With a sudden change of mood she laughs gaily and naturally.*) But you're forgiven—that is, if you can explain why you've never been to see us.

DARRELL

Honestly, Nina, I've been so rushed with work I haven't had a chance to go anywhere.

NINA

Or an inclination!

DARRELL

(*Smiling*). Well—maybe.

NINA

Do you like the Institute so much? (*He nods gravely.*) Is it the big opportunity you wanted?

DARRELL

(*Simply*). I think it is.

NINA

(*With a smile*). Well, you're the taking kind for whom opportunities are made!

DARRELL

(*Smiling*). I hope so.

NINA

(*Sighing*). I wish that could be said of more of us—(*then quickly*)—meaning myself.

DARRELL

(*Thinking with a certain satisfaction*). Meaning Sam . . . that doesn't look hopeful for future wedded bliss! (*Teasingly*). But I heard you were "taking an opportunity" to go in for literature—collaborating with Marsden.

NINA

No, Charlie is only going to advise. He'd never deign to appear as co-author. And besides, he never appreciated the real Gordon. No one did except me.

DARRELL

(*Thinking caustically*). Gordon myth strong as ever . . . root of her trouble still . . .
(*Keenly inquisitive*). Sam certainly appreciated him, didn't he?

NINA

(*Not remembering to hide her contempt*). Sam? Why, he's the exact opposite in every way!

DARRELL

(*Caustically thinking*). These heroes die hard . . . but perhaps she can write him out of her system. . . .
(*Persuasively*). Well, you're going ahead with the biography, aren't you? I think you ought to.

NINA

(*Dryly*). For my soul, Doctor? (*Listlessly.*) I suppose I will. I don't know. I haven't much time. The duties of a wife—(*Teasingly.*) By the way, if it isn't too rude to inquire, aren't you getting yourself engaged to some fair lady or other?

DARRELL

(*Smiling—but emphatically*). Not on your life! Not until after I'm thirty-five, at least!

NINA

(*Sarcastically*). Then you don't believe in taking your own medicine? Why, Doctor! Think of how much good it would do you!—(*excitedly with a hectic sarcasm*)—if you had a nice girl to love—or was it learn to love?—and take care of—whose character you could shape and whose life you could guide and make what you

pleased, in whose unselfish devotion you could find peace! (*More and more bitterly sarcastic.*) And you ought to have a baby, Doctor! You will never know what life is, you'll never be really happy until you've had a baby, Doctor—a fine, healthy baby! (*She laughs a bitter, sneering laugh.*)

DARRELL

(*After a quick, keen glance, thinking*). Good! . . . she's going to tell . . .
(*Meekly*). I recognize my arguments. Was I really wrong on every point, Nina?

NINA

(*Harshly*). On every single point, Doctor!

DARRELL

(*Glancing at her keenly*). But how? You haven't given the baby end of it a chance yet, have you?

NINA

(*Bitterly*). Oh, haven't I? (*Then bursts out with intense bitterness.*) I'll have you know I'm not destined to bear babies, Doctor!

DARRELL

(*Startledly*). What's that? . . . why not? . . . (*Again with a certain satisfaction.*) Can she mean Sam? . . . that he . . .
(*Soothingly—but plainly disturbed*). Why don't you begin at the beginning and tell me all about it? I feel responsible.

NINA

(*Fiercely*). You are! (*Then wearily.*) And you're not. No one is. You didn't know. No one could know.

DARRELL

(*In same tone*). Know what?
(*Thinking with the same eagerness to believe something he hopes*). She must mean no one could know that Sam wasn't . . . but I might have guessed it . . . from his general weakness . . . poor unlucky devil . . .
(*Then as she remains silent—urgingly*). Tell me. I want to help you, Nina.

NINA

(*Touched*). It's too late, Ned. (*Then suddenly.*) I've just thought—Sam said he happened to run into you. That isn't so, is it? He went to see you and told you how worried he was about me and asked you out to see me, didn't he? (*As* DARRELL *nods.*) Oh, I don't mind! It's even rather touching. (*Then mockingly.*) Well, since you're out here professionally, and my husband wants me to consult you, I might as well give you the whole case history! (*Wearily.*) I warn you it isn't pretty, Doctor! But then life doesn't seem to be pretty, does it? And, after all, you aided and abetted God the Father in making this mess. I hope it'll teach you not to be so cocksure in future. (*More and more bitterly.*) I must say you proceeded very unscientifically, Doctor! (*Then suddenly starts her story in a dull monotonous tone recalling that of* EVANS' *mother in the previous Act.*) When we went to visit Sam's mother I'd known for two months that I was going to have a baby.

DARRELL

(*Startled—unable to hide a trace of disappointment*). Oh, then you actually were?
(*Thinking disappointedly and ashamed of himself for being disappointed*). All wrong, what I thought . . . she was going to . . . then why didn't she? . . .

NINA

(*With a strange happy intensity*). Oh, Ned, I loved it more than I've ever loved anything in my life—even Gordon! I loved it so it seemed at times that Gordon must be its real father, that Gordon must have come to me in a dream while I was lying asleep beside Sam! And I was happy! I almost loved Sam then! I felt he was a good husband!

DARRELL

(*Instantly repelled—thinking with scornful jealousy*). Ha! . . . the hero again! . . . comes to her bed! . . . puts horns on poor Sam! . . . becomes the father of his child! . . . I'll be damned if hers isn't the most idiotic obsession I ever . . .

NINA

(*Her voice suddenly becoming flat and lifeless*). And then Sam's mother told me I couldn't have my baby. You see, Doc-

tor, Sam's great-grandfather was insane, and Sam's grandmother died in an asylum, and Sam's father had lost his mind for years before he died, and an aunt who is still alive is crazy. So of course I had to agree it would be wrong—and I had an operation.

DARRELL

(*Who has listened with amazed horror— profoundly shocked and stunned*). Good God! Are you crazy, Nina? I simply can't believe! It would be too hellish! Poor Sam, of all people! (*Bewilderedly.*) Nina! Are you absolutely sure?

NINA

(*Immediately defensive and mocking*). Absolutely, Doctor! Why? Do you think it's I who am crazy? Sam looks so healthy and sane, doesn't he? He fooled you completely, didn't he? You thought he'd be an ideal husband for me! And poor Sam's fooling himself too because he doesn't know anything about all this—so you can't blame him, Doctor!

DARRELL

(*Thinking in a real panic of horror— and a flood of protective affection for her*). God, this is too awful! . . . on top of all the rest! . . . how did she ever stand it! . . . she'll lose her mind too! . . . and it's my fault! . . .
(*Getting up, comes to her and puts his hands on her shoulders, standing behind her—tenderly*). Nina! I'm so damned sorry! There's only one possible thing to do now. You'll have to make Sam give you a divorce.

NINA

(*Bitterly*). Yes? Then what do you suppose would be his finish? No, I've enough guilt in my memory now, thank you! I've got to stick to Sam! (*Then with a strange monotonous insistence.*) I've promised Sam's mother I'd make him happy! He's unhappy now because he thinks he isn't able to give me a child. And I'm unhappy because I've lost my child. So I must have another baby—somehow—don't you think, Doctor?—to make us both happy? (*She looks up at him pleadingly. For a moment they stare into each other's eyes— then both turn away in guilty confusion.*)

DARRELL

(*Bewilderedly thinking*). That look in her eyes . . . what does she want me to think? . . . why does she talk so much about being happy? . . . am I happy? . . . I don't know . . . what is happiness? . . .
(*Confusedly*). Nina, I don't know what to think.

NINA

(*Thinking strangely*). That look in his eyes . . . what did he mean? . . .
(*With the same monotonous insistence*). You must know what to think. I can't think it out myself any more. I need your advice—your *scientific* advice this time, if you please, Doctor. I've thought and thought about it. I've told myself it's what I ought to do. Sam's own mother urged me to do it. It's sensible and kind and just and good. I've told myself this a thousand times and yet I can't quite convince something in me that's afraid of something. I need the courage of someone who can stand outside and reason it out as if Sam and I were no more than guinea pigs. You've got to help me, Doctor! You've got to show me what's the sane—the truly sane, you understand! —thing I must do for Sam's sake, and my own.

DARRELL

(*Thinking confusedly*). What do I have to do? . . . this was all my fault . . . I owe her something in return . . . I owe Sam something . . . I owe them happiness! . . . (*Irritably.*) Damn it, there's a humming in my ears! . . . I've caught some fever . . . I swore to live coolly . . . let me see. . . .
(*In a cold, emotionless professional voice, his face like a mask of a doctor*). A doctor must be in full possession of the facts, if he is to advise. What is it precisely that Sam's wife has thought so much of doing?

NINA

(*In the same insistent tone*). Of picking out a healthy male about whom she cared nothing and having a child by him that Sam would believe was his child, whose life would give him confidence in his own living, who would be for him a living proof that his wife loved him.

(*Confusedly, strangely and purposefully*). This doctor is healthy. . . .

DARRELL

(*In his ultra-professional manner—like an automaton of a doctor*). I see. But this needs a lot of thinking over. It isn't easy to prescribe—
(*Thinking*). I have a friend who has a wife . . . I was envious at his wedding . . . but what has that to do with it? . . . damn it, my mind won't work! . . . it keeps running away to her . . . it wants to mate with her mind . . . in the interest of Science? . . . what damned rot I'm thinking! . . .

NINA

(*Thinking as before*). This doctor is nothing to me but a healthy male . . . when he was Ned he once kissed me . . . but I cared nothing about him . . . so that's all right, isn't it, Sam's mother?

DARRELL

(*Thinking*). Let me see. . . . I am in the laboratory and they are guinea pigs . . . in fact, in the interest of science, I can be for the purpose of this experiment, a healthy guinea pig myself and still remain an observer . . . I observe my pulse is high, for example, and that's obviously because I am stricken with a recurrence of an old desire . . . desire is a natural male reaction to the beauty of the female . . . her husband is my friend. . . . I have always tried to help him . . .
(*Coldly*). I've been considering what Sam's wife told me and her reasoning is quite sound. The child can't be her husband's.

NINA

Then you agree with Sam's mother? She said: "Being happy is the nearest we can ever come to knowing what good is!"

DARRELL

I agree with her decidedly. Sam's wife should find a healthy father for Sam's child at once. It is her sane duty to her husband.
(*Worriedly thinking*). Have I ever been happy? . . . I have studied to cure

the body's unhappiness . . . I have watched happy smiles form on the lips of the dying . . . I have experienced pleasure with a number of women I desired but never loved . . . I have known a bit of honor and a trifle of self-satisfaction . . . this talk of happiness seems to me extraneous . . .

NINA

(*Beginning to adopt a timid, diffident, guilty tone*). This will have to be hidden from Sam so he can never know! Oh, Doctor, Sam's wife is afraid!

DARRELL

(*Sharply professional*). Nonsense! This is no time for timidity! Happiness hates the timid! So does Science! Certainly Sam's wife must conceal her action! To let Sam know would be insanely cruel of her—and stupid, for then no one could be the happier for her act!
(*Anxiously thinking*). Am I right to advise this? . . . yes, it is clearly the rational thing to do . . . but this advice betrays my friend! . . . no, it saves him! . . . it saves his wife . . . and if a third party should know a little happiness . . . is he any poorer, am I any the less his friend because I saved him? . . . no, my duty to him is plain . . . and my duty as an experimental searcher after truth . . . to observe these three guinea pigs, of which I am one . . .

NINA

(*Thinking determinedly*). I must have my baby! . . .
(*Timidly—gets from her chair and half-turns toward him—pleadingly*). You must give his wife courage, Doctor. You must free her from her feeling of guilt.

DARRELL

There can only be guilt when one deliberately neglects one's manifest duty to life. Anything else is rot! This woman's duty is to save her husband and herself by begetting a healthy child!
(*Thinking guiltily and instinctively moving away from her*). I am healthy . . . but he is my friend . . . there is such a thing as honor! . . .

NINA

(*Determinedly*). I must take my happiness! . . .
(*Frightenedly—comes after him*). But she is ashamed. It's adultery. It's wrong.

DARRELL

(*Moving away again—with a cold sneering laugh of impatience*). Wrong! Would she rather see her husband wind up in an asylum? Would she rather face the prospect of going to pot mentally, morally, physically herself through year after year of devilling herself and him? Really, Madame, if you can't throw overboard all such irrelevant moral ideas, I'll have to give up this case here and now!
(*Thinking frightenedly*). Who is talking? . . . is he suggesting me? . . . but you know very well I can't be the one, Doctor! . . . why not, you're healthy and it's a friendly act for all concerned.

NINA

(*Thinking determinedly*). I must have my baby! . . .
(*Going further toward him—she can now touch him with her hand*). Please, Doctor, you must give her strength to do this right thing that seems to her so right and then so wrong! (*She puts out her hand and takes one of his.*)

DARRELL

(*Thinking frightenedly*). Whose hand is this? . . . it burns me . . . I kissed her once . . . her lips were cold . . . now they would burn with happiness for me! . . .

NINA

(*Taking his other hand and slowly pulling him around to face her, although he does not look at her—pleadingly*). Now she feels your strength. It gives her the courage to ask you, Doctor, to suggest the father. She has changed, Doctor, since she became Sam's wife. She can't bear the thought now of giving herself to any man she could neither desire nor respect. So each time her thoughts come to the man she must select they are afraid to go on! She needs your courage to choose!

DARRELL

(*As if listening to himself*). Sam is my friend . . . well, and isn't she your friend? . . . her two hands are so warm! . . . I must not even hint at my desire! . . .

(*Judicially calm*). Well, the man must be someone who is not unattractive to her physically, of course.

NINA

Ned always attracted her.

DARRELL

(*Thinking frightenedly*). What's that she said? . . . Ned? . . . attracts? . . . (*In same tone*). And the man should have a mind that can truly understand—a scientific mind superior to the moral scruples that cause so much human blundering and unhappiness.

NINA

She always thought Ned had a superior mind.

DARRELL

(*Thinking frightenedly*). Did she say Ned? . . . she thinks Ned . . . ? (*In same tone*). The man should like and admire her, he should be her good friend and want to help her, but he should not love her—although he might, without harm to anyone, desire her.

NINA

Ned does not love her—but he used to like her and, I think, desire her. Does he now, Doctor?

DARRELL

(*Thinking*). Does he? . . . who is he? . . . he is Ned! . . . Ned is I! . . . I desire her! . . . I desire happiness! . . . (*Trembling now—gently*). But, Madame, I must confess the Ned you are speaking of is I, and I am Ned.

NINA

(*Gently*). And I am Nina, who wants her baby. (*Then she reaches out and turns his head until his face faces hers but he keeps his eyes down—she bends her head meekly and submissively—softly.*) I should be so grateful, Ned. (*He starts, looks up at her wildly, makes a motion as though to take her in his arms, then remains fixed for a moment in that attitude, staring at her bowed head as she repeats submissively.*) I should be so humbly grateful.

DARRELL

(*Suddenly falling on his knees and taking her hand in both of his and kissing it humbly—with a sob*). Yes—yes, Nina—yes—for your happiness—in that spirit! (*Thinking—fiercely triumphant*). I shall be happy for a while! . . .

NINA

(*Raising her head—thinking—proudly triumphant*). I shall be happy! . . . I shall make my husband happy! . . .

Curtain.

ACT FIVE

SCENE: *The sitting room of a small house* EVANS *has rented in a seashore suburb near New York. It is a bright morning in the following April.*

The room is a typical sitting room of the quantity-production bungalow type. Windows on the left look out on a broad porch. A double doorway in rear leads into the hall. A door on right, to the dining room. NINA *has tried to take the curse of offensive, banal newness off the room with some of her own things from her old home but the attempt has been half-hearted in the face of such overpowering commonness, and the result is a room as disorganized in character as was the* PROFESSOR'S *study in the last Act.*

The arrangement of the furniture follows the same pattern as in preceding scenes. There is a Morris chair and a round golden-oak table at left of center, an upholstered chair, covered with bright chintz at center, a sofa covered with the same chintz at right.

NINA *is sitting in the chair at center. She has been trying to read a book but has let this drop listlessly on her lap. A great change is noticeable in her face and bearing. She is again the pregnant woman of Act Three but this time there is a triumphant strength about her expression, a ruthless self-confidence in her eyes. She has grown stouter, her face has filled out. One gets no impression of neurotic strain from her now, she seems nerveless and deeply calm.*

NINA

(*As if listening for something within her—joyfully*). There! . . . that can't be my imagination . . . I felt it plainly . . . life . . . my baby . . . my only baby . . . the other never really lived . . . this is the child of my love! . . . I love Ned! . . . I've loved him ever since that first afternoon . . . when I went to him . . . so scientifically! . . . (*She laughs at herself.*) Oh, what a goose I was! . . . then love came to me . . . in his arms . . . happiness! . . . I hid it from him . . . I saw he was frightened . . . his own joy frightened him . . . I could feel him fighting with himself . . . during all those afternoons . . . our wonderful afternoons of happiness! . . . and I said nothing . . . I made myself be calculating . . . so when he finally said . . . dreadfully disturbed . . . "Look here, Nina, we've done all that is necessary, playing with fire is dangerous" . . . I said, "You're quite right, Ned, of all things I don't want to fall in love with you!" . . . (*She laughs.*) He didn't like that! . . . he looked angry . . . and afraid . . . then for weeks he never even phoned . . . I waited . . . it was prudent to wait . . . but every day I grew more terrified . . . then just as my will was breaking, his broke . . . he suddenly appeared again . . . but I held him to his aloof doctor's pose and sent him away, proud of his will power . . . and sick of himself with desire for me! . . . every week since then he's been coming out here . . . as my doctor . . . we've talked about our child wisely, dispassionately . . . as if it were Sam's child . . . we've never given in to our desire . . . and I've watched love grow

in him until I'm sure . . . (*With sudden alarm.*) But am I? . . . he's never once mentioned love . . . perhaps I've been a fool to play the part I've played . . . it may have turned him against me . . . (*Suddenly with calm confidence.*) No . . . he does . . . I feel it . . . it's only when I start thinking, I begin to doubt . . . (*She settles back and stares dreamily before her—a pause.*) There . . . again . . . his child! . . . my child moving in my life . . . my life moving in my child . . . the world is whole and perfect . . . all things are each other's . . . life is . . . and the is is beyond reason . . . questions die in the silence of this peace . . . I am living a dream within the great dream of the tide . . . breathing in the tide I dream and breathe back my dream into the tide . . . suspended in the movement of the tide, I feel life move in me, suspended in me . . . no whys matter . . . there is no why . . . I am a mother . . . God is a Mother . . . (*She sighs happily, closing her eyes. A pause.*)

(EVANS *enters from the hallway in rear. He is dressed carefully but his clothes are old ones—shabby collegiate gentility—and he has forgotten to shave. His eyes look pitiably harried, his manner has become a distressingly obvious attempt to cover up a chronic state of nervous panic and guilty conscience. He stops inside the doorway and looks at her with a pitiable furtiveness, arguing with himself, trying to get up his courage.*)

EVANS

Tell her! . . . go on! . . . you made up your mind to, didn't you? . . . don't quit

now! . . . tell her you've decided . . . for her sake . . . to face the truth . . . that she can't love you . . . she's tried . . . she's acted like a good sport — but she's beginning to hate you . . . and you can't blame her . . . she wanted children . . . and you haven't been able . . . (*Protesting feebly.*) But I don't know for certain . . . that that's my fault . . . (*Then bitterly.*) Aw, don't kid yourself, if she'd married someone else . . . if Gordon had lived and married her . . . I'll bet in the first month she'd . . . you'd better resign from the whole game . . . with a gun! . . . (*He swallows hard as if he were choking back a sob—then savagely.*) Stop whining! . . . go on and wake her up! . . . say you're willing to give her a divorce so she can marry some real guy who can give her what she ought to have! . . . (*Then with sudden terror.*) And if she says yes? . . . I couldn't bear it! . . . I'd die without her! . . . (*Then with a somber alien forcefulness.*) All right . . . good riddance! . . . I'd have the guts to bump off then, all right! . . . that'd set her free . . . come on now! . . . ask her! . . .
(*But his voice begins to tremble uncertainly again as he calls*). Nina.

NINA

(*Opens her eyes and gazes calmly, indifferently at him*). Yes?

EVANS

(*Immediately terrified and beaten—thinking*). I can't! . . . the way she looks at me! . . . she'd say yes! . . .
(*Stammering*). I hate to wake you up but —it's about time for Ned to come, isn't it?

NINA

(*Calmly*). I wasn't asleep.
(*Thinking as if she found it hard to concentrate on him, to realize his existence*). This man is my husband . . . it's hard to remember that . . . people will say he's the father of my child. . . . (*With revulsion.*) That's shameful! . . . and yet that's exactly what I wanted! . . . wanted! . . . not now! . . . now I love Ned! . . . I won't lose him! . . . Sam must give me a divorce . . .

I've sacrificed enough of my life . . . what has he given me? . . . not even a home . . . I had to sell my father's home to get money so we could move near his job . . . and then he lost his job! . . . now he's depending on Ned to help him get another! . . . my love! . . . how shameless! . . . (*Then contritely.*) Oh, I'm unjust . . . poor Sam doesn't know about Ned . . . and it was I who wanted to sell the place . . . I was lonely there . . . I wanted to be near Ned.

EVANS

(*Thinking in agony*). What's she thinking? . . . probably lucky for me I don't know! . . .
(*Forcing a brisk air as he turns away from her*). I hope Ned brings that letter he promised me to the manager of the Globe company. I'm keen to get on the job again.

NINA

(*With scornful pity*). Oh, I guess Ned will bring the letter. I asked him not to forget.

EVANS

I hope they'll have an opening right off. We can use the money. (*Hanging his head.*) I feel rotten, living on you when you've got so little.

NINA

(*Indifferently but with authority, like a governess to a small boy*). Now, now!

EVANS

(*Relieved*). Well, it's true. (*Then coming to her—humbly ingratiating.*) You've felt a lot better lately, haven't you, Nina?

NINA

(*With a start—sharply*). Why?

EVANS

You look ever so much better. You're getting fat. (*He forces a grin.*)

NINA

(*Curtly*). Don't be absurd, please! As a matter of fact, I don't feel a bit better.

EVANS

(*Thinking despondently*). Lately, she jumps on me every chance she gets . . . as if everything I did disgusted her!

(*He strays over to the window and looks out listlessly*). I thought we'd get some word from Charlie this morning saying if he was coming down or not. But I suppose he's still too broken up over his mother's death to write.

NINA

(*Indifferently*). He'll probably come without bothering to write.
　　(*Vaguely—wonderingly*). Charlie . . . dear old Charlie . . . I've forgotten him, too. . . .

EVANS

I think that's Ned's car now. Yes. It's stopping. I'll go out and meet him. (*He starts for the door in rear.*)

NINA

(*Sharply, before she can restrain the impulse*). Don't be such a fool!

EVANS

(*Stops—stammers confusedly*). What—what's the matter?

NINA

(*Controlling herself—but irritably*). Don't mind me. I'm nervous.
　　(*Thinking guiltily*). One minute I feel ashamed of him for making such a fool of himself over my lover . . . the next minute something hateful urges me to drive him into doing it!
(*The maid has answered the ring and opened the outer door. NED DARRELL comes in from the rear. His face looks older. There is an expression of defensive bitterness and self-resentment about his mouth and eyes. This vanishes into one of desire and joy as he sees NINA. He starts toward her impulsively.*) Nina! (*Then stops short as he sees EVANS.*)

NINA

(*Forgetting EVANS, gets to her feet as if to receive DARRELL in her arms—with love*). Ned!

EVANS

(*Affectionately and gratefully*). Hello, Ned! (*He holds out his hand, which DARRELL takes mechanically.*)

DARRELL

(*Trying to overcome his guilty embarrassment*). Hello, Sam. Didn't see you. (*Hurriedly reaching in his coat pocket.*) Before I forget, here's that letter. I had a talk over the phone with Appleby yesterday. He's pretty sure there's an opening—(*with a condescension he can't help*)—but you'll have to get your nose on the grindstone to make good with him.

EVANS

(*Flushing guiltily—forcing a confident tone*). You bet I will! (*Then gratefully and humbly.*) Gosh, Ned, I can't tell you how grateful I am!

DARRELL

(*Brusquely, to hide his embarrassment*). Oh, shut up! I'm only too glad.

NINA

(*Watching EVANS with a contempt that is almost gloating—in a tone of curt dismissal*). You'd better go and shave, hadn't you, if you're going to town?

EVANS

(*Guiltily, passing his hand over his face—forcing a brisk, purposeful air*). Yes, of course. I forgot I hadn't. Excuse me, will you? (*This to DARRELL. EVANS hurries out, rear.*)

DARRELL

(*As soon as he is out of earshot—turning on NINA accusingly*). How can you treat him that way? It makes me feel—like a swine!

NINA

(*Flushing guiltily—protestingly*). What way? (*Then inconsequentially.*) He's always forgetting to shave lately.

DARRELL

You know what I mean, Nina!
　　(*Turns away from her—thinking bitterly*). What a rotten liar I've become! . . . and he trusts me absolutely! . . .

NINA

(*Thinking frightenedly*). Why doesn't he take me in his arms? . . . oh, I

feel he doesn't love me now! . . . he's so bitter! . . .
(*Trying to be matter-of-fact*). I'm sorry, Ned. I don't mean to be cross but Sam does get on my nerves.

DARRELL

(*Thinking bitterly*). Sometimes I almost hate her! . . . if it wasn't for her I'd have kept my peace of mind . . . no good for anything lately, damn it! . . . but it's idiotic to feel guilty . . . if Sam only didn't trust me! . . . (*Then impatiently.*) Bosh! . . . sentimental nonsense! . . . end justifies means! . . . this will have a good end for Sam, I swear to that! . . . why doesn't she tell him she's pregnant? . . . what's she waiting for? . . .

NINA

(*Thinking passionately, looking at him*). Oh, my lover, why don't you kiss me? . . .
(*Imploringly*) Ned! Don't be cross with me, please!

DARRELL

(*Fighting to control himself—coldly*). I'm not cross, Nina. Only you must admit these triangular scenes are to say the least, humiliating. (*Resentfully.*) I won't come out here again!

NINA

(*With a cry of pain*). Ned!

DARRELL

(*Thinking exultingly at first*). She loves me! . . . she's forgotten Gordon! . . . I'm happy! . . . do I love her? . . . no! . . . I won't! . . . I can't! . . . think what it would mean to Sam! . . . to my career! . . . be objective about it . . . you guinea pig! . . . I'm her doctor . . . and Sam's . . . I prescribed child for them . . . that's all there is to it! . . .

NINA

(*Torn between hope and fear*). What is he thinking? . . . he's fighting his love . . . oh, my lover! . . .
(*Again with longing*). Ned!

DARRELL

(*Putting on his best professional air, going to her*). How do you feel today? You look as if you might have a little fever. (*He takes her hand as if to feel her pulse. Her hand closes over his. She looks up into his face. He keeps his turned away.*)

NINA

(*Straining up toward him—with intense longing—thinking*). I love you! . . . take me! . . . what do I care for anything in the world but you! . . . let Sam die! . . .

DARRELL

(*Fighting himself—t h i n k i n g*). Christ! . . . touch of her skin! . . . her nakedness! . . . those afternoons in her arms! happiness! . . . what do I care for anything else? . . . to hell with Sam! . . .

NINA

(*Breaking out passionately*). Ned! I love you! I can't hide it any more! I won't! I love you, Ned!

DARRELL

(*Suddenly taking her in his arms and kissing her frantically*). Nina! Beautiful!

NINA

(*Triumphantly—between kisses*). You love me, don't you? Say you do, Ned!

DARRELL

(*Passionately*). Yes! Yes!

NINA

(*With a cry of triumph*). Thank God! At last you've told me! You've confessed it to yourself! Oh, Ned, you've made me so happy! (*There is a ring from the front door bell.* DARRELL *hears it. It acts like an electric shock on him. He tears himself away from her. Instinctively she gets up too and moves to the lounge at right.*)

DARRELL

(*Stupidly*). Someone—at the door.
(*He sinks down in the chair by the table at left. Thinking torturedly*). I said I loved her! . . . she won! . . . she used my desire! . . . but I don't love

her! . . . I won't! . . . she can't own my
life! . . .
(*Violently—almost shouts at her*). I don't,
Nina! I tell you I don't!

NINA

(*The maid has just gone to the front door*).
Sshh! (*Then in a triumphant whisper.*)
You do, Ned! You do!

DARRELL

(*With dogged stupidity*). I don't!
(*The front door has been opened.* MARSDEN
*appears in the rear, walks slowly and
woodenly like a man in a trance into the
room. He is dressed immaculately in deep
mourning. His face is pale, drawn, haggard with loneliness and grief. His eyes
have a dazed look as if he were still too
stunned to comprehend clearly what has
happened to him. He does not seem conscious of* DARRELL'S *presence at first. His
shoulders are bowed, his whole figure
droops.*)

NINA

(*Thinking—in a strange superstitious panic*). Black . . . in the midst of
happiness . . . black comes . . . again
. . . death . . . my father . . . comes
between me and happiness! . . . (*Then
recovering herself, scornfully.*) You
silly coward! . . . it's only Charlie! . . .
(*Then with furious resentment.*) The
old fool! . . . what does he mean coming in on us without warning? . . .

MARSDEN

(*Forcing a pitiful smile to his lips*). Hello,
Nina. I know it's an imposition—but—
I've been in such a terrible state since Mother—(*He falters, his face becomes distorted into an ugly mask of grief, his eyes
water.*)

NINA

(*Immediately sympathetic, gets up and
goes to him impulsively*). There's no question of imposition, Charlie. We were expecting you. (*She has come to him and
put her arms around him. He gives way
and sobs, his head against her shoulder.*)

MARSDEN

(*Brokenly*). You don't know, Nina—how
terrible—it's terrible!—

NINA

(*Leading him to the chair at center, soothingly*). I know, Charlie.
(*Thinking with helpless annoyance*).
Oh, dear, what can I say? . . . his
mother hated me . . . I'm not glad she's
dead . . . but neither am I sorry . . .
(*With a trace of contempt.*) Poor
Charlie . . . he was so tied to her apron
strings . . .
(*Then kindly but condescendingly, comforting him*). Poor old Charlie!

MARSDEN

(*The words and the tone shock his
pride to life. He raises his head and
half-pushes her away—resentfully,
thinking*). Poor old Charlie! . . . damn
it, what am I to her? . . . her old dog
who's lost his mother? . . . Mother
hated her . . . no, poor dear Mother
was so sweet, she never hated anyone . . . she simply disapproved . . .
(*Coldly*). I'm all right, Nina. Quite all
right now, thank you. I apologize for making a scene.

DARRELL

(*Has gotten up from his chair—with
relief—thinking*). Thank God for
Marsden . . . I feel sane again . . .
(*He comes to* MARSDEN—*cordially*). How
are you, Marsden? (*Then offering conventional, consolation, pats* MARSDEN'S
shoulder.) I'm sorry, Marsden.

MARSDEN

(*Startled, looks up at him in amazement*).
Darrell! (*Then with instant hostility.*)
There's nothing to be sorry about that I can
discover! (*Then as they both look at him
in surprise he realizes what he has said—
stammeringly.*) I mean—sorry—is hardly the right word—hardly—is it?

NINA

(*Worriedly*). Sit down, Charlie. You look
so tired.
(*He slumps down in the chair at center mechanically.* NINA *and* DARRELL
return to their chairs. NINA *looks across
him at* DARRELL—*triumphantly—
thinking*). You do love me, Ned! . . .

DARRELL

(*Thinking—answering her look—defiantly*). I don't love you! . . .

MARSDEN

(*Stares intensely before him. Thinking suspiciously—morbidly agitated*). Darrell! . . . and Nina! . . . there's something in this room! . . . something disgusting! . . . like a brutal, hairy hand, raw and red, at my throat! . . . stench of human life! . . . heavy and rank! . . . outside it's April . . . green buds on the slim trees . . . the sadness of spring . . . my loss at peace in Nature . . . her sorrow of birth consoling my sorrow of death . . . something human and unnatural in this room! . . . love and hate and passion and possession! . . . cruelly indifferent to my loss! . . . mocking my loneliness! . . . no longer any love for me in any room! . . . lust in this room! . . . lust with a loathsome jeer taunting my sensitive timidities! . . . my purity! . . . purity? . . . ha! yes, if you say prurient purity! . . . lust ogling me for a dollar with oily shoe-button Italian eyes! . . . (*In terror.*) What thoughts! . . . what a low scoundrel you are! . . . and your mother dead only two weeks! . . . I hate Nina! . . . that Darrell in this room! . . . I feel their desires! . . . where is Sam? . . . I'll tell him! . . . no, he wouldn't believe . . . he's such a trusting fool . . . I must punish her some other way . . . (*Remorsefully.*) What? . . . punish Nina? . . . my little Nina? . . . why, I want her to be happy! . . . even with Darrell? . . . it's all so confused! . . . I must stop thinking! . . . I must talk! . . . forget! . . . say something! . . . forget everything! . . .

(*He suddenly bursts into a flood of garrulity*). Mother asked for you, Nina—three days before the end. She said, "Where is Nina Leeds now, Charlie? When is she going to marry Gordon Shaw?" Her mind was wandering, poor woman! You remember how fond she always was of Gordon. She used to love to watch the football games when he was playing. He was so handsome and graceful, she always

thought. She always loved a strong, healthy body. She took such strict care of her own, she walked miles every day, she loved bathing and boating in the summer even after she was sixty, she was never sick a day in her life until—(*He turns on* DARRELL—*coldly.*) You were right, Doctor Darrell. It was cancer. (*Then angrily.*) But the doctor you sent me to, and. the others he called in could do nothing for her—absolutely nothing! I might just as well have imported some witch doctors from the Solomon Islands! They at least would have diverted her in her last hours with their singing and dancing, but your specialists were a total loss! (*Suddenly with an insulting, ugly sneer, raising his voice.*) I think you doctors are a pack of God-damned ignorant liars and hypocrites!

NINA

(*Sharply*). Charlie!

MARSDEN

(*Coming to himself—with a groan—shamefacedly*). Don't mind me. I'm not myself, Nina. I've been through hell! (*He seems about to sob—then abruptly springs to his feet, wildly.*) It's this room! I can't stand this room! There's something repulsive about it!

NINA

(*Soothingly*). I know it's ugly, Charlie. I haven't had a chance to fix it up yet. We've been too broke.

MARSDEN

(*Confusedly*). Oh, it's all right. I'm ugly, too! Where's Sam?

NINA

(*Eagerly*). Right upstairs. Go on up. He'll be delighted to see you.

MARSDEN

(*Vaguely*). Very well. (*He goes to the door, then stops mournfully.*) But from what I saw on that visit to his home, he doesn't love his mother much. I don't think he'll understand, Nina. He never writes to her, does he?

NINA

(*Uneasily*). No—I don't know.

MARSDEN

She seemed lonely. He'll be sorry for it some day after she—(*He gulps.*) Well—(*He goes.*)

NINA

(*In a sudden panic—thinking*). Sam's mother! . . . "Make my boy, Sammy, happy!" . . . I promised . . . oh, why did Charlie have to remember her? . . . (*Then resolutely.*) I can't remember her now! . . . I won't! . . . I've got to be happy! . . .

DARRELL

(*Uneasily trying to force a casual conversation*). Poor Marsden is completely knocked off balance, isn't he? (*A pause.*) My mother died when I was away at school. I hadn't seen her in some time, so her death was never very real to me; but in Marsden's case—

NINA

(*With a possessive smile of tolerance*). Never mind Charlie, Ned. What do I care about Charlie? I love you! And you love me!

DARRELL

(*Apprehensively, forcing a tone of annoyed rebuke*). But I don't! And you don't! You're simply letting your romantic imagination run away with you—(*showing his jealous resentment in spite of himself.*) —as you did once before with Gordon Shaw!

NINA

(*Thinking*). He is jealous of Gordon! . . . how wonderful that is! . . .
(*With provoking calm*). I loved Gordon.

DARRELL

(*Irritably ignoring this as if he didn't want to hear it*). Romantic imagination! It has ruined more lives than all the diseases! Other diseases, I should say! It's a form of insanity! (*He gets up forcefully and begins to pace about the room.*)
(*Thinking uneasily*). Mustn't look at her . . . find an excuse and get away . . . and this time never come back! . . .
(*Avoiding looking at her, trying to argue reasonably—coldly*). You're acting fool-

ishly, Nina—and very unfairly. The agreement we made has no more to do with love than a contract for building a house. In fact, you know we agreed it was essential that love mustn't enter into it. And it hasn't, in spite of what you say. (*A pause. He walks about. She watches him.*)
(*Thinking*). She's got to come back to earth! . . . I've got to break with her! . . . bad enough now! . . . but to go on with it! . . . what a mess it'd make of all our lives! . . .

NINA

(*Thinking tenderly*). Let his pride put all the blame on me! . . . I'll accept it gladly! . . .

DARRELL

(*Irritably*). Of course, I realize I've been to blame, too. I haven't been able to be as impersonal as I thought I could be. The trouble is there's been a dangerous physical attraction. Since I first met you, I've always desired you physically. I admit that now.

NINA

(*Smiling tenderly—thinking*). Oh, he admits that, does he? . . . poor darling! . . .
(*Enticingly*). And you still do desire me, don't you, Ned?

DARRELL

(*Keeping his back turned to her—roughly*). No! That part of it is finished! (NINA *laughs softly, possessively. He whirls around to face her—angrily.*) Look here! You're going to have the child you wanted, aren't you?

NINA

(*Implacably*). My child wants its father!

DARRELL

(*Coming a little toward her—desperately*). But you're crazy! You're forgetting Sam! It may be stupid but I've got a guilty conscience! I'm beginning to think we've wronged the very one we were trying to help!

NINA

You were trying to help me, too, Ned!

DARRELL

(*Stammering*). Well—all right—let's say that part of it was all right then. But it's got to stop! It can't go on!

NINA

(*Implacably*). Only your love can make me happy now! Sam must give me a divorce so I can marry you.

DARRELL

(*Thinking suspiciously*). Look out! ... there it is! ... marry! ... own me! ... ruin my career! ...
(*Scornfully*). Marry? Do you think I'm a fool? Get that out of your head quick! I wouldn't marry anyone—no matter what! (*As she continues to look at him with unmoved determination—pleadingly.*) Be sensible, for God's sake! We're absolutely unsuited to each other! I don't admire your character! I don't respect you! I know too much about your past! (*Then indignantly.*) And how about Sam? Divorce him? Have you forgotten all his mother told you? Do you mean to say you'd deliberately—? And you expect me to—? What do you think I am?

NINA

(*Inflexibly*). You're my lover! Nothing else matters. Yes, I remember what Sam's mother said. She said, "being happy is the nearest we can come to knowing what good is." And I'm going to be happy! I've lost everything in life so far because I didn't have the courage to take it—and I've hurt everyone around me. There's no use trying to think of others. One human being can't think of another. It's impossible. (*Gently and caressingly.*) But this time I'm going to think of my own happiness—and that means you—and our child! That's quite enough for one human being to think of, dear, isn't it? (*She reaches out and takes his hand. A pause. With her other hand she gently pulls him around until he is forced to look into her eyes.*)

DARRELL

(*Thinking fascinatedly*). I see my happiness in her eyes ... the touch of her soft skin! ... those afternoons! ... God, I was happy! ...
(*In a strange dazed voice—as if it were forced out of him by an impulse stronger than his will*). Yes, Nina.

NINA

(*In a determined voice*). I've given Sam enough of my life! And it hasn't made him happy, not the least bit! So what's the good? And how can we really know that his thinking our child was his would do him any good? We can't! It's all guesswork. The only thing sure is that we love each other.

DARRELL

(*Dazedly*). Yes. (*A noise from the hall and EVANS comes in from the rear. He sees their two hands together but mistakes their meaning.*)

EVANS

(*Genially—with a forced self-confident air*). Well, Doc, how's the patient? I think she's much better, don't you—although she won't admit it.

DARRELL

(*At the first sound of EVANS' voice, pulls his hand from NINA's as if it were a hot coal—avoiding EVANS' eyes, moving away from her jerkily and self-consciously*). Yes. Much better.

EVANS

Good! (*He pats NINA on the back. She shrinks away. His confidence vanishes in a flash.*)
(*Thinking miserably*). Why does she shrink away ... if I even touch her? ...

NINA

(*Matter-of-factly*). I must see how lunch is coming on. You'll stay, of course, Ned?

DARRELL

(*Struggling—shakenly*). No, I think I'd better—
(*Thinking desperately*). Got to go! ... can't go! ... got to go! ...

EVANS

Oh, come on, old man!

NINA

(*Thinking*). He must stay ... and after lunch we'll tell Sam. ...

(*With certainty*). He'll stay. (*Meaningly.*)
And we want to have a long talk with you
after lunch, Sam—don't we, Ned? (DAR-
RELL *does not answer. She goes out, right.*)

EVANS

(*Vaguely making talk*). I got Charlie
to lie down. He's all in, poor guy. (*Then
trying to face* DARRELL *who keeps looking
away from him.*) What did Nina mean,
you want a long talk with me? Or is it a
secret, Ned?

DARRELL

(*Controlling an impulse toward hysterical
laughter*). A secret? Yes, you bet it's a secret! (*He flings himself in the chair at left,
keeping his face averted.*)
(*His thoughts bitter and desperate
like a cornered fugitive's.*) This is horrible! . . . Sam thinks I'm finest fellow in world . . . and I do this to him!
. . . as if he hadn't enough! . . . born
under a curse! . . . I finish him! . . . a
doctor! . . . God damn it! . . . I can see
his end! . . . never forgive myself! . . .
never forget! . . . break me! . . . ruin
my career! . . . (*More desperately.*)
Got to stop this! . . . while there's
time! . . . she said . . . after lunch, talk
. . . she meant, tell him . . . that means
kill him . . . then she'll marry me! . . .
(*Beginning to be angry.*) By God, I
won't! . . . she'll find out! . . . smiling!
. . . got me where she wants me! . . .
then be as cruel to me as she is to him!
. . . love me? . . . liar! . . . still loves
Gordon! . . . her body is a trap! . . . I'm
caught in it! . . . she touches my hand,
her eyes get in mine, I lose my will! . . .
(*Furiously.*) By God, she can't make
a fool of me that way! . . . I'll go away
some place! . . . go to Europe! . . .
study! . . . forget her in work! . . . keep
hidden until boat sails so she can't
reach me! . . . (*He is in a state of
strange elation by this time.*) Go now!
. . . no! . . . got to spike her guns with
Sam! . . . by God, I see! . . . tell him
about baby! . . . that'll stop her! . . .
when she knows I've told him that,
she'll see it's hopeless! . . . she'll stick
to him! . . . poor Nina! . . . I'm sorry!
. . . she does love me! . . . hell! . . . she'll

forget! . . . she'll have her child! . . .
she'll be happy! . . . and Sam'll be
happy! . . .
(*He suddenly turns to* EVANS *who has been
staring at him, puzzledly—in a whisper*).
Look here, Sam. I can't stay to lunch. I
haven't time, I've got a million things to
do. I'm sailing for Europe in a few days.

EVANS

(*Surprised*). You're sailing?

DARRELL

(*Very hurriedly*). Yes—going to study
over there for a year or so. I haven't told
anyone. I came out today to say good-bye.
You won't be able to reach me again. I'll
be out of town visiting. (*Then elatedly.*)
And now for your secret! It ought to make
you very happy, Sam. I know how much
you've wished for it, so I'm going to tell
you although Nina'll be furious with me.
She was saving it to surprise you with at
her own proper time—(*still more elatedly*)—but I'm selfish enough to want to
see you happy before I go!

EVANS

(*Not daring to believe what he hopes—
stammering*). What—what is it, Ned?

DARRELL

(*Clapping him on the back—with strange
joviality*). You're going to be a father, old
scout, that's the secret! (*Then as* EVANS
*just stares at him dumbly in a blissful satis-
faction, he rattles on.*) And now I've got
to run. See you again in a year or so. I've
said good-bye to Nina. Good-bye, Sam.
(*He takes his hand and clasps it.*) Good
luck! Buckle down to work now! You've
got the stuff in you! When I get back I'll
expect to hear you're on the highroad to
success! And tell Nina I'll expect to find
you both happy in your child—both of
you, tell her!—happy in your child! Tell
her that, Sam! (*He turns and goes to the
door.*)
(*Thinking as he goes*). That does it!
. . . honorably! . . . I'm free! . . . (*He
goes out—then out the front door—a
moment later his motor is heard starting—dies away.*)

EVANS

(*Stares after him dumbly in the same state of happy stupefaction—mumbles*). Thank you—Ned.

(*Thinking disjointedly*). Why did I doubt myself? . . . now she loves me . . . she's loved me right along . . . I've been a fool . . . (*He suddenly falls on his knees.*) Oh, God, I thank you!

(NINA *comes in from the kitchen. She stops in amazement when she sees him on his knees. He jumps to his feet and takes her in his arms with confident happiness and kisses her*). Oh, Nina, I love you so! And now I know you love me! I'll never be afraid of anything again!

NINA

(*Bewildered and terror-stricken, trying feebly to push him away—thinking*). Has he . . . has he gone crazy? . . .

(*Weakly*). Sam! What's come over you, Sam?

EVANS

(*Tenderly*). Ned told me—the secret—and I'm so happy, dear! (*He kisses her again.*)

NINA

(*Stammering*). Ned told you—what?

EVANS

(*Tenderly*). That we're going to have a child, dear. You mustn't be sore at him. Why did you want to keep it a secret from me? Didn't you know how happy it would make me, Nina?

NINA

He told you we—we—you, the father—? (*Then suddenly breaking from him—wildly.*) Ned! Where is Ned?

EVANS

He left a moment ago.

NINA

(*Stupidly*). Left? Call him back. Lunch is ready.

EVANS

He's gone. He couldn't stay. He's got so much to do getting ready to sail.

NINA

Sail?

EVANS

Didn't he tell you he was sailing for Europe? He's going over for a year or so to study.

NINA

A year or so! (*Wildly.*) I've got to call him up! No, I'll go in and see him right now! (*She takes a wavering step toward the door.*)

(*Thinking in anguish*). Go! . . . go to him! . . . find him! . . . my lover! . . .

EVANS

He won't be there, I'm afraid. He said we couldn't reach him, that he'd be visiting friends out of town until he sailed. (*Solicitously.*) Why, do you have to see him about something important, Nina? Perhaps I could locate—

NINA

(*Stammering and swaying*). No. (*She stifles an hysterical laugh.*) No, nothing—nothing important—nothing is important—ha—! (*She stifles another laugh—then on the verge of fainting, weakly.*) Sam! Help me—

EVANS

(*Rushes to her, supports her to sofa at right*). Poor darling! Lie down and rest. (*She remains in a sitting position, staring blankly before her. He chafes her wrists.*) Poor darling!

(*Thinking jubilantly*). Her condition . . . this weakness comes from her condition! . . .

NINA

(*Thinking in anguish*). Ned doesn't love me! . . . he's gone! . . . gone forever! . . . like Gordon! . . . no, not like Gordon! . . . like a sneak, a coward! . . . a liar! . . . oh, I hate him! . . . O Mother God, please let me hate him! . . . he must have been planning this! . . . he must have known it today when he said he loved me! . . . (*Thinking frenziedly.*) I won't bear it . . . he thinks he has palmed me off on Sam forever! . . . and his child! . . . he can't! . . . I'll tell Sam he was lying! . . . I'll make Sam hate him! . . . I'll make Sam kill him! . . . I'll promise to love Sam if he kills him! . . .

(*Suddenly turns to* EVANS—*savagely*). He lied to you!

EVANS

(*Letting her wrists drop—appalled—stammers*). You mean—Ned lied about—?

NINA

(*In same tone*). Ned lied to you!

EVANS

(*Stammers*). You're not—going to have a child—

NINA

(*Savagely*). Oh, yes! Oh, yes, I am! Nothing can keep me from that! But you're—you're—I mean, you . . .
(*Thinking in anguish*). I can't say that to him! . . . I can't tell him without Ned to help me! . . . I can't! . . . look at his face! . . . oh, poor Sammy! . . . poor little boy! . . . poor little boy! . . . (*She takes his head and presses it to her breast and begins to weep.*)
(*Weeping*). I mean, you weren't to know about it, Sammy.

EVANS

(*Immediately on the crest again—tenderly*). Why? Don't you want me to be happy, Nina?

NINA

Yes—yes, I do, Sammy.
(*Thinking strangely*). Little boy! . . little boy! . . . one gives birth to little boys! . . . one doesn't drive them mad and kill them! . . .

EVANS

(*Thinking*). She's never called me Sammy before . . . someone used to . . . oh, yes, Mother . . .

(*Tenderly and boyishly*). And I'm going to make you happy from now on, Nina. I tell you, the moment Ned told me, something happened to me! I can't explain it, but—I'll make good now, Nina! I know I've said that before but I was only boasting. I was only trying to make myself think so. But now I say it knowing I can do it! (*Softly.*) It's because we're going to have a child, Nina. I knew that you'd never come to really love me without that. That's what I was down on my knees for when you came in. I was thanking God—for our baby!

NINA

(*Tremblingly*). Sammy! Poor boy!

EVANS

Ned said when he came back he'd expect to find us both happy—in our baby. He said to tell you that. You will be happy now, won't you, Nina?

NINA

(*Brokenly and exhaustedly*). I'll try to make you happy, Sammy. (*He kisses her, then hides his head on her breast. She stares out over his head. She seems to grow older.*)
(*Thinking as if she were repeating the words of some inner voice of life*). Not Ned's child! . . . not Sam's child! . . . mine! . . . there! . . . again! . . . I feel my child live . . . moving in my life . . . my life moving in my child . . . breathing in the tide I dream and breathe my dream back into the tide . . . God is a Mother. . . . (*Then with sudden anguish.*) Oh, afternoons . . . dear wonderful afternoons of love with you, my lover . . . you are lost . . . gone from me forever! . . .

Curtain.

ACT SIX

SCENE: *The same—an evening a little over a year later. The room has undergone a significant change. There is a comfortable, homey atmosphere as though now it definitely belonged to the type of person it was built for. It has a proud air of modest prosperity.*

It is soon after dinner—about eight o'clock. EVANS *is sitting by the table at left, glancing through a newspaper at headlines and reading an article here and there.* NINA *is in the chair at center, knitting a tiny sweater.* MARSDEN *is sitting on the sofa at right, holding a book which he pretends to be looking through, but glancing wonderingly at* EVANS *and* NINA.

There is a startling change in EVANS. *He is stouter, the haggard look of worry and self-conscious inferiority has gone from his face, it is full and healthy and satisfied. There is also, what is more remarkable, a decided look of solidity about him, of a determination moving toward ends it is confident it can achieve. He has matured, found his place in the world.*

The change in NINA *is also perceptible. She looks noticeably older, the traces of former suffering are marked on her face, but there is also an expression of present contentment and calm.*

MARSDEN *has aged greatly. His hair is gray, his expression one of a deep grief that is dying out into a resignation resentful of itself. He is dressed immaculately in dark tweed.*

NINA

(*Thinking*). I wonder if there's a draft in the baby's room? . . . maybe I'd better close the window? . . . oh, I guess it's all right . . . he needs lots of fresh air . . . little Gordon . . . he does remind me of Gordon . . . something in his eyes . . . my romantic imagination? . . . Ned said that . . . why hasn't Ned ever written? . . . it's better he hasn't . . . how he made me suffer! . . . but I forgive him . . . he gave me my baby . . . the baby certainly doesn't look like him . . . everyone says he looks like Sam . . . how absurd! . . . but Sam makes a wonderful father . . . he's become a new man in the past year . . . and I've helped him . . . he asks me about everything . . . I have a genuine respect for him now . . . I can give myself without repulsion . . . I am making him happy . . . I've written ten his mother I'm making him happy . . . I was proud to be able to write her that . . . how queerly things work out! . . . all for the best . . . and I don't feel wicked . . . I feel good . . . (*She smiles strangely.*)

MARSDEN

(*Thinking*). What a change! . . . the last time I was here the air was poisoned . . . Darrell . . . I was sure he was her lover . . . but I was in a morbid state . . . why did Darrell run away? . . . Nina could have got Sam to divorce her if she really loved Darrell . . . then it's evident she couldn't have loved him . . . and she was going to have Sam's baby . . . Darrell's love must have seemed like treachery . . . so she sent him away . . . that must be it . . . (*With satisfaction.*) Yes, I've got it straight now. . . . (*With contemptuous pity.*) Poor Darrell . . . I have no use for him but I did pity him when I ran across him in Munich . . . he was going the pace . . . looked desperate . . . (*Then gloomily.*) My running away was about as successful as his . . . as if one could leave one's memory behind! . . . I couldn't forget

Mother . . . she haunted me through every city of Europe . . . (*Then irritatedly.*) I must get back to work! . . . not a line written in over a year! . . . my public will be forgetting me! . . . a plot came to me yesterday . . . my mind is coming around again . . . I am beginning to forget, thank God! . . . (*Then remorsefully.*) No, I don't want to forget you, Mother! . . . but let me remember . . . without pain! . . .

EVANS

(*Turning over a page of his paper*). There's going to be the biggest boom before long this country has ever known, or I miss my guess, Nina.

NINA

(*With great seriousness*). Do you think so, Sammy?

EVANS

(*Decidedly*). I'm dead sure of it.

NINA

(*With a maternal pride and amusement*). Dear Sam . . . I can't quite believe in this self-confident business man yet . . . but I have to admit he's proved it . . . he asked for more money and they gave it without question . . . they're anxious to keep him . . . they ought to be . . . how he's slaved! . . . for me and my baby! . . .

EVANS

(*Has been looking at* MARSDEN *surreptitiously over his paper*). Charlie's mother must have hoarded up a half million . . . he'll let it rot in government bonds . . . wonder what he'd say if I proposed that he back me? . . . he's always taken a friendly interest . . . well, it's worth a bet, anyway . . . he'd be an easy partner to handle . . .

MARSDEN

(*Staring at* EVANS *wonderingly*). What a changed Sam! . . . I preferred him the old way . . . futile but he had a sensitive quality . . . now he's brash . . . a little success . . . oh, he'll succeed all right . . . his kind are inheriting the earth . . . hogging it, cramming it down their tasteless gullets!

. . . and he's happy! . . . actually happy! . . . he has Nina . . . a beautiful baby . . . a comfortable home . . . no sorrow, no tragic memories . . . and I have nothing! . . . but utter loneliness! . . . (*With grieving self-pity.*) If only Mother had lived! . . . how horribly I miss her! . . . my lonely home . . . who will keep house for me now? . . . it has got to be done sympathetically or I won't be able to work . . . I must write to Jane . . . she'll probably be only too glad . . .

(*Turning to* NINA). I think I'll write to my sister in California and ask her to come on and live with me. She's alone now that her youngest daughter is married, and she has very little money. And my hands are tied as far as sharing the estate with her is concerned. According to Mother's will, I'm cut off too if I give her a penny. Mother never got over her bitter feeling about Jane's marriage. In a way, she was right. Jane's husband wasn't much—no family or position or ability—and I doubt if she was ever happy with him. (*Sarcastically.*) It was one of those love matches!

NINA

(*Smiling—teasingly*). There's no danger of your ever making a love match, is there, Charlie?

MARSDEN

(*Wincing—thinking*). She can't believe any woman could possibly love me! . . .

(*Caustically*). I trust I'll never make that kind of a fool of myself, Nina!

NINA

(*Teasingly*). Pooh! Aren't you the superior bachelor! I don't see anything to be so proud of! You're simply shirking, Charlie!

MARSDEN

(*Wincing but forcing a teasing air*). You were my only true love, Nina. I made a vow of perpetual bachelorhood when you threw me over in Sam's favor!

EVANS

(*Has listened to this last—jokingly*). Hello! What's this? I never knew you were my hated rival, Charlie!

MARSDEN

(*Dryly*). Oh—didn't you really? (*But* EVANS *has turned back to his paper.*)

(*Thinking savagely*). That fool, too! ... he jokes about it! ... as if I were the last one in the world he could imagine ...

NINA

(*Teasingly*). Well, if I'm responsible, Charlie, I feel I ought to do something about it. I'll pick out a wife for you—guaranteed to suit! She must be at least ten years older than you, large and matronly and placid, and a wonderful cook and housekeeper—

MARSDEN

(*Sharply*). Don't be stupid!

(*Thinking angrily*). She picks someone beyond the age! ... she never imagines sex could enter into it! ...

NINA

(*Placatingly—seeing he is really angry*). Why, I was only picking out a type I thought would be good for you, Charlie— and for your work.

MARSDEN

(*Sneeringly—with a meaning emphasis*). You didn't mention chaste. I couldn't respect a woman who hadn't respected herself!

NINA

(*Thinking—stung*). He's thinking of those men in the hospital ... what a fool I was ever to tell him! ...

(*Cuttingly*). Oh, so you think you deserve an innocent virgin!

MARSDEN

(*Coldly—controlling his anger*). Let's drop me, if you please. (*With a look at her that is challenging and malicious.*) Did I tell you I ran into Doctor Darrell in Munich?

NINA

(*Startled—thinking frightenedly and confusedly*). Ned! ... he saw Ned! ... why hasn't he told me before? ... why did he look at me like that? ... does he suspect? ...

(*Trying to be calm but stammering*). You saw—Ned?

MARSDEN

(*With savage satisfaction*). That struck home! ... look at her! ... guilty! ... then I was right that day! ...

(*Casually*). Yes, I chanced to run into him.

NINA

(*More calmly now*). Why on earth didn't you tell us before, Charlie?

MARSDEN

(*Coolly*). Why? Is it such important news? You knew he was there, didn't you? I supposed he'd written you.

EVANS

(*Looking up from his paper—affectionately*). How was the old scout?

MARSDEN

(*Maliciously*). He seemed in fine feather —said he was having a gay time. When I saw him he was with a startling-looking female—quite beautiful, if you like that type. I gathered they were living together.

NINA

(*Cannot restrain herself—breaks out*). I don't believe it! (*Then immediately controlling herself and forcing a laugh.*) I mean, Ned was always so serious-minded it's hard to imagine him messed up in that sort of thing.

(*Thinking in a queer state of jealous confusion*). Hard to imagine! ... my lover! ... oh, pain again! ... why? ... I don't love him now ... be careful! ... Charlie's staring at me. ...

MARSDEN

(*Thinking—jealously*). Then she did love him! ... does she still? ...

(*Hopefully.*) Or is it only pique? ... no woman likes to lose a man even when she no longer loves him. ...

(*With malicious insistence*). Why is that hard to imagine, Nina? Darrell never struck me as a Galahad. After all, why shouldn't he have a mistress? (*Meaningly.*) He has no tie over here to remain faithful to, has he?

NINA

(*Struggling with herself—thinking pitiably*). He's right . . . why shouldn't Ned? . . . is that why he's never written? . . .
(*Airily*). I don't know what ties he has or hasn't got. It's nothing to me if he has fifty mistresses. I suppose he's no better than the rest of you.

EVANS

(*Looking over at her—tenderly reproachful*). That isn't fair, Nina.
(*Thinking proudly*). I'm proud of that . . . never anyone before her . . .

NINA

(*Looking at him—with real gratitude*). I didn't mean you, dear.
(*Thinking—proudly*). Thank God for Sammy! . . . I know he's mine . . . no jealousy . . . no fear . . . no pain . . . I've found peace . . . (*Then distractedly.*) Oh, Ned, why haven't you written? . . . stop it! . . . what a fool I am! . . . Ned's dead for me! . . . oh, I hate Charlie! . . . why did he tell me? . . .

MARSDEN

(*Looking at* EVANS—*contemptuously thinking*). What a poor simpleton Sam is! . . . boasting of his virtue! . . . as if women loved you for that! . . . they despise it! . . . I don't want Nina to think I've had no experiences with women. . . .
(*Mockingly*). So then it's Sam who is the Galahad, eh? Really, Nina, you should have put him in the Museum among the prehistoric mammals!

EVANS

(*Pleased—comes back kiddingly*). Well, I never had your chances, Charlie! I couldn't run over to Europe and get away with murder the way you have!

MARSDEN

(*Foolishly pleased—admitting while denying*). Oh, I wasn't quite as bad as all that, Sam!
(*Scornfully ashamed of himself—thinking*). Poor sick ass that I am! . . . I want them to think I've been a Don Juan! . . . how pitiful and dis-

gusting! . . . I wouldn't have a mistress if I could! . . . if I could? . . . of course I could! . . . I've simply never cared to degrade myself! . . .

NINA

(*Thinking — tormentedly*). The thought of that woman! . . . Ned forgetting our afternoons in nights with her! . . . stop these thoughts! . . . I won't give in to them! . . . why did Charlie want to hurt me? . . . is he jealous of Ned? . . . Charlie has always loved me in some queer way of his own . . . how ridiculous! . . . look at him! . . . he's so proud of being thought a Don Juan! . . . I'm sure he never even dared to kiss a woman except his mother! . . .
(*Mockingly*). Do tell us about all your various mistresses in foreign parts, Charlie!

MARSDEN

(*In confusion now*). I—I really don't remember, Nina!

NINA

Why, you're the most heartless person I've ever heard of, Charlie! Not remember even one! And I suppose there are little Marsdens—and you've forgotten all about them too! (*She laughs maliciously—*EVANS *laughs with her.*)

MARSDEN

(*Still more confused—with a silly idiotic smirk*). I can't say about that, Nina. It's a wise father who knows his own child, you know!

NINA

(*Frightenedly — thinking*). What does he mean? . . does he suspect about the baby too? . . . I must be terribly careful of Charlie! . . .

EVANS

(*Looking up from his paper again*). Did Ned say anything about coming back?

NINA

(*Thinking—longingly*) Come back? . . . oh, Ned, how I wish! . . .

MARSDEN

(*Looking at her—meaningly*). No, he didn't say. I gathered he was staying over indefinitely.

EVANS

I'd sure like to see him again.

NINA

(*Thinking*). He has forgotten me . . . if he did come, he'd probably avoid me. . . .

MARSDEN

He spoke of you. He asked if I'd heard whether Nina had had her baby yet or not. I told him I hadn't.

EVANS

(*Heartily*). Too bad you didn't know. You could have told him what a world-beater we've got! Eh, Nina?

NINA

(*Mechanically*). Yes.
(*Joyfully—thinking*). Ned asked about my baby! . . . then he hadn't forgotten! . . . if he came back he'd come to see his baby! . . .

EVANS

(*Solicitously*). Isn't it time to nurse him again?

NINA

(*Starts to her feet automatically*). Yes, I'm going now.
(*She glances at* MARSDEN, *thinking calculatingly*). I must win Charlie over again . . . I don't feel safe . . . (*She stops by his chair and takes his hand and looks into his eyes gently and reproachfully.*)

MARSDEN

(*Thinking shamefacedly*). Why have I been trying to hurt her? . . . my Nina! . . . I am nearer to her than anyone! . . . I'd give my life to make her happy! . . .

NINA

(*Triumphantly*). How his hand trembles! . . . what a fool to be afraid of Charlie! . . . I can always twist him round my finger! . . .

(*She runs her hand through his hair, and speaks as though she were hiding a hurt reproach beneath a joking tone*). I shouldn't like you any more, do you know it, after you've practically admitted you've philandered all over Europe! And I thought you were absolutely true to me, Charlie!

MARSDEN

(*So pleased he can hardly believe his ears*). Then she did believe me! . . . she's actually hurt! . . . but I can't let her think . . .
(*With passionate earnestness, clasping her hand in both of his, looking into her eyes*). No, Nina! I swear to you!

NINA

(*Thinking—cruelly*). Pah! . . . how limp his hands are! . . . his eyes are so shrinking! . . . is it possible he loves me? . . . like that? . . . what a sickening idea! . . . it seems incestuous somehow! . . . no, it's too absurd! . . .
(*Smiling, gently releases her hand*). All right. I forgive you, Charlie. (*Then matter-of-factly.*) Excuse me, please, while I go up and feed my infant, or we're due to hear some lusty howling in a moment. (*She turns away, then impulsively turns back and kisses* MARSDEN *with real affection.*) You're an old dear, do you know it, Charlie? I don't know what I'd do without you!
(*Thinking*). It's true, too! . . . he's my only dependable friend . . . I must never lose him . . . never let him suspect about little Gordon . . . (*She turns to go.*)

EVANS

(*Jumping up, throwing his paper aside*). Wait a second. I'll come with you. I want to say good night to him. (*He comes, puts his arm about her waist, kisses her and they go out together.*)

MARSDEN

(*Thinking excitedly*). I almost confessed I loved her! . . . a queer expression came over her face . . . what was it? . . . was it satisfaction? . . . she didn't mind? . . . was it pleasure? . . . then I can hope? (*Then miserably.*) Hope for what . . . what do I want?

. . . If Nina were free, what would I do? . . . would I do anything? . . . would I wish to? . . . what would I offer her? . . . money? . . . she could get that from others . . . myself? (*Bitterly*.) What a prize! . . . my ugly body . . . there's nothing in me to attract her . . . my fame? . . . God, what a shoddy, pitiful! . . . but I might have done something big . . . I might still . . . if I had the courage to write the truth . . . but I was born afraid . . . afraid of myself . . . I've given my talent to making fools feel pleased with themselves in order that they'd feel pleased with me . . . and like me . . . I'm neither hated nor loved . . . I'm liked . . . women like me . . . Nina likes me! . . . (*Resentfully*.) She can't help letting the truth escape her! . . . "You're an old dear, do you know it, Charlie?" Oh, yes, I know it . . . too damned well! . . . dear old Charlie! . . . (*In anguish*.) Dear old Rover, nice old doggie, we've had him for years, he's so affectionate and faithful but he's growing old, he's getting cross, we'll have to get rid of him soon! . . . (*In a strange rage, threateningly*.) But you won't get rid of me so easily, Nina! . . . (*Then confusedly and shamefacedly*.) Good God, what's the matter with me! . . . since Mother's death I've become a regular idiot! . . .

EVANS

(*Comes back from the right, a beaming look of proud parenthood on his face*). He was sleeping so soundly an earthquake wouldn't have made him peep! (*He goes back to his chair—earnestly*.) He sure is healthy and husky, Charlie. That tickles me more than anything else. I'm going to start in training him as soon as he's old enough—so he'll be a crack athlete when he goes to college—what I wanted to be and couldn't. I want him to justify the name of Gordon and be a bigger star than Gordon ever was, if that's possible.

MARSDEN

(*With a sort of pity—thinking*). His is an adolescent mind . . . he'll never grow up . . . well, in this adolescent country, what greater blessing could he wish for? . . .
(*Forcing a smile*). How about training his mind?

EVANS

(*Confidently*). Oh, that'll take care of itself. Gordon was always near the top in his studies, wasn't he? And with Nina for a mother, his namesake ought to inherit a full set of brains.

MARSDEN

(*Amused*). You're the only genuinely modest person I know, Sam.

EVANS

(*Embarrassed*). Oh—me—I'm the boob of the family. (*Then hastily*.) Except when it comes to business. I'll make the money. (*Confidently*.) And you can bet your sweet life I will make it!

MARSDEN

I'm quite sure of that.

EVANS

(*Very seriously—in a confidential tone*). I couldn't have said that two years ago—and believed it. I've changed a hell of a lot! Since the baby was born, I've felt as if I had a shot of dynamite in each arm. They can't pile on the work fast enough. (*He grins—then seriously*.) It was about time I got hold of myself. I wasn't much for Nina to feel proud about having around the house in those days. Now—well—at least I've improved. I'm not afraid of my own shadow any more.

MARSDEN

(*Thinking strangely*). Not to be afraid of one's shadow! . . . that must be the highest happiness of heaven! . . .
(*Flatteringly*). Yes, you've done wonders in the past year.

EVANS

Oh, I haven't even started yet. Wait till I get my chance! (*Glances at* MARSDEN *sharply, makes up his mind and leans forward toward him confidentially*.) And I see my real chance, Charlie—lying right ahead, waiting for me to grab it—an agency that's been allowed to run down and go to seed.

Within a year or so they'll be willing to sell out cheap. One of their people who's become a good pal of mine told me that in confidence, put it up to me. He'd take it on himself but he's sick of the game. But I'm not! I love it! It's great sport! (*Then putting the brake on this exuberance—matter-of-factly.*) But I'll need a hundred thousand—and where will I get it? (*Looking at* MARSDEN *keenly but putting on a joking tone.*) Any suggestion you can make, Charlie, will be gratefully received.

MARSDEN

(*Thinking suspiciously*). Does he actually imagine I . . . ? and a hundred thousand, no less! . . . over one-fifth of my entire . . . by Jove, I'll have to throw cold water on that fancy! . . . (*Shortly*). No, Sam, I can't think of anyone. Sorry.

EVANS

(*Without losing any confidence—with a grin*). Check! . . . That's that! . . . Charlie's out . . . till the next time! . . . but I'll keep after him! . . . (*Contemplating himself with pride.*) Gee, I have changed all right! I can remember when a refusal like that would have ruined my confidence for six months!
(*Heartily*). Nothing to be sorry about, old man. I only mentioned it on the off chance you might know of someone. (*Trying a bold closing stroke—jokingly.*) Why don't you be my partner, Charlie? Never mind the hundred thousand. We'll get that elsewhere. I'll bet you might have darn fine original ideas to contribute.
(*Thinking—satisfied*). There! . . . That'll keep my proposition pinned up in his mind! . . .
(*Then jumping to his feet—briskly*). What do you say to a little stroll down to the shore and back? Come on—do you good. (*Taking his arm and hustling him genially toward the door.*) What you need is exercise. You're soft as putty. Why don't you take up golf?

MARSDEN

(*With sudden resistance pulls away—determinedly*). No, I won't go, Sam. I want to think out a new plot.

EVANS

Oh, all right! If it's a case of work, go to it! See you later. (*He goes out. A moment later the front door is heard closing.*)

MARSDEN

(*Looks after him with a mixture of annoyance and scornful amusement*). What a fount of meaningless energy he's tapped! . . . always on the go . . . typical terrible child of the age . . . universal slogan, keep moving . . . moving where? . . . never mind that . . . don't think of ends . . . the means are the end . . . keep moving! . . . (*He laughs scornfully and sits down in* EVANS' *chair, picking up the paper and glancing at it sneeringly.*) It's in every headline of this daily newer testament . . . going . . . going . . . never mind the gone . . . we won't live to see it . . . and we'll be so rich, we can buy off the deluge anyway! . . . even our new God has His price! . . . must have! . . . aren't we made in His image? . . . or vice-versa? . . . (*He laughs again, letting the paper drop disdainfully—then bitterly.*) But why am I so superior? . . . where am I going? . . . to the same nowhere! . . . worse! . . . I'm not even going! . . . I'm there! . . . (*He laughs with bitter self-pity—then begins to think with amused curiosity.*) Become Sam's partner? . . . there's a grotesque notion! . . . it might revive my sense of humor about myself, at least . . . I'm the logical one to help him . . . I helped him to Nina . . . logical partner . . . partner in Nina? . . . what inane thoughts! . . . (*With a sigh.*) No use trying to think out that plot tonight . . . I'll try to read. . . . (*He sees the book he has been reading on the couch and gets up to get it. There is a ring from the front door.* MARSDEN *turns toward it uncertainly. A pause. Then* NINA'S *voice calls down the stairs.*)

NINA

The maid's out. Will you go to the door, Charlie?

MARSDEN

Surely. (*He goes out and opens the front door. A pause. Then he can be heard say-*

ing resentfully.) Hello, Darrell. (*And someone answering "Hello,* MARSDEN*" and coming in and the door closing.*)

NINA

(*From upstairs, her voice strange and excited*). Who is it, Charlie?

DARRELL

(*Comes into view in the hall, opposite the doorway, at the foot of the stairs—his voice trembling a little with suppressed emotion*). It's I, Nina—Ned Darrell.

NINA

(*With a glad cry*). Ned! (*Then in a voice which shows she is trying to control herself, and is frightened now.*) I—make yourself at home. I'll be down—in a minute or two. (DARRELL *remains standing looking up the stairs in a sort of joyous stupor.* MARSDEN *stares at him.*)

MARSDEN

(*Sharply*). Come on in and sit down. (DARRELL *starts, comes into the room, plainly getting a grip on himself.* MARSDEN *follows him, glaring at his back with enmity and suspicion.* DARRELL *moves as far away from him as possible, sitting down on the sofa at right.* MARSDEN *takes* EVANS' *chair by the table.* DARRELL *is pale, thin, nervous, unhealthy looking. There are lines of desperation in his face, puffy shadows of dissipation and sleeplessness under his restless, harried eyes. He is dressed carelessly, almost shabbily. His eyes wander about the room, greedily taking it in.*)

DARRELL

(*Thinking disjointedly*). Here again! . . . dreamed of this house . . . from here, ran away . . . I've come back . . . my turn to be happy! . . .

MARSDEN

(*Watching him—savagely*) Now I know! . . . absolutely! . . . his face! . . . her voice! . . . they did love each other! . . . they do now . . .
(*Sharply*) When did you get back from Europe?

DARRELL

(*Curtly*). This morning on the Olympic.
(*Thinking—cautiously*). Look out

for this fellow . . . always had it in for me . . . like a woman . . . smells out love . . . he suspected before . . . (*Then boldly*) Well, who gives a damn now? . . . all got to come out! . . . Nina wanted to tell Sam . . . now I'll tell him myself! . . .

MARSDEN

(*Righteously indignant*). What has brought him back? . . . what a devilish, cowardly trick to play on poor unsuspecting Sam! . . . (*Revengefully.*) But I'm not unsuspecting! . . . I'm not their fool! . . .
(*Coldly*). What brought you back so soon? When I saw you in Munich you weren't intending—

DARRELL

(*Shortly*). My father died three weeks ago. I've had to come back about his estate.
(*Thinking*). Lie . . . Father's death just gave me an excuse to myself . . . wouldn't have come back for that . . . came back because I love her! . . . damn his questions! . . . I want to think . . . before I see her . . . sound of her voice . . . seemed to burn inside my head . . . God, I'm licked! . . . no use fighting it . . . I've done my damnedest . . . work . . . booze . . . other women . . . no use . . . I love her! . . . always! . . . to hell with pride! . . .

MARSDEN

(*Thinking*). He has two brothers . . . they'll probably all share equally . . . his father noted Philadelphia surgeon . . . rich, I've heard . . . (*With a bitter grin.*) Wait till Sam hears that! . . . he'll ask Darrell to back him . . . and Darrell will jump at it . . . chance to avert suspicion . . . conscience money, too! . . . it's my duty to protect Sam . . . (*As he hears* NINA *coming down the stairs.*) I must watch them . . . it's my duty to protect Nina from herself . . . Sam is a simpleton . . . I'm all she has . . .

DARRELL

(*Hearing her coming—in a panic—thinking*). Coming! . . . in a second

I'll see her! . . . (*Terrified.*) Does she still love me? . . . she may have forgotten . . . no, it's my child . . . she can never forget that! . . .

(NINA *comes in from the rear. She has put on a fresh dress, her hair is arranged, her face newly rouged and powdered, she looks extremely pretty and this is heightened by the feverish state of mind she is in—a mixture of love, of triumphant egotism in knowing her lover has come back to her, and of fear and uncertainty in feeling her new peace, her certainties, her contented absorption in her child failing her. She hesitates just inside the door, staring into* DARRELL's *eyes, thinking a fierce question.*)

NINA

Does he still love me? . . . (*Then triumphantly as she reads him.*) Yes! . . . he does! . . . he does! . . .

DARRELL

(*Who has jumped to his feet—with a cry of longing*). Nina!
(*Thinking with alarm now*). She's changed! . . . changed! . . . can't tell if she loves!
(*He has started to go to her. Now he hesitates. His voice taking on a pleading uncertain quality*). Nina!

NINA

(*Thinking triumphantly—with a certain cruelty*). He loves me! . . . he's mine . . . now more than ever! . . . he'll never dare leave me again! . . .
(*Certain of herself now, she comes to him and speaks with confident pleasure*). Hello, Ned! This is a wonderful surprise! How are you? (*She takes his hand.*)

DARRELL

(*Taken aback—confusedly*). Oh—all right, Nina.
(*Thinking in a panic*). That tone! . . . as if she didn't care! . . . can't believe that! . . . she's playing a game to fool Marsden! . . .

MARSDEN

(*Who is watching them keenly—thinking*). She loves his love for her . . . she's cruelly confident . . . much as I hate this man I can't help feeling

sorry . . . I know her cruelty . . . it's time I took a hand in this . . . what a plot for a novel! . . .
(*Almost mockingly*). Darrell's father died, Nina. He had to come home to see about the estate.

DARRELL

(*With a glare at* MARSDEN—*protestingly*). I was coming home anyway. I only intended to stay a year, and it's over that since— (*Intensely.*) I was coming back anyway, Nina!

NINA

(*Thinking with triumphant happiness*). You dear, you! . . . as if I didn't know that! . . . oh, how I'd love to take you in my arms! . . .
(*Happily*). I'm awfully glad you've come, Ned. We've missed you terribly.

DARRELL

(*Thinking—more and more at sea*). She looks glad . . . but she's changed . . . I don't understand her . . . "we've missed" . . . that means Sam . . . what does that mean? . . .
(*Intensely, pressing her hand*) And I've missed you—terribly!

MARSDEN

(*Sardonically*). Yes, indeed, Darrell, I can vouch for their missing you—Sam in particular. He was asking about you only a short while ago—how things were going with you when I saw you in Munich. (*Maliciously.*) By the way, who was the lady you were with that day? She was certainly startling looking.

NINA

(*Thinking—triumphantly mocking*). A miss, Charlie! . . . he loves me! . . . what do I care about that woman? . . .
(*Gaily*). Yes, who was the mysterious beauty, Ned? Do tell us! (*She moves away from him and sits down at center.* DARRELL *remains standing.*)

DARRELL

(*Glaring at* MARSDEN, *sullenly*). Oh, I don't remember—
(*Thinking apprehensively with a bitter resentment*). She doesn't give a

damn! . . . if she loved me she'd be
jealous! . . . but she doesn't give a
damn! . . .

(*He blurts out resentfully at* NINA). Well,
she was my mistress—for a time—I was
lonely. (*Then with sudden anger turning
on* MARSDEN.) But what's all this to you,
Marsden?

MARSDEN

(*Coolly*). Absolutely nothing. Pardon me.
It was a tactless question. (*Then with continued open malice.*) But I was starting to
say how Sam had missed you, Darrell. It's
really remarkable. One doesn't encounter
such friendship often in these slack days.
Why, he'd trust you with anything!

NINA

(*Wincing—thinking*). That hurts . . .
hurts Ned . . . Charlie is being
cruel! . . .

DARRELL

(*Wincing—in a forced tone*). And I'd
trust Sam with anything.

MARSDEN

Of course. He is a person one can trust.
They are rare. You're going to be amazed
at the change in Sam, Darrell. Isn't he,
Nina? He's a new man. I never saw such
energy. If ever a man was bound for success Sam is. In fact, I'm so confident he is
that as soon as he thinks the time is ripe to
start his own firm I'm going to furnish the
capital and become his silent partner.

DARRELL

(*Puzzled and irritated—thinking
confusedly*). What's he driving at?
. . . why doesn't he get the hell out and
leave us alone? . . . but I'm glad Sam
is on his feet . . . makes it easier to tell
him the truth. . . .

NINA

(*Thinking — worriedly*). What's
Charlie talking about? . . . it's time I
talked to Ned . . . Oh, Ned, I do love
you! . . . you can be my lover! . . . we
won't hurt Sam! . . . he'll never
know! . . .

MARSDEN

Yes, ever since the baby was born Sam's
been another man—in fact, ever since he
knew there was going to be a baby, isn't it,
Nina?

NINA

(*Agreeing as if she had only half-heard
him*). Yes.
    (*Thinking*). Ned's baby! . . . I must
talk to him about our baby. . . .

MARSDEN

Sam is the proudest parent I've ever seen!

NINA

(*As before*). Yes, Sam makes a wonderful
father, Ned.
    (*Thinking*). Ned doesn't care for chil-
dren . . . I know what you're hoping,
Ned . . . but if you think I'm going to
take Sam's baby from him, you're
mistaken! . . . or if you think I'll run
away with you and leave my baby . . .

MARSDEN

(*With the same strange driving insistence*). If anything happened to that child
I actually believe Sam would lose his reason! Don't you think so, Nina?

NINA

(*With emphasis*). I know I'd lose mine!
Little Gordon has become my whole life.

DARRELL

(*Thinking—with a sad bitter irony*).
Sam . . . wonderful father . . . lose his
reason . . . little Gordon! . . . Nina
called my son after Gordon! . . . romantic imagination! . . . Gordon is
still her lover! . . . Gordon, Sam and
Nina! . . . and my son! . . . closed
corporation! . . . I'm forced out! . . .
(*Then rebelling furiously.*) No! . . .
not yet, by God! . . . I'll smash it up!
. . . I'll tell Sam the truth no matter
what! . . .

NINA

(*Thinking with a strange calculation*). I couldn't find a better husband
than Sam . . . and I couldn't find a
better lover than Ned . . . I need them
both to be happy . . .

MARSDEN

(*With sudden despairing suspicion*). Good God . . . after all, is it Sam's child? . . . mightn't it be Darrell's! . . . why have I never thought of that? . . . No! . . . Nina couldn't be so vile! . . . to go on living with Sam pretending . . . and, after all, why should she, you fool? . . . there's no sense! . . . she could have gone off with Darrell, couldn't she? . . . Sam would have given her a divorce . . . there was no possible reason for her staying with Sam, when she loved Darrell, unless exactly because this was Sam's baby . . . for its sake . . . (*Hectically relieved.*) Of course! . . . of course! . . . that's all right! . . . I love that poor baby now! . . . I'll fight for its sake against these two! (*Smilingly gets to his feet—thinking.*) I can leave them alone now . . . for they won't be alone, thanks to me! . . . I leave Sam and his baby in this room with them . . . and their honor . . . (*Suddenly raging.*) Their honor! . . . what an obscene joke . . . the honor of a harlot and a pimp! . . . I hate them! . . . if only God would strike them dead! . . . now! . . . and I could see them die! . . . I would praise His justice . . . His kindness and mercy to me! . . .

NINA

(*Thinking—with horrified confusion*). Why doesn't Charlie go? . . . What is he thinking? . . . I suddenly feel afraid of him! . . .
(*She gets to her feet with a confused pleading cry*). Charlie!

MARSDEN

(*Immediately urbane and smiling*). It's all right. I'm going out to find Sam. When he knows you're here he'll come on the run, Darrell. (*He goes to the door. They watch him suspiciously.*) And you two probably have a lot to talk over. (*He chuckles pleasantly and goes into the hall—mockingly warning.*) We'll be back before long.
(*The front door is heard slamming.* NINA *and* DARRELL *turn and look at each other guiltily and frightenedly. Then he comes to her and takes both of her hands uncertainly.*)

DARRELL

(*Stammeringly*). Nina—I—I've come back to you—do you—do you still care—Nina?

NINA

(*Giving way to his love passionately, as if to drown her fears*). I love you, Ned!

DARRELL

(*Kisses her awkwardly—stammering*). I —I didn't know—you seemed so cold— damn Marsden—he suspects, doesn't he? —but it makes no difference now, does it? (*Then in a flood of words.*) Oh, it's been hell, Nina! I couldn't forget you! Other women—they only made me love you more! I hated them and loved you even at the moment when—that's honest! It was always you in my arms—as you used to be —those afternoons—God, how I've thought of them—lying awake—recalling every word you said, each movement, each expression on your face, smelling your hair, feeling your soft body— (*Suddenly taking her in his arms and kissing her again and again—passionately.*) Nina! I love you so!

NINA

And I've longed for you so much! Do you think I've forgotten those afternoons? (*Then in anguish.*) Oh, Ned, why did you run away? I can never forgive that! I can never trust you again!

DARRELL

(*Violently*). I was a fool! I thought of Sam! And that wasn't all! Oh, I wasn't all noble, I'll confess! I thought of myself and my career! Damn my career! A lot of good that did it! I didn't study! I didn't live! I longed for you—and suffered! I paid in full, believe me, Nina! But I know better now! I've come back. The time for lying is past! You've got to come away with me! (*He kisses her.*)

NINA

(*Letting herself go, kissing him passionately*). Yes! My lover! (*Then suddenly resisting and pushing him away.*) No! You're forgetting Sam—and Sam's baby!

DARRELL

(*Staring at her wildly*). Sam's baby? Are you joking? Ours, you mean! We'll take him with us, of course!

NINA

(*Sadly*). And Sam?

DARRELL

Damn Sam! He's got to give you a divorce! Let him be generous for a change!

NINA

(*Sadly but determinedly*). He would be. You must be just to Sam. He'd give his life for my happiness. And this would mean his life. Could we be happy then? You know we couldn't! And I've changed, Ned. You've got to realize that. I'm not your old mad Nina. I still love you. I will always love you. But now I love my baby too. His happiness comes first with me!

DARRELL

But—he's mine, too!

NINA

No! You gave him to Sam to save Sam!

DARRELL

To hell with Sam! It was to make you happy!

NINA

So I could make Sam happy! That was in it too! I was sincere in that, Ned! If I hadn't been, I could never have gone to you that first day—or if I had, I'd never have forgiven myself. But as it is I don't feel guilty or wicked. I have made Sam happy! And I'm proud! I love Sam's happiness! I love the devoted husband and father in him! And I feel it's his baby—that we've made it his baby!

DARRELL

(*Distractedly*). Nina! For God's sake! You haven't come to love Sam, have you? Then—I'll go—I'll go away again—I'll never come back—I tried not to this time—but I had to, Nina!

NINA

(*Taking him in her arms—with sudden alarm*). No, don't go away, Ned—ever again. I don't love Sam! I love you!

DARRELL

(*Miserably*). But I don't understand! Sam gets everything—and I have nothing!

NINA

You have my love! (*With a strange, self-assured smile at him.*) It seems to me you're complaining unreasonably!

DARRELL

You mean—I can be—your lover again?

NINA

(*Simply, even matter-of-factly*). Isn't that the nearest we can come to making everyone happy? That's all that counts.

DARRELL

(*With a harsh laugh*). And is that what you call playing fair to Sam?

NINA

(*Simply*). Sam will never know. The happiness I have given him has made him too sure of himself ever to suspect me now. And as long as we can love each other without danger to him, I feel he owes that to us for all we've done for him. (*With finality.*) That's the only possible solution, Ned, for all our sakes, now you've come back to me.

DARRELL

(*Repulsed*). Nina! How can you be so inhuman and calculating!

NINA

(*Stung—mockingly*). It was you who taught me the scientific approach, Doctor!

DARRELL

(*Shrinking back from her—threateningly*). Then I'll leave again! I'll go back to Europe! I won't endure—! (*Then in a queer, futile rage.*) You think I'll stay—to be your lover—watching Sam with my wife and my child—you think that's what I came back to you for? You can go to hell, Nina!

NINA

(*Calmly—sure of him*). But what else can I do, Ned? (*Then warningly.*) I hear them coming, dear. It's Sam, you know.

DARRELL

(*In a frenzy*). What else can you do? Liar! But I can do something else! I can smash your calculating game for you! I can tell Sam—and I will—right now—by God, I will!

NINA

(*Quietly*). No. you won't, Ned. You can't do that to Sam.

DARRELL

(*Savagely*). Like hell I can't!
(*The front door is opened.* EVANS' *voice is immediately heard, even before he bounds into the room. He rushes up to* NED *hilariously, shakes his hand and pounds his back, oblivious to* DARRELL'S *wild expression.*)

EVANS

You old son of a gun! Why didn't you let a guy know you were coming? We'd have met you at the dock, and brought the baby. Let me have a look at you! You look thinner. We'll fatten you up, won't we, Nina? Let us do the prescribing this time! Why didn't you let us know where you were, you old bum? We wanted to write you about the baby. And I wanted to boast about how I was getting on! You're the only person in the world—except Nina and Charlie—I would boast about that to.

NINA

(*Affectionately*). Mercy, Sam, give Ned a chance to get a word in! (*Looking at* NED *pityingly but challengingly.*) He wants to tell you something, Sam.

DARRELL

(*Crushed—stammers*). No—I mean, yes —I want to tell you how damn glad I am . . . (*He turns away, his face is screwed up in his effort to hold back his tears.*)
(*Thinking miserably*). I can't tell him! . . . God damn him, I can't! . . .

NINA

(*With a strange triumphant calm*). There! . . . that's settled for all time! . . . poor Ned! . . . how crushed he looks! . . . I mustn't let Sam look at him! . . .
(*She steps between them protectingly*). Where's Charlie, Sam?

MARSDEN

(*Appearing from the hall*). Here, Nina. Always here! (*He comes to her, smiling with assurance.*)

NINA

(*Suddenly with a strange unnatural elation —looking from one to the other with triumphant possession*). Yes, you're here, Charlie—always! And you, Sam—and Ned! (*With a strange gaiety.*) Sit down, all of you! Make yourselves at home! You are my three men! This is your home with me! (*Then in a strange half-whisper.*) Ssshh! I thought I heard the baby. You must all sit down and be very quiet. You must not wake our baby.
(*Mechanically the three sit down, careful to make no noise—*EVANS *in his old place by the table,* MARSDEN *at center,* DARRELL *on the sofa at right. They sit staring before them in silence.* NINA *remains standing, dominating them, a little behind and to the left of* MARSDEN.)

MARSDEN

(*Thinking abjectly*). I couldn't! . . . there are things one may not do and live with oneself afterwards . . . there are things one may not say . . . memory is too full of echoes! . . . there are secrets one must not reveal . . . memory is lined with mirrors! . . . he was too happy! . . . to kill happiness is a worse murder than taking life! . . . I gave him that happiness! . . . Sam deserves my happiness! . . . God bless you, Sam! . . . (*Then in a strange objective tone —thinking.*) My experiment with the guinea pigs has been a success . . . the ailing ones, Sam and the female, Nina, have been restored to health and normal function . . . only the other male, Ned, seems to have suffered deterioration. . . . (*Then bitterly humble.*) Nothing left but to accept her terms . . . I love her . . . I can help to make her happy . . . half a loaf is better . . . to a starving man. . . (*Glancing over at* EVANS—*bitterly gloating*) And your child is mine! . . . your wife is mine! . . . your happiness is mine! . . . may you enjoy my happiness, her husband! . . .

EVANS

(*Looking at* DARRELL *affectionately*). Sure good to see Ned again . . . a real friend if there ever was one . . . looks blue about something . . . oh, that's right, Charlie said his old man had kicked in . . . his old man was rich . . . that's an idea . . . I'll bet he'd put up that capital . . . (*Then ashamed of himself.*) Aw hell, what's the matter with me? . . . he's no sooner here than I start . . . he's done enough . . . forget it! . . . now anyway . . . he looks pretty dissipated . . . too many women . . . ought to get married and settle down . . . tell him that if I didn't think he'd laugh at me giving him advice . . . but he'll soon realize I'm not the old Sam he knew . . . I suppose Nina's been boasting about that already . . . she's proud . . . she's helped me . . . she's a wonderful wife and mother . . . (*Looking up to her—solicitously.*) She acted a bit nervous just now . . . queer . . . like she used to . . . haven't noticed her that way in a long time . . . suppose it's the excitement of Ned turning up . . . mustn't let her get overexcited . . . bad for the baby's milk. . . .

MARSDEN

(*Glancing furtively over his shoulder at* NINA—*broodingly thinking*). She's the old queer Nina now . . . the Nina I could never fathom . . . her three men! . . . and we are! . . . I? . . . yes, more deeply than either of the others since I serve for nothing . . . a queer kind of love, maybe . . . I am not ordinary! . . . our child . . . what could she mean by that? . . . child of us three? . . . on the surface, that's insane . . . but I felt when she said it there was something in it . . . she has strange devious intuitions that tap the hidden currents of life . . . dark intermingling currents that become the one stream of desire . . . I feel, with regard to Nina, my life queerly identified with Sam's and Darrell's . . . her child is the child of our three loves for her . . . I would like to believe that . . . I would like to be her husband in a sense . . . and the father of a child, after my fashion . . . I could forgive her everything . . . permit everything . . . (*Determinedly.*) And I do forgive! . . . and I

will not meddle hereafter more than is necessary to guard her happiness, and Sam's and our baby's . . . as for Darrell, I am no longer jealous of him . . . she is only using his love for her own happiness . . . he can never take her away from me! . . .

NINA

(*More and more strangely triumphant*). My three men! . . . I feel their desires converge in me! . . . to form one complete beautiful male desire which I absorb . . . and am whole . . . they dissolve in me, their life is my life . . . I am pregnant with the three! . . . husband! . . . lover! . . . father! . . . . . . and the fourth man! . . . little Gordon! . . . he is mine too! . . . that makes it perfect! . . . (*With an extravagant suppressed exultance.*) Why, I should be the proudest woman on earth! . . . I should be the happiest woman in the world! . . . (*Then suppressing an outbreak of hysterical triumphant laughter only by a tremendous effort.*) Haha . . . only I better knock wood . . . (*She raps with both knuckles in a fierce tattoo on the table.*) before God the Father hears my happiness! . . .

EVANS

(*As the three turn to her—anxiously*). Nina? What's the matter?

NINA

(*Controlling herself with a great effort comes to him—forcing a smile—puts her arms around him affectionately*). Nothing, dear. Nerves, that's all. I've gotten overtired, I guess.

EVANS

(*Bullying her—with loving authority*). Then you go right to bed, young lady! We'll excuse you.

NINA

(*Quietly and calmly now*). All right, dear. I guess I do need a rest. (*She kisses him as she might kiss a big brother she loved— affectionately.*) Good night, you bossy old thing, **you!**

EVANS

(*With deep tenderness*). Good night, darling.

NINA

(*She goes and kisses Charlie dutifully on the cheek as she might her father—affectionately*). Good night, Charlie.

MARSDEN

(*With a touch of her father's manner*). That's a good girl! Good night, dear.

NINA

(*She goes and kisses* DARRELL *lovingly on the lips as she would kiss her lover*). Good night, Ned.

DARRELL

(*Looks at her with grateful humility*). Thank you. Good night.
(*She turns and walks quietly out of the room. The eyes of the three men follow her.*)

Curtain.

ACT SEVEN

SCENE: *Nearly eleven years later. The sitting room of the* EVAN's *apartment on Park Avenue, New York City—a room that is a tribute to* NINA's *good taste. It is a large, sunny room, the furniture expensive but extremely simple. The arrangement of the furniture shown is as in previous scenes except there are more pieces. Two chairs are by the table at left. There is a smaller table at center, and a chaise longue. A large, magnificently comfortable sofa is at right.*

It is about one in the afternoon of a day in early fall. NINA *and* DARRELL *and their son,* GORDON, *are in the room.* NINA *is reclining on the chaise longue watching* GORDON *who is sitting on the floor near her, turning over the pages of a book.* DARRELL *is sitting by the table at left, watching* NINA.

NINA *is thirty-five, in the full bloom of her womanhood. She is slimmer than in the previous scene. Her skin still retains a trace of summer tan and she appears in the pink of physical condition. But as in the first act of the play, there is beneath this a sense of great mental strain. One notices the many lines in her face at second glance. Her eyes are tragically sad in repose and her expression is set and masklike.*

GORDON *is eleven—a fine boy with, even at this age, the figure of an athlete. He looks older than he is. There is a grave expression to his face. His eyes are full of a quick-tempered sensitiveness. He does not noticeably resemble his mother. He looks nothing at all like his father. He seems to have sprung from a line distinct from any of the people we have seen.*

DARRELL *has aged greatly. His hair is streaked with gray. He has grown stout. His face is a bit jowly and puffy under the eyes. The features have become blurred. He has the look of a man with no definite aim or ambition to which he can relate his living. His eyes are embittered and they hide his inner self-resentment behind a pose of cynical indifference.*

GORDON

(*Thinking as he plays—resentfully*). I wish Darrell'd get out of here! . . . why couldn't Mother let me run my own birthday? . . . I'd never had him here, you bet! . . . what's he always hanging 'round for? . . . why don't he go off on one of his old trips again . . .

last time he was gone more'n a year
... I was hoping he'd died! ... what
makes Mother like him so much? ...
she makes me sick! ... I'd think she'd
get sick of the old fool and tell him
to get out and never come back! ...
I'd kick him out if I was big enough!
... it's good for him he didn't bring
me any birthday present or I'd smash
it first chance I got! ...

NINA

(*Watching him—brooding and loving tenderness—sadly*). No longer
my baby ... my little man ... eleven
... I can't believe it ... I'm thirty-
five ... five years more ... at forty a
woman has finished living ... life
passes her by ... she rots away in
peace! ... (*Intensely.*) I want to rot
away in peace! ... I'm sick of the fight
for happiness! ... (*Smiling with a
wry amusement at herself.*) What ungrateful thoughts on my son's birthday! ... my love for him has been
happiness ... how handsome he is!
... not at all like Ned ... when I was
carrying him I was fighting to forget
Ned ... hoping he might be like Gordon ... and he is ... poor Ned, I've
made him suffer a great deal ... ! (*She
looks over at* DARRELL—*self-mockingly.*) My lover! ... so very rarely now,
those interludes of passion ... what
has bound us together all these years?
... love? ... if he could only have
been contented with what I was able
to give him! ... but he has always
wanted more ... yet never had the
courage to insist on all or nothing ...
proud without being proud enough!
... he has shared me for his comfort's
sake with a little gratitude and a big
bitterness ... and sharing me has corrupted him! ... (*Then bitterly.*) No. I
can't blame myself! ... no woman can
make a man happy who has no purpose in life! ... why did he give up
his career? ... because I had made
him weak? ... (*With resentful scorn.*)
No, it was I who shamed him into
taking up biology and starting the station at Antigua ... if I hadn't he'd
simply have hung around me year af-

ter year, doing nothing ... (*Irritatedly.*) Why does he stay so long? ...
over six months ... I can't stand having him around me that long any
more! ... why doesn't he go back to
the West Indies? ... I always get a
terrible feeling after he's been back a
while that he's waiting for Sam to die!
... or go insane! ...

DARRELL

(*Thinking—with an apathetic bitterness*). What is she thinking? ... we
sit together in silence, thinking ...
thoughts that never know the other's
thoughts ... our love has become the
intimate thinking together of thoughts
that are strangers ... our love! ...
well, whatever it is that has bound us
together, it's strong! ... I've broken
with her, run away, tried to forget her
... running away to come back each
time more abject! ... or, if she saw
there was some chance I might break
loose, she'd find some way to call me
back ... and I'd forget my longing for
freedom, I'd come wagging my tail ...
no, guinea pigs have no tails ... I hope
my experiment has proved something!
... Sam ... happy and wealthy ...
and healthy! ... I used to hope he'd
break down ... I'd watch him and
read symptoms of insanity into every
move he made ... despicable? ... certainly, but love makes one either noble
or despicable! ... he only grew healthier ... now I've given up watching
him ... almost entirely ... now I
watch him grow fat and I laugh! ...
the huge joke has dawned on me! ...
Sam is the only normal one! ... we
lunatics! ... Nina and I! ... have
made a sane life for him out of our
madness! ... (*Watching* NINA—*sadly.*) Always thinking of her son ...
well, I gave him to her ... Gordon ...
I hate that name ... why do I continue hanging around here? ... each
time after a few months my love
changes to bitterness ... I blame Nina
for the mess I've made of life ...

NINA

(*Suddenly turning on him*). When are you
going back to the West Indies, Ned?

DARRELL

(*Determinedly*). Soon!

GORDON

(*Stops playing to listen—thinking*). Gosh, I'm glad! . . . How soon, I wonder? . . .

NINA

(*With a trace of a sneer*). I don't see how you can afford to leave your work for such long periods. Don't you grow rusty?

DARRELL

(*Looking at her meaningly*). My life work is to rust—nicely and unobtrusively! (*He smiles mockingly.*)

NINA

(*Sadly—thinking*). To rot away in peace . . . that's all he wants now, too! . . . and this is what love has done to us! . . .

DARRELL

(*Bitterly*). My work was finished twelve years ago. As I believe you know, I ended it with an experiment which resulted so successfully that any further meddling with human lives would have been superfluous!

NINA

(*Pityingly*). Ned!

DARRELL

(*Indifferent and cynical*). But you meant my present dabbling about. You know better than to call that work. It's merely my hobby. Our backing Sam has made Marsden and me so wealthy that we're forced to take up hobbies. Marsden goes in for his old one of dashing off genteel novels, while I play at biology. Sam argued that golf would be healthier and less nonsensical for me, but you insisted on biology. And give it its due, it has kept me out in the open air and been conducive to travelling and broadening my mind! (*Then forcing a smile.*) But I'm exaggerating. I really am interested, or I'd never keep financing the Station. And when I'm down there I do work hard, helping Preston. He's doing remarkable work already, and he's still in his twenties. He'll be a big man—(*his bitterness cropping up again*) at least if he takes my advice and never carries his experiments as far as human lives!

NINA

(*In a low voice*). How can you be so bitter, Ned—on Gordon's birthday?

DARRELL

(*Thinking cynically*). She expects me to love the child she deliberately took from me and gave to another man! . . . no, thank you, Nina! . . . I've been hurt enough! . . . I'll not leave myself open there! . . .
(*Regarding his son bitterly*). Every day he gets more like Sam, doesn't he?

GORDON

(*Thinking*). He's talking about me . . . he better look out! . . .

NINA

(*Resentfully*). I don't think Gordon resembles Sam at all. He reminds me a great deal of his namesake.

DARRELL

(*Touched on a sore spot—with a nasty laugh—cuttingly*). Gordon Shaw? Not the slightest bit in the world! And you ought to thank God he doesn't! It's the last thing I'd want wished on a boy of mine—to be like that rah-rah hero!

GORDON

(*Thinking contemptuously*). Boy of his! . . . He hasn't got a boy! . . .

NINA

(*Amused and pleased by his jealousy*). Poor Ned! . . . isn't he silly? . . . at his age, after all we've been through, to still feel jealous . . .

DARRELL

I'd much rather have him (*pointing to* GORDON) grow up to be an exact duplicate of the esteemed Samuel!

GORDON

(*Thinking resentfully*). He's always making fun of my father! . . . he better look out! . . .

DARRELL

(*More and more mockingly*). And what could be fairer? The good Samuel is an A One success. He has a charming wife and a darling boy, and a Park Avenue apartment and a membership in an expensive golf club. And, above all, he rests so complacently on the proud assurance that he is self-made!

NINA

(*Sharply*). Ned! You ought to be ashamed! You know how grateful Sam has always been to you!

DARRELL

(*Bitingly*). Would he be grateful if he knew how much I'd really done for him?

NINA

(*Sternly*). Ned!

GORDON

(*Suddenly jumps up and confronts* DARRELL, *his fists clenched, trembling with rage, stammers*). You—shut up—making fun of my father!

NINA

(*In dismay*). Gordon!

DARRELL

(*Mockingly*). My dear boy, I wouldn't make fun of your father for the world!

GORDON

(*Baffledly—his lips trembling*). You—you did, too! (*Then intensely.*) I hate you!

NINA

(*Shocked and indignant*). Gordon! How dare you talk like that to your Uncle Ned!

GORDON

(*Rebelliously*). He's not my uncle! He's not my anything!

NINA

Not another word or you'll be punished, whether it's your birthday or not! If you can't behave better than that, I'll have to phone to all your friends they mustn't come here this afternoon, that you've been so bad you can't have a party!
(*Thinking remorsefully*). Is this my fault? . . . I've done my best to get him

to love Ned! . . . but it only makes him worse! . . . it makes him turn against me! . . . turn from me to Sam! . . .

GORDON

(*Sullenly*). I don't care! I'll tell Dad!

NINA

(*Peremptorily*). Leave the room! And don't come near me again, do you hear, until you've apologized to Uncle Ned!
(*Thinking angrily*). Dad! . . . It's always Dad with him now! . . .

DARRELL

(*Boredly*). Oh, never mind, Nina!

GORDON

(*Going out—mutters*). I won't 'pologize —never!
(*Thinking vindictively*). I hate her too when she sides with him! . . . I don't care if she is my mother! . . . she has no right! . . . (*He goes out, rear.*)

DARRELL

(*Irritably*). What if he does hate me? I don't blame him! He suspects what I know —that I've acted like a coward and a weakling toward him! I should have claimed him no matter what happened to other people! Whose fault is it if he hates me, and I dislike him because he loves another father? Ours! You gave him to Sam and I consented! All right! Then don't blame him for acting like Sam's son!

NINA

But he shouldn't say he hates you.
(*Thinking bitterly*). Sam's! . . . he's becoming all Sam's! . . . I'm getting to mean nothing! . . .

DARRELL

(*Sardonically*). Perhaps he realizes subconsciously that I am his father, his rival in your love; but I'm not his father ostensibly, there are no taboos, so he can come right out and hate me to his heart's content! (*Bitterly.*) If he realized how little you love me any more, he wouldn't bother!

NINA

(*Exasperatedly*). Oh, Ned, do shut up! I can't stand hearing those same old reproaches I've heard a thousand times before! I can't bear to hear myself making the same old bitter counter-accusations. And then there'll be the same old terrible scene of hate and you'll run away—it used to be to drink and women, now it's to the Station. Or I'll send you away, and then after a time I'll call you back, because I'll have gotten so lonely again living this lonely lie of my life, with no one to speak to except Sam's business friends and their deadly wives. (*She laughs helplessly.*) Or else you'll get lonely in your lie a little before I do and come back again of your own desire! And then we'll kiss and cry and love each other again!

DARRELL

(*With an ironical grimace*). Or I might cheat myself into believing I'd fallen in love with some nice girl and get myself engaged to be married again as I did once before! And then you'd be jealous again and have to find some way of getting me to break it off!

NINA

(*Forlornly amused*). Yes—I suppose the thought of a wife taking you away from me would be too much—again! (*Then helplessly.*) Oh, Ned, when are we ever going to learn something about each other? We act like such brainless fools—with our love. It's always so wonderful when you first come back, but you always stay too long—or I always keep you too long! You never leave before we've come to the ugly bitter stage when we blame each other! (*Then suddenly forlornly tender.*) Is it possible you can still love me, Ned?

DARRELL

(*Mournfully smiling*). I must, or I'd never act this fool way, would I?

NINA

(*Smiling back*). And I must love you. (*Then seriously.*) After all, I can never forget that Gordon is the child of your love, Ned.

DARRELL

(*Sadly*). You'd better forget that, for his sake and your own. Children have sure intuitions. He feels cheated of your love— by me. So he's concentrating his affections on Sam whose love he knows is secure, and withdrawing from you.

NINA

(*Frightened—angrily*). Don't be stupid, Ned! That isn't so at all! I hate you when you talk that way!

DARRELL

(*Cynically*). Hate me, exactly. As he does! That's what I'm advising you to do if you want to keep his love! (*He smiles grimly.*)

NINA

(*Sharply*). If Gordon doesn't love you it's because you've never made the slightest attempt to be lovable to him! There's no earthly reason why he should like you, when you come right down to it, Ned! Take today, for instance. It's his birthday but you'd forgotten, or didn't care! You never even brought him a present.

DARRELL

(*With bitter sadness*). I did bring him a present. It's out in the hall. I bought him a costly delicate one so he could get full satisfaction and yet not strain himself when he smashed it, as he's smashed every present of mine in the past! And I left it out in the hall, to be given to him after I've gone because, after all, he is my son and I'd prefer he didn't smash it before my eyes! (*Trying to mock his own emotion back—with savage bitterness.*) I'm selfish, you see! I don't want my son to be too happy at my expense, even on his birthday!

NINA

(*Tormented by love and pity and remorse*). Ned! For God's sake! How can you torture us like that! Oh, it's too dreadful—what I have done to you! Forgive me, Ned!

DARRELL

(*His expression changing to one of pity for her—goes to her and puts his hand on her head—tenderly*). I'm sorry. (*With remorseful tenderness.*) Dreadful, what you've done, Nina? Why, you've given me the only happiness I've ever known! And no matter what I may say or do in bitterness, I'm proud—and grateful, Nina!

NINA

(*Looks up at him with deep tenderness and admiration*). Dearest, it's wonderful of you to say that! (*She gets up and puts her hands on his shoulders and looks into his eyes—tenderly in a sort of pleading.*) Can't we be brave enough—for you to go away —now, on this note—sure of our love —with no ugly bitterness for once?

DARRELL

(*Joyfully*). Yes! I'll go—this minute if you wish!

NINA

(*Playfully*). Oh, you needn't go this minute! Wait and say good-bye to Sam. He'd be terribly hurt if you didn't. (*Then seriously.*) And will you promise to stay away two years—even if I call you back before then—and work this time, really work?

DARRELL

I'll try, Nina!

NINA

And then—surely come back to me!

DARRELL

(*Smiling*). Surely—again!

NINA

Then good-bye, dear! (*She kisses him.*)

DARRELL

Again! (*He smiles and she smiles and they kiss again.* GORDON *appears in the doorway at rear and stands for a moment in a passion of jealousy and rage and grief, watching them.*)

GORDON

(*Thinking with a strange tortured shame*). I mustn't see her! . . . pretend I didn't see her! . . . mustn't never let her know I saw her! . . . (*He vanishes as silently as he had come.*)

NINA

(*Suddenly moving away from* DARRELL, *looking around her uneasily*). Ned, did you see—? I had the queerest feeling just then that someone—

GORDON

(*His voice sounds from the hall with a strained casualness*). Mother! Uncle Charlie's downstairs. Shall he come right up?

NINA

(*Startled, her own voice straining to be casual*). Yes, dear—of course! (*Then worriedly.*) His voice sounded funny. Did it to you? Do you suppose he—?

DARRELL

(*With a wry smile*). It's possible. To be on the safe side, you'd better tell him you kissed me good-bye to get rid of me! (*Then angrily.*) So Marsden's here again! The damned old woman! I simply can't go him any more, Nina! Why Gordon should take such a fancy to that old sissy is beyond me!

NINA

(*Suddenly struck—thinking*). Why, he's jealous of Gordon liking Charlie! . . . (*Immediately all affectionate pity.*) Then he must love Gordon a little! . . . (*Letting her pity escape her*). Poor Ned! (*She makes a movement toward him.*)

DARRELL

(*Startled and afraid she may have guessed something he doesn't acknowledge to himself*). What? Why do you say that? (*Then rudely defensive.*) Don't be silly! (*Resentfully.*) You know well enough what I've always held against him! I wanted to put up all the money to back Sam when he started. I wanted to do it for Sam's sake— but especially for my child's sake. Why did Marsden absolutely insist on Sam letting him in equally? It isn't that I begrudge him the money he's made, but I know there was something queer in his mind and that he did it intentionally to spite me! (*From the hallway comes the sound of* MARSDEN's *voice and* GORDON's *greeting him vociferously as he lets him into the apartment. As* DARRELL *listens his expression becomes furious again. He bursts out angrily.*) You're letting that old ass spoil Gordon, you fool, you!

(MARSDEN *comes in from the rear, smiling, immaculately dressed as usual. He looks hardly any older except that his hair is grayer and his tall figure more stooped. His expression and the general atmosphere he gives out are more nearly like those of Act One. If not happy, he is at least living in comparative peace with himself and his environment.*)

MARSDEN

(*Comes straight to* NINA). Hello, Nina Cara Nina! Congratulations on your son's birthday! (*He kisses her.*) He's grown so much bigger and stronger in the two months since I've seen him. (*He turns and shakes hands with* DARRELL *coldly—with a trace of a patronizing air.*) Hello, Darrell. Last time I was here you were leaving for the West Indies in a week but I see you're still around.

DARRELL

(*Furious—with a mocking air*). And here you are around again, yourself! You're looking comfortable these days, Marsden. I hope your sister is well. It must be a great comfort, having her to take your mother's place! (*Then with a harsh laugh.*) Yes, we're two bad pennies, eh, Marsden?— counterfeits—fakes—Sam's silent partners!

NINA

(*Thinking irritably*). Ned's getting hateful again! . . . Poor Charlie! . . . I won't have him insulted! . . . he's become such a comfort . . . he understands so much . . . without my having to tell him . . .
(*Looking rebukingly at* DARRELL) Ned is sailing this week, Charlie.

MARSDEN

(*Thinking triumphantly*). He's trying to insult me . . . I know all he means . . . but what do I care what he says . . . she's sending him away! . . . intentionally before me! . . . it means he's finished! . . .

DARRELL

(*Thinking resentfully*). Is she trying to humiliate me before him? . . . I'll teach her! . . . (*Then struggling with himself—remorsefully.*) No . . . not this time . . . I promised . . . no quarrel . . . remember . . .
(*Acquiescing—with a pleasant nod to* MARSDEN). Yes, I'm going this week and I except to be gone at least two years this time—two years of hard work.

MARSDEN

(*Thinking with scornful pity*). His work! . . . what a pretense! . . a scientific dilettante! . . . could anything be more pitiable? . . . poor chap! . . .
(*Perfunctorily*). Biology must be an interesting study. I wish I knew more about it.

DARRELL

(*Stung yet amused by the other's tone— ironically*). Yes, so do I wish you did, Marsden! Then you might write more about life and less about dear old ladies and devilish bachelors! Why don't you write a novel about life sometime, Marsden? (*He turns his back on* MARSDEN *with a glance of repulsion and walks to the window and stares out.*)

MARSDEN

(*Confusedly*). Yes—decidedly—but hardly in my line—
(*Thinking in anguish—picking up a magazine and turning over the pages aimlessly*). That . . . is . . . true! . . . he's full of poison! . . . I've never married the word to life! . . . I've been a timid bachelor of Arts, not an artist! . . . my poor pleasant books! . . . all is well! . . . is this well, the three of us? . . . Darrell has become less and less her lover . . . Nina has turned more and more to me . . . we have built up a secret life of subtle sympathies and confidences . . . she has known I have understood about her mere physical passion for Darrell . . . what woman could be expected to love Sam passionately? . . . some day she'll confide all about Darrell to me . . . now that he's finished . . . she knows that I love her without my telling . . . she even knows the sort of love it is. . . . (*Passionately—thinking.*) My love is finer than any she has known! . . . I do not lust for her! . . . I would be content if our marriage should be purely the placing of our ashes in the same tomb . . . our urns side by side and touching one another . . . could the others say as much, could they love so deeply? . . . (*Then suddenly miserably self-contemptuous.*) What! . . . platonic heroics at my age! . . . do I believe a word of that? . . . look at her beautiful eyes! . . . wouldn't I give anything in life to see them desire me? . . . and the intimacy I'm boasting about, what more

does it mean than that I've been playing the dear old Charlie of her girl-
hood again? . . . (*Thinking in anguish.*) Damned coward and weakling! . . .

NINA

(*Looking at him—pityingly—thinking*). What does he always want of
me? . . . me? . . . I am the only one
who senses his deep hurt . . . I feel
how life has wounded him . . . is that
partly my fault, too? . . . I have
wounded everyone . . . poor Charlie,
what can I do for you? . . . if giving
myself to you would bring you a moment's happiness, could I? . . . the idea
used to be revolting . . . now, nothing
about love seems important enough to
be revolting . . . poor Charlie, he only
thinks he ought to desire me! . . . dear
Charlie, what a perfect lover he would
make for one's old age! . . . what a
perfect lover when one was past passion! . . . (*Then with sudden scornful
revulsion.*) These men make me sick!
. . . I hate all three of them! . . . they
disgust me! . . . the wife and mistress
in me has been killed by them! . . .
thank God, I am only a mother now!
. . . Gordon is my little man, my only
man! . . .
(*Suddenly*). I've got a job for you, Charlie
—make the salad dressing for lunch. You
know, the one I'm so crazy about.

MARSDEN

(*Springs to his feet*). Righto! (*He puts his
arm about her waist and they go out together laughingly, without a glance at* DAR-
RELL.)

DARRELL

(*Thinking dully*). I mustn't stay to
lunch . . . ghost at my son's feast! . . .
I better go now . . . why wait for Sam?
. . . what is there to say to him I can
say? . . . and there's nothing about him
I want to see . . . he's as healthy as a
pig . . . and as sane . . . I was afraid
once his mother had lied to Nina . . . I
went upstate and investigated . . . true,
every word of it . . . his great-grandfather, his grandmother, his father,
were all insane . . . (*Moving uneas-

ily.*) Stop it! . . . time to go when
those thoughts come . . . sail on Saturday . . . not come here again . . . Nina
will soon be fighting Sam for my son's
love! . . . I'm better out of that! . . . O
Christ, what a mess it all is! . . .

GORDON

(*Appears in the doorway in rear. He
carries a small, expensive yacht's model
of a sloop with the sails set. He is in a
terrific state of conflicting emotions,
on the verge of tears yet stubbornly determined*). I got to do it! . . . Gosh, it's
awful . . . this boat is so pretty . . . why
did it have to come from him? . . . I
can get Dad to buy me another boat
. . . but now I love this one . . . but he
kissed Mother . . . she kissed him . . .
(*He walks up defiantly and confronts* DAR-
RELL *who turns to him in surprise*). Hey—
Darrell—did you—? (*He stops chokingly.*)

DARRELL

(*Immediately realizing what is coming—thinking with somber anguish*).
So this has to happen! . . . what I
dreaded! . . . my fate is merciless, it
seems! . . .
(*With strained kindliness*). Did what?

GORDON

(*Growing hard—stammers angrily*). I
found this—out in the hall. It can't be
from anybody else. Is this—your present?

DARRELL

(*Hard and defiant himself*). Yes.

GORDON

(*In a rage—tremblingly*). Then—here's
what—I think of you! (*Beginning to cry,
he breaks off the mast, bowsprit, breaks
the mast in two, tears the rigging off and
throws the dismantled hull at* DARRELL's
feet.) There! You can keep it!

DARRELL

(*His anger overcoming him for an instant*). You—you mean little devil, you!
You don't get that from me—(*He has tak-
en a threatening step forward.* GORDON
stands white-faced, defying him. DARRELL
*pulls himself up short—then in a trem-

bling voice of deeply wounded affection.)
You shouldn't have done that, son. What
difference do I make? It was never my
boat. But it was your boat. You should
consider the boat, not me. Don't you like
boats for themselves? It was a beautiful little boat, I thought. That's why I—

GORDON

(*Sobbing miserably*). It was awful pretty!
I didn't want to do it! (*He kneels down
and gathers up the boat into his arms
again.*) Honest I didn't. I love boats! But I
hate you! (*This last with passionate intensity.*)

DARRELL

(*Dryly*). So I've observed.
(*Thinking with angry anguish*). He
hurts, damn him! . . . .

GORDON

No, you don't know! More'n ever now!
More'n ever! (*The secret escaping him.*)
I saw you kissing Mother! I saw Mother,
too!

DARRELL

(*Startled, but immediately forcing a
smile*). But I was saying good-bye. We're
old friends. You know that.

GORDON

You can't fool me! This was different!
(*Explosively.*) It would serve you good
and right—and Mother, too—if I was to
tell Dad on you!

DARRELL

Why, I'm Sam's oldest friend. Don't make
a little fool of yourself!

GORDON

You are not his friend. You've always been
hanging around cheating him—hanging
around Mother!

DARRELL

Keep still! What do you mean cheating
him?

GORDON

I don't know. But I know you aren't his
friend. And sometime I'm going to tell him
I saw you—

DARRELL

(*With great seriousness now—deeply
moved*). Listen! There are things a man of
honor doesn't tell anyone—not even his
mother or father. You want to be a man of
honor, don't you? (*Intensely.*) There are
things we don't tell, you and I!
(*He has put his hand around* GORDON's
shoulder impulsively.) This is my son!
. . . I love him! . . .

GORDON

(*Thinking—terribly torn*). Why do I
like him now? . . . I like him awful! . . .
(*Crying*). We?—who d'you mean?—I've
got honor!—more'n you!—you don't have
to tell me!—I wasn't going to tell Dad
anyway, honest I wasn't! We?—what
d'you mean, we?—I'm not like you! I
don't want to be ever like you! (*There is
the sound of a door being flung open and
shut and* EVANS' *hearty voice.*)

EVANS

(*From the entrance hall*). Hello, everybody!

DARRELL

(*Slapping* GORDON *on the back*). Buck up,
son! Here he is! Hide that boat or he'll ask
questions.
(GORDON *runs and hides the boat under the
sofa. When* EVANS *enters,* GORDON *is entirely
composed and runs to him joyfully.* EVANS
*has grown stouter, his face is heavy now, he
has grown executive and used to command,
he automatically takes charge wherever he
is. He does not look his age except that his
hair has grown scanty and there is a perceptible bald spot on top. He is expensively
tailored.*)

EVANS

(*Hugging* GORDON *to him—lovingly*).
How's the old son? How's the birthday
coming along?

GORDON

Fine, Dad!

EVANS

Hello, Ned! Isn't this kid of mine a whop-
per for his age, though!

DARRELL

(*Smiling strainedly*). Yes.

> (*Writing—thinking*). It hurts now!
> . . . to see my son his son! . . . I've had
> enough! . . . get out! . . . any excuse!
> . . . I can phone afterwards! . . . I'll yell
> out the whole business if I stay! . . .

I was just going, Sam. I've got to step
around and see a fellow who lives near—
biologist. (*He has gone to the door.*)

EVANS

(*Disappointedly*). Then you won't be here
for lunch?

DARRELL

> (*Thinking*). I'll yell the truth into
> your ears if I stay a second longer . . .
> you damned lunatic! . . .

Can't stay. Sorry. This is important. I'm
sailing in a few days—lots to do—see you
later, Sam. So long—Gordon.

GORDON

(*As he goes out with awkward haste*).
Good-bye—Uncle Ned.

> (*Thinking confusedly*). Why did I
> call him that when I said I never
> would! . . . I know . . . must be be-
> cause he said he's sailing and I'm
> glad . . .

EVANS

So long, Ned.

> (*Thinking—good-naturedly super-
> ior.*) Ned and his biology! . . . He
> takes his hobby pretty seriously! . . .
> (*With satisfaction.*) Well, he can af-
> ford to have hobbies now! . . . his in-
> vestment with me has made him a
> pile. . . .

Where's Mother, son?

GORDON

Out in the kitchen with Uncle Charlie.

> (*Thinking*). I hope he never comes
> back! . . . why did I like him then?
> . . . it was only for a second . . . I didn't
> really . . . I never could! . . . why does
> he always call me Gordon as if he
> hated to? . . .

EVANS

(*Sitting down at left*). I hope lunch is
ready soon. I'm hungry as the devil, aren't
you?

GORDON

(*Absent-mindedly*). Yes, Dad.

EVANS

Come over here and tell me about your
birthday. (GORDON *comes over.* EVANS *pulls
him up on his lap.*) How'd you like your
presents? What'd you get from Uncle
Ned?

GORDON

(*Evasively*). They were all dandy. (*Suddenly.*) Why was I named Gordon?

EVANS

Oh, you know all about that—all about
Gordon Shaw. I've told you time and again.

GORDON

You told me once he was Mother's beau—
when she was a girl.

EVANS

(*Teasingly*). What do you know about
beaus? You're growing up!

GORDON

Did Mother love him a lot?

EVANS

(*Embarrassedly*). I guess so.

GORDON

> (*Thinking keenly*). That's why Dar-
> rell hates me being called Gordon . . .
> he knows Mother loved Gordon bet-
> ter'n she does him . . . now I know
> how to get back at him . . . I'll be just
> like Gordon was and Mother'll love
> me better'n him! . . .

And then that Gordon was killed, wasn't
he? Am I anything like him?

EVANS

I hope you are. If when you go to college
you can play football or row like Gordon
did, I'll—I'll give you anything you ask
for! I mean that!

GORDON

(*Dreamily*). Tell me about him again, will
you, Dad—about the time he was stroking
the crew and the fellow who was Number
Seven began to crack, and he couldn't see
him but he felt him cracking somehow,
and he began talking back to him all the

time and sort of gave him his strength so that when the race was over and they'd won Gordon fainted and the other fellow didn't.

EVANS

(*With a fond laugh*). Why, you know it all by heart! What's the use of my telling you?

NINA

(*Comes in from the rear while they are talking. She comes forward slowly. Thinking resentfully*). Does he love Sam more than he does me? . . . oh, no, he can't! . . . but he trusts him more! . . . he confides in him more! . . .

GORDON

Did you ever used to fight fellows, Dad?

EVANS

(*Embarrassedly*). Oh, a little—when I had to.

GORDON

Could you lick Darrell?

NINA

(*Thinking frightenedly*). Why does he ask that? . . .

EVANS

(*Surprised*). Your Uncle Ned? What for? We've always been friends.

GORDON

I mean, if you weren't friends, could you?

EVANS

(*Boastfully*). Oh, yes, I guess so. Ned was never as strong as I was.

NINA

(*Thinking contemptuously*). Ned is weak. . . . (*Then apprehensively.*) But you're getting too strong, Sam. . . .

GORDON

But Gordon could have licked you, couldn't he?

EVANS

You bet he could!

GORDON

(*Thinking*). She must have loved Gordon better'n Dad even! . . .

NINA

(*She comes forward to the chair at center, forcing a smile*). What's all this talk about fighting? That's not nice. For heaven's sake, Sam, don't encourage him—

EVANS

(*Grinning*). Never mind the women, Gordon. You've got to know how to fight to get on in this world.

NINA

(*Thinking pityingly*). You poor booby! . . . how brave you are now! . . . (*Softly*). Perhaps you're right, dear. (*Looking around.*) Has Ned gone?

GORDON

(*Defiantly*). Yes—and he's not coming back—and he's sailing soon!

NINA

(*With a shudder*). Why does he challenge me that way? . . . and cling to Sam? . . . he must have seen Ned and me . . . he doesn't offer to come to my lap . . . he used to . . . Ned was right . . . I've got to lie to him . . . get him back . . . here . . . on my lap! . . . (*With a sneer—to* EVANS). I'm glad Ned's gone. I was afraid he was going to be on our hands all day.

GORDON

(*Eagerly, half-getting down from his father's lap*). You're glad—? (*Then cautiously thinking*). She's cheating . . . I saw her kiss him. . . .

NINA

Ned's getting to be an awful bore. He's so weak. He can't get started on anything unless he's pushed.

GORDON

(*Moving a little nearer—searching her face—thinking*). She doesn't seem to like him so much . . . but I saw her kiss him! . . .

EVANS

(*Surprised*). Oh, come now, Nina, aren't you being a little hard on Ned? It's true he's sort of lost his grip in a way but he's our best friend.

GORDON

(*Moving away from his father again — resentfully — thinking*).   What's Dad standing up for him to her for?

NINA

(*Thinking triumphantly*).   That's right, Sam . . . just what I wanted you to say! . . .
(*Boredly*). Oh, I know he is but he gets on my nerves hanging around all the time. Without being too rude, I urged him to get back to his work, and made him promise me he wouldn't return for two years. Finally he promised—and then he became silly and sentimental and asked me to kiss him good-bye for good luck! So I kissed him to get rid of him! The silly fool!

GORDON

(*Thinking—overjoyed*). Then! . . . that's why! . . . that's why! . . . and he'll be gone two years! . . . oh, I'm so glad! . . .
(*He goes to her and looks up into her face with shining eyes*). Mother!

NINA

Dear! (*She takes him up on her lap and hugs him in her arms.*)

GORDON

(*Kisses her*). There!
(*Triumphantly thinking*).   That makes up for his kiss! . . . That takes it off her mouth. . . .

EVANS

(*Grinning*). Ned must be falling for you— in his old age! (*Then sentimentally.*) Poor guy! He's never married, that's the trouble. He's lonely. I know how he feels. A fellow needs a little feminine encouragement to help him keep his head up.

NINA

(*Snuggling* GORDON's *head against hers— laughing teasingly*). I think your hardheaded Dad is getting mushy and silly! What do you think, Gordon?

GORDON

(*Laughing with her*). Yes, he's mushy, Mother! He's silly! (*He kisses her and whispers.*) I'm going to be like Gordon

Shaw, Mother! (*She hugs him fiercely to her, triumphantly happy.*)

EVANS

(*Grinning*). You two are getting too hardboiled for me. (*He laughs. They all laugh happily together.*)

NINA

(*Suddenly overcome by a wave of conscience-stricken remorse and pity*). Oh, I am hard on Ned! . . . poor dear generous Ned! . . . you told me to lie to your son against you . . . for my sake . . . I'm not worthy of your love! . . . I'm low and selfish! . . . but I do love you! . . . this is the son of our love in my arms! . . . oh, Mother God, grant my prayer that some day we may tell our son the truth and he may love his father! . . .

GORDON

(*Sensing her thoughts, sits in her lap and stares into her face, while she guiltily avoids his eyes—in fear and resentment. Thinking*). She's thinking about that Darrell now! . . . I know! . . . she likes him too! . . . she can't fool me! . . . I saw her kissing! . . . she didn't think he was a silly fool then! . . . she was lying to Dad and me! . . . (*He pushes off her lap and backs away from her.*)

NINA

(*Thinking frightenedly*). He read my thoughts! . . . I mustn't even think of Ned when he's around! . . . poor Ned! . . . no, don't think of him! . . .
(*Leaning forward toward* GORDON *with her arms stretched out entreatingly but adopting a playful tone*). Why, Gordon, what's come over you? You jumped off my lap as though you'd sat on a tack! (*She forces a laugh.*)

GORDON

(*His eyes on the floor—evasively*). I'm hungry. I want to see if lunch is nearly ready. (*He turns abruptly and runs out.*)

EVANS

(*In a tone of superior manly understanding, kindly but laying down the law to womanly weakness*). He's sick of being babied, Nina. You forget he's getting to be a big boy. And we want him to grow up a real he-man and not an old lady like Charlie. (*Sagaciously.*) That's what's made Charlie like he is, I'll bet. His mother never stopped babying him.

NINA

(*Submissively—but with a look of bitter scorn at him*). Perhaps you're right, Sam.

EVANS

(*Confidently*). I know I am!

NINA

(*Thinking with a look of intense hatred*). Oh, Mother God, grant that I may some day tell this fool the truth!

Curtain.

ACT EIGHT

SCENE: *Late afternoon in late June, ten years later—the afterdeck of the* EVANS' *motor cruiser anchored in the lane of yachts near the finish line at Poughkeepsie. The bow and amidship of the cruiser are off right, pointed upstream. The portside rail is in the rear, the curve of the stern at left, the rear of the cabin with broad windows and a door is at right. Two wicker chairs are at left and a chaise longue at right. A wicker table with another chair is at center. The afterdeck is in cool shade, contrasted with the soft golden haze of late afternoon sunlight that glows on the river.*

NINA *is sitting by the table at center,* DARRELL *in the chair farthest left,* MARSDEN *in the chaise longue at right.* EVANS *is leaning over the rail directly back of* NINA, *looking up the river through a pair of binoculars.* MADELINE ARNOLD *is standing by his side.*

NINA'S *hair has turned completely white. She is desperately trying to conceal the obvious inroads of time by an over-emphasis on make-up that defeats its end by drawing attention to what it would conceal. Her face is thin, her cheeks taut, her mouth drawn with forced smiling. There is little left of her face's charm except her eyes which now seem larger and more deeply mysterious than ever. But she has kept her beautiful figure. It has the tragic effect of making her face seem older and more worn-out by contrast. Her general manner recalls instantly the* NINA *of Act Four, neurotic, passionately embittered and torn. She is dressed in a white yachting costume.*

DARRELL *seems to have "thrown back" to the young doctor we had seen at the house of* NINA'S *father in Act Two. He has again the air of the cool, detached scientist regarding himself and the people around him as interesting phenomena. In appearance, he is once more sharply defined, his face and body have grown lean and well-conditioned, the puffiness and jowls of the previous Act are gone. His skin is tanned almost black by his years in the tropics. His thick hair is iron-gray. He wears flannel pants, a blue coat, white buckskin shoes. He looks his fifty-one years, perhaps, but not a day more.* MARSDEN *has aged greatly. The stoop of his tall figure is accentuated, his hair has grown whitish. He is an older image of the* MARSDEN *of Act Five, who was so prostrated by his mother's death. Now it is his sister's death two months before that has plunged him into despair. His present grief, however, is more resigned to its fate than the old. He is dressed immaculately in black, as in Act Five.*

EVANS *is simply* EVANS, *his type logically developed by ten years of continued success and accumulating wealth, jovial and simple and good-natured as ever, but increasingly stubborn and self-opinionated. He has grown very stout. His jowly broad face has a heavy, flushed, apoplectic look. His head has grown quite bald on top. He is wearing a yachting cap, blue yachting coat, white flannel pants, buckskin shoes.*

MADELINE ARNOLD *is a pretty girl of nineteen, with dark hair and eyes. Her skin is deeply tanned, her figure tall and athletic, reminding one of* NINA'S *when we first saw her. Her personality is direct and frank. She gives the impression of a person who always knows exactly what she is after and generally gets it, but is also generous and a good loser, a good sport who is popular with her own sex as well as sought after by men. She is dressed in a bright-colored sport costume.*

EVANS

(*Nervous and excited—on pins and needles—lowering his binoculars impatiently*). Can't see anything up there! There's a damned haze on the river! (*Handing the binoculars to* MADELINE.) Here, Madeline. You've got young eyes.

MADELINE

(*Eagerly*). Thank you. (*She looks up the river through the glasses.*)

NINA

(*Thinking—bitterly*). Young eyes! . . . they look into Gordon's eyes! . . . he sees love in her young eyes! . . . mine are old now! . . .

EVANS

(*Pulling out his watch*). Soon be time for the start. (*Comes forward—exasperatedly.*) Of course, the damned radio has to pick out this time to go dead! Brand new one I had installed especially for this race, too! Just my luck! (*Coming to* NINA *and putting his hand on her shoulder.*) Gosh, I'll bet Gordon's some keyed-up right at this moment, Nina!

MADELINE

(*Without lowering the glasses*). Poor kid! I'll bet he is!

NINA

(*Thinking with intense bitterness*). That tone in her voice! . . . her love already possesses him! . . . my son! . . . (*Vindictively.*) But she won't! . . . as long as I live! . . .
(*Flatly*). Yes, he must be nervous.

EVANS

(*Taking his hand away, sharply*). I didn't mean nervous. He doesn't know what it is to have nerves. Nothing's ever got him rattled yet. (*This last with a resentful look down at her as he moves back to the rail.*)

MADELINE

(*With the calm confidence of one who knows*). Yes, you can bank on Gordon never losing his nerve.

NINA

(*Coldly*). I'm quite aware my son isn't a weakling— (*Meaningly, with a glance at* MADELINE) even though he does do weak things sometimes.

MADELINE

(*Without lowering the glasses from her eyes—thinking good-naturedly*). Ouch! . . . that was meant for me! . . . (*Then hurt.*) Why does she dislike me so? . . . I've done my best, for Gordon's sake, to be nice to her. . . .

EVANS

(*Looking back at* NINA *resentfully—thinking*). Another nasty crack at Madeline! . . . Nina's certainly become the prize bum sport! . . . I thought once her change of life was over she'd be ashamed of her crazy jealousy . . . instead of that it's got worse . . . but I'm not going to let her come between Gordon and Madeline . . . he loves her and she loves him . . . and her folks have got money and position, too . . . and I like her a lot . . . and, by God, I'm going to see to it their marriage goes through on schedule, no matter how much Nina kicks up! . . .

DARRELL

(*Keenly observant—thinking*). Nina hates this young lady . . . of course! . . . Gordon's girl . . . she'll smash their engagement if she can . . . as she did mine once . . . once! . . . thank God my slavery is over! . . . how did she know I was back in town? . . . I wasn't going to see her again . . . but her invitation was so imploring . . . my duty to Gordon, she wrote . . . what duty? . . . pretty late in the day! . . . that's better left dead, too! . . .

EVANS

(*Looking at his watch again*). They ought to be lined up at the start any minute now. (*Pounding his fist on the rail—letting his pent-up feelings explode.*) Come on, Gordon!

NINA

(*Startled—with nervous irritation*). Sam! I told you I have a splitting headache! (*Thinking intensely*). You vulgar boor! . . . Gordon's engagement to her is all your fault! . . .

EVANS

(*Resentfully*). I'm sorry. Why don't you take some aspirin? (*Thinking irritably*). Nina in the dumps! . . . Charlie in mourning! . . . what a pair of killjoys! . . . I wanted to bring Gordon and his friends on board to celebrate . . . no chance! . . . have to take Madeline . . . stage a party in New York . . . leave this outfit flat . . . Nina'll be sore as the devil but she'll have to like it . . .

DARRELL

(*Examining* NINA *critically—thinking*). She's gotten into a fine neurotic state . . . reminds me of when I first knew her . . . (*Then exultantly.*) Thank God, I can watch her objectively again . . . these last three years away have finally done it . . . complete cure! . . . (*Then remorsefully.*) Poor Nina! . . . we're all deserting her . . . (*Then glancing at* MARSDEN—*with a trace of a sneer.*) Even Marsden seems to have left her for the dead! . . .

MARSDEN

(*Vaguely irritated—thinking*). What am I doing here? . . . what do I care about this stupid race? . . . why did I let Nina bully me into coming? . . . I ought to be alone . . . with my memories of dear Jane . . . it will be two months ago Saturday she died . . . (*His lips tremble, tears come to his eyes.*)

MADELINE

(*With an impatient sigh, lowering the glasses*). It's no use, Mr. Evans, I can't see a thing.

EVANS

(*With angry disgust*). If only that damned radio was working!

NINA

(*Exasperatedly*). For heaven's sake, stop swearing so much!

EVANS

(*Hurt—indignantly*). What about it if I am excited? Seems to me you could show a little more interest without it hurting you, when it's Gordon's last race, his last appearance on a varsity! (*He turns away from her.*)

MADELINE

(*Thinking*). He's right . . . she's acting rotten . . . if I were Gordon's mother, I certainly wouldn't . . .

EVANS

(*Turning back to* NINA—*resentfully*). You used to cheer loud enough for Gordon Shaw! And our Gordon's got him beat a mile, as an oarsman, at least! (*Turning to* DARRELL.) And that isn't father stuff either, Ned! All the experts say so!

DARRELL

(*Cynically*). Oh, come on, Sam! Surely no one could ever touch Shaw in anything! (*He glances at* NINA *with a sneer.*) (*Immediately angry at himself*). What an idiot! . . . that popped out of me! . . . old habit! . . . I haven't loved her in years! . . .

NINA

(*Thinking indifferently*). Ned still feels jealous . . . that no longer pleases

me . . . I don't feel anything . . . except that I must get him to help me.
(*She turns to* DARRELL *bitterly*). Sam said
"our" Gordon. He means his. Gordon's become so like Sam, Ned, you won't recognize him!

MADELINE

(*Thinking indignantly*). She's crazy!
. . . he's nothing like his father! . . .
he's so strong and handsome! . . .

EVANS

(*Good-naturedly, with a trace of pride*).
You flatter me, Nina. I wish I thought
that. But he isn't a bit like me, luckily for
him. He's a dead ringer for Gordon Shaw
at his best.

MADELINE

(*Thinking*). Shaw . . . I've seen his
picture in the gym . . . my Gordon is
better looking . . . he once told me
Shaw was an old beau of his mother's
. . . they say she was beautiful once . . .

NINA

(*Shaking her head—scornfully*). Don't be
modest, Sam. Gordon *is* you. He may be a
fine athlete like Gordon Shaw, because
you've held that out to him as your ideal,
but there the resemblance ceases. He isn't
really like him at all, not the slightest bit!

EVANS

(*Restraining his anger with difficulty
—thinking*). I'm getting sick of this!
. . . she's carrying her jealous grouch
too far! . . .
(*Suddenly exploding, pounds his fists on
the rail*). Damn it, Nina, if you had any
feeling you couldn't—right at the moment when he's probably getting into the
shell— (*He stops, trying to control himself, panting, his face red.*)

NINA

(*Staring at him with repulsion—with cool
disdain*). I didn't say anything so dire, did
I—merely that Gordon resembles you in
character. (*With malice.*) Don't get excited. It's bad for your high blood pressure. Ask Ned if it isn't.
(*Intensely—thinking*). If he'd only
die! . . . (*Thinking—immediately.*)
Oh, I don't mean that . . . I mustn't.

DARRELL

(*Thinking keenly*). There's a death
wish . . . things have gone pretty far
. . . Sam does look as if he might have
a bad pressure . . . what hope that
would have given me at one time! . . .
no more, thank God! . . .
(*In a joking tone*). Oh, I guess Sam's all
right, Nina.

EVANS

(*Gruffly*). I never felt better. (*He jerks out
his watch again.*) Time for the start. Come
on in the cabin, Ned, and shoot a drink.
We'll see if McCabe's getting the damned
radio fixed. (*Passing by* MARSDEN *he claps
him on the shoulder exasperatedly.*) Come
on, Charlie! Snap out of it!

MARSDEN

(*Startled out of his trance—bewilderedly*).
Eh?—what is it?—are they coming?

EVANS

(*Recovering his good nature—with a grin,
taking his arm*). You're coming to shoot a
drink. You need about ten, I think, to get
you in the right spirit to see the finish!
(*To* DARRELL *who has gotten up but is still
standing by his chair.*) Come on, Ned.

NINA

(*Quickly*). No, leave Ned with me. I want
to talk to him. Take Madeline—and Charlie.

MARSDEN

(*Looking at her appealingly*). But I'm perfectly contented sitting—
      (*Then after a look in her eyes—think-
ing*). She wants to be alone with Darrell . . . all right . . . doesn't matter
now . . . their love is dead . . . but
there's still some secret between them
she's never told me . . . never mind . . .
she'll tell me sometime . . . I'm all she
will have left . . . soon. . . . (*Then
stricken with guilt.*) Poor dear Jane!
. . . how can I think of anyone but
you! . . . God, I'm contemptible! . . .
I'll get drunk with that fool! . . .
that's all I'm good for! . . .

MADELINE

(*Thinking resentfully*). She takes a fine do-this-little-girl tone toward me! . . . I'll give in to her now . . . but once I'm married! . . .

EVANS

Come on then, Madeline. We'll give you a small one. (*Impatiently.*) Charlie! Head up!

MARSDEN

(*With hectic joviality*). I hope it's strong poison!

EVANS

(*Laughing*). That's the spirit! We'll make a sport out of you yet!

MADELINE

(*Laughing, goes and takes* MARSDEN'S *arm*). I'll see you get home safe, Mr. Marsden!
(*They go into the cabin,* EVANS *following them.* NINA *and* DARRELL *turn and look at each other wonderingly, inquisitively, for a long moment.* DARRELL *remains standing and seems to be a little uneasy.*)

DARRELL

(*Thinking with melancholy interest*). And now? . . . what? . . . I can look into her eyes . . . strange eyes that will never grow old . . . without desire or jealousy or bitterness . . . was she ever my mistress? . . . can she be the mother of my child? . . . is there such a person as my son? . . . I can't think of these things as real any more . . . they must have happened in another life.

NINA

(*Thinking sadly*). My old lover . . . how well and young he looks . . . now we no longer love each other at all . . . our account with God the Father is settled . . . afternoons of happiness paid for with years of pain . . . love, passion, ecstasy . . . in what a far-off life were they alive! . . . the only living life is in the past and future . . . the present is an interlude . . . strange interlude in which we call on past and future to bear witness we are living!
(*With a sad smile*). Sit down, Ned. When I heard you were back I wrote you because

I need a friend. It has been so long since we loved each other we can now be friends again. Don't you feel that?

DARRELL

(*Gratefully*). Yes. I do. (*He sits down in one of the chairs at the left, drawing it up closer to her.*)
(*Thinking cautiously*). I want to be her friend . . . but I will never . . .

NINA

(*Thinking cautiously*). I must keep very cool and sensible or he won't help me. . . .
(*With a friendly smile*). I haven't seen you look so young and handsome since I first knew you. Tell me your secret. (*Bitterly.*) I need it! I'm old! Look at me! And I was actually looking forward to being old! I thought it would mean peace. I've been sadly disillusioned! (*Then forcing a smile.*) So tell me what fountain of youth you've found.

DARRELL

(*Proudly*). That's easy. Work! I've become as interested in biology as I once was in medicine. And not selfishly interested, that's the difference. There's no chance of my becoming a famous biologist and I know it. I'm very much a worker in the ranks. But our Station is a "huge success," as Sam would say. We've made some damned important discoveries. I say "we." I really mean Preston. You may remember I used to write you about him with enthusiasm. He's justified it. He *is* making his name world-famous. He's what I might have been—I did have the brains, Nina!— if I'd had more guts and less vanity, if I'd hewn to the line! (*Then forcing a smile.*) But I'm not lamenting. I've found myself in helping him. In that way I feel I've paid my debt—that his work is partly my work. And he acknowledges it. He possesses the rare virtue of gratitude. (*With proud affection.*) He's a fine boy, Nina! I suppose I should say man now he's in his thirties.

NINA

(*Thinking with bitter sorrow*). So, Ned . . . you remember our love . . . with bitterness! . . . as a stupid mistake! . . . the proof of a gutless vanity that ruined your career! . . . oh! . . . (*Then controlling herself—thinking cynically.*) Well, after all, how do I remember our love? . . . with no emotion at all, not even bitterness! . . . (*Then with sudden alarm.*) He's forgotten Gordon for this Preston! . . . (*Thinking desperately.*) I must make him remember Gordon is his child or I can never persuade him to help me! (*Reproachfully*). So you have found a son while I was losing mine—who is yours, too!

DARRELL

(*Struck by this—impersonally interested*). That's never occurred to me but now I think of it— (*Smiling.*) Yes, perhaps unconsciously Preston is a compensating substitute. Well, it's done both of us good and hasn't harmed anyone.

NINA

(*With bitter emphasis*). Except your real son—and me—but we don't count, I suppose!

DARRELL

(*Coolly*). Harmed Gordon? How? He's all right, isn't he? (*With a sneer.*) I should say from all I've been hearing that he was your ideal of college hero—like his never-to-be-forgotten namesake!

NINA

(*Thinking resentfully*). He's sneering at his own son! . . . (*Then trying to be calculating.*) But I mustn't get angry . . . I must make him help me. . . . (*Speaking with gentle reproach*). And am I the ideal of a happy mother, Ned?

DARRELL

(*Immediately moved by pity and ashamed of himself*). Forgive me, Nina. I haven't quite buried all my bitterness, I'm afraid. (*Gently.*) I'm sorry you're unhappy, Nina.

NINA

(*Thinking with satisfaction*). He means that . . . he still does care a little . . . if only it's enough to . . . ! (*Speaking sadly*). I've lost my son, Ned! Sam has made him all his. And it was done so gradually that, although I realized

what was happening, there was never any way I could interfere. What Sam advised seemed always the best thing for Gordon's future. And it was always what Gordon himself wanted, to escape from me to boarding school and then to college, to become Sam's athletic hero—

DARRELL

(*Impatiently*). Oh, come now, Nina, you know you've always longed for him to be like Gordon Shaw!

NINA

(*Bursting out in spite of herself—violently*). He's not like Gordon! He's forgotten me for that—! (*Trying to be more reasonable.*) What do I care whether he's an athlete or not? It's such nonsense, all this fuss! I'm not the slightest bit interested in this race today, for example! I wouldn't care if he came in last! (*Stopping herself—thinking frightenedly*). Oh, if he should ever guess I said that! . . .

DARRELL

(*Thinking keenly*). Hello! . . . she said that as if she'd like to see him come last! . . . why? . . . (*Then vindictively.*) Well, so would I! . . . it's time these Gordons took a good licking from life! . . .

MADELINE

(*Suddenly appears in the door from the cabin, her face flushed with excitement*). They're off! Mr. Evans is getting something—it's terribly faint but—Navy and Washington are leading—Gordon's third! (*She disappears back in the cabin.*)

NINA

(*Looking after her with hatred*). Her Gordon! . . . she is so sure! . . . how I've come to detest her pretty face! . . .

DARRELL

(*Thinking with a sneer*). "Gordon's third"! . . . you might think there was no one else pulling the shell! . . . what idiots women make of themselves about these Gordons! . . . she's pretty, that Madeline! . . . she's got a figure like Nina's when I first loved her . .

those afternoons . . . age is beginning to tell on Nina's face . . . but she's kept her wonderful body! . . .

(*With a trace of malice—dryly*). There's a young lady who seems to care a lot whether Gordon comes in last or not!

NINA

(*Trying to be sorrowful and appealing*). Yes. Gordon is hers now, Ned. (*But she cannot bear this thought—vindictively.*) That is, they're engaged. But, of course, that doesn't necessarily mean— Can you imagine him throwing himself away on a little fool like that? I simply can't believe he really loves her! Why, she's hardly even pretty and she's deadly stupid. I thought he was only flirting with her—or merely indulging in a passing physical affair. (*She winces.*) At his age, one has to expect— even a mother must face nature. But for Gordon to take her seriously, and propose marriage—it's too idiotic for words!

DARRELL

(*Thinking cynically*). Oh, so you'll compromise on his sleeping with her . . . if you have to . . . but she must have no real claim to dispute your ownership, eh? . . . you'd like to make her the same sort of convenient slave for him that I was for you! . . .

(*Resentfully*). I can't agree with you. I find her quite charming. It seems to me if I were in Gordon's shoes I'd do exactly what he has done.

(*In confusion—thinking bitterly*). In Gordon's shoes! . . . I always was in Gordon Shaw's shoes! . . . and why am I taking this young Gordon's part? . . . what is he to me, for God's sake?

NINA

(*Unheedingly*). If he marries her, it means he'll forget me! He'll forget me as completely as Sam forgot his mother! She'll keep him away from me! Oh, I know what wives can do! She'll use her body until she persuades him to forget me! My son, Ned! And your son, too! (*She suddenly gets up and goes to him and takes one of his hands in both of hers.*) The son of our old love, Ned!

DARRELL

(*Thinking with a strange shudder of mingled attraction and fear as she touches him*). Our love . . . old love . . . old touch of her flesh . . . we're old . . . it's silly and indecent . . . does she think she still can own me? . . .

NINA

(*In the tone a mother takes in speaking to her husband about their boy*). You'll have to give Gordon a good talking to, Ned.

DARRELL

(*Still more disturbed—thinking*). Old . . . but she's kept her wonderful body . . . how many years since? . . . she has the same strange influence over me . . . touch of her flesh . . . it's dangerous . . . bosh, I'm only humoring her as a friend . . . as her doctor . . . and why shouldn't I have a talk with Gordon? . . . a father owes something to his son . . . he ought to advise him. . . . (*Then alarmed.*) But I was never going to meddle again . . .

(*Sternly*). I swore I'd never again meddle with human lives, Nina!

NINA

(*Unheedingly*). You must keep him from ruining his life.

DARRELL

(*Doggedly—struggling with himself*). I won't touch a life that has more than one cell! (*Harshly.*) And I wouldn't help you in this, anyway! You've got to give up owning people, meddling in their lives as if you were God and had created them!

NINA

(*Strangely forlorn*). I don't know what you mean, Ned. Gordon is my son, isn't he?

DARRELL

(*With a sudden strange violence*). And mine! Mine, too! (*He stops himself.*)

(*Thinking*). Shut up, you fool! . . . is that the way to humor her? . . .

NINA

(*With strange quiet*). I think I still love you a little, Ned.

DARRELL

(*In her tone*). And I still love you a little, Nina. (*Then sternly.*) But I will not meddle in your life again! (*With a harsh laugh.*) And you've meddled enough with human love, old lady! Your time for that is over! I'll send you a couple million cells you can torture without harming yourself! (*Regaining control — shamefacedly.*) Nina! Please forgive me!

NINA

(*Starts as if out of a dream—anxiously*). What were you saying, Ned? (*She lets go of his hand and goes back to her chair.*)

DARRELL

(*Dully*). Nothing.

NINA

(*Strangely*). We were talking about Sam, weren't we? How do you think he looks?

DARRELL

(*Confusedly casual*). Fine. A bit too fat, of course. He looks as though his blood pressure might be higher than it ought to be. But that's not unusual in persons of his build and age. It's nothing to hope—I meant, to worry over! (*Then violently.*) God damn it, why did you make me say hope?

NINA

(*Calmly*). It may have been in your mind, too, mayn't it?

DARRELL

No! I've nothing against Sam. I've always been his best friend. He owes his happiness to me.

NINA

(*Strangely*). There are so many curious reasons we dare not think about for thinking things!

DARRELL

(*Rudely*). Thinking doesn't matter a damn! Life is something in one cell that doesn't need to think!

NINA

(*Strangely*). I know! God the Mother!

DARRELL

(*Excitedly*). And all the rest is gutless egotism! But to hell with it! What I started to say was, what possible reason could I have for hoping for Sam's death?

NINA

(*Strangely*). We're always desiring death for ourselves or others, aren't we—while we while away our lives with the old surface ritual of coveting our neighbor's ass?

DARRELL

(*Frightenedly*). You're talking like the old Nina now—when I first loved you. Please don't! It isn't decent—at our age!
    (*Thinking in terror*). The old Nina! . . . am I the old Ned? . . . then that means? . . . but we must not meddle in each other's lives again! . . .

NINA

(*Strangely*). I am the old Nina! And this time I will not let my Gordon go from me forever!

EVANS

(*Appears in the doorway of the cabin—excited and irritated*). Madeline's listening in now. It went dead on me. (*Raising the binoculars as he goes to the rail, he looks up the river.*) Last I got, Gordon third, Navy and Washington leading. They're the ones to fear, he said—Navy especially. (*Putting down the glasses—with a groan.*) Damned haze! My eyes are getting old. (*Then suddenly with a grin.*) You ought to see Charlie! He started throwing Scotch into him as if he were drinking against time. I had to take the bottle away from him. It's hit him an awful wallop. (*Then looking from one to the other—resentfully.*) What's the matter with you two? There's a race going on, don't you know it? And you sit like dead clams!

DARRELL

(*Placatingly*). I thought someone'd better stay out here and let you know when they get in sight.

EVANS

(*Relieved*). Oh, sure, that's right! Here, take the glasses. You always had good eyes.

(DARRELL *gets up and takes the glasses and goes to the rail and begins adjusting them.*)

DARRELL

Which crew was it you said Gordon feared the most?

EVANS

(*Has gone back to the cabin doorway*). Navy. (*Then proudly.*) Oh, he'll beat them! But it'll be damn close. I'll see if Madeline's getting— (*He goes back in the cabin.*)

DARRELL

(*Looking up the river—with vindictive bitterness—thinking*). Come on, Navy! ...

NINA

(*Thinking bitterly*). Madeline's Gordon! ... Sam's Gordon! ... the thanks I get for saving Sam at the sacrifice of my own happiness! ... I won't have it! ... what do I care what happens to Sam now? ... I hate him! ... I'll tell him Gordon isn't his child! ... and threaten to tell Gordon too, unless! ... he'll be in deadly fear of that! ... he'll soon find some excuse to break their engagement! ... he can! ... he has the strangest influence over Gordon! ... but Ned must back me up or Sam won't believe me! ... Ned must tell him too! ... but will Ned? ... he'll be afraid of the insanity! ... I must make him believe Sam's in no danger ...

(*Intensely*). Listen, Ned, I'm absolutely sure, from things she wrote me before she died, that Sam's mother must have been deliberately lying to me about the insanity that time. She was jealous because Sam loved me and she simply wanted to be revenged, I'm sure.

DARRELL

(*Without lowering glasses—dryly*). No. She told you the truth. I never mentioned it, but I went up there once and made a thorough investigation of his family.

NINA

(*With resentful disappointment*). Oh—I suppose you wanted to make sure so you could hope he'd go insane?

DARRELL

(*Simply*). I needed to be able to hope that, then. I loved you horribly at that time, Nina—horribly!

NINA

(*Putting her hands on his arm*). And you don't—any more, Ned?

(*Thinking intensely*). Oh, I must make him love me again ... enough to make him tell Sam! ...

DARRELL

(*Thinking strangely — struggling with himself*). She'd like to own me again ... I wish she wouldn't touch me ... what is this tie of old happiness between our flesh? ...

(*Harshly—weakly struggling to shake off her hands, without lowering the glasses*). I won't meddle again with human lives, I told you!

NINA

(*Unheeding, clinging to him*). And I loved you horribly! I still do love you, Ned! I used to hope he'd go insane myself because I loved you so! But look at Sam! He's sane as a pig! There's absolutely no danger now!

DARRELL

(*Thinking—alarmed*). What is she after now—what does she want me for? ...

(*Stiffly*). I'm no longer a doctor but I should say he's a healthy miss of Nature's. It's a thousand to one against it at this late day.

NINA

(*With sudden fierce intensity*). Then it's time to tell him the truth, isn't it? We've suffered all our lives for his sake! We've made him rich and happy! It's time he gave us back our son!

DARRELL

(*Thinking*). Aha ... so that's it! ... tell Sam the truth? ... at last! ... by God, I'd like to tell him, at that! ...

(*With a sneer*). Our son? You mean yours, my dear! Kindly count me out of any further meddling with—

NINA

(*Unruffledly—obsessed*). But Sam won't believe me if I'm the only one to tell him! He'll think I'm lying for spite, that it's only my crazy jealousy! He'll ask you! You've got to tell him too, Ned!

DARRELL

(*Thinking*). I'd like to see his face when I told him this famous oarsman isn't his son but mine! . . . that might pay me back a little for all he's taken from me! . . .
(*Harshly*). I've stopped meddling in Sam's life, I tell you!

NINA

(*Insistently*). Think of what Sam has made us go through, of how he's made us suffer! You've got to tell him! You still love me a little, don't you, Ned? You must when you remember the happiness we've known in each other's arms! You were the only happiness I've ever known in life!

DARRELL

(*Struggling weakly—thinking*). She lies! . . . there was her old lover, Gordon! . . . he was always first! . . . then her son, Gordon! . . . (*With desperate rancor—thinking*). Come on, Navy! . . . beat her Gordons for me! . . .

NINA

(*Intensely*). Oh, if I'd only gone away with you that time when you came back from Europe! How happy we would have been, dear! How our boy would have loved you —if it hadn't been for Sam!

DARRELL

(*Thinking—weakly*). Yes, if it hadn't been for Sam I would have been happy! . . . I would have been the world's greatest neurologist! . . . my boy would have loved me and I'd have loved him! . . .

NINA

(*With a crowning intensity to break down his last resistance*). You must tell him, Ned! For my sake! Because I love you! Because you remember our afternoons—our mad happiness! Because you love me!

DARRELL

(*Beaten—dazedly*). Yes—what must I do?—meddle again?
(*The noise of* MADELINE'S *excited voice cheering and clapping her hands, of* MARSDEN'S *voice yelling drunkenly, of* EVANS', *all shouting "Gordon! Gordon! Come on, Gordon!" comes from the cabin.* MARSDEN *appears swaying in the cabin doorway yelling "Gordon!" He is hectically tipsy.* DARRELL *gives a violent shudder as if he were coming out of a nightmare and pushes* NINA *away from him.*)

DARRELL

(*Thinking—dazedly still, but in a tone of relief*). Marsden again! . . . thank God! . . . he's saved me! . . . from her! . . . and her Gordons! . . .
(*Turning on her triumphantly*). No, Nina —sorry—but I can't help you. I told you I'd never meddle again with human lives! (*More and more confidently.*) Besides, I'm quite sure Gordon isn't my son, if the real deep core of the truth were known! I was only a body to you. Your first Gordon used to come back to life. I was never more to you than a substitute for your dead lover! Gordon is really Gordon's son! So you see I'd be telling Sam a lie if I boasted that I— And I'm a man of honor! I've proved that, at least! (*He raises his glasses and looks up the river.*)
(*Thinking exultantly*). I'm free! . . . I've beaten her at last! . . . now come on, Navy! . . . you've got to beat her Gordons for me! . . .

NINA

(*After staring at him for a moment— walking away from him—thinking with a dull fatalism*). I've lost him . . . he'll never tell Sam now . . . is what he said right? . . . is Gordon Gordon's? . . . oh, I hope so! . . . oh, dear, dead Gordon, help me to get back your son! . . . I must find some way. . . . (*She sits down again.*)

MARSDEN

(*Who has been staring at them with a foolish grin*). Hello, you two! Why do you look so guilty? You don't love each other any more! It's all nonsense! I don't feel the slightest twinge of jealousy. That's proof enough, isn't it? (*Then blandly apologetic.*) Pardon me if I sound a bit pipped—a good bit! Sam said ten and then took the bottle away when I'd had only five! But it's enough! I've forgotten sorrow! There's nothing in life worth grieving about, I assure you, Nina! And I've gotten interested in this race now. (*He sings raucously.*) "Oh we'll row, row, row, right down the river! And we'll row, row, row—" Remember that old tune—when you were a little girl, Nina? Oh, I'm forgetting Sam said to tell you Gordon was on even terms with the leaders! A gallant spurt did it! Nip and tuck now! I don't care who wins —as long as it isn't Gordon! I don't like him since he's grown up! He thinks I'm an old woman! (*Sings.*) "Row, row, row." The field against Gordon!

DARRELL

(*Hectically*). Right! (*He looks through the glasses—excitedly.*) I see a flashing in the water way up there! Must be their oars! They're coming! I'll tell Sam! (*He hurries into the cabin.*)

NINA

(*Thinking dully*). He'll tell Sam . . . no, he doesn't mean that . . . I must find some other way . . .

MARSDEN

(*Walks a bit uncertainly to* NINA's *chair*). Gordon really should get beaten today— for the good of his soul, Nina. That Madeline is pretty, isn't she? These Gordons are too infernally lucky—while we others— (*He almost starts to blubber—angrily*) we others have got to beat him today! (*He slumps clumsily down to a sitting position on the deck by her chair and takes her hand and pats it.*) There, there, Nina Cara Nina! Don't worry your pretty head! It will all come out all right! We'll only have a little while longer to wait and then you and I'll be quietly married!
(*Thinking frightenedly*). The devil! . . . what am I saying? . . . I'm drunk! . . . all right, all the better! . . . I've wanted all my life to tell her! . . .
Of course, I realize you've got a husband at present but, never mind, I can wait. I've waited a lifetime already; but for a long

while now I've had a keen psychic intuition that I wasn't born to die before—
(EVANS *and* MADELINE *and* DARRELL *come rushing out of the cabin. They all have binoculars. They run to the rail and train their glasses up the river.*)

MADELINE

(*Excitedly*). I see them! (*Grabbing his arm and pointing.*) Look, Mr. Evans—there— don't you see?

EVANS

(*Excitedly*). No—not yet— Yes! Now I see them! (*Pounding on the rail.*) Come on, Gordon boy!

MADELINE

Come on, Gordon!
(*The whistles and sirens from the yachts up the river begin to be heard. This grows momentarily louder as one after another other yachts join in the chorus as the crews approach nearer and nearer until toward the close of the scene there is a perfect pandemonium of sound.*)

NINA

(*With bitter hatred—thinking*). How I hate her! . . . (*Then suddenly with a deadly calculation—thinking.*) Why not tell her? . . . as Sam's mother told me? . . . of the insanity? . . . she thinks Gordon is Sam's son. (*With a deadly smile of triumph.*) That will be poetic justice! . . . that will solve everything! . . . she won't marry him! . . . he will turn to me for comfort! . . . but I must plan it out carefully! . . .

MARSDEN

(*Driven on—extravagantly*). Listen, Nina! After we're married I'm going to write a novel—my first real novel! All the twenty-odd books I've written have been long-winded fairy tales for grown-ups— about dear old ladies and witty, cynical bachelors and quaint characters with dialects, and married folk who always admire and respect each other, and lovers who avoid love in hushed whispers! That's what I've been, Nina—a hush-hush whisperer of lies! Now I'm going to give an honest healthy yell—turn on the sun into the shadows of lies—shout "This is life and this is sex, and here are passion and hatred and regret and joy and pain and ecstasy, and these are men and women and sons and daughters whose hearts are weak and strong, whose blood is blood and not a soothing syrup!" Oh, I can do it, Nina! I can write the truth! I've seen it in you, your father, my mother, sister, Gordon, Sam, Darrell and myself. I'll write the book of us! But here I am talking while my last chapters are in the making—right here and now— (*Hurriedly.*) You'll excuse me, won't you, Nina? I must watch—my duty as an artist! (*He scrambles to his feet and peers about him with a hectic eagerness.* NINA *pays no attention to him.*)

EVANS

(*Exasperatedly, taking down his glasses*). You can't tell a damn thing—which is which or who's ahead—I'm going to listen in again. (*He hurries into the cabin.*)

NINA

(*With a smile of cruel triumph— thinking*). I can tell her . . . confidentially . . . I can pretend I'm forced to tell her . . . as Sam's mother did with me . . . because I feel it's due to her happiness and Gordon's . . . It will explain my objection to the engagement . . . oh, it can't help succeeding . . . my Gordon will come back! . . . I'll see he never gets away again! . . .
(*She calls*). Madeline!

MARSDEN

(*Thinking*). Why is she calling Madeline? . . . I must watch all this carefully! . . .

EVANS

(*Comes rushing out in wild alarm*). Bad news! Navy has drawn ahead—half a length—looks like Navy's race, he said— (*Then violently.*) But what does he know, that damn fool announcer—some poor boob—!

MADELINE

(*Excitedly*). He doesn't know Gordon! He's always best when he's pushed to the limit!

NINA

(*She calls more sharply*). Madeline!

DARRELL

(*Turns around to stare at her—thinking*). Why is she calling Madeline? . . . she's bound she'll meddle in their lives . . . I've got to watch her . . . well, let's see. . . .
(*He touches* MADELINE *on the shoulder*). Mrs. Evans is calling you, Miss Arnold.

MADELINE

(*Impatiently*). Yes, Mrs. Evans. But they're getting closer. Why don't you come and watch?

NINA

(*Not heeding — impressively*). There's something I must tell you.

MADELINE

(*In hopeless irritation*). But— Oh, all right. (*She hurries over to her, glancing eagerly over her shoulder towards the river.*) Yes, Mrs. Evans?

DARRELL

(*Moves from the rail toward them— thinking keenly*). I must watch this . . . she's in a desperate meddling mood! . . .

NINA

(*Impressively*). First, give me your word of honor that you'll never reveal a word of what I'm going to tell you to a living soul —above all not to Gordon!

MADELINE

(*Looking at her in amazement—soothingly*). Couldn't you tell me later, Mrs. Evans —after the race?

NINA

(*Sternly—grabbing her by the wrists*). No, now! Do you promise?

MADELINE

(*With helpless annoyance*). Yes, Mrs. Evans.

NINA

(*Sternly*). For the sake of your future happiness and my son's I've got to speak! Your engagement forces me to! You've probably wondered why I objected. It's because the marriage is impossible. You can't marry Gordon! I speak as your friend! You must break your engagement with him at once!

MADELINE

(*Cannot believe her ears—suddenly panic-stricken*). But why—why?

DARRELL

(*Who has come closer—resentfully thinking*). She wants to ruin my son's life as she ruined mine! . . .

NINA

(*Relentlessly*). Why? Because—

DARRELL

(*Steps up suddenly beside them—sharply and sternly commanding*). No, Nina! (*He taps* MADELINE *on the shoulder and draws her aside.* NINA *lets go of her wrist and stares after them in a sort of stunned stupor.*) Miss Arnold, as a doctor I feel it my duty to tell you that Mrs. Evans isn't herself. Pay no attention to anything she may say to you. She's just passed through a crucial period in a woman's life and she's morbidly jealous of you and subject to queer delusions! (*He smiles kindly at her.*) So get back to the race! And God bless you! (*He grips her hand, strangely moved.*)

MADELINE

(*Gratefully*). Thank you. I understand, I think. Poor Mrs. Evans! (*She hurries back to the rail, raising her glasses.*)

NINA

(*Springing to her feet and finding her voice—with despairing accusation*). Ned!

DARRELL

(*Steps quickly to her side*). I'm sorry, Nina, but I warned you not to meddle. (*Then affectionately.*) And Gordon is—well—sort of my stepson, isn't he? I really want him to be happy. (*Then smiling good-naturedly.*) All the same, I can't help hoping he'll be beaten in this race. As an oarsman he recalls his father, Gordon Shaw, to me. (*He turns away and raises his glasses, going back to the rail.* NINA *slumps down in her chair again.*)

EVANS

Damn! They all look even from here! Can you tell which is which, Madeline?

MADELINE

No—not yet—oh, dear, this is awful! Gordon!

NINA

(*Looking about her in the air—with a dazed question*). Gordon?

MARSDEN

(*Thinking*). Damn that Darrell! . . . if he hadn't interfered Nina would have told . . . something of infinite importance, I know! . . .
(*He comes and again sits on the deck by her chair and takes her hand*). Because what, Nina—my dear little Nina Cara Nina—because what? Let me help you!

NINA

(*Staring before her as if she were in a trance—simply, like a young girl*). Yes, Charlie. Yes, Father. Because all of Sam's father's family have been insane. His mother told me that time so I wouldn't have his baby. I was going to tell Madeline that so she wouldn't marry Gordon. But it would have been a lie because Gordon isn't really Sam's child at all, he's Ned's. Ned gave him to me and I gave him to Sam so Sam could have a healthy child and be well and happy. And Sam is well and happy, don't you think? (*Childishly.*) So I haven't been such an awfully wicked girl, have I, Father?

MARSDEN

(*Horrified and completely sobered by what he has heard—stares at her with stunned eyes*). Nina! Good God! Do you know what you're saying?

MADELINE

(*Excitedly*). There! The one on this side! I saw the color on their blades just now!

EVANS

(*Anxiously*). Are you sure? Then he's a little behind the other two!

DARRELL

(*Excitedly*). The one in the middle seems to be ahead! Is that the Navy?
(*But the others pay no attention to him. All three are leaning over the rail, their glasses glued to their eyes, looking up the*

*river. The noise from the whistles is now
very loud. The cheering from the observation trains can be heard.*)

MARSDEN

(*Stares into her face with great pity now*).
Merciful God, Nina! Then you've lived all
these years—with this horror! And you
and Darrell deliberately—?

NINA

(*Without looking at him—to the air*).
Sam's mother said I had a right to be happy too.

MARSDEN

And you didn't love Darrell then—?

NINA

(*As before*). I did afterwards. I don't now.
Ned is dead, too. (*Softly.*) Only you are
alive now, Father—and Gordon.

MARSDEN

(*Gets up and bends over her paternally,
stroking her hair with a strange, wild, joyous pity*). Oh, Nina—poor little Nina—
my Nina—how you must have suffered! I
forgive you! I forgive you everything! I
forgive even your trying to tell Madeline—
you wanted to keep Gordon—oh, I understand that—and I forgive you!

NINA

(*As before—affectionately and strangely*).
And I forgive you, Father. It was all your
fault in the beginning, wasn't it? You
mustn't ever meddle with human lives
again!

EVANS

(*Wildly excited*). Gordon's sprinting, isn't
he? He's drawing up on that middle one!

MADELINE

Yes! Oh, come on, Gordon!

DARRELL

(*Exultantly*). Come on, Navy!

EVANS

(*Who is standing next to* NED, *whirls on
him in a furious passion*). What's that?
What the hell's the matter with you?

DARRELL

(*Facing him—with a strange friendliness
slaps him on the back*). We've got to beat
these Gordons, Sam! We've got to beat—

EVANS

(*Raging*). You—! (*He draws back his
fist—then suddenly horrified at what he is
doing but still angry, grabs* DARRELL *by both
shoulders and shakes him.*) Wake up!
What the hell's got into you? Have you
gone crazy?

DARRELL

(*Mockingly*). Probably! It runs in my family! All of my father's people were happy
lunatics—not healthy, country folk like
yours, Sam! Ha!

EVANS

(*Staring at him*). Ned, old man, what's the
trouble? You said "Navy."

DARRELL

(*Ironically—with a bitter hopeless laugh*).
Slip of the tongue! I meant Gordon! Meant
Gordon, of course! Gordon is always meant
—meant to win! Come on, Gordon! It's
fate!

MADELINE

Here they come! They're both spurting! I
can see Gordon's back!

EVANS

(*Forgetting everything else, turns back to
the race*). Come on, boy! Come on, son!
(*The chorus of noise is now a bedlam as
the crews near the finish line. The people
have to yell and scream to make themselves
heard.*)

NINA

(*Getting up—thinking with a strange,
strident, wild passion*). I hear the
Father laughing! . . . O Mother God,
protect my son! . . . let Gordon fly to
you in heaven! . . . quick, Gordon!
. . . love is the Father's lightning! . . .
Madeline will bring you down in
flames! . . . I hear His screaming
laughter! . . . fly back to me! . . . (*She
is looking desperately up into the sky
as if some race of life and death were
happening there for her.*)

EVANS

(*Holding on to a stanchion and leaning far out at the imminent risk of falling in*). One spurt more will do it! Come on, boy, come on! It took death to beat Gordon Shaw! You can't be beaten either, Gordon! Lift her out of the water, son! Stroke! Stroke! He's gaining! Now! Over the line, boy! Over with her! Stroke! That's done it! He's won! He's won!

MADELINE

(*Has been shrieking at the same time*). Gordon! Gordon! He's won! Oh, he's fainted! Poor dear darling! (*She remains standing on the rail, leaning out dangerously, holding on with one hand, looking down longingly toward his shell.*)

EVANS

(*Bounding back to the deck, his face congested and purple with a frenzy of joy, dancing about*). He's won! By God, it was close! Greatest race in the history of rowing! He's the greatest oarsman God ever made! (*Embracing* NINA *and kissing her frantically.*) Aren't you happy, Nina? Our Gordon! The greatest ever!

NINA

(*Torturedly—trying incoherently to force out a last despairing protest*). No!—not yours!—mine!—and Gordon's!—Gordon is Gordon's!—he was my Gordon!—his Gordon is mine!

EVANS

(*Soothingly, humoring her—kissing her again*). Of course he's yours, dear—and a dead ringer for Gordon Shaw, too! Gordon's body! Gordon's spirit! Your body and spirit, too, Nina! He's not like me, lucky for him! I'm a poor boob! I never could row worth a damn! (*He suddenly staggers as if he were very drunk, leaning on* MARSDEN—*then gives a gasp and collapses inertly to the deck, lying on his back.*)

MARSDEN

(*Stares down at him stupidly—then thinking strangely*). I knew it! . . . I saw the end beginning! . . .
(*He touches* NINA's *arm—in a low voice*). Nina—your husband! (*Touching* DARRELL *who has stood staring straight before him*

with a bitter ironical smile on his lips.*) Ned—your friend! Doctor Darrell—a patient!

NINA

(*Stares down at* EVANS—*slowly, as if trying to bring her mind back to him*). My husband? (*Suddenly with a cry of pain, sinks on her knees beside the body.*) Sam!

DARRELL

(*Looking down at him—thinking yearningly*). Is her husband dead . . . at last? . . . (*Then with a shudder at his thoughts.*) No! . . . I don't hope! . . . I don't! . . .
(*He cries*). Sam! (*He kneels down, feels of his heart, pulse, looks into his face—with a change to a strictly professional manner.*) He's not dead. Only a bad stroke.

NINA

(*With a cry of grief*). Oh, Ned, did all our old secret hopes do this at last?

DARRELL

(*Professionally, staring at her coldly*). Bosh, Mrs. Evans! We're not in the Congo that we can believe in evil charms! (*Sternly.*) In his condition, Mr. Evans must have absolute quiet and peace of mind or— And perfect care! You must tend him night and day! And I will! We've got to keep him happy!

NINA

(*Dully*). Again? (*Then sternly in her turn, as if swearing a pledge to herself.*) I will never leave his side! I will never tell him anything that might disturb his peace!

MARSDEN

(*Standing above them—thinking exultantly*). I will not have long to wait now! . . . (*Then ashamed.*) How can I think such things . . . poor Sam! . . . he was . . . I mean he is my friend . . . (*With assertive loyalty*). A rare spirit! A pure and simple soul! A good man—yes, a good man! God bless him! (*He makes a motion over the body like a priest blessing.*)

DARRELL

(*His voice suddenly breaking with a sincere human grief*). Sam, old boy! I'm so damned sorry! I will give my life to save you!

NINA

(*In dull anguish*). Save—again? (*Then lovingly, kissing* EVANS' *face.*) Dear husband, you have tried to make me happy, I will give you my happiness again! I will give you Gordon to give to Madeline!

MADELINE

(*Still standing on the rail, staring after* GORDON's *shell*). Gordon! . . . dear lover . . . how tired . . . but you'll rest in my arms . . . your head will lie on my breast . . . soon! . . .

Curtain

ACT NINE

SCENE: *Several months later. A terrace on the* EVANS' *estate on Long Island. In the rear, the terrace overlooks a small harbor with the ocean beyond. On the right is a side entrance of the pretentious villa. On the left is a hedge with an arched gateway leading to a garden. The terrace is paved with rough stone. There is a stone bench at center, a recliner at right, a wicker table and armchair at left.*

It is late afternoon of a day in early fall. GORDON EVANS *is sitting on the stone bench, his chin propped on his hands,* MADELINE *standing behind him, her arm about his shoulders.* GORDON *is over six feet tall with the figure of a trained athlete. His sun-bronzed face is extremely handsome after the fashion of the magazine-cover American collegian. It is a strong face but of a strength wholly material in quality. He has been too thoroughly trained to progress along a certain groove to success ever to question it or be dissatisfied with its rewards. At the same time, although entirely an unimaginative code-bound gentleman of his groove, he is boyish and likable, of an even, modest, sporting disposition. His expression is boyishly forlorn, but he is making a manly effort to conceal his grief.*

MADELINE *is much the same as in the previous Act except that there is now a distinct maternal older feeling in her attitude toward* GORDON *as she endeavors to console him.*

MADELINE

(*Tenderly, smoothing his hair*). There, dear! I know how horribly hard it is for you. I loved him, too. He was so wonderful and sweet to me.

GORDON

(*His voice trembling*). I didn't really realize he was gone—until out at the cemetery—(*His voice breaks.*)

MADELINE

(*Kissing his hair*). Darling! Please don't!

GORDON

(*Rebelliously*). Damn it, I don't see why

he had to die! (*With a groan.*) It was that constant grind at the office! I ought to have insisted on his taking better care of himself. But I wasn't home enough, that's the trouble. I couldn't watch him. (*Then bitterly.*) But I can't see why Mother didn't!

MADELINE

(*Reprovingly but showing she shares his feeling*). Now! You mustn't start feeling bitter toward her.

GORDON

(*Contritely*). I know I shouldn't. (*But returning to his bitter tone.*) But I can't help remembering how unreasonably she's acted about our engagement.

MADELINE

Not since your father was taken sick, she hasn't, dear. She's been wonderfully nice.

GORDON

(*In the same tone*). Nice? Indifferent, you mean! She doesn't seem to care a damn one way or the other any more!

MADELINE

You could hardly expect her to think of anyone but your father. She's been with him every minute. I never saw such devotion. (*Thinking*). Will Gordon ever get old and sick like that? ... oh, I hope we'll both die before! ... but I'd nurse him just as she did his father ... I'll always love him! ...

GORDON

(*Consoled—proudly*). Yes, she sure was wonderful to him, all right! (*Then coming back to his old tone.*) But—this may sound rotten of me—I always had a queer feeling she was doing it as a duty. And when he died, I felt her grief was—not from love for him—at least, only the love of a friend, not a wife's love. (*As if under some urgent compulsion from within.*) I've never told you, but I've always felt, ever since I was a little kid, that she didn't really love Dad. She liked him and respected him. She was a wonderful wife. But I'm sure she didn't love him. (*Blurting it out as if he couldn't help it.*) I'll tell you, Madeline! I've always felt she cared a lot for—Darrell. (*Hastily.*) Of course, I might be wrong. (*Then bursting out.*) No, I'm not wrong! I've felt it too strongly, ever since I was a kid. And then when I was eleven—something happened. I've been sure of it since then.

MADELINE

(*Thinking in amazement, but not without a queer satisfaction*). Does he mean that she was unfaithful to his father? ... no, he'd never believe that ... but what else could he mean? ... (*Wonderingly*). Gordon! Do you mean you've been sure that your mother was—

GORDON

(*Outraged by something in her tone—jumping to his feet and flinging her hand off—roughly*). Was what? What do you mean, Madeline?

MADELINE

(*Frightened—placatingly puts her arms around him*). I didn't mean anything, dear. I simply thought you meant—

GORDON

(*Still indignant*). All I meant was that she must have fallen in love with Darrell long after she was married—and then she sent him away for Dad's sake—and mine, too, I suppose. He kept coming back every couple of years. He didn't have guts enough to stay away for good! Oh, I suppose I'm unfair. I suppose it was damned hard on him. He fought it down, too, on account of his friendship for Dad. (*Then with a bitter laugh.*) I suppose they'll be getting married now! And I'll have to wish them good luck. Dad would want me to. He was game. (*With a bitter gloomy air.*) Life is damn queer, that's all I've got to say!

MADELINE

(*Thinking with a sort of tender, loving scorn for his boyish naïveté*). How little he knows her! ... Mr. Evans was a fine man but ... Darrell must have been fascinating once ... if she loved anyone she isn't the kind who would hesitate ... any more than I have with Gordon ... oh, I'll never be unfaithful to Gordon ... I'll love him always! ... (*She runs her fingers through his hair caressingly—comfortingly.*) You must never blame them, dear. No one can help love. We couldn't, could we? (*She sits beside him. He takes her in his arms. They kiss each other with rising passion.* MARSDEN *comes in noiselessly from the garden, a bunch of roses and a pair of shears in his hands. He looks younger, calm and contented. He is dressed in his all-black, meticulous, perfectly tailored mourning costume. He stands looking at the two lovers, a queer agitation coming into his face.*)

MARSDEN

(*Scandalized as an old maid—thinking*). I must say! . . . his father hardly cold in his grave! . . . it's positively bestial! . . . (*Then struggling with himself—with a defensive self-mockery.*) Only it wasn't his father . . . what is Sam to Darrell's son? . . . and even if he were Sam's son, what have the living to do with the dead? . . . his duty is to love that life may keep on living . . . and what has their loving to do with me? . . . my life is cool green shade wherein comes no scorching zenith sun of passion and possession to wither the heart with bitter poisons . . . my life gathers roses, coolly crimson, in sheltered gardens, on late afternoons in love with evening . . . roses heavy with after-blooming of the long day, desiring evening . . . my life is an evening . . . Nina is a rose, my rose, exhausted by the long, hot day, leaning wearily toward peace. . . . (*He kisses one of the roses with a simple sentimental smile—then still smiling, makes a gesture toward the two lovers.*) That is on another planet, called the world . . . Nina and I have moved on to the moon. . . .

MADELINE

(*Passionately*). Dear one! Sweetheart!

GORDON

Madeline! I love you!

MARSDEN

(*Looking at them—gaily mocking—thinking*). Once I'd have felt jealous . . . cheated . . . swindled by God out of joy! . . . I would have thought bitterly, "The Gordons have all the luck!" . . . but now I know that dear old Charlie . . . yes, poor dear old Charlie!—passed beyond desire, has all the luck at last! . . . (*Then matter-of-factly.*) But I'll have to interrupt their biological preparations . . . there are many things still to be done this evening . . . Age's terms of peace, after the long interlude of war with life, have still to be concluded . . . Youth must keep decently away . . . so many old wounds may have to be unbound,

and old scars pointed to with pride, to prove to ourselves we have been brave and noble! . . .

(*He lets the shears drop to the ground. They jump startledly and turn around. He smiles quietly*). Sorry to disturb you. I've been picking some roses for your mother, Gordon. Flowers really have the power to soothe grief. I suppose it was that discovery that led to their general use at funerals—and weddings! (*He hands a rose to* MADELINE.) Here, Madeline, here's a rose for you. Hail, Love, we who have died salute you! (*He smiles strangely. She takes the rose automatically, staring at him uncomprehendingly*).

MADELINE

(*Thinking suspiciously*). What a queer creature! . . . there's something uncanny! . . . oh, don't be silly! . . . it's only poor old Charlie! . . .

(*She makes him a mocking curtsey*). Thank you, Uncle Charlie!

GORDON

(*Thinking with sneering pity*). Poor old guy! . . . he means well . . . Dad liked him. . . .

(*Pretending an interest in the roses*). They're pretty. (*Then suddenly.*) Where's Mother—still in the house?

MARSDEN

She was trying to get rid of the last of the people. I'm going in. Shall I tell her you want to see her? It would give her an excuse to get away.

GORDON

Yes. Will you? (MARSDEN *goes into the house on right.*)

MADELINE

You'd better see your mother alone. I'll go down to the plane and wait for you. You want to fly back before dark, don't you?

GORDON

Yes, and we ought to get started soon. (*Moodily.*) Maybe it would be better if you weren't here. There are some things I feel I ought to say to her—and Darrell. I've got to do what I know Dad would have wanted. I've got to be fair. He always was to everyone all his life

MADELINE

You dear, you! You couldn't be unfair to anyone if you tried! (*She kisses him.*) Don't be too long.

GORDON

(*Moodily*). You bet I won't! It won't be so pleasant I'll want to drag it out!

MADELINE

Good-bye for a while then.

GORDON

So long. (*He looks after her lovingly as she goes out right, rear, around the corner of the house.*)
(*Thinking*). Madeline's wonderful! . . . I don't deserve my luck . . . but, God, I sure do love her! . . . (*He sits down on the bench again, his chin on his hands.*) It seems rotten and selfish to be happy . . . when Dad . . . oh, he understands, he'd want me to be . . . it's funny how I got to care more for Dad than for Mother . . . I suppose it was finding out she loved Darrell . . . I can remember that day seeing her kiss him . . . it did something to me I never got over . . . but she made Dad happy . . . she gave up her own happiness for his sake . . . that was certainly damn fine . . . that was playing the game . . . I'm a hell of a one to criticize . . . my own mother! . . . (*Changing the subject of his thoughts abruptly.*) Forget it! . . . think of Madeline . . . we'll be married . . . then two months' honeymoon in Europe . . . God, that'll be great! . . . then back and dive into the business . . . Dad relied on me to carry on where he left off . . . I'll have to start at the bottom but I'll get to the top in a hurry, I promise you that, Dad! . . .
(NINA *and* DARRELL *come out of the house on the right. He hears the sound of the door and looks around.*)
(*Thinking resentfully*). Funny! . . . I can't stand it even now! . . . when I see him with Mother! . . . I'd like to beat him up! . . . (*He gets to his feet, his face unconsciously becoming older and cold and severe. He stares accusingly at them as they come slowly toward him in silence.* NINA *looks much*

older than in the preceding Act. Resignation has come into her face, a resignation that uses no make-up, that has given up the struggle to be sexually attractive and look younger. She is dressed in deep black. DARRELL's deep sunburn of the tropics has faded, leaving his skin a Mongolian yellow. He, too, looks much older. His expression is sad and bitter.*)

NINA

(*Glancing at* GORDON *searchingly—thinking sadly*). He sent for me to say good-bye . . . really good-bye forever this time . . . he's not my son now, nor Gordon's son, nor Sam's, nor Ned's . . . he has become that stranger, another woman's lover. . . .

DARRELL

(*Also after a quick keen glance at* GORDON's *face—thinking*). There's something up . . . some final accounting . . . (*Thinking resignedly.*) Well, let's get it over . . . then I can go back to work. . . . I've stayed too long up here . . . Preston must be wondering if I've deserted him. . . . (*Then with a wondering sadness.*) Is that my son? . . . my flesh and blood? . . . staring at me with such cold enmity? . . . how sad and idiotic this all is! . . .

NINA

(*Putting on a tone of joking annoyance*). Your message was a godsend, Gordon. Those stupid people with their social condolences were killing me. Perhaps I'm morbid but I always have the feeling that they're secretly glad someone is dead—that it flatters their vanity and makes them feel superior because they're living. (*She sits wearily on the bench.* DARRELL *sits on side of the recliner at right.*)

GORDON

(*Repelled by this idea—stiffly*). They were all good friends of Dad's. Why shouldn't they be sincerely sorry? His death ought to be a loss to everyone who knew him. (*His voice trembles. He turns away and walks to the table.*)
(*Thinking bitterly*). She doesn't care a damn! . . . she's free to marry Darrell now! . . .

NINA

(*Thinking sadly, looking at his back*). He's accusing me because I'm not weeping . . . well, I did weep . . . all I could . . . there aren't many tears left . . . it was too bad Sam had to die . . . living suited him . . . he was so contented with himself . . . but I can't feel guilty . . . I helped him to live . . . I made him believe I loved him . . . his mind was perfectly sane to the end . . . and just before he died, he smiled at me . . . so gratefully and forgivingly, I thought . . . closing our life together with that smile . . . that life is dead . . . its regrets are dead . . . I am sad but there's comfort in the thought that now I am free at last to rot away in peace . . . I'll go and live in Father's old home . . . Sam bought that back . . . I suppose he left it to me . . . Charlie will come in every day to visit . . . he'll comfort and amuse me . . . we can talk together of the old days . . . when I was a girl . . . when I was happy . . . before I fell in love with Gordon Shaw and all this tangled mess of love and hate and pain and birth began! . . .

DARRELL

(*Staring at* GORDON'S *back resentfully*). It gets under my skin to see him act so unfeelingly toward his mother! . . . if he only knew what she's suffered for his sake! . . . the Gordon Shaw ideal passed on through Sam has certainly made my son an insensitive clod! . . . (*With disgust.*) Bah, what has that young man to do with me? . . . compared to Preston he's only a well-muscled, handsome fool! . . . (*With a trace of anger.*) But I'd like to jolt his stupid self-complacency! . . . if he knew the facts about himself, he wouldn't be sobbing sentimentally about Sam . . . he'd better change his tune or I'll certainly be tempted to tell him . . . there's no reason for his not knowing now . . . (*His face is flushed. He has worked himself into a real anger.*)

GORDON

(*Suddenly, having got back his control, turns to them—coldly*). There are certain things connected with Dad's will I thought I ought to— (*With a tinge of satisfied superiority.*) I don't believe Dad told you about his will, did he, Mother?

NINA

(*Indifferently*). No.

GORDON

Well, the whole estate goes to you and me, of course. I didn't mean that. (*With a resentful look at* DARRELL.) But there is one provision that is peculiar, to say the least. It concerns you, Doctor Darrell—a half-million for your Station to be used in biological research work.

DARRELL

(*His face suddenly flushing with anger*). What's that? That's a joke, isn't it?
(*Thinking furiously*). It's worse! . . . it's a deliberate insult! . . . a last sneer of ownership! . . . of my life! . . .

GORDON

(*Coldly sneering*). I thought it must be a joke myself—but Dad insisted.

DARRELL

(*Angrily*). Well, I won't accept it—and that's final!

GORDON

(*Coldly*). It's not left to you but to the Station. Your supervision is mentioned but I suppose if you won't carry on, whoever is in real charge down there will be only too glad to accept it.

DARRELL

(*Stupefied*). That means Preston! But Sam didn't even know Preston—except from hearing me talk about him! What had Sam to do with Preston? Preston is none of his business! I'll advise Preston to refuse it!
(*Thinking torturedly*). But it's for science! . . . he has no right to refuse! . . . I have no right to ask him to! . . . God damn Sam! . . . wasn't it enough for him to own my wife, my son, in his lifetime? . . . now in death he reaches out to steal Preston! . . . to steal my work! . . .

NINA

(*Thinking bitterly*). Even in death
Sam makes people suffer . . .
(*Sympathetically*). It isn't for you—nor
for Preston. It's for science, Ned. You must
look at it that way.

GORDON

(*Thinking resentfully*). What a tender tone she takes toward him! . . .
she's forgotten Dad already! . . .
(*With a sneer*). You'd better accept. Half-
millions aren't being thrown away for
nothing every day.

NINA

(*In anguish—thinking*). How can
Gordon insult poor Ned like that! . . .
his own father! . . . Ned has suffered
too much! . . .
(*Sharply*). I think you've said about
enough, Gordon!

GORDON

(*Bitterly, but trying to control himself—
meaningly*). I haven't said all I'm going to
say, Mother!

NINA

(*Thinking—at first frightenedly*).
What does he mean? . . . does he know
about Ned being . . . ? (*Then with a
sort of defiant relief.*) Well, what does
it matter what he thinks of me? . . .
he's hers now, anyway. . . .

DARRELL

(*Thinking vindictively*). I hope he
knows the truth, for if he doesn't, by
God, I'll tell him! . . . if only to get
something back from Sam of all he's
stolen from me! . . .
(*Authoritatively—as* GORDON *hesitates*).
Well, what have you got to say? Your
mother and I are waiting.

GORDON

(*Furiously, taking a threatening step toward him*). Shut up, you! Don't take that
tone with me or I'll forget your age—
(*contemptuously*) and give you a spanking!

NINA

(*Thinking hysterically*). Spanking!
. . . the son spanks the father! . . .

(*Laughing hysterically*). Oh, Gordon,
don't make me laugh! It's all so funny!

DARRELL

(*Jumps from his chair and goes to her—
solicitously*). Nina! Don't mind him! He
doesn't realize—

GORDON

(*Maddened, comes closer*). I realize a lot!
I realize you've acted like a cur! (*He steps
forward and slaps* DARRELL *across the face
viciously.* DARRELL *staggers back from the
force of the blow, his hands to his face.*
NINA *screams and flings herself on* GOR-
DON, *holding his arms.*)

NINA

(*Piteously—hysterically*). For God's sake,
Gordon! What would your father say?
You don't know what you're doing! You're
hitting your father!

DARRELL

(*Suddenly breaking down—chokingly*).
No—it's all right, son—all right—you
didn't know—

GORDON

(*Crushed, overcome by remorse for his
blow*). I'm sorry—sorry—you're right,
Mother—Dad would feel as if I'd hit him
—just as bad as if I'd hit him!

DARRELL

It's nothing, son—nothing!

GORDON

(*Brokenly*). That's damn fine, Darrell—
damn fine and sporting of you! It was a
rotten, dirty trick! Accept my apology, Darrell, won't you?

DARRELL

(*Staring at him stupidly—thinking*).
Darrell? . . . he calls me Darrell! . . .
but doesn't he know? . . . I thought she
told him. . . .

NINA

(*Laughing hysterically—thinking*). I
told him he hit his father . . . but he
can't understand me! . . . why, of
course he can't! . . . how could he? . . .

GORDON

(*Insistently holding out his hand*). I'm damned sorry! I didn't mean it! Shake hands, won't you?

DARRELL

(*Doing so mechanically—stupidly*). Only too glad—pleased to meet you—know you by reputation—the famous oarsman—great race you stroked last June—but I was hoping the Navy would give you a beating.

NINA

(*Thinking in desperate hysterical anguish*). Oh, I wish Ned would go away and stay away forever! . . . I can't bear to watch him suffer any more! . . . it's too frightful! . . . yes, God the Father, I hear you laughing . . . you see the joke . . . I'm laughing too . . . it's all so crazy, isn't it? . . . (*Laughing hysterically*). Oh, Ned! Poor Ned! You were born unlucky!

GORDON

(*Making her sit down again—soothing her*). Mother! Stop laughing! Please! It's all right—all right between us! I've apologized! (*As she has grown calmer.*) And now I want to say what I was going to say. It wasn't anything bad. It was just that I want you to know how fine I think you've both acted. I've known ever since I was a kid that you and Darrell were in love with each other. I hated the idea on Father's account—that's only natural, isn't it?—but I knew it was unfair, that people can't help loving each other any more than Madeline and I could have helped ourselves. And I saw how fair you both were to Dad—what a good wife you were, Mother—what a true friend you were, Darrell—and how damn much he loved you both! So all I wanted to say is, now he's dead, I hope you'll get married and I hope you'll be as happy as you both deserve— (*Here he breaks down, kissing her and then breaking away.*) I've got to say good-bye—got to fly back before dark—Madeline's waiting. (*He takes* DARRELL's *hand and shakes it again. They have both been staring at him stupidly.*) Good-bye Darrell! Good luck!

DARRELL

(*Thinking sufferingly*). Why does he keep on calling me Darrell . . . he's my boy . . . I'm his father . . . I've got to make him realize I'm his father! . . . (*Holding* GORDON's *hand*). Listen, son. It's my turn. I've got to tell you something—

NINA

(*Thinking torturedly*). Oh, he mustn't! . . . I feel he mustn't! . . . (*Sharply*). Ned! First let me ask Gordon a question. (*Then looking her son in the eyes, slowly and impressively.*) Do you think I was ever unfaithful to your father, Gordon?

GORDON

(*Startled, stares at her—shocked and horrified—then suddenly he blurts out indignantly*). Mother, what do you think I am —as rotten-minded as that! (*Pleadingly.*) Please, Mother, I'm not as bad as that! I know you're the best woman that ever lived —the best of all! I don't even except Madeline!

NINA

(*With a sobbing triumphant cry*). My dear Gordon! You do love me, don't you?

GORDON

(*Kneeling beside her and kissing her*). Of course!

NINA

(*Pushing him away—tenderly*). And now go! Hurry! Madeline is waiting! Give her my love! Come to see me once in a while in the years to come! Good-bye, dear! (*Turning to* DARRELL, *who is standing with a sad resigned expression—imploringly.*) Did you still want to tell Gordon something, Ned?

DARRELL

(*Forcing a tortured smile*). Not for anything in the world! Good-bye, son.

GORDON

Good-bye, sir.

(*He hurries off around the corner of the house at left, rear, thinking troubledly.*) What does she think I am? . . . I've never thought that! . . . I couldn't! . . . my own mother! I'd kill myself if I ever even caught myself thinking . . . ! (*He is gone.*)

NINA

(*Turns to* NED, *gratefully taking his hand and pressing it*). Poor dear Ned, you've always had to give! How can I ever thank you?

DARRELL

(*With an ironical smile—forcing a joking tone*). By refusing me when I ask you to marry me! For I've got to ask you! Gordon expects it! And he'll be so pleased when he knows you turned me down. (MARSDEN *comes out of the house.*) Hello, here comes Charlie. I must hurry. Will you marry me, Nina?

NINA

(*With a sad smile*). No. Certainly not. Our ghosts would torture us to death! (*Then forlornly.*) But I wish I did love you, Ned! Those were wonderful afternoons long ago! The Nina of those afternoons will always live in me, will always love her lover, Ned, the father of her baby!

DARRELL

(*Lifting her hand to his lips—tenderly*). Thank you for that! And that Ned will always adore his beautiful Nina! Remember him! Forget me! I'm going back to work. (*He laughs softly and sadly.*) I leave you to Charlie. You'd better marry him, Nina—if you want peace. And after all, I think you owe it to him for his life-long devotion.

MARSDEN

(*Thinking uneasily*). They're talking about me ... why doesn't he go? ... she doesn't love him any more ... even now he's all heat and energy and the tormenting drive of noon ... can't he see she is in love with evening? ... (*Clearing his throat uneasily*). Do I hear my name taken in vain?

NINA

(*Looking at* MARSDEN *with a strange yearning*). Peace! ... yes ... that is all I desire ... I can no longer imagine happiness ... Charlie has found peace ... he will be tender ... as my father was when I was a girl ... when I could imagine happiness ... (*With a girlish coquettishness and embarrassment—making way for him on the*

bench *beside her—strangely*). Ned's just proposed to me. I refused him, Charlie. I don't love him any more.

MARSDEN

(*Sitting down beside her*). I suspected as much. Then whom do you love, Nina Cara Nina?

NINA

(*Sadly smiling*). You, Charlie, I suppose. I have always loved your love for me. (*She kisses him—wistfully.*) Will you let me rot away in peace?

MARSDEN

(*Strongly*). All my life I've waited to bring you peace.

NINA

(*Sadly teasing*). If you've waited that long, Charlie, we'd better get married tomorrow. But I forgot. You haven't asked me yet, have you? Do you want me to marry you, Charlie?

MARSDEN

(*Humbly*). Yes, Nina.
(*Thinking with a strange ecstasy*). I knew the time would come at last when I would hear her ask that! ... I could never have said it, never! ... oh, russet-golden afternoon, you are a mellow fruit of happiness ripely falling!

DARRELL

(*Amused—with a sad smile*). Bless you, my children! (*He turns to go.*)

NINA

I don't suppose we'll ever see you again, Ned.

DARRELL

I hope not, Nina. A scientist shouldn't believe in ghosts. (*With a mocking smile.*) But perhaps we'll become part of cosmic positive and negative electric charges and meet again.

NINA

In our afternoons—again?

DARRELL

(*Smiling sadly*). Again. In our afternoons.

MARSDEN

(*Coming out of his day dream*). We'll be married in the afternoon, decidedly. I've already picked out the church, Nina—a gray ivied chapel, full of restful shadow, symbolical of the peace we have found. The crimsons and purples in the windows will stain our faces with faded passion. It must be in the hour before sunset when the earth dreams in afterthoughts and mystic premonitions of life's beauty. And then we'll go up to your old home to live. Mine wouldn't be suitable for us. Mother and Jane live there in memory. And I'll work in your father's old study. He won't mind me.

(*From the bay below comes the roaring hum of an airplane motor.* NINA *and* DARRELL *jump startledly and go to the rear of the terrace to watch the plane ascend from the water, standing side by side.* MARSDEN *remains oblivious.*)

NINA

(*With anguish*). Gordon! Good-bye, dear! (*Pointing as the plane climbs higher moving away off to the left—bitterly.*) See, Ned! He's leaving me without a backward look!

DARRELL

(*Joyfully*). No! He's circling. He's coming back! (*The roar of the engine grows steadily nearer now.*) He's going to pass directly over us! (*Their eyes follow the plane as it comes swiftly nearer and passes directly over them.*) See! He's waving to us!

NINA

Oh, Gordon! My dear son! (*She waves frantically.*)

DARRELL

(*With a last tortured protest*). Nina! Are you forgetting? He's my son, too! (*He shouts up at the sky.*) You're my son, Gordon! You're my— (*He controls himself abruptly—with a smile of cynical self-pity.*) He can't hear! Well, at least I've done my duty! (*Then with a grim fatalism —with a final wave of his hand at the sky.*) Good-bye, Gordon's son!

NINA

(*With tortured exultance*). Fly up to heaven, Gordon! Fly with your love to heaven! Fly always! Never crash to earth like my old Gordon! Be happy, dear! You've got to be happy!

DARRELL

(*Sardonically*). I've heard that cry for happiness before, Nina! I remember hearing myself cry it—once—it must have been long ago! I'll get back to my cells—sensible unicellular life that floats in the sea and has never learned to cry for happiness! I'm going, Nina.

(*As she remains oblivious, staring after the plane—thinking fatalistically*). She doesn't hear, either. . . . (*He laughs up at the sky.*) Oh, God, so deaf and dumb and blind! . . . teach me to be resigned to be an atom! . . . (*He walks off, right, and enters the house.*)

NINA

(*Finally lowering her eyes—confusedly*). Gone. My eyes are growing dim. Where is Ned? Gone, too. And Sam is gone. They're all dead. Where are Father and Charlie? (*With a shiver of fear she hurries over and sits on the bench beside* MARSDEN, *huddling against him.*) Gordon is dead, Father. I've just had a cable. What I mean is, he flew away to another life—my son, Gordon, Charlie. So we're alone again—just as we used to be.

MARSDEN

(*Putting his arm around her—affectionately*). Just as we used to be, dear Nina Cara Nina, before Gordon came.

NINA

(*Looking up at the sky—strangely*). My having a son was a failure, wasn't it? He couldn't give me happiness. Sons are always their fathers. They pass through the mother to become their father again. The Sons of the Father have all been failures! Failing they died for us, they flew away to other lives, they could not stay with us, they could not give us happiness!

MARSDEN

(*Paternally—in her father's tone*). You had best forget the whole affair of your association with the Gordons. After all, dear Nina, there was something unreal in all that has happened since you first met Gordon Shaw, something extravagant and fantastic, the sort of thing that isn't done, really, in our afternoons. So let's you and me forget the whole distressing episode, regard it as an interlude, of trial and preparation, say, in which our souls have been scraped clean of impure flesh and made worthy to bleach in peace.

NINA

(*With a strange smile*). Strange interlude! Yes, our lives are merely strange dark interludes in the electrical display of God the Father! (*Resting her head on his shoulder.*) You're so restful, Charlie. I feel as if I were a girl again and you were my father and the Charlie of those days made into one. I wonder is our old garden the same? We'll pick flowers together in the aging afternoons of spring and summer, won't we? It will be a comfort to get home—to be old and to be home again at last—to be in love with peace together—to love each other's peace—to sleep with peace together—! (*She kisses him—then shuts her eyes with a deep sigh of requited weariness*) —to die in peace! I'm so contentedly weary with life!

MARSDEN

(*With a serene peace*). Rest, dear Nina. (*Then tenderly.*) It has been a long day. Why don't you sleep now—as you used to, remember?—for a little while?

NINA

(*Murmurs with drowsy gratitude*). Thank you, Father—have I been wicked?—you're so good—dear old Charlie!

MARSDEN

(*Reacting automatically and wincing with pain—thinking mechanically*). God damn dear old . . . ! (*Then with a glance down at* NINA's *face, with a happy smile.*) No, God bless dear old Charlie . . . who, passed beyond desire, has all the luck at last! . . . (NINA *has fallen asleep. He watches with contented eyes the evening shadows closing in around them.*)

Curtain.

Street Scene

BY ELMER RICE

ELMER RICE

Elmer Rice was born in New York City in 1892. He received the LL.B. degree cum laude from the New York Law School in 1912, and was admitted to the New York Bar in 1913. His marriage to Hazel Levy occurred in 1915.

Mr. Rice's first novel, *A Voyage to Purilia,* a satire on motion pictures, was published in 1930. He is a member of the governing boards of the Authors' League of America, the American Dramatists, the American Civil Liberties Union, the League of British Dramatists, the Inter-Professional Association for Social Insurance, etc.

Mr. Rice's first play, *On Trial,* introduced the now-familiar movie flash-back in time and action to the stage. *The Adding Machine,* one of his best-known successes, was the first expressionistic drama to employ a native American background.

Despite his previous successes, *Street Scene* was rejected by nearly every theatrical manager in New York. Produced by William A. Brady at the Playhouse, New York, January 10, 1929, *Street Scene* received the Pulitzer award for 1928-1929.

CHARACTERS

ABRAHAM KAPLAN

GRETA FIORENTINO

EMMA JONES

OLGA OLSEN

WILLIE MAURRANT

ANNA MAURRANT

DANIEL BUCHANAN

FRANK MAURRANT

GEORGE JONES

STEVE SANKEY

AGNES CUSHING

CARL OLSEN

SHIRLEY KAPLAN

FILIPPO FIORENTINO

ALICE SIMPSON

LAURA HILDEBRAND

MARY HILDEBRAND

CHARLIE HILDEBRAND

SAMUEL KAPLAN

ROSE MAURRANT

HARRY EASTER

MAE JONES

DICK McGANN

VINCENT JONES

Dr. JOHN WILSON

OFFICER HARRY MURPHY

A MILKMAN

A LETTER CARRIER

AN ICE-MAN

TWO COLLEGE GIRLS

A MUSIC STUDENT

MARSHAL JAMES HENRY

FRED CULLEN

AN OLD-CLOTHES MAN

AN INTERNE

AN AMBULANCE DRIVER

A FURNITURE MOVER

TWO NURSE-MAIDS

POLICEMEN

TWO APARTMENT-HUNTERS

PASSERS-BY

SCENE

There is only one setting which is described in detail in the text.

The action takes place on an evening in June, and on the morning and afternoon of the following day.

STREET SCENE

ACT ONE

SCENE: *The exterior of a "walk-up" apartment-house, in a mean quarter of New York. It is of ugly brownstone and was built in the '90's. Between the pavement of large, gray flagstones and the front of the house, is a deep and narrow "area-way," guarded by a rusted, ornamental iron railing. At the right, a steep flight of rotting wooden steps leads down to the cellar and to the janitor's apartment, the windows of which are just visible above the street level. Spanning the area-way is a "stoop" of four shallow, stone steps, flanked on either side by a curved stone balustrade. Beyond the broad fourth step, another step leads to the double wooden outer doors of the house; and as these are open, the vestibule, and the wide, heavy glass-panelled entrance door beyond are visible. Above the outer doors, is a glass fanlight, upon which appears the half-obliterated house number. At the left side of the doorway is a sign which reads: "Flat To-Let. 6 Rooms. Steam Heat."*

On either side of the stoop, are the two narrow windows of the ground-floor apartments. In one of the windows, at the left, is a sign bearing the legend: "Prof. Filippo Fiorentino. Music for all occasions. Also instruction." Above, are the six narrow windows of the first-floor apartments, and above that, the stone sills of the second-floor windows can just be seen.

To the left of the house, part of the adjoining building is visible: the motor entrance to a storage warehouse. Crude boarding across the large driveway and rough planks across the sidewalk and curb indicate that an excavation is in progress. On the boarding is painted in rude lettering: "Keep Out"; and at the curb is a small barrel bearing a sign with the words: "Street Closed." To the wall of the warehouse is affixed a brass plate, bearing the name: "Patrick Mulcahy Storage Warehouse Co. Inc."

To the right of the house, scaffolding and a wooden sidewalk indicate that the house next door is being demolished. On the scaffolding is a large, wooden sign reading: "Manhattan House-Wrecking Corp."

In the close foreground, below the level of the curb, is a mere suggestion of the street.

At rise: The house is seen in the white glare of an arc-light, which is just off-stage to the right. The windows in the janitor's apartment are lighted, as are also those of the ground-floor apartment, at the right, and the two windows at the extreme left of the first-floor. A dim, red light is affixed to the boarding of the excavation at the left.

In the lighted ground-floor window, at the right of the doorway, ABRAHAM KAPLAN *is seated, in a rocking-chair, reading a Yiddish newspaper. He is a Russian Jew, well past sixty: clean-shaven, thick gray hair, hooked nose, horn-rimmed spectacles. To the left of the doorway,* GRETA FIORENTINO *is leaning out of the window. She is forty, blonde, ruddy-faced and stout. She wears a wrapper of light, flowered material and a large pillow supports her left arm and her ample, uncorseted bosom. In her right hand is a folding paper fan, which she waves languidly.*

Throughout the act and, indeed, throughout the play, there is constant noise. The noises of the city rise, fall, intermingle: the distant roar of "L" trains, automobile sirens and the whistles of boats on the river; the rattle of trucks and the indeterminate clanking of metals; fire-engines, ambulances, musical instruments, a radio, dogs barking and hu-

545

man voices calling, quarrelling and screaming with laughter. The noises are subdued and in the background, but they never wholly cease.

A moment after the rise of the curtain, an elderly man enters at the right and walks into the house, exchanging a nod with MRS. FIORENTINO. A MAN, *munching peanuts, crosses the stage from left to right.*

A VOICE (*off-stage*). Char-lie!
(EMMA JONES *appears at the left. She is middle-aged, tall and rather bony. She carries a small parcel.*)

MRS. FIORENTINO (*she speaks with a faint German accent*). Good evening, Mrs. Jones.

MRS. JONES (*stopping beneath* MRS. FIORENTINO'S *window*). Good evenin', Mrs. F. Well, I hope it's hot enough for you.

MRS. FIORENTINO. Ain't it joost awful? When I was through with the dishes, you could take my clothes and joost wring them out.

MRS. JONES. Me, too. I ain't got a dry stitch on me.

MRS. FIORENTINO. I took off my shoes and my corset and made myself nice and comfortable, and tonight before I go to bed, I take a nice bath.

MRS. JONES. The trouble with a bath is, by the time you're all through, you're as hot as when you started. (*As* OLGA OLSEN, *a thin, anemic Scandinavian, with untidy fair hair, comes up the cellar steps and onto the sidewalk.*) Good evenin', Mrs. Olsen. Awful hot, ain't it?

MRS. OLSEN (*coming over to the front of the stoop*). Yust awful. Mrs. Forentiner, my hoosban' say vill you put de garbage on de doom-vaider?

MRS. FIORENTINO. Oh, sure, sure! I didn't hear him vistle. (*As* MRS. JONES *starts to cross to the stoop.*) Don't go 'vay, Mrs. Jónes. (*She disappears from the window.*)

MRS. OLSEN (*Pushing back some wisps of hair*). I tank is more cooler in de cellar.

MRS. JONES (*sitting on the stoop and fanning herself with her parcel*). Phew! I'm just about ready to pass out.

MRS. OLSEN. My baby is crying, crying all day.

MRS. JONES. Yeah, I often say they mind the heat more'n we do. It's the same with dogs. My Queenie has jes' been layin' aroun' all day.

MRS. OLSEN. The baby get new teet'. It hurt her.

MRS. JONES. Don't tell me! If you was to know what I went t'roo with my Vincent. Half the time, he used to have convulsions. (WILLIE MAURRANT, *a disorderly boy of twelve, appears at the left, on roller skates. He stops at the left of the stoop and takes hold of the railing with both hands.*)

WILLIE (*raising his head and bawling*). Hey, ma!

MRS. JONES (*disapprovingly*). If you want your mother, why don't you go upstairs, instead o' yellin' like that?

WILLIE (*without paying the slightest attention to her, bawls louder*). Hey, ma!

MRS. MAURRANT (*appearing at one of the lighted first-floor windows*). What do you want, Willie?
(*She is a fair woman of forty, who looks her age, but is by no means unattractive.*)

WILLIE. Gimme a dime, will ya? I wanna git a cone.

MRS. MAURRANT (*to* MRS. OLSEN *and* MRS. JONES). Good evening.

MRS. OLSEN *and* MRS. JONES. Good evenin', Mrs. Maurrant.

MRS. MAURRANT (*to* WILLIE). How many cones did you have today, already?

WILLIE (*belligerently*). I'm hot! All de other guys is havin' cones. Come on, gimme a dime.

MRS. MAURRANT. Well, it's the last one. (*She disappears.*)

MRS. JONES. You certainly don't talk very nice to your mother. (*To* MRS. OLSEN.) I'd like to hear one o' mine talkin' that way to me!

MRS. MAURRANT (*appearing at the window*). Remember, this is the last one.

VILLIE. Aw right. T'row it down. (MRS. FIORENTINO *reappears and leans out of the window again.*)

MRS. MAURRANT. Catch it! (*She throws out a twist of newspaper.* WILLIE *scrambles for it, hastily extracts the dime, drops the newspaper on the pavement and skates off, at the left.*)

MRS. FIORENTINO (*twisting her neck upwards*). Good evening, Mrs. Maurrant.

MRS. MAURRANT. Good evening, Mrs. Fiorentino. (*Calling after* WILLIE.) And don't come home too late, Willie! (*But* WILLIE *is already out of earshot.*)

MRS. FIORENTINO. Why don't you come down and be sociable?

MRS. MAURRANT. I'm keeping some supper warm for my husband. (*A slight pause.*) Well, maybe I will for just a minute. (*She leaves the window. The lights in her apartment go out.*)

MRS. FIORENTINO. She has her troubles with dot Willie.

MRS. JONES. I guess it don't bother her much. (*Significantly.*) She's got her mind on other things.

MRS. OLSEN (*looking about cautiously and coming over to the left of the stoop between the two women*). He vas comin' again today to see her.

MRS. JONES (*rising excitedly, and leaning over the balustrade*). Who—Sankey?

MRS. OLSEN (*nodding*). Yes.

MRS. FIORENTINO. Are you sure, Mrs. Olsen?

MRS. OLSEN. I seen him. I vas doostin' de halls.

MRS. FIORENTINO. Dat's terrible!

MRS. JONES. Wouldn't you think a woman her age, with a grown-up daughter—!

MRS. OLSEN. Two times already dis veek, I see him here.

MRS. JONES. I seen him, meself, one day last week. He was comin' out o' the house, jest as I was comin' in wit' de dog. "Good mornin', Mrs. Jones," he says to me, as if butter wouldn't melt in his mouth. "Good mornin'," says I, lookin' him straight in the eye— (*Breaking off suddenly, as the vestibule door opens.*) Be careful, she's comin'. (MRS. MAURRANT *comes out of the house and stops, for a moment, on the top step.*)

MRS. MAURRANT. Goodness, ain't it hot! I think it's really cooler upstairs. (*She comes down the steps to the sidewalk.*)

MRS. JONES. Yeah, jes' what I was sayin', meself. I feel like a wet dish-rag.

MRS. MAURRANT. I would have liked to go to the Park concert tonight, if Rose had got home in time. I don't get much chance to go to concerts. My husband don't care for music. But Rose is more like me—just crazy about it.

MRS. JONES. Ain't she home yet?

MRS. MAURRANT. No. I think maybe she had to work overtime.

MRS. JONES. Well, all mine ever comes home for is to sleep.

MRS. FIORENTINO. The young girls nowadays—!

MRS. OLSEN. My sister was writin' me in Schweden is same t'ing—

MRS. JONES. It ain't only the young ones, either. (*A baby is heard crying in the cellar.*)

OLSEN'S VOICE (*from the cellar*). Ol-ga! (*A* MAN, *in a dinner jacket and straw hat, appears at the left, whistling a jazz tune. He crosses the stage and goes off at the right.*)

MRS. OLSEN (*hurrying to the right*). I betcha the baby, she's cryin' again.

OLSEN'S VOICE. Ol-ga!

MRS. OLSEN. Yes. I come right away. (*She goes down the cellar steps.*)

MRS. JONES. What them foreigners don't know about bringin' up babies would fill a book.

MRS. FIORENTINO (*a little huffily*). Foreigners know joost as much as other people, Mrs. Jones. My mother had eight children and she brought up seven.

MRS. JONES (*tactfully*). Well, I'm not sayin' anythin' about the Joimans. The Joimans is different—more like the Irish. What I'm talkin' about is all them square-heads an' Polacks—(*with a glance in* KAPLAN's *direction*)—an' Jews.

BUCHANAN'S VOICE (*from a third story window*). Good evening, ladies.

THE WOMEN (*in unison, looking upward*). Oh, good evening, Mr. Buchanan.

BUCHANAN'S VOICE. Well, is it hot enough for you?

MRS. JONES. I'll say!

BUCHANAN'S VOICE. I was just saying to my wife, it's not the heat I mind as much as it is the humidity.

MRS. JONES. Yeah, that's it! Makes everything stick to you.

MRS. MAURRANT. How's your wife feeling in this weather?

BUCHANAN'S VOICE. She don't complain about the weather. But she's afraid to go out of the house. Thinks maybe she couldn't get back in time, in case—you know.

MRS. JONES (*to the other women*). I was the same way, with my Vincent—afraid to take a step. But with Mae, I was up an' out till the very last minute.

MRS. FIORENTINO (*craning her neck upward*). Mr. Buchanan, do you think she would eat some nice minestrone—good Italian vegetable-soup?

BUCHANAN'S VOICE. Why, much obliged, Mrs. F., but I really can't get her to eat a thing.

MRS. JONES (*rising and looking upward*). Tell her she ought to keep up her strength. She's got two to feed, you know.

BUCHANAN'S VOICE. Excuse me, she's calling.

MRS. JONES (*crossing to the railing, at the left of* MRS. FIORENTINO). You'd think it was him that was havin' the baby.

MRS. MAURRANT. She's such a puny little thing.

MRS. FIORENTINO (*with a sigh*). Well, that's the way it goes. The little skinny ones have them and the big strong ones don't.

MRS. MAURRANT. Don't take it that way, Mrs. Fiorentino. You're a young woman, yet.

MRS. FIORENTINO (*shaking her head*). Oh, well!

MRS. JONES. My aunt, Mrs. Barclay, was forty-two— (*Breaking off.*) Oh, good evenin', Mr. Maurrant!

(FRANK MAURRANT *appears, at the left, with his coat on his arm. He is a tall, powerfully-built man of forty-five, with a rugged, grim face.*)

MRS. FIORENTINO. Good evening, Mr. Maurrant.

MAURRANT. 'Evenin'. (*He goes to the stoop and seats himself, mopping his face.*) Some baby of a day!

MRS. MAURRANT. Have you been working all this while, Frank?

MAURRANT. I'll say I've been workin'. Dress-rehearsin' since twelve o'clock, with lights —in this weather. An' tomorra I gotta go to Stamford, for the try-out.

MRS. MAURRANT. Oh, you're going to Stamford tomorrow?

MAURRANT. Yeah, the whole crew's goin'. (*Looking at her.*) What about it?

MRS. MAURRANT. Why, nothing. Oh, I've got some cabbage and potatoes on the stove for you.

MAURRANT. I just had a plate o' beans at the Coffee Pot. All I want is a good wash. I been sweatin' like a horse, all day. (*He rises and goes up the steps.*)

MRS. FIORENTINO. My husband, too; he's sweating terrible.

MRS. JONES. Mine don't. There's some people that just naturally do, and then there's others that don't.

MAURRANT (*to* MRS. MAURRANT). Is anybody upstairs?

MRS. MAURRANT. No. Willie's off playing with the boys. I can't keep him home.

MAURRANT. What about Rose?

MRS. MAURRANT. I think maybe she's working overtime.

MAURRANT. I never heard o' nobody workin' nights in a real estate office .

MRS. MAURRANT. I thought maybe on account of the office being closed to-morrow — (*To the others.*) Mr. Jacobson, the head of the firm, died Tuesday, and tomorrow's the funeral, so I thought maybe—

MRS. JONES. Yeah. Leave it to the Jews not to lose a workin' day, without makin' up for it.

MAURRANT (*to* MRS. MAURRANT). She shouldn't be stayin' out nights without us knowin' where she is.

MRS. MAURRANT. She didn't say a word about not coming home.

MAURRANT. That's what I'm sayin', ain't it? It's a mother's place to know what her daughter's doin'.

MRS. FIORENTINO (*soothingly*). Things are different nowadays, Mr. Maurrant, from what they used to be.

MAURRANT. Not in my family, they're not goin' to be no different. Not so long as I got somethin' to say.

A GIRL'S VOICE (*off-stage*). Red Rover! Red Rover! Let Freddie come over!
(GEORGE JONES, *a short, rather plump, red-faced man, cigar in mouth, comes out of the house, as* MAURRANT *enters the vestibule.*)

JONES. Hello, Mr. Maurrant.

MAURRANT (*curtly*). 'Evenin'. (*He enters the house.* JONES *looks after him in surprise, for a moment.* MRS. MAURRANT *seats herself on the stoop.*)

JONES. Good evenin', ladies.

MRS. FIORENTINO *and* MRS. MAURRANT. Good evening, Mr. Jones.

JONES (*seating himself on the left balustrade*). What's the matter with your hubby, Mrs. Maurrant? Guess he's feelin' the heat, huh?

MRS. MAURRANT. He's been working till just now and I guess he's a little tired.

MRS. JONES. Men are all alike. They're all easy to get along with, so long as everythin's goin' the way they want it to. But once it don't—good night!

MRS. FIORENTINO. Yes, dot's true, Mrs. Jones.

JONES. Yeah, an' what about the women?

MRS. MAURRANT. I guess it's just the same with the women. I often think it's a shame that people don't get along better, together. People ought to be able to live together in peace and quiet, without making each other miserable.

MRS. JONES. The way I look at it, you get married for better or worse, an' if it turns out to be worse, why all you can do is make the best of it.

MRS. MAURRANT. I think the trouble is people don't make allowances. They don't realize that everybody wants a kind word, now and then. After all, we're all human, and we can't just go along by ourselves, all the time, without ever getting a kind word. (*While she is speaking,* STEVE SANKEY *appears at the right. He is in the early thirties, and is prematurely bald. He is rather flashily dressed, in a patently cheap, light-gray suit, and a straw hat, with a plaid band. As he appears,* MRS. JONES *and* MRS. FIORENTINO *exchange a swift, significant look.*)

SANKEY (*stopping at the right of the stoop and removing his hat*). Good evening, folks! Is it hot enough for you?

THE OTHERS. Good evening.

MRS. MAURRANT (*self-consciously*). Good evening, Mr. Sankey.
(*Throughout the scene, MRS. MAURRANT and SANKEY try vainly to avoid looking at each other.*)

SANKEY. I don't know when we've had a day like this. Hottest June fifteenth in forty-one years. It was up to ninety-four at three p. m.

JONES. Six dead in Chicago. An' no relief in sight, the evenin' paper says.
(*MAURRANT appears at the window of his apartment and stands there, looking out.*)

MRS. FIORENTINO. It's joost awful!

SANKEY. Well, it's good for the milk business. You know the old saying, it's an ill wind that blows nobody any good.

MRS. MAURRANT. Yes. You hardly get the milk in the morning, before it turns sour.

MRS. JONES. I'm just after pourin' half-a-bottle down the sink.
(*MAURRANT leaves the window.*)

MRS. FIORENTINO. You shouldn't throw it avay. You should make—what do you call it?—schmier-käs'.

SANKEY. Oh, I know what you mean—pot-cheese. My wife makes it, too, once in a while.

MRS. MAURRANT. Is your wife all right again, Mr. Sankey? You were telling me last time, she had a cold.
(*MRS. JONES and MRS. FIORENTINO exchange another look.*)

SANKEY. Was I? Oh, sure, sure. That was a couple of weeks ago. Yes, sure, she's all right again. That didn't amount to anything much.

MRS. JONES. You got a family, too, ain't you?

SANKEY. Yes. Yes, I have. Two little girls. Well, I got to be going along. (*He goes to the left of the stoop and stops again.*) I told my wife I'd go down to the drug-store and get her some nice cold ginger-ale. You want something to cool you off in this kind of weather.

MRS. JONES (*as SANKEY passes her*). If you ask me, all that gassy stuff don't do you a bit of good.

SANKEY. I guess you're right, at that. Still it cools you off. Well, good-night, folks. See you all again. (*He strolls off, at the left, with affected nonchalance; but when he is almost out of sight, he casts a swift look back at MRS. MAURRANT.*)
(*A dowdy WOMAN, wheeling a dilapidated baby carriage, appears at the left, and crosses the stage.*)

JONES. What's his name—Sankey?

MRS. JONES. Yeah—Mr. Sankey.

MRS. MAURRANT. He's the collector for the milk company.
(*AGNES CUSHING comes out of the house. She is a thin, dried-up woman, past fifty.*)

MISS CUSHING (*coming down the steps*). Good evening.

THE OTHERS. Good evening, Miss Cushing.

MRS. MAURRANT. How is your mother to-day, Miss Cushing?

MISS CUSHING (*pausing at the left of the stoop*). Why, she complains of the heat. But I'm afraid it's really her heart. She's seventy-two, you know. I'm just going down to the corner to get her a little ice-cream. (*As she goes off at the left, OLSEN, the janitor, a lanky Swede, struggles up the cellar steps with a large, covered, tin garbage-barrel. The others look around in annoyance, as he bangs the garbage-barrel upon the pavement.*)

OLSEN. Phew! Hot! (*He mops his face and neck with a dingy handkerchief, then lights his pipe and leans against the railing.*)

MRS. JONES (*significantly, as she crosses to the center of the stoop and sits*). Between you and I, I don't think her mother's got long for this world. Once the heart starts goin' back on you—!

MRS. FIORENTINO. It's too bad.

MRS. MAURRANT. Poor soul! She'll have nothing at all when her mother dies. She's just spent her whole life looking after her mother.

MRS. JONES. It's no more than her duty, is it?

MRS. FIORENTINO. You could not expect that she should neglect her mother.

A VOICE (*off-stage*). Char-lie!

MRS. MAURRANT. It's not a matter of neglecting. Only—it seems as if a person should get more out of life than just looking after somebody else.

MRS. JONES. Well, I hope to tell you, after all I've done for mine, I expect 'em to look after me, in my old age.

MRS. MAURRANT. I don't know. It seems to me you might just as well not live at all, as the way she does. (*Rising, with affected casualness.*) I don't know what's become of Willie. I think I'd better walk down to the corner and look for him. My husband don't like it if he stays out late. (*She goes off, at the left. They all watch her, in dead silence, until she is out of earshot. Then the storm breaks.*)

MRS. JONES (*rising excitedly*). Didja get that? Goin' to look for Willie! Can ya beat it?

MRS. FIORENTINO. It's joost terrible!

JONES. You think she's just goin' out lookin' for this guy Sankey?

MRS. JONES (*scornfully*). Ain't men the limit? What do you think he came walkin' by here for? (*Mincingly.*) Just strolled by to get the wife a little ginger-ale. A fat lot he cares whether his wife has ginger-ale!

MRS. FIORENTINO. Two little girls he's got, too!

JONES. Yeah, that ain't right—a bird like that, wit' a wife an' two kids of his own.

MRS. FIORENTINO. The way he stands there and looks and looks at her!

MRS. JONES. An' what about the looks she was givin' him! (*Seating herself again.*) You'd think he was the Prince of Wales, instead of a milk-collector. And didja get the crack about not seein' him for two weeks?

MRS. FIORENTINO. And joost today he was upstairs, Mrs. Olsen says.
(OLSEN *approaches the stoop and removes his pipe from his mouth.*)

OLSEN (*pointing upwards*). Some day, her hoosban' is killing him. (*He replaces his pipe and goes back to his former position.*)

MRS. FIORENTINO. Dot would be terrible!

JONES. He's li'ble to, at that. You know, he's got a wicked look in his eye, dat baby has.

MRS. JONES. Well, it's no more than he deserves, the little rabbit—goin' around breakin' up people's homes. (*Mockingly.*) Good evenin', folks! Jes' like Whozis on the radio.

JONES. D'ya think Maurrant is wise to what's goin' on?

MRS. JONES. Well, if he ain't, there must be somethin' the matter with him. But you never can tell about men. They're as blind as bats. An' what I always say is, in a case like that, the husband or the wife is always the last one to find out.
(MISS CUSHING, *carrying a small paper bag, hurries on, at the left, in a state of great excitement.*)

MISS CUSHING (*breathlessly, as she comes up the left of the stoop*). Say, what do you think! I just saw them together—the two of them!

MRS. JONES (*rising excitedly*). What did I tell you?

MRS. FIORENTINO. Where did you see them, Miss Cushing?

MISS CUSHING. Why, right next door, in the entrance to the warehouse. They were standing right close together. And he had his hands up on her shoulders. It's awful, isn't it?

JONES. Looks to me like this thing is gettin' pretty serious.

MRS. JONES. You didn't notice if they was kissin' or anythin', did you?

MISS CUSHING. Well, to tell you the truth, Mrs. Jones, I was so ashamed for her, that I hardly looked at all.

JONES (*sotto voce, as the house door opens*). Look out! Maurrant's comin'.
(*A conspirators' silence falls upon them, as* MAURRANT, *pipe in mouth, comes out of the house.*)

MISS CUSHING (*tremulously*). Good evening, Mr. Maurrant.

MAURRANT (*on the top step*). 'Evenin'. (*To the others.*) What's become of me wife?

MRS. JONES. Why, she said she was goin' around the corner to look for Willie.

MAURRANT (*grunts*). Oh.

MRS. JONES. They need a lot of lookin' after, when they're that age.
(*A momentary silence.*)

MISS CUSHING. Well, I think I'd better get back to my mother. (*She goes up the steps.*)

MRS. JONES, MRS. FIORENTINO *and* JONES. Good night, Miss Cushing.

MISS CUSHING. Good night. (*As she passes* MAURRANT.) Good night, Mr. Maurrant.

MAURRANT. 'Night.
(*She looks at him swiftly, and goes into the vestibule.*)

A BOY'S VOICE (*off-stage*). Red Rover! Red Rover! Let Mary come over!
(*As* MISS CUSHING *enters the house,* SHIRLEY KAPLAN *appears at the ground-floor window, at the extreme right, with a glass of steaming tea in her hand. She is a dark, unattractive Jewess, past thirty. She wears a light house-dress.* KAPLAN *goes on reading.*)

SHIRLEY (*to the neighbors outside; she speaks with the faintest trace of accent*). Good evening.

THE OTHERS (*not very cordially*). Good evenin'.

SHIRLEY. It's been a terrible day, hasn't it?

JONES *and* MRS. JONES. Yeah.

SHIRLEY (*going to the other window*). Papa, here's your tea. Haven't you finished your paper yet? It makes it so hot, with the lights on.

KAPLAN (*lowering his newspaper*). Oll right! Oll right! Put it out! Put it out! There is anahoo, notting to read in de papers. Notting but deevorce, skendal, and moiders. (*He speaks with a strong accent, over-emphatically and with much gesticulation. He puts his paper away, removes his glasses, and starts to drink his tea.*)

SHIRLEY. There doesn't seem to be a breath of air, anywhere.
(*No one answers.* SHIRLEY *goes away from the window and puts out the lights.*)

MRS. JONES (*sotto voce*). You wouldn't think anybody would want to read that Hebrew writin', would ya? I don't see how they make head or tail of it, meself.

JONES. I guess if you learn it when you're a kid—

MRS. JONES (*suddenly*). Well, will you look at your hubby, Mrs. F.! He's sure got his hands full! (*She looks towards the left, greatly amused.*)
(SHIRLEY *reappears at the window at the extreme right, and seats herself on the sill.*)

MRS. FIORENTINO (*leaning far out*). Joost look at him! (*Calling.*) Lippo, be careful you don't drop any!

LIPPO (*off-stage*). 'Allo, Margherita!
(*They all watch in amusement, as* FILIPPO FIORENTINO, *a fat Italian, with thick black hair and moustache, comes on at the left. He is clutching a violin in his left arm and balancing five ice-cream cones in his right hand.*)

LIPPO (*shouting*). Who wantsa da ice-cream cone? Nice fresha ice-cream cone!

MRS. FIORENTINO. Lippo, you will drop them!

MRS. JONES (*going up to him*). Here, gimme your violin. (*She relieves him of the violin and he shifts two of the cones to his left hand.*)

LIPPO (*as* MRS. JONES *hands the violin to* MRS. FIORENTINO). T'ank you, Meeses Jones. 'Ere's for you a nica, fresha ice-cream cone.
(MRS. FIORENTINO *puts the violin on a chair behind her.*)

MRS. JONES (*taking a cone*). Why thank you very much, Mr. F.

LIPPO (*going up to the window*). Meeses Fiorentino, 'ere's for you a nica, fresha ice-cream cone.

MRS. FIORENTINO (*taking the cone*). It makes me too fat.

LIPPO. Ah, no! Five, ten poun' more, nobody can tell da deef! (*He laughs aloud at his own joke and crosses to the stoop.*)

MRS. JONES (*enjoying her cone*). Ain't he a sketch, though?

LIPPO. Meester Jones, you eata da cone, ha?

JONES. Why, yeah, I will at that. Thanks. Thanks.

LIPPO. Meester Maurrant?

MAURRANT. Naw; I got me pipe.

LIPPO. You lika better da pipe den da ice-cream? (*Crossing the stoop.*) Meesa Kaplan, nica, fresha cone, yes?

SHIRLEY. No, thanks. I really don't want any.

LIPPO. Meester Kaplan, yes?

KAPLAN (*waving his hand*). No, no. Tenks, tenks!

MRS. JONES (*to* JONES). You oughta pay Mr. F. for the cones.

JONES (*reluctantly reaching into his pocket*). Why, sure.

LIPPO (*excitedly*). Ah, no, no! I don' taka da mon'. I'm treata da whole crowd. I deedn' know was gona be such a biga crowd or I bringa doz'. (*Crossing to* OLSEN.) Meester Olsen, you lika da cone, ha?

OLSEN. Sure. Much oblige'. (*He takes the pipe from his mouth and stolidly licks the cone.*)

LIPPO (*seating himself on the stoop; with a long sigh of relaxation*). Aaah! (*He tastes the cone and smacking his lips, looks about for approval.*) Ees tasta good, ha?

JONES (*His mouth full*). You betcha!

MRS. JONES. It cools you off a little.

LIPPO. Sure. Dassa right. Cool you off. (*He pulls at his clothing and sits on the stoop.*) I'ma wat, wat—like I jus' come outa da bad-tub. Ees 'ota like hal in da Park. Two, t'ree t'ousan' people, everybody sweatin'—ees smal lika menageria.

(*While he is speaking,* ALICE SIMPSON, *a tall, spare spinster, appears at the right. She goes up the steps, enters the vestibule, and is about to push one of the buttons on the side wall.*)

MRS. JONES (*sotto voce*). She's from the Charities. (*Coming over to the stoop and calling into the vestibule.*) If you're lookin' for Mrs. Hildebrand, she ain't home yet.

MISS SIMPSON (*coming to the doorway*). Do you know when she'll be back?

MRS. JONES. Well, she oughta be here by now. She jus' went aroun' to the Livingston. That's the pitcher-theayter.

MISS SIMPSON (*outraged.*) You mean she's gone to a moving-picture show?

OLSEN (*calmly*). She's comin' now.

LIPPO (*rising to his feet and calling vehemently*). Mees Hil'brand! Hurry up! Hurry up! Ees a lady here. (*He motions violently to her to hurry.* LAURA HILDEBRAND *appears at the right, with her two children,* CHARLIE *and* MARY. *She is a small, rather young woman, with a manner of perpetual bewilderment. Both children are chewing gum, and* MARY *comes on skipping a rope and chanting: "Apple, peach, pear, plum, banana."* CHARLIE *carefully avoids all the cracks in the sidewalk.*)

MISS SIMPSON (*coming out on the steps*). Well, good evening, Mrs. Hildebrand!

MRS. HILDEBRAND (*flustered*). Good evening, Miss Simpson.

MISS SIMPSON. Where have you been?—to a moving-picture show?

MRS. HILDEBRAND. Yes ma'am.

MISS SIMPSON. And where did you get the money?

MRS. HILDEBRAND. It was only seventy-five cents.

MISS SIMPSON. Seventy-five cents is a lot, when you're being dispossessed and dependent upon charity. I suppose it came out of the money I gave you to buy groceries with.

MRS. HILDEBRAND. We always went, Thursday nights, to the pictures when my husband was home.

MISS SIMPSON. Yes, but your husband isn't home. And as far as anybody knows, he has no intention of coming home.

KAPLAN (*leaning forward out of his window*). Ees dis your conception of cherity?

SHIRLEY. Papa, why do you interfere?

MISS SIMPSON (*to* KAPLAN). You'll please be good enough to mind your own business.

KAPLAN. You should go home and read in your Bible de life of Christ.

MRS. JONES (*to* MRS. FIORENTINO). Will you listen to who's talkin' about Christ!

MISS SIMPSON (*turning her back on* KAPLAN *and speaking to* MRS. HILDEBRAND). You may as well understand right now that nobody's going to give you any money to spend on moving-picture shows.

LIPPO. Ah, wotsa da matter, lady? (*He thrusts his hand into his pocket and takes out a fistful of coins.*) 'Ere, you taka da mon', you go to da pitcha, ever' night. (*He forces the coins into* MRS. HILDEBRAND'S *hand.*) An' here's for da bambini. (*He gives each child a nickel.*)

MRS. FIORENTINO (*to* MRS. JONES). Dot's why we never have money.

MRS. HILDEBRAND (*bewildered*). I really oughtn't to take it.

LIPPO. Sure! Sure! I got plenta mon'.

MISS SIMPSON (*disgustedly*). We'd better go inside. I can't talk to you here, with all these people.

MRS. HILDEBRAND (*meekly*). Yes ma'am. (*She follows* MISS SIMPSON *into the house, her children clinging to her.*)

MRS. JONES. Wouldn't she give you a pain?

LIPPO. I tella you da whola troub'. She's a don' gotta nobody to sleepa wit'.
(*The men laugh.*)

MRS. JONES (*to* MRS. FIORENTINO). Ain't he the limit!

MRS. FIORENTINO (*greatly pleased*). Tt!

LIPPO. Somebody go sleepa wit' her, she's alla right, Meester Jones, 'ow 'bout you?
(SHIRLEY, *embarrassed, leaves the window.*)

JONES (*with a sheepish grin*). Naw, I guess not.

LIPPO. Wot'sa matter? You 'fraid you' wife, ha? Meester Maurrant, how 'bout you?
(MAURRANT *emits a short laugh.*)

MRS. FIORENTINO (*delighted*). Lippo, you're joost awful.

LIPPO (*enjoying himself hugely*). Alla ri'. Ahma gonna go myself! (*He laughs boisterously. The others laugh too.*)

MRS. JONES (*suddenly*). Here's your wife, now, Mr. Maurrant.
(*A sudden silence falls upon them all, as* MRS. MAURRANT *approaches at the left. A swift glance apprises her of* MAURRANT'S *presence.*)

LIPPO. 'Allo, Meeses Maurrant. Why you don' come to da concerto?

MRS. MAURRANT. Well, I was waiting for Rose, but she didn't get home. (*To* MAURRANT, *as she starts to go up the steps.*) Is she home yet, Frank?

MAURRANT. No, she ain't. Where you been all this while?

MRS. MAURRANT. Why, I've been out looking for Willie.

MAURRANT. I'll give him a good fannin', when I get hold of him.

MRS. MAURRANT. Ah, don't whip him, Frank, please don't. All boys are wild like that, when they're that age.

JONES. Sure! My boy Vincent was the same way. An' look at him, today—drivin' his own taxi an' makin' a good livin'.

LIPPO (*leaning on the balustrade*). Ees jussa same t'ing wit' me. W'en Ahm twelva year, I run away—I don' never see my parent again.

MAURRANT. That's all right about that. But it ain't gonna be that way in my family.

MRS. MAURRANT (*as* MISS SIMPSON *comes out of the house*). Look out, Frank. Let the lady pass.

MISS SIMPSON. Excuse me.
(*They make way for her, as she comes down the steps.* MRS. MAURRANT *seats herself on the stoop.*)

LIPPO. Meeses Hil'brand, she gotta de tougha luck, ha? Tomorra, dey gonna t'row 'er out in da street, ha?

MISS SIMPSON (*stopping at the right of the stoop and turning towards him*). Yes, they are. And if she has any place to sleep, it will only be because the Charities find her a place. And you'd be doing her a much more neighborly act, if you helped her to realize the value of money, instead of encouraging her to throw it away.

LIPPO (*with a deprecatory shrug*). Ah, lady, no! I give 'er coupla dollar, maka 'er feel good, maka me feel good—dat don' 'urt nobody.
(SHIRLEY *reappears at the window.*)

MISS SIMPSON. Yes it does. It's bad for her character.

KAPLAN (*throwing away his cigarette and laughing aloud*). Ha! You mek me leff!

MISS SIMPSON (*turning, angrily*). Nobody's asking your opinion.

KAPLAN. Dot's oll right. I'm taling you wit'out esking. You hoid maybe already dot poem:
"Organized cherity, measured and iced,
In der name of a kushus, stetistical Christ."

MISS SIMPSON (*fiercely*). All the same, you Jews are the first to run to the Charities. (*She strides angrily off at the right.* LIPPO, *affecting a mincing gait, pretends to follow her.*)

KAPLAN (*leaning out of the window*). Come back and I'll tal you somet'ing will maybe do good your kerecter.

MRS. FIORENTINO. Lippo!

MRS. JONES (*highly amused*). Look at him, will ya?

LIPPO (*laughing and waving his hand*). Gooda-bye, lady! (*He comes back to the stoop.*)

KAPLAN (*to the others*). Dey toin out in de street a mudder vit' two children, and dis female comes and preaches to her bourgeois morelity.

MRS. JONES (*to* MRS. FIORENTINO). He's shootin' off his face again.

SHIRLEY. Papa, it's time to go to bed!

KAPLAN (*irritably*). Lat me alone, Shoiley. (*Rising and addressing the others.*) Dees cherities are notting but anudder dewise for popperizing de verking-klesses. W'en de lendlords steal from de verkers a million dollars, dey give to de Cherities a t'ousand.

MAURRANT. Yeah? Well, who's puttin' her out on the street? What about the lan'lord here? He's a Jew, ain't he?

MRS. JONES. I'll say he's a Jew! Isaac Cohen!

KAPLAN. Jews oder not Jews—wot has dis got to do vit' de quastion? I'm not toking releegion, I'm toking economics. So long as de kepitalist klesses—

MAURRANT (*interrupting*). I'm talkin' about if you don't pay your rent, you gotta move.

MRS. MAURRANT. It doesn't seem right, though, to put a poor woman out of her home.

MRS. FIORENTINO. And for her husband to run away—dot vos not right either.

LIPPO. I betcha 'e's got 'nudder woman. He find a nice blonda chicken, 'e run away.

MRS. JONES. There ought to be a law against women goin' around, stealin' other women's husbands.

MRS. FIORENTINO. Yes, dot's right, Mrs. Jones.

MAURRANT. Well, what I'm sayin' is, it ain't the landlord's fault.

KAPLAN. Eet's de folt of our economic system. So long as de institution of priwate property exeests, de verkers vill be at de moicy of de property-owning klesses.

MAURRANT. That's a lot o' bushwa! I'm a woikin' man, see? I been payin' dues for twenty-two years in the Stage-Hands Union. If we're not gettin' what we want, we call a strike, see?—and then we get it.

LIPPO. Sure! Ees same wit' me. We gotta Musician Union. We getta pay for da rehears', we getta pay for da overtime—

SHIRLEY. That's all right when you belong to a strong union. But when a union is weak, like the Teachers' Union, it doesn't do you any good.

MRS. JONES (*to* MRS. FIORENTINO). Can y' imagine that?—teachers belongin' to a union!

KAPLAN (*impatiently*). Oll dese unions eccomplish notting wotever. Oll dis does not toch de fondamental problem. So long as de tuls of industry are in de hands of de ke*pit*alist klesses, ve vill hev exploitation and sloms and—

MAURRANT. T' hell wit' all dat hooey! I'm makin' a good livin' an' I'm not doin' any kickin'.

OLSEN (*removing his pipe from his mouth*). Ve got prosperity, dis country.

JONES. You said somethin'!

KAPLAN. Sure, for de reech is planty prosperity! Mister Morgan rides in his yacht and upstairs dey toin a voman vit' two children in de street.

MAURRANT. And if you was to elect a Socialist president tomorra, it would be the same thing.

MRS. FIORENTINO. Yes, dot's right, Mr. Maurrant.

JONES. You're right!

KAPLAN. Who's toking about electing presidents? Ve must put de tuls of industry in de hands of de vorking-klesses and dis ken be accomplished only by a sushal revolution!

MAURRANT. Yeah? Well, we don't want no revolutions in this country, see?
(*General chorus of assent.*)

MRS. JONES. I know all about that stuff—teachin' kids there ain't no Gawd an' that their gran'fathers was monkeys.

JONES (*rising, angrily*). Free love, like they got in Russia, huh?
(KAPLAN *makes a gesture of impatient disgust, and sinks back into his chair.*)

MAURRANT. There's too goddam many o' you Bolshevikis runnin' aroun' loose. If you don't like the way things is run here, why in hell don't you go back where you came from?

SHIRLEY. Everybody has a right to his own opinion, Mr. Maurrant.

MAURRANT. Not if they're against law and order, they ain't. We don't want no foreigners comin' in, tellin' us how to run things.

MRS. FIORENTINO. It's nothing wrong to be a foreigner. Many good people are foreigners.

LIPPO. Sure! Looka Eetalians. Looka Cristoforo Colombo! 'E'sa firs' man discov' America—'e's Eetalian, jussa like me.

MAURRANT. I'm not sayin' anythin' about that—

OLSEN (*removing his pipe*). Firs' man is Lief Ericson.

LIPPO (*excitedly, going towards* OLSEN). Wassa dat?

OLSEN. Firs' man is Lief Ericson.

LIPPO. No! No! Colombo! Cristoforo Colomb'—'e'sa firs' man discov' America—ever'body knowa dat! (*He looks about appealingly.*)

MRS. JONES. Why, sure, everybody knows that.

JONES. Every kid learns that in school.

SHIRLEY. Ericson was really the first discoverer—

LIPPO (*yelling*). No! Colomb'!

SHIRLEY. But Columbus was the first to open America to settlement.

LIPPO (*happily, as he goes back to the stoop*). Sure, dassa wot Ahm say—Colomb' is firs'.

OLSEN. Firs' man is Lief Ericson.
(LIPPO *taps his forehead, significantly.*)

LIPPO. Looka wot Eetalian do for America—'e build bridge, 'e build railroad, 'e build subway, 'e dig sewer. Wit'out Eetalian, ees no America.

JONES. Like I heard a feller sayin': the Eye-talians built New York, the Irish run it an' the Jews own it.
(*Laughter.*)

MRS. FIORENTINO (*convulsed*). Oh! Dot's funny!

JONES (*pleased with his success*). Yep; the Jews own it all right.

MAURRANT. Yeah, an' they're the ones that's doin' all the kickin'.

SHIRLEY. It's no disgrace to be a Jew, Mr. Maurrant.

MAURRANT. I'm not sayin' it is. All I'm sayin' is, what we need in this country is a little more respect for law an' order. Look at what's happenin' to people's homes, with all this divorce an' one thing an' another. Young girls goin' around smokin' cigarettes an' their skirts up around their necks. An' a lot o' long-haired guys talkin' about free love an' birth control an' breakin' up decent people's homes. I tell you it's time somethin' was done to put the fear o' God into people!

MRS. JONES. Good for you, Mr. Maurrant!

JONES. You're damn right.

MRS. FIORENTINO. Dot's right, Mr. Maurrant!

MRS. MAURRANT. Sometimes, I think maybe they're only trying to get something out of life.

MAURRANT. Get somethin', huh? Somethin' they oughtn't to have, is that it?

MRS. MAURRANT. No; I was only thinking—

MAURRANT. Yeah, you were only thinkin', huh?

KAPLAN (*rising to his feet again*). De femily is primerily an economic institution.

MRS. JONES (*to* MRS. FIORENTINO). He's in again.

KAPLAN. W'en priwate property is ebolished, de femily will no longer hev eny reason to exeest.

SHIRLEY. Can't you keep quiet, papa?

MAURRANT (*belligerently*). Yeah? Is that so? No reason to exist, huh? Well, it's gonna exist, see? Children respectin' their parents an' doin' what they're told, get me? An' husbands an' wives, lovin' an' honorin' each other, like they said they would, when they was spliced—an' any dirty sheeny that says different is li'ble to get his head busted open, see?

MRS. MAURRANT (*springing to her feet*). Frank!

SHIRLEY (*trying to restrain* KAPLAN). Papa!

KAPLAN. Oll right! I should argue vit' a low-kless gengster.

MAURRANT (*raging*). Who's a gangster? Why, you goddam—! (*He makes for the balustrade.*)

MRS. MAURRANT (*seizing his arm*). Frank!

JONES (*seizing the other arm*). Hey! Wait a minute! Wait a minute!

MAURRANT. Lemme go!

SHIRLEY (*interposing herself*). You should be ashamed to talk like that to an old man! (*She slams down the window.*)

MAURRANT. Yeah? (*To* MRS. MAURRANT *and* JONES.) All right, lemme go! I ain't gonna do nothin'.
(*They release him.* SHIRLEY *expostulates with* KAPLAN *and leads him away from the window.*)

MRS. JONES (*who has run over to the right of the stoop*). Maybe if somebody handed him one, he'd shut up with his talk for a while.

LIPPO. 'E talka lika dat een Eetaly, Mussolini's gonna geeve 'eem da castor-oil.

MRS. JONES (*laughing*). Yeah? Say, that's a funny idea! (*Still chuckling, she goes to the railing at the left of the stoop.*)

JONES. No kiddin', is that what they do?

MRS. FIORENTINO. Yes, dot's true. My husband read it to me in the Italian paper.

MRS. MAURRANT. Why must people always be hurting and injuring each other? Why can't they live together in peace?

MAURRANT (*mockingly*). Live in peace! You're always talkin' about livin' in peace!

MRS. MAURRANT. Well, it's true, Frank. Why can't people just as well be kind to each other?

MAURRANT. Then let 'im go live with his own kind.

JONES (*coming down the steps*). Yeah, that's what I say. (*As* MRS. JONES *laughs aloud.*) What's eatin' you?

MRS. JONES. I was just thinkin' about the castor-oil.
(MAURRANT *seats himself on the right balustrade.*)

LIPPO. Sure, 'esa funny fell', Mussolini. (*Doubling up in mock pain.*) 'E geeve 'em da pain in da belly, dey no can talk. (*Suddenly.*) Look! 'Eresa da boy. 'Esa walk along da street an' read da book. Datsa da whola troub': reada too much book.
(*While* LIPPO *is speaking,* SAMUEL KAPLAN *appears at the left. He is twenty-one, slender, with dark, unruly hair and a sensitive, mobile face. He is hatless, and his coat is slung over one shoulder. He walks along slowly, absorbed in a book. As he approaches the stoop,* SHIRLEY, *in a kimono, appears at the closed window, opens it, and is about to go away again, when she sees* SAM.)

SHIRLEY (*calling*). Sam!

SAM (*looking up*). Hello, Shirley.

SHIRLEY. Are you coming in?

SAM. No, not yet. It's too hot to go to bed.

SHIRLEY. Well, I'm tired. And papa's going to bed, too. So don't make a noise when you come in.

SAM. I won't.

SHIRLEY. Good night.

SAM. Good night.
(SHIRLEY *goes away from the window.*)

SAM (*to the others, as he seats himself on the curb to the right of the stoop*). Good evening!

SEVERAL. 'Evening.

LIPPO (*approaching* SAM). 'Ow you lika da concerto? I see you sittin' in da fronta seat.

SAM. I didn't like it. Why don't they play some real music, instead of all those Italian organ-grinder's tunes?

LIPPO (*excitedly*). Wotsa da matter? You don't lika da Verdi?

SAM. No, I don't. It's not music!

LIPPO. Wot you call music—da Tschaikov', ha? (*He hums derisively a few bars from the first movement of the Symphonie Pathetique.*)

SAM. Yes, Tschaikovsky—and Beethoven. Music that comes from the soul.

MRS. MAURRANT. The one I like is— (*She hums the opening bars of Mendelssohn's Spring Song.*)

LIPPO. Dotsa da Spring Song from da Mendelson.

MRS. MAURRANT. Yes! I love that. (*She goes on humming sotfly.*)

MRS. FIORENTINO. And the walzer von Johann Strauss. (*She hums the Wienerwald Waltz.*)

MRS. JONES. Well, gimme a good jazz band, every time.

LIPPO (*protestingly*). Ah no! Ees not music, da jazz. Ees breaka your ear. (*He imitates the discordant blaring of a saxophone.*)

JONES (*bored*). Well, I guess I'll be on me way.

MRS. JONES. Where are *you* goin'?

JONES. Just around to Callahan's to shoot a little pool. Are you comin' along, Mr. Maurrant?

MAURRANT. I'm gonna wait awhile.
(*A* MAN, *with a club-foot, appears at the right and crosses the stage.*)

MRS. JONES (*as* JONES *goes toward the right*). Don't be comin' home lit, at all hours o' the mornin'.

JONES (*over his shoulder*). Aw, lay off dat stuff! I'll be back in a half-an-hour. (*He goes off, at the right.*)

A VOICE (*off-stage*). Char-lie!

MRS. JONES. Him an' his pool! Tomorra he won't be fit to go to work, again.

SAM (*who has been awaiting a chance to interrupt*). When you hear Beethoven, it expresses the struggles and emotions of the human soul.

LIPPO (*waving him aside*). Ah, ees no good, da Beethoven. Ees alla time sad, sad. Ees wann maka you cry. I don' wanna cry, I wanna laugh. Eetalian music ees make you 'appy. Ees make you feel good. (*He sings several bars of Donna é mobile.*)

MRS. MAURRANT (*applauding*). Yes, I like that, too.

LIPPO. Ah, ees bew-tiful! Ees maka you feela fine. Ees maka you wanna dance. (*He executes several dance steps.*)

MRS. FIORENTINO (*rising*). Vait, Lippo, I vill give you music. (*She goes away from the window. The lights go on, in the Fiorentino apartment.*)

LIPPO (*calling after her*). Playa Puccini, Margherita! (*He hums an air from Madame Butterfly. Then as* MRS. FIORENTINO *begins to play the waltz from La Bohème on the piano.*) Ah! La Bohème! Bew-tiful! Who'sa gonna dance wit' me? Meeses Maurrant, 'ow 'bout you?

MRS. MAURRANT (*with an embarrassed laugh*). Well, I don't know. (*She looks timidly at* MAURRANT, *who gives no sign.*)

LIPPO. Ah, come on! Dansa wit' me! (*He takes her by the hand.*)

MRS. MAURRANT. Well, all right, I will.

LIPPO. Sure, we hava nica dance.
(*They begin to dance on the sidewalk.*)

LIPPO (*to* MAURRANT). Your wife ees dansa swell.

MRS. MAURRANT (*laughing*). Oh, go on, Mr. Fiorentino! But I always loved to dance!
(*They dance on.* SANKEY *appears, at the left, carrying a paper-bag, from which the neck of a ginger-ale bottle protrudes.* MAURRANT *sees him and rises.*)

MRS. JONES (*following* MAURRANT's *stare and seeing* SANKEY). Look out! You're blockin' traffic!

SANKEY (*stopping at the left of the stoop*). I see you're having a little dance.
(MRS. MAURRANT *sees him and stops dancing.* LIPPO *leans against the right balustrade, panting. The music goes on.*)

SANKEY. Say, go right ahead. Don't let me stop you.

MRS. MAURRANT. Oh, that's all right. I guess we've danced about enough. (*She goes up the steps, ill at ease.*)

SANKEY. It's a pretty hot night for dancing.

MRS. MAURRANT. Yes, it is.

SANKEY (*going towards the right*). Well, I got to be going along. Good night, folks.

THE OTHERS (*except* MAURRANT). Good night.

LIPPO (*as he seats himself at the left of the stoop*). Stoppa da music, Margherita!
(*The music stops.* SANKEY *goes off, at the right.* MRS. MAURRANT *goes quickly up the steps.*)

MAURRANT (*stopping her*). Who's that bird?

MRS. MAURRANT. Why, that's Mr. Sankey. He's the milk-collector.

MAURRANT. Oh, he is, is he? Well, what's he hangin' around here for?

MRS. MAURRANT. Well, he lives just down the block, somewhere.

MRS. JONES. He's just been down to the drug-store, gettin' some ginger-ale for his wife.

MAURRANT. Yeah? Well, what I want to know is, why ain't Rose home yet?

MRS. MAURRANT. I told you, Frank—

MAURRANT. I know all about what you told me. What I'm sayin' is, you oughta be lookin' after your kids, instead of doin' so much dancin'.

MRS. MAURRANT. Why, it's the first time I've danced, in I don't know when.

MAURRANT. That's all right, about that. But I want 'em home, instead o' battin' around the streets, hear me?
(*While he is speaking*, WILLIE *appears sobbing, at the left, his clothes torn and his face scratched. He is carrying his skates.*)

MRS. MAURRANT (*coming down the steps*). Why, Willie, what's the matter? (*Reproachfully, as* WILLIE *comes up to her, sniffling.*) Have you been fighting again?

WILLIE (*with a burst of indignation*). Well, dat big bum ain't gonna say dat to me. I'll knock da stuffin's out o' him, dat's what I'll do!

MAURRANT (*tensely, as he comes down the steps*). Who's been sayin' things to you?

WILLIE. Dat big bum, Joe Connolly, dat's who! (*Blubbering.*) I'll knock his goddam eye out, next time!

MRS. MAURRANT. Willie!

MAURRANT (*seizing* WILLIE'S *arm*). Shut up your swearin', do you hear?—or I'll give you somethin' to bawl for. What did he say to you, huh? What did he say to you?

WILLIE (*struggling*). Ow! Leggo my arm!

MRS. MAURRANT. What difference does it make what a little street-loafer like that says?

MAURRANT. Nobody's askin' you! (*To* WILLIE.) What did he say? (*He and* MRS. MAURRANT *exchange a swift involuntary look; then* MAURRANT *releases the boy.*) G'wan up to bed now, an' don't let me

hear no more out o' you. (*Raising his hand.*) G'wan now. Beat it!
(WILLIE *ducks past* MAURRANT *and hurries up the steps and into the vestibule.*)

MRS. MAURRANT. Wait, Willie, I'll go with you. (*She goes up the steps, then stops and turns.*) Are you coming up, Frank?

MAURRANT. No I ain't. I'm goin' around to Callahan's for a drink, an' if Rose ain't home, when I get back, there's gonna be trouble. (*Without another glance or word, he goes off at the right.* MRS. MAURRANT *looks after him for a moment, with a troubled expression.*)

MRS. MAURRANT (*entering the vestibule*). Well, good night, all.

THE OTHERS. Good night.
(SAM *rises. As* MRS. MAURRANT *and* WILLIE *enter the house,* MRS. FIORENTINO *reappears at the window.*)

MRS. FIORENTINO. Lippo! (*She sees that something is wrong.*)

MRS. JONES. Say, you missed it all!
(SAM, *about to go up the steps, stops at the right of the stoop.*)

MRS. FIORENTINO (*eagerly*). Vat?

MRS. JONES (*volubly*). Well, they was dancin', see? An' who should come along but Sankey!

MRS. FIORENTINO. Tt!
(*A light appears in the Maurrant apartment.*)

MRS. JONES. Well, there was the three o' them—Mr. Maurrant lookin' at Sankey as if he was ready to kill him, an' Mrs. Maurrant as white as a sheet, an' Sankey, as innocent as the babe unborn.

MRS. FIORENTINO. Did he say something?

MRS. JONES. No, not till after Sankey was gone. Then he wanted to know who he was an' what he was doin' here. "He's the milk-collector," she says.

MRS. FIORENTINO. It's joost awful.

MRS. JONES. Oh, an' then Willie comes home.

LIPPO. Da boy tella 'eem 'is mamma ees a whore an' Weelie leeck 'im.

MRS. JONES. Well, an' what else is she?

SAM (*unable longer to restrain himself*). Stop it! Stop it! Can't you let her alone? Have you no hearts? Why do you tear her to pieces, like a pack of wolves? It's cruel, cruel! (*He chokes back a sob, then dashes abruptly into the house.*)

LIPPO (*rising to his feet and yelling after him*). Wotsa matter you?

MRS. JONES. Well, listen to him, will you! He must be goin' off his nut, too.

LIPPO. 'Esa reada too mucha book. Ees bad for you.

MRS. FIORENTINO. I think he is loving the girl.

MRS. JONES. Yeah? Well, that's all the Maurrants need is to have their daughter get hooked up wit' a Jew. It's a fine house to be livin' in, ain't it, between the Maurrants upstairs, an' that bunch o' crazy Jews down here.
(*A GIRL appears at the left, glancing apprehensively, over her shoulder, at a MAN who is walking down the street behind her. They cross the stage and go off, at the right.*)

MRS. JONES (*as MRS. OLSEN comes up the cellar steps and over to the stoop*). Well, good night.

MRS. FIORENTINO. Good night, Mrs. Jones.

LIPPO. Goo' night, Meeses Jones.

MRS. JONES. Wait a minute, Mrs. Olsen. I'll go with you.
(*MRS. JONES and MRS. OLSEN enter the house. OLSEN yawns mightily, knocks the ashes from his pipe, and goes down the cellar steps. WILLIE MAURRANT leans out of the window and spits into the areaway. Then he leaves the window and turns out the light. A POLICEMAN appears, at the right, and strolls across the stage.*)

LIPPO (*who has gone up the steps*). Margherita, eef I ever ketcha you sleepin' wit' da meelkaman, Ahm gonna breaka your neck.

MRS. FIORENTINO (*yawning*). Stop your foolishness, Lippo, and come to bed!
(*LIPPO laughs and enters the house. MRS. FIORENTINO takes the pillow off the window-sill, closes the window, and starts to pull down the shade. ROSE MAURRANT and HARRY EASTER appear at the left. ROSE is a pretty girl of twenty, cheaply but rather tastefully dressed. EASTER is about thirty-five, good-looking, and obviously prosperous.*)

MRS. FIORENTINO. Good evening, Miss Maurrant.

ROSE (*as they pass the window*). Oh, good evening, Mrs. Fiorentino.
(*ROSE and EASTER cross to the stoop. MRS. FIORENTINO looks at them a moment, then pulls down the shade and turns out the lights.*)

ROSE (*stopping at the foot of the steps*). Well, this is where I live, Mr. Easter. (*She extends her hand.*) I've had a lovely time.

EASTER (*taking her hand*). Why, you're not going to leave me like this, are you? I've hardly had a chance to talk to you.

ROSE (*laughing*). We've been doing nothing but talking since six o'clock. (*She tries gently to extricate her hand.*)

EASTER (*still holding it*). No, we haven't. We've been eating and dancing. And now, just when I want to talk to you— (*He puts his other arm around her.*) Rose—

ROSE (*rather nervously*). Please don't, Mr. Easter. Please let go. I think there's somebody coming. (*She frees herself, as the house-door opens and MRS. OLSEN appears in the vestibule. They stand in silence, as MRS. OLSEN puts the door off the latch, tries it to see that it is locked, dims the light in the vestibule and comes out on the stoop.*)

MRS. OLSEN (*as she comes down the steps*). Good evening, Miss Maurrant. (*She darts a swift look at EASTER and crosses to the cellar steps.*)

ROSE. Good evening, Mrs. Olsen. How's the baby?

MRS. OLSEN. She vas cryin' all the time. I tank she vas gettin' new teet'.

ROSE. Oh, the poor little thing! What a shame!

MRS. OLSEN (*as she goes down the steps*). Yes, ma'am. Goot night, Miss Maurrant.

ROSE. Good night, Mrs. Olsen. (*To* EASTER.) She's got the cutest little baby you ever saw.

EASTER (*rather peevishly*). Yeah? That's great. (*Taking* ROSE's *hand again*.) Rose, listen—

ROSE. I've really got to go upstairs now, Mr. Easter. It's awfully late.

EASTER. Well, can't I come up with you, for a minute?

ROSE (*positively*). No, of course not!

EASTER. Why not?

ROSE. Why, we'd wake everybody up. Anyhow, my father wouldn't like it.

EASTER. Aren't you old enough to do what you like?

ROSE. It's not that. Only I think when you're living with people, there's no use doing things you know they don't like. (*Embarrassed.*) Anyhow, there's only the front room and my little brother sleeps there. So good night, Mr. Easter.

EASTER (*taking both her hands*). Rose— I'm crazy about you.

ROSE. Please let me go, now.

EASTER. Kiss me good-night.

ROSE. No.

EASTER. Why not, hm?

ROSE. I don't want to.

EASTER. Just one kiss.

ROSE. No.

EASTER. Yes! (*He takes her in his arms and kisses her.* ROSE *frees herself and goes to the right of the stoop.*)

ROSE (*her bosom heaving*). It wasn't nice of you to do that.

EASTER (*going over to her*). Why not? Didn't you like it? Hm?

ROSE. Oh, it's not that.

EASTER. Then what is it, hm?

ROSE (*turning and facing him*). You know very well what it is. You've got a wife, haven't you?

EASTER. What of it? I tell you I'm clean off my nut about you.

ROSE (*nervously, as the house-door opens*). Look out! Somebody's coming.
(EASTER *goes to the other side of the stoop and they fall into a self-conscious silence, as* MRS. JONES *comes out of the house, leading an ill-conditioned dog.*)

MRS. JONES (*as she comes down the steps*). Oh, good evenin'. (*She stares at* EASTER, *then goes towards the right.*)

ROSE. Good evening, Mrs. Jones. It's been a terrible day, hasn't it.

MRS. JONES. Yeah. Awful. (*Stopping.*) I think your father's been kinda worried about you.

ROSE. Oh, has he?

MRS. JONES. Yeah. Well, I gotta give Queenie her exercise. Good night. (*She stares at* EASTER *again, then goes off at right.*)

ROSE. Good night, Mrs. Jones. (*To* EASTER.) I'll soon have all the neighbors talking about me.

EASTER (*going over to her again*). What can they say, hm?—that they saw you saying good-night to somebody on the front door-step?

ROSE. They can say worse than that—and what's more, they will, too.

EASTER. Well, why not snap out of it all?

ROSE. Out of what?

EASTER (*indicating the house*). This! The whole business. Living in a dirty old tenement like this; working all day in a real-estate office, for a measly twenty-five a week. You're not going to try to tell me you like living this way, are you?

ROSE. No, I can't say that I like it, especially. But maybe it won't always be this way. Anyhow, I guess I'm not so much better than anybody else.

EASTER (*taking her hand*). Do you know what's the matter with you? You're not wise to yourself. Why, you've got just about everything, you have. You've got looks and personality and a bean on your shoulders—there's nothing you haven't got. You've got It, I tell you.

ROSE. You shouldn't keep looking at me, all the time, at the office. The other girls are beginning to pass hints about it.

EASTER (*releasing her hand, genuinely perturbed*). Is that a fact? You see, that shows you! I never even knew I was looking at you. I guess I just can't keep my eyes off you. Well, we've got to do something about it.

ROSE (*nervously snapping the clasp of her hand-bag*). I guess the only thing for me to do is to look for another job.

EASTER. Yes, that's what I've been thinking, too. (*As she is about to demur.*) Wait a minute, honey! I've been doing a little thinking and I've got it all doped out. The first thing you do is throw up your job, see?

ROSE. But—

EASTER. Then you find yourself a nice, cozy little apartment somewhere. (*As she is about to interrupt again.*) Just a minute, now! Then you get yourself a job on the stage.

ROSE. How could I get a job on the stage?

EASTER. Why, as easy as walking around the block. I've got three or four friends in the show-business. Ever hear of Harry Porkins?

ROSE. No.

EASTER. Well, he's the boy that put on Mademoiselle Marie last year. He's an old pal of mine, and all I'd have to say to him is: (*putting his arm around her shoulder*) "Harry, here's a little girl I'm interested in," and he'd sign you up in a minute.

ROSE. I don't think I'd be any good on the stage.

EASTER. Why, what are you talking about, sweetheart? There's a dozen girls, right now, with their names up in electric lights, that haven't got half your stuff. All you got to do is go about it in the right way—put up a little front, see? Why, half the game is nothing but bluff. Get yourself a classy little apartment, and fill it up with trick furniture, see? Then you doll yourself up in a flock of Paris clothes and you throw a couple or three parties and you're all set. (*Taking her arm.*) Wouldn't you *like* to be on Broadway?

ROSE. I don't believe I ever could be.

EASTER. Isn't it worth trying? What have you got here, hm? This is no kind of a racket for a girl like you. (*Taking her hand.*) You do like me a little, don't you?

ROSE. I don't know if I do or not.

EASTER. Why, sure you do. And once you get to know me better, you'd like me even more. I'm no Valentino, but I'm not a bad scout. Why, think of all the good times we could have together—you with a little apartment and all. And maybe we could get us a little car—

ROSE. And what about your wife?

EASTER (*letting go her hand*). The way I figure it is, she doesn't have to know anything about it. She stays up there in Bronxville, and there are lots of times when business keeps me in New York. Then, in the Summer, she goes to the mountains. Matter of fact, she's going next week and won't be back until September.

ROSE (*shaking her head and going towards the stoop*). I don't think it's the way I'd want things to be.

EASTER. Why, there's nothing really wrong about it.

ROSE. Maybe there isn't. But it's just the way I feel about it, I guess.

EASTER. Why, you'd get over that in no time. There's lots of girls—

ROSE. Yes, I know there are. But you've been telling me all along I'm different.

EASTER. Sure, you're different. You're in a class by yourself. Why, sweetheart— (*He tries to take her in his arms.*)

ROSE (*pushing him away*). No. And you mustn't call me sweetheart.

EASTER. Why not?

ROSE. Because I'm not your sweetheart.

EASTER. I want you to be—
(*A sudden yell of pain is heard from upstairs. They both look up, greatly startled.*)

EASTER. My God, what's that—a murder?

ROSE. It must be poor Mrs. Buchanan. She's expecting a baby.

EASTER. Why does she yell like that? God, I thought somebody was being killed.

ROSE. The poor thing! (*With sudden impatience, she starts up the steps.*) I've got to go, now. Good night.

EASTER (*taking her hand*). But, Rose—

ROSE (*freeing her hand quickly*). No, I've got to go. (*Suddenly.*) Look, there's my father. There'll only be an argument, if he sees you.

EASTER. All right, I'll go. (*He goes towards the left, as* MAURRANT *appears at the right.*)

ROSE (*going up to the top step*). Good night.

EASTER. Good night. (*He goes off, at the left.* ROSE *begins searching in her hand-bag for her latch-key.*)

ROSE (*as* MAURRANT *approaches*). Hello, pop.

MAURRANT (*stopping at the foot of the steps*). Who was that you was talkin' to?

ROSE. That's Mr. Easter. He's the manager of the office.

MAURRANT. What's he doin' here? You been out wit' him?

ROSE. Yes, he took me out to dinner.

MAURRANT. Oh, he did, huh?

ROSE. Yes, I had to stay late to get out some letters. You see, pop, the office is closed tomorrow, on account of Mr. Jacobson's funeral—

MAURRANT. Yeah, I know all about that. This is a hell of a time to be gettin' home from dinner.

ROSE. Well, we danced afterwards.

MAURRANT. Oh, you danced, huh? With a little pettin' on the side, is that it?

ROSE (*rather angrily, as she seats herself on the left balustrade*). I don't see why you can never talk to me in a nice way.

MAURRANT. So you're startin' to go on pettin' parties, are you?

ROSE. Who said I was on a petting-party?

MAURRANT. I suppose he didn't kiss you or nothin', huh?

ROSE. No, he didn't! And if he did—

MAURRANT. It's your own business, is that it? (*Going up the steps.*) Well, I'm gonna make it my business, see? Is this bird married? (ROSE *does not answer.*) I t'ought so! They're all alike, them guys—all after the one thing. Well, get this straight. No married men ain't gonna come nosin' around my family, get me?

ROSE (*rising agitatedly, as the house-door opens*). Be quiet, pop! There's somebody coming.

MAURRANT. I don't care!
(BUCHANAN *hurries out of the house. He is a small and pasty young man—a typical, "white-collar slave." He has hastily put on his coat and trousers over his pajamas and his bare feet are in slippers.*)

BUCHANAN (*as he comes down the steps*). I think the baby's coming!

ROSE (*solicitously*). Can I do anything, Mr. Buchanan?

BUCHANAN (*as he hurries toward the left*). No, I'm just going to phone for the doctor.

ROSE (*coming down the steps*). Let me do it, and you go back to your wife.

BUCHANAN. Well, if you wouldn't mind. It's Doctor John Wilson. (*Handing her a slip of paper.*) Here's his number. And the other number is her sister, Mrs. Thomas. And here's two nickels. Tell them both to come right away. She's got terrible pains. (*Another scream from upstairs.*) Listen to her! I better go back. (*He dashes up the steps and into the house.*)

ROSE. Oh, the poor woman! Pop, tell ma to go up to her. Hurry!

MAURRANT. Aw, all right.
(*He follows* BUCHANAN *into the house.* ROSE *hurries off at the left, just as* MAE JONES *and* DICK MCGANN *appear.* MAE *is a vulgar shop-girl of twenty-one;* DICK, *a vacuous youth of about the same age.* MAE *is wearing* DICK'S *straw hat and they are both quite drunk.*)

MAE (*to* ROSE). Hello, Rose. What's your hurry?

ROSE (*without stopping*). It's Mrs. Buchanan. I've got to phone to the doctor. (*She hurries off.*)

DICK (*as they approach the stoop*). Say, who's your little friend?

MAE. Oh, that's Rose Maurrant. She lives in the house.

DICK. She's kinda cute, ain't she?

MAE (*seating herself on the stoop*). Say, accordin' to you, anythin' in a skirt is kinda cute—providin' the skirt is short enough.

DICK. Yeah, but they ain't any of 'em as cute as you, Mae.

MAE (*yawning and scratching her leg*). Yeah?

DICK. Honest, I mean it. How 'bout a little kiss? (*He puts his arms about her and plants a long kiss upon her lips. She submits, with an air of intense boredom.*)

DICK (*removing his lips*). Say, you might show a little en-thoo-siasm.

MAE (*rouging her lips*). Say, you seem to think I oughta hang out a flag, every time some bozo decides to wipe off his mouth on me.

DICK. De trouble wit' you is you need another little snifter. (*He reaches for his flask.*)

MAE. Nope! I can't swaller any more o' that rotten gin o' yours.

DICK. Why, it ain't so worse. I don't mind it no more since I had that brass linin' put in me stomach. Well, happy days! (*He takes a long drink.*)

MAE (*rising indignantly*). Hey, for God's sake, what are you doin'—emptyin' the flask?

DICK (*removing the flask from his lips*). I t'ought you didn't want none.

MAE. Can't you take a joke? (*She snatches the flask from him and drains it, kicking out at* DICK, *to prevent his taking it from her.*)

DICK (*snatching the empty flask*). Say, you wanna watch your step, baby, or you're li'ble to go right up in a puff o' smoke.

MAE (*whistling*). Phew! Boy! I feel like a t'ree alarm fire! Say, what de hell do dey make dat stuff out of?

DICK. T'ree parts dynamite an' one part army-mule. Dey use it for blastin' out West.

MAE (*bursting raucously into a jazz tune*). Da-da-da-da-dee! Da-da-da-da-dee! (*She executes some dance steps.*)

DICK. Say, shut up, will ya? You'll be wakin' the whole neighborhood.

MAE (*boisterously*). What the hell do I care? Da-da-da-da-dee! Da-da-da-da-dee! (*Suddenly amorous, as she turns an unsteady pirouette.*) Kiss me, kid!

DICK. I'll say!
(*They lock in a long embrace.* SAM, *coatless, his shirt-collar open, appears at the window, watches the pair for a moment, and then turns away, obviously disgusted. They do not see him.*)

DICK (*taking* MAE'S *arm*). Come on!

MAE. Wait a minute! Where y' goin'?

DICK. Come on, I'm tellin' ya! Fred Hennessey gimme de key to his apartment. Dere won't be nobody dere.

MAE (*protesting feebly*). I oughta go home. (*Her hand to her head.*) Oh, baby! Say, nail down dat sidewalk, will ya?

DICK. Come on!
(ROSE *appears, at the left.*)

MAE. Sweet papa! (*She kisses DICK noisily; then bursts into song again.*) Da-da-da-da-dee! Da-da-da-da-dee! (*As they pass ROSE.*) Hello, Rose. How's de milkman?

DICK (*raising his hat with drunken politeness*). Goo' night, sweetheart.
(*They go off, at the left,* MAE's *snatches of song dying away in the distance.* ROSE *stands still, for a moment, choking back her mortification.*)

BUCHANAN's VOICE. Miss Maurrant, did you get them?

ROSE (*looking up*). Why yes, I did. The doctor will be here right away. And Mrs. Thomas said it would take her about an hour.
(VINCENT JONES *appears at the right and stops near the stoop. He is a typical New York taxicab driver, in a cap.* ROSE *does not see him.*)

BUCHANAN's VOICE. She's got terrible pains. Your mother's up here, with her. (MRS. BUCHANAN *is heard calling faintly.*) I think she's calling me.
(ROSE *goes towards the stoop and sees* VINCENT.)

VINCENT. Hello, Rosie.

ROSE. Good evening. (*She tries to pass, but he blocks her way.*)

VINCENT. What's your hurry?

ROSE. It's late.

VINCENT. You don' wanna go to bed, yet. Come on, I'll take you for a ride in me hack. (*He puts his arm about her.*)

ROSE. Please let me pass.
(SAM *appears at the window. They do not see him.*)

VINCENT (*enjoying* ROSE's *struggle to escape*). You got a lot o' stren'th, ain't you? Say, do you know, you're gettin' fat? (*He passes one hand over her body.*)

ROSE. Let me go, you big tough.

SAM (*simultaneously*). Take your hands off her!
(*He climbs quickly out of the window and onto the stoop.* VINCENT, *surprised, releases* ROSE *and steps to the sidewalk.* ROSE *goes up the steps.* SAM, *trembling with excitement and fear, stands on the top step.* VINCENT *glowers up at him.*)

VINCENT. Well, look who's here! (*Mockingly.*) Haster gesehn de fish in de Bowery? (*Menacingly.*) What de hell do you want?

SAM (*chokingly*). You keep your hands off her!

VINCENT. Yeah? (*Sawing the air with his hands.*) Oi, Jakie! (*He suddenly lunges forward, seizes* SAM's *arm, pulls him violently by the right hand down the steps and swings him about, so that they stand face to face, to the left of the stoop.* ROSE *comes down between them.*) Now what o' ya got t' say?

ROSE. Let him alone!

SAM (*inarticulately*). If you touch her again—

VINCENT (*mockingly*). If I touch her again—! (*Savagely.*) Aw, shut up, you little kike bastard! (*He brushes* ROSE *aside and putting his open hand against* SAM's *face, sends him sprawling to the pavement.*)

ROSE (*her fists clenched*). You big coward.

VINCENT (*standing over* SAM). Get up, why don't you?

ROSE (*crossing to* SAM). If you hit him again, I'll call my father.

VINCENT (*as* MRS. JONES *and the dog appear at the right*). Gee, don't frighten me like dat. I got a weak heart. (*He is sobered, nevertheless.* SAM *picks himself up. As* MRS. JONES *approaches*). Hello, ma.

MRS. JONES (*with maternal pride*). Hello, Vincent. What's goin' on here?

VINCENT. Oh, jus' a little friendly argument. Ikey Finkelstein don't like me to say good evenin' to his girl friend.

ROSE. You'd better keep your hands to yourself, hereafter.

VINCENT. Is dat so? Who said so, huh?

MRS. JONES. Come on, Vincent. Come on upstairs. I saved some stew for you.

VINCENT. All right, I'm comin'. (*To* ROSE.) Good night, dearie. (*He makes a feint at* SAM, *who starts back in terror.* VINCENT *laughs.*)

MRS. JONES. Aw, let 'im alone, Vincent.

VINCENT (*as he goes up the steps*). Who's touchin' him? A little cockroach like dat, ain't woit' my time. (*To* ROSE.) Some sheik you picked out for yourself! (*He enters the vestibule and opens the door with his latchkey.*)

MRS. JONES (*going up the steps*). You seem to have plenty of admirers, Miss Maurrant. (*Pausing on the top step.*) But I guess you come by it natural.
(ROSE *does not reply.* MRS. JONES *follows* VINCENT *into the house.* ROSE *averts her head to keep back the tears.* SAM, *stands facing the house, his whole body quivering with emotion. Suddenly he raises his arms, his fists clenched.*)

SAM (*hysterically, as he rushes to the foot of the stoop*). The dirty bum! I'll kill him!

ROSE (*turning and going to him*). It's all right, Sam. Never mind.

SAM (*sobbing*). I'll kill him! I'll kill him! (*He throws himself on the stoop and, burying his head in his arms, sobs hysterically.* ROSE *sits beside him and puts her arm about him.*)

ROSE. It's all right, Sam. Everything's all right. Why should you pay any attention to a big tough like that? (SAM *does not answer.* ROSE *caresses his hair and he grows calmer.*) He's nothing but a loafer, you know that. What do you care what he says?

SAM (*without raising his head*). I'm a coward.

ROSE. Why no, you're not, Sam.

SAM. Yes, I am. I'm a coward.

ROSE. Why, he's not worth your little finger, Sam. You wait and see. Ten years from now, he'll still be driving a taxi and you—why, you'll be so far above him, you won't even remember he's alive.

SAM. I'll never be anything.

ROSE. Why, don't talk like that, Sam. A boy with your brains and ability. Graduating from college with honors and all that! Why, if I were half as smart as you, I'd be just so proud of myself!

SAM. What's the good of having brains, if nobody ever looks at you—if nobody knows you exist?

ROSE (*gently*). I know you exist, Sam.

SAM. It wouldn't take much to make you forget me.

ROSE. I'm not so sure about that. Why do you say that, Sam?

SAM. Because I know. It's different with you. You have beauty—people look at you —you have a place in the world—

ROSE. I don't know. It's not always so easy, being a girl—I often wish I were a man. It seems to me that when you're a man, it's so much easier to sort of—be yourself, to kind of be the way you feel. But when you're a girl, it's different. It doesn't seem to matter what you are, or what you're thinking or feeling—all that men seem to care about is just the one thing. And when you're sort of trying to find out, just where you're at, it makes it hard. Do you see what I mean? (*Hesitantly.*) Sam, there's something I want to ask you— (*She stops.*)

SAM (*turning to her*). What is it, Rose?

ROSE. I wouldn't dream of asking anybody but you. (*With a great effort.*) Sam, do you think it's true—what they're saying about my mother?
(SAM *averts his head, without answering.*)

ROSE (*wretchedly*). I guess it is, isn't it?

SAM (*agitatedly*). They were talking here, before—I couldn't stand it any more! (*He clasps his head and, springing to his feet, goes to the right of the stoop.*) Oh, God, why do we go on living in this sewer?

ROSE (*appealingly*). What can I do, Sam? (SAM *makes a helpless gesture.*) You see, my father means well enough, and all that, but he's always been sort of strict and—I don't know—sort of making you freeze up, when you really wanted to be nice and loving. That's the whole trouble, I guess; my mother never had anybody to really love her. She's sort of gay and happy-like —you know, she likes having a good time and all that. But my father is different. Only—the way things are now—everybody talking and making remarks, all the neighbors spying and whispering—it sort of makes me feel— (*She shudders.*) I don't know—!

SAM (*coming over to her again*). I wish I could help you, Rose.

ROSE. You do help me, Sam—just by being nice and sympathetic and talking things over with me. There's so few people you can really talk to, do you know what I mean? Sometimes, I get the feeling that I'm all alone in the world and that— (*A scream of pain from* MRS. BUCHANAN.)

ROSE (*springing to her feet*). Oh, just listen to her!

SAM. Oh, God!

ROSE. The poor thing! She must be having terrible pains.

SAM. That's all there is in life—nothing but pain. From before we're born, until we die! Everywhere you look, oppression and cruelty! If it doesn't come from Nature, it comes from humanity—humanity trampling on itself and tearing at its own throat. The whole world is nothing but a bloodstained arena, filled with misery and suffering. It's too high a price to pay for life —life isn't worth it! (*He seats himself despairingly on the stoop.*)

ROSE (*putting her hand on his shoulder*). Oh, I don't know, Sam. I feel blue and discouraged, sometimes, too. And I get a sort of feeling of, oh, what's the use. Like last night. I hardly slept all night, on account of the heat and on account of thinking about—well, all sorts of things. And this morning, when I got up, I felt so miserable. Well, all of a sudden, I decided I'd walk to the office. And when I got to the Park, everything looked so green and fresh, that I got a kind of feeling of, well, maybe it's not so bad, after all. And then, what do you think?—all of a sudden, I saw a big lilac-bush, with some flowers still on it. It made me think about the poem you said for me—remember?—the one about the lilacs.

SAM (*quoting*).
"When lilacs last in the dooryard bloom'd
And the great star early droop'd in the
    western sky in the night,
I mourn'd and yet shall mourn, with ever-
    returning Spring."
(*He repeats the last line.*)
I mourn'd and yet shall mourn, with ever-
    returning Spring? Yes!

ROSE. No, not that part. I mean the part about the farmhouse. Say it for me, Sam. (*She sits at his feet.*)

SAM.
"In the door-yard, fronting an old farm-
    house, near the white-washed palings,
Stands the lilac-bush, tall-growing, with
    heart-shaped leaves of rich green,
With many a pointed blossom, rising del-
    icate, with the perfume strong I love,
With every leaf a miracle—and from this
    bush in the door-yard,
With delicate-color'd blossoms and heart-
    shaped leaves of rich green,
A sprig with its flower I break."

ROSE (*eagerly*). Yes, that's it! That's just what I felt like doing—breaking off a little bunch of the flowers. But then I thought, maybe a policeman or somebody would see me, and then I'd get into trouble; so I didn't.

BUCHANAN'S VOICE. Miss Maurrant! Miss Maurrant!
(SAM *and* ROSE *spring to their feet and look up.*)

ROSE. Yes?

BUCHANAN'S VOICE. Do you mind phoning to the doctor again? She's getting worse.

ROSE. Yes, sure I will. (*She starts to go.*) Wait! Maybe this is the doctor now.

BUCHANAN'S VOICE (*excitedly as* DR. WILSON *appears at the left*). Yes, that's him. Mrs. Maurrant! Tell her the doctor's here! Doctor, I guess you're none too soon.

DR. WILSON (*a seedy, middle-aged man in a crumpled Panama*). Plenty of time. Just don't get excited. (*He throws away his cigarette and enters the vestibule. The mechanical clicking of the door-latch is heard as* DR. WILSON *goes into the house.*)

ROSE. I hope she won't have to suffer much longer.

MAURRANT (*appearing at the window, in his under-shirt*). Rose!

ROSE (*rather startled*). Yes, pop, I'll be right up.

MAURRANT. Well, don't be makin' me call you again, d'ya hear?

ROSE. I'm coming right away.
(MAURRANT *leaves the window.*)

ROSE. I'd better go up now, Sam.

SAM. Do you have to go to bed, when you're told, like a child?

ROSE. I know, Sam, but there's so much wrangling goes on, all the time, as it is, what's the use of having any more? Good night, Sam. There was something I wanted to talk to you about, but it will have to be another time. (*She holds out her hand.* SAM *takes it and holds it in his.*)

SAM (*trembling and rising to his feet*). Rose, will you kiss me?

ROSE (*simply*). Why, of course I will, Sam. (*She offers him her lips. He clasps*

her in a fervent embrace, to which she submits but does not respond.)

ROSE (*freeing herself gently*). Don't be discouraged about things, Sam. You wait and see—you're going to do big things, some day. I've got lots of confidence in you.

SAM (*turning away his head*). I wonder if you really have, Rose?

ROSE. Why, of course, I have! And don't forget it! Good night. I hope it won't be too hot to sleep.

SAM. Good night, Rose. (*He watches her, as she opens the door with her latch-key and goes into the house. Then he goes to the stoop and seating himself, falls into a reverie. A* POLICEMAN *appears at the right and strolls across, but* SAM *is oblivious to him. In the distance, a home-comer sings drunkenly. A light appears, in the Maurrant hall-bedroom, and a moment later,* ROSE *comes to the window and leans out.*)

ROSE (*calling softly*). Hoo-hoo! Sam! (SAM *looks up, then rises.*) Good night, Sam. (*She wafts him a kiss.*)

SAM (*with deep feeling*). Good night, Rose dear.
(*She smiles at him. Then she pulls down the shade.* SAM *looks up for a moment, then resumes his seat. A scream from* MRS. BUCHANAN *makes him shudder. A deep rhythmic snoring emanates from the Fiorentino apartment. A steamboat whistle is heard. The snoring in the Fiorentino apartment continues.* SAM *raises his clenched hands to heaven. A distant clock begins to strike twelve.* SAM'S *arms and head drop forward.*)

The curtain falls slowly.

ACT TWO

Daybreak, the next morning. It is still quite dark and comparatively quiet. The rhythmic snoring in the Fiorentino apartment is still heard, and now and then, a distant "L" train or speeding automobile. A moment after the rise of the curtain, JONES *appears, at the right, on his way home from the speakeasy. He reels, slightly, but negotiates the steps and entrance-door, without too much difficulty. It grows lighter—and noisier. The street-light goes out. The* OLSEN *baby begins to cry. An alarm clock rings. A dog barks. A canary begins to sing. Voices are heard in the distance. They die out and other voices are heard. The house-door opens and* DR. WILSON *comes out, passing* JONES, *at the top of the stoop.* DR. WILSON *stands on the steps and yawns the yawn of an over-tired man. Then he lights a cigarette and goes towards the left.*

BUCHANAN'S VOICE. Doctor!

DR. WILSON (*stopping and looking up*). Well?

BUCHANAN'S VOICE. What if she does wake up?

DR. WILSON (*sharply*). She won't, I've told you! She's too exhausted. The best thing you can do is lie down and get some sleep yourself.
(*As he goes off at the left,* MAE *and* DICK *appear. They walk slowly and listlessly and far apart.*)

DICK (*as they reach the stoop*). Well, goo' night.

MAE (*with a yawn, as she finds her latch-key*). Goo' night. (*Going up the steps and looking towards the Fiorentino apartment*). Aw, shut up, you wop!

DICK (*his dignity wounded*). How 'bout kissin' me good-night?

MAE (*venomously, from the top step*). For God's sake, ain't you had enough kissin' for one night! (*She enters the vestibule and puts the key in the lock. The ringing of an alarm clock is heard.*)

DICK (*raising his voice*). Well, say, if that's the way you feel about it—

MAE. Aw, go to hell! (*She enters the house. The alarm clock has stopped ringing.*)

DICK. You dirty little tart! (*He stands, muttering to himself, for a moment, then goes off at the right, passing the* POLICE-MAN, *who looks at him, suspiciously. The sounds of a Swedish quarrel are heard from the janitor's apartment. The baby is still crying. As the* POLICEMAN *goes left, a* MILKMAN *appears, whistling and carrying a rack of full milk-bottles.*)

THE POLICEMAN. Hello, Louie.
(*The snoring in the Fiorentino apartment stops.*)

THE MILKMAN. Hello, Harry. Goin' to be another scorcher.

THE POLICEMAN. You said it. (*He goes off at the left.*)
(*The* MILKMAN *crosses to the cellar steps.* MAE *appears, at the hall bedroom window of the Jones apartment, and removes her dress over her head. The* MILKMAN, *about to go down the steps, sees her and stops to watch.* MAE, *about to slip out of her step-in, sees him, throws him an angry look and pulls down the shade. The* MILKMAN *grins and goes down the cellar steps.* CHARLIE HILDEBRAND *comes out of the house. He is chewing gum and as he comes out to the top of the stoop, he scatters the wrappings of the stick of gum on the stoop. Then he jumps down the four steps of the stoop, in one jump, and goes off at the left, pulling the chewing-gum out in a long ribbon, and carefully avoiding all the cracks in the pavement. A* YOUNG WORKMAN, *carrying a kit of tools and a tin lunch-box, appears at the left, extinguishes the red light on the excavation, and opening the door, goes in. A* TRAMP *comes on at the right and shuffles across. He sees a cigar butt on the pavement, picks it up and pockets it, as he exits at the left.* ROSE, *in her nightgown, appears at the window, yawns slightly and disappears. It is daylight now. The baby stops crying.* MRS. OLSEN *comes up the cellar steps. She goes up the stoop, turns out the light in the vestibule, and takes the door off the latch. The* MILKMAN *comes up the cellar steps, his tray laden with empty bottles and goes off, whistling, at the left.* SAM, *coatless, a book in his hand, appears at the window. He looks out for a moment, then climbs out on the stoop, looks up at* ROSE'S *window, then seats himself and be-*

gins to read. WILLIE *comes out of the house.*)

WILLIE (*chanting, as he comes down the steps*). Fat, Fat the water-rat, Fifty bullets in his hat.

SAM. Hello, Willie. Is Rose up yet?

WILLIE (*without stopping or looking at him*). Yeah. I don't know. I guess so. (*He turns a somersault and goes off at left, continuing his chanting.* SAM *glances up at* ROSE'S *window again, then resumes his book.* MRS. JONES *and her dog come out of the house.*)

MRS. JONES (*haughtily, as she comes down the steps*). Mornin'.

SAM (*scarcely looking up from his book*). Good morning.
(MRS. JONES *and the dog go off at the right. A middle-aged workman, carrying a large coil of wire, appears at the left and goes to the door of the excavation.* MRS. OLSEN *comes out of the house and exits into the basement.*)

THE WORKMAN (*calling*). You down there, Eddie?

A VOICE (*from the depths*). Yeah!

THE WORKMAN. All right! (*He climbs down into the excavation.* ROSE *comes to window and pulls up the shade.* WILLIE *and* CHARLIE *can be heard, off-stage left, engaged in an earnest conversation.*)

CHARLIE (*off-stage*). He could not!

WILLIE (*off-stage*). He could so!
(*They appear at left. Each has under his arm, a paper-bag, from which a loaf of bread protrudes.*)

CHARLIE. I'll betcha he couldn't.

WILLIE. I'll betcha he could.

CHARLIE. I'll betcha a million dollars he couldn't.

WILLIE. I'll betcha five million dollars he could. Hold that! (*He hands* CHARLIE *his loaf of bread and turns a cart-wheel.*) Bet you can't do it.

CHARLIE. Bet I can. (*He puts both loaves of bread on the pavement, attempts a cart-wheel and fails.*)

WILLIE (*laughing raucously*). Haw-haw! Told you you couldn't!

CHARLIE. Can you do this? (*He turns a back somersault.*)

WILLIE. Sure—easy! (*He turns a back somersault. They pick up their loaves again.* WILLIE'S *drops out of the bag, but he dusts it, with his hand, and replaces it.*) How many steps can you jump up?

CHARLIE. Three. (*He jumps up three steps.*)

WILLIE. I can do four.

CHARLIE. Let's see you.
(WILLIE, *the bread under his arm, jumps up the four steps, undisturbed by* SAM'S *presence. He drops the bread, and is about to replace it in the bag, but gets a better idea. He inflates the bag and explodes it with a blow of his fist.* CHARLIE *looks on, in admiration and envy.*)

ROSE (*appearing at the window*). Willie, we're waiting for the bread.

WILLIE (*holding it up*). All right! Cantcha see I got it? (*He enters the house, followed by* CHARLIE.)

SAM (*rising*). Hello, Rose.

ROSE. Hello, Sam.

SAM. Come down.

ROSE. I haven't had breakfast yet. (*Calling into the room.*) Yes! He's on his way up.

MISS CUSHING (*coming out of the house*). Good morning. (*She looks inquiringly from* SAM *to* ROSE.)

SAM (*impatiently*). Good morning.
(*A middle-aged nun appears at the right, accompanied by a scrawny child of about fourteen. They walk across the stage.*)

ROSE. Good morning, Miss Cushing.
(MISS CUSHING *goes off, at the left, glancing back at* ROSE *and* SAM.)

ROSE. I'm going to Mr. Jacobson's funeral. (*Calling into the room.*) Yes, I'm coming.

(*To* SAM.) Breakfast's ready. I'll be down as soon as the dishes are done.
(*She disappears.* SAM *looks up at the window, for a moment, then begins to read again.* MRS. FIORENTINO *appears at the window, at the extreme left, with a double armful of bedding, which she deposits upon the window-sill. Then she goes away again.*)

SHIRLEY (*appearing at the window*). Sam, breakfast is ready.

SAM. I don't want any breakfast.

SHIRLEY. What do you mean, you don't want any breakfast? What kind of a business is that, not to eat breakfast?

SAM. Do I have to eat breakfast, if I don't want to?

SHIRLEY. You've got your head so full of that Rose Maurrant upstairs, that you don't want to eat or sleep or anything, any more.

SAM. If I don't feel like eating, why should I eat? (*Bursting out.*) You're always telling me: "Eat!" "Don't eat!" "Get up!" "Go to bed!" I know what I want to do, without being told.

SHIRLEY. I don't see, just when you're graduating from college, why you want to get mixed up with a little batzimer like that!

SAM. It's always the same thing over again with you. You never can get over your race prejudice. I've told you a hundred times that the Jews are no better than anybody else.

SHIRLEY. I'm not talking about that! Look at the kind of family she comes from. What's her father? Nothing but an illiterate rough-neck. And her mother—

SAM (*indignantly*). Are you starting, too?

KAPLAN'S VOICE. Shoi-ley!

SHIRLEY. Wait a minute, papa's calling. (*Into the room.*) All right, papa! (*To* SAM.) Come in, Sam, or papa will be making long speeches again.

SAM (*impatiently*). All right! All right! I'll come.
(*A young shopgirl, smiling to herself, appears at the right and walks across the*

stage. SAM *rises and goes into the house.* SHIRLEY *leaves the window.* BUCHANAN, *emerging from the house, collarless and unshaven, encounters* SAM *in the vestibule.*)

BUCHANAN (*eagerly*). Good morning!

SAM (*abruptly*). Good morning. (*He enters the house.* BUCHANAN *looks back at him, then comes down the steps.* MRS. FIORENTINO *raises the drawn shade and opens the window.*)

MRS. FIORENTINO. Good morning, Mr. Buchanan.

BUCHANAN. Oh, good morning, Mrs. Fiorentino. (*Going over to the left balustrade.*) I guess you know that the baby came last night, don't you?

MRS. FIORENTINO. No! I did not hear a vord about it.

BUCHANAN. Why, I thought she'd wake up the whole neighborhood, the way she was yelling. Three-thirty this morning, the baby came. I been up the whole night. (*An old* LETTER-CARRIER, *coatless, appears at the right.*)

MRS. FIORENTINO. A boy, is it?

BUCHANAN. No, it's a little girl. I guess we'll call her Mary, after my mother.

LETTER-CARRIER (*going up the steps*). Mornin'.

MRS. FIORENTINO. Good morning. Any letters for me?

LETTER-CARRIER (*from the top of the steps*). No, not a thing.

BUCHANAN (*turning toward him*). I was just telling Mrs. Fiorentino, I had a little addition to my family last night.

LETTER-CARRIER. Your first, is it?

BUCHANAN (*hastening to explain*). Well, we've only been married a little over a year.

LETTER-CARRIER. Well, I've had seven, an' I'm still luggin' a mail-bag at sixty-two. (*He goes into the vestibule and puts the mail into the letter-boxes.*)

MRS. FIORENTINO. How is your wife?

BUCHANAN. Well, she had a pretty hard time of it. Her sister's up there with her. And Mrs. Maurrant was up, nearly all night. I don't know what we'd have done without her.

LETTER-CARRIER (*coming down the steps*). It don't pay to let 'em have their own way, too much. That's where I made my mistake. (*As the* LETTER-CARRIER *goes off, at the left,* LIPPO *appears at the window behind his wife, and tickles her.*)

MRS. FIORENTINO (*startled*). Lippo!

BUCHANAN. Morning. I was just telling your wife—

MRS. FIORENTINO. Lippo, what do you think? Mr. Buchanan has a little girl!

LIPPO. Ah, dotsa fine! Margherita, why you don' have da baby, ha?

MRS. FIORENTINO (*abruptly*). I must go and make the coffee. (*She goes away from the window.* OLSEN *comes half-way up the steps and leans against the railing, smoking his pipe.*)

A VOICE (*off-stage left*). Oh-h! Corn! Sweet corn!

LIPPO. Ees funny t'ing. You gotta da leetle, skeeny wife and she's hava da baby. My Margherita, she's beeg an' fat an' she no can hava da baby.

BUCHANAN. Well, that's the way o' the world, I guess. (*As he goes off, at the left, an* ICE-MAN *appears, trundling a three-wheeled cart, filled with ice.*)

LIPPO. Buon giorno, Mike.

MIKE. Buon giorno, signore. Come sta?

LIPPO. Benissimo. Fa molto caldo ancora, oggi.

MIKE. Si, si signore. Bisognera abbastanza ghiaccio. Twen'y fi' cent, ha?

LIPPO. No, no, e troppo.

MIKE. Twen'y cent? Eesa melta fas'.

LIPPO. Alla right. Gimme twen'y cent.

MIKE. Si, si signore. Sure. (*As he wheels the cart to the cellar-entrance and begins*

to chop a block of ice, a MAN in shirt-sleeves strides in from the left and stops at the curb, as though seeing someone in a house across the street.*)

THE MAN (*angrily*). Well, what about it? We've been waiting a half an hour!

A VOICE. I'll be right over!

THE MAN. Yeah? Well, make it snappy! (*He strides off at the left, muttering angrily.* ROSE *comes out of the house and stands in the doorway, looking for* SAM. *Then she comes out on the stoop and peers in the* KAPLAN *apartment. As she turns away, she sees* LIPPO.*)

ROSE (*crossing to the left of the stoop*). Good morning.

LIPPO. Gooda mornin', Meesa Maurrant. (MIKE *goes down into the cellar, with a chunk of ice.*)

ROSE. It's awful hot again, isn't it?

LIPPO. You don' like?

ROSE. I don't sleep very well, when it's so hot.

LIPPO. No? Ahm sleepa fine. Een Eetaly, where Ahm born, is much more 'ot like 'ere. Een summer, ees too 'ot for workin'. Ees too 'ot only for sleepin'. W'en Ahm leetla boy, Ahm sleepa, sleepa, whola day. I don't wear no clo's—nawthin' only leetle short pair pants. I lay down on groun' under da lemon-tree, Ahm sleepa whola day.

ROSE. Under a lemon-tree! That must have been nice.

LIPPO. Ees smella sweet, lemon-tree. Where Ahm born ees t'ousan' lemon-tree. Lemon an' olive an' arancia.

ROSE. Oh, that must be lovely!

LIPPO. Ah, ees bew-tiful! Ees most bewtiful place in whole worl'. You hear about Sorrent', ha?

ROSE. No, I don't think I ever did.

LIPPO (*incredulously*). You never hear about Sorrent'?

ROSE. No, I don't know much about geography. Is it a big place?

LIPPO. Ees not vera beeg—but ever'body know Sorrent'. Sorrento gentile! La bella Sorrento! You hear about Napoli—Baia di Napoli?

ROSE. Oh yes, the Bay of Naples! Is it near there?

LIPPO. Sure, ees on Bay of Napoli. Ees bew-tiful! Ees alla blue. Sky blue, water blue, sun ees shine alla time.

ROSE. Oh, how lovely.
(MIKE comes up the cellar-steps, chops another block of ice, and goes down the cellar-steps with it.)

LIPPO. An' ees Vesuvio, too. You hear about Vesuvio?—ees beeg volcano.

ROSE. Oh yes, sure. I saw a picture once, called The Last Days of Pompeii, and it showed Mount Vesuvius, with smoke coming out of the top.

LIPPO. Da's right. An' night-time, ees fire come out, maka da sky red.

ROSE. Didn't it frighten you?

LIPPO. Ah no, ees nawthin' to be afraid. Ees jus' volcano.

ROSE. I'd love to go to Italy. It must be awfully pretty. But I don't suppose I ever will.

LIPPO. W'y sure! Some day you gonna marry reech fella; 'e's taka you Eetaly—ever'where.

ROSE. I guess there's not much chance of that. Rich fellows aren't going around looking for girls like me to marry. Anyhow, I don't think money is everything, do you?

LIPPO. Ees good to hava money. Da's w'y Ahm come to America. Een Eetaly, ees bewtiful, but ees no money. 'Ere ees not bewtiful, but ees plenty money. Ees better to 'ave money.
(An elderly man, in the gray uniform of a special officer, comes out of the house, filling his pipe from a tobacco-box.)

THE MAN. Good mornin'.

ROSE. Good morning, Mr. Callahan. (The MAN drops the empty tobacco-tin on the sidewalk and goes off slowly at the left.) I don't think I'd be happy, just marrying a man with money, if I didn't care for him, too.

LIPPO (laughing). Wotsa matter, ha? You lova da leetla kike, ha?

ROSE. Why no, I don't. I don't love anybody—at least, I don't think I do. But it's not on account of his being a Jew.

LIPPO. No, ees no good—Jew. 'E's only t'ink about money, money—alla time money.

ROSE. But Sam isn't like that, a bit. He's only interested in poetry and things like that.
(The ICE-MAN comes up out of the cellar and trundles off his cart at the right.)

MRS. FIORENTINO (calling). Lippo! Breakfast!

LIPPO (calling). Alla right, Margherita!
(To ROSE.) You marry fella wit' lot o' money. Ees much better. (He goes away from the window, as MISS CUSHING appears, at the left, carrying a paper-bag.)

ROSE. How's your mother today, Miss Cushing?

MISS CUSHING. She's not feeling so good today.

ROSE. It's too bad she's not feeling well.

MISS CUSHING. I'm afraid it's her heart. At her age, you know—! (As she enters the house, TWO COLLEGE GIRLS of nineteen appear at the right.)

FIRST GIRL (as they appear). I don't understand it.

SECOND GIRL. Convex is this way; and concave is this way.

FIRST GIRL. That I know.

SECOND GIRL. When you're near-sighted, they give you convex glasses, and when you're far-sighted, they give you concave.

FIRST GIRL. That I didn't know.

SECOND GIRL. Of course, you know it. Didn't we have it in psychology?

FIRST GIRL (*as they disappear at the left*). I don't remember.

(WILLIE *comes out of the house, on his way to school. He is hatless, and carries his books under his arm.*)

ROSE (*intercepting him at the top of the stoop*). Why, Willie, the way you look! Your collar's all open.

WILLIE. I know it! De button came off.

ROSE. Why didn't you ask ma to sew it on for you?

WILLIE. She ain't dere. She's up at Buchanan's.

ROSE. Well, wait till I see if I have a pin. (*She searches in her hand-bag.*)

WILLIE (*starting down the steps*). Aw, it's all right de way it is.

ROSE (*following him to the sidewalk*). No, it isn't. You can't go to school like that. (*Producing a safety-pin.*) Now, hold still, while I fix it.

WILLIE (*squirming*). Aw, fer de love o' Mike—!

ROSE. You'll get stuck, if you don't hold still. There, that looks better, now. And you didn't comb your hair, either.

WILLIE (*trying to escape*). Say, lemme alone, cantcha?

ROSE (*taking a comb out of her hand-bag and combing his hair.*) You can't go to school looking like a little street-loafer.

WILLIE. Aw, you gimme a pain in de—

ROSE. You're getting big enough to comb your own hair, without being told. There! Now you look very nice.

WILLIE. So's your old man! (*He runs towards the left kicking the empty tobacco tin ahead of him, then stops, turns and deliberately rumples his hair.*)

ROSE (*indignantly, as WILLIE runs off*). Why, Willie!

(MRS. JONES *and the dog appear at the right.* OLSEN *knocks the ashes out of his pipe and goes down into the cellar.* MRS. MAURRANT *comes out of the house.*)

ROSE. Hello, ma.

MRS. JONES (*at the steps*). Good mornin'.

ROSE *and* MRS. MAURRANT. Good morning, Mrs. Jones.

MRS. JONES. How's little Mrs. Buchanan gettin' on?

MRS. MAURRANT. Well, she's sleeping now, poor thing. She was so worn out, she just went off into a sound sleep. I really didn't think, last night, she'd have the strength to pull through it.

MRS. JONES. Well, it's somethin', we all got to go through. I been through enough with mine, I hope to tell you. Not that they didn't turn out all right.

MRS. MAURRANT. I wouldn't give up having mine for anything in the world.

MRS. JONES. Well, after all, what more does any woman want than watchin' her kids grow up an' a husband to look out for her?

MRS. MAURRANT. Yes, that's true.

MRS. JONES. Yes, and the world would be a whole lot better off, if there was more that lived up to it. (*Starting up the steps.*) Well, I gotta get my Mae up out o' bed. Gawd knows what time she got in, this mornin'. (*She enters the vestibule, then stops and turns.*) If you don't mind my bein' so bold, Mrs. Maurrant—an' I don't mind sayin' it in front of your daughter, either—I'd think twice before I'd let any child o' mine bring a Jew into the family.

ROSE (*with a show of temper*). I don't see what it has to do with you, Mrs. Jones.

MRS. JONES. There's no need to get huffy about it. I'm only advisin' you for your own good. I'm sure it don't make no difference to me what you do. Come on, Queenie. (*She goes into the house.*)

ROSE. Well, of all the nerve I ever heard in my life—! She and those wonderful children of hers!

MRS. MAURRANT (*coming half way down the steps*). The best way is not to pay any attention to her. There's lots of people like that, in the world—they never seem to be happy, unless they're making trouble for somebody. Did Willie go to school?

ROSE. Yes, he did. It's awful the way he goes around, looking like a little tough. And the language he uses, too.

MRS. MAURRANT. I know. I just don't seem able to manage him, any more.

ROSE. I sometimes wonder if it wouldn't be better for us all, if we moved out to the suburbs somewhere—you know, some place in Jersey or Staten Island.

MRS. MAURRANT. I don't think pop would do it. (*As* MAURRANT *comes out of the house, carrying a much-battered satchel.*) Are you leaving now, Frank?

MAURRANT (*from the top of the stoop*). Looks like it, don't it. Where you been all this while?

MRS. MAURRANT. Why, you know where I've been, Frank—up to Mrs. Buchanan's.

MAURRANT. Yeah? An' where you goin' now?

MRS. MAURRANT. Just around to Kraus's to get a chicken. I thought I'd make her some chicken-soup, to give her strength.

MAURRANT. Say, how about lookin' after your own home an' lettin' the Buchanans look after theirs.

MRS. MAURRANT. All I'm trying to do is to be a little neighborly. It's the least anybody can do, with the poor thing hardly able to lift her hand.

MAURRANT. That's all right about that! (*Coming down the steps.*) A woman's got a right to stay in her own home, lookin' after her husband an' children.

MRS. MAURRANT (*going towards him*). What else have I been doing all these years, I'd like to know?

MAURRANT. Well, just see that you don't forget it, that's all—or there's li'ble to be trouble.

MRS. MAURRANT (*putting her hand on his arm*). All right, Frank. Don't say any more, please. When will you be back—tomorrow?

MAURRANT. I don' know when I'll be back. Whenever I'm t'roo wit' me work—that's when. What are you so anxious to know for, huh?

MRS. MAURRANT. Why, I just asked, that's all.

MAURRANT. Oh, you just asked, huh? Just in case somebody wanted to come aroun' callin', is that it?

MRS. MAURRANT. No, it isn't. It isn't anything of the kind. You got no right to talk to me like that, in front of my own daughter. You got no right. No, you haven't! (*She turns away and hurries off, abruptly, at the left.*)

ROSE. Ma! (*She starts to run after her mother.*)

MAURRANT (*imperiously*) Come back here, you! (ROSE *hesitates.*) Come back, hear me? (ROSE *turns and comes slowly back.*) You stay right here. (*He puts down his satchel and takes a flask from his pocket.*)

ROSE. Why do you talk to her like that?

MAURRANT. Nobody's askin' you.

ROSE. If you were only a little nicer to her, maybe everything would be different.

MAURRANT. Yeah? Where's she got any kick comin'. Ain't I always been a good husband to her? Ain't I always looked after her?·(*He takes a drink.*)

ROSE. It's not that, pop. It's somebody to be sort of nice to her that she wants—sort of nice and gentle, the way she is to you. That's all it is.

MAURRANT (*turning to her*). So she's got you headed the same way, has she? Goin' out nights with married men, huh?

ROSE. You don't need to worry about me, pop. I can take care of myself, all right.

MAURRANT. No daughter o' mine ain't gonna go that way. I seen too many o' those kind around the theayter.

ROSE. Things are different, nowadays, Pop. I guess maybe you don't realize that. Girls aren't the way they used to be—sort of soft and helpless. A girl nowadays knows how to look out for herself. But not her, pop; she needs somebody to look after her.

MAURRANT. Aw, can all that talk! You been listenin' to them bolshevikis, that's the trouble. But I'm gonna keep you straight, by God, or I'll know the reason why.

ROSE. I guess I've got a right to think about things for myself.

MAURRANT. Yeah? Well, don't let me ketch that other bozo comin' around here, either —that's all I got to say.

ROSE (*hesitantly, going up to him*). Pop, listen—couldn't we get a little house some-where—Queens or somewhere like that?

MAURRANT. What's the idea?

ROSE. Well, I don't know. I sort of thought it would be nice for all of us. And maybe if ma had a nice little home and some real nice neighbors—do you see what I mean?

MAURRANT. This place suits me all right.

ROSE. You can get some real nice little houses, that don't cost such an awful lot. And I wouldn't mind helping to pay for it. And once we had it all fixed up—

MAURRANT. Forget it! I don' know when I'll be back. (*As he starts to go right.*) An' remember what I tol' you, hear?

MRS. JONES (*appearing at her window, with a tin dust-pan*). Good mornin', Mr. Maur-rant. You off on a little trip?

MAURRANT (*curtly*). Yeah. (*He goes off. MRS. JONES empties the dust-pan out of the window and goes away. KAPLAN comes out of the house, a bundle of newspapers, un-der his arm. He walks slowly and pain-fully, with the aid of a heavy stick.*)

KAPLAN (*at the foot of the steps*). Vy do you look so sed, hm?

ROSE (*turning, and sitting on the right bal-ustrade*). Oh, good morning, Mr. Kaplan.

KAPLAN. A young girl, like you, should not look so sed.

ROSE. I'm not sad, especially, only—

KAPLAN. You got troubles, hm?

ROSE. I don't know. It's just sort of every-thing.

KAPLAN. Velt-schmerz you got, hm? Vit' my boy Sem is de same t'ing. Dees vay you feel only ven you are yong. Ven you gat old like me, you tink only: "Moch longer I von't be here."

ROSE. Why should things be the way they are, Mr. Kaplan? Why must people al-ways be fighting and having troubles, in-stead of just sort of being happy together.

KAPLAN. My dear yong leddy, ef I could enser dis quastion, I would be de greatest benefactor thet de verld hes ever known. Dees is som't'ing, vich all de philosophers hev been unable to enser. De ones thet be-lieve in God, say de davil is responsible; and de ones thet don't believe in God, say 'uman nature is responsible. It is my opin-ion thet most unheppiness can be traced to economic cosses and thet—
(CHARLIE *and* MARY HILDEBRAND *have come out of the house, carrying their school-books.*)

MARY. Hello.

ROSE. Hello, Mary. Hello, Charlie.

CHARLIE. Hello.

MARY (*chattily, as they reach the sidewalk*). We're going to be dispossessed today.

ROSE. What a shame!

MARY. Yes, ma'am. My father went away and so we couldn't pay the rent.

CHARLIE (*tugging at her arm*). Aw, come on, Mary.

ROSE. Have you another place to live, Mary?

MARY. No ma'am. But Miss Simpson, from the Charities, says she'll find us a place. She says we must learn to be less extrava-gant.

CHARLIE. Come ahead, will you?

MARY. I'm going to school now. Good-bye.

ROSE. Good-bye.
(*The children go off, at the left.*)

KAPLAN. More troubles!

ROSE. I know. Isn't it awful to think of them being turned out in the street like that?

KAPLAN. In a ciwilized verld, soch t'ings could not heppen.

ROSE. You mean if there were different laws?

KAPLAN. Not laws! We got already too many laws. Ve must hev ection, not laws. De verking-klesses must t'row off de yoke of kepitalism, and ebolish wage-slavery.

ROSE. But wouldn't people still be unkind to each other and fight and quarrel among themselves?

KAPLAN. My dear young leddy, so long as ve keep men in slevery, dey vill behave like sleves. But wance ve establish a verld based upon 'uman needs and not upon 'uman greed—

ROSE. You mean people will begin being nice to each other and making allowances and all?

KAPLAN. All dees vill come. Wot ve hev now is a wicious soicle. On de one hend, ve hev a rotten economic system—

ROSE. Excuse me, here's my mother. (*She goes toward the left, as* MRS. MAURRANT *approaches, a paper package in her hand.* KAPLAN *goes off, at the right.*)

MRS. MAURRANT (*as* ROSE *comes up to her*). Did he go? (*They stop on the pavement, at the left of the stoop.*)

ROSE. Yes.

MRS. MAURRANT. I got a little chicken, to make Mrs. Buchanan some soup.

ROSE. He had a flask with him, ma. I hope he doesn't start drinking.

MRS. MAURRANT. What did he say—anything?

ROSE. No, only the way he always talks. I tried to talk to him about buying a house, somewheres, but he wouldn't listen.

MRS. MAURRANT. No, I knew he wouldn't.

ROSE. It doesn't seem to be any use trying to get him to listen to anything.

MRS. MAURRANT. It's always been that way. I've always tried to be a good wife to him, Rose. But it never seemed to make any difference to him.

ROSE. I know, ma.

MRS. MAURRANT. And I've tried to be a good mother, too.

ROSE. I know, ma. I know just the way you feel about it.

MRS. MAURRANT (*appealingly*). Do you, Rose?

ROSE. Yes, ma, I do. Honest I do.

MRS. MAURRANT. I've always tried to make a nice home for him and to do what's right. But it doesn't seem to be any use.

ROSE. I know, ma. (*Hesitantly.*) But it's on account of—(*She stops.*)

MRS. MAURRANT. Are you going to start, too? Are you going to start like all the others? (*She turns away and bursts into tears.*)

ROSE (*fondling her*). Don't ma. Please don't.

MRS. MAURRANT. I thought you'd be the one that would feel different.

ROSE. I do, ma—really I do.

MRS. MAURRANT. What's the good of being alive, if you can't get a little something out of life? You might just as well be dead.

ROSE. Look out, ma. Somebody's coming. (*A smartly-dressed girl, with one side of her face covered with cotton and adhesive tape, appears at the left and crosses the stage. At the same time,* JONES *comes out of the house.* ROSE *and* MRS. MAURRANT *stand in awkward silence, as he comes down the stoop and approaches them.*)

JONES. Well, is it hot enough for you, today?

ROSE. It's awful, isn't it?

JONES (*as he goes towards the left*). You said it. Still along about January, we'll all be wishin' we had a little o' this weather. (*He exits.* MRS. MAURRANT *goes towards the stoop.*)

ROSE. Ma, listen. If I say something, will you listen to me?

MRS. MAURRANT. Yes, sure I will, Rose. I'll listen to anything you say, only—

ROSE. Well, what I was thinking was, if he didn't come around here so much, maybe. Do you see what I mean, ma?

MRS. MAURRANT (*constrainedly*). Yes, Rose.

ROSE (*putting her arm around her*). It's on account of all that's going around—everybody in the whole house. You see what I mean, don't you, ma?

MRS. MAURRANT. Every person in the world has to have somebody to talk to. You can't live without somebody to talk to. I'm not saying that I can't talk to you, Rose, but you're only a young girl and it's not the same thing.

ROSE. It's only on account of pop. I'm scared of what he's likely to do, if he starts drinking.

MRS. MAURRANT. Well, I'll see, Rose. Sometimes I think I'd be better off if I was dead.

ROSE. If there was only something I could do.

MRS. MAURRANT. There isn't anything anybody could do. It's just the way things are, that's all.
(BUCHANAN *appears at the left. They turn and face him, as he approaches.*)

MRS. MAURRANT. Oh, Mr. Buchanan, I got a little chicken, so that I could make her some good, nourishing soup.

BUCHANAN. Well, say, you got to let me pay you for it.

MRS. MAURRANT. Oh, never mind about that. We'll have the chicken for supper tonight. Did you have her medicine made up?

BUCHANAN. Yes, I got it right here. I called up the office and they told me not to come down today.

MRS. MAURRANT. Well, that's very nice. It'll be a comfort to her to have you around.

BUCHANAN. Yes, that's what I thought, too. Well, I'd better be getting upstairs. (*He goes up the steps.*)

MRS. MAURRANT. I'll be up later, with the soup.

BUCHANAN. Well, thanks. (*Stopping at the top of the stoop and turning to her.*) You've been a mighty good neighbor, Mrs. Maurrant. (*He enters the house.*)

MRS. MAURRANT. He's an awful nice, young feller—so nice and gentle. And he's always trying to be so helpful. It makes you feel sort of sorry for him.
(SHIRLEY *comes out of the house, carrying a large wicker bag, which contains her lunch and schoolbooks. She takes a postcard out of the mail-box.*)

MRS. MAURRANT (*going up the steps*). Well, I'd better go and start this chicken. Are you coming home for lunch, Rose?

ROSE. Yes. I'll be back, as soon as the funeral's over.

MRS. MAURRANT. Oh, all right. (*As she sees* SHIRLEY.) Good morning.

SHIRLEY (*coming out of the vestibule, reading the post-card*). Good morning.

ROSE. Good morning.
(MRS. MAURRANT *goes into the house. The shade of* MAE'S *window flies up and she is seen, for an instant, dressed only in her step-in. She yawns noisily and turns away from the window.*)

ROSE (*seating herself on the stoop*). It's another awful day, isn't it.

SHIRLEY. Yes, and when you have to keep forty children quiet—! Well, thank goodness, in two weeks, school closes. Otherwise, I think I'd go crazy.

ROSE. Well, you get a nice, long vacation, anyhow.

SHIRLEY. Not much vacation for me. I'm taking Summer courses at Teachers College. (*She looks at* ROSE *a moment, hesitates, and then comes down the steps.*) Miss Maurrant, if you don't mind, I want to talk to you about my brother, Sam.

ROSE. Why, certainly, Miss Kaplan.

SHIRLEY. I guess you know he's only finishing college, this month—

ROSE. Yes, of course, I do.

SHIRLEY. Then he has to go three years to law-school and pass the bar examination. before he can be a full-fledged lawyer.

ROSE. Yes, it takes a long time.

SHIRLEY. A long time and lots of money. And before a young lawyer begins to make his own living, that takes a long time, too. It will be ten years, maybe, before he's making enough to support himself and a family. (*Looking away.*) Then, it's time enough for him to think about marriage.

ROSE. You don't mean me and Sam, Miss Kaplan?

SHIRLEY. Yes, that's just what I mean.

ROSE. Why, we're just good friends, that's all.

SHIRLEY. I know how it is with a boy like Sam, Miss Maurrant. He thinks he's a man, already; but he's nothing but a boy. If you're such a good friend, you shouldn't take his mind away from his work.

ROSE. But I haven't meant to, Miss Kaplan—honest I haven't.

SHIRLEY. I've had to work hard enough to get him as far as he is. And I have my father to take care of, too. The few dollars he makes, writing for the radical papers, don't even pay the rent. Believe me, every dollar I make goes.

ROSE. I know. Sam's often told me how much he owes to you.

SHIRLEY. He doesn't owe me anything. I don't care about the money. Only he should be thinking about his work and not about other things.

ROSE. Yes, he should be thinking about his work. But don't you think there are other things in the world, too, besides just work?

SHIRLEY. Don't you think I know that? I know that just as well as you do. Maybe, you think I'm only an old-maid school-teacher, without any feelings.

ROSE. Oh, I don't—really I don't!

SHIRLEY (*turning her head away*). Maybe I'm not a movie vamp, with dimples—but I could have had my chances, too. Only I wanted to give Sam an education.

ROSE. I haven't tried to vamp Sam, honestly I haven't. We just seemed sort of naturally to like each other.

SHIRLEY. Why must you pick out Sam? You could get other fellows. Anyhow, it's much better to marry with your own kind. When you marry outside your own people, nothing good ever comes of it. You can't mix oil and water.

ROSE. I don't know. I think if people really care about each other—

SHIRLEY. He's nothing but a baby. He sees a pretty face and, right away, he forgets about everything else.

ROSE (*with a flash of temper*). I know I haven't as much brains as Sam, or as you, either, if that's what you mean.

SHIRLEY (*contritely, going towards her*). I didn't mean to hurt your feelings. I haven't got anything against you. Only, he's all I've got in the world. What else have I got to live for?

SAM (*appearing at the extreme right window, with a cup of coffee and a piece of coffee-cake*). Hello, Rose.

ROSE. Hello, Sam.

SHIRLEY (*in a low tone*). Please don't tell him what I said. (SAM *goes to the other window.*)

ROSE. Oh no, I won't. (SHIRLEY *hurries off, at the left.*)

ROSE (*rising and turning towards Sam*). Sam—

SAM (*holding out the coffee-cake*). Want some coffee-cake?

ROSE. No. (*Going up the steps.*) Sam, there's something I want to ask you, before I forget. Is there any special way you have to act in a synagogue?

SAM (*eating throughout*). In a synagogue?

ROSE. Yes. The funeral I'm going to, is in a synagogue, and I thought there might be some special thing you have to do. Like in church, you know, a girl is always supposed to keep her hat on.

SAM. I don't know. I've never in my life been in a synagogue.

ROSE. Didn't you ever go to Sunday-school, or anything like that?

SAM. No.

ROSE. That's funny. I thought everybody went, once in a while. How about when your mother died?

SAM. She was cremated. My parents were always rationalists.

ROSE. Didn't they believe in God or anything?

SAM. What do you mean by God?

ROSE (*puzzled*). Well—you know what I mean. What anybody means—God. Somebody that sort of loves us and looks after us, when we're in trouble.

SAM (*sitting on the window-sill*). That's nothing but superstition—the lies that people tell themselves, because reality is too terrible for them to face.

ROSE. But, Sam, don't you think it's better to believe in something that makes you a little happy, than not to believe in anything and be miserable all the time?

SAM. There's no such thing as happiness. That's an illusion, like all the rest.

ROSE. Then, what's the use of living?

SAM (*brushing the last crumbs off his hands*). Yes, what is the use?

ROSE. Why, you oughtn't to talk like that, Sam—a person with all the talent and brains that you've got. I know things aren't just the way you want them to be. But they aren't for anybody. They aren't for me, either.

SAM. Then, why don't we get out of it, together?

ROSE. I don't see just how we could do that, Sam.

SAM. It would be easy enough—ten cents' worth of carbolic acid.

ROSE. Why, Sam, you don't mean kill ourselves!

SAM. Is your life so precious to you that you want to cling to it?

ROSE. Well, yes. I guess it is.

SAM. Why? Why? What is there in life to compensate for the pain of living?

ROSE. There's a lot. Just being alive—breathing and walking around. Just looking at the faces of people you like and hearing them laugh. And seeing the pretty things in the store-windows. And rough-housing with your kid brother. And—oh, I don't know—listening to a good band, and dancing—Oh, I'd hate to die! (*Earnestly.*) Sam, promise you won't talk about killing yourself, any more.

SAM. What difference would it make to you, if I did?

ROSE. Don't talk like that, Sam! You're the best friend I've ever had. (*She puts her hand on his.*)

SAM. I can't think of anything but you.

ROSE. There's something I want to ask your advice about, Sam. It's about what I started to tell you about, last night. A man I know wants to put me on the stage.

SAM (*releasing her hand and drawing back*). What man?

ROSE. A man that works in the office. He knows a manager and he says he'll help me get started. You see, what I thought was, that if I could only get out of here and have a decent place to live and make a lot of money, maybe everything would be different, not only for me, but for ma and pop and Willie.

SAM. But don't you know what he wants, this man?

ROSE. Nobody gives you anything for nothing, Sam. If you don't pay for things in one way, you do in another.

SAM. Rose, for God's sake, you mustn't! (VINCENT JONES *comes out of the house.*)

ROSE (*seeing* VINCENT *in the vestibule*). Look out, Sam, here's that tough, from upstairs. (*She goes over to the left of the stoop.*)

VINCENT (*in the doorway*). Hello, Rosie. Been here, all night, talkin' to the little yit? (ROSE *does not answer.*)

VINCENT (*turning to* SAM). Hello, motzers! Shake! (*He leans over the balustrade and seizes* SAM's *hand, in a crushing grip.*)

SAM (*writhing with pain*). Let me go!

ROSE. Let him alone!
(VINCENT *gives* SAM's *hand another vicious squeeze and then releases him.* SAM *cowers back in the window, nursing his hand.*)

VINCENT (*waving his hand about in mock pain*). Jesus, what a grip dat little kike's got! I'd hate to get into a mix-up wit' him. (*To* ROSE.) Got a date for to-night, kid?

ROSE. Yes, I have.

VINCENT. Yeah? Gee, ain't dat too bad. I'll give you two dollars, if you let me snap your garter.

ROSE. Shut up, you!
(VINCENT *laughs.* SAM *makes an inarticulate sound.*)

VINCENT (*threateningly*). Whadja say? I t'ought I hoid you say sumpin. (*He makes a threatening gesture.* SAM *shrinks back.*)

VINCENT (*with a loud laugh, as he goes down the steps*). Fightin' Kaplan, de pride o' Jerusalem! (*He looks at them both, then laughs again.*) Fer cryin' out loud! (*He goes off at the left.*)

ROSE. Oh, if there was only some way of getting out of here! (SAM *puts the back of his hand to his forehead and turns away.*) I sometimes think I'd just like to run away.

SAM (*without turning*). Yes!

ROSE. Anywhere—it wouldn't matter where—just to get out of this.

SAM (*turning*). Why shouldn't we do it?

ROSE (*rather startled coming over to the right balustrade*). Would you go with me, Sam?

SAM. Yes—anywhere.

ROSE. I've heard that people are much nicer and friendlier, when you get outside of New York. There's not so much of a mad rush, other places. And being alone, you could sort of work things out for yourself. (*Suddenly.*) Only, what would you do, Sam?

SAM. I could get a job, too.

ROSE. And give up your law-work?

SAM. I'd give up everything, to be with you.

ROSE. No. I wouldn't let you do that, Sam. It's different with me—
(EASTER *appears at the right.*)

EASTER (*stopping at the right of the stoop*). Good morning, Miss Maurrant.
(*Startled,* ROSE *turns and sees him, for the first time.*)

ROSE (*none too pleased*). Oh, good morning, Mr. Easter. What brings you in this neighborhood?

EASTER (*not very plausibly*). Well, I just happened to have a little business, right around the corner. So, I thought as long as you were going to the funeral, we might just as well go together.

ROSE. Well, I hardly expected to see you around here. (*An awkward pause.*) Oh, I'd like you to meet my friend, Mr. Kaplan.

EASTER. How do you do, Mr. Kaplan? Glad to know you.
(SAM *murmurs something inaudible. An awkward silence.*)

ROSE (*to* SAM). Mr. Easter is the manager of the office. (SAM *does not reply. Another silence.*)

ROSE (*to* EASTER). It's awful hot again, isn't it?

EASTER. Worse than yesterday. (*Approaching the stoop.*) Tell you what I was thinking. I was thinking, that after the funeral, we might take a run down to the beach, somewhere, and cool off a little.

ROSE. I can't today. I've got a lot of things I want to do.

EASTER. Oh, you can do 'em some other day.

ROSE. No, really, I can't. (*Looking at her watch.*) Well, I guess it's time we got started. (*She comes down the steps.*)

EASTER. Yes, it is. We'll pick up a cab at the corner.
(MRS. MAURRANT *appears at her window, looks out, and sees* ROSE *and* EASTER.)

ROSE. Why, I thought I'd walk. It's not far.

EASTER. Too hot, today, for any walking.

ROSE (*starting to go towards the left*). Not if you keep in the shade.

EASTER. Much more comfortable taking a cab.

ROSE. I'd rather walk.

EASTER. Well, whatever you say. Good morning, Mr. Kaplan. Glad to have met you.
(SAM *murmurs an inaudible reply.*)

ROSE. Good-bye, Sam. I'll see you, later.
(SAM *does not answer.* ROSE *and* EASTER *go towards the left, in silence.* SAM *watches them, intently, trembling with jealousy.* MRS. MAURRANT, *surprised and disturbed, watches* ROSE *and* EASTER.)

ROSE (*to* EASTER, *as they disappear*). It's a lucky thing my father wasn't around.
(SAM *suddenly turns and goes into the house.* MRS. MAURRANT *remains at the window, looking out, with obvious expectancy.*)

A DISTANT VOICE (*off-stage left*). Strawberries! Straw-*berries!*
(*An anemic girl of eighteen, with a music-roll under her arm, appears at the left. She enters the house and pushes one of the buttons, in the vestibule, then goes to the entrance-door and waits. A moment later,* MRS. FIORENTINO *appears hastily, at the window, and whisks away the bed-clothes. After another moment, the latch clicks and the girl enters the house.*)

THE VOICE (*a little nearer*). Oh-h! Straw-berries! Straw-*berries!*
(SANKEY *appears at the right. He carries a pencil behind his ear, wears a round cap*

with a metal name-plate and a stiff visor, and carries a large black-covered bill-holder. He and* MRS. MAURRANT *see each other and both become tense with excitement.* MRS. MAURRANT *beckons to him and he comes over to the railing, under her window.*)

MRS. MAURRANT (*in a low, tense voice*). Come up.

SANKEY (*looking about, nervously*). Now?

MRS. MAURRANT. Yes. I got to talk to you.

SANKEY. Is it all right?

MRS. MAURRANT. Yes. He's gone to Stamford.

SANKEY. How about later?

MRS. MAURRANT. No. Rose'll be home in an hour. She's not working today.

SANKEY. All right. (*He looks about again, then goes quickly towards the steps.* SAM *appears, at the entrance-door. He is about to step out, when he sees* SANKEY. *He stops and looks at him.* SANKEY *sees* SAM, *hesitates a moment, then goes quickly into the house. Meanwhile,* MRS. MAURRANT *has closed both windows and pulled down the shades.* SAM *takes a periodical out of the mail-box, then comes out of the house and down the steps. He looks up at the* MAURRANT *windows, sees the drawn shades, and looks about, in perturbed perplexity, not knowing what to do. At length, he sits down on the steps of the stoop, tears the wrapper off the periodical—The Nation —and begins to read. The girl in* LIPPO's *apartment begins playing the piano. This continues throughout the scene. Two untidy and rather coarse-looking men appear, at the left and approach the stoop:* JAMES HENRY, *a city marshal, and* FRED CULLEN, *his assistant. They stop in front of the house.* SAM *pays no attention to them.*)

THE MARSHAL (*crossing to the left of the stoop, and taking a paper from his pocket*). Dis is it. (*To* SAM.) Hildebrand live here?

SAM (*startled*). What?

THE MARSHAL. I'm askin' you if Hildebrand lives here.

SAM. Yes. Fourth floor.

THE MARSHAL. Better give de janitor a buzz, Fred.
(FRED *goes up the steps and rings the janitors' bell, then leans over the left balustrade.*)

FRED (*bawling*). Hey, janitor.

OLSEN (*below*). Vell?

FRED. Come on out, a minute. (*As* OLSEN *appears below.*) We got a warrant for Hildebrand.

OLSEN. Fourt' floor—Hildebrand.

FRED. Yeah, I know. We got a warrant for her.

THE MARSHAL. I'm City Marshal Henry. We got a dispossess warrant.

OLSEN (*coming up the steps*). Oh, sure. You gonna put 'em out?

THE MARSHAL. Yeah, dat's it. Has she got anybody to take de foinicher away?

OLSEN (*with a shrug*). I don' know.

THE MARSHAL. Well, we'll have t' dump it on de side-walk, den. Go ahead, Fred.
(*They enter the house.* OLSEN *leans his elbows on the coping, and smokes his pipe.* SAM *sits on the steps, deep in troubled thought. A grocery boy, with a full basket, appears at the right, and goes down the cellar-steps.* MAE JONES *comes out of the house. She stands on the top step, yawns noisily, and goes off, at left. She and* SAM *do not pay the slightest attention to each other.*)

A VOICE (*a little nearer*). Straw-berries! Straw-*berries!*
(MRS. OLSEN *comes up the cellar-steps, with a heavy pail of water.* OLSEN *leans forward to make room for her. She staggers over to the stoop, almost dropping the pail, and goes up the steps, into the vestibule.* OLSEN *yawns and goes down into the cellar.* MRS. JONES *appears, at the window, her hair wet and stringy, a towel pinned about her shoulders, and leans out to dry her hair.*)

AN OLD-CLOTHES MAN (*appearing at left*). I kesh ko! I kesh ko! (*He wears a battered derby and carries a folded newspaper under his arm.* MRS. OLSEN, *on her knees, begins washing up the vestibule.* FRED *comes out of the house, carrying a worn chair and a large gilt-framed picture, which he deposits on the side-walk, against the railing, to the left of the stoop.*)

AN OLD-CLOTHES MAN (*as if to someone across the street*). Kesh ko? (*To* SAM.) Any old klose, mister?
(SAM *pays no attention to him.*)
(FRED *re-enters the house.*)

THE OLD-CLOTHES MAN (*to* MRS. JONES). Any ol' klose, leddy?

MRS. JONES. Naw, nawthin'.

THE OLD-CLOTHES MAN. Hets? Shoes? Ol' stockings?

MRS. JONES. Nawthin' I tell you.
(*As the* OLD CLOTHES MAN *goes off, at the right,* MAURRANT *appears, still carrying his satchel.*)

MRS. JONES. Why, hello, Mr. Maurrant.
(MAURRANT *looks up without replying and comes over to the stoop.*) I thought you was off to Stamford.

MAURRANT. I changed me—(*He stops, to the right of the stoop, and looks up at the drawn shades of his apartment.* SAM *rises, slowly and rigidly, his eyes glued in fascination, upon* MAURRANT. MAURRANT'S *movements take on a lithe and cat-like quality. Then, slowly and deliberately, he goes towards the steps, his back arched, like a tiger ready to spring.*)

SAM (*suddenly blocking the steps*). No! No! For God's sake—!

MAURRANT (*raging*). Out o' me way, you goddam little rat! (*He flings* SAM *violently aside, almost knocking him down.* MRS. OLSEN, *terrified, rises and shrinks into a corner, as* MAURRANT *with swift stealthiness, enters the house.* MRS. JONES *leans out, to see what is wrong.* SAM *rushes down the steps and stands under the* MAURRANT *windows. The* MARSHAL *comes out of the house, carrying a wash-boiler, filled with pots.*)

SAM (*hysterically*). Mrs. Maurrant! Mrs. Maurrant!

MRS. JONES. What's the matter?
(*The* MARSHAL *puts the wash-boiler on the balustrade and looks on, in amazement.*)

SAM (*to* MRS. JONES). Quick! Run and tell her! Quick!

MRS. JONES. What is it? (*Suddenly.*) Oh, Gawd, is he in there? (*She leaves the window, hastily.*)

SAM. Yes! Mrs. Maurrant! Mrs. Maurrant!
(*A scream of terror is heard, from the* MAURRANT *apartment.*)

MRS. MAURRANT'S VOICE. Frank! Frank!
(*Two shots are heard, in quick succession, and then a heavy fall.* MRS. OLSEN *runs out of the vestibule and down into the cellar.* SANKEY'S *voice is heard, inarticulate with fear. Then, one of the shades shoots up, and* SANKEY *appears at the window, coatless, his face deformed by terror. He tries to open the window, but succeeds only in shattering the pane with his elbow.* MAURRANT *appears behind him and pulls him away from the window. Then another shot is heard.*)

THE MARSHAL. For Chris' sake, what's happenin'? Get an ambulance, you! (*He pushes* SAM *towards the left, then hurries off, at the right. As* SAM *runs off, a crowd begins to form.* OLSEN *comes up from the cellar, followed by the* GROCER-BOY. *The two workmen come up, out of the excavation. Two or three of the workmen from the demolished building run on at the right.*)

A WORKMAN. What's happening?

A MAN. What is it? A murder?
(*Still others join the crowd: A huckster, a janitor from a neighboring house, a mulatto girl, six or eight women of the neighborhood, some in street-dresses, others in house-dresses or dingy wrappers.* LIPPO'S *pupil appears, at the window, badly frightened. The crowd surges about, uncertainly, not knowing what has happened, and buzzing with questions, which nobody can answer. While the crowd is still forming,* FRED, *the* MARSHAL'S *assistant, appears at the broken window.*)

FRED (*excitedly*). Grab dat boid! He's comin' down!

A WORKMAN. What boid?

A MAN. Here he is, now!
(*The crowd murmurs with excitement and surges about the stoop, as the house-door opens and* MAURRANT *appears. His coat is open and his shirt is torn almost to shreds. His face, hands and clothing are covered with blood. He stands, in the door-way, for a moment, surveying the crowd, his eyes glaring.*)

FRED. Grab him! Don't let him get away!
(*As the crowd makes a concerted movement towards* MAURRANT, *he whips out an automatic revolver and levels it. The crowd shrinks back. Some of the women scream.*)

MAURRANT. Git back! Git back, all o' you!
(*The crowd falls back towards the left, to make way for him. With his back to the balustrade, he comes quickly down the steps, and still leveling his revolver at the crowd, retreats backwards to the cellar steps. A man, approaching at the right, comes stealthily up behind him, but* MAURRANT *senses his presence in time, wheels quickly, menaces the man with his revolver, then rushes down the cellar steps. While all this is happening, the other shade in the* MAURRANT *apartment flies up and* MISS CUSHING *opens the window and leans out.*)

MISS CUSHING. Hurry up! Get an ambulance!
(*No one pays any attention to her, as they are all watching* MAURRANT. *As* MAURRANT *runs down the cellar steps, the crowd surges forward to the railing, on both sides of the stoop and leans over. A scream from* MRS. OLSEN *is heard from the basement.* FRED *goes away from the window.*)

MISS CUSHING. Get an ambulance, somebody! (*Unable to attract anyone's attention, she leaves the window.*)

OLSEN. Olga! (*He hurries down the cellar steps.*)

A MAN (*calling*). Here's a cop! (*The crowd looks to the right.*) Hey! Hurry up!
(*A* POLICEMAN *runs on from the right.*)

THE POLICEMAN. Where is he?

VOICES IN THE CROWD. He's down the cellar! He ran down the cellar! He went down the steps!

THE POLICEMAN. Get out of the way! (THE POLICEMAN *and two men in the crowd go down the cellar steps.*)

VOICES IN THE CROWD. Watch yourself! Look out, he's got a gun! He's a big guy with his shirt torn! (*The rest of the crowd peers over the railing.*)

MISS CUSHING (*leaning out of* ROSE'S *window*). Hey, don't you hear me? Get an ambulance!

ANOTHER MAN (*looking up*). What's de matter? You want de ambulance?

MISS CUSHING. Yes! Right away.

ANOTHER MAN (*to the* GROCERY-BOY). Run aroun' de corner to de horspital, Johnny, an' tell 'em to send de ambulance!

THE GROCERY-BOY. Sure!

MISS CUSHING. Run!
(*The* GROCERY-BOY *runs off swiftly at the left.* MISS CUSHING *leaves the window. Meanwhile, as the* POLICEMAN *and the* TWO MEN *have gone down the cellar steps, the* MARSHAL *has run on, from the right, panting.*)

THE MARSHAL (*as the* GROCERY-BOY *runs off*). Did dey git 'm?

A MAN. He beat it down de cellar.

A WORKMAN. De cop's gone after him.

THE MARSHAL. Why de hell didn' you stop 'im?
(FRED *comes out of the house.*)

A WORKMAN. He had a gun.

FRED. Did somebody go for de ambulance.

A MAN. Yeah. De kid went.

A WOMAN. It's only aroun' de corner.

ANOTHER MAN. Dey'll be here, right away.
(*The crowd moves over towards* FRED.)

THE MARSHAL (*pushing his way through the crowd and up the steps*). What de hell happened, Fred?

FRED (*as the crowd moves toward the stoop*). It's a moider. Dis boid's wife an' some other guy. Jesus, you oughta see de blood.
(*Another* POLICEMAN *runs up, at the left, closely followed by* SAM.)

FRED. Upstairs, officer! Dere's two of 'em got shot.

THE POLICEMAN (*elbowing his way through the crowd*). Look out o' de way, youse! (*He goes up the stoop and crosses to the door.*) Where's de guy dat did it?

VOICES IN THE CROWD. Down de cellar! He beat it down de steps!

FRED. Dere's another cop after 'im. You better look after dem, upstairs. Foist floor.

SAM (*agonized*). Are they dead?
(*No one pays any attention to him.*)

THE MARSHAL (*stopping the* POLICEMAN, *and exhibiting his badge*). I'm City Marshal Henry. Kin I do anythin'?

POLICEMAN. Don' let anybody in or out! Hear?

THE MARSHAL. Yeah, sure! (*The* POLICEMAN *exits quickly, into the house.*)

SAM. Are they dead?
(*No one notices him. The* MARSHAL *takes up his position in the doorway.*)

BUCHANAN (*appearing at the* MAURRANT *window*). Where's the ambulance?

THE MARSHAL. It'll be here, right away. Dere's a cop on his way up.

SAM. Mr. Buchanan! Mr. Buchanan! Are they dead? (*But* BUCHANAN *has already disappeared. The* TWO MEN, *who followed the first* POLICEMAN *into the cellar, now come up the steps. The crowd moves over to the railing, at the right.*)

THE MARSHAL. Did you get him, boys?

ONE OF THE MEN. He must be hidin', somewheres. De cop's lookin' for 'im.

ANOTHER MAN. Somebody better call de resoives.
(SAM *runs up the steps and tries to enter the house.*)

THE MARSHAL (*seizing him roughly*). You can't get in now! Get back dere! (*He pushes* SAM *back into the crowd, at the foot of the steps.*)

THE POLICEMAN (*appearing at the* MAURRANT *window*). Hey, call up headquarters an' tell 'em to send the resoives. Make it quick! (*He goes away from the window.*)

THE MARSHAL. You go, Fred.

FRED. Sure!

A MAN. Dere's a phone in de warehouse. (*An ambulance bell is heard at the left, as* FRED *goes quickly towards the left. Another spectator hurries on and joins the crowd.*)

VOICES IN THE CROWD. Dere it is! Dere's de ambulance now! Here dey come! (*The* CROWD *moves over towards the left.*)

A MAN. Dey won't be able to git past.

THE POLICEMAN (*reappearing at the window*). Is dat de ambulance?

THE MARSHAL. Yeah.
(BUCHANAN *and* MRS. JONES *crowd to the window, behind the* POLICEMAN, *and, at the other window,* LIPPO, MISS CUSHING *and* MRS. HILDEBRAND *appear. A hospital interne and an ambulance-driver come on at the left.*)

THE POLICEMAN. Hurry up, Doc! She's still breathin.'

THE INTERNE (*forcing his way through the crowd*). All right! Better bring the stretcher, Harry.

THE AMBULANCE-DRIVER. Yes, sir. (*He hurries off, at the left. The* INTERNE *goes quickly into the house. The crowd attempts to follow, several of its members going up the steps.*)

THE MARSHAL (*pushing them back*). Keep back, now! Back off de stoop, everybody! (*The crowd forms a compact mass, about the foot of the steps. The persons at the* MAURRANT *windows have disappeared.* FRED *hurries on, at the left.*)

FRED (*pushing his way through the crowd and up the steps*). I got 'em. Dey'll be right up. Anudder cop jes' wen' in t'roo de warehouse cellar.

THE MARSHAL. Dey'll git 'im all right. (*Looking at his watch.*) Better git busy wit' dat foinicher, Fred. We got two udder jobs today.

FRED. Yeah, sure, Jimmy. (*He enters the house. The* AMBULANCE-DRIVER *appears at left, carrying a canvas stretcher.*)

THE AMBULANCE-DRIVER. Get out o' the way!

THE MARSHAL. Git back, can't youse? What de hell's de matter wit' youse? (*He comes down the steps and violently pushes the crowd back. The* AMBULANCE-DRIVER *enters the house.*)

THE POLICEMAN (*at the window*). Are dey bringin' dat stretcher?

THE MARSHAL. On de way up! (*To the crowd.*) Keep back!
(*The* POLICEMAN *leaves the window.* LIPPO'S PUPIL, *her music-roll under her arm, appears timidly in the doorway.*)

THE MARSHAL (*grabbing her arm roughly*). Where you goin'?

THE GIRL (*nervously*). I'm going home.

THE MARSHAL. Home? Where do you live?

THE GIRL. Ninety-first Street.

THE MARSHAL. What are you doin' here?

THE GIRL. I just came for a music-lesson, that's all.

THE MARSHAL. Yeah? Well, you can't go now.

THE GIRL (*beginning to whimper*). I want to go home.

THE MARSHAL. You can't go, now. Nobody can't leave de house, now.

THE POLICEMAN (*coming out of the house*). Who's dis kid?

THE MARSHAL. Says she come here to take a music-lesson an' she wants to go home.

THE POLICEMAN (*to the girl*). Do you know anythin' about this killin'?

THE GIRL. No, I don't. I just heard some shooting, that's all. My mother will be worried, if I don't come home.

THE POLICEMAN. Well, you can't go, now. Get inside dere, out o' de way. Dey'll be bringin' her down, in a minute. (*He pushes the girl inside the house a. 1 comes down the steps.*)

THE POLICEMAN. Come on, git back from dem steps! Back now, all o' youse! (*He and the* MARSHAL *push the crowd back to the right of the stoop, leaving the steps and the sidewalk in front of them clear. Then he goes up the steps again.*)

THE MARSHAL. What did he do? Shoot two of 'em?

THE POLICEMAN. I'll say he did! His wife an' her sweetie. A guy named Sankey. He was dead when I got up dere.

THE MARSHAL. I seen him tryin' to climb out t'roo de winder. An' dis guy grabs 'im an' pulls 'im back.

THE INTERNE (*from the* MAURRANT *window*). Officer! Come on up! (*He leaves the window, as the* POLICEMAN *exits into the house. Suddenly* SAM *utters an exclamation of anguish and, pushing his way out of the crowd, hurries over to the left.*)

THE MARSHAL. Hey, you! Where you goin'? (SAM *ignores him and hurries on.*)

A WOMAN. Look! There's the Maurrant girl!

ANOTHER WOMAN. Who?

A WOMAN. It's her daughter.
(*The crowd murmurs, excitedly, as* ROSE *comes on quickly, at the left.*)

ROSE. What's the matter, Sam? What's the ambulance for? Did anybody get hurt?

SAM. Go away, Rose. Go away.

ROSE. Who is it, Sam? What's the matter? Is it my mother? It's not my mother, is it? (*Clinging to him.*) Sam, is it?

SAM. There's been an accident. Go away, Rose. (*He tries to force her away.*)

ROSE. Tell me what's happened! Tell me!

MISS CUSHING (*appearing at the window*). They're bringing her down!

ROSE (*with a cry*). It *is* my mother!

MISS CUSHING (*seeing her*). Oh, my God, there's Rose!
(MRS. FIORENTINO, MRS. JONES, MRS. HILDEBRAND, LIPPO *and* BUCHANAN *crowd to the* MAURRANT *windows.*)

SAM. Rose! Go away!
(*She pays no attention to him, but stands watching the door, transfixed. The* INTERNE *comes briskly out of the house.*)

THE INTERNE (*to the* MARSHAL). Hold the door open, will you? (*He comes down the steps.*)

THE MARSHAL. Sure, doc! (*He hurries into the vestibule.*)

THE INTERNE (*to the crowd*). Keep back, now!

ROSE (*seizing the* INTERNE'S *arm*). Doctor! Is she dead?

THE INTERNE. Who are you? Her daughter?

ROSE. Yes, sir. I'm her daughter.

THE INTERNE. She's pretty badly hurt. Step aside, now!
(*They step aside, as the* AMBULANCE-DRIVER *and the* POLICEMAN *come out of the house, carrying* MRS. MAURRANT *on the stretcher There is a low murmur from the crowd.*)

THE AMBULANCE-DRIVER. Easy, now.

THE POLICEMAN. All right. (*They come down the steps and go towards the left.*)

ROSE (*running forward and gripping the side of the stretcher*). Mother! Mother!

MRS. MAURRANT (*opening her eyes, feebly*). Rose! (*She tries to lift her hand, but it falls back.*)

THE INTERNE (*pulling* ROSE *back*). You mustn't talk to her, now.
(SAM *takes her about the shoulders. They and the* INTERNE *follow the stretcher off, at the left.*)
(*The crowd swarms after them.* FRED *comes out of the house, carrying one end of an iron bedstead.*)

Curtain.

ACT THREE

Mid-afternoon of the same day. At the left of the stoop, is a large roll of bedding. Before the rise of the curtain, and continuing faintly thereafter, a woman can be heard singing scales. OLSEN, *pipe in mouth, is leaning against the railing. Two* MEN, *furniture-movers, appear at the left.*

ONE OF THE MEN (*picking up the bedding*). All right. Dat's all, Charlie! (*The* MEN *exit left.*)
(*A* POLICEMAN *comes out of the house, carrying the blood-stained dress of* MRS. MAURRANT, *and* SANKEY'S *coat, cap, and bill-holder. He comes down the steps, and exits at the right.*)
(*At the left,* TWO YOUNG NURSE-MAIDS, *in smart uniforms, appear, each wheeling a de-luxe baby-carriage.*)

FIRST NURSE-MAID (*seeing the house-number*). This must be the place, right here—346. (*They stop, under the* MAURRANT *windows.*)

SECOND NURSE-MAID. Yes, I guess it is.

FIRST NURSE-MAID. Yes, this is it, all right. (*Looking up.*) Must be right up there, on the first floor, see?

SECOND NURSE-MAID. Yes, sure. (*Excitedly.*) Say, look! You can see where the glass is out of the window. That's where this feller What's-his-name tried to climb out.

FIRST NURSE-MAID. Oh, yes, I see it! Say, what do you know about that!

SECOND NURSE-MAID (*taking a pink tabloid newspaper from under the hood of the baby-buggy*). Wait! There's a picture of it, somewhere. (*Turning the pages.*) Here it is. (*They excitedly examine it together, as she reads.*) "Composograph showing Sankey, scantily clad, in a last vain attempt to escape the vengeance of the jealousy-crazed husband, whose home he had destroyed." And there's Maurrant pulling him back. And Mrs. Maurrant trying to get the pistol away from him, see? Look at the blood running down her face, will you?

FIRST NURSE-MAID. It's worse than awful! Can you *imagine* what those two must have felt like, when he walked in on them like that?

SECOND NURSE-MAID. Well, he just happened to be one of the ones that finds out! Believe me, there's lots and lots of husbands that don't know the half of what goes on up-town, while they're down-town making a living.

FIRST NURSE-MAID. Say, you're not telling me, are you? If I was to spill all I know, there'd be many a happy home busted up. I wonder if they caught him.

SECOND NURSE-MAID (*as her* BABY *begins a thin wailing*). Oh, God, he's in again! (*To the unseen* BABY.) Shut up, a little while, can't you? (*She shakes the carriage.*)

A POLICEMAN (*appearing at the* MAURRANT *windows, a tabloid in his hand*). Keep movin', ladies. No loiterin' aroun' here.

FIRST NURSE-MAID (*eagerly*). Say, have they caught him, yet?

THE POLICEMAN. Why, ain't you hoid? He was last seen, flyin' over Nova Scotia, on his way to Paris.

FIRST NURSE-MAID. Who are you trying to string, anyhow?

SECOND NURSE-MAID (*coquettishly*). Say, will you let us come up and look around?

THE POLICEMAN. Why, sure, sure! Bring de babies, too. De commissioner is soivin' tea, up here, at four-thoity.

SECOND NURSE-MAID. You're awful smart, aren't you?

THE POLICEMAN. Yeah, dat's why dey put me on de entertainment committee. I'm Handsome Harry Moiphy, de boy comedian o' Brooklyn.

FIRST NURSE-MAID (*looking at her watch*). Oh, say, I ought to be getting back. (*Turning her carriage.*) Clarice darling would throw a duck-fit, if she knew I brought her precious Dumplings to a neighborhood like this.

SECOND NURSE-MAID (*turning her carriage*). There's not so much to see, anyhow. It's nothing but a cheap, common dump. (*They go towards the left.*)

THE POLICEMAN. Over de river, goils. See you in de funny paper.

SECOND NURSE-MAID. Don't you get so fresh.

THE POLICEMAN. Drop in again, when you're in de neighborhood. An' tell Mrs. Vanderbilt, Harry was askin' for her. (*As the* NURSE-MAIDS *go off, at the left,* EASTER *hurries on at the right, several folded newspapers under his arm.*)

EASTER (*to the* POLICEMAN, *going to the left of the stoop*). Is Miss Maurrant up there, officer?

THE POLICEMAN. No. There ain't nobody up here but me.

EASTER. You don't happen to know where she is, do you?

THE POLICEMEN. No, I don't. Are you a reporter?

EASTER. Who, me? I'm just a friend of hers. I've got to see her.

THE POLICEMAN. Well, I ain't seen her since she went off to the horspital this mornin'. She ain't been back since. (*He starts to leave the window.*)

EASTER. Oh, officer!

THE POLICEMAN. Yeah?

EASTER. Have they caught him, yet?

THE POLICEMAN. Naw, not yet. But we'll get 'im, all right! (*He leaves the window.* EASTER *remains at the left of the stoop, uncertain whether to go or not.* MRS. JONES

appears, at the right, carrying several newspapers.)

MRS. JONES (*to* OLSEN). Have they caught him yet?

OLSEN (*shaking his head*). No.

MRS. JONES. I been down at Police Headquarters, all this while—(*Breaking off, as she notices* EASTER.) Say, what's he want here? (OLSEN *shrugs his shoulders.*)

EASTER (*approaching them*). Pardon me, but maybe you can tell me where I can find Miss Maurrant? (OLSEN *shakes his head.*)

MRS. JONES. Why no, I can't. I jus' this minute got back from Police Headquarters. Maybe she's aroun' at the horspital.

EASTER. No, I just came from there.

MRS. JONES. Well, I really couldn't say where she is. Was there somethin' special you wanted to see her about?

EASTER. I'm a friend of hers—

MRS. JONES. Yeah, I noticed you talkin' to her, last night, when I took the dog out. (*Staring at him.*) Well, I guess she'll need all the friends she's got, now. Imagine a thing like that happenin' right here in this house, at ten o'clock in the mornin'! Everythin' goin' on just as usual, and then, all of a sudden, before you know it, there's two people murdered.

OLSEN. I tal everybody some day he kill her.

MRS. JONES. Well, I ain't sayin' it's right to kill anybody, but if anybody had a reason, he certainly had. You oughta heard some o' the questions they was askin' me down at the Police. I could feel myself gettin' redder an' redder. "Say," I says, "how do you expect me to know things like that?" (*Suddenly, as she looks left.*) Here's Rose now!

EASTER. Where? (*He turns quickly and hurries to the left, as* ROSE *appears, carrying four or five packages.*)

MRS. JONES (*to* OLSEN). He seems to take a pretty friendly interest in her. (OLSEN *nods.*)

ROSE (*anxiously, as she comes up to* EASTER, *at the left of the stoop*). Have they caught him yet?

EASTER. Why no, they haven't. I just asked the officer, upstairs.

ROSE. Oh, I hope he got away! If they get him, there's no telling what they'll do to him. And what would be the good of that? He never would have done it, if he'd been in his right mind.

EASTER. I only heard about it, a little while ago. So I went right around to the hospital. But they said you'd left.

ROSE (*going to the steps*). She never opened her eyes again. They did everything they could for her, but it didn't help.

EASTER. Here, let me take your bundles.

ROSE. No, it's all right. I think I'll just sit down for a minute. (*She sits on the stoop and puts the packages beside her.*)

EASTER. Can't I get you something? A drink or something?

ROSE. No, I'm all right. It's so hot. (*She puts her hand to her head.*) And all those people asking me a lot of questions.

MRS. JONES (*approaching the stoop*). Are you feelin' dizzy or anythin'?

ROSE. No, I'll be all right in a minute.

MRS. JONES. Well, I was gonna say, if you want to go up to my flat an' lay down for a minute—

ROSE. No, thanks; I don't want to lie down. I've got to go upstairs to get some things.

EASTER. Why, say, you don't want to go up there!

ROSE. I've got to; there's some things I need.

EASTER. Well, let me get them for you. Or this lady here.

MRS. JONES. Yeah, sure. The place is a sight, up there. You're li'ble to go into a faint or somethin'.

ROSE. I guess nothing can be any worse than what's happened already. (*Indicating the bundles.*) I got to change my dress. I bought a white dress for her. And white silk stockings. I want her to look pretty.

MRS. JONES. Yeah, white is the nicest.

ROSE. She looks so quiet and natural. You'd think she was asleep.

MRS. JONES. It was the same way with my mother. You'd of thought she was gonna get up, the next minute. (*Starting to go up the steps.*) Well, I gotta go up an' get me some lunch. Between everythin' happenin' an' goin' down to Police Headquarters an' all, I ain't had a bite to eat since breakfast. (*Stopping on the top step, and looking from* ROSE *to* EASTER.) Well, you certainly never know, when you get up in the mornin', what the day is gonna bring. (*She enters the house.*)

ROSE (*rising*). Well, I'd better be going up, too. There's a lot of things to attend to.

EASTER. You better let me come up with you.

ROSE. Why thanks, Mr. Easter. But I'd rather go alone, if you don't mind.

EASTER. But, listen here—you can't go through all this alone—a kid like you. That's why I came around. I knew you'd be needing a helping hand.

ROSE. That's awfully nice of you, Mr. Easter. But I don't need any help, honest I don't. (*She opens one of the packages.*)

EASTER. Why, you can't handle everything yourself! What about a place to live and all that?

ROSE (*taking a rosette of black crape out of the package*). Well, I don't exactly know, yet. I'll have to find some place where Willie and I can live. I'd like it to be some place where he wouldn't be running around the streets all the time. You see, there's nobody but me to look out for him, now.

(OLSEN *crosses to the cellar.* MRS. JONES *appears at her window and furtively peeps out, at* ROSE *and* EASTER.)

ROSE (*as she sees that* OLSEN *is about to descend the cellar steps*). Oh, Mr. Olsen!

OLSEN (*stopping*). Yes ma'am.

ROSE. Would you mind lending me a hammer and some tacks? I want to put up this crape.

OLSEN. Yes ma'am; I bring 'em right away. (*He goes down into the cellar.* MRS. JONES *leaves the window.*)

EASTER (*insistently*). But why won't you let me help you out?

ROSE. It's terribly nice of you, Mr. Easter. But I'll be able to manage alone, really I will. It isn't as if I wasn't young and strong and able to take care of myself. But as it is, I'd sort of rather not be under obligations.

EASTER. Why, you wouldn't be under any obligations. I just mean it in a friendly way, that's all.

ROSE. You've been very nice to me and all that, Mr. Easter. But—well, I've been sort of thinking things over—you know, about what we talked about last night and all. And I honestly don't think I'd care about going on the stage.

EASTER. Say, you've got me all wrong, Rose! Just forget all about that, will you? I just want to help you out, that's all. (*Taking a step towards her.*) I think you're one swell kid, and I want to do something for you. I'm not trying to put anything over on you. (SHIRLEY *appears, at the left, carrying her school-bag, from which a newspaper protrudes.*)

ROSE. Well, that's nice and friendly of you, Mr. Easter. If I ever do need any help—

SHIRLEY (*catching sight of* ROSE). Rose! You poor thing! (*She runs up to* ROSE *and throws her arms about her.*) It's terrible—terrible!

ROSE. Yes, it is. But I sort of had a feeling, all along, that something terrible was going to happen.
(OLSEN *comes up the steps, with a hammer and a box of tacks.*)

SHIRLEY. How could he do such a thing! I couldn't believe it when I read it.

ROSE. He was out of his mind, when he did it. Oh, I only hope he got away! (*As* OLSEN *approaches.*) Oh, thanks, Mr. Olsen.

OLSEN. I do it.

ROSE (*giving him the crape*). Oh, would you, please? Right up there, I think. (*She indicates the left of the doorway.*)

OLSEN (*going up the steps*). Sure.

ROSE (*going to* EASTER *and extending her hand*). Thanks for coming around, Mr. Easter. I don't know when I'll be able to get back to the office.

EASTER. Why, that's all right about that. Only, in the meantime, I wish—

ROSE. If I need any help, I'll let you know. (*With a tone of finality in her voice.*) Good-bye.

EASTER. All right; but don't forget. (*He hesitates, then decides to go.*) Well, good-bye. (*He goes off at left.*)

ROSE. I've got to go up and get some things that Willie and I need. Sam went to call for him at school and take him around to my aunt's. You see, I didn't want him coming back here. He's only a little kid, after all.

SHIRLEY. Oh, it's such a terrible thing! I can't believe it yet.

OLSEN (*holding up the crape*). Dis vay?

ROSE. Yes, like that. (*Hesitantly, as she picks up her bundles.*) Miss Kaplan, it's sort of silly of me, I guess. But I'm kind of afraid to go up there alone. I wonder if you'd mind coming up with me.
(OLSEN *tacks up the crape.*)

SHIRLEY. Anything I can do for you, poor child!
(*She and* ROSE *go up the steps.*)

ROSE. Thanks ever so much. (*To* OLSEN.) Thanks, Mr. Olsen. It's awfully nice of you. (*She and* SHIRLEY *enter the house.* OLSEN *exits down the cellar steps.* KAPLAN *appears, at his window, and seating himself, begins to read a newspaper. An under-sized* MAN *and a tall, athletic* WOMAN *appear at the right. They are dressed for tennis, and carry tennis-rackets.*)

A MAN (*as they cross*). He *would* say that.

A WOMAN. So I just looked at him for a moment, without saying anything. And then, I said: "My dear boy," I said. "What do you expect anyhow, in this day and age?" I said, "Why even Frankl has to do a black bathroom, occasionally," I said.

A MAN (*as they disappear at the left*). Exactly! And what did he say to that?
(BUCHANAN *comes out of the house, and, seeing* KAPLAN *at the window, stops at the right balustrade.*)

BUCHANAN. Well, there's been *some* excitement around here, today.

KAPLAN (*looking up from his paper*). Dees is a terrible t'ing vich hes heppened.

BUCHANAN. I'll say it is! You know, the way I look at it, he didn't have a right to kill the both of them like that. Of course I'm not saying what she did was right, either.

KAPLAN. How ken ve call ourselves ciwilized, ven ve see thet sax jealousy hes de power to avaken in us de primitive pessions of de sevege?

BUCHANAN (*rather bewildered by this*). Yes, that's crue, too. Of course, you can't expect a man to stand by and see his home broken up. But murdering them, like that, is going a little too far. Well, I got to go and phone the doctor. This thing's given my wife a kind of a relapse. She thought a lot of Mrs. Maurrant. (*He goes down the steps, and off at the left, as* LIPPO *appears, at the right.*)

LIPPO (*stopping in front of* KAPLAN's *window*). Dey don' ketcha Maurrant, ha?

KAPLAN. I hevn't hoid anyt'ing foider.

LIPPO. He'sa gonna gat da 'lectrica-chair, ha?

KAPLAN. De blood-lust of our enlightened population must be setisfied! De Chreestian state will kerry out to de last letter de Mosaic law.

LIPPO. Eef Ahm ketcha my wife sleepin' wit' 'nudder man, Ahm gonna keela 'er, too.
(SAM *hurries on at the left.*)

KAPLAN. So you t'ink thet merriage should give to de husband de power of life and det' and thet—

SAM (*going up the steps*). Papa, is there any news of Maurrant?

KAPLAN. I hev heard notting.

SAM. The police are going to make me testify against him. What can I do, papa?

KAPLAN. You ken do notting.

SAM. How can I send a man to the electric-chair? How can I? I tried to stop him, papa. I tried to warn her— (*He stops short, as several shots are heard off-stage, at the left.*) What's that?

LIPPO (*excitedly*). Dey finda 'im!
(*He runs off, at the left, followed by* SAM. KAPLAN *leans out of the window. At the same moment,* MRS. JONES *leans out of her window and, a moment later,* MRS. FIORENTINO *out of hers. In the Maurrant apartment, the* POLICEMAN *leans out and* ROSE *and* SHIRLEY *appear in the hall bed-room window.* ROSE *is wearing a mourning-dress.* OLSEN *comes up the cellar steps and runs off at the left.* MRS. OLSEN *comes up the steps. Several* MEN *and* WOMEN *appear, at the right, and run off, at the left.*)

ROSE (*agitatedly*). Is that him?

THE POLICEMAN. Must be!
(*Voices are heard shouting, in the distance, and then another shot. The* POLICEMAN *leaves the window.*)

ROSE. Oh, God! They wouldn't shoot him, would they? (*She leaves the window.*)

SHIRLEY (*following her*). Rose!
(*Two or three more persons appear at the right and run off at the left. The* POLICEMAN *runs out of the house, as* BUCHANAN *appears at the left.*)

BUCHANAN (*excitedly*). They got him!
(*The* POLICEMAN *runs off, at the left.* SHIRLEY *reappears at the Maurrant window.*)

MRS. JONES (*calling*). Have they got him?

BUCHANAN. Yes! He was hiding in the furnace, down at 322. (*As* ROSE *comes out of the house.*) They found him, Miss Maurrant!

ROSE (*her hand to her heart*). Oh! Is he hurt?

BUCHANAN. I don't know. He fired at the cops and they fired back at him. I was just passing the house, when it happened.

MRS. JONES (*leaning far out*). Here they come! (*She leaves the window.*)
(*The low murmur of the approaching crowd can be heard, off-stage left.*)

ROSE. Where? (*She comes down the stoop and looks off, at the left.*) Oh! (*She covers her eyes and turns away.*)

MRS. FIORENTINO. You better come inside.

SHIRLEY. Come up, Rose.

BUCHANAN. Yes, you better. (*He takes her by the arm.*)

ROSE (*resisting*). No. No. Please let me alone. I want to see him. (*She leans against the railing. Meanwhile, the murmur and tramp of the approaching crowd has grown nearer and nearer.*)

MRS. FIORENTINO. Look at him, vill you! (*MISS CUSHING comes out of the house, and stands on the stoop, followed a moment later, by MRS. JONES. MAURRANT appears at the left, between two policemen. Behind him a third POLICEMAN holds back a swarming crowd, which includes SAM and LIPPO. MAURRANT's clothes are torn, and his right arm is in a crude sling. Sweat, blood and grime have made him almost unrecognizable. The POLICEMEN, too, show evidences of a struggle.*)

ROSE (*running forward*). Pop! Are you hurt?

MAURRANT (*seeing her for the first time*). Rose!

ONE OF THE POLICEMEN (*to whom MAURRANT is manacled*). Keep back, miss!

MAURRANT. It's me daughter! Fer Chris' sake, boys, lemme talk to me daughter! Maybe I'll never be seein' her again!

FIRST POLICEMAN. Give 'im a woid wit' her. (*He is the OFFICER who was on duty in the Maurrant apartment.*)

SECOND POLICEMAN (*after a moment's hesitation*). Well, all right. (*Savagely to MAURRANT.*) But don't try to pull nothin', hear? (*There is a forward movement in the crowd.*)

FIRST POLICEMAN (*to the crowd*). Keep back, youse!

MAURRANT. Rose! You're wearin' a black dress, Rose!

ROSE. Oh, pop, why did you do it? Why did you?

MAURRANT. I must o' been out o' me head, Rose. Did she say anythin'?

ROSE. She never opened her eyes again.

MAURRANT. I'd been drinkin', Rose—see what I mean?—an' all the talk that was goin' around. I just went clean off me nut, that's all.

ROSE. What'll they do to you, pop?

MAURRANT. It's the chair for me, I guess. But I don't care—let 'em give me the chair. I deserve it all right. But it's her, I'm thinkin' of, Rose—the way she looked at me. I oughtn't to done it, Rose.

ROSE. She was always so good and sweet.

MAURRANT. Don't I know it? I ain't no murderer—you ought to be the one to know that, Rose. I just went out o' me head, that's all it was.

SECOND POLICEMAN. All right, that's all now. Come on!

MAURRANT. Gimme a minute, can't you? She's me daughter. Gimme a chance, can't you? What's gonna happen to you, Rose?

ROSE. I'll be all right, pop. You don't need to worry about me.

MAURRANT. I ain't been a very good father, have I?

ROSE. Don't worry about that, pop.

MAURRANT. It ain't that I ain't meant to be. It's just the way things happened to turn out, that's all. Keep your eye on Willie, Rose. Don't let Willie grow up to be a murderer, like his pop.

ROSE. I'm going to do all I can for him, pop.

MAURRANT. You're a good girl, Rose. You was always a good girl.

ROSE (*breaking down*). Oh, pop! (*She throws her arms about his neck and buries her head against him.* MAURRANT *sobs hoarsely.*)

FIRST POLICEMAN (*gently*). Come on, now, miss.
(*He and* SAM *take* ROSE *away from* MAURRANT.)

SECOND POLICEMAN. All right. Come on, Charlie.
(*They go towards the right, the crowd swarming behind them. Straggling along at the very end of the crowd, is an unkempt* WOMAN, *wheeling a ramshackle baby-carriage.* MRS. JONES *and* MISS CUSHING *fall in with the crowd.* ROSE *gradually recovers her self-control, and stands at the stoop, with* SAM *beside her. The others watch the receding crowd for a moment. Then* KAPLAN *and* MRS. FIORENTINO *leave their windows. The* FIRST POLICEMAN *enters the house, followed by* LIPPO. MRS. OLSEN *goes to the cellar.* SHIRLEY *looks down at* ROSE *and* SAM, *for a moment, then abruptly leaves the window.*)

SAM (*taking* ROSE *by the arm*). Rose, you better come inside.

ROSE. No, I'm all right again, Sam—honestly I am. (*Trying to regain her self-composure.*) What about Willie, Sam?

SAM. I told him an accident had happened.

ROSE. It's better to break it to him, that way. But I'll have to tell him, I guess. He'd only find it out himself, tomorrow, with the papers all full of it. I saw Mrs. Sankey, down at Police Headquarters. It's terrible for her, with two little children.

SHIRLEY (*appearing at the Maurrant window, a covered pot in her hand*). Rose!

ROSE (*looking up*). Yes, Miss Kaplan?

SHIRLEY. There's a chicken here, that I found on the gas-stove.

ROSE. A chicken?

SHIRLEY. Yes. The policeman says he smelt it cooking, this morning, so he turned out the gas.

ROSE. Oh, I remember, now. My mother said she was going to make some soup for poor Mrs. Buchanan, upstairs.

SHIRLEY. It won't keep long, in this weather.

ROSE. No. I really think Mrs. Buchanan ought to have the good of it.

SHIRLEY. All right. I'll take it up to her.

ROSE. Thanks ever so much, Miss Kaplan. (SHIRLEY *leaves the window.*) It's only a few hours ago that she was standing right here, telling me about the chicken. And then, she went upstairs, and the next I saw of her, they were carrying her out. (*Abruptly, as she starts to go up the steps.*) Well, I've got to go up and get my things.

SAM. I must talk to you! What are you going to do, Rose?

ROSE. Well, I haven't really had any time to do much thinking. But I really think the best thing I could do, would be to get out of New York. You know, like we were saying, this morning—how things might be different, if you only had a chance to breathe and spread out a little. Only when I said it, I never dreamt it would be this way.

SAM. If you go, I'll go with you.

ROSE. But, Sam dear—

SAM. I don't care anything about my career. It's you—you—I care about. Do you think I can stay here, stifling to death, in this slum, and never seeing you? Do you think my life means anything to me, without you?

ROSE. But, Sam, we've got to be practical about it. How would we manage?

SAM. I don't care what I do. I'll be a day-laborer; I'll dig sewers—anything. (*Taking her passionately in his arms.*) Rose, don't leave me!

ROSE. I like you so much, Sam. I like you better than anybody I know.

SAM. I love you, Rose. Let me go with you!

ROSE. It would be so nice to be with you. You're different from anybody I know. But I'm just wondering how it would work out.

SAM. If we have each other, that's the vital thing, isn't it? What else matters but that?

ROSE. Lots of things, Sam. There's lots of things to be considered. Suppose something was to happen—well, suppose I was to have a baby, say. That sometimes happens, even when you don't want it to. What would we do, then? We'd be tied down then, for life, just like all the other people around here. They all start out loving each other and thinking that everything is going to be fine—and before you know it, they find out they haven't got anything . and they wish they could do it all over again—only it's too late.

SAM. It's to escape all that, that we must be together. It's only because we love each other and belong to each other, that we can find the strength to escape.

ROSE (*shaking her head*). No, Sam.

SAM. Why do you say no?

ROSE. It's what you said just now—about people belonging to each other. I don't think people ought to belong to anybody but themselves. I was thinking, that if my mother had really belonged to herself, and that if my father had really belonged to himself, it never would have happened. It was only because they were always depending on somebody else, for what they ought to have had inside themselves. Do you see what I mean, Sam? That's why I don't want to belong to anybody, and why I don't want anybody to belong to me.

SAM. You want to go through life alone? — never loving anyone, never having anyone love you?

ROSE. Why, of course not, Sam! I want love more than anything else in the world. But loving and belonging aren't the same thing. (*Putting her arms about him.*) Sam dear, listen. If we say good-bye, now, it doesn't mean that it has to be forever. Maybe some day, when we're older and wiser, things will be different. Don't look as if it was the end of the world, Sam!

SAM. It *is* the end of my world.

ROSE. It isn't, Sam! If you'd only believe in yourself, a little more, things wouldn't look nearly so bad. Because once you're sure of yourself, the things that happen to you, aren't so important. The way I look at it, it's not what you do that matters so much; it's what you are. (*Warmly.*) I'm so fond of you, Sam. And I've got such a lot of confidence in you. (*Impulsively.*) Give me a nice kiss!

(SAM *takes her in his arms and kisses her, passionately. A gawky* GIRL *of seventeen— one of* LIPPO'S *pupils, appears at the left, and looks at them, scandalized. Then she goes into the vestibule and rings the bell. The door clicks and she enters the house, as* SHIRLEY *comes out, carrying a wicker suit-case.* SHIRLEY *looks at* SAM *and* ROSE.)

ROSE (*to* SHIRLEY). I was just telling Sam, that I think I'll soon be going away from New York.

(SAM *looks at her, for a moment, in agony, then goes abruptly into the house.*)

SHIRLEY. I put your things in this suit-case. (*She comes down to the pavement. The* GIRL, *in the Fiorentino apartment, begins tuning her violin.*)

ROSE (*taking the suit-case*). You've been awfully nice to me. Don't worry about Sam, Miss Kaplan. Everything will be all right with him.

SHIRLEY. I hope so. (*From the Fiorentino apartment, come the strains of Dvořák's Humoresque, jerkily played on a violin.*)

ROSE. Oh, I just know it will! (*Extending her hand.*) Good-bye, Miss Kaplan.

SHIRLEY. Good-bye, Rose. (*Impulsively.*) You're a sweet girl! (*She hugs and kisses her.*)

ROSE. I hope I'll see you, again.

SHIRLEY (*crying*). I hope so, Rose. (ROSE *takes up the suit-case and goes off at the left.* SHIRLEY *stands watching her.*)

KAPLAN (*re-appearing at his window*). Shoiley, vot's de metter again vit Sam? He's crying on de bed.

SHIRLEY. Let him alone, papa, can't you? (*She turns and enters the house.* KAPLAN *sighs and, seating himself at the window, opens a newspaper. A shabby, middle-aged* COUPLE *appear at the right, and approach the stoop.*)

THE MAN (*reading the To-Let sign*). Here's a place. Six rooms. Want to take a look at it?
(*A group of* CHILDREN *off-stage left, begin singing The Farmer in the Dell. This continues until after the curtain is down.*)

THE WOMAN. All right. No harm lookin'. Ring for the janitor. (*The* MAN *goes up the stoop and rings the janitor's bell.*) Somebody must o' just died.

THE MAN. Yeah, maybe that's why they're movin' out. (*Wiping his face with a hand-kerchief.*) Phoo! Seems to be gettin' hotter every minute.
(MRS. FIORENTINO *seats herself, at her window, a sewing-basket in her lap.* MRS. JONES *and* MISS CUSHING *appear at the right, busily engaged in conversation.*)

MISS CUSHING. The poor little thing!

MRS. JONES (*as they go up the steps*). Well, you never can tell with them quiet ones. It wouldn't surprise me a bit, if she turned out the same way as her mother. She's got a gentleman friend, that I guess ain't hangin' around for nothin'. I seen him, late last night, and this afternoon, when I come home from the police— (*She is still talking, as they enter the house.*)
(MRS. OLSEN *comes up the cellar steps. A* SAILOR *appears at the left, with two girls, an arm about the waist of each. They stroll slowly across.*)

The curtain falls.

The Green Pastures

BY MARC CONNELLY

TO MY MOTHER

AUTHOR'S NOTE

"The Green Pastures" is an attempt to present certain aspects of a living religion in the terms of its believers. The religion is that of thousands of Negroes in the deep South. With terrific spiritual hunger and the greatest humility these untutored black Christians—many of whom cannot even read the book which is the treasure house of their faith—have adapted the contents of the Bible to the consistencies of their everyday lives.

Unburdened by the differences of more educated theologians they accept the Old Testament as a chronicle of wonders which happened to people like themselves in vague but actual places, and of rules of conduct, true acceptance of which will lead them to a tangible, three-dimensional Heaven. In this Heaven, if one has been born in a district where fish frys are popular, the angels do have magnificent fish frys through an eternity somewhat resembling a series of earthly holidays. The Lord Jehovah will be the promised comforter, a just but compassionate patriarch, the summation of all the virtues His follower has observed in the human beings about him. The Lord may look like the Reverend Mr. Dubois as our Sunday School teacher speculates in the play, or he may resemble another believer's own grandfather. In any event, His face will be familiar to the one who has come for his reward.

The author is indebted to Mr. Roark Bradford, whose retelling of several of the Old Testament stories in "Ol' Man Adam an' His Chillun" first stimulated his interest in this point of view.

One need not blame a hazy memory of the Bible for the failure to recall the characters of Hezdrel, Zeba and others in the play. They are the author's apocrypha, but he believes persons much like them have figured in the meditations of some of the old Negro preachers, whose simple faith he has tried to translate into a play.

MARC CONNELLY

Marc Connelly was born in McKeesport, Pennsylvania, in 1890. He was educated in the public schools and at Trinity Hall, Washington, Pennsylvania. Beginning as a reporter on the *Pittsburgh Sun* in 1910, Mr. Connelly transferred to the *Pittsburgh Dispatch,* and later contributed a humorous column to the *Gazette Times*. In 1915 he came to New York to see the production of a musical comedy for which he had written the lyrics. Upon the failure of the production, and lacking the return fare to Pittsburgh, Mr. Connelly stayed on in New York. He has contributed verse and articles to a number of magazines. He is president of the Authors' League of America.

Prior to the production of *The Green Pastures,* Marc Connelly was known chiefly for the productions upon which he and George S. Kaufman collaborated, including several musical comedies. The outstanding plays of their joint authorship were *Dulcy, Merton of the Movies,* and *Beggar on Horseback.*

Suggested by *Ol' Man Adam and His Chillun* by Roark Bradford, *The Green Pastures* has been called the "divine comedy of the modern theatre." The popular reception of the drama is demonstrated by the fact that the production of *The Green Pastures* has continued for six years, and has been presented throughout Europe.

Produced by Laurence Rivers, Inc., at the Mansfield Theatre, New York, February 26, 1930, *The Green Pastures* won the 1929-1930 Pulitzer award.

CHARACTERS

MR. DESHEE, THE PREACHER
MYRTLE
FIRST BOY
SECOND BOY
FIRST COOK
A VOICE
SECOND COOK
FIRST MAN ANGEL
FIRST MAMMY ANGEL
A STOUT ANGEL
A SLENDER ANGEL
ARCHANGEL
GABRIEL
GOD
CHOIR LEADER
CUSTARD MAKER
ADAM
EVE
CAIN
CAIN'S GIRL
ZEBA
CAIN THE SIXTH
BOY GAMBLER
FIRST GAMBLER
SECOND GAMBLER
VOICE IN SHANTY
NOAH
NOAH'S WIFE
SHEM
FIRST WOMAN
SECOND WOMAN

THIRD WOMAN
FIRST MAN
FLATFOOT
HAM
JAPHETH
FIRST CLEANER
SECOND CLEANER
ABRAHAM
ISAAC
JACOB
MOSES
ZIPPORAH
AARON
A CANDIDATE
  MAGICIAN
PHARAOH
GENERAL
HEAD MAGICIAN
FIRST WIZARD
SECOND WIZARD
JOSHUA
FIRST SCOUT
MASTER OF
  CEREMONIES
KING OF BABYLON
PROPHET
HIGH PRIEST
CORPORAL
HEZDREL
SECOND OFFICER

SCENES

PART ONE

PART TWO

THE GREEN PASTURES

PART ONE

SCENE I

A corner in a Negro church.

Ten children and an elderly preacher.

The costumes are those that might be seen in any lower Louisiana town at Sunday-School time. As the curtain rises, MR. DESHEE, *the preacher, is reading from a Bible. The* CHILDREN *are listening with varied degrees of interest. Three or four are wide-eyed in their attention. Two or three are obviously puzzled, but interested, and the smallest ones are engaged in more physical concerns. One is playing with a little doll, and another runs his finger on all the angles of his chair.*

DESHEE. "An' Adam lived a hundred and thirty years, an' begat a son in his own likeness, after his image; an' called his name Seth. An' de days of Adam, after he had begotten Seth, were eight hundred years; an' he begat sons an' daughters; an' all de days dat Adam lived were nine hundred an' thirty years; an' he died. An' Seth lived a hundred an' five years an' begat Enos; an' Seth lived after he begat Enos eight hundred an' seven years and begat sons and daughters. An' all de days of Seth were nine hundred and twelve years; an' he died." An' it go on like dat till we come to Enoch an' de book say: "An' Enoch lived sixty an' five years and begat Methuselah." Den it say: "An' all de days of Methuselah were nine hund'ed an' sixty an' nine years an' he died." An' dat was de oldest man dat ever was. Dat's why we call ol' Mr. Gurney's mammy ol' Mrs. Methuselah, caize she's so ol'. Den a little later it tell about another member of de fam'ly. His name was Noah. Maybe some of you know about him already. I'm gonter tell you all about him next Sunday. Anyway dat's de meat an' substance of de first five chapters of Genesis. Now, how you think you gonter like de Bible?

MYRTLE. I think it's jest wonderful, Mr. Deshee. I cain't understand any of it.

FIRST BOY. Why did dey live so long, Mr. Deshee?

DESHEE. Why? Caize dat was de way God felt.

SECOND BOY. Dat made Adam a way back.

DESHEE. Yes, he certainly 'way back by de time Noah come along. Want to ask me any mo' questions?

SECOND BOY. What de worl' look like when de Lawd begin, Mr. Deshee?

DESHEE. How yo' mean what it look like?

MYRTLE. Carlisle mean who was in N'Orleans den.

DESHEE. Dey wasn't nobody in N'Orleans on 'count dey wasn't any N'Orleans. Dat's de whole idea I tol' you at de end of de first Chapter. Yo' got to git yo' minds fixed. Dey wasn't any Rampart Street. Dey wasn't any Canal Street. Dey wasn't any Louisiana. Dey wasn't nothin' on de earth at all caize fo' de reason dey wasn't any earth.

MYRTLE. Yes, but what Carlisle wanter know is—

DESHEE (*interrupting and addressing little boy who has been playing with his chair and paying no attention*). Now Randolph, if you don't listen, how yo' gonter grow up and be a good man? Yo' wanter grow up an' be a transgressor?

LITTLE BOY (*frightened*). No.

DESHEE. You tell yo' mammy yo' sister got to come wid you next time. She kin git de things done in time to bring you to de school. You content yo'self. (*The* LITTLE

BOY *straightens up in his chair.*) Now, what do Carlisle want to know?

CARLISLE. How he decide he want de worl' to be right yere and how he git de idea he wanted it?

MYRTLE. Caize de Book say, don't it, Mr. Deshee?

DESHEE. De Book say, but at de same time dat's a good question. I remember when I was a little boy de same thing recurred to me. An' ol' Mr. Dubois, he was a wonderful preacher at New Hope Chapel over in East Gretna, he said: "De answer is dat de Book ain't got time to go into all de details." And he was right. You know sometimes I think de Lawd expects us to figure out a few things for ourselves. We know that at one time dey wasn't anything except Heaven, we don't know jest where it was but we know it was dere. Maybe it was everywhere. Den one day de Lawd got the idea he'd like to make some places. He made de sun and de moon, de stars. An' he made de earth.

MYRTLE. Who was aroun' den, nothin' but angels?

DESHEE. I suppose so.

FIRST BOY. What was de angels doin' up dere?

DESHEE. I suppose dey jest flew aroun' and had a good time. Dey wasn't no sin, so dey musta had a good time.

FIRST BOY. Did dey have picnics?

DESHEE. Sho, dey had the nicest kind of picnics. Dey probably had fish frys, wid b'iled custard and ten cent seegars for de adults. God gives us humans lotsa ideas about havin' good times. Maybe dey were

things he'd seen de angels do. Yes, sir, I bet dey had a fish fry every week.

MYRTLE. Did dey have Sunday School, too?

DESHEE. Yes, dey musta had Sunday School for de cherubs.

MYRTLE. What did God look like, Mr. Deshee?

DESHEE. Well, nobody knows exactly what God looked like. But when I was a little boy I used to imagine dat he looked like de Reverend Dubois. He was de finest looking ol' man I ever knew. Yes, I used to bet de Lawd looked exactly like Mr. Dubois in de days when he walked de earth in de shape of a natchel man.

MYRTLE. When was dat, Mr. Deshee?

DESHEE. Why, when he was gettin' things started down heah. When He talked to Adam and Eve and Noah and Moses and all dem. He made mighty men in dem days. But aldo they was awful mighty dey always knew dat He was beyond dem all. Pretty near one o'clock, time fo' you chillun to go home to dinner, but before I let you go I wan' you to go over wid me de main facts of de first lesson. What's the name of de book?

CHILDREN. Genesis.

DESHEE. Dat's right. And what's de other name?

CHILDREN. First Book of Moses.

DESHEE. Dat's right. And dis yere's Chapter One. (*The lights begin to dim.*) "In de beginnin' God created de heaven an' de earth. An' de earth was widout form an' void. An' de darkness was upon de face of de deep."

SCENE II

In the darkness many voices are heard singing "Rise, Shine, Give God The Glory." They sing it gayly and rapidly. The lights go up as the second verse ends. The chorus is being sung diminuendo by a mixed company of angels. That is they are angels in that they wear brightly colored robes and have wings protruding from their backs. Otherwise they look and act like a company of happy Negroes at a fish fry. The scene itself is a pre-Creation Heaven with compromises. In the distance is an unbroken stretch of blue sky. Companionable varicolored clouds billow down to the floor of the stage and roll overhead to the branches of a live oak tree which is up left. The tree is leafy and dripping with Spanish moss, and with the clouds makes a frame for the scene. In the cool shade of the tree are the usual appurtenances of a fish fry; a large kettle of hot fat set on two small parallel logs, with a fire going underneath, and a large rustic table formed by driving four stakes into the ground and placing planks on top of the small connecting boards. On the table are piles of biscuits and corn bread and the cooked fish in dish pans. There are one or two fairly large cedar or crock "churns" containing boiled custard, which looks like milk. There is a gourd dipper beside the churns and several glasses and cups of various sizes and shapes from which the custard is drunk.

The principal singers are marching two by two in a small area at the right of the stage. Two MAMMY ANGELS *are attending to the frying beside the kettle. Behind the table a* MAN ANGEL *is skinning fish and passing them to the cooks. Another is ladling out the custard. A* MAMMY ANGEL *is putting fish on bread for a brood of cherubs, and during the first scene they seat themselves on a grassy bank upstage. Another* MAMMY ANGEL *is clapping her hands disapprovingly and beckoning a laughing* BOY CHERUB *down from a cloud a little out of her reach. Another* MAMMY ANGEL *is solicitously slapping the back of a girl cherub who has a large fish sandwich in her hand and a bone in her throat. There is much movement about the table, and during the first few minutes several individuals go up to the table to help themselves to the food and drink. Many of the women angels wear hats and a few of the men are smoking cigars. A large boxful is on the table. There is much laughter and chatter as the music softens, but continues, during the early part of the action. The following short scenes are played almost simultaneously.*

FIRST COOK (*at kettle; calling off*). Hurry up, Cajey. Dis yere fat's cryin' fo' mo' feesh.

A VOICE (*off stage*). We comin', fas' we kin. Dey got to be ketched, ain't dey? We cain't say, "C'm'on little fish. C'm'on an' git fried," kin we?

SECOND COOK (*at table*). De trouble is de mens is all worm fishin'.

FIRST MAN ANGEL (*at table*). Whut dif'runce do it make? Yo' all de time got to make out like somebody's doin' somethin' de wrong way.

SECOND COOK (*near table*). I s'pose you got de per'fec' way fo' makin' bait.

FIRST MAN ANGEL. I ain't sayin' dat. I is sayin' what's wrong wid worm fishin'.

SECOND COOK. Whut's wrong wid worm fishin'? Ever'thing, dat's all. Dey's only one good way fo' catfishin', an' dats minny fishin'. Anybody know dat.

FIRST MAN ANGEL. Well, it jest so happen dat minny fishin' is de doggondest fool way of fishin' dey is. You kin try minny fishin' to de cows come home an' all you catch'll be de backache. De trouble wid you, sister, is you jest got minny fishin' on de brain.

SECOND COOK. Go right on, loud mouf. You tell me de news. My, my! You jest de wisest person in de worl'. First you, den de Lawd God.

FIRST MAN ANGEL (*to the custard ladler*). You cain't tell dem nothin'. (*Walks away to the custard churn.*) Does you try to 'splain some simple fac' dey git man-deaf.

FIRST MAMMY ANGEL (*to* CHERUB *on the cloud*). Now, you heerd me. (*The* CHERUB *assumes several mocking poses, as she speaks*.) You fly down yere. You wanter be put down in de sin book? (*She goes to the table, gets a drink for herself and points out the* CHERUB *to one of the men behind the table*.) Dat baby must got imp blood in him he so vexin'. (*She returns to her position under the cloud*.) You want me to fly up dere an' slap you down? Now, I tol' you. (*The* CHERUB *starts to come down*.)

STOUT ANGEL (*to the* CHERUB *with a bone in her throat*). I tol' you you was too little fo' cat fish. What you wanter git a bone in yo' froat fo'? (*She slaps he* CHERUB'S *back*.)

SLENDER ANGEL (*leisurely eating a sandwich as she watches the back-slapping*). What de trouble wid Leonetta?

STOUT ANGEL. She got a catfish bone down her froat. (*To the* CHERUB.) Doggone, I tol' you to eat grinnel instead.

SLENDER ANGEL. Ef'n she do git all dat et, she gonter have de bellyache.

STOUT ANGEL. Ain't I tol' her dat? (*To* CHERUB.) Come on now; let go dat bone. (*She slaps* CHERUB'S *back again. The bone is dislodged and the* CHERUB *grins her relief*.) Dat's good.

SLENDER ANGEL (*comfortingly*). Now she all right.

STOUT ANGEL. Go on an' play wid yo' cousins. (*The* CHERUB *joins the* CHERUBS *sitting on the embankment. The concurrency of scenes ends here*.) I ain't see you lately, Lily. How you been?

SLENDER ANGEL. Me, I'm fine. I been visitin' my mammy. She waitin' on de welcome table over by de throne of grace.

STOUT ANGEL. She always was pretty holy.

SLENDER ANGEL. Yes, ma'am. She like it dere. I guess de Lawd's took quite a fancy to her.

STOUT ANGEL. Well, dat's natural. I declare yo' mammy one of de finest lady angels I know.

SLENDER ANGEL. She claim you de best one she know.

STOUT ANGEL. Well, when you come right down to it, I suppose we is all pretty near perfec'.

SLENDER ANGEL. Yes, ma'am. Why is dat, Mis' Jenny?

STOUT ANGEL. I s'pose it's caize de Lawd he don' 'low us 'sociatin' wid de devil any mo' so dat dey cain' be no mo' sinnin'.

SLENDER ANGEL. Po' ol' Satan. Whutevah become of him?

STOUT ANGEL. De Lawd put him some place I s'pose.

SLENDER ANGEL. But dey ain't any place but Heaven, is dey?

STOUT ANGEL. De Lawd could make a place, couldn't he?

SLENDER ANGEL. Dat's de truth. Dey's one thing confuses me though.

STOUT ANGEL. What's dat?

SLENDER ANGEL. I do a great deal of travelin' an' I ain't never come across any place but Heaven anywhere. So if de Lawd kick Satan out of Heaven jest whereat did he go? Dat's my question.

STOUT ANGEL. You bettah let de Lawd keep his own secrets, Lily. De way things is goin' now dey ain't been no sinnin' since dey give dat scamp a kick in de pants. Nowadays Heaven's free of sin an' if a lady wants a little constitutional she kin fly till she wing-weary widout gittin' insulted.

SLENDER ANGEL. I was jest a baby when Satan lef'. I don't even 'member what he look like.

STOUT ANGEL. He was jest right fo' a devil. (*An* ARCHANGEL *enters. He is older than the others and wears a white beard. His clothing is much darker than that of the others and his wings a trifle more imposing*.) Good mo'nin', Archangel.
(*Others say good morning*.)

ARCHANGEL. Good mo'nin', folks. I wonder kin I interrup' de fish fry an' give out de Sunday school cyards? (*Cries of "Sutting-ly!" "Mah goodness, yes"—etc. The marching* CHOIR *stops*.) You kin keep singin' if you want to. Why don' you sing

"When de Saints Come Marchin' In?" Seem to me I ain' heard dat lately. (*The* CHOIR *begins* "*When the Saints Come Marching In*," *rather softly, but does not resume marching. The* ARCHANGEL *looks off left.*) All right, bring 'em yere. (*A prim-looking* WOMAN TEACHER-ANGEL *enters, shepherding ten* BOY *and* GIRL CHERUBS. *The* TEACHER *carries ten beribboned diplomas, which she gives to the* ARCHANGEL. *The* CHERUBS *are dressed in stiffly starched white suits and dresses, the little girls having enormous ribbons at the backs of their dresses and smaller ones in their hair and on the tips of their wings. They line up in front of the* ARCHANGEL *and receive the attention of the rest of the company. The* CHOIR *sings through the ceremony.*) Now den cherubs, why is you yere?

CHILDREN. Because we so good.

ARCHANGEL. Dat's right. Now who de big boss?

CHILDREN. Our dear Lawd.

ARCHANGEL. Dat's right. When you all grow up what you gonter be?

CHILDREN. Holy angels at de throne of grace.

ARCHANGEL. Dat's right. Now, you passed yo' 'xaminations and it gives me great pleasure to hand out de cyards for de whole class. Gineeva Chaproe. (*The* FIRST GIRL CHERUB *goes to him and gets her diploma. The* CHOIR *sings loudly and resumes marching, as the* ARCHANGEL *calls out another name—and presents diplomas.*) Corey Moulter. (SECOND GIRL CHERUB *gets her diploma.*) Nootzie Winebush. (THIRD GIRL CHERUB.) Harriet Prancy. (FOURTH GIRL CHERUB.) I guess you is Brozain Stew't. (*He gives the* FIFTH GIRL CHERUB *the paper. Each of the presentations has been accompanied by hand-clapping from the bystanders.*) Now you boys know yo' own names. Suppose you come yere and help me git dese 'sorted right? (BOY CHERUBS *gather about him and receive their diplomas. The little* GIRLS *have scattered about the stage, joining groups of the adult angels. The angel* GABRIEL *enters. He is bigger and more elaborately winged than even the* ARCHANGEL, *but he is also* much younger and beardless. His costume is less conventional than that of the other men, resembling more the Gabriel of the Doré drawings. His appearance causes a flutter among the others. They stop their chattering with the children. The* CHOIR *stops as three or four audible whispers of* "Gabriel!" *are heard. In a moment the heavenly company is all attention.*)

GABRIEL (*lifting his hand*). Gangway! Gangway for de Lawd God Jehovah! (*There is a reverent hush as* GOD *enters. He is the tallest and biggest of them all. He wears a white shirt with a white bow tie, a long Prince Albert coat of black alpaca, black trousers and congress gaiters. He looks at the assemblage. There is a pause. He speaks in a rich, bass voice.*)

GOD. Is you been baptized?

OTHERS (*chanting*). Certainly, Lawd.

GOD. Is you been baptized?

OTHERS. Certainly, Lawd.

GOD (*with the beginning of musical notation*). Is you been baptized?

OTHERS (*now half-singing*). Certainly, Lawd. Certainly, certainly, certainly, Lawd. (*They sing the last two verses with equivalent part division.*)

Is you been redeemed?
  Certainly, Lawd.
Is you been redeemed?
  Certainly, Lawd.
Is you been redeemed?
  Certainly, Lawd. Certainly, certainly, certainly, Lawd.

Do you bow mighty low?
  Certainly, Lawd.
Do you bow mighty low?
  Certainly, Lawd.
Do you bow mighty low?
  Certainly, Lawd. Certainly, certainly, certainly, Lawd.

(*As the last response ends all heads are bowed.* GOD *looks at them for a moment; then lifts His hand.*)

GOD. Let de fish fry proceed. (EVERYONE *rises. The* ANGELS *relax and resume their inaudible conversations. The activity behind the table and about the cauldron is resumed. Some of the* CHOIR *members cross to the table and get sandwiches and cups of the boiled custard. Three or four of the* CHILDREN *in the Sunday School class and the* LITTLE GIRL *who had the bone in her throat affectionately group themselves about* GOD *as he speaks with the* ARCHANGEL. *He pats their heads, they hang to his coat-tails, etc.*)

ARCHANGEL. Good mo'nin', Lawd.

GOD. Good mo'nin', Deacon. You lookin' pretty spry.

ARCHANGEL. I cain' complain. We jest been givin' our cyards to de chillun.

GOD. Dat's good.
(*A small* CHERUB, *his feet braced against one of* GOD's *shoes is using* GOD's *coat tail as a trapeze. One of the* COOKS *offers a fish sandwich which* GOD *politely declines.*)

FIRST MAMMY ANGEL. Now, you leave go de Lawd's coat, Herman. You heah me?

GOD. Dat's all right, sister. He jest playin'.

FIRST MAMMY ANGEL. He playin' too rough. (GOD *picks up the* CHERUB *and spanks him good-naturedly. The* CHERUB *squeals with delight and runs to his mother.* GABRIEL *advances to* GOD *with a glass of the custard.*)

GABRIEL. Little b'iled custud, Lawd?

GOD. Thank you very kindly. Dis looks nice.

CUSTARD MAKER (*offering a box*). Ten cent seegar, Lawd?

GOD (*taking it*). Thank you, thank you. How de fish fry goin'? (*Ad lib. cries of* "O. K. Lawd," "Fine an' dandy, Lawd," "De best one yit, Lawd," *etc. To the* CHOIR.) How you shouters gittin' on?

CHOIR LEADER. We been marchin' and singin' de whole mo'nin'.

GOD. I heerd you. You gettin' better all de time. You gittin' as good as de one at de throne. Why don' you give us one dem ol' time jump-ups?

CHOIR LEADER. Anythin' you say, Lawd. (*To the others.*) "So High!"
(*The* CHOIR *begins to sing* "So High You Can't Get Over It." *They sing softly, but do not march. An* ANGEL *offers his cigar to* GOD *from which He can light His own.*)

GOD. No, thanks. I'm gonter save dis a bit. (*He puts the cigar in his pocket and listens to the singers a moment. Then he sips his custard. After a second sip, a look of displeasure comes on his face.*)

GABRIEL. What's de matter, Lawd?

GOD (*sipping again*). I ain't jest sure, yit. Dey's something 'bout dis custard. (*Takes another sip.*)

CUSTARD MAKER. Ain't it all right, Lawd?

GOD. It don't seem seasoned jest right. You make it?

CUSTARD MAKER. Yes, Lawd. I put everythin' in it like I allus do. It's supposed to be perfec'.

GOD. Yeah. I kin taste de eggs and de cream and de sugar. (*Suddenly.*) I know what it is. It needs jest a little bit mo' firmament.

CUSTARD MAKER. Dey's firmament in it, Lawd.

GOD. Maybe, but it ain' enough.

CUSTARD MAKER. It's all we had, Lawd. Dey ain't a drap in de jug.

GOD. Dat's all right. I'll jest r'ar back an' pass a miracle. (CHOIR *stops singing.*) Let it be some firmament! An' when I say let it be some firmament, I don't want jest a little bitty dab o' firmament caize I'm sick an' tired of runnin' out of it when we need it. Let it be a whole mess of firmament! (*The stage has become misty until* GOD *and the heavenly company are obscured. As he finishes the speech there is a burst of thunder. As the stage grows darker.*) Dat's de way I like it.
(*Murmurs from the others;* "Dat's a lot of firmament." "My, dat is firmament!" "Look to me like he's created rain," *etc.*)

FIRST MAMMY ANGEL (*when the stage is dark*). Now, look Lawd, dat's too much firmament. De cherubs is gettin' all wet.

SECOND MAMMY ANGEL. Look at my Carlotta, Lawd. She's soaked to de skin. Dat's *plenty* too much firmament.

GOD. Well, 'co'se we don't want de chillun to ketch cold. Can't you dreen it off?

GABRIEL. Dey's no place to dreen it, Lawd.

FIRST MAMMY ANGEL. Why don't we jest take de babies home, Lawd?

GOD. No, I don' wanta bust up de fish fry. You angels keep quiet an' I'll pass another miracle. Dat's always de trouble wid miracles. When you pass one you always gotta r'ar back an' pass another. (*There is a hush.*) Let dere be a place to dreen off dis firmament. Let dere be mountains and valleys an' let dere be oceans an' lakes. An' let dere be rivers and bayous to dreen it off in, too. As a matter of fac' let dere be de earth. An' when dat's done let dere be de sun, an' let it come out and dry my cherubs' wings. (*The lights go up until the stage is bathed in sunlight. On the embankment upstage there is now a waist-high wrought-iron railing such as one sees on the galleries of houses in the French quarter of New Orleans. The* CHERUBS *are being examined by their parents and there is an ad lib. murmur of,* "You all right, honey?" "You feel better now, Albert?" "Now you all dry, Vangy?" *until the* ARCHANGEL, *who has been gazing in awe at the railing, drowns them out.*)

ARCHANGEL. Look yere!
(*There is a rush to the embankment accompanied by exclamations,* "My goodness!" "What's dis?" "I declah!" *etc.* GABRIEL *towers above the group on the middle of the embankment.* GOD *is wrapped in thought, facing the audience. The* CHOIR *resumes singing* "So High You Can't Get Over It" *softly. The babbling at the balustrade dies away as the people lean over the railing.* GABRIEL *turns and faces* GOD *indicating the earth below the railing with his left hand.*)

GABRIEL. Do you see it, Lawd?

GOD (*quietly, without turning his head upstage*). Yes, Gabriel.

GABRIEL. Looks mighty nice, Lawd.

GOD. Yes.
(GABRIEL *turns and looks over the railing.*)

GABRIEL (*gazing down*). Yes, suh. Dat'd make mighty nice farming country. Jest look at dat South forty over dere. You ain't going to let dat go to waste is you Lawd? Dat would be a pity an' a shame.

GOD (*not turning*). It's a good earth. (GOD *turns, room is made for him beside* GABRIEL *on the embankment.*) Yes. I ought to have somebody to enjoy it. (*He turns, facing the audience. The others, save for the* CHOIR *who are lined up in two rows of six on an angle up right, continue to look over the embankment.*) Gabriel! (GOD *steps down from the embankment two paces.*)

GABRIEL (*joining him*). Yes, Lawd.

GOD. Gabriel, I'm goin' down dere.

GABRIEL. Yes, Lawd.

GOD. I want you to be my working boss yere while I'm gone.

GABRIEL. Yes, Lawd.

GOD. You know dat matter of dem two stars?

GABRIEL. Yes, Lawd.

GOD. Git dat fixed up! You know dat sparrow dat fell a little while ago? 'Tend to dat, too.

GABRIEL. Yes, Lawd.

GOD. I guess dat's about all. I'll be back Saddy. (*To the* CHOIR.) Quiet, angels. (*The* CHOIR *stops singing. Those on the embankment circle down stage.* GOD *goes to embankment. Turns and faces the company.*) I'm gonter pass one more miracle. You all gonter help me an' not make a soun' caize it's one of de most impo'tant miracles of all. (*Nobody moves.* GOD *turns, facing the sky and raises his arms above his head.*) Let there be man.
(*There is growing roll of thunder as stage grows dark. The* CHOIR *bursts into* "Hallelujah," *and continues until the lights go up on the next scene.*)

SCENE III

Enclosing the stage is a heterogeneous cluster of cottonwood, camphor, live oak and syca-more trees, yaupon and turkey-berry bushes, with their purple and red berries, sprays of fern-like indigo fiera and splashes of various Louisiana flowers. In the middle of the stage, disclosed when the mistiness at rise grows into warm sunlight, stands ADAM. *He is a puzzled man of 30, of medium height, dressed in the clothing of the average field hand: He is bare-headed. In the distance can be heard the choir continuing. "Bright Mansions Above." A bird begins to sing.* ADAM *smiles and turns to look at the source of this novel sound. He senses his strength and raises his forearms, his fists clenched. With his left hand he carefully touches the muscles of his upper right arm. He smiles again, realizing his power. He looks at his feet which are stretched wide apart. He stamps once or twice and now almost laughs in his enjoyment. Other birds begin trilling and* ADAM *glances up joyfully toward the foliage.* GOD *enters.*

GOD. Good mo'nin', Son.

ADAM (*with a little awe*). Good mo'nin', Lawd.

GOD. What's yo' name, Son?

ADAM. Adam.

GOD. Adam which?

ADAM (*frankly, after a moment's puzzled groping*). Jest Adam, Lawd.

GOD. Well, Adam, how dey treatin' you? How things goin'?

ADAM. Well, Lawd, you know it's kind of a new line of wukk.

GOD. You'll soon get de hang of it. You know yo' kind of a new style with me.

ADAM. Oh, I guess I'm gonter make out all right soon as I learn de ropes.

GOD. Yes, I guess you will. Yo' a nice job.

ADAM. Yes, Lawd.

GOD. Dey's jest one little thing de matter with you. Did you notice it?

ADAM. Well, now you mentioned it, Lawd, I kind of thought dey was somethin' wrong.

GOD. Yes suh, you ain't quite right. Adam, you need a family. De reason for dat is in yo' heart you is a family man. (*Flicking*

the ash off his cigar.*) I'd say dat was de main trouble at de moment.

ADAM (*smiling*). Yes sir. (*His smile fades and he is puzzled again.*) At de same time —dey's one thing puzzlin' me, Lawd. Could I ask you a question?

GOD. Why, certainly, Adam.

ADAM. Lawd, jest what *is* a family?

GOD. I'm gonter show you. (*Indicates a spot.*) Jest lie down dere, Adam. Make out you was goin' to slumber.

ADAM (*gently*). Yes, Lawd. (*He lies down.* GOD *stands beside him and as he raises his arms above his head the lights go down. In the darkness* GOD *speaks.*)

GOD. Eve. (*Lights go up.* EVE *is standing beside* ADAM. *She is about twenty-six, and quite pretty. She is dressed like a country girl. Her gingham dress is quite new and clean.* GOD *is now at the other side of the stage, looking at them critically.* EVE *looks at* ADAM *in timid wonder and slowly turns her head until she meets the glance of* GOD. ADAM *stands beside* EVE. *They gaze at each other for a moment.* GOD *smiles.*) Now you all right, Eve. (ADAM *and* EVE *face him.*) Now I'll tell you what I'm gonter do. I'm gonter put you in charge here. I'm gonter give you de run of dis whole garden. Eve, you take care of dis man an' Adam you take care of dis woman. You belong to each other. I don' want you to try to do too much caize yo' both 'kind of experiment wid me an' I ain't sho' whether you could make it. You two jest enjoy yo'self. Drink de water from de little brooks an' de wine from de grapes an' de berries, an' eat de food dat's hangin' for you in de trees. (*He pauses, startled by a painful thought.*) Dat is, in all but one tree. (*He pauses. Then, not looking at them.*) You know what I mean, my children?

ADAM *and* EVE. Yes, Lawd. (*They slowly turn their heads left, toward the branches of an off-stage tree. Then they look back at* GOD.)

ADAM. Thank you, Lawd.

EVE. Thank you, Lawd.

GOD. I gotter be gittin' along now. I got a hund'ed thousan' things to do 'fo' you take you' nex' breath. Enjoy yo'selves— (GOD *exits.*)
(ADAM *and* EVE *stand looking after Him for a moment, then each looks down and watches their hands meet and clasp. After a moment they lift their heads slowly until they are again gazing at the tree.*)

EVE. Adam.

ADAM (*looking at the tree, almost in terror*). What?

EVE (*softly as she too continues to look at the tree*). Adam.
(*The* CHOIR *begins singing "Turn You Round" and as the lights go down the* CHOIR *continues until there is blackness. The* CHOIR *suddenly stops. The following scene is played in the darkness.*)

MR. DESHEE'S VOICE. Now, I s'pose you chil-
lun know what happened after God made Adam 'n' Eve. Do you?

FIRST GIRL'S VOICE. I know, Mr. Deshee.

MR. DESHEE'S VOICE. Jest a minute, Randolph. Didn't I tell you you gotta tell yo' mammy let yo' sister bring you. Carlisle, take way dat truck he's eatin'. You sit by him, see kin you keep him quiet. Now, den, Myrtle what happened?

FIRST GIRL'S VOICE. Why, den dey ate de fo'bidden fruit and den dey got driv' out de garden.

MR. DESHEE'S VOICE. An' den what happened?

FIRST GIRL'S VOICE. Den dey felt ver bad.

MR. DESHEE'S VOICE. I don' mean how dey feel, I mean how dey do. Do dey have any children or anything like dat?

FIRST GIRL'S VOICE. Oh, yes, suh, dey have Cain 'n' Abel.

MR. DESHEE'S VOICE. Dat's right, dey have Cain an' Abel.

BOY'S VOICE. Dat was a long time after dey got married, wasn't it, Mr. Deshee? My mammy say it was a hund'ed years.

MR. DESHEE'S VOICE. Well, nobody kin be so sure. As I tol' you befo' dey was jest beginnin' to be able to tell de time an' nobody was any too sure 'bout anythin' even den. So de bes' thing to do is jest realize dat de thing happened an' don't bother 'bout how many years it was. Jest remember what I told you about it gittin' dark when you go to sleep an' it bein' light when you wake up. Dat's de way time went by in dem days. One thing we do know an' dat was dis boy Cain was a mean rascal.
(*The lights go up on the next scene.*)

SCENE IV

A roadside.
    CAIN, *a husky young Negro, stands over the body of the dead* ABEL. *Both are dressed as laborers.* CAIN *is looking at the body in awe, a rock in his right hand.* GOD *enters.*

GOD. Cain, look what you done to Abel.

CAIN. Lawd, I was min'in' my own business and he come monkeyin' aroun' wit' me. I was wukkin' in de fiel' an he was sittin' in de shade of de tree. He say "Me, I'd be skeered to git out in dis hot sun. I be 'fraid my brains git cooked. Co'se you ain't got no brains so you ain't in no danger." An' so I up and flang de rock. If it miss 'im all right, an' if it hit 'im, all right. Dat's the way I feel.

GOD. All right, but I'm yere to tell you dat's called a crime. When de new Judge is done talkin' to you you'll be draggin' a ball and chain de rest of yo' life.

CAIN. Well, what'd he want to come monkeyin' aroun' me fo' den? I was jest plowin', min'in' my own business, and not payin him no min', and yere he come makin' me de fool. I'd bust anybody what make me de fool.

GOD. Well, I ain't sayin' you right an' I ain't sayin' you wrong. But I do say was I you I'd jest git myself down de road 'til I was clean out of de county. An' you better take an' git married an' settle down an' raise some chillun. Dey ain't nothin' to make a man fo'git his troubles like raisin' a family. Now, you better git.

CAIN. Yessuh. (CAIN *walks off.*)
(GOD *watches him from the forestage and as the lights begin to dim looks off. The* CHOIR *begins "Run, Sinner, Run."*)

GOD. Adam an' Eve you better try again. You better have Seth an' a lot mo' chillun. (*There is darkness. The* CHOIR *continues until the lights go up on the next scene.*)

SCENE V

CAIN *is discovered walking on an unseen treadmill. A middle distance of trees, hillsides and shrubbery passes him on an upper treadmill. Behind is the blue sky. He stops under the branches of a tree to look at a sign on a fence railing. Only half the tree is visible on the stage. The sign reads,* "NOD PARISH. COUNTY LINE."

CAIN (*sitting down with a sigh of relief under the tree*). At las'! Phew! (*Wipes his forehead with a handkerchief.*) Feels like I been walkin' fo'ty years. (*He looks back.*) Well, dey cain' git me now. Now I kin raise a fam'ly. (*An idea occurs to him, and suddenly he begins looking right and left.*) Well, I'll be hit by a mule! Knock me down for a trustin' baby! Where I gonter git dat fam'ly? Dat preacher fooled me. (*He is quite dejected.*) Doggone!

CAIN's GIRL (*off-stage*). Hello, Country Boy!
(CAIN *glances up to the off-stage branches of the tree.*)

CAIN. Hey-ho, Good lookin'! Which way is it to town?

CAIN's GIRL (*off-stage*). What you tryin' to do? You tryin' to mash me? I be doggone if it ain't gittin' so a gal cain't hardly leave de house 'out some of dese fast men ain' passin' remarks at her.

CAIN. I ain' passin' remarks.

CAIN's GIRL (*off-stage*). If I thought you was tryin' to mash me, I'd call de police an' git you tooken to de first precinct.

CAIN. Look yere, gal, I ast you a question, an' if you don' answer me I'm gonter bend you 'cross my pants an' burn you up.

CAIN's GIRL (*off-stage*). I'm comin' down. (CAIN *takes his eyes from the tree.*)

CAIN. Yes, an' you better hurry.
(CAIN's GIRL *enters. She is as large as* CAIN, *wickedly pretty, and somewhat flashily dressed. She smiles at* CAIN.)

CAIN'S GIRL. I bet you kin handle a gal mean wid dem big stout arms of your'n. I sho' would hate to git you mad at me, Country Boy.

CAIN (*smiling*). Come yere. (*She goes a little closer to him.*) Don't be 'fraid, I ain' so mean.

CAIN'S GIRL. You got two bad lookin' eyes. I bet yo' hot coffee 'mong de women folks.

CAIN. I ain' never find out. What was you doin' in dat tree?

CAIN'S GIRL. Jest coolin' myself in de element.

CAIN. Is you a Nod Parish gal?

CAIN'S GIRL. Bo'n an' bred.

CAIN. You know yo' kinda pretty.

CAIN'S GIRL. Who tol' you dat?

CAIN. Dese yere two bad eyes of mine.

CAIN'S GIRL. I bet you say dat to everybody all de way down de road.

CAIN. Comin' down dat road I didn't talk to nobody.

CAIN'S GIRL. Where you boun' for, Beautiful?

CAIN. I'm jest seein' de country. I thought I might settle down yere fo' a spell. You live wit' yo' people?

CAIN'S GIRL. Co'se I does.

CAIN. 'Spose dey'd like to take in a boarder?

CAIN'S GIRL. Be nice if dey would, wouldn't it?

CAIN. I think so. You got a beau?

CAIN'S GIRL. Huh-uh!

CAIN (*smiling*). You has *now*.

CAIN'S GIRL. I guess—I guess if you wanted to kiss me an' I tried to stop you, you could pretty nearly crush me wit' dem stout arms.

CAIN. You wouldn't try too much, would you?

CAIN'S GIRL. Maybe for a little while.

CAIN. An' den what?

CAIN'S GIRL. Why don' we wait an' see?

CAIN. When would dat be?

CAIN'S GIRL. Tonight. After supper. Think you kin walk a little further now, City Boy?

CAIN. Yeh, I ain't so weary now.
(*She takes his hand.*)

CAIN'S GIRL. What yo' name? (*Takes his arm.*)

CAIN. Cain.

CAIN'S GIRL. Then I'm Cain's Gal. Come on, honey, an' meet de folks.
(*They exit. The* CHOIR *is heard singing "You Better Mind," as* GOD *enters.* GOD *watches the vanished* CAIN *and his girl.*)

GOD (*after shaking his head*). Bad business. I don' like de way things is goin' atall.
(*The stage is darkened. The* CHOIR *continues singing until the lights go up on the next scene.*)

SCENE VI

GOD's *private office in Heaven. It is a small room, framed by tableau curtains. A large window up center looks out on the sky. There is a battered roll-top desk. On the wall next to the window is a framed religious oleograph with a calendar attached to it underneath. A door is at the left. A hat rack is on the wall above the door. There are two or three cheap pine chairs beside the window, and beyond the door. In front of the desk is an old swivel armchair which creaks every time* GOD *leans back in it. The desk is open and various papers are stuck in the pigeonholes. Writing implements, etc. are on the desk. On a shelf above the desk is a row of law books. A cuspidor is near the desk, and a waste basket by it. The general atmosphere is that of the office of a Negro lawyer in a Louisiana town. As the lights go up* GOD *takes a fresh cigar from a box on the desk and begins puffing it without bothering to light it. There is no comment on this minor miracle from* GABRIEL *who is sitting in one of the chairs with a pencil and several papers in his hand. The singing becomes pianissimo.*

GABRIEL (*looking at the papers*). Well, I guess dat's about all de impo'tant business this mornin', Lawd.

GOD. How 'bou' dat cherub over to Archangel Montgomery's house?

GABRIEL. Where do dey live, Lawd? (*The singing stops.*)

GOD. Dat little two story gold house, over by de pearly gates.

GABRIEL. Oh, *dat* Montgomery. I thought you was referrin' to de ol' gentleman. Oh, yeh. (*He sorts through the papers and finds one he is looking for.*) Yere it 'tis. (*Reads.*) "Cherub Christina Montgomery; wings is moltin' out of season an' nobody knows what to do."

GOD. Well, now, take keer of dat. You gotter be more careful, Gabe.

GABRIEL. Yes, Lawd. (*Folds the papers and puts them in a pocket.* GOD *turns to his desk, takes another puff or two of the cigar, and with a pencil, begins checking off items on a sheet of paper before him. His back is turned toward* GABRIEL. GABRIEL *takes his trumpet from the hat rack and burnishes it with his robe. He then wets his lips and puts the mouthpiece to his mouth.*)

GOD (*without turning around*). Now, watch yo'self, Gabriel.

GABRIEL. I wasn't goin' to blow, Lawd. I jest do dat every now an' den so I can keep de feel of it. (*He leans trumpet against the wall.* GOD *picks up the papers and swings his chair around toward* GABRIEL.)

GOD. What's dis yere about de moon?

GABRIEL (*suddenly remembering*). Oh! De moon people say it's beginnin' to melt a little, on 'count caize de sun's so hot.

GOD. It's goin' 'roun' 'cordin' to schedule, ain't it?

GABRIEL. Yes, Lawd.

GOD. Well, tell 'em to stop groanin'. Dere's nothin' de matter wid dat moon. Trouble is so many angels is flyin' over dere on Saddy night. Dey git to beatin' dere wings when dey dancin' an' dat makes de heat. Tell dem dat from now on dancin' 'roun' de moon is sinnin'. Dey got to stop it. Dat'll cool off de moon. (*He swings back and puts the paper on the desk. He leans back in the chair comfortably, his hands clasped behind his head.*) Is dere anythin' else you ought to remin' me of?

GABRIEL. De prayers, Lawd.

GOD (*puzzled, slowly swinging chair around again*). De prayers?

GABRIEL. From mankind. You know, down on de earth.

GOD. Oh, yeh, de poor little earth. Bless my soul, I almos' forgot about dat. Mus' be three or four hund'ed years since I been down dere. I wasn't any too pleased wid dat job.

GABRIEL (*laughing*). You know you don' make mistakes, Lawd.

GOD (*soberly, with introspective detachment*). So dey tell me. (*He looks at* GABRIEL, *then through the window again.*) So dey tell me. I fin' I kin be displeased though, an' I was displeased wid de mankind I las' seen. Maybe I ought to go down dere again—I need a little holiday.

GABRIEL. Might do you good, Lawd.

GOD. I think I will. I'll go down an' walk de earth agin an' see how dem poor humans is makin' out. What time is it, by de sun an' de stars?

GABRIEL (*glancing out of the window*). Jest exactly half-past, Lawd.

(GOD *is taking his hat and stick from the hat rack.*)

GOD (*opening the door*). Well, take keer o' yo'self. I'll be back Saddy. (*He exits.*)

(*The stage is darkened. The* CHOIR *begins "Dere's no Hidin' Place," and continues until the lights go up on the next scene.*)

SCENE VII

GOD *is walking along a country road. He stops to listen. Church bells are heard in the distance.*

GOD. Dat's nice. Nice an' quiet. Dat's de way I like Sunday to be. (*The sound is broken by a shrill voice of a girl. It is* ZEBA *singing a "blues."*) Now, dat ain't so good. (GOD *resumes his walk and the upper treadmill brings on a tree stump on which* ZEBA *is sitting. She is accompanying her song with a ukulele.* GOD *and the treadmill stop. When the stump reaches the center of the stage, it is seen that* ZEBA *is a rouged and extremely flashily dressed chippy of about eighteen.*) Stop dat!

ZEBA. What's de matter wid you, Country Boy? Pull up yo' pants. (*She resumes singing.*)

GOD. Stop dat!

ZEBA (*stops again*). Say, listen to me, Banjo Eyes. What right you got to stop a lady enjoyin' herself?

GOD. Don't you know dis is de Sabbath? Da's no kin' o' song to sing on de Lawd's day.

ZEBA. Who care 'bout de Lawd's day, anymo'? People jest use Sunday now to git over Saddy.

GOD. You a awful sassy little girl.

ZEBA. I come fum sassy people! We even speak mean of de dead.

GOD. What's yo' name?

ZEBA (*flirtatiously*). "What's my name?" Ain't you de ol'-time gal hunter! Fust, "What's my name?" den I s'pose, what would it be like if you tried to kiss me? You preachers is de debbils.

GOD. I ain't aimin' to touch you daughter. (*A sudden sternness frightens* ZEBA. *She looks at him sharply.*) What is yo' name?

ZEBA. Zeba.

GOD. Who's yo' fam'ly?

ZEBA. I'm de great-great gran' daughter of Seth.

GOD. Of Seth? But Seth was a good man.

ZEBA. Yeh, he too good, he die of holiness.

GOD. An' yere's his little gran' daughter reekin' wid cologne. Ain't nobody ever tol' you yo' on de road to Hell?

ZEBA (*smiling*). Sho' dat's what de preacher say. Exceptin' of course, I happens to know dat I'm on de road to de picnic groun's, an' at de present time I'm waitin' to keep a engagement wid my sweet papa. He don' like people talkin' to me.

(CAIN THE SIXTH *enters. He is a young buck, wearing a "box" coat and the other flashy garments of a Rampart Street swell.*)

CAIN THE SIXTH. Hello, sugah! (*He crosses in front of* GOD *and faces* ZEBA.) Hello, mamma! Sorry I'm late baby, but de gals in

de barrel-house jest wouldn't let me go. Doggone, one little wirehead swore she'd tear me down.
(ZEBA *smiles and takes his hand.*)

GOD. What's yo' name, son?

CAIN THE SIXTH (*contemptuously; without turning*). Soap 'n water, Country Boy.

GOD (*sternly*). What's yo' name, son?
(CAIN *slowly turns and for a moment his manner is civil.*)

CAIN THE SIXTH. Cain the Sixth.

GOD. I was afraid so.

CAIN THE SIXTH (*his impudence returning*). You a new preacher?

GOD. Where you live?

CAIN THE SIXTH. Me, I live mos' any place.

GOD. Yes, an' you gonter see dem all. Is de udder young men all like you?

CAIN THE SIXTH (*smiling*). De gals don' think so. (*He turns towards* ZEBA *again, picks her up and sits on the stump with the laughing* ZEBA *on his lap.*)

ZEBA. Dey ain't nobody in de worl' like my honey-cake.
(CAIN *kisses her and she resumes her song.* GOD *watches them.* ZEBA *finishes a verse of the song and begins another softly.* CAIN THE SIXTH'S *eyes have been closed during the singing.*)

CAIN THE SIXTH (*his eyes closed*). Is de preacher gone?
(ZEBA *looks quickly at* GOD *without seeing him, and then looks off. She stops the song.*)

ZEBA. Yeh, I guess he walks fast.
(CAIN *pushes her off his lap and rises.*)

CAIN THE SIXTH (*with acid sweetness*). Dey tell me las' night you was talkin' to a creeper man, baby.

ZEBA. Why, you know dey ain't nobody in de world fo' me but you.

CAIN THE SIXTH (*smiling*). I know dey ain't. I even got dat guaranteed. (*Takes a revolver from his pocket.*) See dat, baby?

ZEBA. Sho' I see it, honey.

CAIN THE SIXTH. Dat jest makes me positive. (*Puts the gun back.*)

ZEBA (*pushing him back on the stump*). You don' wanter believe dem stories, papa.

CAIN THE SIXTH (*with sinister lightness*). No, I didn't believe dem, baby. Co'se dat big gorilla, Flatfoot, from de other side of de river *is* in town ag'in.

ZEBA. Dat don' mean nothin'. Flatfoot ain't nothin' to me.

CAIN THE SIXTH (*sitting again*). Co'se he ain't. Go 'head, sing some mo', baby.
(ZEBA *resumes singing.*)

GOD. Bad business. (*The treadmills start turning.* GOD *resumes his walk.* ZEBA, *still singing, and* CAIN THE SIXTH *recede with the landscape.* GOD *is again alone on the country road. There is a twitter of birds.* GOD *looks up and smiles.*) De birds is goin' 'bout dere business, all right. (*A patch of flowers goes by, black-eyed Susans, conspicuously.*) How you flowers makin' out? (CHILDREN'S *voices answer,* "We O. K., Lawd.") Yes, an' you looks very pretty. (CHILDREN'S *voices:* "Thank you, Lawd." *The flowers pass out of sight.*) It's only de human bein's makes me downhearted. Yere's as nice a Sunday as dey is turnin' out anywhere, an' nobody makin' de right use of it. (*Something ahead of him attracts his attention. His face brightens.*) Well, now dis is mo' like it. Now dat's nice to see people prayin'. It's a wonder dey don' do it in de church. But I fin' I don' min' it if dey do it outdoors.
(*A group of five adult Negroes and a boy on their knees in a semicircle appears. The treadmills stop. The* BOY, *his head bent, swings his hands rhythmically up to his head three or four times. There is a hush.*)

GAMBLER. Oh, Lawd, de smoke-house is empty. Oh, Lawd, lemme git dem groeries. Oh, Lawd, lemme see dat little *six*. (*He casts the dice.*) Wham! Dere she is, frien's.
(*Exclamations from the others:* "Well damn my eyes!" "Doggone, dat's de eighth pass he make." "For God's sake, can't you ever crap?" *etc. The* BOY *is picking up the money.*)

GOD. Gamblin'! (*Looks over the group's shoulders.*) An' wid frozen dice!

BOY GAMBLER. Dey's a dolla' 'n' a half talkin' fo' me. How much you want of it, Riney?

FIRST GAMBLER. I take fo' bits. Wait a minute. Mebbe I take a little mo'. (*He counts some money in his hand.*)

SECOND GAMBLER (*glancing up at* GOD). Hello, Liver Lips. (*To the others.*) Looka ol' Liver Lips.
(*The others look up and laugh good-naturedly, repeating "Liver Lips."*)

FIRST GAMBLER. Ain't his pockets high from de groun'? Ol' High-Pockets.
(*The others keep saying "Ol' Liver Lips." "Ol' Liver Lips don't like to see people dicin'." "Dat's a good name, 'High Pockets'."*)

BOY GAMBLER (*to others*). Come on, you gonter fade me or not?
(GOD *seizes the* BOY's *ears and drags him to his feet. The others do not move, but watch amused.*)

GOD. Come yere, son. Why, yo' jest a little boy. Gamblin' an' sinnin'. (GOD *looks at the* BOY's *face.*) You been chewin' tobacco, too, like you was yo' daddy. (GOD *sniffs.*) An' you been drinkin' sonny-kick-mammy-wine. You oughta be 'shamed. (*To the others.*) An' you gamblers oughta be 'shamed, leadin' dis boy to sin.

FIRST GAMBLER. He de bes' crap shooter in town, mister.

GOD. I'm gonter tell his mammy. I bet she don' know 'bout dis.

FIRST GAMBLER. No, she don' know. (*The others laugh.*) She don' know anythin'.

SECOND GAMBLER. Das de God's truth.

FIRST GAMBLER. See kin you beat 'im, High Pockets. Dey's a dolla' open yere.

GOD. I ain't gonter beat 'im. I'm gonter teach 'im. I may have to teach you all. (*He starts walking from them. The* BOY *sticks out his tongue the moment* GOD's *back is turned.*)

BOY GAMBLER. If you fin' my mammy you do mo'n I kin. Come on, gamblers, see kin you gimme a little action. Who wants any part of dat dollar?
(*The treadmill carries them off. The* FIRST GAMBLER *is heard saying: "I'll take another two bits," and the others, "Gimme a dime's wo'th," "I ain't only got fifteen cents left," etc. as they disappear.*)

GOD (*walking*). Where's dat little boy's home? (*The front of a shanty appears and* GOD *stops in front of the door.*) Yere's de place. It ain't any too clean, either. (*Knocks on the door with his cane.*)

VOICE IN SHANTY. Who dar?

GOD. Never you min' who's yere. Open de door.

VOICE IN SHANTY. You gotta search warrant?

GOD. I don' need one.

VOICE IN SHANTY. Who you wanter see?

GOD. I wanter see de mammy of de little gamblin' boy.

VOICE IN SHANTY. You mean little Johnny Rucker?

GOD. Dat may be his name.

VOICE IN SHANTY. Well, Mrs. Rucker ain't home.

GOD. Where's she at?

VOICE IN SHANTY. Who, Mrs. Rucker?

GOD. You heerd me.

VOICE IN SHANTY. Oh, she run away las' night wid a railroad man. She's eloped.

GOD. Where's Rucker?

VOICE IN SHANTY. He's flat under de table. He so drunk he cain't move.

GOD. Who are you?

VOICE IN SHANTY. I'se jest a fren' an' neighbor. I come in las' night to de party, an' everybody in yere's dead drunk but me. De only reason I kin talk is I drank some new white mule I made myself, an' it burn my throat so I cain't drink no mo'. You got any mo' questions?

GOD. Not for you.

(*The shanty begins to move off as* GOD *starts walking again.*)

VOICE IN SHANTY. Good riddance, I say.
(*Shanty disappears.*)

GOD. Dis ain't gittin' me nowheres. All I gotta say dis yere mankind I been peoplin' my earth wid sho' ain't much. (*He stops and looks back.*) I got good min' to wipe 'em all off an' people de earth wid angels. No. Angels is all right, singin' an' playin' an' flyin' around, but dey ain't much on workin' de crops and buildin' de levees. No, suh, mankind's jest right for my earth, if he wasn't so doggone sinful. I'd rather have my earth peopled wit' a bunch of channel catfish, dan I would mankin' an' his sin. I jest can't stan' sin. (*He is about to resume his walk when* NOAH *enters.* NOAH *is dressed like a country preacher. His coat is of the "hammer-tail" variety. He carries a prayer book under his arm.*)

NOAH. Mo'nin', brother.

GOD. Mo'nin', brother. I declare you look like a good man.

NOAH. I try to be, brother. I'm de preacher yere. I don't think I seen you to de meetin'.
(*They resume walking.*)

GOD. I jest come to town a little while ago an' I been pretty busy.

NOAH. Yeh, mos' everybody say dey's pretty busy dese days. Dey so busy dey cain't come to meetin'. It seem like de mo' I preaches de mo' people ain't got time to come to church. I ain't hardly got enough members to fill up de choir. I gotta do de preachin' an' de bassin' too.

GOD. Is dat a fac'?

NOAH. Yes, suh, brother. Everybody is mighty busy, gamblin', good-timin', an' goin' on. You jest wait, though. When Gabriel blow de horn you gonter fin' dey got plenty of time to punch chunks down in Hell. Yes, suh.

GOD. Seems a pity. Dey all perfec'ly healthy?

NOAH. Oh, dey healthy, all right. Dey jest all lazy, and mean, and full of sin. You look like a preacher, too, brother.

GOD. Well, I am, in a way.

NOAH. You jest passin' through de neighborhood?

GOD. Yes. I wanted to see how things was goin' in yo' part of de country, an' I been feelin' jest 'bout de way you do. It's enough to discourage you.

NOAH. Yes, but I gotta keep wres'lin' wid 'em. Where you boun' for right now, brother?

GOD. I was jest walkin' along. I thought I might stroll on to de nex' town.

NOAH. Well, dat's a pretty good distance. I live right yere. (*He stops walking.*) Why don' you stop an' give us de pleasure of yo' comp'ny for dinner? I believe my ol' woman has kilt a chicken.

GOD. Why, dat's mighty nice of you, brother. I don' believe I caught yo' name.

NOAH. Noah, jest brother Noah. Dis is my home, brother. Come right in.
(GOD *and* NOAH *start walking towards Noah's house which is just coming into view on the treadmill. The stage darkens, the* CHOIR *sings "Feastin' Table," and when the lights go up again, the next scene is disclosed.*)

SCENE VIII

Interior of NOAH's *house. The ensemble suggests the combination living-dining room in a fairly prosperous Negro's cabin. Clean white curtains hang at the window. A table and chairs are in the center of the room. There is a cheerful checked tablecloth on the table, and on the wall, a framed, highly colored picture reading "God Bless Our Home."*

NOAH's WIFE, *an elderly Negress, simply and neatly dressed,* GOD *and* NOAH *are discovered grouped about the table.*

NOAH. Company, darlin'. (NOAH's WIFE *takes* NOAH's *and* GOD's *hats.*) Dis gemman's a preacher, too. He's jest passin' through de country.

GOD. Good mo'nin', sister.

NOAH's WIFE. Good mo'nin'. You jest ketch me when I'm gittin' dinner ready. You gonter stay with us?

GOD. If I ain't intrudin'. Brother Noah suggested—

NOAH's WIFE. You set right down yere. I got a chicken in de pot an' it'll be ready in 'bout five minutes. I'll go out de back an' call Shem, Ham an' Japheth. (*To* GOD.) Dey's our sons. Dey live right acrost de way but always have Sunday dinner wid us. You mens make yo'selves comf'table.

GOD. Thank you, thank you very kindly.

NOAH. You run along, we all right. (GOD *and* NOAH *seat themselves.* NOAH's WIFE *exits.*)

GOD. You got a fine wife, Brother Noah.

NOAH. She pretty good woman.

GOD. Yes, suh, an' you got a nice little home. Have a ten cent seegar? (GOD *offers him one.*)

NOAH. Thank you, much obliged. (*Both men lean back restfully in their chairs.*)

GOD. Jest what seems to be de main trouble 'mong mankind, Noah?

NOAH. Well, it seems to me de main trouble is dat de whol' distric' is wide open. Now you know dat makes fo' loose livin'. Men folks spen's all dere time fightin', loafin' an' gamblin', an' makin' bad likker.

GOD. What about de women?

NOAH. De women is worse dan de men. If dey ain't makin' love powder dey out beg, borrow an' stealin' money for policy tickets. Doggone, I come in de church Sunday 'fo' las' 'bout an hour befo' de meetin' was to start, and dere was a woman stealin' de altar cloth. She was goin' to hock it. Dey ain't got no moral sense. Now you take dat case las' month, over in East Putney. Case of dat young Willy Roback.

GOD. What about him?

NOAH. Dere is a boy seventeen years old. Doggone, if he didn't elope with his aunt. Now, you know, dat kin' of goin' on is bad fo' a neighborhood.

GOD. Terrible, terrible.

NOAH. Yes, suh. Dis use' to be a nice, decent community. I been doin' my best to preach de Word, but seems like every time I preach de place jest goes a little mo' to de dogs. De good Lawd only knows what's gonter happen.

GOD. Dat is de truth. (*There is a pause. Each puffs his cigar. Suddenly* NOAH *grasps his knee, as if it were paining him, and twists his foot.*)

NOAH. Huh!

GOD. What's de matter?

NOAH. I jest got a twitch. My buck-aguer I guess. Every now and den I gets a twitch in de knee. Might be a sign of rain.

GOD. That's just what it is. Noah, what's de mos' rain you ever had 'round dese parts?

NOAH. Well, de water come down fo' six days steady last April an' de ribber got so swole it bust down de levee up 'bove Freeport. Raise cain all de way down to de delta.

GOD. What would you say was it to rain for forty days and forty nights?

NOAH. I'd say dat was a *complete* rain!

GOD. Noah, you don't know who I is, do you?

NOAH (*puzzled*). Yo' face looks easy, but I don' think I recall de name. (GOD *rises slowly, and as he reaches his full height there is a crash of lightning, a moment's darkness, and a roll of thunder. It grows light again.* NOAH *is on his knees in front of* GOD.) I should have known you. I should have seen de glory.

GOD. Dat's all right, Noah. You didn't know who I was.

NOAH. I'm jes' ol' preacher Noah, Lawd, an' I'm yo' servant. I ain' very much, but I'se all I got.

GOD. Sit down, Noah. Don' let me hear you shamin' yo'se'f, caize yo' a good man. (*Timidly* NOAH *waits until* GOD *is seated, and then sits, himself.*) I jest wanted to fin' out if you was good, Noah. Dat's why I'm walkin' de earth in de shape of a natchel man. I wish dey was mo' people like you. But, far as I kin see you and yo' fam'ly is de only respectable people in de worl'.

NOAH. Dey jest all poor sinners, Lawd.

GOD. I know. I am your Lawd. I am a god of wrath and vengeance an' dat's why I'm gonter destroy dis worl'.

NOAH (*almost in a whisper; drawing back*). Jest as you say, Lawd.

GOD. I ain't gonter destroy you, Noah. You and yo' fam'ly, yo' sheep an' cattle, an' all de udder things dat ain't human I'm gonter preserve. But de rest is gotta go. (*Takes a pencil and a sheet of paper from his pocket.*) Look yere, Noah. (NOAH *comes over and looks over his shoulder.*) I want you

to build me a boat. I want you to call it de "Ark," and I want it to look like dis. (*He is drawing on the paper. Continues to write as he speaks.*) I want you to take two of every kind of animal and bird dat's in de country. I want you to take seeds an' sprouts an' everythin' like dat an' put dem on dat Ark, because dere is gonter be all dat rain. Dey's gonter to be a deluge, Noah, an' dey's goin' to be a flood. De levees is gonter bust an' everything dat's fastened down is comin' loose, but it ain't gonter float long, caize I'm gonter make a storm dat'll sink everythin' from a hencoop to a barn. Dey ain't a ship on de sea dat'll be able to fight dat tempest. Dey all got to go. Everythin'. Everythin' in dis pretty worl' I made, except one thing, Noah. You an' yo' fam'ly an' de things I said are going to ride dat storm in de Ark. Yere's de way it's to be. (*He hands* NOAH *the paper.* NOAH *takes it and reads.*)

NOAH (*pause; looks at paper again*). Yes, suh, dis seems to be complete. Now 'bout the animals, Lawd, you say you want everythin'?

GOD. Two of everythin'.

NOAH. Dat would include jayraffes an' hippopotamusses?

GOD. Everythin' dat is.

NOAH. Dey was a circus in town las' week. I guess I kin fin' dem. Co'se I kin git all de rabbits an' possums an' wil' turkeys easy. I'll sen' de boys out. Hum, I'm jest wonderin'—

GOD. 'Bout what?

NOAH. 'Bout snakes. Think you'd like snakes, too?

GOD. Certainly, I want snakes.

NOAH. Oh, I kin git snakes, lots of 'em. Co'se, some of 'em's a little dangerous. Maybe I better take a kag of likker, too?

GOD. You kin have a kag of likker.

NOAH (*musingly*). Yes, suh, dey's a awful lot of differ'nt kin's of snakes, come to think about it. Dey's water moccasins, cotton-moufs, rattlers—mus' be a hund'ed kin's of other snakes down in de swamps. Maybe I better take two kags of likker.

GOD (*mildly*). I think de one kag's enough.

NOAH. No. I better take two kags. Besides I kin put one on each side of de boat, an' balance de ship wid dem as well as havin' dem fo' medicinal use.

GOD. You kin put one kag in de middle of de ship.

NOAH (*buoyantly*). Jest as easy to take de two kags, Lawd.

GOD. I think one kag's enough.

NOAH. Yes, Lawd, but you see forty days an' forty nights—
(*There is a distant roll of thunder.*)

GOD (*firmly*). One kag, Noah.

NOAH. Yes, Lawd. One kag.
(*The door in the back opens and* NOAH's WIFE *enters with a tray of dishes and food.*)

NOAH's WIFE. Now, den, gen'lemen, if you'll jest draw up cheers.
(*The stage is darkened. The* CHOIR *is heard singing "I Want to Be Ready." They continue in the darkness until the lights go up on the next scene.*)

SCENE IX

In the middle of the stage is the Ark. On the hillside, below the Ark, a dozen or more men and women, townspeople, are watching NOAH, SHEM, HAM *and* JAPHETH *on the deck of the Ark. The three sons are busily nailing boards on the cabin.* NOAH *is smoking a pipe. He wears a silk hat, captain's uniform and a "slicker."*

NOAH (*to* SHEM). You, Shem, tote up some ol' rough lumber, don' bring up any planed up lumber, caize dat ain't fo' de main deck.

SHEM. Pretty near supper time, daddy.

NOAH. Maybe 'tis, but I got de feelin' we ought to keep goin'.

FIRST WOMAN. You gonter work all night, Noah, maybe, huh?

NOAH (*without looking at her*). If de sperrit move me.

SECOND WOMAN. Look yere, Noah, whyn't you give up all dis damn foolishness? Don' you know people sayin' yo' crazy? What you think you doin' anyway?

NOAH. I'se buildin' a Ark. (*Other men and women join those in the foreground.*) Ham, you better stop for a while 'n' see whether dey bringin' de animals up all right. (*He looks at his watch.*) Dey ought to be pretty near de foot o' de hill by dis time; if dey ain't you wait fo' dem and bring 'em yo'se'f.

(HAM *goes down a ladder at the side of the ship and exits during the following scene. The newcomers in group have been speaking to some of the early arrivals.*)

SECOND WOMAN (*to* THIRD WOMAN, *one of the newcomers*). No, you don't mean it!

THIRD WOMAN. I do so. Dat's what de talk is in de town.

FIRST WOMAN. You hear dat, Noah? Dey say yo' ol' lady is tellin' everybody it's gonter rain fo' fo'ty days and fo'ty nights. You know people soon gonter git de idea you all crazy.

NOAH. Lot I keer what you think. (*To* JAPHETH.) Straighten up dem boards down dere, Japheth. (*Indicates floor of deck.*)

FIRST WOMAN (*to* THIRD WOMAN). Was I you, I wouldn' go 'round with Mrs. Noah anymore, lady. Fust thing you know you'll be gittin' a hard name, too.

THIRD WOMAN. Don' I know?

SECOND WOMAN. A lady cain't be too partic'-lar dese days.

(ZEBA *and* FLATFOOT, *a tall, black, wicked-looking buck, enter, their arms around each other's waists.*)

ZEBA. Dere it is baby. Was I lyin'?

FLATFOOT. Well, I'll be split in two!

FIRST MAN. What you think of it, Flatfoot?

FLATFOOT. I must say! Look like a house wit' a warpin' cellar.

NOAH. Dis yere vessel is a boat.

FLATFOOT. When I was a little boy dey used to build boats down near de ribber, where de water was.
(*The others laugh.*)

NOAH. Dis time it's been arranged to have de water come up to de boat. (JAPHETH *looks belligerently over the rail of the Ark at* FLATFOOT. *To* JAPHETH.) Keep yo' shirt on, son.

SECOND WOMAN (*to* THIRD WOMAN). Now, you see de whole fam'ly's crazy.

THIRD WOMAN. Listen, dey ain't gonter 'taminate me. It was me dat started re-solvin' dem both out o' de buryin' society.

ZEBA. When all dis water due up yere, Noah?

NOAH. You won't know when it gits yere, daughter.

ZEBA. Is she goin' to be a side-wheeler, like de Bessy-Belle?

FLATFOOT. No! If she was a side-wheeler she'd get her wheels all clogged wid sharks. She gonter have jus' one great big stern wheel, like de Commodore. Den if dey ain't 'nuf water why de big wheel kin stir some up.
(*General laughter. Two or three of the* GAMBLERS *enter and join the group, followed by* CAIN THE SIXTH.)

CAIN THE SIXTH. Dere's de fool an' his mon-ument, jest like I said.
(*The* GAMBLERS *and* CAIN THE SIXTH *roar with laughter, slap their legs, etc., the members of the main group talk sotto voce to each other as* CAIN THE SIXTH *catches*

ZEBA's *eye.* FLATFOOT *is on her right and is not aware of* CAIN THE SIXTH's *presence.*)

NOAH. See how dey makin' out inside, son. (*Stops hammering.* JAPHETH *exits into Ark.* NOAH *turns and gazes towards the east.*)

CAIN THE SIXTH. Hello, honey.

ZEBA (*frightened but smiling*). Hello, sug-ah.

CAIN THE SIXTH (*pleasantly*). Ain' dat my ol' frien' Flatfoot wid you?

ZEBA. Why, so 'tis! (FLATFOOT *is now listen-ing. To* FLATFOOT.) He's got a gun.

CAIN THE SIXTH. No, I ain't. (*He lifts his hands over his head.* ZEBA *quickly advances and runs her hands lightly over his pock-ets.*)

ZEBA (*relieved*). I guess he ain't.

CAIN THE SIXTH. No, I ain't got a gun for my ol' friend, Flatfoot. (*He walks up to him.*)

FLATFOOT (*smiling*). Hi, Cain. How's de boy?
(CAIN *quickly presses his chest against* FLAT-FOOT's, *his down-stage arm sweeps around* FLATFOOT's *body and his hand goes up to the small of* FLATFOOT's *back.*)

CAIN THE SIXTH (*quietly, but triumphant-ly*). I got a little *knife* fo' him.
(FLATFOOT *falls dead. The laughter of the others stops and they look at the scene.* ZEBA *for a moment is terrified, her clenched hand pressed to her mouth. She looks at* CAIN THE SIXTH, *who is smiling at her. He tosses the knife on the ground and holds his hands out to her. She goes to him, smil-ing.*)

ZEBA. You sho' take keer of me, honey.

CAIN THE SIXTH. Dat's caize I think yo' wo'th takin' keer of. (*To the others.*) It's all right, folks. I jest had to do a little cleanin' up.

FIRST WOMAN (*smiling*). You is de quickes' scoundrel.

FIRST GAMBLER. It was a nice quick killin'. Who was he?

SECOND WOMAN (*casually*). Dey called him Flatfoot. From over de river. He wa'nt any good. He owed me for washin' for over a year.

THIRD WOMAN. Used to peddle muggles. Said it had a kick like reg'lar snow. Wasn't no good.

SECOND GAMBLER. Think we ought to bury him?

FIRST MAN. No, just leave him dere. Nobody comes up yere, 'cept ol' Manatee. (*Indicates* NOAH. *Cries of "Ol' Manatee! Ol' Manatee, dat's good!"*)

NOAH (*stilling looking off*). You bettah pray, you po' chillun.
(*They all laugh.*)

FIRST WOMAN. We bettah pray? You bettah pray, Ol' Manatee!

ZEBA. You bettah pray for rain.
(*Laughter again.*)

NOAH. Dat's what I ain't doin', sinners. Shem! Japheth! (*To others, as he points off. Patter of rain.*) Listen!

CAIN THE SIXTH (*casually*). Doggone, I believe it *is* gonter shower a little.

FIRST GAMBLER. It do look like rain.

FIRST WOMAN. I think I'll git on home. I got a new dress on.

ZEBA. Me, too. I wants to keep lookin' nice fo' my sweet papa. (*She pats* CAIN THE SIXTH's *cheek.* CAIN THE SIXTH *hugs her.*)

NOAH (*almost frantically*). Ham! Is de animals dere?

HAM (*off-stage*). Yes, sir, dere yere. We're comin'.

NOAH. Den bring 'em on.
(SHEM *and* JAPHETH *come on deck with*

their hammers. The stage begins to darken.*)

THIRD WOMAN. I guess we all might go home 'til de shower's over. Come on, papa.

SECOND GAMBLER. See you after supper, Noah.
(*Crowd starts moving off, right.*)

NOAH. God's gittin' ready to start, my sons. Let's git dis plankin' done.

ZEBA. Put a big Texas on it, Noah, an' we'll use it fo' excursions.
(*There is a distant roll of thunder, there are cries of "Good night, Admiral." "See you later." "So long, Manatee," as the crowd goes off. The thunder rumbles again. There is the sound of increasing rain. The hammers of* SHEM *and* JAPHETH *sound louder and are joined by the sounds of other hammerers. There is a flash of lightning. The* CHOIR *begins "Dey Ol' Ark's a-Movering," the sounds on the Ark become faster and louder. The rush of rain grows heavier.*)

NOAH. Hurry! Hurry! Where are you, Ham?

HAM (*just off-stage*). Yere I am, father, wid de animals.

NOAH. God's give us his sign. Send 'em up de gangplank.
(*An inclined plane is thrown against the Ark from the side of the stage by* HAM, *who cracks a whip.*)

HAM. Get on, dere.
(*The heads of two elephants are seen.*)

NOAH. Bring 'em on board! De Lawd is strikin' down de worl'!
(*The singing and the noises reach fortissimo as* HAM *cracks his whip again, and the rain falls on the stage. The stage is darkened. The* CHOIR *continues singing in the darkness.*)

SCENE X

*When the lights go up on scene, the Ark is at sea. Stationary waves run in front of it.
The hillside has disappeored. The Ark is in the only lighted area.*

*   SHEM *is smoking a pipe on the deck, leaning on the rail. A steamboat whistle blows
three short and one long blast.* SHEM *is surprised. In a moment* HAM *appears, also with a
pipe, and joins* SHEM *at the rail.*

SHEM. Who'd you think you was signallin'?

HAM. Dat wasn't me, dat was daddy.

SHEM. He think he gonter git a reply?

HAM. I don' know. He's been gittin a heap of comfort out of dat likker.

SHEM. De kag's nearly empty, ain't it?

HAM. Pretty nearly almos'. (*They look over the rail. A pause.*) Seen anythin'?

SHEM. Dis mornin' I seen somethin' over dere might' a' been a fish.

HAM. Dat's de big news of de week.

SHEM. How long you think dis trip's gonter las'?

HAM. I don' know! Rain fo'ty days 'n' fo'ty nights an' when dat stop' I thought sho' we'd come up ag'inst a san' bar o' somethin'. Looks now like all dat rain was jest a little incident of de trip. (*The whistle blows again.*) Doggone! I wish he wouldn't do dat. Fust thing we know he'll wake up dem animals ag'in.

(JAPHETH *appears.*)

SHEM. What de matter wit' de ol' man, Jape?

JAPHETH. Doggone, he say he had a dream dat we're nearly dere. Dat's why he pullin' de whistle cord. See kin he git a' answer. (*He looks over the rail.*) Look to me like de same ol' territory.

(MRS. NOAH *appears on deck.*)

NOAH'S WIFE. You boys go stop yo' paw pullin' dat cord. He so full of likker he think he's in a race.

JAPHETH. He claim he know what he's doin'.

NOAH'S WIFE. I claim he gittin' to be a perfec' nuisance. Me an' yo' wives cain't hardly heah ou'sel'es think. (NOAH *appears, his hat rakishly tilted on his head. He goes to the railing and looks out.*) You 'spectin' company?

NOAH. Leave me be, woman. De watah don' look so rough today. De ol' boat's ridin' easier.

NOAH'S WIFE. Ridin' like a ol' mule!

NOAH. Yes, suh, de air don't feel so wet. Shem! 'Spose you sen' out 'nother dove. (SHEM *goes into the Ark.*) Ham, go git de soundin' line. Jape, keep yo' eye on de East.

(JAPHETH *goes to the end of the boat.*)

NOAH'S WIFE. As fo' you, I s'pose you'll help things along by takin' a little drink.

NOAH. Look yere, who's de pilot of dis vessel?

NOAH'S WIFE. Ol' Mister Dumb Luck.

NOAH. Well, see dat's where you don' know anythin'.

NOAH'S WIFE. I s'pose you ain't drunk as a fool?

NOAH (*cordially*). I feel congenial.

NOAH'S WIFE. An' you look it. You look jest wonderful. I wonder if you'd feel so congenial if de Lawd was to show up?

NOAH. De Lawd knows what I'm doin', don' you worry 'bout dat.

NOAH'S WIFE. I wouldn't say anythin' ag'inst de Lawd. He suttinly let us know dey'd be a change in de weather. But I bet even de Lawd wonders sometimes why he ever put you in charge.

NOAH. Well, you let de Lawd worry 'bout dat.
(SHEM *appears with the dove*).

SHEM. Will I leave her go, Paw?

NOAH. Leave 'er go. (*There is a chorus of "Good Luck, Dove," from the group as the dove flies off-stage.* HAM *appears with the sounding line.*) Throw 'er over, Boy.
(HAM *proceeds to do so.*)

NOAH'S WIFE. An' another thing—

HAM. Hey!

NOAH (*rushing to his side*). What is it?

HAM. Only 'bout a inch! Look!
(*They lean over.*)

JAPHETH. It's gettin' light in de East.
(*As* HAM *works the cord up and down,* NOAH *and* NOAH'S WIFE *turn toward* JAPHETH. *The* CHOIR *begins "My Soul Is a Witness for the Lord."*)

NOAH. Praise de Lawd, so it is.

NOAH'S WIFE. Oh, dat's pretty.

NOAH (*to* HAM). An' de boat's stopped. We've landed. Shem, go down 'n' drag de fires an' dreen de boiler. Yo go help 'im, Ham.

JAPHETH. Look, Paw.
(*The dove wings back to the Ark with an olive branch in its mouth.*)

NOAH. 'N' yere's de little dove wid greenery in its mouth! Take 'er down, Jape, so she kin tell de animals. (JAPHETH *exits after* SHEM *and* HAM *carrying the dove. To* MRS. NOAH.) Now, maybe you feel little different.

NOAH'S WIFE (*contritely*). It was jes' gittin' to be so tiresome. I'm sorry, Noah.

NOAH. Dat's all right, ol' woman. (NOAH'S WIFE *exits.* NOAH *looks about him. The lights have changed and the water piece is gone and the Ark is again on the hillside. Two mountains can be seen in the distance and a rainbow slowly appears over the Ark.*)

The singing has grown louder.) Thank you, Lawd, thank you very much indeed. Amen.
(*The singing stops with the "Amen."* GOD *appears on the deck.*)

GOD. Yo' welcome, Noah.
(NOAH *turns and sees him.*)

NOAH. O, Lawd, it's wonderful.

GOD (*looking about him*). I sort of like it. I like de way you handled de ship, too, Noah.

NOAH. Was you watchin', Lawd?

GOD. Every minute. (*He smiles.*) Didn't de ol' lady light into you?

NOAH (*apologetically*). She was kinda restless.

GOD. That's all right. I ain't blamin' nobody. I don' even min' you' cussin' an' drinkin'. I figure a steamboat cap'n on a long trip like you had has a right to a little redeye, jest so he don' go crazy.

NOAH. Thank you, Lawd. What's de orders now?

GOD. All de animals safe?

NOAH. Dey all fin'n' dandy, Lawd.

GOD. Den I want you to open dat starboard door, an' leave 'em all out. Let 'em go down de hill. Den you an' de family take all de seeds 'n' de sprouts an' begin plantin' ag'in. I'm startin' all over, Noah.
(NOAH *exits.* GOD *looks around.*)

GOD. Well, now we'll see what happens. (GOD *listens with a smile, as noises accompanying the debarking of the animals are heard. There are the cracks of whips, the voices of the men on the Ark, shouting: "Git along dere." "Whoa, take it easy." "Duck yo' head." "Keep in line dere," etc. Over the Ark there is a burst of centrifugal shadows, and the sound of a myriad of wings.* GOD *smiles at the shadows.*) Dat's right, birds, fin' yo' new homes. (*Bird twitters are heard again.* GOD *listens a moment and rests an arm on the railing. He speaks softly.*) Gabriel, kin you spare a minute?
(GABRIEL *appears.*)

GABRIEL. Yes, Lawd?

(*The sounds from the other side of the Ark are by now almost hushed.* GOD *indicates the new world with a wave of the hand.*)

GOD. Well, it's did.

GABRIEL (*respectfully, but with no enthusiasm*). So I take notice.

GOD. Yes, suh, startin' all over again.

GABRIEL. So I see.

GOD (*looking at him suddenly*). Don' seem to set you up much.

GABRIEL. Well, Lawd, you see— (*He hesitates.*) 'Tain't none of my business.

GOD. What?

GABRIEL. I say, I don' know very much about it.

GOD. I know you don'. I jest wanted you to see it. (*A thought strikes him.*) Co'se, it ain' yo' business, Gabe. It's my business. 'Twas my idea. De whole thing was my idea. An' every bit of it's my business 'n' nobody else's. De whole thing rests on my shoulders. I declare, I guess *dat's* why I feel so solemn an' serious, at dis particklar time. You know *dis* thing's turned into quite a proposition.

GABRIEL (*tenderly*). But, it's all right, Lawd, as you say, it's did.

GOD. Yes, suh, it's did. (*Sighs deeply. Looks slowly to the right and the left. Then softly.*) I only hope it's goin' to work out all right.

Curtain.

PART TWO

SCENE I

GOD's *office again.*

Somewhere the CHOIR *is singing:* "*A City Called Heaven.*" *In the office are two* WOMEN CLEANERS. *One is scrubbing the floor, the other dusting the furniture. The one dusting stops and looks out the window. There is a whirr and a distant faint Boom. The* CHOIR *stops.*

FIRST CLEANER. Dat was a long way off.

SECOND CLEANER (*at window*). Yes, ma'am. An' dat must a' been a big one. Doggone, de Lawd mus' be mad fo' sho', dis mo'nin'. Dat's de fo'ty-six' thunde'-bolt since breakfast.

FIRST CLEANER. I wonder where at He's pitchin' dem.

SECOND CLEANER. My goodness, don' you know?

FIRST CLEANER (*a little hurt*). Did I know I wouldn't ask de question.

SECOND CLEANER. Every one of dem's bound fo' de earth.

FIRST CLEANER. De earth? You mean dat little ol' dreenin' place?

SECOND CLEANER. Dat's de planet. (*Another faint whirr and boom.*) Dere goes another.

FIRST CLEANER. Well, bless me. *I* didn't know dey was thunde'-bolts.

SECOND CLEANER. Wha'd you think dey was?

FIRST CLEANER (*above desk*). I wasn't sho', but I thought maybe He might be whittlin' a new star o' two, an' de noise was jest de chips fallin'.

SECOND CLEANER. Carrie, where you been? Don' you know de earth is de new scandal? Ever'body's talkin' about it.

FIRST CLEANER. Dey kep' it from me.

SECOND CLEANER. Ain't you noticed de Lawd's been unhappy lately?

FIRST CLEANER (*thoughtfully*). Yeah, He ain't been his old self.

SECOND CLEANER. What did you think was de matteh? Lumbago?

FIRST CLEANER (*petulantly*). I didn't know. I didn't think it was fo' me t'inquieh.

SECOND CLEANER. Well, it jest so happens dat de Lawd is riled as kin be by dat measly little earth. Or I should say de scum dat's on it.

FIRST CLEANER. Dat's mankind down dere.

SECOND CLEANER. Dey mus' be scum, too, to git de Lawd so wukked up.

FIRST CLEANER. I s'pose so. (*Another whirr and boom.*) Looks like He's lettin' dem feel de wrath. Ain' dat a shame to plague de Lawd dat way?

SECOND CLEANER. From what I hear dey been beggin' fo' what dey're gittin'. My brother flew down to bring up a saint de other day and he say from what he see mos' of de population down dere has made de debbil king an' dey wukkin' in three shifts fo' him.

FIRST CLEANER. You cain't blame de Lawd.

SECOND CLEANER. Co'se you cain't. Dem human bein's 'd make anybody bile oveh. Ev'rytime de Lawd try to do sompin' fo' dem, doggone if dey don't staht some new ruckus.

FIRST CLEANER. I take notice He's been wukkin' in yere mo' dan usual.

SECOND CLEANER. I wish He'd let us ladies fix it up. Wouldn't take a minute to make dis desk gold-plated.

FIRST CLEANER. I s'pose He likes it dis way. De Lawd's kind o' ol' fashioned in some ways. I s'pose He keeps dis office plain an' simple on purpose.

SECOND CLEANER (*finishing her work*). I don' see why.

FIRST CLEANER (*looking off*). Well, it's kind of a nice place to come to when He's studyin' somethin' impo'tant. 'Most evah-thin' else in heaven's so fin' 'n' gran', maybe ev'ry now an' den He jest gits sick an' tired of de glory. (*She is also collecting her utensils.*)

SECOND CLEANER. Maybe so. Jest de same I'd like to have a free hand wid dis place for a while, so's I could gold it up.
(GOD *appears in the doorway.*)

GOD. Good mo'nin', daughters.

FIRST *and* SECOND CLEANERS. Good mo'nin', Lawd. We was jest finishin'.

GOD. Go ahead den, daughters. (*Goes to the window.*)

FIRST *and* SECOND CLEANERS. Yes, Lawd. (*They exeunt. Off-stage.*) Good mo'nin', Gabriel.
(*Off-stage* GABRIEL *says, "Good mo'nin', sisters," and enters immediately. He stands in the doorway for a moment watching* GOD—*a notebook and pencil in his hand.*)

GOD. What's de total?

GABRIEL (*consulting the book*). Eighteen thousand nine hund'ed an' sixty for de mo'nin'. Dat's includin' de village wid de fo'tune tellers. Dey certainly kin breed fast.

GOD (*softly*). Dey displease me. Dey displease me greatly.

GABRIEL. Want some more bolts, Lawd?

GOD (*looking through window*). Look at 'em dere. Squirmin' an' fightin' an' bearin' false witness. Listen to dat liar, dere. He don' intend to marry dat little gal. He don' even love her. What did you say?

GABRIEL. Should I git mo' bolts?

GOD. Wait a minute. (*He carefully points his finger down through the window.*) I'm goin' to git dat wicked man myself. (*From a great distance comes an agonized cry: "Oh, Lawd!"* GOD *turns from the window.*) No use gittin' mo' thunde'-bolts. Dey don' do de trick. (*He goes to the swivel chair and sits.*) It's got to be somethin' else.

GABRIEL. How would it be if you was to doom 'em all ag'in, like dat time you sent down de flood? I bet dat would make dem mind.

GOD. You see how much good de flood did. Dere dey is, jest as bad as ever.

GABRIEL. How about cleanin' up de whole mess of 'em and sta'tin' all over ag'in wid some new kind of animal?

GOD. An' admit I'm licked?

GABRIEL (ashamedly). No, of co'se not, Lawd.

GOD. No, suh. No, suh. Man is a kind of pet of mine and it ain't right fo' me to give up tryin' to do somethin' wid him. Doggone, mankin' *mus'* be all right at de core or else why did I ever bother wid him in de first place? (Sits at desk.)

GABRIEL. It's jest dat I hates to see you worryin' about it, Lawd.

GOD. Gabe, dere ain't anythin' worth while anywheres dat didn't cause somebody some worryin'. I ain't never tol' you de trouble I had gittin' things started up yere. Dat's a story in itself. No, suh, de more I keep on bein' de Lawd de more I know I got to keep improvin' things. An' dat takes time and worry. De main trouble wid mankin' is he takes up so much of my time. He ought to be able to help hisself a little. (He stops suddenly and cogitates.) Hey, dere! I think I got it!

GABRIEL (eagerly). What's de news?

GOD (still cogitating). Yes, suh, dat seems like an awful good idea.

GABRIEL. Tell me, Lawd.

GOD. Gabriel, have you noticed dat every now an' den, mankin' turns out some pretty good specimens?

GABRIEL. Dat's de truth.

GOD. Yes, suh. Dey's ol' Abraham and Isaac an' Jacob an' all dat family.

GABRIEL. Dat so, Lawd.

GOD. An' everyone of dem boys was a hard wukker an' a good citizen. We got to admit dat.

GABRIEL. Dey wouldn't be up yere flyin' wid us if dey hadn't been.

GOD. No, suh. An' I don' know but what de answer to de whole trouble is right dere.

GABRIEL. How you mean, Lawd?

GOD. Why, doggone it, de good man is de man dat keeps busy. I mean I been goin' along on de principle dat he was something like you angels—dat you ought to be able to give him somethin' an' den jest let him sit back an' enjoy it. Dat ain't so. Now dat I recollec' I put de first one down dere to take keer o' dat garden an' den I let him go ahead an' do nothin' but git into mischief. (He rises.) Sure, *dat's* it. He ain't *built* jest to fool 'roun' an' not do nothin'. Gabe, I'm gonter try a new scheme.

GABRIEL (eagerly). What's de scheme, Lawd?

GOD. I'll tell you later. Send in Abraham, Isaac an' Jacob. (A voice outside calls: "Right away, Lawd.") You go tell dem to put dem bolts back in de boxes. I ain' gonter use dem ag'in a while.

GABRIEL. O. K., Lawd.

GOD. Was you goin' anywhere near de Big Pit?

GABRIEL. I could go.

GOD. Lean over de brink and tell Satan he's jest a plain fool if he thinks he kin beat anybody as big as me.

GABRIEL. Yes, suh, Lawd. Den I'll spit right in his eye. (GABRIEL exits.)
(GOD looks down through the window again to the earth below.)

GOD. Dat new polish on de sun makes it powerful hot. (He "r'ars back.") Let it be jest a little bit cooler. (He feels the air.) Dat's nice. (Goes to His desk. A knock on the door.) Come in.
(ABRAHAM, ISAAC and JACOB enter. All are very old men, but the beard of ABRAHAM is the longest and whitest, and they suggest their three generations. They have wings that are not quite so big as those of the native angels.)

ISAAC. Sorry we so long comin', Lawd. But Pappy and me had to take de boy (*pointing to* JACOB) over to git him a can of wing ointment.

GOD. What was de matter, son?

JACOB. Dey was chafin' me a little. Dey fine now, thank you, Lawd.

GOD. Dat's good. Sit down an' make yo'-selves comf'table. (*The three sit.* MEN: "*Thank you, Lawd.*") Men, I'm goin' to talk about a little scheme I got. It's one dat's goin' to affec' yo' fam'lies an' dat's why I 'cided I'd talk it over wid you, 'fo it goes into ee-fect. I don' know whether you boys know it or not, but you is about de three best men of one fam'ly dat's come up yere since I made little apples. Now I tell you what I'm gonter do. Seein' dat you human bein's cain't 'preciate anythin' lessen you fust wukk to git it and den keep strugglin' to hold it, why I'm gonter turn over a very valuable piece of property to yo' fam'ly, and den see what kin dey do with it. De rest of de worl' kin go jump in de river fo' all I keer. I'm gonter be lookin' out fo' yo' descendants only. Now den, seein' dat you boys know de country pretty tho'ly, where at does you think is de choice piece of property in de whole worl'? Think it over for a minute. I'm gonter let you make de s'lection.

ABRAHAM. If you was to ask me, Lawd, I don't think dey come any better dan de Land of Canaan.

GOD (*to* ISAAC *and* JACOB). What's yo' feelin' in de matter?

JACOB (*after a nod from* ISAAC). Pappy an' me think do we get a pick, dat would be it.

GOD (*goes to window again; looks out*). De Land of Canaan. Yes, I guess dat's a likely neighborhood. It's all run over wid Philistines and things right now, but we kin clean dat up. (*He turns from the window and resumes his seat.*) All right. Now who do you boys think is de best of yo' men to put in charge down dere? You see I ain't been payin' much attention to anybody in partic'lar lately.

ISAAC. Does you want de brainiest or de holiest, Lawd?
(MEN *look up.*)

GOD. I want de holiest. I'll make him brainy.
(MEN *appreciate the miracle.*)

ISAAC (*as* ABRAHAM *and* JACOB *nod to him*). Well, if you want A Number One goodness, Lawd, I don't know where you'll git more satisfaction dan in a great-great-great-great grandson of mine.

GOD. Where's he at?

ISAAC. At de moment I b'lieve he's in de sheep business over in Midian County. He got in a little trouble down in Egypt, but t'wan't his doin'. He killed a man dat was abusin' one of our boys in de brick works. Of co'se you know old King Pharaoh's got all our people in bondage.

GOD. I heard of it. (*With some ire.*) Who did you think put them dere? (*The visitors lower their heads.*) It's all right, boys. (*All rise.*) I'm gonter take dem out of it. An' I'm gonter turn over de whole Land of Canaan to dem. An' do you know whose gonter lead dem dere? Yo' great, great, great, great grandson. Moses, ain't it?

ISAAC. Yes, Lawd.

GOD (*smiling*). Yes. I been noticin' *him*.

ABRAHAM. It's quite a favor fo' de fam'ly, Lawd.

GOD. Dat's why I tol' you. You see, it so happens I love yo' fam'ly, an' I delight to honor it. Dat's all, gen'lemen. (*The three others rise and cross to the door, murmuring,* "Yes, Lawd," "Thank you, Lawd," "Much obliged, Lawd," *etc. The* CHOIR *begins,* "My Lord's A-Writin' All De Time" *pianissimo.* GOD *stands watching the men leave.*) Enjoy yo'selves. (*He goes to the window. The singing grows softer. He speaks through the window to the earth.*) I'm comin' down to see you, Moses, an' dis time my scheme's got to wukk.
(*The stage is darkened. The singing grows louder and continues until the lights go up on the next scene.*)

SCENE II

The tableau curtains frame the opening of a cave, which is dimly lighted. A large turkey-berry bush is somewhere near the foreground. MOSES *is seated on the grass eating his lunch from a basket in his lap.* ZIPPORAH, *his wife, stands watching him. He is about forty,* ZIPPORAH *somewhat younger. They are dressed inconspicuously.* MOSES *stutters slightly when he speaks. He looks up to see* ZIPPORAH *smiling.*

MOSES. What you smilin' at, Zipporah?

ZIPPORAH. Caize you enjoyin' yo'self.

MOSES. You is a good wife, Zipporah.

ZIPPORAH. You is a good husband, Moses. (MOSES *wipes his mouth with a handkerchief and begins putting into the basket the various implements of the meal which had been on the ground about him.*) Why you suppose it's so dark yere today? Dey's no rain in de air.

MOSES. Seems like it's jest aroun' dis cave. Yo' father's house is got de sun on it. (*He looks in another direction.*) Looks all clear down toward Egypt.

ZIPPORAH. Co'se it *would* be fine weather in Egypt. De sky looks all right. Maybe it's gonter rain jest right yere. Why don't you move de sheep over to de other pasture?

MOSES (*a bit puzzled*). I don' know. It got dark like dis befo' you come along wid de dinner an' I was gonter stop you on de top of de hill. Den somethin' kep' me yere.

ZIPPORAH. S'pose it could be de Lawd warnin' you dat dey's 'Gyptians hangin' 'roun'?

MOSES. Dey may have fo'gotten all about dat killin' by now. Dey got a new Pharaoh down dere.

ZIPPORAH. An' I hear he's jest as mean to yo' people as his pappy was. I wouldn't put it pas' him to send soljahs all the way up yere fo' you.

MOSES. Dat's all right. De Lawd's looked after me so far, I don't 'spect him to fall down on me now. You better be gittin' home.

ZIPPORAH (*taking the basket*). I'll be worryin' about you.

MOSES (*kissing her and then smiling*). 'Parently de Lawd ain't. He knows I'm safe as kin be. Lemme see you feel dat way.

ZIPPORAH. You is a good man, Moses.

MOSES. I's a lucky man. (ZIPPORAH *exits with the basket.* MOSES *looks up at the sky.*) Dat's funny. De sun seems to be shinin' everyplace but right yere. It's shinin' on de sheep. Why ain't dey no cloud dere?

GOD (*off-stage*). Caize I want it to be like dat, Moses.

MOSES (*looking about him*). Who's dat?

GOD (*off-stage again*). I'm de Lawd, Moses.

MOSES (*smiling*). Dat's what you say. Dis yere shadow may be de Lawd's wukk, but dat voice soun' pretty much to me like my ol' brother Aaron.

GOD (*off-stage*). Den keep yo' eyes open, son. (*The turkey-berry bush begins to glow and then turns completely red.* MOSES *looks at it fascinated.*) Maybe you notice de bush ain't burnin' up.

MOSES. Dat's de truth. (MOSES *is full of awe but not frightened.*)

GOD (*off-stage*). Now you believe me?

MOSES. Co'se I does. It's wonderful. (*The light in the bush dies and* GOD *appears from behind it.*)

GOD. No, it ain't, Moses. It was jest a trick.

MOSES. 'Scuse me doubtin' you, Lawd. I always had be feelin' you wuz takin' keer of me, but I never 'spected you'd fin' de time to talk wid me pussunly. (*He laughs.*) Dat was a good trick, Lawd. I'se seen some good ones, but dat was de beatenest.

GOD. Yo' gonter see lots bigger tricks dan dat, Moses. In fac', yo' gonter perfo'm dem.

MOSES (*incredulously*). Me? I'm gonter be a tricker?

GOD. Yes, suh.

MOSES. An' do magic? Lawd, my mouth ain't got de quick talk to go wid it.

GOD. It'll come to you now.

MOSES (*now cured of stuttering*). Is I goin' wid a circus?

GOD (*slowly and solemnly*). Yo' is goin' down into Egypt, Moses, and lead my people out of bondage. To do dat I'm gonter make you de bes' tricker in de worl'.

MOSES (*a little frightened*). Egypt! You know I killed a man dere, Lawd. Won't dey kill me?

GOD. Not when dey see yo' tricks. You ain't skeered, is you?

MOSES (*simply and bravely*). No, suh, Lawd.

GOD. Den yere's what I'm gonter do. Yo' people is my chillun, Moses. I'm sick and tired o' the way ol' King Pharaoh is treatin' dem, so I'se gonter take dem away, and yo' gonter lead dem. You gonter lead 'em out of Egypt an' across de river Jordan. It's gonter take a long time, and you ain't goin' on no excursion train. Yo' gonter wukk awful hard for somethin' yo' goin' to fin' when de trip's over.

MOSES. What's dat, Lawd?

GOD. It's de Land of Canaan. It's de bes' land I got. I've promised it to yo' people, an' I'm gonter give it to dem.

MOSES. Co'se, ol' King Pharaoh will do everything he kin to stop it.

GOD. Yes, an' dat's where de tricks come in. Dey tell me he's awful fond of tricks.

MOSES. I hear dat's *all* he's fon' of. Dey say if you can't take a rabbit out of a hat you cain't even git in to see him.

GOD. Wait'll you see de tricks you an' me's goin' to show him.

MOSES (*delightedly*). Doggone! Huh, Lawd?

GOD. Yes, suh. Now de first trick— (GOD *is lifting a stick which he carries.*)

MOSES. Jest a minute, Lawd. (GOD *halts the demonstration.*) I'm gonter learn de tricks and do just like you tell me, but I *know* it's gonter take me a little time to learn all dat quick talkin'. Cain't I have my brother Aaron go wid me? He's a good man.

GOD. I was gonter have him help you wid de Exodus. I guess he can watch, too.

MOSES. I'll call 'im. (*He turns as if to shout.*)

GOD. Wait. (MOSES *turns and looks at* GOD.) I'll *bring* him. (*Softly.*) Aaron!
(AARON *appears between* GOD *and* MOSES *in the mouth of the cave. He is a little taller than* MOSES *and slightly older. He, too, is dressed like a field hand.*)

AARON (*blankly*). Hey!
(MOSES *goes to him, takes his hand and leads him, bewildered, down to where* MOSES *had been standing alone.* AARON *then sees* GOD.)

MOSES (*almost in a whisper*). It's all right.

GOD. Don't worry, son, I'm jest showin' some tricks. Bringin' you yere was one of dem. (AARON *stares at* GOD *as if hypnotized.*) Now den, you see dis yere rod? Looks like a ordinary walking stick, don' it?

MOSES. Yes, Lawd.

GOD. Well, it ain't no ordinary walkin' stick, caize look. (MOSES *leans forward.*) When I lays it down on de groun'—
(*The stage is darkened. The* CHOIR *begins, "Go Down, Moses," and continues until the lights go up on the next scene.*)

SCENE III

The throne room of PHARAOH. *It suggests a Negro lodge room. The plain board walls are covered by several large parade banners of varying sizes, colors and materials, bordered with gold fringe and tassels on them. Some of the inscriptions on them read:*

SUBLIME ORDER OF PRINCES OF THE HOUSE OF PHARAOH
HOME CHAPTER

MYSTIC BROTHERS OF THE EGYPTIAN HOME GUARD
LADIES AUXILIARY, NO. I

SUPREME MAGICIANS AND WIZARDS OF THE UNIVERSE

PRIVATE FLAG OF HIS HONOR OLD KING PHARAOH

ROYAL YOUNG PEOPLE'S PLEASURE CLUB

ENCHANTED AND INVISIBLE CADETS OF EGYPT BOYS' BRIGADE

There is one door up right and a window. The throne, an ordinary armchair with a drapery over its back, is on a dais. PHARAOH *is seated on the throne. His crown and garments might be those worn by a high officer in a Negro lodge during a ritual. About the throne itself are high officials, several of them with plumed hats, clothing that suggests military uniforms, and rather elaborate sword belts, swords and scabbards. A few soldiers carrying spears are also in his neighborhood and one or two bearded ancients in brightly colored robes with the word "Wizard" on their conical hats. In the general group of men and women scattered elsewhere in the room Sunday finery is noticeable everywhere. Most of the civilians have bright "parade" ribbons and wear medals. In a cleared space immediately before the throne a* CANDIDATE MAGICIAN *is performing a sleight-of-hand trick with cards.* PHARAOH *watches him apathetically. He is receiving earnest attention from a few of the others, but the majority of the men and women are talking quietly among themselves. Beside the* CANDIDATE MAGICIAN *are several paraphernalia of previously demonstrated tricks.*

CANDIDATE MAGICIAN (*holding up some cards*). Now den, ol' King Pharaoh, watch dis. (*He completes a trick. There is a murmur of "Not Bad." "Pretty Good," etc. from a few of the watchers.* PHARAOH *makes no comment.*) Now, I believe de cyard I ast you to keep sittin' on was de trey of diamonds, wasn't it?

PHARAOH. Yeah.

CANDIDATE MAGICIAN. Den kin I trouble you to take a look at it now? (PHARAOH *half rises to pick up a card he has been sitting on, and looks at it.*) I believe you'll now notice dat it's de King of Clubs? (PHARAOH

nods and shows the card to those nearest him. The CANDIDATE MAGICIAN waits for an audible approval and gets practically none.) An' dat, ol' King Pharaoh, completes de puffohmance.
(*An elderly man in a uniform steps forward.*)

GENERAL. On behalf of my nephew I beg Yo' Honor to let him jine de ranks of de royal trickers and magicians.

PHARAOH (*to the two* WIZARDS). What do de committee think? (*The* WIZARDS *shake their heads.*) Dat's what I thought. He ain't good enough. I'd like to help you out,

General, but you know a man's got to be a awful good tricker to git in de royal society dese days. You better go back an' steddy some mo', son. (*He lifts his voice and directs two* SOLDIERS *guarding the door.*) Is de head magician reached de royal waitin' room yit? (*One of the* SOLDIERS *opens the door to look out.*) If he is, send him in.

(*The* SOLDIER *beckons to some one offstage, throws the door open, and announces to the court.*)

SOLDIER. De Head Magician of de land of Egypt.

(*A very old and villainous man enters. His costume is covered with cabalistic and zodiacal signs. He advances to the King, the other magician and his uncle making way for him. He bows curtly to* PHARAOH.)

HEAD MAGICIAN. Good mo'nin', ol' King Pharaoh.

PHARAOH. Mo'nin', Professor. What's de news?

HEAD MAGICIAN. Evahthing's bein' carried out like you said.

PHARAOH. How's de killin' of de babies 'mongst de Hebrews comin' along?

HEAD MAGICIAN. Jes' like you ordered.

PHARAOH (*genially*). Dey killed all of 'em, huh?

HEAD MAGICIAN. Do dey see one, dey kill 'im. You teachin' 'em a great lesson. Dey don' like it a-tall.

PHARAOH (*smiling*). What do dey say?

HEAD MAGICIAN (*pawing the air inarticulately*). I hates to tell in front of de ladies.

PHARAOH. Dey feels pretty bad, huh?

HEAD MAGICIAN. Dat's jest de beginnin' of it. Betwixt de poleece and de soljahs we killed about a thousan' of 'em las' night. Dat's purty good.

PHARAOH (*thoughtfully*). Yeh, it's fair. I guess you boys is doin' all you kin. But I fin' I ain't satisfied, though.

HEAD MAGICIAN. How you mean, Yo' Honor?

PHARAOH. I mean I'd like to make dose Hebrew chillun realize dat I kin be even mo' of a pest. I mean I hates dem chillun. An' I'm gonter think of a way of makin' 'em even mo' mizzable.

HEAD MAGICIAN. But dey *ain't* anythin' meaner dan killin' de babies, King.

PHARAOH. Dey must be sump'n. Doggone, you is my head tricker, you put yo' brains on it. (*To the others.*) Quiet, whilst de Head Magician go into de silence.

HEAD MAGICIAN (*after turning completely around twice, and a moment's cogitation*). I tell you what I kin do. All de Hebrews dat ain't out to de buryin' grounds or in the hospitals is laborin' in de brick wukks.

PHARAOH. Yeh?

HEAD MAGICIAN (*after a cackling laugh*). How would it be to take de straw away from 'em and tell 'em dey's got to turn out jest as many bricks as usual? Ain't dat nasty?

PHARAOH. Purty triflin', but I s'pose it'll have to do for de time bein'. Where's de extreme inner guard? (*One of the military attendants comes forward.*) Go on out an' tell de sup'intendent to put dat into eeffect. (*The attendant bows and starts for the door. He stops as* PHARAOH *calls to him.*) Wait a minute! Tell 'im to chop off de hands of anybody dat say he cain't make de bricks dat way. (*The attendant salutes and exits, the door being opened and closed by one of the* SOLDIERS.) Now what's de news in de magic line?

HEAD MAGICIAN. I ain't got very many novelties today, King, I bin wukkin' too hard on de killin's. I'm so tired I don' believe I could lift a wand.

(*There are murmurs of protest from the assemblage.*)

PHARAOH. Doggone, you was to 'a been de chief feature o' de meetin' dis mornin'. Look at de turn-out you got account of me tellin' 'em you was comin'.

HEAD MAGICIAN. Well, dat's de way it is, King. Why don' you git de wizards to do some spell castin'?

PHARAOH. Dey say it's in de cyards dat dey cain't wukk till high noon. (*He glances at the* WIZARDS.) Think mebbe you kin cheat a little?

FIRST WIZARD. Oh dat cain't be done, King.

PHARAOH. Well, we might as well adjourn, den. Looks to me like de whole program's shot to pieces. (*He starts to rise, when there is a furious banging on the door.*) What's de idea, dere? See who dat is. (*The* SOLDIERS *open the door.* MOSES *and* AARON *enter, pushing the two* SOLDIERS *aside and coming down in front of* PHARAOH. *The* SOLDIERS *are bewildered and* PHARAOH *is angry.*) Say, who tol' you two baboons you could come in yere?

MOSES. Is you ol' King Pharaoh?

PHARAOH. Dat's me. Did you hear what I asked you?

MOSES. My name is Moses, and dis is my brother Aaron.
(*Murmur of "Hebrews" spreads through the room.*)

PHARAOH (*in a rage*). Is you Hebrews?

MOSES. Yes, suh.

PHARAOH (*almost screaming*). Put 'em to de sword!
(*As the courtiers approach,* AARON *suddenly discloses the rod, which he swings once over his head. The courtiers draw back as if their hands had been stung. Cries of "Hey!" "Look out," etc.*)

MOSES. Keep outside dat circle.
(*The courtiers nearest* MOSES *and* AARON *look at each other, exclaiming ad lib., "Did you feel dat?" "What is dat?" "What's goin' on, heah?" "My hands is stingin'!" etc.*)

PHARAOH (*puzzled but threatening*). What's de idea yere?

MOSES. We is magicians, ol' King Pharaoh.

PHARAOH (*to the* HEAD MAGICIAN). Put a spell on 'em. (*The* HEAD MAGICIAN *stands looking at them bewildered. To* MOSES.) I got some magicians, too. We'll see who's got de bes' magic. (MOSES *and* AARON *laugh. Most of the courtiers are cowering. To the* HEAD MAGICIAN.) Go ahead, give 'em grigri.

MOSES. Sure, go ahead.

PHARAOH. Hurry up, dey's laughin' at you. What's de matter?

HEAD MAGICIAN. I cain't think of de right spell.

PHARAOH (*now frightened himself*). You mean dey got even *you* whupped?

HEAD MAGICIAN. Dey's got a new kind of magic.

PHARAOH (*gazes at* HEAD MAGICIAN *a moment, bewildered. To the* WIZARDS.) I s'pose if de Professor cain't, you cain't.

FIRST WIZARD. Dat's a new trick, King.

HEAD MAGICIAN (*rubbing his fingers along his palms*). It's got 'lectricity in it!

PHARAOH. Hm, well dat may make it a little diff'rent. So you boys is magicians, too?

MOSES. Yes, suh.

PHARAOH. Well, we's always glad to see some new trickers in de co't, dat is if dey good. (*He glances about him.*) You look like you is O. K.

MOSES. Dat's what we claims, ol' King Pharaoh. We think we's de best in de worl'.

PHARAOH. You certainly kin talk big. Jest what is it you boys would like?

MOSES. We came to show you some tricks. Den we's goin' to ask you to do somethin' for us.

PHARAOH. Well, I s'pose you know I'm a fool for conjurin'. If a man kin show me some tricks I ain't seen, I goes out of my way to do him a favor.

MOSES. Dat's good. Want to see de first trick?

PHARAOH. It ain't goin' to hurt nobody?

MOSES. Dis one won't.

PHARAOH. Go ahead.

MOSES. Dis yere rod my brother has looks jes' like a walkin' stick, don't it?
(*The courtiers now join the King in interest.*)

PHARAOH. Uh huh. Le's see.
(AARON *hands him the rod, which* PHARAOH *inspects and returns.*)

MOSES. Well, look what happens when he lays it on de groun'.
(AARON *places the rod on the second step of the throne. It turns into a lifelike snake. There are exclamations from the assemblage.*)

PHARAOH. Dat's a good trick! Now turn it back into a walkin' stick again. (AARON *picks it up and it is again a rod. Exclamations of "Purty good!" "Dat's all right!" "What do you think of that!" etc.*) Say, you is good trickers!

MOSES. You ain't never seen de beat of us. Now I'm goin' to ask de favor.

PHARAOH. Sure, what is it?

MOSES (*solemnly*). Let de Hebrew chillun go!

PHARAOH (*rises and stares at them. There is a murmur of "Listen to 'im!" "He's got nerve!" "I never in my life!" "My goodness!" etc.*). What did you say?

MOSES. Let de Hebrew chillun go.
(PHARAOH *seats himself again.*)

PHARAOH (*slowly*). Don' you know de Hebrews is my slaves?

MOSES. Yes, suh.

PHARAOH. Yes, suh, my slaves. (*There is a distant groaning.*) Listen, and you kin hear 'em bein' treated like slaves. (*He calls toward the window.*) What was dey doin' den?

MAN NEAR THE WINDOW. Dey's jest gettin' de news down in de brick-yard.

PHARAOH. I won't let them go. (*He snorts contemptuously.*) Let's see another trick.

MOSES. Yes, suh, yere's a better one. (*He lowers his head.*) Let's have a plague of de flies.
(AARON *raises the rod. The room grows*

dark and a great buzzing of flies is heard. The courtiers break out in cries of "Get away fum me!" "Take 'em away!" "De place is filled with flies!" "Dis is terrible!" "Do sump'n, Pharaoh!"*)

PHARAOH (*topping the others*). All right—stop de trick!

MOSES. Will you let de Hebrews go?

PHARAOH. Sho I will. Go ahead stop it!

MOSES (*also above the others*). Begone!
(*The buzzing stops and the room is filled with light again, as* AARON *lowers the rod. All except* MOSES *and* AARON *are brushing the flies from their persons.*)

PHARAOH (*laughing*). Doggone, dat was a good trick! (*The others, seeing they are uninjured, join in the laughter, with exclamations of "Doggone!" "You all right?" "Sho' I'm all right." "Didn' hurt me," etc.*) You *is* good trickers.

MOSES. Will you let de Hebrew chillun go?

PHARAOH (*sitting down again*). Well, I'll tell you, boys. I'll tell you sump'n you didn' know. You take me, *I'm* a pretty good tricker, an' I jest outtricked you. So, bein' de bes' tricker, I don' think I will let 'em go. You got any mo' tricks yo'self?

MOSES. Yes, suh. Dis is a little harder one. (AARON *lifts the rod.*) Gnats in de mill pon', gnats in de clover, gnats in de tater patch, stingin' all over.
(*The stage grows dark again. There is the humming of gnats and the slapping of hands against faces and arms, and the same protests as were heard with the flies, but with more feeling. "I'm gittin' stung to death!" "I'm all stung!" "Dey'r like hornets!" "Dey's on my face!" etc.*)

PHARAOH. Take 'em away, Moses!

MOSES (*his voice drowning the others*). If I do, will you let 'em go?

PHARAOH. Sho' I will, dis time.

MOSES. Do you mean it?

PHARAOH. Co'se I mean it! Doggone, one just stang me on de nose.

MOSES. Begone! (*Lights come up as* AARON *lowers the rod. There is a moment of general recovery again.* PHARAOH *rubs his nose, looks at his hands, etc., as do the others.*) Now, how about it?

PHARAOH (*smiling*). Well, I'll tell you, Moses. Now dat de trick's over—
(MOSES *takes a step toward* PHARAOH.)

MOSES. Listen, Pharaoh. You been lyin' to me, and I'm gittin' tired of it.

PHARAOH. I ain't lyin', I'm trickin', too. You been trickin' me and I been trickin' you.

MOSES. I see. Well, I got one mo' trick up my sleeve which I didn't aim to wukk unless I had to. Caize when I does it, I cain't undo it.

PHARAOH. Wukk it an' I'll trick you right back. I don' say you ain't a good tricker, Moses. You is one of de best I ever seen But I kin outtrick you. Dat's all.

MOSES. It ain't only me dat's goin' to wukk dis trick. It's me an' de Lawd.

PHARAOH. Who?

MOSES. De Lawd God of Israel.

PHARAOH. I kin outtrick you an' de Lawd too!

MOSES (*angrily*). Now you done it, ol' King Pharaoh. You been mean to de Lawd's people, and de Lawd's been easy on you caize you didn't know no better. You been givin' me a lot of say-so and no do-so, and I didn' min' dat. But now you've got to braggin' dat you's better dan de Lawd, and dat's too many.

PHARAOH. You talk like a preacher, an' I never did like to hear preachers talk.

MOSES. You ain't goin' to like it any better, when I strikes down de oldes' boy in every one of yo' people's houses.

PHARAOH. Now you've given up trickin' and is jest lyin'. (*He rises.*) Listen, I'm Pharaoh. I do de strikin' down yere. I strike down my enemies, and dere's no one in all Egypt kin kill who he wants to, 'ceptin' me.

MOSES. I'm sorry, Pharaoh. Will you let de Hebrews go?

PHARAOH. You heard my word. (AARON *is lifting his rod again at a signal from* MOSES.) Now, no more tricks or I'll—

MOSES. Oh, Lawd, you'll have to do it, I guess. Aaron, lift de rod.
(*There is a thunderclap, darkness and screams. The lights go up. Several of the younger men on the stage have fallen to the ground or are being held in the arms of the horrified elders.*)

PHARAOH. What have you done yere? Where's my boy?
(*Through the door come four* MEN *bearing a young man's body.*)

FIRST OF THE FOUR MEN. King Pharaoh.
(PHARAOH *drops into his chair, stunned, as the dead boy is brought to the throne.*)

PHARAOH (*grief-stricken*). Oh, my son, my fine son.
(*The courtiers look at him with mute appeal.*)

MOSES. I'm sorry, Pharaoh, but you cain't fight de Lawd. Will you let his people go?

PHARAOH. Let them go.
(*The lights go out. The* CHOIR *begins, "Mary Don't You Weep," and continues until it is broken by the strains of "I'm Noways Weary and I'm Noways Tired." The latter is sung by many more voices than the former, and the cacophony ends as the latter grows in volume and the lights go up on the next scene.*)

SCENE IV

The CHILDREN OF ISRAEL are marching on the treadmill and now singing fortissimo. They are of all ages and most of them are ragged. The men have packs on their shoulders, one or two have hand carts. The line stretches across the stage. It is nearing twilight, and the faces of the assemblage are illumined by the rays of the late afternoon sun. The upper treadmill carries a gradually rising and falling middle distance past the marchers. The foot of a mountain appears; a trumpet call is heard as the foot of the mountain reaches stage center. The marchers halt. The picture now shows the mountain running up out of sight off right. The singing stops. A babel of "What's de matter?" "Why do we stop?" "Tain't sundown yet!" "What's happened?" "What's goin' on?" "What are they blowin' for?" etc. Those looking ahead begin to murmur. "It's Moses," "Moses." "What's happened to him?" The others take up the repetition of "Moses," and MOSES enters, on the arm of AARON. He is now an old man, as is his brother, and he totters toward the center of the stage. Cries of "What's de matter, Moses?" "You ain't hurt, is you?" "Ain't that too bad?" etc. He slowly seats himself on the rock at the foot of the mountain.

AARON. How you feelin' now, brother?

MOSES. I'm so weary, Aaron. Seems like I was took all of a sudden.

AARON. Do we camp yere?

MOSES (*pathetically*). No, you got to keep goin'.

AARON. But you cain't go no further tonight, brother.

MOSES. Dis never happened to me befo'.

A YOUNG WOMAN. But you's a ol' man, now, Father Moses. You cain't expect to go as fas' as we kin.

MOSES. But de Lawd said I'd do it. He said I was to show you de Promised Land. Fo'ty years I bin leadin' you. I led you out o' Egypt. I led you past Sinai, and through de wilderness. Oh, I cain't fall down on you now!

AARON. Le's res' yere fo' de night. Den we'll see how you feel in de mo'nin'.

MOSES. We tol' de scouts we'd meet 'em three miles furder on. I hate fo' 'em to come back all dis way to report. 'Tis gettin' a little dark, ain't it?

AARON. It ain't dark, Brother.

MOSES. No, it's my eyes.

AARON. Maybe it's de dust.

MOSES. No, I jest cain't seem to see. Oh, Lawd, dey cain't have a blind man leadin' 'em! Where is you, Aaron?

AARON. I'se right yere, Moses.

MOSES. Do you think— (*Pause.*) Oh! Do you think it's de time He said?

AARON. How you mean, Moses?
(*Crowd look from one to another in wonder.*)

MOSES. He said I could lead 'em to de Jordan, dat I'd *see* de Promised Land, and dat's all de further I could go, on account I broke de laws. Little while back I thought *I did* see a river ahead, and a pretty land on de other side. (*Distant shouts "Hooray!"* "Yere dey are!" "Dey travelled quick." *etc.*) Where's de young leader of de troops? Where's Joshua?
(*The call "Joshua" is taken up by those on the right of the stage, followed almost immediately by "Yere he is!" "Moses wants you!" etc. JOSHUA enters. He is a fine-looking Negro of about thirty.*)

JOSHUA (*going to MOSES' side*). Yes, suh.

MOSES. What's de shoutin' 'bout, Joshua?

JOSHUA. De scouts is back wid de news. De Jordan is right ahead of us, and Jericho is jest on de other side. Moses, we're dere! (*There are cries of "Hallelujah!" "De Lawd be praised!" "Hooray!" "De Kingdom's comin'!" etc. With a considerable stir among the marchers, several new arrivals crowd in from right, shouting, "Moses, we're dere!"* JOSHUA *seeing the newcomers.*) Yere's de scouts! (*Three very ragged and dusty young men advance to* MOSES.)

MOSES (*as the shouting dies*). So it's de River Jordan?

FIRST SCOUT. Yes, suh.

MOSES. All we got to take is de city of Jericho.

FIRST SCOUT. Yes, suh.

MOSES. Joshua, you got to take charge of de fightin' men, an' Aaron's gotta stay by de priests.

JOSHUA. What about you?

MOSES. You are leavin' me behind. Joshua, you gonter get de fightin' men together and take dat city befo' sundown.

JOSHUA. It's a big city, Moses, wid walls all 'round it. We ain't got enough men.

MOSES. You'll take it, Joshua.

JOSHUA. Yes, suh, but how?

MOSES. Move up to de walls wid our people. Tell de priests to go wid you with de rams' horns. You start marchin' 'roun' dem walls, and den—

JOSHUA. Yes, suh.

MOSES. De Lawd'll take charge, jest as he's took charge ev'y time I've led you against a city. He ain't never failed, has he?

SEVERAL VOICES. No, Moses. (*All raise their heads.*)

MOSES. And he ain't goin' to fail us now. (*He prays. All bow.*) Oh, Lawd, I'm turnin' over our brave young men to you, caize I know you don' want me to lead 'em any further. (*Rises.*) Jest like you said, I've got to de Jordan but I cain't git over it. An' yere dey goin' now to take de city of Jericho. In a little while dey'll be marchin' 'roun' it. An' would you please be so good as to tell 'em what to do? Amen. (*To* JOSHUA.) Go ahead. Ev'ybody follows Joshua now. Give de signal to move on wid e'vything. (*A trumpet is heard.*) You camp fo' de night in de City of Jericho. (MOSES *seats himself on the rock.*)

JOSHUA. Cain't we help you, Moses?

MOSES. You go ahead. De Lawd's got his plans fo' me. Soun' de signal to march. (*Another trumpet call is heard. The company starts marching off.* AARON *lingers a moment.*) Take care of de Ark of de Covenant, Aaron.

AARON. Yes, Brother. Good-bye.

MOSES. Good-bye, Aaron. (*The singing is resumed softly and dies away. The last of the marchers has disappeared.*) Yere I is, Lawd. De chillun is goin' into de Promised Land. (GOD *enters from behind the hill. He walks to* MOSES, *puts his hands on his shoulders.*) You's with me, ain't you, Lawd?

GOD. Co'se I is.

MOSES. Guess I'm through, Lawd. Jest like you said I'd be, when I broke de tablets of de law. De ol' machine's broke down.

GOD. Jest what was it I said to you, Moses? Do you remember?

MOSES. You said I couldn't go into de Promised Land.

GOD. Dat's so. But dat ain't all dey was to it.

MOSES. How you mean, Lawd?

GOD. Moses, you been a good man. You been a good leader of my people. You got me angry once, dat's true. And when you anger me I'm a God of Wrath. But I never meant you wasn't gonter have what was comin' to you. An' I ain't goin' to do you out of it, Moses. It's jest de country acrost de River dat you ain't gonter enter. You gonter have a Promised Land. I been gettin' it ready fo' you, fo' a long time. Kin you stand up?

MOSES (*rising, with* GOD's *help*). Yes, suh, Lawd.

GOD. Come on, I'm goin' to show it to you. We goin' up dis hill to see it. Moses, it's a million times nicer dan de Land of Canaan. (*They start up the hill.*)

MOSES. I cain't hardly see.

GOD. Don't worry. Dat's jest caize you so old.
(*They take a step or two up the hill, when* MOSES *stops suddenly.*)

MOSES. Oh!

GOD. What's de matter?

MOSES. We cain't be doin' dis!

GOD. Co'se we kin!

MOSES. But I fo'got! I fo'got about Joshua and de fightin' men!

GOD. How about 'em?

MOSES. Dey're marchin' on Jericho. I tol' 'em to march aroun' de walls and den de Lawd would be dere to tell 'em what to do.

GOD. Dat's all right. He's der.

MOSES. Den who's dis helpin' me up de hill?

GOD. Yo' faith, yo' God.

MOSES. And is you over dere helpin' them too, Lawd? Is you goin' to tell dem poor chillun what to do?

GOD. Co'se I is. Listen, Moses. I'll show you how I'm helpin' dem.
(*From the distance comes the blast of the rams' horns, the sound of crumbling walls, a roar, and a moment's silence. The* CHOIR *begins "Joshua Fit De Battle of Jericho" and continues through the rest of the scene.*)

MOSES. You did it, Lawd! You've tooken it! Listen to de chillun—dey's in de Land of Canaan at last! You's de only God dey ever was, ain't you, Lawd?

GOD (*quietly*). Come on, ol' man.
(*They continue up the hill. The stage is darkened.*)

MR. DESHEE (*in the dark*). But even dat scheme didn' work. Caize after dey got into the Land of Canaan dey went to de dogs again. And dey went into bondage again. Only dis time it was in de City of Babylon.
(*The* CHOIR, *which has been singing "Cain't Stay Away," stops as the next scene begins.*)

SCENE V

Under a low ceiling is a room vaguely resembling a Negro night club in New Orleans. Two or three long tables run across the room, and on the left is a table on a dais with a gaudy canopy above it. The table bears a card marked "Reserved for King and guests."

Flashy young men and women are seated at the tables. About a dozen couples are dancing in the foreground to the tune of a jazz orchestra. The costumes are what would be worn at a Negro masquerade to represent the debauchees of Babylon.

FIRST MAN. When did yuh git to Babylon?

SECOND MAN. I jes' got in yesterday.

THIRD MAN (*dancing*). How do you like dis baby, Joe?

FOURTH MAN. Hot damn! She could be de King's pet!

A WOMAN. Anybody seen my papa?

THIRD MAN. Don' fo'git de dance at de High Priest's house tomorrow.
(*The dance stops as a bugle call is heard. Enter* MASTER OF CEREMONIES.)

MASTER OF CEREMONIES. Stop! Tonight's guest of honor, de King of Babylon an' party of five.

(*Enter the* KING *and five* GIRLS. *The* KING *has on an imitation ermine cloak over his conventional evening clothes and wears a diamond tiara. All rise as the* KING *enters, and sing,* "Hail, de King of Bab—Bab—Babylon.")

KING. Wait till you see de swell table I got. (*He crosses the stage to his table. The* GIRLS *are jabbering.*) Remind me to send you a peck of rubies in de mo'nin'.

MASTER OF CEREMONIES. Ev'nin', King!

KING. Good ev'nin'. How's de party goin'?

MASTER OF CEREMONIES. Bes' one we ever had in Babylon, King.

KING. Any Jew boys yere?

MASTER OF CEREMONIES (*indicating some of the others*). Lot o' dem yere. I kin go git mo' if you want 'em.

KING. I was really referrin' to de High Priest. He's a 'ticlar frien' o' mine an' he might drop in. You know what he look like?

MASTER OF CEREMONIES. No, suh, but I'll be on de look-out fo' him.

KING. O. K. Now le's have a li'l good time.

MASTER OF CEREMONIES. Yes, suh. (*To the orchestra.*) Let 'er go, boys.
(*The music begins, waiters appear with food and great urns painted gold and silver, from which they pour out wine for the guests. The* MASTER OF CEREMONIES *exits. The* KING'*s dancing-girls go to the middle of the floor, and start to dance. The* KING *puts his arms about the waists of two* GIRLS, *and draws them to him.*)

KING. Hot damn! Da's de way! Let de Jew boys see our gals kin dance better'n dere's. (*There is an ad lib. babel of* "Da's de truth, King!" "I don' know—we got some good gals, too!" *etc.*) Dey ain' nobody in de worl' like de Babylon gals.
(*The dancing grows faster, the watchers keep time with hand-claps. The door at the left opens suddenly, and the* PROPHET, *a patriarchal, ragged figure enters. He looks belligerently about the room, and is followed almost immediately by the* MASTER OF CEREMONIES.)

PROPHET. Stop!
(*The music and the dancers halt.*)

KING. What's the idea, bustin' up my party?

MASTER OF CEREMONIES. He said he was expected, King. I thought mebbe he was de—

KING. Did you think he was de High Priest of de Hebrews? Why, he's jest an ol' bum! De High Priest is a fashion plate. T'row dis ole bum out o' yere!

PROPHET. Stop!
(*Those who have been advancing to seize him stop, somewhat amused.*)

KING. Wait a minute. Don't throw him out. Let's see what he has to say.

PROPHET. Listen to me, King of Babylon! I've been sent yere by de Lawd God Jehovah. Don't you dare lay a hand on de Prophet!

KING. Oh, you're a prophet, is yuh? Well, you know we don' keer much fo' prophets in dis part of de country.

PROPHET. Listen to me, sons and daughters of Babylon! Listen, you children of Israel dat's given yo'selves over to de evil ways of yo' oppressors! You're all wallowin' like hogs in sin, an' de wrath of Gawd ain' goin' to be held back much longer! I'm tellin' you, repent befo' it's too late. Repent befo' Jehovah casts down de same fire dat burned up Sodom and Gomorrah. Repent befo' de— (*During this scene yells increase as the* PROPHET *continues.*)
(*The* HIGH PRIEST *enters left. He is a fat voluptuary, elaborately clothed in brightly colored robes. He walks in hand in hand with a gaudily dressed* "chippy.")

HIGH PRIEST (*noise stops*). Whoa, dere! What you botherin' the King fo'?

PROPHET (*wheeling*). And you, de High Priest of all Israel, walkin' de town wid a dirty li'l tramp.

KING. Seems to be a frien' o' yours, Jake.

HIGH PRIEST (*crossing to the* KING *with his girl*). Aw, he's one of dem wild men, like Jeremiah and Isaiah. Don' let him bother you none. (*Pushes* PROPHET *aside and goes to* KING'*s table.*)

PROPHET. You consort with harlots, an' yo' pollution in the sight of de Lawd. De Lawd God's goin' to smite you down, jest as he's goin' to smite down all dis wicked world! (*Grabs* HIGH PRIEST *and turns him around.*)

KING (*angrily against the last part of the preceding speech*). Wait a minute. I'm getting tired of this. Don' throw him out. Jest kill him!
(*There is the sound of a shot. The* PROPHET *falls.*)

PROPHET. Smite 'em down, Lawd, like you said. Dey ain't a decent person left in de whole world. (*He dies.* MASTER OF CEREMONIES, *revolver in hand, looks down at the* PROPHET.)

MASTER OF CEREMONIES. He's dead, King.

KING. Some of you boys take him out.
(*A couple of young men come from the background and walk off with the body.*)

HIGH PRIEST. Don' know whether you should'a done that, King.

KING. Why not?

HIGH PRIEST. I don' know whether de Lawd would like it.

KING. Now, listen, Jake. You know yo' Lawd ain't payin' much attention to dis man's town. Except fo' you boys, it's tho'ly protected by de Gawds o' Babylon.

HIGH PRIEST. I know, but jest de same—

KING. Look yere, s'pose I give you a couple hund'ed pieces of silver. Don' you s'pose you kin arrange to persuade yo' Gawd to keep his hands off?

HIGH PRIEST (*oilily*). Well of co'se we could try. I dunno how well it would work. (*As* the HIGH PRIEST *speaks, the* KING *claps his hands.* MASTER OF CEREMONIES *enters with bag of money.*)

KING. Yere it is.

HIGH PRIEST (*smiling*). I guess we kin square things up. (*He prays—whiningly.*) Oh Lawd, please forgive my po' frien' de King o' Babylon. He didn't know what he was doin' an—
(*There is a clap of thunder, darkness for a second. The lights go up and* GOD *is standing in the center of the room.*)

GOD (*in a voice of doom*). Dat's about enough. (*The guests are horrified.*) I's stood all I kin from you. I tried to make dis a good earth. I helped Adam, I helped Noah, I helped Moses, an' I helped David. What's de grain dat grew out of de seed? Sin! Nothin' but sin throughout de whole world. I've given you ev'y chance. I sent you warriors and prophets. I've given you laws and commandments, an' you betrayed my trust. Ev'ything I've given you, you've defiled. Ev'y time I've fo'given you, you've mocked me. An' now de High Priest of Israel tries to trifle wid my name. Listen, you chillun of darkness, yo' Lawd is tired. I'm tired of de struggle to make you worthy of de breath I gave you. I put you in bondage ag'in to cure you an' yo' worse dan you was amongst de flesh pots of Egypt. So I renounce you. Listen to the words of yo' Lawd God Jehovah, for dey is de last words yo' ever hear from me. I repent of dese people dat I have made and I will deliver dem no more.
(*There is darkness and cries of "Mercy!" "Have pity, Lawd!" "We didn' mean it, Lawd!" "Forgive us, Lawd!" etc. The* CHOIR *sings "Death's Gwineter Lay His Cold Icy Hands On Me" until the lights go up on the next scene.*)

SCENE VI

GOD *is writing at his desk. Outside, past the door, goes* HOSEA, *a dignified old man, with wings like* JACOB'S. GOD, *sensing his presence, looks up from the paper he is examining, and follows him out of the corner of his eye. Angrily he resumes his work as soon as* HOSEA *is out of sight. There is a knock on the door.*

GOD. Who is it?
(GABRIEL *enters.*)

GABRIEL. It's de delegation, Lawd.

GOD (*wearily*). Tell 'em to come in. (ABRAHAM, ISAAC, JACOB, *and* MOSES *enter.*) Good mo'nin', gen'lemen.

THE VISITORS. Good mo'nin', Lawd.

GOD. What kin I do for you?

MOSES. You know, Lawd. Go back to our people.

GOD (*shaking his head*). Ev'ry day fo' hund'eds of years you boys have come in to ask dat same thing. De answer is still de same. I repented of de people I made. I said I would deliver dem no more. Good mo'nin', gen'lemen. (*The four* VISITORS *rise and exeunt.* GABRIEL *remains.*) Gabe, why do dey do it?

GABRIEL. I 'spect dey think you gonter change yo' mind.

GOD (*sadly*). Dey don' know me. (HOSEA *again passes the door. His shadow shows on wall.* GABRIEL *is perplexed, as he watches.* GOD *again looks surreptitiously over His shoulder at the passing figure.*) I don' like dat, either.

GABRIEL. What, Lawd?

GOD. Dat man.

GABRIEL. He's jest a prophet, Lawd. Dat's jest old Hosea. He jest come up the other day.

GOD. I know. He's one of de few dat's come up yere since I was on de earth last time.

GABRIEL. Ain' been annoyin' you, has he?

GOD. I don' like him walkin' past de door.

GABRIEL. All you got to do is tell him to stop, Lawd.

GOD. Yes, I know. I don' want to tell him. He's got a right up yere or he wouldn't be yere.

GABRIEL. You needn' be bothered by him hangin' aroun' de office all de time. I'll tell 'im. Who's he think he—

GOD. No, Gabe. I find it ain't in me to stop him. I sometimes jest wonder why he don' come in and say hello.

GABRIEL. You want him to do dat? (*He moves as if to go to the door.*)

GOD. He never has spoke to me, and if he don' wanta come in, I ain't gonter make him. But dat ain't de worst of it, Gabriel.

GABRIEL. What is, Lawd?

GOD. Ev'y time he goes past de door I hears a voice.

GABRIEL. One of de angels?

GOD (*shaking his head*). It's from de earth. It's a man.

GABRIEL. You mean he's prayin'?

GOD. No, he ain't exactly prayin'. He's jest talkin' in such a way dat I got to lissen. His name is Hezdrel.

GABRIEL. Is he on de books?

GOD. No, not yet. But ev'y time dat Hosea goes past I hear dat voice.

GABRIEL. Den tell *it* to stop.

GOD. I find I don' want to do that, either. Dey's gettin' ready to take Jerusalem down dere. Dat was my big fine city. Dis Hezdrel, he's jest one of de defenders. (*Sud-*

denly and passionately, almost wildly.) I ain't comin' down. You hear me? I ain't comin' down. (He looks at GABRIEL.) Go ahead, Gabriel. 'Tend to yo' chores. I'm gonter keep wukkin' yere.

GABRIEL. I hates to see you feelin' like dis, Lawd.

GOD. Dat's all right. Even bein' Gawd ain't a bed of roses. (GABRIEL exits. HOSEA's shadow is on the wall. For a second HOSEA hesitates. GOD looks at the wall. Goes to window.) I hear you. I know yo' fightin' bravely, but I ain't comin' down. Oh, why don' you leave me alone? You know you ain't talkin' to me. Is you talkin' to me? I cain't stand yo' talkin' dat way. I kin only hear part of what you' sayin', and it puzzles me. Don' you know you cain't puzzle God? (A pause. Then tenderly.) Do you want me to come down dere ve'y much? You know I said I wouldn't come down? (Fiercely.) Why don' he answer me a little? (With clenched fists, looks down through the window.) Listen! I'll tell you what I'll do. I ain't goin' to promise you anythin', and I ain't goin' to do nothin' to help you. I'm jest feelin' a little low, an' I'm only comin down to make myself feel a little better, dat's all.

(The stage is darkened. CHOIR begins "A Blind Man Stood In De Middle of De Road," and continues until the lights go up on the next scene.)

SCENE VII

It is a shadowed corner beside the walls of the temple in Jerusalem. The light of camp fires flickers on the figure of HEZDREL, who was ADAM in Part I. He stands in the same position ADAM held when first discovered but in his right hand is a sword, and his left is in a sling. Around him are several prostrate bodies. Pistol and cannon shots, then a trumpet call. Six YOUNG MEN enter from left in command of a CORPORAL. They are all armed.

CORPORAL. De fightin's stopped fo' de night, Hezdrel.

HEZDREL. Yes?

CORPORAL. Dey're goin' to begin ag'in at cockcrow. (MAN enters, crosses the stage and exits.) Herod say he's goin' to take de temple tomorrow, burn de books and de Ark of de Covenant, and put us all to de sword.

HEZDREL. Yo' ready, ain't you?

EVERYBODY. Yes, Hezdrel.

HEZDREL. Did de food get in through de hole in de city wall?
(Two SOLDIERS enter, cross the stage and exit.)

CORPORAL. Yessuh, we's goin' back to pass it out now.

HEZDREL. Good. Any mo' of our people escape today?

CORPORAL. Ol' Herod's got de ol' hole covered up now, but fifteen of our people got out a new one we made.
(Other SOLDIERS enter, cross the stage and exit.)

HEZDREL. Good. Take dese yere wounded men back and git 'em took care of.

CORPORAL. Yes, suh.
(They pick up the bodies on the ground and carry them off-stage as HEZDREL speaks.)

HEZDREL. So dey gonter take de temple in de mo'nin'? We'll be waitin' for 'em. Jest remember, boys, when dey kill us we leap out of our skins, right into de lap of God.
(The men disappear with the wounded; from the deep shadow upstage comes GOD.)

GOD. Hello, Hezdrel—Adam.

HEZDREL (*rubbing his forehead*). Who is you?

GOD. Me? I'm jest an' ol' preacher, from back in de hills.

HEZDREL. What you doin' yere?

GOD. I heard you boys was fightin'. I jest wanted to see how it was goin'.

HEZDREL. Well, it ain't goin' so well.

GOD. Dey got you skeered, huh?

HEZDREL. Look yere, who is you, a spy in my brain?

GOD. Cain't you see I'se one of yo' people?

HEZDREL. Listen, Preacher, we ain't skeered. We's gonter be killed, but we ain't skeered.

GOD. I's glad to hear dat. Kin I ask you a question, Hezdrel?

HEZDREL. What is it?

GOD. How is it you is so brave?

HEZDREL. Caize we got faith, dat's why!

GOD. Faith? In who?

HEZDREL. In our dear Lawd God.

GOD. But God say he abandoned ev' one down yere.

HEZDREL. Who say dat? Who dare say dat of de Lawd God of Hosea?

GOD. De God of Hosea?

HEZDREL. You heard me. Look yere, you *is* a spy in my brain!

GOD. No, I ain't, Hezdrel. I'm jest puzzled. You ought to know dat.

HEZDREL. How come you so puzzled 'bout de God of Hosea?

GOD. I don' know. Maybe I jest don' hear things. You see, I live 'way back in de hills.

HEZDREL. What you wanter find out?

GOD. Ain't de God of Hosea de same Jehovah dat was de God of Moses?

HEZDREL (*contemptuously*). No. Dat ol' God of wrath and vengeance? We have de God dat Hosea preached to us. He's de one God.

GOD. Who's he?

HEZDREL (*reverently*). De God of mercy.

GOD. Hezdrel, don' you think dey must be de same God?

HEZDREL. I don' know. I ain't bothered to think much about it. Maybe dey is. Maybe our God is de same ol' God. I guess we jest got tired of his appearance dat ol' way.

GOD. What you mean, Hezdrel?

HEZDREL. Oh, dat ol' God dat walked de earth in de shape of a man. I guess he lived wid man so much dat all he seen was de sins in man. Dat's what made him de God of wrath and vengeance. Co'se he made Hosea. An' Hosea never would a found what mercy was unless dere was a little of it in God, too. Anyway, he ain't a fearsome God no mo'. Hosea showed us dat.

GOD. How you s'pose Hosea found dat mercy?

HEZDREL. De only way he could find it. De only way I found it. De only way anyone kin find it.

GOD. How's dat?

HEZDREL. Through sufferin'.

GOD (*after a pause*). What if dey kill you in de mo'nin', Hezdrel.

HEZDREL. If dey do, dey do. Dat's all.

GOD. Herod say he's goin' to burn de temple—

HEZDREL. So he say.

GOD. And burn de Ark an' de books. Den dat's de end of de books, ain't it?

HEZDREL (*buoyantly*). What you mean? If he burns dem things in dere? Naw. Dem's jest copies.

GOD. Where is de others?

HEZDREL (*tapping his head*). Dey's a set in yere. Fifteen got out through de hole in the city wall today. A hundred and fifty got out durin' de week. Each of 'em is a set of de books. Dey's scattered safe all over de countryside now, jest waitin' to git pen and paper fo' to put 'em down ag'in.

GOD (*proudly*). Dey cain't lick you, kin dey Hezdrel?

HEZDREL (*smiling*). I' know dey cain't. (*Trumpet.*) You better get out o' yere, Preacher, if you wanter carry de news to yo' people. It'll soon be daylight.

GOD. I'm goin'. (*He takes a step upstage and stops.*) Want me to take any message?

HEZDREL. Tell de people in de hills dey ain't nobody like de Lawd God of Hosea.

GOD. I will. If dey kill you tomorrow I'll bet dat God of Hosea'll be waitin' for you.

HEZDREL. I *know* he will.

GOD (*quietly*). Thank you, Hezdrel.

HEZDREL. Fo' what?

GOD. Fo' tellin' me so much. You see I been so far away, I guess I was jest way behin' de times. (*He exits. Pause, then trumpet sounds.*)

(HEZDREL *paces back and forth once or twice. Another young* SOLDIER *appears. Other men enter and stand grouped about* HEZDREL.)

SECOND OFFICER (*excitedly*). De cock's jest crowed, Hezdrel. Dey started de fightin' ag'in.

HEZDREL. We's ready fo' 'em. Come on, boys. (*From the darkness upstage comes another group of* SOLDIERS.) Dis is de day dey say dey'll git us. Le's fight till de last man goes. What d'you say?

CORPORAL. Le's go, Hezdrel!

HEZDREL (*calling left*). Give 'em ev'ything, boys!

(*There is a movement toward the left, a bugle call and the sound of distant battle. The lights go out. The* CHOIR *is heard singing, "March On," triumphantly. They continue to sing after the lights go up on the next scene.*)

SCENE VIII

It is the same setting as the Fish Fry Scene in Part I. The same angels are present but the CHOIR, *instead of marching, is standing in a double row on an angle upstage right.* GOD *is seated in an armchair near center. He faces the audience. As the* CHOIR *continues to sing,* GABRIEL *enters, unnoticed by the chattering angels. He looks at* GOD *who is staring thoughtfully toward the audience.*

GABRIEL. You look a little pensive, Lawd. (GOD *nods his head.*) Have a seegar, Lawd?

GOD. No thanks, Gabriel.
(GABRIEL *goes to the table, accepts a cup of custard; chats with the angel behind the table for a moment as he sips, puts the cup down and returns to the side of* GOD.)

GABRIEL. You look awful pensive, Lawd. You been sittin' yere, lookin' dis way, an awful long time. Is it somethin' serious, Lawd?

GOD. Very serious, Gabriel.

GABRIEL (*awed by His tone*). Lawd, is de time come for me to blow?

GOD. Not yet, Gabriel. I'm just thinkin'.

GABRIEL. What about, Lawd? (*Puts up hand. Singing stops.*)

GOD. 'Bout somethin' de boy tol' me. Somethin' 'bout Hosea, and himself. How dey foun' somethin'.

GABRIEL. What, Lawd?

GOD. Mercy. (*A pause.*) Through *sufferin'*, he said.

GABRIEL. Yes, Lawd.

GOD. I'm tryin' to find it, too. It's awful impo'tant. It's awful impo'tant to all de people on my earth. Did he mean dat even God must suffer? (GOD *continues to look out over the audience for a moment and then a look of surprise comes into his face. He sighs. In the distance a voice cries.*)

THE VOICE. Oh, look at him! Oh, look, dey goin' to make him carry it up dat high hill! Dey goin' to nail him to it! Oh, dat's a terrible burden for one man to carry! (GOD *rises and murmurs "Yes!" as if in recognition. The heavenly beings have been watching him closely, and now, seeing him smile gently, draw back, relieved. All the angels burst into "Hallelujah, King Jesus." GOD continues to smile as the lights fade away. The singing becomes fortissimo.*)

Curtain.

Alison's House

BY SUSAN GLASPELL

SUSAN GLASPELL

Susan Glaspell was born at Davenport, Iowa, in 1882. She holds the Ph.B. degree from Drake University, Iowa, and did post-graduate work at the University of Chicago. In 1913 she married George Cram Cook, now deceased. In Des Moines she served as legislative reporter for *The News and the Capitol*.

Among her books are *The Road to the Temple, Brook Evans, The Fugitive's Return,* and *Ambrose Holt and Family*. Miss Glaspell was prominently identified with the Little Theatre movement through the Provincetown Players. In 1925 she was married to Norman H. Matson.

Miss Glaspell's one-act plays received wide critical acclaim when they were produced by the Provincetown Players.

Staged by Eva Le Gallienne and produced at the Civic Repertory Theatre, Inc., New York City, December 1, 1930, *Alison's House* was awarded the 1930-1931 Pulitzer Prize.

CHARACTERS

ANN LESLIE.

JENNIE.

RICHARD KNOWLES.

TED STANHOPE.

LOUISE.

THE FATHER.

EBEN.

ELSA.

MISS AGATHA.

HODGES.

MRS. HODGES.

Period—December 31, 1899

SCENES

ACT ONE

The Library of the old Stanhope homestead in Iowa, on the Mississippi.

ACT TWO

The same as Act One.

ACT THREE

Alison's room.

ALISON'S HOUSE

ACT ONE

SCENE: *The library of the old Stanhope homestead in Iowa, on the Mississippi, where* MISS AGATHA STANHOPE *still lives. There is a river village near-by, and the small city where the other* STANHOPES *now live is about ten miles up the river.*

It is the room of people who have lived in comfortable circumstances and signifies a family of traditions and cultivation.

Left, just rear of center, a door into the hall. In the rear corner, left, a stone fireplace. In the rear wall a bay-window, the windows coming down to a low seat, and curtained with old plum-colored velvet. Right of this are books, which are continued into an alcove. There is an easy chair near the bay-window, by it a foot-stool and a low table; front, right, a long table. At the left, front of door, a desk. The room is carpeted, a tone deeper than the curtains. On the walls are portraits of an older generation.

The time is eleven in the morning of the last day of the nineteenth century, December 31, 1899. But the furnishings of the library are of a period earlier than this.

As the curtain rises ANN *is seated before her Oliver typewriter, near the alcove, behind the long table. She is fair, sensitive looking. She wears a shirt waist and blue skirt, in the manner of 1900. She is about twenty-three, and has gentle manners. She reaches down and takes another old paper from a small horse-hair trunk beside her. Makes a type-written note.*

Enter JENNIE.

JENNIE (*speaking to some one behind her*). You had better come in here. Everything is so upset—with the moving. Oh, here is Miss Ann. He says he's a reporter, Miss. I don't know anything about it. (*Enter* KNOWLES, *a young man*. JENNIE *goes out*.)

ANN. You wished to see Mr. Stanhope?

KNOWLES. Well—yes, some of the family. But most of all, the house.

ANN. The house is being broken up.

KNOWLES. I want to see it before it's broken up. Especially the room that was used by Miss Alison Stanhope.

ANN. I think no one goes in that room, except the family.

KNOWLES. You are not—of the family?

ANN. Oh, no. I am Mr. Stanhope's secretary.

KNOWLES (*going a little nearer*). Those papers you're working with—are they by any chance the papers of Miss Alison Stanhope?

ANN. They are not.

KNOWLES (*with his very nice smile*). And it's none of my business what they are. I'm from the Chicago Record Herald. Down to get a little story about the house, because it is being broken up.

ANN (*with a smile*). Isn't there anything going on in Chicago?

KNOWLES. Perhaps not as much as went on in this house.

ANN. I'm surprised a metropolitan paper should be interested in the fact Miss Agatha Stanhope is moving up to town to live with her brother.

KNOWLES. It isn't Miss Agatha. It's Miss Alison.

ANN. But aren't you a little late? Miss Alison has been dead eighteen years.

KNOWLES. She isn't dead. Anything about her is alive. She belongs to the world. But the family doesn't seem to know that.

ANN. They published her poems.

653

KNOWLES. But anything about where— how—they were written. The desk she sat at. The window she looked from. Is there a bird singing in that tree now? Well, no, probably not, the last day of December. But looking through the dead branches, to meadows sloping to the Mississippi, as she looked.

ANN. You cared for the poems?

KNOWLES. I'll never forget the day I got them—at the bookshop on the Midway, and walked down through Jackson Park, and saw the lake—because she had seen the river. I write a little poetry myself.

ANN. I wish I could. But I can't write it. That's why I'm so grateful to Alison.

KNOWLES. I know. Do you read the Record Herald?

ANN. Usually.

KNOWLES. Did you see it last Wednesday?

ANN. I don't remember.

KNOWLES. Do you remember a poem—no, verses—Michigan Avenue?

ANN. I'm afraid I didn't see that.

KNOWLES (*grinning*). Well, I did.

ANN. You get your poems printed?

KNOWLES. I'm no Alison, but—

ANN. I suppose you haven't it with you?

KNOWLES. Well, since you mention it, I don't seem to remember taking it out of my vest pocket.

ANN. I'd love to see it.

KNOWLES. You would? Oh, well, I don't mind. (*Taking a clipping from his pocket, he hands it to her.*) Don't *expect* anything.

ANN (*who is reading*). Oh, I think that's nice.

KNOWLES (*eagerly looking over her shoulder*). Which part?

ANN. The lake. "Through all the years you waited for your city—"

KNOWLES. Just a fancy. I like best—"Lights snuffed in fog as—"

(TED *comes in, whistling "A hot time in the old town tonight."*)

ANN. Ted! Here is a poem about— (*To* KNOWLES.) Oh, here is a member of the family, Mr. Edward Stanhope. This gentleman—

KNOWLES. Knowles.

ANN. Mr. Knowles is a reporter. He's from the Record Herald.

TED. Honest?

KNOWLES (*laughing*). Honest.

ANN. He wants to see the house.

TED. Should have come sooner. Everything's topsy-turvy. Anyway—why?

KNOWLES. Because Alison Stanhope lived and died here.

TED. I see. Well, they haven't started on Alison's room yet. Aunt Agatha won't let them.

KNOWLES. Won't you let me see it? It isn't just the story. It's—a feeling about it. (*To* ANN.) You know. And since it's going to be broken up, and won't be any more, why not some one who has a feeling about it to —to hold it in memory, you might say.

TED (*uncertainly*). Well, I dunno.

ANN. I've been in there. Mr. Stanhope took me when I got here this morning. He said he wanted me to be there—before it ceased. It's just the same. It's as if she might come in the door.

KNOWLES. We understand. We three. Why trouble the older folks about it? This is the last day of the nineteenth century.

TED. Well, there's no lie, but—

KNOWLES. I can't tell you how I'd appreciate it. How much it would mean to me.

TED (*at the door, looking into the hall*). They're all in the dining-room, counting dishes.

KNOWLES. Fine!

TED. But if Louise finds out.

KNOWLES. She won't. We'll see to it.

TED (*attracted by the idea of stealing a march*). S—h. (*Goes out, softly, followed by* KNOWLES. ANN *returns to the poem she had not finished.*)
(*Enter* LOUISE.)

LOUISE (*sharply*). What is this story of Jennie's—about a reporter?

ANN. There was a reporter.

LOUISE. Did you talk to him?

ANN. Not much.

LOUISE. Where is he?

ANN. He went out just now.

LOUISE. Where?

ANN. Why, just out.

LOUISE. You refuse to talk to me—about a family matter?

ANN (*examining a paper from the trunk*). There is so much for me to do.

LOUISE. Well—really. We'll see about this! (*Goes to the door.*) Father! Father Stanhope!

ANN. Oh—please! Surely that isn't necessary, when he's so busy—troubled.

LOUISE. So am I busy—troubled. Yes, Father. Just a moment, please.
(*Enter* STANHOPE. *He has the look of a man who has made a place for himself, who is acquainted with responsibilities. He is vigorous for a man of sixty-three, though troubled at the moment. One soon feels he has a feeling for others that makes him tolerant, though firm.*)

STANHOPE (*good humoredly*). What's the trouble now?

LOUISE. Father, I think you ought to know there's a reporter in the house. Ann knows about it, and won't tell.

STANHOPE. Yes? Well, when you've seen as many reporters as I have you'll know they don't usually shoot, or even bite. He probably came down about the Mahoney case.

LOUISE (*to* ANN). Where was he from?

ANN. Chicago.

LOUISE. Chicago! You see? "The Mahoney case"!

STANHOPE. What did he want, Ann?

ANN. To see the house.

LOUISE. Why? Why should he see the house?

ANN. Because Alison lived here.

LOUISE. I knew that!

STANHOPE. Well, and what of it? My dear, you can't have a distinguished person in the family without running into a little public interest. (*He takes one of the papers from the trunk.*)

LOUISE. Father! Please let's try to do this without—stirring things up. Just because we're breaking up the house do we have to revive the stories about Alison?

STANHOPE. To what stories about my sister do you refer?

LOUISE. Now please don't be vexed with me. You know as well as I do—the whole story they've harped on so long—that she was different—a rebel—goodness, I don't know what they do mean.

STANHOPE. I think the worst they can say about my dear sister is that she was a great soul, and a poet. It isn't going to hurt my feelings to have it said again.

LOUISE. But you know how they talk—it makes the whole family seem—different. And after Elsa— (*At this change.*) Oh, forgive me, but you must know how the town does talk about Elsa. You can't run away with a married man—live with a man who has a wife and children and not be talked about.

ANN. In making the memoranda of these old contracts am I to—
(STANHOPE *moves to her.*)

LOUISE. And they do link it up with something queer about Alison.

STANHOPE (*checking anger, and speaking easily*). That would be most unjust to Alison. She never lived with a man who had a wife and children.

LOUISE (*knowing she shouldn't say it*). She wanted to, didn't she?

STANHOPE (*again checking anger, speaking humorously*). Oh we want to do lots of things we don't do. I might want to ask my daughter-in-law to keep still. In fact, I think I shall.

LOUISE (*rather angry, and made the more persistent by it*). Where did he go—this reporter?

ANN. Why they went out—just a moment ago.

LOUISE. They? Who's with him?

ANN. He's with Ted.

LOUISE. Ted! He's already told him enough to fill a page! Where did they go?

STANHOPE (*as ANN peers at a paper*). Well, where did they go, Ann—the roof—the cellar?

ANN. He wanted to see the Alison room.

LOUISE. And you dared—and Ted dared— Oh, what *management!* (*She moves to the door, but STANHOPE follows.*)

STANHOPE. No. Not up there. No disturbance in Alison's room. It is to keep its— serenity, the one day it has left.

LOUISE. Serenity! With reporters prowling around?

ANN. He writes poetry himself.

LOUISE. How absurd!

ANN. No, it was quite good.

LOUISE. The trouble is, Father, the family has too many—on the outskirts, who like to snatch a little of the sensationalism. I'm amazed you can't see my point. Just now, after Elsa—

STANHOPE. I have told you before I did not wish to discuss my daughter with you.

LOUISE. But you act as if I had nothing to do with it. Your daughter is my husband's sister—I'm sorry to say. My children are Stanhopes. I don't want them taunted.

STANHOPE. Have they been taunted? They're rather young for that.

LOUISE. They will be.

STANHOPE. Well, sufficient unto the day is the taunting thereof.

LOUISE. But if we stir it all up again—

STANHOPE. The family china and silver seem more important at the moment than the family disgraces. I hadn't thought you need come down here, Louise, but you were anxious to get your Aunt Agatha moved with the least friction. Now why not a little management in the dining-room? Poor Agatha's all upset.

LOUISE (*starting to go, but turning*). It isn't good for Eben, either!

STANHOPE (*occupied with a paper*). The dining-room?

LOUISE. Oh, Father, why won't you be serious with me?

STANHOPE. Because you make me feel too serious, perhaps.

LOUISE. Eben isn't any too well grounded.

STANHOPE. Oh Eben has a very good hold on the law.

LOUISE. I mean the law of *life*.

STANHOPE. Oh. Law of life.

LOUISE. He has that same thing. He could just—shake everything loose. I'm sorry to talk before outsiders.

STANHOPE. I don't regard Ann an outsider. It was you came where she was working, not Ann who intruded. Now Ann, take these notes, please.

LOUISE. I think a family should stand together.

STANHOPE. That's right. Stand by your Aunt Agatha.

LOUISE (*murmuring as she goes out*). What can I *do?*

STANHOPE (*sitting down by ANN, she with her pad for dictation*). Sometimes I wish I weren't the head of a family. Sometimes I wish there weren't any family. (ANN *had begun to take this, tears off the page.*) Quite so. Some things we never put down.

Even Alison didn't put it all down. (*Listening to footsteps in the hall.*) Ted! (TED *comes to the door.*) Come in here. Both of you.

(KNOWLES *follows* TED *into the room.*)

TED. This is Mr. Knowles, Father.

STANHOPE (*curtly*). How do you do?

KNOWLES. How do you do, sir.

STANHOPE (*to* TED). What have you been doing?

TED. Just walking around.

STANHOPE. Where?

TED. Round the house.

STANHOPE. What room of the house?

KNOWLES. My fault, sir. I wanted to see Miss Alison's room.

STANHOPE. You did, did you? A great many people have wanted to see it, and haven't.

KNOWLES (*to* TED). I want to thank you for letting me see it.

STANHOPE. He had no business to let you see it!

KNOWLES. Nevertheless I shall remember it always.

STANHOPE (*momentarily touched by the sincerity of his tone*). And now you're going to write a lurid story about it.

KNOWLES. Not lurid. (*With a smile.*) That wouldn't be the way to handle this story. But that room belongs to the world, don't you think so? Alison Stanhope's room— holds something.

(AGATHA STANHOPE *has appeared in the doorway; she retains the manner of strength, though obviously feeble. She is carrying a china tea-pot, and a sugar bowl. She is arrested by* KNOWLES' *last words.*)

AGATHA. What does it hold? (*Fearful of dropping the tea-pot she holds it against her.*) What does it hold?

STANHOPE. Never mind, Agatha. (*He tries to take the pieces she carries, but she does not give them to him.*)

AGATHA. What is he here for?

STANHOPE. It's all right, Agatha. (*He guides her to the big chair, would help her seat herself.*)

AGATHA. What does he know about it?

STANHOPE. Nothing. Nothing at all.

(*Enter* JENNIE, *carrying a large basket filled with straw, on the top of which is another piece of the tea set.*)

JENNIE. I think this will be all right, Miss Agatha. (*She puts it down, goes out.* AGATHA *still looking at the reporter. With* STANHOPE'S *help she is seated, as if not knowing it has happened.*)

STANHOPE (*pulling up the law table for the tea things*). You needn't do these things yourself.

AGATHA. What does it hold? It holds nothing, I tell you—nothing. (*Making as if to rise.*) Did you take something?

KNOWLES. Oh, no. Indeed I did not.

AGATHA (*to* STANHOPE). He's looking for something.

STANHOPE. No, Agatha. Just some one here with Ted. (*Low, to* TED.) You haven't done so well, you see.

AGATHA. I won't have people looking through Alison's room. I've guarded it for eighteen years. (*Changing, cunning.*) All right, look. Look again. See what you find.

STANHOPE. We'll say good day now, young man.

KNOWLES. One question, please. Sorry. I was told to ask it. Have all the poems of Alison Stanhope been published?

AGATHA (*who had begun taking out the straw for packing*). What's that? What does he mean?

STANHOPE (*soothing her*). Never mind. I will answer your question, though I've answered it many times before. All the poems of Alison Stanhope have been published.

AGATHA. Now. You see? He answered you, didn't he?

KNOWLES. In going through the house—going through old papers—did you—

STANHOPE. It was one question you were to ask.

KNOWLES. Please, just this. It is a matter of public concern, you know. Did you find any papers—

AGATHA. What papers? What papers is he talking about?

STANHOPE. My sister is not equal to this. No, we found nothing that brings any new light to bear on the life of Alison Stanhope. Everything had been gone through long before.

AGATHA. Everything had been gone through long before.

KNOWLES. Thank you, sir. (*To* AGATHA.) Sorry to have disturbed you.

AGATHA (*sharply*). You didn't disturb me.

KNOWLES (*to* ANN, *with a smile*). Good-bye.

ANN (*holding it out to him*). I like the poem.

KNOWLES. Would you like to keep it?

ANN. Thank you.
(KNOWLES *goes out, followed by* TED.)

AGATHA. Where did he come from? What does he want?

STANHOPE. It's nothing—nothing at all. (*To himself.*) We're lucky to get off this easy.

AGATHA. That's why I didn't want to move. Stirring it all up! I wish they'd let Alison alone.

STANHOPE. They will, dear—in time.

AGATHA. Why can't they let her rest in peace?

STANHOPE. They will—soon. Though it wasn't in peace Alison rested.

AGATHA. What do you mean? I knew her better than you did.

STANHOPE. No you didn't, Agatha. But never mind. Now you don't have to pack these things yourself.

AGATHA. Mother's tea set? I'll pack it myself, and take it with me myself.

ANN. Perhaps I could help you, Miss Agatha. (*To* STANHOPE.) Have I time?

STANHOPE (*nodding*). We don't make much headway, anywhere. (*He sits at the table, discouraged.*) It's harder than I thought.

AGATHA. I wouldn't have believed it, John. I just wouldn't have believed that you—our brother John—would break up the old place, turning me out of home.

STANHOPE. That's because I want to turn you into my own home. You have to take care of me now, Agatha.

AGATHA. Elsa went away and left you.

STANHOPE (*hurt, but again speaking brightly*). So you have to step into the breach, as usual.

AGATHA. I looked after Alison—so long. Then looked after what Alison left. Now you're turning her out of home.

STANHOPE. Don't say that. She wouldn't say it. Alison was at home in the universe.

AGATHA. Elsa shouldn't have gone away and left her father.

STANHOPE. No.

AGATHA. Alison wouldn't have.

STANHOPE. No, Alison didn't do it—that way. But we differ. We're all different.

AGATHA. Alison stayed.

STANHOPE. Yes.
(ANN *has been packing the tea set.*)

AGATHA (*looking down at it*). No—no, those are too near together.

ANN (*taking one out*). Then I'll fix it—this way. (TED *returns.*)

TED. Nice fellow.

STANHOPE (*at the table, looking through papers*). You exceeded your authority, young man.

TED. We can't keep Alison in a prison.

AGATHA. Who kept Alison in a prison? What do you mean—a prison? She was where she wanted to be, wasn't she?

TED. She doesn't belong to just us. She belongs to the world.

STANHOPE. Oh, come Ted. We've heard that times enough, and acted on it.

AGATHA. I say she does not belong to the world! I say she belongs to us. And I'll keep her from the world—I'll keep the world from getting her—if it kills me—and kills you all!

TED (*at first standing there, astonished by the outburst*). Well, I hope it doesn't. (*Sits at the desk, taking paper and pen.*)

STANHOPE (*going over to* TED). Now that is enough. One more word to agitate her, and you'll answer to me. (*Low.*) I told you what the doctor said. (*As* ANN *rises, after packing the tea set.*) Well, that's in good shape, isn't it, Agatha? Now you finish up here, Ann, and Ted will help you list the books.

TED. Soon's I finish this letter. He won't give me the grade unless I tell him.

AGATHA. Who are you writing to?

TED. My English prof.

AGATHA. What about?

TED. Alison.

STANHOPE. Keep quiet or leave the room!

TED. Gee, Father, there's no other room to go to. They're all torn up.

AGATHA. What's he telling him?

STANHOPE. Nothing. He's just acting important. Now Agatha—Michael is here with the carriage. There's no reason for your sitting in this confusion. I'm going to have him drive you to the village for the noon train. That will get you to town in twenty minutes. Louise can go with you; or Ann, if you prefer. There you'll be comfortable, and can rest.

AGATHA. Me leave this house—while it is still this house? I shall be the last to step from the **door.**

STANHOPE. Oh, Agatha. You make it so hard for yourself, and for us all.

AGATHA. Leave things for every one else to pry into—looking—prying.

TED. What kind of a pen did Alison use, and where is the pen?

STANHOPE. Be still!

TED. Well, gee, she's my aunt, isn't she, and you want me to be flunked in English?

AGATHA (*low, gloatingly*). He doesn't know what kind of a pen she used—and I won't tell.

STANHOPE. No; why should you? (*He goes over to the books. Is looking at titles. For a moment* AGATHA *watches* TED. *She gets an idea, shrinks from it; it is terrible to her, but it grows, she faces it, and for a time she is aware of nothing else, does not move.*)

STANHOPE (*as* ANN *puts aside papers*). You are through there now?

ANN. I think so.

STANHOPE. Suppose we start on the books. We don't have to do it very minutely, but must have something of a catalogue, as they go to different people. (ANN *gets ready for this.* STANHOPE *glances at his sister, but a little bent now, turned from him, he does not see her eyes, their horror, and purpose. Low.*) Poetry. The Mermaid series, twelve volumes.
(TED *tears off his sheet of paper, crumples it, kicks the leg of the desk, rubs his head.*)

TED (*muttering*). What's anybody go to college for? Gee! (*Takes another sheet, considers.*) Gee, whiz!

STANHOPE. Chaucer. (*Taking one out.*) These are old. (*Reads a little.*) Alison read it aloud—beautifully. Her voice—(*Stands as if listening. Abruptly breaks from this.*) Two volumes. (*Puts the book back.* AGATHA *begins to unpack the tea set. Looks around to see that her brother is not watching her. Works carefully, to make no noise. Puts the pieces at the side of her chair, where the others will not see. Presses the straw back in the basket.*) Spencer, The Faery Queen.

(*Waits for her to write.*) Greene, Marlowe, Jonson.

ANN. All one volume?

STANHOPE. Yes.

TED. Oh—*rats.* (*Rubs his head.*)

STANHOPE. Shakespeare, five volumes. (*Takes out the next book, examines it.*) This is a nice old edition of Milton. See? (*Showing it to* ANN.) Alison was fond of this book.

ANN. Funny old pictures, aren't they? (AGATHA *gets her hands under the basket, which is on the low table. With difficulty rises, and takes it from the room.*)

STANHOPE. But we must get on with it. (*Hearing his sister as she is leaving the room.*) Agatha? (*As she does not pause.*) Well, her last day here. Now we come to Robert Burns—good Bobbie.

ANN. One volume?

STANHOPE. Yes. And Browning—Robert, four volumes; Mrs. Browning— (*Enter* LOUISE.)

LOUISE. This is the table to be sent to cousin Marion, isn't it? (*Her hand on the low table from which* AGATHA *has taken the basket.*)

STANHOPE. Do we need to tear up this room just now?

LOUISE. The man is here—and if we are to finish by day after tomorrow.

TED. Did Alison sleep well?

STANHOPE. Really, Ted, sometimes I think you haven't good sense.

TED. I've got sense enough to know how I can make this grade. You ought to hear *him.* He takes me out for dinner—fills me up on wine—

LOUISE. Who?

TED. Styles—English prof.

LOUISE. Your teachers at Harvard take you out and give you wine?

TED. Only Styles. Ever since he heard I was her nephew. Nearly dropped dead first time he asked me. But it always ends telling me I got no soul—insensitive family— unworthy. He's crazy. Got to get this grade though.

LOUISE. Father, you surely won't permit Ted to write a stranger—telling things— stirring it all up.

STANHOPE. Take the table out for Louise, Ted.

LOUISE. What is the tea set doing on the floor? Not a very safe place for valuable old china. (*She picks up the tea-pot and puts it on the big table, is getting the other pieces.*)

STANHOPE (*to* ANN). Why I thought you packed that tea set.

ANN. I did.

STANHOPE. And she unpacked it?

LOUISE. And left it on the floor.

ANN. But she was so anxious about it.

STANHOPE. I'm afraid. Afraid for Agatha.

TED. Now about what Alison ate.

LOUISE. Seems to me it's Ted whose mind is failing.

STANHOPE. We're not in the mood for this nonsense.

TED. It's no nonsense to me—after flunking history. What did she eat, Father? Did she like sweets?

LOUISE. Ted might as well be in town.

TED. Meat. How about meat?

STANHOPE (*going back to the books*). No one is paying any attention to you. (*Firmly.*) Tennyson.

TED. Then how am I to get through college?

LOUISE (*who is dusting the small table*). I always said Ted should be sent to a western school. At least the professors don't intoxicate the students.

TED. He never got me full but once. Then he was trying to find out about her love affair.

STANHOPE (*angrily*). Shelley. Four volumes.

LOUISE. You see? All this prying. Why it's as if the family weren't anything *else*. Why not tell him your grandfather was governor of the state and that your uncle is in Congress?

TED. He says the rest of the family is of interest only because it's so vacuous. Vacuous, is that the word? But about the food, Father. I got to get this letter off before he reads what I handed in. Meat. Sweets. Fruit. (*Writes.*) Lots of fruit.

STANHOPE. And Keats. (*He stands looking through the Keats.*)
(*A door closes outside.*)

EBEN (*off*). How are you, Jennie?

STANHOPE. Why, that's Eben.

EBEN (*off*). Oh, but you'll like it in town. Lots more going on. You can go to church.

JENNIE (*off, in a dismal voice*). I'm out of the habit.
(*EBEN enters. He is self-assured in manner, though soon one feels the inner uncertainties, hesitations, and the inner beauty.*)

EBEN. How are you, Father? Working hard, Louise?

LOUISE. Certainly.

EBEN. Hello, Ann. (*To TED who stares moodily.*) Well, I see you're energetically on the job.

TED (*solemnly*). I am doing my best.

EBEN. Who could do more?

TED (*gloomily*). Who?

LOUISE. I thought you weren't coming down till the office closed.

EBEN. I closed it. Nobody wants to do anything—last day of the year—last day of the century. Nobody's busy but Cousin Marion. She telephoned three times. Thinks her club women might take the house for a museum.

STANHOPE. She's thought that for two years. They haven't the money.

EBEN. She says they could get a little, and pay gradually—give a kermiss or something.

STANHOPE. We'll close with Hodges, who doesn't have to give a kermiss.

EBEN. Her idea would hold the place together.

STANHOPE. Hold it together for the public. Agatha would never submit to it.

EBEN. How is she?

STANHOPE. Not well. Over-excited, which is just what the doctor warned against. I want to tell you, all of you—are you listening, Ted?—nothing must be said to agitate her. Everything possible must be kept from her. Dr. Lange told me last night her heart is more and more uncertain. And she's getting—well, queer. Ann packed that tea set, and soon as we turned our backs she unpacked it.

LOUISE (*who is looking through articles in a small cabinet, left, rear*). Oh, I hope she doesn't get too queer. We've had enough. I hate the idea of people thinking we're different.

EBEN. Nothing very funny about an old lady, who's lived alone too long, getting a bit childish. She'll be all right, once she's up at father's.

STANHOPE. It's important to keep telling her she must do it for me. Don't let her think we feel she isn't able to live down here alone. Tell her I'm alone.

EBEN (*sympathetically*). Yes. (*Looking around.*) Hate like the dickens to see the place go, Father.

STANHOPE. Do you think I don't?

EBEN. The fun we used to have down here as kids—Elsa and I. Especially when Alison was here. Remember how she was always making us presents?

STANHOPE. I remember.

EBEN. An apple—pebbles from the river—little cakes she'd baked. And always her jolly little verses with them. "Alison won't tell," she'd say, when Elsa and I had run off to the river. "Alison knows," she'd say.

TED (*repeating softly as he writes*). Alison knows.

EBEN. It was all so darn real today, coming down here for the last time. And the century going—her century. When I got the first glimpse of the place through the trees I had a feeling of the whole century being piled on top of her, that she couldn't get out from under.

LOUISE. How *morbid*. Don't *let* your mind run on such things!

EBEN. Who am I—to tell my mind where to run? You know, Father, I'd like to hear her say once more—right now—here—Alison understands, because — I'll be darned if I do.

TED. Was Alison a virgin?

LOUISE. *Father!*

STANHOPE. See here now!

EBEN. Getting fresh, aren't you?

TED. It isn't me. Why won't you understand? *He* wants to *know*—and I got to make this grade.

STANHOPE. There is such a thing as taste, young man.

TED. Just what I told him—women of one's family—and he almost slapped me. Well, was she a virgin?

STANHOPE (*violently*). Yes!

TED. Oh, gee, I hoped she wasn't. (*Starting to write, turning.*) How do you know?

STANHOPE. Leave the room!

TED. Where'll I go? I don't see how you can be sure—

EBEN (*going to him, taking him by the collar, lifting him to his feet and shaking him back and forth*). You miserable little fool! And you're the baby Alison used to say got through from heaven. The hell you did! Didn't you get *anything* from her? (*Shaking him.*) Didn't you?

TED. Say! Leave me alone, will you? I guess I was only two years old when she died! What do I know about her?

EBEN. Nothing. Absolutely nothing, and never will. Why that prof ought to kill you. If your soul wasn't a shriveled peanut something from her would have made you a human being!

STANHOPE. Come now, Eben. That's enough.

EBEN. What's the use of having had an Alison in the family? Sometimes I think I'll run away from all this—and find her.

LOUISE. You haven't been drinking, have you?

EBEN. No, but I will.

LOUISE. If you haven't been drinking there's even less excuse for this raving.

EBEN. You think it's raving, Father?

STANHOPE. I think it is too uncontrolled.

EBEN. The last day we'll ever be in her house—the last day it will be her house—how can we help but think of her—and feel her—and wonder what's the matter with us—that something from her didn't —oh Lord, *make* us something!
(ELSA, *wearing coat, furs, hat, has stepped inside the door. She has beauty, a soft radiance.*)

ELSA (*in a low thrilling voice*). Yes, Eben. Yes!

EBEN. Elsa!

STANHOPE. Elsa!

ELSA. Father, may I—come in? (*One hand, palm up. Goes out toward him, timidly, but eloquent.*)

LOUISE. Certainly you may not—not while — (*But is afraid to go on,* STANHOPE *is staring so strangely at his daughter.*)

TED. Hello, Elsa. How'd you get here?

ELSA (*gratefully*). Hello, Ted. (*To her father.*) Perhaps I shouldn't have come. But Eben wrote me the place was being broken up and—

LOUISE. You wrote to her?

EBEN. Yes, I write to my sister.

ELSA. I had to be here once more. I thought —perhaps it's too much to ask—but I hoped you would let me stay here. Just tonight. It would—do me good.

LOUISE (*with a shrill laugh*). Now that's —funny. (*Laughs again.*)

ELSA (*advancing a little to her father*). It doesn't mean you forgive me, Father, if— if you don't. If you can't. But won't you just do it—because Alison would do it? She'd take my hands. She'd say—Little Elsa. She'd say—Elsa has come home. (*From upstairs a wild cry from* JENNIE.)

JENNIE (*above*). Mr. Stanhope—everybody!—help!
(EBEN *hurries out.*)

JENNIE (*off*). Everybody—quick—the house—burning!

TED. Fire! I smelled it! (*He runs out,* LOUISE *goes, and* ANN. STANHOPE *does not pass his daughter without pausing a moment, looking at her.*)
(*Outside a confusion of voices, a running about. Only* ELSA *remains as she was, as if she cannot move.*)

ELSA. Just as I stepped into the house. As if—as if— (*Shaking this off.*) Oh, no— no. (*She looks around the room. Softly.*) Don't burn. Don't. (*After another moment, having looked from one thing to another, she goes to the books, runs her hand over them. Stands there. But at a noise of something falling upstairs, she becomes frightened, suddenly takes an armful of books. Is starting out, but stopped by a confident shout from* EBEN.)

EBEN (*off*). It's all right. We're getting it! Two more buckets, Ted!
(ELSA *sits down where* ANN *had sat, still holding the books, bent over them, her back to the door. After a moment,* AGATHA *comes in.* ELSA *does not hear her, and* AGATHA, *in a curious, fixed state has not seen* ELSA. *She sits where she sat before. She is white, rigid.* ELSA, *moving a little, drops one of the books.*)

AGATHA (*not turning*). What's that? Who's here?

ELSA. Aunt Agatha!

AGATHA (*still not turning, as if she can not*). Who's that? Who's here? (ELSA *goes to her, and as still* AGATHA *does not look up, sits on a stool beside her.*) Elsa.

ELSA. Yes—Elsa.

AGATHA. Elsa went away.

ELSA. She came back. (*Timidly.*) Are you —glad?

AGATHA. Alison was so afraid of fire.

TED (*off*). That fixes it!

ELSA. They are getting the fire out.

AGATHA. No. Burning. All burning. All at once.

ELSA (*trying to take her hand*). No, Aunt Agatha. You see the boys are here. They are getting the fire out. There's nothing to be afraid of.

AGATHA. I am not afraid—now.

STANHOPE (*outside*). Agatha! Where is she?
(ELSA *starts up, but* AGATHA *takes her hand in a fierce grip, forcing her down.*)

STANHOPE (*still off*). Jennie! Where's Miss Agatha? Agatha!

ELSA (*freeing herself, going to the door*). Here, Father. Aunt Agatha is in here with me.
(STANHOPE *comes in.*)

STANHOPE (*gently, as he sees her there rigid, white*). It's all right, Agatha. Just a little blaze. Nothing whatever to worry about. The boys have it out already. (*After staring at him,* AGATHA *leans back with a wail that goes into a whimper.*) You understand, don't you, Agatha? They have put the fire out.

AGATHA (*with horror*). They have put the fire out.
(*Enter* EBEN, *coat off, flushed, much excited.*)

EBEN. That fire was set, Father.

STANHOPE. *What?*

EBEN. We found the charred straw—in the closet that breaks through to Alison's room

—coal oil there—and in Alison's room. Some one was trying to burn the house.

STANHOPE. But that's—incredible. *Why?* Oh, no—you're mistaken.

EBEN. It's undeniable. The evidence is right there.

STANHOPE (*going to the door*). Jennie! (AGATHA *leans away, as if avoiding something.* ELSA *holds her hands.*) Jennie! (*Turning.*) I don't believe a word of it! (*Enter* JENNIE.) What do you know about this fire?

JENNIE (*distraught, almost crying*). I don't know anything about it. I smelled the smoke. I ran up. It was burning—in the closet.
(*Enter* LOUISE.)

LOUISE. The fire was set. Some one tried to burn the house.

STANHOPE (*to* JENNIE). Who's been here?

JENNIE. Nobody. Nobody. Just the family —and me—and Michael.

STANHOPE. Who's been upstairs?

LOUISE. That reporter was upstairs.

STANHOPE. Why you've all lost your wits! What possible reason?

LOUISE. But no other stranger was upstairs. (STANHOPE *looks at her a moment, incredulous, dazed. Starts for the door.* ANN *comes in.*)

STANHOPE. Ann, what do you know about this reporter?

ANN. Why, I don't know anything about him.

LOUISE. Perhaps it isn't a reporter. Perhaps it's—some hostility to the family.

STANHOPE (*angrily*). That is ridiculous.

LOUISE. Well, who did it? Why?

STANHOPE. How did the fellow seem to you?

ANN. He seemed all right. I thought he was—just what he said he was. I'm sure he's all right. He showed me a poem he had written.

LOUISE. As if that proves anything! Had you known him before?

ANN (*indignant at the tone*). I had never seen him before.

STANHOPE (*going to the door; sharply*). Ted!

TED (*from above*). Staying up here to make sure!

STANHOPE. Leave Michael on watch. Come down here at once!

EBEN. I can't make head or tail of it. Who would want to burn the house?

ANN (*distressed*). Mightn't it have just—happened?

LOUISE (*scornfully*). "Happened?" Straw —saturated with kerosene?
(*Enter* TED.)

STANHOPE. Now what about you and this reporter?

TED. Well, what about us?

STANHOPE. Answer my question!

TED. What question, Father? What about us?

STANHOPE. You were the only people in that part of the house—and a fire was set.

TED. For—Pete's—sake! Talk about *me* being crazy! You think I set a fire to burn the house?

STANHOPE (*violently*). No! I don't think anything of the kind! But what did you do up there?

TED. We looked at Aunt Alison's room. And he talked about her that crazy way people do talk about her. And that's all.

STANHOPE. Did you have any straw up there?

TED (*tolerantly*). Oh, Father, what would I be doing with straw?

STANHOPE (*furiously*). I don't know what you'd be doing with straw! You just might have had some idea of making yourself useful!

TED. Useful enough to burn the house.

STANHOPE. Be still! (*Turning to* JENNIE *who stands by the door, frightened*). Who had straw upstairs?

JENNIE. Nobody. Nobody's I know of.

STANHOPE. Did you take coal oil upstairs?

JENNIE (*beginning to cry*). I did not. I did not take coal oil upstairs.

STANHOPE. Very well, Jennie. I believe you. But who— (*In looking around, bewildered, his eye falls on the tea set. Slowly he moves over to it, then looks at his sister, who is still in that strange, fixed state. An idea comes to him that is a shock. Ponders, incredulous, but the idea is growing.*)

STANHOPE (*to* EBEN). Straw—you say? (*Moves nearer* AGATHA. *Speaks gently.*) Agatha, why did you unpack the tea set, after Ann had packed it for you?

JENNIE. Oh!
(*All look at her. She goes from the room.*)

AGATHA. What? What's that you say? Tea set?

STANHOPE. Yes. Why did you unpack it, after Ann had packed it for you?

AGATHA. I can pack my own mother's tea set, can't I?

STANHOPE (*gently*). But you let her do it for you. (*Silence, after which he speaks carefully.*) Agatha, what did you do with the straw the dishes were packed in?

AGATHA (*in a wail*). O-h! I wish you'd all go away—and leave me here alone! Why couldn't you *let it burn*?

STANHOPE (*slowly*). You love the house so much you would *burn* it—rather than—leave it?

AGATHA (*not speaking to any of them now*). What could I *do*? I tried—and tried. Burn them? All by themselves? (*In a whisper.*) It was—too lonely. (*She falls back.*)

STANHOPE. Get brandy, quick. And the doctor.
(LOUISE *goes out, and* TED.)

AGATHA (*resolutely sitting up*). I don't want the doctor. (*But she again falls back.*)

ELSA. Are you all right, Aunt Agatha?

AGATHA (*looking up at* ELSA). Couldn't take them away—and couldn't—*couldn't*.

Curtain.

ACT TWO

SCENE: *The scene is as Act I. It is the same day, three o'clock in the afternoon.* ANN *is at her typewriter,* STANHOPE *at the table, on which is a box of papers. He crumples the one he was looking at, throws it to the floor, where there is a heap of discarded papers. He takes some of them to the fireplace, stands watching them burn.*

STANHOPE (*turning*). Well, we must get on with it. (*Sitting down, examines another paper.*) Receipt for a carriage, twenty-eight years old. People used to keep everything. (*Crumples it, throws it to the floor.*) I sometimes took your mother driving in that carriage.

ANN. You were so good to Mother.

STANHOPE (*softly, with a sigh*). I hope so. (*After a moment of dreaming.*) Remember how she used to come toward you—her hands out?

ANN (*her hands out*). I can see them.

STANHOPE. And sitting by the fire, in the blue velvet dress, in that chair she liked—

ANN. Chippendale.

STANHOPE. Leaning back a little, yet erect, her hands, so long and white, loosely clasped on an arm of it.

ANN. I can see her.

STANHOPE. You look like her, Ann.

ANN. Not so good-looking.

STANHOPE (*smiling*). Not quite. But who could be?

ANN. It will be nine years in January.

STANHOPE. Nine years. (*With an effort coming from this, handing her a package of old papers.*) Just make the lists of what these deeds are, keep the latest one of each and put the others in an envelope marked Old Deeds.
(EBEN *enters carrying a large box.*)

EBEN. This finishes in the attic. Seems to be mostly old newspapers.

STANHOPE (*taking one*). James G. Blaine.

EBEN (*who is looking at another*). Why the old hotel was standing then. The one that burned when I was a kid. Remember going to the fire. (*Turning a page, laughing.*) Did you know the Baileys had sued the McMasters—about stealing a stallion for breeding?

STANHOPE. That stallion was in the courts a long time.

EBEN. And now the McMasters are worth —more than we'll ever see. Shall we keep these?

STANHOPE. Where?

EBEN. I don't know. I think they ought to stay right here. That everything should stay where it is.

STANHOPE. Don't start that again. Don't you think it's harder for me than you? I was born here. Grew up here.

EBEN. That's why. And Alison.

STANHOPE. And Agatha. She can't be left here any longer. You can see that now. And she's won't go while we keep the place. Too bad we got that fire out.

EBEN. That was a funny thing. Aunt Agatha must be—pretty bad—trying that with us all right here.

STANHOPE. She kept talking about anything else being too lonely.

EBEN. I think she had something she wanted to burn, and couldn't.

STANHOPE. Yes.

EBEN. What?

STANHOPE. I don't know. Just some old thing she cherished, and didn't want to take from the house.

EBEN. Something about Alison?

STANHOPE. Perhaps.

EBEN. Father, we did publish all the poems, didn't we?

STANHOPE. We gave them all to Professor Burroughs. He took all except a few he thought weren't so good. Those I have, as you know.

EBEN. Letters from Alison, perhaps.

STANHOPE. Each of us has his own. Agatha has the letters Alison wrote to her. They're not many, for they were so seldom apart. Of course if she wants to burn her own letters, she has that right. Though I wish she wouldn't. She should leave them to the children.

EBEN. Seems very strange to me.

STANHOPE. Yes. Well, it's just because she has become strange. The Centennial Exposition—1876. Oh, we can't burn these papers. They've been kept too long. Save them for the children.

EBEN. We're keeping more now than we know where to put.

STANHOPE. Louise can find a place for them. Tomorrow these will be the newspapers of a former century.

EBEN. You going up to the dance, Ann?

ANN (*shaking her head*). No.

STANHOPE (*putting down his paper*). Why I never thought of the dance. Of course you must go, Ann.

ANN. There's so much to do here. I'd rather help.

EBEN. Turned Walter down, didn't you?

STANHOPE. What's that? Have you quarreled with Walter?

ANN. No, I didn't quarrel with him. I just got tired hearing how fast he could run.

STANHOPE. Ted's going up with the Logans. You go with them, and go to the dance with Ted.

ANN. Ted's taking May McMasters.

STANHOPE. Sometimes I think that boy hasn't a grain of sense. But it's New Year's Eve. You must go to the dance.

ANN (*smiling*). Please, Mr. Stanhope, if you don't mind my staying here, to begin early in the morning—

EBEN. Shouldn't have given Walter the sack till he was started back to New Haven.

ANN. I didn't give him the sack. We just decided to run in different directions.

STANHOPE. But aren't you and Louise going to the dance, Eben?

EBEN (*shaking his head*). I'm bored with their dances.

STANHOPE. I fear you're bored with too much, son.

EBEN. Fear so. But anyway, with Elsa here —and the last night in the old place—

STANHOPE. It's good of you.

EBEN (*brightly*). Oh, no.
(STANHOPE *again begins looking through the box of papers on the table.* TED *comes in, sits at the desk, takes his unfinished letter from the pigeon-hole, glares at it.*)

TED. I'll be flunked.

EBEN (*not looking up from his newspaper*). Might try a little study, for a change.

TED. Tell me something to tell him, Father.

STANHOPE. Have you begun that again?

TED. About her conservatory. Keeping her flowers warm in winter. How did she keep them warm? (*The others go on with what they are doing.*) Well, how do you keep flowers warm? Do you wrap them in cotton? Straw, maybe. What do you suppose Aunt Agatha wanted to burn the house for?

STANHOPE. Because she is feeble, and very sad.

TED. But I thought she liked the house. (*To* ANN.) Make a good story for that reporter!

EBEN. Run out and find him. Tell him all the news!

TED. He's still around. He's down by the river, walking where Alison walked. He's crazy. Nice, though. What flowers, Father? Geraniums? (*Writes.*) Loved geraniums.

STANHOPE (*so sharply* TED *jumps*). Edward! You have very little sense of family, or very little sense of anything. But perhaps you have sense enough to know what it would mean if your allowance stopped.

TED. Yes, Father. I have the kind of sense can understand that.

STANHOPE. Very well then! No stories about the family—about the fire—to this reporter—or your teacher—or any one else.

TED. You don't know my situation, Father. It's dark. (*Returns to his letter; turns, meekly.*) It's all right to write about flowers, isn't it? (*Turning back to the letter.*) Violets. (*Begins to sing "Every morn I bring thee violets."*)
(*There are voices in the hall.* JENNIE *enters.*)

JENNIE. Mr. and Mrs. Hodges are here.

STANHOPE (*low, with irritation*). They weren't to come again until we were out of the house.

EBEN. Send them away.

STANHOPE (*decisively, after hesitation*). No. Perhaps we can close the deal. Very well, Jennie. Ask them to come in. (*She goes.*) But Agatha mustn't know.

EBEN. She's still lying down in her room.

STANHOPE. Who's with her?

EBEN. Elsa.

TED. How do you spell mignonette?

EBEN. F-o-o-l.

TED. That spells E-b-e-n.

(*Enter* MR. *and* MRS. HODGES. *He is a small, lean, shrewd-faced man. His wife is larger and has a big rather foolish face.*)

HODGES. Well! How'd do, everybody.

STANHOPE. How do you do, Mr. Hodges? How are you today, Mrs. Hodges?

MRS. HODGES. Oh, I keep going.
(EBEN *brings a chair for her.*)

HODGES. Well, guess you weren't expecting us.

STANHOPE. No, not today.

HODGES. Like to decide between this place and another we got in mind. Other's in better repair.

EBEN. Then you'd better take that one.

HODGES. Well, I dunno. My wife kind of turns to this one. Thinks she could fix it up pretty—woman's notions.

MRS. HODGES. I think with piazzas down stairs and up it would be nice for my summer boarders.

STANHOPE (*rather faintly*). Summer boarders?

HODGES. That's how we calculate. Don't think a poor man like me'd buy this ramshackle old place for just my old woman and those two young uns, do you? But we'd have to fix it all up. Paint her a bright yellow, maybe, with green edgin'—somethin' you can *see*. Summer boarders wouldn't take to a gray house edged with red you can't tell for red.

MRS. HODGES. I could make that conservatory into a sun parlor where they could sit when it rained.

HODGES. But 'twould mean a big outlay, 'cause we'd have to cut it up in more rooms.
(*The* STANHOPES *are silent.*)

MRS. HODGES (*feeling she must break the pause*). Nobody could pay what'd be right to pay for rooms that big.

HODGES. Well, folks don't need rooms so big now.

MRS. HODGES. Hard to take care of.

HODGES. But it's in bad repair, Mr. Stanhope.

STANHOPE (*with effort*). Oh, I don't think so. The roof needs just a little mending, but the foundations are good.

MRS. HODGES. Looks a good deal run down, Mr. Stanhope. (*Fearing she has been impolite.*) Of course you haven't been living here yourself. You have your nice place in town. But for summer boarders 'twould need a lot of paint and varnish, and that new wall-paper that's more lively like.

HODGES. All those things cost. They cost.

STANHOPE. Certainly. But we feel our price is low. The house has—character.

HODGES. Character. (*Rubbing his chin.*) Well, maybe so. But *what* character? Not the character for summer boarders. That's what I tell the old lady here. And how do I know there'd be any boarders?

EBEN (*cheerfully*). There might not.

HODGES. Just what I say. Folks like to go up the river now-a-days, not down the river. And with the old Mississippi rising higher every year, seems like she'd wash this place away 'fore we could get dead and buried.

EBEN. Then you could have a house boat.

HODGES. How? (*Laughs loudly.*) Yes, that's a joke. (*To his wife.*) Summer boarders on a house boat.

STANHOPE (*courteous, but cold*). Just why did you come in today, Mr. Hodges?

HODGES. Want to take one more look at her, 'fore we give her up. Try to figure out where we could put in partitions—modernize. Outside, too—needs a lot. Too many trees make a place gloomy.

EBEN. Those trees have been growing a long time.

HODGES. Well, then they've been growing long enough, haven't they? (*Laughing, waiting for* EBEN *to join him, but* EBEN *does not.*) And that lilac hedge—shuts the place in too much. What's the use putting your money in a place nobody can see?

Take out some of that tangled old stuff and put in flower beds in fancy shapes— heart-shaped, maybe—you'd be surprised the difference it would make.

EBEN (*softly*). No, I wouldn't be surprised. (*Speaking more brightly.*) Now here's an interesting thing, Mr. Hodges. You aren't sure you want to buy, and we aren't sure we want to sell.

HODGES (*to* STANHOPE, *sharply*). Not want to sell? But you made me a proposition, and I've gone to the expense of getting a carpenter to figure on it.

STANHOPE. I will stand by what I said. But you will have to make up your minds. We have other possibilities for the place.

HODGES. Now there you surprise me, Mr. Stanhope. You certainly do surprise me. And I'm very much afraid you'd be disappointed in those other parties. Don't think anybody else 'd be fool enough to buy it. Now that's my opinion, if you want my opinion. Know darn well I wouldn't buy it, 'cept my old woman's got the idea, and when a woman gets an idea, you might as well give up.

STANHOPE. I think Mrs. Hodges' idea is— practical.

MRS. HODGES (*nodding and smiling*). They could go out in row boats. Take their lunch over to the Island, and that would get them out of the house, part of the time.

EBEN. I think you'd make more leaving the house as it is, and getting people who would—

STANHOPE (*low*). Never mind, Eben.

HODGES. No. No, there you're wrong, young man. Summer boarders want things modern, and cheerful. But I tell you what bothers me, Mr. Stanhope. The place ain't healthy.

STANHOPE. I grew up here. I'm healthy.

HODGES. Seems like the river had something against this place. Right here on this bend's where she washes in more and more.

EBEN. Yes, Mr. Hodges, I really think you would die of rheumatism, shortly before you were drowned.

HODGES. How? (*Laughing.*) He jokes, don't he? Well, my brother Ed used to joke. Never could figure out what Ed was getting at.

STANHOPE. I can't figure out just what you are getting at, Mr. Hodges. We are very busy here today. Do you want the place, or not?

HODGES. Well, now, that depends.

STANHOPE. You weren't coming again until we had left the house.

HODGES. That's right—so we weren't. But the carpenter's coming Friday—make an estimate. Like to look it over once more ourselves, get a few ideas of our own, for I know damn well—excuse me, Miss— (*bending over to nod to* ANN, *who has been going ahead with her work*) —what he'll try to do.

EBEN (*softly*). Yes. Carpenters are very expensive now.

HODGES. They are that. So we'll just have a look at them upstairs rooms, Mr. Stanhope. See how we can portion 'em out.

STANHOPE. I am sorry not to fall in with your plans, but my sister is up there, and she is ill.

MRS. HODGES. That so? Miss Stanhope ailing? Well, she's—getting along, isn't she?

STANHOPE. Yes. She is.

HODGES. Well, we all got to get old some time. That's what I say. No use to fret.

MRS. HODGES. We wouldn't ask to go in her room, Mr. Stanhope. And we'd keep quiet —just whisper. I have sick headaches, myself.

STANHOPE (*giving up, after considering*). I suppose it can't be helped. Will you go with them, Eben?

EBEN. Awfully busy here.

STANHOPE. Ted! No, Ann, please. And very quietly, that I ask you.

MRS. HODGES (*in a whisper, and tip-toeing*). We'll go—like this.
(*Exit the* HODGES, *with* ANN.)

EBEN. I don't think we could possibly do worse.

STANHOPE. I don't think we could do better.

EBEN. They'll destroy it.

STANHOPE. I want it destroyed.

EBEN (*coldly*). You do? I care for it.

STANHOPE. I care for it so much I don't want—itself, to go to some one else.

EBEN. That sounds more like Aunt Agatha than you, Father.

STANHOPE. Very well. Agatha and I are the only two left. Listen now! Ted! Leave that foolishness! Try and do something with your own brains—not trading on your Aunt Alison! Are you listening?

TED. Yes, sir.

STANHOPE. And don't ask me how to spell anything!

TED. No, sir.

STANHOPE. Some day, when I'm gone, you'll talk about this again, and wonder why I sold it, and blame me. And perhaps you'll be right, but I'm using the best judgment I've got. Agatha can not be left here. Her heart's feeble, and her mind—not what it was. If the place remained, she'd come back here, and you know it as well as I do.

EBEN. She couldn't be left here—with a nurse?

STANHOPE. That might be all right about her heart. Not her mind.

EBEN. She's old to transplant.

STANHOPE. And we're not doing it well. All the confusion. And now—Elsa.

EBEN. She loves Elsa. Elsa doesn't harm anybody—except herself.

STANHOPE. She harmed all of us. She disgraced us.

EBEN. Maybe she couldn't help it.

STANHOPE. "Couldn't help it"! What a weak defense. Alison helped it—and so did I.

EBEN. What did you say, Father?

STANHOPE. Never mind what I said. The only person in this family who has any sense of family is Louise—and she's another family.

EBEN. Oh Louise takes it too hard.

STANHOPE. She goes at it wrong, but she's the only one wants what I want.

TED (*hopefully entering the conversation*). And what is that, Father?

STANHOPE. Hold a family together. Have some pride.

TED. I got a great idea. Redeem family fortune. Fellow at school's worked out a new idea for putting on rubber tires. Like to go in with him, soon 's our sentence expires at Cambridge.

STANHOPE. You will go in your father's office, which was his father's before him, and you will try and show more interest in the business than your brother does.

TED. Sometimes I think I haven't just the mind that makes a lawyer.

EBEN. Oh, I think you have.

STANHOPE. What do you mean? The law is a noble profession.

TED. Thought I might do better in some kind of a rubber wheel business.

EBEN. I tell you, Father, suppose I take a year off.

STANHOPE. Seems to me you've taken ten years off.

EBEN. Sometimes I feel I want something else.

STANHOPE. What?

EBEN. I don't know.

STANHOPE. And what about your family?

EBEN. Oh that's why I'm going.

STANHOPE. You are not going!

EBEN. Probably not.

STANHOPE. Going where?

EBEN. I don't know. Somewhere—where things are different.

STANHOPE. Things are not different anywhere.

EBEN. Sometimes I think if I didn't have to do anything for a while—I could do something.

STANHOPE. What?

EBEN. Don't know yet.

STANHOPE. You have your children.

EBEN. Louise's.

STANHOPE. Well, you couldn't very well have had them alone, could you? Come, Eben, don't talk like a weakling. What if you aren't perfectly happy with Louise? I wasn't happy with your mother, either, but I didn't run away, leaving my children to shift for themselves.

EBEN. It isn't just Louise—or, I suppose not. It's things I used to think about when I was with Alison. And still think about— when she's with me.

STANHOPE. Alison didn't desert her family.

EBEN. No, but I don't write poetry.

STANHOPE. Oh, dear.

EBEN. Never mind, Father—guess I'm just talking foolishly, because the old place is being broken up.

STANHOPE. It's a time to put your shoulder to the wheel.

EBEN. All right. Where's the wheel?

STANHOPE. Here. (*Pushing toward him the box of papers on the table.*)
(EBEN *begins on these, his father too has taken out a handful of them.*)

TED (*after crumpling a sheet of his letter*). Tell you what, Eben, I got an idea.

EBEN. Doubt it.

TED. You do something for me, I'll do something for you.

EBEN. What?

TED. Well, give you an interest in taking off rubber tires.

EBEN. Thanks. Got too many interests already. (*Showing a paper to his father.*) This any good?

TED. Well, I'll run away with Louise.

EBEN. That's better.

STANHOPE. Don't talk such nonsense.

TED. Kidnap her. And you write me a theme—about Alison. I'm two behind. "Alison knows" you could call it.

EBEN. So I could.

TED. Just write the way you talk. Sounds funny in talk, but written it would look all right.

EBEN (*with a real interest, which makes his father look at him*). Do you think so?

TED. About the little presents, and—oh the things she used to say to you. How she looked—and moved around—and why she was different from other folks.

EBEN. I would like to do that.

TED. Fine! Dandy!

STANHOPE. Did you ever try to write, Eben?

EBEN. I used to write things—and show them to Alison.

STANHOPE. I never knew that.

EBEN. No. No one else knew—except Elsa.

STANHOPE. And did you keep it up?

EBEN. Not after I was married.

TED. It's a bargain! You help me get through college, and I'll put you on your feet—financially speaking, on your feet.

EBEN (*thinking of something else*). Thanks, awfully.

TED. Don't mention it.
(*Enter* LOUISE.)

LOUISE. Elsa isn't staying here, is she?

STANHOPE. Tonight.

LOUISE. Then I'm not staying.

EBEN. Family feeling.

LOUISE. Exactly. I'm sorry, Father Stanhope, but I can't stay in the house with Elsa. She ran away with the husband of my best friend, leaving—

EBEN. Father knows just what she did, Louise.

LOUISE. How could I ever face Margaret again, if I'd stayed under the same roof with Elsa?

EBEN. Monstrous idea—staying under the same roof with Elsa.

LOUISE. I'm sorry to say it is.

STANHOPE. And I am sorry, Louise, but in that case you will have to go up with the Logans and Ted.

LOUISE. I don't think I should be the one to be turned out!

STANHOPE. I am not turning you out; but neither am I turning Elsa out—not tonight.

LOUISE. Was there any reason for her coming—other than to make trouble?

STANHOPE. She felt there was a reason, apparently.

TED. And I'm glad she came. Why shouldn't she?

LOUISE. Yes—indeed—why shouldn't she! Much you know about it—or care—what the town says. It will be known she's here, and just stir it all up!

EBEN. This isn't very pleasant for Father, Louise.

LOUISE. Did I create the situation?

EBEN. You seem to be creating this one.

LOUISE. I am sorry for Father—sorrier than any one. But there is nothing to do about Elsa except condemn her.

EBEN. The Logans are coming at four, aren't they, Ted?

LOUISE. You side with her—against me, your wife?

EBEN. You take too much pleasure in siding against her. She's had enough, hasn't she?

LOUISE. She brought it on herself.

EBEN. If you're so thick with Margaret, you might persuade her to be decent enough to get a divorce.

LOUISE. She does not believe in divorce. She is standing by her principles.

EBEN. She is standing by her thirst for revenge.

LOUISE. Oh, of course you think *she's* the one in the wrong! You think—

STANHOPE. Don't quarrel, children. Elsa did wrong—Louise is right there. But I am not turning her out—not tonight.

LOUISE. Then I go.

EBEN (*cheerfully*). Goodbye.

LOUISE. A husband should be loyal to his wife!

EBEN. Who says so?

LOUISE. Now you're talking foolishly again! As if you hadn't good sense. Every one says so—every one.

EBEN (*after turning a paper*). No they don't.

LOUISE. But they *do*. A husband should be loyal to his wife. Isn't that so, Father Stanhope?

STANHOPE. Certainly.

EBEN. Why "certainly," Father? If a wife steals—murders—

LOUISE. Steals? Murders? Do I steal—murder? (*She waits for a reply which does not come.*)

TED. Tell you what, Louise, let's you and me take a little trip. (LOUISE *can only stare.*) Take you to Cambridge with me. Quite a good deal going on. You'd probably like it.

LOUISE (*slowly, to* STANHOPE). I just don't know what to make of this family. I do not know what to make of them.

EBEN. You can't make anything of them, Louise. I think the idea of a little trip with Ted—

STANHOPE (*bringing down his hand*). Stop that nonsense!

LOUISE (*observing* HODGES' *cap and muffler on the chair*). Who is here?

STANHOPE. The Hodges.

LOUISE. Where are they?

STANHOPE. They are looking over the house.

LOUISE. Who's with them? Who is showing them round?

STANHOPE. Ann.

LOUISE. Ann? But why Ann? Why an outsider?

STANHOPE. Oh I don't consider Ann an outsider.

LOUISE (*forcing herself to speak respectfully*). But she is an outsider, Father Stanhope. She's your secretary. She's not a member of the family. (*After a silence.*) Is she?

STANHOPE. She is as dear to me as my own daughter. Well—no, not that.

LOUISE (*gently*). Of course, Father, I know Elsa can't be dear to you—now.

STANHOPE. Elsa is dear to me, though I've lost her.

EBEN. Don't say that, Father.

STANHOPE. Isn't it true?

LOUISE. You have me, Father.

STANHOPE. Yes. Yes, thank you, Louise. (*There are voices on the stairs. The* HODGES *enter.* ANN *leaving them at the door.*)

LOUISE (*capably taking hold of things*). How do you do, Mrs. Hodges? Though perhaps you don't know me. I am Mrs. Eben Stanhope.

MRS. HODGES. How'd do, Mrs. Stanhope.

HODGES. Pleased to meet you, mam.

LOUISE. Of course you are seeing the house in great confusion. But we'll have everything out of here soon.

MRS. HODGES. Oh, that's all right.

HODGES. Quite a chore—moving.

LOUISE. It's a *dear* old place, isn't it?

HODGES. Well, we think it's dear enough. (*Looks slyly at* EBEN.)

LOUISE. So roomy, and well built. And such *traditions*.

HODGES. How?

MRS. HODGES. It's for my summer boarders —if we take it.

LOUISE. Now Mrs. Hodges, I think that's an *excellent* idea. So practical. Do you know, I've thought the same thing myself. It's really too big for a family, but for summer boarders—right here on the river— the woods all around. Quite likely I can send you some people.

MRS. HODGES. Oh, *that* would be nice.

HODGES. Right clever of you, mam.

LOUISE. And that big cheerful kitchen to cook for them! I wonder how many people used to be cooked for in that kitchen, Father?

STANHOPE. A good many.

LOUISE. And now again the house will be full of people having a good time. That's a nice idea for us, too, isn't it, Father? (STANHOPE *tries to reply, but does not speak.*) You see we love the house. It's a real grief to us, giving it up. But it's too big for a family. That's why we're letting you have it.

HODGES (*slyly*). Very good of you, mam.

EBEN. Quite philanthropic.

HODGES. How? (*Bursting out laughing.*) He jokes, don't he?

LOUISE. Yes. Jokes.

STANHOPE (*abruptly*). Do you want the house, Hodges?

HODGES. Yes.

STANHOPE (*who seems stunned*). Good. (*With effort.*) Sign up for it now?

HODGES (*sitting down at the table, taking out his check book*). Bind the bargain.

STANHOPE (*resolutely*). Good. Then come in the office—tomorrow's New Year's—come Thursday, and we'll go over the deed. You'll find everything in order.

LOUISE (*to* MRS. HODGES). You see there are no complications. The place has been in the family from the first.
(STANHOPE *is staring ahead, and does not see the check* HODGES *holds out to him.*)

HODGES. A hundred fifty. That all right?

STANHOPE. Yes. Quite all right.

HODGES. Well, now we'll be out of your way. Soon's you go out, we come in.

STANHOPE. Very good.

LOUISE. And I know you're going to enjoy it—just as much as we did.

MRS. HODGES. You must come to see us sometime.

LOUISE. Indeed we will.

HODGES. Guess you won't hardly know the old place, once we take hold.

MRS. HODGES. We're going to paint—modernize.

LOUISE. That's just what it needs.

HODGES. Well, Thursday then.

STANHOPE. Thursday.

HODGES. How's ten?

STANHOPE. Let us say ten. (*Rising.*) Goodday, Mrs. Hodges.

MRS. HODGES. Good day, Mr. Stanhope. And I hope your sister will find herself more smart for the moving.

STANHOPE. Thank you. I hope so.

HODGES. Well, 'bye folks. (*To* EBEN, *laughing.*) Couldn't crack another joke, could you?

EBEN. Couldn't possibly.

HODGES (*to* LOUISE). Always nice to have a cheerful member of the family.

LOUISE. Yes, isn't it nice? (LOUISE *starts out with them.*)

HODGES. We go out the back way. Got the team there.
(STANHOPE, *sinking to his chair, holds the check, staring at it.*)

EBEN (*bitterly*). So that ends— (*But observing his father, doesn't go on.*)

TED. Well, so it's sold. Gee! Now it isn't ours any more. What you getting for it, Father?
(*His father does not seem to hear. Enter* JENNIE.)

JENNIE. He's here again.

EBEN. Who?

JENNIE. Him. That reporter that didn't set fire to the house.

EBEN. We can't see a reporter now.

JENNIE. It isn't you he wants. It's Miss Ann.

STANHOPE (*sharply*). What for?

KNOWLES (*stepping inside the door*). Afraid I'll have to explain that myself. Only, well, you see— (*Confused.*) Awfully sorry to bother you, but what else could I do?
(JENNIE, *wanting to linger, is putting to rights some things on the window seat.*)

STANHOPE. I can think of a number of other things you might have done.

KNOWLES (*smiling*). What?

STANHOPE. Gone back to Chicago.

KNOWLES. Without seeing her, you mean?

STANHOPE. But why do you wish to see Miss Leslie?

KNOWLES. Is *that* her name?

STANHOPE. That is her name, but you haven't said why you wish to see her.

KNOWLES (*flushing*). Well, that's hard to say—to you.

STANHOPE. Then I'm afraid you can't see her.

TED (*in warning voice*). Be kind, Father. Be kind.

STANHOPE. Anything you wish to ask my secretary you can ask me.

KNOWLES. Sorry to disagree, Mr. Stanhope, but, really, I can't.

STANHOPE. Something about my sister Alison?

KNOWLES. Well—yes, indirectly.

STANHOPE. Oh we've had enough of that.

KNOWLES. I haven't.

STANHOPE. We are unable to give you more time.

KNOWLES. But excuse me again, it isn't your time I want.

TED. You'll just have to tell him straight out. When people get older they have to be told.

STANHOPE (*angrily*). Is that so?

TED. Yes, sir.

KNOWLES. It hasn't anything to do with the paper.

STANHOPE. Then I understand it even less.

KNOWLES. I wanted to ask her to take a walk with me.

STANHOPE. You don't even know her name, and you expect her to take a walk with you?

KNOWLES. I don't expect, exactly. I hope.

TED. There's a difference.

STANHOPE. Indeed?

TED (*meekly*). Yes, sir.

STANHOPE (*heatedly*). But why do you want to take a walk with her?

TED. Oh—*gee*. 'Cause he *likes* her. You don't have to know a girl's name to like her.

KNOWLES. No, you don't. Though it's a very nice name, Ann Leslie. It suits her, I think.

STANHOPE (*after looking at him some time*). Jennie, tell Miss Ann a gentleman is here to see her.
(JENNIE *goes*.)

KNOWLES. Thank you, sir. I thought about it a long time, and I didn't know any way to see her, but just walk in and ask for her.

STANHOPE (*who seems confused*). No doubt it was better than throwing stones at the window.

TED. Or you might have set fire to the house. (*As his father pushes his chair back*.) Well, then she would have run out, wouldn't she? (*He and* KNOWLES *laugh*.)

STANHOPE. Eben, have you decided which books you want to take?
(*They walk over to the books, into the alcove*.)

KNOWLES. You know, I think all your family have something of the spirit of Alison Stanhope.

TED. Oh, gee, I don't.

KNOWLES. Yes, coming in fresh, I can tell better than you. It's as if something of her remained here, in you all, in—in quite a different form.

TED. Different, all right.

KNOWLES. A—playfulness.

TED. Golly, you think we're playful? Why man, we're going through the blackest page of our history. As for me, I can't decide which room to choose.

KNOWLES. Choose?

TED. To hang myself.

KNOWLES. The river's handy.

TED. Good swimmer. Can you write themes?

KNOWLES. You bet.

TED. Write one for me—about playfulness, or suicide, or something, and I'll—I got a lot of influence with Ann.

KNOWLES. Maybe you're in love with her.

TED. No. Always been around the house a lot. Too much like a sister. Anyway, Ann's pretty old.

KNOWLES. She is not old!

TED. She's twenty-three!

KNOWLES. I'm twenty-five.

TED. Well, then she isn't old for you.

KNOWLES. I'm glad she has this nice position.

TED. It isn't a position.

KNOWLES. What is it then?

TED. Oh it's just—the way it is.
(*Enter* ANN; TED *returns to his letter, whistling "The Stars and Stripes."*)

KNOWLES. I thought perhaps you'd take a walk with me.

ANN (*startled, confused*). You did?

KNOWLES. Got my nerve, haven't I?

ANN. Why, I don't know.

TED. Better not go, Ann. You might take cold.

KNOWLES. No theme.

TED (*softly*). Oh, yes. Clever work. (*Rising.*) Well, I'm not going to take a walk, thank you just as much. Got to two-step a hundred miles tonight. (*Goes to the door, whistling two-step.*) My advice to you, Ann, as one of your natural protectors, is not to go. What do we know about this young man? Never trust anybody from Chicago.

KNOWLES. I was born in Grand Rapids.

TED. You see? We hadn't even known where he was born. And we don't know yet what his grandfather did.

KNOWLES. He made shoes.

TED. That's why he has to walk. Bum joke.

ANN. No joke at all.

TED (*sadly*). No joke at all. (*He goes.*)

KNOWLES. It's true you don't know anything about me. But how will you ever know, if I don't have a chance to tell you? Now don't say you don't want to know.

ANN. I haven't said it.

KNOWLES. If we don't take a walk now, we'll never take a walk in this century. Had you thought of that?

ANN. I hadn't, to tell the truth.
(EBEN *comes in with an armful of books.*)

KNOWLES. The sun of this century is setting. (*He has said it as matter of fact, but is himself caught into its large implication.* EBEN, *who has put his books on the table stands, a little bowed, in thought.*)

ANN (*softly*). Yes.
(EBEN *goes back into the alcove.*)

KNOWLES. I was walking down there by the river. (*While he is speaking* STANHOPE *is seen at the opening of the alcove, his back to them, looking at books. He takes out a small volume, opening it.*) And I didn't know whether I was thinking of Alison Stanhope, or thinking of you. Well, guess you were part of the same thing. And I was thinking of the last day of the century getting dim. (STANHOPE *is listening, though he has not turned.*) You know, how you think of a lot of things at once. I thought of how she used to walk where I was walking. (STANHOPE *turns, though they do not see him.*) And never will again. But it was as if her thoughts were there. They must have been hers—for they were better than mine. And it seemed to me if you would walk there with me—you and I together—well, that she wouldn't be gone. (*Abruptly.*) You think I'm crazy?

ANN. No. No, I don't.

KNOWLES. Perhaps I could even write a poem about it—how the river flowed by the sea, as her century flowed—to eternity.

STANHOPE (*quietly*). I think a walk might do you good, Ann.

KNOWLES. Thank you, sir.

ANN. Well, just a little walk. I'll get my things.

KNOWLES. Fine! (*She goes. Rather timidly, to* STANHOPE *who stands as he was, and holding open the little book.*) It must be hard for you, leaving this old house.

STANHOPE. It is hard. (*He feels the book in his hand, looks at it, looks at the young man, goes to him, holding it out.*) This is a book my sister Alison loved and used.

KNOWLES (*taking it*). Emerson's Poems. (*Looking through it.*) Did *she* mark it? (STANHOPE *nods.*)

STANHOPE. I was going to take it for myself. But she loved to make her little gifts. So—for her—on the last day of her century—I would like to give it to you.

KNOWLES (*incredulous*). You *would*? Oh, *thank* you, sir. (*Feeling the book as something precious.*) I can't tell you how— Why, I can hardly believe it! I never in my life heard of anything more generous.

STANHOPE (*a little embarrassed*). Oh, no; not at all.

KNOWLES (*looking at the book, begins to read aloud what he sees*).

"Hast thou named all the birds without a
        gun;
Loved the wood-rose and left it on its stalk;
At rich men's tables eaten bread and pulse;
Unarmed, faced danger with a heart of
        trust;
And loved so well a high behavior
In man or maid, that thou from speech
        refrained,
Nobility more nobly to repay? —
O be my friend, and teach me to be thine!"

(*Pause.*) It's called Forbearance.

STANHOPE (*simply*). Thank you. (*Holds out his hand for the book.*) I will read you one—because you are a poet. (*Turns a few pages.*)

KNOWLES. I'm afraid—

STANHOPE. It is called "The House."

    "There is no architect
    Can build as the muse can;
    She is skilful to select
    Materials for her plan;

    Slow and warily to choose
    Rafters of immortal pine,
(*He glances up to the beamed ceiling above.*)
    Or cedar incorruptible,
    Worthy her design."

Some other things, and then— (*Looking ahead.*)

    "She lays her beams in music,
      In music every one,
    To the cadence of the whirling world
      Which dances round the sun.

    That so they shall not be displaced
      By lapses or by wars,
    But for the love of happy souls
      Outlive the newest stars."

(*He hands back the book.*)

KNOWLES. Alison's house.

STANHOPE. Yes.
(EBEN *comes from the alcove with more books.*)

EBEN. These all right for me, Father! (*They look at them,* ANN *returns.*)

ANN. All ready.

KNOWLES. Fine! Well—goodbye. And thank you—again.

STANHOPE. Goodbye.

ANN. I'll be back.
(*They laugh, go out.*)

EBEN. Did you notice Ann?

STANHOPE. Yes, I noticed her. She never looked more like her mother.

EBEN. Happy.

STANHOPE. She's in love.

EBEN. In *love*? (*Laughing.*) Oh, come, Father! She doesn't know him!

STANHOPE. Neither did Alison know him.

EBEN. It must have been—pretty tough for Alison—giving him up.

STANHOPE. You'll never know. I know a little—no one will ever know the half. Yes, you can have the Plato, and what you want. Who will value them more than you?

EBEN. Shall I ask Aunt Agatha, too?

STANHOPE (*shaking his head*). What are books to Agatha—now?
(ELSA *comes in.*)

EBEN. We're looking through the books. You must take some of them, mustn't she, Father?

STANHOPE. If she likes.

ELSA. Could I have the David Copperfield Alison read to us?

EBEN (*taking it from the books he has selected*). Here it is.

ELSA. But you were taking it.

EBEN. I have others. (*Giving it.*) Take it. She read it to us when you had sprained your ankle jumping from the hayloft. Remember?

ELSA (*looking through the book*). I remember. (*Reads on, smiles at something she sees.*) Aunt Agatha wants to come in here, Father.

STANHOPE. The doctor said she should stay in bed.

ELSA. She won't. She's up, and she says she wants to be down here.

STANHOPE. Oh, I wish it were tomorrow.

ELSA. Shall I let her come?

STANHOPE. I don't suppose you can stop her. I'll speak to her. (*He goes.*)

EBEN. You staying long, Elsa?

ELSA. No. How could I? (EBEN *is silent.*) I suppose I shouldn't have come.

EBEN. Far as I'm concerned, you should. Father—

ELSA. He looks so much older.

EBEN. You made him older. Nothing ever hit him as hard.

ELSA. Oh, Eben—don't.

EBEN. Well, you've got to take it.

ELSA. Of course. But if only I could take it —all.

EBEN. You can't. That's why you had no right to do it. Alison didn't.

ELSA. No. But she was Alison. She had God.

EBEN. Afraid God left her pretty lonely at times.

ELSA. Yes. That's why she wrote about Him as if He ought to be more.

EBEN. How's Bill?

ELSA. Bill's all right. He misses the business, and his friends, and the children. I can see him missing them.

EBEN. Lucky he has enough to live on.

ELSA. Yes. But that isn't enough.

EBEN. But you're happy?

ELSA. Happy, and unhappy.

EBEN. What did you run away like that for? Why didn't you talk it over with me?

ELSA. You would have kept me from going.

EBEN. Of course I would!

ELSA. But I had to go, Eben. Don't you see? That was the way I loved him.

EBEN (*after watching her face*). Wish I loved some one.

ELSA. I wish you did. (*Listening.*) They're coming. (*She arranges the big chair.*)

AGATHA (*as they come in*). I'm no prisoner, am I? Why should I stay up in my room if I don't want to?
(*Her brother is steadying her arm; on her other arm swings a silk bag, closed by a draw-string. Both* EBEN *and* STANHOPE *help in seating her, more feeble than in the morning. As soon as she is seated she clutches for the bag, holding it.* ELSA *brings a footstool, which her aunt disregards.*)

EBEN (*cheerfully*). All right now?

AGATHA. If it's the last day I'll ever be here, then I want to *be* here.

EBEN. That's right, Aunt Agatha, and here we all are.

AGATHA. But tomorrow. We won't be here tomorrow.

ELSA. Then let's think about our being here today. (*She sits on the footstool.* EBEN *throws more papers on the fire from the heap on the floor.*)

AGATHA. Yes. Make it burn. (*Turning a little to see.*) Burn them. Burn them all. (*She clutches the bag.*) What are they?

EBEN. Old things we don't need any more.

AGATHA. Old things we don't need any more.
(STANHOPE, *who has been watching her, can bear it no longer, goes out.*)

ELSA. You'll have your tea now, won't you, Aunt Agatha?

AGATHA (*after a moment of not coming from her own thought*). What? No. No, I don't want it. (*She turns her head to the fire, taking the bag from her arm, holding it in her hands.*) Put on—old things we don't need any more.
(*After an anxious look at her,* EBEN *puts more papers on the fire.*)

EBEN (*briskly*). It's going to be fine for you up at Father's. That's going to be the most comfortable room you ever had.

AGATHA. If Elsa hadn't run away and left her father I wouldn't be turned out.

ELSA. I'm sorry, Aunt Agatha.

AGATHA (*quite differently*). Little Elsa. (*With a low sob* ELSA *leans against her aunt.* EBEN *goes softly out. So they sit a moment,* AGATHA's *hand on* ELSA's *hair. But from this she goes into a curious, fixed state.*) Where is Alison?

ELSA. She isn't here. Though she seemed here, just a moment ago.

AGATHA. I have to take care of Alison.

ELSA. Yes. You always did.

AGATHA. I always did.

ELSA. Always.

AGATHA. But she—went away. How could I tell—what she wanted me to do? (*Pause.*) Who is looking at us?

ELSA. No one is looking at us. You and I are here alone.

AGATHA. You are Elsa?

ELSA. I am Elsa.
(*With trembling fingers* AGATHA *undoes the* string *of her bag and takes out a small portfolio. Looks fearfully around, looks at the fire. She tries to rise.*)

ELSA. What is it, Aunt Agatha? I will do anything you want done.

AGATHA. You will—do anything—I want done?

ELSA. Why yes, Aunt Agatha. I will do anything in the world for you.

AGATHA. Elsa will do it. Elsa.

ELSA. Yes. Elsa will do it.

AGATHA. Then— (*She holds out the leather case, but withdraws it. Then suddenly gives it.*) Take it! For— Elsa. (*She falls forward.*

ELSA (*frightened*). Aunt Agatha! (*She leans her back in the chair, though not letting go the small portfolio* AGATHA *has given her. Becomes more frightened as she looks.*) Aunt Agatha! What is it? Speak to me! (*After another moment of growing fear she runs to the door.*) Father! Eben!
(EBEN *hurries in.*)

EBEN. What is it?
(STANHOPE *enters.*)

ELSA. She—has she fainted?

STANHOPE (*bending over her*). Agatha! Agatha!
(*On the other side* EBEN *takes one of her hands, he is feeling for her pulse.* EBEN *lays his head against her heart.*)

EBEN (*looking up*). Why, Father, I don't—
(*Her eyes are closed.* STANHOPE *lifts one of the lids, looking at the eye.*)

ELSA. Has she—fainted?

STANHOPE. She has died.
(ELSA, *who has not let go the leather case, presses it against her breast.*)

EBEN. It is better.

STANHOPE (*who is kneeling by her*). My sister! Agatha! Forgive me. (*Lifting his head, taking her two hands, looking into her face. Softly, as if putting her to sleep.*) Yes. Yes. Find Alison, dear. Find Alison.

Curtain.

ACT THREE

SCENE: *Alison's room. The door into the hall is rear, toward left; center, rear, a fireplace. Beyond this is a smaller door, as if opening into dressing-room or closet. At right, extending from rear, a single, four-poster bed. It has a light, flowered counter-pane. Right, front, a desk. There is a small stand near the head of the bed; between the bed and fireplace, a low easy chair. In the rear corner, left, an old bureau. In the middle of the room, though somewhat front, and left, an old-fashioned walnut table.*

The curtains are white. The carpet is the color of gray-green moss.

A fire is burning, and the room is lighted by a lamp on the stand near the bed.

It nears the last hour of the century, a little after half past ten, evening of the same day. The door opens slowly, and ELSA *comes in. She waits a moment by the door, as if to be asked to enter. Then goes to the fire, holding out her hands. She looks at the clock, on the fireplace mantel. Winds, sets it, consulting her watch. Turns, standing uncertainly a moment. Goes slowly to the desk. Looks at a picture in a gold, oval frame, which hangs over the desk. She opens a drawer and takes out the portfolio her Aunt Agatha gave her. Stands there holding it. She is about to sit at the desk, but steps back from it, as if it is not for her to sit there. Goes to the table; putting the portfolio there, she goes to the mantel, where are two silver candle sticks. Lights them, and takes them to the table. She sits down, and after holding the portfolio a moment, spreads it out as if to open the pockets. (It is one of those flexible cases which doubles over.) She is opening one side when there is a knock at the door.*

ELSA (*putting the portfolio on the table*). Come in.

ANN. May I? Just a moment?

ELSA. Of course, Ann.

ANN (*looking around*). Alison's room. As if—as if she might be going to bed here.

ELSA. I have been thinking of that. Father said I might sleep here tonight. Eben asked him. (*Pause.*) Won't you sit down, dear? (ANN *comes to the table, sits.*)

ANN. I feel I shouldn't be here. I know you are tired, and want to be alone in this room. I'll only stay a minute.

ELSA. I'm glad you came.

ANN (*impulsively, yet timid*). I was so glad to see you, Elsa, when you came.

ELSA (*gratefully*). You were?

ANN. Oh, yes. So were Eben and Ted.

ELSA. But Father—

ANN. He can't help it, can he?

ELSA. No. Of course not. But—I did so want to come. (*Shaking her head.*) It wasn't that I wanted to. I had to.

ANN. You had to be here once more.

ELSA. The last time.

ANN. It's hard.

ELSA. I used to come to this room when things went wrong. "Come to Alison, dear," she'd say. Or "Whatever is wrong, Alison will make it right." (*Pause.*) If only she could!

ANN. Perhaps she can.

ELSA. I fear not. I have gone—out of her world.

ANN. I'm not sure she would think so.

ELSA. Perhaps not. For—really—you couldn't go out of her world. She was everywhere. She knew.

ANN. I didn't know her but—it does seem that way. What did I say? I didn't know her? But I do know her. Her poems let me know her. And now—tonight—I know her better than before. (ELSA *only waits in inquiry*.) Elsa! Can you fall in love, all at once, with somebody you don't know?

ELSA (*looking at the picture over the desk*). Ask Alison.

ANN (*following her look*). Is that—his picture?

ELSA. Yes. It was always there—as long as I can remember.

ANN (*going to it*). How strange the clothes look.

ELSA. Ours will look strange too, in thirty years.

ANN. Why I suppose they will. They seem so right now.

ELSA. Nothing stays right—forever.

ANN (*turning to her*). Love does.

ELSA (*with a little laugh*). Love doesn't have to clothe itself.

ANN (*coming back to her*). Then you think it really can be love, though it happens—all at once?

ELSA. It has happened too often for me to say it can't be true. Though it wasn't that way with me.

ANN. You and Bill had known each other a long time.

ELSA. Since I had braids down my back. And he never used to be—different from any one else. And then—all of a sudden—We had been dancing; we stopped by the door. We just looked at each other—stared, rather and he said— "Why, Elsa!" We stood there, and then he said, "It is Elsa." And we went out to the verandah, and everything was different, because he was Bill and I was Elsa.

ANN. So it did happen suddenly, after all.

ELSA. And everything we had together in the past—when we used to slide down hill together—was there, alive, giving us a past we hadn't known we were making for ourselves.

ANN. I think it is a miracle, don't you?

ELSA. Yes, I think it is a miracle. Though it's a miracle you have to pay for, sometimes.

ANN. Always, perhaps.

ELSA. I don't know. Often it goes happily. It's nice that you don't have to hurt any one.

ANN. But I do, I fear. He was almost engaged. Not quite. Elsa! His name is Richard.

ELSA. Richard is a nice name.

ANN. I shall never call him Dick. Richard I think is better for him. (ELSA *nods gravely*.) And to think it was Alison brought us together! That is like a blessing, don't you think?

ELSA. I do think so.

ANN. It was wonderful—down by the river, thinking of all that happened in this century that is going, of all that will happen in the century that is right here now, for us. (*She is lost in this a moment.*) Perhaps it seems cruel we should be sitting here talking of love, with poor Miss Agatha dead just across the hall.

ELSA. It is the way it is.

ANN. And it is strange: She was so good but she does seem dead, and Alison, dead eighteen years, is here. (ELSA's *hand moves, rests on the portfolio*.) Elsa, I came to ask you something, and I'm sorry it seems I came for a purpose—a favor, because I stayed down here hoping to have a talk with you, but—

ELSA. What is it, dear? I will do it, if I can.

ANN. You see Richard has to think of—the story. In spite of— (*an excited little laugh*) everything else, he has to think of the paper. And it's more of a story now, Alison's sister dying just as she is leaving the house where she and Alison lived together.

ELSA. Yes, I suppose it is more of a story.

ANN. And he needs a picture of Miss Agatha.

ELSA. You would have to ask Father about that.

ANN. How could I? He's with *her.*

ELSA. But you see I haven't—the right. Ask Eben.

ANN. Eben is so strange. He's down in the library, reading the books, and he doesn't look up when you come in, or hear you when you speak. So I thought—I can't talk to the others, but I believe I could talk to Elsa. I always wanted to talk to you. I always had—sounds foolish—a sort of case on you. All the younger girls did. Elsa Stanhope—they'd say. As if you were what they wanted to be.

ELSA. Oh—Ann.

ANN. It seemed you had everything. Beautiful—a Stanhope—so nice to everyone, yet always holding yourself a little apart. We used to think of you as a princess.

ELSA (*after looking at her in silence a moment*). And then I—went back on you, didn't I?

ANN. It was—a shock. But we thought you were brave.

ELSA. I wasn't brave. I was trapped. I didn't think it was right—but I couldn't help myself. And Bill. When you love, you want to give your man—everything in the world.

ANN. Everything.

ELSA. But in giving to him, I took so much away from him.

ANN (*for a moment not intruding on all* ELSA *is feeling*). But you love each other— as much as ever.

ELSA. Our love is a flame—burning fiercely —in sorrow. (*Coming from this.*) I wish I could say yes about the picture, Ann. There is one here. (*She goes to the desk, takes a picture from the drawer.* ANN *goes to her, they look at it.*)

ANN. Oh, it's a *dear.* She was much younger then.

ELSA. Taken years ago, before Alison died.

ANN. When she was Agatha, while Alison was Alison.

ELSA (*nodding*). It never would have occurred to her to have one taken afterwards. She thought she was just for Alison.

ANN. She worshipped her.

ELSA. And guarded her, her whole life through. I'd really like to give it to you, for her own sake. Aunt Agatha, who lived always in this house, now wanted, for a moment, by the world. She was so good. And she will pass—so soon. I'd like to talk to your Richard, and tell him how good she was.

ANN. Oh, *would* you, Elsa?

ELSA. But I haven't the right to speak for the family. (*A knock.*) Come in. (EBEN *enters.*) I thought you'd come, Eben.

EBEN (*with an emotional, rather reckless laugh*). See the New Year in.

ANN (*softly*). Will you ask him?

ELSA. Eben, Ann wants this picture of Aunt Agatha, to give to her reporter.

EBEN. She's in love with him.

ELSA (*laughing*). It certainly looks that way.

EBEN. Are you going to marry him, Ann?

ANN. What else can I do?
(*They all laugh a little.*)

EBEN. And go away and leave Father?

ANN. What else can I do?

EBEN. Poor Father. We all want to go away and leave him.

ELSA. You won't, Eben.

EBEN. What else can I do—but stay? (*Pause.*) I don't know about the picture. You'd have to ask Father.

ANN. He's with his sister.

EBEN. And she too—went away and left him. (*He holds out his hand for the picture.*) Remember her that way, Elsa?

ELSA. I remember.

EBEN. And then she got old, and strange. Yes—yes, take it. Let her have—one moment of youth.

ANN. Oh, *thank* you, Eben. You know, I think you are right.

EBEN. Oh, yes, you would think so. Easy to call it right, when it's what you want to do. Don't mind me, Ann. Just talking to myself.

ANN. I do thank you. And I do think you are right.

EBEN. Well, that's good.

ANN. Good night.

ELSA. Good night, Ann. Many happy new years.

ANN. Thank you. And to you.

ELSA. Thank you.
(ANN *goes.*)

EBEN. You've no idea how Father will miss her. Seems a pretty sudden decision. You see, I don't *get* it. You are yourself for years and years, and then some other self, you don't know at all, is more to you than anything else. It's like building up something—only to throw it down.

ELSA. And then it all means something.

EBEN. Does it? Poor Father. It isn't only that Ann is so helpful to him, but he has a particular feeling about her. I wonder how long Mother and Father were happy together?

ELSA. I don't remember them as happy.

EBEN. I suspect he gave up a lot. I almost know it—felt I shouldn't know. And what's he left with? I don't see Ted comforting any one's old age.

ELSA. But I think he may. He's so much like every one else.

EBEN. Dreary picture of the world.

ELSA. Though you are Father's greatest comfort, Eben.

EBEN. Then I can only say again—poor Father.

ELSA. What's the matter, Eben?

EBEN (*considering talking to her, putting it off*). It's a good thing you were here—when it happened. Father would have sent for you.

ELSA. Yes, I think he would want me to be here—now.

EBEN (*standing by the fire*). The clock is going.

ELSA. I wanted it to tell—the last hour.

EBEN. As it told the hours for Alison. Don't you suppose they seemed pretty long at times?

ELSA. Here—she should be sitting. (*Her hand on the chair by the fire.*)

EBEN. Unless— (*He goes over to the desk, puts his hand on that chair.*) Here. (*Standing back, as if looking at* ALISON.) She is sitting here with her papers—with her thoughts, and the words for her thoughts. She is wearing a white dress. The full skirt spreads out from the chair. The sleeves too are full, and her small hands hover over what she has. Her eyes— Heavens! Have I forgotten them?

ELSA. They are clear—like golden wine.

EBEN. Her brown hair is parted in the middle, and held loosely at the neck. She is looking straight ahead, as if into something. But she is really waiting for the right word to come. They came, you can tell that. They were willing visitors. She didn't have to go out and pull them in. There is a knock at the door. It's me. I am crying. She makes a funny little face. She says— Tell Alison. I tell her Jimmy Miles has knocked over my mud house. She says — You can build a fort, and put him in it. She tells me the story of the bumble bee that got drunk on larkspur and set out to see how drunk you could get in heaven. And what became of her thoughts—the thought I interrupted?

ELSA. Oh, it waited for her, and the bumble bee came into it.

EBEN. And that was his heaven.

ELSA. Why not? (*They are both brighter.*) Then another knock. No, a pounding with fists—Alison—Alison. Little Elsa! Aunt Agatha won't give me a cookie, because I pulled the cat's tail. She tells me Aunt Agatha can't help being like that, and that the cat would agree with her. And she says —what if I had pulled the tail off, and we laugh; and she writes me a little poem, about a cookie that had no tail. She gives me candy, and stands at the door so Aunt Agatha can't get in, but God, she says, could come down the chimney. (*They both laugh.* ELSA *goes over to the table, takes up the portfolio she was about to open when* ANN *came in. Slowly.*) I don't know what is in this.

EBEN. Where did you get it? (*A knock at the door.*) Come in.
(STANHOPE *opens the door. Stands there a moment before closing it. Continues to stand near the door.*)

STANHOPE (*as if to himself*). I wish I could talk with Alison.

EBEN. Come into her room, Father. Do sit down. You look tired out.
(STANHOPE *sits in the chair near the fire;* EBEN *sits by the desk,* ELSA *at the table. A long pause.*)

STANHOPE. The funeral must be down here.

EBEN. Yes. I think so too.

STANHOPE. It means a good deal of work, but I won't take her out of her house. Not into another—house.

EBEN. Things can be straightened around enough—for that.

STANHOPE. How badly we did it.

EBEN. We did the best we could.

STANHOPE. Poor consolation. (*After a moment he turns directly to* ELSA.) You were alone with your aunt when she died.

ELSA. Yes, Father.

STANHOPE. What did she say?

ELSA. The last thing?

STANHOPE. Yes.

ELSA. She said— For Elsa.

STANHOPE. What did she mean?

ELSA. I don't know—yet.

STANHOPE. You were holding a little leather case that Alison used.

ELSA. Yes.

STANHOPE. Where did you get it?

ELSA. Aunt Agatha gave it to me.

STANHOPE. And it was then she said—

ELSA. For Elsa.

STANHOPE. What is in it?

ELSA. I don't know yet.

STANHOPE. Open it and see.
(ELSA *hesitates, looks to* EBEN.)

EBEN. But it's Elsa's, isn't it, Father, if Aunt Agatha gave it to her?

STANHOPE. It belongs to the family. Agatha didn't know what she was doing. Where is it? (ELSA *takes it from the table.*) Open it.
(*There is a knock at the door.*)

ELSA (*after waiting for one of the others to speak*). Come.
(JENNIE *enters.*)

JENNIE (*who seems confused at seeing the two men*). Oh, I thought it was just Miss Elsa. (*Stands uncertainly, troubled.*)

ELSA. What is it, Jennie?

JENNIE. Never mind—now. (*But stands there.*)

EBEN. Did you want something?

JENNIE. Yes.

EBEN. Well, what?

JENNIE. She told me to.

STANHOPE. Who?

JENNIE. Her. Miss Agatha.

EBEN. Told you what?

(JENNIE *goes to the desk, starts to open a drawer, turns to* STANHOPE.)

JENNIE. Excuse me, but I gave my promise. (*Looks.*) It's gone! Where is it?

STANHOPE. Where is what, Jennie?

JENNIE. Give it to me! I gave my promise.

EBEN. You'll have to tell us a little more, Jennie. We don't know what you are talking about.

JENNIE. All these last days—after she got the idea—and couldn't—it was always the same— "Make the fire, Jennie. Put on more wood—make it burn" —and she'd sit by it—and couldn't.

STANHOPE. Couldn't *what*?

JENNIE. Do it herself. So she'd tell me— and each time I'd promise.

EBEN. What did you promise, Jennie?

JENNIE (*a little impatiently*). To do it for her, if she died before— Where *is* it? It isn't here— (*looking again in the drawer, then in the pigeon-holes*) or here. (STANHOPE, *rising, takes the portfolio from* ELSA, *who almost resists, and rises.*)

ELSA. No! It is mine!

STANHOPE (*to* JENNIE). Is this what you are looking for?

JENNIE. That's it! Oh, give it to me! Please give it to me—so's I can carry out my promise. I could never draw another easy breath if—

STANHOPE. What did Miss Agatha say about it?

JENNIE. Nothing. Only she'd try—and couldn't. Get it—then bring it back here. Give it to me—so I can carry out my promise!

EBEN. Just what did you promise, Jennie?

STANHOPE (*as* JENNIE *does not reply*). Answer, please. What did you promise?

JENNIE. I promised to burn it.

ELSA (*low*). Oh, no!

STANHOPE. My sister must have changed her mind. She gave this to Miss Elsa.

JENNIE. Then she wanted *you* to—

STANHOPE. Is that it? Did she ask you to burn it?

ELSA (*shaking her head*). She held it out to me—started to take it back—then gave it, said— For Elsa, and died.

EBEN. That certainly makes it Elsa's.

JENNIE. I was to do it, the very night she —couldn't. I won't sleep a wink tonight unless—

STANHOPE. Yes you will sleep, Jennie. This is a family matter. You may rest assured I will see that the right thing is done.

JENNIE (*after standing there helplessly*). Well, I can't help it, can I?

STANHOPE. No, it is out of your hands now.

EBEN. It's after half past ten, Jennie. Better get some rest. You'll have a hard day tomorrow.

JENNIE (*looking from him to his father*). I looked after her—thirty years. And I did for Miss Alison, when we had Miss Alison. What am I going to do—now?

STANHOPE. Of course you know we will always look after you, Jennie.

JENNIE. But who—who will I look after?

STANHOPE. Oh you'll have to look after me.

JENNIE. You have so many.

STANHOPE. Have I?

JENNIE (*moving to the door*). Well— (*Turning back.*) That was why she tried to burn the house—burn it altogether, because she couldn't burn it alone. You can tell by that—how much she wanted to do it.

EBEN. And how impossible it was to do it.

JENNIE. But I could do it. I wouldn't even look at it. I promised not to. I would put it in the kitchen stove, put down the lid, and wait. Then I was to stir the ashes, to make sure.

STANHOPE. Good night, Jennie. I promise you again, the right thing will be done.

JENNIE. Good night.

EBEN. Good night, Jennie. (*She goes.*) Poor old thing. Remember all the good things she used to make for us, Elsa?

ELSA. Cookies with nuts in them.

EBEN. Doughnuts sprinkled with sugar. (*Looking at his father, who has returned to his chair, spread the portfolio on his lap, and is about to open it.*) If you will forgive me, Father, you're awfully tired now, I think you would feel better about it—afterwards, to let Elsa open the package Aunt Agatha gave her and see whether it is for all of us.
(STANHOPE, *after considering, holds the portfolio out to* ELSA.)

ELSA (*taking it*). Thank you, Father. (*She sits at the table. Uncertainly, to* EBEN.) Shall I open it now?

EBEN. If you will. Why not?

ELSA (*she puts the case on the table, spreads it out. Nervously, to* EBEN). Perhaps you had better do it.

EBEN. No, open it.
(*She unfastens one side, takes out a slender package of old papers, tied with a thread.*)

EBEN. Why that's like—

ELSA (*feeling it*). It's the paper Alison used for—for her— (*Taking out others.*) All tied—that same way.

EBEN. The way *she* tied them. (*After a pause.*) Undo one of them.
(ELSA *tries to untie the knot, has trouble with it.*)

STANHOPE. Break that thread!
(ELSA *does so, and unfolds a long sheet of old paper.*)

EBEN. Alison's writing!

STANHOPE (*sharply*). What are they?

ELSA (*reading*). Why—they are—they are—

EBEN (*reading over her shoulder*). Are they—*poems?* (*He takes one from another package, then opens still another. As if he cannot believe it.*) All of them. (*He takes a package to his father.*) They are Alison's. They are poems. Poems we never saw. (STANHOPE *examines one.*) They are her poems, aren't they?

STANHOPE (*slowly*). No one else—that ever lived—would say it just that way.

EBEN. But Father—had you known about them?

STANHOPE. I did not know they existed.

EBEN. But *why?* (*Showing one he is himself reading.*) See? She never wrote a thing —more Alison.

STANHOPE (*reading it*). Alison—at her best.

EBEN. Then I just can't understand it! Where have they been? *Why?* My *God*— was it *this* Aunt Agatha thought she must burn?

STANHOPE. I don't understand it.

ELSA (*who has been reading*). O-h, I think I do.

EBEN (*about to speak to her, but she is deeply absorbed, turns again to his father*). But Father—this is of immense importance! Look at them! Why I believe it's almost as many as we published! Coming now— when she has her place—you know all they say about her—now—so much later—all of these— But *why?*

ELSA. *Alison!* (*Her head goes down among the papers. The two men look at her. There is a tap at the door.* TED *comes in, wearing outdoor things. At the interruption,* ELSA *raises her head, and while he is there goes on reading.*)

TED (*going to his father*). I'm sorry, Father —about Aunt Agatha. Know how you feel. I'm— (*Feels awkward.*) Gee, I had an awful time getting here. Awfully sorry not to have been here before. You see I was at the Martin's, and Louise didn't know that, so I didn't get the word till I got to the dance. (*Turning to* EBEN, *as his father does not seem to hear him.*) Started on my bike. Gee, those ruts, in the dark. Had to walk from the Swartz'. Thought I was never going to get here.

EBEN (*still dazed*). You were good to try so hard. Glad you're here.

TED. Must have happened just after I left.

EBEN. Yes. At four-fifteen.

TED. Louise'll be down first thing in the morning. She's awfully sorry she can't be here tonight.

EBEN. It's just as— That's all right.

TED (*looking at his father*). Well, gee I'm — (*Looking from one to the other.*) Course I know how you all feel. (*As no one speaks he stoops to pick up a paper* ELSA *has brushed to the floor.*) That's Alison's writing. (*Reading.*) It's a poem. Guess I don't know that one. (*Looking up at* EBEN.) Why I thought the manuscripts were all at the State Historical Society. (*Putting it on the table he takes up another.*) Don't seem to remember this one, either. (*Turning over others.*) Say! Where did these come from?

EBEN. We have just found them.

TED. *Found* them? Where were they?

EBEN. Aunt Agatha had them.

TED. And never— For Pete's sake! (*Suddenly excited.*) Why say, that's important, isn't it?

EBEN (*nodding, speaking low*). Father's pretty—done up by this, after—everything else. Just leave him here with us now. You can look at those tomorrow.

TED (*looking at his father*). Well—all right. (*Going reluctantly to the door.*) But gee, what did Aunt Agatha want to hide them for?

EBEN. We don't know. She must have thought it was the right thing to do.

TED. Don't see how she figured *that* out.

EBEN. We can talk about it tomorrow. (*As* TED *is closing the door.*) Don't say anything about it!

STANHOPE (*looking up*). No!

TED. Gee! (*He goes.*)

EBEN (*regarding his father*). Don't you think we'd better put them away for tonight! They're too important for now. Hadn't you better get to bed, Father?

STANHOPE (*to* ELSA). Why did you say her name like that?

ELSA. Because she was telling me her story. It's here—the story she never told. She has written it, as it was never written before. The love that never died—loneliness that never died—anguish and beauty of her love! I said her name because she was with me.

(STANHOPE *holds out his hand.*)

EBEN. Not tonight.

(*But as* STANHOPE *continues to hold out his hand* EBEN *gives him the poems* ELSA *had been reading. He and* ELSA *sit by the table, bending over others.*)

EBEN (*low, and in beautiful excitement*). Why that bird sang—thirty years ago, and sings now.

ELSA. But *her—her.*

EBEN. But the way she kept it all in life. I can see that flower bend, and smell it.

STANHOPE (*simply*). I can not bear it.

EBEN (*going to him and trying to take the poems*). Don't read them tonight, Father. (*But* STANHOPE *keeps them, and takes up another.* EBEN *goes back to the table.*)

ELSA (*speaking to what she reads*). Yes. I know.

(*The clock strikes eleven. A dimming of the lights indicates the passing of time. A moment's darkness. When the lights rise* ELSA *still sits at the table, as if she has had a great experience, as if she has come to know something, and has the courage to know it.* EBEN *has moved, and is standing by the fire.* STANHOPE *sits as he was, bowed over the papers still in his lap. After a moment the clock strikes the half hour.*)

EBEN (*slowly, as if trying to realize it*). And all of that—went on in this room.

STANHOPE. If I had known it was as much as this—I would not have asked her to stay.

ELSA. You did ask her to stay?

STANHOPE. In this room I asked her to stay. He was below. He had come for her.

EBEN. I never really knew the story.

STANHOPE. She had gone East, with Father, to Cambridge, Thirtieth reunion of Father's class. She met him there. He was a teacher of English, at Harvard. At once they seemed to recognize each other. He was for her. She was for him. That was— without question. But he was married. He had children. They parted. But—they were one. I know that now.

EBEN. And it was after that—all those years after that—she played with us, Elsa— loved her flowers—comforted us and gave us the little presents.

ELSA. It was death for her. But she made it —life eternal.

EBEN (so moved it is hard to speak). Never mind, Alison. We have found you.

ELSA. You will never be alone again. (A knock. TED comes in.)

TED. I want to read some of the poems. (As no one speaks.) Well, gee, I'm of the family too, ain't I? If you don't want me here I'll take some of them down to the library.

STANHOPE. They will not be taken from this room.

TED. All right, then I'll read them here.

EBEN. Not now.

TED. They're mine as much as yours, aren't they?

STANHOPE. I will protect my sister. I will do —what Agatha could not do.

EBEN (sharply). What do you mean?

STANHOPE. They were for her alone. She does not have to show her heart to the world.

ELSA. Father! You don't mean— Tell us you don't mean—!

STANHOPE. I mean that I am going to burn them in her own fireplace—before her century goes.

EBEN. Father!

ELSA (gathering up the papers). No!

TED. And I say— No! They're ours too, aren't they?

STANHOPE. I shall protect my sister, if it's the last thing I do on earth.

EBEN. She isn't just your sister, Father.

TED. I should say not! She's Alison.

STANHOPE. And she could help get you through Harvard, couldn't she? What luck! Send a wire to your teacher! Get your grade!

EBEN. Steady now, Father. There's been too much today. No decisions can be made to-night.

STANHOPE. If they're not made tonight, they will never be made. (He rises.)

TED. Now here I object. Here I step in. I'll protect Alison. I'm younger than you are. I can do it better.

EBEN. Leave it to us, Ted.

TED. I'll not leave it to anybody! I am Alison Stanhope's nephew and I will not have her poems burned. Understand?

STANHOPE. Leave the room!

TED. Oh no, Father, you can't go on doing that. I'll be alive when the rest of you are dead. Then I'm the one to look after them. (With a swift movement he puts some of the papers in his pocket, reaches for others.)

STANHOPE (springing at him). Drop them! Drop them or I'll kill you!

EBEN. Father!
(STANHOPE, overcome by what he has said, steps back. EBEN comes between him and TED.)

EBEN (to TED). I agree with you. I want what you want. The poems must be kept. But the way you go at it would make anybody want to knock you down.

TED. All right. Knock me down. Try it.

EBEN. Shut up. Use some judgment. Can't you see Father's worn out?

TED. I'm not.

ELSA. Oh, Ted! *Please*. Here in Alison's room, Aunt Agatha dead across the hall, must we *quarrel*?

EBEN. Go away, Ted. Elsa and I will talk to Father. You have no sense.

TED. I've got enough sense to know the value of things.

STANHOPE. They're almost as valuable as rubber tires, aren't they?

ELSA. Please go away now. We promise you it will be all right.

STANHOPE. I promise you my sister's intimate papers are not going into your vulgar world.
(TED *snatches for more of them*. EBEN *seizes him*.)

EBEN. I'm a match for you yet! Don't be so damned sure you'll be alive when I am dead! And what if you are? You're alive now, and what of it. What do you amount to?

TED. I'll show you what I amount to! (*He tries to break from* EBEN's *grip*. ELSA *comes behind them, one hand on* EBEN's *shoulder, the other on* TED's.)

ELSA (*quietly*). Oh, this isn't the way we act in our family. (EBEN *steps back*.) Come, Ted dear. I ask you to go. And leave them to me. I know their value—as no one else knows.

TED (*looking hard at her*). All right, Elsa. I trust them to you. Not Eben.Not Father. I leave them with Elsa. (*He goes*.)

STANHOPE. He has some of them.

EBEN. It's all right, Father. Ted is really all right.
(*With a groan*, STANHOPE *sinks to his chair, burying his face in his hands*.)

EBEN (*looking anxiously at him*). Let's have a little sherry—for the New Year. (*He goes*.)

ELSA (*after he has raised his head*). Ted's exasperating, but of course you didn't mean it, Father. You couldn't mean it. It's Alison's heart. You wouldn't keep that from—living in the world she loved.

STANHOPE. Living in *your* world? Linked with—*you*? As if—

ELSA. Don't say it, Father. She wouldn't. She would understand. Alison knew. And do you know, I think she would be glad?

STANHOPE. Glad you ran away with a married man—living in shame and leaving misery behind you?

ELSA. Glad I have my love. In spite of—all the rest. Knowing what it is to be alone, I think she would be glad I am not alone. What could I do—alone? How could I— Elsa—find victory in defeat? For you see, I am not enough. She would know that. She would be tolerant. She would be gentle —oh, so gentle. If she were here now—in her own room—she would say— Happy? Are you happy? Be happy, little Elsa, she would say.
(EBEN *returns with the tray of bottle and glasses*.)

EBEN (*pouring the wine, trying to speak naturally*). Well, it's a trial, having Ted in the family. It's a chore. Though do you know—I rather liked him. (*Giving his father the glass*.) Keep in mind, Father, how Alison loved the kids of the family.

ELSA (*holding her drink before the candle*). That was the color of her eyes.

EBEN (*raising his glass*). To Alison's love of youth!

ELSA (*as if speaking to her*). Alison.

STANHOPE. To my sister, who loved to the uttermost, and denied, because it was right. (*After drinking a little*, EBEN *begins arranging the papers, which are in confusion*.)

STANHOPE. Gather them up. Put them as they were.
(ELSA *helps him*.)

EBEN (*who has paused to read, and smiles at something he sees*). No question about it. They were too big for just us. They are for the world.

STANHOPE. In justification of myself—I am so tired of justifying myself that I wish—I wish I were with Agatha—but I ask you, did she give them to the world?

EBEN. She didn't give the others to the world, either. She was too timid of the world. She just left them, and we did the right thing, as in her heart she knew we would.

STANHOPE. These were not left with the others. Where were they left? What did she tell Agatha?

EBEN. We don't know their story, and now we won't know it, for Aunt Agatha can't tell us. But we know they are here, alive, and we know we will do the right thing.

STANHOPE. Yes. We will do the right thing. (*He goes to the fire, stirs it. There is a knock.* ANN *comes in followed by* TED *and* KNOWLES.)

ANN. I'm sorry to come in here now. But I couldn't help it.
(STANHOPE, *as if unable to bear the thought there is more to meet, sinks to his chair.*)

KNOWLES. And I'm sorry. You've been so good to me, and I've been such a nuisance on a hard day. But when I realized I was the only one from the outside who knew, I—I had to come. It was my duty, sir.

EBEN (*to* TED). So you told.

TED. You think you can keep them to yourself. Ask *anybody. Anybody.*

ANN (*going to* STANHOPE, *and sitting in a low seat beside him*). You were so good to me, always. I feel as if you were my father, though I know you're not, really. You were so good to Mother. (*Low.*) You loved her. And she loved you. Through years. And you denied your love, because of me, and Eben, and Elsa, and Ted. Well, here we all are—the children—Eben, Elsa, Ted, and Ann. Can't you let us, now when you are old, and sad, tell you what to do—for us? Won't you let Alison's words pass on—as a gift to all love—let them *be* here—when you are not here?

STANHOPE. Ann! Don't!

ANN. I must. It is too important. I know that now. I know tonight, better than I would have known last night.

STANHOPE (*his hands falling at his sides*). I cannot make it plain to you, but she was

of an age when people did not tell their loves. She held it deep in her heart. Then can I let her tell it now, to serve you?

ANN. Yes.

STANHOPE (*turning his face away*). I cannot bear—your youth.

ANN. Will you promise me to leave it to Elsa?

STANHOPE. Elsa! Why should I leave it to Elsa?

ANN. To a woman. Because Alison said it—for women.

STANHOPE. Alison was not like Elsa. Alison stayed.

ANN. Then let her speak for Elsa, and Mother, and me. Let her have *that* from it. For her own sake—let her have that from it!

EBEN. Yes. I think Father will leave it to Elsa. And now the rest of you, please go.

ANN (*making a move to go, but turning back*). I don't want you to do it, because I have a great love for you, and I don't want you, when dying, to feel, I am guilty, I took life. (*She goes out.* TED *starts after her, but as* KNOWLES *steps forward* TED *stands in the doorway.*)

KNOWLES (*very simply, but as if the words have a great mission*).

"She lays her beams in music,
  In music every one,
  To the cadence of the whirling world
  Which dances round the sun.
  That so they shall not be displaced
  By lapses or by wars,
  But for the love of happy souls
  Outlive the newest stars."

(*Stands silent, motionless a moment, goes.*)

EBEN (*after a little time*). Enough for one night, isn't it? One thing we know. Aunt Agatha left the poems to Elsa. For the time being then, they are with Elsa. After—after the funeral, we can decide just what to do. (*Pause.*) Good night, Father. (*No reply.*) Good night, Elsa.

ELSA. Eben! Don't leave me.

EBEN (*with a nod, as to say, it is better*). Yes. (*He goes.*)

ELSA (*after a pause, low*). I didn't know, Father, that you had gone through it too.

STANHOPE. Did you think I was happy with your mother?

ELSA. No.

STANHOPE. And why did I stay? For you, and your brothers. Mostly, for you.

ELSA. And then I—

STANHOPE. Then you—made it all nothing.

ELSA. I must seem—all wrong to you, Father.

STANHOPE. You are wrong. You did not think of others, and that is wrong. And don't you know what this would say? It would say— They are like that. They were always like that. Louise is right there.

ELSA. Oh, Father—Louise! Our little town! Is that the thing to think of—when Alison has spoken?

STANHOPE. Our little town is our lives. It's Eben's children.

ELSA. And what will be wrong with Eben's children—that they can't love, and understand? You do. Eben does. Have faith, Father. Trust them to understand.

STANHOPE (*as a cry from deep*). Oh, Elsa! Why did you go away—and besmirch the name Alison held high? (*A sound from ELSA, a sobbing under her breath.*) And now—because of you—

ELSA. Don't, Father. Don't say it. She wouldn't. You ought to hurt me—some. But don't be that cruel, to make me feel— because of me—she can't go on. I loved, Father. I loved so much that—

STANHOPE. It is possible to love so much you can live without your love.

ELSA. I suppose it is possible, if you are a very great soul, or have a very stern sense of duty. But do you know, Father, I feel Alison wrote those poems for me.

STANHOPE. I feel she wrote them for me.

ELSA. And there will be those in the future to say, She wrote them for me.

STANHOPE. I feel—something right, something that all the time had to be, in you and me, here alone in her room, giving back to her century what she felt and did not say.

ELSA. But she did say.

STANHOPE. For herself alone.

ELSA. How can you know that? And even so— What has been brought into life cannot be taken from life.
(*STANHOPE goes to the fire, puts on more wood.*)

STANHOPE. I never thought you and I would do another thing together. But she did love you. Then shield her. Join with me. What went on in this room—let it end in this room. It is right. (*He goes to the table and takes the portfolio.*)

ELSA (*standing between him and the fire*). Father! The birds that sang thirty years ago. (*Her hands go out, as birds.*) The flower that bent in the wind. (*She bends, as in the wind. The clock gives the first stroke of twelve. He stands motionless, listening.*)

ELSA (*choked with tears*). Happy New Year, Father.

STANHOPE (*mechanically*). Happy — (*From a distance are bells in the village, whistles, a few shots. He looks around the room, hearing the bells. He looks long at ELSA.*) It isn't—what you said. Or even, what Ann said. But her. It goes. It is going. It is gone. She loved to make her little gifts. If she can make one more, from her century to yours, then she isn't gone. Anything else is—too lonely. (*He holds the poems out to her.*) For Elsa— From Alison.

ELSA (*taking them*). Father! My Father!

STANHOPE (*his arms around her*). Little Elsa.)*He holds her close while distant bells ring in the century.*)

Curtain.

Of Thee I Sing

BY GEORGE S. KAUFMAN
AND
MORRIE RYSKIND

GEORGE S. KAUFMAN

George S. Kaufman was born in Pittsburgh, Pennsylvania, in 1889, and was educated in the public schools of that city. After conducting a daily humorous column on the *Washington Times,* Mr. Kaufman worked for the *New York Evening Mail* for a year. Subsequently he served on the dramatic staffs of the *New York Tribune* and the *New York Times,* quitting the latter several years ago in order to devote his entire time to playwriting. Mr. Kaufman has had perhaps the greatest commercial success among contemporary American dramatists.

Of Thee I Sing was written in collaboration with Morrie Ryskind, with lyrics and music by Ira and George Gershwin. It was hailed by one critic as "America's most sophisticated and intelligent musical comedy, the first of a new genus of satires with music—comedies of manners designed to laugh out of existence the silly practices of modern life."

Produced by Sam H. Harris at the Music Box Theatre, New York, December 26, 1931, *Of Thee I Sing* was awarded the Pulitzer Prize for 1931-1932.

MORRIE RYSKIND

Morrie Ryskind was born in New York City in 1895. He attended the public schools and Columbia University. Six weeks before he would have been graduated he was expelled from college because of an anti-war editorial he wrote for the Columbia *Jester.* He was a reporter on the *World* under Herbert Bayard Swope. His first stage writings included some lyrics for the first *Americana,* produced by Richard Herndon, and some sketches for the *Garrick Gaieties.* Mr. Ryskind has collaborated with George S. Kaufman on such musical comedies as *Animal Crackers* (starring the Marx Brothers), *Strike Up the Band,* and *Let 'Em Eat Cake,* the last a sequel to *Of Thee I Sing.* He wrote the first two motion pictures for the Marx Brothers, adaptations of *Cocoanuts* and *Animal Crackers,* and had a hand in Eddie Cantor's *Palmy Days.* His published work includes *Unaccustomed As I Am,* a book of verse, and *Diary of an Ex-President,* which contains further adventures of the Messrs. Wintergreen and Throttlebottom.

CHARACTERS

LOUIS LIPPMAN.

FRANCIS X. GILHOOLEY.

MAID.

MATTHEW ARNOLD FULTON.

SENATOR ROBERT E. LYONS.

SENATOR CARVER JONES.

ALEXANDER THROTTLEBOTTOM.

JOHN P. WINTERGREEN.

SAM JENKINS.

DIANA DEVEREAUX.

MARY TURNER.

MISS BENSON.

VLADIMIR VIDOVITCH.

YUSSEF YUSSEVITCH.

THE CHIEF JUSTICE.

SCRUBWOMAN.

THE FRENCH AMBASSADOR.

SENATE CLERK.

GUIDE.

Photographers, Policemen, Supreme Court Justices, Secretaries,
Sight-seers, Newspapermen, Senators, Flunkeys, Guests, etc.

SCENES

ACT ONE

SCENE   I: Main Street.

SCENE   II: A hotel room.

SCENE   III: Atlantic City.

SCENE   IV: Madison Square Garden.

SCENE   V: Election night.

SCENE   VI: Washington.

ACT TWO

SCENE   I: The White House.

SCENE   II: The Capitol.

SCENE   III: The Senate.

SCENE   IV: Again the White House.

SCENE   V: The Yellow Room.

OF THEE I SING

ACT ONE

SCENE I

Any city in America—with a political parade in progress. The marchers, with their torchlights and banners, move against a shadowy background of skyscrapers, churches, and—almost certainly—speakeasies. Across this background is flung a huge election banner, on which are gargantuan reproductions of the faces of the party's candidates. Highlit and prominent is the party battlecry:

FOR PRESIDENT: JOHN P. WINTERGREEN

The name of the vice-presidential candidate, however, is lost in shadow. As for the countenances of the candidates, it is a little hard to pick them out in the general blur, and the chances are that that's a break for the party.

The procession shambles across the scene, singing as it goes. The song is a combination of all the campaign tunes of the past, into most of which the recurrent phrase, "Wintergreen for President," seems mysteriously to fit. This brilliant slogan is repeated on many of the banners, with "Win With Wintergreen" another favorite. On other banners are such sentiments as:

> "Vote for Prosperity and See What You Get."
> "A Vote for Wintergreen Is a Vote for Wintergreen."
> "Hawaii Wants Wintergreen."
> "Turn the Reformers Out."
> "Wintergreen—A Man's Man's Man."
> "Wintergreen—The Flavor Lasts."
> "He Kept Us Out of Jail."
> "Even Your Dog Loves John P. Wintergreen."
> "The Full Dinner Jacket."

As the procession wends its way a line or two of lyric emerges from the general singing:

> "He's the man the people choose—
> Loves the Irish and the Jews."

It passes on into darkness, band playing, banners flying, torches flaring.

SCENE II

A room in a hotel, and a pretty shabby room it is. It is, however, the temporary head-quarters of those mysterious politicians who make up the National Campaign Committee. It's not that they couldn't afford a better hotel, for the party is notoriously rich, but somehow this room seems thoroughly in keeping with the men who occupy it.

Two of the committeemen are present when the curtain goes up. Their names are FRANCIS X. GILHOOLEY *and* LOUIS LIPPMAN, *and they are, of course, representatives of those two races which the candidate so loves.* MR. GILHOOLEY *sits in his shirtsleeves at a small*

697

table, and between drinks of White Rock—well, maybe not White Rock—he is trying to work out a game of solitaire. MR. LIPPMAN, *also coatless, sprawls on the bed with a newspaper.*

The room is thick with cigar smoke.

MR. LIPPMAN *yawns, stretches, and puts down his newspaper. There comes a knock on the door.*

LIPPMAN. Come in.
(*A* CHAMBERMAID *enters, carrying towels.*)

CHAMBERMAID. I brought you some towels. (*To* GILHOOLEY, *as she passes him.*) I'm just going to the bathroom.

GILHOOLEY. First door to the left.
(*The* MAID *disappears into the bathroom as the telephone rings.*)

LIPPMAN (*at the 'phone*). So what? . . . Who? . . . What's his name? . . . Trottle *what*? . . . Must have the wrong room. This is the National Committee . . . I say this is the National Campaign Committee. (*Hangs up.*) Some fellow downstairs.
(*The* CHAMBERMAID *re-enters.*)

GILHOOLEY. Did you find it?

CHAMBERMAID. Shall I turn the bed down now?

LIPPMAN. Sure. Go ahead.

CHAMBERMAID. I can't turn it down unless you get off it.

LIPPMAN. Oh, then the hell with it!

CHAMBERMAID. Yes, sir. Shall I come back later?

LIPPMAN. Why not?

CHAMBERMAID. Yes, sir. (*She goes.*)

LIPPMAN. Nice girl.

GILHOOLEY (*rising and stretching*). Ho-hum! Certainly is great to take it easy for a while.

LIPPMAN. Yep. It was a tough convention, all right.

GILHOOLEY. I'll say it was tough. Sixty-three ballots.

LIPPMAN. But we put the ticket over. That's the big thing.

GILHOOLEY. Well, there's still the election. I don't mind telling you I'm a little bit worried.

LIPPMAN. Say, we never lost an election yet, and we've had a lot worse candidates.

GILHOOLEY. It ain't just the candidates—it's the whole party.

LIPPMAN. What do you mean the whole party?

GILHOOLEY. Mm. I think maybe they're kind of getting wise to us.

LIPPMAN. Say! If they haven't got wise to us in forty years they'll never get wise.

GILHOOLEY. Yah, but I don't like the way they've been acting lately. You know, we never should have sold Rhode Island.

LIPPMAN. We've got a great ticket, haven't we? For President: John P. Wintergreen. He even *sounds* like a President.

GILHOOLEY. That's why we picked him.

LIPPMAN. And for vice-president—(*hesitates*)—what's the name of that fellow we nominated for vice-president?

GILHOOLEY. Ah—Pitts, wasn't it?

LIPPMAN. No, no—it was a longer name.

GILHOOLEY. Barbinelli?

LIPPMAN. No.

GILHOOLEY. Well, that's longer.

LIPPMAN. You're a hell of a National Committeeman. Don't even know the name of the vice-president we nominated.
(MATTHEW ARNOLD FULTON *enters.* MR. FULTON *owns a string of newspapers, and he is not without power in this land of ours. There are the customary greetings.*)

LIPPMAN. Hey, Fulton! To decide a bet: what's the name of that fellow we nominated for vice-president?

FULTON. What? Oh—Schaeffer, wasn't it?

GILHOOLEY. That's right!

LIPPMAN. No, no! Schaeffer turned it down.

FULTON. Oh, yes.

GILHOOLEY. Wait a minute! Wait a minute! Are you sure we nominated a vice-president?

FULTON. Of course. Didn't I make the nominating speech?

GILHOOLEY. Oh, yeah.

FULTON (*thoughtful*). What was his name again?

GILHOOLEY. Well, think a minute. How did you come to nominate him?

LIPPMAN. Who introduced him to you?

FULTON. Nobody introduced him. I picked his name out of a hat. We put a lot of names in a hat, and this fellow lost.
(*The telephone again.*)

LIPPMAN. Hello . . . No, no, you've got the wrong room. . . . What's his name again? . . . Gotabottle? . . . Oh, Throttlebottom. Wait a minute. (*To the others.*) Guy named Bottlethrottle says he has an appointment with somebody here.

FULTON. Never heard of him.

GILHOOLEY. Not me.

LIPPMAN (*into 'phone*). Must have the wrong room. Tell him this is the National Committee . . . Well, then tell him it *isn't* the National Committee. . . . Hello. And give me room service, will you?

GILHOOLEY (*lighting a cigar*). What do you know, Matty?

FULTON. I know I'm thirsty.

GILHOOLEY (*producing a bottle*). Got just the ticket.

FULTON. Had it analyzed?

GILHOOLEY. Had it psycho-analyzed.

LIPPMAN. Room Service? This is 413. Listen—send up a half a dozen bottles of White Rock, a couple of ginger ales— (*To the others.*) Who's paying for this?

GILHOOLEY. General party expense.

LIPPMAN (*into 'phone*). Make that a dozen White Rock. And some dill pickles. (*Hangs up.*) Well, Matty, how's the newspaper king?

FULTON. Well, if you want to know, a little bit worried.

LIPPMAN. What's the matter?

FULTON. Well, I've just been over to the office doing some long distance 'phoning. Called up about twenty of my editors all over the country, and it's not going to be the cinch we figured on.

GILHOOLEY (*to* LIPPMAN). What did I tell you?

LIPPMAN. What did you find out?

FULTON. Just that. It isn't going to be the cinch we—
(*Enter* SENATORS CARVER JONES *and* ROBERT E. LYONS. SENATOR JONES *is from the West, and* SENATOR LYONS *is from the South. And maybe you don't think they know it.*)

JONES. Ah, gentlemen, good evening!

LYONS. Gentlemen!

GILHOOLEY. Hello, Senator!

LIPPMAN. Senator!

FULTON. How about Wintergreen? Is he coming over?

JONES (*right up on the rostrum*). My friends, I am informed on excellent authority that John P. Wintergreen will shortly honor us with his presence.

FULTON. Fine! Gentlemen, you probably wonder why I asked you over here.

LYONS (*sighting the liquor and pouring himself a good one*). Something about a drink, wasn't it?

FULTON. Senator Jones—

JONES (*bounding to his feet*). My friends!

FULTON. Senator Jones—

JONES. My good friends—

FULTON. You're a man that keeps his ear close to the ground. What do you think about the ticket in the West?

JONES. My very good friends. (*He clears his throat.*) John P. Wintergreen is a great man—one of the greatest that the party has nominated since Alexander Franklin. . . .

LYONS. And Robert E. Lee.

JONES. Unfortunately, however, while the people of the West admire our party, and love our party, and respect our party, they do not trust our party. And so, gentlemen, in the name of those gallant boys who fought overseas, and the brave mothers who sent them, we must not, we cannot, we dare not allow Russian Bolshevism to dump cheap Chinese labor on these free American shores! Gentlemen, I thank you. (*He finishes his drink, and sits.*)

FULTON. Thank *you*, sir. And now, Senator Lyons, tell us about the South.

LYONS (*who doesn't need to be asked twice*). Gentlemen, you ask me about the South. It is the land of romance, of roses and honeysuckle, of Southern chivalry and hospitality, fried chicken and waffles, salad and coffee.

LIPPMAN. No dessert?

FULTON. Thank you, gentlemen. That just about confirms what my editors have been telling me. The people of this country demand John P. Wintergreen for president, and they're going to get him whether they like it or not. And between you and me, gentlemen, I don't think they like it. (*There is a knock on the door.*) Come in. (*The door is slowly opened. Enter a timid little man—hopefully smiling. His name, believe it or not, is* ALEXANDER THROTTLE-BOTTOM.)

THROTTLEBOTTOM. Hi, gentlemen!

FULTON. Yes, sir. What can we do for you?

THROTTLEBOTTOM (*all smiles*). Hello, Mr. Fulton.

FULTON. I'm afraid I don't quite place you. Your face is familiar, but—

THROTTLEBOTTOM. I'm Throttlebottom.

FULTON. What?

THROTTLEBOTTOM. Alexander Throttlebot-tom.

JONES (*pushing him right out*). We're very busy, my good man. If you'll just—

THROTTLEBOTTOM. But I'm Throttlebottom.

FULTON. I understand, Mr. Teitelbaum, but just at present—

GILHOOLEY. You come back later on.

LIPPMAN. After we're gone.

THROTTLEBOTTOM (*insistent about it*). But I'm Throttlebottom. I'm the candidate for vice-president.

FULTON. That's the fellow!

GILHOOLEY. Of course!

LIPPMAN. Sure!

FULTON. What's your name again?

THROTTLEBOTTOM. Alexander—

FULTON. Of course! I nominated you! Alexander! Boys, this is— What's your first name, Mr. Alexander?

THROTTLEBOTTOM. That's my first name. Alexander.

FULTON. Well, well, Alexander Alexander.

GILHOOLEY. Well, that certainly is a coincidence.
(*A* WAITER *has arrived with the accessories. Check in hand, he looks uncertainly around for the victim.*)

THROTTLEBOTTOM. But that isn't my last name. It's Throttlebottom.

LIPPMAN. Throttle what?

THROTTLEBOTTOM. Bottom.

LIPPMAN. How do you spell it?

THROTTLEBOTTOM (*as he starts to spell* LIPP-MAN *takes the check from the* WAITER *and writes*). "T-h-r-o-t-t-l-e-b-o-t-t-o-m."

LIPPMAN. Right! And thank you very much.
(*The* WAITER *goes, and with him the signed check.*)

FULTON. Well, sir, we're very glad indeed to see you, and very proud to have you on our ticket. Sit down.
(*They all sit, leaving no place for* THROTTLEBOTTOM.)

THROTTLEBOTTOM. Thanks. I won't sit. I'm only going to stay a minute. There's something I came up to see you about.

FULTON. What's that?

THROTTLEBOTTOM. Being vice-president. I want to know if you won't let me off.

FULTON. What!

GILHOOLEY. What do you mean?

THROTTLEBOTTOM. I don't want to be vice-president. I want to resign.

FULTON. Why, you can't do that!

JONES. That's treason!

LYONS. Absurd, suh!

LIPPMAN. Why don't you want to be vice-president? That's a good job.

THROTTLEBOTTOM. It's—it's on account of my mother. Suppose she found out?

FULTON. You've got a mother?

GILHOOLEY. He's got a mother.

LIPPMAN. This is a fine time to tell us!

FULTON. Yes, why didn't you tell us? You can't back out now. Everything's printed.

GILHOOLEY. Listen—she'll never hear about it.

JONES. Of course not.

THROTTLEBOTTOM. But maybe she will. Somebody may tell her.

LIPPMAN. Who'll tell her?

FULTON. Nobody'll know!

GILHOOLEY. You'll forget it yourself in three months.

FULTON. Of course!

LIPPMAN (*ever the salesman*). Besides, suppose something should happen to the president?

THROTTLEBOTTOM. What?

LIPPMAN. Suppose something should happen to the president? Then you become president.

THROTTLEBOTTOM. Me?

LIPPMAN. Sure.

THROTTLEBOTTOM. President! Say!

LIPPMAN. Let's drink to that! To our next president!
(*There is a great passing of glasses, and* THROTTLEBOTTOM *comes out of it without one. He dashes into the bathroom, and emerges with one of those green tumblers.*)

GILHOOLEY. Our next president!

JONES. Our next president!
(*And he enters.* JOHN P. WINTERGREEN *himself.*)

WINTERGREEN. I'll drink to that!
(*Takes the glass from the extended arm of* JONES *and drinks.*)

JONES (*as the others greet him*). You dirty crook!

WINTERGREEN. I'll drink to that too!

LIPPMAN. Well, how's the candidate?

WINTERGREEN. Thirsty. Say, doesn't a fellow get a drink? (*He sees the drink* THROTTLEBOTTOM *has just poured for himself, and takes it from his hand.*) Ah! Thank you, waiter. And get me one of those dill pickles, will you?

THROTTLEBOTTOM. But I'm not—

WINTERGREEN. There they are—right over there. (THROTTLEBOTTOM *obediently goes for the pickle.*) Well, gentlemen, it certainly was a great convention. I never expected to get the nomination. Didn't *want* the nomination. Never was so surprised as when my name came up. (*Takes pickle from* THROTTLEBOTTOM, *and gives him the empty glass.*)

GILHOOLEY. Who brought it up, anyhow?

FULTON. Yah. Who was that in the back calling "Wintergreen!"

WINTERGREEN. That was me. Most spontaneous thing you ever saw. So here I am, gentlemen—nominated by the people, absolutely my own master, and ready to do any dirty work the committee suggests. (*In one quick movement he takes the full glass* THROTTLEBOTTOM *has finally succeeded in getting for himself, and replaces it with the pickle.*)

LYONS. *Mr.* President—

WINTERGREEN. I'll drink to that too! Anything else, gentlemen? Anything at all! (FULTON, *meanwhile, is nervously pacing.*) What's the matter, Fulton? Something wrong? You're not sober, are you?

FULTON (*his tone belying the words*). No, no! I'm all right.

WINTERGREEN. Must be something up. (*A look at the others.*) What's the matter?

LIPPMAN (*deprecatingly*). A lot of schmoos.

FULTON. Well, it's this way. Begins to look as though there may be a little trouble ahead.

WINTERGREEN. Trouble?

FULTON. I don't think the people are quite satisfied with the party record.

WINTERGREEN. Who said they *were?*

FULTON. Well, you know what Lincoln said.

WINTERGREEN. Who?

FULTON. Lincoln.

GILHOOLEY. What did he say?

WINTERGREEN. Was it funny?

FULTON. "You can fool some of the people all the time, and you can fool all of the people some of the time, but you can't fool all of the people all of the time."

WINTERGREEN. Was that Lincoln?

THROTTLEBOTTOM. Abraham J. Lincoln.

WINTERGREEN. It's different nowadays. People are bigger suckers.

GILHOOLEY. We made one bad mistake. Never should have sold Rhode Island.

WINTERGREEN. Rhode Island! Nobody missed it! (*A gesture indicating its size.*) Where is Rhode Island now? Anybody know?

FULTON. New York some place. Never get it back.

WINTERGREEN (*a slap of the hands*). I'll tell you what! We'll leave it out of the campaign—not mention it! (*There is a chorus of approval.*) Yes, sir, that's the idea—we won't mention it!

THROTTLEBOTTOM. But suppose somebody else brings it up?

WINTERGREEN. Don't answer 'em! It takes two to make an argument. (*Gazes curiously at* THROTTLEBOTTOM.) I thought this was a closed meeting.

FULTON. Sure it is. Why?

WINTERGREEN (*whispering*). Who's that?

FULTON (*also whispering*). Vice-president.

WINTERGREEN (*whispers*). What?

FULTON. This is Mr. Wintergreen. Mr.—ah—ah—

THROTTLEBOTTOM (*who has also forgotten it*). Ah—ah—Throttlebottom. (*They shake hands.*)

WINTERGREEN. Haven't I seen you before some place?

THROTTLEBOTTOM. I gave you that dill pickle.

WINTERGREEN. Of course!

FULTON. But look here, Mr. President—it's not only Rhode Island. There've been a whole lot of things the last four years.

GILHOOLEY. How about the fours years before that?

WINTERGREEN. I'll tell you what—let's stick to the party record of 1776. That was a good year.

LIPPMAN. What's the matter with 1492?

WINTERGREEN. We can use that year too. We won't mention anything before 1492, or after 1776. That gives us pretty nearly three hundred years.

FULTON. Say, that's great!

LYONS. Just a minute, suh! Down South the people want to hear about the Civil War.

WINTERGREEN. What year was that?

LYONS (*exploring his pockets*). I haven't got the exact figures with me, but it was around 1812.

WINTERGREEN. 1812—let's see. . . .

THROTTLEBOTTOM. What year was 1812?

WINTERGREEN. Well, how about putting the Civil War back in 1776?

LYONS. Perfectly satisfactory, suh. Perfectly satisfactory.

JONES. Eminently fair.

FULTON. Yah, but it isn't enough.

GILHOOLEY. No! What we need is a good live issue!

FULTON. Yes! That's what we need—an issue. Something that everybody is interested in, and that doesn't matter a damn. Something the party can stand on.

THROTTLEBOTTOM (*who has to know everything*). Excuse me, gentlemen, but what party are we?

WINTERGREEN. We've got plenty of time for that. The important thing is to get elected.

JONES. You see, we're Republicans in most states.

LYONS. But the South is Democratic.

JONES. Oh, sure! We're Democrats down there.

THROTTLEBOTTOM (*to* WINTERGREEN). I had a dog that was bitten by a Democrat.

WINTERGREEN (*whispers to* JONES). Who the hell is that?

JONES (*whispers*). Vice-president. (*The* CHAMBERMAID *returns.*)

CHAMBERMAID. Excuse me. (*She goes through the bathroom door.*)

FULTON. Boys, I tell you this is serious. We've got to get something that'll take hold of the popular imagination—sweep the country.

LIPPMAN. The country could stand a good sweeping.

JONES. Mr. Fulton is quite correct.

CHAMBERMAID (*emerging from the bathroom*). Can I turn the bed down now?

FULTON. What?

CHAMBERMAID. Can I turn the bed down now?

FULTON. Say—come here a minute. (*The* MAID *and* THROTTLEBOTTOM *both start toward* FULTON. *To* THROTTLEBOTTOM.) No, not you! (*To the* MAID.) You're an American citizen?

CHAMBERMAID. Yes, sir.

FULTON. Ever vote?

CHAMBERMAID (*what an idea!*). Oh, no, sir.

FULTON. What do you care more about than anything else in the world?

CHAMBERMAID. I don't know. Money, I guess.

GILHOOLEY. That's no good.

WINTERGREEN. Brings up Rhode Island.

FULTON. Of course, money. We all want money. But there must be something else, isn't there?

CHAMBERMAID (*thinks*). No—I like money.

FULTON (*exasperated*). But after money, what?

CHAMBERMAID. Well, maybe love.

FULTON. Love?

CHAMBERMAID. Yeh. *You* know, to meet a nice young fellow that's crazy about you, and you're crazy about him, and you get engaged, and then you get married, and— *you* know—love.

THROTTLEBOTTOM (*a trifle fussed*). Sure.

FULTON (*rather thoughtful*). Oh, yes. Thank you. Thank you very much.

CHAMBERMAID. Shall I turn the bed down now, sir?

FULTON. Not now. Come back later on.

CHAMBERMAID. Yes, sir. (*Starts to go.*)

FULTON. Ah—here you are. (*Starts to give her a coin.* THROTTLEBOTTOM *reaches for it.*) No, not you.

CHAMBERMAID. Thank you, sir. (*Goes.*)

LIPPMAN. Well, you got a lot out of that.

WINTERGREEN. Put women into politics and that's what you get. Love.

GILHOOLEY. Love!

FULTON (*slowly*). What's the matter with love?

THROTTLEBOTTOM. I like love!

FULTON. People *do* care more about love than anything else. Why, they steal for it, they even kill for it.

WINTERGREEN. But will they vote for it?

FULTON. You bet they will! If we could find some way to put it over—why, we could get every vote. Everybody loves a lover; the whole world loves a— (*Stops as he gets an idea; looks fixedly at* WINTERGREEN.)

WINTERGREEN. What's the matter?

FULTON. I've got it!

THROTTLEBOTTOM. He's got it!

FULTON. You've got to fall in love!

WINTERGREEN. You're crazy!

FULTON. You've got to fall in love with a typical American girl!

WINTERGREEN. Huh?

LIPPMAN. What good's that?

GILHOOLEY. What are you talking about?

JONES. What for?

FULTON. Wait a minute! You make love to her from now till Election Day as no girl was ever made love to before!

WINTERGREEN. What's the gag?

GILHOOLEY. Yeah!

LIPPMAN. So what?

FULTON. My God, are you blind? You do this right and you'll get elected by the greatest majority that the American people ever gave a candidate! You'll get every vote!

WINTERGREEN. But wait a minute—

GILHOOLEY. I think there's something in it.

JONES. It sounds good!

LYONS. Certainly does!

LIPPMAN. Say!

FULTON. I tell you it's great!

WINTERGREEN. But look here—

FULTON. You'll go down in history as the greatest lover this country has ever known! You'll be the romantic ideal of every man, woman and child in America!

WINTERGREEN. Oh, no! I don't want anything like that!

FULTON. But man, it's the biggest thing in the world! A hundred million hearts will beat as one; they'll follow your courtship in every State in the Union! You meet the girl, you fall in love with her, you propose, you're accepted, and you're swept into the White House on a tidal wave of love!

WINTERGREEN. But there's nobody I'm in love with! I'm not in love with anybody!

FULTON. We'll get the girl! That'll be easy!

LIPPMAN. My wife's sister!

FULTON. I've got the idea! We'll have a contest—a nation-wide contest to select Miss White House—choose the most beautiful girl from every State—get them all together at Atlantic City, pick the winner and you fall in love with her!
(*Chorus: "Yah!" "Great!" "That's it!"*)

WINTERGREEN. But suppose I *don't* fall in love with her!

THROTTLEBOTTOM. Then *I* get her!

FULTON. You can't *help* falling in love with her! The most beautiful girl in America! I tell you this is wonderful! (*Into the telephone.*) Give me Beekman 5000.

WINTERGREEN. Give me another drink!

LIPPMAN. Let's all have another drink! Scotch or rye, Jack?

WINTERGREEN. Both!

FULTON. Give me Jenkins! Hello!

LIPPMAN. Say when!

FULTON. That's what I said—Jenkins!

WINTERGREEN. That's enough! (*Takes the bottle instead of the glass.*)

FULTON. Jenkins? Fulton! Stop the presses! John P. Wintergreen will run for President on a one-word platform: Love! National beauty contest in Atlantic City to select Miss White House! Now listen! I want a love cartoon on the front page of every one of my papers from now till Election Day! Right! And call up Coolidge and tell him I want a thousand words on love tomorrow morning!

Curtain.

SCENE III

Atlantic City—with the beauty contest in full swing. The scene is a section of the boardwalk, and the various candidates for First Lady are in about three-quarter-piece bathing suits. For it is notorious, of course, that the prime requisite for a First Lady is that she should look well in a bathing suit.

To music and lyric the candidates introduce themselves:

Who is the lucky girl to be?
Ruler of Washington, D. C.?
Who is to be the blushing bride?
Who will sleep at the President's side?
Strike up the cymbals, drum and fife!
One of us is the President's future wife!

We're in Atlantic City
To meet with the committee,
And when they've made their mind up
The winner will be signed up.
The prize is consequential—
    Presidential!
Our bodies will bear witness
    To our fitness.

If a girl is sexy
She may be Mrs. Prexy!
One of us is the President's future wife!

Enter the GENTLEMEN OF THE PRESS, *cameras in hand.*

PHOTOGRAPHERS.
More important than a photograph of Parliament,
Or a shipwreck on the sea—
What'll raise the circulation
Of our paper through the nation
Is the dimple on your knee.

More important than a photograph of Parliament,
Or a Western spelling bee,
Or the latest thing in science,
For our pleasure-loving clients
Is the dimple on your knee.

GIRLS.
More important than a photograph of Parliament
Is the dimple on my knee:
But supposing I am losing
When the judges are a-choosing—
What will my poor future be?

Do I have to go back to the cafeteria

With my lovely dimpled knee?
Does a girl who's so ambitious
Have to work at washing dishes?
I'm afraid that worries me.

PHOTOGRAPHERS.
Don't worry, little girl,
For even if you lose the prize—
Don't worry, little girl,
Myself, I can't resist your eyes.

GIRLS.
I'll worry, if you please,
Until you tell what's on your mind.

PHOTOGRAPHERS.
Don't worry, little girl—
I've asked my heart and this is what I
    find—
Don't worry, little girl,
Don't worry, little girl.

GIRLS.
Why shouldn't we worry?

PHOTOGRAPHERS.
Because, because, because, because,
Because you're in the money
With a smile that's sweet and sunny
    I could fall for you myself.

Because, because, because, because
Your looks are so appealing
They have given me a feeling
    I could fall for you myself.
        The thrills you're sending through me
        Are doing something to me
        The opposite of gloomy,—
If they don't want you, *I* want you!

Because, because, because, because,
Because your ways are simple,
And your knee can show a dimple
    I could fall for you myself.

Next: The Committee headquarters in one of the grander Boardwalk hostelries. A few banners on the walls proclaim the fact that this is no longer just a hotel parlor, but the center of national interest. A few dozen GIRLS, *still in bathing suits, are scattered around the room.*

Enter MR. FULTON, *followed by the faithful* GILHOOLEY *and a handful of newspapermen and newsreelers.*

GILHOOLEY (*to the movie men*). Come on, boys! Set 'em up right here—that'll give you a good angle! Hello, ladies!

FULTON. Well, well! What a crowd! How are you, ladies? This certainly is a big day, all right! Must be ten thousand people outside this hotel! Never saw so much excitement in all my life!

ONE OF THE GIRLS. Say! What does a President's wife have to do, anyhow?

GILHOOLEY. That depends on the President. (*A young* WOMAN *comes forward to greet* MR. FULTON. *She is chiefly distinguished from the other girls by the fact that she is dressed. Her name is* MARY TURNER.)

MARY. Good morning, Mr. Fulton.

FULTON. Well, Miss Turner! Having quite a day, huh?

MARY. Quite a day, Mr. Fulton.

FULTON. Heard some very nice things about the way you've been handling this. Afraid I'll have to give you a raise.

MARY. Well, I'm afraid I'll have to take it. (*Enter those two pillars of the government* —SENATORS JONES *and* LYONS.)

LYONS. Afternoon, gentlemen! Ladies!

FULTON. Ah, here's some of the committee now! Good afternoon, gentlemen!

JONES. Mr. Fulton! Good afternoon, ladies! Good afternoon. (*Beams on the* PHOTOGRAPHERS.) Well! Quite a battery you have here—quite a battery!

LYONS. Gentlemen of the press!

JONES. Very glad to see you, gentlemen! Always glad to meet the newspaper boys! (*Enter a lad named* JENKINS, *who is one of* FULTON's *various assistants.*)

JENKINS. Good morning, Chief!

FULTON. Oh, hello, Jenkins!

JONES. Hello, there! I've met you before! Never forget a face! Just tell me—we've met before? Am I right?

JENKINS. Right you are, Senator!

JONES (*SO pleased with himself*). Right! Where was it?

JENKINS. San Francisco. That opium joint on 4th Street.

JONES (*not so pleased*). Well, I guess I got the wrong man. Remarkable resemblance, though, remarkable resemblance. (THROTTLEBOTTOM *enters. Still hoping.*)

THROTTLEBOTTOM. Hello, everybody! Hello, Mr. Fulton!

GILHOOLEY. Hello, there!

JONES. How are you?

LYONS. Good morning, suh!

FULTON. Who is that guy?

GILHOOLEY. Vice-president.

FULTON. Oh, yes. Hello! How are you?

THROTTLEBOTTOM. Are these the girls? I'm Mr. Throttlebottom. (*Sights a promising girl.*) Hello! How are you?

THE GIRL. Fine!

THROTTLEBOTTOM. Is your mother down here with you?

THE GIRL (*she's no fool*). Yes, sir.

THROTTLEBOTTOM. Oh! Well! Never mind!

FULTON (*goes to* THROTTLEBOTTOM). Say, look here a minute. You know, vice-presidents don't usually go around in public. They're not supposed to be seen.

THROTTLEBOTTOM. But I'm not vice-president yet. Couldn't I go around a little longer?

GILHOOLEY. That isn't the point. If you're going to be vice-president you've got to practice up for it. You've got to go in hiding.

THROTTLEBOTTOM. But I came up the back way.

FULTON. You shouldn't have come at all. Suppose somebody sees you?

GILHOOLEY. We'd lose the election.

THROTTLEBOTTOM. You mean you want me to hide from everybody?

JONES. That's it!

FULTON. Right!

THROTTLEBOTTOM (*gets an idea*). I could go back to my old business.

FULTON. What's that?

THROTTLEBOTTOM. I used to be a hermit.

FULTON. Great!

GILHOOLEY. That's the idea!

THROTTLEBOTTOM. The only thing is, I thought you might want me to make some speeches.

FULTON. No, no!

GILHOOLEY. You just go and sit in your cave.

THROTTLEBOTTOM (*thinks it over*). I know. I could go back to the cave and write my speeches there.

FULTON. That's the idea!

JONES. Perfect!

GILHOOLEY. And make 'em there, too!

JONES. Don't let anybody find you—don't let anybody see you.

THROTTLEBOTTOM. I won't. I won't even come out in February to cast my shadow. (*He goes.*)
(*Enter, then, a particularly beauteous girl named* DIANA DEVEREAUX. *She is from the South, as one speedily discovers when she speaks.*)

DIANA. Mo'nin', Senator Lyons.

LYONS. Well, Miss Devereaux! And how is the fairest flower of the South?

DIANA. Senator Lyons, that's the prettiest thing been said to me since I left Louisiana. I sure been gettin' pow'ful homesick.

ONE OF THE GIRLS (*who seems to be a little embittered*). She sure is getting pow'ful Southern.

LYONS. You're just a breath of the old Southland.

DIANA. Senator, you keep on sayin' sweet things like that and I'm just going to throw my arms right around your neck.

FULTON. You never made me an offer like that, Miss Devereaux.

DIANA. Why, Mr. Fulton!

FULTON. Yes, sir, when I look around I'm sorry I didn't run for President myself.

DIANA. You'd make a mighty nice consolation prize. Wouldn't he, girls?

FULTON. Now, now! Matter of fact, we're getting up some consolation prizes. Got that list, Jenkins?

JENKINS. Here you are, sir.

FULTON. Of course the first prize, as you all know, is Mr. Wintergreen himself. The second prize is a season pass to Coney Island. And the third prize is an autographed photograph of Clara Bow, or ten cents in gold. (*There is a burst of cheering in the distance. Enter* WINTERGREEN, *followed by* LIPPMAN *and practically all the reporters in the world.*) Well, well! The candidate himself! Hello, Jack!

WINTERGREEN. Hello, there!

FULTON. Ladies, permit me to introduce your future husband, John P. Wintergreen! Here they are, Jack. How do you like 'em?

WINTERGREEN (*a trifle nervously*). Why, they're wonderful. Hello! How are you?

FULTON. Say something to them.

WINTERGREEN. Well, ladies, this certainly is a pleasure. All I can say is I love you, and you're the only girls I have ever loved. (*With growing nervousness.*) And after we're married, I hope you'll all be happy, and—listen, Fulton, I can't go through with this.

FULTON. You've got to go through with it.

WINTERGREEN. But I don't know any of these girls! How can I marry them? If it was only somebody I knew, like—Lippman, whatever became of your wife's sister?

LIPPMAN (*with a shake of the head*). Not in a bathing suit.

FULTON. By the way, Jack, I want you to meet Miss Diana Devereaux.

LYONS. Miss Devereaux, may I have the honor—

DIANA. Mr. President, I'm mighty happy to meet you! I hope we're going to see a lot of each other.

WINTERGREEN. Any hope of yours, Miss Devereaux, is a hope of mine, I hope.

DIANA. You keep on saying sweet things like that and I'm just going to throw my arms right around your neck.
(*The* GIRLS *chime in when she is half-way through the sentence and finish it right with her, Southern accent and all.*)

WINTERGREEN. Seems to be quite an echo here.

DIANA (*playing with his lapel*). Have you-all got a fraternity pin?

WINTERGREEN. Well, would a safety pin do?

DIANA. Mr. Wintergreen, you've got the grandest sense of humor.

MARY. All right, Mr. Fulton.

FULTON. And now, ladies—attention, please! The time has come for the final test. (*The* GIRLS *start a general primping and there is an excited buzz.*) It has been a grueling contest—you have been under a great strain. And we of the committee want to thank you—and through you the three million others who took part in this contest, only ninety-eight per cent of whom had to be sent home for misbehavior. And now, ladies, the judges await you. And may the best girl win.

GIRLS (*to music*).
    Who is the lucky girl to be—
    Ruler of Washington, D. C.?

DIANA.
    Bye-bye, Mr. President—I'm a-prayin'
    I'm the little lady they're okayin'.

GIRLS.
Strike up the cymbals, drum and fife:
One of us is the President's future wife!
(*They go.* WINTERGREEN, *his nervousness mounting, is left alone in the room. But not quite alone, for at her desk in the corner* MARY TURNER *is quietly working.*)

WINTERGREEN (*as he sees her*). Oh! (*Takes a moment.*) Say! (*She turns.*) You haven't got a drink on you, have you?

MARY. Why, no. I'm sorry.

WINTERGREEN. That's all right. Didn't want it anyhow. (*Pacing.*)

MARY. Little bit nervous?

WINTERGREEN (*whirling*). Who? Me? What have I got to be nervous about?

MARY. That's what I was wondering. Twenty-four of the most beautiful girls in the country—and you get the winner. Lot of men would like to be in your shoes.

WINTERGREEN. Yeah, but it's my bedroom slippers I'm worrying about. . . . Say, you've been watching them—who do you think it's going to be?

MARY. I couldn't say. Likely to be any one of them.

WINTERGREEN. That's what I was afraid of. But which one? What's your guess?

MARY. Well, don't hold me to it, but I shouldn't be surprised if it were Miss Devereaux.

WINTERGREEN. Devereaux! I thought so! That's the one with the Southern exposure?

MARY. That's Miss Devereaux. She's a good-looking girl, don't you think?

WINTERGREEN (*in heavy Southern accent*). Yes, she's a good-looking gal, all right.

MARY (*falling right into line*). Don't you-all like good-looking gals?

WINTERGREEN. Down Carolina way we're all a-crazy about good-looking gals, but we-all don't like 'em talking that-a-way.

MARY. How do you-all like 'em to talk, sure enough?

WINTERGREEN (*abandons the dialect*). Say, that's terrible, isn't it? If she wins would I have to listen to that all the time?

MARY. But she does it charmingly. And she's very beautiful.

WINTERGREEN. Beautiful, yeah—I like a beautiful girl—they're all right, but—(*he stumbles*)—when a fellow gets married he wants a home, a mother for his children.

MARY. You've got children?

WINTERGREEN. No, no, I mean if I was married. You see, when you're married—well, *you* know.

MARY. Well, I think Miss Devereaux might listen to reason. And she'd make a very beautiful mother for your children.

WINTERGREEN. Will you stop saying beautiful? I don't know anything about these girls, any of them. What kind of wives they'd make—whether they could sew, or make a bed, or cook. They don't look as though they'd ever had a skillet in their hands. Say, what *is* a skillet?

MARY. You wouldn't have to worry about that in the White House. They have plenty of servants there.

WINTERGREEN. The White House—yeah, but some day we'll have to move out of the White House. Then what? The Old President's Home? There'll be no servants there. She'll *have* to cook

MARY. Then she'll cook. And like it.

WINTERGREEN. But will *I* like it? Why, the average girl today can't cook—she can't even broil an egg.

MARY. Nonsense! Every girl can cook.

WINTERGREEN (*scornfully*). Every girl can cook—can *you*?

MARY. I certainly can!

WINTERGREEN. Then what are you doing here?

MARY (*right back at him*). I'm holding down a job! And I can cook, and sew, and make lace curtains, and bake the best darned corn muffins you ever ate! And what do you know about that?

WINTERGREEN. Did you say corn muffins?

MARY. Yes, corn muffins!

WINTERGREEN. Corn muffins! You haven't got one on you, have you?

MARY. I haven't far to go. (*Opens a drawer in her desk.*) It's lunch, but you can have it.

WINTERGREEN. Oh, I couldn't do that!

MARY. Please! (*As he reaches.*) The second from the left is a corn muffin. That's an apple.

WINTERGREEN (*taking muffin*). Well! You must let me take *you* to lunch some day. (*Samples it.*) Why—it melts in the mouth! It's—it's marvelous.

MARY. And I'm the only person in the world who can make them without corn.

WINTERGREEN. What a muffin! Say, I don't even know your name.

MARY. That's right—you don't.

WINTERGREEN. Mine's Wintergreen.

MARY. I know. Mine's Turner.

WINTERGREEN. Just Turner?

MARY. Mary Turner.

WINTERGREEN (*suddenly*). Say, why in God's name didn't you get into this contest?

MARY. One of the three million?

WINTERGREEN. Well, you know what the first prize is?

MARY. Yeah, can you imagine?

WINTERGREEN. And you get your picture in the paper.

MARY. Having tea on the lawn with the Filipino delegation. And you throwing the medicine ball at the cabinet.

WINTERGREEN. Oh, do we have to have a cabinet?

MARY. What would you throw the medicine ball at? Me?

WINTERGREEN (*suddenly sobered*). Gosh, it'd be fun with you. We could have a grand time.

MARY (*the Southern accent*). Why, Mr. Wintergreen—

WINTERGREEN. No, I mean it! Listen—I've only got a minute—maybe less than that! I love you! I know it's awful sudden, but in a minute it'll be too late! Let's elope—let's get out of here!

MARY. But—but wait a minute! You don't know me!

WINTERGREEN. I know you better than those girls! (*A gesture.*) You can make corn muffins, and—you're darned cute-looking, and—I love you!

MARY. But I don't know *you!*

WINTERGREEN. What's there to know? I'm young, I'm a swell conversationalist, and I've got a chance to be President! And besides that you love me!

MARY. But it's absurd! Why, you can't—

WINTERGREEN. The hell I can't! (*He seizes her and starts kissing her.*) It's fate, Mary, that's what it is—fate! (*Kisses her again.*) Why, we were meant for each other—you and me!

MARY. You and *I!*

WINTERGREEN. All right, you and I!
(*A burst of music. The sound of many voices as the doors are thrown open. Enter* FULTON *and the* COMMITTEE, *full of importance.*)

FULTON (*sings*).
As the chairman of the committee,
I announce we've made our choice;
Ev'ry lover from Dubuque to Jersey City
    Should rejoice!

COMMITTEE.
    We rejoice!
When the angels up there designed her,
    They designed a thoroughbred;
And on March the Fourth the President
    will find her
    Worthy of his board and bed.

FULTON. And now it thrills me to introduce the rarest of American beauties, the future first lady of the land—a fit consort for the ruler of our country. Gentlemen—Miss Diana Devereaux!
(DIANA *appears, a golden crown on her head, followed by all the other* GIRLS.)

ALL.
How beautiful, beautiful, beautiful!
    How utterly, utterly so!
The charming, the gracious, the dutiful
    Diana Devereaux.

FULTON. The committee will now tell why
she was chosen—with music!

ALL.
    Never was there a girl so fair;
    Never was there a form so rare;

DIANA. I could throw my arms right around
your neck!

ALL.
    A voice so lyrical
        Is given few;
    Her eyes a miracle
        Of Prussian blue;
    Ruby lips and a foot so small;
    As for hips—she has none at all!

    What a charming epiglottis!
        What a lovely coat of tan!
    Oh, the man who isn't hot is
        Not a man!

    She's a bargain to whom she's wed;
    More than worthy his board and bed!

FULTON.
Says the chairman of the committee.
Let the newsmen now come in.
(*To* DIANA.)
For the sound reels you must look your
    best, my pretty.
Have the interviews begin!

COMMITTEE.
    We shall go and bring them in!

WINTERGREEN.
    Stop! No!
    Though this may be a blow,
    I simply cannot marry
        Diana Devereaux!

ALL.
    What's this? What's this?
    He says he cannot marry
        Diana Devereaux!

COMMITTEE.
    You mean you will not marry
        Diana Devereaux!

WINTERGREEN.
Please understand—it isn't that I would
    jilt or spurn 'er:
It's just that I love someone else.

ALL. Who?

WINTERGREEN (*reprovingly*). Whom! . . .
Mary Turner.

ALL.
    The man is mad!
    Or else a cad!
    He'll have to take her—
    He can't forsake her!

DIANA.
    This jilting me,
    It cannot be!
    This lousy action
    Calls for retraction!

COMMITTEE.
    We must know why
    You should prefer
    Instead of Di
    A girl like her.

GIRLS.
    Yes, tell us why
    You should prefer
    Instead of Di
    A girl like her.

WINTERGREEN.
    All that I can say of Mary Turner
    Is that I love Mary Turner.

COMMITTEE.
    What's to be done?
    Though she has won,
    Though she is signed up,
    He's made his mind up!
    His love he'd ruther
    Give to the other.
    What shall we do now?
    What is our cue now?

DIANA.
He will do nothing of the sort;
First we'll settle this thing in court.
(*To* WINTERGREEN.)
You seem to think Miss Turner hits the
    spot;
But what has she got that I haven't got?

ALL.
Yes, what has *she* got that *she* hasn't got!

WINTERGREEN.
     My Mary makes corn muffins!
(*To* DIANA.)
     Can *you* make corn muffins?

DIANA.
     I can't make corn muffins!

ALL.
     She can't make corn muffins!

WINTERGREEN.
     Some girls can bake a pie,
     Made up of prunes and quinces;
     Some make an oyster fry—
     Others are good at blintzes.
     Some lovely girls have done
     Wonders with turkey stuffin's,
     But I have found the one
     Who can really make corn muffins.
(*He passes muffins to the* COMMITTEE.)

DIANA. Who cares about corn muffins? All
I demand is justice!

COMMITTEE.
     Corn muffins—

Though other girls are good at turkey stuf-
     fin's,
She takes the cake, for she can bake corn
     muffins
          Corn muffins—
     He's not to blame for falling if she's able
     To serve them at his table.
(*The* COMMITTEE *samples the muffins, and
is overwhelmed.*)
          Great, great!
     It really must be fate!
     We must declare these muffins
     The best we ever ate!

ALL.
     There's none but Mary Turner
     Could ever be his mate!

     There's none but Mary Turner
     Could ever be his mate!

     Let's all rejoice!
(*One and all, with the exception of* DIANA,
*they burst into a joyous dance, expressing
the ecstasy that is theirs at the very existence of so remarkable a young woman.
On this pæan of joy the curtain falls.*)

SCENE IV

*Madison Square Garden—the height of the campaign. One sees first the outside of the
Garden, and across it a great banner bearing the pictures of* WINTERGREEN *and* MARY
TURNER. WOO WITH WINTERGREEN, *the slogan now runs, and beneath it:* LOV-
ERS! VOTE FOR JOHN AND MARY! *Of* MR. THROTTLEBOTTOM, *or whatever his
name is, there is just no mention at all.*

*A band plays. Drawn by the ballyhoo, a crowd gathers and goes gayly into the Garden,
singing and cheering.*

*Inside the Garden, then, with the proceedings in full swing. A Garden that is packed
to the rafters with cheering humanity, alive with cold-drink vendors, and hot dog salesmen, and everything that goes with so great an occasion. Over the rostrum there hangs
the inevitable loud speaker, set in a cluster of lights that send a concentrated glow down
on the platform. The various committeemen occupy the platform seats, and the two center chairs are conspicuously empty, obviously waiting for the stellar pair. When the scene
starts* FULTON *is in the midst of an impassioned address.*

FULTON. . . . seventeen hundred and seven-
ty-six, eighteen hundred and twelve, eighteen hundred and sixty-one, eighteen hundred and ninety-eight, and nineteen hundred and seventeen! (*There is loud ap-*
plause as he stops for a sip of water.*) And
so, my friends, on Tuesday next yours is a
great privilege. You will cast your ballots
for the greatest cause and the greatest emotion known to the heart of mankind! Love!

(*Applause.*) Yes, my good friends, for love! For love and for the greatest of all lovers! John P. Wintergreen! (*He sits down to great applause.*)

LOUD SPEAKER (*through the cluster of megaphones that hang overhead*). Attention, please! Next Wednesday night: Jack Sharkey, American champion of the world, versus Max Schmeling, German champion of the world, for the championship of the world! (*Applause.*)

FULTON (*again to his feet*). And, my friends, as a good American, I believe that Jack Sharkey will win! (*Applause; he sits.*)

LOUD SPEAKER. Attention, please! Message for Dr. Hugo Kristmacher! Dr. Kristmacher! Your wife just telephoned the box-office and says not to come home tonight. (*Applause.*)

FULTON. And now, my good people, it is my great pleasure and privilege to introduce a man who has served his country long and gloriously, a man who has for many years waged a great and single-handed fight for what he considered his own interests. The silver-tongued orator of the golden West, Senator Carver Crockett Jones! (*Applause.*)

(SENATOR JONES *rises.*)

LOUD SPEAKER. Attention, please! While Senator Jones is speaking you will be entertained by the world's greatest wrestlers. Vladimir Vidovitch, the Harlem Heaver, and Yussef Yussevitch, the Terrible Turk, in a match for the world's championship. (*Two* ATTENDANTS *dash out and quickly unroll a mat. Then enter, from opposite sides,* VIDOVITCH *and* YUSSEVITCH. *As they reach the arena they drop their bathrobes and stand revealed as great three-hundred pounders, with arms like tree trunks. There is the sound of a gong. Simultaneously the* WRESTLERS *go into action and* SENATOR JONES *starts his speech.*)

JONES. My friends! We have arrived at a great moment in our history. Magnificent though our past has been, it dwindles into utter insignificance beside the brilliance of our future destiny. Gaze into that future, my friends, and what do you see? What do you see? (*At this moment what one chiefly sees is the rear elevation of* VIDOVITCH, *which is being stared at by something akin to admiration by* YUSSEVITCH.) There it is, my friends, for all the world to envy. (*The* WRESTLERS *reverse, and it is now* YUSSEVITCH *that is starred. They break, and resume wrestling as* JONES *resumes talking.*) Not for us the entangling alliances of Europe, not for us the allying entanglances of Asia. (*A burst of applause. The* WRESTLERS, *at the moment, have a complicated double scissors hold on each other, but their arms are free. Pausing in their labors, they join in the applause.*) Here then we stand, alone in our strength, solitary in our splendor, the greatest and most glorious country that God Almighty put upon earth—the United States of AMERICA!!! (*The* WRESTLERS, *relinquishing a complicated hold, jump to their feet and salute. The* CROWD *bursts into applause.*) And so, my friends—

(*One of the* WRESTLERS *makes a sensational dive for the other's leg, throwing him to the mat with a crash. The* CROWD *sets up a cheering and yelling, egging on the* WRESTLERS. *The* COMMITTEEMEN *sitting behind* JONES *crowd to the edge of the rail to look on; the whole* CROWD *is on its feet.* JONES *tries bravely to talk against this for a moment, but his own interest in the* WRESTLERS *finally gets the better of him. He joins the cheerers. It all comes to a climax as one of the men finally gets the other down. Cheers. Applause. Bows. The* WRESTLERS *exit; the* ATTENDANTS *roll up the mat; the* CROWD *settles back.*)

FULTON. And now, my friends, while we are waiting for our beloved candidate— (*There is a hullabaloo at the entrance— the sound of a scuffle, voices, etc. The* CROWD *gets to its feet as the noise mounts. Enter* THROTTLEBOTTOM, *trying to fight off four* POLICEMEN *and a couple of Garden* ATTENDANTS. *As he comes into view it is seen that he is practically in tatters, his coat off, his collar askew. He struggles to the foot of the platform stairs.*) Here, here, here! What's all this? Who is this man? Stop that noise! What is this? (*The noise quiets down. The* POLICEMEN *stand holding tightly onto* THROTTLEBOTTOM, *two to each arm. Behind him stand the Garden* ATTENDANTS, *one of whom has picked up a huge iron bar somewhere.*) What is all this? What do you want here?

THROTTLEBOTTOM (*tears himself loose and gets half-way up the steps*). But wait, wait! I'm Throttlebottom! I'm the vice-president. Here—look! I'm Throttlebottom! (*Takes a banner from his pocket and unrolls it. Sure enough, it reads: For Vice-President: Alexander Throttlebottom.*)

FULTON. Oh, yes! Yes! It's all right, officers. This man is all right! (THROTTLEBOTTOM *gets up on the platform. The other* COMMITTEEMEN *come forward to greet him, but not too cordially.* THROTTLEBOTTOM, *meanwhile, is trying to get his clothes together, stuffing his shirt into his trousers, getting his collar back on.*) What are you doing here? Why didn't you stay in your cave?

THROTTLEBOTTOM. The other hermits objected.

FULTON (*at the rostrum, reluctantly*). My friends, we have an unexpected surprise for you. It is your great and rare privilege to hear a few words from— (THROTTLEBOTTOM *prompts him*) Alexander Throttlebottom— (*he pronounces the name with great care*) candidate for— (THROTTLEBOTTOM *prompts him again, first looking at the banner himself*) vice-president. (*Then, as an afterthought.*) Of the United States of America.
(*The* CROWD *is silent.* THROTTLEBOTTOM *advances to the rostrum; takes his speech from his pocket. It unrolls all the way to the ground, turning out to be about ten feet long. A pleased expression spreads over his face; recognition is his at last.*)

LOUD SPEAKER (*just as* THROTTLEBOTTOM *opens his mouth to speak*). Attention, please! At the end of the first period in Montreal: Boston Bruins, 3: Chicago White Sox, 1. (*The machine clanks off;* THROTTLEBOTTOM *again gets ready to speak. Once more a slow smile comes over his face.*) Attention, please! There will now be an intermission of fifteen minutes.
(*There is a great pushing back of chairs; everybody gets up and starts to leave.*)

THROTTLEBOTTOM. No, no, no! No!
(*The various noises merge into a greater and growing noise. Cries of "Wintergreen!" "Here comes Wintergreen!" Flashlights. Cheering. Music. Enter* WINTERGREEN *and* MARY TURNER, *preceded by* POLICEMEN. *To the accompaniment of cheers and handshaking they advance to the platform and go up the stairs. There is a great shaking of hands with the* COMMITTEEMEN. THROTTLEBOTTOM, *as the presidential procession gets up onto the platform, is simply pushed right out of the way by the* POLICEMEN, *and practically falls down the stairs on the other side. Here he is met by other* POLICEMEN, *and is ignominiously dragged out of the place, kicking and protesting. Meanwhile, as the noise subsides,* WINTERGREEN *and* MARY *take their seats, and* FULTON *advances to the rostrum to introduce them.*)

FULTON (*stilling the tumult with upraised hand*). No need to tell you who the next speakers will be. They are the most beloved couple in America today, the most beloved couple that have ever run for the highest office in the gift of the American people. There have been many great lovers in history. But Romeo never loved Juliet, Dante never loved Beatrice, Damon never loved Pythias, as John P. Wintergreen loves Mary Turner. (*Applause.*) My friends, the issue of this campaign is a simple one. We do not talk to you about war debts or wheat or immigration—we appeal to your hearts, not your intelligence. It is the old, old story, yet ever new—the sweetest story ever told. John P. Wintergreen, candidate for President of the United States of America, loves Mary Turner. Mary Turner, the most beautiful, the loveliest example of typical American womanhood—and I defy our opponents to say otherwise—loves John P. Wintergreen. He has proposed to her in 47 States of the Union, and in 47 States she has accepted him. Tonight she will give him her answer in the great Empire State of New York! John and Mary, stand up! (*They do so.*) Can you look at them and not be thrilled by their youth, their charm, their passion? Ladies and gentlemen, I give you John P. Wintergreen and Mary Turner! (FULTON *sits down as pandemonium breaks loose.* WINTERGREEN *and* MARY *come forward; the tumult slowly dies.*)

WINTERGREEN. My friends, I come before you in this final rally of the campaign not as John P. Wintergreen the candidate, not as John P. Wintergreen the statesman, but as a simple man in love. So I beg you to bear with me for a moment, while I ask the girl of my dreams if she will be my heart's delight. (*There is applause as he turns to* MARY.) Miss Turner, there has been something on my mind for a long, long time.

MARY. Yes, Mr. Wintergreen?

WINTERGREEN (*the hesitant lover*). May I not call you—Mary?

MARY. I wish you would—John.

WINTERGREEN. Do you remember that night we first walked together, on the boardwalk in Atlantic City?

MARY. With the moon shining overhead?

WINTERGREEN. And the lights rippling on the water. Do you remember what I said to you, Mary, as I took your dear hand in mine?

MARY. You said— (*she drops her eyes*) — that I reminded you of your mother, who had been dead these many years.

WINTERGREEN. And in the cornfields of Kansas, on the plains of Arizona, in the mountains of Nebraska, I whispered to you how much you were beginning to mean to me.

MARY. Our friendship has been a wonderful thing to me.

WINTERGREEN. And in the cave in Kentucky — (*Two* PHOTOGRAPHERS *dash on.* WINTERGREEN *stops until picture is taken.*) —when you were frightened of the darkness, I put my arm around your trembling shoulder and drew you to me.

MARY. You were so brave, so strong.

WINTERGREEN. Mary, I can conceal it from you no longer. Look at me, darling. (*He tilts her face up.*) I love you. (*The* CROWD *breaks into great cheers and applause.* WIN-TERGREEN *stops them with a gesture.*) Yes, Mary, I love you. (*A gesture to halt applause that has not come.*)

MARY. Why, John! I hardly know what to say.

WINTERGREEN. Say that you love me, Mary, and that you will be mine.

MARY. I do love you, John.
(*Applause. The* CROWD *on its feet.* WINTERGREEN *again checks them.*)

WINTERGREEN. And if I am elected President, you will marry me?

MARY (*with simple determination*). I will.

WINTERGREEN (*turns quickly to the crowd, his arm still around* MARY). Citizens, it is up to you! Can you let this glorious romance end unhappily!

MARY. Can you tear asunder two loving hearts whom God hath joined together!

WINTERGREEN. I put my faith and trust in the American people! Go then to the polls on Tuesday and show the whole world that the United States of America stands first, last and always for Love! Are you with me?

ALL (*on their feet*). YES!

FULTON. Sing 'em the campaign song, Jack! Sing the campaign love song!

WINTERGREEN.
　　　Of thee I sing, baby,
　　Summer, autumn, winter, spring, baby
　　　　You're my silver lining,
　　　　　You're my sky of blue,
　　　　There's a love light shining,
　　　　　All because of you.

　　　Of thee I sing, baby,
　　You have got that certain thing, baby,
　　　　Shining star and inspiration,
　　　　Worthy of a mighty nation,
　　　　　Of thee I sing!
(*The* CROWD *yells itself blue in the face. When they are good and blue, the curtain falls.*)

SCENE V

Election Night. The roar of the CROWD, *the blowing of horns, the tooting of sirens. A band that plays furiously. The voice of a nation is speaking, and the results are being thrown upon a motion picture screen. Faster and faster they come—bulletins from here, there, and everywhere; photographs of the candidate, photographs of* MARY TURNER, *photographs of people that have nothing to do with anything. And returns, returns, returns:*

WHITESIDE, VERMONT. Indications are that Wintergreen has swept the town by a plurality of 154.

———

WATERVILLE, MASS. Early returns show Wintergreen well ahead. First Election district gives:

Wintergreen 12
Scattering 1

———

A picture of JOHN P. WINTERGREEN.

———

A picture of MARY TURNER.

———

ATLANTA, GA. 16 election districts out of 184 give:

Wintergreen 12,736
Jefferson Davis 1,653

———

NEW YORK, N. Y. 126 election districts report:

Wintergreen 72,639
Bryan 128
Absent 4
Late 2

———

A picture of MARY TURNER.

———

A picture of WINTERGREEN.

———

A picture of GEORGE WASHINGTON, *of all people.*

———

LANDSLIDE, NEB.
John P. Wintergreen 12,538
A Man Named Wilkins 1

———

A picture of PATRICK HENRY.

———

HOLLYWOOD, CAL.
Wintergreen 160,000

Mickey Mouse 159,000
Gloria Swanson's First Husband   84,638

———

John P. Wintergreen Casting Ballot No. 8 at Public School 63 at 6:05 o'clock this morning. (*And a picture of him doing so.*)

John P. Wintergreen Casting Ballot No. 168 at Public School 145 at 8:10 o'clock this morning and 2:25 this afternoon.

———

NEW YORK, N. Y. Alexander Throttlebottom, vice-presidential candidate, gets his shoes shined preparatory to entering election booth. (*But one sees only the feet.*)

———

A picture of the WHITE HOUSE.

———

WINTERGREEN *again.*

———

NEW YORK, N. Y. 8 Rubbers Out of 150 Give:

Culbertson 300
Lenz 200
Grand Slam 1,000
Vulnerable 1,500

———

More pictures:
   BENJAMIN FRANKLIN.
   BABE RUTH (*just for good measure*).

———

NEW YORK, N. Y. 41 Election Districts give:

Wintergreen 46,572
Walter Hampden 136
Mae West 82

———

LEXINGTON, KENTUCKY.
Wintergreen 27,637
Light Wines and Beer 14
Straight Whiskey 1,850,827

Pictures again:

JOHN P. WINTERGREEN.
PATRICK HENRY.
PRIMO CARNERA.
MAN O' WAR.

MANCHESTER, ENGLAND.
Wintergreen 14,653
King George 3
Queen Mary 1

ROME, ITALY. 127 Election Districts give:
Wintergreen 0
Mussolini 828,638

NEW YORK, N. Y. Empire States gives Wintergreen plurality of 1,627,535, with only three counties missing.

LATER. Three missing New York counties located by Pinkerton men in Northeast Nebraska.

More pictures:

GEORGE WASHINGTON.
THE MARX BROTHERS.

NEW YORK, N. Y. First Returns from Wall St. Give:
Wintergreen 192,000
Radio 5¾
Goldman, Sachs 2⅛

And still more pictures:

THE WHITE HOUSE.
THE CAPITOL.
THE ROXY.
ROXY HIMSELF.
A FRIEND OF ROXY'S.
AN UNIDENTIFIED MAN (*who looks suspiciously like the vice-presidential candidate*).

MACY'S BASEMENT.
Wintergreen ...... $~~1.50~~ 97c
(Only one to a customer)

RICHMOND, VA.
Wintergreen 98,728
Mason 499

Dixon 1
Mason & Dixon 500

ST. LOUIS, MO.

				R	H	E
Cardinals	000	010	000	1	4	1
Giants	000	000	002	2	5	0

All returns indicate that
Wintergreen is sweeping
Country!

Wintergreen lacks
only four votes
to win!

WINTERGREEN CASTS LAST FOUR VOTES!

WINTERGREEN ELECTED!

Our Next President!
(*A beaming picture of* WINTERGREEN.)

Our Next First Lady!
(MISS TURNER *at her gayest.*)

BULLETIN. At a late hour to-night the defeated candidate sent the following telegram to John P. Wintergreen, the winner: "Heartily congratulate you on your splendid victory and charge fraud in Indiana, Illinois, Nebraska, Montana, Washington, Ohio and Massachusetts."

BULLETIN. At midnight to-night Alexander Throttlebottom refused to concede his election as Vice-President.

NEXT WEEK:
NORMA SHEARER
in
"THE LOVE GIRL"

And, to finish off, the Metro-Goldwyn lion. It opens its mouth. It crows.

Curtain.

SCENE VI

On the steps of the Capitol, Washington, D. C. It is Inauguration Day, and the scene is one of flashing uniforms and surging crowds. Except for a cleared space in which the all-important ceremony is to take place—two ceremonies, as a matter of fact—the steps are packed with diplomats, Army and Navy attachés, Cabinet members, Senators, Congressmen and anyone else who could get a ticket. As background for all this there looms the Capitol itself, with the great dome polishing it all off.

A hush falls on the crowd. The proceedings are about to begin.

Enter, to music, the nine JUDGES *of the Supreme Court of the United States—wrapped in their black robes, and all looking astonishingly like a certain Chief Justice who shall be nameless.*

The JUDGES *sing.*

JUDGES. We're the one—
                two—
                 three—
                  four—
                   five—
                    six—
                     seven—
                      eight—
        nine Supreme Court judges;
As the super-Solomons of this great nation,
We will supervise to-day's inauguration,
And we'll superintend the wedding celebration,
   In a manner official
   And judicial.

ALL.
One, two three, four, five, six, seven, eight,
   nine Supreme Court judges!

JUDGES.
We have powers that are positively regal—
Only we can take a law and make it legal.

ALL.
They're the A. K.s who give the O. K.s—
One, two, three, four, five, six, seven, eight,
   nine Supreme Court judges!
(*There is a great fanfare of trumpets in the distance—a swelling cheer.*)

ALL.
Hail, hail, the ruler of our gov'ment!
Hail, hail, the man who taught what love meant!
   Clear, clear the way
On his inaugural and wedding day!

Hail, hail, the mighty ruler of love!
Hail, hail, the man who made us love!
   Hip, hip, hooray!
For his inaugural and wedding day!
   Hurray!
(*Enter, to terrific cheering,* WINTERGREEN *and the* COMMITTEE. *High-hatted, frock-coated.*)

CHIEF JUSTICE. And now, Mr. President, if you don't mind, we'd like your inaugural address.

WINTERGREEN (*to music*).
I have definite ideas about the Philippines,
   And the herring situation up in Bismarck;
I have notions on the salaries of movie queens,
   And the men who sign their signatures with *this* mark! (*He makes a cross.*)
But on this glorious day I find
I'm sentimentally inclined,
   And so—
I sing this to the girls I used to know:

Here's a kiss for Cinderella,
   And a parting kiss for May;
Toodle-oo, good-bye! This is my wedding day!
Here's a final smile for Della,
   And the lady known as Lou;
Toodle-oo, good-bye! With bach'lor days I'm through!
(*And the girls in question, believe it or not, parade tantalizingly by him.*)

Though I really never knew them,
  It's a rule I must obey;
I am singing good-bye to them
  In the customary way.
My regards to Arabella,
  And to Emmaline and Kay;
Toodle-oo, dear girls, good-bye! This is my
  wedding day!

ALL.
He is toodle-ooing all his lady loves,
  All the girls he didn't know so well;
All the innocent and all the shady loves—
  Oh, dinga donga dell!

Bride and groom! Their future should be
  glorious;
  What a happy story they will tell!
Let the welkin now become uproarious—
  Oh, dinga donga, dinga donga dell!
(*On a platform at the head of the stairs, as
if by magic, there appears* MARY TURNER,
gorgeous in bridal attire.)

    Clear the way!
    Hail the bride!
    Sweet and gay—
    Here comes the bride!

MARY.
Is it true or am I dreaming?
  Do I go to Heav'n to stay?
Never was a girl so happy on her wedding
  day!

CHIEF JUSTICE. Do you, John P. Wintergreen, solemnly swear to uphold the Constitution of the United States of America
and to love, honor and cherish this woman
so long as you two shall live?

WINTERGREEN. I do.

CHIEF JUSTICE. Do you, Mary Turner,
promise to love, honor and cherish this
man so long as you two shall live?

MARY. I do.

CHIEF JUSTICE. Therefore, by virtue of the
power that is vested in me as Chief Justice, I hereby pronounce you President of
the United States, man and wife.

WINTERGREEN. Mary!

MARY. John! (*They embrace; the* CROWD
yells its head off.)

WINTERGREEN *and* MARY.
Is it true or am I dreaming?
  Do I go to Heav'n to stay?
Never was a girl so happy on her wed-
  ding—
(*Enter, of all people,* DIANA DEVEREAUX.
And is she annoyed?)

DIANA. Stop! Halt! Pause! Wait!

ALL.
    Who is this intruder?
    There's no one could be ruder!
    What's your silly notion
    In causing this commotion?

DIANA (*recitative, and with highly operatic
interludes*). I was the most beautiful blossom in all the Southland. I was sent up
North to enter the contest, with the understanding that the winner was to be the
President's wife. The committee examined
me. My lily white body fascinated them. I
was chosen. It was the happiest moment
of my life.

ALL. Yes, yes, go on! Yes, yes, go on!

DIANA. Suddenly the sky fell—suddenly
for no reason at all, no reason at all, this
man rejected me. All my castles came
tumbling down. And so I am serving him
with a summons—for breach of promise!

ALL.
    What! What!
    The water's getting hot!
    She says he made a promise—
    A promise he forgot!

DIANA. It's true! It's true!

CHIEF JUSTICE.
    The day he's getting married,
    You put him on the spot!

ALL.
    It's dirty work of Russia—
    A communistic plot!

WINTERGREEN.
Please understand! It wasn't that I would
  jilt or spurn 'er;
It's just that there was someone else!

ALL. Whom?

WINTERGREEN (*correcting them*). Who!
Mary Turner!

CHIEF JUSTICE.
We're having fits!
The man admits
This little sinner
Was really winner!

DIANA.
I couldn't see
His jilting me,
And so I'm doing
A bit of suing.

ALL.
And if it's true she has a claim
You should be called a dirty name!
Yes, if it's true, she has a claim
Then you're a dirty, dirty name!

MARY.
John, no matter what they do to hurt
  you,
The one you love won't desert you.

DIANA.
I'm a queen who has lost her king:
Why should she wear the wedding
  ring?

WINTERGREEN.
Some girls can bake a pie,
  Made up of prunes and quinces,
Some make an oyster fry—
  Others are good at blintzes.
Some lovely girls have done
  Wonders with turkey stuffin's,
But I have found the one
  Who can really make corn muffins!

ALL.
Yes, he has found the one
Who can really make corn muffins.

DIANA. Who cares about corn muffins? All
I demand is justice!

WINTERGREEN and MARY. Which is more
important—corn muffins or justice?

ALL. Which is more important—corn muffins or justice?

CHIEF JUSTICE. If you will wait a moment
—you'll have our decision. Forty—seven
—eleven—(The JUSTICES leap into a football huddle. After a moment they resume
their positions.)

CHIEF JUSTICE. The decision of the Supreme Court is—corn muffins!

ALL.
  Great! Great!
It's written on the slate!
There's none but Mary Turner
Could ever be his mate!

DIANA.
It's I, not Mary Turner
Who should have been his mate;
I'm off to tell my story
In ev'ry single state!

CHIEF JUSTICE.
Be off with you, young woman,
He's married to his mate!
Be off with you, young woman,
He's married to his mate!
(DIANA goes, but she'll be heard from
again.)

ALL.
There's none but Mary Turner
Could ever be his mate!
There's none but Mary Turner
Could ever be his mate!

WINTERGREEN.
  Of thee I sing, baby,
Summer, autumn, winter, spring, baby—
  Shining star and inspiration,
  Worthy of a mighty nation,
    Of thee I sing!
        Curtain.

ACT TWO

SCENE I

The PRESIDENT's *office, in the White House. And not only the* PRESIDENT's *office, but the* PRESIDENT's WIFE's *office, too. There are several indications of this joint occupancy. The Presidential desk, for example, is divided into two sections—one piled high with various state papers, and the other lined with perfumes, powders, and the other perquisites of femininity. Great portraits of George and Martha Washington look down from on high; the governmental eagle adorns the curtains.*

The same JENKINS *who used to work for* MR. FULTON *is now secretary to the* PRESIDENT, *and with* MRS. WINTERGREEN's *secretary*, MISS BENSON, *he is hard at work when the curtain rises. Enter, to music, about two dozen more* SECRETARIES. *They all get together in a little song and dance—an old White House custom:*

> Oh, it's great to be a secret'ry
> In the White House, D. C.
> You get inside information on Algeria:
> You know ev'ry move they're making in Liberia.
> You learn what's what and what is not
> In the land of the free.
> Ev'ry corner that you turn you meet a notable
> With a statement that is eminently quotable—
> Oh, it's great to be a secret'ry
> In the White House, D. C.

A White House GUIDE *enters, followed by a crowd of* SIGHTSEERS. *They are plainly from the country—men with loosely wrapped umbrellas, women with waistlines not in the right place, and a terrible child or two.*

GUIDE. And this, ladies and gentlemen, is the executive office. This is the room in which the President discharges his official duties, and has been occupied by every President since Hoover. On your right stands the famous double desk used by the President and Mrs. Wintergreen in administering the affairs of the country. During the 1912 coal shortage this room was used as a garage. Right this way, please. We are now entering the room from which, on an historic occasion, the Spanish Ambassador jumped out of the window, in the very nick of time. Here the diplomatic corps gathers once a month to pay its formal respects to the Chief Executive, and here too the cabinet assembles when— (*The last* SIGHTSEER *is through the door. The telephone on the desk rings.*)

JENKINS. Hello. . . . Who? . . . No, the Coolidges don't live here any more!

MISS BENSON (*holding a perfume bottle up to the light*). Mrs. Wintergreen is running low on Chanel No. 5.

JENKINS (*consulting a schedule*). Looks like a pretty full day. (*Reads.*) Delegation from South America—

MISS BENSON. What's eating them?

JENKINS. Usual thing. Want Hollywood cleaned up. (*Looking at list.*) Delegation of Camisole Indians—they want scalping restored. Committee of cotton manufacturers—that's for Mrs. Wintergreen. They want her to bring back cotton stockings.

MISS BENSON. Oh, they do, eh?

JENKINS. Mayors of fourteen American cities—(*Another* SECRETARY *enters with newspaper clippings.*) Well?

SECRETARY. Morning editorials. (*He goes.* JENKINS *looks the clippings over; shakes his head.*)

MISS BENSON. What's the matter?

JENKINS. Same thing. They're still harping on it.

MISS BENSON. You mean Devereaux?

JENKINS (*as he reads*). Mm.

MISS BENSON. What's it say?

JENKINS. Nothing new. They just think she got a raw deal.

MISS BENSON. A lot of people think that.

JENKINS (*crumpling a clipping*). Just as well if he doesn't see this one. You know, it wouldn't surprise me a bit—(*Another* SECRETARY *enters.*)

SECRETARY. Mr. Jenkins—

JENKINS. Yes?

SECRETARY. Those people are here now. Can you see them?

JENKINS. Show them into the Blue Room.

SECRETARY. Yes, sir. (*Goes.*)

JENKINS. Want to come along? Delegation from the Virgin Islands.

MISS BENSON. Well, well! And what are they after?

JENKINS. They want their name changed. They claim it's hurting business. (*They go, as another* GUIDE *enters with a sightseeing party. A* SAILOR *or two. A* SWEDE. *A* DUTCHMAN.)

GUIDE. Right this way, please—follow me. This, ladies and gentlemen, is the executive office. It is in this room that the President signs the many laws that govern your every-day life, and from which he controls the various departmental activities. (*One of the* SIGHTSEERS *emerges a bit from the crowd, eagerly taking in the scene. He turns out to be, of all people,* ALEXANDER

THROTTLEBOTTOM.) Here come the various heads of government for daily consultation with the Executive, and to receive from him the benefit of his wide experience. It is in this room—(*To* THROTTLEBOTTOM, *who has strayed a little too far from the group.*) I beg your pardon, sir, but would you please stay over there with the others? You see, we're personally responsible in case anything is stolen.

THROTTLEBOTTOM (*meekly rejoining the group*). Yes, sir.

GUIDE (*opens door*). Thank you. (*Resuming his formal tone.*) Now, are there any questions?

A SIGHTSEER. Does the President live here all year round?

GUIDE. All year round. Except when Congress is in session.

SIGHTSEER. Where does the vice-president live?

GUIDE. Who?

SIGHTSEER. The vice-president. Where does he live?

GUIDE (*taking a little red book out of his pocket*). Just one moment, please. Vice regent, viceroy, vice societies—I'm sorry, but he doesn't seem to be in here.

THROTTLEBOTTOM (*so mildly*). I can tell you about that.

GUIDE. What?

THROTTLEBOTTOM. I know where the vice-president lives.

GUIDE. Where?

THROTTLEBOTTOM. He lives at 1448 Z Street.

GUIDE. Well, that's very interesting. He has a house there, has he?

THROTTLEBOTTOM. Well, he lives there.

GUIDE. All by himself?

THROTTLEBOTTOM. No, with the other boarders. It's an awfully good place. Mrs. Spiegelbaum's. It's a great place, if you like Kosher cooking.

GUIDE. Think of your knowing all that! Are you a Washingtonian?

THROTTLEBOTTOM. Well, I've been here since March 4. I came down for the inauguration, but I lost my ticket.

GUIDE. You don't say? Well! First time you've been to the White House?

THROTTLEBOTTOM (*nods*). I didn't know people were allowed in.

GUIDE. You seem to know the vice-president pretty well. What kind of fellow is he?

THROTTLEBOTTOM. He's all right. He's a nice fellow when you get to know him, but nobody wants to know him.

GUIDE. What's the matter with him?

THROTTLEBOTTOM. There's nothing the matter with him. Just vice-president.

GUIDE. Well, what does he do all the time?

THROTTLEBOTTOM. He sits around in the parks, and feeds the pigeons, and takes walks, and goes to the movies. The other day he was going to join the library, but he had to have two references, so he couldn't get in.

GUIDE. But when does he do all his work?

THROTTLEBOTTOM. What work?

SIGHTSEER. Doesn't he preside over the Senate?

THROTTLEBOTTOM. What?

GUIDE. Sure he does! That's the vice-president's job.

THROTTLEBOTTOM. What is?

GUIDE. To preside over the Senate.

THROTTLEBOTTOM. Over what?

GUIDE. The Senate. You know what Senators are, don't you?

THROTTLEBOTTOM. Sure—I saw them play yesterday.

GUIDE. No, no! The vice-president presides over the Senate. It meets in the Capitol.

THROTTLEBOTTOM. When does it?

GUIDE. Right now! It's going on now!

THROTTLEBOTTOM (*frenzied*). How do you get there?

GUIDE. The Capitol?

THROTTLEBOTTOM. Yeah!

GUIDE. Street car at the door—right up Pennsylvania Avenue.

THROTTLEBOTTOM (*hurrying out*). Street car at the door—right up Pennsyl— (*Turns back.*)—what's the name of that place?

GUIDE. The Senate!

THROTTLEBOTTOM. The Senate! (*He dashes out*).

GUIDE. Right this way, please. (*Opens door.*) Here the diplomatic corps gathers monthly to pay its formal respects to the Chief Executive, and here too the cabinet assembles upon the occasion of its weekly meetings— (*They go. In the distance there is a fanfare of trumpets;* JENKINS *and* MISS BENSON *enter and take their places at the Presidential chairs. Enter, then, the* PRESIDENT *and* MARY.)

WINTERGREEN *and* MARY. Good morning!

JENKINS *and* MISS BENSON. Good morning! (WINTERGREEN *looks out the window, through which is visible the panorama of Washington, with Washington's Monument prominent in the foreground.*)

WINTERGREEN. What a country—what a country! Jenkins, what monument is that?

JENKINS (*promptly*). Grant's Tomb.

WINTERGREEN. Oh, yes. Well, what's on the schedule this morning? Ah, here we are! (*Takes up some letters.*) Tell the Secretary of the Navy to scrap two battleships.

JENKINS. What?

WINTERGREEN. Scrap two and build four. Disarmament.

JENKINS. Yes, sir.

WINTERGREEN. Cablegram to the President of San Domingo: "Congratulations on beginning your second day in office. That's five I owe you, and will bet you double or nothing on tomorrow."

JENKINS. Yes, sir.

WINTERGREEN. Tell the Secretary of War to stand ready to collect that bet.

JENKINS. Yes, sir.

WINTERGREEN. Letter to the Friars' Club, 48th St., New York City. "Dear Brother Friars: Regret very much I cannot take part in this year's minstrel show. Owing to conditions in the South, I do not think it would be wise for me to black up." (*Looks through the pile of letters.*) I get the lousiest mail for a President!

MARY. Emily! Take a cablegram to the Queen of Roumania.

MISS BENSON. Yes, ma'am.

MARY. Queen of Roumania. "Dear Marie: I have been trying out that new soap you are selling, and I predict an even greater success for it than you had with the shaving cream. Jack joins me in sending love. Do write and tell us all about Carol."

WINTERGREEN. And that French girl. . . . Jenkins!

JENKINS. Yes, sir.

WINTERGREEN. Take a memo to the Secretary of State: "Referring to last Tuesday night's poker game, please note that the Liberian minister's check for twelve dollars and forty-five cents has been returned for lack of funds. Kindly get a new minister for next Tuesday night's game, and add $12.45 to the Liberian National Debt."

JENKINS. Yes, sir.

WINTERGREEN. Get the Governor of Maryland on the phone and ask him what horse he likes in the fourth at Pimlico.

JENKINS. Yes, sir.

WINTERGREEN (*brandishing a telephone bill*). And tell the telephone company that this is not my bill. (*Hands it to secretary.*) That long distance call was March 3rd.

JENKINS. Yes, sir.

WINTERGREEN. Anybody in the ante-room?

JENKINS. Yes, sir. Secretary of the Navy, Secretary of Agriculture, and four zebras.

WINTERGREEN. Zebras?

JENKINS. There's a man who wants to give them to you.

WINTERGREEN (*thinking it over*). Well, I could use two. (*A SECRETARY enters with a wooden board, covered with electric buttons. A long wire is attached to it.*)

JENKINS. All ready, Mr. President. Time to press a button.

WINTERGREEN. So early in the morning?

JENKINS. Opening of the International Corn Growing Exposition. Button No. 1. . . . Ready. . . . Press.

WINTERGREEN (*presses button, then laughs*). Say, Jenkins, I never will forget the time I reopened the Bank of United States by mistake. (JENKINS *beats a hasty retreat. The telephone rings.*) Hello! (*Annoyed, hands the instrument to MARY.*) For you!

MARY. Who is it?

WINTERGREEN. The butcher!

MARY. Hello! . . . Oh, good morning, Mr. Schneidermann. . . . Fine, thank you. . . . Now, let me see. What have you got that's good? . . . Well, we had lamb chops yesterday. . . . They *are*? Well, wait a minute. (*To* WINTERGREEN.) John, who's coming to dinner to-night?

WINTERGREEN. What? Let me see—the Chief Justice, the Attorney General, Jackie Cooper, and those three judges that got paroled. That's six.

MARY (*as she returns to 'phone*). That's eight with us. . . . Hello, Mr. Schneidermann. Make it sixteen lamb chops—

WINTERGREEN. Wait a minute! What about that dirigible?

MARY. What?

WINTERGREEN. That dirigible from Germany. If that gets in we've got to have *them*.

MARY. Oh, dear! How many are there?

WINTERGREEN. Ah—sixty-four passengers, and of course two stowaways—that's sixty-six.

MARY. That's seventy-four in all.

WINTERGREEN. But they may not get here.

MARY. But when'll we know? . . . Just a minute, Mr. Schneidermann. (*Back to* WINTERGREEN, *pretty testily.*) I've got to know whether they're going to get here.

WINTERGREEN. How do I know? Take a chance! You can always use lamb chops.

MARY (*back to 'phone, wearily*). Listen, Mr. Schneidermann. A hundred and forty-eight lamb chops. . . . That's right. . . . Now, how is your asparagus? . . . Well, make it a carload of asparagus, and about seventy-five loaves of rye bread. That's all, thank you.

JENKINS (*entering*). Beg pardon, sir. Another button.

WINTERGREEN. What's this? (*Reads.*) Opening of a new speakeasy on 52d Street, New York. Didn't I open that yesterday?

JENKINS. Yes, sir. This is the re-opening. They closed it last night. (*He goes.*)

MARY (*coming to* WINTERGREEN *with a stack of bills in her hand*). John, look at these grocery bills!

WINTERGREEN. Well, what about it?

MARY. I've simply got to have a bigger allowance.

WINTERGREEN. Again! For God's sake, Mary!

MARY. Well, I can't help it. Fifty people to dinner every night. And Senators to breakfast every morning. It mounts up.

WINTERGREEN. I've got to have them! It's business!

MARY. Then you've got to give me enough to feed them.

WINTERGREEN. Where am I going to get it from?

MARY. Get it from! If you had any gumption you'd ask Congress for a raise.

WINTERGREEN. Ask Congress for a raise! I'm lucky they don't lay me off! (JENKINS *enters.*)

JENKINS. I beg your pardon.

WINTERGREEN. It's all right. What is it?

JENKINS. The Secretary of Agriculture and the Secretary of the Navy are still waiting.

WINTERGREEN. I forgot. Have them come in.

SECRETARY. The Secretary of Agriculture! (*He enters. It turns out to be our old friend* LIPPMAN.)

LIPPMAN. Hello, Jack! Hello, Mary!

WINTERGREEN. Hello, Secretary!

SECRETARY. The Secretary of the Navy! (*Enter* GILHOOLEY. *It seems that* WINTERGREEN *took care of the boys.*)

WINTERGREEN. Sit down, boys. Sorry I kept you waiting.

LIPPMAN. That's all right.

GILHOOLEY. O K., Chief.

WINTERGREEN. Well, what's on your mind, Loujs? How's agriculture?

LIPPMAN. That's what I came to talk to you about. Listen, Jack! I don't know anything about agriculture. I told you I wanted the Treasury.

WINTERGREEN. What's the matter with agriculture?

LIPPMAN. Agriculture's all right—it's those farmers. Wheat, wheat! All they know is raise wheat! And then they raise hell with me because nobody wants it.

WINTERGREEN. Why do you let them raise so much?

LIPPMAN. How can you stop 'em? I did all I could. I invited the seven-year-locusts, but they didn't come. Even the locusts don't want their lousy wheat. And they're always complaining about being in one place all the time—they want to travel.

GILHOOLEY. You call that trouble. How'd you like to have a lot of sailors on your neck?

WINTERGREEN. What do *they* want—*two* wives in every port?

GILHOOLEY. Yeah. And any port in a storm. And no storms. And they won't stand for those bells any more. They want to know what time it is the same as anybody else. But that's not the big thing.

WINTERGREEN. Well?

GILHOOLEY. It's the ocean They don't like the ocean.

WINTERGREEN. Which ocean don't they like?

GILHOOLEY. All of them. They say it's a nice place to visit, but they don't want to live there. It's no place to bring up a family.

WINTERGREEN (*thinking it over*). The farmers want to travel and the sailors want to settle down. . . . I've got it! Have them change places!

LIPPMAN. What?

WINTERGREEN. It'll solve the whole problem! Sailors don't know anything about farming—in two years there won't *be* any wheat! You'll have a wheat shortage!

LIPPMAN. And I'll get hell again!

WINTERGREEN. And look what it does for business! You get the farmers on the boats; the traveling salesmen will come back to the farmhouses—*you* know, to stay over night! Why, I haven't heard a good story in years!
(*A* SECRETARY *enters.*)

SECRETARY. The Secretary of State! (*He comes in. It is* FULTON.)

FULTON. Hello, boys. Everybody.

WINTERGREEN. How are you, Matty?

FULTON (*all business*). What are you doing, Jack? Important?

WINTERGREEN. Just chinning.

FULTON (*a look toward the doors*). Can you keep the room clear for a little while?

WINTERGREEN. Sure. What's up?

FULTON (*starts toward door*). Shall I tell 'em?

WINTERGREEN. No, here we are. (*Presses a buzzer.*)

LIPPMAN (*starting off*). See you later.

FULTON. No, no. Want you fellows to stay. (JENKINS *enters.*)

WINTERGREEN. I don't want to be disturbed for a little while.

JENKINS. Yes, sir.

FULTON. Just a minute. When Senators Jones and Lyons get here, bring 'em in.

JENKINS. Yes, sir.

FULTON. And nobody else.

JENKINS. Yes, sir. What shall I do about the press conference?

FULTON. Have 'em wait!' (JENKINS *goes.* FULTON *waits for the doors to close.*) There's hell to pay!

WINTERGREEN. What's the matter?

FULTON. Devereaux!

MARY. John! (*He puts an arm around her.*)

WINTERGREEN. What about her?

FULTON. The thing has been growing for weeks—*you* know that, boys—(*This to* LIPPMAN *and* GILHOOLEY.)

WINTERGREEN. What has?

FULTON. Well, you know there's always been a certain bunch that said Devereaux didn't get a square deal.

WINTERGREEN. A handful of Southerners!

FULTON. At the beginning, yes. But now it's spreading all over the country!

WINTERGREEN. What do you mean?

MARY. What's happened?

FULTON. I'll tell you what I mean. Yesterday the Federation of New Jersey Woman's Clubs came out solid for Devereaux.

MARY. John! (*A sob from* MARY.)

FULTON. And this morning I got a petition from the Kansas City Elks—demanding Devereaux! And the same thing'll happen with the Moose and the Shriners!
(*Enter* SENATORS JONES *and* LYONS. *A nod or two from the others.*)

FULTON. Good! I've just been telling the President how things stand!

JONES. Mr. President, I cannot overstate the case. The West is up in arms.

LYONS. The South, suh, is on fire!

JONES. Nebraska has just declared martial law! A posse has been formed!

LYONS. In Louisiana you have been hanged in effigy!

WINTERGREEN (*defiant*). How do the Philippines feel about it?

MARY. It's all my fault!

WINTERGREEN. No! I'd rather have you than Nebraska!

FULTON. It doesn't matter whose fault it is. We've got to do something! We've got to do something to counteract this Devereaux propaganda!

WINTERGREEN. I'll tell you what we'll do! (*Presses a buzzer.*) We carried 48 States in the campaign, didn't we? Mary and I?

FULTON. Yeah!

WINTERGREEN. And there was Devereaux propaganda then! But we licked it before and we can do it again! (*As* JENKINS *enters.*) Those newspaper men still out there?

JENKINS. Yes, sir.

WINTERGREEN. Bring 'em in when I ring!

JENKINS. Yes, sir. (*Goes.*)

WINTERGREEN. The trouble with you boys is you're yellow!

FULTON. Now look here!

WINTERGREEN. One sock and you're ready to quit! We've got to fight, that's all! I'm as good as I ever was! And so's Mary! And we still love each other! (*Turning to her.*) Don't we?

MARY (*with spirit*). You bet we do!

WINTERGREEN (*swinging back onto the men*). There you are! We're not through! We haven't begun to fight! By God, we can tour again if we have to! I can still sing! Once a trouper always a trouper! (MARY *is freshening the lip-stick and powdering the face.*) What do you say, boys? Are you with me?

ALL. Yes!
(WINTERGREEN *presses the buzzer.*)

FULTON. You got to put it over, Jack!

WINTERGREEN. I'll put it over! I'll give them the best performance since Richard Mansfield! Are you ready, Mary?

MARY (*finishing the make-up job*). Ready!

WINTERGREEN (*as a* SECRETARY *enters*). Bring in those newspapermen! (*Music strikes up. Enter the* NEWSPAPERMEN.)

WINTERGREEN. Well, gentlemen, what's on your mind?

REPORTERS (*singing it, of course*).
We don't want to know about the moratorium,
  Or how near we are to beer,
    Or about the League of Nations,
    Or the seventeen vacations
You have had since you've been here.

Here's the one thing that the people of America
Are beside themselves to know:
  They would like to know what's doing
  On the lady who is suing
You—Diana Devereaux?

  Ev'rybody wants to know:
  What about Miss Devereaux?
  From the highest to the low:
  What about Miss Devereaux?

WINTERGREEN.
  It's a pleasant day—
  That's all I can say!

MARY.
  Here's the one thing we'll announce:
  Love's the only thing that counts!

REPORTERS.
　　　　People want to know:
　　　　What of Devereaux?

WINTERGREEN.
　　When the one you love is near
　　Nothing else can interfere.

ALL.
　　When the one you love is near
　　Nothing else can interfere.

WINTERGREEN.
　　Here's some information
　　I will gladly give the nation:
　　I am for the true love,
　　Here's the only girl I do love.

MARY.
　　I love him and he loves me
　　And that's how it will always be,
　　So what care we about Miss Devereaux?

　　Who cares what the public chatters?
　　Love's the only thing that matters.

WINTERGREEN.
　　Who cares
　　If the sky cares to fall in the sea?
　　Who cares what banks fail in Yonkers,
　　Long as you've got a kiss that conquers?
　　Why should I sigh?
　　Life is one long jubilee,
　　So long as I care for you
　　And you care for me.

(*This argument being unanswerable, the* REPORTERS *go, completely convinced. The* COMMITTEE, *highly pleased, surrounds* WINTERGREEN *and congratulates him.*)

WINTERGREEN. Nothing at all, boys! I owe it all to the little woman!

MARY. You were grand, John!

FULTON. I never heard you in better voice!

WINTERGREEN. Did you hear that F sharp I gave them?

GILHOOLEY. Great!

WINTERGREEN (*letting his voice loose for a second in a snatch of operatic aria*). Do you know what I'll do? I'll go on the radio every night! Mary and I!

FULTON. National Biscuit Co.! They've been after you!

JONES. National Biscuit! That's a very popular hour in the West!

WINTERGREEN. A new song every night! I'll even get a megaphone!

MARY. And we can make records!

WINTERGREEN (*ever practical*). No, dear. They don't sell any more!

FULTON. Well, every little helps!

MARY. And I can still bake!

WINTERGREEN. What!

MARY. Corn muffins! Corn muffins for the unemployed!

WINTERGREEN. That's my girl! You feed 'em and I'll sing to them! We'll get the country back! Give us a week and they'll forget that Devereaux ever lived! (*A chorus of approval from the* COMMITTEE.) And you fellows wanted to quit! Why, we haven't begun to fight! This is a cinch! What would you do if a real fight came along! (*Enter a dozen* SECRETARIES.) What's this?

SECRETARIES. The French Ambassador!

WINTERGREEN. I can't see him! (*Enter another dozen* SECRETARIES.) And what's this?

SECRETARIES. The French Ambassador!

WINTERGREEN. I can't see him! (*Enter half a dozen French* SOLDIERS, *in full uniforms and Oh! what beards. They line up and sing, it being an old rule that French* SOLDIERS *always sing when they line up.*)

　　Garçon, s'il vous plait,
　　Encore Chevrolet Coupé;
　　Papah, pooh, pooh, pooh!
　　À vous toot dir vay, à vous?
　　Garçon, q'est-ce que c'est?
　　Tra la, Maurice Chevalier!
　　J'adore crêpes Suzette
　　Et aussi Lafayette!

And now we give the meaning of our song: We're six of the fifty million and we can't be wrong! (*Enter the* FRENCH AMBASSADOR. *You never saw so many medals.*)

FRENCH SOLDIERS. Ze French Ambassador!

WINTERGREEN. I still can't see him!

FRENCH AMBASSADOR (*sings*). I am the Ambassador of France!

WINTERGREEN. Europe?

FRENCH AMBASSADOR (*recitative*). And I have come here to see a grievous wrong righted. My country is deeply hurt. Not since the days of Louis the Seventh, the Eighth, the Ninth, the Tenth, and possibly the Eleventh have such a thing happen!

WINTERGREEN. What's troubling you?

FRENCH AMBASSADOR. You have done a great injustice to a French descendent—a lovely girl whose rights have been trampled in the dust!

ALL. Who is she? What's her name?

FRENCH AMBASSADOR. Her name is Diana Devereaux.

ALL. Diana Devereaux! Diana Devereaux! Since when is she of French descent?

FRENCH AMBASSADOR.
I've been looking up her family tree,
And I have found a most important pedigree!

She's the illegitimate daughter
Of an illegitimate son
Of an illegitimate nephew
Of Napoleon!

ALL (*awed*). Napoleon!

FRENCH AMBASSADOR.
She offers aristocracy
To this bizarre democracy,
Where naught is sacred but the old simoleon!
I must know why
You crucify
My native country
With this effront'ry,
To the illegitimate daughter of an illegitimate son
Of an illegitimate nephew of Napoleon!

ALL.
To the illegitimate daughter of an illegitimate son
Of an illegitimate nephew of Napoleon!

COMMITTEE.
You so-and-so!
We didn't know
She had a tie-up
So very high up.

She's the illegitimate daughter of an illegitimate son
Of an illegitimate nephew of Napoleon!
(*The voice of* DIANA *is heard in the distance. A snatch of aria. She enters, singing.*)

DIANA.
I was the most beautiful blossom in all the Southland.

WINTERGREEN *and* MARY. We know all that.

FRENCH AMBASSADOR. You know all that—but you *don't* know the misery of this poor little girl who has suffered. Because—

COMMITTEE. Because—

WINTERGREEN *and* MARY. Because?

FRENCH AMBASSADOR. Because?

DIANA (*it seems to be a reprise*).
Because, because, because, because—
I won the competition
But I got no recognition
And because he broke my heart!
Because, because, because, because—
The man who ought to love me
Tried to make a monkey of me;
Double-crossing from the start!
I might have been First Lady,
But now my past is shady;
Oh, pity this poor maidie!

FRENCH AMBASSADOR. And there's the man who ought to pay!

ALL.
Because, because, because, because—
She won the prize for beauty
And he didn't do his duty,
He has broken her poor heart!

FRENCH AMBASSADOR. You see how this poor child has suffered. And so, on behalf of France, I demand that your marriage be annulled and that you marry Diana!

WINTERGREEN. Never! Never!

FRENCH AMBASSADOR. Then you will arouse the anger of France and you must be prepared to face the consequences! (*The French contingent, with* DIANA, *marches off, singing "Garçon, S'il Vous Plait." There is a momentous pause.*)

FULTON. Jack, you've got to do something about this!

WINTERGREEN. Leave my Mary? Never!

FULTON.
We are all in this together;
We are birdies of a feather;
And if you don't change your thesis,
Then our party goes to pieces!

LYONS.
All our jobs you'll be destroying
With your attitude annoying.

GILHOOLEY.
You will get us all in trouble!
And in spades, sir, which is double!

WINTERGREEN. I will never leave my Mary!

LYONS.
Since he's acting so contrary,
Send him off on a vacation!

GILHOOLEY. I suggest his resignation!

WINTERGREEN. Resignation?

ALL. Resignation!

FULTON.
You've got to face it—this is a crisis!
To leave your Mary, you may decline,
But to save us, my good advice is—
    You resign!

ALL. Yes, resign!

WINTERGREEN.
I assure you, though it's a crisis,
To leave my Mary I must decline
And I don't care what your advice is,
    I decline to resign!

MARY. We decline to resign!

ALL.
He is stubborn—we must teach him;
I'm afraid we must impeach him!
He is stubborn—we must teach him;
He has forced us to impeach him!
    You decline to resign,
    So we'll teach you!
    We'll impeach you!
    You decline to resign—
    We don't envy you at all!
    You decline to resign,
    So we'll teach you,
    We'll impeach you!
    You decline to resign—
Humpty Dumpty has to fall!
(*They go—leaving* WINTERGREEN *and* MARY *alone. In the circumstances there is only one thing to do—and they do it. They sing a reprise.*)
    Who cares
    If the sky cares to fall in the sea?
    We two together can win out;
    Just remember to stick your chin out.
    Why should we sigh?
    Life is one long jubilee—
    So long as I care for you.
    And you care for me.
(*The lights dim; the curtains come together.*)

SCENE II

A Capitol corridor, just outside the United States Senate. A smartly dressed PAGE *comes out of the Senate door; another goes in.*
    Enter, then, the COMMITTEE—*those same five boys. As they come in* FULTON *is doing the talking.*

FULTON. Say, I'm just as sorry as anybody. I like Jack as much as you do, and I'd give my shirt not to have to do this.

JONES. We can't be sentimental at a time like this.

GILHOOLEY. Say! Wait a minute! If he's put out of office who becomes the President?

JONES. Why, the vice-president, of course.

LIPPMAN. Who's that?

FULTON (*as it dawns on him*). We haven't got a vice-president.

GILHOOLEY. Sure we have! He came up to the room!
(*Enter* ALEXANDER THROTTLEBOTTOM. *He is panting, having run all the way from the White House. The* COMMITTEE *continues its argument.*)

FULTON (*suddenly remembering*). Pitts! I nominated him!
(*A chorus of dissent.* LIPPMAN: "*No, that wasn't his name!*" JONES: "*It was Schaefferl*" LYONS: "*No, Pitts!*" GILHOOLEY: "*No, it was a longer name. Barbinelli!*")
(THROTTLEBOTTOM, *who has been listening to all this in full expectation of imminent discovery, now comes over to them.*)

THROTTLEBOTTOM. Hello, gentlemen!

FULTON. It was Alexander Something.

GILHOOLEY. Yah, that's it!

THROTTLEBOTTOM. Throttlebottom.

GILHOOLEY. That's right! (*A chorus from the others. "Yes, that's right!"*)

FULTON (*realizing that it is a stranger who has spoken*). Oh! Thank you. (*Hands him a cigar.*)

THROTTLEBOTTOM. Oh, thank you, Mr. Fulton.

FULTON (*looking at him*). Haven't I seen you before some place?

THROTTLEBOTTOM. I'm Throttlebottom.

FULTON. Huh?

THROTTLEBOTTOM. Throttlebottom. The vice-president. That's how I knew the name.
(*A chorus of greetings. "Well, hello!" "Where have you been?" "Well, for God's sake!" "Here! Have a light!"*)

FULTON. Well, for heaven's sake! Just the fellow we were looking for!

GILHOOLEY. Yes, *sir!*

FULTON. We want to talk to you!

THROTTLEBOTTOM. Me?

LYONS. That's what!

FULTON. We've got a surprise for you!

THROTTLEBOTTOM (*covering his eyes*). A surprise?

LIPPMAN. Sure! Remember I told you you had a chance to be President?

THROTTLEBOTTOM. Yeah!

FULTON. Well, we've been thinking it over and we're going to make you President!

GILHOOLEY. That's what we are!

THROTTLEBOTTOM. President! Say! You mean of the United States?

JONES. That's what we do!

THROTTLEBOTTOM. But what was the matter with the other fellow?

FULTON. We're going to impeach him!

GILHOOLEY. He wouldn't play ball with us!

THROTTLEBOTTOM. Well, I don't play very well—you see this finger—

FULTON. Come on! Let's get started!

GILHOOLEY. Yeah, we've got work to do!

THROTTLEBOTTOM. You really mean it? I'm not vice-president any more?

JONES. Not if we impeach the President!

THROTTLEBOTTOM. Well, when do we do that?

JONES. Right now! Come on!

FULTON. You've got to preside over the Senate!

THROTTLEBOTTOM. And after that I'll be President?

LYONS. That's what you will! (*The* COMMITTEE *enters the Senate.* THROTTLEBOTTOM *is about to follow when a* SCRUBWOMAN *comes along the corridor.*)

THROTTLEBOTTOM. President! Say! (*To the* SCRUBWOMAN.) How will that sound? President Alexander Bottlethrottom. (*Corrects himself.*) Throttlebottom.

SCRUBWOMAN. Huh?

THROTTLEBOTTOM (*he has to tell someone*). I'm going to be President!

SCRUBWOMAN. I'd rather have this job. It's steady. (*She goes, just as* WINTERGREEN *and* JENKINS *arrive from the other side.*)

JENKINS. Well, it's a dirty trick, Chief. That's all I've got to say.

WINTERGREEN. It's politics. They've got to eat, too.

JENKINS. Want me to go in with you?

WINTERGREEN. No. I want to handle this alone.

JENKINS. More power to you, Chief. (*Takes his hand; holds it during the following speech.*) And I want you to know that if the worst comes to the worst, and they fire you out—

WINTERGREEN. I know—if they fire me out you want a job with the next President.

JENKINS. Right! (*He goes.*)
(WINTERGREEN *starts for the door into the Senate.*)

THROTTLEBOTTOM. Hello, Mr. President. Hey!

WINTERGREEN. Hey?

THROTTLEBOTTOM. I'll bet you don't remember me, do you?

WINTERGREEN (*after a searching gaze*). You're the fellow that gave me that dill pickle.

THROTTLEBOTTOM. That's right.

WINTERGREEN. What are you doing now?

THROTTLEBOTTOM. I'm vice-president.

WINTERGREEN. You don't say? Lost your other job, huh?

THROTTLEBOTTOM. Well, I'm going to have a good job now, because I'm going to be President.

WINTERGREEN (*realizing it*). Say, that's right! If they kick me out that makes you President.

THROTTLEBOTTOM. Say, I wonder if you'd mind doing me a favor?

WINTERGREEN. Sure!

THROTTLEBOTTOM. You see, I don't know anything about being President. I just found out today how to be vice-president.

WINTERGREEN. Well, that's something.

THROTTLEBOTTOM. Isn't there some book I could read?

WINTERGREEN. Yes. I'm writing one. "What Every Young President Ought to Know."

THROTTLEBOTTOM. Has it got pictures?

WINTERGREEN. It's got everything! Tells you just what to do! Of course the first four years are easy. You don't do anything except try to get re-elected.

THROTTLEBOTTOM. That's pretty hard these days.

WINTERGREEN. It looks that way. The next four years you wonder why the hell you wanted to be re-elected. And after that you go into the insurance business and you're all set.

THROTTLEBOTTOM. Well, couldn't I save a lot of time and go right into the insurance business?

WINTERGREEN. No, you've got to work yourself up.

THROTTLEBOTTOM. Yeah, but it's a pretty hard job, being President. You've got to keep on writing those Thanksgiving proclamations, no matter what—and then there's that other bunch, Congress. I guess there isn't anything you can really do about Congress, is there?

WINTERGREEN. Take my advice and keep them out of Washington.

THROTTLEBOTTOM. Can you do that?

WINTERGREEN. St. Patrick did it. Keep them out if you have to quarantine the place. Get the measles.

THROTTLEBOTTOM. I had measles once.

WINTERGREEN. Yeah, but you never had Congress. That's worse.

THROTTLEBOTTOM. Oh! What about those messages that the President is always sending to Congress—who reads those, anyway?

WINTERGREEN. The fellow who prints 'em.

THROTTLEBOTTOM. Well, wouldn't everybody read them if you made 'em funnier?

WINTERGREEN. No, we've had some pretty funny ones.

THROTTLEBOTTOM. Couldn't you make a speech instead? Then they'd *have* to listen.

WINTERGREEN. No, no! You've got to be careful about speeches. You only make a speech when you want the stock market to go down.

THROTTLEBOTTOM. What do you do when you want the stock market to go up?

WINTERGREEN (*fairly falling on his neck*). Oh! wouldn't I like to know!

Curtain.

SCENE III

Inside the Senate Chamber. The great desk of the presiding officer, mounted on a dais; in circles around him the desks of the SENATORS. *Senators with Dundrearies, Senators with long white beards, Senators of all kinds and descriptions.*

When the curtain rises they are all in their places, and THROTTLEBOTTOM *is on high. The roll is being called, to music, of course, and the* SENATORS *sway rhythmically back and forth in time to the music, humming as they do so.*

THROTTLEBOTTOM. The Senator from North Dakota!

SENATOR. Present!

THROTTLEBOTTOM. Check! . . . The Senator from Minnesota!

SENATOR. Present!

THROTTLEBOTTOM. Check! . . . The Senator from Lou'siana!

SENATOR. Present!

THROTTLEBOTTOM. Check! . . . The Senator who's from Montana!

SENATOR. Present!

THROTTLEBOTTOM. Check! . . . The Senator who's from Alaska! (*A new State, by the way.*)

SENATOR. Present!

THROTTLEBOTTOM. Check! . . . The Senator who's from Nebraska!

SENATOR. Present!

THROTTLEBOTTOM. Check! . . .
　　The Senators from other States
　　　　Will have to bide their time,
　　For I simply can't be bothered
　　　　When the names don't rhyme!
(*The* SENATORS *continue to hum and to sway; led by* THROTTLEBOTTOM, *they now go into song.*)
　　The country thinks it's got depression;
　　　　Ha! Ha! Ha!
　　Just wait until we get in session!
　　　　Ha! Ha! Ha!
　　The people want a lot of action;
　　　　Ho! Ho! Ho!
　　We're here to give them satisfaction!
　　　　Ho! Ho! Ho!
　　Today is really full of laughter,
　　　　Ha! Ha! Ha!
　　Compared to what will follow after!
　　　　Ha! Ha! Ha!
There's action ev'ry minute when this happy group convenes:
　　To get business into tangles
　　We can guarantee more angles
Than the town of Boston guarantees in beans!

If you think you've got depression
Wait until we get in session
And you'll find out what depression really
    means!

CLERK. It is now twelve o'clock noon and
the Senate of the United States is hereby
declared in session.

THROTTLEBOTTOM. Thanks. Gentlemen,
when you hear the musical note it will be
exactly twelve o'clock noon. (*And he
brings the gavel down—right on his
watch.*) Well, gentlemen, I'm glad to meet
you all. You'll have to excuse me for not
knowing much about this job. I see I made
one mistake already—I went and got
shaved. Now let's get at things—I'm only
going to be with you one day, so let's make
it a pip.

CLERK. The first thing before the Senate is
unfinished business!

THROTTLEBOTTOM. But aren't we going to
impeach the President?

CLERK. Unfinished business!

SENATOR FROM MASSACHUSETTS. Mr. Chairman! Mr. Chairman!

CLERK (*to* THROTTLEBOTTOM). That's you.

THROTTLEBOTTOM. Oh, I thought I was just
vice-president.

CLERK. You must recognize the Senator
from Massachusetts.

THROTTLEBOTTOM. Oh, hello! How's everything in Massachusetts?

SENATOR FROM MASSACHUSETTS. Mr. Chairman! I rise to protest against a great injustice! In seventeen hundred and seventy-
five Paul Revere made the famous ride that
saved his country from the greedy clutch of
England.

THROTTLEBOTTOM. That's right—I read
about that. (*Informally, to the* CLERK.)
He went from one house to another, and
he knocked on the door, and by the time
they came out he was at the next house.

SENATOR FROM MASSACHUSETTS. Paul Revere's name has been given the affectionate
tribute of a grateful people. But what of

that gallant figure who is even more responsible? Gentlemen: what about Jenny,
Paul Revere's horse? (*Applause.*) Surely,
gentlemen, Jenny is entitled to the protection of a governmental pension. A bill
providing such a pension was introduced
into this body in the year 1804, and came
up for its first reading in 1852.

THROTTLEBOTTOM. I wasn't here then.

SENATOR FROM MASSACHUSETTS. Gentlemen,
in these hundred and fifty-five years Jenny
has not been getting any younger. I ask
you, gentlemen, what are we going to do
about Jenny?

THROTTLEBOTTOM. Well, that's unfinished
business if I ever heard it.

SENATOR JONES. May I point out to the
Senator from Massachusetts that Jenny is
dead?

THROTTLEBOTTOM. She is? What do you
think of that? Good old Jenny! When did
she die?

SENATOR JONES. She died in 1805.

THROTTLEBOTTOM. The Senate will rise for
one minute in silent tribute to the departed
horse from Massachusetts. (*They rise: he
bangs the gavel.*) Well, that finishes Jenny.
Is there any other unfinished business?

SENATOR LYONS. Mr. Chairman! Gentlemen! I crave the indulgence of this august
body while I say a few words in honor of
my wife's birthday. (*Applause.*) And I
move you, Mr. Chairman, that the Senate
appropriate $5,000 for flowers to be sent
her on this historic occasion.

A SENATOR. Second the motion!

THROTTLEBOTTOM. All in favor say "Aye!"
(*A full-throated "Aye" from the assemblage.*) Motion carried! (*To the* CLERK.)
Put in my card. . . . Now, what comes
next? How about impeaching the President?

CLERK (*handing him a sheet of paper*).
Mr. Vice-President—

THROTTLEBOTTOM. What's this?

CLERK. The following committees are
ready to report.

THROTTLEBOTTOM (*consulting the paper*). Committee on Aviation. . . . Airedales. . . . Bloomingdale's. . . . (*Closes his eyes, one finger suspended over the paper.*) Eenie, meenie, minie, mo. Catch a committee by the toe. If they holler give 'em dough, eenie, meenie, minie, mo. (*Places his finger on the paper, looks to see which committee he has selected.*) Committee on Unemployment.

SENATOR JONES. The Committee on Unemployment is gratified to report that due to its unremitting efforts there is now more unemployment in the United States than ever before.

THROTTLEBOTTOM. Now we're getting some place! Now let's impeach the President!

SENATOR FROM MASSACHUSETTS. Mr. Chairman! I would like to call the attention of the Senate to a matter that has been puzzling me for some time. It has to do with a very interesting bridge hand, in which the cards were distributed as follows: East held the four aces, West the four kings, North the four queens, and South—ah—nothing of any importance.

LYONS (*rising indignantly*). Mr. Chairman! The South will never be satisfied with a hand like that!
(*A fanfare of trumpets.*)

PAGES (*announcing*). The President of the United States!

THROTTLEBOTTOM. Who?

CLERK. The President of the United States!
(*He enters.*)

CLERK. The next business before the Senate is the resolution on the impeachment of the President!

THROTTLEBOTTOM (*to* WINTERGREEN). Won't you sit down while we kick you out?
(*Enter, to music,* FULTON *and the* COMMITTEE.)

COMMITTEE (*in harmony*). Whereas—

LYONS. At a meeting of the Senate at which a quorum was present a motion was made and it was proposed that—

COMMITTEE. Whereas—

LYONS. John P. Wintergreen had undertaken to marry the winner of a contest held at Atlantic City—

COMMITTEE. Whereas—

LYONS. His subsequent refusal to marry the winner, Miss Diana Devereaux, will lead to dire international complications—

COMMITTEE. Whereas—

LYONS. Now therefore be it resolved that President John P. Wintergreen be, and he hereby is, impeached from the said office of President of these United States.

JONES. I second the resolution.

FULTON. Our first witness—the French Ambassador.
(*Enter the six* FRENCH SOLDIERS.)

SOLDIERS.
　　Garçon, s'il vous plait,
　　Encore, Chevrolet Coupé;
　　　Papah, pooh, pooh pooh!
　　A vous toot dir vay, à vous?

SENATORS.
　　We say how d'you do,
　　Which means that we welcome you;
　　We're glad of the chance
　　To say hello to France.
(*The* FRENCH AMBASSADOR *enters.*)

FRENCH AMBASSADOR.
　　You've dealt a lovely maid
　　　A blow that is injurious;
　　A very dirty trick was played
　　　And France is simply furious!

SENATORS.
　　He says a lovely maid
　　　Was dealt a blow injurious;
　　He says a dirty trick was played
　　　And France is simply furious!

FULTON. Ambassador, please explain why France should be concerned about the plaintiff.

FRENCH AMBASSADOR.
She's the illegitimate daughter of an illegitimate son
　　Of an illegitimate nephew of Napoleon!

ALL. Napoleon!

FRENCH AMBASSADOR.
She's contemplating suicide
Because that man he threw aside
A lady with the blue blood of Napoleon.
　　What sort of man
　　Is this who can
　　Insult my country
　　With this effront'ry

ALL.
To the illegitimate daughter of an illegitimate son
　　Of an illegitimate nephew of Napoleon!

FRENCH AMBASSADOR. The Atlantic City witnesses! (*Enter the* GIRLS *in bathing suits.*) And Miss Diana Devereaux!

DIANA. I have come all ze way from France to bring ze greetings.

FRENCH AMBASSADOR. Tell your story, little one. Commencez, s'il vous plait.

DIANA (*sings*).
　　Jilted, jilted,
　　I'm a flow'r that's wilted;
　　　Blighted, blighted,
　　Till the wrong is righted;
　　　Broken, broken,
　　By a man soft-spoken;
　　　Faded, faded,
　　Heaven knows why.
When men are deceivers, I'm afraid,
'Tis sad to be a trusting maid.
　　Jilted, jilted, jilted am I,
　　Oh, what is there left but to die?

ALL.
Just as in the Frankie and Johnnie song—

THROTTLEBOTTOM.
He done her wrong, he done her wrong—

ALL.
　　Jilted, jilted, jilted is she!
　　Oh, what is there left but—to dee?
(*The* SENATE *is visibly affected.*)

THROTTLEBOTTOM. And now, Mr. President, what have you to say for yourself?

WINTERGREEN.
Impeach me! Fine me! Jail me! Sue me!
My Mary's love means much more to me!

THROTTLEBOTTOM.
Enough, enough! We want no preachment!
It's time to vote on his impeachment!

ALL.
It's time to vote on his impeachment!

THROTTLEBOTTOM. The Senator from Minnesota?

SENATOR. Guilty!

THROTTLEBOTTOM. Check! . . . The Senator from North Dakota?

SENATOR. Guilty!

THROTTLEBOTTOM. Check! . . .The Senator from Lou'siana?

SENATOR. Guilty!

THROTTLEBOTTOM. Check! . . . The Senator who's from Montana?
(*And at this dramatic moment, in breaks* MARY TURNER WINTERGREEN.)

MARY. Stop! stop! stop!

WINTERGREEN. Mary!

MARY (*to music*).
Before you go any further, with your permission,
I must tell you of my husband's delicate condition.

ALL. Delicate condition! What do you mean?

MARY (*such a gay song*).
　　I'm about to be a mother;
　　He's about to be a father;
　　　We're about to have a baby:
　　　　I must tell it,
　　　　These doings compel it!
　　Oh, I'm about to be a mother;
　　He's about to be a father;
　　　We're about to have a baby—

ALL. A baby!

MARY.
　　A baby to love and adore—
　　Who could ask for anything more?

ALL (*dancing happily*).
　　She's about to be a mother;
　　He's about to be a father;
　　　They're about to have a baby:
　　　　We can't bother
　　　　A budding young father!

WINTERGREEN. Mary, is it true? Am I to have a baby?

MARY. It's true, John, it's true!

WINTERGREEN. It's wonderful, it's wonderful—water! Water! (*He faints.*)

DIANA. It eez a fine countree—I am compromised and she has ze babee!

THROTTLEBOTTOM. Gentlemen, gentlemen—this country has never yet impeached an expectant father. What do you say?

SENATORS. Not guilty!

THROTTLEBOTTOM (*to the* CLERK). Check that!

FRENCH AMBASSADOR.
Sacre! I go to the telegraph office to cable my report:
This is American trickery of the most reprehensible sort!

DIANA. I was the most beautiful blossom—(*the* AMBASSADOR *takes her by the hand; leads her away*) —in all the Southland.

SENATOR FROM MASSACHUSETTS. Great work, Jack! You'll be reinstated in the hearts of the American people.

SENATOR JONES. You're doing your duty by posterity.

WINTERGREEN. Posterity? Why, posterity is just around the corner.

ALL.
Posterity is just around the corner!
(SENATORS *bring out tambourines.*)
Posterity is just around the corner!
It really doesn't pay to be a mourner.
Posterity is just around the corner!
Posterity is here—I don't mean maybe!
There's nothing guarantees it like a baby!
Posterity is here and will continue!
We really didn't know you had it in you!
Posterity
Is in its infancy!

WINTERGREEN.
I sing to ev'ry citizen and for'gner:
Posterity is just around the corner!
(THROTTLEBOTTOM, *with a bass drum, is leading a march around the room.*)
We'll soon be pulling plums, like Jackie Horner!
Posterity is just around the—

ALL.
Oomposterity, oomp-osterity, oompah, oompah, oomp-posterity.
Oomp-posterity, oomp-posterity, oompah, oompah oom-
Posterity is just around the corner!
Around the corner!
Curtain.

SCENE IV

A corridor in the White House.
Enter JENKINS *and* MISS BENSON.

JENKINS. It'll certainly be great to have a baby in the White House. I wonder when it'll be born.

MISS BENSON. Let's see—they were married March 4, weren't they?

JENKINS. That's right.

MISS BENSON (*counting on her fingers*). April, May, June, July, August, September, October, November, DECEMBER! It'll be born in December.

JENKINS. How do you know?

MISS BENSON. Well, it won't be born *before* December.

JENKINS. How do you know?

MISS BENSON. Oh, the President wouldn't do a thing like that. He'd never be re-elected.

JENKINS. You can't tell. Might be the very thing that would re-elect him.

MISS BENSON. It's certainly wonderful the way this has lined people up behind the President.

JENKINS. Yeah, but we don't know what France is going to do. She's still liable to make trouble.

MISS BENSON. My, you'd think a woman could have a baby without France butting in.

JENKINS. Well, fifty million Frenchmen— they've got to do something.

MISS BENSON. Let 'em do it in Paris. Why should they come over here and—

WINTERGREEN (*singing as he enters*). "Somebody's coming to our house; somebody's coming to stay—" Oh, hello.

JENKINS. Hi, Chief!

MISS BENSON. Good morning, Mr. President. And how is Mrs. Wintergreen this morning?

WINTERGREEN (*vaguely*). Who? Mrs. Wintergreen? (*Realizes that there is such a person.*) Oh, she's fine! Fine! Yes, sir! (*Tapping his own chest.*) Should have seen the breakfast I ate!

MISS BENSON. Tell me, Mr. President. Ah — (*hesitantly*) —when is the baby expected?

WINTERGREEN. Well, of course you can't tell about such things, but we think sometime in Novem—December. (*Another quick correction.*) December.

MISS BENSON (*with a look at* JENKINS). Oh, December.

WINTERGREEN. Yes, we sort of thought December would be a nice month. End the old year right and all that sort of thing. Have a cigar? Oh, pardon me, the baby isn't born yet.
(*Enter* FULTON.)

FULTON. Hello, Jack!

WINTERGREEN. Hello, there! Should have seen the breakfast I ate. (*To the* SECRETARIES.) See you later.

MISS BENSON (*to* JENKINS). I told you December.

JENKINS. Well, I'd still like to make a bet on it.
(*The* SECRETARIES *go.*)

FULTON. Well, Jack, how are you? And how's the wife?

WINTERGREEN. Fine, fine! Never felt better.

FULTON. Mighty smart girl, Mary. She certainly saved the day for us.

WINTERGREEN. *She* saved the day? I suppose I was just an innocent bystander?

FULTON. I don't mean that, but I thought it sort of came as a surprise to you.

WINTERGREEN. Surprise? Why, I planned the whole thing. I foresaw the situation months ago.

FULTON. Anyway, it settled France. They're still yelling, but there's nothing they can do about it. The American people are behind you to a man. How'd you ever get the idea, Jack?

WINTERGREEN. Why, it wasn't anything. Nothing at all. Anybody in my place would have done the same.

FULTON. Yes, sir, it'll be a wonderful thing to have a baby in the White House.

WINTERGREEN. You mean instead of a President?

FULTON. No, no, Jack—I mean it. I tell you, there's something about the patter of baby feet, trickling down the stairs. . . . (*Enter the* FRENCH AMBASSADOR.)

FRENCH AMBASSADOR. Gentlemen!

FULTON (*with a bow*). Monsieur!

FRENCH AMBASSADOR (*with an elaborate bow*). Monsieur President.

WINTERGREEN. You all alone?

FRENCH AMBASSADOR. But yes.

WINTERGREEN. Where are those six guys who used to march in ahead of you— (*his gesture carries out the idea of crossed bayonets, and even goes a bit further by bringing thumb and nose into close juxtaposition*) —you know.

FRENCH AMBASSADOR. They could not come today. They have dancing lesson.

WINTERGREEN. You look kind of naked without them.

FRENCH AMBASSADOR (*acknowledges this with a bow*). You will pardon this intrusion, Monsieur, but I have received another note from my country.

WINTERGREEN. That's all right. We've got a lot of notes from your country, and some of them were due ten years ago.

FRENCH AMBASSADOR. But this is not a promise to pay—this is serious.

WINTERGREEN. Shoot!

FRENCH AMBASSADOR (*bows*). Monsieur, I have good news for you. France consents to your having the child.

FULTON. Ah!

WINTERGREEN. France consents?

FRENCH AMBASSADOR. Freely.

WINTERGREEN. Why, that's wonderful of her. Good old France! Do you mind if I tell my wife, so she can go ahead? (AMBASSADOR *bows*.) You've no idea how this will please her. Won't take me a minute—I'll be right back.

FRENCH AMBASSADOR. But one moment, Monsieur. (WINTERGREEN *pauses*.) France consents, but on one condition.

WINTERGREEN. Yeah?

FRENCH AMBASSADOR. France must have the baby!

FULTON *and* WINTERGREEN. WHAT?

FRENCH AMBASSADOR. Do not be hasty, Monsieur. You must understand the desperate situation of my country. For fifty years the birth rate of France has been declining, declining, declining.

WINTERGREEN. What's that got to do with me?

FRENCH AMBASSADOR. You must see, Monsieur. If you had married Mlle. Devereaux, as you have promise, the baby she is French. But now you have taken away from France one baby, and she demand replacement.

WINTERGREEN. Never!

FULTON. I should say not!

FRENCH AMBASSADOR. It is the old law, Monsieur; an eye for an eye, a tooth for a tooth, and a baby for a baby.

WINTERGREEN. You'll get no tooth from my baby!

FRENCH AMBASSADOR. The tooth, the whole tooth, and nothing but the tooth!

WINTERGREEN. Not one tooth!

FRENCH AMBASSADOR. That is your final word?

WINTERGREEN. It is! Good day, Monsieur!

FRENCH AMBASSADOR. Good day! (*Clicks his heels; salutes; turns and starts out.*) Lafayette, we are coming! (*Goes.*)

FULTON. What do you think France'll do?

WINTERGREEN. What's the worst she can do? Sue us for what she owes us?

FULTON. But that other thing! France is awful touchy about her birth rate!

WINTERGREEN. What are you worrying about? I fixed *this* up, didn't I?

FULTON. What?

WINTERGREEN. Well, Mary's going to have a baby, isn't she?

FULTON. Yes!

WINTERGREEN. Well! Next year I make a tour of France! Lafayette! (*He salutes.*)

Curtain.

SCENE V

The Yellow Room of the White House. And is it yellow? But it is also very beautiful—and endless. It extends as far as the eye can reach—a vista of hallway, and polished floor, and chandeliers, and ladies in evening clothes, and men in magnificent uniforms. White-wigged FLUNKIES *move in and out of the assemblage.*

At the rise of the curtain an endless line of diplomats is presenting the WINTERGREENS *with an endless line of baby carriages. The* FLUNKIES *bellow the names as they accept the carriages—"Compliments of Ecuador," "Compliments of Bolivia," "Compliments of Spain," "Compliments of Lithuania." And then, for finale, an exceedingly small baby carriage. You've guessed it—"Compliments of Scotland."*

There is a burst of music.

ALL.
Oh, trumpeter, trumpeter, blow your golden horn!
Oh, trumpeter, trumpeter, blow your golden horn!
A White House baby will very soon be born,
A White House baby will very soon be born!
    Blow your horn!
With a hey, nonny nonny, and a ha cha cha!
With a hey, nonny nonny, and a ha cha cha!
There's something glorious happening today
For all the citizens of the U. S. A.
A White House baby will very soon be born!
Oh, trumpeter, blow your horn,
Oh, trumpeter, blow your horn,
Oh, trumpeter, blow your horn,
Your golden horn, your golden horn!
(*The* DOCTOR *enters.*)
Oh, doctor, doctor, what's the news, we pray?
We've waited for your bulletin all day.

DOCTOR.
The baby of the President and frau
Will be here almost any minute now.

ALL.
With a hey, nonny nonny, and a ha cha cha!
With a hey, nonny nonny, and a ha cha cha!

Oh, doctor, here is the one thing we must know,
We're all of us anxious and we've got to know:
The baby, is it to be a girl or boy?
    A baby girl or boy?
    A nation's pride and joy!
We must know whether it's a girl or boy—
    A girl or boy?

DOCTOR.
    On that matter no one budges,
    For all cases of the sort
    Are decided by the judges
    Of the *Supreme* Court.

FLUNKIES. The *Supreme* Court!
(*Enter the* SUPREME COURT.)

JUDGES. We're the one, two, three, four, five, six, seven, eight, nine Supreme Court Judges.

ALL.
With a hey, nonny nonny, and a ha cha cha!
With a hey, nonny nonny, and a ha cha cha!
About the baby—will it be
A boy or girl—a he or she?

JUDGES.
    On that matter no one budges
    For all cases of the sort
    Are decided by the judges
    Of the *Supreme* Court.

FLUNKIES. The Secretary of Agriculture!
(*Enter* LIPPMAN.)

LIPPMAN.
> The farmers in the dell,
> The farmers in the dell,
> They all keep a-asking me:
> A boy or a gel?

FLUNKIES. The Secretary of the Navy!
(*Enter* GILHOOLEY.)

GILHOOLEY.
> All the sailors in the Navy
> Of these great United States,
> Do not eat their bowls of gravy,
> Nor the captains nor the mates.
> They refuse to jib an anchor,
> Strike a boom or heave a sail,
> Till you've satisfied their hanker:
> Is it female or a male?

FLUNKIES. Senator Carver Jones!
(*Enter* JONES.)

JONES.
> Out on the prairie,
> The cowboys all keep asking of me:
> He or a she—
> She or a he?
> Out on the prairie,
> For baby boy or girl they are keen,
> But they want nothing in between.

FLUNKIES. Senator Robert E. Lyons!
(*Enter* LYONS.)

LYONS.
> Way down upon the Swanee River
> Folks are filled with joy,
> But they want to know what will the stork
>   deliver?
> Will it be a girl or boy?

ALL.
> There's something glorious happening to-
>   day;
> A baby will be born,
> A baby will be born.
> Oh, trumpeter, trumpeter, blow your gold-
>   en horn!
(*Enter* WINTERGREEN, *followed by* FULTON *and* JENKINS.)

FULTON. Take it easy, Jack! Nothing can happen to her.

WINTERGREEN. I know, but at a time like this—Mary in there alone— (*A chorus of greeting from all.*) Oh! Hello! God, I'm nervous! Anybody got a drink? (*Every man brings out a flask.*) Thanks. When I think of Mary in there alone— (*Takes a drink.*) Well, I guess it's not going to be so hard for her.

GILHOOLEY. How is Mary?

WINTERGREEN. Finest little woman in the world! When I think of what she's got to —anybody got a drink? (*The flasks come out again. He takes* GILHOOLEY's, *although he still has* FULTON's *in his hand.*) Well, I guess I'd better not mix them.

MISS BENSON. Oh, Mr. Wintergreen!

WINTERGREEN (*wheeling*). Any news?

MISS BENSON. The baby will be here at any moment.
(*An excited buzz from the crowd.*)

WINTERGREEN. Tell 'em I'm ready. (MISS BENSON *goes.*) My God! You hear that? What do I do now? Anybody got a drink?

CHIEF JUSTICE. Gentlemen, duty calls. The baby is now being born. We must decide the sex.

WINTERGREEN. *You* decide?

CHIEF JUSTICE. We do, sir.

JUDGES.
> On that matter no one budges,
>   For all cases of the sort
> Are decided by the judges
>   Of the Supreme Court!
(*They retire.*)

WINTERGREEN. I shouldn't be drinking at a time like this. (*To* JENKINS *and the* COMMITTEE.) Here! Take it away! (JENKINS *reaches for the flask.* WINTERGREEN *pulls away.*) Oh, no, you don't. My wife's the finest little woman in the world! And I can lick anybody that says she ain't!

FLUNKIES (*announcing*). The French Ambassador!

WINTERGREEN. Bring him in!

FRENCH AMBASSADOR. Your Excellency! I have another message from France!

WINTERGREEN. Not a nickel!

FRENCH AMBASSADOR. Will you surrender the baby?

WINTERGREEN. Never! Give my baby to France and have it eat snails and get ptomaine poisoning! Never!

FRENCH AMBASSADOR. Then, sir, I am instructed to say that with the birth of the child France severs diplomatic relations!

WINTERGREEN. Hurray!

FRENCH AMBASSADOR. And that is not all, sir. I wish furthermore to report—
(*Two* FLUNKIES *enter and blow a fanfare on their trumpets. The* SUPREME COURT *re-enters.*)

JUDGES. Whereas—

CHIEF JUSTICE. A child has been born to the President of the United States and his consort—

JUDGES. Whereas—

CHIEF JUSTICE. The Supreme Court of the United States has been called upon to determine the sex of the aforesaid infant—

JUDGES. Whereas—

CHIEF JUSTICE. By a strict party vote it has been decided that—

JUDGES. It's a boy!
(*The* COMMITTEE *and* GUESTS *press around* WINTERGREEN *to congratulate him.*)

WINTERGREEN. A boy! That makes me a father! Thank you! Thank you very much! I certainly am a lucky man! Boy, the cigars! Smoke up, everybody! Here you are, ladies and gentlemen! Have a cigar, Frenchy!

FRENCH AMBASSADOR. My thanks, Monsieur. On behalf of France permit me to offer my felicitations.

WINTERGREEN. Attaboy! Let bygones be bygones! Have another cigar!

FRENCH AMBASSADOR. And permit me also to inform you that France hereby severs diplomatic relations. (*He reaches for the cigar.*)

WINTERGREEN (*closes the humidor with a bang*). Then the hell with you!

FRENCH AMBASSADOR. You understand what this means, Monsieur?

WINTERGREEN. I do! (*Takes back the first cigar.*) It means no smoke!

FRENCH AMBASSADOR. Precisely. And where there is no smoke there is fire. I am instructed to say, Monsieur, that this means that the French government will—
(*The* FLUNKIES *re-enter. Another fanfare. The* JUSTICES *re-enter.*)

JUDGES. Whereas—

CHIEF JUSTICE. A child has been born to the President of the United States and his consort—

WINTERGREEN. Hey! We had that.

CHIEF JUSTICE. But you are having it again, sir. This one is a girl!
(*ALL crowd around* WINTERGREEN *to congratulate him again.*)

WINTERGREEN. A girl! That makes me a father *and* a mother. Twins! That's a little more than I counted on!

JENKINS. Cigars, sir?

WINTERGREEN. No. Cigarettes this time! A boy *and* a girl! Well!

FRENCH AMBASSADOR (*sings*).
    Oh, I can stand no more,
    My temper's getting gingery;
    This certainly will lead to war!
    This insult added to injury!

You realize what you have done, sir? You have taken away from France not one baby, but two!

WINTERGREEN. That's it! Blame me for everything!

FRENCH AMBASSADOR. What you have done to Mlle. Devereaux! That poor little girl! Where is she? What is she doing?
(*In the distance* DIANA *is heard singing "I was the most beautiful blossom."*)

WINTERGREEN. She's still singing. (DIANA *enters.*) You like that song, don't you?

FRENCH AMBASSADOR. My poor motherless one! My sweet blossom of the Southland!

FLUNKIES (*announcing*). The Vice-President of the United States!

THROTTLEBOTTOM (*knitting a baby's sweater*). Is the baby born yet? I just got this finished!

WINTERGREEN. Only one? Where's the other one?

THROTTLEBOTTOM (*pulls out second sweater*). I thought something like that might happen!

FRENCH AMBASSADOR. Once and for all, Monsieur, what are you going to do? What are you going to do about Mlle. Devereaux and her babies?

WINTERGREEN. Well, she can have her own babies.

DIANA. But I am not married, Monsieur.

WINTERGREEN. What's that got to do with it?

FRENCH AMBASSADOR. Everything. The family has been illegitimate long enough.

WINTERGREEN. Then let her get married! .

FRENCH AMBASSADOR. Exactly! But it was agreed, Monsieur, that she was to marry the President of the United States.

WINTERGREEN. But she can't have me! I'm married!

FRENCH AMBASSADOR. Then it is war, sir! When the President of the United States fails to fulfil his duty—

WINTERGREEN. That's it! I've got it!

ALL. Got what?

WINTERGREEN. It's in the Constitution! When the President of theUnited States is unable to fulfil his duties, his obligations are assumed by—

THROTTLEBOTTOM. The vice-president! I get her!

CHIEF JUSTICE. Article Twelve!

FRENCH AMBASSADOR. Monsieur, you are a genius!

THROTTLEBOTTOM (*to* WINTERGREEN). I could throw my arms right around your neck!

WINTERGREEN. Oh, no, you don't! Hers! (*The* TRUMPETERS *re-enter. Another fanfare.*)

WINTERGREEN. Oh, my God!

CHIEF JUSTICE. It's all right. The boys are merely practicing.
(*There is a great burst of music, and from the more intimate quarters of the White House there comes into the room a great canopied bed, hung with gold, and silver, and bald-headed eagles. In it is* MARY TURNER WINTERGREEN, *a twin on each arm.* WINTERGREEN *advances to greet her; the* CROWD *bursts into song. And of all the songs in the world, you'd never guess what they pick out. It's "Of Thee I Sing, Baby."*)

The Curtain Falls.

Both Your Houses

BY MAXWELL ANDERSON

MAXWELL ANDERSON

Maxwell Anderson was born in Atlantic, Pennsylvania, in 1888. In 1911 he received his A.B. from the University of North Dakota, in 1914 his M.A. from Stanford University. Following his graduation he served on the faculties of Whittier College in Southern California, Leland Stanford University, and the University of North Dakota. In 1911 he married Margaret Haskett. He worked successively on the staffs of the *Grand Forks* (North Dakota) *Herald, San Francisco Chronicle, San Francisco Bulletin, New Republic, New York Evening Globe,* and *New York Morning World.* While on the latter newspaper he met Laurence Stallings, with whom he collaborated on the popular *What Price Glory?*

"The spirit of the play is idealistic," the Pulitzer Prize Committee said of *Both Your Houses;* "it breathes a fine indignation, but it is so conducted that legitimate entertainment values are not lost, and the characters speak and act with convincing naturalness."

Produced by the Theatre Guild at the Royale Theatre, New York, March 6, 1933, *Both Your Houses* received the Pulitzer award for 1932-1933.

CHARACTERS

MARJORIE GRAY

BUS

EDDIE WISTER

SOLOMON FITZMAURICE

MARK

SIMEON GRAY

LEVERING

MERTON

DELL

SNEDEN

MISS McMURTRY

WINGBLATT

PEEBLES

FARNUM

ALAN McCLEAN

EBNER

ACTION AND SCENE

The play takes place in the House Office Building, Washington, D. C.

ACT ONE

SCENE I: The office of the Chairman of the Appropriations Committee. A morning in early spring.

SCENE II: The Committee Room. The action of this scene begins three minutes before the close of Scene I.

ACT TWO

SCENE I: The office of the Chairman of the Appropriations Committee. Late afternoon. Three days later.

SCENE II: The Committee Room. One hour later.

ACT THREE

SCENE I: The Committee Room. Evening. Three days later.

SCENE II: The same. Three hours later.

BOTH YOUR HOUSES

ACT ONE

SCENE I

SCENE: *The Reception Room in the offices of the Chairman of the Appropriations Committee in the House Office Building, Washington, D. C. The entrance from the hall is at the rear. A window and the door of the Chairman's private office on the right. To the left is the door to the Appropriations Committee room. A stenographer's desk with a typewriter, telephone and a small letter file is placed on the right, and the filing case and a safe on the left.*

MARJORIE GRAY, *secretary to and daughter of the Chairman, is at the telephone.* GRETA NILLSON, *better known as* BUS, *enters with coat and hat on.*

MARJORIE. Hello—Mr. Gray's office! Oh, hello, Alan. Where are you? The Dahl Agency? What are you doing there? But I thought you were going to be here for the meeting this morning.—You what?— You want to see Dad? Well, you can't unless you get here before they go into session and they're due right now.—Then you'd better hurry right over or you'll miss him!

BUS. Morning, Marjorie.

MARJORIE. Well, Bussy—aren't you working today?

BUS. No, dearest—I'm fired.

MARJORIE. What? What do you mean?

BUS. It was a surprise to me, too. I sat right down hard on my fifty yard line.

MARJORIE. Eddie fired you? By telephone?

BUS. By proxy. Oh, he's back from New York, but I haven't seen him.

MARJORIE. Can I do anything, do you suppose?

BUS. At the moment I don't think your dad's whole committee could. And I liked that job—and I needed it.

MARJORIE. But what's supposed to be the explanation?

BUS. It's dirty! You remember last session when Eddie was practically keeping house with the steel lobby—

MARJORIE. I remember Dad raising the devil about it—

BUS. Remember the secretary old man Sprague brought down with him—the one that franked out that speech of Eddie's on naval parity and the Japanese menace? She came in here one day—tall, blond, never been in Washington before—

MARJORIE. Oh yes—

BUS. Well, I think that's the baby.

MARJORIE. You don't mean the steel company's moving right into the House Office Building?

BUS. Certainly—To help Mr. Wister with his home work. What else was he doing in New York? Why didn't he get back here yesterday?

MARJORIE. That's what dad wants to know.

BUS. Of course, illicit passion may have raised its pretty tousled head.

MARJORIE. Better to be swallowed by passion than by the Appalachian Steel Company. In any case you won't have trouble getting a job, Bus.

BUS. Trouble enough if I wind up with one of these new Congressmen, spending all my time cleaning up after him, and never knowing when he'll make a mess on the floor of the House.

MARJORIE. Of course the new ones don't pay quite so much—

BUS. The worst of them is they've mostly never been away from home before, and all they know about having a secretary is what they've learned from the moving pictures. They try holding you on their laps the first day and assault the second.

MARJORIE. You're romancing, Bus.

BUS. Well—you've always worked for your father, so you wouldn't know.

MARJORIE. No, I suppose not.

BUS. Not that I hold it too much against them. I'm not exactly at an age to choose my pleasures—and assault at first sight isn't always to be despised—

MARJORIE. Bus, you're a devil—

BUS. Do you know how many specimens I've had under my personal microscope? Nine. Two fired me for honesty, I fired five for dishonesty—and the other two met natural deaths by electorate. Oh wouldn't I like to get even with one or two of those corporation statesmen! Just give me half a chance, and I'm just good and sure I would.—By the way, how's your Nevada school teacher working out?

MARJORIE. Alan? He's a little out of hand! I'm going to have to give him lessons in how to juggle dynamite.

BUS. Is that all? I thought I detected adoration in his eyes!

MARJORIE. I wouldn't really mind! Adoration is rare these days—and a bit embarrassing. However—

BUS. However!

MARJORIE. I'll manage.

BUS. Of course you will.
(EDDIE WISTER *enters, a well-dressed man of thirty-eight, with a Racquet Club manner.*)

EDDIE. Hello! Sorry you got here first, Bussy. Good morning, Marjorie. (MARJORIE *waves her hand.*) What did Miss Corey tell you?

BUS. Well, I got the impression, I don't know why—that I'd lost my job.

EDDIE. Why? There's plenty of work for both of you—

BUS. In Washington, maybe—

EDDIE. Don't be sour, Bus. Do you really want to know why I've taken her on?

MARJORIE. There seem to be two schools of thought.

EDDIE. Well, it's for the same reason I wasn't here yesterday. Wasn't that pretty obvious?

MARJORIE. Not at all. The committee sat here from two to five, waiting for you, and blasting your hide.

EDDIE (*to* BUS). No kidding! Didn't you tell them I was detained?

BUS. I did. It was my last official act.

MARJORIE. Bussy didn't know you were looking for a new secretary!

EDDIE. Well, I wasn't—but I couldn't help myself. She's been the secretary of an old friend of mine.

BUS. Sure—Col. Sprague—of Appalachian Steel.

EDDIE. How did you know that?

BUS. She was down here with him last spring.

EDDIE. Look here, Bus—I'm going to need you, you know. Miss Corey doesn't know the district—nor the routine either—you'll certainly have to finish the work on the bill—

BUS. She's to be in charge of the office, isn't she?

EDDIE. I suppose so, unfortunately—

BUS. Then I'm sorry, but you'll have to excuse me. I'll take the notes in the committee, and then I'm through.
(SOLOMON FITZMAURICE *enters.*)

SOL. More wenches!

MARJORIE. Good morning, Sol!

SOL. Hell-on-fire! You can't turn a corner without skirts blowing in your eye! By God, when I come up to this town it was a man's town, and a statesman could arrive at his office when he felt damn good and like it, without a squad of females waiting for him with their legs crossed and pads open on their knees, yawning for dictation!

MARJORIE. Had a bad night, Sol?

SOL. In the old days, when government was government, a couple of men could sit down over a jug of whiskey and decide something—(*He has opened the lower drawer of the filing case, extracted a jug, and replaced it with another from his satchel. The empty jug he now drops in the waste basket.*)

MARJORIE. Sol—you can't put that there!

SOL. I always have.

MARJORIE. Well, from now on it's out. The janitor's complained about it, and threatened to report it—leave it in your own waste-basket, darling.

SOL. And now a gentleman can't have his liquor because a janitor complains!

EDDIE. It's only the empty ones they complain about.

SOL. Why, the lousy reds, I'll show 'em— (*He picks up the empty jug, walks with it to the window, and drops it out.*)

MARJORIE. Sol, you pig! It'll break on the coping!

SOL. Let 'em sweep it up, the Soviets! You got to bear with an old man, Clover. The changes of this world are too much for him, and he's growing testy and short-tempered.

MARJORIE. Drunk and delirious, I'd say.

SOL (*pourng a drink into a paper cup*). On my soul, I haven't touched liquor since befor breakfast.
(*There is a knock at the door and* MARK *enters with a basket piled high with letters.*)

BUS. Somebody's hearing from the folks back home!

MARJORIE. Now Mark—you're not bringing all that in here?

MARK (*looking at a letter*). Congressman Gray—Yes, ma'am.

MARJORIE (*to* BUS). That's another night's work!

MARK. Ain't no fun for me either, Miss Marjorie.

MARJORIE. Take 'em inside, Mark.

MARK. O. K. What good is all this—that's what I want to know?

SOL. What good is it? Mark, a question like that spoken at the right time might blow this government right over, right over— don't you know that?

MARK. Tell you the truth—I don't even care. If it went over—maybe I'd be on the up-side. (*He goes into the inner office.*)

EDDIE. Call the janitor and sweep 'em out.

MARJORIE. We're not from a corporation district—we have to be pleasant to the constituents. Will you help me, Bus?

BUS. Well, come on—(*She moves toward inner office.*) My God, and they say the art of letter-writing is dead—(*She goes in.*)

MARJORIE. It is. (*She follows* BUS *out.*)

SOL. Have a little one? You're going to need it.

EDDIE. Is something hanging over me, Solomon?

SOL. When Simeon gets through with you you're going to be so low you can look up and see the depression all around you.

EDDIE. What's troubling the honorable Chairman?

SOL. Boy—(*The door opens and* GRAY *and* LEVERING *enter from the hall.*)

GRAY. Oh, there you are!

EDDIE. Morning, Simeon. Now wait—I know I'm in bad, but—

GRAY. You're a help, aren't you? One day in the term I need you here—and you choose that day to climb the Statue of Liberty.

EDDIE. No truth in it, Simeon. Merely had to go to New York. It was a crisis.

GRAY. In steel?

LEVERING. I noticed it dropped seven points!

EDDIE. Well, that may have had something to do with it.

GRAY. Well, we're a week late with this bill already, and I came back yesterday for nothing else but to get it set.

EDDIE. We'll get it set today, won't we?

GRAY. Did you ever hear of a bill being put in shape in one day with a new member sitting there and asking questions?

SOL. Is that young cub coming in with the caucus today?
(MARJORIE *enters from the inner office.*)

LEVERING. That's just what I want to talk to you about, boys. He's been dodging me for a week now.

SOL. Dodges the party whip, does he? Well, that shows intelligence.

GRAY. Well, why—

LEVERING. That's what I'd like to know.

SOL. We're going to need a solid caucus to push this thing through the committee. You'd better get hold of him, Disraeli.

LEVERING. I've been trying to, but I can't find him.

GRAY. Don't tell me we've got another problem on our hands. The less they know the more hell they raise.

MARJORIE. Mr. McClean was just on the phone. He's on his way over here now.

GRAY. Good. You'd better see him, Dizzy, and straighten him out.

LEVERING. Isn't McClean your man, Sime? Wasn't it you brought his name up when we had that deadlock in the committee?

GRAY. I never saw him in my life, but as the case was presented to me, it looked like a set-up. He was from the district of the dam, he'd have to vote for it, and he wouldn't dare add any more to it.

SOL. What did you say his name was? Mc-Clean?

GRAY. Yes, Alan McClean.

EDDIE. The sooner we get him in and talk to him the better.

SOL. McClean. There's a McClean owns a newspaper in Nevada—used to sow a lot of headaches around here. Any relation?

GRAY. I don't know.

MARJORIE. Yes. This is his son.

SOL. If he's anything like the old man, you'd better keep him under your cold speculative eye, Dizzy.

EDDIE. Oh, we're watching him! Didn't I tell you Merton is his secretary? Well, I have an understanding with Merton.

GRAY. Well, get Merton in here and let's hear what he has to say.
(MARK *enters from the private office, crosses to the hall door and goes out.*)

EDDIE. O. K. Get me Merton. Personally I think he's harmless. He doesn't know what it's all about.

SOL. Maybe.
(MARJORIE *goes into the inner office.*)

EDDIE. Merton?—Wister. Come into Mr. Gray's office, will you?

SOL. About that little item of mine, Simeon. Are we going to be able to get that in?

GRAY. No, we aren't.

SOL. Give out something, Simeon! They've got to finish that dam, no matter what its name is. Everybody in Washington has tacked something onto the bill except yours truly—and I'm the one man that deserves it.

GRAY. Well, next time try to tack on something smaller than the Atlantic Fleet, and perhaps you'll get it.

EDDIE. What does he want this time?

GRAY. He wants the Atlantic Fleet to spend its vacation at that real estate development of his. How's it going to read in the newspapers—"The Atlantic Fleet is anchored for the summer at Rocky Point, Long Island, to boom Representative Fitzmaurice's summer resort and chain of speakeasies!"

SOL. The Atlantic Fleet's got to spend its summer somewhere, hasn't it? It might just as well be at Rocky Point as at Hampton Roads, and they'd have a damn sight better time, too. Even the navy likes good liquor, and the girls are a hell of a lot fresher on Long Island than down there at the naval base where the gobs have been chasing them since 1812. We owe something to our navy, Simeon; let 'em ashore once in a while in a neighborhood where they won't need prophylactics.

GRAY. Well, it carries two hundred thousand extra, and it sounds fishy, and we can't do it.

SOL. Fishy! My God, a little honest smell of fish on that bill would hang over it like an odor of sanctity! It's loaded down with post offices and subsidies and river and harbor dredging and insane asylums and smaller miscellaneous graft till it stinks clear out on the Pacific! That Ohio gang of Harding's was a perfume compared to this!

GRAY. You won't get it by arguing.

SOL. I don't know anything else you've balked at. The bill started out as a forty million dollar appropriation to finish that goddamn dam which was supposed to cost four hundred million over all—

GRAY. You're telling me!

SOL. And which has already come to seven hundred and ninety on account of the inside gouging you stood for! Why, damn it, Simeon, you've let 'em pile odds and ends of boodle onto this last forty million until you've run it up to two hundred and seventy-five—and still going strong! There isn't a lobby in Washington that hasn't got a section all to itself! Dell's in it, Eddie's in it—

EDDIE. I am like hell—

SOL. Well, you will be if I know you! Everybody has a cut in it except old Sol

himself, who did all the work. I'm the contact man for the whole kit and caboodle in this dirty House—I spend my days soft-soaping the middle-westerners and my nights drinking with the Southern colonels and my mornings eating apple pie with leather-bellies from New England —and what do I get? A rain-check—come back tomorrow!

GRAY. Too bad about you, Sol!

SOL. I'm getting to be an old man, Sime— we've worked together a long time, and I don't ask much. All I need's a jug of liquor every day and a lot of hard work. But I've got to make a little to retire on. Why, goddamn it, I haven't even paid last year's income tax yet.

GRAY. Save the goddamns for the radio. Listen, Sol, a lot of that junk's coming out, and coming out today. You've got to help me. They've got it loaded down till the old man'll have to veto his own measure. Anyway, we're not going to be caught short in front of any new member—

(MERTON, *a sharp-faced young man, enters without preliminaries.*)

MERTON. Morning—

GRAY.—and you can lay that to Eddie and his New York crisis.

EDDIE. Hello, Merton. Come in and tell us what you know about McClean. Mr. Levering is worried about him.

MERTON. Oh, I wouldn't be, sir. He's a nice fellow.

LEVERING. No doubt, but what's his history?

MERTON. Tell you that in a nut-shell. He was a teacher in an agricultural college in Nevada. Kicked up a row over the misappropriation of endowment funds—hell of a stink—got himself fired. His father made an issue of it in his paper—and the upshot was, elected to Congress. Tell me he ran a pretty smart campaign, too. But he wouldn't have been elected if a lot of contractors hadn't got back of him and put up the funds.

GRAY. Oh, he's in with the contractors?

MERTON. No, he isn't. He's straight. It never enters that head not to be straight. But the farmers out there are waiting for water, and he promised them he'd work to get the Nevada dam finished. He'll be for the bill. You needn't worry about that.

EDDIE. Good.

GRAY. What's he like?

MERTON. Serious. Wears mail-order clothes. Reads Thomas Jefferson. He came down to Washington three months ago, and he's spent all his time in the Congressional Library.

LEVERING. But that doesn't answer my question, Mr. Merton. What's he doing that is so important that he can't make an appointment with me?

MERTON. That's the funny thing about it. You won't believe this. He's been working day and night having his own election investigated. (*A pause.*)

SOL. Say that again.

MERTON. That's true. He's having his own election investigated.

SOL. Now for the love of—How?

MERTON. He's having a detective agency look it up.

SOL. At his own expense?

MERTON. At his own expense.

SOL. Comes from Nevada, intellectual, reads Jefferson, having his own election investigated. Simeon, call your meeting to order and for God's sake muzzle him. This is William Jennings Bryan! (*He goes into the committee room.*)

MERTON. Leave him to me, Mr. Gray. I'll steer him right.

EDDIE. Are you staying right with him, Merton?

MERTON. I follow him—and he believes everything I tell him. Just leave him to me.

LEVERING. Is he in his office now?

MERTON. Not yet, sir.

LEVERING. Well, when he comes in, will you tell him again and very definitely that I want to see him at once in my office?

MERTON. Yes, sir. (*They go out.*)

GRAY. Marjorie, will you come with me. (MARJORIE *and* GRAY *start toward the inner office.* DELL, SNEDEN *and* MISS MCMURTRY *enter the hall.*) Go right in, everybody—be with you in a minute. (*He and* MARJORIE *go into the office.*)

DELL. So you got here at last!

SNEDEN. We were meeting in Washington, you know—not in New York.

EDDIE. I'm damned sorry, boys—

DELL. Well, you're only a day late—

MCMURTRY. We waited all afternoon, Mr. Wister. I must say—

EDDIE. I'm awfully sorry, Miss McMurtry, you must believe me—

MCMURTRY. I suppose I'll have to—

DELL. After all, what's twenty-four hours? (GRAY *reenters from the office.*)

SNEDEN. I could have shot eighteen holes yesterday.

EDDIE. You couldn't walk eighteen holes— (*They all go into the committee room.* WINGBLATT, PEEBLES *and* FARNUM *enter from the hall.*)

WINGBLATT. Well, why shouldn't Nevada get it?

FARNUM. Now, wait a minute! You Easterners treat California like a foreign country! If they let those Fresno banks fail, the whole Imperial Valley'll fail—California'll go straight to hell and the moving pictures along with it—

WINGBLATT. That's a good idea too. (BUS *enters from the inner office.*)

PEEBLES. The whole South went to hell after the Civil War, and nobody seemed to care much—We've been unemployed since 1865 and we get along, don't we?

BUS. Go right in, gentlemen, the meeting's beginning.

WINGBLATT. You're a complaining man, Peebles. I don't know what to do about you! (*The men pass into the committee room.* ALAN MCCLEAN *enters from the hall.*)

BUS. Good morning, Mr. McClean.

ALAN. Good morning, Miss Nillson.

BUS. Looking for someone? She's in there.

ALAN. Thanks. I hope things haven't started yet.

BUS. Oh, the hyenas are in conference. I've already missed words of wisdom. (BUS *goes into the committee room.* MARJORIE *comes out of the inner office.*)

MARJORIE. Hello, Alan. Do you know people are looking for you?

ALAN. Who?

MARJORIE. Levering, for one.

ALAN. Oh, he's been looking for me for days. Am I too late to see your father?

MARJORIE. I'm afraid so. The committee's in session. You should have been here an hour ago.

ALAN. I did my best. I got some information yesterday which had to be verified, and it took time—it took all night.

MARJORIE. And that's why I haven't seen you—

ALAN. Yes. It's something I'm not quite ready to talk about yet.

MARJORIE. Not even with me?

ALAN. Not even with you.

MARJORIE. Well, you are late, but it can't be helped now. You'll have to walk in and sit down and tell them who you are.

ALAN. I think I'd better meet your father first and get started regularly. I'm not at all sure I know how to deal with these facts I've gathered. That's why I tried to see him yesterday.

MARJORIE. He simply couldn't manage it, Alan. He'd just got back and didn't have a free moment. Most of this bill was framed while he was ill and away, and it was a day's work checking up on it.

ALAN. Then—there might be some clauses he hasn't had time to look into?

MARJORIE. Oh, that's possible—there are an awful lot of clauses.

ALAN. I see. I'd better see him before I sit on the committee.

MARJORIE. You mean—you mean you aren't going in today?

ALAN. No, I don't think so.

MARJORIE. Merton's been advising you, hasn't he? They know about you, Alan. And if some of them didn't have a lot of faith in you why would you be here at all?

ALAN. I wouldn't be too sure that's the reason. They may have wanted somebody that looked easy and didn't know too much.

MARJORIE. Do you think you're like that?

ALAN. I probably don't know how to be very dangerous, even if I do know more than they think I do. And appointments are made that way sometimes, aren't they?

MARJORIE. All the time. I played among the pork barrels as a child! That's what one learns. In fact, you're quite right. Yours was made that way.

ALAN. Well, I don't like it—really Marjorie.

MARJORIE. Dad will take you right under his wing, Alan, and help you any way he can. He's like that.

ALAN. I know—I know. I've been counting on him.
(LEVERING *enters from the hall.*)

LEVERING. Ah, there you are, McClean. I've been looking for you!

ALAN. How are you, Mr. Levering?

LEVERING. Just a little perturbed, if you don't mind my saying so. I wanted to have a chat with you before you took up your duties on the committee.

ALAN. Oh, I'm sorry.

LEVERING (*to* MARJORIE). My dear—could Mr. McClean and I have a word in private anywhere?

MARJORIE (*looking at her notes*). Oh, I have some calls to make—I don't think you'll be interrupted here. (*She goes into the inner office.*)

LEVERING. Thank you, my dear—we won't be a minute. Well, young man, no doubt you've been amusing yourself?

ALAN. I've been studying a little—

LEVERING. Hard at your books as usual? Didn't you miss an appointment with the committee yesterday?

ALAN. Yes, I did.

LEVERING. Now I don't know what your ideas are, my boy, but a good party man doesn't make important decisions, as a rule, without consulting his party leaders—

ALAN. I'm not really sure I am a good party man, Mr. Levering.

LEVERING. What? You were elected on a reform ticket, I know. But you don't want to count as one of these sons of the wild jackass, do you?

ALAN. I don't especially like the name—no.

LEVERING. If you want to get anything done you have to cooperate.

ALAN. I know that.

LEVERING. But you don't cooperate, McClean. We knew you were a sensible, reliable young man, and we put you on the Appropriations Committee for that reason. I had one talk with you and then you disappeared. I haven't seen you. You've either avoided me, or I've had unbelievable luck with the telephone service. Now what's the matter?

ALAN. I guess I've just been uncertain of a number of things—and I didn't want to try to talk about them till I felt sure—

LEVERING. That's a good answer. I can see your point of view. But if you're puzzled, just put your questions to me. Now the caucus this morning is considering the deficiency bill for the Nevada dam. You're naturally for that project; it'll make a nice start for you.

ALAN. Well, I don't know—

LEVERING. You don't know what?

ALAN. I've discovered that some of the people who backed me for office were the contractors who have handled the work on the whole project.

LEVERING. Can you be sure of that?

ALAN. Oh, yes. I've looked it up and they don't really need forty millions to finish it. There's a lot of water in this business besides what's to be used for irrigation.

LEVERING. If you're sure of that, we ought to go over it. We certainly should. And I want to do it.

ALAN. But I didn't want to go over it with anyone, Mr. Levering. And I felt almost certain that if I went over it with you, it would lead to a compromise.

LEVERING. You amaze me, McClean. There could be no question of compromise in such a case. This comes of your working alone and taking no advice.

ALAN. It puts me in a sort of hyphenated position, because I realize I owe it to the people who elected me to put the dam through. But I also ran on an economy platform, and that concerns the whole country. I've been thinking about it a good deal and the two things just don't go together. But I guess I'll just have to decide that for myself.

LEVERING. The dam must go through, of course. (*The telephone bell rings.*)

ALAN. But why must there be so many expensive and unnecessary things attached to it?

LEVERING. You wouldn't break your word to the people? That would be flatly dishonest.

ALAN. But isn't the whole affair dishonest? (MARJORIE *enters and goes to the phone.*)

MARJORIE. Hello—Yes.

LEVERING. Now, look here—

MARJORIE. I'm sorry—he's in conference.

LEVERING. We must go over your information in detail. Suppose you come with me now?

ALAN. I'm sorry but there's another matter I must take care of first.

LEVERING. How long will it take?

ALAN. About half an hour, I think.

LEVERING. Very well, I'll expect you in my office in half an hour. (*He goes out.*)

MARJORIE. Anything unpleasant?

ALAN. He seemed to find it so.

MARJORIE. What led up to it?

ALAN. I told him I hadn't consulted him on a certain matter because I didn't want his advice.

MARJORIE. You said that? To Levering? Why, you couldn't have been more insulting!

ALAN. Well, it just happened—I suppose if I'd been better prepared, but I couldn't think of how to get around it—

MARJORIE. You've got to keep on good terms with him. He's the presidential mouthpiece—the official whipper-in of the administration.

ALAN. I could bring myself to dislike him. I don't like taking advice from him and I don't like his face. And I certainly don't care to be—whipped in.

MARJORIE. But Alan—

ALAN. I've changed my mind. I think I'll sit with the committee after all.

MARJORIE. But you have an appointment with Levering—

ALAN. I didn't make an appointment. If he did, he can keep it. What's it like in there? A table—with chairs around it?

MARJORIE. That's right.

ALAN. There'll be an extra chair, I hope.

MARJORIE. Oh, yes.

ALAN. We're having lunch together, aren't we?

MARJORIE. Yes.

ALAN. Here goes.

MARJORIE. Alan, you aren't a wild radical, are you?

ALAN. No, just a farmer.

MARJORIE. Well, this first time it might be better just to listen.

ALAN. Oh, I'm not going to say anything.

MARJORIE. All right!

Curtain.

ACT ONE

SCENE II

SCENE: *The Committee Room. A large entrance at the rear, the office door at the right. The Committee, with* GRAY *presiding, is seated around the table.* GRAY *is speaking.* BUS *sits at his left taking notes.*

GRAY. Also, in my humble opinion, subject to correction from superior minds, Section 42 had better be struck out in toto, just to avoid possible remarks from the gallery. When you want money for river dredging it's better to pick a stream that doesn't dry up completely in the summer. I don't insist that your rivers be navigable, but it would look better if they had water in them.

PEEBLES. Isn't that the Big Belly Creek improvement?

GRAY. That's it.

PEEBLES. Well, listen, Mr. Chairman, we had to concede that to get the majority for the Iowa drainage business. It's going to mess up a lot of deals if that's out.

GRAY. And now who wants Iowa drained?

PEEBLES. That's the jackass Senator's pet notion, Simeon. It seems there's some of Iowa under water, and he wants to put up levees and drain it. I've never been in Iowa myself.

GRAY. The jackass, huh. I don't suppose there happens to be any patronage mixed up in that?

PEEBLES. Well, there you are.

GRAY. All right. I suppose we'll have to leave that in. Section 74, enlarging the nursing force under the Department of the Interior. I suppose you'll have the appointing of those nurses, Miss McMurtry?

MCMURTRY. Why, as a matter of fact, they do usually ask me for the names—

GRAY. I'm sorry—but that's out.

MCMURTRY. Why, Mr. Gray!

GRAY. It's out, Miss McMurtry.

MCMURTRY. But those nurses are so badly needed! You have no idea of the problems of the maternity bureau. In the first place—

GRAY. Let's not go into them now.

MCMURTRY. I suppose it's because I'm a woman, and—

GRAY. It's more than that; this section has been changed since I saw it last. What does this mean, this addendum, allotting fifteen thousand for the dissemination of birth control information and contraceptives?

SOL. Why look at me?

GRAY. Don't you know that's clearly against the law?

MCMURTRY. Only in cases of real necessity, Mr. Chairman. You see, so much of the difficulty in maternity cases arises from too many children, and after devoting years to a study of the subject I have formed the deliberate opinion that one should strike at the seat of the trouble.

SNEDEN. That certainly is the seat of it!

MCMURTRY. Moreover, I don't consider it a subject for jesting—especially at a time when so many men are unemployed and are constantly at home and women don't know how to protect themselves and the result is even more mouths to feed and even greater destitution!

PEEBLES. I declare that angle never occurred to me before—

MCMURTRY. There are a lot of things that don't occur to men, but women know that during periods of unemployment the men have nothing else to do and no other outlet for their energy.

WINGBLATT. What!

PEEBLES. Energy!

MCMURTRY. It's purely scientific—

GRAY. Genius, Miss McMurtry. Downright genius. Nevertheless, that section is out in entirety. Mr. Farnum, what was the reason you gave for wanting to establish a national park around the home of Joaquin Miller? Who was Joaquin Miller?

FARNUM. Didn't he write poetry?

GRAY. I'm asking you. I don't know whether he wrote poetry or a joke-book.

WINGBLATT. Certainly he wrote poetry. "Sail on! Sail on! Sail on!"

GRAY. Is that all you remember, Mr. Wingblatt?

WINGBLATT. That's all.

GRAY. Then that's out.

FARNUM. Suit yourself. You lose three opposition votes on the St. Lawrence if you drop it, though.

GRAY. We can afford it. And 65 is out.

EDDIE. What's 65?

GRAY. Establishing a patrol of the Canadian border for the Japanese beetle.

WINGBLATT. What! Oh, say, listen—

GRAY. Who wants it?

WINGBLATT. Some of the Non-Partisan League and Farmer-Labor contingent. They want to employ a lot of farmers.

GRAY. Do we need the Non-Partisans to push this bill through, Dell?

DELL. Not according to my figures.

GRAY. Then we'll drop that.

SOL. Now wait! What makes you think Dell's figures are better than mine? I say we do need 'em—and what's more those pretty little golden bugs are a god-send. They're coming down like a plague from the northwest, and it gives a chance to control the Non-Partisans by voting a little something to exterminate 'em.

DELL. They're coming from the southwest, Sol, not the northwest. There are no Japanese beetles along the Canadian border.

SOL. Well, what of it? Is this geography or politics?

GRAY. If Dell says we don't need 'em, they're out, and that's that.

SOL. Just the watch-dog of the Treasury, earning his name.

GRAY. Sol, I promised the President to bring this one down under two hundred millions and we're going to do it. You can outvote me on it if you want to, but if you do I swear I'll attack it on the floor and have it sent back here.

SOL. I've got no deal on with the Non-Partisans, Simeon! They're no friends of mine!

GRAY. Then why are they bombarding me with arguments against leaving the Atlantic Fleet at Hampton Roads this summer?

SOL. How would I know? Maybe they've got children on some of those vessels and they want 'em protected—

GRAY. Well, you can hardly blame me if it puts me on my guard—

SOL. By God, if there's anything I hate more than store liquor it's an honest politician! There's something slimy about a man being honest in your position. You spend your days and nights arranging deals among a pack of thieves, and just because you won't take anything for yourself, you think your hands are clean.

GRAY (*busy with his papers*). I get the impression you're talking a lot, Sol.

SOL. The whole damn government's a gang of liver flukes, sucking the blood out of the body politic—and there you sit, an honest liver fluke, arranging the graft for everybody else and refusing to do any blood sucking on your own account! God, it makes me sick!

MCMURTRY. Mr. Fitzmaurice—there are some of us here who would rather not be compared to animal parasites—and moreover the government is here for the good of the people! It does a great deal of good—

SOL. It does a four billion dollar business in taxes, and I'll say that's pretty good. For God's sake why don't you folks admit it, and take your bribes like men and go home and invest 'em?

GRAY. You all through, Sol?

SOL. No!

GRAY. Section 57—I don't find it in this copy. Lend me your notes, Dell. (*He looks at* DELL's *copy.* ALAN *enters. They all look up.*) Yes?

ALAN. Im—I'm Mr. McClean.

GRAY. My name's Gray. Do you want to meet the members of the committee?

ALAN. I don't want to disturb anything. I'll just listen, thank you. (*He sits.*)

GRAY. Why, surely. (*A smile goes around the Committee.*)

SOL. Young man, my name's Fitzmaurice, Solomon Fitzmaurice, and I welcome you to our festive board. You'll find us all too damned friendly here.

ALAN. Thank you.

GRAY. Section 57—yes, that's the one. That's out.

DELL. But listen, Sime, that's the new veterans' hospital at Baton Rouge.

GRAY. Right.

DELL. Well—that—you'd better think twice about that, Sime.

GRAY. I understand that hospital isn't really needed—

DELL. No, but you see—

FARNUM. Oh, Sime—have you got a copy of the bill? Mr. McClean would like to look up certain items.

GRAY. Certainly. Take mine. (*He hands it over.* ALAN *studies it, turning the pages.*)

DELL. I don't quite see how that can be eliminated, after our very definite talk with Klein.

GRAY. I. J.? Is that Klein's district?

DELL. It is, indeed—and you remember what the Legion told him—

GRAY. Yes, I see. Well, we'll have to make up for it somewhere else. That'll have to stay in.

DELL. Right.

GRAY. But for God's sake give me a hand with some of these cuts, some of you. There's about thirty-three million still to come out.

WINGBLATT. What are you going to eliminate? You've cut enough already to get it killed in the Senate—

GRAY. It'll pass the Senate—

PEEBLES. It may not even get by the House if you pare it any more.

GRAY. It's got to come down, I tell you! Whether the House likes it or not, it's got to get used to spending less money.

WINGBLATT. It can't be done!

GRAY. It's going to be done! There's no way of raising the money! Talk to the Ways and Means Committee!

WINGBLATT. Oh, hell.

GRAY. Section 200. Appropriating an additional million for extending irrigation service from the Nevada dam. That can go over to the next session.

ALAN. Mr. Chairman—

GRAY. Yes?

ALAN. Could I have a word?

GRAY. I can tell you right now, Mr. McClean, that section's out but go ahead.

ALAN. It wasn't my intention, Mr. Gray, to argue about the appropriation, but there are a few questions I would like to ask.

SOL. I knew it!

GRAY. It's all right. Don't mind us.

ALAN. What I wanted to ask was—

EDDIE. Louder, please.

ALAN. What I wanted to ask was—am I correct in assuming two hundred millions is the total which the bill will carry?

GRAY. I hope so.

ALAN. And is it the intention of the committee to put the bill in final shape today?

GRAY. Yes—that's what we're shooting at.

ALAN. Oh—well I just want to say, Mr. Chairman, that I'm in sympathy with you on this. When you say the bill ought to be cut down, I agree with you. But I'd go farther than that. I think the whole bill—and I hope you'll realize that I say this quite sincerely—not for effect at all—and I know it's a radical suggestion—but I think the whole bill ought to be dropped.

SOL. Now that's something! (*There is a general gasp.*)

WINGBLATT. You'll have to take that up somewhere else, sir.

ALAN. I think it ought to be dropped right here and now.

GRAY. You've made a study of this, I presume?

ALAN. I've been looking into it for some time, Mr. Chairman.

GRAY. I have been in charge of House appropriations for something like fifteen years, sir, and I say that this bill can't be dropped, and it's like sweating blood to get it down within limits. If you have any suggestions along that line—

ALAN. I come from an agricultural district, Mr. Chairman, where the farmers haven't got any money, and they're taxed beyond what they can stand already. Not only that but in the town I come from there used to be thirty eight stores on the main street. There are now fifteen—because people have no money to buy. When stores get judgments against the farmers and put up their cattle and machinery at auction, nothing is sold. And the whole country's like that. Nobody can buy anything, at any price. Now, I was elected and sent here because I told my people I'd do what I could to reduce taxes and cut down even necessary expenditures. And there's nothing in this bill that can't be done without. So I'm against it.

GRAY. We'll take the vote later. If you wish to vote against it, that's your privilege. Meanwhile, we have little enough time, and I'd like to proceed with the business in hand.

ALAN. I beg your pardon, Mr. Chairman, but I thought this was the business in hand.

GRAY. At the moment you're out of order.

WINGBLATT. Do you expect to run the House and dictate to the government the first time you step into a committee room?

ALAN. It may be that I've had exceptional opportunites for studying this particular bill. You see, in looking up a certain matter that concerned me closely I was astonished to come upon several instances of lobbyist influence. There's private graft in this bill, Mr. Chairman.

SOL. My God, that's a bombshell!

GRAY. What do you mean, Mr. McClean?

ALAN. I mean that in at least three instances, the people who are asking for certain appropriations stand to benefit in a monetary way.

GRAY. Will you kindly name the sections concerned?

ALAN. Well—the gentlemen I mean are no doubt aware of the situation. They are on this committee.

SOL (*rising*). By the eternal, we'll have their heart's blood! I been suspecting for years there was something crooked going on here!

GRAY. Sit down, Sol. You'll have to make your charges a little more concrete, Mr. McClean, if you expect any credence.

ALAN. Well, that's a little difficult. I prefer not to do that at present.

GRAY. Then you'll pardon us if the committee goes ahead with its program.

DELL. I happen to be somewhat familiar with your campaign for office in Nevada, Mr. McClean. It seems to me that you pledged yourself to work for the completion of the Nevada dam. Am I correct?

ALAN. Yes.

DELL. Then you must know that this bill was framed for the special purpose of supplying funds to complete that dam.

ALAN. Well, yes, but I am no longer in favor of it.

DELL. No?

ALAN. I have discovered that my backer and campaign manager had an understanding concerning the contracts. Naturally that puts a different face on the scheme.

SOL. Why don't you ask him why, some of you gouging miscreants, lost to honor and truth! I fear we stand alone here, Mr. McClean, absolutely alone!

ALAN. Pardon me, Mr. Fitzmaurice, but you are one of the gentlemen I had in mind. There is an appropriation listed here in connection with the maintenance of the Atlantic Fleet.

SOL. They took it away from me—took it away from an old man—and here I stand in my honesty—naked to every breeze! Everybody else gets his pickings, but old

Sol gets shoved away from the trough. It's nothing less than conspiracy!

ALAN. Are you also making charges against the committee?

SNEDEN. Wait a minute! Let me ask you something, Mr. McClean. You say we should drop this whole bill. You must know that that Nevada dam is a half billion dollar investment, and it's been waiting there for a year and a half for this forty millions to finish it.

PEEBLES. Three thousand people stranded in construction camps!

WINGBLATT. A hundred thousand farmers waiting for water!

SNEDEN. What's more, they're your own constituents!

MCMURTRY. No wonder the stores are closed on your own main street!

DELL. And after all you owe something to your district.

ALAN. But I say there's an understanding with the contractors! That forty million is too much because the work could be done for less if the bidding were honest! And even if the whole forty millions were necessary, why must the bill carry over two hundred millions for other projects—most of them quite unneccesary—

WINGBLATT. How unnecessary?

ALAN. Wasteful, useless, extravagant, ridiculous—

WINGBLATT. And how are you going to pass a bill giving forty millions to Nevada if the rest of the country gets nothing out of it? Nobody'd vote for it but Nevada's own Congressmen and by God you'd look pretty lonely.

ALAN. Does Congress have to be bribed to pass a bill?

SOL. Boy, they're laughing at you. Maybe I'm laughing at you myself. Don't you know about the government of the United States?

GRAY. That's enough, Sol.

SOL. Sime, this boy is suffering!

GRAY. I say it's enough.

SOL. Wait a minute. Let me put it to him in two words. Mr. McClean, you can't do anything in Congress without arranging matters. Everybody wants something, everybody's trying to put something over for his voters, or his friends, or the folks he's working for. So they all get together, and they put all those things in bills, and everybody votes for 'em. All except the opposition. They don't vote for 'em because they don't get anything. That's all there is to it. That's the whole government. Is that crooked?

ALAN. Yes, it is.

SOL. That's what I say. I've been saying it for years. (*The committee laughs.*) What are you laughing at? You all came up to this Congress fighting mad, full of juice and high purpose—just like him. Well, look what happened to you. You run into people making deals! Money changers in the temple of public righteousness!

MCMURTRY. Indeed!

SOL. Yes, and it happened to me too, and I was shocked and I started making radical remarks. Why, before I knew where I was I was an outsider. I couldn't get anything for my district, I couldn't get recognized to make a speech—I couldn't even get into a poker game. My constituents complained and I wasn't going to be re-elected. So I began to play ball, just to pacify the folks back home. And it worked. They've been re-electing me ever since—re-electing a fat crook because he gets what they want out of the Treasury, and fixes the Tariff for 'em, and sees that they don't get gypped out of their share of the plunder. That's what happened to every man of us here, but that's the way the government's run. If you want to be in Congress you have to do it. You let us finish that dam for you, and you'll be re-elected—talk against it and you won't be.

MCMURTRY. I won't listen to this!(*Half the committee is standing.*)

ALAN. What right have I to think about being re-elected?

SOL. I'm saying it only because you're going to make yourself a lot of trouble, boy. If you don't fall in line and help pass the pie—and do it quick—you'll be no better than a ghost in these historic halls. Nobody'll see you or hear what you say—and when you leave it'll be as if you'd never been here.

ALAN. Maybe it's been so in the past—but I can't believe it's true now. Times are different—the people—

SOL. All right, look around you and see how many friends you've got among us. Talk to 'em—ask 'em how many'll support you in blocking a bill or even cutting it down! State your principles!

ALAN. Mr. Chairman!

GRAY. I'm through! Go on—talk your heads off!

ALAN. I'm sorry this came up this way, Mr. Chairman, and members of the Committee —but I didn't expect to say anything today. I came here really to sit and listen. So I've probably gone at everything wrong end to and broken all the rules there are— but now it's started I would like to ask you something. Isn't it true the country's pretty desperate about taxes now—and wouldn't it do more good than harm to cancel this bill? There may be necessary expenses in it, and I know my own district stands to benefit more than any other —but when you just haven't got any money, you have to do without what you've been used to.

SNEDEN. Well, this country has long been in need of some bright young college graduate who was willing to take over the burdens of the administration.

MCMURTRY. Young man, you've been dreadfully misled.

ALAN. I think maybe you've all been misled for a long time—you think there's still money to spend—but there isn't, and you're all going to find it out!

DELL. Meeting over, Simeon?

GRAY. Adjourned till tomorrow. Usual time.

FARNUM. Wait a minute, Hi. I want to see you.

PEEBLES. It's all gone. I tell you.
(*The members have begun to straggle out.* ALAN *watches them go until only* SOL *and* GRAY *remain.* BUS *is still at the table putting papers together.*)

SOL. Want to talk it over with me, McClean?

ALAN. No. I—I'd rather be alone for a while.

SOL. Do you ever take a drink in the middle of the day?

ALAN. No, thanks.

SOL. All right, all right—only don't make a virtue of it. (*He goes out.*)

GRAY. All right, Miss Nillson, Marjorie will take it over tomorrow.
(BUS *goes out.*)

ALAN. Mr. Gray.

GRAY. Yes?

ALAN. I wanted to see you before the meeting—

GRAY. I'll make it just as soon as I can, McClean, but at this moment I'm helpless. Do me a favor. Talk to Miss Gray about it.

ALAN. I need somebody's help very much, Mr. Gray, and I'd rather it was you than anybody else—

GRAY. You will need help if you're to carry through your program. More help than I can give you.

ALAN. I've been led to believe that you'd be in sympathy with me.

GRAY. I am. But I would suggest that you've been a bit too heavy-handed to be effective. We all get hot about things when we're first here, McClean. But it doesn't help any, and after a while we find out that—

ALAN. I know I should apologize for the mess I made of it, but I really wasn't prepared to broach the matter at all, and besides I was bothered by the fact that some of my evidence might seem to reflect — well, on even your integrity.

(MARJORIE *has entered from the office.*)

GRAY. My integrity?

ALAN. Yes, sir.

GRAY. Well, that's something I've always taken care of myself, my boy, and I can't remember that anything's ever been said against it. You have the advantage of novelty.

ALAN. I realize that you were away at the time the bill was framed, but I have it on fairly competent authority that you own stock in a Culver bank, which is in shaky condition, and that the location of a penitentiary there and the spending of federal money would probably save it.

GRAY. I hadn't thought of that, but now you mention it, I hope it does save it.

ALAN. But if all this came out it might look strange —

GRAY. You think so?

ALAN. And it's such a simple thing to eliminate —

GRAY. Sometimes it's not so simple, McClean.

ALAN. But, Mr. Gray, if I really make a fight on this bill, I'll have to use all the ammunition I've got —

GRAY. If there's anything wrong with the penitentiary at Culver, Mr. McClean, I'll be glad to go over it with you, but not just now, please. It's an asylum, isn't it, an asylum for the criminal insane?

ALAN. Yes.

GRAY. Yes, I remember. But it had slipped my mind that it went to Culver. You know, I think I met your father when he was in Washington once. Not exactly a patient man himself, but valuable. You ought to have some gift for politics if you're like him.

ALAN. I hope I'm not impatient.

GRAY. You are, though. Now, shall we say as soon as possible? At the very earliest opportunity?

ALAN. Yes, sir. Thank you. (*He goes out.*)

MARJORIE. Was he right? Is the bank really in bad condition?

GRAY. I don't know of any bank in good condition.

MARJORIE. Then it could be made to look —strange?

GRAY. I suppose it could. The papers would go after it like a pack of wolves. Oh, a lot of people would have plenty of fun believing I was crooked. You look as if you half believed it yourself.

MARJORIE. No, darling. But the penitentiary had better go somewhere else.

GRAY. That's a difficulty. It's hooked up with so many agreements and promises. It's a week's work to untangle a thing like that. Maybe we shouldn't have laughed at his detectives!

MARJORIE. Maybe I shouldn't have made out such a good case for his appointment. How did you ever let that penitentiary clause slip by?

GRAY. That thing was fixed up while I was away, Marjorie, and there wasn't much point in ruling it out because it benefited my home town. That would have been bending backwards. Well, I guess you have to bend backwards in this business.

MARJORIE. I knew it was something like that. You shouldn't be working so hard.

GRAY. I'll have a few minutes for lunch if you could go out with me now.

MARJORIE. I had a—no, I'll go with you. I'll put a few things away here while you get your coat.

GRAY. Be right with you. (*He goes out. ALAN enters from the hall.*)

ALAN. Are we going to lunch, Marjorie? I didn't tell you what was on my mind, because it seemed best to talk to him about it.

MARJORIE. I don't know what you think you're here for nor what you want to do, but you've forfeited my respect for whatever it is.

ALAN. Why?

MARJORIE. And it's not that he's my father, but he's the one person who's really on your side! He's fought all his life to cut down appropriations and maintain a standard of honesty! And he's never got anything out of it.

ALAN. But I always believed that, Marjorie.

MARJORIE. But the first step you take in your campaign is to turn on him! Threatening to expose an innocent coincidence that would make it impossible for him to go on with his work! Don't you know every form of corruption in the country would take on new life if he were crowded off the committee? Don't you know every lobbyist in the city's waiting for just such a chance?

ALAN. But Marjorie—if he's made himself a part of the system so much that I can't attack any part of it without attacking him, I can't help it.

MARJORIE. But he hasn't! He isn't part of it. The clause means nothing to him personally, but it can't be thrown out at the last minute.

ALAN. He told you that?

MARJORIE. Yes. It might look as if he were to blame if it were brought out. But it would be unfair, terribly unfair. You don't know how hard it is to keep up a reputation like his over a long period of years in Washington.

ALAN. But Marjorie, I do realize it.

MARJORIE. Did you actually set detectives on him?
(BUS *and* GRAY *enter from the office.*)

ALAN. No, I didn't.

MARJORIE. Then how did you know all this?

ALAN. Oh, it doesn't matter.

GRAY. Well, Marjorie.

MARJORIE. Yes—let's go. (GRAY *and* MARJORIE *go out together.*)

BUS. I beg your pardon.

ALAN. It's all right.

BUS. I thought I heard a repercussion as I came in here.

ALAN. You did.

BUS. It sounded final. I hope it wasn't.

ALAN. I don't know.

BUS. That's no way to win a girl, you know. Opposing her father.

ALAN. No. I know it isn't.

BUS. I wish I'd met somebody like you when I was young and inflammable. I'd be a better woman today. However, now that I'm here, let me congratulate you on your disgraceful conduct in the committee. You were swell.

ALAN. Was I?

BUS. I haven't heard such a row since the debate over taking the couches out of the House Office Building. That was an uproar.

ALAN. I suppose I might as well go ahead with it.

BUS. With what?

ALAN. Well, I'm against this bill—it's crooked from beginning to end—and I've got enough information to kill it.

BUS. Where, if I may ask, did you get all this stuff?

ALAN. Well, I was having my election investigated.

BUS. I heard that—I didn't believe it.

ALAN. Well, I was. And day before yesterday I got some extra pages from the bureau—and they weren't about myself—they were about some of the others on the committee.

BUS. Someone else is doing some investigating.

ALAN. Yes. Well, they sent right over for the pages but not before I'd read them. I didn't realize at first how important it was, but now that I do, I'm certainly going to use it.

BUS. How?

ALAN. On the floor of the House, if necessary.

BUS. But what gave you the idea they'd let you make a speech?

ALAN. Why not?

BUS. They've got machinery down here especially designed for keeping people from speaking. No, you won't get a chance to open your mouth. The Speaker'll be tipped off, the parliamentary experts will have your number, they'll know everything you're planning to say before you say it. Why, damn it, your own secretary is working for them and turning in regular reports.

ALAN. My secretary? Merton?

BUS. Yes, Merton.

ALAN. But that can't be.

BUS. It is, I assure you.

ALAN. And you think I won't be allowed to speak?

BUS. I know you won't. Alan, you're up against a gang of professional empire wreckers. If you added up the conquerors of all time, from Alexander to Napoleon, the lump of what they got wouldn't touch what's dragged down annually by this gang out of our national treasury. And that being the case, do you think they'd hesitate to make things difficult for you? So far as they're concerned, you just aren't here. You don't exist. You aren't even a fly in the ointment. And the ointment business around here runs, believe me, into something staggering.

ALAN. I guess I might just as well go home.

BUS. You might just as well. It's a bad time for idealists. I'm out of a job myself.

ALAN. And everybody just lets them sit here—ruining things! Why, who are they, anyway? Who gives orders like that?

BUS. Oh, those on the inside—

ALAN. And anybody that isn't on the inside is supposed to stand around and wait till they give the word?

BUS. Yes, indeed.

ALAN. By God, I'm not as easy as that. And I won't do it! No, and I'm not going home—

BUS. No, you'll stay and draw your salary. They all do. They've done it for years.

ALAN. They won't drive me out, and they won't give me orders! I know how the country feels whether they do or not, and they're going to find some of this money red-hot when they pick it up!

BUS. I wonder—

ALAN. You don't think it can be done—

BUS. I don't think you can do it.

ALAN. I've been on a crooked school board and I know how they jump for cover when you start looking at their books!

BUS. Well, it isn't exactly a school board.

ALAN. Oh, yes it is! Only a damn sight less intelligent! And they've all got weak spots! They can be had—and they're going to be—right on this bill they are! Why damn their goddamn eyes—

BUS. Mr. McClean, there's something about you that vaguely begins to appeal to me. Do you want any help?

ALAN. What kind?

BUS. I need a job. I was fired this morning. I know all about everything. Have you got any plans?

ALAN. No, I haven't yet.

BUS. What of it? What I've forgotten is plenty for both of us, and if we could include the setting off of a few bombs, I'd find it a fascinating and congenial occupation.

ALAN. Go on!

BUS. The House is split just about fifty-fifty on this bill. A little finegling here and there, and a few promises, and you might —yes sir, you might find yourself with the deciding vote in your own little hands.

ALAN. I wouldn't know how to do that.

BUS. But I would. Oh, they made a foolish move today. They left the Non-Partisans out of this bill. There are four or five of 'em and they could swing Congress if they could stick in a lump for once. If we could find—Beetles!

ALAN. What?

BUS. Beetles! The committee didn't give 'em their beetles, Mr. McClean.

ALAN. Oh, I begin to get you!

BUS. Of course you do. Now you go out and talk with a few Non-Partisans and you'll find yourself among friends.

ALAN. You think it will work?

BUS. I'm sure it will!

ALAN. Listen—you're hired!

BUS. Salary?

ALAN. Whatever it's been. (*She puts out her hand. He takes it.*)

BUS. Shall we go to lunch?

ALAN. Why not? I'm hollow.
(MERTON *enters from the office.*)

MERTON. Oh, Mr. McClean, I wondered where you'd escaped to. I thought perhaps you'd like to lunch with me—

ALAN. What do you mean by escaped, Mr. Merton?

MERTON. Why—uh—we have several things to talk over—

ALAN. I rather doubt that. You're fired.

MERTON. Sir?

ALAN. I said, you're fired.

MERTON. I don't quite get it—

ALAN. Maybe you're a bit slow in the head. You're fired!

MERTON. But Mr. McClean! I've been secretary to the Congressmen from your district for many years now—if there's been any mistake made which I could rectify—

ALAN. You'd have to go back too far! You'd probably have to talk to your father and mother. You'd also have to make a lot of changes in your education and subsequent career. I said you're fired, and when I said it, I meant it good and plenty! (*He turns to* BUS.) Are you ready, Miss Nillson?

BUS. Hello, Merton!

Curtain.

ACT TWO

SCENE I

SCENE: *The Office, three days later. Afternoon.* MARJORIE *is at the desk.* SOL *enters with a letter in his hand, and looks at her morosely.*

SOL. Sons and heirs of boll-weevils and inch-worms. The lousy, filthy, air-polluting spoor of a mongrel dog. Did you hear what I said?

MARJORIE. What?

SOL. I said, those sons and heirs of a weak-minded seventh generation of boll-weevils and inch-worms—

MARJORIE. What's the matter, Sol?

SOL. Do you know what those quadruple asses have done?

MARJORIE. Who?

SOL. The federal income tax bureau. They've disallowed enough exemptions over a period of four years to soak me forty-five thousand dollars extra. Those web-footed, ass-faced, water-drinking, ossified descendants of a bad smell. What have you got to be in this carrion government to get your income tax fixed? A Secretary of the Treasury?

MARJORIE. That helps. It helped before.

SOL. God, what a government! It's bad enough to have to have it, but imagine having to pay for it! Tomorrow I'm going to take a tin-cup and stand at the corner of N Street and Pennsylvania Avenue. I'm going to stand there with my hat off and a tin-cup in my hand, asking alms from passers-by.

MARJORIE. You'd better take a jug along to go with the tin-cup.

SOL. We're ruined, Marjorie, ruined. My real estate equities are wiped out, the speakeasies are in the red, the Playground's deserted, the bill isn't going to pass, and I haven't got any more navy than Paraguay.

MARJORIE. What do you mean, the bill won't pass? What's the matter, Sol?

SOL. It's a rebellion. This McClean's a little David, Marjorie, and he's got six strings on his harp, six Farmer-Labor and Non-Partisan Leaguers lined up with him to control the House and ride our bill to destruction. And he'll do it, Marjorie, he'll do it!

MARJORIE. Oh, nonsense!

SOL. Wait and see. The old oracle's corns are hurting.

MARJORIE. How close is it?

SOL. We're dangling by a spider web, Clover. According to my figures, there are eighteen members that could go either way. The rest are pretty well nailed down, for or against. Well, that eighteen has been talked to, and the best I can make it, McClean's just one vote behind. Let one more man swing over, and there'll be a majority against us.

MARJORIE. Did Alan do all this?

SOL. He couldn't fail. We put the ammunition right into his hands. And that's something for old Simeon Gray to worry about.

MARJORIE. Sol, you've got to stop hammering at Dad. He's a nervous wreck, and I'm worried about him. And you do him no good!

SOL. I do him no good! What is he doing for me?

MARJORIE. What you don't get one way, you get another. (EDDIE *comes in from the hall.*) You're an artist at that, Sol—you know you are.

EDDIE. Hello, Sol! Say, Marjorie, could you do me a big favor?

MARJORIE. If it can be done quickly.

EDDIE. It's quite a job. That damn bill is lying in pieces all over my office.

SOL. Sure—they're sitting up nights slashing it to bits.

EDDIE. Miss Corey's been trying to paste it together, and confidentially, she's done one of the finest pasting jobs I've seen in years. If you help her for a few minutes you can name your price—

MARJORIE. I'll take a cigarette—but you'll have to wait till Dad gets here.

EDDIE. The committee meeting's in half an hour, remember.
(LEVERING *and* WINGBLATT *enter.*)

LEVERING. Eddie, I ought to take that flask of Sol's and hang a few glass medals on that glass brain of yours!

EDDIE. What's the matter?

LEVERING. I thought you were supposed to be watching McClean. What other use are you?

EDDIE. What's he done now?

WINGBLATT. Aren't we counting Trumper for one of our votes?

SOL. Yes—if he's still supposed to be sane.

WINGBLATT. Well, I happen to know he's been in McClean's office since one o'clock. (MARJORIE *goes into the inner office.*)

LEVERING. We lost two other votes this morning, and if he gets Trumper, he's over the line. I thought you said he was harmless!

EDDIE. Are you trying to make me the goat? I've done all I can! He got away from you too, didn't he? If this bill doesn't pass, I stand to lose a large amount of actual money.

WINGBLATT. And what kind of fake money do you think we stand to lose?

EDDIE. Well, I didn't put him on the committee, did I?

LEVERING. That's done with and let's not rake it up!

EDDIE. I suggest you'd better talk to Simeon.
(GRAY *enters from the hall.*)

LEVERING. That's what I'm here for. He'll have to postpone this meeting long enough to give us a chance to attack those fellows one by one.

GRAY. Postpone the meeting? What for?

LEVERING. Because we may have to add something to that bill, Sime, to push it through Congress.

GRAY. Add to it? Why?

SOL. A lot's been happening around here since we saw you last! McClean's got Trumper in his office right now, and if he brings him over we're one vote behind.

GRAY. What? Why you're crazy, Sol!

SOL. It's enough to drive a man crazy! Where have you been?

GRAY. At the White House.

SOL. Hell, you've been there for two days now. What have you been doing? Taking lessons in smiling?

GRAY. We've been trying to cut down on this bill.

SOL. Cutting it down! If you don't start building it up pretty soon, this is going to be a purely imaginary bill, a mere wraith of legislation in all its functions and effects.

GRAY. Drop the oratory, Sol!

SOL. All right! But you'd better listen to me. I tell you this boy prodigy from Nevada is lifting every stone in Washington and tipping the worms off to their big chance. And they're turning, Sime, they're turning. Congratulate yourself!

GRAY. Me? Why didn't you go out after those Non-Partisans? You've handled 'em before.

SOL. It was you wouldn't give 'em that Japanese beetle patronage.

GRAY. McClean can't give it to them, either, can he?

SOL. I got down on my knees and begged you to let 'em have it! It's the first burning issue they've had since the Indian raids of '75. But you wouldn't give it to 'em. Now McClean's sold 'em on the idea that they can control the whole damn Congress if they stick together—and they're wild—there's no stopping them.

GRAY. I wish I'd known we were dealing with a maniac.

SOL. Why don't you give the bastards their beetles! You and the old man sitting up there and slicing off five dollars here and two ninety-eight there—

EDDIE. Sure, tell 'em they can have their beetles! What difference does it make?

GRAY. What do you think, Disraeli?

LEVERING. There's nothing else to do.

GRAY. All right. Go ahead.

WINGBLATT. If we want to do any more scouting before the committee meets, we'd better do it now! The whole damn Farmer-Labor geselshaft is in conference downstairs!

LEVERING. Let Sol tackle them, Wingie! You'd better go after Trumper!

WINGBLATT. But what can I promise him? Nobody's told me how far I can go—outside of the beetles!

GRAY. Do you need more than that?

LEVERING. If you do, let him have it!

WINGBLATT. And can he take it? Let's go.

GRAY. Sol, are you dead on your feet?

SOL. I don't think it'll do any good. They say even God has his price—but there's no arguing with these Scandinavians! Come on, Wingie. (SOL *and* WINGBLATT *go out.*)

LEVERING. You and the President may have to loosen up a bit on this bill, Sime.

GRAY. I wouldn't be too optimistic. We sat six solid hours over this thing today, and I give you my word, he won't stand for a dollar we don't need for the vote.

ĐEVERING. Yes, but a few more dollars may be needed, Sime! In any case you'd better hold off your meeting till we know where we are!

GRAY. Right!
(LEVERING *goes out.*)

EDDIE. Forget about those Non-Partisans, Sime. We've got more trouble than that!

GRAY. Yes? Where?

EDDIE. I just had a call from the cuttlefish. He's threatened to withdraw his support, and you know what that'd mean! the whole middle west against us! Why, we wouldn't have a prayer. You know why, of course.

GRAY. No.—why?

EDDIE. He's in with this Committee of 48 on National Defense.

GRAY. What's that got to do with it?

EDDIE. Well, National Defense, Simeon—

GRAY. The Committee of 48 on National Defense is another name for about 48 steel companies.

EDDIE. I didn't mention it before, Sime, because I figured on holding out on them for your sake. But I can't do it. They were sore about being left out of the omnibus bill, and they mean to get in on this or know the reason why.

GRAY. What do they want?

EDDIE. Rehabilitation of two battleships.

GRAY. Two battleships! That's fifteen millions!

EDDIE. Might be about that.

GRAY. Why, you're insane!

EDDIE. You don't know how this one interlocks—the steel crowd, the cuttlefish, the Pennsylvania machine, the aluminum boys—I can't fight 'em all.

GRAY. Tell 'em it can't be done.

EDDIE. They won't listen.

GRAY. Then let 'em wait. Why should they try to unload Navy stuff onto a deficiency bill?

EDDIE. They think it's a good spot.

GRAY. A battleship's no damn good any more—in peace or war—and they know it. And yet they spend fortunes to wreck disarmament conferences and keep the high seas cluttered with their antediluvian tin cans.

EDDIE. I know all that, Sime—but they're pinching me.

GRAY. You'll be re-elected, Eddie!

EDDIE. Not if I flop on this. They can pick their own man.

GRAY. I hate to refuse you, Eddie, but it's too much.

EDDIE. I'll have to have it, Simeon.

GRAY. It's impossible! If you can't get it, you can't—and that ends the argument.

EDDIE. Now listen, Simeon—everybody's in on this bill.

GRAY. Oh, no.

EDDIE. That river dredging scheme. Where does that come in—

GRAY. That's out. I saw the general

EDDIE. Well, that Veterans' Bureau—what about that?

GRAY. Why pick on that? Do you expect me to fight the American Legion?

EDDIE. I suppose not. And there's that Massachusetts crowd—and that penitentiary at Culver—

GRAY. What?

EDDIE. That penitentiary at Culver— How did that get in there?

GRAY. It was put there in Committee—why?

EDDIE. By whom?
(*A pause.*)

GRAY (*slowly*). By me.

EDDIE. Why?

GRAY. What's wrong with it?

EDDIE. I'm asking you.

GRAY. Nothing.

EDDIE. I hear different. Who's the majority stock holder of the Culver bank? Who knows that it's bound to crash?

GRAY. So, it was you—

EDDIE. What?

GRAY. I thought McClean had been looking me up—it was you.

EDDIE. You're wrong, Sime—

GRAY. Don't Sime me, God damn you! I thought you were a friend of mine—

EDDIE. I am—anything I know about you I must have heard in a perfectly open way.

GRAY. You had the Dahl Agency look up what I owned.

EDDIE. You're wrong, Sime—dead wrong!

GRAY. Don't lie to me! I made it my business to find out.

EDDIE. You were looked up, but not by me. Sprague had it done for the company.

GRAY. It comes to the same thing. You're Sprague's hired man!

EDDIE. Well, where do you get this stuff of walking around here as if you were God's favorite archangel dispensing favors in the lower regions! It's rather nice to know that you're just one of us after all!

GRAY. Would you expect me to publish a thing like that to the hyenas on the committee?

EDDIE. Well, what are you going to do about it?

GRAY. We haven't got a majority anyway and a couple of battleships ought to sink us cold—so put 'em in. Just to make sure we lose!

EDDIE. We certainly will lose if they aren't in. So what's my answer?

GRAY. You get your fifteen million! And you can take your rake-off out of it—and you know what I think of you!

EDDIE. Well, I've been puzzled about you, Simeon—but not now.

GRAY. That all you want?

EDDIE. It'll do for the time being. No hard feelings?

GRAY. You think not!
(BUS *enters from the committee room.*)

BUS. It's no business of mine, Eddie, but your Miss Corey is up to her eyebrows in mucilage and hysterics. She'll never untangle that bill in time—

EDDIE. Marjorie said she'd lend a hand—

GRAY. Marjorie's going to be busy. (*He goes into the office.*)

EDDIE. Give Miss Corey a lift with that copy, will you, Bus?

BUS. Sure—why not?

EDDIE. Thanks. Don't make it too permanent. There may be another change or two. (ALAN *enters from the hall.*) Hello, McClean!

ALAN. How are you, Mr. Wister? (EDDIE *goes out.*) Oh, my God—Bus!

BUS. Well, I thought that confab with Trumper would never end. How did it come out?

ALAN. That man's crazy!

BUS. Don't say that. What did he want?

ALAN. Free seeds and free silver!

BUS. I don't believe it!

ALAN. It's true. He wants to flood the country with free silver.

BUS. Well—good Lord—give the country free silver. I say it ought to have free silver.

ALAN. It's not funny, Bus.

BUS. Well, give it free gasoline, then, and fiat money! We need Trumper's vote.

ALAN. You don't know what he's like!

BUS. Oh, yes, I do. He thinks he's the logical candidate for the next Presidential nomination.

ALAN. Exactly! He spent three-quarters of an hour reading me his speech of acceptance.

BUS. That was a short one—God, the ones I've heard of his. Is he still there?

ALAN. Yes.

BUS. Nobody with him?

ALAN. No, he's just sitting there!

BUS. Alan, this is our moment! Go back and talk to him—tell him you've been thinking things over—"Mr. Trumper, you're a great statesman, and I consider it a privilege to support you!"

ALAN. You don't know what I've let myself in for with the rest of them to get the votes we've got! I've had to pledge myself to an increased tariff on lumber and an increased tariff on wheat, a new system of landbanks, an embargo on circus animals —including Siamese cats!

BUS. Cats?

ALAN. Cats!

BUS. Cats and beetles! Well, what of it? What we want is to defeat this bill. You don't need to worry about those promises, because you'll never be called on to deliver. Why not one of them will even get out of committee.

ALAN. But Bus—

BUS. We've done everything but give it the final push-over! You're not going to fall down on that! What's a promise or two— this is Washington!

ALAN. Bus, this is funny up to a point—but I simply will not and cannot go near Trumper again. I can't work this way.

BUS. Well, what are you going to do?

ALAN. I don't know, but I've got to think of someone else.

BUS. Why? Trumper's ideal—he's a jelly fish!

ALAN. But there's nothing ideal about the way you want me to get him. You've been swell, Bus—I couldn't have got started at all without you, but our methods turn my stomach over. They're just like everyone else's, and I'm calling a halt right now.

BUS. There's no other method in this place, Alan.

ALAN. God, what happens to people here?

BUS. You'll find out some day. You can't just go to a Congressman and say, "Please mister, vote on our side because it's honest!"

ALAN. I'm not quite that naive. But there must be a few here who see—as well as I do—that this regime is damn near over! There must be a few who're sick of the way things are being done and ready to take a chance for once.

BUS. For instance—who?

ALAN. Well—Sol, for one!

BUS. Sol!

ALAN. Yes, Sol! He knows it! And more than that he has a damn good reason to be sore right at the moment!

BUS. Alan, the strain's begun to tell on you!

ALAN. No, I've got to do this my way. It may seem crazy to you but it doesn't to me! I'm going to talk to him!

BUS. Alan, you're in for a terrible headache! I'd better go clean up after the efficient Miss Corey.

(SOL *enters from the hall.*)

sol. Hello! How's the opposition?

bus. In beautiful shape, Sol—beautiful! You're wasting your time, Alan. (*She goes into the committee room.*)

sol. Alan, that was a smooth piece of work, picking up Bussy the way you did—and I won't keep it from you, you've got us worried.

alan. I hope so, Sol.

sol. I've got a proposition for you, Alan. Show me your lists and you can see mine —all open and above board. Because I'll tell you the truth, according to my reckoning we've got you. That is, unless you've seen somebody else I'm not figuring on—

alan. I've seen everybody!

sol. Tell me one thing and I'll know the whole story. Have you seen Trumper?

alan. Oh, yes, I've seen him.

sol. And he came over to you?

alan. Well, he offered to.

sol. Then I'm wrong. Sol's wrong again, and you're one vote ahead. Is that the way you dope it?

alan. If I sell out for what he wants.

sol. But you aren't going to do it? A man of your principles? You wouldn't trade back and forth like the rest of us?

alan. Sol, I want to ask you something.

sol. Anything, Alan, anything.

alan. You think we're enemies now— we're working against each other—and you don't trust me—but we're really on the same side.

sol. Well, frankly, I didn't know I'd been playing into your hands to that extent.

alan. You remember what you said to me in the committee room, the first time I saw you? You said when you first came to Washington, you were young and a radical and the whole system made you sick—didn't you?

sol. Did I say that?

alan. And it was true—wasn't it?

sol. You aren't making an appeal to my virtue, Alan? My lost virtue?

alan. I'm saying that you know I'm right about this thing—and you're wrong.

sol. There's a simple formula for deciding what's right and wrong in politics, lad. It comes down to one rule! God's always in the money. He don't lose.

alan. But suppose God's changed sides! The thing you'd better start worrying about is that you're going to wake up some morning and find yourself an old man— and not only old, but out—down and out.

sol. Why boy, you're eloquent! Only isn't it kind of a last resort to come to old Sol and try to win him over?

alan. You know this gang isn't going to last. They're afraid—Gray's afraid and the President's afraid. They feel that something's happened and something has— something's snapped!

sol. God, boy—you make me wonder. You shake me, Alan, and I haven't been shaken for a long time. You think the people are changing—waking up?

alan. I know they are.

sol. Now it's been my firm conviction, fortified by thirty years' experience, that the people don't change—and they seldom or never wake up. In fact, I have found no word in the English language and no simile or figure of speech that would express the complete and illimitable ignorance and incompetence of the voting population. But maybe I don't go back far enough. Maybe it's a longer cycle than I take in.

alan. They're awake now—and they're going to throw you all out—all of you.

sol. Wait a minute—wait till I pour myself a drink. (*He does so.*) Now, what do you want me to do?

alan. I want you to vote against the bill.

sol. Give me reasons, Alan, give me reasons.

ALAN. You get nothing out of it, even if it passes, do you?

SOL. No. But if I voted against it I'd be out with all my friends.

ALAN. What of it? You and I could control the House now, Sol. We could wreck their machine, we could wreck their bill. Think of it—we could show them there are more honest men than thieves for once.

SOL. It ain't true though. There ain't half as many honest men as thieves. Never have been. There's just one fallacy in this argument of yours. Would it be your plan, in case we got control, to run this government honest—as being the best policy?

ALAN. Why not?

SOL. Then there wouldn't be anything in it for anybody, would there? Nothing beyond his salary?

ALAN. Well—no.

SOL. You see, that's the fatal flaw!

ALAN. You want to come with me, Sol. You know you do. And I'm counting on you.

SOL. You're counting on me! I'd better tell you about myself, boy, before you say any more! Long ago when I was slim and eagle-eyed, I had a good angel. You wouldn't believe it to look at me now, but old Sol had a good angel by his side back there in the morning of time. And when a question like this came up this angel of light would come shouldering round him, arguing for righteousness, arguing against evil courses and the selling of his soul. If I was going to do wrong I had a wrestle with that angel. Like Jacob of old I wrestled with him in the night, and like Jacob of old I often came out ahead. It got so that the angel didn't have a chance with me, Alan, and after a while he got tired. Temptation would come upon me and I'd look around for this here spirit to wrestle with, and he wouldn't be there. He ought to be here wrestling with me now, Alan, but he's quit me. He don't even brush his wings by me, let alone give me a struggle. So I'm just an old man soaked in tobacco and fusel oil, and no help to anybody. No, if it's up to me to stop the bill, it'll pass.

You never get anywhere by taking things away from people, Alan. You've got to give them something.

ALAN. Why?

SOL. Because the sole business of government is graft, special privilege and corruption—with a by-product of order. They have to keep order or they can't make collections.

ALAN. Oh—oh, I see. Sol—

SOL. Don't say it, Alan, don't say it.

ALAN. Sol, you know—you may be right.

SOL. No, I'm all wrong. But what I'm mostly wrong about is I don't steal in a big enough way. Steal apples and they put you in jail—steal a nation and the hosts of heaven come down and line up under your banners.

ALAN. That's what I mean.

SOL. What?

ALAN. That's exactly what I mean!

SOL. I don't get you!

ALAN. I guess you're right, that's all. I guess you're right.

SOL. I'm right as far as I'm concerned. Sol's dyed in the wool—a black sheep—and whitewash won't cover him.
(WINGBLATT enters from the hall.)

WINGBLATT. Sol, can you come out here a minute?

SOL. Good news, Wingie?

WINGBLATT. Not especially good news for McClean—but good news!

SOL. You haven't been promising things?

WINGBLATT. No—no! Just free seeds and free silver! God, the punishment I've been taking. Campaign speeches for Christ's sake!

SOL. That's better than having to make 'em!
(They exit laughing. ALAN goes to the phone.)

ALAN. Get me Mr. Wister's office. Hello! Bus?—Alan! Are you where you can talk?—No, you were right about Sol. And they've grabbed Trumper too!—No, I'm not licked! But I've got another idea! No, no—I don't like what it means a damn bit. It's as rotten as every other method in this place, but it's the only chance I've got left. I want to get copies of everything ever proposed for H.R. 2007.—I'm going to use my information—you know what.—Oh, God, Bus, I know that! I know it's a dirty thing to do! I have more reasons than you have for not liking it! But I've got to do it, nobody's going to stop me! Oh, let's not talk about it! Just get me the copies of those things, and get 'em here quick!
(SOL *enters from the hall.*)

SOL. Tact, boy, tact! Now you see, Alan, with a little tact and longsuffering, Wingie's just brought Trumper into camp—and we've got you licked. Has it ever occurred to you that you might be conducting your life on too high a moral plane?

ALAN. That's just what I have been thinking!

SOL. What?

ALAN. I guess your methods are better than mine, that's all. If I'm not on the inside I'll be out altogether.

SOL. Now, don't let me overpersuade you, Alan. You stick to your line.

ALAN. You don't want me on your side?

SOL. Good Lord! I wouldn't believe it for a minute.

ALAN. Well, you may when it happens. I'm going to ask for something in the bill myself.

SOL. You're going to ask for something? Don't do it, Alan.

ALAN. I'm going to ask for that extra million for Nevada irrigation.

SOL. And vote on our side?

ALAN. Yes.

SOL. But you're away late asking for it now, Alan. You should have put in your bid earlier.

ALAN. Don't you think I have a certain amount of influence—just for the moment?

SOL. Now, look here—was this whole setup of yours a badger game? It's going to look that way.

ALAN. But what does it matter how it looks? Dell's in it—and Sneden and the veterans' lobby—and even Mr. Gray—

SOL. No—not Gray.

ALAN. I thought so. Isn't he? That prison at Culver's his, isn't it? I thought it was.

SOL. Oh, no, no, no! You're off the beat there. Simeon's never been hooked up with anything.

ALAN. But as I understand it, the bank's mainly his, and the money's badly needed.

SOL. As you understand it? Where did you hear this?

ALAN. It was an accident.

SOL. Oh, it was—

ALAN. But it's certain enough to get me anything I'd ask for. I wouldn't tell this to anyone else, Sol, but you're a friend of mine, and I know it won't get spread around.

SOL. Alan, you paralyze me. I get sober listening to you. Or am I sober? I take it you're not a drinking man?

ALAN. Not a heavy one!

SOL. Things like that don't come out by accident. You looked into it.

ALAN. Not intentionally. But you might as well have your fleet on the strength of it.

SOL. Boy, when I look at you and reflect on how I wasted my young time! The cunning of the serpent with the outward appearance of the dove! By God, I've never been up against it before!

ALAN. But Sol, if I'm going to make capital of it, you may as well do the same.

SOL. No. No, I can't use it on Simeon, Alan. You go in and make your own deal. I'm not a man to take an unfair advantage of a friend—never was a man to do that.

ALAN. Well, don't use it if it's against your conscience.

SOL. No, no! I couldn't do it. Not to save my soul from perdition! On the other hand —I ought to do it, Alan. This generation that's growing up now, it's a generation of vipers. You can't compete with 'em without being a viper. Why, they're born with teeth and claws nowadays. I'll just step in and see him a minute.

ALAN. You really might as well.

SOL. Not about that. Just in a friendly way.

ALAN. Surely.

SOL. And I stood there telling you about my angel. An old man's got to look out for himself. He's got to. (*He goes into the office.* BUS *enters.*)

BUS. Well?

ALAN. Are they complete copies?

BUS. Solid pork! What are you up to?

ALAN. I've been talking to Sol. He's in there getting his navy right now.

BUS. What?

ALAN. I'll catch the rest of them when the caucus meets, and advise them to ask for anything they want. They won't be refused.

BUS. What are you going to do?

ALAN. I'm going to overload the bill! I'm going to fill that thing with rubbish till no one will have the face to vote for it. Till it's a monstrosity and no one will dare sponsor it!

BUS. And this came to you all by yourself? Let me gaze on you, Alan. Let me contemplate the contours of that Nevada profile!

ALAN. Oh, you don't think it will work out?

BUS. On the contrary, I think it might. I think it will if you can carry it off. I resign, Alan. I abdicate. Take my hand and lead me. I'm a little child!

Curtain.

ACT TWO

SCENE II

SCENE: *The Committee Room.* MARJORIE *is taking the report.* DELL, SNEDEN, WINGBLATT *and* PEEBLES *are conversing.* MISS MCMURTRY *is just entering through the hall door.* BUS *is just finishing putting papers together and looks up as* EDDIE *comes in from the office.*

BUS (*to* MARJORIE). It's all here. You may find it a bit sticky. (*She goes out to the office, closing the door.* EDDIE *picks up the sheaf and leafs it through.*)

WINGBLATT. No—if we've got Trumper, he hasn't got a chance—look here. (*He shows his figuring to* FARNUM.)

PEEBLES. Was Trumper wobbling?

FARNUM. Good Lord, anyone can have Trumper that'll listen to him.
(GRAY *comes in from the office.*)

GRAY. Have you got it together?

EDDIE. Seems to be all here. Six copies. I'm stepping out for a minute, Sime, but you can go ahead. I've okayed everything. (*He goes out.*)

WINGBLATT. Sime—where's Sol?

GRAY. I don't know. It doesn't matter. He's been over it with me.

SNEDEN. Is it going to pass, Simeon?

GRAY. So far as I know it is. Do you want to take a look at it?

SNEDEN. Sure.

MCMURTRY. Could I see a schedule of the accepted items?

GRAY. I beg your pardon. Certainly. (*He hands her the remaining copy.* ALAN *comes in and seats himself.*) Now, boys, I don't want this session to take too much time.

SNEDEN. Neither do I. This bill's ruining my game.

GRAY. Look them over and we can take the vote. We've been on the thing entirely too long.

FARNUM. Why should we spoil our day looking at it? It's all cut and dried anyway.

WINGBLATT. Put it in type, Simeon. There aren't any changes, are there?

GRAY. A few. I went over it with the President.

PEEBLES. One thing you can be sure of then—there's no good news in it.

MCMURTRY. I think the other members should be here.

DELL. Just for the hell of it?

GRAY. They will be. Look it over first, if you like.

DELL. Say, that veterans' hospital isn't eliminated, is it?

GRAY. It had to be, I saw Klein about that myself.

DELL. Well, what the hell!

PEEBLES. You can't do things this way, Sime. You've cut out that Iowa drainage.

GRAY. Had to do it—

FARNUM. Hey, boy—Sol got his navy.

GRAY. And Sol gets his navy. I had to admit it.

PEEBLES. You mean the President slashed that Iowa thing—and leased Sol the Atlantic Fleet?

GRAY. Right.

WINGBLATT. Sol got his Navy? Well, in that case—

SNEDEN. Look here, Sime—what's this "Naval rehabilitation"? Is that the fifteen million slice Eddie's been trying to get for his committee?

GRAY. That's it, and I couldn't avoid it. Those two, and the Japanese beetle, which we had to have for the Dakota vote, are the only items the committee hadn't concurred in.

WINGBLATT. Damn swell items, if you ask me.

PEEBLES. That's what I say. We're a long way over the budget.

GRAY. I don't like it any better than you do.

WINGBLATT. Well, why was it, then? The rest of us have had to surrender on one clause after another! You don't intend to rush this thing through without explaining?

GRAY. Not at all. If you want me to enumerate the reasons for every inclusion, it can be done. It'll take a lot of time, but—

DELL. We wouldn't be much ahead, Sime. But it certainly looks this time as if there were a few people on the inside who were getting what they wanted at the expense of the rest of us.

WINGBLATT. And personally I'm tired of taking one man's word for what we can have and what we can't! This caucus is supposed to be governed by majority vote —and by God, I think it should be!

GRAY. A fine mess you'd send over to the White House.
(SOL *and* EDDIE *enter.*)

FARNUM. I'd like to ask Sol there how he wangled that Navy out of you! I'd also like to ask Eddie why he's able to slip things in after the dead-line!

GRAY. If you wanted to influence this legislation you should have made a study of it.

WINGBLATT. I know—as you have.

GRAY. Yes, as I have. If you want this thing kicked back here—

SNEDEN. Oh, what the hell! There's no use jawing with him. It's always this way.

Let's get it over with. (*He picks up his golf cap.*)

ALAN (*rising*). Mr. Chairman.

PEEBLES. Oh, let it ride! (*He starts to rise.*)

WINGBLATT. What do you say, Farnum?

FARNUM. What's the good? Let it go. I give up. (*He gets up.*)

ALAN. Mr. Chairman.
(*The committee is ready to go.*)

GRAY. Mr. McClean?

ALAN. As you all know, I have been engaged, perhaps mistakenly, in attempting to defeat H.R. 2007. As matters stand now, it seems it will pass, and in the light of that knowledge I have been reconsidering a number of questions concerning it. I have gone over the Nevada project again—and I am convinced that, since the bill is to pass anyway, it would be wise to include the extra million for irrigation which was put over to next year.

MCMURTRY. An extra million! Well, I must say—

GRAY. You should have spoken earlier, Mr. McClean.

ALAN. Also, in looking over this project, I was drawn into a perusal of other items which have been offered for the bill and rejected—and with Miss Nillson's help I have made a list of all requests which were denied in preliminary discussions of the legislation. The list is long, longer, I believe, than the list of those accepted, but I have been amazed, and I think you will be amazed, to find that they are practically all measures of considerable value, calculated to relieve a great deal of unemployment—

SNEDEN. Are we going to finish up or not?

ALAN. Just one moment. I have copies of those rejected items. Would you care to look at the schedule?

GRAY. Thanks, I'm sufficiently familiar with them.

ALAN. Now, my point is simply this: these appear to me to be reasonable and justifiable proposals, quite as applicable to the present state of the country as any now incorporated. In consequence I am reversing my previous stand in the committee on this subject, and hereby move that this list, which I now offer, be added to H.R. 2007 in due form. (*He hands up a sheaf of papers.*)

DELL. Yeah?

PEEBLES. What's that?

GRAY. You're asking that all that junk go back in the bill?

ALAN. I am.

GRAY. I had enough grief getting it out and I have no intention of going through it again. The bill's in shape, and it's going to the house tomorrow just as it is. (*He turns.*)

ALAN. I'm making it as a motion, Mr. Chairman.

GRAY. Who put you up to this?

ALAN. I'm acting on my own initiative. The plan originated with me.

GRAY. You're welcome to it.

ALAN. I shall be much obliged if someone will second my motion—

GRAY. I'm entertaining no such nonsense— as a motion or anything else—

WINGBLATT. What have you got here— everything that's been cut out of the bill?

ALAN. Absolutely everything, I think. (*He goes about the room distributing copies.*)

PEEBLES. Let's see it.

DELL. But what's the idea?

ALAN. To put everything in that's been asked for.

DELL. Everything?

ALAN. Why not? I find nothing unworthy of inclusion, and the decision rests with the majority.

FARNUM. Christ! That's Napoleonic!

WINGBLATT. You know, I'd be almost inclined to second that motion.

GRAY. I haven't recognized any motion.

SNEDEN. Is the veterans' administration in here?

FARNUM. My God, this one's got everything.

DELL. How about the uniforms for postal employees?

MCMURTRY. The appropriation for the nursing bureau—has it been included in this version?

WINGBLATT. God yes! All the infant industries are in it—including bastardy! I tell you it's all here, boys! If anything was ever complete, this is.

GRAY. Have you had enough of this tomfoolery?

PEEBLES. What's the total, Mr. McClean?

ALAN. Including everything, four hundred and seventy-five millions.

SNEDEN. That's impossible. It's a lovely dream, but it's not for us.

ALAN. It's not impossible! I give you my word, gentlemen, that if you pass the motion Mr. Gray will do everything in his power to see that the bill is made law. He's pledged himself to get this dam completed.

GRAY. Are you making promises for me, now?

EDDIE. What do you mean, McClean? You give your word?

GRAY. Can't you see what he's trying to do? He's trying to hang enough junk on this thing to sink it!

ALAN. Pardon me, Mr. Gray—I'm merely trying to follow your lead—when you included the navy and the steel company—

SOL. Oh, you feathered serpent! That's what you were doing!

GRAY. Are you setting up as an expert now?

ALAN. I hardly think, Mr. Gray, that you were functioning as an expert when you allowed those two items to be included.

GRAY. Oh, you don't?

ALAN. No, sir.

GRAY. Perhaps you consider this maniacal proposal of yours a constructive solution?

ALAN. I am not trying to be constructive, Mr. Chairman—merely logical.

SNEDEN. Wait a minute! You call a four hundred and seventy-five million dollar bill for a forty million dollar appropriation logical?

ALAN. Not at all. I only say that if it is logical to include Mr. Wister's rehabilitated battleships on this bill, it is just as logical to include your veterans' administration.

SNEDEN. Well, that sounds reasonable.

SOL. Boys—he's slipping something over on you!

FARNUM. We've had plenty slipped over on us! The Atlantic Fleet for one thing!

GRAY. We're not including what we like here—we're including what we have to for the vote—and that's all!

PEEBLES. Well, suppose you had to include something useful—just had to? Certainly draining those Iowa swamps is at least a thousand times more sensible than appropriating good money to drag that fleet over to Sol's front yard—I leave it to the conference!

GRAY. There's a tremendous difference in the amounts.

ALAN. Exactly eight thousand five hundred dollars—to be precise.

EDDIE. And that's important information too.

PEEBLES. My God, is that all?

MCMURTRY. Well, surely there's considerable difference between fifteen thousand dollars appropriated to provide nurses for the poor—and fifteen millions to repair two battleships!

EDDIE. If you imbeciles don't recognize this thing as the most obvious damned trick in the world—Christ! I'd have drawn up the bill myself without bothering—

WINGBLATT. It looks like you did anyway. What I still want to know is—

GRAY. Ask it later! Are we going to settle this bill or not? It's got to go to the House tomorrow and McClean comes in here with a Civil War grandstand play and sets you by the ears!

ALAN. I assure you that was not my intention, Mr. Chairman.

GRAY. Will someone please make a motion to put this bill to a vote so we can get out of here?

ALAN. I move that the bill is unanimously accepted—with all items, clauses and appropriations which I have included—

GRAY. I don't know whether you're insane or you've been put up to it. Will someone move to put this bill to a vote?

SOL. I so move.

EDDIE. I second the motion.

WINGBLATT. Now, wait a minute, Simeon! Don't pull a fast one on us. I still want to get to the bottom of how and why Sol got his fleet.

FARNUM. Yeah! And I still want to know why Eddie was allowed to push his steel company in after the deadline! What about that?

GRAY. The President agreed—at the urging of the Committee of 48 on National Defense—

DELL. My God, is the cuttlefish super-chairman of this committee too?

EDDIE. He was certainly going to swing the whole Middle West against us if we didn't do something for the Committee of 48!

WINGBLATT. Says you! I second Mr. McClean's motion!

GRAY. For God's sake, Wingie!

EDDIE. There's a motion before the committee, unless I'm wrong.

MCMURTRY. I hardly see why the rest of us should be put aside to accommodate Mr. Wister and Mr. Fitzmaurice. If the Chairman found it necessary to trade for votes

there are others on the committee who might have had votes to offer!

SOL (muttering). Angels! Jacob of Old! You double-crossing little—

SNEDEN. Certainly. Why didn't you let us in on it, and give us a chance?

MCMURTRY. Doesn't the President consider uncared for babies an item in national defense? (She snorts.)

GRAY. Why don't you address all these questions to Mr. McClean?

ALAN. Mr. Chairman—

GRAY. Are you trying to filibuster the whole damn day away! Now I ask you again to bring it to a vote.

WINGBLATT. All right! Let McClean talk!

PEEBLES. What did Sol have up his sleeve, Mr. McClean?

ALAN. Since, as Mr. Gray reminds us, there is already a question before the committee, I call for that question. Let us first vote on the bill without the additions—

WINGBLATT. And that's an idea, too. Question.

GRAY. If you are under the impression that we can make decisions of this character in any off-hand and childish spirit—

WINGBLATT. We know all that—and you've been asking for a vote! Well, put it!

PEEBLES. Sure, question!

SEVERAL. Question!

GRAY. Very well. Those in favor of sending 2007 to the House as it stands—

EDDIE and SOL. Aye.

GRAY. Opposed.

REST OF THE COMMITTEE. No.

WINGBLATT. I guess that's fairly obvious.

GRAY. And now, having reached what is probably a new low for all time in common-sense, I suggest that we adjourn till tomorrow.

EDDIE. I move we adjourn.

ALAN. I made a motion a little while ago which was not recognized, Mr. Chairman —a motion for the inclusion of the items in this copy of the bill. I wish to offer that motion again.

WINGBLATT. And I wish to second it!

GRAY. Not today.

WINGBLATT. Yes, today!

SNEDEN. You can't adjourn the meeting!

FARNUM. Personally, I'd like to vote on McClean's motion, and before I do I'd like to hear McClean's reason why Sol and Eddie can get away with murder.

PEEBLES. So would I. And we're not leaving till we find out. I want to hear the rest of the story. (*To* ALAN.) Go ahead and talk.

ALAN (*his eye on* GRAY). I don't see that any explanations are needed. Ask for what you want, and you'll get it, that's all.

GRAY. If Mr. McClean will pardon me, I'll do a little talking myself about his inspired suggestion. It's obvious that he has nothing in mind except to make this bill look like a raid on the treasury. You all know my position in such matters. I am the one man among you who has given his time to government finances over a period of years. I've carried the work and made the decisions because I know what can and what cannot be done. Now McClean has come in here with the deliberate intention of stampeding you into a log-rolling vote that will look like an organized steal, and he thinks he can get away with it—and he thinks I don't dare say anything because he's discovered that I have stock in a bank at Culver, and Culver is affected by one of the allotments in this bill. That's his whole case. If that gives him status as an expert and puts him in control here, why pass his resolution. If you still trust my judgment or think my word's any good, you'll send the measure to the House as it stands.
(*A pause.*)

PEEBLES. How much stock do you hold in the Culver bank, Mr. Chairman?

GRAY. A third interest. Anything else?

PEEBLES. No. Not from this side—
(*A pause.*)

GRAY. Now, I should like to call for another vote on the bill as it stands.

FARNUM. Does that mean including Sol and Eddie?

GRAY. It does.

SNEDEN. They get what they're asking for?

GRAY. They do.

SNEDEN. Then I don't see why we shouldn't.

WINGBLATT. Nor I. How come, Simeon?

GRAY. Those items have been accepted—

SNEDEN. How much more will the bill stand?

GRAY. It won't stand a nickel.

WINGBLATT. In other words—just because a couple of guys got in under the wire with this information—they're the white-headed boys.

GRAY. The bill is carrying every possible cent it can. What's more, it'll absolutely be vetoed if you add anything to it—anything.

PEEBLES. I don't quite believe that. As a matter of fact, boys, I don't believe that at all. It won't be vetoed.

GRAY. All right, hang yourselves.

WINGBLATT. We've been rooked by an inside gang—that's what's happened.

FARNUM. And now they're trying to tell us the House won't pass it and the Old Man'll veto it if we ask for what they got.

SNEDEN. Why, this bill's all set to pass, and the President's all set to sign it.

WINGBLATT. I seconded a motion here a minute ago!

PEEBLES. What's that steel business but highway robbery?

WINGBLATT. That's all! I call for the question.

FARNUM. Question!

PEEBLES. And what happens? Nothing—except the bill carries more than expected. Sure—Question!

GRAY. Dell?

DELL. There's nothing in here I could object to, Simeon.

GRAY. Very well. All in favor of including the items in Mr. McClean's list will signify by saying aye.

THE COMMITTEE (*except* SOL, EDDIE *and* GRAY). Aye.

GRAY. The motion is carried. Adjourned. (*There is a silence, the members begin to stir.*)

MCMURTRY. I'm afraid we've done a most appalling thing. Shouldn't we reconsider?

PEEBLES. We should not. (SOL *rises.*)

FARNUM. It's all right, Sol. You're getting yours too.

SOL. Nobody's getting anything if you ask me! Imagine me trusting a missionary! And at my age! Angels! (SOL *and* EDDIE *go out.*)

FARNUM. Listen, Sneden—keep this away from the reporters tonight. Keep it dark till it's read.

SNEDEN. Yeah! That's a thought, too.

MCMURTRY. I'm sure we've done a most appalling thing.
(*They go out.* ALAN, MARJORIE *and* GRAY *are alone.* ALAN *goes toward the door.*)

GRAY. Just a moment, Mr. McClean. You've beaten me here this afternoon, and made a good job of it. No doubt it looks to you as if no man with a remnant of honesty would have the face to present the thing to the House.

ALAN. Yes, that is the way I feel, Mr. Gray.

GRAY. That is one way of looking at it, McClean. But you once told us about a little town where the people had no money to buy. I want to tell you about another town. I grew up in Culver and I know the people there—the storekeepers and the

professional men and the people in the street. I know them by their first names—and I know what they've been through. They've lost nearly everything they had. Business is gone and two banks have failed. The third one's mine, and people think it's sound, and what money is left is in it. But the bank isn't sound; and if the bill's defeated and the penitentiary doesn't go to Culver, the bank will fail, and a lot of people will lose their life savings and their jobs.

ALAN. But, Mr. Gray, isn't it a little unfair to support Culver by taxing other places which are just as badly off?

GRAY. Yes, it is unfair! But I'm here to represent a certain district, McClean, and they need what I can do for them as they've never needed it before. I don't hold what you've done against you, but I am going to fight you. I'm going to fight you every inch of the way. You've made it damn difficult! You've dumped 275 extra millions on the bill, and you expect that to kill it in the House. But I don't intend to let that kill it. This fight hasn't even begun. I'm not asking you to call off your dogs, and I'm not apologizing. I'm going to use every weapon I can lay my hands on, and I won't be very squeamish where or how I find them.

ALAN. You don't leave me much choice, do you?

GRAY. And you leave me no choice!

ALAN. That's going to make it very interesting! (*He goes out.*)

MARJORIE. Dad, what is it?

GRAY. Nothing!

MARJORIE. If you wanted to make him believe the worst possible about you—What does it mean? Why do you want that bill to pass as much as all that?

GRAY. It's nothing that concerns you, Marjorie.

MARJORIE. It does concern me. If I didn't believe in you right now, more than anything in the world, I'd be with Alan against you.

GRAY. Perhaps you should be!

MARJORIE. It isn't fair to tell me just that much! I want an answer! You must give me an answer!

GRAY. The third national bank of Culver is not merely in difficulties, Marjorie. It has borrowed twice on federal securities. In its vaults are three packages of bonds which, if examined, would prove to be blank paper. If the bank fails those securities will be examined at once. I am chairman of the board. I was away when it was done, but I've known of it for some time! To put it baldly, I'm guilty. So you see, if I don't get my penitentiary one way, I'll get it another! Does that answer your question?

Curtain.

ACT THREE

SCENE I

SCENE: *The Committee Room. Evening. Three days later.* SNEDEN *and* DELL *are seated at the table.* PEEBLES *is near the door, having just entered to make a report, and* WINGBLATT *is standing at the small table.*

WINGBLATT. Do you mean to tell me you spent three hours with that Rhode Island bunch and couldn't even get a rise out of them?

PEEBLES. They said they'd vote for it if it looked like it was going through—

WINGBLATT. Well, good God, what good's that going to do?

PEEBLES. I haven't had any sleep for two nights, Wingie!

WINGBLATT. You go back there and tell them it is going through and quit boasting about the late hours you keep! Nobody's had any sleep as far as I know. Did you tell 'em about that federal base at Newport?

PEEBLES. I did. They're scared of it.

WINGBLATT. Scared of federal money? Don't make me laugh.

DELL. The President's bringing pressure, Wingie.

WINGBLATT. What kind of pressure?

DELL. Patronage pressure.

WINGBLATT. So that's it. That's why we keep losing votes as fast as we bring 'em in.

DELL. Sure it is. He wants it sent back to the committee and scaled down.

PEEBLES. And that's what's going to happen.

SNEDEN. It is not. We've had twenty thousand telegrams favoring this bill the last two days!

DELL. Yeah, but listen to this. Editorial in the Washington Tribune: "The plunderbund at the Capitol is overreaching itself. One more big grab—"

WINGBLATT. That's an administration organ, that sheet. Plays any tune the President sets for it!

DELL. You won't find many papers don't say the same thing, no matter what their politics are.

WINGBLATT. Are you going haywire on us?

DELL. I don't want to be spanked in public, Wingie. I'd rather take my licking in the solitude of my own boudoir.

PEEBLES. You sure Dizzy's meeting us here?

DELL. That's what he said.

WINGBLATT. Who's been working on that Massachusetts crowd?

DELL. Farnum. They're all right! They'll be for it on account of the new lighthouse and harbor work.

WINGBLATT. That puts us four votes ahead.

SNEDEN. And then add in Illinois and it puts us four votes behind.

DELL. That's right.

PEEBLES. All I know is if this bill don't pass, I don't come back here no more, and I haven't even got enough left to buy me a hunting and fishing license.

DELL. What would a poacher like you want with a hunting and fishing license? (*The telephone rings.*)

WINGBLATT. Damn it, they'll be calling the roll within an hour and we don't know anything—we don't even know how we're going to vote.

SNEDEN (*at the phone*). Yeah. Well, why not? Eddie's supposed to handle Delaware, isn't he? I don't know what more they could ask for. All right, Dave. (*He hangs up.* MARJORIE *enters from the office.*)

MARJORIE. Where's Sol?

DELL. Downstairs, Marjorie. The manufacturing states are holding a conference, and he's down there with Farnum and Eddie.

MARJORIE. Dad just got a call from the Speaker. He says he can't keep the debate going more than half an hour longer. He'll have to let it come to a vote. (*She goes out.*)

WINGBLATT. Anything we want to do we better do right now.
(LEVERING *enters.*)

LEVERING. Hello, boys.

SNEDEN. There he is.

WINGBLATT. Dizzy, for God's sake come in here and give us a line on what's going to happen. These babes in the wood think we're going to have to oppose our own bill. (MARK *opens the hall door and brings in a large sack of telegrams.*)

LEVERING. They may be right.

WINGBLATT. But why? Every organization in the country wants it.

MARK. More telegrams, gentlemen. (*He goes out.*)

WINGBLATT. Look at what Mark's just brought in. And look at those telegrams. Open any one of them! The country's screaming its head off for the thing!

LEVERING. Not the country. Don't confuse the country with the people that still have money left to send telegrams. They represent a very small fraction of the country.

DELL. He's right.

WINGBLATT. Everybody stands to benefit! Every state in the Union!
(EBNER *enters from the hall.*)

EBNER. McClean isn't around here, is he?

SNEDEN. No, haven't seen McClean.

EBNER. Sorry, just looking for him.

WINGBLATT. Listen, Joe, while you're here will you tell me one thing?

EBNER. Sure!

WINGBLATT. What's got into this little Jesus McClean that makes you guys stick to him?

EBNER. He certainly put it over on you, Wingie.

WINGBLATT. Well, what are you radicals fighting us for? You've got clauses in that bill!

SNEDEN. You're just cutting your own throats voting against it.

EBNER. We don't want those clauses. You're in a hole, you boys, and McClean put you there, and we're going to keep you there. Personally, I think you never will get out of it—and I think we'll blow this government higher than a kite before you know what's happened to you! I guess you never heard of a revolution, did you? Well, you're going to hear of one. And you can write that on your list, or print it on the wall, or put it up in lights over the Capitol! (*He goes out.*)

WINGBLATT. Gone Bolshevik, have they? Well, they won't get far with that.

SNEDEN. He's been reading the life of Trotzky in two volumes.

DELL. They've got an organization now, boys. They think this McClean's a new Bob LaFollette.

LEVERING. Unless we can make sure of a decisive majority for the bill, we'll all have to throw our weight against it. If we offend the country once more—

PEEBLES. Now don't say that, Dizzy. Don't say that.

LEVERING. It's out of my hands!

SOL (*outside*).

> And how can man die better
> Than facing fearful odds
> For the ashes of his fathers
> And the altars of his gods?

(SOL *enters.* MARJORIE *comes in from the office.*) Dizzy, I've been out gathering recruits to stand at my right hand and keep the bridge with me!

WINGBLATT. What's the news, Sol?

SNEDEN. How do we rate, Sol?

DELL. Oh, Sol, what was that Rhode Island business?

LEVERING. Let's have it, Sol. How did you come out?

MARJORIE. Sol, what happened?

SOL. Well, Clover, the situation called for a good deal of oratory!
(FARNUM *and* EDDIE *enter.*)

FARNUM. Oratory! What do you say to Pennsylvania!

MARJORIE. What do you mean? Did they come over?

EDDIE. What do you say to Indiana and Illinois?

FARNUM. What do you say to that vast and glorious Empire State—New York to you!

WINGBLATT. Cut the comedy!

EDDIE. They came over!

FARNUM. Sol brought 'em over!

MARJORIE. We've got a majority?

FARNUM. A majority? We've got the damnedest, sweetest, most beautiful majority I ever saw delivered in one package! (MARJORIE *runs out.*)

EDDIE. The whole blatting conference voted to go for it solid!

SNEDEN. The rosy-fingered dawn appears!

LEVERING. That's Sol's work?

EDDIE. Sol's work!

FARNUM. And beautiful!

LEVERING. What did you to do 'em, Sol?

SOL. I talked to 'em. Where are appropriations supposed to originate in the government of the United States? In the House of Representatives. Then by what right does the President try to dictate how much we can appropriate, or where, or how? That's all.

DELL. What did you do? Give 'em your word of honor?

SOL. Honor? Pennsylvania gets twenty-one millions. Illinois gets those Lake Michigan docks—

SNEDEN. How can you promise docks on Lake Michigan?

WINGBLATT. Yeah, who gave you authority to do that?

SOL. It's in the bill!

DELL. Sure. Don't you remember?

SNEDEN. No, I do not. And I'll never believe it.

SOL. This is an extraordinary bill! It will keep a million people out of the bread lines!

LEVERING. If it isn't vetoed.

(GRAY *and* MARJORIE *enter from the office.*)

GRAY. Well, I hear we've got a majority!

DELL. We certainly have!

WINGBLATT. What's the news from the White House, Sime?

GRAY. Well, no news is good news, I suppose. So far he hasn't said a word. Collier promised to let me know if there was any decision. (*The buzzer sounds twice.*)

DELL. There goes the buzzer. Half an hour, Disraeli! How do we vote?

WINGBLATT. My God, is there any question any more? To hell with the country. We're climbing on the bandwagon!

FARNUM. Come on, Dizzy, don't hold up the procession.

PEEBLES. How about it?

LEVERING. How much of a majority have we got?

DELL. Fifty-five or sixty to the good!

LEVERING. We're breaking with the President, Sime!

GRAY. With that majority it's an act of God. He can't blame us for going along.

LEVERING. O. K., boys, we're voting "Aye."

DELL. Right.

(*There is a general sigh of relief. The crowd goes out through the hall door.* SOL, MARJORIE *and* GRAY *are left alone.*)

SOL. Well, Sime, we're riding high.

MARJORIE. Sol, you're a genius!

SOL. I had to be! (*The telephone rings.*)

GRAY. You deserve your fleet—can I get you the Army for next summer?

SOL. Certainly, and you can throw in the Marines!

MARJORIE. Hello! What? Oh, just a minute. It's for you, Dad.

GRAY. Oh! (*He goes to the phone.*)

SOL. A wee nip, Clover? Just to celebrate?

MARJORIE. Why not?

GRAY. Hello!—Hello, Collier! What?—What!—You heard him say that? (SOL *and* MARJORIE *stop.*) Then it's definite—I see!—All right, thanks, Collier—The President's decided to veto the measure if it passes.

MARJORIE. Where does that leave us, Sol? (SOL *sits down to figure.*)

SOL. About twelve votes shy of a two-thirds majority.

MARJORIE. We've got to get them, Sol. We've got to!

GRAY. There's never quite enough time, is there?

SOL. If I had an hour more, I might be able to fetch in those Californians.

GRAY. But there is less than half an hour, Sol.

MARJORIE. It can't go this way. Sol, you know what this means—it just can't happen.

GRAY. Maybe there's no way out of it.

MARJORIE. There must be—it takes so little to make them go one way or another.

SOL. It's so close right now, that if Alan was to forget his principles, we'd have our two-thirds and could beat the veto.

MARJORIE. Then something can still be done!

SOL. That's what I was thinking. Sime, are you going to mind if I put the case to him?

GRAY. I wouldn't do it, Sol—I'd rather nobody did it. I have some messages to send off.

SOL. Have it your own way, Sime. I think it's worth trying.

GRAY. Well, I don't. Nobody could deliver fifteen men in the time that's left. And that being the case, I'd rather you didn't mention the subject. I don't particularly like the idea of people feeling sorry for me.

SOL. I get you.
(GRAY *goes into the office*.)

MARJORIE. How many votes are there in that group of Alan's?

SOL. About twenty under his wing—more than enough.

MARJORIE. Then I am going down to his office and get him. But Sol, you will have to talk to him—this is something I can't ask him, but you can.

SOL. I'm going to.

MARJORIE. I wish it were anybody else.

SOL. I'm glad it isn't anybody else.
(MARK *enters with a cup of coffee, sugar, paper napkins and crackers*.)

MARK. Oh! Excuse me!

MARJORIE. I'll be right back. (*She goes out*.)

MARK. I brought your coffee, sir.

SOL. Leave it there, Mark.

MARK. And Mr. Fitzmaurice?

SOL. Yes.

MARK. Do you know anything about this here money bill the papers is talking about? Taking all that money out of the Treasury?

SOL. I've heard about it, Mark.

MARK. Well, I was hoping you would be against that bill.

SOL. Why, boy?

MARK. Because this government's costing a sight too much. A sight!

SOL. I'd hate to see you go, Mark. But if you can stand it —

MARK. Me!

SOL. Don't you know the service in this building will be cut in half if the deficiency bill don't pass?

MARK. No, sir! I didn't know that. I certainly didn't. Maybe I spoke out of turn, Mr. Fitzmaurice!

SOL. Now it's high-minded of you to consider the good of the country.

MARK. I ain't really high-minded, Mr. Fitzmaurice. I ain't high-minded at all. No— I was just swayed by reading matter.

SOL. You aren't really against it?

MARK. On the whole, I ain't really against it at all. I'm really for it on the whole. I want to drop the whole matter, Mr. Fitzmaurice.
(BUS *enters from the office*.)

SOL. Fine—we'll drop it. 'Evening, Bussy!

BUS. 'Evening, Sol. How's the opposition tonight?

SOL. Well, Bussy—We view our prospects with a certain amount of optimism. I think we can safely say that.

BUS. Sounds like a brokerage firm with its back to the wall. How's Atlantic Fleet common?

SOL. You're dancing on the grave of an old man, Bussy.

BUS. You do look a bit low.

SOL. Not as low as I was this afternoon, though. We've taken over four manufacturing states from you since then.

BUS. What!

SOL. It's true—we're too far ahead to catch now.

BUS. That's a jolt! I might as well admit that jolts me pretty hard—if true!

SOL. How's the middle western bloc?

BUS. Oh, that's holding together in great shape. You weren't thinking of going after our farmers, Sol?

SOL. We're going to be too many for you on the vote, Bussy. So why hold out? Why not fall in line and get some of the credit?

BUS. Baby! Do you know what I think?

SOL. No.

BUS. By your tone of voice I think you're expecting a veto!

SOL. Serpent of Eden—I am!

BUS. And we can still hold you up?

SOL. That's the situation.

BUS. Then of course we will!
(ALAN *enters with* MARJORIE.)

ALAN. Hello, Sol!

BUS. Alan, there's news! The President's going to veto the bill and that's our winning card!

ALAN. Great, Bus! Marjorie said you wanted to see me, Sol.

SOL. Alan, we're going over there to vote in about five minutes and I want you to do something for me.

ALAN. What is it?

SOL. I want you to release that middle western bloc of yours.

ALAN. Give me reasons, Sol—give me reasons!

BUS. Now what makes you think you'll get any help from us?

SOL. From Alan!

BUS. You have an eminent nerve! We may be just beginners, Sol; we may be putty in your hands, but we know better than that.

SOL. Alan, you're going to wish you had. Sometime you are going to wish as you've never wished anything before.

BUS. Threats?

SOL. No, not threats. But you've got some people in a jam, Alan, and I can't get them out of it. Houdini couldn't get them out of it, but with your influence I think maybe you could.

ALAN. Who?

SOL. Simeon.

ALAN. I'm sorry, Sol, but I don't see why you come to me about this.

SOL. I only want to say one thing—you won't reform anything by defeating this one bill. Parties may come and parties may go—administrations come in and go out, but the graft varies only in amount, not in kind. Now you can defeat this one appropriation bill, just for your own noble satisfaction, but you won't reform anything, and it might be more to the point to be human—this once. I had a share in it, Alan, I helped you wreck him. Neither one of us knew what we were doing, but by God, we ought to do what we can to take it back.

ALAN. Just what do you mean by wreck, Sol?

SOL. I mean something you won't rest easy knowing, Alan. I mean a term in jail.

ALAN. What?

SOL. I mean just what I said.
(EBNER *enters from the hall.*)

EBNER. Oh, good evening. We're all waiting for you downstairs, McClean. Thought we'd go over in a body.

ALAN. Just a minute, Joe!

EBNER. And before we go down—one or two of the boys are wavering a bit. It's hard for some people to turn down patronage when it's offered on a platter. So it might be a good idea to stick close to them. I'll do what I can, and I'll expect you to back me up.

BUS. Run along, Joe, Alan will catch you downstairs.

EBNER. We'll go down in history! This is the day the Old Guard meets its Waterloo!

ALAN. Give me three minutes, will you, Joe?

EBNER. Say, you aren't letting yourself be talked to?

ALAN. No. I'll be with you in a minute—but for God's sake, get out now! Marjorie, is it true?
(EBNER *goes out.*)

MARJORIE. Yes. I don't know whether you will ever forgive me or not, Alan. I'm going back on everything I believed, but things look different when there is a prison staring someone in the face. I don't care any more whether it's honest or not. I don't want him to go through with it.

ALAN. But what has your father done?

MARJORIE. I've loved him and almost worshipped him—because he was honest and just, and they couldn't corrupt him—somebody had to be honest in this place, or you couldn't breathe the air—and he isn't really guilty even now.

ALAN. Guilty of what, Marjorie?

MARJORIE. Something at the bank, Alan. Some misuse of funds that he wasn't concerned in at all. Only it falls on him. (*The buzzer sounds twice.*)

ALAN. I'm afraid it's impossible—even if there were time.

SOL. There must be two or three key men, Alan, who could bring the others around if you worked with them.

ALAN. Worked with them? Go to those farmers and ask them to vote for the bill, after what I've done to it?

BUS. We've wasted a week's work, Alan. You'd better turn those votes loose.

SOL. We're counting on you! (*The buzzer sounds three times.*)

ALAN. Counting on me! Why, I couldn't find words to say it to them. I'm sorry, Marjorie, but I can't think of any one person now. I'm not fighting you or your father. I'm fighting this machine!

MARJORIE. But think what it means to him!

ALAN. I hope you're wrong about it and the blame doesn't fall on him, but even if it does, I can't stop now. If I were wiser, I might know how to compromise. I may be sending an innocent man to prison and I wish to Christ I knew how to avoid it, but I don't! (*The buzzer sounds four times.*)

MARJORIE. Alan! Alan!

ALAN. Don't ask it of me and don't tell me what I've lost! I know what I've lost from all of you. And it's not my choice to lose it —but I'm in a fight that's got to be won —and you're asking for something I've no right to give!

Curtain.

ACT THREE

SCENE II

SCENE: *The Committee Room. Later the same evening.* SNEDEN, FARNUM, PEEBLES, WINGBLATT, EDDIE, SOL *and* DELL *appear in the doorway singing.*

THE CROWD.
Take it away, my boys—take it away!
When we get started everybody has to pay,
Pay, pay, pay!
Take it away, my boys—take it away!
We hear the eagle screaming:
Pht the army! Pht the navy! Hey!

PEEBLES. Who said "Pht the army"? Who said that?

SNEDEN. Good old Peebles! Peebles is in the R.O.T.C. A lieutenant, by God!

PEEBLES. Do you realize you're talking to a son of the American Revolution?

WINGBLATT. A son of what?

DELL. I'm not a drinking man—but I'm drinking.

WINGBLATT. Shut up, will you? I want to know what Peebles is a son of?

CROWD (*singing*).
Take it away, my boys—take it away!
Mama loves papa almost every other day,
Day, day, day!

Take it away, my boys—salt it in brine!
Please pass the bacon, Elmer!
Pht the people, pht the people, hey!

FARNUM. Well, boys—who won?

THE CROWD. We did!

FARNUM. Who lost?

THE CROWD. Nobody!

SOL. Have you all got your bribes? Everybody satisfied? Hold up your hands, them that didn't get their bribes!

PEEBLES. Bribes! Bribes! Sir, I don't care for your choice of words.

WINGBLATT. Yes, suh! We both resent that, suh! As professional Southerners, we resent that! You'll take that back, suh, and you'll couch it in less invidious terms, suh!

SOL. How's times, boys? Everybody prosperous? Everybody flying high?

WINGBLATT. Oh, yes, suh, massah! Everybody prosperous.

SOL. Corn in the crib and sorghum in the barrel?

WINGBLATT. Oh, yes, suh, massah! Corn in de crib and sorghum in de barrel!

SOL. And how-all's Miss Meadows and the gals? Sitting pretty on the front porch, I take oath. Eating pork?

WINGBLATT. Um-um, massah!

SOL. And riding horses, plenty of riding horses for a gentleman?

WINGBLATT. Massah, did you-all say riding horses?
(BUS *enters from the office.*)

BUS. Have you all gone crazy? What happened?

SEVERAL. They passed the bill!

BUS. One at a time—what?

SOL. They passed the bill!

BUS. Well, what of it? It's going to be vetoed, anyway.

WINGBLATT. Good God, it passed with a two-thirds majority—and it can't be vetoed!
(MARJORIE *enters from the office.*)

BUS. Alan released those votes!

SOL. He didn't! His farmers stuck together. But they weren't enough—not near enough!

MARJORIE. How much of a majority was there?

SOL. It was a landslide! Maybe fifteen or twenty stood out against it!

MARJORIE. Then—it's certain.

WINGBLATT. Certain! The whole House went crazy!

FARNUM. It looked like the Klondike gold rush!

MARJORIE. Has Dad come back yet? (*She goes into the office.*)

SOL. It was Alan who did it, Bus, and we're giving him credit for it!

BUS. He'll like that a lot.
(ALAN *enters from the hall.*)

SOL. Alan, my boy, I've been appointed by this delegation to tender you a little message. Tonight you feast at our expense with sparkling burgundy and venison pie.

ALAN. No thanks, Sol. Is Marjorie in the office, Bus?

BUS. Yes, Alan.

SOL. Boy, it was a stunning job!

WINGBLATT. It's a system!

SOL. You give everybody what he wants, including the opposition, and lo! there ain't no opposition.

DELL. It can be applied to all appropriation bills!

WINGBLATT. Yes, and I'm willing to bet it will be!

ALAN. I know I lost, Sol. You don't need to tell me.

DELL. Don't you feel bad about this, Mr. McClean.

SNEDEN. We made more mistakes than you did. We only won by accident!
(MISS MCMURTRY *enters*.)

WINGBLATT. Why, you damn near beat us at our own game.
(*The crowd greets* MCMURTRY.)

MCMURTRY. Mr. McClean, I want to thank you from my heart for the poor and the stricken who will turn to the bureau for relief!

SNEDEN. You aren't going to spurn us, are you, Bess?

MCMURTRY. Well, I don't as a rule—but on this occasion—(*She takes a drink.* LEVERING *enters*.)

LEVERING. Alan, my boy—many a man in Congress promises more than he performs; but few indeed perform more than they promise. You're one of the few!

ALAN. You know I put those things in the bill to kill it!

WINGBLATT. But it didn't kill it. That's what put it through!

SNEDEN. And you were careful to stick in your own extra million, weren't you?

ALAN. I had a personal reason for doing that!

WINGBLATT. Well, so did we all! We all had personal reasons! Sol had his navy! Farnum had his national park! And I had —I won't say what I had, but it was damn good and personal!

LEVERING. We want you to come in and work with us, McClean.

ALAN. I'm afraid you're under a misapprehension. I'm not the kind of person to trust on the inside.

WINGBLATT. Oh, give us a whirl, brother. You can't buck the game single-handed. Are we going to celebrate?

FARNUM. Sit in with us a couple of months! You'll be the right kind of person!

LEVERING. You really have no choice now, McClean. You're one of us, or you have no friends in Congress.

ALAN. You want me in with you because I know too much and you're afraid I may tell what I know. Well, I'm not accepting the invitation.

PEEBLES. Does that mean you're thinking of letting newspaper correspondents in on confidential matters that took place in secret session?

ALAN. I don't know.

PEEBLES. That means he is.

WINGBLATT. Don't be a sorehead. We're quite willing to listen to suggestions. What do you think we ought to do?

ALAN. I think we all ought to get up and go home.

DELL. Go home!

ALAN. We've cost the country about four hundred millions today, and the least we can do is clear out of here before we cost them any more.

SNEDEN. You're suggesting that we all resign?

ALAN. I am.

FARNUM. Boys, am I losing my mind?

MCMURTRY. I never heard such talk!

WINGBLATT. Oh, I've had enough!

SNEDEN. I'm not much of a home boy myself!
(MARJORIE *and* GRAY *enter from the office*.)

ALAN. How long do you think a governing body can go on when it's made itself a laughing stock, the length and breadth of the country, the way this one has?

WINGBLATT. Why, you simple-minded cub, that's treason!

ALAN. How can one speak treason about this government or Congress? It's one vast, continuous, nation-wide disaster!

EDDIE. Just another red, boys!

WINGBLATT. A bull-fighter!

EDDIE. He's following Ebner's trail!

ALAN. And I'm not a red! I don't like communism or fascism or any other political patent medicine! If I did, I'd say what Ebner says—go right ahead the way you're going. You're doing all you can to bring it on!

FARNUM. There's never been a better government on the face of the earth! Our forefathers fought and died to give us the government we have today!

ALAN. And look at it now!

PEEBLES. What he means is, he don't like us much.

GRAY. You may not believe me, but I respect what you're trying to do—I respect it profoundly. Tell me what you would like to see here, Alan. If you know of anything better, I wouldn't mind working toward it myself. I don't care for this system any more than you do.

ALAN. Is honesty possible here at all?

GRAY. I'd say that honesty was so rare as to be almost unknown in any government, and impossible under our system.

PEEBLES. Now what the hell is our system?

GRAY. Our system is every man for himself —and the nation be damned!

SOL. And it works! It works when you give it a chance. Do you want me to point you the road to prosperity? Loot the treasury, loot the national resources, hang fortunes on the Wall Street Christmas tree! Graft, gigantic graft brought us our prosperity in the past and will lift us out of the present depths of parsimony and despair!

DELL. You're pushing it a little far, Sol!

SOL. I'm understating it! Brigands built up this nation from the beginning, brigands of a gigantic Silurian breed that don't grow in a piddling age like ours! They stole billions and gutted whole states and empires, but they dug our oil-wells, built our railroads, built up everything we've got, and invented prosperity as they went along!

Let 'em go back to work! We can't have an honest government, so let 'em steal plenty and get us started again. Let the behemoths plunder so the rest of us can eat!

LEVERING. Oh, turn it off, Sol!

DELL. That don't sound so good!

GRAY. Allowing for Sol's usual exaggeration—it is true!

ALAN. Then aren't you against it?

GRAY. I am.

ALAN. And isn't it time to say that it can't go on?

FARNUM. Can't go on?

PEEBLES. Who's going to stop it?

WINGBLATT. Don Quixote!

SOL. Take it easy, boys. I heard Alan say once before that something couldn't go on, and the hell he raised gave you all heart-failure. If you've got anything on your mind, Alan, give us fair warning.

ALAN. More people are open-minded nowadays than you'd believe. A lot of them aren't so sure we found the final answer a hundred and fifty years ago. Who knows what's the best kind of government? Maybe they all get rotten after a while and have to be replaced. It doesn't matter about you or me. We had a little set-to here over a minor matter, and you've won, but I want to tell you I'm not even a premonition of what you're going to hear crashing around you if the voters who elect you ever find out what you're like and what you do to them. The best I can do is just to help them find it out.

EDDIE. Let him shoot his mouth off. He'll start talking wild and the papers won't give him three lines.

SOL. That's true too, Alan. Nobody'll believe you. What happens here is incredible, absolutely incredible.

ALAN. I'm not the person to give you a warning. I'm not a politician. I'm a Nevada school-teacher. I don't know your tricks—you showed me that tonight, and

I won't forget it. But I didn't lose because I was wrong. I lost because I tried to beat you at your own game—and you can always win at that. You think you're good and secure in this charlatan's sanctuary you've built for yourselves. You think the sacred and senseless legend poured into the people of this country from childhood will protect you. It won't. It takes about a hundred years to tire this country of trickery—and we're fifty years overdue right now. That's my warning. And I'd feel pretty damn pitiful and lonely saying it to you, if I didn't believe there are a hundred million people who are with me, a hundred million people who are disgusted enough to turn from you to something else. Anything else but this. (*He turns and goes out.*)

GRAY. And good luck to him! (*He goes into his office.* MARJORIE *goes out after* ALAN.)

LEVERING. Think the papers'll give him a break, Sol?

BUS. They'll give him a break! On every front page in the country!

SOL. They'll have to—if he hands them that line.

PEEBLES. May be a little nasty for some of us.

SOL. It'll blow over, it'll blow over. As a matter of fact, the natural resources of this country in political apathy and indifference have hardly been touched. They're just learning how to pay taxes. In a few more years you'll really give 'em taxes to pay.

WINGBLATT. You think so?

SOL. I know it. On the other hand, he's right about you. I always told you boys you were a bunch of crooks, and you are. The whole blistering blasphemous batch of you! And some day they're going to catch up with you.

WINGBLATT. Well, how about youself, you two-faced swindler?

SOL. I'm too old, Wingie. They won't get me. No—I don't hardly expect it in my time. (*He pours himself a drink.*)

BUS. Maybe.

Curtain.

Men In White

BY SIDNEY KINGSLEY

TO THE MEN IN MEDICINE
WHO DEDICATE THEMSELVES,
WITH QUIET HEROISM,
TO MAN

Caution: Professionals and amateurs are hereby warned that *Men in White*, being fully protected under the Copyright Laws of the United States of America, the British Empire, including the Dominion of Canada, and all other countries of the Copyright Union, is subject to royalty. All rights, including professional, amateur, motion picture, recitation, lecturing, public reading, radio broadcasting, and the rights of translation into foreign languages are strictly reserved. Particular emphasis is laid on the question of readings, permission for which must be secured from the author's agent in writing. All inquiries should be addressed to the author's agent, Harold Freedman, 101 Park Avenue, New York City.

SIDNEY KINGSLEY

Sidney Kingsley was born in New York in 1907 and graduated from Cornell University in 1928, having achieved distinction as an actor in the Cornell Dramatic Club. He also wrote and directed plays during his college days. After graduation he acted for six months in the Tremont Stock Company in the Bronx and later had a small part in the Broadway production of *Subway Express*.

Mr. Kingsley devoted himself during the next five years to the writing of plays. Following many disappointments and after five options had been taken on it within three years, *Men in White* was finally produced by the experimental Group Theatre.

Presented at the Broadhurst Theatre, New York, September 26, 1933, by the Group Theatre, Sidney Harmon and James R. Ullman, *Men in White* received the 1933-1934 Pulitzer award.

"I swear by Apollo, the physician, and Aesculapius, and Hygieia, and Panacea and all the gods and all the goddesses—and make them my judges—that this mine oath and this my written engagement I will fulfill as far as power and discernment shall be mine. . . .

"I will carry out regimen for the benefit of the sick, and I will keep them from harm and wrong. To none will I give a deadly drug even if solicited, nor offer counsel to such an end; but guiltless and hallowed will I keep my life and mine art.

"Into whatsoever houses I shall enter I will work for the benefit of the sick, holding aloof from all voluntary wrong and corruption. Whatsoever in my practice, or not in my practice, I shall see or hear amid the lives of men which ought not to be noised abroad—as to this I will keep silent, holding such things unfitting to be spoken.

"And now, if I shall fulfill this oath and break it not, may the fruits of art and life be mine, may I be honored of all men for all time; the opposite if I transgress and be foresworn."

—*Excerpts from the Hippocratic oath, to which physicians have bound themselves since the days of antique Greece.*

CHARACTERS

DR. GORDON, attending in medicine.

DR. HOCHBERG, attending chief of surgical staff.

DR. MICHAELSON, interne.

DR. VITALE, young practitioner.

DR. McCABE, retired surgeon.

DR. FERGUSON, interne, house surgeon.

DR. WREN, attending in medicine.

DR. OTIS ("SHORTY"), interne.

DR. BRADLEY ("PETE"), interne.

DR. CRAWFORD ("MAC"), interne.

BARBARA DENNIN, student nurse.

NURSE JAMISON.

NURSE MARY RYAN.

FIRST NURSE.

SECOND NURSE.

ORDERLY.

MR. HUDSON, a wealthy patient.

JAMES MOONEY, his business associate.

LAURA HUDSON, his daughter.

DR. LEVINE, in general practice.

DR. CUNNINGHAM, a "courtesy" physician at St. George's.

DOROTHY SMITH, a young patient.

MRS. SMITH, her mother.

MR. SMITH, her father.

MR. HOUGHTON, a trustee of the hospital.

MR. SPENCER, a trustee of the hospital.

MR. RUMMOND, a trustee of the hospital.

MRS. D'ANDREA, the mother of a patient.

SCENES

The entire action takes place within the walls of St. George's Hospital.

MEN IN WHITE

ACT ONE

SCENE I

The library of St. George's Hospital. The staff of the hospital gather here to read, to smoke, and to discuss many things—primarily Medicine.

This is a large, comfortable room flanked on the left by tall windows, on the right by ceiling-high bookcases crammed with heavy tomes. There is a bulletin-board in one corner, on which various notices, announcements, advertisements, schedules, etc., are tacked; there is a long table, an abandon of professional magazines and pamphlets strewn upon it; there are many plump leather club chairs, some of which are occupied at the moment by members of the staff. In a series of stalls against the back wall are a number of phones.

Niched high in the wall is a marble bust of Hippocrates,[1] the father of Medicine, his kindly, brooding spirit looking down upon the scene. At the base of the bust is engraved a quotation from his Precepts: "Where the love of man is, there also is the love of the art of healing."

A number of the staff are smoking and chatting in small groups, the nucleus of each group being an older man in civilian clothes—an attending physician; the young men, internes, recognizable by their white short-sleeved summer uniforms, are doing most of the listening, the older ones most of the talking, the hush of the room on their voices.

One elderly white-haired physician, seated well to the right, is straining his eyes over a thick medical volume. A number of other books and pamphlets are on a stool beside him. A middle-aged physician, his back to us, is searching the bookcase for a desired volume. A younger practitioner is standing by the window, looking out into the street.

Through a wide, glass-panelled, double door, set in the rear wall, we see a section of the corridor alive with its steady cavalcade of nurses, internes, etc., all hurrying by to their separate tasks. The quick activity of the hospital outside contrasts noticeably with the classical repose of the library.

The loud speaker at the head of the corridor calls: "DR. RAMSEY! DR. RAMSEY! DR. RAMSEY!"

Phone rings. An interne crosses to the phones, picks one up, talks in low tones.

Enter DR. HOCHBERG, *a short, vital man, whose large head is crowned by a shock of graying hair. He carries himself with quiet, simple dignity. There is strength in the set of his jaw; but the predominating quality expressed in his face is a sweet compassion—a simple goodness.[2] That he is a man of importance is at once apparent in the respectful attention bestowed on him by the others.*

---

[1] *Hippocrates* (460 to 359 B.C.): ancient Greek physician whose figure is revered by all medical men as that of the ideal physician. He has left a group of writings known as the "Hippocratic Collection," and an oath which is the beacon for all ages of the incorruptibility of medicine.

[2] "All knowledge attains its ethical value and its human significance only by the humane sense in which it is employed. Only a good man can be a great physician."—Nothnagel.

DR. GORDON (*the middle-aged physician, who has just found his book. Sees* HOCH-BERG). Ah, Doctor Hochberg! I've been waiting for you. (*He quickly replaces the volume and goes to* HOCHBERG.)
(*The young practitioner by the window wheels round at the mention of* HOCHBERG'S *name.*)

DR. GORDON. There's a patient I want you to see.

DR. HOCHBERG. Certainly, Josh. We'll look at him in a minute. I just—(*His eye sweeps the room.*) George Ferguson isn't here, is he?

MICHAELSON (*one of the internes seated; looks up from his reading*). No, Dr. Hochberg. Shall I call him?

HOCHBERG (*nods*). Please.
(MICHAELSON *rises and goes to a telephone.*)

DR. VITALE (*the young practitioner, leaves the window and approaches* HOCHBERG). Er . . . Dr. Hochberg—

HOCHBERG. Good morning, doctor.

VITALE. I sent a patient of mine to your clinic yesterday. Did you have a chance to . . . ?

HOCHBERG (*recollecting*). Oh—yes, yes. (*Reassuringly, knowing that this is perhaps* VITALE's *first private patient, and most likely a relative at that.*) No rush to operate there. You try to cure him medically first.

VITALE (*relieved*). I see. All right, doctor. Thank you. Thank you.

HOCHBERG. Not at all. Keep in touch with me. Let me know what progress you make.

VITALE. I will.

HOCHBERG. If we have to, we'll operate. But I think if we wait on nature this case will respond to expectant treatment.

VITALE. Right! (*He goes.*)

GORDON (*shakes his head, kidding* HOCH-BERG). Fine surgeon you are—advising against operation!

HOCHBERG (*smiles and shrugs his shoulders*). Why not give the patient the benefit of the doubt? You can always operate! That's easy, Josh.

MICHAELSON (*returning from the phone*). Dr. Ferguson'll be right down, sir.

HOCHBERG. Thanks.

GORDON. I hear you've some interesting cases at your clinic.

HOCHBERG. Yes, yes—er—suppose you have dinner with me tonight. We'll talk, hm? I discovered a little place on Eighty-fourth Street where they serve the most delicious schnitzel and a glass of beer (*measuring it with his hands*)—that high! . . . But beer!

GORDON. Sounds good. I'll just phone my wife and—

HOCHBERG. It won't upset her plans?

GORDON. Oh, no! (*He crosses to the phone.*)

HOCHBERG (*approaches the white-haired physician and places a hand gently on his shoulder*). And how is Dr. McCabe to-day?

MCCABE. My eyes are bothering me! (*He indicates the pyramid of books beside his chair.*) Trying to read all of this new medical literature. It certainly keeps piling up! (*He shakes his head.*) Has me worried!

HOCHBERG. But, why?

MCCABE (*nods toward internes*). These young men today—How can they ever catch up with all this?[1]

[1] "The amount of human labor and ingenuity that is now being thrown into the investigation of Nature is almost incredible even to men of science. Some conception of the enormous and un-readable bulk of scientific literature may be gained by a glance at the 'International Catalogue of Scientific Literature.' This gives the *titles alone* of original articles in the various departments of physical science. These titles for the year 1914 alone occupied seventeen closely printed volumes! The rate of publication has accelerated considerably since then. There are very few departments of science which do not have some bearing on Medicine. It is evident that no human mind can possibly compass even a year's output of this material."—Charles Singer in "A Short History of Medicine."

HOCHBERG. These young men are all right. They're serious—hard-working boys. I've a lot of faith in them.

MCCABE. But there's so much. (*He shakes his head.*) We've gone so far since I was a boy.[1] In those days appendicitis was a fatal disease. Today it's nothing. These youngsters take all that for granted. They don't know the men who dreamed and sweated—to give them anaesthesia and sterilization and surgery, and X-ray. All in my lifetime. I worked with Spencer Wells in London,[2] and Murphy at Mercy Hospital.[3] Great men. None of these youngsters will equal them. They can't. There's too much! I'm afraid it will all end in confusion.

HOCHBERG. Where the sciences *in general* are going to end, with their mass of detail—nobody knows. But, good men in medicine . . . we'll always have. Don't worry, Dr. McCabe . . . one or two of these boys may surprise you yet, and turn out another Murphy or another Spencer Wells.

MCCABE (*shaking his head*). Not a Spencer Wells! No! Not a Spencer Wells! (HOCHBERG *helps him rise.*) Chilly in here, isn't it? (*He walks slowly to the door.*) I'm always cold these days. (*He shakes his head.*) Bad circulation!
(GORDON *finishes his phone call, hangs up and crosses to* HOCHBERG.)

HOCHBERG. All right for dinner, Josh?

GORDON. Oh, of course. Certainly!
(*An interne,* GEORGE FERGUSON, *and an attending physician,* DR. WREN, *come up the corridor engaged in discussion. The interne stops outside the door to give some instructions to a passing nurse, who hastens to obey them. He pauses in the doorway of the library, still talking to* DR.

WREN. GEORGE FERGUSON *is about twenty-eight; handsome in an angular, manly fashion, tall, wiry, broad-shouldered, slightly stooped from bending over books and patients; a fine sensitive face, a bit tightened by strain, eager eyes, an engaging earnestness and a ready boyish grin.*)

FERGUSON. If we used Dakin tubes[4] it might help. . . .

DR. WREN. They're worth a trial!

FERGUSON. And, this afternoon, first chance I have, I'll take him up to the O.R.[5] and debride all that dead tissue.

WREN. Good idea! (*And he marches on down the corridor.*)
(DR. MCCABE *reaches the door.* FERGUSON *holds it open for him.* MCCABE *returns* FERGUSON's *smile and nod.* MCCABE *goes on.* FERGUSON *enters and approaches* HOCHBERG.)

MICHAELSON. They've been ringing you here, George.

FERGUSON. Thanks, Mike! (*To* DR. HOCHBERG.) Good morning, Dr. Hochberg.

HOCHBERG. Good morning, George.

FERGUSON. I was down in the record room this morning. (*He takes a pack of index-cards out of his pocket.*) The first forty-five cases seem to bear you out. . . .

HOCHBERG (*smiles*). Uh, hm! . . .

FERGUSON. Some three hundred more charts to go through yet, but. . . .

GORDON. What's this?

HOCHBERG. Oh, Ferguson and I are doing a little research. I have some crazy notions about modern surgical technique. Ferguson, here, is writing a paper to prove that I'm right!

---

[1] Medicine has advanced farther in the last fifty years than in the preceding fifty centuries.
   Without anaesthesia, asepsis and X-ray, all of which were developed during the last half-century, major surgery would have remained an impossible dream.
[2] Thomas Spencer Wells (1818-1897): pioneer in abdominal surgery—noted for his simple and effective methods.
[3] J. B. Murphy (1857-1916): outstanding among the men who developed the technique of abdominal surgery.
[4] Dakin tubes: arrangement of tubes invented during the World War by Dr. H. D. Dakin to provide constant flushing of deep and gangrenous wounds with an effective antiseptic (Dakin's solution) also devised by him.
[5] O.R.: hospital jargon for operating-room.

FERGUSON. As a matter of fact, Dr. Hochberg is writing the paper. I'm just helping collect the data and arrange it.

HOCHBERG. Oh! You're doing all the hard work! How's 217?

FERGUSON. Pretty restless during the night, but her temperature's down to normal now.

HOCHBERG. Good! And Ward B—bed three?

FERGUSON. Fine! Asked for a drink of whiskey.

HOCHBERG (*smiles*). He'll be all right.

FERGUSON. He is all right! (*He grins.*) I gave him the drink.

HOCHBERG (*laughs*). Won't hurt him. . . .

FERGUSON (*becomes serious, turns to* DR. GORDON). I wish you'd have another look at 401, Doctor.

GORDON. Any worse today?

FERGUSON. I'm afraid so. He's putting up a fight, though. He may pull through.

GORDON (*shaking his head dubiously*). Mm, I don't know.

FERGUSON. I hope so. He's a fine fellow. He's planning great things for himself— when he gets out. . . .
(*The phone rings. A short interne crosses to phones and picks one up.*)

HOCHBERG. Oh, by the way, George, we're sending Mr. Hudson home Tuesday.

FERGUSON (*suddenly excited*). Tuesday? Great! Does Laura know, yet?

HOCHBERG (*nods*). I phoned her this morning.

FERGUSON. She happy?

HOCHBERG. Naturally!

FERGUSON. I wish you had let me tell her.

HOCHBERG (*twinkling*). Ah—I should have thought of that!

SHORTY (*at phone*). One second. (*Calls.*) Ferguson! For you.

HOCHBERG. Go on! Call for you. (FERGUSON *goes to phone.* HOCHBERG *beams at* GORDON.) Good boy! Lots of ability! We're going to be proud of him some day.
(*Enter a lean, shabby man who at first glance appears out of place here. His coat is rusty, and rough weather has left its stain on the hat he carries so deferentially. Tucked under one arm is a large envelope of the type used for X-ray pictures. He has a timid, beaten manner. He is a fairly young man, but worry has lined his forehead, and prematurely grayed his hair, making him seem years older. He hesitates at* DR. HOCHBERG'S *elbow, and finally ventures to touch it.*)

HOCHBERG (*turns, looks at him. Politely, as to a stranger*). Yes? (*Suddenly he recognizes the man.*) Why . . . Levine! (*He grips* LEVINE'S *arms with both hands, almost in an embrace.*) My dear Levine! . . . I didn't recognize you. . . .

LEVINE (*nods and smiles sadly*). I know.

HOCHBERG. Dr. Gordon! You remember Dr. Levine?

GORDON (*hesitates a moment*). Why, of course. (*They shake hands.*)

HOCHBERG. Such a stranger! Where have you been hiding all this time? Why, it must be . . . five years since. . . .

LEVINE. Six!

HOCHBERG. Six? My! Mm. . . . (*To* GORDON.) We're getting old. (*Then, affectionately.*) Ah! It's good to see you again.

LEVINE. It's nice to get back, but. . . . (*He looks around.*) Things here seem pretty much the same. New faces—that's all.

GORDON. Nothing much changes in a hospital.

LEVINE. Only people! We change . . . get old . . . break up so quickly. (*The tragic quality in his voice affects the others. Pause.*)

GORDON. Well. . . . (To HOCHBERG.) I'm going up to look at that boy in 401. (HOCHBERG *nods.* GORDON *turns to* LEVINE.) I'm glad to have seen you again. (*Exit* GORDON.)

HOCHBERG. Tell me . . . how are things with you?

LEVINE. Oh. . . . (*He shrugs his shoulders.*) Just about getting along.

HOCHBERG. And how is Katherine?

LEVINE (*his brow wrinkles*). Not so well.

HOCHBERG (*concerned*). What seems to be the trouble?

LEVINE. Her lungs. . . . She has a slight persistent cough! Some X-rays[1] here. . . . (*He opens the large envelope he is carrying and from it takes two X-ray plates. HOCHBERG holds up the plates to the window and examines them.*) (FERGUSON *hangs up and returns to* HOCHBERG.)

HOCHBERG (*holds the plates so that FERGUSON can see them*). George . . . ?

FERGUSON. That shadow there! The right apex.

LEVINE. Yes—I was afraid of. . . .

HOCHBERG. Now, don't be an alarmist! (*Sees something.*) Mm! (*Squints at the plate, and asks, gravely.*) Have you examined the sputum? (*Pause.*)

LEVINE. I brought a specimen. (*He takes out a bottle, wrapped in paper, and explains apologetically.*) My microscope is broken.

HOCHBERG. We'll look at it here!

FERGUSON. Certainly! (*He takes the bottle.*) I'll have the path lab[2] check up on this. Is it anything important?

LEVINE. My wife.

FERGUSON. Oh.

HOCHBERG. Er . . . Dr. Ferguson, Dr. Levine! (*They shake hands and exchange greetings.*)

FERGUSON. I'll tend to this at once, Doctor.

LEVINE. Thanks. Do you think if I came back this evening—?

FERGUSON. Oh, yes, the report will be ready then. Drop into my room—106.

LEVINE. 106? (*He turns to* HOCHBERG. *With nostalgia.*) My old room.

FERGUSON. You interned here? Are you the—Oh, of course. Bellevue, aren't you?

LEVINE (*nods*). '23!

FERGUSON. Professor Dury mentions you quite often.

LEVINE. Dury? (*To* HOCHBERG.) He still remembers me. . . .

FERGUSON. He thinks a great deal of you.

HOCHBERG. George, here, is one of his prize pupils, too.

LEVINE. And does he want you to study abroad?

FERGUSON. Yes. I planned to go with Sauerbruch, but he has been forced to leave Germany.[3] So, instead of that, I'm going to study under von Eiselsberg[4] in Vienna.

HOCHBERG. Hm! I remember when I was a student in Berlin, one of my classmates came to an examination in military uniform . . . sabre and all. Virchow looked at

---

[1] X-ray: discovered by Wilhelm Konrad Röntgen (1845-1922). It has since become so important an accessory that today a good physician would not set a broken finger without it.

[2] Path lab: hospital jargon for pathology laboratory.

[3] "In the physician's professional relations, though divided by national lines, there remains the feeling that he belongs to a Guild that owes no local allegiance, which has neither king nor country, but whose work is in the world."—Sir William Osler, in "Counsels and Ideals."

Attempting to make the physician deny this, his fundamental creed, Hitler's Reich has merely succeeded in halting the progress of modern German medicine. Nazi intolerance forced not only all the prominent Jewish figures in medicine, but also non-Jews like Ernst Ferdinand Sauerbruch, greatest living German surgeon, to close their clinics and leave Germany in despair. Not satisfied with expatriating their finest surgeons, the Nazis, with peculiar compassion, enforced anti-vivisection laws restricting their young surgeons from practicing . . . except on human subjects! Surgery, which is a fine art requiring, in addition to other things, the digital sensitivity of a pianist, demands incessant practice. Germany will see no more Sauerbruchs till she learns to respect the autonomy, the humanity, and the tolerance which are the spirit of medicine, and without it cannot exist.

[4] Anton von Eiselsberg: the foremost living Viennese surgeon.

him, and said, "You! What are you doing here in that monkey suit? Your business is with death! Ours is with life!" Virchow was a man of science. He knew.[1] (*He shakes his head.*) I wonder what he would say to our beloved Germany today.

LEVINE. Yes. . . .

FERGUSON (*to* HOCHBERG). Well, Laura prefers Vienna, anyway, so. . . . (*To* LEVINE.) I'm going on my honeymoon too, you see.

LEVINE. You'll find it difficult mixing the two. I know von Eiselsberg.

HOCHBERG. It's going to be very difficult. You don't know Laura.

FERGUSON. After a year in Vienna I'm working with Dr. Hochberg. So the real labor won't begin till I come back from Europe.

HOCHBERG. Oh, I'll drive you, George! With a whip, eh?

LEVINE. Lucky! (*Retrospectively.*) Yes. . . . I once looked forward to all that. (*He sighs.*)

HOCHBERG. Well, come, Levine. We'll go down to X-ray and read these pictures properly.

FERGUSON (*holds up bottle*). And don't worry about this.

LEVINE. Thank you . . . thank you. (*Exit* HOCHBERG. LEVINE *turns to* FERGUSON.) Remember, there's only one Hochberg. Every minute with him is precious.

FERGUSON. I won't miss a second of it.

(LEVINE *goes.* FERGUSON *crosses to a long table at which* MICHAELSON *and* SHORTY *are seated.*)

MICHAELSON (*who has been watching* LEVINE *and* FERGUSON). He's telling *you,* huh?

FERGUSON (*nods, smiles and looks for a particular book in the shelves*). Say, there's a damned interesting article on Hochberg in this week's A.M.A.[2]

FERGUSON. I know. (*He finds the magazine and hands it over to* SHORTY, *a small, chubby, good-natured, irresponsible, wisecracking fellow, who takes life in his stride.*) Here it is. You want to read this, Shorty.
(SHORTY *sits down to read it.*)

MICHAELSON. Yep. I wish I could get in with him for a year. . . .

FERGUSON (*to* SHORTY). What do you think of that first case? The way he handled it? Beautiful job, isn't it? Beautiful!

PETE (*interne, a tall, gawky lad, slow moving and casual about everything but food, enters, fixing his stethoscope. He drawls*). Say, George. . . .

SHORTY. Pete! Sweetheart! You're just the man I've been looking for.

PETE (*drily*). The answer is no.

SHORTY. Will you lend me your white tux vest for tonight? I've got. . . .

PETE (*abruptly*). The answer is still no. (*He turns to* FERGUSON.) That little—

SHORTY (*sits down again*). Thanks!

PETE. You're welcome. (*To* FERGUSON *again.*) The little girl we just operated on is coming out of her ether nicely. I was kind of worried about that preop [3] Insulin.[4]

FERGUSON. Why? How much did you give her?

PETE. Forty units.

FERGUSON. Twenty would have been enough.

---

[1] Rudolf Virchow, pathologist and anthropologist (1821-1902) made many important contributions to modern medicine.
Though I have taken some liberties in the telling, this anecdote has its basis in fact and was recounted to me with relish by an old pupil of the great Virchow.
[2] A.M.A.: the journal of the American Medical Association. The most widely read medical publication in the United States; published with the purpose of welding the medical profession into an efficient, competent body to guard against quackery and to preserve the highest standards of ethics and education.
[3] Preop: hospital jargon meaning "before operation."
[4] Insulin: an extract from the pancreas used in the treatment of diabetes.
The patient referred to has diabetes, and hence special preoperative treatment is required.

PETE. I know.

FERGUSON. Then why the hell did you give her forty? You might have hurt the kid.

PETE. Dr. Cunningham ordered it.

SHORTY. That dope—Cunningham!

FERGUSON. You should have told me before you gave it to her. I'm not going to have patients go into shock on the operating table![1] Understand?

PETE. O. K.

FERGUSON (*good-naturedly, slapping* PETE *on the head with a pamphlet*). If this happens again, Pete, you get your behind kicked in . . . and not by Cunningham!

PETE. O. K.
(A NURSE, *passing by, carrying a tray of medication, halts in the doorway, looks in and calls.*)

NURSE. Oh, Doctor Ferguson, that drink worked wonders. Bed three is sitting up and taking notice.

FERGUSON (*laughs*). A new school of therapy!

SHORTY. Say, Jamison, you're not looking so hot. You ought to stay home one night and get some sleep.

JAMISON. Oh, I'm doing all right. (*She laughs and goes.*)

SHORTY. Yeah? I'll bet you are.
(*The loud speaker starts calling,* "DR. BRADLEY! DR. BRADLEY!")

PETE. Say, I'm hungry! Somebody got something to eat?

SHORTY. What, again? (PETE *looks at him with scorn.*) Lend me your white vest for tonight, will you, Pete? I'll fix up a date for you with that red-head.
(*Phone rings.*)

PETE (*nodding at* FERGUSON). Fix him up.
(FERGUSON *laughs.*)

SHORTY. It'd do him good. That's the trouble with love—it kills your sex-life. . . . (*Indicates the phone.*) Pete! Phone!

PETE. I was once in love myself. (*He starts for phone.*) But when it began to interfere with my appetite. . . . Hell! No woman's worth that!
(*They laugh.*)

FERGUSON. Thing I like about you, Pete, is your romantic nature.

PETE (*on phone*). Dr. Bradley! O.K. I'll be right up! (*He hangs up.*) Yep. At heart I'm just a dreamer.

SHORTY. At heart you're just a stinker!

PETE. Thanks.

SHORTY (*quickly*). You're welcome!
(PETE *goes toward the door.*)

FERGUSON. Going upstairs, Pete?

PETE. Yep.

FERGUSON (*gives him the bottle of sputum*). Will you take this to the path lab? Ask Finn to examine it and draw up a report.

PETE. O.K.
(*Enter* DR. GORDON.)

FERGUSON. Tell him to give it special attention! It's a friend of Hochberg's.

SHORTY (*follows* PETE *to door*). I take back what I said, Pete. You're a great guy, and I like you. Now, if you'll only lend me that white vest. . . .

PETE. No!

SHORTY. Stinker! (*They exit.*)
(GORDON *comes over to* FERGUSON.)

GORDON (*his face grave*). Well . . . I just saw 401. He's a mighty sick boy. He may need another transfusion.

FERGUSON. We'll have to go pretty deep to find a good vein.

---

[1] Insulin shock: In diabetes, insulin is used to enable the body to utilize the abnormal amounts of sugar in the blood. Too much insulin, however, will reduce the sugar content of the blood below normal and throw the patient into a condition of shock.

GORDON. That's what I'm worried about. If it comes up tonight I want you to be here to do it.

FERGUSON. Tonight?

GORDON. There are three donors on call.

FERGUSON. This is my night out. . . . My fiancée has made arrangements. . . . So I'm afraid I won't be here.

GORDON. I'm sorry, Ferguson. When the House needs you. . . .

FERGUSON. I'd like to, Doctor, but the same thing happened last week. I can't disappoint my fiancée again . . . or . . . (*He smiles.*) . . . I won't have any.

MICHAELSON. Er—Dr. Gordon, couldn't I do that transfusion?

GORDON. I'm afraid not—the superficial veins are all thrombosed.[1] Ferguson has followed the case from the start; he knows the veins we've used.

FERGUSON. Laidlaw knows the veins. . . .

GORDON. Frankly, I don't trust any of the other men on this case. I know I'm imposing, but I want this boy to have every possible chance. . . . (*Pause.*) He's a sick boy, Ferguson. What do you say?

FERGUSON. All right! I'll stay.

GORDON. Thanks! (*He starts to go—turns back.*) And if your sweetheart kicks up a fuss send her around to me. I'll tell her about my wife. Up at four-thirty this morning to answer the phone. Somebody had a bellyache. . . (*He laughs, nods and goes.* FERGUSON *remains, dejected.*)

FERGUSON. Damn it! I wanted to be with Laura, tonight.

MICHAELSON. That's tough, George. I'm sorry I couldn't help you out.

(*The loud speaker starts calling:* "DR. MANNING! DR. MANNING!")

FERGUSON (*rises and walks about*). Laura's going to be hurt. You'd think they'd have a little. . . .

NURSE (*comes quickly down the corridor, looks in, and calls, a bit breathless*). Dr. Ferguson? (*She sees him.*) Dr. Ferguson, a woman just came in on emergency with a lacerated throat. She's bleeding terribly! Dr. Crane told me to tell you he can't stop it.

FERGUSON. Get her up to the operating-room. (*He snaps his fingers.*) Stat.[2] (*She hurries off. He turns to* MAC.) Drop that Mac, and order the O.R.! Come on! (MAC *goes to a phone. To* MICHAELSON.) Call an anaesthetist, will you? And locate Dr. Hochberg! Try the X-ray room!

MICHAELSON. Right! (*He jumps to a phone. Exit* FERGUSON.)

MAC—MICHAELSON (*On phones simultaneously*).
MAC. Operating-room! . . . Emergency B! . . . Quick! . . . O.R.? . . . Set up the O.R. right away! Lacerated throat! Dr. Ferguson! Yes!

MICHAELSON. Find Dr. Hochberg! Right away! Emergency! . . . (*The loud speaker, which has been calling,* "DR. MANNING!" *changes to a louder and more persistent,* "DR HOCHBERG! DR. HOCHBERG, DR. HOCHBERG!"*) Well, try the X-ray room! . . . And locate the staff anaesthetist!

(*In the back corridor we catch a glimpse of an orderly hurriedly pushing a rolling-stretcher on which the emergency patient is lying, crying hysterically. An interne on one side, and the nurse at the other are holding pads to her throat and trying to calm her.*)

Fade Out.

---

[1] Thrombosed vein: a plugged or occluded vein.
[2] Stat: hospital jargon for immediately.

SCENE II

The largest and the most expensive private room in the hospital. It is luxuriously fur-nished in the best of taste and tries hard to drive all clinical atmosphere out into the corridor. What the room can't eliminate, it attempts to disguise; not, however, with complete success. For there, behind a large, flowered screen, the foot of a hospital "gatch" bed peeps out, and in the corner we see a table with bottles of medication on it.

MR. HUDSON, *a large man, haunched, paunched and jowled, clad in pajamas and a lounging robe, is sitting up on a divan being shaved by the hospital barber.[1] He is talk-ing to one of his business associates, a* MR. MOONEY, *who is a smaller, nattier, less im-pressive, and, at the moment, highly nervous edition of* HUDSON.

HUDSON (*through a face full of lather*). We'll get that property, Mooney! And we'll get it now . . . on our own terms.

MOONEY (*marching impatiently to and fro*). How are you going to break that Clinton Street boom?

HUDSON. You get in touch with the real estate editor of every paper in town. Tell them we've decided to change the location of Hudson City from Clinton to . . . say Third Street. Map out a territory! Make it convincing!
(*A nurse enters with a bowl of flowers, places it on a small table, arranges the flowers, and departs.*)

MOONEY (*hesitantly*). Think they'll believe it?

HUDSON. Sure. . . . Got a cigar?

MOONEY (*produces one, then hesitates*). You're not supposed to smoke, you know.

HUDSON. I'm all right! Can't think without a cigar! (*He takes it. The barber gives him a light. He puffs once or twice with huge relish.*) Start negotiations with every real-ty owner in the new territory. Buy op-tions! They'll believe that!
(*The barber finishes, starts to powder* HUD-SON's *face, but is waved away.*)

MOONEY. Oh yes. . . .

HUDSON. In the meantime sell ten of our houses on Clinton Street—including cor-ners. Sell low!

MOONEY. Hey! We want that stuff!

HUDSON. Get Henderson! Form two dum-my corporations—and sell to them.

MOONEY. Oh! . . . Yes, I think it'll work . . . that ought to bring down those prices. (*The barber packs his shaving kit, and exits.*)

HUDSON. We'll wait till they're ready to take nickels . . . then our dummy cor-porations can grab all that property. . . . Mooney, we'll be excavating this Spring, yet.
(*Enter* DR. HOCHBERG. *He sees* HUDSON *smoking, frowns, goes to him, takes the cigar out of his mouth, and throws it away.*)

HOCHBERG. Didn't Doctor Whitman say no more cigars?

HUDSON (*startled, his first impulse one of extreme annoyance*). Hochberg, please. . . . (*He controls himself, turns to Moon-ey.*)

MOONEY (*glances at* HOCHBERG, *picks up his coat and hat*). Well, I'll be going now.

HUDSON (*helps him into his coat*). Phone me!

[1] The barber of mediaeval days is the great-granddaddy of the modern surgeon. He let blood, cupped, leeched, gave enemas, extracted teeth and treated wounds.
This particular barber would be delighted to learn the honorable antecedence of his profession, for, with the help of his white jacket, he tries, like many of his brethren, to resemble an interne, and is delighted when occasionally some near-sighted visitor does call him "Doctor."

MOONEY. I will. . . . Don't worry! (*Shakes* HUDSON's *hand.*) Take care of yourself! (*To* HOCHBERG.) Goodbye, Doctor! (HOCHBERG *nods. Exit* MOONEY.)

(HOCHBERG *watches* MOONEY *go, then turns to* HUDSON *and shakes his head.*)

HUDSON. Whitman's sending me home Tuesday, isn't he? What do you want to do? Make an invalid of me? (*He goes to the phone.*) Operator! Get me Vanderbilt 2-34—(*He gasps, an expression of pain crosses his face, his free hand goes to his breast.*)

HOCHBERG (*nods grimly*). Uh, huh! (HUDSON *glances at* HOCHBERG *guiltily, controls himself, continues on the phone.*)

HUDSON. 3471!

HOCHBERG (*goes to him, takes the phone out of his hand, puts it down, with an abrupt nod of the head toward the bed*). You better lie down!

HUDSON. It's nothing. Just a . . .

HOCHBERG (*softly*). I know. Get into bed. (HUDSON *shakes his head and smiles to himself at* HOCHBERG's *persistence. Then he goes to the bed and lies down.* HOCHBERG *feels his pulse.*)

HUDSON. I tell you, I'm all right!

HOCHBERG. I don't understand people like you, John. Whitman is the best cardiac man in the country, but he can't give you a new heart! Don't you know that? Are you such a fool?

(*Enter* LAURA, *a spirited, chic young lady; lithe, fresh, quick, modern, a trifle spoiled perhaps, but withal eminently warm, lovable and human.*)

LAURA. What's he done now, Hocky?

HUDSON. Hello, honey!

HOCHBERG. Laura!

LAURA (*kissing* HUDSON). How's my dad today?

HUDSON. I'm fine, dear, just fine.

LAURA (*takes* HOCHBERG's *hand*) And Hocky, wie geht's?

HOCHBERG. Laura, my dear, can't you do anything with him?

LAURA. Why? . . . Smoking again?

HOCHBERG. Yes.

LAURA. Oh, Dad!

HUDSON. Now, don't you start, Laura!

LAURA. But it's so foolish.

HUDSON. I have an important deal on, honey. Besides I'm all right. Whitman's sending me home Tuesday.

LAURA. I know, dear, and that's great! But it isn't going to do any good if you act this way. Can't you forget the office? Close it up! I mean that.

HOCHBERG. She's right, John—absolutely.

LAURA. What good is your money, damn it! if you can't enjoy it?

HUDSON. Well, it can still buy my little girl a honeymoon.

LAURA. I could spend my honeymoon right here! And have a swell time. As long as it's with George. . . . (*To* HOCHBERG.) Where is that man?

HOCHBERG. Upstairs—busy!

LAURA. Oh! (*To her father.*) So, are you going to behave yourself, Dad?

HUDSON (*smiles and pinches her cheek*). Don't worry about me! I'm all right. . . . I'll live. (*Deliberately changing the subject.*) How was Doris' party last night?

LAURA. Noisy.

HUDSON. Not much fun, eh?

LAURA. Not much.

HUDSON. Too bad George couldn't be there.

LAURA. I spent most of the time upstairs with Doris' baby. It woke and wanted some attention. Babies are awfully human that way, aren't they? Do you know that Doris was going to let him cry himself to sleep? Can you imagine? . . . Believe me, when I have my baby, it's going to get all the care and love and attention it can use.

HOCHBERG (*chuckles*). You have the right instincts, Laura.

LAURA. Have I? (*Rises.*) I haven't had a real kiss in days. . . . Can I get George on the phone, Hocky?

HOCHBERG. He'll be down soon.

LAURA (*goes to phone*). I want to see that man! (*She picks up the phone.*)

HOCHBERG (*brusquely*). Better wait! (LAURA *looks at him, a bit resentfully.*) He's in the operating room.

LAURA. Oh!

HUDSON. Er . . . while you're there, Laura, will you call the office like a good girl, and ask Henderson if . . .

LAURA. No! (*She hangs up sharply.*)

HUDSON. But this is on my mind.

HOCHBERG. Again? John, you're a madman!

LAURA (*quickly, with a tinge of bitterness.*) And he's not the only one, Doctor Hochberg.

HUDSON (*looks up at her quizzically, sees what's eating her, then turns to* HOCHBERG). God, they make a slave of that boy. And he doesn't get a dime! I can't see it.

HOCHBERG (*smiles at that one*). He's not here for the money! He's here to learn. The harder he works the more he learns. If he wanted to make money he wouldn't have chosen medicine in the first place. You know, when he comes with me, his pay is only going to be $20 a week, but there's a chance to work. The man who's there with me now works from 16 to 18 hours a day. He even has a cot rigged up in one of the laboratories, where he sleeps sometimes.[1]

HUDSON. For $20 a week?

HOCHBERG (*nods vigorously*). Yes, yes. . . . (*He turns to* LAURA.) George is a fine boy with great promise. The next five years are crucial years in that boy's life. They're going to tell whether he becomes an important man or not.[2]

LAURA. George is an important man right now, Hocky, to me.

HOCHBERG. To *you*. . . .

LAURA. Well . . . I don't count?

HOCHBERG. Of course you do, dear!

LAURA (*controls herself, turns to her father, abruptly changing the conversation*). What time shall I call for you Tuesday?

HUDSON (*to* HOCHBERG). When can I get out of here?

HOCHBERG. In the morning. Eight—nine o'clock.

HUDSON. Good! (*To* LAURA.) Have Martha prepare a big juicy steak—they've been starving me here.

HOCHBERG. No big steaks!
(HUDSON *groans.* FERGUSON *enters, tired and upset.*)

LAURA. Hello, darling! (*He kisses her.*)

LAURA. Why so glum, dear—toothache?

FERGUSON (*grins—looks at her hat*). Where did you get that hat?

LAURA. Don't you like it?

FERGUSON. Looks like a sailboat! (LAURA *wrinkles her face, pretending to be on the verge of tears.*) No, it's becoming! You look beautiful . . . doesn't she, Doctor Hochberg?

HOCHBERG (*disparagingly*). Hm—she looks all right.

LAURA (*laughs*). I'll kill that man.

HOCHBERG. You should have seen the brat when I delivered her. (*The recollection is too much for him. He looks at* LAURA, *shakes his head, and chuckles.*)

[1] Following the eminent example of Sir William Osler.
[2] "The education of most people ends upon graduation; that of the physician means a lifetime of incessant study."—Marx in Garrison's "History of Medicine."
How much truer this is, then, for a man in medicine who wishes to extend himself in special fields above and beyond those normally trodden by his colleagues!

FERGUSON (*goes to the bedside*). And Dad —I guess we're going to lose our best patient Tuesday.

LAURA. Isn't it marvelous?

FERGUSON. Did you ever see him look so healthy?

HUDSON. I feel fine, George! Good enough to eat a big steak!

HOCHBERG (*grunts*). Mm!

HUDSON. Oh, by the way, George, my secretary's tending to the wedding invitations. Better get your list in to him. And see him about your visas, too. He'll tend to all that.

FERGUSON (*to* LAURA). You know—I still can't believe it's going to happen! I mean just happen!

LAURA. Neither can I.

FERGUSON. Vienna's going to be lots of fun.

LAURA. Fun? You don't know. Wait till you've seen the Prater. It's Coney Island with a lift! Lights all over . . . and those lovely people all laughing and happy . . . and the whole place just tinkling with music.

FERGUSON. I've always had a yen to hear Strauss on his home grounds.

HOCHBERG (*softly*). When I visited Von Eiselsberg his students spent all their time working—with an occasional glass of beer for relaxation. That's what George's Vienna is going to be, Laura.
(GEORGE *and* LAURA *are brought up sharp. Enter a nurse with a wheel-chair.*)

NURSE. Time for your sun bath, sir.

HUDSON. Oh—go away!

HOCHBERG. Come on, Mr. Hudson, no nonsense.

HUDSON. Aw, hell, I can walk, I'm no cripple!

LAURA. Sit down, dad.

HUDSON (*sits in the chair. The nurse tucks a blanket around him.* HUDSON *grumbles to himself*). Treat me like a God damned baby! . . . (*To* NURSE.) Get me that report, will you?

HOCHBERG. John. . . .

HUDSON. I can read, can't I? There's nothing the matter with my eyes. . . . For God's sake. . . . (*He turns to* GEORGE *and* LAURA.) Don't you listen to that old fogey! You kids enjoy yourselves. You're only young once.
(*The* NURSE *wheels him out.* HOCHBERG *watches him go and nods.*)

HOCHBERG. Yes, that's true enough! (*He looks at* FERGUSON *and* LAURA, *a twinkle in his eyes, and sits down as if he were there to stay.*)

FERGUSON. You don't need me yet, Doctor Hochberg, do you?

HOCHBERG. Why not?

LAURA (*threateningly*). Hocky!

HOCHBERG (*rises, grinning like a little boy who's had his joke*). All right! (*To* FERGUSON.) I'll call you when I want you. (*He goes.*)

LAURA (*softly*). Sweetheart! (*She holds out her hands to him.*)

FERGUSON (*taking them*). Darling! (*He draws her up out of the chair to him.*)

LAURA. How's my boy?

FERGUSON (*stares at her in adoration. He almost whispers*). You're lovely. . . . Lovely, Laura. (*Big hug.*)

LAURA. If you knew how I've been aching for this. (*Silence for a moment, as she clings to him.*) Three months! (*She sighs deeply.*) I don't know how I can live till then.

FERGUSON (*tenderly*). Sweet! They're going to be long—those three months—terribly.

LAURA. Yes, I know—I hate to think of them! (*She takes his hand, leads him to a huge easy-chair.*) Come here and—

FERGUSON. Ah!

LAURA. Sit down! (*She pushes him down into the chair and curls up on his lap. Then she takes his head in her hands and scrutinizes his face*). Let me look at you.

(*She shakes her head.*) You're getting thin, young man! And your eyes are tired.

FERGUSON. I didn't have much sleep last night. It was a pretty sick house.

LAURA. You're overworked. . . . (*Pulls his head over on her shoulder.*) And I don't like it one bit. (*Pause.*) You know, you've spoiled everything for me. (FERGUSON *raises his head,* LAURA *pushes his head back.*) I was thinking last night, all the music and noise and fun . . . didn't mean a thing without you. I don't seem to get a kick out of life any more, unless you're around. (*She pauses.*) And that's not very often, is it?

FERGUSON. Darling, we'll make up for it all . . . later on. Honestly.

LAURA. I don't know if we can, George. Last night, for instance. If you had been there—perfect! Now's it's—gone. You see, dearest, the way I feel, if I had you every minute from now on, it wouldn't be enough. (FERGUSON *starts to speak, she puts her hands over his lips.*) I wish I'd lived all my life with you. I wish I'd been born in the same room with you, and played in the same streets.

FERGUSON (*smiles*). I'm glad you missed them. They were ordinary and gloomy. They might have touched you . . . changed you. . . . (*He cups her face in his hands and looks at her.*) About seven months ago there was a boy here who'd been blind from birth. We operated on him—successfully. One night I showed him the stars—for the first time. He looked at them a moment and began to cry like a baby, because, he said, they were so lovely, and—he might never have seen them. When I look at you, Laura, I get something of that feeling. I . . . I can't tell you how large a part of me you've become, Laura! You're. . . . (*The loud speaker is heard calling: "Dr. Ferguson! Dr. Ferguson. . . ."*) Oh, damn it! . . .

LAURA. Don't move! (*She clutches him tightly.*)

FERGUSON. It's no use, Laura! That's my call! Let me up!

LAURA. No!

FERGUSON. Come on! (*He rises, lifting her in his arms, kisses her, sets her on her feet.*)

LAURA. Oh! You spoiled it. (*He goes to the phone, picks up the receiver.* LAURA *finds her vanity case . . . powder and lipstick.*)

FERGUSON. Dr. Ferguson! . . . Yes! . . . Oh! Yes, sir! . . . Yes, doctor! I'll be ready. . . . I'll tend to all that. Right! (*He hangs up— turns to* LAURA.)

LAURA. All right, go on—go to work!

FERGUSON. I won't be needed for half an hour yet.

LAURA. Well, I have to go to my hairdresser's and make myself beautiful for tonight.

FERGUSON. Laura, dear, I. . . .

LAURA. And what a night we're going to have! Doris asked us over there, but I want you to myself. I want to go to that cute little road house where the food and the music were so good—then a long drive up the Hudson—and, darling, there's a full moon, tonight!

FERGUSON. Laura, I've some bad news. You won't be upset, will you?

LAURA. Why?

FERGUSON. I can't make it tonight. I have to stay in. . . .

LAURA (*almost in tears*). Again?

FERGUSON. I'm so sorry, dear. I tried to duck out of it, but I couldn't. There's a transfusion I have to do.

LAURA. What time? I'll wait.

FERGUSON. Better not! It depends on the patient. I've just got to be around and ready!

LAURA. Are you the only one here who can do that transfusion?

FERGUSON. Dr. Gordon seems to think so!

LAURA. George! They're overworking you. It's not fair. . . .

FERGUSON. I don't mind it so much for myself . . . only . . .

LAURA (dully). No? Well I do. (Pause. Then LAURA continues in a low voice, suddenly hoarse.) I was planning so much on tonight.

FERGUSON. Don't you think I was, Laura? All week I've been looking forward to it.

LAURA. Sure. I know.

FERGUSON. You're not sore?

LAURA. It's not your fault. I don't imagine it's much fun for you, either—

FERGUSON. Fun! If you knew how fed up I can be with this place sometimes. . . .

LAURA. George, I'm so low—I've been this way for weeks.

FERGUSON. Damn Gordon! Laidlaw could have done that transfusion.

LAURA. Oh, George, what's our life going to be like?

FERGUSON (gently). Pretty grand, I should say.

LAURA. How can it be? How can it?

FERGUSON. Dear . . . we'll go out tomorrow instead. Mac promised to take my floor. And we'll have a swell time. Saturday's more fun anyway.

LAURA. It's not just tonight! It's all the nights.

FERGUSON. Darling! You're exaggerating! You're. . . .

LAURA. No, I'm not.

FERGUSON. What do you expect me to do? I want to get out . . . I want to enjoy myself . . . but I can't, that's all. I can't.

LAURA. George, I know this is important to you . . . and if it's going to help you . . . I can go on like this for another three months . . . for another year and three months; but when we come back to New York, let's arrange our lives like human beings. You can open up an office and have regular hours . . . specialize!

FERGUSON. If I work with Hochberg, darling, I won't have the time to go into practice.

LAURA. That's just it. I know Hocky. I'll never see you then, George.

FERGUSON. But, Laura. . . . (He laughs nervously.) I've plugged all my life just in the hope that some day I'd have a chance to work with a man like Hochberg. . . . Why. . .

LAURA. I couldn't go on this way. I just couldn't. . . . I'd rather break off now, and try to forget you. . . .

FERGUSON. Laura! Don't ever say a thing like that!

LAURA. I mean it—it would kill me. But I'd rather die quickly than by slow torture. I can't. . . . (The loud speaker is calling him. FERGUSON and LAURA stand there both in anguish.) They're calling you.

FERGUSON. I know. (He hesitates a moment . . . goes to the phone.) Dr. Ferguson! Yes . . . who? South 218 . . . yes? . . . well, call Dr. Cunningham. It's his case . . . let him. (Suddenly his voice becomes brittle.) When? What's her temperature? . . . Pulse? . . . Is she pale? . . . Perspiring? . . . Did she ask for food before she became unconscious? . . . No! No more insulin! Absolutely. I'll be right down. (He hangs up.) I have to go now, Laura. And please—please don't worry. (He bends down to kiss her. She turns her face away. He straightens up and regards her with a worried expression.)

FERGUSON. As bad as that?

LAURA (in a low voice—a bit husky with emotion). Yes.

FERGUSON (forcing a smile). Things will straighten themselves out.

LAURA. No, they won't.
(Pause. FERGUSON pulls himself together, looks toward the door.)

FERGUSON. I'll see you tomorrow night dear? Right?

LAURA. Yes. (*She puts on her hat.*) Think it over, George! We'll have to come to some decision!

FERGUSON. Oh, Laura, will you please. . .

LAURA. I mean it! Absolutely!

FERGUSON (*pauses for a moment in the doorway*). All right . . . all right! (FERGUSON *goes.* LAURA *stands there a moment, the picture of frustration and woe, then she walks in a little circle, crying quietly.*)

Black Out.

SCENE III

A bed, screened off from the others, in a corner of the children's ward. The entire wall, separating ward from corridor, is framed in glass panels, so that the nurse on duty out there can always keep a watchful eye over the youngsters.

A little girl of ten is lying back, eyes closed, skin pale and clammy. Her father stands at the foot of the bed, gazing fearfully at his little daughter. He is wan and unkempt, his hair disheveled, his eyes sunken, his collar open, tie awry—the picture of despair. His wife is standing beside the child, weeping.

At the phone is a young student-nurse, BARBARA DENNIN. *She is speaking rapidly into the phone.*

NURSE. South 218! . . . Calling Dr. Ferguson! At once!

MRS. SMITH. She's so pale, Barney. . . . She's so pale!

MR. SMITH. Where's Cunningham? . . . Why isn't he here? (*To the* NURSE.) Miss Dennin! Can't you do something?

NURSE. Dr. Ferguson will be right here, sir!
(*Enter* DR. CUNNINGHAM, *a dignified, impressive-looking gentleman, immaculately attired, goatee, pince-nez, throaty voice— just a bit too much of the "professional manner," arrived at in this instance by a certain false philosophy which one occasionally finds in the profession.* CUNNINGHAM *believes that nine patients out of ten will be cured by nature anyway, and the tenth will die no matter what the physician does for him. This system of logic concludes that impressing the patient and assuaging his fears are more important than keeping up with medical journals and the march of treatment. The sad part of it is that* CUNNINGHAM *is a successful practitioner—successful, that is, in terms of bank account. True, most of his colleagues look* down on him with scorn, but he has a magnificent Park Avenue office, with all the impressive equipment, wealthy patients, and political influence—which, although he is not a member of the staff, has gained him the "courtesy" of the hospital—meaning that he may bring his patients here for hospitalization.*)

NURSE. Dr. Cunningham! Thank God you're here!

MRS. SMITH. Dr. Cunningham! My baby! She's fainted! She's. . . .

CUNNINGHAM. Now please . . . please, Mrs. Smith! (*He takes off his coat, turns to* BARBARA.) What's happened here?

NURSE. Complete collapse . . . about two minutes ago. . . .

CUNNINGHAM. Let's see the chart! (*She hands him the chart. He looks at it, frowns, shakes his head.*) Hm! This is bad! (*He takes* DOT's *wrist and feels the pulse, closing his eyes.*)

NURSE. Pulse is barely. . . .

CUNNINGHAM. Sh! Quiet, please! . . . (*Silence.*) Hm! . . . Let me have my stethoscope! (*She takes his stethoscope out of his bag and hands it to him. He listens to* DOT's *heart. His frown deepens.*) Diabetic coma!

MRS. SMITH. Doctor! . . . you've got to save her!

MR. SMITH. Rose . . . come here!

CUNNINGHAM. Miss Dennin— (*He indicates* MRS. SMITH *with a gesture of the head.*)

NURSE (*takes* MRS. SMITH's *arm*). You'll have to wait outside. . . . Just a moment.

MRS. SMITH. Oh, my God!
(BARBARA *leads them out, then returns.*)

CUNNINGHAM. Prepare some insulin! At once . . . forty units . . . with fifty grams of glucose.

BARBARA. But, sir, Dr. Ferguson advised against insulin. . . .

CUNNINGHAM. Ferguson? You please take your orders from me . . . forty units! Quick!

BARBARA. Yes, sir.
(FERGUSON *enters the room.* DR. CUNNINGHAM *glances at him, nods curtly, and turns to* BARBABA.)

CUNNINGHAM. Please, hurry that!

FERGUSON (*looks at the patient, shakes his head*). I was afraid of shock!

CUNNINGHAM. This isn't shock! It's diabetic coma!

FERGUSON (*his brow wrinkled, looks at the patient again*). Her temperature subnormal?

CUNNINGHAM (*impatiently*). Yes! (*To* BARBARA.) Is that insulin ready yet?

FERGUSON. I beg your pardon, Doctor, but isn't insulin contra-indicated here?

CUNNINGHAM. No. It's our last chance.
(FERGUSON *bites his lips to restrain himself.* CUNNINGHAM *takes the hypo from* BARBARA *and presses out the air bubbles.*)

FERGUSON. Doctor, I mean no offense, but I've studied this case history, and it looks like shock . . . not coma!

CUNNINGHAM (*pauses—looks at the patient, shakes his head*). No . . . no. . . .

FERGUSON. But, the clinical picture is so clear-cut. . . . Look at the patient! She's pale, cold, clammy, temperature subnormal. She's complained of hunger! Sudden onset!

CUNNINGHAM (*angrily*). Suppose you let me handle this case, young man. (*To* BARBARA.) Prepare that arm!
(BARBARA *swabs the arm.* CUNNINGHAM *leans over the patient.* FERGUSON *hesitates a moment, then goes to* CUNNINGHAM, *puts his hand on* CUNNINGHAM's *arm.*)

FERGUSON. Please, Doctor! Call in one of the other men! . . . Ask them! Anybody!

CUNNINGHAM. There's no time! Take your hand off!

FERGUSON. That insulin's going to prove fatal.

CUNNINGHAM (*wavers a moment, uncertain, hesitant, then he turns on* FERGUSON). Get out of here, will you? I don't want any interruption while I'm treating my patient! (*He shakes* FERGUSON's *arm off.* . . . *Bends to administer the hypo, hesitates a moment, then straightens up . . . confused and worried.* FERGUSON, *with sudden resolve, takes the hypo from* CUNNINGHAM's *fingers and squirts out the insulin.*) Here! What are you. . . . Why did you do that, you fool?

FERGUSON (*ignores him, turns to* BARBARA, *his voice crisp and cool*). Shock position! (BARBARA *goes to the foot of the bed, turns the ratchet that elevates the foot of the bed.* FERGUSON *dashes to the door, looks out, calls down the corridor.*) Nurse! Nurse!

A NURSE (*answers from down the corridor*). Yes, sir?

FERGUSON. Sterile glucose! Quick! And a thirty c.c. syringe.

BARBARA. Some glucose here, sir, all ready!

FERGUSON. How much?

BARBARA. Fifty grams!

FERGUSON. Good! Half of that will do! Apply a tourniquet . . . right arm!

BARBARA. Yes, sir!

FERGUSON (*calls down the corridor*). Never mind the glucose—a hypo of adrenalin! (*The* NURSE's *voice answers.* Yes, sir.)

FERGUSON (*turns up the corridor*). Nurse, nurse! Some hot packs . . . and blankets! Quick . . . come on . . . hurry! (*He starts to return to the patient, but* DR. CUNNINGHAM, *who has sufficiently recovered from his shock, blocks* FERGUSON's *path.*)

CUNNINGHAM. What do you think you're doing? I'll have you brought up before the medical board. . . . I'll have you thrown out of this hospital . . . you can't. . . .

FERGUSON. All right! Have me thrown out! I don't give a damn! I don't care! I really don't . . . pardon me! (*He brushes* CUNNINGHAM *aside and hurries to patient.*)

CUNNINGHAM (*flustered and impotent*). I never heard of such a thing . . . why. . . .

FERGUSON. Ready?

BARBARA. Yes, sir!

FERGUSON (*quickly*). Let's have that glucose. (BARBARA *gives it to him.*) Swab that arm! Never mind the iodine! Just the alcohol! (BARBARA *swabs the arm.*) Thank God! A good vein! (*He administers the hypo.*)

CUNNINGHAM. You'll pay for this, young man! . . . That patient's life is on your hands. . . .
(*A* NURSE *enters with blankets and hot packs.*)

NURSE. Blankets and hot packs, Doctor!

FERGUSON. Yes. . . . (*He and* BARBARA *place the hot packs on* DOT, *then* BARBARA *covers her with the blankets.*)
(*Enter another* NURSE.)

SECOND NURSE. A hypo of adrenalin!

FERGUSON. Here! (*He takes it from her, administers it. Then straightens up, sighs, turns to two* NURSES.) That's all. Thank you! (*They go.* FERGUSON, BARBARA *and* CUNNINGHAM *watch the patient intently. There is no change in her condition.*)

FERGUSON. That's about all we can do!

CUNNINGHAM. You report downstairs . . . at once!
(*They watch the patient, strained, tense. After a long moment* DOT's *arm, which has been hanging limp over the bedside, moves. She raises her hand to her forehead, opens her eyes. She looks at* FERGUSON.)

DOROTHY (*faintly*). Dr. George. . . .

FERGUSON. Yes, baby?

DOROTHY. I'm thirsty . . . I want a drink.

FERGUSON. You bet, sweetheart. (*To* BARBARA.) Water!
(BARBARA *gives the child a glass of water,* DOT *sits up and sips it, still rubbing her eyes sleepily.*)

DOROTHY. I feel so funny . . . Dr. George! Dizzy-like. . . .

FERGUSON. Drink that!

DOROTHY. What happened?

FERGUSON. Nothing! You just fell asleep, that's all. (DOT *has stopped sipping her water to stare at* FERGUSON *with huge blue eyes, wide open now. He grins at her and points to the glass.*) Come on! Bottoms up! (*She smiles back at him, and drains the glass.*) Atta girl!
(BARBARA *lowers foot and raises head of bed.*)

DOROTHY. Barbara!

BARBARA. Yes, dear?

DOROTHY. I want mother. Where's mother?

BARBARA. She's just outside, dear.

DOROTHY. I want mother. . . .

BARBARA. I'm bringing her right in.
(FERGUSON *meanwhile has turned to face* CUNNINGHAM *who is nervously fidgeting with his pince-nez.*)

DOROTHY. Dr. George . . . my operation hurts me here. . . .

FERGUSON (*sympathetically*). Oh! We'll fix that up in a minute! (*To* CUNNINGHAM.) An opium suppository, Doctor?

CUNNINGHAM. No! (*To* BARBARA.) Morphine! A twelfth!

BARBARA. Yes, sir. (*She goes.*)

CUNNINGHAM (*turns his glance on* FERGUSON). I ought to report you, of course! You're a damned, meddling young puppy. . . . (*He hesitates a moment.*) However . . . under the circumstances, I guess I can afford to be lenient . . . this time. But if you ever dare interfere again in any of my cases . . . !
(MR. *and* MRS. SMITH *enter. They rush to the bedside.*)

MRS. SMITH (*crying and laughing*). Dorothy, my darling.

MR. SMITH. Dots! Dots!

MRS. SMITH. Are you all right, my baby? (*She kisses* DOT.) My baby!

DOROTHY. Oh! . . . my operation, mother.

CUNNINGHAM. Careful, Mrs. Smith. . . .

MR. SMITH. Careful, Rose!

MRS. SMITH. Yes . . . yes . . . of course. Did I hurt my darling?

CUNNINGHAM. Now, the child's been through quite an ordeal. You mustn't excite her. I want her to have some rest . . . you'd better. . . . (*Indicating the door with his hand.*)

MR. SMITH. Yes, come, Rose. . . . She's weak. . . . (*To* DOT.) Go to sleep, darling.

MRS. SMITH. Goodbye, dear! (*She kisses her.*) Is there anything mother can bring you, darling?

DOROTHY (*sleepily*). No, mama. . . .
(MR. SMITH *kisses the child, takes his wife's arm and leads her away.*)

CUNNINGHAM (*turns to* FERGUSON). Order a blood sugar! If there are any new developments phone my secretary at once!

MRS. SMITH (*to* CUNNINGHAM). She'll be all right, Doctor?

CUNNINGHAM. Yes . . . yes. . . . You call me tonight!
(DR. CUNNINGHAM, MR. *and* MRS. SMITH *start to go.*)

MRS. SMITH (*as they exit, to* CUNNINGHAM). Doctor, how can I ever thank you enough for this?

FERGUSON (*goes to* DOROTHY). Well, young lady, how about getting some sleep?

DOROTHY. O.K. Dr. George!

FERGUSON. Close your eyes!

DOROTHY. But don't go away!

FERGUSON (*sits on bedside*). No. . . . I'll sit right here! Come on! (DOROTHY *takes his hand, shuts her eyes, and dozes off. Enter* BARBARA *with hypo.* FERGUSON *whispers.*) She won't need that!

BARBARA. Did Dr. Cunningham say anything to you?

FERGUSON. No. (*He stares down at* DOROTHY.) Pretty kid, isn't she?

BARBARA. I was scared we were going to lose her.

FERGUSON (*touches the sleeping child's hair, and murmurs*). She has hair like Laura's.

BARBARA. What, Doctor?

FERGUSON. Nothing. . . . Nothing. . . .

BARBARA. I think it was wonderful of you to stand up against Dr. Cunningham that way! I. . . .

FERGUSON (*annoyed, turns to hypo, etc., and says a bit curtly*). Better clean up that mess.

BARBARA. Yes, sir. (*She puts hypos, etc., on trays. Suddenly her trembling fingers drop the hypo. It splinters with a crash.*)

FERGUSON (*angrily*). Here! (*Glances over at the sleeping child.*) What's the matter with you?

BARBARA. I'm sorry. I was just . . . nervous, I guess. . . .

FERGUSON (*looks at her a moment. She is a soft, feminine girl. . . . Her jet black hair and serious, large brown eyes are set off to pretty advantage by the blue-and-white student-nurse uniform. She has a simple, naive quality that lends her an air of appealing wistfulness. He sees how genuinely nervous she is . . . and smiles to reassure her*). Has Cunningham been treating you too?

BARBARA (*smiles*). No, sir. This is my first case with a sick child and I got to like her an awful lot. I guess that was. . . .

FERGUSON. I see. What's your name?

BARBARA. Barbara Dennin.

FERGUSON. You're going to be a swell nurse, Barbara!

BARBARA. Thanks!

FERGUSON. Now, take my advice! I know just how you feel—nerves all tied up in a knot . . . want to yell! Feel the same way myself. . . . You get as far away from here as you can, tonight. Have a good time! Relax! Forget hospital! Tomorrow you'll be all right.

BARBARA. I . . . I can't. I have an exam in Materia Medica tomorrow.

FERGUSON. Materia Medica? . . . Hm! . . . I think I have some notes that may help you. . . . I'll leave them with the orderly on the first floor, and you can get them on your way down.

BARBARA. Thanks.

FERGUSON. May help you a bit. You won't have to cram all night, anyway.
(*The loud speaker is calling "Dr. Ferguson."* MARY, *another and much older nurse, enters with a basin, etc.*)

MARY. Your call, Dr. Ferguson?

FERGUSON (*listening*). Yes. Are you on duty here now?

MARY. Yes, sir.

FERGUSON. If she wakes with any pain, give her an opium suppository! If her temperature goes below normal, call me! I'll be in.

MARY. Tonight, too?

FERGUSON (*almost savagely*). Yes, tonight, too! (*His name is called louder, more insistent. He turns to the door, mutters to the loud speaker.*) All right! All right! I'm coming! (*He goes.* MARY *turns to stare after him, her eyebrows raised in surprise.*)

MARY. Gee! Ain't he snappy today?
(BARBARA *simply stares after him.*)

Black Out.

SCENE IV

A tiny, sombre, austere, cell-like room, with hardly enough space for its simple furnishings—a cot-bed, a bureau, a desk, a chair, a small book-case and a wash-basin. On the bureau is a small radio—the one luxury in the room. On the walls are two framed diplomas—the sole decorations. The room is untidy—as all internes' rooms are; the bed is messed, it being customary for internes to use it as a lounge; the books are piled irregularly on the book-shelves, on the desk, on the bureau, and on the floor.

A moonlit night filters in through a single square window.

FERGUSON, *wearing spectacles, is at his desk, reading, by the light of a desk lamp, a ponderous medical tome. Occasionally he jots down a note.*

A knock at the door.

FERGUSON (*without looking up, in a tired voice*). Come in!
(*Enter* SHORTY *in a stiff-bosom shirt, collar, white vest.*)

SHORTY (*triumphantly*). Well, I got the vest. . . .

FERGUSON. That's good.

SHORTY. Can you lend me a tie, George? Mine is—er—
(FERGUSON *rises and wearily goes to his dresser, finds a tux bow tie, hands it to* SHORTY.)

FERGUSON. Here you are, Shorty. (*He sits down again to his book.*)

SHORTY. Thanks! Say, do you mind making a bow for me? I can never get these things straight.

FERGUSON. Come here! I'll try. (*He starts to tie* SHORTY's *bow.*)

SHORTY. Drink in my room . . . if you want one.

FERGUSON. I don't think so, Shorty!

SHORTY. Good drink! . . . Ginger ale, sugar and alcohol . . . out of the large jar in the path lab. . . .

FERGUSON. Stand still, will you? (*After fumbling nervously with the tie, he makes a bad job of it.*) Oh, hell! I can't do it! Sorry! (*He undoes the tie.*) Ask Laidlaw!

SHORTY (*looks askance at* FERGUSON). Nerves, young fellow! . . . Better see a doctor about that!

PETE (*pokes in his head*). Anything to eat in here?

FERGUSON. Some chocolate!

PETE. Good! (*Enters—comes up to desk.*)

FERGUSON. Here! (*Gives him a chunk.* SHORTY *starts to go.*) Have a good time, Shorty!

SHORTY (*confidently*). I will.

PETE (*stands there, eating chocolate*). Hope she gives in without a struggle.

SHORTY. No fun, you dope—without a struggle. (*Exits.*)

PETE. Oh, yeah? (*Calls after him.*) Well, take off my vest before you start. I don't want any stains on it. (*He returns to the desk and points to the chocolate.*) Now can I have some of that myself? (*He reaches over and breaks off a piece of chocolate.*)

FERGUSON (*smiles*). Who was the first piece for?

PETE. Oh, that? That was for my tapeworm. (*He holds up the chocolate.*) This is for me. (*Pops it into his mouth.* FERGUSON *laughs a tired laugh, and hands him*

the rest of the large bar, anxious to get rid of him.)

FERGUSON. Here, take it all, Pete!

PETE. Thanks! What a lousy dinner we had tonight! Fish! . . . Oh, how I hate fish!

FERGUSON. Friday night.

PETE. Yeah! Say! What are *you* doing in?

FERGUSON. 341 may need a transfusion. . . .

PETE. A lot of good that'll do him. (*Stuffs his mouth with chocolate.*) For Christ's sake . . . he passed out. . . .

FERGUSON. No?

PETE. About ten minutes ago.

FERGUSON (*slowly*). Gee, that's too bad!

PETE (*jamming in a huge chunk of chocolate*). Yeah! Say, I'm hungry. . . . I'm going to run out to Fleischer's and grab a sandwich. Will you keep an eye on my floor till I get back?

FERGUSON. All right! Hurry it, will you? . . . I may be going out myself.

PETE. Be right back! (*Exits.*)

(FERGUSON *sits there a moment, staring blankly at the wall. Finally he sighs, wearily closes the book, pushes it away, takes off his spectacles, puts them in a case, and reaches for the phone.*)

FERGUSON. Outside wire, please! . . . Atwater 9-0032. . . . Yes. . . . Hello! Hello! Is Miss Hudson there? Dr. Ferguson calling. . . . Yes. . . . Hello, Laura! . . . How are you dear? . . . Feeling better? . . . Oh! . . . Well, look dear, I can make it tonight, after all. What? . . . Oh, don't be silly! . . . But darling . . . we'll work that out! We'll find some. . . . It's so far away, yet. . . . Why talk about . . . ? Listen Laura! That chance to work with Hochberg is one of the best breaks I've ever had! You don't expect me to throw it over, like that, at a moment's notice, simply because you have some crazy idea that. . . . No, no! I don't want to even talk about it, tonight. I'm tired, Laura. It's been a hell of a day! Three operations and . . . I can't think! I can't make an important decision tonight

. . . in a minute! Oh, Laura! What the hell are you doing? Punishing me? . . . All right, Laura. (*A knock at the door.*) All right. . . . I'll see you tomorrow night! . . . Yes . . . yes . . . good-bye! (*He hangs up, somewhat sharply, then wearily goes to the door, opens it.* DR. LEVINE *is standing there.*)

LEVINE. I'm sorry if I. . . .

FERGUSON. Oh, no! Come on in, Dr. Levine!

LEVINE (*murmurs a hardly audible thanks and enters. He looks about, touches the desk, smiles, nods, and murmurs almost to himself*). Yes. . . . Yes . . . it certainly is nice! Six years . . . like yesterday. (*Looks at his watch.*) Think that report is ready?

FERGUSON. I'll see. (*Takes phone.*)

LEVINE. Oh, don't trouble!

FERGUSON. That's. . . . (*Into phone.*) Hello! Path-lab, please! (*To* DR. LEVINE.) What did Dr. Hochberg find?

LEVINE. He left it for the X-ray man to read.

FERGUSON (*into phone*). Hello! . . . Dr. Finn? . . . Ferguson! What about that sputum? . . . Oh! (*To* DR. LEVINE.) Under the microscope, now. (*Into phone.*) Fine! Hurry that through, will you? . . . And send it down to my room! . . . Yes. Thanks! (*He hangs up.*) A few minutes . . . I hope it's nothing. . . .

LEVINE (*nods*). Poor Katherine! She's had so much. Things were so different when I was here . . . before I married.

FERGUSON. Yes . . . Professor Dury told me.

LEVINE. Dury? I know just what he says: Levine—the fool!—wealthy mother— chance to work with Hochberg—to be somebody. Threw it all away . . . for a pretty face. (*He laughs to himself, sadly.*) Hm . . . Dury!

FERGUSON. Your mother? Hasn't she . . . ? (DR. LEVINE *shakes his head.*) Not yet? . . . Well, she'll come around to your way.

LEVINE (*shakes his head again*). No.

When I married Katherine, a gentile, and my mother disowned me . . . it must have broken her heart. But still, she was doing the right thing from her point of view. . . . (*He sighs.*) Poor Katherine! I didn't count on that! East side! Tenements! Fifty-cent patients! Poverty! Dirt! Struggle! (*He shakes his head.*) I don't know. Maybe it would have been better for her the other way . . . maybe. (*He smiles sadly at* FERGUSON.) Burnt offerings! Jehovah and Aesculapius![1] They both demand their human sacrifice. . . . (*Pauses.*) Medicine! Why do we kill ourselves for it?

FERGUSON. I don't know. I often wonder, myself, whether it was worth the grind of working my way through college and med school. . . .

LEVINE. Med school, too?

FERGUSON. Yes.

LEVINE. I don't see how you kept up with classes.

FERGUSON. I managed.

LEVINE. Terrific grind!

FERGUSON. It wasn't much fun . . . but, still . . . I guess it's the only thing I really want to do. . . . (*Pause.*) My dad used to say, "Above all is humanity!" He was a fine man—my dad. A small town physician— upstate. When I was about thirteen, he came to my room one night and apologized because he was going to die. His heart had gone bad on him. He knew if he gave up medicine and took it easy he could live for twenty years. But he wanted to go right on, wanted to die in harness. . . . And he did. (*Pause.*) Above all else is humanity— that's a big thought. So big that alongside of it you and I don't really matter very much. That's why we do it, I guess.

LEVINE. You're right of course! Ah . . . it's not good—too much suffering! Kills things in you. . . . A doctor shouldn't have to worry about money! That's one disease he's not trained to fight. It either corrupts him . . . or it destroys him. (*He sighs.*) Well . . . maybe some day the State will take over Medicine. . . .

[1] Aesculapius: Greek God of Medicine.

FERGUSON. Before we let the State control medicine, we'd have to put every politician on the operating table, and cut out his acquisitive instincts.

LEVINE (*laughs*). That, I'm afraid, would be a major operation!

FERGUSON (*smiles*). Yes. . . . (*Then he becomes serious again, working himself up, thinking of* LAURA.) But, it *is* a danger! We can't allow outside forces, or things . . . or people to interfere with us. . . . We can't! And, if they do, we've got to bar them out . . . even if we have to tear out our hearts to do it. . . . (LEVINE *looks puzzled. He can't quite follow this.* FERGUSON *suddenly realizes the personal turn his thoughts have taken, sees* LEVINE's *bewilderment, and stops short. He laughs, a bit self-conscious.*) I'm sorry. I guess that's a bit off the track . . . just something personal.

LEVINE (*smiles*). Oh! Yes. . . .
(*A knock at the door.* FERGUSON *goes to the door. An* ORDERLY *is there.*)

ORDERLY. Dr. Ferguson?

FERGUSON. Yes?

ORDERLY. Dr. Finn sent this down! (*He hands* FERGUSON *a printed report.*)

FERGUSON. Oh, yes, thanks! (ORDERLY *goes.* FERGUSON *is about to hand it to* LEVINE.) Doctor. . . . (FERGUSON *glances at it and suddenly stiffens.*) One second!

LEVINE (*suddenly becomes tense, too*). Dr. Ferguson! Is that. . . . ?

FERGUSON (*in a strained, brittle voice*). Wait! (*He goes to the phone.*) Path Lab!

LEVINE. Is that for me?
(FERGUSON *doesn't answer him.*)

FERGUSON. Path Lab? . . . Dr. Finn? . . . Ferguson! That report you just sent me . . . are you positive? . . . Make sure! Look again. . . .

LEVINE. Is that the finding on my? . . .

FERGUSON (*over the phone*). Yes . . . Yes. . . . Clear as that? (*Slowly.*) I'm afraid you're right. (*He hangs up slowly, turns to* LEVINE, *hands him the card in silence.*)

LEVINE (*takes it, reads it. He droops. His fingers tremble, the card falls to the ground. After a moment's silence he wets his lips and murmurs, almost inaudibly*). I knew it . . . I knew it. . . .

FERGUSON. Gee, I wish I could tell you how sorry I. . . .

LEVINE. Tuberculosis! Oh, my poor Katherine! (*He sits down on the bed and stares vacantly ahead.*) What are we going to do, now?

FERGUSON (*goes to the bed, sits down next to him, tenderly puts a hand on his shoulder*). She'll come through, all right! You'll see. (*A silence.* DR. LEVINE *pulls himself together.*) Perhaps if you took her to a drier climate. . . .

LEVINE. Maybe . . . maybe! (*He rises.*) That means . . . giving up the little practice I have . . . means starting all over again. I don't know if we can do it. We're not young, any longer. I don't know. . . . (DR. LEVINE *turns toward the door.*)

FERGUSON. Is there anything I can do?

LEVINE. No, thanks! Thanks! (*Exit* DR. LEVINE.)
(FERGUSON *stands there a moment, staring after him. Enter* PETE.)

PETE (*sucking his teeth with great gusto*). Boy, what a roast-beef sandwich I had! Mm! (*He sucks his teeth louder.*) Have you got a . . . oh, yeah! (*He reaches over, and takes a tongue-depressor out of* FERGUSON's *breast pocket.* PETE *splits the depresser, and using one of the splinters as a tooth-pick, continues to make even a greater noise with his lips.* FERGUSON, *pretty near the cracking point, turns his back on* PETE. PETE *goes to the radio, and tunes in on a loud jazz number. He flops down onto the bed—sucks his teeth.*) Going out?

FERGUSON. No!

PETE. Change your mind?

FERGUSON. Yes.

PETE. Boy, you know that Miss Simpson down in the X-ray lab— She was over at Fleischer's. Next table to mine. Say—she's swell all dressed up in street clothes. I looked at her for ten minutes without recognizing her. I guess maybe it was because I wasn't looking at her face. (*Sucks his teeth.*) Luscious! She had one of those tight black silk dresses . . . absolutely nothing else on underneath—you could see that. And a pair of mammaries! Mm!

FERGUSON (*tensely*). Pete! I want to do some reading. Will you get the hell out?

PETE (*sits up, looks at* FERGUSON, *rises quickly*). Sure! (*With a puzzled, backward glance at* FERGUSON, *he goes.* FERGUSON *switches off the radio; walks up and down the room, almost frantic, then throws himself face down, on the bed. There is a timid little knock at the door.*)

FERGUSON. Come in! (*The knock is repeated.* FERGUSON *rises, calling impatiently.*) Come in. Come in! (BARBARA *opens the door and slips in, breathless with the adventure.*) What . . . er?

BARBARA. I came down for those notes . . .

FERGUSON. Oh! Of course. I forgot . . . stupid of me. Let's see—what was it? Materia Medica?

BARBARA. Yes.

FERGUSON (*looks through drawer in his desk*). I had them here some place.

BARBARA. I suppose I oughtn't to have come in.

FERGUSON (*assorting notes*). Pathology, Histology—no—no.

BARBARA. I hope nobody saw me.

FERGUSON. Materia Medica. Here! (*He takes a notebook out of the drawer, glances through it, hands it to her.*) There you are!

BARBARA. Thanks!

FERGUSON. Not at all! . . . Hope they're some help. (*He goes to the window, looks out—dismissing her. Still in his old mood.*)

BARBARA (*stands there a moment, waiting. Finally she asks timidly*). Is there . . . anything wrong?

FERGUSON. What?

BARBARA. Anything wrong?

FERGUSON. Oh! No! No! (*He turns to the window again.* BARBARA *hesitates a moment—sees that he has already forgotten her in the intensity of his mood. She slowly turns, opens the door, looks out, and suddenly shuts it with an exclamation of fright.*) What—

BARBARA (*breathless . . . frightened*). Headnurse! Outside!

FERGUSON. See you? Wait a minute! She'll be gone! Better sit down!

BARBARA. Thanks! (*She watches him a moment.*) Are you sure Doctor Cunningham didn't— (FERGUSON *shakes his head.*) Because . . . if it would mean anything . . . I'd go right down and tell them all—everybody—just what happened. . . .

FERGUSON. No, it's not Cunningham—

BARBARA. What is it, then?

FERGUSON. It's just— (*With an effort he shakes off his mood.*) Don't mind me, tonight.

BARBARA. You work very hard, don't you?

FERGUSON (*almost savagely*). Work? Sure! What else is there but *work*—and *work!* (*He suddenly realizes* BARBARA *is staring at him. He pulls himself together.*) Let's see those notes! (*She brings them to him. He places the book on the desk, leans over it, and turns the pages.*) There! (BARBARA *is next to him, leaning over the notes, her head near his.*) These pages synopsize the whole business. Read through the notes carefully; memorize these pages—and you've got it! I think you'll find it lots easier that way.

BARBARA (*pointing to a word*). What's this?

FERGUSON. Calomel!

BARBARA (*her head almost touching his*). Oh, of course! It's a C.

FERGUSON (*hands her the book*). Clear?

BARBARA. Yes. (*As she reaches for the book, her hand meets his, and she clings to it.*) You know, when I thought Dots was going to die . . . I got the feeling like I . . . I . . . God! . . . I can't put it into words!

FERGUSON. I know. I know that feeling. . . .

BARBARA. You, too?

FERGUSON. Me, too? (*Clutching his throat.*) Up to here, Barbara! Right now! Christ! I'm tired of work, and blood and sweat and pain! And the chap in 341 is dead! And Levine's wife is going to die . . . and one begins to wonder where in Heaven's God, and what in Hell's it all about, and why on earth does everything make any difference.

BARBARA (*clutches his arm with her hand*). Yes, that's the feeling . . . and you get so lonely . . . and you feel . . . tomorrow it's me . . . and the only thing that matters is just being alive . . . just being alive. Now! . . . Isn't it? (*She is very close to* GEORGE *now, clutching his arm with her hand.*)

FERGUSON (*looks at her sympathetically*). You kids have a pretty tough time of it, don't you? Grind all day and lights out at ten o'clock.

BARBARA. And only one night out till twelve-thirty . . . and I haven't taken mine in two months. There's just nobody. . . .

(*They are very close, now. She almost whispers the last words to him.*)

FERGUSON. You're a sweet girl, Barbara. (*Suddenly he takes her in his arms and kisses her. She clings to him for a moment. Then they separate. He is confused and upset.*) I'm sorry, Barbara . . . I. . . . (*He goes to the notes, opens them—after a pause.*) These diagrams here go with this page. Aside from that, I guess they'll be pretty clear. (*He gives the book to her . . . grips her shoulder.*) Please don't feel that I . . . just. . . .

BARBARA. Oh! No! No!

FERGUSON. Thanks. (*Goes to the door . . . opens it . . . looks out.*) I'm going up to Ward C, to look around for a few seconds. The coast is clear—you'd better go now. (*Exit* FERGUSON.)

(BARBARA *takes up the notes . . . walks slowly to the door . . . hesitates there a moment . . . is about to go out, suddenly stops . . . decides to stay. For a moment she leans against the door, breathless, then she goes back into the room, slowly drops the notes on the table, goes to the bed, sits down, takes off her cap, throws it on the bed and sits there . . . waiting.*)

Curtain.

ACT TWO

Three months later

SCENE I

A softly lit room, the main feature of which is a long table. Seated about it are the members of the Joint Committee—three laymen representing the Lay Board and four doctors representing the Medical Board. Beyond them, we see mahogany panels, a huge fireplace and an oil portrait hanging over it, dark plush portières drawn to conceal windows and doors—in effect, a rich board-room of the same general conspiratorial appearance as the board-room of a railroad, a steel, oil, banking or other big business institution.

At rise: MR. HOUGHTON, *short, stodgy, aggressive . . . the economist, has just finished reading a report.*

MR. HOUGHTON. . . . 28,000—19,000—33,-500 which adds up to a total deficit of 163,-000 dollars so far, Doctors. (*He shakes his head.*) You'll have to cut down those expenses, Doctors.

DR. GORDON. How?

DR. WREN. We're to the bone, already. We've cut—

MR. SPENCER (*presiding, gray templed, sure, suave, six generations of Harvard! He gives* DR. WREN *the floor*). Dr. Wren!

DR. WREN (*rises*). Everything—our staff, nurses, technicians, salaries, meals—telephones even! Our internes are allowed only two outside calls. . . .

DR. HOCHBERG. An absurd economy!

MR. HOUGHTON (*taking some papers out of his briefcase*). Mm! . . . It seems to me we've a lot of people in our laboratories. Couldn't we reduce—

DR. HOCHBERG. No, no— (*To the chairman.*) Mr. Spencer!

MR. SPENCER (*giving* HOCHBERG *the floor*). Doctor Hochberg.

DR. HOCHBERG (*rises, and explains, very patiently*). Those laboratories, Mr. Houghton, *are* the hospital. Most of our *real* work is done in them. (*He smiles and shakes his head.*) Without that pathology lab and the chemistry lab and the X-ray lab we're helpless.

MR. RUMMOND (*rather old and dim-witted, trying very hard to be a constructive part of this business, but not quite able to grasp it*). You are? . . . Really?

DR. HOCHBERG. Absolutely.

MR. RUMMOND. Hm. Interesting. I didn't realize they were that important.

DR. HOCHBERG. Oh, yes.

DR. GORDON. I should say so.

MR. HOUGHTON. Well, then. . . . (*He looks at his papers, and shakes his head.*) I don't know. 163,000 dollars—these days! The Board of Trustees is—

MR. SPENCER. Er. . . . We'll come back to that later, Mr. Houghton. I want to clear away all . . . er . . . Dr. Gordon! Any reports from the Medical Board to this joint committee?

DR. GORDON. Appointments! Two-year interneships, gentlemen—recommended on the basis of competitive examinations. (*Starts looking through some papers for the list.*) Internes. . . . Ah, yes. (*Finds his list and reads from it.*) Aubert, Dickinson, Flickers, Frankey, Gordon, Kern, Monroe! The Medical Board awaits your approval of these men.

MR. HOUGHTON (*quickly*). Where's Ten Eyck?

MR. SPENCER. You still can't do anything for Ten Eyck?

DR. GORDON. Ten Eyck? (*He glances over his lists, murmuring.*) Ten Eyck, Ten Eyck, Ten Eyck. Oh, yes—here it is. Gentlemen! Charles Arthur Ten Eyck finished fourth from the bottom—on a list of three hundred men examined.

MR. HOUGHTON. Senator Ten Eyck's going to be sore as hell. . . .

DR. LARROW (*pompous pedant, cut pretty much from the same pattern as* DR. CUNNINGHAM). I met the boy. Seems well-bred. Good family. . . .

DR. WREN. He doesn't *know* anything. I gave him his oral in medicine. An ignoramus.

DR. LARROW. Examinations! Bah! He graduated at an approved medical school, didn't he?

DR. WREN *and* DR. GORDON (*together*). DR. WREN. How he managed it is a mystery to me. DR. GORDON. We gave him special consideration, Mr. Spencer. But he just won't do.

MR. SPENCER. Well—his uncle's kicking up a fuss, but if the boy's that bad. . . . After all, you know best. The appointments are in your hands. Which brings me to the real purpose of this special meeting. (*He organizes his papers, clears his throat, and looks at them a moment. Then portentously.*) Mr. Houghton has just . . . er . . . read the bad news.

DR. WREN. We usually run up a much larger deficit.

MR. SPENCER (*smiles at this naiveté, so typical of the doctor in business*). Yes . . . but these are unusual times, Doctor. As you, no doubt, have heard, there has been a depression.

DR. GORDON. *Has* been? I like that. You try and collect some of my bills.

DR. LARROW. Yes. People are too poor to get sick these days.

DR. HOCHBERG. That's something no matter how poor a man is he can always get—sick!
(GORDON *and* WREN *enjoy a laugh at* LARROW's *discomfiture.*)

MR. SPENCER. Er . . . Doctors! Please! This is a very important matter! (*They quiet down, and lean forward. There is no escaping the note of impending ill news in* SPENCER's *manner.*) Two of our Trustees are very shaky, and may not be able to meet their usual subscription at all. They've already spoken to me about resigning. (*The doctors look at each other. This is bad.*) And so, I've been looking around carefully for a new Trustee—and believe me, Doctors, it was a mighty hard search. But, finally— (*he smiles*) I found someone to underwrite our deficit. (*Sighs of relief and approval from the doctors.*) A man well known for his philanthropies, his generous soul, his civic and social services—John Hudson—the real estate Hudson. (HOCHBERG *grunts.*) A friend of yours, I believe, Doctor!

DR. HOCHBERG. Yes. But I didn't recognize him by the description. (MR. SPENCER *laughs.*) He'll be useful. The only real estate man I heard of who's made money the last few years. Good business head. He'll put St. George's on a paying basis.

MR. SPENCER (*laughs*). If he can do that, he's a wizard. Mr. Houghton will resign in favor of him tomorrow.

MR. HOUGHTON. With pleasure.

MR. SPENCER. I've talked the matter over with him, and he's definitely interested.
(*Chorus of approval from the Committee.*)

MR. HOUGHTON. If we can get him to subscribe for. . . .

MR. SPENCER. Mr. Houghton! Please!

MR. HOUGHTON. Sorry!

MR. SPENCER. Now, it happens that one of our internes is marrying John Hudson's daughter—in a few weeks, I believe. Of course, Doctors, appointments lie completely in your hands, but we feel here is an opportunity. We suggest the medical-board offer Dr. Ferguson an associateship.

DR. HOCHBERG. What? Impossible!

MR. SPENCER. Impossible? A serious student, capable, going to study a year abroad under a well-known man—why impossible?

DR. HOCHBERG. He won't be *ready* for the job!

MR. SPENCER. Have you any personal prejudice against the boy?

DR. HOCHBERG (*annoyed*). No . . . no! (*He rises.*) As a matter of fact I'm very fond of that boy. I think he has promise of becoming a good surgeon, some day. But not over night. He has years of intensive study ahead of him. I don't care what strength of character is native to a man—he will not work for something he can get for nothing —and Ferguson's no exception. An associateship here now simply means he'll go into practice and drop his studies.

DR. LARROW. And why shouldn't he? He's marrying well. . . . With his wife's connections, he ought to . . . er . . . do very nicely.

DR. HOCHBERG. If he doesn't continue his studies, he'll never be worth a damn as far as medicine goes.

MR. SPENCER. After all, Doctor Hochberg, that's *his* concern, not ours.

DR. LARROW *and* MR. SPENCER (*together*).
DR. LARROW. Oh! (*Dubiously.*) He's all right. . . . But (*with conviction*) he's no infant Cushing[1] by any means. MR. SPENCER.

---

[1] Harvey Cushing (1869-   ): professor of surgery at the Johns Hopkins and Harvard Universities—the most eminent brain surgeon in the world.

We must think of the hospital, doctors! That's our job.

DR. HOCHBERG (*losing his temper. To* DR. LARROW). You're wrong, Doctor. That boy has *unusual* ability. Yes, yes—another Cushing, perhaps! (*Controls himself—to* MR. SPENCER *quietly.*) Exactly, Mr. Spencer! The hospital! Do you realize the responsibility in precious human life that lies in an associate's hands? Ferguson doesn't know enough, yet; he's apt to make mistakes that will hurt not only himself, but the integrity of St. George's Hospital.

MR. SPENCER. Oh, come now, Dr. Hochberg!

MR. HOUGHTON *and* RUMMOND (*together*). MR. HOUGHTON. Oh, for Christ's sake. . . . RUMMOND. Nothing to be thrown away so lightly!

MR. SPENCER. What do you think, Dr. Wren?

DR. WREN (*slowly*). Well . . . he won't be ready for it, of course, but—er—we could see to it that he'd always be covered by an older man!

DR. HOCHBERG. And give him nothing to do! Make a figure-head of him. Fine! That's fine!

MR. HOUGHTON. What of it?

DR. GORDON. Of course, we don't exactly approve of the appointment, however . . .

MR. HOUGHTON (*exploding*). Approve! Approve!

MR. SPENCER (*irritably*). Mr. Houghton! Please! (HOUGHTON *subsides with a grunt.*) Dr. Gordon! Go on!

DR. GORDON. Of course, we don't exactly approve the appointment of such a young man; however, we do need Hudson. And Ferguson's not a fool, by any means.

MR. SPENCER. Exactly, Dr. Gordon.

MR. HOUGHTON. But, Josh, don't you see—?

DR. GORDON. Leo, we've got to face the facts. There's hardly a hospital in this city that hasn't shut down on its charity wards. I know a dozen that have completely closed off entire floors and wings! If we have to economize any more, our wealthy patients will take care of themselves, but who's going to take care of all your charity cases? The wards upstairs are full, right now.

MR. HOUGHTON *and* DR. HOCHBERG (*together*). MR. HOUGHTON. It takes money to run a hospital, Doctor! DR. HOCHBERG (*to* GORDON). You're right, Josh . . . you're . . . (*To* HOUGHTON.) I know, Mr. Houghton, I know. And believe me, we're deeply grateful to you gentlemen for your help.

MR. RUMMOND *and* MR. SPENCER (*together*). MR. RUMMOND. A good cause. MR. SPENCER. I only wish I could subscribe more, Doctor! I would.

DR. HOCHBERG. Yes. Deeply grateful. . . . Although, it's a social crime, gentlemen, that hospitals should depend on the charity of a few individuals.

(*The Trustees look at each other, not quite sure whether they've been attacked or flattered.*)

DR. LARROW. The fact remains that we can't afford to refuse Hudson's help.

DR. HOCHBERG. I don't say that.

DR. LARROW. We need him.

DR. HOCHBERG. We do. And till hospitals are subsidized by the community and run by men in medicine, we'll continue to need our wealthy friends. I realize that. I say by all means make Hudson a Trustee. Take all the help he can give. And promise Ferguson an associateship as soon as he's *ready* to go into practice.

SPENCER. And that'll be—when?

DR. HOCHBERG. In five or six years.

MR. HOUGHTON, MR. RUMMOND *and* MR. SPENCER (*together*). MR. HOUGHTON. Oh, for Christ's sake! You're dealing with a business man there, not a child! MR. RUMMOND. You can't expect the man to— MR. SPENCER (*smiling wryly*). I'm very much afraid Hudson will tell us to come around ourselves in five or six years.

HOCHBERG (*to* SPENCER). How do you know?

MR. SPENCER. He wants the boy to open an office and settle down.

DR. HOCHBERG. He does? That's nice. Well, Ferguson won't be ready.

MR. SPENCER. If we don't appoint the boy we can't expect Hudson to be interested.

DR. WREN. There you are right, probably.

MR. SPENCER. Well, that's—er—the important thing, after all, isn't it? Hudson's interest.

MR. HOUGHTON. I should say it was his *capital!* (HOUGHTON *roars with laughter at his own quip.*)

MR. SPENCER. Then you'll submit our recommendation to the medical board?

DR. WREN. Yes. And they'll O.K. it, too. I'm pretty sure it'll go through.
(DR. HOCHBERG *throws up his hands.*)

MR. SPENCER. Fine! Fine! After all, Doctor Hochberg, as you say, we're here in a common cause—the hospital. (*He smiles. Looks over his papers.*) Mm! . . . Guess that's about all! (*He glances around.*) Anything else, gentlemen? Mr. Houghton? (HOUGHTON *gathers his papers, shakes his head "No," puts his papers in portfolio.*) Dr. Wren?

DR. WREN (*looks at his watch*). No. Nothing!

MR. RUMMOND. What time have you there? (*Compares watches, nods, rises, and gets his coat.*)

MR. SPENCER. Anybody? Then the meeting is—

DR. GORDON. One second, Mr. Spencer! Since you're discussing this with Mr. Hudson, I think it would be a fine thing if we could extend our X-ray therapy department.

MR. SPENCER. First give him the associateship, then we'll talk about equipment.

DR. HOCHBERG (*rises*). Don't count your chickens, Josh!

DR. GORDON. Oh, he'll get the appointment!

DR. HOCHBERG. Yes. But he won't accept it.

MR. SPENCER (*smiles*). What makes you say that?

DR. HOCHBERG. I know the boy! He's too honest, too wise, to sacrifice his career for a nice office and an easy practice. Besides he won't have the time. He's going to work with me! And . . . er . . . well. . . . (*He laughs.*) It was perhaps a bit foolish to waste so much energy arguing the matter. (*He starts for the door.*)

MR. SPENCER (*laughs*). As a matter of fact —I had dinner last night at the Hudsons' and I spoke to Ferguson about the appointment. He's delighted with the idea. . . .

DR. HOCHBERG (*stops—returns—incredulous*). He said that?

MR. SPENCER. Certainly! And, why not? It's a fine opportunity for him. (*Looks around.*) Nothing else, gentlemen? No? . . . (*Bangs his mallet on the table.*) Meeting is adjourned!
(*All except* HOCHBERG *move toward the door. He stands there, stock-still, palpably hit.*)

Black Out.

SCENE II

The library. DR. MCCABE *is sitting in arm-chair reading.* MICHAELSON *is seated at the long table. Nearby* SHORTY *is swinging an imaginary golf club.*

SHORTY. My stance was all wrong, see? That's one reason I sliced so much.
(MCCABE *looks up, grunts, and goes back to his book.*)

MICHAELSON. I wouldn't even know how to hold a club any more.

SHORTY. You'd be surprised. A couple of

games, and you're right back in form. Look at Ferguson! He hasn't played tennis in years—since high school, I think he said—and yet, last week he beat Laura two sets in a row. And that girl swings a mean racquet.

PETE (*enters, sour-faced*). That patient in 310! Boy, I'd like to give him two dozen spinal taps and bite the point off the needle to make sure he feels them.

MICHAELSON. Whoa! (*Laughs.*) Your gall-bladder needs draining, Pete!

PETE. Ah! The smart alec! He invited me to share this special lunch with him. When I heard *lunch,* I accepted—(*he snaps his fingers*)—like that! (*Then, morosely.*) Smart alec!

SHORTY. Well, what's the matter with that?

PETE. Do you know what 310's here for? (*Shrilly.*) Rectal feeding! (*The others laugh.*)

MCCABE (*looks up, annoyed*). Sh! Sh! Quiet! (*They glance over at him and quiet down. He goes back to his books. They kid* PETE *in an undertone, muffling their laughter.*)

CUNNINGHAM (*enters—looks around irritably*). Where's Ferguson?

SHORTY. Not here, Doctor.

CUNNINGHAM. I've been trying to find him since twelve o'clock. What kind of house-service is this? Where is he?

MICHAELSON. Why, you see, Doctor—Ferguson's being married next week, and he's at a ceremony rehearsal or something.

CUNNINGHAM. I told him not to let 327's bladder become distended.

MICHAELSON. 327? Ferguson catheterized him this morning.

CUNNINGHAM. Well, he needs another.

SHORTY. I'll get one of the juniors to do it, right away.

CUNNINGHAM. Never mind! I'll do it myself. (*He goes to the door, grumbling.*)

¹ Pancreatitis: inflammation of the pancreas.

Fine house-service you get around here. 327 is full of urine.

PETE. And so are you.

MCCABE (*looks up*). What's that?

PETE. I'm sorry, Doctor.

MCCABE. What for? You're quite right. He is. (*The internes grin.* MCCABE *looks at them quizzically. He turns to* SHORTY.) Young man! How would you treat the different forms of acute pancreatitis?¹

SHORTY (*a study in blankness*). Er . . . acute pancrea . . . mm. . . . Why, the same way. I'd—

MCCABE. Wrong! (*Pause, he shakes his head at* SHORTY.) You play golf, huh? (*He tosses a pamphlet to* SHORTY.) Read that, and find out something about pancreatitis. (*He suddenly draws his shoulders together and looks over at the windows.*) There's a— (*He turns to* MICHAELSON.) Will you see if that window's open? There's a draught in here, some place. (MICHAELSON *crosses to the window. Through the glass-paned door, we see* FERGUSON *in civilian clothes, and* LAURA *coming up the corridor. They are in high spirits, joking and laughing.* FERGUSON *starts to enter the library, but* LAURA *hesitates in the doorway.*)

PETE. How was it?

FERGUSON (*grinning*). Terrible.

MICHAELSON (*to* FERGUSON *and* LAURA). Ho' there! (*To* MCCABE.) They're all closed, Doctor.

FERGUSON (*to* LAURA). Come on in!

LAURA. Well—is it all right for me to—? (*The Internes assure her in chorus that it's quite all right.* FERGUSON *takes her arm and pulls her into the room.*)

FERGUSON. Sure. Come on! (*To others.*) Any calls for me?

MICHAELSON. Yes. Quite a few, George.

LAURA. You should have seen my hero! He was scared to death.

FERGUSON. Who wouldn't be?

SHORTY. What was it like?

FERGUSON. Every step a major operation. Next time I take spinal anaesthesia first. (SHORTY *sings a funereal wedding march.*) Exactly, Shorty! The last mile.
(*They laugh.* MCCABE *looks up very much annoyed. He snorts, shuts his book with a bang. The others stop laughing and glance at him.* MCCABE *reaches for his cane, rises rustily, and goes out mumbling.*)

LAURA (*watches him go, then turns to the others, who grin*). Perhaps I shouldn't have come in here.

SHORTY. Nonsense!

MAC. It's perfectly O.K.

PETE. Don't mind old Doc McCabe! He thinks the world ended in 1917 when he retired.

LAURA. Retired!

FERGUSON. Yes, but he still comes around to talk, read, watch operations. Gives us hell for not knowing anything. Medicine's not just his profession—it's his life. (*He shakes his head admiringly.*) Great guy! If I live to be eighty, that's the way I want to grow old!

LAURA. Not I. When I'm too old to enjoy life first hand I want to lie down, and say "Laura, it was good while it lasted. Now, *fini!*"

SHORTY. My idea exactly. Why sit around and listen to your arteries hardening?

PETE. Don't worry, sweetheart! The chances are none of us will live to grow that old. (*To* LAURA.) Most doctors die pretty young, you know.
(LAURA *looks pained.*)

MICHAELSON. That's right. The strain gets them around forty-five. Heart goes bad.

LAURA (*glances at* FERGUSON *and grimaces*). There's a pleasant thought.

FERGUSON (*laughs*). Cheerful bunch!

PETE. So I say—eat, drink and be merry— for tomorrow you . . . (*With a gesture.*) Pht!

MICHAELSON. George! Better phone in! Cunningham's been looking for you!

FERGUSON. What's he want now?

SHORTY. His shoes shined, or something. I don't know.

PETE. 327 catheterized!

FERGUSON. Again? He'll wind up by— (*goes to phone*)—giving that patient a urethritis.[1] (*Picks up the phone.*) Dr. Ferguson! I just came in. Any calls for me? Find him, will you? Library!

PETE. He's certainly been giving you all the dirty work lately.

MICHAELSON. Yes!

SHORTY. What'd you do? Kick his mother?

FERGUSON. What's the difference? Four more days and I'll be *aus* interne.

LAURA. Who is this charming fellow?

FERGUSON. He doesn't matter, darling! Nothing matters, now—except Vienna!

MICHAELSON. I bet you'll have a swell time over there.

FERGUSON. You bet right! (*The phone rings.* FERGUSON *goes to it. On phone.*) Yes, Doctor Cunningham? . . . Yes, Doctor Cunningham! . . . Yes. . . . Oh, you're quite right! . . . Yes. . . . Yes. . . . (*He winks at the boys, who smile and shake their heads.*) Uh, huh! . . . Yes . . . yes. . . . All right, Doctor! Sure.

MAC. Will you have lunch with us, Laura?

PETE. A lousy lunch.

LAURA (*laughs*). Just had one, thanks! George and I dropped into Rumpelmayer's after the rehearsal!

SHORTY. Rumpelmayer? At the St. Moritz?

LAURA. Yes.

PETE (*hungrily*). How was the food? Good?

---

[1] Urethritis: inflammation of the urethra.

LAURA. Delicious!

PETE. Oh? (*Sighs enviously, then in a resigned tone.*) Well—guess I'll go down and eat slop.

MAC. Sure we can't coax you?

LAURA. I'm full up to here! Thanks!

MAC. Sorry. So long.
(MAC, SHORTY *and* PETE *go.*)

FERGUSON (*still on the phone*). Yes. . . . Absolutely right, Doctor. I'll tend to it. (*He hangs up, wrings the phone as if it were* CUNNINGHAM'S *neck and grins at* LAURA.)

LAURA. Can I smoke in here?

FERGUSON. Sure.

LAURA (*puts a cigarette in her mouth and waits for a light*). Well?

FERGUSON. What? (*She points to her cigarette.*) Oh! (*He laughs, fishes out a packet of matches and lights her cigarette.*)

LAURA. Darling! You're marvelous this way. I've never seen you so high.

FERGUSON. I've never been so high! You know, dear, I love this old place, and yet, my God, I can't wait to get out of here.

LAURA. I was worried last night, after Mr. Spencer spoke to you—you looked so glum. I was afraid you might change your mind.

FERGUSON. Not a chance!

LAURA. Not bothered about that appointment?

FERGUSON. No. That'll be all right—if I get it.

LAURA. You'll get it.

FERGUSON. What do you know about it?

LAURA. I know you, you fish!

FERGUSON (*grins, then suddenly becomes serious*). I wonder if . . . Mr. Spencer spoke to the committee, yet?

LAURA. If he did, it's quick work.

FERGUSON. I hope he hasn't yet.

LAURA. Why?

FERGUSON. Well, I—want to talk to Dr. Hochberg first.

LAURA (*laughs*). Why are you so afraid of Hocky? He won't bite you! Or, do you think by delaying it, you can change my mind—and work with Hocky when we come back?

FERGUSON. No, that's not it.

LAURA. Because if you do, I'm warning you! I'll just drop out of the picture, George. Even if we're married—you'll come home one day, and I just won't be there.

FERGUSON (*takes her in his arms. Tenderly*). Shut up, will you? It's just that I don't want to seem ungrateful.

LAURA. Oh, he'll probably find somebody else.

FERGUSON. Of course he will. (*Smiles, somewhat wistfully.*) There isn't a man I know who wouldn't give a right eye for the chance to work with Dr. Hochberg. You don't realize it, dear, he's an important man. He . . .

LAURA (*impatiently*). The important man, George, is the man who knows how to live. I love Hocky, I think an awful lot of him. But, he's like my father. They have no outside interests at all. They're flat—they're colorless. They're not men—they're caricatures! Oh, don't become like them, George! Don't be an important man and crack up at forty-five. I want our lives together to be full and rich and beautiful! I want it so much.

FERGUSON (*fervently*). Oh, my dear, so do I. . . . And believe me, that's the way it's going to be. (*He looks at her fondly.*) And I once thought I could live without you.

LAURA. What? When?

FERGUSON. Never! (*He kisses her.* NURSE JAMISON *enters, smiles embarrassed.* FERGUSON *turns around, sees her, grins.*) Yes?

NURSE. Mrs. D'Andrea—the mother of that boy—the automobile accident that came in this morning—she's outside, raising an awful rumpus. Wants to see you.

FERGUSON. Take her to Michaelson!

NURSE. I did! She wants to see you!

FERGUSON. There's nothing I can tell her now.

NURSE. I know, Doctor, but she insists on seeing you.

FERGUSON. What for? We won't know till tomorrow whether he'll live or die. (*The* ITALIAN WOMAN *tries to enter.* NURSE JAMISON *restrains her.*) All right! Let her in, Jamison! Let her in!

ITALIAN WOMAN. Dottori. . . . Dottori. . . . Heeza all right? Yes? Heeza all right?

FERGUSON. I'm sorry! There's nothing I can tell you now.

ITALIAN WOMAN. Heeza gonna . . . live? Dottori?

FERGUSON. Tomorrow! Tomorrow! You come back tomorrow! We'll know then—tomorrow.

ITALIAN WOMAN. Tomorrow?

FERGUSON. Yes.

ITALIAN WOMAN. Mamma mia! Tomorrow! . . . Oh, Dottori! Pleeza! Pleeza! Don't let my boy die! Pleeza! . . .

FERGUSON. I'll do everything I can, mother. And you, try not to worry too much.

NURSE. Come! You'd better . . .

ITALIAN WOMAN (*to* NURSE). Oh, lady, heeza my boy. . . . (*To* LAURA.) Heeza my boy! Heeza besta boy I got. Heeza besta boy in the world. If he's gonna die I'm gonna die, too. . . . (*She prays in Italian.*)

NURSE. Come! Come! (*She leads out* ITALIAN WOMAN.)
(*As they go to the door,* DR. HOCHBERG *enters, passing them. He pauses to watch them go, then turns to* FERGUSON.)

LAURA. Hello, Hocky!

DR. HOCHBERG. Hello, Laura! (*To* FERGUSON.) Who was that?

FERGUSON. Mrs. D'Andrea, mother of that case . . . automobile accident . . . this morning.

DR. HOCHBERG. Oh, yes, yes, yes, I know—you gave him a shot of tetanus anti-toxin?

FERGUSON. Doctor Michaelson took care of that.

DR. HOCHBERG. He did? Good! (*Glances at his watch.*) Where have you been since twelve o'clock?

FERGUSON. I was gone a little longer than I expected to be.

LAURA. It was awfully important, Hocky.

DR. HOCHBERG. It must have been.

FERGUSON. I left Michaelson in charge to cover me. I only meant to be gone half an hour. . . .

DR. HOCHBERG. In the meantime it was two.

FERGUSON. Sorry, Doctor! This won't happen again.

DR. HOCHBERG. I hope not. (*He relaxes— becomes the old familiar again.*) Watch it! A few more days to go. Your record is clean. Keep it that way! (*There is a pause.* HOCHBERG *looks at* GEORGE, *steadily for a moment.* GEORGE *becomes self-conscious and uneasy. Finally* DR. HOCHBERG *speaks.*) George . . . I heard something this morning—I didn't know quite what to make of it. (*Pause.*) You still want to accomplish something in medicine?

FERGUSON. Certainly.

DR. HOCHBERG. You mean that?

FERGUSON. Yes.

DR. HOCHBERG (*to* LAURA). You love George, don't you, Laura?

LAURA. You know I do.

HOCHBERG. Of course you do and you want to help him—but that's not the way, Laura. Believe me, nobody can help George but himself—and hard work! He cannot buy this; he must earn it. (*To* FERGUSON.) That appointment they talked to you about, George . . . you won't be ready for it. . . .

FERGUSON. After a year with Von Eiselsberg, I thought. . . .

HOCHBERG. One year? (*He shakes his head.*)

FERGUSON. It's not as if I were going to drop my studies. I intend to keep on. (HOCHBERG *shakes his head.*)

LAURA. I don't see why not!

HOCHBERG (*to* LAURA). My dear child. . . .

LAURA. After all, George has worked so terribly hard till now, Hocky. If it's going to make things easier. . . .

HOCHBERG. There are no easy roads in medicine.

FERGUSON. I didn't expect it to be easy. I counted on work. Hard work!

DR. HOCHBERG. Ten years of it! Then . . . yes.

LAURA. I can't see how it's going to hurt George.

DR. HOCHBERG. There are a great many things you can't see, Laura.

LAURA. If he goes into practice, we'll have some time for ourselves, Hocky.

DR. HOCHBERG. Time? How? There are only twenty-four hours in a day. He's working with me and if— (*He suddenly stops short as the truth strikes him.*) Or is he—? (*To* FERGUSON.) Are you?

FERGUSON. Doctor Hochberg, I haven't loafed yet, and I don't intend to start now. But Laura and I are young, we love each other. I want a little *more* out of life than just my work. I don't think that's asking too much.

DR. HOCHBERG. I see. I see. (*Pause.*) So. you've decided not to come with me next year.
(*There's a long silence. Finally* LAURA *answers apologetically.*)

LAURA. After all, Hocky, we feel that we'll be happier that way—and . . .

DR. HOCHBERG. Of course, Laura. It's George's life and yours. You've a right to decide for yourselves—what you're going to do with it. I didn't mean to meddle. . . .

LAURA. Oh, Hocky, you know we don't feel that way about you.

DR. HOCHBERG. I'm glad you don't. . . . (*Pause. Trying to hide his hurt, he continues.*) How's papa?

LAURA. So so. . . . He still has an occasional attack.

DR. HOCHBERG. Still smokes, I suppose.

LAURA (*nods*). When I'm not around. He's building again.

DR. HOCHBERG. Well—don't let him work too hard!

LAURA. As if I have anything to say about that! You know dad! He usually has his way.

DR. HOCHBERG (*glances at* FERGUSON, *then nods significantly*). Yes. . . . (DR. HOCHBERG *turns to* GEORGE *and says gently.*) You'd better get into your uniform, George. We may have to operate shortly. A new case just came in on the surgical service. One of our own nurses. What's her name—? That nice little girl up in pediatrics? Oh, yes—Dennin! Barbara Dennin! You remember her? Pediatrics.

FERGUSON (*embarrassed*). Oh, yes, yes. I remember her—an excellent nurse.

DR. HOCHBERG. Poor child! Such a nice little girl, too. . . . Sepsis! [1]

FERGUSON (*sympathetically*). Oh! That's awful! She bad?

DR. HOCHBERG. Temperature 105, blood count way up.

FERGUSON. Tch! What was it—ruptured appendix?

DR. HOCHBERG (*shakes his head*). Septic abortion!

FERGUSON. Abortion?

DR. HOCHBERG. Yes. Poor girl—it's a shame. Well, we'll see what we can do. Meet me up there. (*He starts towards the door.* FERGUSON *stands there, his brow wrinkling.*)

[1] *Sepsis:* septic poisoning—the presence of various pathogenic organisms or their toxins in the blood or tissues.

MICHAELSON (*entering*). That D'Andrea fellow is still unconscious. Seems to be something the matter with his lower jaw.

DR. HOCHBERG. What!

MICHAELSON. Protruding—somewhat rigid. Thought it might be tetanus.

DR. HOCHBERG. No! Not so soon! Anyway, you gave him anti-toxin, didn't you?

MICHAELSON. Why—er. . . . (*He shoots a quick glance at* FERGUSON.) No!

DR. HOCHBERG. What? (*Angrily.*) Don't you know yet that T.A.T.[1] is routine in this hospital?

MICHAELSON. Yes, sir. . . . But I thought— (*To* FERGUSON.) You didn't tell me. I thought you gave it!

DR. HOCHBERG (*to* FERGUSON). Doctor Ferguson!

FERGUSON. I intended to . . . to mention it to him. I guess—I—forgot. . . .

DR. HOCHBERG. Forgot? Is that a thing to forget? You should have given the anti-toxin yourself!

LAURA. It's my fault, Hocky, I dragged him away—we were late.

DR. HOCHBERG. That's no excuse. He's not supposed to leave the house at all! And a very sick house, too. You know that, Dr. Ferguson!

FERGUSON. Yes, sir.

LAURA. Oh, Hocky—it was important!

Terribly important! It was a rehearsal of our wedding.

DR. HOCHBERG. A rehearsal? Yes, Laura, that's nice. A rehearsal of your wedding. But, do you realize, upstairs, there is a boy all smashed to bits. There'll be no wedding for him, if he develops tetanus. (*To* FERGUSON.) Doctor Ferguson! Inject that anti-toxin at once!

FERGUSON. Yes, sir! (*He goes.*)

DR. HOCHBERG (*turns to* LAURA, *looks at her a moment, then shakes his head and says slowly*). Laura, you deserve to be spanked! (LAURA's *face becomes angry and defiant. Her jaw tightens, but she says nothing.*) Don't you realize what that boy's work means?

LAURA. Of course I do, Hocky.

DR. HOCHBERG (*very softly, almost to himself*). No . . . no, you don't! (*Then, louder.*) Would you like to see perhaps?

LAURA. Yes . . . why not? . . .

DR. HOCHBERG (*glances toward the corridor where* MICHAELSON *is standing, talking to a nurse*). Doctor Michaelson! (MICHAELSON *enters.*) Take Miss Hudson here upstairs, see that she gets a cap and gown, and have her in the operating room in about— (*with a sharp jerk of his arm he bares his wrist watch and looks at it*) twenty minutes! (*Without so much as another glance at* LAURA, *he marches briskly out of the library.*)

Black Out.

[1] T. A. T.: Hospital jargon for tetanus-antitoxin.

Tetanus, the disease commonly known as "lockjaw," follows the contamination of a wound with dirt, which frequently contains tetanus bacilli. Antitoxin given shortly after such contamination is capable of preventing the disease. In most hospitals this antitoxin is administered routinely to all patients who sustain lacerations in automobile accidents, etc., where there is a chance of dirt gaining entrance into the wound.

SCENE III

The end of the corridor. In the corner are the night-desk and a medicine cabinet. To the left of them is a room, numbered 401.

To the right are the elevator doors. A woman and a boy are waiting for the elevator.

A nurse carrying a basin, some towels, etc., enters from the left. MARY *comes out of 401, crosses to the night desk—takes a hypodermic needle and some bottles from the chest. The nurse with the basin enters 401. The elevator whirs, and the doors open with a clang. An aged couple step out first, then* FERGUSON. *The woman and the boy enter the elevator. The door clangs shut, and the elevator whirs. The aged couple cross to the left and disappear off.* FERGUSON *starts to go into 401, stops, turns to* MARY. MARY, *who has been eyeing him, looks away.*

FERGUSON. How is she? (MARY *shakes her head. She is pale, grim, restrained.*) Temperature?

MARY. 106.

FERGUSON. 106?

MARY. Yeah!

FERGUSON. Delirious?

MARY. She was—before— (*Pause, as she lights a small alcohol lamp, and sterilizes a hypodermic needle by boiling it in a spoon held over the flame.*) She kept calling—for you.

FERGUSON (*suddenly rigid*). For me?

MARY. Yeah!

FERGUSON (*stunned*). Oh! (*He turns to enter the room.*)

MARY. Better wait! Doctor Hochberg's in there. She's quiet, now. If you went in she might start talking again.
(*The nurse with the basin and towels comes out of the room, sees* FERGUSON, *smiles at him, and as she crosses left, throws a cheery hello to him over her shoulder. He doesn't answer. Nurse, puzzled, exits left.*)

FERGUSON. God! I never dreamed this would happen.

MARY. Men don't—usually. . . .

FERGUSON. Why didn't she come to me? Why didn't she tell me? Why did she keep away?

MARY. I guess that was my fault. Long time ago I saw she was falling for you. I told her you were in love with someone else, and engaged to be married—and to keep away from you. I didn't know then, that she already . . .

FERGUSON. I see! I see! That's why she—I thought after that night . . . she'd just realized how crazy we'd both been. . . . Crazy! I thought she at least knew how to take care of herself. But when this happened . . . she should have told me! You should have told me! Why did you let her do this?

MARY. I didn't know . . . till last night. It was . . . too late, then! She was just a green kid! Didn't realize what it was all about!

FERGUSON. God! I wouldn't have let this happen! I wouldn't have let this happen!

MARY. I suppose you'd have helped her—

FERGUSON. Yes! Yes! Yes . . . rather than this. . . .

DR. HOCHBERG (*pokes his head out of the door of 401*). Where's that hypo?

MARY. In a second, Doctor!

HOCHBERG (*to* FERGUSON). Did you tend to D'Andrea?

FERGUSON. Yes, sir! Gave him the T.A.T. He's conscious, now.

HOCHBERG. That business with his jaw—?

FERGUSON (*mechanically*). Slight dislocation. Put it back into place. Bandaged it! No further evidence of internal injury. . . . Although there may be a slight fracture of the tibia or the fibula of the left leg. I'll have some X-ray pictures taken this afternoon!

HOCHBERG. Uh huh! Pain?

FERGUSON. Complained of slight pain . . . general.

HOCHBERG. Did you give him some morphine?

FERGUSON. No, sir. . . .

HOCHBERG. Why not?

FERGUSON. Accident case! Didn't want to mask any possible internal injuries.

HOCHBERG. Ah! Yes. Very good, very good. (*To* MARY.) Er . . . tell me . . . was this Miss Dennin a friend of yours?

MARY. Yeah . . . in a way. I sort a . . . liked her.

HOCHBERG. Well, she's a mighty sick girl. You'd better notify her relatives. . . .

MARY. Ain't none . . . that would be interested.

HOCHBERG. No? Her friends, then? (MARY *shakes her head.*) My . . . my! (*To* FERGUSON.) What a pity! Tch, tch! (*He turns back into the room.*) Oh, Wren, I want you to— (*He disappears into the room.*)

MARY. Nobody! Nobody to turn to!

FERGUSON. Her folks? Her people? At home! Surely there's—

MARY. Yeah!—a stepfather! And to top it all, she's going to be kicked out of here!

FERGUSON. They wouldn't do that!

MARY. Wouldn't they, though? Ask Miss Hackett! And she won't get into any other hospital, either. They'll see to that!

FERGUSON. Poor kid!

MARY. It might be a lucky break for her if she just passed out!

FERGUSON. What are you talking about? She can't die! She's got to pull through! She's got to!

MARY. And then, what? . . . She hasn't got a dime to her name.
(HOCHBERG *and* WREN *come out of the room.*)

DR. HOCHBERG. Tch! Poor girl! . . . Why do they go to butchers like that?

DR. WREN. Well . . . she couldn't have come to us.

DR. HOCHBERG. No . . . that's the shame! Ah, Wren, some of our laws belong to the Dark Ages! Why can't we help the poor and the ignorant? The others will always help themselves—law or no law.[1]

FERGUSON. What are your findings on the case, Doctor?

HOCHBERG. Definite evidence of sepsis. . . . Better order the operating room, at once! A hysterectomy![2]

FERGUSON. Don't you think operation is contra-indicated?

HOCHBERG. Not in this case.

FERGUSON. If we put her in Fowler's position and . . .

HOCHBERG. You see, the infection is localized in the uterus . . . and it's been my experience in cases like this . . . the only way to save the patient is to remove the focus of infection.[3] Otherwise she hasn't a chance.

---

[1] Dr. Rongey, former president of the A. M. A., estimates that there are more illegal abortions every year in New York and Chicago than there are children actually born in those cities. Most of these operations are performed on otherwise respectable, law-abiding, married women. Proof enough that here is another social problem that can't be eliminated by legislation. No one wants to encourage the indiscriminate use of this grim practice. However, the lash of the law, instead of correcting the evil, only whips it into dark corners, creating a vicious class of criminal practitioner—bootleg doctors and ignorant midwives who work in dark, back-room apartments. A saner, healthier attitude is that adopted by the Soviet government, which is fostering birth control education, and instituting legal abortion clinics in a spirit best expressed by the motto inscribed over the door of one such clinic: "You are welcome this time, but we hope you will never have to come here again."

[2] Hysterectomy: removal of the uterus.

[3] Those who question this surgical procedure, see: Robinson, M. R.—Revaluation of the prevailing theories and principles of Puerperal Infection—*Am. Jour. of Surg.* 20:131:1933.

FERGUSON. The girl was up in the children's ward. She asked to be put there, because she loves them. It seems a terrible shame to deprive her of the chance of ever having any of her own.

HOCHBERG. It is. It is a terrible shame—yes. But, it's future life or her life. We'll save hers . . . if we can. Order the operating-room!

FERGUSON. Yes, sir.

HOCHBERG (*to* MARY). And, the man, who —was responsible— (FERGUSON *stiffens.*) Does he realize what's happened?

MARY. I suppose so.

HOCHBERG. Mmm, hmm! . . . Who is the man?

MARY. I don't know!

HOCHBERG. Well—if you can find out he should be notified, at least. (*To* FERGUSON.) What are you waiting for? Order the operating-room!

FERGUSON. Yes, sir. (*He goes to the phone.*) Operating-room! . . . Hello! . . . How soon can you have the O.R. ready for a hysterectomy? Dr. Hochberg! Yes. . . . (*Turns to* HOCHBERG.) Ready now.

HOCHBERG. Good! (*To* MARY.) Patient prepared?

MARY. Yes!

HOCHBERG. Fine! Er—give her that hypo!

MARY. Yes, sir! (*Goes into* BARBARA's *room.*)

HOCHBERG (*to* FERGUSON). Have her brought up at once.

FERGUSON (*into phone*). Patient ready! Send a rolling stretcher down to 401, at once! (*He hangs up.*)

HOCHBERG. Call the staff anaesthetist!

WREN. I'll give the anaesthesia, if you want me to, Hochberg.

HOCHBERG. There's no one I'd rather have.

WREN. General?

HOCHBERG. No—no. I'm afraid to give her ether. . . . We can work better under spinal anaesthesia.[1]

WREN. Spinal?—Good!

HOCHBERG. Come! I'd like to take a quick look at that D'Andrea boy.

WREN. I want to prepare my—

HOCHBERG. A second! Come. (*To* FERGUSON.) You can start scrubbing, now. (*Exit* HOCHBERG *and* WREN.)

(FERGUSON *stands there a moment.* MARY *comes out. She puts the alcohol and iodine back on the emergency shelf.*)

MARY. Well, that's—

(*The elevator begins to whine.* MARY *and* FERGUSON *glance over at the indicator dial over the elevator door. It slowly comes round from O.R. to 3, where it stops. The door opens with a clang. An orderly steps out, backward, pulling a rolling stretcher after him. He turns to* MARY *and grins.*)

ORDERLY. Well, here I am, sweetheart!

MARY (*suddenly bursts into tears*). Who the hell are you calling sweetheart? (*She hurries into the room.*)

ORDERLY (*puzzled*). What the— (*He looks at* FERGUSON, *embarrassed, smiles, and shakes his head in bewilderment. Then he wheels the stretcher into the room.*)

THE ELEVATOR MAN (*who has kept the elevator-door open, calls to* FERGUSON *in a monotone*). Going down?

FERGUSON (*slowly enters the elevator, then, in a low, harsh voice*). Up! Operating-room! (*The door clangs shut, the elevator whines siren-like, rising to a crescendo, as the indicator dial goes up.*)

Black Out.

[1] Anaesthesia: Ethyl ether and nitrous oxide, both intoxicants, were to the early part of the nineteenth century what rye, scotch and gin are to the twentieth. No hectic party was complete without an "ether frolic." An American dentist, noticing the numbness and insensibility to pain produced by "ether jag," applied the principle to the extraction of teeth. In 1846 he successfully demonstrated the simplicity and safety of ether in this type of minor operation. Before the year was up, ether was being used for many kinds of operation. "Shock" was now minimized, and speed became less important than good, neat, complete surgery. Then, for superficial operations, Halsted and Cushing, American surgeons, developed anaesthesia of a partial area by injecting solutions of cocaine into the tissue around that area. Another surgeon, J. L. Corning, introduced "spinal anaesthesia" by injecting cocaine derivatives into the spinal canal. This process gives the patient complete insensitivity to pain below the site of injection, without rendering him unconscious. The technique of spinal anaesthesia has been developed to a high degree and is now being used by many hospitals in preference to "general anaesthesia."

SCENE IV

The operating-room. A feeling of sharp, white gleaming cleanliness! Back center, the huge, hanging, kettle-drum lamp, with its hundreds of reflecting mirrors, throws a brilliant, shadowless light on the chromium operating table. All the nooks and corners of the room are rounded off to facilitate cleansing, and to prevent the accumulation of dust.

To the right is the sterilizing room with its polished nickel auto-claves, bubbling and steaming.

To the left is a long North skylight, double paned.

There is one sterile nurse, wearing cap and gown, mask and long rubber gloves; there are two unsterile nurses, similarly clothed but wearing no gloves. They move to and fro like so many pistons, efficiently, quickly, quietly—ghost-like automata.

In the right-hand corner nearest us, stands a row of half a dozen sinks, the faucets in them turned on and off by means of knee-stirrups attached underneath. Above, a shelf holds cans of sterile brushes, pans of liquid soap, and eight-minute glasses—one to each sink. Well apart from these sinks, and to the right, are two basins in a white-enamel stand; one contains blue bichloride, the other alcohol. Beyond them again stands a foot-pedal gown drum, scarred from its purifying baths of steam.

To the left is a long glove table, on which are the gloves wrapped in canvas "books", sterile powder can, and towels covered by a sterile sheet.

WREN, in cap and mask, is dipping his hands in the bichloride pan; PETE, at the wash-basin, is cleaning his nails with an orange-stick, and MICHAELSON is scrubbing his hands with long, easy rhythmic strokes of the brush. They are chatting quietly.

The sterile nurse goes to the glove table and folds over the sheet, uncovering the glove books, etc.

A NURSE comes from the sterilizing-room, carrying a steaming tray of instruments to the instrument table at the foot of the operating-table. The sterile nurse returns to the instrument table and there is a clink of instruments as she arranges them.

WREN holds up his hands so that the bichloride rolls down the forearm and off the elbow; he repeats this once more in the bichloride, and twice in the alcohol pan, then walks away, holding his dripping hands high and away from him.

A sterile nurse gives him a sterile towel. He dries his hands, using the separate sides and ends of the towel for each hand, then he tosses the towel to the floor, and crosses to the glove table.

An unsterile nurse quickly crosses, picks up the towel, and takes it away. WREN powders his hands, opens a glove book, gingerly plucks out a glove, handling it by the cuff, careful not to touch the outside of the glove, as that might still soil it (since the hands themselves can never be completely sterilized) and slips it on. The second glove he slips on, careful not to touch his wrist with his already gloved hand. He then snaps the gloves over the cuffs of his jacket, wraps a sterile towel about his hands and walks over to the operating table.

PETE finishes scrubbing, goes to the bichloride basin, and dips his hands, using the same technique as WREN. When he is through with the alcohol, however, he turns to the gown "drum". The sterile nurse crosses to the drum, steps on the pedal which raises the lid, and deftly extracts a folded gown, without touching the drum itself. She releases her foot, and the lid clunks back. She hands the folded gown to him; he takes a corner of it, unrolls it, and slips into it. An unsterile nurse comes up behind, careful not to touch him, and ties the gown for him.[1]

The whole effect is that of a smooth, well-oiled machine, a routine so studied that the people in the operating room can afford to be casual—as they are.

One of the unsterile nurses enters with LAURA, *whom she has just helped into a cap and gown.*

NURSE. All right?

LAURA. Yes.

MICHAELSON (*to* LAURA). Well, you're all set, now!

LAURA (*smiles nervously*). Yes—thanks!

MICHAELSON. Not at all! A pleasure!

LAURA (*doubtfully*). Oh! The pleasure's all mine!

MICHAELSON (*laughs*). I'll bet it is.

LAURA. This gown seems awfully wrinkled.

NURSE. They're never pressed. That would unsterilize them.

LAURA. Oh! I see. (*Enter* DR. HOCHBERG *and* FERGUSON *in operating pajamas. They are putting on their masks.*) Hello!

HOCHBERG. Oh, hello! (*To* FERGUSON.) We have a guest! (*He turns over the eight-minute glass and begins to scrub up.*)

FERGUSON (*stands stock-still for a moment*). Laura! What? . . .

LAURA. Surprise! (*She starts to go toward* GEORGE.)

HOCHBERG (*warning her back with a quick gesture*). Uh, uh! (*She stops.*) Stand over there—in the corner! Don't come near us! We're getting clean! You're full of contamination.

LAURA. Oh—am I?
(FERGUSON *begins to scrub up.*)

HOCHBERG. Yes. (*A long pause while they scrub.* HOCHBERG, *still scrubbing, turns to* LAURA.) Well—how do you feel?

LAURA (*trying to bluff off her nervousness*). Great!

HOCHBERG. Mm, hm!

LAURA. How do I look? (*She holds out her gown at both sides.*)

---

[1] Behind the fascinating ritual of this "sterile" or "aseptic" technique, which has the beat and the rhythm of some mechanical dance composition, lies the whole story of modern surgery and, indeed, the modern hospital.

Less than eighty years ago, hospitals were festering death-houses. It was far safer to be operated on in a private home than in a hospital, where the slightest surgical cases almost inevitably developed infection. So high was the fatality that surgeons began to discuss seriously the demolition of all hospitals.

Medicine pondered, "Where did infection spring from; and, how to combat it?" Dr. Oliver Wendell Holmes, appalled at the devastating mortality in child-birth, was one of the first to suggest that the physician himself might be the carrier of infection. Semmelweis, a Hungarian doctor, cleaned up his assistants' hands, and lo—he transformed a Viennese delivery ward from a chamber of almost certain death to one of birth and hope. Then the Frenchman, Pasteur, looked through a microscope, and the whole course of medicine was changed. He saw the vast, invisible armies of microbes that ride the dust of the air, and realized they were the cause of decay and fermentation. But the great name in this story is that of Lister, the British surgeon, who took the torch from Pasteur and led surgery out of darkness into light. Realizing that infection of a wound was nothing more than a fermentation caused by Pasteur's tiny creatures, he sought about for a means of destroying these agents of destruction. He found a powerful weapon in carbolic acid. This was the beginning of "antisepsis" and a new epoch in surgery.

Gradually the "antiseptic" method was replaced by another which grew out of it. A technique evolved whereby instruments, dressings, gowns, gloves, etc., all steam-sterilized, precluded the necessity for powerful antiseptics, which often destroy human tissue as well as the enemy germs. No living bacteria are allowed near the wound. This gentler, if more elaborate technique is the "sterile" or "aseptic" one in use today.

HOCHBERG. Very becoming!

LAURA. Think, so, George?

FERGUSON. Yes—very!

HOCHBERG. You can look around, but keep out of the way! Don't touch anything! Put your hands behind your back! (*A long silence, broken only by the rasping sound of scrubbing brushes.* LAURA *stares, fascinated.*)

HOCHBERG. Oh, nurse. (*A* NURSE *comes over.*) See that Miss Hudson here gets a mask before she goes in. Find a stool for her—and put it near the operating table! I don't want her to miss anything!

LAURA (*wryly*). Thanks, Hocky!

HOCHBERG. Don't mention it, Laura!
(DR. HOCHBERG *finishes scrubbing, and goes through the same routine as the others. When he gets his gown he disappears to a corner of the operating-room, hidden by the basins.* FERGUSON, *also, goes through the routine of gown and gloves, etc.*)

WREN. Orderly! Orderly!

ORDÉRLY (*enters from anaesthesia-room*). Yes, sir?

WREN. Bring the patient in!
(BARBARA *is wheeled in by the* ORDERLY. *As she enters,* WREN *bends over to look at her.* FERGUSON *comes over.*)

FERGUSON. How is she, Doctor?

BARBARA. George!

FERGUSON. Yes?

BARBARA. What are they going to do to me?

FERGUSON. There's nothing to be afraid of, Barbara!

BARBARA. You won't let them hurt me?

FERGUSON. No, of course not.

BARBARA. Will you be there? George, darling, please be there!

FERGUSON. I'll be there.

BARBARA. Thanks, dear. . . . I loved you. . . . I don't care. . . . (*Her head goes back.*)

WREN (*looks at* FERGUSON, *who is rigid. Then at* LAURA, *who is equally rigid. He turns to orderly and says, sharply*). Come on! Come on!
(*The* ORDERLY *wheels* BARBARA *to the operating table.* WREN *follows. The patient is transferred to the operating table.*)

LAURA. What was that all about?

FERGUSON. Laura, I'm sorry as hell—I wish I. . . .

LAURA. George! Is it—? (*She clutches his arm.*)

FERGUSON (*recoiling from her touch*). Don't! You mustn't! Stand away! Over there! You've unsterilized the gown! (*He tears off his gown and gloves, throws them on the floor, and calls into the sterilizing-room.*) Nurse! Nurse! Sterile gown, gloves, towels! Quick! (*He turns to* LAURA, *explains, apologetically.*) We've got to be very careful. . . . You know . . . germs are . . .
(*A* NURSE *enters, picks up the gown and gloves. He dips his hands into the bichloride pan, and then the alcohol pan. A sterile nurse brings him a sterile gown, he unfolds it and slides into it. And the sterile nurse, behind him, ties it. In the meantime another nurse returns with a sterile towel. He dries his hands, and throws the towel on the floor. The unsterile nurse picks it up and takes it away. The sterile nurse powders his hands, brings him a sterile glove book and opens it. He plucks out a glove, and puts it on, the nurse helping him, in approved aseptic technique, by thrusting her fingers under the cuff, and pushing home the glove. In the meantime the patient, concealed by the people around her, has been anaesthetized, and is being draped. All the time* LAURA *has been staring at* FERGUSON. FERGUSON, *working the fingers of the gloves, looks at* LAURA. *Exit the* ORDERLY *with the rolling stretcher.*)

LAURA. Did you. . . . Did you have an affair with that girl—or what?

FERGUSON (*almost inaudibly*). Yes. . . .

LAURA. Oh! (*A bitter little laugh.*) That's a funny one!

DR. HOCHBERG (*on a foot-stool, bends over the patient—calls*). Dr. Ferguson . . . ! (*The call is taken up by a number of voices. A* NURSE *crosses to* FERGUSON.)

NURSE. Dr. Ferguson! The patient is draped and ready!

FERGUSON. All right! I'm coming! (*He goes to the operating table.*)

NURSE (*to* LAURA). If you want to watch —you'd better go over. I'll get a stool for you—mask!

LAURA. No, thanks . . . ! I've had enough . . . ! I've had enough!

A 2ND NURSE (*enters*). Here! Here! Get busy! (*Notices* LAURA.) You! What's the matter? You look so. . . . Feel ill, dear? (*To* 1ST NURSE.) Take her out! Near a window! Give her some water!

LAURA. No . . . ! No . . . ! I'm . . . I'm fine . . . ! Thanks! (*She tears off the tight cap, begins to sob, and exits. The* NURSES *look at each other and grin.*)

1ST NURSE. Med-student?

2ND NURSE. Of course! First time! What else?

1ST NURSE. She's got a long way to go, yet! (*They laugh.*)
(NURSE *and* DOCTORS *about the table turn and say, "Sh! Sh!" The nurses immediately hush.*)

HOCHBERG. Ready, Dr. Wren?

WREN. All set!

HOCHBERG. Ready, Dr. Ferguson?

FERGUSON. Ready!

HOCHBERG (*reaching out his hand, without looking up*). Scalpel!
(*The operating nurse hands over the scalpel, cutting a gleaming arc through the air, then she clumps it into* DR. HOCHBERG'S *hand. He bends over the patient. There is a sudden burst of activity and gleam of clamps about the table. The unsterile nurses, hands behind their backs, stand on tip-toes, and crane their necks to see over the shoulders of the assistant. All lights dim down, except the operating light, which bathes the tableau in a fierce, merciless, white brilliance.*)

Curtain.

ACT THREE

SCENE I

FERGUSON'S *room. The next morning. The shade is drawn, the room dark, except for the small lamp at the bed.* FERGUSON *is sitting on the bed, his head in his hands. His clothes are wrinkled—he hasn't changed them all night. His hair is mussed, his eyes red.*

A knock at the door.

FERGUSON *doesn't stir. The knock is repeated.* FERGUSON *still remains motionless. The door slowly opens.* HOCHBERG *enters.*

HOCHBERG. Good morning, George.

FERGUSON. Oh, good morning. (HOCHBERG *pulls up the shade. A great burst of sunlight streams in, blinding* GEORGE. *He turns his face away, rubs his eyes.*) What time? (*He picks up the clock.*) Oh—I didn't know it was so late.

HOCHBERG. Lovely out, isn't it?

FERGUSON. Yes. . . . (*He rises wearily, goes to the wash-basin, washes himself, and combs his hair.*)

HOCHBERG (*examining a brain in a jar on the desk*). Hm. . . . That's a fine specimen.

Ah . . . yes . . . you've been doing some study on brain surgery?

FERGUSON Yes. . . .

HOCHBERG. Fascinating work. Miss Dennin's temperature is down this morning

FERGUSON. I know.

HOCHBERG. The nurse tells me you watched the case all last night. That's very nice. . . . Hm. Excellent book—this. You should read all of Cushing's reports. How is er—D'Andrea?

FERGUSON. Examined those pictures. He did have a fracture of the tibia of the left leg. No further evidence of internal injury. He'll be all right, I guess.

HOCHBERG. Good. Good. He's a lucky boy. He looked badly hurt.

FERGUSON. Doctor Hochberg. There's something I've got to tell you. . . .

HOCHBERG (*quickly*). I know. Wren told me. (*Pause.* HOCHBERG *looks at the specimen.*) Great field—brain surgery—for a young man.

FERGUSON. You must think it was pretty low of me.

HOCHBERG. George . . . George!

FERGUSON. I didn't know anything about it till yesterday. I wouldn't have let her. . . . I swear I wouldn't have. . . .

HOCHBERG. It was a bad job. . . .

FERGUSON. Oh, that poor kid. God, I ought to be shot.

HOCHBERG. Did you force her to have an affair with you; or did she come to you of her own free will? Then why do you blame yourself so?

FERGUSON. That has nothing to do with it.

HOCHBERG. That has everything to do with it!

FERGUSON. Dr. Hochberg, you don't know what she's up against.

HOCHBERG. I know.

FERGUSON. It's not as if she were just a tramp. . . . She's a fine, sensitive girl! God! What a mess I've gotten her into! She can't bear any children. Thrown out of the hospital—nowhere to go—no one to turn to. What's she going to do?

HOCHBERG. Don't worry. We'll find something for her.

FERGUSON. Just giving her a job—isn't going to help her very much. There's only one decent thing . . . I'm going to . . . marry her . . . if she'll have me.

HOCHBERG. George! Stop talking like an idiot! Pull yourself together! What about Laura?

FERGUSON. She's through with me, Dr. Hochberg.

HOCHBERG. She knows?

FERGUSON. Yes. I kept phoning her all day yesterday—all last night. She wouldn't come to the phone . . . wouldn't even talk to me, Dr. Hochberg.

HOCHBERG. Hm . . . that's too bad. Yet you know, George, in a way—that's not the worst that could have happened to you. . . .

FERGUSON. No! Don't say that!

HOCHBERG. Well, now there's work, my boy. Remember that's the master word—work.

FERGUSON. I'm going to marry that girl.

HOCHBERG. What for?

FERGUSON. I have to take care of her, don't I?

HOCHBERG. I see. You've saved some money then?

FERGUSON. Out of what?

HOCHBERG. Then how are you going to help her? How are you going to take care of her?

FERGUSON. I'm going into practice. . . .

HOCHBERG. Mid-Victorian idealism won't solve this problem, George. . . .

FERGUSON. That girl is human, isn't she? She needs me.

HOCHBERG. If you think you can provide for both of you by first starting practice—then you just don't know. . . .

FERGUSON. I'll manage somehow. I'm not afraid of that.

HOCHBERG. Remember Levine? I got a letter from him yesterday. Colorado. He's trying to build up a practice. . . . (*The loud speaker in the corridor starts calling* DR. HOCHBERG.) They're starving, George. He begs me to lend him twenty dollars.

FERGUSON. I don't see what that has to do with me.

HOCHBERG. You didn't know him six years ago. He wouldn't *let* me help him, then. He was sure! So confident! And, better equipped for practice than you are.

FERGUSON. Possibly!

HOCHBERG. I won't answer for Levine . . . at least he loved Katherine. But you don't love this girl. It was an accident—and for that you want to ruin yourself.—the rest of your life—destroy your ambition, your ideals—fill yourself with bitterness, live day and night with a woman who will grow to despise you. . . .

FERGUSON. Dr. Hochberg. Please—it's no use. I've thought of all that! It doesn't make any difference. There's only one decent thing to do—and I'm going to do it.

HOCHBERG (*picks up the phone*). Yes? . . . Dr. Hochberg. . . . Yes, hello. . . . That's all right. Wait for me down in the—no. . . . Come up here to 106, 106. Yes. Is the man there at the desk? Yes. Hello, Arthur. Please ask one of the orderlies to show this young lady up to 106. Yes, thank you.

FERGUSON. Is that Laura?

HOCHBERG. Yes.

FERGUSON. I can't see her now! I can't talk to her.

HOCHBERG. Don't be a child! You've got to see her and have this out. (*Pause.*)

FERGUSON. Dr. Hochberg, I want you to know that . . . I appreciate all you've done for me.

HOCHBERG. What have I done?

FERGUSON. I mean yesterday. I . . . I must have seemed very ungrateful. But it's just because there are so many other things that I thought I wanted.

HOCHBERG. I know. It's our instinct to live, to enjoy ourselves. All of us.

FERGUSON. I love Laura so much. She's so full of life and fun, and all the things I've missed for so many years. I just didn't have the guts to give them up. I kidded myself that I could have that, and still go on. And last night, I realized I kidded myself out of the most important thing that ever happened to me, a chance to work with you. . . .

HOCHBERG. Do you still want to? You can, if you do.

FERGUSON. No—not now.

HOCHBERG. But why? If you realize, now, what you really want. . . .

FERGUSON. I'm going into practice, I told you. . . .

HOCHBERG. Now, George, calm down. Give yourself a chance to think it over.

FERGUSON. I've thought it over.

HOCHBERG. I warn you, George. You'll be sorry.

FERGUSON. I can't just ignore this!

HOCHBERG. In that case, you're through— you're finished—you're. . . .

FERGUSON. All right! Then I am. Why not? What good's a profession that can't give you bread and butter after you've sweated out ten years of your life on it? And if I can't make a go of practice, I'll find a job at something else—and to hell with medicine! I won't starve. I'll always make a living. . . .
(LAURA *appears in the doorway accompanied by an* ORDERLY.)

ORDERLY. Right here, Miss.

FERGUSON. Good morning, Laura.

LAURA (*deliberately ignoring* GEORGE, *looking only at* HOCHBERG, *clipping every word*). Hello, Hocky. . . . Did you want me up here?

HOCHBERG. Yes. Come in, Laura.

LAURA. Sorry to call you so early but. . . .

HOCHBERG. It isn't early for me, Laura. . . . (*She's still standing in the doorway, tense and hard. Impatiently.*) Come in, come in. . . . (*She wavers a moment, then enters.*) Sit down.

LAURA. No. I'm in a hurry, Hocky. I just wanted to see you for a minute . . . alone.

HOCHBERG. Sit down, Laura.

LAURA. I suppose you wondered why I disappeared, yesterday.

HOCHBERG. No. . . . I heard all about it. . . .

LAURA. Oh, you did? A laugh, isn't it?

HOCHBERG. Not particularly.

LAURA. Well, you spanked me all right.

HOCHBERG. Harder than I meant, Laura. . . . Forgive me.

LAURA. Oh, that's all right. Better now than later, Hocky.

HOCHBERG. Will you please sit down, Laura? (LAURA, *suddenly limp, sits down.* HOCHBERG, *scrutinizing her face closely.*) Sleep much last night?

LAURA. Sure. Why not? (*She puts a cigarette into her mouth, searches for a match.* GEORGE's *hand automatically goes to his pocket, to find a match for her.*) Light, Hocky? (HOCHBERG *gives her a light. She exhales a huge puff of smoke.*) I'm washed up with the whole business, Hocky.

HOCHBERG. Yes, of course you are . . . of course.

FERGUSON. I'm sorry you feel so bitter about it, Laura. . . .

LAURA. How did you expect me to feel?

FERGUSON. I don't blame you. I. . . .

LAURA. Thanks. That's sweet of you.

HOCHBERG. Neither do I blame him, Laura.

LAURA. There's no excuse for a thing like that—you know it, Hocky. None at all.

HOCHBERG. I know nothing—except the human body, a little. And I haven't met the wise man or woman, Laura, whom impulse couldn't make a fool of. . . .

LAURA. If you want to reason that way, there isn't anything you couldn't justify.

HOCHBERG. I'm not trying to, Laura. It's so far beyond that. . . . (FERGUSON *starts for the door.*) Where are you going?

FERGUSON. Upstairs.

HOCHBERG. Wait, George! Wait a minute!

FERGUSON. There's nothing more to be said, Dr. Hochberg. Laura's perfectly right.

LAURA (*rises*). Don't leave on my account. I've got to go, now, anyway. I've got to pack. I'm sailing on the Olympic, tonight. Going to get as far away from all this as I can. (*She laughs.*) Humph! I was making plans. I was worried all the time. . . . God! What a fool I was. . . .

HOCHBERG. Do you think he's having such an easy time of it?

LAURA. Oh, he'll take care of himself.

HOCHBERG. Maybe you'd better go home now, Laura.

LAURA. I think it was a pretty rotten trick.

HOCHBERG. Stop it! Laura, stop it!

LAURA. He had no time for me—he was too busy for me—but he did find time to. . . . That's what hurts, Hocky! Hurts like the devil!

HOCHBERG. Don't you think I know how you feel, Laura?
(*The loud speaker is calling* DR. HOCHBERG.)

LAURA. You think I still care? Well, I don't!

HOCHBERG. That's fine! Then it doesn't make any difference to you that right now he's throwing his life away. (*Goes to the phone, picks it up, speaks into it.*) Yes? Dr. Hochberg! (*To* LAURA.) He's going to marry her, Laura.

LAURA. No?

FERGUSON. Dr. Hochberg! Please!

HOCHBERG. Yes. And go into practice, and starve and give up his studies and maybe get out of medicine altogether. The thing he's meant for! And worked so hard for. (*Into the phone, suddenly tense.*) Yes! What! Prepare a hypo of caffeine, and adrenalin, long needle! At once! (*He hangs up and hurries to the door.*)

FERGUSON. Do you want me—?

HOCHBERG. No . . . no . . . no. . . . You stay here! (*He hurries out.* LAURA *stands there a moment looking at* GEORGE, *then starts to go.*)

FERGUSON. Laura!

LAURA. What?

FERGUSON. I don't want you to go away feeling like this. . . .

LAURA. What difference does it make how I feel?

FERGUSON. A great deal . . . to me.

LAURA (*pause*). You love her, don't you?

FERGUSON. I love you, Laura.

LAURA (*laughs bitterly*). Yes, I'm sure you do.

FERGUSON (*grasps both of* LAURA'S *arms tightly*). I don't care whether you believe it or not, Laura, it just happens that I do.

LAURA. Let go—let go my arm! You're. . . .

FERGUSON. Sorry! (*He turns from her and sinks down despondently on the bed.*)

LAURA (*after a pause*). Then how? I don't quite understand . . . I didn't sleep a wink last night, George. I was trying to figure this out. But it doesn't make sense . . . except that . . . I don't know. If you cared for me how could you do that?

FERGUSON. I don't know myself, Laura. Everything had gone wrong that day. Six long operations. I had a battle with Cunningham, I lost a patient. . . . Things sort of kept piling up till I thought I'd bust . . . this kid came to my room for some notes . . . she was sympathetic and lonely herself, and . . . well. . . . But after that I didn't see her around, and . . . I just forgot about it. You'd think she'd come to me when this happened. But, she didn't. I know I should have looked her up. I know I was pretty small and rotten. I thought . . . I thought it didn't mean very much to her. But it did, Laura! Now she's up against it, and. . . .

LAURA. If we meant anything at all to each other, you'd have come to me. I don't give a damn about ceremony! But the point is you didn't really care about me, George. Not for a minute.

FERGUSON. I wanted you more than anything else in the world that night, Laura. But we'd quarrelled and—you wouldn't even go out with me.

LAURA. It was that night?

FERGUSON. Yes.

LAURA. Oh!

FERGUSON. I didn't want to give up Hocky . . . and I didn't want to give you up . . . and I was fighting you . . . and. . . .

LAURA. Through her?

FERGUSON. Yes. . . .

LAURA (*laughs bitterly*). And you say you loved me!

FERGUSON. If I hadn't, I'd have called quits then and there, Laura. I'd have gone to Vienna and worked my way through. That's what I was planning to do . . . before I met you. Alone in Vienna I'd really accomplish something. . . .

LAURA. Well, why don't you go on? Go on and do it, now. If it's so important to you. I won't be around to distract you! Go on! . . . But you're not, you see. You're going to marry a girl you say you don't care for. You're going to let a casual incident rob you of all the things you say are important.

FERGUSON. It's not a casual incident, *any more*, Laura.

LAURA. All right, make your beautiful gestures. Marry her!

FERGUSON. I'm going to.

LAURA. Go ahead! And inside of a year you'll be hating the sight of each other.

FERGUSON. That's a chance I'll have to take.

LAURA. You think you're being brave and strong, I suppose. But you're not. You're a coward. You're doing it because it's the easiest way out. Because you're afraid people'll say things about you. You have no backbone.

FERGUSON. Yes, Laura. You're right. I had no backbone when I let myself be talked out of a chance to work with Hocky. And maybe to do something fine some day. But right now I have no choice. I'm not doing this because I give a good God damn what anybody says or thinks; I'm doing it because that girl's life is smashed, and I'm responsible, and I want to try and help her pick up the pieces and put them together again. (*He stops short.* LAURA *is weeping quietly.*) Oh, Laura . . . ! Don't!

LAURA. I knew how you felt about Hocky and I shouldn't have . . . insisted. I've been selfish, but it was only because I loved you so much. And . . . I still do. That's the way I am, George. I can't help it. I. . . .
(*Enter* HOCHBERG, *slowly, his face drawn and grave, something tragic written on it. He looks at* FERGUSON.)

FERGUSON (*sensing* HOCHBERG'S *look*). What is it, Doctor?

HOCHBERG. Miss Dennin died.

FERGUSON (*dazed*). What . . . ?

LAURA. Oh, God!

HOCHBERG. A few minutes ago.
(FERGUSON *looks blankly at* DR. HOCHBERG, *glances, as if for corroboration, at* LAURA, *and suddenly starts for the door.* HOCHBERG *catches his arm and holds it tightly.*)

HOCHBERG (*softly*). There's nothing you can do, George. Embolism! Went into collapse! Died instantly.

FERGUSON (*almost inaudibly*). Oh! (*He sinks down on the bed, his back to them.*)

HOCHBERG. George!

LAURA. Darling!

FERGUSON. Only a few hours ago . . . she was pleading with me for a chance to live. . . . She was so young. She didn't want to die. . . .

LAURA. Stop it, George! Stop torturing yourself. Please! These things happen. It might have happened to anybody.

FERGUSON. Couldn't you do anything, Dr. Hochberg?

HOCHBERG. I tried . . . everything. Caffein intravenously. Adrenalin directly into the heart. Useless! That little blood-clot in the lung . . . and we're helpless. Forty years I've spent in medicine . . . and I couldn't help her.

FERGUSON. Then what's the use? What good is it all? Why go on? It takes everything from you and when you need it most it leaves you helpless. We don't know anything. . . . We're only guessing.

HOCHBERG. We've been doing a little work on embolism . . . getting some results. It's slow, though . . . slow. Maybe, some day, George. . . .

FERGUSON. Some day . . . . ?

HOCHBERG There isn't a man in medicine who hasn't said what you've said and meant it for a minute—all of us, George. And you're right. We are groping. We are guessing. But, at least our guesses today are closer than they were twenty years ago. And twenty years from now, they'll be still closer. That's what we're here for. Mm . . . there's so much to be done. And so little time in which to do it . . . that one life is never long enough. . . . (*He sighs.*) It's not easy for any of us. But in the end our reward is something richer than simply living. Maybe it's a kind of success that world out there can't measure . . . maybe it's a kind of glory, George. (*Pause.*) Yes, question as much as we will—when the test comes we know—don't we, George?

FERGUSON. Yes. . . .

HOCHBERG (*goes slowly to the door, pauses there*). Er . . . we'll reduce that fracture at ten. Schedule the appendix at three . . . the gastric-ulcer immediately afterwards.

FERGUSON. Yes, sir.

(HOCHBERG *goes.* LAURA *turns to* FERGUSON.)

LAURA. Oh, darling! I'm so sorry! (*Pause.*) George, let's get away from here. Let's go some place where we can talk this thing over quietly and sanely.

FERGUSON. No, Laura. This is where I belong!

LAURA. Yes. . . . (*Pause.*)

FERGUSON. You see. . . .

LAURA. I understand. . . . (*Pause.*) Well . . . when you come back from Vienna, if Hocky'll let you off for a night give me a ring! I'll be around. And, maybe some day we'll get together, anyway.

(*The loud speaker is heard calling* DR. FERGUSON!)

LAURA (*smiles wryly*). They're calling you.

FERGUSON. Yes.

LAURA. Work hard.

FERGUSON. So long, Laura. (LAURA *tears herself away, and hurries out.* FERGUSON *stares after her till she disappears. The loud speaker calls him back. He goes to the phone, slowly, a bit stunned. He picks up the phone.*) Yes? Dr. Ferguson! . . . Who? . . . Oh, Mrs. D'Andrea? Sure! Your boy's all right! Yes. Now, you mustn't cry, Mother! You mustn't! He's all right! (*With his free hand he is brushing the tears from his own eyes and nose, for he is beginning to weep himself. But you could never tell it by his voice, which is strong with professional reassurance.*) We'll fix his leg this morning, and he'll be home in a week. Yes . . . he's going to live . . . don't cry! (*He is still reassuring her as the curtain descends.*)

BIBLIOGRAPHY

BIBLIOGRAPHY

MAXWELL ANDERSON

White Desert, 1923.

What Price Glory? (in collaboration with Laurence Stallings), 1924; included in Mantle's *Best Plays*, 1924-1925.

The Buccaneer (in collaboration with Laurence Stallings), 1925.

First Flight (in collaboration with Laurence Stallings), 1925.

Outside Looking In, 1925.

Saturday's Children, 1927; included in Mantle's *Best Plays*, 1926-1927.

Gods of the Lightning (in collaboration with Harold Hickerson), 1928.

Gypsy, 1928; included in Mantle's *Best Plays*, 1928-1929.

Elizabeth the Queen, 1930; included in Mantle's *Best Plays*, 1930-1931.

Night Over Taos, 1932.

Both Your Houses, 1932; included in Mantle's *Best Plays*, 1932-1933; Pulitzer prize drama for 1932-1933.

Mary of Scotland, 1933; included in Mantle's *Best Plays*, 1933-1934.

Valley Forge, 1934; included in Mantle's *Best Plays*, 1934-1935.

MARC CONNELLY

Dulcy (in collaboration with George S. Kaufman), 1921; included in Mantle's *Best Plays*, 1921-1922.

To the Ladies! (in collaboration with George S. Kaufman), 1922.

Merton of the Movies (in collaboration with George S. Kaufman, from the novel by Harry Leon Wilson), 1922; included in Mantle's *Best Plays*, 1922-1923.

Helen of Troy, New York (in collaboration with George S. Kaufman), 1923, a musical comedy.

The Deep Tangled Wildwood (in collaboration with George S. Kaufman), 1923.

Be Yourself (in collaboration with George S. Kaufman), 1924, a musical comedy.

Beggar on Horseback (in collaboration with George S. Kaufman), 1924; included in Mantle's *Best Plays*, 1923-1924.

The Wisdom Tooth, 1926; included in Mantle's *Best Plays*, 1925-1926.

The Wild Man of Borneo (in collaboration with Herman J. Mankiewicz), 1927.

The Green Pastures (suggested by *Ol' Man Adam an' His Chillun* by Roark Bradford), 1930; included in Mantle's *Best Plays*, 1929-1930; Pulitzer prize drama for 1929-1930.

The Farmer Takes a Wife (in collaboration with Frank B. Elser, adapted from *Rome Haul* by Walter D. Edmonds), 1934; included in Mantle's *Best Plays*, 1934-1935.

OWEN DAVIS

Forever After, 1918.

At 9:45, 1919.

Opportunity, 1920.

The Detour, 1921.

Icebound, 1922; included in Mantle's *Best Plays*, 1922-1923, Pulitzer prize drama for 1922-1923.

The World We Live In, 1922.

Up the Ladder, 1922.

Robin Hood, 1923.

The Nervous Wreck, 1923.

Lazybones, 1924.

Easy Come, Easy Go, 1924.

The Haunted House, 1924.

Beware of Widows, 1925.

The Great Gatsby, 1926.
Blow Your Own Horn, 1926.
The Donovan Affair, 1926.
Sandalwood (adapted from the novel by Fulton Oursler), 1926.
The Triumphant Bachelor, 1927.
Carry On, 1928.
Mile-a-Minute Kendall, 1931.
Just to Remind You, 1931.
The Good Earth (in collaboration with Donald Davis, from the novel by Pearl S.
    Buck), 1932.
The Ninth Guest, 1932.
Jezebel, 1933.
Saturday Night, 1933.
Too Many Boats, 1934.
Spring Freshet, 1934.

ZONA GALE

Miss Lulu Bett (a dramatization of the novel of the same name), 1920; Pulitzer
    prize drama for 1920-1921.
Uncle Jimmy, 1922, one-act.
Mister Pitt (a dramatization of the novel, *Birth*), 1924.
The Neighbors, 1926, one-act.
Faint Perfume (a dramatization of the novel of the same name), 1934.
Evening Clothes, one-act.
The Clouds, one-act.

SUSAN GLASPELL

Trifles, 1917, one-act.
Suppressed Desires (in collaboration with George Cram Cook), 1917.
Woman's Honor, 1918, one-act.
Bernice, 1920.
The People, 1920, one-act.
Close the Book, 1920, one-act.
The Outside, 1920, one-act.
Tickless Time (in collaboration with George Cram Cook), 1920, one-act.
Inheritors, 1921.
Verge, 1922.
The Comic Artist (in collaboration with Norman Matson), 1927.
Alison's House, 1930; included in Mantle's *Best Plays,* 1930-1931; Pulitzer prize
    drama for 1930-1031.

PAUL GREEN

Surrender to the Enemy, 1917.
Supper for the Dead, 1920, one-act.
The Old Man of Edenton, 1920, one-act.
Old Wash Lucas, 1920, one-act.
White Dresses, 1920, one-act.
The Last of the Lowries, 1920, one-act.
The Long Night, 1920, one-act.
Blue Thunder, 1921, one-act.
The Good-Bye, 1921, one-act.
Granny Boling, 1921, one-act.
Fixins (in collaboration with Erma Green), 1921, one-act.
Blackbeard (in collaboration with Elizabeth Lay Green), 1921, one-act.
The Man in the House, 1921, one-act.

Old Christmas, 1921, one-act.
The Picnic, 1921, one-act.
Bread and Butter Comes to Supper, 1921, one-act.
Wrack P'int, 1921, one-act.
Sam Tucker, 1921, one-act.
The Lord's Will, 1921, one-act.
The No 'Count Boy, 1923, one-act.
Day by Day, 1923, one-act.
The Cup of Fury, 1923, one-act.
The Man Who Died at Twelve O'Clock, 1923, one-act.
The End of the Row, 1923, one-act.
The Hot Iron, 1923, one-act.
The Prayer Meeting, 1923, one-act (*Granny Boling* revised).
Your Fiery Furnace, 1923, one-act (*Sam Tucker* revised).
In Aunt Mahaly's Cabin, 1924, one-act.
In Abraham's Bosom, 1925; included in Mantle's *Best Plays*, 1926-1927; Pulitzer
    prize drama for 1926-1927.
Quare Medicine, 1925, one-act.
The Dry Tree, 1925, one-act.
The Field God, 1927.
Tread the Green Grass, 1927.
Unto Such Glory, 1927, one-act.
The House of Connelly, 1927; included in Mantle's *Best Plays*, 1931-1932.
In the Valley, 1928, one-act.
Potter's Field, 1931.
The Southern Cross, 1933.
Roll, Sweet Chariot, 1934.

SIDNEY HOWARD

Swords, 1921.
The Labor Spy (in collaboration with Robert Dunn), 1924.
Bewitched (in collaboration with Edward Sheldon), 1924.
Lexington: A Pageant Drama, 1924.
They Knew What They Wanted, 1924; included in Mantle's *Best Plays*, 1924-1925;
    Pulitzer prize drama for 1924-1925.
Lucky Sam McCarver, 1925.
Ned McCobb's Daughter, 1926.
The Silver Cord, 1926; included in Mantle's *Best Plays*, 1926-1927.
Salvation (in collaboration with Charles MacArthur), 1927.
Half Gods, 1929.
Alien Corn, 1931; included in Mantle's *Best Plays*, 1932-1933.
Lute Song (in collaboration with Will Irwin), 1931.
Yellowjack (in collaboration with P. H. De Kruif), 1933.
Dodsworth (in collaboration with Sinclair Lewis), 1934; included in Mantle's *Best
    Plays*, 1933-1934.
Gather Ye Rosebuds (in collaboration with Robert Littell), 1934.

TRANSLATIONS AND. ADAPTATIONS
S. S. Tenacity (from the French of Charles Vildrac), 1922.
Sancho Panza (from the Hungarian of Melchior Lengyel), 1923.
Casanova (from the Spanish of de Azertis), 1923.
Michel Auclair (from the French of Charles Vildrac), 1924.
The Last Night of Don Juan (from the French of Edmond Rostand), 1925.
Morals (from the German of Ludwig Thoma), 1925.
Olympia (from the Hungarian of Ferenc Molnàr), 1929.

One, Two, Three (from the Hungarian of Ferenc Molnàr), 1929.

Marius (from the French of Marcel Pagnol), 1930.

The Late Christopher Bean (from the French of René Fauchois), 1933; included in Mantle's *Best Plays*, 1932-1933.

Ode to Liberty (from the French of Michel Duran), 1934.

HATCHER HUGHES

A Marriage Made in Heaven, 1918.

Ruint, 1920.

Wake Up, Jonathan (in collaboration with Elmer Rice), 1921.

Hell-Bent fer Heaven, 1922; included in Mantle's *Best Plays*, 1923-1924; Pulitzer prize drama for 1923-1924.

It's a Grand Life (in collaboration with Alan Williams), 1930.

The Lord Blesses the Bishop, 1934.

GEORGE S. KAUFMAN

Someone in the House (in collaboration with Larry Evans and Walter Percival), 1918.

Jacques Duval (adapted from the German), 1920.

Dulcy (in collaboration with Marc Connelly), 1921; included in Mantle's *Best Plays*, 1921-1922.

To the Ladies! (in collaboration with Marc Connelly), 1922.

Merton of the Movies (in collaboration with Marc Connelly, from the novel by Harry Leon Wilson), 1922; included in Mantle's *Best Plays*, 1922-1923.

Helen of Troy, New York (in collaboration with Marc Connelly), 1923, a musical comedy.

The Deep Tangled Wildwood (in collaboration with Marc Connelly), 1923.

Beggar on Horseback (in collaboration with Marc Connelly), 1924; included in Mantle's *Best Plays*, 1923-1924.

Be Yourself (in collaboration with Marc Connelly), 1924, a musical comedy.

Minick (in collaboration with Edna Ferber), 1924; included in Mantle's *Best Plays*, 1924-1925.

The Cocoanuts, 1925, a musical comedy.

The Butter and Egg Man, 1925; included in Mantle's *Best Plays*, 1925-1926.

The Good Fellow (in collaboration with Herman J. Mankiewicz), 1926.

If Men Played Cards as Women Do, 1926, one-act.

The Royal Family (in collaboration with Edna Ferber), 1927; included in Mantle's *Best Plays*, 1927-1928.

Animal Crackers (in collaboration with Morrie Ryskind), 1928, a musical comedy.

The Channel Road (in collaboration with Alexander Woollcott), 1929.

June Moon (in collaboration with Ring Lardner), 1929; included in Mantle's *Best Plays*, 1929-1930.

Strike Up the Band, 1929, musical comedy; music and lyrics by George and Ira Gershwin.

Once in a Lifetime (in collaboration with Moss Hart), 1930; included in Mantle's *Best Plays*, 1930-1931.

The Band Wagon (in collaboration with Howard Dietz), 1931, a revue.

Eldorado (in collaboration with Laurence Stallings), 1931.

Of Thee I Sing (in collaboration with Morrie Ryskind; music and lyrics by George and Ira Gershwin), 1931; included in Mantle's *Best Plays*, 1931-1932; Pulitzer prize drama for 1931-1932.

Dinner at Eight (in collaboration with Edna Ferber), 1932; included in Mantle's *Best Plays*, 1932-1933.

Let 'Em Eat Cake (in collaboration with Morrie Ryskind, lyrics by Ira Gershwin), 1933, a musical comedy.

The Dark Tower (in collaboration with Alexander Woollcott), 1933.

Merrily We Roll Along (in collaboration with Moss Hart), 1934; included in Mantle's *Best Plays*, 1934-1935.

Still Alarm, 1934, one-act.

Bring On the Girls (in collaboration with Morrie Ryskind), 1934.

GEORGE KELLY

Finders Keepers, 1922, one-act.

The Torch-Bearers, 1922.

The Flattering Word, 1924, one-act.

Smarty's Party, 1924, one-act.

The Weak Spot, 1924, one-act.

Poor Aubrey, 1924, one-act.

The Show-Off, 1924; included in Mantle's *Best Plays*, 1923-1924.

Craig's Wife, 1925; included in Mantle's *Best Plays*, 1925-1926; Pulitzer prize drama for 1925-1926.

Daisy Mayme, 1926; included in Mantle's *Best Plays*, 1926-1927.

Behold the Bridegroom, 1927; included in Mantle's *Best Plays*, 1927-1928.

One of Those Things, 1927, one-act.

Maggie the Magnificent, 1929.

Philip Goes Forth, 1931.

SIDNEY KINGSLEY

Wonder-dark Epilogue, 1927, one-act, included in *Cornell University Plays*.

Men in White, 1933; included in Mantle's *Best Plays*, 1933-1934; Pulitzer prize drama for 1933-1934.

EUGENE O'NEILL

The Web, 1913, one-act.

Thirst, 1913, one-act.

Warnings, 1914, one-act.

Recklessness, 1914, one-act.

Fog, 1914, one-act.

Bound East for Cardiff, 1914, one-act.

Before Breakfast, 1916, one-act.

Ile, 1917, one-act.

In the Zone, 1917, one-act.

The Long Voyage Home, 1917, one-act.

The Moon of the Carribees, 1917, one-act.

The Rope, 1918, one-act.

Beyond the Horizon, 1918; included in Mantle's *Best Plays*, 1919-1920; Pulitzer prize drama for 1919-1920.

Where the Cross Is Made, 1918, one-act.

The Dreamy Kid, 1918, one-act.

The Straw, 1919.

Gold, 1920 (an expansion of the one-act *Where the Cross Is Made*).

"Anna Christie," 1920 (revised edition of Chris Christopherson); included in Mantle's *Best Plays*, 1921-1922; Pulitzer prize drama for 1921-1922.

The Emperor Jones, 1920; included in Mantle's *Best Plays*, 1920-1921.

Diff'rent, 1920.

The First Man, 1921.

The Hairy Ape, 1921.

The Fountain, 1922.

Welded, 1923.

All God's Chillun Got Wings, 1923.

Desire Under the Elms, 1924; included in **Mantle's** *Best Plays*, 1924-1925.

Marco Millions, 1924.

The Great God Brown, 1925; included in **Mantle's** *Best Plays*, 1925-1926.

Lazarus Laughed, 1926.

Strange Interlude, 1927; included in **Mantle's** *Best Plays*, 1927-1928; Pulitzer prize drama for 1927-1928.

Dynamo, 1928.

Mourning Becomes Electra, 1929-1931 (a trilogy); included in **Mantle's** *Best Plays*, 1931-1932.

Ah, Wilderness! 1932; included in Mantle's *Best Plays*, 1933-1934.

Days Without End, 1933.

ELMER RICE

On Trial, 1914; included in Mantle's *Best Plays*, 1909-1919.

The Iron Cross, 1917.

The Home of the Free, 1917, one-act.

For the Defense, 1919.

Wake Up, Jonathan (in collaboration with Hatcher Hughes), 1921.

It Is the Law (in collaboration with Hayden Talbot), 1922.

The Adding Machine, 1923.

Close Harmony (or *The Lady Next Door*, in collaboration with Dorothy Parker), 1924.

The Mongrel (an adaptation), 1924.

Cock Robin (in collaboration with Philip Barry), 1927.

Street Scene, 1929; included in Mantle's *Best Plays*, 1928-1929; Pulitzer prize drama for 1928-1929.

The Subway, 1929.

See Naples and Die, 1929.

The Left Bank, 1931; included in Mantle's *Best Plays*, 1931-1932.

Counsellor-at-Law, 1931.

Black Sheep, 1932.

The House in Blind Alley, 1932.

We, The People, 1933; included in Mantle's *Best Plays*, 1932-1933.

Between Two Worlds, 1934.

Judgment Day, 1934.

Not for Children, 1935.

MORRIE RYSKIND

Animal Crackers (in collaboration with George S. Kaufman), 1928, a musical comedy.

Strike Up the Band (based on a libretto by George S. Kaufman; lyrics by Ira Gershwin; music by George Gershwin), 1930, a musical comedy.

Of Thee I Sing (in collaboration with George S. Kaufman; lyrics and music by Ira and George Gershwin), 1931; included in Mantle's *Best Plays*, 1931-1932; Pulitzer prize drama for 1931-1932, a musical comedy.

Let 'Em Eat Cake (in collaboration with George S. Kaufman, lyrics by Ira Gershwin), 1933, a musical comedy.

JESSE LYNCH WILLIAMS

The Stolen Story, 1906 (a dramatization of the short story of the same name).

And So They Were Married, 1914.

Why Marry? 1917 (revised edition of *And So They Were Married*); included in Mantle's *Best Plays*, 1909-1919; Pulitzer prize drama for 1917-1918.

Why Not? 1922 (a dramatization of the novelette, *Remating Time*); included in Mantle's *Best Plays*, 1922-1923.

Lovely Lady, 1925.

APPENDIX

Delight

ET SHERWOOD

This Play Is Lovingly Dedicated to
Lynn Fontanne
and
Alfred Lunt

ROBERT EMMET SHERWOOD

Robert Sherwood confesses that his literary career began in 1903, when, at the age of seven, he edited a magazine called *Children's Life*. From then until the time he won the Pulitzer Prize with *Idiot's Delight* in 1936, his career has been chiefly literary, with interludes for an elementary and college education at Harvard, service in the World War with the 42nd Battalion of the Canadian Black Watch, with journalistic ventures as dramatic critic of *Vanity Fair*, and motion-picture editor of *Life* and the *New York Herald*. His first play, *The Road to Rome*, was an immediate success. It was followed by *The Queen's Husband*, *Waterloo Bridge*, *This Is New York*, *Acropolis*, *Reunion in Vienna* and the 1936 Pulitzer Prize choice *Idiot's Delight*. Robert Sherwood is also the author of *The Virtuous Knight*, an historical novel dealing with the period of the Third Crusade.

CHARACTERS

DUMPTSY
ORCHESTRA LEADER
DONALD NAVADEL
PITTALUGA
AUGUSTE
CAPTAIN LOCICERO
DR. WALDERSEE
MR. CHERRY
MRS. CHERRY
HARRY VAN
SHIRLEY
BEULAH
BEBE
FRANCINE
ELAINE
EDNA
MAJOR
FIRST OFFICER
SECOND OFFICER
THIRD OFFICER
FOURTH OFFICER
QUILLERY
SIGNOR ROSSI
SIGNORA ROSSI
MAID
ACHILLE WEBER
IRENE

SCENES

ACT ONE

Afternoon of a winter day in any imminent year.

ACT TWO

SCENE I: Eight o'clock that evening.
SCENE II: Eleven o'clock that evening.
SCENE III: After midnight.

ACT THREE

The following afternoon.

ness, all the way from Santa Barbara to St. Moritz. And you lured me away from a superb job . . .

PITTALUGA (*as* DON *continues*)

Lazzarone, briccone, bestione. Perdio.

DON

. . . with your glowing descriptions of this handsome place, and the crowds of sportlovers, gay, mad, desperately chic, who were flocking here from London, Paris, New York. . . .

PITTALUGA

Did *I* know what was going to happen? Am *I* the king of Europe?

DON

You are the proprietor of this obscure tavern. You're presumably responsible for the fact that it's a deadly, boring dump!

PITTALUGA

Yes! And I engaged you because I thought you had friends—rich friends— and they would come here after you instead of St. Moritz, and Muerren, and Chamonix. And where are your friends? What am I paying you for? To countermand my orders and tell me you are fed . . . (*Wails from warning sirens are heard from off-stage right.* PITTALUGA *stops short. Both listen.*) Che cosa succede?

DON

That's from down on the flying field.

PITTALUGA

It is the warning for the air raids! (AUGUSTE, *the barman, is heard in bar off-stage, left.*)

AUGUSTE'S VOICE

Che cosa? (PITTALUGA *and* DON *rush to the window.*)

PITTALUGA

Segnali d'incursione. La guerra e incominiciata e il nemico viene. (*Airplane motors are heard off right.*)

DON (*looking through window*)

Look! The planes are taking off. They're the little ones—the combat planes. (CAPTAIN LOCICERO *enters from the lobby.*

He is the officer in charge of the frontier station. He is tired, quiet, nice. AUGUSTE *enters from the bar.* DUMPTSY *follows the* CAPTAIN.)

AUGUSTE

Signor Capitano!

CAPTAIN

Buona sera! (AUGUSTE *helps him take off his coat.*)

DUMPTSY

Che cosa succede, Signor Capitano? È la guerra?

CAPTAIN

No—no—datemi cognac. (DUMPTSY *puts coat on chair right of table and goes up and exits through arch center.* CAPTAIN *sits chair left of table.*)

AUGUSTE (*as he goes out*)

Si, Signor Capitano. (*The* CAPTAIN *sits down at a table.* PITTALUGA *and* DON *cross to him.* DUMPTSY *goes.*)

PITTALUGA

Che cosa significano quei terribili segnali? È, forse, il nemico che arriva?

DON

What's happened, Captain? Is there an air raid? Has the war started?

CAPTAIN (*smiling*)

Who knows? But there is no raid. (*The porter's hand-bell in the lobby is heard.*) They're only testing the sirens, to see how fast the combat planes can go into action. You understand—it's like life-boat drill on a ship. (DUMPTSY *enters.*)

DUMPTSY

Scusi, padrone. Due Inglesi arrivati. (*He hurries out.*)

PITTALUGA

Scusi. Vengo subito. Presto, presto! (*He goes.*)

CAPTAIN

Have a drink, Mr. Navadel?

DON

Thank you very much—but some guests are actually arriving. I must go and be very affable. (*He goes.* DR. WALDERSEE *appears on the gallery above and comes down the stairs as* AUGUSTE *enters from the bar and serves the* CAPTAIN *with brandy and soda. The* DOCTOR *is an elderly, stout, crotchetty, sad German.*)

CAPTAIN

Good afternoon, Doctor. Have a drink?

DOCTOR

Thank you very much—no. What is all that aeroplanes?
(AUGUSTE *goes.*)

CAPTAIN

This is a crucial spot, Dr. Waldersee. We must be prepared for visits from the enemy.

DOCTOR

Enemy, eh? And who is that?

CAPTAIN

I don't quite know, yet. The map of Europe supplies us with a wide choice of opponents. I suppose, in due time, our government will announce its selection—and we shall know just whom we are to shoot at.

DOCTOR

Nonsense! Obscene nonsense!

CAPTAIN

Yes—yes. But the taste for obscenity is incurable, isn't it?

DOCTOR

When will you let me go into Switzerland?

CAPTAIN

Again I am powerless to answer you. My orders are that no one for the time being shall cross the frontiers, either into Switzerland or Austria.

DOCTOR

And when will this "time being" end?

CAPTAIN

When Rome makes its decision between friend and foe.

DOCTOR

I am a German subject. I am not your foe.

CAPTAIN

I am sure of that, Dr. Waldersee. The two great Fascist states stand together, against the world.

DOCTOR (*passionately*)

Fascism has nothing to do with it! I am a scientist. I am a servant of the whole damn stupid human race. (*He crosses toward the* CAPTAIN.) If you delay me any longer here, my experiments will be ruined. Can't you appreciate that? I must get my rats at once to the laboratory in Zurich, or all my months and years of research will have gone for nothing.
(DON *enters, followed by* MR. *and* MRS. CHERRY—*a pleasant young English couple in the first flush of their honeymoon.*)

DON

This is our cocktail lounge. There is the American bar. We have a thé dansant here every afternoon at 4:30—supper dancing in the evening.

CHERRY

Charming.

DON

All this part of the hotel is new. Your rooms are up there. (*He crosses to the window.*) I think you'll concede that the view from here is unparalleled. We can look into four countries. (*The* CHERRYS *follow him to the window.*) Here in the foreground, of course, is Italy. This was formerly Austrian territory, transferred by the treaty of Versailles. It's called Monte Gabriele in honor of D'Annunzio, Italian poet and patriot. Off there is Switzerland and there is Austria. And far off, you can just see the tip of a mountain peak that is in the Bavarian Tyrol. Rather gorgeous, isn't it?

CHERRY

Yes.

MRS. CHERRY

Darling—*look* at that sky!

CHERRY

I say, it *is* rather good.

DON

Do you go in for winter sports, Mrs. Cherry?

MRS. CHERRY

Oh, yes—I—we're very keen on them.

DON

Splendid! We have everything here.

CHERRY

I've usually gone to Kitzbuhel.
(PITTALUGA *and* DUMPTSY *appear upstage and speak in Italian through the dialogue.*)

PITTALUGA

Dumptsy, il bagaglio è stato portato su?

DUMPTSY

Si, signore, è già sopra.

PITTALUGA

Sta bene, vattene.

DON

It's lovely there, too.

CHERRY

But I hear it has become much too crowded there now. I—my wife and I hoped it would be quieter here.

DON

Well—at the moment—it is rather quiet here.

PITTALUGA (*coming down*)

Your luggage has been sent up, Signor. Would you care to see your room now?

CHERRY

Yes. Thank you.

PITTALUGA

If you will have the goodness to step this way. (*He goes up the stairs.*) 'Scuse me.

CHERRY (*pauses at the window on the way up*)

What's that big bare patch down there?

DON (*casually*)

Oh, that's the airport. (PITTALUGA *coughs discreetly.*) We have a great deal of flying here.

PITTALUGA

Right this way, please.

CHERRY

Oh—I see. (*They continue on up, preceded by* PITTALUGA.)

DON

And do come down for the thé dansant.

MRS. CHERRY

We should love to.

PITTALUGA

Right straight ahead, please. (*They exit through gallery.*)

DON (*standing on first step*)

Honeymooners.

CAPTAIN

Yes—poor creatures.

DON

They wanted quiet.

DOCTOR (*rises*)

Ach Gott! When will you know when I can cross into Switzerland?

CAPTAIN

The instant that word comes through from Rome. (*The hand-bell is heard.*) You understand that I am only an obscure frontier official. And here in Italy, as in your own Germany, authority is centralized.

DOCTOR

But you can send a telegram to Rome, explaining the urgency of my position.
(DUMPTSY *appears, greatly excited.*)

DUMPTSY

More guests from the bus, Mr. Navadel. Seven of them! (*He goes.*)

DON

Good God! (*He goes out.*)

DOCTOR

Ach, es gibt kein Ruhe hier.

CAPTAIN

I assure you, Dr. Waldersee, I shall do all in my power.

DOCTOR

They must be made to understand that time is of vital importance.

CAPTAIN

Yes, I know.

DOCTOR

I have no equipment here to examine them properly—no assistant for the constant observation that is essential if my experiments are to succeed . . .

CAPTAIN (*a trifle wearily*)

I'm so sorry . . .

DOCTOR

Yes! You say you are so sorry. But what do you *do*? You have no comprehension of what is at stake. You are a soldier and indifferent to death. You say you are sorry, but it is nothing to you that hundreds of thousands, *millions,* are dying from a disease that it is within my power to cure!

CAPTAIN

Again, I assure you, Dr. Waldersee, that I . . .

DON'S VOICE

Our Mr. Pittaluga will be down in a moment. In the meantime, perhaps you and the—the others . . . (*He comes in, followed by* HARRY VAN, *a wan, thoughtful, lonely American vaudevillian promoter, press agent, book-agent, crooner, hoofer, barker or shill, who has undertaken all sorts of jobs in his time, all of them capitalizing his powers of salesmanship, and none of them entirely honest. He wears a snappy, belted, polo coat and a brown felt hat with brim turned down on all sides*) . . . would care to sit here in the cocktail lounge. We have a thé dansant here at 4:30 . . . supper dancing in the evening . . .

HARRY

Do you run this hotel?

DON

I'm the Social Manager.

HARRY

What?

DON

The Social Manager.

HARRY

Oh! American, aren't you?

DON

I am. Santa Barbara's my home, and Donald Navadel is my name.

HARRY

Happy to know you. My name's Harry Van. (*They shake hands.*)

DON

Glad to have you here, Mr. Van. Are you—staying with us long?

DOCTOR (*rising*)

I shall myself send a telegram to Rome, to the German Embassy.

CAPTAIN

They might well be able to expedite matters.

(*The* DOCTOR *goes.*)

HARRY

I've got to get over that border. When I came in on the train from Fiume, they told me the border is closed, and the train is stuck here for tonight and maybe longer. I asked them why, but they either didn't know or they refused to divulge their secrets to me. What seems to be the trouble?

DON

Perhaps Captain Locicero can help you. He's the commander of Italian Headquarters here. This is Mr. Van, Captain.

CAPTAIN (*rising*)

Mr. Van, my compliments.

HARRY

And mine to you, Captain. We're trying to get to Geneva.

CAPTAIN

You have an American passport?

HARRY

I have. Several of them. (*He reaches in his pocket and takes out seven passports, bound together with elastic. He fans them like a deck of cards and hands them to the* CAPTAIN.)

CAPTAIN

You have your family with you?

HARRY

Well—it isn't exactly a family. (*He goes to the right.*) Come in here, girls!

SHIRLEY (*from off-stage*)

Come on in, kids. Harry wants us.

(*Six blonde chorus girls come in. They are named:* SHIRLEY, BEULAH, BEBE, FRANCINE, EDNA *and* ELAINE. *Of these,* SHIRLEY *is the principal, a frank, knowing fan dancer.* BEULAH *is a bubble dancer, and therefore ethereal.* BEBE *is a hard, harsh little number who shimmies.* DON *doesn't know quite how to take this surprising troupe, but the* CAPTAIN *is impressed, favorably.*)

HARRY

Allow me to introduce the girls, Captain. We call them "Les Blondes." We've been playing the Balkan circuit—Budapest, Bucharest, Sofia, Belgrade, and Zagreb. (*He turns to* DON.) Back home, that would be the equivalent of "Pan Time." (*He laughs nervously, to indicate that the foregoing was a gag.*)

CAPTAIN (*bowing*)

How do you do?

HARRY

The Captain is head man, girls.

GIRLS

How do you do? . . . Pleased to meet you. . . . Etc.

HARRY

The situation in brief is this, Captain. We've got very attractive bookings at a night spot in Geneva. Undoubtedly they feel that the League of Nations needs us. (*Another laugh.*) It's important that we get there at once. So, Captain, I'll be grateful for prompt action.

CAPTAIN (*looking at the first passport*)

Miss Shirley Laughlin.

HARRY

Laughlin. This is Shirley. Step up, honey.

(SHIRLEY *steps forward.*)

CAPTAIN (*pleased with* SHIRLEY)

How do you do?

SHIRLEY

Pleased to meet you.

CAPTAIN

This photograph hardly does you justice.

SHIRLEY

I know. It's terrible, isn't it!

HARRY (*interrupting*)

Who's next, Captain?

CAPTAIN

Miss Beulah Tremoyne.

HARRY

Come on, Beulah. (*She comes forward in a wide sweep, as* SHIRLEY *goes up and joins the group.*) Beulah is our bubble dancer, a product of the æsthetic school, and therefore more of a dreamer.

CAPTAIN

Exquisite!

BEULAH

Thank you *ever* so much. (*She starts to sit down by the* CAPTAIN. *She is turning it on.*)

HARRY

That'll be all, Beulah.

CAPTAIN

Miss Elaine Messiger——

HARRY

Come on, babe.

CAPTAIN

Miss Francine Merle——

HARRY

No tricks, Francine. This is just identification.

CAPTAIN

Miss Edna Creesh——

HARRY

Turn it off, honey.

CAPTAIN

And Miss Bebe Gould.

HARRY

You'll find Bebe a very, very lovely girl.

BEBE (*remonstrating*)

Harry!

HARRY

A shimmy artiste, and incorrigibly unsophisticated.

CAPTAIN (*summing up*)

Very beautiful. Very, very beautiful. Mr. Van, I congratulate you.

HARRY

That's nice of you, Captain. Now, can we . . .

CAPTAIN

And I wish I, too, were going to Geneva. (*He hands back the passports to* HARRY.)

HARRY

Then it's O.K. for us to pass?

CAPTAIN

But won't you young ladies sit down?

SHIRLEY

Thanks, Captain.

BEULAH

We'd love to.

FRANCINE

He's cute.

EDNA

I'll say.
(*They all sit.*)

HARRY

I don't want to seem oblivious of your courtesy, Captain, but the fact is we can't afford to hang around here any longer. That train may pull out and leave us.

CAPTAIN

I give you my word, that train will not move tonight, and maybe not tomorrow night, and maybe never. (*He bows deeply.*) It is a matter of the deepest personal regret to me, Mr. Van, but——

HARRY

Listen, pal. Could you stop being polite for just a moment, and tell us how do we get to Geneva?

CAPTAIN

That is not for me to say. I am as powerless as you are, Mr. Van. I, too, am a pawn.

(*He picks up his coat and hat.*) But, speaking for myself, I shall not be sorry if you and your beautiful companions are forced to remain here indefin:tely. (*He salutes the girls, smiles and goes out.*)

HARRY

Did you hear that? He says he's a pawn.

BEBE

He's a Wop.

BEULAH

But he's cute!

SHIRLEY

Personally, I'd just as soon stay here. I'm sick of the slats on those stinking day coaches.

HARRY

After the way we've been betrayed in the Balkans, we can't afford to stay any place. (*He turns to* DON.) What's the matter, anyway? Why can't decent respectable people be allowed to go about their legitimate business?

DON

Evidently you're not fully aware of the international situation.

HARRY

I'm fully aware that the international situation is always regrettable. But what's wrong now?

DON

Haven't you been reading the papers?

HARRY

In Bulgaria and Jugo-Slavia? (*He looks around at the girls, who laugh.*) No.

DON

It may be difficult for you to understand, Mr. Van, but we happen to be on the brink of a frightful calamity.

HARRY

What?

DON

We're on the verge of war.

SHIRLEY

War?

BEBE

What about?

HARRY

You mean—that business in Africa?

DON

Far more serious than that! *World* war! All of them!

HARRY

No lie! You mean—it'll be started by people like that? (*Points after the* CAPTAIN.) Italians?

DON

Yes. They've reached the breaking point.

HARRY

I don't believe it. I don't believe that people like that would take on the job of licking the world. They're too romantic.
(PITTALUGA *steps forward.*)

PITTALUGA

Do you wish rooms, Signor?

HARRY

What have you got?

PITTALUGA

We can give you grande luxe accommodations, rooms with baths. . . .

HARRY

What's your scale of prices?

PITTALUGA

From fifty lira up.

DON

That's about five dollars a day.

HARRY (*wincing*)

What?

DON

Meals included.

HARRY

I take it there's the usual professional discount.

PITTALUGA (*to* DON)

Che cosa significa?

DON

Mr. Van and the young ladies are artists.

PITTALUGA

Ebbene?

DON (*scornfully*)

In America we give special rates to artists.

PITTALUGA (*grimly*)

Non posso, non posso.
(*The* CHERRYS *appear on the balcony above.*)

DON

I'm sure Mr. Pittaluga will take care of you nicely, Mr. Van. He will show you attractive rooms on the *other* side of the hotel. They're delightful.

HARRY

No doubt. But I want to see the accommodations.

PITTALUGA

Step this way, please.

HARRY

Come on, girls. Now—I want two girls to a room, and a single room for me adjoining. I promised their mothers I'd always be within ear-shot. Put on your shoes, Beulah. (*He goes out right, followed by the* GIRLS, *and* DON.)

BEULAH (*as they go*)

Why's he kicking? I think this place is *attractive!*

SHIRLEY

Oh—you know Harry. He's always got to have something to worry about. (*They have gone.*)

MRS. CHERRY (*coming down*)

What an extraordinary gathering!

CHERRY

There's something I've never been able to understand—the tendency of Americans to travel en masse. (*They pause to admire the view and each other. He takes her in his arms and kisses her.*) Darling!

MRS. CHERRY

What?

CHERRY

Nothing. I just said, "Darling"! (*He kisses her again.*) My sweet. I love you.

MRS. CHERRY

That's right. (*She kisses him.*)

CHERRY

I think we're going to like it here, aren't we, darling?

MRS. CHERRY

Yes. You'll find a lot to paint.

CHERRY

No doubt. But I'm not going to waste any time painting.

MRS. CHERRY

Why not, Jimmy? You've got to work and——

CHERRY

Don't ask "why not" in that laboriously girlish tone! You know damned well why not!

MRS. CHERRY (*laughing*)

Now really, darling. We don't have to be maudlin. We're old enough to be sensible about it, aren't we!

CHERRY

God forbid that we should spoil everything by being sensible! This is an occasion for pure and beautiful foolishness. So don't irritate me by any further mention of work.

MRS. CHERRY

Very well, darling. If you're going to be stinking about it . . . (*He kisses her again.*)
(*The* DOCTOR *comes in from the right and regards their love-making with scant enthusiasm. They look up and see him. They aren't embarrassed.*)

CHERRY

How do you do?

DOCTOR

Don't let me interrupt you. (*He rings a bell and sits down.*)

CHERRY

It's quite all right. We were just starting out for a walk.

MRS. CHERRY

The air is so marvellous up here, isn't it?

DOCTOR (*doubtfully*)

Yes.
(DUMPTSY *comes in from the right.*)

CHERRY

Yes—we think so. Come on, darling. (*They go out at the back.*)

DOCTOR

Mineral water.

DUMPTSY

Yes, sir.
(QUILLERY *comes in and sits at the left. He is small, dark, brooding and French— an extreme-radical-socialist, but still, French.*)

DOCTOR

Not iced—warm.

DUMPTSY

If you please, sir. (*He goes out, left.*)
(*A group of five Italian flying corps officers come in, talking gaily in Italian. They cross to the bar entrance and go out.*)

FIRST OFFICER

Sono Americane.

SECOND OFFICER

Sono belle, proprio da far strabiliare.

THIRD OFFICER

Forse sarrano stelle cinematografiche di Hollyvood.

SECOND OFFICER

E forse ora non ci rincrescerà che abbiano cancellato la nostra licenza. (*They go into the bar.*)

HARRY (*coming in*)

Good afternoon.

DOCTOR

Good afternoon.

HARRY

Have a drink?

DOCTOR

I am about to have one.

HARRY

Mind if I join you? (*He sits down near the* DOCTOR.)

DOCTOR

This is a public room.

HARRY (*whistles a snatch of a tune*)

It's a funny kind of situation, isn't it?

DOCTOR

To what situation do you refer?

HARRY

All this stopping of trains . . .
(DUMPTSY *enters from the bar and serves
the* DOCTOR *with a glass of mineral water*)
and orders from Rome and we are on the
threshold of calamity.

DOCTOR

To me it is not funny. (*He rises with his
mineral water.*)

HARRY

Get me a Scotch.

DUMPTSY

With soda, sir?

HARRY

Yes.

DUMPTSY

If you please, sir.

QUILLERY

I will have a beer.

DUMPTSY

We have native or imported, sir.

QUILLERY

Native will do.

DUMPTSY

If you please, sir. (*He goes out.*)

DOCTOR

I repeat—to me it is *not* funny! (*He
bows.*) You will excuse me.

HARRY

Certainly. . . . See you later, pal. (*The*
DOCTOR *goes.* HARRY *turns to* QUILLERY.)
Friendly old bastard!

QUILLERY

Quite! But you were right. The situation
is funny. There is always something essentially laughable in the thought of a

lunatic asylum. Although, it may perhaps
seem less funny when you are inside.

HARRY

I guess so. I guess it isn't easy for Germans to see the comical side of things
these days. Do you mind if I join you?
(*He rises and crosses to the left.*)

QUILLERY

I beg of you to do so, my comrade.

HARRY

I don't like to thrust myself forward—
(*He sits down*)—but, you see, I travel with
a group of blondes, and it's always a relief
to find somebody to talk to. Have you seen
the girls?

QUILLERY

Oh, yes.

HARRY

Alluring, aren't they?

QUILLERY

Very alluring.
(DUMPTSY *comes in with the drinks and
goes.*)
(HARRY *takes out his chewing gum,
wraps it in paper, places it in a silver snuff
box, which he shows to* QUILLERY.)

HARRY

That's a genuine antique snuff box of
the period of Louis Quinze.

QUILLERY

Very interesting.

HARRY

It's a museum piece. (*Puts the box in his
pocket.*) You've got to hoard your gum
here in Europe.

QUILLERY

You've travelled far?

HARRY

Yeah—I've been a long way with that
gorgeous array of beautiful girls. I took
'em from New York to Monte Carlo. To
say we were a sensation in Monte Carlo
would be to state a simple incontrovertible
fact. But then I made the mistake of accepting an offer from the manager of the
Club Arizona in Budapest. I found that

conditions in the South-East are not so good.

QUILLERY

I travelled on the train with you from Zagreb.

HARRY

Zagreb! A plague spot! What were you doing there?

QUILLERY

I was attending the Labor Congress.

HARRY

Yeah—I heard about that. The night club people thought that the congress would bring in a lot of business. They were wrong. But—excuse me—(*Rises.*) My name is Harry Van.

QUILLERY (*rises*)

Quillery is my name.

HARRY

Glad to know you, Mr.——?

QUILLERY

Quillery.

HARRY

Quillery. (*Sits.*) I'm an American. What's your nationality?

QUILLERY

I have no nationality. (*Sits.*) I drink to your good health.

HARRY

And to your lack of nationality, of which I approve.
(*They drink.* SIGNOR *and* SIGNORA ROSSI *come in and cross to the bar.* ROSSI *is a consumptive.*)

ROSSI

Abbiamo trascorso una bella giornata, Nina. Beviamo un po'?

SIGNORA ROSSI

Dopo tutto quell' esercizio ti farebbe male. Meglio che tu ti ripcsi per un'oretta.

ROSSI

Ma, no mi sento proprio bene. Andiamo. Mi riposerò più tardi. (*They go into the bar.*)

HARRY

I get an awful kick hearing Italian. It's beautiful. Do you speak it?

QUILLERY

Only a little. I was born in France. And I love my home. Perhaps if I had raised pigs—like my father, and all his fathers, back to the time when Cæsar's Roman legions came—perhaps, if I had done that, I should have been a Frenchman, as they were. But I went to work in a factory— and machinery is international.

HARRY

And I suppose pigs are exclusively French?

QUILLERY

My father's pigs are! (HARRY *laughs.*) The factory where I have worked made artificial limbs—an industry that has been prosperous the last twenty years. But sometimes—in the evening—after my work—I would go out into the fields and help my father. And then, for a little while, I would become again a Frenchman.

HARRY (*takes out his cigarette case*)

That's a nice thought, pal. (*Offers* QUILLERY *a cigarette.*) Have a smoke?

QUILLERY

No, thank you.

HARRY

I don't blame you. These Jugo-Slav cigarettes are not made of the same high-grade quality of manure to which I grew accustomed in Bulgaria.

QUILLERY

You know, my comrade—you seem to have a long view of things.

HARRY

So long that it gets very tiresome.

QUILLERY

The long view is not easy to sustain in this short-sighted world.

HARRY

You're right about that, pal.

QUILLERY

Let me give you an instance: There we were—gathered in Zagreb, representatives of the workers of all Europe. All brothers, collaborating harmoniously for the United Front! And now—we are rushing to our homes to prevent our people from plunging into mass murder—mass suicide!

HARRY

You're going to try to stop the war?

QUILLERY

Yes.

HARRY

Do you think you'll succeed?

QUILLERY

Unquestionably! This is not 1914, remember! Since then, some new voices have been heard in this world—loud voices. I need mention only one of them—Lenin—Nikolai Lenin!

(*A ferocious looking* MAJOR *of the Italian flying corps comes in and goes quickly to the bar. As he opens the door, he calls "Attention!" He goes into the bar, the door swinging to behind him.*)

HARRY

Yes—but what are you going to do about people like *that*?

QUILLERY

Expose them! That's all we have to do. Expose them—for what they are—atavistic children! Occupying their undeveloped minds playing with out-moded toys.

HARRY

Have you *seen* any of those toys?

QUILLERY

Yes! France is full of them. But there is a force more potent than all the bombing planes and submarines and tanks. And that is the mature intelligence of the workers of the world! There is one antidote for war—Revolution! And the cause of Revolution gains steadily in strength. Even here in Italy, despite all the repressive power of Fascism, sanity has survived, and it becomes more and more articulate. . . .

HARRY

Well, pal—you've got a fine point there. And I hope you stick to it.

QUILLERY

I'm afraid you think it is all futile idealism!

HARRY

No—I don't. And what if I did? I am an idealist myself.

QUILLERY

You too believe in the revolution?

HARRY

Not necessarily in *the* revolution. I'm just in favor of any revolution. Anything that will make people wake up, and get themselves some convictions. Have you ever taken cocaine?

QUILLERY

Why—I imagine that I have—at the dentist's.

HARRY

No—I mean, for pleasure. You know—a vice.

QUILLERY

No! I've never indulged in that folly.

HARRY

I have—during a stage of my career when luck was bad and confusion prevailed.

QUILLERY

Ah, yes. You needed delusions of grandeur.

HARRY

That's just what they were.

QUILLERY

It must have been an interesting experience.

HARRY

It was illuminating. It taught me what is the precise trouble with the world today. We have become a race of drug addicts—hopped up with false beliefs—false fears—false enthusiasms. . . .

(*The four* OFFICERS *emerge from the bar, talking excitedly.*)

SECOND OFFICER

Ma, è state fatta la dichiarazone di guerra attuale?

FIRST OFFICER

Caricheremo delle bombe esplosive?

THIRD OFFICER

Se la guerra è veramente in cominciata, allora vuol dire che noi. . . .

FOURTH OFFICER

La guerra è in cominciata fra l'Italia e la Francia.
(*All the above speeches are said together, as the* MAJOR *enters from the bar.*)

MAJOR

Silenzio! Solo il vostro commandante conosce gli ordini. Andiamo!
(*All five go out hurriedly.*)

QUILLERY (*jumps up*)

Mother of God! Did you hear what they were saying?

HARRY (*rises*)

I heard, but I couldn't understand.

QUILLERY

It was about war. I know only a little Italian—but I thought they were saying that war has already been declared. (*He grabs his hat.*) I must go and demand that they let me cross the border! At once! (*He starts to go.*)

HARRY

That's right, pal. There's no time to lose.

QUILLERY

Wait—I haven't paid. . . . (*He is fumbling for money.*)

HARRY

No, no. This was my drink. You've got to hurry!

QUILLERY

Thank you, my comrade. (*He goes out quickly. Airplane motors are heard, off at the right.* HARRY *crosses to the window.* DUMPTSY *comes in to remove the empty glasses.*)

DUMPTSY

Fine view, isn't it, sir?

HARRY

I've seen worse.

DUMPTSY

Nothing quite like it, sir. From here, we look into four nations. Where you see that little village, at the far end of the valley—that is Austria. Isn't that beautiful over there?

HARRY

Are you Italian?

DUMPTSY

Well, yes, sir. That is to say, I didn't used to be.

HARRY

What did you used to be?

DUMPTSY

Austrian. All this part was Austria, until after the big war, when they decided these mountains must go to Italy, and I went with them. In one day, I became a foreigner. So now, my children learn only Italian in school, and when I and my wife talk our own language they can't understand us. (*He gets* HARRY's *drink and brings it over to him.*) They changed the name of this mountain. Monte Gabriele—that's what it is now. They named it after an Italian who dropped poems on Vienna. Even my old father—he's dead—but all the writing on the gravestones was in German, so they rubbed it out and translated it. So now he's Italian, too. But they didn't get my sister. She married a Swiss. She lives over there, in Schleins.

HARRY

She's lucky.

DUMPTSY

Yes—those Swiss are smart.

HARRY

Yeah, they had sense enough to get over there in the first place.

DUMPTSY (*laughs*)

But it doesn't make much difference who your masters are. When you get used to them, they're all the same.
(*The Porter's bell rings.* PITTALUGA *appears.*)

PITTALUGA

Dumptsy! Dumptsy! Una gentildonna arriva. Prendi i suoi bagagli. Affretati!

DUMPTSY

Si, Signore. Vengo subito. (*He goes.*)

PITTALUGA (*clasps his hands*)

Sciocco! Anna, Per Dio! Dove sei stata, va sopra a preparare la stanza.
(ANNA, *the maid, enters with towels.*)
Presto, presto!
(ANNA *runs up the steps, exits.* PITTALUGA *goes back into the lobby.*)

IRENE'S VOICE

Vieni, Achille.

DON (*coming in*)

This is our cocktail lounge, madame.
(IRENE *enters. She is somewhere between thirty and forty, beautiful, heavily and smartly furred in the Russian manner. Her hair is blonde and quite straight. She is a model of worldly wisdom, chic, and carefully applied graciousness. Her name is pronounced "EAR-RAY-NA." . . . She surveys the room with polite appreciation, glancing briefly at* HARRY.)

DON

Your suite is up there, madame. All this part of the hotel is quite new.

IRENE

How very nice!

DON

We have our best view from this side of the hotel. (*He goes to the window.* IRENE *follows slowly.*) You can see four countries—Italy, Switzerland, Austria and Bavaria.

IRENE

Magnificent!

DON

Yes—we're very proud of it.

IRENE

All those countries. And they all look so very much alike, don't they!

DON

Yes—they do really—from this distance.

IRENE

All covered with the beautiful snow. I think the whole world should be always covered with snow. It would be so much more clean, wouldn't it?

DON

By all means!

IRENE

Like in my Russia. White Russia. (*Sighs, and goes up to the next landing.*) Oh, and—how exciting! A flying field. Look! They're bringing out the big bombers.

DON

Madame is interested in aviation?

IRENE

No, no. Just ordinary flying bores me. But there is no experience in life quite so thrilling as a parachute jump, is there!

DON

I've never had that thrill, I'm ashamed to say.

IRENE

Once I had to jump when I was flying over the jungle in Indo-China. It was indescribable. Drifting down, sinking into that great green sea of enchantment and hidden danger.
(DUMPTSY *comes in.*)

DON

And you weren't afraid?

IRENE

No—no—I was not afraid. In moments like that, one is given the sense of eternity.

HARRY (*viciously*)

Dumptsy! Get me another Scotch.

DUMPTSY

Yes, sir.

HARRY

And put ice in it, this time. If you haven't got any ice, go out and scoop up some snow.

DUMPTSY

If you please, sir. (*He goes into the bar.*)

IRENE (*her gaze wandering about the room*)

But your place is really charming.

DON

You're very kind.

IRENE

I must tell every one in Paris about it. There's something about this design—it suggests a—an amusing kind of horror.

DON (*not knowing quite how to interpret that*)

Madame is a student of decoration?

IRENE

No, no. Only an amateur, my friend. An amateur, I'm afraid, in everything.
(*The siren sounds from off at the right.* IRENE, *near the top of the staircase, stops to listen.*)

IRENE

What is that?

DON

Oh—it's merely some kind of warning. They've been testing it.

IRENE

Warning? Warning against what?

DON

I believe it's for use in case of war.

IRENE

War? But there will be no war.
(PITTALUGA *enters from the lobby, escorting* ACHILLE WEBER—*which is pronounced* "VAY-BAIR." *He is a thin, keen executive, wearing a neat little mustache and excellent clothes. In his lapel is the rosette of the Legion of Honor. He carries a brief case.*)

PITTALUGA (*as they come in*)

Par ici, Monsieur Weber. Vous trouverez Madam ici . . .

IRENE (*leaning over the railing*)

Achille!

WEBER (*pausing and looking up*)

Yes, my dear?

IRENE

Achille—there will be no war, will there?

WEBER (*amused*)

No, no—Irene. There will be no war. They're all much too well prepared for it. (*He turns to* PITTALUGA.) Where are our rooms?

PITTALUGA

Votre suite est par ici, Monsieur. La plus belle de la maison! La vue est superbe!

IRENE (*to* DON)

There, you see! They will not fight. They are all much too much afraid of each other.
(WEBER *is going up the staircase, ignoring the view.* PITTALUGA *is following.*)

IRENE (*to* WEBER)

Achille—I am mad about this place! Je rafolle de cette place!

WEBER (*calmly*)

Yes, my dear.

IRENE

We must be sure to tell the Maharajah of Rajpipla, Achille. Can't you imagine how dear little "Pip" would love this? (*They go out on the landing above.*)

HARRY

Who was that?

DON (*impressed*)

That was Achille Weber. One of the biggest men in France. I used to see him a lot at St. Moritz.
(*There is a sound of airplane motors off at the right.*)

HARRY

And the dame? Do you assume that is his wife?

DON (*curtly*)

Are you implying that she's not?

HARRY

No, no—I'm not implying a thing. (*He wanders to the piano.*) I'm just kind of—kind of baffled.

DON

Evidently. (*He goes out.*)
(HARRY *at the piano strikes a chord of the Russian song, "Kak Stranna." * DUMPTSY *enters from the bar and serves* HARRY *with Scotch. The off-stage noise increases as more planes take the air.*)

DUMPTSY (*at the window*)

Do you see them—those aeroplanes—flying up from the field down there?

HARRY (*glances toward window, without interest*)

Yes—I see them.

DUMPTSY

Those are the big ones. They're full of bombs, to drop on people. Look! They're going north. Maybe Berlin. Maybe Paris.
(HARRY *strikes a few chords.*)

HARRY

Did you ever jump with a parachute?

DUMPTSY

Why, no—sir. (*He looks questioningly at* HARRY.)

HARRY

Well, I have a couple of times. And it's nothing. But—I didn't land in any jungle. I landed where I was supposed to—in the Fair Grounds.

DUMPTSY (*seriously*)

That's interesting, sir.
(*The* ROSSIS *enter from the bar. He is holding a handkerchief to his mouth. She is supporting him as they cross.*)

SIGNORA ROSSI

Non t'ho detto che dovevi fare attenzione? Te l'ho detto, te l'ho detto che sarebbe accaduto ciò. Vedi, ora ti piglia un accesso di tosse.

ROSSI

'Scusatemi, Mina. (*Another coughing fit.*)

SIGNORA ROSSI

Va a sdraiarti. Dovresti riposarti a lungo. E adopera il termometro. Scommetto che t'è aumentata la temperatura. (*They go out.*)

DUMPTSY

That Signor Rossi—he has tuberculosis.

HARRY

Is he getting cured up here?
(*The* DOCTOR *appears on the landing above.*)

DUMPTSY

Ja. This used to be a sanatorium, in the old days. But the Fascisti—they don't like to admit that any one can be sick! (*He starts to go.*)

DOCTOR

Dumptsy!

DUMPTSY

Herr Doctor.

DOCTOR (*coming down*)

Mineral water.

DUMPTSY

Ja wohl, Herr Doctor.
(DUMPTSY *goes out, left. The* DOCTOR *sits down.* HARRY *takes one more look toward the gallery, where* IRENE *had been. He then looks at the* DOCTOR, *and decides not to suggest joining him. He starts to play "Kak Stranna." The* DOCTOR *turns and looks at him, with some surprise. The uproar of planes is now terrific, but it starts to dwindle as the planes depart.*)

DOCTOR

What is that you are playing?

HARRY

A Russian song, entitled "Kak Stranna," meaning "how strange!" One of those morose ballads about how once we met, for one immortal moment, like ships that pass in the night. Or maybe like a couple of trucks, side-swiping each other. And now we meet again! How strange!

DOCTOR

You are a musician?

HARRY

Certainly. I used to play the piano in picture theatres—when that was the only kind of sound they had—except the peanuts.

(DUMPTSY *brings in the mineral water and stops to listen, admiringly.*)

DOCTOR

Do you know Bach?

HARRY

With pleasure. (*He shifts into something or other by Bach.*)

DOCTOR (*after a moment*)

You have good appreciation, but not much skill.

HARRY

What do you mean, not much skill? Listen to this. (*He goes into a trick arrangement of* "The Waters of the Minnetonka.") "The Waters of the Minnetonka" —Cadman. (*He goes on playing.*) Suitable for Scenics—Niagara Falls by moonlight. Or—if you play it this way—it goes fine with the scene where the young Indian chief turns out to be a Yale man, so it's O.K. for him to marry Lillian ("Dimples") Walker. (*Starts playing* "Boola, Boola.")

DOCTOR

Will you have a drink?

HARRY

Oh! So you want me to stop playing?

DOCTOR

No, no! I like your music very much.

HARRY

Then, in that case, I'd be delighted to drink with you. Another Scotch, Dumptsy.

DUMPTSY

If you please, sir. (*He goes out.*)

DOCTOR

I'm afraid I was rude to you.

HARRY

That's all right, pal. I've been rude to lots of people, and never regretted it. (*He plays on, shifting back into* "Kak Stranna."

DOCTOR

The fact is, I am a man who is very gravely distressed.

HARRY

I can see that, Doctor. And I sympathize with you.

DOCTOR (*fiercely*)

You cannot sympathize with me, because you do not know!

HARRY

No—I guess I don't know—except in a general way.

DOCTOR

You are familiar with the writings of Thomas Mann. (*It is a challenge, rather than a question.*)

HARRY

I'm afraid not, pal.
(*The* DOCTOR *opens* "The Magic Mountain," *which he has been reading.*)

DOCTOR

"Backsliding"—he said—"spiritual backsliding to that dark and tortured age— that, believe me, is disease! A degradation of mankind—a degradation painful and offensive to conceive." True words, eh?

HARRY

Absolutely!
(DUMPTSY *comes in with the Scotch.* HARRY *gets up from the piano and crosses.* DUMPTSY *goes.* HARRY *sits down with the* DOCTOR.)

DOCTOR

Have you had any experience with the disease of cancer?

HARRY

Certainly. I once sold a remedy for it.

DOCTOR (*exploding*)

There *is* no remedy for it, so far!

HARRY

Well—this was kind of a remedy for everything.

DOCTOR

I am within *that* of finding the cure for cancer! You probably have not heard of Fibiger, I suppose?

HARRY

I may have. I'm not sure.

DOCTOR

He was a Dane—experimented with rats. He did good work, but he died before it could be completed. I carry it on. I have been working with Oriental rats, in Bologna. But because of this war scare, I must go to neutral territory. You see, nothing must be allowed to interfere with my experiments. Nothing!

HARRY

No. They're important.

DOCTOR

The laboratory of the University of Zurich has been placed at my disposal—and in Switzerland, I can work, undisturbed. I have twenty-eight rats with me, all in various carefully tabulated stages of the disease. It is the disease of civilization—and I can cure it. And now they say I must not cross the border.

HARRY

You know, Doctor, it *is* funny.

DOCTOR

What's funny? To you, everything is funny!

HARRY

No—it's just that you and I are in the same fix. Both trying to get across that line. You with rats—me with girls. Of course—I appreciate the fact that civilization at large won't suffer much if *we* get stuck in the war zone. Whereas with you, there's a lot at stake . . .

DOCTOR

It is for me to win one of the greatest victories of all time. And the victory belongs to Germany.

HARRY

Sure it does!

DOCTOR

Unfortunately, just now the situation in Germany is not good for research. They are infected with the same virus as here, chauvinistic nationalism! They expect all bacteriologists to work on germs to put in bombs to drop from airplanes. To fill people with death! When we've given our lives to *save* people. Oh—God in heaven—why don't they let me do what is good? Good for the whole world? Forgive me. I become excited.

HARRY

I know just how you feel, Doctor. Back in 1918, I was a shill with a carnival show, and I was doing fine. The boss thought very highly of me. He offered to give me a piece of the show, and I had a chance to get somewhere. And then what do you think happened? Along comes the United States Government and they drafted me! You're in the army now! They slapped me into a uniform and for three whole months before the Armistice, I was parading up and down guarding the Ashokan Reservoir. They were afraid your people might poison it. I've always figured that that little interruption ruined my career. But I've remained an optimist, Doctor.

DOCTOR

You can afford to.

HARRY

I've remained an optimist because I'm essentially a student of human nature. You dissect corpses and rats and similar unpleasant things. Well—it has been my job to dissect suckers! I've probed into the souls of some of the God-damnedest specimens. And what have I found? Now, don't sneer at me, Doctor—but above everything else I've found Faith. Faith in peace on earth and good will to men—and faith that "Muma," "Muma" the three-legged girl, really has got three legs. All my life, Doctor, I've been selling phony goods to people of meagre intelligence and great faith. You'd think that would make me contemptuous of the human race, wouldn't you? But—on the contrary—it has given *me* Faith. It has made me sure that no matter how much the meek may be bulldozed or gypped they *will* eventually inherit the earth.

(SHIRLEY *and* BEBE *come in from the lobby.*)

SHIRLEY

Harry!

HARRY

What is it, honey?
(SHIRLEY *goes to* HARRY *and hands him a printed notice.*)

SHIRLEY (*excited*)

Did you see this?

HARRY

Doctor—let me introduce Miss Shirley Laughlin and Miss Bebe Gould.

SHIRLEY

How do you do?

DOCTOR (*grunts*)

How do you do?

BEBE

Pleased to know you, Doctor.
(HARRY *looks at the notice.*)

SHIRLEY

They got one of those put up in every one of our rooms.

HARRY (*showing it to the* DOCTOR)

Look—"What to do in case of air-raids" —in all languages.

DOCTOR

Ja—I saw that.

SHIRLEY

Give it back to me, Harry. I'm going to send it to Mama.

HARRY (*handing it to her*)

Souvenir of Europe.

SHIRLEY

It'll scare the hell out of her.

BEBE

What's the matter with these people over here? Are they all screwy?

HARRY

Bebe—you hit it right on the nose!
(*Turns to the* DOCTOR.) I tell you, Doctor —these are very wonderful, profound girls. The mothers of tomorrow!
(*He beams on them.* BEULAH *comes in.*)

SHIRLEY

Oh—shut up!

BEULAH

Say—Harry . . .

HARRY

What is it, honey?

BEULAH

Is it all right if I go out with Mr. Navadel and try to learn how to do this skiing?
(WEBER *comes out on the gallery and starts down.*)

HARRY

What? And risk those pretty legs? Emphatically—no!

BEULAH

But it's healthy.

HARRY

Not for me, dear. Those gams of yours are my bread and butter. (WEBER *crosses. They look at him. He glances briefly at them.*) Sit down, girls, and amuse yourselves with your own thoughts.
(*The* GIRLS *sit.* WEBER, *at the left, lights his cigar. The* CAPTAIN *comes in, quickly, obviously worried.*)

CAPTAIN

I have been trying to get through to headquarters, Monsieur Weber.

WEBER

And when can we leave?

CAPTAIN

Not before tomorrow, I regret to say.
(IRENE *appears on the gallery.*)

WEBER

Signor Lanza in Venice assured me there would be no delay.

CAPTAIN

There would be none, if only I could get into communication with the proper authorities. But—the wires are crowded. The whole nation is in a state of uproar.

WEBER

It's absurd lack of organization.
(*The* PIANIST *and* DRUMMER *come in from the lobby. The* VIOLINIST *and* SAXOPHONIST *follow.*)

CAPTAIN (*with tense solemnity*)

There is good excuse for the excitement now, Monsieur Weber. The report has just come to us that a state of war exists between Italy and France.

HARRY

What?

CAPTAIN

There is a rumor of war between Italy and France!

HARRY

Rumors—rumors—everything's rumors! When are we going to *know*?

CAPTAIN

Soon enough, my friend.

DOCTOR

And what of Germany?

CAPTAIN

Germany has mobilized. (IRENE *pauses to listen.*) But I don't know if any decision has been reached. Nor do I know anything of the situation anywhere else. But—God help us—it will be serious enough for everyone on this earth.
(IRENE *joins* WEBER, *who has sat down at the left.*)

IRENE (*to* WEBER, *and straight at him*)

But I thought they were all too well prepared, Achille. Has there been some mistake somewhere?

WEBER (*confidentially*)

We can only attribute it to spontaneous combustion of the dictatorial ego.

IRENE (*grimly*)

I can imagine how thrilling it must be in Paris at this moment. Just like 1914. All the lovely soldiers—singing—marching—marching! We must go at once to Paris, Achille.

HARRY (*rises*)

What's the matter with the music, professor? Us young folks want to dance.
(ELAINE *and* FRANCINE *come in.*)

ELAINE

Can we have a drink now, Harry?

HARRY

Sure. Sit down.
(DON *enters, exuding gratification at the sight of this gay, chic throng. The* ORCHESTRA *starts to play* "Valencia.")

WEBER

Will you have a drink, Irene?

IRENE

No, thank you.

WEBER

Will you, Captain Locicero?

CAPTAIN

Thank you. Brandy and soda, Dumptsy.

DUMPTSY

Si, Signor.

BEBE (*yells*)

Edna! We're going to have a drink!
(EDNA *comes in.*)

WEBER

For me, Cinzano.

DUMPTSY

Oui, Monsieur. (*He goes into the bar.*)

DOCTOR

It is all incredible.

HARRY

Nevertheless, Doctor, I remain an optimist. (*He looks at* IRENE.) Let doubt prevail throughout this night—with dawn will come again the light of truth! (*He turns to* SHIRLEY.) Come on, honey—let's dance.
(*They dance.* DON *dances with* BEULAH. *The* ORCHESTRA *continues with its spirited but frail performance of* "Valencia." *There are probably* "border incidents" *in Lorraine, the Riviera, Poland, Czecho-Slovakia and Mongolia.*)

Curtain.

ACT TWO

SCENE I

It is about 7:30 in the evening of the same day.
The CHERRYS *are seated, both of them dressed for dinner.* AUGUSTE *is serving them cocktails.*

CHERRY

Thank you.

AUGUSTE

Thank you, Signor.

CHERRY

Has any more news come through?

AUGUSTE

No, Signor. They permit the wireless to say nothing.

CHERRY

I suppose nothing really will happen.

AUGUSTE

Let us pray that is so, Signor. (AUGUSTE *goes into the bar.* CHERRY *leans over and kisses his wife.*)

CHERRY

My sweet . . . you're really very lovely.

MRS. CHERRY

Yes. (*He kisses her again, then lifts his glass.*)

CHERRY

Here's to us, darling.

MRS. CHERRY

And to hell with all the rest.

CHERRY

And to hell with all the rest. (*They drink, solemnly.*)

MRS. CHERRY

Jimmy—

CHERRY

What is it, darling?

MRS. CHERRY

Were you just saying that—or do you believe it?

CHERRY

That you're lovely? I can give you the most solemn assurance. . . .

MRS. CHERRY

No—that nothing is going to happen.

CHERRY

Oh.

MRS. CHERRY

Do you believe that?

CHERRY

I know this much: they can't start any real war without England. And no matter how stupid and blundering our government may be, our people simply won't stand for it.

MRS. CHERRY

But people can be such complete fools.

CHERRY

I know it, darling. Why can't they all be like us?

MRS. CHERRY

You mean—nice.

CHERRY

Yes—nice—and intelligent—and happy.

MRS. CHERRY

We're very conceited, aren't we?

CHERRY

Of course. And for good and sufficient reason.

MRS. CHERRY

I'm glad we're so superior, darling. It's comforting.

(HARRY *comes in from bar.*)

CHERRY

Oh—good evening, Mr. Van.

HARRY

Good evening. Pardon me—(*He starts to go.*)

CHERRY

Oh—don't run away, Mr. Van. Let's have some music.

MRS. CHERRY

Won't you have a drink with us?

HARRY

No, thanks, Mrs. Cherry—if you don't mind. (*Sits down at the piano.*) I'm afraid I put down too many Scotches this afternoon. As a result of which, I've just had to treat myself to a bicarbonate of soda. (*Starts playing* "Some of these days.")

MRS. CHERRY

I love that.

HARRY

Thanks, pal—always grateful for applause from the discriminating. (*Finishes the chorus and stops.*)

CHERRY

Do play some more.

HARRY

No. The mood isn't right.

MRS. CHERRY

I can't tell you what a relief it is to have you here in this hotel.

HARRY

It's kind of you to say that, Mrs. Cherry. But I don't deserve your handsome tribute. Frequently, I can be an asset to any gathering—contributing humorous anecdotes and bits of homely philosophy. But here and now, I'm far from my best.

CHERRY

You're the only one here who seems to have retained any degree of sanity.

MRS. CHERRY

You and your young ladies.

HARRY

The girls are lucky. They don't know anything. And the trouble with me is that I just don't give a damn.

MRS. CHERRY

We've been trying hard not to know anything—or not to give a damn. But it isn't easy.

HARRY

You haven't been married very long, have you? I hope you don't mind my asking. . . .

CHERRY

We were married the day before yesterday.

HARRY

Let me offer my congratulations.

CHERRY

Thank you very much.

HARRY

It's my purely intuitive hunch that you two ought to get along fine.

CHERRY

That's our intention, Mr. Van.

MRS. CHERRY

And we'll do it, what's more. You see— we have one supreme thing in common:

HARRY

Yeah?

MRS. CHERRY

We're both independent.

CHERRY

We're like you Americans, in that respect.

HARRY

You flatter us.

MRS. CHERRY

Jimmy's a painter.

HARRY

You don't say!

MRS. CHERRY

He has been out in Australia, doing colossal murals for some government building. He won't show me the photographs of them, but I'm sure they're simply awful. (*She laughs fondly.*)

CHERRY

They're allegorical. (*He laughs, too.*)

HARRY

I'll bet they're good, at that. What do you do, Mrs. Cherry?

MRS. CHERRY

Oh, I work in the gift department at Fortnum's——

HARRY

Behind a counter, eh!

MRS. CHERRY

Yes—wearing a smock, and disgracing my family.

HARRY

Well, what d'ye know!

MRS. CHERRY

Both our families hoped we'd be married in some nice little church, and settle down in a nice little cottage, in a nice little state of decay. But when I heard Jimmy was on the way home I just dropped everything and rushed down here to meet him —and we were married, in Florence.

CHERRY

We hadn't seen each other for nearly a year—so, you can imagine, it was all rather exciting.

HARRY

I can imagine.

MRS. CHERRY

Florence is the most perfect place in the world to be married in.

HARRY

I guess that's true of any place.

CHERRY

We both happen to love Italy. And—I suppose—we're both rather on the romantic side.

HARRY

You stay on that side, no matter what happens.

MRS. CHERRY (*quickly*)

What do you think is going to happen?

HARRY

Me? I haven't the slightest idea.

CHERRY

We've looked forward so much to being here with no one bothering us, and plenty of winter sports. We're both keen on skiing. And now—we may have to go dashing back to England at any moment.

MRS. CHERRY

It's rotten luck, isn't it?

HARRY

Yes, Mrs. Cherry. That's what it is—it's rotten. (QUILLERY *enters from the bar, reading a newspaper.*) So they wouldn't let you cross?

QUILLERY

No!

HARRY

Is there any news?

QUILLERY (*glaring*)

News! Not in this patriotic journal! "Unconfirmed rumors"—from Vienna, London, Berlin, Moscow, Tokyo. And a lot of confirmed lies from Fascist headquarters in Rome. (*He slaps the paper down and sits.*) If you want to know what is really happening, ask *him*—up there! (*Indicates the rooms above.*)

CHERRY

Who?

QUILLERY

Weber! The great Monsieur Achille Weber, of the Comité des Forges! He can give you all the war news. Because he *made* it. You don't know who he is, eh? Or what he has been doing here in Italy? I'll tell you. (*He rises and comes close to them.*) He has been organizing the arms industry. Munitions. To kill French babies. And English babies. France and Italy are at war. England joins France. Germany joins Italy. And that will drag in the Soviet Union and the Japanese Empire and the United States. In every part of the world, the good desire of men for peace and decency is undermined by the dynamite of jingoism. And it needs only one spark, set off anywhere by one egomaniac, to send it all up in one final, fatal explosion. Then love becomes hatred, courage becomes terror, hope becomes despair. (*The* DOCTOR *appears on the gallery above.*) But—it will all be very nice for Achille Weber. Because he is a master of the one *real League of Nations*—(The DOCTOR *slowly comes down steps.*) The League of Schneider-Creusot, and Krupp, and Skoda, and Vickers and Dupont. The League of Death! And the workers of the world are expected to pay him for it, with their sweat, and their life's blood.

DOCTOR

Marxian nonsense!

QUILLERY

Ah! Who speaks?

DOCTOR

I speak.

QUILLERY

Yes! The eminent Dr. Hugo Waldersee. A wearer of the sacred swastika. Down with the Communists! Off with their heads! So that the world may be safe for the Nazi murderers.

DOCTOR

So that Germany may be safe from its oppressors! It is the same with all of you—Englishmen, Frenchmen, Marxists—you manage to forget that Germany, too, has a right to live! (*Rings handbell on the table.*)

QUILLERY

If you love Germany so much, why aren't you there, now—with your rats?

DOCTOR (*sitting*)

I am not concerned with politics. (*Auguste enters from the bar.*) I am a scientist. (*To* AUGUSTE.) Mineral water! (AUGUSTE *bows and exits into the bar.*)

QUILLERY

That's it, Herr Doctor! A scientist—a servant of humanity! And you know that if you were in your dear Fatherland, the Nazis would make you abandon your cure of cancer. It might benefit too many people outside of Germany—even maybe some Jews. They would force you to devote yourself to breeding malignant bacteria—millions of little germs, each one trained to give the Nazi salute and then go out and poison the enemy. You—a fighter against disease and death—you would become a Judas goat in a slaughter house. (DON *has appeared during this.*)

CHERRY

I say, Quillery, old chap—do we have to have so much blood and sweat just before dinner?

QUILLERY (*turning on him*)

Just before dinner! And now we hear the voice of England! The great, well-fed, pious hypocrite! The grabber—the exploiter—the immaculate butcher! It was *you* forced this war, because miserable little Italy dared to drag its black shirt across your trail of Empire. What do *you* care if civilization goes to pieces—as long as you have your dinner—and your dinner jacket!

CHERRY (*rising*)

I'm sorry, Quillery—but I think we'd better conclude this discussion out on the terrace.

MRS. CHERRY

Don't be a damned fool, Jimmy. You'll prove nothing by thrashing him.

QUILLERY

It's the Anglo-Saxon method of proving everything! Very well—I am at your disposal.

DON

No! I beg of you, Mr. Cherry. We mustn't have any of that sort of thing. (*He turns to* QUILLERY.) I must ask you to leave. If you're unable to conduct yourself as a gentleman, then . . .

QUILLERY

Don't say any more. Evidently I cannot

conduct myself properly! I offer my apologies, Mr. Cherry.

CHERRY

That's quite all right, old man. Have a drink. (*He extends his hand. They shake.*)

QUILLERY

No, thank you. And my apologies to you, Herr Doctor.

DOCTOR

There is no need for apologizing. I am accustomed to all that.

QUILLERY

If I let my speech run away with me, it is because I have hatred for certain things. And you should hate them, too. They are the things that make us blind—and ignorant—and—and dirty. (*He turns and goes out quickly.* DON *goes with him.*)

MRS. CHERRY

He's so right about everything.

CHERRY

I know, poor chap. Will you have another cocktail, darling?

MRS. CHERRY

I don't think so. Will you, Doctor? (*He shakes his head, indicates the mineral water. She rises.*) Let's dine.

CHERRY

It will be a bit difficult to summon up much relish. (*They go out, hand in hand.*)

HARRY

I find them very appealing, don't you, Doctor? (*The* DOCTOR *doesn't announce his findings.*) Did you know they were married only the day before yesterday? Yeah—they got themselves sealed in Florence—because they love Italy. And they came here hoping to spend their honeymoon on skis. . . . Kind of pathetic, isn't it?

DOCTOR

What did you say?

HARRY

Nothing, pal. (DON *comes in.*) Only making conversation.

DOCTOR (*rising*)

That Communist! Making me a criminal because I am a German!

DON

I'm dreadfully sorry, Dr. Waldersee. We never should have allowed the ill-bred little cad to come in here.

DOCTOR

Oh— It's no matter. I have heard too many Hymns of Hate before this. To be a German is to be used to insults, and injuries. (*He goes out.* DON *starts to go out left.*)

HARRY

Just a minute, Don.

DON

Well?

HARRY

Have you found out yet who that dame is?

DON

What "dame"?

HARRY

That Russian number with Weber.

DON

I have not enquired as to her identity.

HARRY

But did he register her as his wife?

DON

They registered separately! And if it's not too much to ask, might I suggest that you mind your own damned business?

HARRY

You might suggest just that. And I should still be troubled by one of the most tantalizing of questions—namely, "Where have I seen that face before?" Generally, it turns out to be someone who was in the second row one night, yawning.

DON

I'm sure that such is the case now. (*He starts again to go.*)

HARRY

One moment, Don. There's something else.

DON (*impatiently*)

What is it?

HARRY

I take it that your job here is something like that of a professional greeter.

DON

You're at liberty to call it that, if you choose.

HARRY

You're a sort of Y.M.C.A. secretary—who sees to it that all the guests get together and have a good time.

DON

Well?

HARRY

Well—do you think you're doing a very good job of it right now?

DON (*simply furious*)

Have you any suggestions for improving the performance of my duties?

HARRY

Yes, Don—I have.

DON

And I'd very much like to know just exactly who the hell do you think you are to be offering criticism of my work?

HARRY

Please, please! You needn't scream at me. I'm merely trying to be helpful. I'm making you an offer.

DON

What is it?

HARRY (*looking around*)

I see you've got a color wheel here. (*Referring to the light.*)

DON

We use it during the supper dance. But —if you don't mind, I——

HARRY

I see—well—how would it be if I and the girls put on part of our act here, tonight? For purposes of wholesome merriment and relieving the general tension?

DON

What kind of an act is it?

HARRY

And don't say, "What kind of an act," in that tone of voice. It's good enough for this place. Those girls have played before the King of Rumania. And if some of my suspicions are correct—but I won't pursue that subject. All that need concern you is that we can adjust ourselves to our audience, and tonight we'll omit the bubble dance and the number in which little Bebe does a shimmy in a costume composed of detachable gardenias, unless there's a special request for it.

DON

Do you expect to be paid for this?

HARRY

Certainly not. I'm making this offer out of the goodness of my heart. Of course, if you want to make any appropriate adjustment on our hotel bill . . .

DON

And you'll give me your guarantee that there'll be no vulgarity?

(IRENE *appears on the gallery and starts to come down. She is wearing a dinner dress.*)

HARRY

Now be careful, Don. One more word like that and the offer is withdrawn . . .

(DON *cautions him to silence.*)

DON

It's a splendid idea, Mr. Van. We'll all greatly appreciate your little entertainment, I'm sure. (*To* IRENE.) Good evening, Madame.

IRENE (*with the utmost graciousness*)

Good evening, Mr. Navadel. (*She pauses at the window.*) It *is* a lovely view. It's like a landscape on the moon.

DON

Yes—yes. That's exactly what it's like. (*She comes down.*)

HARRY

You understand, we'll have to rehearse with the orchestra.

DON

Oh, yes—Mr. Van. Our staff will be glad to co-operate in every way. . . . Do sit down, Madame.

IRENE (*sitting*)

What became of those planes that flew off this afternoon? I haven't heard them come back. (*Takes out a cigarette.*)

DON

I imagine they were moving to some base farther from the frontier. I hope so. They always made the most appalling racket. (*Lights her cigarette for her.*)

HARRY

About eleven o'clock?
(WEBER *appears on the gallery.*)

DON

Yes, Mr. Van. Eleven will do nicely. You'll have a cocktail, Madame?
(HARRY *goes into the lobby.*)

IRENE

No, no. Vodka, if you please.

DON

I shall have it sent right in. (*He goes off at the left into bar.* IRENE *looks slowly off, after* HARRY. *She smiles slightly.* WEBER *comes down the stairs quickly. He is not in evening dress. He too pauses at the window.*)

WEBER

A perfectly cloudless night! They're very lucky. (*He comes on down.*)

IRENE

Did you get your call?

WEBER

Yes. I talked to Lanza.

IRENE

I gather the news is, as usual, good.

WEBER

It is extremely serious! You saw those bombers that left here this afternoon?

IRENE

Yes.

WEBER

They were headed for Paris. Italy is evidently in a great hurry to deliver the first blow.

IRENE

How soon may we leave here?

WEBER

None too soon, I can assure you. The French high command will know that the bombers come from this field. There will be reprisals—probably within the next twenty-four hours.

IRENE

That will be exciting to see.

WEBER

An air raid?

IRENE

Yes—with bombs bursting in the snow. Sending up great geysers of diamonds.

WEBER

Or perhaps great geysers of us.

IRENE (*after a moment*)

I suppose many people in Paris are being killed now.

WEBER

I'm afraid so. Unless the Italians bungle it.

IRENE

Perhaps your sister—Madame d'Hilaire —perhaps she and her darling little children are now dying.

WEBER (*sharply*)

My sister and her family are in Montbeliard.

IRENE

But you said the Italians might bungle it. They might drop their bombs on the wrong place.

WEBER

I appreciate your solicitude, my dear. But you can save your condolences until they are needed. (DUMPTSY *comes in from the bar and serves the vodka.* WEBER *rises.*) I must telegraph to Joseph to have the house ready. It will be rather cold in Biarritz now—but far healthier than Paris. You are going in to dinner now?

IRENE

Yes.

WEBER

I shall join you later. (*He goes out.* DUMPTSY *picks up the* CHERRYS' *glasses.*)

DUMPTSY

We will have a great treat to-night, Madame.

IRENE

Really?

DUMPTSY

That American impresario, that Mr. Harry Van—he will give us an entertainment with his dancing girls.

IRENE

Is he employed here regularly?

DUMPTSY

Oh, no, Madame. He is just passing, like you. This is a special treat. It will be very fine.

IRENE

Let us hope so. (*She downs the vodka.*)

DUMPTSY

Madame is Russian, if I may say so.

IRENE (*pleased*)

How did you know that I am Russian? Just because I am having vodka?

DUMPTSY

No, Madame. Many people try to drink vodka. But only true Russians can do it gracefully. You see—I was a prisoner with your people in the war. I liked them.

IRENE

You're very charming. What is your name?

DUMPTSY

I am called Dumptsy, Madame.

IRENE

Are you going again to the war, Dumptsy?

DUMPTSY

If they tell me to, Madame.

IRENE

You will enjoy being a soldier?

DUMPTSY

Yes—if I'm taken prisoner soon enough.

IRENE

And who do you think will win?

DUMPTSY

I can't think, Madame. It is all very doubtful. But one thing I can tell you: whoever wins, it will be the same as last time—Austria will lose.

IRENE

They will all lose, Dumptsy. (*The* CHERRYS *come in. She greets them pleasantly.*) Good evening.

CHERRY

Good evening, Madame.
(*The* CHERRYS *start to sit, across from* IRENE.)

IRENE

Bring some more vodka, Dumptsy. Perhaps Mr. and Mrs. Cherry will have some, too.

CHERRY

Why, thank you—we . . .

MRS. CHERRY

I'd love to. I've never tasted vodka.

IRENE

Ah—then it's high time. Bring in the bottle, Dumptsy.

DUMPTSY

Yes, Madame. (*He goes in to the bar.*)

IRENE

Come, sit down here. (*The* CHERRYS *sit by her.*) You will find vodka a perfect stimulant to the appetite. So much better than that hybrid atrocity, the American cocktail!

CHERRY

To tell you the truth, Madame—we've already dined.

IRENE

It is no matter. It is just as good as a liqueur.

MRS. CHERRY

We didn't really dine at all. We merely looked at the minestrone and the Parmesan cheese—and we felt too depressed to eat anything.

IRENE

It's the altitude. After the first exhilaration there comes a depressive reaction, especially for you, who are accustomed to the heavy, Pigwiggian atmosphere of England.

CHERRY

Pigwiggian?

IRENE

Yes, Pigwig—Oliver Twist—you know, your Dickens?

(DUMPTSY *enters from bar with a bottle of vodka and two more glasses, which he places on the table. He returns to the bar.*)

CHERRY

You know England, Madame?

IRENE (*fondly*)

Of course I know England! My governess was a sweet old ogre from your north country—and when I was a little girl I used to visit often at Sandringham.

CHERRY (*impressed*)

Sandringham?

MRS. CHERRY

The palace?

IRENE

Yes. That was before your time. It was in the reign of dear, gay King Edward, and the beautiful Alexandra. (*She sighs a little for those days.*) I used to have such fun playing with my cousin David. He used to try to teach me to play cricket, and when I couldn't swing the bat properly, he said, "Oh, you Russians will never be civilized!" (*Laughs.*) When I went home to Petersburg I told my uncle, the Tsar, what David had said, and he was so amused! But now—you must drink your vodka. (*They rise, and lift their glasses.*) A toast!

To his most gracious Majesty the King. (*They clink glasses.*) God bless him.

CHERRY

Thank you, Madame.

(*All three drink and* MRS. CHERRY *coughs violently.*)

IRENE (*to* MRS. CHERRY)

No—no! Drink it right down. Like this. (*She swallows it in a gulp.*) So! (*Refills the glasses from the bottle.*) The second glass will go more easily. (*They sit.*) I used to laugh so at your funny British Tommies in Archangel. They all hated vodka until one of them thought of mixing it with beer.

MRS. CHERRY

How loathsome!

IRENE

It was! But I shall be forever grateful to them—those Tommies. They saved my life when I escaped from the Soviets. For days and nights—I don't know how many —I was driving through the snow—snow —snow—snow—, in a little sleigh, with the body of my father beside me, and the wolves running along like an escort of dragoons. You know—you always think of wolves as howling constantly, don't you?

CHERRY

Why, yes—I suppose one does.

IRENE

Well, they don't. No, these wolves didn't howl! They were horribly, confidently silent. I think silence is much more terrifying, don't you?

CHERRY

You must have been dreadfully afraid.

IRENE

No, I was not afraid for myself. It was the thought of my father. . . .

MRS. CHERRY

Please! I know you don't want to talk about it any more.

IRENE

Oh, no—it is so far away now. But I shall never forget the moment when I came through the haze of delirium, and saw the faces of those Tommies. Those simple, friendly faces. And the snow—and the wolves—and the terrible cold—they were all gone—and I was looking at Kew Gardens on a Sunday afternoon, and the sea of golden daffodils—"fluttering and dancing in the breezes."

(WEBER *has come in with the daffodils.*)

WEBER

Shall we go in to dinner now, Irene?

IRENE

Yes, yes, Achille. In a minute. I am coming. (WEBER *goes.* IRENE *rises.*) Now—we must finish our vodka. (CHERRY *rises.*) And you must make another try to eat something.

CHERRY

Thank you so much, Madame. (*They drink.*)

IRENE

And later on, we must all be here for Mr. Van's entertainment—and we must all applaud vigorously.

MRS. CHERRY

We shall, Madame.

CHERRY

He's such a nice chap, isn't he?

IRENE (*going*)

Yes—and a real artist, too.

CHERRY

Oh—you've seen him?

IRENE

Why—yes—I've seen him, in some café chantant, somewhere. I forget just where it was. (*The three of them have gone out together. The light is dimmed to extinction. The curtain falls.*)

ACT TWO

SCENE II

About two hours later.
WEBER *is drinking brandy.* The CAPTAIN *is standing.*

CAPTAIN

I have been listening to the radio. Utter bedlam! Of course, every government has imposed the strictest censorship—but it is very frightening—like one of those films where ghostly hands suddenly reach in and switch off all the lights.

WEBER

Any suggestions of air raids?

CAPTAIN

None. But there is ominous quiet from Paris. Think of it—Paris—utterly silent! Only one station there is sending messages, and they are in code.

WEBER

Probably instructions to the frontier.

CAPTAIN

I heard a man in Prague saying something that sounded interesting, but him I could not understand. Then I turned to London, hopefully, and listened to a gentleman describing the disastrous effects of ivy upon that traditional institution, the oak.

WEBER

Well—we shall soon know. . . . There'll be no trouble about crossing the frontier tomorrow?

CAPTAIN

Oh, no. Except that—I am still a little worried about Madame's passport.

WEBER

We'll arrange about that. Have a cigar, Captain?

CAPTAIN

Thank you.
(IRENE *comes in as the* CAPTAIN *starts to light the cigar.*)

IRENE

Do you hear the sound of airplanes?
(*All stop to listen, intently. The sound becomes audible. The* CAPTAIN *shakes out the match, throws the unlit cigar on the table, and dashes to the window and looks upward.*)

CAPTAIN

It is our bombers. One—two—three. Seven of them. Seven out of eighteen. You will excuse me? (*He salutes and dashes out.*)

WEBER

Seven out of eighteen! Not bad, for Italians.
(IRENE *has gone to the window to look out.*)

IRENE

I'm so happy for you, Achille.

WEBER

What was that, my dear?

IRENE

I said—I'm so happy for you.

WEBER

But—just why am I an object of congratulation?

IRENE

All this great, wonderful death and destruction, everywhere. And you promoted it!

WEBER

Don't give me too much credit, Irene.

IRENE

But I *know* what you've done.

WEBER

Yes, my dear. You know a great deal. But don't forget to do honor to Him—up there—who put fear into man. I am but the humble instrument of His divine will.

IRENE (*looking upward, sympathetically*)

Yes—that's quite true. We don't do half enough justice to Him. Poor, lonely old soul. Sitting up in heaven, with nothing to do but play solitaire. Poor, dear God. Playing Idiot's Delight. The game that never means anything, and never ends.

WEBER

You have an engaging fancy, my dear.

IRENE

Yes.

WEBER

It's the quality in you that fascinates me most. Limitless imagination! It is what has made you such an admirable, brilliant liar. And so very helpful to me! Am I right?

IRENE

Of course you are right, Achille. Had I been bound by any stuffy respect for the truth, I should never have escaped from the Soviets.

WEBER

I'm sure of it.

IRENE

Did I ever tell you of my escape from the Soviets?

WEBER

You have told me about it at least eleven times. And each time it was different.

IRENE

Well, I made several escapes. I am always making escapes, Achille. When I am worrying about you, and your career. I have to run away from the terror of my own thoughts. So I amuse myself by studying the faces of the people I see. Just ordinary, casual, dull people. (*She is speaking in a tone that is sweetly sadistic.*) That young English couple, for instance. I was watching them during dinner, sitting there, close together, holding hands, and rubbing their knees together under the table. And I saw him in his nice, smart, British uniform, shooting a little pistol at a huge tank. And the tank rolls over him. And his fine strong body, that was so full of the capacity for ecstasy, is a mass of mashed flesh and bones—a smear of purple blood—like a stepped-on snail. But before the moment of death, he consoles himself by thinking, "Thank God *she* is safe! She is bearing the child I gave her, and he will live to see a better world." (*She walks behind* WEBER *and leans over his shoulder.*) But I know where she is. She is lying in a cellar that has been wrecked by an air raid, and her firm young breasts are all mixed up with the bowels of a dismembered policeman, and the embryo from her womb is splattered against the face of a dead bishop. That is the kind of thought with which I amuse myself, Achille. And it makes me so proud to think that I am so close to you—who make all this possible.

(WEBER *rises and walks about the room. At length he turns to her.*)

WEBER

Do you talk in this whimsical vein to many people?

IRENE

No. I betray my thoughts to no one but you. You know that I am shut off from the world. I am a contented prisoner in your ivory tower.

WEBER

I'm beginning to wonder about that.

IRENE

What? You think I could interest myself in some one else——?

WEBER

No—no, my dear. I am merely wondering whether the time has come for you to turn commonplace, like all the others?

IRENE

The others?

WEBER

All those who have shared my life. My former wife, for instance. She now boasts that she abandoned me because part of my income is derived from the sale of poison gas. Revolvers and rifles and bullets she didn't mind—because they are also used by sportsmen. Battleships too are permissible; they look so splendid in the news films. But she couldn't stomach poison gas. So now she is married to an anemic Duke, and the large fortune that she obtained from me enables the Duke to indulge his principal passion, which is the slaughtering of wild animals, like rabbits, and pigeons and rather small deer. My wife is presumably happy with him. I have always been glad you are not a fool as she was, Irene.

IRENE

No. I don't care even for battleships. And I shall not marry an anemic Duke.

WEBER

But—there was something unpleasantly reminiscent in that gaudy picture you painted. I gather that this silly young couple has touched a tender spot, eh?

IRENE

Perhaps, Achille. Perhaps I am softening.

WEBER

Then apply your intelligence, my dear. Ask yourself: why shouldn't they die? And who are the greater criminals—those who sell the instruments of death, or those who buy them, and use them? You know there is no logical reply to that. But all these little people—like your new friends —all of them consider me an arch-villain because I furnish them with what they want, which is the illusion of power. That is what they vote for in their frightened governments—what they cheer for on their national holidays—what they glorify in their anthems, and their monuments, and their waving flags! Yes—they shout bravely about something they call "national honor." And what does it amount to? Mistrust of the motives of every one else! Dog in the manger defense of what they've got, and greed for the other fellow's possessions! Honor among thieves! I assure you, Irene—for such little people the deadliest weapons are the most merciful.

(*The* CHERRYS *enter. He is whistling* "Minnie the Moocher.")

IRENE

Ah! Mr. and Mrs. Cherry!

CHERRY

Hello there. (*They come down.*)

IRENE

You have dined well!

MRS. CHERRY

Superbly!

CHERRY

We ate everything—up to and including the zabaglione.

IRENE

You can thank the vodka for that. Vodka never fails in an emergency.

CHERRY

And we can thank you, Madame, and do so.

IRENE

But—permit me to introduce Monsieur Weber. (WEBER *rises.*) Mrs. Cherry—Mr. Cherry.
(*They are exchanging greetings as* DON *comes in.*)

DON

We're going to have a little cabaret show for you now, Madame.

WEBER

I don't think I shall wait for it, my dear.

IRENE

But you must——

WEBER

I really should look over Lanza's estimates——

IRENE

Please, Achille—Mr. Van is an artist. You will be so amused.

WEBER (*resuming seat*)

Very well, Irene.

DON (*his tone blandly confidential*)

Between ourselves, I don't vouch for the quality of it. But it may be unintentionally amusing.

IRENE

I shall love it.

CHERRY

This is the most marvellous idea, Mr. Navadel.

DON

Oh, thank you. We try to contrive some novelty each evening. If you'll be good enough to sit here——
(DON *goes up to usher in the* ROSSIS *and direct them to their seats. The musicians come in and take their places. The* DOCTOR *comes in.* DUMPTSY *is busily moving chairs about, clearing a space for the act.* IRENE *and the* CHERRYS *chat pleasantly.* ANNA, *the maid, appears on the gallery above to watch the entertainment.*)
(HARRY *comes in. He is wearing a tight-fitting dinner jacket, and carries a cane and a straw hat.*)

HARRY

Áll set, Don?

DON

Quite ready, whenever you are.

HARRY

Okey-doke. Give us a fanfare, professor. (*He goes out. The band obliges with a fanfare.* HARRY *returns, all smiles.*) Before we start, folks, I just want to explain that we haven't had much chance to rehearse with my good friend, Signor Palota, and his talented little team here. (*He indicates the orchestra with a handsome gesture.*) So we must crave your indulgence and beg you to give us a break if the rhythm isn't all strictly kosher. (*He waits for his laugh.*) All we ask of you, kind friends, is "The Christian pearl of Charity," to quote our great American poet, John Greenleaf Whittier. We thank you. Take it away! (*He bows. All applaud. He then sings a song—The girls come on in costume and dance.*)
(*During the latter part of the act, the* CAPTAIN, *the* MAJOR, *and four flying corps* OFFICERS *come in. The latter are dirty and in a fever of heroically restrained excitement. They survey the scene with wonderment and then with delight, saying, in Italian, "What's all this?" and "What brought these blonde bambinos to Monte Gabriele?" etc.* HARRY *interrupts the act and orders the orchestra to play the Fascist*

anthem, "Giovinezza." *The officers acknowledge this graceful gesture with the
Fascist salute. The* GIRLS *wave back. The*
CAPTAIN *gets the* OFFICERS *seated and then
goes to order drinks.* HARRY *and the* GIRLS
resume.)

(*At the end of the act, all applaud and
the* OFFICERS *shout "Brava—Bravissima"
and stamp their feet with enthusiasm. The*
GIRLS *take several bows and go.* HARRY *returns for a solo bow, waving his straw hat.
One of the* OFFICERS *shouts, in Italian, "We
want the young ladies!"*)

CAPTAIN (*to* HARRY)

My friends wish to know respectfully if
the young ladies will care to join them in
a little drink?

HARRY

Certainly! Come back in, girls. Get over
there and join the army! (*The* GIRLS *do
so.*) Now, folks—with your kind permission—I shall give the girls an interlude of
rest and refreshment and treat you to a
little piano specialty of my own. Your
strict attention is not obligatory.

(*He starts his specialty, assisted by* SHIR-
LEY *and* EDNA. *The* OFFICERS *don't pay
much attention. Bottles of champagne are
brought for them and the* GIRLS.)

(WEBER *goes and speaks to the* CAPTAIN.
*He beckons him up to the landing of the
stairs where they converse in low tones, the*
CAPTAIN *telling him about the air-raid.*)

(HARRY'S *act is interrupted by the entrance of* QUILLERY.)

QUILLERY (*to* HARRY)

Do you know what has happened?

DON

I told you we didn't want you here.

PITTALUGA

We're having an entertainment here.

QUILLERY

Yes! An entertainment!

HARRY

If you'll just sit down, pal. . . . (*He
and the* GIRLS *continue with their singing.*)

QUILLERY

An entertainment—while Paris is in
ruins!

CHERRY (*rises*)

What?

DOCTOR

What are you saying?

QUILLERY

They have bombed Paris! The Fascisti
have bombed Paris!

DON

What? But it can't be possible——

HARRY

Go on, Shirley. Keep on singing.

QUILLERY

I tell you—tonight their planes flew
over and——

CHERRY

But how do you know this?

QUILLERY

It is on the wireless—everywhere. And I
have just talked to one of their mechanics,
who was on the flight, and saw, with his
own eyes——

HARRY

Won't you please sit down, pal? We're
trying to give you a little entertainment—
(*Stops playing.*)

QUILLERY

For the love of God—listen to me!
While you sit here eating and drinking, tonight, Italian planes dropped twenty thousand kilos of bombs on Paris. God knows
how many they killed. God knows how
much of life and beauty is forever destroyed! And you sit here, drinking, laughing, with *them*—the murderers. (*Points to
the flyers, who ask each other, in Italian,
what the hell is he talking about.*) They
did it! It was their planes, from that field
down there. Assassins!

(*The* OFFICERS *make a move toward*
QUILLERY—*one of them arming himself
with a champagne bottle.*)

HARRY (*comes down from the piano*)

We can't have any skull-cracking in this
club. Hey, Captain, speak to your men before anything starts.

(*The* CAPTAIN *comes down to the* OF-

FICERS *and pacifies them.* CHERRY *comes down to stand by* QUILLERY.)

MRS. CHERRY

Jimmy! . . . You keep out of this!

QUILLERY

I say, God damn you! Assassins!

MAJOR AND FIRST AND THIRD OFFICERS
(*jump up*)

Assassini!

HARRY

Now listen, pal. . . .

SHIRLEY

Harry! Don't get yourself mixed up in this mess!

QUILLERY

You see, we stand together! France— England—America! Allies!

HARRY

Shut up, France! It's O. K., Captain. We can handle this——

QUILLERY

They don't dare fight against the power of England and France! The free democracies against the Fascist tyranny!

HARRY

Now, for God's sake stop fluctuating!

QUILLERY

England and France are fighting for the hopes of mankind!

HARRY

A minute ago, England was a butcher in a dress suit. Now we're Allies!

QUILLERY

We stand together. We stand together forever. (*Turns to* OFFICERS.) I say God damn you. God damn the villains that sent you on this errand of death.

CAPTAIN (*takes a few steps toward* QUILLERY)

If you don't close your mouth, Frenchman, we shall be forced to arrest you.

QUILLERY

Go on, Fascisti! Commit national sui-

cide. That's the last gesture left to you toy soldiers.

HARRY

It's all right, Captain. Mr. Quillery is for peace. He's going back to France to stop the war.

QUILLERY (*turns on* HARRY)

You're not authorized to speak for me. I am competent to say what I feel. And what I say is "Down with Fascism! Abbasso Fascismo!"
(*There is an uproar from the* OFFICERS.)

CAPTAIN (*ordinarily gentle, is now white hot with rage*)

Attenzione!

QUILLERY

Vive la France! Viv——

CAPTAIN

E agli arresti.

QUILLERY

Call out the firing squad! Shoot me dead! But do not think you can silence the truth that's in me.

CAPTAIN (*grabs* QUILLERY *from the left and calls the* FIRST OFFICER)

Molinari!
(FIRST OFFICER *grabs* QUILLERY *from the right. They start to take him out.*)

QUILLERY (*as he is being led out*)

The Empire of the Fascisti will join the Empire of the Cæsars in smoking ruins. Vive la France! Vive la France!
(WEBER *goes upstairs and exits. They have gone.*)

CHERRY (*to* HARRY)

You'd better carry on with your turn, old boy.

HARRY

No, pal. The act is cold. (*To the orchestra leader.*) Give us some music, Signor. (*The orchestra starts playing.*) Let dancing become general.

CHERRY

Let's dance, my sweet.

MRS. CHERRY

I can't bear to, Jimmy.

CHERRY

I think we should.

MRS. CHERRY

Very well, darling. (*They dance. The* OFFICERS *dance with the* GIRLS.)

HARRY (*goes over to* IRENE)

Would you care to dance?

IRENE

Why—why, thank you. (*She stands up, and they join the slowly moving mob.* SHIRLEY *is singing as loud as she can. The color wheel turns so that the dancers are bathed in blue, then amber, then red.*)

CURTAIN.

ACT TWO

SCENE III

Later that night.
IRENE *and* HARRY *are alone. She is sitting, telling the story of her life. He is listening with fascination and doubt.*

IRENE

My father was old. The hardships of that terrible journey had broken his body. But his spirit was wrong—the spirit that is Russia. He lay there, in that little boat, and he looked up at me. Never can I forget his face, so thin, so white, so beautiful, in the starlight. And he said to me, "Irene—little daughter," and then—he died. For four days I was alone, with his body, sailing through the storms of the Black Sea. I had no food—no water—I was in agony from the bayonet wounds of the Bolsheviki. I knew I must die. But then—an American cruiser rescued me. May God bless those good men! (*She sighs.*) I've talked too much about myself. What about you, my friend?

HARRY

Oh—I'm not very interesting. I'm just what I seem to be.

IRENE

C'est impossible!

HARRY

C'est possible! The facts of my case are eloquent. I'm a potential genius—reduced to piloting six blondes through the Balkans.

IRENE

But there is something that you hide from the world—even, I suspect, from yourself. Where did you acquire your superior education?

HARRY

I worked my way through college selling encyclopædias.

IRENE

I knew you had culture! What college was it?

HARRY

Oh—just any college. But my sales talk was so good that I fell for it myself. I bought the God-damned encyclopædia. And I read it all, travelling around, in day coaches, and depot hotels, and Fox-time dressing rooms. It was worth the money.

IRENE

And how much of all this have you retained?

HARRY (*significantly*)

I? I—never forget anything.

IRENE

How unfortunate for you! Does your encyclopædia help you in your dealings with the girls?

HARRY

Yes, Mrs. Weber. . . . I got considerable benefit from studying the lives of the great courtesans, and getting to understand their technique. . . .

IRENE

Forgive me for interrupting you—but that is not my name.

HARRY

Oh—pardon me, I thought . . .

IRENE

I know what you thought. Monsieur Weber and I are associated in a sort of business way.

HARRY

I see.

IRENE

He does me the honor to consult me in matters of policy.

HARRY

That's quite an honor! Business is pretty good, isn't it!

IRENE

I gather that you are one of those noble souls who does not entirely approve of the munitions industry?

HARRY

Oh, no—I'm not noble. Your friend is just another salesman. And I make it a point never to criticize anybody else's racket.

IRENE

Monsieur Weber is a very distinguished man. He has rendered very distinguished services to all the governments of the world. He is decorated with the Legion of Honor, the Order of the White Eagle, the Order of St. James of the Sword, and the Military Order of Christ!

HARRY

The Military Order of Christ. I never heard of that one.

IRENE

It is from Portugal. He has many orders.

HARRY

Have you ever been in America?

IRENE

Oh, yes—I've seen it all—New York, Washington, Palm Beach . . .

HARRY

I said America. Have you ever been in the West?

IRENE

Certainly I have. I flew across your continent. There are many White Russians in California.

HARRY

Did you ever happen to make any parachute landings in any places like Kansas, or Iowa, or Nebraska?

IRENE (laughing)

I have seen enough of your countrymen to know that you are typical.

HARRY

Me? I'm not typical of anything.

IRENE

Oh, yes, you are. You are just like all of them—an ingenuous, sentimental idealist. You believe in the goodness of human nature, don't you?

HARRY

And what if I do? I've known millions of people, intimately—and I never found more than one out of a hundred that I didn't like, once you got to know them.

IRENE

That is very charming—but it is naïve.

HARRY

Maybe so. But experience prevents me from working up much enthusiasm over any one who considers the human race as just so many clay pigeons, even if he does belong to the Military Order of Christ.

IRENE

If you came from an older culture, you would realize that men like Monsieur Weber are necessary to civilization.

HARRY

You don't say.

IRENE

I mean, of course, the sort of civilization

that we have got. (*She smiles upon him benevolently. It is as though she were explaining patiently but with secret enjoyment the facts of life to a backward nephew.*) Stupid people consider him an archvillain because it is his duty to stir up a little trouble here and there to stimulate the sale of his products. Do you understand me, my friend?

HARRY

I shouldn't wonder.

IRENE

Monsieur Weber is a true man of the world. He is above petty nationalism; he can be a Frenchman in France—a German in Germany—a Greek—a Turk—whatever the occasion demands.

HARRY

Yes—that little Quillery was an Internationalist, too. He believed in brotherhood, but the moment he got a whiff of gunpowder he began to spout hate and revenge. And now those nice, polite Wops will probably have to shut him up with a firing squad.

IRENE (*takes out a cigarette from her case*)

It is a painful necessity.

HARRY

And it demonstrates the sort of little trouble that your friend stirs up. (*He takes out his lighter and lights her cigarette.*)

IRENE

Do you know that you can be extremely rude?

HARRY

I'm sorry if I've hurt your feelings about Mr. Weber, but he just happens to be a specimen of the one per cent that I *don't* like.

IRENE

I was not referring to that. Why do you stare at me so?

HARRY

Have I been staring?

IRENE

Steadily. Ever since we arrived here this afternoon. Why do you do it?

HARRY

I've been thinking I could notice a funny resemblance to some one I used to know.

IRENE

You should know better than to tell any woman that she resembles somebody else. We none of us like to think that our appearance is commonplace.

HARRY

The one you look like wasn't commonplace.

IRENE

Oh! She was some one near and dear to you?

HARRY

It was somebody that occupies a unique shrine in the temple of my memory.

IRENE

That *is* a glowing tribute. The temple of your memory must be so crowded! But I am keeping you from your duties.

HARRY

What duties?

IRENE

Shouldn't you be worrying about your young ladies?

HARRY

They're all right; they've gone to bed.

IRENE

Yes—but there are several Italian officers about. Aren't you supposed to be the chaperone?

HARRY

I leave the girls to their own resources, of which they have plenty. (*He stares hard at her.*) Have you always been a blonde?

IRENE

Yes—as far as I can remember.

HARRY

You don't mind my asking?

IRENE

Not at all. And now, may I ask you something?

HARRY

Please do so.

IRENE

Why do you waste yourself in this de-graded work? Touring about with those obvious little harlots?

HARRY

You mean you think I'm fitted for some-thing that requires a little more mentality?

IRENE

Yes.

HARRY

How do you know so much about me? (*It should be remembered that all through this scene* HARRY *is studying her, trying to fit together the pieces of the jig-saw puzzle of his memory.*)

IRENE

For one thing, I saw your performance tonight.

HARRY

You thought it was punk?

IRENE

I thought it was unworthy.

HARRY

It was unfortunately interrupted. You should have seen . . .

IRENE

I saw enough. You are a very bad dancer.

HARRY

The King of Rumania thought I was pretty good.

IRENE

He is entitled to his opinion—and I to mine.

HARRY

I'll admit that I've done better things in my time. Would it surprise you to know that I was once with a mind-reading act?

IRENE

Really?

HARRY

Yeah.

IRENE

Now you're staring at me again.

HARRY

Have you ever been in Omaha?

IRENE

Omaha? Where is that? Persia?

HARRY

No. Nebraska. That's one of our states. I played there once with the greatest act of my career. I was a stooge for Zuleika, the Mind Reader. At least she called me her stooge. But I was the one who had to do all the brain work.

IRENE

And she read people's minds?

HARRY

I did it for her. I passed through the audience and fed her the cues. We were sensational, playing the finest picture houses in all the key cities. Zuleika sat up on the stage, blindfolded—and usually blind drunk.

IRENE

Oh, dear. And was *she* the one that I re-semble?

HARRY

No! There was another act on the same bill. A troupe of Russians . . .

IRENE

Russians?

HARRY

Singers, mandolin players, and squat dancers. One of them was a red-headed girl. She was fascinated by our act, and she kept pestering me to teach her the code. She said she could do it better than Zuleika.

IRENE

Those poor Russians. There are so many of them all over the world. And so many of them completely counterfeit!

HARRY

This dame was counterfeit all right. In fact, she was the God-damnedest liar I ever saw. She lied just for the sheer artistry of it. She kept after me so much that I told her finally to come up to my hotel room one night, and we'd talk it over.

IRENE

I hope you didn't tell her the code.

HARRY

No. After the week in Omaha the bill split. The Russians went to Sioux Falls and we went on the Interstate Time. I played with Zuleika for another year and then the drink got her and she couldn't retain. So the act busted up. I've always hoped I'd catch up with that red-headed Russian again sometimes. She might have been good. She had the voice for it, and a kind of overtone of mystery.

IRENE

It's a characteristic gypsy quality. And you never saw her again?

HARRY

No.

IRENE

Perhaps it is just as well. She couldn't have been so clever—being duped so easily into going to your room.

HARRY

She wasn't being duped! She knew what she was doing. If there was any duping going on, she was the one that did it.

IRENE

She *did* make an impression!

HARRY (*looking straight at her*)

I was crazy about her. She was womanhood at its most desirable—and most unreliable.

IRENE

And you such a connoisseur. But—it's getting late.

HARRY (*rises*)

Do you know any Russian music? (*He crosses to the piano.*)

IRENE (*rises*)

Oh, yes. When I was a little girl my father used to engage Chaliapin to come often to our house. He taught me many songs.

HARRY

Chaliapin, eh? Your father spared no expense. (*He sits at the piano.*)

IRENE

That was in *old* Russia. (*He plays a few bars of "Kak Stranna."*) Kak Stranna!

HARRY

Yeah! How strange! (*He starts to play "Prostchai."*) Do you know this one? (IRENE *sings some of it in Russian.*) How do you spell that name—Irene?

IRENE

I-R-E-N-E. (HARRY *pounds the piano and jumps up.*) What's the matter?

HARRY

That's it! Irene! (*He pronounces it* I-REEN.)

IRENE

But what——?

HARRY

I knew it! You're the one!

IRENE

What one?

HARRY

That red-headed liar! Irene! I knew I could never be mistaken. . . .

IRENE

Irene is a very usual name in Russia. (*She laughs heartily.*)

HARRY

I don't care how usual it is. Everything fits together perfectly now. The name—the face—the voice—Chaliapin for a teacher! Certainly it's you! And it's no good shaking your head and looking amazed! No matter how much you may lie, you can't deny the fact that you slept with me in the Governor Bryan Hotel in Omaha in the fall of 1925. (IRENE *laughs heartily again.*) All right—go ahead and laugh. That blonde hair had me fooled for a while— but now I know it's just as phony as the bayonet wounds, and the parachute jumps into the jungle. . . .

IRENE (*still laughing*)

Oh—you amuse me.

HARRY

It's a pleasure to be entertaining. But you can't get away with it.

IRENE

You amuse me very much indeed. Here we are—on a mountain peak in Bedlam. Tonight, the Italians are bombing Paris. At this moment, the French may be bombing Rome, and the English bombing Germany—and the Soviets bombing Tokyo, and all you worry about is whether I am a girl you once met casually in Omaha.

HARRY

Did I say it was casual?

IRENE (*laughing*)

Oh—it *is* amusing!

HARRY (*angrily*)

I know you're amused. I admit it's all very funny. I've admitted everything. I told you I was crazy about you. Now when are you going to give me a break and tell me——

IRENE

You! You are so troubled—so—so uncertain about everything.

HARRY

I'm not uncertain about it any more, Babe. I had you tagged from the start. There was something about you that was indelible . . . something I couldn't forget all these years.
(WEBER *appears on the gallery, wearing his Sulka dressing gown.*)

WEBER

Forgive me for intruding, my dear. But I suggest that it's time for you to go to bed.

IRENE

Yes, Achille. At once. (WEBER *treats* HARRY *to a rather disparaging glance and exits.* IRENE *starts upstairs.*) Poor Achille! He suffers with the most dreadful insomnia—it is something on his mind. (*She*

goes up a few more steps.) He is like Macbeth. Good night, my friend—my funny friend.

HARRY

Good night.

IRENE

And thank you for making me laugh so much—tonight.

HARRY

I could still teach you that code.

IRENE

Perhaps—we shall meet again in—what was the name of the hotel?

HARRY

It was the Governor Bryan.

IRENE

Oh, yes! The Governor Bryan! (*Laughing heartily, she exits.* HARRY *goes to the piano, sits down and starts to play "Kak Stranna."* DUMPTSY *enters from the bar.*)

DUMPTSY

That was wonderful—that singing and dancing.

HARRY (*still playing*)

Thanks, pal. Glad you enjoyed it.

DUMPTSY

Oh, yes, Mr. Van—that was good.

HARRY (*bangs a chord*)

Chaliapin—for God's *sake!*

DUMPTSY

I beg your pardon, sir?

HARRY (*rises*)

It's nothing. Good night, Dumptsy. (*He goes out into the lobby.*)

DUMPTSY

Good night, sir. (*He starts for the bar.*)

CURTAIN.

ACT THREE

The following afternoon.
HARRY *is at the piano, idly playing the* "Caprice Viennoise," *or something similar. His thoughts are elsewhere.*
SHIRLEY *is darning some stockings and humming the tune.* BEBE *is plucking her eyebrows.*
BEULAH, ELAINE, FRANCINE *and* EDNA *are seated at a table.* BEULAH *is telling* ELAINE'S *fortune with cards. The others are watching. All are intensely serious, and all chewing gum.*

SHIRLEY
What's that number, Harry?

HARRY
The "Caprice Viennoise"—Kreisler.

SHIRLEY
It's pretty.

HARRY
You think so? (*He shifts to something jazzier.*)

BEULAH
You are going to marry.

ELAINE
Again?

BEULAH
The cards indicate dis*tinctly* two marriages, and maybe a third.

ELAINE (*chewing furiously*)
For *God's* sake!

SHIRLEY (*to* HARRY)
We certainly need some new stockings.

HARRY
We'll renovate the wardrobe in Geneva.

BEULAH
Now—let's see what the fates tell us next.

BEBE
Say, Harry—when do we lam it out of here?

HARRY
Ask Beulah. Maybe she can get it out of the cards.

BEBE
I hate this place. It's spooky.

BEULAH (*to* HARRY)
What'd you say, honey?

ELAINE
Ah—don't pay any attention to him. What else do they say about me?

BEULAH
Well . . . you'll enter upon a period of very poor health.

ELAINE
When?

BEULAH
Along about your thirty-seventh year.

SHIRLEY
That means any day now. (*She winks broadly at* BEBE, *who laughs.*)

HARRY (*vehemently*)
Listen to me, you nymphs! We can't be wasting our time with card tricks. We've got to do a little rehearsing.

SHIRLEY
Why, Harry—what are you mad about now?

HARRY
Who said I was mad about anything?

SHIRLEY
Well—every time you get yourself into a peeve, you take it out on us. You start in hollering, "Listen, girls—we got to rehearse."

HARRY

I am not peeved. Merely a little disgusted. The act needs brushing up.

BEBE

Honestly, Harry—don't you think we know the routine by now?

HARRY

I'm not saying you don't know it. I'm just saying that your performance last night grieved me and shocked me. You had your eyes on those officers and not on your work. That kind of attitude went big in Rumania, but now we're going to a town where artistry counts. Some day, I'll take the whole bunch of you to watch the Russian ballet, just to give you an idea of what dancing is.

(CAPTAIN LOCICERO comes in.)

CAPTAIN

Your pardon, Mr. Van.

HARRY

Ah, Captain. Good afternoon. . . . Rest, girls.

CAPTAIN (to the GIRLS)

Good afternoon.

GIRLS

Good afternoon, Captain.

HARRY

You bring us news?

CAPTAIN

Good news, I hope. May I have your passports?

HARRY

Certainly. (He gets them out of his coat and hands them to the CAPTAIN.)

CAPTAIN

Thank you. I hope to have definite word for you very shortly. (He salutes and starts to go.)

HARRY

What about Mr. Quillery, Captain? What's happened to him?

CAPTAIN

Mr. Quillery was very injudicious. Very injudicious. I am glad that you are so much more intelligent. (He goes out.)

SHIRLEY

I don't think they could have done anything cruel to him. They're awfully sweet boys, those Wops.

HARRY

So I observed. . . . Now listen to me, girls. Geneva's a key spot, and we've got to be good. Your audiences there won't be a lot of hunkies, who don't care what you do as long as you don't wear practically any pants. These people are accustomed to the best. They're mains—big people, like prime ministers, and maharajahs and archbishops. If we click with them, we'll be set for London and Paris. We may even make enough money to get us home.

BEBE

Oh—don't speak of such a thing! Home!

EDNA

To get a real decent henna wash again!

HARRY

The trouble with all of you is, you're thinking too much about your own specialties. You're trying to steal the act, and wreck it. Remember what the late Knute Rockne said: "Somebody else can have the all-star, all-American aggregations. All I want is a team!" Now, you—Beulah. You've got plenty of chance to score individually in the bubble number. But when we're doing the chorus routine, you've got to submerge your genius in the mass.

BEULAH

What do I do wrong, honey?

HARRY

Your Maxie Ford is lacklustre. Here— I'll show you. . . . (HARRY gets up to demonstrate the Maxie Ford.)

SHIRLEY (laughs)

If you do it that way, Beulah, you'll go flat on your face. Here—I'll show you.

HARRY

Just a minute, Miss Laughlin. Who's the director of this act, you or me?

SHIRLEY (*amiably*)

You are, you old poop. But you just don't know the steps.

ELAINE

Don't let her get fresh, Harry.

BEBE

Slap her down!

SHIRLEY

Give us the music, Harry.

BEULAH

Please, Harry. Shirley just wants to be helpful.

HARRY

I feel I should resent this—but— (*He returns to the piano.*) Go ahead, Miss Laughlin. Carry on. (*He plays.* SHIRLEY *demonstrates.* BEULAH *tries it.*)

BEULAH

Have I got it right?

SHIRLEY

Sure! He's just shooting his face off! (*During this, the following conversation goes on:*)

ELAINE

You know that Wop that was giving me a play last night?

FRANCINE

You mean the one with the bent nose?

BEBE

I thought he was terrible. But that boy I had is a Count.

ELAINE

Well, look what he gave me.

EDNA

What is it?

BEBE

Let me see it.

ELAINE

I don't know what it is.

BEBE

Looks like money. What kind of money is that, Harry?

HARRY

It's an old Roman coin.

SHIRLEY

How much is it worth?

HARRY

I haven't looked up the latest rate of exchange on dinars. But I think, dear, you've been betrayed. Now, pay attention, girls. . . . As I said, we've got to improve the act, and with that in view, I'm going to retire from all the dance routine.

BEBE

What?

BEULAH

Why, *Harry*—we couldn't. . . .

SHIRLEY

Oh! I hurt you, didn't I! (*She rushes to him, coos over him.*) Yes, I did, you poor baby. I hurt his feelings—and I'm sorry— I'm very, very sorry.

HARRY

All right, Shirley. We can dispense with the regrets. Save your lipstick. (*He thrusts her away.*)

SHIRLEY

But why . . .?

HARRY

I've decided that I'm a thinker, rather than a performer. From now on, I shall devote myself to the purely creative end of the act, and, of course, the negotiation of contracts.

BEULAH

But when did you make up your mind to this, honey?

HARRY

I've been considering it for a long time.

SHIRLEY

Say! What were you talking about to that Russian dame?

HARRY

We discussed world politics.

FRANCINE

Oh!

SHIRLEY

And how are politics these days?

BEBE

Did you get anywheres near to first base, Harry?

HARRY

I find it impossible to explain certain things to you girls. You're children of nature.

SHIRLEY

We're *what*?

BEULAH

He means we're natural.

HARRY

Never mind, sweetheart. You'll sing the number, Shirley.

SHIRLEY

Me?

BEBE

With that terrible voice?

HARRY

She handled it fine that time I had bronchitis in Belgrade. And with a little rehearsal, you'll have the whole League of Nations rooting for you. Now—let's have it. (*He plays,* SHIRLEY *sings,* BEBE *disapproves.*)

(DON *comes in, dressed for travelling.*)

DON

Captain Locicero has got the orders to let us through and the train is due to leave about four o'clock. What a relief to be out of this foul place!

HARRY

You going too, Don?

DON

Yes. There's nothing for me here. In fact, I'm sick and tired of Europe as a whole. I was in town this morning when they shot Quillery.

BEBE

Who?

SHIRLEY

It was that little guy that bawled out the Wops.

BEULAH

They *shot* him? Why did they have to do that?

DON

Of course, he asked for it. But even so, it's pretty sickening to see one of your fellow human beings crumpled up in horrible, violent death. Well—there'll be plenty more like him, and right here, too. The French know all about this air base, and they'll be over any minute with their bombs. So—it's California here I come!

HARRY

And run right into the Japs? Better stop off at Wichita.

DON

I'll see you all on the train. (*He goes up the stairs.*)

HARRY

You girls go get yourselves ready.
(*The* CHERRYS *appear on the gallery.* DON *speaks to them, then goes out. The* CHERRYS *come down.*)

ELAINE

O.K., Harry.

EDNA (*going*)

I'm surprised at those Wops. They seemed like such sweet boys.

BEBE

Sure—when they talk they sound like opera. But they're awful excitable. (BEBE, ELAINE, EDNA *and* FRANCINE *have gone out.*)

BEULAH

But I can't understand—why did they have to shoot that poor boy?

HARRY

It's hard to explain, Beulah. But it seems there's some kind of argument going on over here, and the only way they can settle it is by murdering a lot of people.

BEBE

You don't need to tell *me* what it's like. I was in the Club Grotto the night the Purple Gang shot it out with the G's. And was that terrible! Blood all over everything! (*She and* SHIRLEY *and* BEULAH *have gone out.*)

HARRY

You heard what they did to Quillery?

CHERRY

Yes. It seems that he died like a true patriot, shouting "Vive La France."

HARRY

Better if he died like a man—sticking to what he knew was right.

CHERRY

He was a nice little chap.

MRS. CHERRY

The Italians are swine!
(DON *reappears on the balcony and comes down.*)

CHERRY

Oh, they had a perfect right to do it.

MRS. CHERRY

But to kill a man for saying what he thinks!

CHERRY

Many people will be killed for less than that.

HARRY

I'll have to be saying good-bye pretty soon. Did you say the train goes at four, Don?

DON

Four o'clock. Correct! (*He goes.*)

HARRY

I hope all this unpleasantness won't spoil your winter sports.

CHERRY

Oh, that's all washed up. We're going, too—if they'll let us cross the border.

HARRY

So the honeymoon has ended already?

MRS. CHERRY

Yes—I suppose so.

CHERRY

England is coming into this business. We have to stand by France, of course And so there's nothing for it but . . .

MRS. CHERRY

And so Jimmy will have to do his bit, manning the guns, for civilization. Perhaps he'll join in the bombardment of Florence, where we were married.

CHERRY

You know—after the ceremony we went into the Baptistery and prayed to the soul of Leonardo da Vinci that we might never fail in our devotion to that which is beautiful and true. I told you we were a bit on the romantic side. We forgot what Leonardo said about war. Bestial frenzy, he called it. And bestial frenzy it is.

MRS. CHERRY

But we mustn't think about that now. We have to stand by France. We have to make the world a decent place for heroes to live in. Oh, Christ! (*She starts to sob.* CHERRY *rushes to her.*)

CHERRY

Now, now, darling. We've got to make a pretense of being sporting about it. Please, darling. Don't cry.

HARRY

Let her cry, the poor kid. Let her sob her heart out—for all the God-damned good it will do her. You know what I often think? (*He is trying to be tactful.*) I often think we ought to get together and elect somebody else God. Me, for instance. I'll bet I'd do a much better job.

MRS. CHERRY

You'd be fine, Mr. Van.

HARRY

I believe I would. There'd be a lot of people who would object to my methods. That Mr. Weber, for instance. I'd certainly begin my administration by beating the can off him.

CHERRY

Let's start the campaign now! Vote for good old Harry Van, and his Six Angels!
(*The* CAPTAIN *comes in with a brief-case full of papers and passports. He takes these out and puts them on a table.*)

CAPTAIN

Good afternoon, Mrs. Cherry. Gentlemen.

HARRY

Do we get across?

CAPTAIN

Here is your passport, Mr. Van—and the young ladies, with my compliments. They have been duly stamped. (*He hands them over.*)

HARRY

Thanks, Captain. And how about Mr Weber and his—friend? Are they going, too?

CAPTAIN

I have their passports here. I advise you to make ready, Mr. Van. The train will leave in about forty-five minutes.

HARRY

O.K., Captain. See you later, Mr. and Mrs. Cherry. (*He goes.*)

CHERRY

O.K., Harry.

MRS. CHERRY

And what about us, Captain?

CAPTAIN

Due to a slight technicality, you will be permitted to cross the frontier. Here are your passports.

CHERRY

I can't tell you how grateful we are. (WEBER *appears on the gallery.*)

CAPTAIN

You needn't be grateful to me, Mr. Cherry. The fact that you are allowed to pass is due to the superb centralization of authority in my country. The telegram authorizing your release was filed at 11:43 today, just seventeen minutes before a state of war was declared between Great Britain and Italy. I must obey the order of Rome, even though I know it's out of date. Is your luggage ready?

CHERRY

It's all out here in the hall. We're off now, Captain. Well, good-bye and good luck!

CAPTAIN

And good luck to you—both of you.

CHERRY

I need hardly say that I'm sorry about all this. It's really a damned rotten shame.

CAPTAIN

It is. All of that. Good-bye, my friend. (*He extends his hand and* CHERRY *shakes it.*) Madame. . . . (*He extends his hand to* MRS. CHERRY.)

MRS. CHERRY

Don't call *me* your friend, because I say what Quillery said—damn you—damn your whole country of mad dogs for having started this horror.

CAPTAIN (*bows*)

It is not my fault, Mrs. Cherry.

CHERRY

It's utterly unfair to talk that way, darling. The Captain is doing his miserable duty as decently as he possibly can.

CAPTAIN (*tactfully*)

In this unhappy situation, we are all in danger of losing our heads.

MRS. CHERRY

I know . I know. Forgive me for the outburst. (*She extends her hand to the* CAPTAIN *and they shake.*) I should have remembered that it's everybody's fault.

CHERRY

That's right, my sweet. Come along. (*They go out.*)

CAPTAIN (*to* WEBER)

Frankly; my heart bleeds for them.

WEBER

They're young. They'll live through it, and be happy.

CAPTAIN

Will they? I was their age, and in their situation, twenty years ago, when I was sent to the Isonzo front. And people said just that to me: "Never mind, you are young—and youth will survive and come to triumph." And I believed it. That is why I couldn't say such deceiving words to them now.

WEBER

The cultivation of hope never does any immediate harm. Is everything in order?

CAPTAIN (*rises*)

Quite, Monsieur Weber. Here it is. (*He hands over* WEBER'S *passport.*)

WEBER

And Madame's?

(*The* CAPTAIN *picks up a document on foolscap.*)

CAPTAIN

This is an unusual kind of passport. It has given us some worry.

WEBER

The League of Nations issues documents like that to those whose nationality is uncertain.

CAPTAIN

I understand—but the attitude of Italy toward the League of Nations is not at the moment cordial.

WEBER

Then you refuse to honor Madame's passport?

CAPTAIN

My instructions are to accord you every consideration, Monsieur Weber. In view of the fact that Madame is travelling with you, I shall be glad to approve her visa.

WEBER

Madame is not travelling with me. She has her own passport.

CAPTAIN

But it is understood that you vouch for her, and that is enough to satisfy the authorities.

WEBER (*with cold authority*)

Vouch for her? It is not necessary for anyone to vouch for Madame! She is entirely capable of taking care of herself. If her passport is not entirely in order, it is no affair of mine.

CAPTAIN (*genuinely distressed*)

But—I must tell you, Monsieur Weber —this is something I do not like. This places me in a most embarrassing position. I shall be forced to detain her.

WEBER

You are a soldier, my dear Captain, and you should be used to embarrassing positions. Undoubtedly you were embarrassed this morning, when you had to shoot that confused pacifist, Quillery. But this is war, and unpleasant responsibilities descend upon you and on me as well. However . . . (*He sees* HARRY, *who is coming in.*) I shall attend to my luggage. Thank you, Captain. (*He goes out.*)

CAPTAIN

Don't mention it. (*to* HARRY.) The young ladies are ready?

HARRY

Yes—they're ready. And some of your aviators are out there trying to talk them into staying here permanently.

CAPTAIN (*smiling*)

And I add my entreaties to theirs.

HARRY

We won't have any more trouble, will we?

(*The* DOCTOR *appears on the gallery with coat, hat, books done in a bundle, and umbrella. He comes downstairs.*)

CAPTAIN

Oh, no, Mr. Van. Geneva is a lovely spot. All of Switzerland is beautiful, these days. I envy you going there, in such charming company.

HARRY

Hi, Doctor. Have you got the rats all packed?

DOCTOR

Good afternoon. I am privileged to go now? (*He puts down all of his belongings and crosses.*)

CAPTAIN

Yes, Dr. Waldersee. Here is your passport.

DOCTOR

Thank you. (*He examines the passport carefully.*)

HARRY

I can tell you, Doctor—I'm going to be proud to have known you. When I read in the papers that you've wiped out cancer and won the Nobel prize, and you're the greatest hero on earth, I'll be able to say, "He's a personal friend of mine. He once admired my music."

DOCTOR (*solemnly*)

Thank you very much. (*To the* CAP- TAIN.) This visa is good for crossing the Austrian border?

CAPTAIN

Certainly. But you are going to Zurich?

DOCTOR (*rises*)

I have changed my plans. I am going back into Germany. Germany is at war. Perhaps I am needed. (*He crosses to pick up his coat.*)

HARRY

Needed for what?

DOCTOR

I shall offer my services for what they are worth.

(HARRY *goes to help him on with his coat.*)

HARRY

But what about the rats?

DOCTOR (*fiercely*)

Why should I save people who don't want to be saved—so that they can go out and exterminate each other? Obscene maniacs! (*Starts to put on his gloves.*) Then I'll be a maniac, too. Only I'll be more dangerous than most of them. For I know all the tricks of death! And—as for my rats, maybe they'll be useful. Britain will put down the blockade again, and we shall be starving—and maybe I'll cut my rats into filets and eat them. (*He laughs, not pleasantly, and picks up his umbrella and books.*)

HARRY

Wait a minute, Doctor. You're doing this without thinking. . . .

DOCTOR

I'm thinking probably that remedy you sold is better than mine. Hasten to apply it. We are all diseased. . . .

HARRY

But you can't change around like this! Have you forgotten all the things you told me? All that about backsliding?

DOCTOR

No, I have not forgotten the degradation of mankind—that is painful and offensive to conceive. (*He is going out.*) I am sorry to disappoint you about the Nobel prize. (*He has gone.*)

HARRY

Good-bye, Doctor. (*He sits down, wearily.*) Why in the name of God can't somebody answer the question that every- body asks? Why? Why? Oh—I know the obvious answers, but they aren't good enough. Weber—and a million like him— they can't take the credit for *all* of this! Who is it that did this dirty trick on a lot of decent people? And why do you let them get away with it? That's the thing that I'd like to know!

CAPTAIN

We have avalanches up here, my friend. They are disastrous. They start with a little crack in the ice, so tiny that one cannot see it, until, suddenly, it bursts wide open. And then it is too late.

HARRY

That's very effective, Captain. But it don't satisfy me, because this avalanche isn't made out of ice. It's made out of flesh and blood—and—and *brains*. . . . It's God-damned bad management—that's what it is! (*This last is half to himself.*)

(IRENE *has appeared on the gallery and started to come down.*)

IRENE

Still upset about the situation, Mr. Van? Ah—good afternoon, my dear Captain Locicero.

CAPTAIN

Good afternoon, Madame.

IRENE

I have had the most superb rest here. The atmosphere is so calm, and imper- sonal, and soothing. I can't bear to think that we're going to Biarritz, with the dull, dismal old sea pounding in my ears.

(WEBER *comes in.*)

IRENE

We are leaving now, Achille?

WEBER

I believe that some difficulties have arisen. (*He looks toward the* CAPTAIN.)

IRENE

Difficulties?

CAPTAIN

I regret, Madame, that there must be some further delay.

IRENE

Oh! Then the train is not going through, after all?

CAPTAIN

The train is going, Madame. But this passport of yours presents problems which, under the circumstances——

IRENE

Monsieur Weber will settle the problems, whatever they are. Won't you, Achille?

WEBER

There is some question about your nationality, Irene.

CAPTAIN (*referring to the passport*)

It states here, Madame, that your birthplace is uncertain, but assumed to be Armenia.

IRENE

That is a province of Russia!

CAPTAIN

You subsequently became a resident of England, then of the United States, and then of France.

IRENE (*angrily*)

Yes—it's all there—clearly stated. I have never before had the slightest difficulty about my passport. It was issued by the League of Nations.

WEBER

I'm afraid the standing of the League of Nations is not very high in Italy at this moment.

CAPTAIN

The fact is, Madame, the very existence of the League is no longer recognized by our government. For that reason, we can not permit you to cross the frontier at this time. (*She looks at him and then at* WEBER. *The* CAPTAIN *hands her the passport.*) I'm sure you will appreciate the delicacy of my position. Perhaps we shall be able to adjust the matter tomorrow. (*He salutes and goes out, glad to escape.* HARRY *goes with him, asking "What's the trouble, Captain? Can't something be done about it?"*)

WEBER

I should of course wait over, Irene. But you know how dangerous it is for me to delay my return to France by so much as one day. I have been in touch with our agents. The premier is demanding that production be doubled—trebled—at once.

IRENE

Of course.

WEBER

Here—(*He takes out an envelope containing money.*) This will cover all possible expenses. (*He gives her the envelope.*) There is a train for Venice this evening. You must go there and see Lanza. I have already sent him full instructions.

IRENE

Yes, Achille. And I thank you for having managed this very, very tactfully.

WEBER (*smiles*)

You are a genuinely superior person, my dear. It is a privilege to have known you.

IRENE

Thank you again, Achille. Good-bye.

WEBER

Good-bye, Irene. (*He kisses her hand.* HARRY *returns.*) Coming, Mr. Van?

HARRY

In a minute. (WEBER *goes.* IRENE *puts the money in her handbag.*) Tough luck, babe.

IRENE

It's no matter.

HARRY

I just talked to the Captain and he isn't going to be as brutal as the Bolsheviks were. I mean, you won't suffer any bayonet wounds. He'll fix it for you to get through tomorrow.

IRENE

You want to be encouraging, my dear friend. But it's no use. The Italian government has too many reasons for wishing to detain me. They'll see to it that I disappear —quietly—and completely.

HARRY

Yes—I know all about that.

IRENE

All about what?

HARRY

You're a person of tremendous significance. You always were.
(SHIRLEY *appears at the left.*)

SHIRLEY

Hey, Harry! It's time for us to go.

HARRY

I'll be right out.
(SHIRLEY *goes.*)

IRENE

Go away—go away with your friends. If I am to die, it is no concern of yours!

HARRY

Listen, babe—I haven't any wish to . . .

IRENE (*flaming*)

And please don't call me *babe!* (*She stands up and walks away from him. He follows her.*)

HARRY

My apologies, Madame. I just call everybody "babe."

IRENE

Perhaps that's why I do not like it!

HARRY

Even if I don't believe anything you say, I can see pretty plainly that you're in a tough spot. And considering what we were to each other in the old Governor Bryan Hotel——

IRENE

Must you always be in Omaha?

HARRY

I'd like to help you, Irene. Isn't there something I can do?

IRENE

I thank you, from my heart, I thank you, for that offer. But it's useless. . . .

HARRY

You don't have to thank me. Tell me— what can I do?

IRENE

You're very kind, and very gallant. But, unfortunately, you're no match for Achille Weber. He has decided that I shall remain here and his decision is final!

HARRY

Is he responsible for them stopping you?

IRENE

Of course he is. I knew it the moment I saw that ashamed look on Captain Locicero's face, when he refused to permit me . . .

HARRY

So Weber double-crossed you, did he! What has the son of a bitch got against you?

IRENE

He's afraid of me. I know too much about his methods of promoting his own business.

HARRY

Everybody knows about his methods. Little Quillery was talking about them last night. . . .

IRENE

Yes—and what happened to Quillery? That's what happens to every one who dares to criticize him. Last night I did the one thing he could never forgive. I told him the truth! At last I told him just what I think. And now—you see how quickly he strikes back!
(SHIRLEY *and* BEBE *appear.*)

SHIRLEY

Harry! The bus is going to leave.

HARRY

All right—all right!

BEBE
But we got to go this *minute!*

HARRY
I'll be with you. Get out!

SHIRLEY (*as they go*)
Can you imagine? He stops everything to make another pass at that Russian. (*They have gone.*)

IRENE
Go ahead—go ahead! You can't help me! No one can! (*He picks up his coat and hat.*) But—if it will make you any happier in your future travels with Les Blondes, I'll tell you, yes—I did know you. slightly, in Omaha!

HARRY (*peering at her*)
Are you lying again?

IRENE
It was Room 974. Does that convince you?

HARRY (*ferociously*)
How can I remember what room it was?

IRENE (*smiling*)
Well, then—you'll never be sure, Mr. Van.

BEBE'S VOICE
Harry!

SHIRLEY'S VOICE
For God's sake, Harry!

DON (*appearing*)
We can't wait another instant! (DON goes.)

SHIRLEY'S VOICE
Come *on!*

HARRY
(*He turns and starts for the door, addressing the* GIRLS *en route.*) All right, God damn it! (*He goes out.*)
(IRENE *takes out her vanity case, and does something to her face. She takes off her hat and cloak.* DUMPTSY *comes in from the back. He is wearing the uniform of a private in the Italian army, with gas mask at the alert, and a full pack on his back.*)

DUMPTSY
Good afternoon, Madame.

IRENE (*turning*)
Why, Dumptsy—what is that costume?

DUMPTSY
They called me up. Look! I'm an Italian soldier.

IRENE
You look splendid!

DUMPTSY
If you please, Madame. But why didn't you go on that bus?

IRENE
I've decided to stay and enjoy the winter sports.

DUMPTSY
I don't think this is a good place any more, Madame. They say the war is very big—bigger than last time.

IRENE
Yes—I hear that on all sides.

DUMPTSY
The French will be here to drop bombs on everybody.

IRENE
It will be thrilling for us if they do. Won't it, Dumptsy?

DUMPTSY
Maybe it will, Madame. But—I came to say good-bye to Auguste, the barman, and Anna, the maid. They're both cousins of mine. They'll laugh when they see me in these clothes. (*He goes to the left.*) Can I get you anything, Madame?

IRENE
Yes, Dumptsy. I'll have a bottle of champagne. Bring two glasses. We'll have a drink together.

DUMPTSY
If you please, Madame. (DUMPTSY *goes into the bar.* IRENE *lights a cigarette and goes up to the window to look out.* PITTALUGA *comes in.*)

PITTALUGA

Your luggage is in the hall, Madame. Will you wish it taken to the same suite?

IRENE

No—I didn't really care much for those rooms. Have you anything smaller?

PITTALUGA (*in a less deferential tone*)

We have smaller rooms on the other side of the hotel.

IRENE

I'll have the smallest. It will be cozier.

PITTALUGA

You wish to go to it now?

IRENE

No. You can send up the luggage. I'll look at it later.
(PITTALUGA *bows and goes.* DUMPTSY *returns with the champagne.*)

DUMPTSY

I was right, Madame. Auguste laughed very much.

IRENE (*coming down*)

What will happen to your wife and children, Dumptsy?

DUMPTSY

Oh—I suppose the Fascisti will feed them. They promised to feed all the families with a man who is out fighting for their country. (*He has filled her glass. She sits down.*)

IRENE

Go ahead and pour yourself one, Dumptsy.

DUMPTSY

Thank you so much, Madame. I wasn't sure I heard correctly.

IRENE

Here's to you, Dumptsy—and to Austria.

DUMPTSY

And to you, Madame, if you please.

IRENE

Thank you. (*They drink.*)

DUMPTSY

And may you soon be restored to your home in Petersburg.

IRENE

Petersburg?

DUMPTSY

Yes, Madame. Your home.

IRENE (*with a slight smile*)

Ah, yes. My home! (*They drink again.*) And have no fear for the future, Dumptsy. Whatever happens—have no fear!

DUMPTSY

If you please, Madame. (*He finishes his drink.*) And now I must go find Anna, if you will excuse me.

IRENE

Here, Dumptsy. (*She hands him a note of money.*) Good-bye, and God bless you.

DUMPTSY

Thank you so much, Madame. (DUMPTSY *leans over and kisses her hand.*) Kiss die hand, Madame.
(*The* CAPTAIN *and* MAJOR *come in from the lobby.* DUMPTSY *salutes, strenuously, and goes out. The* MAJOR *goes across and into the bar. The* CAPTAIN *is following him.*)

IRENE

Some champagne, Captain?

CAPTAIN

No, thank you very much.

IRENE

You needn't be anxious to avoid me, Captain. I know perfectly well that it wasn't your fault.

CAPTAIN

You are very understanding, Madame.

IRENE

Yes—that's true. I am one of the most remarkably understanding people on earth. (*She swallows her drink.*) I understand so damned much that I am here, alone, on this cold mountain, and I have no one to turn to, nowhere to go . . .

CAPTAIN

If I can be of service to you in any way . . .

IRENE

I know you'll be kind, Captain Locicero. And faultlessly polite.

CAPTAIN (*with genuine sympathy*)

I realize, Madame, that politeness means nothing now. But—under these tragic circumstances—what else can I do?

IRENE. (*deliberately*)

What else can you do? I'll tell you what else you can do in these tragic circumstances. You can refuse to fight! Have you ever thought of that possibility? You can refuse to use those weapons that they have sold you! But—you were going into the bar. Please don't let me detain you.

CAPTAIN

You will forgive me, Madame?

IRENE

Fully, my dear Captain. . . . Fully.

CAPTAIN

Thank you. (*He salutes and goes into the bar.*)
(IRENE *pours herself another drink. Then she picks it up, goes to the piano, and starts to play a sketchy accompaniment for* "Kak Stranna." *She seems to be pretty close to tears. Perhaps she does cry a little, thoroughly enjoying the emotion.* HARRY *comes in wearing his snappy overcoat and his hat. He pays no attention to her, as he takes off his coat and hat and throws them down somewhere.*)

IRENE

Did you have some trouble?

HARRY

No. Whose is that champagne?

IRENE

Mine. Won't you have some?

HARRY

Thanks.

IRENE

Dumptsy used that glass.

HARRY

That's all right. (*He fills the glass and drinks.*)

IRENE

What happened? Didn't the train go?

HARRY

Yes—the train went. . . . I got the girls on board. Mr. and Mrs. Cherry promised to look out for them. They'll be O.K.

IRENE

And you came back—to me?

HARRY (*curtly*)

It seems fairly obvious that I did come back. (*He refills his glass.*)

IRENE

You meant it when you said that you wanted to help me.

HARRY

You said I'd never be sure. Well—I came back to tell you I *am* sure! I got thinking back, in the bus, and I came to the conclusion that it *was* Room 974 or close to it, anyway. And somehow or other, I couldn't help feeling rather flattered, and touched, to think that with all the sordid hotel rooms you've been in, you should have remembered that one. (*He has some more champagne.*)

IRENE (*after a moment*)

Bayard is not dead!

HARRY

Who?

IRENE

The Chevalier Bayard.

HARRY

Oh?

IRENE

Somewhere in that funny, music-hall soul of yours is the spirit of Leander, and Abelard, and Galahad. You give up everything—risk your life—walk unafraid into the valley of the shadow—to aid and comfort a damsel in distress. Isn't that the truth?

HARRY

Yes—it's the truth—plainly and simply put. (*He pours himself more champagne and drinks it quickly.*) Listen to me, babe —when are you going to break down and tell me who the hell are you?

IRENE

Does it matter so very much who I am?

HARRY

No.

IRENE

Give me some more champagne. (HARRY *goes to her and pours.*) My father was not one of the Romanoffs. But for many years, he was their guest—in Siberia. From him I learned that it is no use telling the truth to people whose whole life is a lie. But you—Harry—you are different. You are an honest man.

HARRY (*after a short pause*)

I am—am I? (*He crosses to the bar.*) Another bottle of champagne. . . . Hi, Captain.

CAPTAIN'S VOICE (*offstage in bar*)

What has happened, Mr. Van? Did you miss the train?

HARRY

No—just a God-damned fool. (*He closes the bar door.* IRENE *is gazing at him. He goes to her and kisses her.*)

IRENE

All these years—you've been surrounded by blondes—and you've loved only me!

HARRY

Now listen—we don't want to have any misunderstanding. If you're hooking up with me, it's only for professional reasons —see?

IRENE

Yes—I see.

HARRY

And what's more, I'm the manager. I'll fix it with the Captain for us to cross the border tomorrow, or the next day, or soon. We'll join up with the girls in Geneva— and that's as good a place as any to re-hearse the code.

IRENE

The code! Of *course*—the code! I shall learn it easily.

HARRY

It's a very deep complicated scientific problem.

IRENE

You must tell it to me at once.

HARRY

At once! If you're unusually smart and apply yourself you'll have a fairly good idea of it after six months of study and re-hearsal.

IRENE

A mind reader! Yes—you're quite right. I shall be able to do that very well!

(AUGUSTE *enters from the bar with a bottle of champagne. He refills their glasses, then refills* HARRY'S *glass, gives* HARRY *the bottle and goes back in to the bar.*)

HARRY

And, another thing, if you're going to qualify for this act with me, you've got to lay off liquor. I mean, after we finish this. It's a well-known fact that booze and sci-ence don't mix. (*He has another drink.* IRENE *is as one in a trance.*)

IRENE

I don't think I shall use my own name. No—Americans would mispronounce it horribly. No, I shall call myself—Na-moura . . . Namoura the Great—assisted by Harry Van.

HARRY

You've got nice billing there.

IRENE

I shall wear a black velvet dress—very plain—My skin, ivory white. I must have something to hold. One white flower. No! A little white prayer book. That's it. A little white . . . (*The warning siren is heard.*) What's that?

HARRY

Sounds like a fire. (*The* CAPTAIN *and* MAJOR *burst out of the bar and rush to the big window, talking excitedly in Italian and pointing to the northwestern sky. The siren shrieks continue. The* MAJOR *then rushes out, the* CAPTAIN *about to follow him.*) What's up, Captain?

CAPTAIN

French airplanes. It is reprisal for last night. They are coming to destroy our base here.

HARRY

I see.

CAPTAIN

They have no reason to attack this hotel. But—there may easily be accidents. I advise the cellar.

(AUGUSTE *rushes in from the bar,* PITTALUGA *from the lobby. The latter orders* AUGUSTE *to lower the Venetian blinds.*)

IRENE

Oh, no, Captain. We must stay here and watch the spectacle.

CAPTAIN

I entreat you not to be reckless, Madame. I have enough on my conscience now, without adding to it your innocent life!

IRENE

Don't worry, Captain. Death and I are old friends.

CAPTAIN

God be with you, Madame.

(*He goes out.* HARRY *and* IRENE *empty their glasses.* HARRY *refills them. Airplane motors are heard, increasing. Then the sound of machine guns.*)

(*Bombs are heard bursting at some distance.* AUGUSTE *and* PITTALUGA *go.*)

IRENE

Those are bombs.

HARRY

I guess so.

IRENE

We're in the war, Harry.

HARRY

What do you think we ought to do about it? Go out and say "Boo"?

IRENE

Let them be idiotic if they wish. We are sane. Why don't you try singing something?

HARRY

The voice don't feel appropriate. Too bad we haven't got Chaliapin here. (*She laughs.*) You know, babe—you look better blonde.

IRENE

Thank you.

(PITTALUGA *runs in.*)

PITTALUGA

The French beasts are bombing us! Every one goes into the cellar.

HARRY

Thanks very much, Signor.

PITTALUGA

You have been warned! (*He rushes out.*)

IRENE

Ridiculous! Here we are, on top of the world—and he asks us to go down into the cellar. . . . Do you want to go into the cellar?

HARRY

Do you?

IRENE

No. If a bomb hits, it will be worse in the cellar. (*He holds her close to him. She kisses him.*) I love you, Harry.

HARRY

You do, eh!

IRENE

Ever since that night—in the Governor Bryan Hotel—I've loved you. Because I knew that you have a heart that I can trust. And that whatever I would say to you, I would never—*never* be misunderstood.

HARRY

That's right, babe. I told you I had you tagged, right from the beginning.

IRENE

And you adore me, don't you, darling?

HARRY

No! Now lay off——

IRENE

No—of course not—you mustn't admit it!

HARRY

Will you please stop pawing me?
(*She laughs and lets go of him.*)
(HARRY *pours more champagne, as she crosses to the window, opens the slats of the blinds, and looks out. There is now great noise of planes, machine guns and bombs.*)

IRENE

Oh, you must see this! It's superb! (*He crosses to the window with his glass and looks out. The light on the stage is growing dimmer, but a weird light comes from the window. The scream of many gas bombs is heard.*) It's positively Wagnerian —isn't it?

HARRY

It looks to me exactly like "Hell's Angels." Did you ever see that picture, babe?

IRENE

No. I don't care for films.

HARRY

I *do.* I love 'em—every one of them. (*He is dragging her to the piano—a comparatively safe retreat.*) Did you know I used to play the piano in picture theatres? Oh, sure—I know all the music there is.
(*They are now at the piano—*HARRY *sitting,* IRENE *standing close by him. She is looking toward the window. He starts to accompany the air-raid with the* "Ride of the Walkyries." *There is a loud explosion.*)

IRENE

Harry . . .

HARRY

Yes, babe?

IRENE

Harry—do you realize that the whole world has gone to war? The *whole world!*

HARRY

I realize it. But don't ask me why. Because I've stopped trying to figure it out.

IRENE

I know why it is. It's just for the purpose of killing *us* . . . you and me. (*There is another loud explosion.* HARRY *stops playing.*) Because we are the little people— and for us the deadliest weapons are the most merciful. . . .
(*Another loud explosion.* HARRY *drinks.*)

HARRY

They're getting closer.

IRENE

Play some more. (*He resumes the* "Walkyrie.") Harry—do you know any hymns?

HARRY

What?

IRENE

Do you know any hymns?

HARRY

Certainly. (*He starts to play* "Onward, Christian Soldiers" *in furious jazz time, working in strains of* "Dixie." *There is another fearful crash, shattering the pane of the big window. He drags her down beside him at the piano.* HARRY *resumes* "Onward, Christian Soldiers" *in a slow, solemn tempo.*)

HARRY (*sings*)

Onward, Christian Soldiers——
(*Irene joins the loud singing.*)

BOTH (*singing*)

Marching as to war—
With the Cross of Jesus
Going on before. . . .
(*The din is now terrific. Demolition-bombs, gas-bombs, airplanes, shrapnel, machine guns.*)

Curtain.

POSTSCRIPT

During the past two weeks (this is March 16, 1936) the Italians have made a great offensive in Ethiopia; there has been an outburst of assassination and hara kiri by Fascists in Japan; the British Foreign Secretary, Mr. Eden, has said in the House of Commons that the current situation is "dreadfully similar to 1914"; a mutual assistance treaty has been ratified between republican France and Soviet Russia, and the German army has occupied the Rhineland, thereby shattering all that remained of the treaties of Versailles and Locarno.

What will happen before this play reaches print or a New York audience, I do not know. But let me express here the conviction that those who shrug and say, "War is inevitable," are false prophets. I believe that the world is populated largely by decent people, and decent people don't want war. Nor do they make war. They fight and die, to be sure—but that is because they have been deluded by their exploiters, who are members of the indecent minority.

Of course, this delusion may still go on. If decent people will continue to be intoxicated by the synthetic spirit of patriotism, pumped into them by megalomaniac leaders, and will continue to have faith in the "security" provided by those lethal weapons sold to them by the armaments industry, then war *is* inevitable; and the world will soon resolve itself into the semblance of an ant hill, governed by commissars who owe their power to the profundity of their contempt for the individual members of their species.

But I don't believe this will be so. I believe that a sufficient number of people are aware of the persistent validity of the Sermon on the Mount, and they remember that, between 1914 and 1918, twelve million men died in violence to make safe for democracy the world which we see about us today. That awareness and remembrance can be strong enough to resist the forces which would drive us back into the confusion and the darkness and the filth of No Man's Land.

The megalomaniac, to live, must inspire excitement, fear and awe. If, instead, he is greeted with calmness, courage and ridicule, he becomes a figure of supreme insignificance. A display of the three latter qualities by England, France, the Soviet Union, and the United States will defeat Fascism in Germany, Italy, and Japan, and will remove the threat of war which is Fascism's last gesture of self-justification.

By refusing to imitate the Fascists in their policies of heavily fortified isolation, their hysterical self-worship and psychopathic hatred of others, we may achieve the enjoyment of peaceful life on earth, rather than degraded death in the cellar.

R. E. S.

You Can't Take It With You

BY MOSS HART
and
GEORGE S. KAUFMAN

CHARACTERS

PENELOPE SYCAMORE
ESSIE
RHEBA
PAUL SYCAMORE
MR. DE PINNA
ED
DONALD
MARTIN VANDERHOF
ALICE
HENDERSON
TONY KIRBY
BORIS KOLENKHOV
GAY WELLINGTON
MR. KIRBY
MRS. KIRBY
THREE MEN
OLGA

The Scene Is the Home of Martin Vanderhof, New York

ACT ONE

A Wednesday Evening

During this act the curtain is lowered to denote the passing of several hours.

ACT TWO

A Week Later

ACT THREE

The Next Day

YOU CAN'T TAKE IT WITH YOU

ACT ONE

SCENE I

The home of MARTIN VANDERHOF—*just around the corner from Columbia University, but don't go looking for it. The room we see is what is customarily described as a living room, but in this house the term is something of an understatement. The every-man-for-himself room would be more like it. For here meals are eaten, plays are written, snakes collected, ballet steps practiced, xylophones played, printing presses operated—if there were room enough there would probably be ice skating. In short, the brood presided over by* MARTIN VANDERHOF *goes on about the business of living in the fullest sense of the word. This is a house where you do as you like, and no questions asked.*

At the moment, GRANDPA VANDERHOF'S *daughter,* MRS. PENELOPE SYCAMORE, *is doing what she likes more than anything else in the world. She is writing a play—her eleventh. Comfortably ensconced in what is affectionately known as Mother's Corner, she is pounding away on a typewriter perched precariously on a rickety card table. Also on the table is one of those plaster-paris skulls ordinarily used as an ash tray, but which serves* PENELOPE *as a candy jar. And, because* PENNY *likes companionship, there are two kittens on the table, busily lapping at a saucer of milk.*

PENELOPE VANDERHOF SYCAMORE *is a round little woman in her early fifties, comfortable looking, gentle, homey. One would not suspect that under that placid exterior there surges the Divine Urge—but it does, it does.*

After a moment her fingers lag on the keys; a thoughtful expression comes over her face. Abstractedly she takes a piece of candy out of the skull, pops it into her mouth. As always, it furnishes the needed inspiration—with a furious burst of speed she finishes a page and whips it out of the machine. Quite mechanically, she picks up one of the kittens, adds the sheet of paper to the pile underneath, replaces the kitten.

As she goes back to' work, ESSIE CARMICHAEL, MRS. SYCAMORE'S *eldest daughter, comes in from the kitchen. A girl of about twenty-nine, very slight, a curious air of the pixie about her. She is wearing ballet slippers—in fact, she wears them throughout the play.*

ESSIE (*fanning herself*)
My, that kitchen's hot.

PENNY (*finishing a bit of typing*)
What, Essie?

ESSIE
I say the kitchen's awful hot. That new candy I'm making—it just won't ever get cool.

PENNY
Do you have to make candy today, Essie? It's such a hot day.

ESSIE
Well, I got all those new orders. Ed went out and got a bunch of new orders.

PENNY
My, if it keeps on I suppose you'll be opening up a store.

ESSIE
That's what Ed was saying last night, but I said No, I want to be a dancer.
(*Bracing herself against the table, she manipulates her legs, ballet fashion.*)

PENNY
The only trouble with dancing is, it takes so long. You've been studying such a long time.

ESSIE (*slowly drawing a leg up behind her as she talks*)
Only—eight—years. After all, mother, you've been writing plays for eight years.

927

We started about the same time, didn't
we?

PENNY

Yes, but you shouldn't count my first
two years, because I was learning to type.
(*From the kitchen comes a colored maid
named* RHEBA—*a very black girl somewhere
in her thirties. She carries a white tablecloth, and presently starts to spread it over
the table.*)

RHEBA (*as she enters*)

I think the candy's hardening up now,
Miss Essie.

ESSIE

Oh, thanks, Rheba. I'll bring some in,
mother—I want you to try it.
(*She goes into the kitchen.*)
(PENNY *returns to her work as* RHEBA
busies herself with the table.)

RHEBA

Finish the second act, Mrs. Sycamore?

PENNY

Oh, no, Rheba. I've just got Cynthia entering the monastery.

RHEBA

Monastery? How'd she get there? She
was at the El Morocco, wasn't she?

PENNY

Well, she gets tired of the El Morocco,
and there's this monastery, so she goes
there.

RHEBA

Do they let her in?

PENNY

Yes, I made it Visitors' Day, so of course
anybody can come.

RHEBA

Oh.

PENNY

So she arrives on Visitors' Day, and—
just stays.

RHEBA

All night?

PENNY

Oh, yes. She stays six years.

RHEBA (*as she goes into the kitchen*)

Six years? My, I bet she busts that monastery wide open.

PENNY (*half to herself, as she types*)

"Six Years Later." . . .
(PAUL SYCAMORE *comes up from the cellar. Mid-fifties, but with a kind of youthful
air. His quiet charm and mild manner are
distinctly engaging.*)

PAUL (*turning back as he comes through
the door*)

Mr. De Pinna! (*A voice from below.
"Yah?"*) Mr. De Pinna, will you bring up
one of those new skyrockets, please? I
want to show them to Mrs. Sycamore. (*An
answering monosyllable from the cellar as
he turns toward* PENNY.) Look, Penny—
what do you think of these little fire
crackers? Ten strings for a nickel. Listen.
(*He puts one down on the center table
and lights it. It goes off with a good bang.*)
Nice, huh?

PENNY

Paul, dear, were you ever in a monastery?

PAUL (*quite calmly*)

No, I wasn't. . . . Wait till you see the
new rockets. Gold stars, then blue stars,
then some bombs, and then a balloon. Mr.
De Pinna thought of the balloon.

PENNY

Sounds lovely. Did you do all that today?

PAUL

Sure. We made up—oh, here we are.
(MR. DE PINNA *comes up from the cellar. A
bald-headed little man with a serious manner, and carrying two good-sized skyrockets.*) Look, Penny. Cost us eighteen
cents to make and we sell 'em for fifty.
How many do you figure we can make
before the Fourth, Mr. De Pinna?

DE PINNA

Well, we've got two weeks yet—what
day you going to take the stuff up to
Mount Vernon?

PAUL

Oh, I don't know—about a week. You know, we're going to need a larger booth this year—got a lot of stuff made up.

DE PINNA (*examining the rocket in his hand*)

Look, Mr. Sycamore, the only thing that bothers me is, I'm afraid the powder chamber is just a little bit close to the balloon.

PAUL

Well, we've got the stars and the bombs in between.

DE PINNA

But that don't give the balloon time enough. A balloon needs plenty of time.

PAUL

Want to go down in the cellar and try it?

DE PINNA

All right.

PAUL (*as he disappears through the cellar door*)

That's the only way you'll really tell.

PENNY (*halting* DE PINNA *in the cellar doorway*)

Mr. De Pinna, if a girl you loved entered a monastery, what would you do?

DE PINNA (*he wasn't expecting that one*)

Oh, I don't know, Mrs. Sycamore—it's been so long.
(*He goes.*)
(RHEBA *returns from the kitchen, bringing a pile of plates.*)

RHEBA

Miss Alice going to be home to dinner tonight, Mrs. Sycamore?

PENNY (*deep in her thinking*)

What? I don't know, Rheba. Maybe.

RHEBA

Well, I'll set a place for her, but she's only been home one night this week. (*She puts down a plate or two.*) Miss Essie's making some mighty good candy today.

She's doing something new with cocoanuts. (*More plates.*) Let's see—six, and Mr. De Pinna, and if Mr. Kolenkhov comes that makes eight, don't it? (*At which point a muffled sound, reminiscent of the Battle of the Marne, comes up from the cellar. It is the skyrocket, of course. The great preliminary hiss, followed by a series of explosions.* PENNY *and* RHEBA, *however, don't even notice it.* RHEBA *goes right on.*) Yes, I'd better set for eight.

PENNY

I think I'll put this play away for a while, Rheba, and go back to the war play.

RHEBA

Oh, I always liked that one—the war play.
(ESSIE *returns from the kitchen, carrying a plate of freshly made candy.*)

ESSIE

They'll be better when they're harder, mother, but try one—I want to know what you think.

PENNY

Oh, they look awfully good. (*She takes one.*) What do you call them?

ESSIE

I think I'll call 'em Love Dreams.

PENNY

Oh, that's nice. . . . I'm going back to my war play, Essie. What do you think?

ESSIE

Oh, are you, mother?

PENNY

Yes, I sort of got myself into a monastery and I can't get out.

ESSIE

Oh, well, it'll come to you, mother. Remember how you got out of that brothel. . . . Hello, boys. (*This little greeting is idly tossed toward the snake solarium, a glass structure looking something like a goldfish aquarium, but containing, believe it or not, snakes.*) The snakes look hungry. Did Rheba feed them?

PENNY (*as* RHEBA *re-enters*)

I don't know. Rheba, did you feed the snakes yet?

RHEBA

No, Donald's coming and he always brings flies with him.

PENNY

Well, try to feed them before Grandpa gets home. You know how fussy he is about them.

RHEBA

Yes'm.

PENNY (*handing her the kittens*)

And take Groucho and Harpo into the kitchen with you. . . . I think I'll have another Love Dream.

(MR. SYCAMORE *emerges from the cellar again.*)

PAUL

Mr. De Pinna was right about the balloon. It was too close to the powder.

ESSIE (*practicing a dance step*)

Want a Love Dream, father? They're on the table.

PAUL

No, thanks. I gotta wash.

PENNY

I'm going back to the war play, Paul.

PAUL

Oh, that's nice. We're putting some red stars after the blue stars, then come the bombs and *then* the balloon. That ought to do it.

(*He goes up the stairs.*)

ESSIE (*another dance step*)

Mr. Kolenkhov says I'm his most promising pupil.

PENNY (*absorbed in her own troubles*)

You know, with forty monks and one girl, something ought to happen.

(ED CARMICHAEL *comes down the stairs. A nondescript young man in his mid-thirties. In shirtsleeves at the moment.*)

ED

Listen!

(*He hums a snatch of melody as he heads for the far corner of the room—the xylophone corner. Arriving there, he picks up the sticks and continues the melody on the xylophone. Immediately* ESSIE *is up on her toes, performing intricate ballet steps to* ED'S *accompaniment.*)

ESSIE (*dancing*)

I like that, Ed. Yours?

ED (*shakes his head*)

Beethoven.

ESSIE (*never coming down off her toes*)

Lovely. Got a lot of *you* in it. . . . I made those new candies this afternoon, Ed.

ED (*playing away*)

Yah?

ESSIE

You can take 'em around tonight.

ED

All right. . . . Now, here's the finish. This is me.

(*He works up to an elaborate crescendo, but* ESSIE *keeps pace with him right to the finish.*)

ESSIE

That's fine. Remember it when Kolenkhov comes, will you?

PENNY (*who has been busy with her papers*)

Ed, dear, why don't you and Essie have a baby? I was thinking about it just the other day.

ED

I don't know—we could have one if you wanted us to. What about it, Essie? Do you want to have a baby?

ESSIE

Oh, I don't care. I'm willing if Grandpa is.

ED

Let's ask him.

(ESSIE *goes into the kitchen as* PENNY *goes back to her manuscripts.*)

PENNY (*running through the pile*)

Labor play . . . religious play . . . sex play. I know it's here some place.

(ED, *meanwhile, has transferred his attention from the xylophone to a printing press that stands handily by, and now gives it a preliminary workout.*)

(MR. DE PINNA *comes out of the cellar, bound for the kitchen to wash up.*)

DE PINNA

I was right about the balloon. It was too close to the powder.

ED

Anything you want printed, Mr. De Pinna? How about some more calling cards?

DE PINNA (*as he passes into the kitchen*)

No, thanks. I've still got the *first* thousand.

ED (*calling after him*)

Well, call on somebody, will you? (*He then gives his attention to* RHEBA, *who is busy with the table again.*) What have we got for dinner, Rheba? I'm ready to print the menu.

RHEBA

Cornflakes, watermelon, some of those candies Miss Essie made, and some kind of meat—I forget.

ED

I think I'll set it up in boldface Cheltenham tonight. (*He starts to pick out the letters.*) If I'm going to take those new candies around I'd better print up some descriptive matter after dinner.

PENNY

Do you think anybody reads those things, Ed—that you put in the candy boxes? . . . Oh, here it is. (*She pulls a manuscript out of a pile.*) "Poison Gas." (*The door bell sounds.*) I guess that's Donald. (*As* RHEBA *breaks into a broad grin.*) Look at Rheba smile.

ED

The boy friend, eh, Rheba?

PENNY (*as* RHEBA *disappears into the hallway*)

Donald and Rheba are awfully cute together. Sort of like Porgy and Bess.

(RHEBA *having opened the door, the gentleman named* DONALD *now looms up in the doorway—darkly. He is a colored man of no uncertain hue.*)

DONALD

Good evening, everybody!

ED

Hi, Donald! How've you been?

DONALD

I'm pretty good, Mr. Ed. How you been, Mrs. Sycamore?

PENNY

Very well, thank you. (*She looks at him, appraisingly.*) Donald, were you ever in a monastery?

DONALD

No-o. I don't go no place much. I'm on relief.

PENNY

Oh, yes, of course.

DONALD (*pulling a bottle out of each side pocket*)

Here's the flies, Rheba. Caught a big mess of them today.

RHEBA (*taking the jars.*)

You sure did.

DONALD

I see you've been working, Mrs. Sycamore.

PENNY

Yes, indeed, Donald.

DONALD

How's Grandpa?

PENNY

Just fine. He's over at Columbia this afternoon. The Commencement exercises.

DONALD

My, the years certainly do roll 'round.

ED (*with his typesetting*)

M — E — A — T. . . . What's he go there for all the time, Penny?

PENNY

I don't know. It's so handy—just around the corner.

(PAUL *comes downstairs.*)

PAUL

Oh, Donald! Mr. De Pinna and I are going to take the fireworks up to Mount Vernon next week. Do you think you could give us a hand?

DONALD

Yes, sir, only I can't take no money for it this year, because if the Government finds out I'm working they'll get sore.

PAUL

Oh! . . . Ed, I got a wonderful idea in the bathroom just now. I was reading Trotzky. (*He produces a book from under his arm.*) It's yours, isn't it?

ED

Yah, I left it there.

PENNY

Who is it?

PAUL

You know, Trotzky. The Russian Revolution.

PENNY

Oh.

PAUL

Anyhow, it struck me it was a great fireworks idea. Remember "The Last Days of Pompeii"?

PENNY

Oh, yes. Palisades Park. (*With a gesture of her arms she loosely describes a couple of arcs, indicative of the eruption of Mt. Vesuvius.*) That's where we met.

PAUL

Well, I'm going to do the Revolution! A full hour display.

DONALD

Say!

PENNY

Paul, that's wonderful!

ED

The red fire is the flag, huh?

PAUL

Sure! And the Czar, and the Cossacks!

DONALD

And the freeing of the slaves?

PAUL

No, no, Donald—

(*The sound of the front door slamming. A second's pause, and then* GRANDPA *enters the living room.* GRANDPA *is about 75, a wiry little man whom the years have treated kindly. His face is youthful, despite the lines that sear it; his eyes are very much alive. He is a man who made his peace with the world long, long ago, and his whole attitude and manner are quietly persuasive of this.*)

GRANDPA (*surveying the group*)

Well, sir, you should have been there. That's all I can say—you should have been there.

PENNY

Was it a nice Commencement, Grandpa?

GRANDPA

Wonderful. They get better every year. (*He peers into the snake solarium.*) You don't know how lucky you are you're snakes.

ED

Big class this year, Grandpa? How many were there?

GRANDPA

Oh, must have been two acres. *Everybody* graduated. And much funnier speeches than they had last year.

DONALD

You want to listen to a good speech you go up and hear Father Divine.

GRANDPA

I'll wait—they'll have him at Columbia.

PENNY

Donald, will you tell Rheba Grandpa's home now and we won't wait for Miss Alice.

DONALD

Yes'm. . . . (*As he goes through the kitchen door.*) Rheba, Grandpa's home—we can have dinner.

PAUL

Got a new skyrocket today, Grandpa. Wait till you see it. . . . Wonder why they don't have fireworks at Commencements.

GRANDPA

Don't make enough noise. You take a good Commencement orator and he'll drown out a whole carload of fireworks. And say just as much, too.

PENNY

Don't the graduates ever say anything?

GRANDPA

No, they just sit there in cap and night-gown, get their diplomas, and then along about forty years from now they suddenly say, "Where am I?"
(ESSIE *comes in from the kitchen, bringing a plate of tomatoes for the evening meal.*)

ESSIE

Hello, Grandpa. Have a nice day?

GRANDPA (*watching* ESSIE *as she puts the tomatoes on the table*)
Hello-have-a-nice-day. (*Suddenly he roars at the top of his voice.*) Don't I even get kissed?

ESSIE (*kissing him*)
Excuse me, Grandpa.

GRANDPA

I'll take a tomato, too. (ESSIE *passes the plate;* GRANDPA *takes one and sits with it in his hand, solemnly weighing it.*) You know, I could have used a couple of these this afternoon. . . . Play something, Ed.

(ED *at once obliges on the xylophone—something on the dreamy side. Immediately* ESSIE *is up on her toes again, drifting through the mazes of a toe dance.*)

ESSIE (*after a moment*)
There was a letter came for you, Grandpa. Did you get it?

GRANDPA

Letter for me? I don't know anybody.

ESSIE

It was for you, though. Had your name on it.

GRANDPA

That's funny. Where is it?

ESSIE

I don't know. Where's Grandpa's letter, mother?

PENNY (*who has been deep in her work*)
What, dear?

ESSIE (*dancing dreamily away*)
Where's that letter that came for Grandpa last week?

PENNY

I don't know. (*Then brightly*) I remember seeing the kittens on it.

GRANDPA

Who was it from? Did you notice?

ESSIE

Yes, it was on the outside.

GRANDPA

Well, who was it?

ESSIE (*first finishing the graceful flutterings of the Dying Swan*)
United States Government.

GRANDPA

Really? Wonder what *they* wanted.

ESSIE

There was one before that, too, from the same people. There was a couple of them.

GRANDPA

Well, if any more come I wish you'd give them to me.

ESSIE

Yes, Grandpa.
(*A fresh flurry of dancing; the xylophone grows a little louder.*)

GRANDPA

I think I'll go out to Westchester tomorrow and do a little snake-hunting.

PAUL (*who has settled down with his book some time before this*)
"God is the State; the State is God."

GRANDPA

What's that?

PAUL

"God is the State; the State is God."

GRANDPA

Who says that?

PAUL

Trotzky.

GRANDPA

Well, that's all right—I thought *you* said it.

ED

It's nice for printing, you know. Good and short. (*He reaches into the type case.*)
G — O — D — space — I — S — space — T — H — E
(*The sound of the outer door closing, and* ALICE SYCAMORE *enters the room. A lovely, fresh young girl of about twenty-two. She is plainly* GRANDPA's *granddaughter, but there is something that sets her apart from the rest of the family. For one thing, she is in daily contact with the world; in addition, she seems to have escaped the tinge of mild insanity that pervades the rest of them. But she is a Sycamore for all that, and her devotion and love for them are plainly apparent. At the moment she is in a small nervous flutter, but she is doing her best to conceal it.*)

ALICE (*as she makes the rounds, kissing her grandfather, her father, her mother*)
And so the beautiful princess came into the palace, and kissed her mother, and her father, and her grandfather—hi, Grandpa —and what do you think? They turned into the Sycamore family. Surprised?

ESSIE (*examining* ALICE's *dress*)
Oh, Alice, I like it. It's new, isn't it?

PENNY

Looks nice and summery.

ESSIE

Where'd you get it?

ALICE

Oh, I took a walk during lunch hour.

GRANDPA

You've been taking a lot of walks lately. That's the second new dress this week.

ALICE

Oh, I just like to brighten up the office once in a while. I'm known as the Kay Francis of Kirby & Co. . . . Well, what's new around here? In the way of plays, snakes, ballet dancing or fireworks. Dad, I'll bet you've been down in that cellar all day.

PAUL

Huh?

PENNY

I'm going back to the war play, Alice.

ESSIE

Ed, play Alice that Beethoven thing you wrote. Listen, Alice.
(*Like a shot* ED *is at the xylophone again,* ESSIE *up on her toes.*)
(GRANDPA, *meanwhile, has unearthed his stamp album from under a pile of oddments in the corner, and is now busy with his magnifying glass.*)

GRANDPA

Do you know that you can mail a letter all the way from Nicaragua for two pesetos?

PENNY (*meanwhile dramatically reading one of her own deathless lines*)
"Kenneth, my virginity is a priceless thing to me."

ALICE (*finding it hard to break through all this*)

Listen, people. . . . Listen. (*A break in the music; she gets a scattered sort of attention.*) I'm not home to dinner. A young gentleman is calling for me.

ESSIE

Really? Who is it?

PENNY

Well, isn't that nice?

ALICE (*with quiet humor*)

I did everything possible to keep him from coming here, but he's calling for me.

PENNY

Why don't you both stay to dinner?

ALICE

No, I want him to take you in easy doses. I've tried to prepare him a little, but don't make it any worse than you can help. Don't read him any plays, Mother, and don't let a snake bite him, Grandpa, because I like him. And I wouldn't dance for him, Essie, because we're going to the Monte Carlo ballet tonight.

GRANDPA

Can't do *anything*. Who *is* he—President of the United States?

ALICE

No, he's vice-president of Kirby & Co. Mr. Anthony Kirby, Jr.

ESSIE

The Boss' son?

PENNY

Well!

ALICE

The Boss' son. Just like the movies.

ESSIE

That explains the new dresses.

ED

And not being home to dinner for three weeks.

ALICE

Why, you're wonderful!

PENNY (*all aglow*)

Are you going to marry him?

ALICE

Oh, of course. Tonight! Meanwhile I have to go up and put on my wedding dress.

ESSIE

Is he good-looking?

ALICE (*vainly consulting her watch*)

Yes, in a word. Oh, dear! What time is it?

PENNY

I don't know. Anybody know what time it is?

PAUL

Mr. De Pinna might know.

ED

It was about five o'clock a couple of hours ago.

ALICE

Oh, I ought to know better than to ask you people. . . . Will you let me know the minute he comes, please?

PENNY

Of course, Alice.

ALICE

Yes, I know, but I mean the *minute* he comes.

PENNY

Why, of course. (ALICE *looks apprehensively from one to the other; then disappears up the stairs.*) Well, what do you think of that?

GRANDPA

She seems to like him, if you ask me.

ESSIE

I should say so. She's got it bad.

PENNY

Wouldn't it be wonderful if she married him? We could have the wedding right in this room.

PAUL

Now, wait a minute, Penny. This is the first time he's ever called for the girl.

PENNY

You only called for me once.

PAUL

Young people are different nowadays.

ESSIE

Oh, I don't know. Look at Ed and me. He came to dinner *once* and just stayed.

PENNY

Anyhow, I think it's wonderful. I'll bet he's crazy about her. It must be he that's been taking her out every night. (*The door bell rings.*) There he is! Never mind, Rheba, I'll answer it. (*She is fluttering to the door.*) Now remember what Alice said, and be *very* nice to him.

GRANDPA (*rising*)

All right—let's take a look at him.

PENNY (*at the front door; milk and honey in her voice*)

Well! Welcome to our little home! I'm Alice's mother. Do come right in! Here we are! (*She reappears in the archway, piloting the stranger.*) This is Grandpa, and that's Alice's father, and Alice's sister, and her husband, Ed Carmichael. (*The family all give courteous little nods and smiles as they are introduced.*) Well! Now give me your hat and make yourself right at home.

THE MAN

I'm afraid you must be making a mistake.

PENNY

How's that?

THE MAN

My card.

PENNY (*reading*)

"Wilbur C. Henderson. Internal Revenue Department."

HENDERSON

That's right.

GRANDPA

What can we do for you?

HENDERSON

Does a Mr. Martin Vanderhof live here?

GRANDPA

Yes, sir. That's me.

HENDERSON (*all milk and honey*)

Well, Mr. Vanderhof, the Government wants to talk to you about a little matter of income tax.

PENNY

Income tax?

HENDERSON

Do you mind if I sit down?

GRANDPA

No, no. Just go right ahead.

HENDERSON (*settling himself*)

Thank you.
(*From above stairs the voice of* ALICE *floats down.*)

ALICE

Mother! Is that Mr. Kirby?

PENNY (*going to the stairs*)

No. No, it isn't, darling. It's—an internal something or other. (*To* MR. HENDERSON.) Pardon me.

HENDERSON (*pulling a sheaf of papers from his pocket*)

We've written you several letters about this, Mr. Vanderhof, but have not had any reply.

GRANDPA

Oh, that's what those letters were.

ESSIE

I told you they were from the Government.
(MR. DE PINNA *comes up from the cellar, bearing a couple of giant firecrackers. He pauses as he sees a stranger.*)

DE PINNA

Oh, pardon me.

PAUL

Yes, Mr. De Pinna?

DE PINNA

These things are not going off, Mr. Syca-more. Look.

(*He prepares to apply a match to one of them, as a startled income tax man nearly has a conniption fit. But* PAUL *is too quick for him.*)

PAUL

Ah—not here, Mr. De Pinna. Grandpa's busy.

DE PINNA

Oh.

(MR. DE PINNA *and* PAUL *hurry into the hall with their firecrackers.*)

HENDERSON (*now that order has been re-stored.*)

According to our records, Mr. Vander-hof, you have never paid an income tax.

GRANDPA

That's right.

HENDERSON

Why not?

GRANDPA

I don't believe in it.

HENDERSON

Well—you own property, don't you?

GRANDPA

Yes, sir.

HENDERSON

And you receive a yearly income from it?

GRANDPA

I do.

HENDERSON

Of—(*He consults his records.*)—be-tween three and four thousand dollars.

GRANDPA

About that.

HENDERSON

You've been receiving it for years.

GRANDPA

I have. 1901, if you want the exact date.

HENDERSON

Well, the Government is only concerned from 1914 on. That's when the income tax started.

GRANDPA

Well?

HENDERSON

Well—it seems, Mr. Vanderhof, that you owe the Government twenty-two years' back income tax.

ED

Wait a minute! You can't go back that far—that's outlawed.

HENDERSON (*calmly regarding him*)

What's *your* name?

ED

What difference does that make?

HENDERSON

Ever file an income tax return?

ED

No, sir.

HENDERSON

What was your income last year?

ED

Ah—twenty-eight dollars and fifty cents, wasn't it, Essie?

(ESSIE *gives quick assent; the income tax man dismisses the whole matter with an impatient wave of the hand and returns to bigger game.*)

HENDERSON

Now, Mr. Vanderhof, you know there's quite a penalty for not filing an income tax return.

PENNY

Penalty?

GRANDPA

Look, Mr. Henderson, let me ask you something.

HENDERSON

Well?

GRANDPA

Suppose I pay you this money—mind you, I don't say I'm going to do it—but just for the sake of argument—what's the Government going to do with it?

HENDERSON

How do you mean?

GRANDPA

Well, what do I get for my money? If I go into Macy's and buy something, there it *is*—I see it. What's the Government give me?

HENDERSON

Why, the Government gives you everything. It protects you.

GRANDPA

What from?

HENDERSON

Well—invasion. Foreigners that might come over here and take everything you've got.

GRANDPA

Oh, I don't think they're going to do that.

HENDERSON

If you didn't pay an income tax, they would. How do you think the Government keeps up the Army and Navy? All those battleships . . .

GRANDPA

Last time we used battleships was in the Spanish-American War, and what did we get out of it? Cuba—and we gave that back. I wouldn't mind paying if it were something sensible.

HENDERSON (*beginning to get annoyed*)

Well, what about Congress, and the Supreme Court, and the President? We've got to pay *them*, don't we?

GRANDPA (*ever so calmly*)

Not with my money—no, sir.

HENDERSON (*furious*)

Now wait a minute! I'm not here to argue with you. All I know is that you haven't paid an income tax and you've got to pay it!

GRANDPA

They've got to show me.

HENDERSON (*yelling*)

We *don't* have to show you! I just told you! All those buildings down in Washington, and Interstate Commerce, and the Constitution!

GRANDPA

The Constitution was paid for long ago. And Interstate Commerce—what *is* Interstate Commerce, anyhow?

HENDERSON (*with murderous calm*)

There are forty-eight States—see? And if there weren't Interstate Commerce, nothing could go from one State to another. See?

GRANDPA

Why not? They got fences?

HENDERSON

No, they haven't got fences! They've got *laws!* . . . My God, I never came across anything like this before!

GRANDPA

Well, I might pay about seventy-five dollars, but that's all it's worth.

HENDERSON

You'll pay every cent of it, like everybody else!

ED (*who has lost interest*)

Listen, Essie—listen to this a minute.
(*The xylophone again;* ESSIE *goes into her dance.*)

HENDERSON (*going right ahead, battling against the music*)

And let me tell you something else! You'll go to jail if you don't pay, do you hear that? There's a law, and if you think you're bigger than the law, you've got another think coming! You'll hear from

the United States Government, that's all I can say!
(*He is backing out of the room.*)

GRANDPA (*quietly*)
Look out for those snakes.

HENDERSON (*jumping*)
Jesus!
(*Out in the hall, and not more than a foot or two behind* MR. HENDERSON, *the firecracker boys are now ready to test that little bomber. It goes off with a terrific detonation, and* MR. HENDERSON *jumps a full foot. He wastes no time at all in getting out of there.*)

PAUL (*coming back into the room.*)
How did that sound to you folks?

GRANDPA (*quite judicially*)
I liked it.

PENNY
My goodness, he was mad, wasn't he?

GRANDPA
Oh, it wasn't his fault. It's just that the whole thing is so silly.

PENNY (*suddenly finding herself with a perfectly good Panama in her hand*)
He forgot his hat.

GRANDPA
What size is it?

PENNY (*peering into its insides*)
Seven and an eighth.

GRANDPA
Just right for me.

DE PINNA
Who was that fellow, anyhow?
(*Again the door bell.*)

PENNY
This *must* be Mr. Kirby.

PAUL
Better make sure this time.

PENNY
Yes, I will.
(*She disappears.*)

ESSIE
I hope he's good-looking.

PENNY (*heard at the door*)
How do you do?

A MAN'S VOICE
Good evening.

PENNY (*taking no chances*)
Is this Mr. Anthony Kirby, Jr.?

TONY
Yes.

PENNY (*giving her all*)
Well, Mr. Kirby, come right in! We've been expecting you. Come right in! (*They come into sight;* PENNY *expansively addresses the family.*) This is *really* Mr. Kirby! Now, I'm Alice's mother, and that's Mr. Sycamore, and Alice's grandfather, and her sister Essie, and Essie's husband. (*There are a few mumbled greetings.*) There! Now you know *all* of us, Mr. Kirby. Give me your hat and make yourself right at home.
(TONY KIRBY *comes a few steps into the room. He is a personable young man, not long out of Yale, and, as we will presently learn, even more recently out of Cambridge. Although he fits all the physical requirements of a Boss' son, his face has something of the idealist in it. All in all, a very nice young man.*)

TONY
How do you do?
(*Again the voice of the vigilant* ALICE *floats down from upstairs. "Is that Mr. Kirby, mother?"*)

PENNY (*shouting up the stairs*)
Yes, Alice. He's *lovely!*

ALICE (*aware of storm signals*)
I'll be right down.

PENNY
Do sit down, Mr. Kirby.

TONY
Thank you. (*A glance at the dinner table.*) I hope I'm not keeping you from dinner?

GRANDPA

No, no. Have a tomato?

TONY

No, thank you.

PENNY (*producing the candy-filled skull*)

How about a piece of candy?

TONY (*eyeing the container*)

Ah—no, thanks.

PENNY

Oh, I forgot to introduce Mr. De Pinna. This is Mr. De Pinna, Mr. Kirby. (*An exchange of "How do you do's?"*)

DE PINNA

Wasn't I reading about your father in the newspaper the other day? Didn't he get indicted or something?

TONY (*smiling*)

Hardly that. He just testified before the Securities Commission.

DE PINNA

Oh.

PENNY (*sharply*)

Yes, of course. I'm sure there was nothing crooked about it, Mr. De Pinna. As a matter of fact—(*She is now addressing* TONY.)—Alice has often told us what a lovely man your father is.

TONY

Well, I know father couldn't get along without Alice. She knows more about the business than any of us.

ESSIE

You're awful young, Mr. Kirby, aren't you, to be vice-president of a big place like that.

TONY

Well, you know what that means, vice-president. All I have is a desk with my name on it.

PENNY

Is that all? Don't you get any salary?

TONY (*with a laugh*)

Well, a little. More than I'm worth, I'm afraid.

PENNY

Now you're just being modest.

GRANDPA

Sounds kind of dull to me—Wall Street. Do you like it?

TONY

Well, the hours are short. And I haven't been there very long.

GRANDPA

Just out of college, huh?

TONY

Well, I knocked around for a while first. Just sort of had fun.

GRANDPA

What did you do? Travel?

TONY

For a while. Then I went to Cambridge for a year.

GRANDPA (*nodding*)

England.

TONY

That's right.

GRANDPA

Say, what's an English commencement like? Did you see any?

TONY

Oh, very impressive.

GRANDPA

They are, huh?

TONY

Anyhow, now the fun's over, and—I'm facing the world.

PENNY

You've certainly got a good start, Mr. Kirby. Vice-president, and a rich father.

TONY

Well, that's hardly my fault.

PENNY (*brightly*)

So now I suppose you're all ready to settle down and—get married.

PAUL

Come now, Penny, I'm sure Mr. Kirby knows his own mind.

PENNY

I wasn't making up his mind for him— was I, Mr. Kirby?

TONY

That's quite all right, Mrs. Sycamore.

PENNY (*to the others*)

You see?

ESSIE

You mustn't rush him, Mother.

PENNY

Well, all I meant was he's bound to get married, and suppose the wrong girl gets him?
(*The descending* ALICE *mercifully comes to* TONY'S *rescue at this moment. Her voice is heard from the stairs.*)

ALICE

Well, here I am, a vision in white.
(*She comes into the room—and very lovely indeed.*)
Apparently you've had time to get acquainted.

PENNY

Oh, yes, indeed. We were just having a delightful talk about love and marriage.

ALICE

Oh, dear.
(*She turns to* TONY.)
I'm sorry. I came down as fast as I could.

RHEBA (*bringing a platter of sliced watermelon*)

God damn those flies in the kitchen. . . . Oh, Miss Alice, you look beautiful. Where you going?

ALICE (*making the best of it*)

I'm going out, Rheba.

RHEBA (*noticing* TONY)

Stepping, huh?
(*The door bell sounds.*)

ESSIE

That must be Kolenkhov.

ALICE (*uneasily*)

I think we'd better go, Tony.

TONY

All right.
(*Before they can escape, however,* DONALD *emerges from the kitchen, bearing a tray.*)

DONALD

Grandpa, you take cream on your cornflakes? I forget.

GRANDPA

Half and half, Donald.
(*The voice of* BORIS KOLENKHOV *booms from the outer door.*)

KOLENKHOV

Ah, my little Rhebishka!

RHEBA (*with a scream of laughter*)

Yassuh, Mr. Kolenkhov!

KOLENKHOV

I am so hungry I could even eat my little Rhebishka!
(*He appears in the archway, his great arm completely encircling the delighted* RHEBA. MR. KOLENKHOV *is one of* RHEBA'S *pets, and if you like Russians he might be one of yours. He is enormous, hairy, loud, and very, very Russian. His appearance in the archway still further traps* ALICE *and* TONY.)
Grandpa, what do you think? I have had a letter from Russia! The Second Five Year Plan is a failure!
(*He lets out a laugh that shakes the rafters.*)

ESSIE

I practiced today, Mr. Kolenkhov!

KOLENKHOV (*with a deep Russian bow*)

My Pavlowa!
(*Another bow.*)

Madame Sycamore! . . . My little Alice!
(*He kisses her hand.*)
Never have I seen you look so magnificent.

ALICE

Thank you, Mr. Kolenkhov. Tony, this is Mr. Kolenkhov, Essie's dancing teacher. Mr. Kirby.

TONY

How do you do?
(*A click of the heels and a bow from* KOLENKHOV.)

ALICE (*determined, this time*)

And now we really *must* go. Excuse us, Mr. Kolenkhov—we're going to the Monte Carlo ballet.

KOLENKHOV (*at the top of his tremendous voice*)

The Monte Carlo ballet! It *stinks!*

ALICE (*panicky now*)

Yes. . . . Well—goodbye, everybody. Goodbye.

TONY

Goodbye. I'm so glad to have met you all.
(*A chorus of answering "Good-byes" from the family. The young people are gone.*)

KOLENKHOV (*still furious*)

The Monte Carlo ballet!

PENNY

Isn't Mr. Kirby lovely? . . . Come on, everybody! Dinner's ready!

ED (*pulling up a chair*)

I thought he was a nice fellow, didn't you?

ESSIE

Mm. And so good-looking.

PENNY

And he had such nice manners. Did you notice, Paul? Did you notice his manners?

PAUL

I certainly did. You were getting pretty personal with him.

PENNY

Oh, now, Paul . . . Anyhow, he's a very nice young man.

DE PINNA (*as he seats himself*)

He looks kind of like a cousin of mine.

KOLENKHOV

Bakst! Diaghlieff! *Then* you had the *ballet!*

PENNY

I think if they get married here I'll put the altar right where the snakes are. You wouldn't mind, Grandpa, would you?

ESSIE

Oh, they'll want to get married in a church. His family and everything.

GRANDPA (*tapping on a plate for silence*)

Quiet, everybody! Quiet!
(*They are immediately silent—Grace is about to be pronounced.* GRANDPA *pauses a moment for heads to bow, then raises his eyes heavenward. He clears his throat and proceeds to say Grace.*)
Well, Sir, we've been getting along pretty good for quite a while now, and we're certainly much obliged. Remember, all we ask is just to go along and be happy in our own sort of way. Of course we want to keep our health, but as far as anything else is concerned, we'll leave it to You. Thank You.
(*The heads come up as* RHEBA *comes through the door with a steaming platter.*)
So the Second Five Year Plan is a failure, eh, Kolenkhov?

KOLENKHOV (*booming*)

Catastrophic!
(*He reaches across the table and spears a piece of bread. The family, too, is busily plunging in.*)

THE CURTAIN IS DOWN.

SCENE II

Late the same night. The house is in darkness save for a light in the hall.

Somewhere in the back regions an accordion is being played. Then quiet. Then the stillness of the night is suddenly broken again by a good loud BANG! from the cellar. Somewhere in the nether regions, one of the Sycamores is still at work.

Once more all is quiet, then the sound of a key in the outer door. The voices of ALICE *and* TONY *drift through.*

ALICE

I could see them dance every night of the week. I think they're marvelous.

TONY

They are, aren't they? But of course just walking inside *any* theatre gives *me* a thrill.

ALICE (*as they come into sight in the hallway*)

It's been *so* lovely, Tony. I hate to have it over.

TONY

Oh, is it over? Do I have to go right away?

ALICE

Not if you don't want to.

TONY

I don't.

ALICE

Would you like a cold drink?

TONY

Wonderful.

ALICE (*pausing to switch on the light*)

I'll see what's in the ice-box. Want to come along?

TONY

I'd follow you to the ends of the earth.

ALICE

Oh, just the kitchen is enough.

(*They go out. A pause, a ripple of gay laughter from the kitchen, then they return.* ALICE *is carrying a couple of glasses,* TONY *brings two bottles of ginger ale and an opener.*)

Lucky you're not hungry, Mr. K. An ice-box full of cornflakes. That gives you a rough idea of the Sycamores.

TONY (*working away with the opener*)

Of course, why they make these bottle openers for Singer midgets I never *was* able to—ah!

(*As the bottle opens.*)

All over my coat.

ALICE

I'll take mine in a glass, if you don't mind.

TONY (*pouring*)

There you are. A foaming beaker.

ALICE

Anyhow, it's cold.

TONY (*pouring his own*)

Now if you'll please be seated, I'd like to offer a toast.

ALICE (*settling herself*)

We are seated.

TONY

Miss Sycamore—

(*He raises his glass on high.*)

—to you.

ALICE

Thank you, Mr. Kirby.

(*Lifting her own glass.*)

To you.

(*They both drink.*)

TONY (*happily*)

I wouldn't trade one minute of this evening for—all the rice in China.

ALICE

Really?

TONY

Cross my heart.

ALICE (*a little sigh of contentment. Then shyly*)

Is there much rice in China?

TONY

Terrific. Didn't you read "The Good Earth?"

(*She laughs. They are silent for a moment.*)

I suppose I ought to go.

ALICE

Is it very late?

TONY (*looks at his watch*)

Very.

(*Alice gives a little nod. Time doesn't matter.*)

I don't want to go.

ALICE

I don't want you to.

TONY

All right, I won't.

(*Silence again.*)

When do you get your vacation?

ALICE

Last two weeks in August.

TONY

I might take mine then, too.

ALICE

Really?

TONY

What are you going to do?

ALICE

I don't know. I hadn't thought much about it.

TONY

Going away, do you think?

ALICE

I might not. I like the city in the summer time.

TONY

I do too.

ALICE

But you always go up to Maine, don't you?

TONY

Why—yes, but I'm sure I *would* like the city in the summer time. That is, I'd like it if—Oh, you know what I mean, Alice. I'd love it if *you* were here.

ALICE

Well—it'd be nice if you were here, Tony.

TONY

You know what you're saying, don't you?

ALICE

What?

TONY

That you'd rather spend the summer with me than anybody else.

ALICE

It looks that way, doesn't it?

TONY

Well, if it's true about the summer, how would you feel about—the winter?

ALICE (*seeming to weigh the matter*)

Yes. I'd—like that too.

TONY (*tremulous*)

Then comes spring—and autumn. If you could—see your way clear about those, Miss Sycamore. . . .

ALICE (*again a little pause*)

Yes.

TONY

I guess that's the whole year. We haven't forgotten anything, have we?

ALICE

No.

TONY

Well, then—
(*Another pause; their eyes meet. And at this moment,* PENNY *is heard from the stairway.*)

PENNY

Is that you, Alice? What time is it?
(*She comes into the room, wrapped in a bathrobe.*)
Oh!
(*In sudden embarrassment.*)
Excuse me, Mr. Kirby. I had no idea—that is, I—
(*She senses the situation.*)
—I didn't mean to interrupt anything.

TONY

Not at all, Mrs. Sycamore.

ALICE (*quietly*)

No, Mother.

PENNY

I just came down for a manuscript—(*fumbling at her table*)—then you can go right ahead. Ah, here it is. "Sex Takes a Holiday." Well—goodnight, Mr. Kirby.

TONY

Good-night, Mrs. Sycamore.

PENNY

Oh, I think you can call me Penny, don't you, Alice? At least I hope so.
(*With a little laugh she vanishes up the stairs.*)
(*Before* PENNY'S *rippling laugh quite dies, BANG! from the cellar.* TONY *jumps.*)

ALICE (*quietly*)

It's all right, Tony. That's father.

TONY

This time of night?

ALICE (*ominously*)

Any time of night. Any time of *day.*
(*She stands silent. In the pause,* TONY *gazes at her fondly.*)

TONY

You're more beautiful, more lovely, more adorable than anyone else in the whole world.

ALICE (*as he starts to embrace her*)

Don't, Tony. I can't.

TONY

What?

ALICE

I can't, Tony.

TONY

My dear, just because your mother—all mothers are like that, Alice, and Penny's a darling. You see, I'm even calling her Penny.

ALICE

I don't mean that.
(*She faces him squarely.*)
Look, Tony. This is something I should have said a long time ago, but I didn't have the courage. I let myself be swept away because—because I loved you so.

TONY

Darling!

ALICE

No, wait, Tony. I want to make it clear to you. You're of a different world—a whole different kind of people. Oh, I don't mean money or socially—that's too silly. But your family and mine—it just wouldn't work, Tony. It just wouldn't work.
(*Again an interruption. This time it is* ED *and* ESSIE, *returning from the neighborhood movie. We hear their voices at the door, deep in an argument.* ED: *"All right, have it your way. She can't dance. That's why they pay her all that money—because she can't dance." And then* ESSIE: *"Well, I don't call that dancing, what she does."*)
(*They come into sight.*)

ESSIE

Oh, hello.
(*There is an exchange of greetings, a note of constraint in* ALICE'S *voice. But* ESSIE *goes right ahead.*)
Look! What do *you* think? Ed and I just saw Fred Astaire and Ginger Rogers. Do you think she can dance, Mr. Kirby?

TONY (*mildly taken aback by this*)

Why, yes—I always thought so.

ESSIE

What does she do, anyhow? Now, look —you're Fred Astaire and I'm Ginger Rogers.

(*She drapes herself against* TONY, *a la Ginger Rogers.*)

ALICE

Essie, please.

ESSIE

I just want to use him for a minute. . . . Look, Mr. Kirby—

(*Her arms go round his neck, her cheek against his.*)

ALICE (*feeling that it's time to take action*)

Essie, you're just as good as Ginger Rogers. We all agree.

ESSIE (*triumphantly*)

You see, Ed?

ED

Yeh. . . . Come on, Essie—we're butting in here.

ESSIE

Oh, they've been together all evening. . . . Good night, Mr. Kirby.

(*An exchange of good-nights—it looks as though the* CARMICHAELS *are really going upstairs before the whole thing gets too embarrassing. Then* ED *turns casually to* ESSIE *in the doorway.*)

ED

Essie, did you ask Grandpa about us having a baby?

ESSIE (*as they ascend the stairs*)

Yes—he said go right ahead.

ALICE (*when they are gone*)

You see? That's what it would be like, always.

TONY

But I didn't mind that. Besides, darling, we're not going to live with our families. It's just you and I.

ALICE

No, it isn't—it's never quite that. I love them, Tony—I love them deeply. Some

people could cut away, but I couldn't. I know they do rather strange things—I never know what to expect next—but they're gay, and they're fun, and—I don't know—there's a kind of nobility about them. That may sound silly, but I mean— the way they just don't care about things that other people give their whole lives to. They're—really wonderful, Tony.

TONY

Alice, you talk as though only you could understand them. That's not true. Why, I fell in love with them tonight.

ALICE

But your family, Tony. I'd want *you,* and everything about you, everything about *me,* to be—one. I couldn't start out with a part of me that you didn't share, and part of you that I didn't share. Unless we were all one—you, and *your* mother and father—I'd be miserable. And they never can be, Tony—I know it. They couldn't be.

TONY

Alice, every family has got curious little traits. What of it? My father raises orchids at ten thousand dollars a bulb. Is that sensible? My mother believes in spiritualism. That's just as bad as your mother writing plays, isn't it?

ALICE

It goes deeper, Tony. Your mother believes in spiritualism because it's fashionable. And your father raises orchids because he can afford to. My mother writes plays because eight years ago a typewriter was delivered here by mistake.

TONY

Darling what *of* it?

ALICE

And look at Grandpa. Thirty-five years ago he just quit business one day. He started up to his office in the elevator and came right down again. He just stopped. He could have been a rich man, but he said it took too much time. So for thirty-five years he's just collected snakes and gone to circuses and commencements. It never occurs to any of them—

(*As if to prove her point, they are suddenly interrupted at this moment by the entrance of* DONALD *from the kitchen. It is a* DONALD *who has plainly not expected to encounter midnight visitors, for he is simply dressed in a long white nightgown and a somewhat shorter bathrobe—a costume that permits a generous expanse of white nightshirt down around the legs, and, below that, a couple of very black shins. His appearance, incidentally, explains where all that music had been coming from, for an accordion is slung over his shoulder.*)

DONALD (*surprised, but not taken aback*)

Oh, excuse me. I didn't know you folks was in here.

ALICE (*resigned*)

It's all right, Donald.

DONALD

Rheba kind of fancied some candy, and—

(*His gaze is roaming the room.*)

oh, there it is.

(*He picks up* PENNY's *skull, if you know what we mean.*)

You-all don't want it, do you?

ALICE

No, Donald. Go right ahead.

DONALD

Thanks.

(*He feels that the occasion calls for certain amenities.*)

Have a nice evening?

ALICE

Yes, Donald.

DONALD

Nice dinner?

ALICE (*restraining herself*)

Yes, Donald.

DONALD

The ballet nice?

ALICE (*entirely too quietly*)

Yes, Donald.

DONALD (*summing it all up*)

That's nice.

(*He goes—and* ALICE *bursts forth.*)

ALICE

Now! Now do you see what I mean? Could you explain Donald to your father? Could you explain Grandpa? You couldn't, Tony, you couldn't! I should have known! I did know! I love you, Tony, but I love them too! And it's no use, Tony! It's no use!

(*She is weeping now in spite of herself.*)

TONY (*quietly*)

There's only one thing you've said that matters—that makes any sense at all. You love me.

ALICE

But, Tony, I know so well . . .

TONY

My darling, don't you think other people have had the same problem? Everybody's got a family.

ALICE (*through her tears*)

But not like mine.

TONY

That doesn't stop people who love each other. . . . Darling! Darling, won't you trust me, and go on loving me, and forget everything else?

ALICE

How can I?

TONY

Because nothing can keep us apart. You know that. You must know it. Just as I know it.

(*He takes her in his arms.*)

They want you to be happy, don't they? They *must*.

ALICE

Of course they do. But they can't change, Tony. I wouldn't want them to change.

TONY

They won't have to change. They're charming, lovable people, just as they are. You're worrying about something that may never come up.

ALICE

Oh, Tony, am I?

TONY

All that matters right now is that we love each other. That's right, isn't it?

ALICE (*whispering*)

Yes.

TONY

Well, then!

ALICE (*in his arms*)

Tony, Tony!

TONY

Now! I'd like to see a little gayety around here. Young gentleman calling, and getting engaged and everything.

ALICE (*smiling up into his face*)

What do I say?

TONY

Well, first you thank the young man for getting engaged to you.

ALICE

Thank you, Mr. Kirby, for getting engaged to me.

TONY

And then you tell him what it was about him that first took your girlish heart.

ALICE

The back of your head.

TONY

Huh?

ALICE

Uh-huh. It wasn't your charm, and it wasn't your money—it was the back of your head. I just happened to like it.

TONY

What happened when I turned around?

ALICE

Oh, I got used to it after a while.

TONY

I see . . . Oh, Alice, think of it. We're pretty lucky, aren't we?

ALICE

I know that *I* am. The luckiest girl in the world.

TONY

I'm not exactly unlucky myself.

ALICE

It's wonderful, isn't it?

TONY

Yes . . . Lord, but I'm happy.

ALICE

Are you, Tony?

TONY

Terribly . . . And now—good-night, my dear. Until tomorrow.

ALICE

Good-night.

TONY

Isn't it wonderful we work in the same office? Otherwise I'd be hanging around *here* all day.

ALICE

Won't it be funny in the office tomorrow—seeing each other and just going on as though nothing had happened?

TONY

Thank God I'm vice-president. I can dictate to you all day. "Dear Miss Sycamore: I love you, I love you, I love you."

ALICE

Oh, darling! You're such a fool.

TONY (*an arm about her as he starts toward the hallway*)

Why don't you meet me in the drugstore in the morning—before you go up to the office? I'll have millions of things to say to you by then.

ALICE

All right.

TONY

And then lunch, and then dinner tomorrow night.

ALICE

Oh, Tony! What will people say?

TONY

It's got to come out some time. In fact, if you know a good housetop, I'd like to do a little shouting.

(*She laughs—a happy little ripple. They are out of sight in the hallway by this time; their voices become inaudible.*)

(PAUL, *at this point, decides to call it a day down in the cellar. He comes through the door, followed by* MR. DE PINNA. *He is carrying a small metal container, filled with powder.*)

PAUL

Yes, sir, Mr. De Pinna, we did a good day's work.

DE PINNA

That's what. Five hundred Black Panthers, three hundred Willow Trees, and eight dozen Junior Kiddie Bombers.

(*Alice comes back from the hallway, still under the spell of her love.*)

PAUL

Why, hello, Alice. You just come in?

ALICE (*softly*)

No. No, I've been home quite a while.

PAUL

Have a nice evening? Say, I'd like to take a look at this new red fire we've got.

ALICE (*almost singing it*)

I had a beautiful evening, father.

PAUL

Will you turn out the lights, Mr. De Pinna? I want Alice to get the full effect.

ALICE (*who hasn't heard a word*)

What, father?

PAUL

Take a look at this new red fire. It's beautiful.

(MR. DE PINNA *switches the lights out;* PAUL *touches a match to the powder. The red fire blazes, shedding a soft glow over the room.*)

There! What do you think of it? Isn't it beautiful?

ALICE (*radiant; her face aglow, her voice soft*)

Yes, father. Everything is beautiful. It's the most beautiful red fire in the world!

(*She rushes to him and throws her arms about him, almost unable to bear her own happiness.*)

CURTAIN.

ACT TWO

A week later, and the family has just risen from the dinner table. Two or three of them have drifted out of the room, but GRANDPA *and* PAUL *still sit over their coffee cups.*

There is, however, a newcomer in the room. Her name is GAY WELLINGTON, *and, as we will presently guess, she is an actress, a nymphomaniac, and a terrible souse. At the moment she sits with a gin bottle in one hand and a glass in the other, and is having a darned good time. Hovering over her, script in hand, is a slightly worried* PENNY. ED *is watching the proceedings from somewhere in the vicinity of the printing press, and* DONALD, *leisurely clearing the table, has paused to see if* MISS WELLINGTON *can really swallow that one more drink of gin that she is about to tackle. She does, and another besides.*

PENNY *finally decides to make a try.*

PENNY

I'm ready to read the play now, Miss Wellington, if you are.

GAY WELLINGTON

Just a minute, dearie—just a minute. (*The gin again.*)

PENNY

The only thing is—I hope you won't mind my mentioning this, but—you don't drink when you're acting, do you, Miss Wellington? I'm just asking, of course.

GAY

I'm glad you brought it up. Once a play opens, I never touch a drop. Minute I enter a stage door, this bottle gets put away till intermission.

GRANDPA (*who plainly has his doubts*)

Have you been on the stage a long time, Miss Wellington?

GAY

All my life. I've played everything. Ever see "Peg o' My Heart?"

GRANDPA

Yes, indeed.

GAY (*with that fine logic for which the inebriated brain is celebrated*)

I saw it too. Great show.
(*She staggers backwards a bit, but recovers herself just in time.*)
My! Hot night, ain't it?

DONALD (*ever helpful*)

Want me to open a window, Miss Wellington?

GAY

No, the hell with the weather.
(*She takes a second look at the dusky* DONALD.)
Say, he's cute.
(RHEBA, *who has entered just in time to overhear this, gives* GAY *a look that tells her in no uncertain terms to keep out of Harlem on dark nights. Then she stalks back into the kitchen,* DONALD *close on her heels.*)

DONALD (*trying to explain it all*)

She's just acting, Rheba. She don't mean anything.

PENNY

Well, any time you're ready, we can go up to my room and start. I thought I'd read the play up in my room.

GAY

All right, dearie, just a minute.
(*She starts to pour one more drink, then suddenly her gaze becomes transfixed. She shakes her head as though to dislodge the image, then looks again, receives verification, and starts to pour the gin back into the bottle.*)
When I see snakes it's time to lay down.
(*She makes for a couch in the corner, and passes right out—cold.*)

PENNY

Oh, but those are real, Miss Wellington. They're Grandpa's. . . . I hope she's not going to—(*shaking her*) Miss Wellington! Miss Wellington!

ED

She's out like a light.

PAUL

Better let her sleep it off.

DONALD (*carrying the news into the kitchen*)

Rheba, Miss Wellington just passed out.
(*From the nether recesses we hear* RHEBA's *reaction—an emphatic "Good!"*)

PENNY

Do you think she'll be all right?

GRANDPA

Yes, but I wouldn't cast her in the religious play.

PENNY

Well, I suppose I'll just have to wait. I wonder if I shouldn't cover her up.

GRANDPA

Next time you meet an actress on the top of a bus, Penny, I think I'd *send* her the play, instead of bringing her home to read it.

ESSIE (*as* ED *starts in with the printing press*)

Ed, I wish you'd stop printing and take those Love Dreams around. They're out in the kitchen.

ED

I will. I just want to finish up these circulars.

ESSIE

Well, do that later, can't you? You've got to get back in time to play for me when Kolenkhov comes.

GRANDPA

Kolenkhov coming tonight?

ESSIE

Yes, tomorrow night's his night, but I had to change it on account of Alice.

GRANDPA

Oh! . . . Big doings around here tomorrow night, huh?

PENNY

Isn't it exciting? You know, I'm so nervous—you'd think it was me he was engaged to, instead of Alice.

ESSIE

What do you think they'll *be* like—his mother and father? . . . Ed, what are you doing *now*?

ED

Penny, did you see the new mask I made last night?
(*He reveals a new side of his character by suddenly holding a homemade mask before his face.*)
Guess who it is.

PENNY

Don't tell me now, Ed. Wait a minute . . . Cleopatra.

ED (*furious*)

It's Mrs. Roosevelt.
(*He goes into the kitchen.*)
(PAUL, *meanwhile, has gone to a table in the corner of the room, from which he now brings a steel-like boat model, two or three feet high, puts it down on the floor, and proceeds to sit down beside it. From a large cardboard box, which he has also brought with him, he proceeds to take out additional pieces of steel and fit them into the model.*)

PAUL

You know, the nice thing about these Erector Sets, you can make so many different things with them. Last week it was the Empire State Building.

GRANDPA

What is it this week?

PAUL

The Queen Mary.

PENNY (*looking it over*)

Hasn't got the right hat on.
(ED *comes in from the kitchen, bringing a pile of about a dozen candy boxes, neatly wrapped, and tied together for purposes of delivery.*)

ED (*as* MR. DE PINNA *comes in from the hall*)

Look. Mr. De Pinna, would you open the door and see if there's a man standing in front of the house?

ESSIE

Why, what for?

ED

Well, the last two days, when I've been out delivering, I think a man's been following me.

ESSIE

Ed, you're crazy.

ED

No, I'm not. He follows me, and he stands and watches the house.

DE PINNA

Really?
(*Striding out.*)
I'll take a look and see.

GRANDPA

I don't see what anybody would follow *you* for, Ed.

PENNY

Well, there's a lot of kidnapping going on, Grandpa.

GRANDPA

Yes, but not of Ed.

ED (*as* MR. DE PINNA *returns from the hall*)

Well? Did you see him?

DE PINNA

There's nobody out there at all.

ED

You're sure?

DE PINNA

Positive. I just saw him walk away.

ED

You see? I told you.

ESSIE

Oh, it might have been anybody, walking along the street. Ed, will you hurry and get back?

ED (*picking up his boxes*)

Oh, all right.

DE PINNA

Want to go down now, Mr. Sycamore, and finish packing up the fireworks?

PAUL (*putting the Queen Mary back on the table*)

Yeh, we've got to take the stuff up to Mt. Vernon in the morning.
(*They go into the cellar. Simultaneously the voice of* ALICE, *happily singing, is heard as she descends the stairs.*)

ALICE

Mother, may I borrow some paper? I'm making out a list for Rheba tomorrow night.

PENNY

Yes, dear. Here's some.

ALICE (*as she sights* MISS WELLINGTON)

Why, what happened to your actress friend? Is she giving a performance?

PENNY

No, she's not acting, Alice. She's really drunk.

ALICE

Essie, you're going to give Rheba the kitchen all day tomorrow, aren't you? Because she'll need it.

ESSIE

Of course, Alice. I'm going to start some Love Dreams now, so I'll be 'way ahead.
(*She goes into the kitchen.*)

ALICE

Thanks, dear . . . Look, mother, I'm coming home at three o'clock tomorrow. Will you have everything down in the cellar by that time? The typewriter, and the snakes, and the xylophone, and the printing press . . .

GRANDPA

And Miss Wellington.

ALICE

And Miss Wellington. That'll give me time to arrange the table, and fix the flowers.

GRANDPA

The Kirbys are certainly going to get the wrong impression of this house.

ALICE

You'll *do* all that, won't you, mother?

PENNY

Of course, dear.

ALICE

And I think we'd better have cocktails ready by seven-fifteen, in case they happen to come a little early. . . . I wonder if I ought to let Rheba cook the dinner. What do you think, Grandpa?

GRANDPA

Now, Alice, I wouldn't worry. From what I've seen of the boy I'm sure the Kirbys are very nice people, and if everything isn't so elaborate tomorrow night, it's all right too.

ALICE

Darling, I'm not trying to impress them, or pretend we're anything that we aren't. I just want everything to—to go off well.

GRANDPA

No reason why it shouldn't, Alice.

PENNY

We're all going to do everything we can to make it a nice party.

ALICE

Oh, my darlings, I love you. You're the most wonderful family in the world, and

I'm the happiest girl in the world. I didn't know anyone could *be* so happy. He's so wonderful, Grandpa. Why, just seeing him —you don't know what it does to me.

GRANDPA

Just seeing him. Just seeing him for lunch, and dinner, and until four o'clock in the morning, and at nine o'clock *next* morning you're at the office again and there he is. You just see him, huh?

ALICE

I don't care! I'm in love!
(*She swings open the kitchen door.*)
Rheba! Rheba!
(*She goes into the kitchen.*)

GRANDPA

Nice, isn't it? Nice to see her so happy.

PENNY

I remember when I was engaged to Paul —how happy I was. And you know, I still feel that way.

GRANDPA

I know . . . Nice the way Ed and Essie get along too, isn't it?

PENNY

And Donald and Rheba, even though they're *not* married. . . . Do you suppose Mr. De Pinna will ever marry anyone, Grandpa?

GRANDPA (*a gesture toward the couch*)
Well, there's Miss Wellington.

PENNY

Oh, dear, I *wish* she'd wake up. If we're going to read the play tonight—
(MR. DE PINNA *comes up from the cellar, bringing along a rather large-sized un-framed painting.*)

DE PINNA

Mrs. Sycamore, look what I found!
(*He turns the canvas around, revealing a portrait of a somewhat lumpy discus thrower, in Roman costume—or was it Greek?*)
Remember?

PENNY

Why, of course. It's my painting of you as The Discus Thrower. Look, Grandpa.

GRANDPA

I remember it. Say, you've gotten a little bald, haven't you, Mr. De Pinna?

DE PINNA (*running a hand over his completely hairless head*)
Is it very noticeable?

PENNY

Well, it was a long time ago—just before I stopped painting. Let me see—that's eight years.

DE PINNA

Too bad you never finished it, Mrs. Sycamore.

PENNY

I always meant to finish it, Mr. De Pinna, but I just started to write a play one day and that was that. I never painted again.

GRANDPA

Just as well, too. *I* was going to have to strip next.

DE PINNA (*meditatively*)
Who would have thought, that day I came to deliver the ice, that I was going to stay here for eight years?

GRANDPA

The milkman was here for five, just ahead of you.

DE PINNA

Why did he leave, anyhow? I forget.

GRANDPA

He didn't leave. He died.

PENNY

He was such a nice man. Remember the funeral, Grandpa? We never knew his name and it was kind of hard to get a certificate.

GRANDPA

What was the name we finally made up for him?

PENNY

Martin Vanderhof. We gave him *your* name.

GRANDPA

Oh, yes, I remember.

PENNY

It was a lovely thought, because otherwise he never would have got all those flowers.

GRANDPA

Certainly was. And it didn't hurt *me* any. Not bothered with mail any more, and I haven't had a telephone call from that day to this.
(*He catches an unwary fly and drops it casually into the snake solarium.*)

PENNY

Yes, it was really a wonderful idea.

DE PINNA (*with the picture*)

I wish you'd finish this sometime, Mrs. Sycamore. I'd kind of like to have it.

PENNY

You know what, Mr. De Pinna? I think I'll do some work on it. Right tonight.

DE PINNA

Say! Will you?
(*The door bell rings.*)

PENNY (*peering at the prostrate* GAY)

I don't think she's going to wake up anyhow. . . . Look, Mr. De Pinna! You go down in the cellar and bring up the easel and get into your costume. Is it still down there?

DE PINNA (*excited*)

I think so!
(*He darts into the cellar.*)

PENNY

Now, where did I put my palette and brushes?
(*She dashes up the stairs as the voice of* KOLENKHOV *is heard at the door, booming, of course.*)

KOLENKHOV

Rhebishka! My little Rhebishka!

RHEBA (*delighted, as usual*)

Yassuh, Mr. Kolenkhov!

PENNY (*as she goes up the stairs*)

Hello, Mr. Kolenkhov. Essie's in the kitchen.

KOLENKHOV

Madame Sycamore, I greet you!
(*His great arm again encircling* RHEBA, *he drags her protestingly into the room.*)
Tell me, Grandpa—what should I do about Rhebishka! I keep telling her she would make a great toe dancer, but she laughs only!

RHEBA (*breaking away*)

No, suh! I couldn't get up on my toes, Mr. Kolenkhov! I got corns!
(*She goes into the kitchen.*)

KOLENKHOV (*calling after her*)

Rhebishka, you could wear diamonds!
(*Suddenly he sights the portrait of* MR. DE PINNA.)
What is that?

GRANDPA (*who has taken up his stamp album again*)

It's a picture of Mr. De Pinna. Penny painted it.

KOLENKHOV (*summing it up*)

It stinks.

GRANDPA

I know.
(*He indicates the figure on the couch.*)
How do you like that?

KOLENKHOV (*peering over*)

What is *that*?

GRANDPA

She's an actress. Friend of Penny's.

KOLENKHOV

She is drunk—no?

GRANDPA

She is drunk—yes. . . . How are *you,* Kolenkhov?

KOLENKHOV

Magnificent! Life is chasing around inside of me, like a squirrel.

GRANDPA

'Tis, huh? . . . What's new in Russia? Any more letters from your friend in Moscow?

KOLENKHOV

I have just heard from him. I saved for you the stamp.
(*He hands it over.*)

GRANDPA (*receiving it with delight*)

Thanks, Kolenkhov.

KOLENKHOV

They have sent him to Siberia.

GRANDPA

That so? How's he like it?

KOLENKHOV

He has escaped. He has escaped and gone back to Moscow. He will get them yet, if they do not get him. The Soviet Government! I could take the whole Soviet Government and—grrh!
(*He crushes Stalin and all in one great paw, just as* ESSIE *comes in from the kitchen.*)

ESSIE

I'm sorry I'm late, Mr. Kolenkhov. I'll get into my dancing clothes right away.

KOLENKHOV

Tonight you will really work, Pavlowa.
(*As* ESSIE *goes up the stairs.*)
Tonight we will take something new.

GRANDPA

Essie making any progress, Kolenkhov?

KOLENKHOV (*first making elaborately sure that* ESSIE *is gone*)

Confidentially, she stinks.

GRANDPA

Well, as long as she's having fun. . . .
(DONALD *ambles in from the kitchen, chuckling.*)

DONALD

You sure do tickle Rheba, Mr. Kolenkhov. She's laughing her head off out there.

KOLENKHOV

She is a great woman. . . . Donald, what do you think of the Soviet Government?

DONALD

The what, Mr. Kolenkhov?

KOLENKHOV

I withdraw the question. What do you think of *this* Government?

DONALD

Oh, I like it fine. I'm on relief, you know.

KOLENKHOV

Oh, yes. And you like it?

DONALD

Yassuh, it's fine. Only thing is you got to go round to the place every week and collect it, and sometimes you got to stand in line pretty near half an hour. Government ought to be run better than that—don't you think, Grandpa?

GRANDPA (*as he fishes an envelope out of his pocket*)

Government ought to stop sending me letters. Want me to be at the United States Marshal's office Tuesday morning at ten o'clock.

KOLENKHOV (*peering at the letter*)

Ah! Income tax! They have got you, Grandpa.

GRANDPA

Mm. I'm supposed to give 'em a lot of money so as to keep Donald on relief.

DONALD

You don't say, Grandpa? You going to pay it now?

GRANDPA

That's what they want.

DONALD

You mean I can come right *here* and get it instead of standing in that line?

GRANDPA

No, Donald. You will have to waste a full half hour of your time every week.

DONALD

Well, I don't like it. It breaks up my week.

(*He goes into the kitchen.*)

KOLENKHOV

He should have been in Russia when the Revolution came. Then he would have stood in line—a bread line.

(*He turns to* GRANDPA.)

Ah, Grandpa, what they have done to Russia. Think of it! The Grand Duchess Olga Katrina, a cousin of the Czar, she is a waitress in Childs' restaurant! I ordered baked beans from her only yesterday. It broke my heart. A crazy world, Grandpa.

GRANDPA

Oh, the world's not so crazy, Kolenkhov. It's the people *in* it. Life's pretty simple if you just relax.

KOLENKHOV

How can you relax in times like these?

GRANDPA

. Well, if they'd relaxed there wouldn't *be* times like these. That's just my point. Life is simple and kind of beautiful if you let it come to you. But the trouble is, people forget that. I know I did. I was right in the thick of it—fighting, and scratching and clawing. Regular jungle. One day it just kind of struck me. I wasn't having any fun.

KOLENKHOV

So you did what?

GRANDPA

Just relaxed. Thirty-five years ago, that was. And I've been a happy man ever since.

(*From somewhere or other* GRANDPA *has brought one of those colored targets that one buys at Schwartz's. He now hangs it up on the cellar door, picks up a handful of feathered darts, and carefully throws one at the target.*)

(*At the same time* ALICE *passes through the room, en route from kitchen to the upstairs region.*)

ALICE

Good evening, Mr. Kolenkhov.

KOLENKHOV (*bowing low over her hand*)

Ah, Miss Alice! I have not seen you to present my congratulations. May you be very happy and have many children. That is my prayer for you.

ALICE

Thank you, Mr. Kolenkhov. That's quite a thought.

(*Singing gayly, she goes up the stairs.*)

KOLENKHOV (*looking after her*)

Ah, love! That is all that is left in the world, Grandpa.

GRANDPA

Yes, but there's plenty of that.

KOLENKHOV

And soon Stalin will take that away, too. I tell you, Grandpa—

(*He stops as* PENNY *comes down the stairs—a living example of what the well-dressed artist should wear. She has on an artist's smock over her dress, a flowing black tie, and a large black velvet tam-o'-shanter, worn at a rakish angle. She carries a palette and an assortment of paints and brushes.*)

PENNY

Seems so nice to get into my art things again. They still look all right, don't they, Grandpa?

GRANDPA

Yes, indeed.

KOLENKHOV

You are a breath of Paris, Madame Sycamore.

PENNY

Oh, thank you, Mr. Kolenkhov.

DONALD (*coming in from the kitchen*)

I didn't know you was working for the WPA.

PENNY

Oh, no, Donald. You see, I used to paint all the time, and then one day—

(*The outer door slams and* ED *comes in.*)

ED (*in considerable excitement*)

It happened again! There was a fellow following me every place I went!

PENNY

Nonsense, Ed. It's your imagination.

ED

No, it isn't. It happens every time I go out to deliver candy.

GRANDPA

Maybe he wants a piece of candy.

ED

It's all right for you to laugh, Grandpa, but he keeps following me.

KOLENKHOV (*somberly*)

You do not know what following is. In Russia *everybody* is followed. I was followed right out of Russia.

PENNY

Of course. You see, Ed—the whole thing is just imagination.

(MR. DE PINNA *comes up from the cellar, ready for posing. He wears the traditional Roman costume, and he certainly cuts a figure. He is carrying* PENNY's *easel, a discus, and a small platform for posing purposes.*)

Ah, here we are! . . . Right here, Mr. De Pinna.

DONALD (*suddenly getting it*)

Oh, is that picture supposed to be Mr. De Pinna?

PENNY (*sharply*)

Of course it is, Donald. What's it look like—me?

DONALD (*studying the portrait*)

Yes, it does—a little bit.

PENNY

Nonsense! What would I be doing with a discus?

KOLENKHOV

Ed, for tonight's lesson we use the first movement of Scheherazade.

ED

Okay.

DE PINNA (*about to mount the platform*)

I hope I haven't forgotten how to pose.

(*He takes up the discus and strikes the classic pose of the Discus Thrower. Somehow, it is not quite convincing.*)

DONALD

What's he going to do with that thing? Throw it?

PENNY

No, no, Donald. He's just posing. . . . Mr. De Pinna, has something happened to your figure during these eight years?

DE PINNA (*pulling in his stomach*)

No, I don't think it's any different.

(*With a sudden snort,* GAY WELLINGTON *comes to.*)

PENNY (*immediately alert*)

Yes, Miss Wellington?

(*For answer,* GAY *peers first at* PENNY, *then at* MR. DE PINNA. *Then, with a strange snort, she just passes right out again.*)

PENNY

Oh, dear.

(ESSIE *comes tripping down the stairs—very much the ballet dancer. She is in full costume—ballet skirt, tight white satin bodice, a garland of roses in her hair.*)

ESSIE

Sorry, Mr. Kolenkhov, I couldn't find my slippers.

KOLENKHOV

(*Having previously removed his coat, he now takes off his shirt, displaying an enormous hairy chest beneath his undershirt.*)

We have a hot night for it, my Pavlowa, but art is only achieved through perspiration.

PENNY

Why, that's wonderful, Mr. Kolenkhov. Did you hear that, Grandpa—art is only achieved through perspiration.

GRANDPA

Yes, but it helps if you've got a little talent with it.

(*He returns to his dart throwing.*)
Only made two bull's-eyes last night.
Got to do better than that.
(*He hurls a dart at the board, then his
eye travels to* MISS WELLINGTON, *whose
posterior offers an even easier target.*)
Mind if I use Miss Wellington, Penny?

PENNY

What, Grandpa?

GRANDPA

(*Shakes his head.*)
Never mind. . . . Too easy.
(GRANDPA *throws another dart at the
target.*)

KOLENKHOV

You are ready? We begin!
(*With a gesture he orders the music
started; under* KOLENKHOV'S *critical eye*
ESSIE *begins the mazes of the dance.*)
Foutte temp el levee.
(ESSIE *obliges with her own idea of
foutte temp el levee.*)
Pirouette! . . . Come, come! You can
do that! It's eight years now. Pirouette!
. . . At last! . . . Entre chat! . . . Entre
chat!
(ESSIE *leaps into the air, her feet twirl-
ing.*)
No, Grandpa, you cannot relax with
Stalin in Russia. The Czar relaxed, and
what happened to *him*?

GRANDPA

He was too late.

ESSIE (*still leaping away*)
Mr. Kolenkhov! Mr. Kolenkhov!

KOLENKHOV

If he had not relaxed the Grand Duchess
Olga Katrina would not be selling baked
beans today.

ESSIE (*imploringly*)
Mr. Kolenkhov!

KOLENKHOV

I am sorry.
(*The door bell rings.*)
We go back to the pirouette.

PENNY

Could you pull in your stomach, Mr.
De Pinna? . . . That's right.

KOLENKHOV

A little freer. A little freer with the
hands. The whole body must work. Ed,
help us with the music. The music must
be free, too.
(*By way of guiding* ED, KOLENKHOV
*hums the music at the pace that it should
go. He is even pirouetting a bit himself.*)
(*From the front door comes the murmur of voices, not quite audible over the
music. Then the stunned figure of* RHEBA
comes into the archway, her eyes popping.)

RHEBA

Mrs. Sycamore. . . . Mrs. Sycamore.
(*With a gesture that has a grim foreboding in it, she motions toward the still
invisible reason for her panic.*)
(*There is a second's pause, and then the
reason is revealed in all its horror. The
KIRBYS, in full evening dress, stand in the
archway. All three of them.* MR. AND MRS.
KIRBY, *and* TONY.)
(PENNY *utters a stifled gasp; the others
are too stunned even to do that. Their surprise at seeing the* KIRBYS, *however, is no
greater than that of the* KIRBYS *at the sight
that is spread before them.*)
(GRANDPA, *alone of them all, rises to the
situation. With a kind of old world grace,
he puts away his darts and makes the
guests welcome.*)

GRANDPA

How do you do?

KIRBY (*uncertainly*)
How do you do?
(*Not that it helps any, but* MR. DE PINNA
is squirming into his bathrobe, KOLENKHOV
is thrusting his shirt into his trousers, and
ED *is hastily getting into his coat.*)

TONY

Are we too early?

GRANDPA

No, no. It's perfectly all right—we're
glad to see you.

PENNY (*getting rid of the smock and tam*)

Why—yes. Only—we thought it was to
be tomorrow night.

MRS. KIRBY

Tomorrow night!

KIRBY

What!

GRANDPA

Now, it's perfectly all right. Please sit
right down and make yourselves at home.
(*His eyes still on the* KIRBYS, *he gives*
DONALD *a good push toward the kitchen,
by way of a hint.* DONALD *goes, promptly,
with a quick little stunned whistle that
sums up HIS feelings.*)

KIRBY

Tony, how could you possibly—

TONY

I—I don't know. I thought—

MRS. KIRBY

Really, Tony! This is most embarrassing.

GRANDPA

Not at all. Why, we weren't doing a
thing.

PENNY

Just spending the evening at home.

GRANDPA

That's all. . . . Now don't let it bother
you. This is Alice's mother, Mrs. Sycamore
. . . Alice's sister, Mrs. Carmichael. . . .
Mr. Carmichael. . . . Mr. Kolenkhov. . . .
(*At this point* MR. DE PINNA *takes an
anticipatory step forward, and* GRANDPA *is
practically compelled to perform the introduction.*)
And—Mr. De Pinna. Mr. De Pinna,
would you tell Mr. Sycamore to come right
up? Tell him that Mr. and Mrs. Kirby are
here.

PENNY (*her voice a heavy whisper*)

And be sure to put his pants on.

DE PINNA (*whispering right back*)

All right. . . . Excuse me.
(*He vanishes—discus and all.*)

GRANDPA

Won't you sit down?

PENNY (*first frantically trying to cover the
prostrate* GAY WELLINGTON)

I'll tell Alice that you're—
(*She is at the foot of the stairs.*)
—Alice! Alice, dear!
(*The voice of* ALICE *from above, "What
is it?"*)
Alice, will you come down, dear? We've
got a surprise for you.
(*She comes back into the room, sum-
moning all her charm.*)
Well!

GRANDPA

Mrs. Kirby, may I take your wrap?

MRS. KIRBY

Well—thank you. If you're perfectly
sure that we're not—
(*Suddenly she sees the snakes and lets
out a scream.*)

GRANDPA

Oh, don't be alarmed, Mrs. Kirby.
They're perfectly harmless.

MRS. KIRBY (*edging away from the
solarium*)

Thank you.
(*She sinks into a chair, weakly.*)

GRANDPA

Ed, take 'em into the kitchen.
(ED *at once obeys.*)

PENNY

Of course we're so used to them around
the house—

MRS. KIRBY

I'm sorry to trouble you, but snakes
happen to be the one thing—

KIRBY

I feel very uncomfortable about this.
Tony, how could you have done such a
thing?

TONY

I'm sorry, Dad. I thought it was tonight.

KIRBY

It was very careless of you. *Very!*

GRANDPA

Now, now, Mr. Kirby—we're delighted.

PENNY

Oh, now, anybody can get mixed up, Mr. Kirby.

GRANDPA

Penny, how about some dinner for these folks? They've come for dinner, you know.

MRS. KIRBY

Oh, please don't bother. We're really not hungry at all.

PENNY

But it's not a bit of bother. Ed!—
(*Her voice drops to a loud whisper.*)
Ed, tell Donald to run down to the A. and P. and get half a dozen bottles of beer, and—ah—some canned salmon—
(*Her voice comes up again.*)
—do you like canned salmon, Mr. Kirby?

KIRBY

Please don't trouble, Mrs. Sycamore. I have a little indigestion, anyway.

PENNY

Oh, I'm sorry . . . How about you, Mrs. Kirby? Do you like canned salmon?

MRS. KIRBY (*you just know that she hates it*)

Oh, I'm very fond of it.

PENNY

You can have frankfurters if you'd rather.

MRS. KIRBY (*regally*)

Either one will do.

PENNY (*to* ED *again*)

Well, make it frankfurters, and some canned corn, and Campbell's Soup.

ED (*going out the kitchen door*)

Okay!

PENNY (*calling after him*)

And tell him to hurry!
(PENNY *again addresses the* KIRBYS.)
The A. and P. is just at the corner, and frankfurters don't take *any* time to boil.

GRANDPA (*as* PAUL *comes through the cellar door*)

And this is Alice's father, *Mr.* Sycamore. Mr. and Mrs. Kirby.

THE KIRBYS

How do you do?

PAUL

I hope you'll forgive my appearance.

PENNY

This is Mr. Sycamore's busiest time of the year. Just before the Fourth of July—
(*And then* ALICE *comes down. She is a step into the room before she realizes what has happened; then she fairly freezes in her tracks.*)

ALICE

Oh!

TONY

Darling, will you ever forgive me? I'm the most dull-witted person in the world. I thought it was tonight.

ALICE (*staggered*)

Why, Tony, I thought you—
(*To the* KIRBYS.)
—I'm so sorry—I can't imagine—why, I wasn't—have you all met each other?

KIRBY

Yes, indeed.

MRS. KIRBY

How do you do, Alice?

ALICE (*not even yet in control of herself*)

How do you do, Mrs. Kirby? I'm afraid I'm not very—presentable.

TONY

Darling, you look lovely.

KIRBY

Of course she does. Don't let this upset you, my dear—we've all just met each other a night sooner, that's all.

MRS. KIRBY

Of course.

ALICE

But I was planning such a nice party tomorrow night . . .

KIRBY (*being the good fellow*)

Well, we'll come again tomorrow night.

TONY

There you are, Alice. Am I forgiven?

ALICE

I guess so. It's just that I—we'd better see about getting you some dinner.

PENNY

Oh, that's all done, Alice. That's all been attended to.
(DONALD, *hat in hand, comes through the kitchen door; hurries across the room and out the front way. The* KIRBYS *graciously pretend not to see.*)

ALICE

But mother—what are you—what did you send out for? Because Mr. Kirby suffers from indigestion—he can only eat certain things.

KIRBY

Now, it's quite all right.

TONY

Of course it is, darling.

KIRBY

I asked him what he wanted, Alice.

ALICE (*doubtfully*)

Yes, but—

KIRBY

Now, now, it's not as serious as all that. Just because I have a little indigestion.

KOLENKHOV (*helping things along*)

Perhaps it is not indigestion at all, Mr. Kirby. Perhaps you have stomach ulcers.

ALICE

Don't be absurd, Mr. Kolenkhov!

GRANDPA

You mustn't mind Mr. Kolenkhov, Mr. Kirby. He's a Russian, and Russians are inclined to look on the dark side.

KOLENKHOV

All right, I am a Russian. But a friend of mine, a Russian, *died* from stomach ulcers.

KIRBY

Really, I—

ALICE (*desperately*)

Please, Mr. Kolenkhov! Mr. Kirby has indigestion and that's all.

KOLENKHOV (*with a Russian shrug of the shoulders*)

All right. Let him wait.

GRANDPA (*leaping into the breach*)

Tell me, Mr. Kirby, how do you find business conditions? Are we pretty well out of the depression?

KIRBY

What? . . . Yes, yes, I think so. Of course, it all depends.

GRANDPA

But you figure that things are going to keep on improving?

KIRBY

Broadly speaking, yes. As a matter of fact, industry is now operating at sixty-four per cent. of full capacity, as against eighty-two per cent. in 1925. Of course in 1929, a peak year—
(*Peak year or no peak year,* GAY WELLINGTON *chooses this moment to come to life. With a series of assorted snorts, she throws the cover back and pulls herself to a sitting position, blinking uncertainly at the assemblage. Then she rises, and weaves unsteadily across the room. The imposing figure of* MR. KIRBY *intrigues her.*)

GAY (*playfully rumpling* MR. KIRBY's *hair as she passes him*)

Hello, Cutie.
(*And with that she lunges on her way —up the stairs.*)
(*The* KIRBYS, *of course, are considerably astounded by this exhibition; the* SYCAMORES *have watched it with varying degrees of frozen horror.* ALICE, *in particular, is speechless; it is* GRANDPA *who comes to her rescue.*)

GRANDPA

That may seem a little strange to you, but she's not quite accountable for her actions. A friend of Mrs. Sycamore's. She came to dinner and was overcome by the heat.

PENNY

Yes, some people feel it, you know, more than others. Perhaps I'd better see if she's all right. Excuse me, please.
(*She goes hastily up the stairs.*)

ALICE

It *is* awfully hot.
(*A fractional pause.*)
You usually escape all this hot weather, don't you, Mrs. Kirby? Up in Maine?

MRS. KIRBY (*on the frigid side*)

As a rule. I had to come down this week, however, for the Flower Show.

TONY

Mother wouldn't miss that for the world. That blue ribbon is the high spot of her year.

ESSIE

I won a ribbon at a Flower Show once. For raising onions. Remember?

ALICE (*quickly*)

That was a Garden Show, Essie.

ESSIE

Oh, yes.
(PENNY *comes bustling down the stairs again.*)

PENNY

I'm so sorry, but I think she'll be all right now. . . . Has Donald come back yet?

ALICE

No, he hasn't.

PENNY

Well, he'll be right back, and it won't take any time at all. I'm afraid you must be starved.

KIRBY

Oh, no. Quite all right.
(*Pacing the room, he suddenly comes upon* PAUL's *Erector Set.*)
Hello! What's this? I didn't know there were little children in the house.

PAUL

Oh, no. That's mine.

KIRBY

Really? Well, I suppose every man has his hobby. Or do you use this as a model of some kind?

PAUL

No, I just play with it.

KIRBY

I see.

TONY

Maybe you'd be better off if *you* had a hobby like that, Dad. Instead of raising orchids.

KIRBY (*indulgently*)

Yes, I wouldn't be surprised.

ALICE (*leaping on this as a safe topic*)

Oh, *do* tell us about your orchids, Mr. Kirby.
(*She addresses the others.*)
You know, they take six years before they blossom. Think of that!

KIRBY

(*Warming to his subject.*)
Oh, some of them take longer than that. I've got one coming along now that I've waited ten years for.

PENNY

(*Making a joke.*)
Believe it or not, I was waiting for an orchid.

KIRBY

Ah—yes. Of course during that time they require the most scrupulous care. I remember a bulb that I was very fond of—
(DONALD *suddenly bulges through the archway, his arms full. The tops of beer*

bottles and two or three large cucumbers peep over the edge of the huge paper bags.)

PENNY

Ah, here we are! Did you get everything, Donald?

DONALD

Yes'm. Only the frankfurters didn't look very good, so I got pickled pigs' feet.
(MR. KIRBY *blanches at the very idea.*)

ALICE (*taking command*)

Never mind, Donald—just bring everything into the kitchen.
(*She turns at the kitchen door.*)
Mr. Kirby, please tell them *all* about the orchids—I know they'd love to hear it. And—excuse me.
(*She goes.*)

GRANDPA

Kind of an expensive hobby, isn't it, Mr. Kirby—raising orchids?

KIRBY

Yes, it is, but I feel that if a hobby gives one sufficient pleasure, it's never expensive.

GRANDPA

That's very true.

KIRBY

You see, I need something to relieve the daily nerve strain. After a week in Wall Street I'd go crazy if I didn't have something like that. Lot of men I know have yachts—just for that very reason.

GRANDPA (*mildly*)

Why don't they give up Wall Street?

KIRBY

How's that?

GRANDPA

I was just joking.

MRS. KIRBY

I think it's necessary for everyone to have a hobby. Of course it's more to me than a hobby, but my great solace is—spiritualism.

PENNY

Now, Mrs. Kirby, don't tell me you fell for that. Why, everybody knows it's a fake.

MRS. KIRBY (*freezing*)

To me, Mrs. Sycamore, spiritualism is—I would rather not discuss it, Mrs. Sycamore.

PAUL

Remember, Penny, you've got one or two hobbies of your own.

PENNY

Yes, but not silly ones.

GRANDPA (*with a little cough*)

I don't think it matters what the hobby is—the important thing is to have one.

KOLENKHOV

To be ideal, a hobby should improve the body as well as the mind. The Romans were a great people! Why! What was their hobby? Wrestling. In wrestling you have to think quick with the mind and act quick with the body.

KIRBY

Yes, but I'm afraid wrestling is not very practical for most of us.
(*He gives a deprecating little laugh.*)
I wouldn't make a very good showing as a wrestler.

KOLENKHOV

You could be a *great* wrestler. You are built for it. Look!
(*With a startlingly quick movement* KOLENKHOV *grabs* MR. KIRBY'S *arms, knocks his legs from under him with a quick movement of a foot, and presto!* MR. KIRBY *is flat on his whatsis. Not only that, but instantaneously* KOLENKHOV *is on top of him.*)
(*Just at this moment* ALICE *re-enters the room—naturally, she stands petrified. Several people, of course, rush immediately to the rescue,* TONY *and* PAUL *arriving at the scene of battle first. Amidst the general confusion they help* MR. KIRBY *to his feet.*)

ALICE

Mr. Kirby! Are you—hurt?

TONY

Are you all right, Father?

KIRBY (*pulling himself together*)

I—I—uh—
(*He blinks, uncertainly.*)
—where are my glasses?

ALICE

Here they are, Mr. Kirby. . . . Oh, Mr. Kirby, they're broken.

KOLENKHOV (*full of apology*)

Oh, I am sorry. But when you wrestle again, Mr. Kirby, you will of course not wear glasses.

KIRBY (*coldly furious*)

I do not intend to wrestle again, Mr. Kolenkhov.
(*He draws himself up, stiffly, and in return gets a sharp pain in the back. He gives a little gasp.*)

TONY

Better sit down, Father.

ALICE

Mr. Kolenkhov, how could you do such a thing? Why didn't somebody stop him?

MRS. KIRBY

I think, if you don't mind, perhaps we had better be going.

TONY

Mother!

ALICE (*close to tears*)

Oh, Mrs. Kirby—please! Please don't go! Mr. Kirby—please! I—I've ordered some scrambled eggs for you, and—plain salad—Oh, please don't go!

KOLENKHOV

I am sorry if I did something wrong. And I apologize.

ALICE

I can't tell you how sorry I am, Mr. Kirby. If I'd been here—

KIRBY (*from a great height*)

That's quite all right.

TONY

Of course it is. It's all right, Alice. We're not going.
(*The* KIRBYS *reluctantly sit down again.*)
(*A moment's silence—no one knows quite what to say.*)

PENNY (*brightly*)

Well! That was exciting for a minute, wasn't it?

GRANDPA (*quickly*)

You were talking about your orchids, Mr. Kirby. Do you raise many different varieties?

KIRBY (*still unbending*)

I'm afraid I've quite forgotten about my orchids.
(*More silence, and everyone very uncomfortable.*)

ALICE

I'm—awfully sorry, Mr. Kirby.

KOLENKHOV (*exploding*)

What did I do that was so terrible? I threw him on the floor! Did it kill him?

ALICE

Please, Mr. Kolenkhov.
(*An annoyed gesture from* KOLENKHOV; *another general pause.*)

PENNY

I'm sure dinner won't be any time at all now.
(*A pained smile from* MRS. KIRBY.)

ESSIE

Would you like some candy while you're waiting? I've got some freshly made.

KIRBY

My doctor does not permit me to eat candy. Thank you.

ESSIE

But these are nothing, Mr. Kirby. Just cocoanut and marshmallow fudge.

ALICE

Don't, Essie.
(*RHEBA appears in the kitchen doorway, beckoning violently to* ALICE.)

RHEBA (*in a loud whisper*)

Miss Alice! Miss Alice!
(ALICE *quickly flies to* RHEBA'S *side.*)
The eggs fell down the sink.

ALICE (*desperately*)

Make some more! Quick!

RHEBA

I ain't got any.

ALICE

Send out for some!

RHEBA (*disappearing*)

All right.

ALICE (*calling after her*)

Tell him to run!
(*She turns back to the* KIRBYS.)
I'm so sorry. There'll be a little delay,
but everything will be ready in just a
minute.
(*At this moment* DONALD *fairly shoots
out of the kitchen door and across the
living room, beating the Olympic record
for all time.*)
(PENNY *tries to ease the situation with a
gay little laugh. It doesn't quite come off,
however.*)

TONY

I've certainly put you people to a lot of
trouble, with my stupidity.

GRANDPA

Not at all, Tony.

PENNY

Look! Why don't we all play a game of
some sort while we're waiting?

TONY

Oh, that'd be fine.

ALICE

Mother, I don't think Mr. and Mrs.
Kirby—

KOLENKHOV

I have an idea. I know a wonderful trick
with a glass of water.
(*He reaches for a full glass that stands
on the table.*)

ALICE (*quickly*)

No, Mr. Kolenkhov.

GRANDPA (*shaking his head*)

No-o.

PENNY

But I'm sure Mr. and Mrs. Kirby would
love this game. It's perfectly harmless.

ALICE

Please, mother. . . .

KIRBY

I'm not very good at games, Mrs. Sycamore.

PENNY

Oh, but *any* fool could play this game,
Mr. Kirby. (*She is bustling around, getting paper and pencil.*) All you do is write
your name on a piece of paper—

ALICE

But mother, Mr. Kirby doesn't want—

PENNY

Oh, he'll love it! (*Going right on*) Here
you are, Mr. Kirby. Write your name on
this piece of paper. And Mrs. Kirby, you
do the same on this one.

ALICE

Mother, what *is* this game?

PENNY

I used to play it at school. It's called
Forget-Me-Not. Now, I'm going to call out
five words—just anything at all—and as
I say each word, you're to put down the
first thing that comes into your mind. Is
that clear? For instance, if I say "grass,"
you might put down "green"—just whatever you think of, see? Or if I call out
"chair," you might put down "table." It
shows the reactions people have to different
things. You see how simple it is, Mr.
Kirby?

TONY

Come on, father! Be a sport!

KIRBY (*stiffly*)

Very well. I shall be happy to play it.

PENNY

You see, Alice? He *does* want to play.

ALICE (*uneasily*)

Well—

PENNY

Now, then! Are we ready?

KOLENKHOV

Ready!

PENNY

Now, remember—you must play fair. Put down the first thing that comes into your mind.

KIRBY (*pencil poised*)

I understand.

PENNY

Everybody ready? . . . The first word is "potatoes." (*she repeats it*) "Potatoes." . . . Ready for the next one? . . . "Bathroom." (ALICE *shifts rather uneasily, but seeing that no one else seems to mind, she relaxes again.*) Got that?

KOLENKHOV

Go ahead.

PENNY

All ready? . . . "Lust."

ALICE

Mother, this is not exactly what you—

PENNY

Nonsense, Alice—that word's all right.

ALICE

Mother, it's *not* all right.

MRS. KIRBY (*unexpectedly*)

Oh, I don't know. It seems to me that's a perfectly fair word.

PENNY (*to* ALICE)

You see? Now, you mustn't interrupt the game.

KIRBY

May I have that last word again, please?

PENNY

"Lust," Mr. Kirby.

KIRBY (*writing*)

I've got it.

GRANDPA

This is quite a game.

PENNY

Sssh, Grandpa. . . . All ready? . . . "Honeymoon." (ESSIE *snickers a little, which is all it takes to start* PENNY *off. Then she suddenly remembers herself.*) Now, Essie! . . . All right. The last word is "sex."

ALICE (*under her breath*)

Mother!

PENNY

Everybody got "sex"? . . . All right— now give me all the papers.

GRANDPA

What happens now?

PENNY

Oh, this is the best part. Now I read out your reactions.

KIRBY

I see. It's really quite an interesting game.

PENNY

I knew you'd like it. I'll read your paper first, Mr. Kirby. (*To the others.*) I'm going to read Mr. Kirby's paper first. Listen, everybody! This is Mr. Kirby. . . . "Potatoes—steak." That's very good. See how they go together? Steak and potatoes?

KIRBY (*modestly, but obviously pleased with himself*)

I just happened to think of it.

PENNY

It's *very* good. . . . "Bathroom—toothpaste." Uh-huh. "Lust—unlawful." Isn't that nice? "Honeymoon—trip." Yes. And "sex—male." Yes, of course . . . That's really a wonderful paper, Mr. Kirby.

KIRBY (*taking a curtain call*)

Thank you . . . It's more than just a game, you know. It's sort of an experiment in psychology, isn't it?

PENNY

Yes, it is—it shows just how your *mind* works. Now we'll see how *Mrs.* Kirby's mind works. . . . Ready? . . . This is *Mrs.* Kirby. . . . "Potatoes—starch." I know just what you mean, Mrs. Kirby. . . . "Bathroom—Mr. Kirby."

KIRBY

What's that?

PENNY

"Bathroom—Mr. Kirby."

KIRBY (*turning to his wife*)

I don't quite follow that, my dear.

MRS. KIRBY

I don't know—I just thought of you in connection with it. After all, you *are* in there a good deal, Anthony. Bathing, and shaving—well, you *do* take a long time.

KIRBY

Indeed? I hadn't realized that I was being selfish in the matter. . . . Go on, Mrs. Sycamore.

ALICE (*worried*)

I think it's a very silly game and we ought to stop it.

KIRBY

No, no. Please go on, Mrs. Sycamore.

PENNY

Where was I . . . Oh, yes. . . . "Lust —human."

KIRBY

Human? (*Thin-lipped.*) Really!

MRS. KIRBY

I just meant, Anthony, that lust is after all a—human emotion.

KIRBY

I don't agree with you, Miriam. Lust is not a human emotion. It is depraved.

MRS. KIRBY

Very well, Anthony. I'm wrong.

ALICE

Really, it's the most pointless game. Suppose we play Twenty Questions?

KIRBY

No, I find this game rather interesting. Will you go on, Mrs. Sycamore? What was the next word?

PENNY (*reluctantly*)

Honeymoon.

KIRBY

Oh, yes. And what was Mrs. Kirby's answer?

PENNY

Ah—"Honeymoon—dull."

KIRBY (*murderously calm*)

Did you say—dull?

MRS. KIRBY

What I meant, Anthony, was that Hot Springs was not very gay that season. All those old people sitting on the porch all afternoon, and—nothing to do at night.

KIRBY

That was not your reaction at the time, as I recall it.

TONY

Father, this is only a *game.*

KIRBY

A very illuminating game. Go on, Mrs. Sycamore!

PENNY (*brightly, having taken a look ahead*)

This one's all right, Mr. Kirby. "Sex— Wall Street."

KIRBY

Wall Street? What do you mean by that, Miriam?

MRS. KIRBY (*nervously*)

I don't know what I meant, Anthony. Nothing.

KIRBY

But you must have meant something, Miriam, or you wouldn't have put it down.

MRS. KIRBY

It was just the first thing that came into my head, that's all.

KIRBY

But what does it mean? Sex—Wall Street.

MRS. KIRBY (*annoyed*)

Oh, I don't know what it means, Anthony. It's just that you're always talking about Wall Street, even when— (*She catches herself.*) I don't know what I meant . . . Would you mind terribly, Alice, if we didn't stay for dinner? I'm afraid this game has given me a headache.

ALICE (*quietly*)

I understand, Mrs. Kirby.

KIRBY (*clearing his throat*)

Yes, possibly we'd better postpone the dinner, if you don't mind.

PENNY

But you're coming tomorrow night, aren't you?

MRS. KIRBY (*quickly*)

I'm afraid we have an engagement tomorrow night.

KIRBY

Perhaps we'd better postpone the whole affair a little while. This hot weather, and —ah—

TONY (*smoldering*)

I think we're being very ungracious, father. Of *course* we'll stay to dinner—tonight.

MRS. KIRBY (*unyielding*)

I have a very bad headache, Tony.

KIRBY

Come, come, Tony, I'm sure everyone understands.

TONY (*flaring*)

Well, *I* don't. I think we ought to stay to dinner.

ALICE (*very low*)

No, Tony.

TONY

What?

ALICE

We were fools, Tony, ever to think it would work. It won't. Mr. Kirby, I won't be at the office tomorrow I—won't be there at all any more.

TONY

Alice, what are you talking about?

KIRBY (*to* ALICE)

I'm sorry, my dear—very sorry . . . Are you ready, Miriam?

MRS. KIRBY (*with enormous dignity*)

Yes, Anthony.

KIRBY

It's been very nice to have met you all. . . . Are you coming, Anthony?

TONY

No, father. I'm not.

KIRBY

I see. . . . Your mother and I will be waiting for you at home. . . . Good-night. (*With* MRS. KIRBY *on his arm, he sweeps toward the outer door.*) (*Before the* KIRBYS *can take more than a step toward the door, however, a new* FIGURE *looms up in the archway. It is a quiet and competent-looking individual with a steely eye, and two more just like him loom up behind him.*)

THE MAN (*very quietly*)

Stay right where you are, everybody. (*There is a little scream from* MRS. KIRBY, *an exclamation from* PENNY.) Don't move.

PENNY

Oh, good heavens!

KIRBY

How dare you? Why, what does this mean?

GRANDPA

What *is* all this?

KIRBY

I demand an explanation!

THE MAN

Keep your mouth shut, you! (*He advances slowly into the room, looking the group over. Then he turns to one of his men.*) Which one is it?

ANOTHER MAN (*goes over and puts a hand on* ED'S *shoulder*)

This is him.

ESSIE

Ed!

ED (*terrified*)

Why, what do you mean?

ALICE

Grandpa, what is it?

KIRBY

This is an outrage!

THE MAN

Shut up! (*He turns to* ED.) What's your name?

ED

Edward—Carmichael. I haven't done anything.

THE MAN

You haven't, huh?

GRANDPA (*not at all scared*)

This seems rather high-handed to me. What's it all about?

THE MAN

Department of Justice.

PENNY

Oh, my goodness! J-men!

ESSIE

Ed, what have you done?

ED

I haven't done anything.

GRANDPA

What's the boy done, Officer?

ALICE

What is it? What's it all about?

THE MAN (*taking his time, and surveying the room*)

That door lead to the cellar?

PENNY

Yes, it does.

PAUL

Yes.

THE MAN (*ordering a man to investigate*)

Mac . . . (MAC *goes into the cellar.*) . . . Jim!

JIM

Yes, sir.

THE MAN

Take a look upstairs and see what you find.

JIM

Okay. (JIM *goes upstairs.*)

ED (*panicky*)

I haven't done anything!

THE MAN

Come here, you! (*He takes some slips of paper out of his pocket.*) Ever see these before?

ED (*gulping*)

They're my—circulars.

THE MAN

You print this stuff, huh?

ED

Yes, sir.

THE MAN

And you put 'em into boxes of candy to get 'em into people's homes.

ESSIE

The Love Dreams!

ED

But I didn't mean anything!

THE MAN

You didn't, huh? (*He reads the circulars.*) "Dynamite the Capitol!" "Dynamite the White House!" "Dynamite the Supreme Court!" "God is the State; the State is God!"

ED

But I didn't mean that. I just like to print. Don't I, Grandpa?
(DONALD *returns with the eggs at this point, and stands quietly watching the proceedings.*)

GRANDPA

Now, Officer, the government's in no danger from Ed. Printing is just his hobby, that's all. He prints anything.

THE MAN

He does, eh?

PENNY

I never heard of such nonsense.

KIRBY

I refuse to stay here and—
(MR. DE PINNA, *at this point, is shoved through the cellar door by* MAC, *protesting as he comes.*)

DE PINNA

Hey, let me get my pipe, will you? Let me get my pipe!

MAC

Shut up, you! . . . We were right, Chief. They've got enough gunpowder down there to blow up the whole city.

PAUL

But we only use that—

THE MAN

Keep still! . . . Everybody in this house is under arrest.

KIRBY

What's that?

MRS. KIRBY

Oh, good heavens!

GRANDPA

Now look here, Officer—this is all nonsense.

DE PINNA

You'd better let me get my pipe. I left it—

THE MAN

Shut up, all of you!

KOLENKHOV

It seems to me, Officer—

THE MAN

Shut up!
(*From the stairs comes the sound of drunken singing—"There was a young lady," etc.* GAY WELLINGTON, *wrapped in* PENNY'S *negligee, is being carried down the stairway by a somewhat bewildered* G-MAN.)

THE G-MAN

Keep still, you! Stop that! Stop it!

THE LEADER (*after* GAY *has been persuaded to quiet down*)
Who's that?

GRANDPA (*pretty tired of the whole business*)
That—is my mother.
(*And then, suddenly, we hear from the cellar.* MR. DE PINNA *seems to have been right about his pipe, to judge from the sounds below. It is a whole year's supply of fireworks—bombs, big crackers, little crackers, sky rockets, pin wheels, everything. The house is fairly rocked by the explosion.*)
(*In the room, of course, pandemonium reigns.* MRS. KIRBY *screams; the* G-MAN *drops* GAY *right where he stands and dashes for the cellar, closely followed by* MR. DE PINNA *and* PAUL; PENNY *dashes for her manuscripts and* ED *rushes to save his xylophone.* KOLENKHOV *waves his arms wildly and dashes in all directions at once; everyone is rushing this way and that.*)
(*All except one. The exception, of course, is* GRANDPA, *who takes all things as they come.* GRANDPA *just says "Well, well, well!"—and sits down. If a lot of people weren't in the way, in fact, you feel he'd like to throw a few darts.*)

CURTAIN

ACT THREE

The following day.
RHEBA *is in the midst of setting the table for dinner, pausing occasionally in her labors to listen to the Edwin C. Hill of the moment—*DONALD. *With intense interest and concentration, he is reading aloud from a newspaper.*

DONALD

". . . for appearance in the West Side Court this morning. After spending the night in jail, the defendants, thirteen in all, were brought before Judge Callahan and given suspended sentences for manufacturing fireworks without a permit."

RHEBA

Yah. Kept me in the same cell with a strip teaser from a burlesque show.

DONALD

I was in the cell with Mr. Kirby. My, he was mad!

RHEBA

Mrs. Kirby and the strip teaser—they were fighting all night.

DONALD

Whole lot about *Mr.* Kirby here. (*Reading again.*) "Anthony W. Kirby, head of Kirby & Co., 62 Wall Street, who was among those apprehended, declared he was in no way interested in the manufacture of fireworks, but refused to state why he was on the premises at the time of the raid. Mr. Kirby is a member of the Union Club, the Racquet Club, the Harvard Club, and the National Geographic Society." My, he certainly is a joiner!

RHEBA

All those rich men are Elks or something.

DONALD (*looking up from his paper*)

I suppose, after all this, Mr. Tony ain't ever going to marry Miss Alice, huh?

RHEBA

No, suh, and it's too bad, too. Miss Alice sure loves that boy.

DONALD

Ever notice how white folks always getting themselves in trouble?

RHEBA

Yassuh, I'm glad I'm colored. (*She sighs, heavily.*) I don't know what I'm going to do with all that food out in the kitchen. Ain't going to be no party tonight, that's sure.

DONALD

Ain't we going to eat it anyhow?

RHEBA

Well, I'm cooking it, but I don't think anybody going to have an appetite.

DONALD

I'm hungry.

RHEBA

Well, *they* ain't. They're all so broke up about Miss Alice.

DONALD

What's she want to go 'way for? Where's she going?

RHEBA

I don't know—mountains some place. And she's *going,* all right, no matter what they say. I know Miss Alice when she gets that look in her eye.

DONALD

Too bad, ain't it?

RHEBA

Sure is.
MR. DE PINNA *comes up from the cellar, bearing the earmarks of the previous day's catastrophe. There is a small bandage*

around his head and over one eye, and another around his right hand. He also limps slightly.)

DE PINNA

Not even a balloon left. (*He exhibits a handful of exploded firecrackers.*) Look.

RHEBA

How's your hand, Mr. De Pinna? Better?

DE PINNA

Yes, it's better. (*A step toward the kitchen.*) Is there some more olive oil out there?

RHEBA (*nods*)

It's in the salad bowl.

DE PINNA

Thanks.
(*He goes out the kitchen door as* PENNY *comes down the stairs. It is a new and rather subdued* PENNY.)

PENNY (*with a sigh*)

Well, she's going. Nothing anybody said could change her.

RHEBA

She ain't going to stay away long, is she, Mrs. Sycamore?

PENNY

I don't know, Rheba. She won't say.

RHEBA

My, going to be lonesome around here without her. (*She goes into the kitchen.*)

DONALD

How *you* feel, Mrs. Sycamore?

PENNY

Oh, I'm all right, Donald. Just kind of upset. (*She is at her desk.*) Perhaps if I do some work maybe I'll feel better.

DONALD

Well, I won't bother you then, Mrs. Sycamore.
(*He goes into the kitchen.*)
(PENNY *puts a sheet of paper into the typewriter; stares at it blankly for a mo-*

ment; types in desultory fashion, gives it up. She leans back and sits staring straight ahead.)
(PAUL *comes slowly down the stairs; stands surveying the room a moment; sighs. He goes over to the Erector Set; absentmindedly pulls out the flag. Then, with another sigh, he drops into a chair.*)

PAUL

She's going, Penny.

PENNY

Yes.
(*She is quiet for a moment; then she starts to weep, softly.*)

PAUL (*going to her*)

Now, now, Penny.

PENNY

I can't help it, Paul. Somehow I feel it's our fault.

PAUL

It's mine more than yours, Penny. All these years I've just been—going along, enjoying myself, when maybe I should have been thinking more about Alice.

PENNY

Don't say that, Paul. You've been a wonderful father. And husband, too.

PAUL

No, I haven't. Maybe if I'd gone ahead and been an architect—I don't know—something Alice could have been proud of. I felt that all last night, looking at Mr. Kirby.

PENNY

But we've been so happy, Paul.

PAUL

I know, but maybe that's not enough. I used to think it was, but—I'm kind of all mixed up now.

PENNY (*after a pause*)

What time is she going?

PAUL

Pretty soon. Train leaves at half past seven.

PENNY

Oh, if only she'd see Tony. I'm sure he could persuade her.

PAUL

But she won't, Penny. He's been trying all day.

PENNY

Where is he now?

PAUL

I don't know—I suppose walking around the block again. Anyhow, she won't talk to him.

PENNY

Maybe Tony can catch her as she's leaving.

PAUL

It won't help, Penny.

PENNY

No, I don't suppose so. . . . I feel so sorry for Tony, too. (GRANDPA *comes down the stairs—unsmiling, but not too depressed by the situation.*) (*Anxiously*) Well?

GRANDPA

Now, Penny, let the girl alone.

PENNY

But, Grandpa—

GRANDPA

Suppose she *goes* to the Adirondacks? She'll be back. You can take just so much Adirondacks, and then you come home.

PENNY

Oh, but it's all so terrible, Grandpa.

GRANDPA

In a way, but it has its bright side, too.

PAUL

How do you mean?

GRANDPA

Well, Mr. Kirby getting into the patrol wagon, for one thing, and the expression on his face when he and Donald had to take a bath together. I'll never forget that

if I live to be a hundred, and I warn you people I intend to. If I can have things like that going on.

PENNY

Oh, it was even worse with Mrs. Kirby. When the matron stripped her. There was a burlesque dancer there and she kept singing a strip song while Mrs. Kirby undressed.

GRANDPA

I'll bet you Bar Harbor is going to seem pretty dull to the Kirbys for the rest of the summer. (*With a determined step,* ALICE *comes swiftly down the stairs. Over her arm she carries a couple of dresses. Looking neither to right nor left, she heads for the kitchen.*)

GRANDPA

Need any help, Alice?

ALICE (*in a strained voice*)

No, thanks, Grandpa. Ed is helping with the bags. I'm just going to press these.

PENNY

Alice, dear—

GRANDPA

Now, Penny.
(ED *has appeared in the hallway with a couple of hatboxes,* ESSIE *behind him.*)

ED

I'll bring the big bag down as soon as you're ready, Alice.

ESSIE

Do you want to take some candy along for the train, Alice?

ALICE

No, thanks, Essie.

PENNY

Really, Alice, you could be just as alone here as you could in the mountains. You could stay right in your room all the time.

ALICE (*quietly*)

No, mother, I want to be by myself—away from everybody. I love you all—you know that. But I just have to go away for a while. I'll be all right. . . . Father, did you 'phone for a cab?

PAUL

No, I didn't know you wanted one.

PENNY

Oh, I told Mr. De Pinna to tell you, Paul. Didn't he tell you?

ED

Oh, he told *me*, but I forgot.

ALICE (*the final straw*)

Oh, I wish I lived in a family that didn't always forget *everything*. That—that behaved the way *other* people's families do. I'm sick of cornflakes, and—Donald, and— (*Unconsciously, in her impatience, she has picked up one of* GRANDPA's *darts; is surprised to find it suddenly in her hand.*) —everything! (*She dashes the dart to the floor.*) Why can't we be like other people? Roast beef, and two green vegetables, and —doilies on the table, and—a place you could bring your friends to—without—
(*Unable to control herself further, she bursts out of the room, into the kitchen.*)

ESSIE

I'll—see if I can do anything.
(*She goes into the kitchen.*)
(*The others look at each other for a moment, helplessly.* PENNY, *with a sigh, drops into her chair again.* PAUL *also sits.* GRANDPA *mechanically picks up the dart from the floor; smooths out the feathers.* ED, *with a futile gesture, runs his fingers idly over the xylophone keys. He stops quickly as every head turns to look at him.*)
(*The sound of the door opening, and* TONY *appears in the archway. A worried and disheveled* TONY.)

PENNY (*quickly*)

Tony, talk to her! She's in the kitchen!

TONY

Thanks. (*He goes immediately into the kitchen. The family, galvanized, listen intently. Almost immediately,* ALICE *emerges from the kitchen again, followed by* TONY. *She crosses the living room and starts quickly up the stairs.*) Alice, won't you listen to me? Please!

ALICE (*not stopping*)

Tony, it's no use.

TONY (*following her*)

Alice, you're not being fair. At least let me talk to you.
(*They are both gone—up the stairs.*)

PENNY

Perhaps if I went upstairs with them . . .

GRANDPA

Now, Penny. Let them alone.
(ESSIE *comes out of the kitchen.*)

ESSIE

Where'd they go? (ED, *with a gesture, indicates the upstairs region.*) She walked right out the minute he came in.
(MR. DE PINNA *also emerges from the kitchen.*)

MR. DE PINNA

Knocked the olive oil right out of my hand. I'm going to smell kind of fishy.

GRANDPA

How're you feeling, Mr. De Pinna? Hand still hurting you?

DE PINNA

No, it's better.

PAUL

Everything burnt up, huh? Downstairs?

DE PINNA (*nodding, sadly*)

Everything. And my Roman costume, too.

GRANDPA (*to* PENNY)

I told you there was a bright side to everything. All except my twenty-two years back income tax. (*He pulls an envelope out of his pocket.*) I get another letter every day.

DE PINNA

Say, what are you going to do about that, Grandpa?

GRANDPA

Well, I had a kind of idea yesterday. It may not work, but I'm trying it, anyhow.

DE PINNA (*eagerly*)

What is it?

(*Suddenly* KOLENKHOV *appears in the doorway*.)

KOLENKHOV (*even he is subdued*)

Good evening, everybody!

PENNY

Why, Mr. Kolenkhov!

GRANDPA

Hello, Kolenkhov.

KOLENKHOV

Forgive me. The door was open.

GRANDPA

Come on in.

KOLENKHOV

You will excuse my coming today. I realize you are—upset.

PENNY

That's all right, Mr. Kolenkhov.

ESSIE

I don't think I can take a lesson, Mr. Kolenkhov. I don't feel up to it.

KOLENKHOV (*uncertainly*)

Well, I—ah—

PENNY

Oh, but do stay to dinner, Mr. Kolenkhov. We've got all that food out there, and somebody's got to eat it.

KOLENKHOV

I will be happy to, Madame Sycamore.

PENNY

Fine.

KOLENKHOV

Thank you. . . . Now, I wonder if I know you well enough to ask of you a great favor.

PENNY

Why, of course, Mr. Kolenkhov. What is it?

KOLENKHOV

You have heard me talk about my friend the Grand Duchess Olga Katrina.

PENNY

Yes?

KOLENKHOV

She is a great woman, the Grand Duchess. Her cousin was the Czar of Russia, and today she is a waitress in Childs' Restaurant. Columbus Circle.

PENNY

Yes, I know. If there's anything at all that we can do, Mr. Kolenkhov . . .

KOLENKHOV

I tell you. The Grand Duchess Olga Katrina has not had a good meal since before the Revolution.

GRANDPA

She must be hungry.

KOLENKHOV

And today the Grand Duchess not only has her day off—Thursday—but it is also the anniversary of Peter the Great. A remarkable man!

PENNY

Mr. Kolenkhov, if you mean you'd like the Grand Duchess to come to dinner, why, we'd be honored.

ESSIE

Oh, yes!

KOLENKHOV (*with a bow*)

In the name of the Grand Duchess, I thank you.

PENNY

I can hardly wait to meet her. When will she be here?

KOLENKHOV

She is outside in the street, waiting. I bring her in.

(*And he goes out.*)

GRANDPA

You know, if this keeps on I want to live to be a hundred and *fifty*.

PENNY (*feverishly*)

Ed, straighten your tie. Essie, look at your dress. How do *I* look? All right?

(KOLENKHOV *appears in the hallway and stands at rigid attention.*)

KOLENKHOV (*his voice booming*)

The Grand Duchess Olga Katrina! (*And the* GRAND DUCHESS OLGA KATRINA, *wheat cakes and maple syrup out of her life for a few hours, sweeps into the room. She wears a dinner gown that has seen better days, and the whole is surmounted by an extremely tacky-looking evening wrap, trimmed with bits of ancient and moth-eaten fur. But once a Grand Duchess, always a Grand Duchess. She rises above everything—Childs', evening wrap, and all.*) Your Highness, permit me to present Madame Sycamore—(PENNY, *having seen a movie or two in her time, knows just what to do. She curtsies right to the floor, and catches hold of a chair just in time.*) Madame Carmichael—(ESSIE *does a curtsy that begins where all others leave off. Starting on her toes, she merges the Dying Swan with an extremely elaborate genuflection.*) Grandpa—

GRANDPA (*with a little bow*)

Madame.

KOLENKHOV

Mr. Sycamore, Mr. Carmichael, and Mr. De Pinna.

(PAUL *and* ED *content themselves with courteous little bows, but not so the social-minded* MR. DE PINNA. *He bows to the floor—and stays there for a moment.*)

GRANDPA

All right now, Mr. De Pinna.

(MR. DE PINNA *gets to his feet again.*)

PENNY

Will you be seated, Your Highness?

THE GRAND DUCHESS

Thank you. You are most kind.

PENNY

We are honored to receive you, Your Highness.

THE GRAND DUCHESS

I am most happy to be here. What time is dinner?

PENNY (*a little startled*)

Oh, it'll be quite soon, Your Highness —very soon.

THE GRAND DUCHESS

I do not mean to be rude, but I must be back at the restaurant by eight o'clock. I am substituting for another waitress.

KOLENKHOV

I will make sure you are on time, Your Highness.

DE PINNA

You know, Highness, I think you waited on me in Childs' once. The Seventy-Second Street place?

THE GRAND DUCHESS

No, no. That was my sister.

KOLENKHOV

The Grand Duchess Natasha.

THE GRAND DUCHESS

I work in Columbus Circle.

GRANDPA

Quite a lot of your family living over here now, aren't there?

THE GRAND DUCHESS

Oh, yes—many. My uncle, the Grand Duke Sergei—he is an elevator man at Macy's. A very nice man. Then there is my cousin, Prince Alexis. He will not speak to the rest of us because he works at Hattie Carnegie's. He has cards printed— Prince Alexis of Hattie Carnegie. Bah!

KOLENKHOV

When he was selling Eskimo Pies at Luna Park he was willing to talk to you.

THE GRAND DUCHESS

Ah, Kolenkhov, our time is coming. My sister Natasha is studying to be a manicure, Uncle Sergei they have promised to make floor-walker, and next month I get transferred to the Fifth Avenue Childs'. From there it is only a step to Schraffts', and *then* we will see what Prince Alexis says!

GRANDPA (*nodding*)

I think you've got him.

THE GRAND DUCHESS

You are telling *me*?
(*She laughs a triumphant Russian laugh, in which* KOLENKHOV *joins.*)

PENNY

Your Highness—did you know the Czar? Personally, I mean.

THE GRAND DUCHESS

Of course—he was my cousin. It was terrible, what happened, but perhaps it was for the best. Where could he get a job now?

KOLENKHOV

That is true.

THE GRAND DUCHESS (*philosophically*)

Yes. And poor relations are poor relations. It is the same in every family. My cousin, the King of Sweden—he was very nice to us for about ten years, but then he said, I just cannot go on. I am not doing so well, either. . . . I do not blame him.

PENNY

No, of course not. . . . Would you excuse me for just a moment?
(*She goes to the foot of the stairs and stands peering up anxiously, hoping for news of* ALICE.)

DE PINNA (*the historian at heart*)

Tell me, Grand Duchess, is it true what they say about Rasputin?

THE GRAND DUCHESS

Everyone wants to know about Rasputin. . . . Yes, my dear sir, it is true. In spades.

DE PINNA

You don't say?

KOLENKHOV

Your Highness, we have to watch the time.

THE GRAND DUCHESS

Yes, I must not be late. The manager does not like me. He is a Communist.

PENNY

We'll hurry things up. Essie, why don't you go out in the kitchen and give Rheba a hand?

THE GRAND DUCHESS (*rising*)

I will help, too. I am a very good cook.

PENNY

Oh, but Your Highness! Not on your day off!

THE GRAND DUCHESS

I do not mind. Where is your kitchen?

ESSIE

Right through here, but you're the guest of honor, Your Highness.

THE GRAND DUCHESS

But I love to cook! Come, Kolenkhov! If they have got sour cream and pot cheese I will make you some blintzes!

KOLENKHOV

Ah! Blintzes! . . . Come, Pavlowa! We show you something!
(*With* ESSIE, *he goes into the kitchen.*)

DE PINNA

Say! The Duchess is all right, isn't she? Hey, Duchess! Can I help?
(*And into the kitchen.*)

PENNY

Really, she's a very nice woman, you know. Considering she's a Grand Duchess.

GRANDPA

Wonderful what people go through, isn't it? And still keep kind of gay, too.

PENNY

Mm. She made me forget about everything for a minute.
(*She returns to the stairs and stands listening.*)

PAUL

I'd better call that cab, I suppose.

PENNY

No, wait, Paul. I think I hear them. Maybe Tony has—

(*She stops as* ALICE's *step is heard on the stair. She enters—dressed for traveling.* TONY *looms up behind her.*)

ALICE

Ed, will you go up and bring my bag down?

TONY (*quickly*)

Don't you do it, Ed!

(ED *hesitates, uncertain.*)

ALICE

Ed, please!

TONY (*a moment's pause; then he gives up*)

All right, Ed. Bring it down.

(ED *goes up the stairs as* TONY *disconsolately stalks across the room. Then he faces the Sycamores.*)

Do you know that you've got the stubbornest daughter in all forty-eight States?

(*The door bell rings.*)

ALICE

That must be the cab.

(*She goes to the door.*)

GRANDPA

If it is, it's certainly wonderful service.

(*To the considerable surprise of everyone, the voice of* MR. KIRBY *is heard at the front door.*)

KIRBY

Is Tony here, Alice?

ALICE

Yes. Yes, he is.

(MR. KIRBY *comes in.*)

KIRBY (*uncomfortably*)

Ah—good afternoon. Forgive my intruding . . . Tony, I want you to come home with me. Your mother is very upset.

TONY (*he looks at* ALICE)

Very well, father . . . Good-bye, Alice.

ALICE (*very low*)

Good-bye, Tony.

KIRBY (*trying to ease the situation*)

I need hardly say that this is as painful to Mrs. Kirby and myself as it is to you people. I—I'm sorry, but I'm sure you understand.

GRANDPA

Well, yes—and in a way, no. Now, I'm not the kind of person tries to run other people's lives, but the fact is, Mr. Kirby, I don't think these two young people have got as much sense as—ah—you and I have.

ALICE (*tense*)

Grandpa, will you please not do this?

GRANDPA (*disarmingly*)

I'm just talking to Mr. Kirby. A cat can look at a king, can't he?

(ALICE, *with no further words, takes up the telephone and dials a number. There is finality in her every movement.*)

PENNY

You—you want me to do that for you, Alice?

ALICE

No, thanks, mother.

PAUL

You've got quite a while before the train goes, Alice.

ALICE (*into the phone*)

Will you send a cab to 761 Claremont, right away, please? . . . That's right, thank you.

(*She hangs up.*)

KIRBY

And now if you'll excuse us . . . are you ready, Tony?

GRANDPA

Mr. Kirby, I suppose after last night you think this family is crazy, don't you?

KIRBY

No, I would not say that, although I am not accustomed to going out to dinner and spending the night in jail.

GRANDPA

Well, you've got to remember, Mr. Kirby, you came on the wrong night. Now tonight, I'll bet you, nothing'll happen at all.

(*There is a great burst of Russian laughter from the kitchen—the mingled voices of* KOLENKHOV *and the* GRAND DUCHESS. GRANDPA *looks off in the direction of the laughter, then decides to play safe.*)

Maybe.

KIRBY

Mr. Vanderhof, it was not merely last night that convinced Mrs. Kirby and myself that this engagement would be unwise.

TONY

Father, I can handle my own affairs.

(*He turns to* ALICE.)

Alice, for the last time, will you marry me?

ALICE

No, Tony. I know exactly what your father means, and he's right.

TONY

No, he's *not*, Alice.

GRANDPA

Alice, you're in love with this boy, and you're not marrying him because we're the kind of people we are.

ALICE

Grandpa—

GRANDPA

I know. You think the two families wouldn't get along. Well, maybe they wouldn't—but who says they're right and we're wrong?

ALICE

I didn't say that, Grandpa. I only feel—

GRANDPA

Well, what *I* feel is that Tony's too nice a boy to wake up twenty years from now with nothing in his life but stocks and bonds.

KIRBY

How's that?

GRANDPA (*turning to* MR. KIRBY)

Yes. Mixed up and unhappy, the way you are.

KIRBY (*outraged*)

I beg your pardon, Mr. Vanderhof, I am a very happy man.

GRANDPA

Are you?

KIRBY

Certainly I am.

GRANDPA

I don't think so. What do you think you get your indigestion from? Happiness? No, sir. You get it because most of your time is spent in doing things you don't want to do.

KIRBY

I don't do anything I don't want to do.

GRANDPA

Yes, you do. You said last night that at the end of a week in Wall Street you're pretty near crazy. Why do you keep on doing it?

KIRBY

Why do I keep on—why, that's my *business*. A man can't give up his business.

GRANDPA

Why not? You've got all the money you need. You can't take it with you.

KIRBY

That's a very easy thing to say, Mr. Vanderhof. But I have spent my entire life building up my business.

GRANDPA

And what's it got you? Same kind of mail every morning, same kind of deals, same kind of meetings, same dinners at night, same indigestion. Where does the fun come in? Don't you think there ought to be something *more*, Mr. Kirby? You must have wanted more than that when you started out. We haven't got too much time, you know—any of us.

KIRBY

What do you expect me to do? Live the way *you* do? Do nothing?

GRANDPA

Well, I have a lot of fun. Time enough for everything—read, talk, visit the zoo now and then, practice my darts, even have time to notice when spring comes around. Don't see anybody I don't want to, don't have six hours of things I *have* to do every day before I get *one* hour to do what I like in—and I haven't taken bicarbonate of soda in thirty-five years. What's the matter with that?

KIRBY

The matter with that? But suppose we *all* did it? A fine world we'd have, everybody going to zoos. Don't be ridiculous, Mr. Vanderhof. Who would do the work?

GRANDPA

There's always people that like to work —you can't *stop* them. Inventions, and they fly the ocean. There're always people to go down to Wall Street, too—because they *like* it. But from what I've seen of you, I don't think you're one of them. I think you're missing something.

KIRBY

I am not aware of missing anything.

GRANDPA

I wasn't either, till I quit. I used to get down to that office nine o'clock sharp, no matter how I felt. Lay awake nights for fear I wouldn't get that contract. Used to worry about the world, too. Got *all* worked up about whether Cleveland or Blaine was going to be elected President—seemed awful important at the time, but who cares now? What I'm trying to say, Mr. Kirby, is that I've had thirty-five years that nobody can take away from me, no matter what they do to the world. See?

KIRBY

Yes, I do see. And it's a very dangerous philosophy, Mr. Vanderhof. It's—it's un-American. And it's exactly why I'm opposed to this marriage. I don't want Tony to come under its influence.

TONY (*a gleam in his eye*).

What's the matter wtih it, father?

KIRBY

Matter with it? Why, it's—it's downright Communism, that's what it is.

TONY

You didn't always think so.

KIRBY

I most certainly did. What are you talking about?

TONY

I'll tell you what I'm talking about. You didn't always think so, because there was a time when you wanted to be a trapeze artist.

KIRBY

Why—why, don't be an idiot, Tony.

TONY

Oh, yes, you did. I came across those letters you wrote to grandfather. Do you remember those?

KIRBY

NO! . . . How dared you read those letters? How dared you?

PENNY

Why, isn't that wonderful? Did you wear tights, Mr. Kirby?

KIRBY

Certainly not! The whole thing is absurd. I was fourteen years old at the time.

TONY

Yes, but at *eighteen* you wanted to be a saxophone player, didn't you?

KIRBY

Tony!

TONY

And at twenty-one you ran away from home because grandfather wanted you to go into the business. It's all down there in black and white. You didn't *always* think so.

GRANDPA

Well, well, well!

KIRBY

I may have had silly notions in my youth, but thank God my father knocked them out of me. I went into the business and forgot about them.

TONY

Not altogether, father. There's still a saxophone in the back of your clothes closet.

GRANDPA

There is?

KIRBY (*quietly*)

That's enough, Tony. We'll discuss this later.

TONY

No, I want to talk about it *now*. I think Mr. Vanderhof is right—dead right. I'm never going back to that office. I've always hated it, and I'm not going on with it. And I'll tell you something else. I didn't make a mistake last night. I knew it was the wrong night. I brought you here on purpose.

ALICE

Tony!

PENNY

Well, for heaven's—

TONY

Because I wanted to wake you up. I wanted you to see a real family—as they really *were*. A family that loved and understood each other. You don't understand *me*. You've never had time. Well, I'm not going to make *your* mistake. I'm clearing out.

KIRBY

Clearing out? What do you mean?

TONY

I mean I'm not going to be pushed into the business just because I'm your son. I'm getting out while there's still time.

KIRBY (*stunned*)

Tony, what are you going to do?

TONY

I don't know. Maybe I'll be a bricklayer, but at least I'll be doing something I want to do.

(*Whereupon the door bell rings.*)

PENNY

That must be the cab.

GRANDPA

Ask him to wait a minute, Ed.

ALICE

Grandpa!

GRANDPA

Do you mind, Alice? . . . You know, Mr. Kirby, Tony is going through just what you and I did when we were his age. I think, if you listen hard enough, you can hear yourself saying the same things to *your* father twenty-five years ago. We all did it. And we were right. How many of us would be willing to settle when we're young for what we eventually get? All those plans we make . . . what happens to them? It's only a handful of the lucky ones that can look back and say that they even came close.

(GRANDPA *has hit home.* MR. KIRBY *turns slowly and looks at his son, as though seeing him for the first time.* GRANDPA *continues.*)

So . . . before they clean out that closet, Mr. Kirby, I think I'd get in a few good hours on that saxophone.

(*A slight pause, then* THE GRAND DUCHESS, *an apron over her evening dress, comes in from the kitchen.*)

THE GRAND DUCHESS

I beg your pardon, but before I make the blintzes, how many will there be for dinner?

PENNY

Why, I don't know—ah—

GRANDPA

Your Highness, may I present Mr. Anthony Kirby, and Mr. Kirby, Junior? The Grand Duchess Olga Katrina.

KIRBY

How's that?

THE GRAND DUCHESS

How do you do? Before I make the blintzes, how many will there be to dinner?

GRANDPA

Oh, I'd make quite a stack of them, Your Highness. Can't ever tell.

THE GRAND DUCHESS

Good! The Czar always said to me, Olga, do not be stingy with the blintzes.
(*She returns to the kitchen, leaving a somewhat stunned* MR. KIRBY *behind her.*)

KIRBY

Ah—who did you say that was, Mr. Vanderhof?

GRANDPA (*very offhand*)

The Grand Duchess Olga Katrina, of Russia. She's cooking the dinner.

KIRBY

Oh!

GRANDPA

And speaking of dinner, Mr. Kirby, why don't you and Tony both stay?

PENNY

Oh, please do, Mr. Kirby. We've got all that stuff we were going to have last night. I mean tonight.

GRANDPA

Looks like a pretty good dinner, Mr. Kirby, and'll kind of give us a chance to get acquainted. Why not stay?

KIRBY

Why—I'd like to very much.
(*He turns to* TONY, *with some trepidation.*)
What do you say, Tony? Shall we stay to dinner?

TONY

Yes, father. I think that would be fine. If—
(*His eyes go to* ALICE.)
—if Alice will send away that cab.

GRANDPA

How about it, Alice? Going to be a nice crowd. Don't you think you ought to stay for dinner?

ALICE

Mr. Kirby—Tony—oh, Tony!
(*And she is in his arms.*)

TONY

Darling!

ALICE

Grandpa, you're wonderful!

GRANDPA

I've been telling you that for years.
(*He kisses her.*)
(ESSIE *enters from the kitchen, laden with dishes.*)

ESSIE

Grandpa, here's a letter for you. It was in the ice-box.

GRANDPA (*looks at the envelope*)

The Government again.

TONY (*happily*)

Won't you step into the office, Miss Sycamore? I'd like to do a little dictating.

GRANDPA (*with his letter*)

Well, well, well!

PENNY

What is it, Grandpa?

GRANDPA

The United States Government apologizes. I don't owe 'em a nickel. It seems I died eight years ago.

ESSIE

Why, what do they mean, Grandpa?

GRANDPA

Remember Charlie, the milkman? Buried under my name?

PENNY

Yes.

GRANDPA

Well, I just told them they made a mistake and I was Martin Vanderhof, Jr. So they're very sorry and I may even get a refund.

ALICE

Why, Grandpa, you're an old crook.

GRANDPA

Sure!

KIRBY (*interested*)

Pardon me, how did you say you escaped
the income tax, Mr. Vanderhof?

KOLENKHOV (*bursting through the kitchen
door, bringing a chair with him.*)

Tonight, my friends, you are going to
eat. . . .
(*He stops short as he catches sight of*
KIRBY.)

KIRBY (*heartily*)

Hello, there!

KOLENKHOV (*stunned*)

How do you do?

KIRBY

Fine! Fine! Never was better.

KOLENKHOV (*to* GRANDPA)

What has happened?

GRANDPA

He's relaxing.
(ED *strikes the keys of the xylophone.*)
That's right. Play something, Ed.
(*He starts to play.* ESSIE *is immediately
up on her toes.*)

THE GRAND DUCHESS (*entering from the
kitchen*)

Everything will be ready in a minute.
You can sit down.

PENNY

Come on, everybody. Dinner!
(*They start to pull up chairs.*)
Come on, Mr. Kirby!

KIRBY (*still interested in the xylophone*)

Yes, yes, I'm coming.

PENNY

Essie, stop dancing and come to dinner.

KOLENKHOV

You will like Russian food, Mr. Kirby.

PENNY

But you must be careful of your indigestion.

KIRBY

Nonsense! I haven't any indigestion.

TONY

Well, Miss Sycamore, how was your trip
to the Adirondacks?

ALICE

Shut your face, Mr. Kirby!

KOLENKHOV

In Russia, when they sit down to dinner
. . .

GRANDPA (*tapping on his plate*)

Quiet! Everybody! Quiet!
(*Immediately the talk ceases. All heads
are lowered as* GRANDPA *starts to say
Grace.*)
Well, Sir, here we are again. We want
to say thanks once more for everything
You've done for us. Things seem to be
going along fine. Alice is going to marry
Tony, and it looks as if they're going to
be very happy. Of course the fireworks
blew up, but that was Mr. De Pinna's
fault, not Yours. We've all got our health
and as far as anything else is concerned,
we'll leave it to You. Thank You.
(*The heads come up again.* RHEBA *and*
DONALD *come through the kitchen door
with stacks and stacks of blintzes. Even
the Czar would have thought there were
enough.*)

Curtain.

Our Town

BY THORNTON WILDER

TO ALEXANDER WOOLLCOTT

OF CASTLETON TOWNSHIP, RUTLAND COUNTY, VERMONT

THORNTON WILDER

Thornton Niven Wilder was born on April 17, 1897, in Madison, Wisconsin. When he was nine years old, he was taken to China by his father, who was American Consul-General at Hong Kong. Young Thornton attended high school at Chefoo, and after his return to the United States continued his schooling in a secondary school at Berkeley, California. Then he entered Oberlin College and later transferred to Yale University. He served as a corporal in the Coast Artillery Corps during the World War. Post-graduate studies at the American Academy in Rome completed his formal education. In 1921 he became a house master and teacher at Lawrenceville. His first novel, *Cabala,* was published in 1925 and received critical, if not a wide public, acclaim. A play, *The Trumpet Shall Sound,* followed in 1926. *The Bridge of San Luis Rey* appeared in the following year and catapulted its author into international fame. In the meantime Thornton Wilder continued his teaching duties at Lawrenceville and subsequently at the University of Chicago. His creative interests have recently turned from the novel to the drama. *Our Town,* which was produced on February 4, 1938, was awarded the Pulitzer Prize for 1937-1938.

CHARACTERS

STAGE MANAGER
DR. GIBBS
JOE CROWELL
HOWIE NEWSOME
MRS. GIBBS
MRS. WEBB
GEORGE GIBBS
REBECCA GIBBS
WALLY WEBB
EMILY WEBB
PROFESSOR WILLARD
MR. WEBB
WOMAN IN THE BALCONY
MAN IN THE AUDITORIUM
LADY IN THE BOX
SIMON STIMSON
MRS. SOAMES
CONSTABLE WARREN
SI CROWELL
BASEBALL PLAYERS
SAM CRAIG
JOE STODDARD
PEOPLE OF THE TOWN

The entire play takes place in Grover's Corners, N. H., 1901 to 1913

OUR TOWN

ACT ONE

No curtain.

No scenery.

The audience, arriving, sees an empty stage in half-light.

Presently the STAGE MANAGER, *hat on and pipe in mouth, enters and begins placing a table and several chairs down stage left, and a table and chairs down stage right.*

"Left" and "right" are from the point of view of the actor facing the audience. "Up" is towards the back wall.

As the house lights go down he has finished setting the stage and leaning against the right proscenium pillar watches the late arrivals in the audience.

When the auditorium is in complete darkness he speaks:

STAGE MANAGER

This play is called "Our Town." It was written by Thornton Wilder; produced and directed by A.... [or: produced by A....; directed by B....]. In it you will see Miss C....; Miss D....; Miss E....; and Mr. F....; Mr. G....; Mr. H....; and many others. The name of the town is Grover's Corners, New Hampshire,—just across the Massachusetts line: longitude 42 degrees 40 minutes; latitude 70 degrees 37 minutes. The First Act shows a day in our town. The day is May 7, 1901. The time is just before dawn. (*A rooster crows.*) The sky is beginning to show some streaks of light over in the East there, behind our mount'in. The morning star always gets wonderful bright the minute before it has to go. (*He stares at it for a moment, then goes up stage.*) Well, I'd better show you how our town lies. Up here— (*That is: parallel with the back wall*) is Main Street. Way back there is the railway station; tracks go that way. Polish Town's across the tracks and some Canuck families. (*Toward the left:*) Over there is the Congregational Church; across the street's the Presbyterian. Methodist and Unitarian are over there. Baptist is down in the holla' by the river. Catholic Church is over beyond the tracks. Here's the Town Hall and Post Office combined; jail's in the basement. Bryan once made a speech from these steps here. Along here's a row of stores. Hitching-posts and horse blocks in front of them. First automobile's going to come along in about five years,—belonged to Banker Cartwright, our richest citizen . . . lives in the big white house· up on the hill. Here's the grocery store and here's Mr. Morgan's drugstore. Most everybody in town manages to look into those two stores once a day. Public School's over yonder. High School's still farther over. Quarter of nine mornings, noontimes, and three o'clock afternoons, the hull town can hear the yelling and screaming from those schoolyards. (*He approaches the table and chairs down stage right:*) This is our doctor's house,—Doc Gibbs. This is the back door. (*Two arched trellises are pushed out, one by each proscenium pillar.*) There's some scenery for those who think they have to have scenery. There's a garden here. Corn . . . peas . . . beans . . . hollyhocks . . . heliotrope . . . and a lot of burdock. (*Crosses the stage.*) In those days our newspaper come out twice a week,—The Grover's Corners *Sentinel*,—and this is Editor Webb's house. And this is Mrs. Webb's garden. Just like Mrs. Gibbs's, only it's got a lot of sunflowers, too. Right here,—big butternut tree. (*He returns to his place by the right proscenium pillar and looks at the audience for a minute.*) Nice town, y'know what I mean? Nobody very remarkable ever come out of it,—s'far as we know. The earliest tombstones in the cemetery up there on the mountain say 1670-1680—they're Grovers and Cartwrights and Gibbses and Herseys —same names as are around here now. Well, as I said: it's about dawn. The only lights on in town are in a cottage over by the tracks where a Polish mother's just had twins. And in the Joe Crowell house, where Joe Junior's getting up so as to deliver the paper. And in the depot, where

Shorty Hawkins is gettin' ready to flag the 5:45 for Boston. (*A train whistle is heard. The* STAGE MANAGER *takes out his watch and nods.*) Naturally, out in the country —all around—they've been lights on for some time, what with milkin's and so on. But town people sleep late. So—another day's begun. There's Doc Gibbs comin' down Main Street now, comin' back from that baby case. And here's his wife comin' downstairs to get breakfast. Doc Gibbs died in 1930. The new hospital's named after him. Mrs. Gibbs died first—long time ago in fact. She went out to visit her daughter, Rebecca, who married an insurance man in Canton, Ohio, and died there—pneumonia—but her body was brought back here. She's up in the cemetery there now—in with a whole mess of Gibbses and Herseys—she was Julia Hersey 'fore she married Doc Gibbs in the Congregational Church over there. In our town we like to know the facts about everybody.—That's Doc Gibbs. And there comes Joe Crowell, Jr., delivering Mr. Webb's *Sentinel*.

(DR. GIBBS *has been coming along Main Street from the left. At the point where he would turn to approach his house, he stops, sets down his—imaginary—black bag, takes off his hat, and rubs his face with fatigue, using an enormous handkerchief.* MRS. GIBBS *has entered her kitchen, gone through the motions of putting wood into a stove, lighting it, and preparing breakfast. Suddenly,* JOE CROWELL, JR., *starts down Main Street from the right, hurling imaginary newspapers into doorways.*)

JOE CROWELL, JR.

Morning, Doc Gibbs.

DR. GIBBS

Morning, Joe.

JOE CROWELL, JR.

Somebody been sick, Doc?

DR. GIBBS

No. Just some twins born over in Polish Town.

JOE CROWELL, JR.

Do you want your paper now?

DR. GIBBS

Yes, I'll take it.—Anything serious goin' on in the world since Wednesday?

JOE CROWELL, JR.

Yessir. My schoolteacher, Miss Foster, 's getting married to a fella over in Concord.

DR. GIBBS

I declare.—How do you boys feel about that?

JOE CROWELL, JR.

Well, of course, it's none of my business,—but I think if a person starts out to be a teacher, she ought to stay one.

DR. GIBBS

How's your knee, Joe?

JOE CROWELL, JR.

Fine, Doc, I never think about it at all. Only like you said, it always tells me when it's going to rain.

DR. GIBBS

What's it telling you today? Goin' to rain?

JOE CROWELL, JR.

No, sir.

DR. GIBBS

Sure?

JOE CROWELL, JR.

Yessir.

DR. GIBBS

Knee ever make a mistake?

JOE CROWELL, JR.

No, sir.

(JOE *goes off.* DR. GIBBS *stands reading his paper.*)

STAGE MANAGER

Here comes Howie Newsome delivering the milk.

(HOWIE NEWSOME *comes along Main Street, passes* DOCTOR GIBBS, *comes down the center of the stage, leaves some bottles at* MRS. WEBB's *back door, and crosses the stage to* MRS. GIBBS's.)

HOWIE NEWSOME

Git-ap, Bessie. What's the matter with you?—Morning, Doc.

DR. GIBBS

Morning, Howie.

HOWIE NEWSOME

Somebody sick?

DR. GIBBS

Pair of twins over to Mrs. Goruslawski's.

HOWIE NEWSOME

Twins, eh? This town's gettin' bigger every year.

DR. GIBBS

Going to rain, Howie?

HOWIE NEWSOME

No, no. Fine day—that'll burn through. Come on, Bessie.

DR. GIBBS

Hello, Bessie. (*He strokes her.*) How old is she, Howie?

HOWIE NEWSOME

Going on seventeen. Bessie's all mixed up about the route ever since the Lockharts stopped takin' their quart of milk every day. She wants to leave 'em a quart just the same—keeps scolding me the hull trip. (*He reaches* MRS. GIBBS's *back door. She is waiting for him.*)

MRS. GIBBS

Good morning, Howie.

HOWIE NEWSOME

Morning, Mrs. Gibbs. Doc's just comin' down the street.

MRS. GIBBS

Is he? Seems like you're late today?

HOWIE NEWSOME

Yes. Somep'n went wrong with the separator. Don't know what 'twas. (*He goes back to Main Street, clucks for Bessie and goes off right.* DR. GIBBS *reaches his home and goes in.*)

MRS. GIBBS

Everything all right?

DR. GIBBS

Yes. I declare—easy as kittens.

MRS. GIBBS

Bacon'll be ready in a minute. Set down and drink your coffee. Child-*run!* Child-*run!* Time to get up.—George! Rebecca! —you can catch a couple hours' sleep this morning, can't you?

DR. GIBBS

Hm! . . . Mrs. Wentworth's coming at eleven. Guess I know what it's about, too. Her stummick ain't what it ought to be.

MRS. GIBBS

All told, you won't get more'n three hours' sleep. Frank Gibbs, I don't know what's goin' to become of you. I do wish I could get you to go away some place and take a rest. I think it would do you good.

MRS. WEBB

Emileeee! Time to get up! Wally! Seven o'clock!

MRS. GIBBS

I declare, you got to speak to George. Seems like something's come over him lately. He's no help to me at all. I can't even get him to cut me some wood.

DR. GIBBS

Is he sassy to you?

MRS. GIBBS

No. He just whines! All he thinks about is that baseball—George! Rebecca! You'll be late for school.

DR. GIBBS

M-m-m. . . .

MRS. GIBBS

George!

DR. GIBBS

George, look sharp!

GEORGE'S VOICE

Yes, Pa!

DR. GIBBS (*as he goes off the stage*)

Don't you hear your mother calling you?

MRS. WEBB

Walleee! Emileee! You'll be late for school! Walleee! You wash yourself good or I'll come up and do it myself.

REBECCA GIBBS'S VOICE

Ma! What dress shall I wear?

MRS. GIBBS

Don't make a noise. Your father's been out all night and needs his sleep. I washed and ironed the blue gingham for you special.

REBECCA

Ma, I hate that dress.

MRS. GIBBS

Oh, hush-up-with-you.

REBECCA

Every day I go to school dressed like a sick turkey.

MRS. GIBBS

Now, Rebecca, don't be impossible. You always look *very* nice.

REBECCA

Mama, George's throwing soap at me.

MRS. GIBBS

I'll come up and slap the both of you,— that's what I'll do.

(*A factory whistle sounds. The children enter and take their places at the breakfast tables:* EMILY *and* WALLY WEBB; GEORGE *and* REBECCA GIBBS.)

STAGE MANAGER

We've got a factory in our town too,— hear it? Makes blankets. Cartwrights own it and it brung 'em a fortune.

MRS. WEBB

Children! Now I won't have it. Breakfast is just as good as any other meal and I won't have you gobbling like wolves. It'll stunt your growth,—that's a fact. Put away your book, Wally.

WALLY

Aw, Ma!

MRS. WEBB

You know the rule's well as I do—no books at table. As for me, I'd rather have my children healthy than bright.

EMILY

I'm both, Mama: you know I am. I'm the brightest girl in school for my age. I have a wonderful memory.

MRS. WEBB

Eat your breakfast.

WALLY

I'm bright, too, when I'm looking at my stamp collection.

MRS. GIBBS

I'll speak to your father about it when he's rested. Seems to me twenty-five cents a week's enough for a boy your age. I declare I don't know how you spend it all.

GEORGE

Aw, Ma,—I gotta lotta things to buy.

MRS. GIBBS

Strawberry phosphates—that's what you spend it on.

GEORGE

I don't see how Rebecca comes to have so much money. She has more'n a dollar.

REBECCA (*spoon in mouth, dreamily*)

I've been saving it up gradual.

MRS. GIBBS

Well, dear, I think it's a good thing every now and then to spend some.

REBECCA

Mama, do you know what I love most in the world—do you?—Money.

MRS. GIBBS

Eat your breakfast.

(*The school bell is heard.*)

THE CHILDREN

Mama, there's first bell.—I gotta hurry. —I don't want any more.

MRS. WEBB

Walk fast, but you don't have to run. Wally, pull up your pants at the knee. Stand up straight, Emily.

MRS. GIBBS

Tell Miss Foster I send her my best congratulations—can you remember that?

REBECCA

Yes, Ma.

MRS. GIBBS

You look real nice, Rebecca. Pick up your feet.

ALL

Good-by.

(*The children from the two houses join at the center of the stage and go up to Main Street, then off left.* MRS. GIBBS *fills her apron with food for the chickens and comes down to the footlights.*)

MRS. GIBBS

Here, chick, chick, chick. No, go away, you. Go away. Here, chick, chick, chick. What's the matter with *you*? Fight, fight, fight,—that's all you do. Hm . . . *you* don't belong to me. Where'd you come from? (*She shakes her apron.*) Oh, don't be so scared. Nobody's going to hurt you.

(MRS. WEBB *is sitting by her trellis, stringing beans.*)

MRS. GIBBS

Good morning, Myrtle. How's your cold?

MRS. WEBB

Well, it's better; but I told Charles I didn't know as I'd go to choir practice tonight. Wouldn't be any use.

MRS. GIBBS

Just the same, you come to choir practice, Myrtle, and try it.

MRS. WEBB

Well, if I don't feel any worse than I do now I probably will. While I'm resting myself I thought I'd string some of these beans.

MRS. GIBBS (*rolling up her sleeves as she crosses the stage for a chat*)

Let me help you. Beans have been good this year.

MRS. WEBB

I've decided to put up forty quarts if it kills me. The children say they hate 'em but I notice they're able to get 'em down all winter.

(*Pause.*)

MRS. GIBBS

Now, Myrtle. I've got to tell you something, because if I don't tell somebody I'll burst.

MRS. WEBB

Why, Julia Gibbs!

MRS. GIBBS

Here, give me some more of those beans. Myrtle, did one of those second-hand furniture men from Boston come to see you last Friday?

MRS. WEBB

No—o.

MRS. GIBBS

Well, he called on me. First I thought he was a patient wantin' to see Dr. Gibbs. 'N he wormed his way into my parlor, and, Myrtle Webb, he offered me three hundred and fifty dollars for Grandmother Wentworth's highboy, as I'm sitting here!

MRS. WEBB

Why, Julia Gibbs!

MRS. GIBBS

He did! That old thing! Why, it was so big I didn't know where to put it and I almost give it to Cousin Hester Wilcox.

MRS. WEBB

Well, you're going to take it, aren't you?

MRS. GIBBS

I don't know.

MRS. WEBB

You don't know—three hundred and fifty dollars. What's come over you?

MRS. GIBBS

Well, if I could get the Doctor to take the money and go away some place on a real trip I'd sell it like that.—Myrtle, ever since I was *that* high I've had the thought that I'd like to see Paris, France. I suppose I'm crazy.

MRS. WEBB

Oh, I know what you mean.—How does the Doctor feel about it?

MRS. GIBBS

Well, I did beat about the bush a little and said that if I got a legacy—that's the

way I put it—I'd make him take me somewhere.

MRS. WEBB

M-m-m. . . . What did he say?

MRS. GIBBS

You know how he is. I haven't heard a
serious word out of him, ever since I've
known him. No, he said, it might make
him discontented with Grover's Corners
to go traipsin' about Europe; better let
well enough alone, he says. Every two
years he makes a trip to the battlefields of
the Civil War and that's enough treat for
anybody, he says.

MRS. WEBB

Well, Mr. Webb just *admires* the way
Dr. Gibbs knows everything about the
Civil War. Mr. Webb's a good mind to
give up Napoleon and move over to the
Civil War, only Dr. Gibbs being one of
the greatest experts in the country just
makes him despair.

MRS. GIBBS

It's a fact! Doctor Gibbs is never so
happy as when he's at Antietam or Gettys-
burg. The times I've walked over those
hills, Myrtle, stopping at every bush and
pacing it all out, like we was going to
buy it.

MRS. WEBB

Well, if that second-hand man's really
serious about buyin' it, Julia, you sell it.
And then you'll get to see Paris, all right.

MRS. GIBBS

Oh, I'm sorry I mentioned it. Only it
seems to me that once in your life before
you die you ought to see a country where
they don't talk and think in English and
don't even want to.

(*The* STAGE MANAGER *returns to the center of the stage.*)

STAGE MANAGER

That'll do. That'll do. Thank you very
much, ladies. (MRS. GIBBS *and* MRS. WEBB
*gather up their things, return into their
homes and disappear.*) Now we're going to
skip a few hours in the day at Grover's
Corners. But before we go on I want you
to know some more things about the town,
—all kinds of things. So I've asked Prof.
Willard of our State University to come
down here and sketch in a few details of
our past history,—kind of scientific account, you might say. Is Prof. Willard
here? (PROF. WILLARD, *a rural savant,
pince-nez on a wide satin ribbon, enters
from the right with some notes in his
hand.*) May I introduce Prof. Willard of
our University. A few brief notes, thank
you, Professor,—unfortunately our time is
limited.

PROF. WILLARD

Grover's Corners . . . let me see . . .
Grover's Corners lies on the old Archaeo-
zoic granite of the Appalachian range. I
may say it's some of the oldest land in the
world. We're very proud of that. A shelf
of Devonian basalt crosses it with vestiges
of Mesozoic shale, and some sandstone
outcroppings; but that's all more recent:
two hundred, three hundred million years
old. Some highly interesting fossils have
been found. . . . I may say: unique fossils . . . two miles out of town, in Silas
Peckham's cow pasture. They can be seen
at the museum in our University at any
time. Did you wish the meteorological
conditions?

STAGE MANAGER

Thank you. We would.

PROF. WILLARD

The mean precipitation is 40 inches.
The mean annual temperature is 43 degrees, ranging between 102 degrees in the
shade, and 38 degrees below zero in winter. The . . . the . . . uh . . .

STAGE MANAGER

Thank you, Professor. And have you
Prof. Gruber's notes on the history of human life here?

PROF. WILLARD

Hm . . . yes . . . anthropological data:
Early Amerindian stock. Cotahatchee
tribes . . . no evidence before the Tenth
Century of this era . . . hm . . . now
entirely disappeared . . . possible traces in
three families. Migration toward the end
of the Seventeenth Century of English
brachycephalic blue-eyed stock . . . for

the most part. Since then some influx of Slav and Mediterranean types. . . .

STAGE MANAGER

And the population, Prof. Willard?

PROF. WILLARD

Within the town limits: 2,640. The postal district brings in 507 more. Mortality and birth-rates are constant; by MacPherson's gauge: 6.032.

STAGE MANAGER

Thank you *very* much, Professor. We're all very much obliged to you, I'm sure.

PROF. WILLARD

Not at all, sir; not at all.

STAGE MANAGER

This way, Professor, and thank you again. (*Exit* PROF. WILLARD.) Now the political and social report: Editor Webb.— Oh, Mr. Webb?
(MRS. WEBB *appears at her back door.*)

MRS. WEBB

He'll be here in a minute. . . . He just cut his hand while he was eatin' an apple.

STAGE MANAGER

Thank you, Mrs. Webb. .

MRS. WEBB

Charles! Everybody's waitin'.
(*Exit* MRS. WEBB.)

STAGE MANAGER

Mr. Webb is Publisher and Editor of The Grover's Corners *Sentinel.* That's our local paper, y'know.
(MR. WEBB *enters from his house, pulling on his coat. His finger is bound in a handkerchief.*)

MR. WEBB

Hm. . . . I don't have to tell you that we're run here by a Board of Selectmen.— All males vote at the age of 21. Women vote indirect. We're lower middle-class, sprinkling of professional men . . . 10% illiterate laborers. Politically, we're 86% Republicans; 6% Democrats; 4% Socialists; rest, indifferent. Religiously, we're 85% Protestants; 12% Catholics; rest, indifferen:. Do you want the poverty and insanity statistics?

STAGE MANAGER

Thank you, no. Have you any comments, Mr. Webb?

MR. WEBB

Very ordinary town, if you ask me. Little better behaved than most. Probably a lot duller. But our young people here seem to like it well enough: 90% of 'em graduating from High School settle down right here to live—even when they've been away to college.

STAGE MANAGER

Thank you, Mr. Webb. Now, is there anyone in the audience who would like to ask Editor Webb anything about the town?

WOMAN IN THE BALCONY

Is there much drinking in Grover's Corners?

MR. WEBB

Well, ma'am, I wouldn't know what you'd call *much.* Satiddy nights the farmhands meet down in Ellery Greenough's stable and holler some. Fourth of July I've been known to taste a drop myself —and Decoration Day, of course. We've got one or two town drunks, but they're always having remorses every time an evangelist comes to town. No, ma'am, I'd say likker ain't a regular thing in the home here, except in the medicine chest. Right good for snake-bite, y'know—always was.

TALL MAN AT BACK OF AUDITORIUM

Is there no one in town aware of—

STAGE MANAGER

Come forward, will you, where we can all hear you— What were you saying?

TALL MAN

Is there no one in town aware of social injustice and industrial inequality?

MR. WEBB

Oh, yes, everybody is,—somethin' terrible. Seems like they spend most of their time talking about who's rich and who's poor.

TALL MAN

Then why don't they do something about it?

MR. WEBB

Well, we're ready to listen to everybody's suggestion as to how you can see that the diligent and sensible 'll rise to the top and the lazy and quarrelsome sink to the bottom. We'll listen to anybody. Meantime until that's settled, we try to take care of those that can't help themselves, and those that can we leave alone. —Are there any more questions?

LADY IN A BOX

Oh, Mr. Webb? Mr. Webb, is there any culture or love of beauty in Grover's Corners?

MR. WEBB

Well, ma'am, there ain't much—not in the sense you mean. Come to think of it, there's some girls that play the piano at High School Commencement; but they ain't happy about it. Yes, and I see where my daughter's been made to read "The Merchant of Venice" over to the school. Seems all pretty remote to 'em, y'know what I mean. No, ma'am, there isn't much culture; but maybe this is the place to tell you that we've got a lot of pleasures of a kind here: we like the sun comin' up over the mountain in the morning, and we all notice a good deal about the birds. We pay a lot of attention to them, and trees and plants. And we watch the change of the seasons: yes, everybody knows about them. But those other things—you're right, ma'am—there ain't much—"Robinson Crusoe" and the Bible; and Handel's "Largo," we all know that; and Whistler's "Mother"—those are just about as far as we go.

LADY IN A BOX

So I thought. Thank you, Mr. Webb.

STAGE MANAGER

All right! All right! Thank you, everybody. (MR. WEBB retires.) We'll go back to the town now. It's middle of the afternoon. All 2,640 have had their dinners and all the dishes have been washed. There's an early afternoon calm in our town: a buzzin' and a hummin' from the school buildings; only a few buggies on Main Street— the horses dozing at the hitching-posts; you all remember what it's like. Doc Gibbs is in his office, tapping people and making them say "ah." Mr. Webb's cuttin' his lawn over there; one man in ten thinks it's a privilege to push his own lawn mower. No, sir. It's later than I thought. There are the children coming home from school already.

(EMILY WEBB comes sedately down Main Street carrying some school books. There are some signs that she is imagining herself to be a lady of striking elegance. Her father's movements to and fro with the lawn mower bring him into her vicinity.)

EMILY

I can't, Lois. I've got to go home and help my mother. I promised.

MR. WEBB

Emily, walk simply. Who do you think you are today?

EMILY

Papa, you're terrible. One minute you tell me to stand up straight and the next minute you call me names. I just don't listen to you.

(She gives him an abrupt kiss.)

MR. WEBB

Golly, I never got a kiss from such a great lady before.

(He goes out of sight. EMILY leans over and picks some flowers by the gate of her house. GEORGE GIBBS comes careening down Main Street. He is throwing a ball up to dizzying heights, and waiting to catch it again. This sometimes requires his taking six steps backward.)

GEORGE

Excuse me, Mrs. Forrest.

STAGE MANAGER (as MRS. FORREST)

Go out and play in the fields, young man. You got no business playing baseball on Main Street.

GEORGE

Awfully sorry, Mrs. Forrest.—Hello, Emily.

EMILY

H'lo.

GEORGE

You made a fine speech in class.

EMILY

Well . . . I was really ready to make a speech about the Monroe Doctrine, but at the last minute Miss Corcoran made me talk about the Louisiana Purchase instead. I worked an awful long time on both of them.

GEORGE

Gee, it's funny, Emily. From my window up there I can just see your head nights when you're doing your homework over in your room.

EMILY

Why, can you?

GEORGE

You certainly do stick to it, Emily. I don't see how you can sit still that long. I guess you like school.

EMILY

Well, I always feel it's something you have to go through.

GEORGE

Yeah.

EMILY

I don't mind it really. It passes the time.

GEORGE

Yeah.—Emily, what do you think? We might work out a kinda telegraph from there to there; and once in a while you could give me a kinda hint or two about one of those Algebra problems. I don't mean the answers, Emily, of course not . . . just some little hint. . . .

EMILY

Oh, I think *hints* are allowed.—So-ah —if you get stuck, George, you whistle to me; and I'll give you some hints.

GEORGE

Emily, you're just naturally bright, I guess.

EMILY

I figure that it's just the way a person's born.

GEORGE

Yeah. But, you see, I want to be a farmer, and my Uncle Luke says whenever I'm ready I can come over and work on his farm and if I'm any good I can just gradually have it.

EMILY

You mean the house and everything? (*Enter* MRS. WEBB.)

GEORGE

Yeah. Well, thanks . . . I better be getting out to the baseball field. Thanks for the talk, Emily.—Good afternoon, Mrs. Webb.

MRS. WEBB

Good afternoon, George.

GEORGE

So-long, Emily.

EMILY

So-long, George.

MRS. WEBB

Emily, come and help me string these beans for the winter. George Gibbs let himself have a real conversation, didn't he? Why, he's growing up. How old would George be?

EMILY

I don't know.

MRS. WEBB

Let's see. He must be almost sixteen.

EMILY

Mama, I made a speech in class today and I was very good.

MRS. WEBB

You must recite it to your father at supper. What was it about?

EMILY

The Louisiana Purchase. It was like silk off a spool. I'm going to make speeches all my life.—Mama, are these big enough?

MRS. WEBB

Try and get them a little bigger if you can.

EMILY

Mama, will you answer me a question, serious?

MRS. WEBB

Seriously, dear—not serious.

EMILY

Seriously,—will you?

MRS. WEBB

Of course, I will.

EMILY

Mama, am I good-looking?

MRS. WEBB

Yes, of course you are. All my children have got good features; I'd be ashamed if they hadn't.

EMILY

Oh, Mama, that's not what I mean. What I mean is: am I *pretty*?

MRS. WEBB

I've already told you, yes. Now that's enough of that. You have a nice young pretty face. I never heard of such foolishness.

EMILY

Oh, Mama, you never tell us the truth about anything.

MRS. WEBB

I *am* telling you the truth.

EMILY

Mama, were *you* pretty?

MRS. WEBB

Yes, I was, if I do say it. I was the prettiest girl in town next to Mamie Cartwright.

EMILY

But, Mama, you've got to say *something* about me. Am I pretty enough . . . to get anybody . . . to get people interested in me?

MRS. WEBB

Emily, you make me tired. Now stop it. You're pretty enough for all normal purposes. Come along now and bring that bowl with you.

EMILY

Oh, Mama, you're no help at all.

STAGE MANAGER

Thank you. Thank you! That'll do. We'll have to interrupt again here. Thank you, Mrs. Webb; thank you, Emily. (MRS. WEBB *and* EMILY *withdraw.*) There are some more things we've got to explore about this town. This time we're going to go about it in another way: we're going to look back on it from the future. I'm not going to tell you what became of these two families we're seeing most of, because the rest of the play will tell you about them. But take some of these others: Take Joe Crowell, Jr.: Joe was a very bright fellow. He graduated with honors and got a scholarship to Boston Tech.,— M.I.T., that is. But the War broke out and Joe died in France. All that education for nothing. Howie Newsome's still delivering milk at Grover's Corners. He's an old man now, has a lot of help, but he still delivers it himself. Says he gets the feel of the town that way. Carries all the accounts in his head; never has to write down a word. Mr. Morgan's drug store ain't the same,—it's all citified. Mr. Morgan retired and went out to live in San Diego, California, where his daughter married a real estate man, name of Kerby. Mr. Morgan died there in 1935 and was buried in a lot of palm trees. Kinda lost his religion at the end and took up New Thought or something. They read some new-fangled poetry over him and cremated him. The New Hampshire in him sort of broke down in him in that climate, seems like. The Cartwrights got richer and richer. The house is closed most of the year. They're off eating big dinners in hotels now,—in Virginia Hot Springs and Miami Beach. They say the winters are cold here. I see where they've become 'Piscopalians. The Cartwright interests have just begun building a new bank in Grover's Corners—had to go to Vermont for the marble, sorry to say. And they've asked a friend of mine what they should put in the cornerstone for people to dig up a thousand years from now. Of course, they've put in a copy of the New York *Times* and a copy of Mr. Webb's *Sentinel*. We're kind of interested in this because some scientific fellas have found a way of painting all that reading matter with a kind of glue—silicate glue—that'll make it keep a thousand—two thousand years. We're putting in a Bible . . . and the Constitution of the United States and a copy of William Shakespeare's plays. What do you say, folks? What do you think? Y'know—Babylon once had two million people in it, and all we know about 'em is the names of the kings and some copies of wheat contracts and . . . the sales of slaves. Yes, every night all those families sat down to supper, and the father came home from his work, and the smoke went up the chimney,—same as here. And even in Greece and Rome, all we know about the real life of the people is what we can piece together out of the joking poems and the comedies they wrote for the theater back then. So I'm going to have a copy of this play put in the cornerstone and the people a thousand years from now'll know a few simple facts about us—more than the Treaty of Versailles and the Lindbergh flight. See what I mean? Well,—you people a thousand years from now,—in the provinces north of New York at the beginning of the Twentieth Century, people et three times a day: soon after sunrise; at noon; and at sunset. Every seventh day, by law and by religion, was a day of rest and all work come to a stop. The religion at that time was Christianity. I guess you have some other records about Christianity. The domestic set-up was marriage: a binding relation between a male and one female that lasted for life. Christianity strictly forbade killing, but you were allowed to kill animals, and you were allowed to kill human beings in war and government punishings. I guess we don't have to tell you about the government and business forms, because that's the kind of thing people seem to hand down first of all. Let me see now if there's anything else. Oh, yes,—at death people were buried in the ground just as they are. So, friends, this is the way we were in our growing up and in our marrying and in our doctoring and in our living and in our dying. Now we'll return to our day in Grover's Corners. A lot of time has gone by. It's evening. You can hear choir practice going on in the Congregational Church. All the children are at home doing their school work. The day is running down like a tired clock.

(*A choir partially concealed in the orchestra pit has begun singing "Blessed be the tie that binds."* SIMON STIMSON *stands directing them. Two ladders have been pushed on to the stage; they serve as indication of the second story in the Gibbs and Webb houses.* GEORGE *and* EMILY *mount them, and apply themselves to their school work.* DR. GIBBS *has entered and is seated in his kitchen reading.*)

SIMON STIMSON

Now look here, everybody. Music come into the world to give pleasure.—Softer! Softer! Get it out of your heads that music's only good when it's loud. You leave loudness to the Methodists. You couldn't beat 'em, even if you wanted to. Now again. Tenors!

GEORGE

Hssst! Emily!

EMILY

Hello.

GEORGE

Hello!

EMILY

I can't work at all. The moonlight's so *terrible.*

GEORGE

Emily, did you get the third problem?

EMILY

Which?

GEORGE

The *third?*

EMILY

Why, yes, George—that's the easiest of them all.

GEORGE

I don't see it. Emily, can you give me a hint?

EMILY

I'll tell you one thing: the answer's in yards.

GEORGE

!!! In yards? How do you mean?

EMILY

In *square* yards.

GEORGE

Oh . . . in square yards.

EMILY

Yes, George, don't you see?

GEORGE

Yeah.

EMILY

In square yards of *wallpaper*.

GEORGE

Wallpaper,—oh, I see. Thanks a lot, Emily.

EMILY

You're welcome. My, isn't the moonlight *terrible?* And choir practice going on.— I think if you hold your breath you can hear the train all the way to Contookuck. Hear it?

GEORGE

M-m-m—What do you know!

EMILY

Well, I guess I better go back and try to work.

GEORGE

Good night, Emily. And thanks.

EMILY

Good night, George.

SIMON STIMSON

Before I forget it: how many of you will be able to come in Tuesday afternoon and sing at Fred Hersey's wedding, —show your hands. That'll be fine; that'll be right nice. We'll do the same music we did for Jane Trowbridge's last month. —Now we'll do: "Art thou weary; art thou languid?" It's a question, ladies and gentlemen, make it talk. Ready.

DR. GIBBS

Oh, George, can you come down a minute?

GEORGE

Yes, Pa.
(*He descends the ladder.*)

DR. GIBBS

Make yourself comfortable, George; I'll only keep you a minute. George, how old are you?

GEORGE

I? I'm sixteen, almost seventeen.

DR. GIBBS

What do you want to do after school's over?

GEORGE

Why, you know, Pa, I want to be a farmer on Uncle Luke's farm.

DR. GIBBS

You'll be willing, will you, to get up early and milk and feed the stock . . . and you'll be able to hoe and hay all day?

GEORGE

Sure, I will. What are you . . . what do you mean, Pa?

DR. GIBBS

Well, George, while I was in my office today I heard a funny sound . . . and what do you think it was? It was your mother chopping wood. There you see your mother—getting up early; cooking meals all day long; washing and ironing; —and still she has to go out in the back yard and chop wood. I suppose she just got tired of asking you. She just gave up and decided it was easier to do it herself. And you eat her meals, and put on the clothes she keeps nice for you, and you run off and play baseball,—like she's some hired girl we keep around the house but that we don't like very much. Well, I knew all I had to do was call your attention to it. Here's a handkerchief, son. George, I've decided to raise your spending money twenty-five cents a week. Not, of course, for chopping wood for your mother, because that's a present you give her, but because you're getting older— and I imagine there are lots of things you must find to do with it.

GEORGE

Thanks, Pa.

DR. GIBBS

Let's see—tomorrow's pay day. You can count on it—Hmm. Probably Rebecca'll feel she ought to have some more too. Wonder what could have happened to your mother. Choir practice never was as late as this before.

GEORGE

It's only half-past eight, Pa.

DR. GIBBS

I don't know why she's in that old choir. She hasn't any more voice than an old crow. . . . Traipsin' around the streets at this hour of the night. . . . Just about time you retired, don't you think?

GEORGE

Yes, Pa.

(GEORGE *mounts to his place on the ladder. Laughter and good nights can be heard on stage left and presently* MRS. GIBBS, MRS. SOAMES *and* MRS. WEBB *come down Main Street. When they arrive at the center of the stage they stop.*)

MRS. SOAMES

Good night, Martha. Good night, Mr. Foster.

MRS. WEBB

I'll tell Mr. Webb; I *know* he'll want to put it in the paper.

MRS. GIBBS

My, it's late!

MRS. SOAMES

Good night, Irma.

MRS. GIBBS

Real nice choir practice, wa'n't it? Myrtle Webb! Look at that moon, will you! Tsk-tsk-tsk. Potato weather, for sure.

MRS. SOAMES

Naturally I didn't want to say a word about it in front of those others, but now we're alone—really, it's the worst scandal that ever was in this town!

MRS. GIBBS

What?

MRS. SOAMES

Simon Stimson!

MRS. GIBBS

Now, Louella!

MRS. SOAMES

But, Julia! To have the organist of a church drink and drunk year after year. You know he was drunk tonight.

MRS. GIBBS

Now, Louella! We all know about Mr. Stimson, and we all know about the troubles he's been through, and Dr. Ferguson knows too, and if Dr. Ferguson keeps him on there in his job the only thing the rest of us can do is just not to notice it.

MRS. SOAMES

Not to notice it! But it's getting worse.

MRS. WEBB

No, it isn't, Louella. It's getting better. I've been in that choir twice as long as you have. It doesn't happen anywhere near so often. . . . My, I hate to go to bed on a night like this.—I better hurry. Those children'll be sitting up till all hours. Good night, Louella.

(*She hurries down stage, enters her house and disappears.*)

MRS. GIBBS

Can you get home safe, Louella?

MRS. SOAMES

It's as bright as day. I can see Mr. Soames scowling at the window now. You'd think we'd been to a dance the way the menfolk carry on.

(*Repeated good nights.* MRS. GIBBS *arrives at her home.*)

MRS. GIBBS

Well, we had a real good time.

DR. GIBBS

You're late enough.

MRS. GIBBS

Why, Frank, it ain't any later 'n usual.

DR. GIBBS

And you stopping at the corner to gossip with a lot of hens.

MRS. GIBBS

Now, Frank, don't be grouchy. Come out and smell my heliotrope in the moonlight. (*They stroll out arm in arm along the footlights.*) Isn't that wonderful? What did you do all the time I was away?

DR. GIBBS

Oh, I read—as usual. What were the girls gossiping about tonight?

MRS. GIBBS

Well, believe me, Frank—there is something to gossip about.

DR. GIBBS

Hmm! Simon Stimson far gone, was he?

MRS. GIBBS

Worst I've ever seen him. How'll that end, Frank? Dr. Ferguson can't forgive him forever.

DR. GIBBS

I guess I know more about Simon Stimson's affairs than anybody in this town. Some people ain't made for small town life. I don't know how that'll end; but there's nothing we can do but just leave it alone. Come, get in.

MRS. GIBBS

No, not yet. . . . Oh, Frank, I'm worried about you.

DR. GIBBS

What are you worried about?

MRS. GIBBS

I think it's my duty to make plans for you to get a real rest and change. And if I get that legacy, well, I'm going to insist on it.

DR. GIBBS

Now, Julia, there's no sense in going over that again.

MRS. GIBBS

Frank, you're just *unreasonable!*

DR. GIBBS

Come on, Julia, it's getting late. First thing you know you'll catch cold. I gave George a piece of my mind tonight. I reckon you'll have your wood chopped for a while anyway. No, no, start getting upstairs.

MRS. GIBBS

Oh, dear. There's always so many things to pick up, seems like. You know, Frank, Mrs. Fairchild always locks her front door every night. All those people up that part of town do.

DR. GIBBS

They're all getting citified, that's the trouble with them. They haven't got nothing fit to burgle and everybody knows it. (*They disappear.* REBECCA *climbs up the ladder beside* GEORGE.)

GEORGE

Get out, Rebecca. There's only room for one at this window. You're always spoiling everything.

REBECCA

Well, let me look just a minute.

GEORGE

Use your own window.

REBECCA

I did; but there's no moon there. . . . George, do you know what I think, do you? I think maybe the moon's getting nearer and nearer and there'll be a big 'splosion.

GEORGE

Rebecca, you don't know anything. If the moon were getting nearer, the guys that sit up all night with telescopes would see it first and they'd tell about it, and it'd be in all the newspapers.

REBECCA

George, is the moon shining on South America, Canada and half the whole world?

GEORGE

Well—prob'ly is. (*The* STAGE MANAGER *strolls on.*)

STAGE MANAGER

Nine-thirty. Most of the lights are out. No, there's Constable Warren trying a few doors on Main Street. And here comes Editor Webb, after putting his newspaper to bed.

MR. WEBB

Good evening, Bill.

CONSTABLE WARREN

Evenin', Mr. Webb.

MR. WEBB

Quite a moon!

CONSTABLE WARREN

Yepp.

MR. WEBB

All quiet tonight?

CONSTABLE WARREN

Simon Stimson is rollin' around a little. Just saw his wife movin' out to hunt for him so I looked the other way—there he is now.

(SIMON STIMSON *comes down Main Street from the left, only a trace of unsteadiness in his walk.*)

MR. WEBB

Good evening, Simon. . . . Town seems to have settled down for the night pretty well. . . . (SIMON STIMSON *comes up to him and pauses a moment.*) Good evening. . . . Yes, most of the town's settled down for the night, Simon. . . . I guess we better do the same. Can I walk along a ways with you? (SIMON STIMSON *continues on his way without a word and disappears at the right.*) Good night.

CONSTABLE WARREN

I don't know how that's goin' to end, Mr. Webb.

MR. WEBB

Well, he's seen a peck of trouble, one thing after another. . . . Oh, Bill . . . if you see my boy smoking cigarettes, just give him a word, will you? He thinks a lot of you, Bill.

CONSTABLE WARREN

I don't think he smokes no cigarettes, Mr. Webb. Leastways, not more'n two or three a year. He don't belong to that crowd that hangs out down by the gully.

MR. WEBB

Hm. . . . I hope not.—Well, good night, Bill.

CONSTABLE WARREN

Good night, Mr. Webb.
(*Exit.*)

MR. WEBB

Who's that up there? Is that you, Myrtle?

EMILY

No, it's me, Papa.

MR. WEBB

Why aren't you in bed?

EMILY

I don't know. I just can't sleep yet, Papa. The moonlight's so *won*-derful. And the smell of Mrs. Gibbs's heliotrope. Can you smell it?

MR. WEBB

Hm. . . . Yes. Haven't any troubles on your mind, have you, Emily?

EMILY

Troubles, Papa. No.

MR. WEBB

Well, enjoy yourself, but don't let your mother catch you. Good night, Emily.

EMILY

Good night, Papa.
(MR. WEBB *crosses into the house, whistling "Blessed Be the Tie that Binds" and disappears.*)

REBECCA

I never told you about that letter Jane Crofut got from her minister when she was sick. The minister of her church in the town she was in before she came here. He wrote Jane a letter and on the envelope the address was like this: It said: Jane Crofut; The Crofut Farm; Grover's Corners; Sutton County; New Hampshire; United States of America.

GEORGE

What's funny about that?

REBECCA

But listen, it's not finished: the United States of America; Continent of North America; Western Hemisphere; the Earth; the Solar System; the Universe; the Mind of God,—that's what it said on the envelope.

GEORGE

What do you know!

REBECCA

And the postman brought it just the same.

GEORGE

What do you know!

STAGE MANAGER

That's the end of the First Act, friends. You can go and smoke now, those that smoke.

ACT TWO

The tables and chairs of the two kitchens are still on the stage.
The ladders have been withdrawn.
The STAGE MANAGER *has been at his accustomed place watching the audience return to its seats.*

STAGE MANAGER

Three years have gone by. Yes, the sun's come up over a thousand times. Summers and winters have cracked the mountains a little bit more and the rains have brought down some of the dirt. Some babies that weren't even born before have begun talking regular sentences already; and a number of people who thought they were right young and spry have noticed that they can't bound up a flight of stairs like they used to, without their heart fluttering a little. Some older sons are sitting at the head of the table, and some people I know are having their meat cut up for them.— All that can happen in a thousand days. Nature's been pushing and contriving in other ways, too: a number of young people fell in love and got married. Yes, the mountain got bit away a few fractions of an inch; millions of gallons of water went by the mill; and here and there a new home was set up under a roof. Almost everybody in the world gets married,— you know what I mean? In our town there aren't hardly any exceptions. Most everybody in the world climbs into their graves married. The First Act was called the Daily Life. This Act is called Love and Marriage. There's another Act coming after this: I reckon you can guess what that's about. So: It's three years later. It's

1904. It's July 7th, just after High School Commencement. That's the time most of our young people jump up and get married. Soon as they've passed their last examinations in solid geometry and Cicero's Orations, looks like they suddenly feel themselves fit to be married. It's early morning. Only this time it's been raining. It's been pouring and thundering. Mrs. Gibbs's garden, and Mrs. Webb's here: drenched. All those bean poles and pea vines: drenched. All yesterday over there on Main Street, the rain looked like curtains being blown along. Hm . . . it may begin again any minute. There! You can hear the 5:45 for Boston. And here comes Howie Newsome delivering the milk. And there's Si Crowell delivering the papers like his brother before him.—You remember about his brother?—all that education he's going to get and that'll be wasted. And there's Mrs. Gibbs and Mrs. Webb come down to make breakfast, just as though it were an ordinary day. I don't have to point out to the women in my audience that those ladies they see before them, both those ladies cooked three meals a day,—one of 'em for twenty years, the other for forty,—and no summer vacation. They brought up two children apiece; washed; cleaned the house,—and never a nervous breakdown. Never thought themselves hard-used, either. It's like what one of those Middle West poets said: You've got to love life to have life, and you've got to have life to love life. . . . It's what they call a vicious circle.

(SI CROWELL *has entered hurling imaginary newspapers into doorways;* HOWIE NEWSOME *has come along Main Street with* BESSIE.)

HOWIE NEWSOME

Git-ap, Bessie.

SI CROWELL

Morning, Howie.

HOWIE NEWSOME

Morning, Si.—Anything in the papers I ought to know?

SI CROWELL

Nothing much, except we're losing about the best baseball pitcher Grover's Corners ever had.

HOWIE NEWSOME

Reckon he was. He's been standing off the whole of South New Hampshire single-handed, looks like.

SI CROWELL

He could hit and run bases, too.

HOWIE NEWSOME

Yep. Mighty fine ball player.—Bessie! I guess I can stop and talk if I've a mind to!

SI CROWELL

I don't see how he could give up a thing like that just to get married. Would you, Howie?

HOWIE NEWSOME

Can't tell, Si. Never had no talent that way. (CONSTABLE WARREN *enters. They exchange mornings.*) You're up early, Bill.

CONSTABLE WARREN

Seein' if there's anything I can do to prevent a flood. River's been risin' all night.

HOWIE NEWSOME

Si Crowell's all worked up here about George Gibbs retiring from baseball.

CONSTABLE WARREN

Yes, sir; that's the way it goes. Back in '84 we had a player, Si,—even George Gibbs couldn't touch him. Name of Hank Todd. Went down to Maine and become a parson. Wonderful ball player.—Howie, how did the weather look to you?

HOWIE NEWSOME

No, 'tain't bad. Think maybe it'll clear up for good.

(CONSTABLE WARREN *and* SI CROWELL *continue on their way.* HOWIE NEWSOME *brings the milk first to* MRS. GIBBS's *house. She meets him by the trellis.*)

MRS. GIBBS

Good morning, Howie. Do you think it's going to rain again?

HOWIE NEWSOME

Morning, Mrs. Gibbs. It rained so heavy, I think maybe it'll clear up.

MRS. GIBBS

Certainly hope it will.

HOWIE NEWSOME

How much did you want today?

MRS. GIBBS

I guess I'll need three-a-milk and two-a-cream, Howie. I'm going to have a house full of relations.

HOWIE NEWSOME

My wife says to tell you we both hope they'll be very happy, Mrs. Gibbs. Know they *will*.

MRS. GIBBS

Thanks a lot, Howie. Tell your wife I hope she gits there to the wedding.

HOWIE NEWSOME

Yes, she'll be there; she'll be there if she kin. (HOWIE NEWSOME *crosses to* MRS. WEBB's *house.*) Morning, Mrs. Webb.

MRS. WEBB

Oh, good morning, Mr. Newsome. I told you four quarts of milk, but I hope you can spare me another.

HOWIE NEWSOME

Yes'm . . . and the two of cream.

MRS. WEBB

Will it rain all day, Mr. Newsome?

HOWIE NEWSOME

No'm. Just sayin' to Mrs. Gibbs as how it may lighten up. Mrs. Newsome told me to tell you as how we hope they'll both be very happy, Mrs. Webb. Know they *will*.

MRS. WEBB

Thank you, and thank Mrs. Newsome and we hope to see you all at the wedding.

HOWIE NEWSOME

Yes, Mrs. Webb. We hope to git there. couldn't miss that. Chck! Bessie!

(*Exit* HOWIE NEWSOME. DR. GIBBS *descends in shirt sleeves, and sits down at his breakfast table.*)

DR. GIBBS

Well, Ma, the day has come. You're losin' one of your chicks.

MRS. GIBBS

Frank Gibbs, don't you say another word. I feel like crying every minute. Sit down and drink your coffee.

DR. GIBBS

The groom's up shaving himself. Whistling and singing, like he's glad to leave us.—Every now and then he says "I do" to the mirror, but it don't sound convincing to me.

MRS. GIBBS

I declare I don't know how he'll get along. I've arranged his clothes and seen to it he's put warm things on,—Frank! they're too young. Emily won't think of such things. He'll catch his death of cold within a week.—Here's something I made for you.

DR. GIBBS

Why, Julia Hersey! French toast!

MRS. GIBBS

'Tain't hard to make, and I had to do something.

DR. GIBBS

I remember my wedding morning, Julia.

MRS. GIBBS

Now don't start that, Frank Gibbs. I tell you I can't stand it.

DR. GIBBS

I was the scardest young fella in the State of New Hampshire. I thought I'd made a mistake for sure. And when I saw you comin' down that aisle I thought you were the prettiest girl I'd ever seen, but the only trouble was that I'd never seen you before. There I was in the Congregational Church marryin' a total stranger.

MRS. GIBBS

And how do you think I felt!—Did you hear Rebecca stirring about upstairs?

DR. GIBBS

Only morning in the year she hasn't been managing everybody's business. She's shut up in her room. I got the impression that maybe she's crying.

MRS. GIBBS

Good Lord! This has got to stop.—Rebecca! Rebecca! Everything's getting cold down here.

(GEORGE *comes rattling down the stairs, very brisk.*)

GEORGE

Good morning, everybody. Only five more hours to live.

(*Makes the gesture of cutting his throat.*)

MRS. GIBBS

Where are you going?

GEORGE

Just stepping across the grass to see my girl.

MRS. GIBBS

Now, George! You take an umbrella or I won't let you out of this house.

GEORGE

Aw, Ma. It's just a *step*!

MRS. GIBBS

From tomorrow on you can kill yourself in all weathers, but while you're in my house you live wisely, thank you. There

are your overshoes right there in the hall.
And here's an umbrella.

GEORGE

Aw, Ma!

DR. GIBBS

George, do as your mother tells you.

MRS. GIBBS

Maybe Mrs. Webb isn't used to callers
at seven in the morning. Take a cup-a
coffee first.

GEORGE

Be back in a minute. (*He crosses the
stage, leaping over the puddles.*) Good
morning, Mother Webb.

MRS. WEBB

Goodness! You frightened me!—Now,
George, you can come in a minute out of
the wet, but you know I can't ask you in.

GEORGE

Why not—?

MRS. WEBB

George, you know's well as I do: the
groom can't see his bride on his wedding
day, not until he sees her in church.

GEORGE

Aw!—that's just a superstition.
(*Enter* MR. WEBB.)

MR. WEBB

Good morning, George.

GEORGE

Mr. Webb, you don't believe in that
superstition, do you?

MR. WEBB

There's a lot of common sense in some
superstitions, George.

MRS. WEBB

Millions have folla'd it, George, and
you don't want to be the first to fly in the
face of custom.

GEORGE

How is Emily?

MRS. WEBB

She hasn't waked up yet. I haven't heard
a sound out of her.

GEORGE

Emily's *asleep!!!*

MRS. WEBB

No wonder! We were up 'till all hours,
—sewing and packing. I'll tell you what
I'll do; you set down here a minute with
Mr. Webb and drink this cup of coffee;
and I'll go upstairs and see she doesn't
come down and surprise you. There's some
bacon, too; but don't be long about it.
(*Exit* MRS. WEBB. *Embarrassed silence.*)

MR. WEBB

Well, George, how are you?

GEORGE

Oh, fine. I'm fine. (*Pause.*) Mr. Webb,
what sense could there be in a superstition like that?

MR. WEBB

Well, you see,—on her wedding morning a girl's head's apt to be full of . . .
clothes and things like that. Don't you
think that's probably it?

GEORGE

Ye-e-s. I never thought of that.

MR. WEBB

A girl's apt to be a mite nervous on her
wedding day.
(*Pause.*)

GEORGE

I wish a fellow could get married without all that marching up and down.

MR. WEBB

Well, every man that's ever lived has
felt that way about it, George; but it hasn't
done much good. It's the women that
have built up weddings, my boy. From
now on they have it pretty much as they
like. . . . All those good women standing
shoulder to shoulder making sure that
the knot's tied in a mighty public way.

GEORGE

But . . . you *believe* in it, don't you,
Mr. Webb?

MR. WEBB

Oh, yes; oh, yes. Don't you misunderstand me, my boy. Marriage is a wonder-

ful thing,—wonderful thing. And don't you forget that, George.

GEORGE

No, sir.—Mr. Webb, how old were you when you got married?

MR. WEBB

Well, you see: I'd been to college and I'd taken a little time to get settled. But Mrs. Webb,—she wasn't much older than what Emily is. Oh, age hasn't much to do with it, George,—not compared to other things.

GEORGE

What were you going to say, Mr. Webb?

MR. WEBB

Oh, I don't know,—was I going to say something? (*Pause.*) George, I was thinking the other night of some advice my father gave me when I got married. Charles, he said, Charles, start out early showing who's boss, he said. Best thing to do is to give an order, even if it don't make sense; just so she'll learn to obey. And he said: if anything about your wife irritates you,—her conversation, or anything,—just get up and leave the house. That'll make it clear to her, he said. And, oh, yes! he said never, *never* let your wife know how much money you have, never.

GEORGE

Well, Mr. Webb . . . I don't think I could . . .

MR. WEBB

So I took the opposite of my father's advice and I've been happy ever since. And let that be a lesson to you, George, never to ask advice on personal matters.— George, are you going to raise chickens on your farm?

GEORGE

What?

MR. WEBB

Are you going to raise chickens on your farm?

GEORGE

Uncle Luke's never been much interested, but I thought—

MR. WEBB

A book came into my office the other day, George, on the Philo System of raising chickens. I want you to read it. I'm thinking of beginning in a small way in the back yard, and I'm going to put an incubator in the cellar—

(*Enter* MRS. WEBB.)

MRS. WEBB

Charles, are you talking about that old incubator again? I thought you two'd be talking about things worth while.

MR. WEBB

Well, Myrtle, if you want to give the boy some good advice, I'll go upstairs and leave you alone with him.

MRS. WEBB

Now, George, I'm sorry, but I've got to send you away so that Emily can come down and get some breakfast. She told me to tell you that she sends you her love but that she doesn't want to lay eyes on you. So good-by, George.

(GEORGE *crosses the stage to his own home and disappears.*)

MR. WEBB

Myrtle, I guess you don't know about that older superstition.

MRS. WEBB

What do you mean, Charles?

MR. WEBB

Since the cave-men: the groom shouldn't be left alone with his father-in-law on the day of the wedding, or near it. Now don't forget that!

STAGE MANAGER

Thank you. Thank you, everybody. Now I have to interrupt again here. You see, we want to know how all this began, —this wedding, this plan to spend a lifetime together. I'm awfully interested in how big things like that begin. You know how it is: you're twenty-one or twenty-two and you make some decisions; then whisssh! you're seventy: you've been a lawyer for fifty years, and that white-haired lady at your side has eaten over fifty thousand meals with you. How do such things begin? George and Emily are going to show you now the conversation they had when they first knew that . . . that . . . as the saying goes . . . they were meant for one another. But before they do it I want you to try and remember what it was like when you were young, when you were fifteen or sixteen. For some reason it is very hard to do: those days when even the little things in life could be almost too exciting to bear. And particularly the days when you were first in love; when you were like a person sleep-walking, and you didn't quite see the street you were in, and didn't quite hear everything that was said to you. You're just a little bit crazy. Will you remember that, please? Now they'll be coming out of High School at three o'clock. George has just been elected President of the Junior Class, and as it's June, that means he'll be President of the Senior Class all next year. And Emily's just been elected Secretary and Treasurer. I don't have to tell you how important that is. (*He places a board across the backs of two chairs, parallel to the footlights, and places two high stools behind it. This is the counter of* MR. MORGAN's *drugstore.*) All ready!

(EMILY, *carrying an armful of—imaginary—school books, comes along Main Street from the left.*)

EMILY

I can't, Louise. I've got to go home. Good-by. Oh, Ernestine! Ernestine! Can you come over tonight and do Algebra? I did the first and third in Study Hall. No, they're not hard. But, Ernestine, that Caesar's awful hard. I don't see why we have to do a thing like that. Come over about seven. Tell your mother you *have* to. G'by. G'by, Helen. G'by, Fred.

(GEORGE, *also carrying books, catches up with her.*)

GEORGE

Can I carry your books home for you, Emily?

EMILY (*coldly*)

Thank you.
(*She gives them to him.*)

GEORGE

Excuse me a minute, Emily.—Say, Bob,

get everything ready. I'll be there in a quarter of an hour. If I'm a little late start practice anyway. And give Herb some long high ones. His eye needs a lot of practice. Seeya later.

EMILY

Good-by, Lizzy.

GEORGE

Good-by, Lizzy.—I'm awfully glad you were elected, too, Emily.

EMILY

Thank you.
(*They have been standing on Main Street, almost against the back wall.* GEORGE *is about to take the first steps towards the audience when he stops again and says:*)

GEORGE

Emily, why are you mad at me?

EMILY

I'm not mad at you.

GEORGE

You . . . you treat me so funny.

EMILY

Well, I might as well say it right out, George. I don't like the whole change that's come over you in the last year. I'm sorry if that hurts your feelings, but I've just got to tell the truth and shame the devil.

GEORGE

I'm awfully sorry, Emily. Wha-a-what do you mean?

EMILY

Well, up to a year ago I used to like you a lot. And I used to watch you as you did everything . . . because we'd been friends so long . . . and then you began spending all your time at baseball . . . and you never even spoke to anybody any more; not even to your own family you didn't . . . and, George, it's a fact, you've got awful conceited and stuck-up, and all the girls say so. They may not say so to your face, but that's what they say about you behind your back, and it hurts me to hear them say it, but I've got to agree with them a little. I'm sorry if it hurts your feelings . . . but I can't be sorry I said it.

GEORGE

I . . . I'm glad you said it, Emily. I never thought that such a thing was happening to me. I guess it's hard for a fella not to have faults creep into his character.
(*They take a step or two in silence, then stand still in misery.*)

EMILY

I always expect a man to be perfect and I think he should be.

GEORGE

Oh . . . I don't think it's possible to be perfect, Emily.

EMILY

Well, my father is, and as far as I can see your father is. There's no reason on earth why you shouldn't be, too.

GEORGE

Well, Emily . . . I feel it's the other way round. That men aren't naturally good; but girls are. Like you and your mother and my mother.

EMILY

Well, you might as well know right now that I'm not perfect. It's not as easy for a girl to be perfect as a man, because we girls are more nervous.—Now I'm sorry I said all that about you. I don't know what made me say it.

GEORGE

No, no,—I guess if it's the truth you ought to say it. You stick to it, Emily.

EMILY

I don't know if it's the truth or not. And I suddenly feel that it isn't important at all.

GEORGE

Emily, would you like an ice-cream soda, or something, before you go home?

EMILY

Well, thank you. . . . I would.
(*They come into the drugstore and seat themselves on the stools.*)

STAGE MANAGER (*as* MR. MORGAN)

Hello, George. Hello, Emily. What'll

you have? Why, Emily Webb, what've you been crying about?

GEORGE (*he gropes for an explanation*)

She . . . she just got an awful scare, Mr. Morgan. She almost got run over by that hardware store wagon. Everybody always says that Tom Huckins drives like a crazy man.

STAGE MANAGER

Here, take a drink of water, Emily. You look all shook up. There!—Now, what'll you have?

EMILY

I'll have a strawberry phosphate, thank you, Mr. Morgan.

GEORGE

No, no. You go and have an ice-cream soda with me, Emily.—Two strawberry ice-cream sodas, Mr. Morgan.

STAGE MANAGER (*working the faucets*)

Yes, sir. I tell you, you've got to look both ways before you cross Main Street these days. Gets worse every year. There are a hundred and twenty-five horses in Grover's Corners this minute I'm talking to you. State Inspector was in here yesterday. And now they're bringing in these auto-mo-biles, the best thing to do is to just stay home. Why, I can remember the time when a dog could lie down all day in the middle of Main Street and nothing would come to disturb him.—Yes, Miss Ellis; be with you in a minute. Here are your sodas. Enjoy 'em.
(*He goes off.*)

EMILY

They're so expensive.

GEORGE

No, no,—don't you think of that. We're celebrating. First, we're celebrating our election. And then do you know what else I'm celebrating?

EMILY

No.

GEORGE

I'm celebrating because I've got a friend

who tells me all the things that ought to be told me.

EMILY

George, *please* don't think of that. I don't know why I said it. It's not true. You're—

GEORGE

No, you stick to it, Emily. I'm glad you spoke to me like you did. But you'll see: I'm going to change so quick—you bet I'm going to change. And, Emily, I want to ask you a favor.

EMILY

What?

GEORGE

Emily, if I go away to State Agriculture College next year, will you write me a letter once in a while?

EMILY

I certainly will. I certainly will, George. . . . (*Pause.*) It certainly seems like being away three years you'd get out of touch with things.

GEORGE

No, no. I mustn't do that. You see I'm not only going to be just a farmer. After a while maybe I'll run for something to get elected. So your letters'll be very important to me; you know, telling me what's going on here and everything. . . .

EMILY

Just the same, three years is a long time. Maybe letters from Grover's Corners wouldn't be so interesting after a while. Grover's Corners isn't a very important place when you think of all New Hampshire; but I think it's a very nice town.

GEORGE

The day wouldn't come when I wouldn't want to know everything that's happening here. I know *that's* true, Emily.

EMILY

Well, I'll try to make my letters interesting.
(*Pause.*)

GEORGE

Y'know, Emily, whenever I meet a farmer I ask him if he thinks it's important to go to Agriculture School to be a good farmer.

EMILY

Why, George—

GEORGE

Yeah, and some of them say that it's even a waste of time. You can get all those things, anyway, out of the pamphlets the government sends out. And Uncle Luke's getting old,—he's about ready for me to start in taking over his farm tomorrow, if I could.

EMILY

My!

GEORGE

And, like you say, being gone all that time . . . in other places and meeting other people . . . If anything like that can happen I don't want to go away. I guess new people aren't any better than old ones. I'll bet they almost never are. Emily . . . I feel that you're as good a friend as I've got. I don't need to go and meet the people in other towns.

EMILY

But, George, maybe it's very important for you to go and learn all that about cattle-judging and soils and those things. And if you're going into politics, maybe you ought to meet people from other parts of the State . . . of course, I don't know.

GEORGE (*after a pause*)

Emily, I'm going to make up my mind right now. I won't go. I'll tell Pa about it tonight.

EMILY

Why, George, I don't see why you have to decide right now. It's a whole year away.

GEORGE

Emily, I'm glad you spoke to me about that . . . that fault in my character. And what you said was right; but there was one thing wrong in it, and that was when you said that for a year I wasn't noticing people, and . . . you, for instance. Listen, Emily . . . you say you were watching me when I did everything. . . . Why, I was doing the same about you all the time. Why, sure,—I always thought about you as one of the chief people I thought about. I always made sure where you were sitting on the bleachers, and who you were with. And we've always had lots of talks . . . and joking, in the halls; and they always meant a lot to me. Of course, they weren't as good as the talk we're having now. Lately I'd been noticing that you'd been acting kind of funny to me, and for three days I've been trying to walk home with you, but something's always got in the way. Yesterday I was standing over against the wall waiting for you, and you walked home with Miss Corcoran.

EMILY

George! . . . Life's awful funny! How could I have known that? Why, I thought—

GEORGE

Listen, Emily, I'm going to tell you why I'm not going to Agriculture School. I think that once you've found a person that you're very fond of . . . I mean a person who's fond of you, too,—at least enough to be interested in your character . . . Well, I think that's just as important as college is, and even more so. That's what I think.

EMILY

I think it's awfully important, too.

GEORGE

Emily.

EMILY

Yes, George.

GEORGE

Emily, if I improve and make a big change . . . would you be . . . I mean: *could* you be . . .

EMILY

I . . . I am now; I always have been.

GEORGE (*pause*)

So I guess this is an important talk we've been having.

EMILY

Yes.

GEORGE (*takes a deep breath and straightens his back*)

Wait just a minute and I'll take you home. (*He rises and goes to the* STAGE MANAGER *who appears and comes toward him.*) Mr. Morgan, I'll have to go home and get the money to pay you for this. It'll only take me a minute.

STAGE MANAGER

What's that? George Gibbs, do you mean to tell me—!

GEORGE

Yes, but I had reasons, Mr. Morgan.— Look, here's my gold watch to keep until I come back with the money.

STAGE MANAGER

That's all right. Keep your watch. I'll trust you.

GEORGE

I'll be back in five minutes.

STAGE MANAGER

I'll trust you ten years, George,—not a day more.—Got all over your shock, Emily?

EMILY

Yes, thank you, Mr. Morgan. It was nothing.

GEORGE (*taking up the books from the counter*)

I'm ready.

(*They walk in grave silence down the stage, turn, and pass through the trellis at the Webbs' back door and disappear.*)

STAGE MANAGER

Thank you, Emily. Thank you, George. Now before we go on to the wedding, there are still some more things we ought to know about this—about this marriage. I want to know some more about how the parents took it; but what I want to know most of all is: oh, you know what I mean, —what Grover's Corners thought about marriage anyway. You know's well as I do: people are never able to say right out what they think of money, or death, or fame, or marriage. You've got to catch it between the lines; you've got to *over*-hear it. Oh, Doctor! Mrs. Gibbs!

(*They appear at their side of the stage and exchange a glance of understanding with him. The* STAGE MANAGER *lays the same plank across two chairs that served as a drugstore counter and it has now become* MRS. GIBBS's *ironing board.* DR. GIBBS *sits down in a rocker and smokes.* MRS. GIBBS *irons a moment in silence; then goes to the foot of the stairs and calls:*)

MRS. GIBBS

Rebecca! It's time you turned out your light and went to sleep. George, you'd better get some sleep, too.

REBECCA'S VOICE

Ma, I haven't finished my English.

MRS. GIBBS

What? Well, I bet you haven't been working, Rebecca. You've been reading that Sears, Roebuck catalogue, that's what you've been doing.—All right, I'll give you ten more minutes. If you haven't finished by then you'll just have to fail the course and be a disgrace to your father and me.—George, what are you doing?

GEORGE'S VOICE (*hurt*)

I'm doing history.

MRS. GIBBS

Well, you'd better go to bed. You're 'probably sleeping at the desk as it is.

(*She casts an amused eye at her husband and returns to her ironing.*)

DR. GIBBS

I had a long talk with the boy today.

MRS. GIBBS

Did you?

DR. GIBBS

I tell you, Mrs. G., there's nothing so terrifying in the world as a son. The relation of a father to a son is the damnedest, awkwardest—. I always come away feeling like a soggy sponge of hypocrisy.

MRS. GIBBS

Well, a mother and a daughter's no picnic, let me tell you.

DR. GIBBS

George is set on it: he wants to marry Emily 'soon as school's out and take her right on to the farm. (*Pause.*) He says he can sit up nights and learn agriculture from government pamphlets, without going to college for it.

MRS. GIBBS

He always was crazy about farming. Gets that from my people.

DR. GIBBS

At a pinch, I guess he could start in farming;—but I swear I think he's too young to get married. Julia, he's just a green half-grown kid. He isn't ready to be a family man.

MRS. GIBBS

No, he ain't. You're right.—But he's a good boy and I wouldn't like to think of him being alone out there . . . coming into town Satiddy nights, like any old farm hand, tuckered out from work and looking for excitement. He might get into bad ways. It wouldn't be enough fun for him to come and sit by our stove,—and holding hands with Emily, for a year mightn't be enough either. He might lose interest in her.

DR. GIBBS

Hm.

MRS. GIBBS

Frank, I' been watching her. George is a lucky boy when you think of all the silly girls in the world.

DR. GIBBS

But, Julia,—George *married*. That great gangling selfish nincompoop.

MRS. GIBBS

Yes, I know. (*She takes up a collar and examines it.*) Frank, what do you do to your collars? Do you gnaw 'em? I never saw such a man for collars.

DR. GIBBS

Julia, when I married you, do you

know what one of my terrors was in getting married?

MRS. GIBBS

Pshaw! Go on with you!

DR. GIBBS

I was afraid we weren't going to have material for conversation more'n 'ld last us a few weeks. I was afraid we'd run out and eat our meals in silence, that's a fact. You and I've been conversing for twenty years now without any noticeable barren spells.

MRS. GIBBS

Well, good weather, bad weather, 'tain't very choice, but I always manage to find something to say.
(*Pause.*)

DR. GIBBS

What do you think? What do you think, Julia? Shall we tell the boy he can go ahead and get married?

MRS. GIBBS

Seems like it's up to us to decide. Myrtle and Charles Webb are willing. They think it's a good idea to throw the young people into the sea and let'm sink or swim, as soon as they're ready.

DR. GIBBS

What does that mean? Must we decide right now? This minute?

MRS. GIBBS

There you go putting the responsibility on me!

DR. GIBBS

Here it is, almost April.—I'll go up and say a word to him right now before he goes to bed. (*He rises.*) You're sure, Julia? You've nothing more to add?

MRS. GIBBS (*stops ironing a moment*)

I don't know what to say. Seems like it's too much to ask, for a big outdoor boy like that to go and get shut up in classrooms for three years. And once he's on the farm, he might just as well have a companion, seeing he's found a fine girl like Emily. . . . People are meant to live two by two in this world. . . . Yes, Frank, go up and tell him it's all right.

DR. GIBBS (*crosses and is about to call when—*)

MRS. GIBBS (*her hands on her cheeks, staring into the audience, in sharp alarm:*)

Wait a minute! Wait a minute!—(*Then resuming her ironing.*) No,—go and tell him.

DR. GIBBS

Why did you stop then, Julia?

MRS. GIBBS

Oh, you know: I thought of all those times we went through in the first years when George and Rebecca were babies,—you walking up and down with them at three in the morning; the whooping-cough; the time George fell off the porch. You and I were twenty-five years old, and more. It's wonderful how one forgets one's troubles, like that.—Yes, Frank, go upstairs and tell him. . . . It's worth it.

DR. GIBBS

Yes, they'll have a lot of troubles, but that's none of our business. Let'm. Everybody has a right to his own troubles.—You ought to be present, Julia,—important occasion like that. I'll call him.—George! Oh, George!

GEORGE'S VOICE

Yes, Pa.

DR. GIBBS

Can you come down a minute? Your mother and I want to speak to you.

GEORGE

Yeah, sure.

MRS. GIBBS (*putting her arm through her husband's*)

Lord, what a fool I am: I'm trembling all over. There's nothing to tremble about.

STAGE MANAGER

Thank you! Thank you! Now we're ready to go on with the wedding. (*While he talks, the actors remove the chair and tables and trellises from the Gibbs and Webb homes. They arrange the pews for the church in the back of the stage. The congregation will sit facing the back wall. The aisle of the church is in the middle of the scene. A small platform is placed against the back wall on which the* STAGE MANAGER *as Minister can stand.*) There are a lot of things to be said about a wedding; there are a lot of thoughts that go on during a wedding. We can't get them all into one wedding, naturally, and especially not into a wedding at Grover's Corners where they're awfully plain and short. In this wedding I play the minister. That gives me the right to say a few more things about it. For a while now, the play gets pretty serious. Y'see, some churches say that marriage is a sacrament. I don't quite know what that means, but I can guess. Like Mrs. Gibbs said a few minutes ago: People were made to live two-by-two. This is a good wedding, but people are so put together that even at a good wedding there's a lot of confusion way down deep in people's minds and we thought that that ought to be in our play, too. The real hero of this scene isn't on the stage at all, and you know who that is. It's like what one of those European fellas said: every child born into the world is Nature's attempt to make a perfect human being. Well, we've seen nature pushing and contriving for some time now. We all know that nature's interested in quantity; but I think she's interested in quality, too,—that's why I'm in the ministry.—Maybe she's trying to make another good governor for New Hampshire. And don't forget the other witnesses at this wedding, —the ancestors. Millions of them. Most of them set out to live two-by-two, also. Millions of them. Well, that's all my sermon. 'Twan't very long, anyway.

(*The organ starts playing Handel's "Largo." The congregation streams into the church and sits in silence.* MRS. WEBB, *on the way to her place, turns back and speaks to the audience.*)

MRS. WEBB

I don't know why on earth I should be crying. I suppose there's nothing to cry about. It came over me at breakfast this morning; there was Emily eating her breakfast as she's done for seventeen years and now she's going off to eat it in someone else's house. I suppose that's it. And Emily! She suddenly said: I can't eat another mouthful, and she put her head down on the table and *she* cried. (*She starts toward her seat in the church, but turns back and adds:*) Oh, I've got to say it: you know, there's something downright cruel about sending our girls out into marriage this way. I hope some of her girl friends have told her a thing or two. It's cruel, I know, but I couldn't bring myself to say anything. I went into it blind as a bat myself. The whole world's wrong, that's what's the matter. There they come.

(*She hurries to her place in the pew.* GEORGE *starts to come down the right aisle of the theater, through the audience. Suddenly three members of his baseball team appear by the right proscenium pillar and start whistling and catcalling to him. They are dressed for the ball field.*)

THE BASEBALL PLAYERS

Eh, George, George! Hsst—yaow! If things don't go right, call us in. We know what to do. Eh, fellas? Yaow! George, don't look so innocent, you old geezer. We know what you're thinking. Don't disgrace the team, big boy. Whoo-oo-oo.

STAGE MANAGER

All right! All right! That'll do. That's enough of that. (*Smiling, he pushes them off the stage. They lean back to shout a few more catcalls.*) There used to be an awful lot of that kind of thing at weddings in the old days,—Rome, and later. We're more civilized now,—so they say.

(*The choir starts singing "Love divine, all love excelling—." George has reached the stage. He stares at the congregation a moment, then takes a few steps of withdrawal, toward the right proscenium pillar.*)

GEORGE (*darkly, to himself*)

I wish I were back at school. . . . I don't want to get married.

(*His mother has left her seat and come toward him. She stops, looking at him anxiously.*).

MRS. GIBBS

George, what's the matter?

GEORGE

Ma, I don't want to grow *old*. Why's everybody pushing me so?

MRS. GIBBS

Why, George . . . you wanted it.

GEORGE

Why do I have to get married at all?
Listen, Ma, for the last time I ask you—

MRS. GIBBS

No, no, George . . . you're a man now.

GEORGE

Listen, Ma, you never listen to me. All I
want to do is to be a fella . . . why do—

MRS. GIBBS

George! If anyone should hear you!
Now stop. Why, I'm ashamed of you!

GEORGE (passing his hand over his forehead)

What's the matter? I've been dreaming.
Where's Emily?

MRS. GIBBS

Gracious! You gave me such a turn.

GEORGE

Cheer up, Ma. What are you looking so
funny for? Cheer up; I'm getting married.

MRS. GIBBS

Let me catch my breath a minute.

GEORGE

Now, Ma, you save Thursday nights.
Emily and I are coming over to dinner
every Thursday night . . . you'll see. Ma,
what are you crying for? Come on; we've
got to get ready for this.

(In the meantime, EMILY, in white and
wearing her wedding veil, has come
through the audience and mounted on to
the stage. She too draws back when she
sees the congregation in the church. The
choir begins: "Blessed be the tie that
binds.")

EMILY

I never felt so alone in my whole life.
And George over there, looking so . . . !
I hate him. I wish I were dead. Papa!
Papa!

MR. WEBB (leaves his seat in the pews and
comes toward her anxiously.)

Emily! Emily! Now don't get upset. . . .

EMILY

But, Papa,—I don't want to get married. . . .

MR. WEBB

Sh-sh—Emily. Everything's all right.

EMILY

Why can't I stay for a while just as I
am? Let's go away.

MR. WEBB

No, no, Emily. Now stop and think.

EMILY

Don't you remember that you used to
say,—all the time you used to say that I
was your girl. There must be lots of
places we can go to. Let's go away. I'll
work for you. I could keep house.

MR. WEBB

Sh. . . . You mustn't think of such
things. You're just nervous, Emily. Now,
now,—you're marrying the best young fellow in the world. George is a fine fellow.

EMILY

But, Papa,—

MR. WEBB

George! George! (MRS. GIBBS returns to
her seat. GEORGE hears MR. WEBB and looks
up. MR. WEBB beckons to him. They move
to the center of the stage.) I'm giving away
my daughter, George. Do you think you
can take care of her?

GEORGE

Mr. Webb, I want to . . . I want to
try. Emily, I'm going to do my best. I
love you, Emily. I need you.

EMILY

Well, if you love me, help me. All I want
is someone to love me.

GEORGE

I will, Emily.

EMILY

If ever I'm sick or in trouble, that's
what I mean.

GEORGE

Emily, I'll try. I'll try.

EMILY

And I mean for *ever*. Do you hear? For ever and ever.

(*They fall into each other's arms. The March from "Lohengrin" is heard.*)

MR. WEBB

Come, they're waiting for us. Now you know it'll be all right. Come, quick.

(GEORGE *slips away and takes his place beside the* STAGE MANAGER-CLERGYMAN. EMILY *proceeds up the aisle on her father's arm.*)

STAGE MANAGER

Do you, George, take this woman, Emily, to be your wedded wife, to have . . .

(MRS. SOAMES *has been sitting in the last row of the congregation. She now turns to her neighbors and in a shrill voice says:*)

MRS. SOAMES

Perfectly lovely wedding! Loveliest wedding I ever saw. Oh, I do love a good wedding, don't you? Doesn't she make a lovely bride?

GEORGE

I do.

STAGE MANAGER

Do you, Emily, take this man, George, to be your wedded husband,—

MRS. SOAMES

Don't know *when* I've seen such a love-ly wedding. But I always cry. Don't know why it is, but I always cry. I just like to see young people happy, don't you? Oh, I think it's lovely.

(*The ring. The kiss. The stage is suddenly arrested into silent tableau. The* STAGE MANAGER, *his eyes on the distance, says to the audience:*)

I've married two hundred couples in my day. Do I believe in it? I don't know. M.... marries N.... millions of them. The cottage, the gocart, the Sunday afternoon drives in the Ford, the first rheumatism, the grandchildren, the second rheumatism, the deathbed, the reading of the will,—Once in a thousand times it's interesting. Well, let's have Mendelssohn's "Wedding March"!

(*The organ picks up the March. The bride and groom come down the aisle, radiant, but trying to be very dignified.*)

MRS. SOAMES

Aren't they a lovely couple? Oh, I've never been to such a nice wedding. I'm sure they'll be happy. I always say: *happiness,* that's the great thing! The important thing is to be happy.

(*The bride and groom reach the steps leading into the audience. A bright light is thrown upon them. They descend into the auditorium and run up the aisle joyously.*)

STAGE MANAGER

That's all the Second Act. Ten minutes' intermission, folks.

ACT THREE

During the intermission the audience has seen the actors arranging the stage. On the right hand side, a little right of the center, ten or twelve ordinary chairs have been placed in three openly spaced rows facing the audience.

These are graves in the cemetery.

Towards the end of the intermission the actors enter and take their places. The front row contains: toward the center of the stage, an empty chair; then MRS. GIBBS; SIMON STIMSON. *The second row contains, among others,* MRS. SOAMES. *The third row has* WALLY WEBB.

The dead sit in a quiet without stiffness, and in a patience without listlessness.
The STAGE MANAGER *takes his accustomed place and waits for the house-lights to go down.*

STAGE MANAGER

This time nine years have gone by, friends—summer, 1913. Gradual changes in Grover's Corners. Horses are getting rarer. Farmers coming into town in Fords. Chief difference is in the young people, far as I can see. They want to go to the moving pictures all the time. They want to wear clothes like they see there . . . want to be citified. Everybody locks their house doors now at night. Ain't been any burglars in town yet, but everybody's heard about 'em. But you'd be surprised though—on the whole, things don't change much at Grover's Corners. Guess you want to know what all these chairs are here fur. Smarter ones have guessed it already. I don't know how you feel about such things; but this certainly is a beautiful place. It's on a hilltop—a windy hilltop—lots of sky, lots of clouds,—often lots of sun and moon and stars. You come up here on a fine afternoon and you can see range on range of hills—awful blue they are—up there by Lake Sunapee and Lake Winnipesaukee . . . and way up, if you've got a glass, you can see the White Mountains and Mt. Washington—where North Conway and Conway is. And, of course, our favorite mountain, Mt. Monadnock's right here—and all around it lie these towns—Jaffrey, 'n East Jaffrey, 'n Peterborough, 'n Dublin and (*Then pointing down in the audience*) there, quite a ways down is Grover's Corners. Yes, beautiful spot up here. Mountain laurel and li-lacks. I often wonder why people like to be buried in Woodlawn and Brooklyn when they might pass the same time up here in New Hampshire. Over in that corner—(*Pointing to stage left*) are the old stones,—1670, 1680. Strong-minded people that come a long way to be independent. Summer people walk around there laughing at the funny words on the tombstones . . . it don't do any harm. And genealogists come up from Boston—get paid by city people for looking up their ancestors. They want to make sure they're Daughters of the American Revolution and of the *Mayflower*. . . . Well, I guess that don't do any harm, either. Wherever you come near the human race, there's layers and layers of nonsense. . . . Over there are some Civil War veterans too. Iron flags on their graves. . . . New Hampshire boys . . . had a notion that the Union ought to be kept together, though they'd never seen more than fifty miles of it themselves. All they knew was the name, friends—the United States of America. The United States of America. And they went and died about it. This here is the new part of the cemetery. Here's your friend, Mrs. Gibbs. 'N let me see—Here's Mr. Stimson, organist at the Congregational Church. And over there's Mrs. Soames who enjoyed the wedding so—you remember? Oh, and a lot of others. And Editor Webb's boy, Wallace, whose appendix burst while he was on a Boy Scout trip to Crawford Notch. Yes, an awful lot of sorrow has sort of quieted down up here. People just wild with grief have brought their relatives up to this hill. We all know how it is . . . and then time . . . and sunny days . . . and rainy days . . . 'n snow . . . tz-tz-tz. We're all glad they're in a beautiful place and we're coming up here ourselves when our fit's over. This certainly is an important part of Grover's Corners. A lot of thoughts come up here, night and day, but there's no post office. Now I'm going to tell you some things you know already. You know'm as well as I do; but you don't take'm out and look at'm very often. I don't care what they say with their mouths—everybody knows that *something* is eternal. And it ain't houses and it ain't names, and it ain't earth, and it ain't even the stars . . . everybody knows in their bones that *something* is eternal, and that something has to do with human beings. All the greatest people ever lived have been telling us that for five thousand years and yet you'd be surprised how people are always losing hold of it. There's something way down deep that's eternal about every human being. (*Pause.*) You know as well as I do that the dead don't stay interested in us living people for very long. Gradually, gradually, they let hold of the earth . . . and the ambitions they had . . . and the pleasures they had . . . and the things they suffered . . . and the people they loved. They get weaned away from earth —that's the way I put it,—weaned away. Yes, they stay here while the earth-part of 'em burns away, burns out, and all that time they slowly get indifferent to what's goin' on in Grover's Corners. They're waitin'. They're waitin' for something that they feel is comin'. Something important and great. Aren't they waitin' for the eternal part in them to come out clear? Some of the things they're going to say maybe'll hurt your feelings—but that's the way it is: mother 'n daughter . . . husband 'n wife . . . enemy 'n enemy . . . money 'n miser . . . all those terribly important things kind of grow pale around here. And what's left? What's left when memory's gone, and your identity, Mrs. Smith?

(*He looks at the audience a minute, then turns to the stage.*) Well! There are some *living* people. There's Joe Stoddard, our undertaker, supervising a new-made grave. And here comes a Grover's Corners boy, that left town to go out West.

(JOE STODDARD *has hovered about in the background.* SAM CRAIG *enters left, wiping his forehead from the exertion. He carries an umbrella and strolls front.*)

SAM CRAIG

Good afternoon, Joe Stoddard.

JOE STODDARD

Good afternoon, good afternoon. Let me see now: do I know you?

SAM CRAIG

I'm Sam Craig.

JOE STODDARD

Gracious sakes alive! Of all people! I should'a knowed you'd be back for the funeral. You've been away a long time, Sam.

SAM CRAIG

Yes, I've been away over twelve years. I'm in business out in Buffalo now, Joe. But I was in the East when I got news of my cousin's death, so I thought I'd combine things a little and come and se[e] old home. You look well.

JOE STODDARD

Yes, yes, can't complain. Very sad, journey today, Samuel.

SAM CRAIG

Yes.

JOE STODDARD

Yes, yes. I always say, I hate to supervise when a young person is taken. I see you brought your umbrella. It's going to rain and make it sadder still, seems like. They'll be here in a few minutes now. I had to come here early today—my son's supervisin' at the home.

SAM CRAIG (*reading stones*)

Old Farmer McCarty, I used to do chores for him—after school. He had the lumbago.

JOE STODDARD

Yes, we brought Farmer McCarty here a number of years ago now.

SAM CRAIG (*staring at* MRS. GIBBS' *knees*)

Why, this is my Aunt Julia. . . . I'd forgotten that she'd . . . of course, of course.

JOE STODDARD

Yes, Doc Gibbs lost his wife two-three years ago . . . about this time. And today's another pretty bad blow for him, too.

MRS. GIBBS (*to* SIMON STIMSON: *in an even voice*)

That's my sister Carey's boy, Sam. . . . Sam Craig.

SIMON STIMSON

I'm always uncomfortable when *they're* around.

MRS. GIBBS

Simon.

SIMON STIMSON

They and their nonsense and their damned glee at being alive. . . .

MRS. GIBBS

Simon, be patient. . . .

SAM CRAIG

[J]o they choose their own verses much,

JOE STODDARD

No . . . not usual. Mostly the bereaved [pi]ck a verse.

SAM CRAIG

Doesn't sound like Aunt Julia. There aren't many of those Hersey sisters left now. Let me see: where are . . . I wanted to look at my father's and mother's . . .

JOE STODDARD

Over there with the Craigs. . . . Avenue F.

SAM CRAIG (*reading* SIMON STIMSON'S *epitaph*)

He was organist at church, wasn't he? —Hm, drank a lot, we used to say.

JOE STODDARD

Nobody was supposed to know about it. He'd seen a peck of trouble. Those musical fellas ain't like the rest of us, I reckon. (*Behind his hand.*) Took his own life, y' know?

SAM CRAIG

Oh, did he?

JOE STODDARD

Hung himself in the attic. They tried to hush it up, but of course it got around. His wife's just married Senator Barstow. Many a time I've seen her, eleven o'clock at night, goin' around the streets huntin' for her husband. Think o' that! Now she's married to Senator Barstow over at Manchester. He chose his own epy-taph. You can see it there. It ain't a verse exactly.

SAM CRAIG

Why, it's just some notes of music— what is it?

JOE STODDARD

Oh, I wouldn't know. It was wrote up in the Boston papers at the time.

SAM CRAIG

Joe, what did she die off?

JOE STODDARD

Who?

SAM CRAIG

My cousin.

JOE STODDARD

Oh, didn't you know? Had some trouble bringing a baby into the world. Let's see, today's Friday—'twas almost a week ago now.

SAM CRAIG (*putting up his umbrella*)

Did the baby live?

JOE STODDARD (*raising his coat collar*)

No. 'Twas her second, though. There's a little boy 'bout four years old.

SAM CRAIG

The grave's going to be over there?

JOE STODDARD

Yes, there ain't much more room over here among the Gibbses, so they're opening up a whole new Gibbs section over by Avenue B. You'll excuse me now. I see they're comin'.

THE DEAD (*not lugubrious; and strongly New England in accent*)

Rain'll do a lot of good.—Yes, reckon things were gettin' downright parched. Don't look like it's goin' to last long, though.—Lemuel, you remember the floods of '79? Carried away all the bridges but one.

(*From left to right, at the back of the stage, comes a procession. Four men carry a casket, invisible to us. All the rest are under umbrellas. One can vaguely see* DR. GIBBS, GEORGE, *the* WEBBS, *etc. They gather about a grave in the back center of the stage, a little to the left of center.*)

MRS. SOAMES

Who is it, Julia?

MRS. GIBBS (*without raising her eyes*)

My daughter-in-law, Emily Webb.

MRS. SOAMES (*a little surprised, but no emotion*)

Well, I declare! The road up here must have been awful muddy. What did she die of, Julia?

MRS. GIBBS

In childbirth.

MRS. SOAMES

Childbirth. (*Almost with a laugh.*) I'd forgotten all about that! My, wasn't life awful—(*With a sigh*) and wonderful.

SIMON STIMSON (*with a sideways glance*)

Wonderful, was it?

MRS. GIBBS

Simon! Now, remember!

MRS. SOAMES

I remember Emily's wedding. Wasn't it a lovely wedding! And I remember her reading the class poem at Graduation Exercises. Emily was one of the brightest girls ever graduated from High School. I've heard Principal Wilkins say so time after time. I called on them at their new farm, just before I died. Perfectly beautiful farm.

A WOMAN FROM AMONG THE DEAD

It's on the same road we lived on.

A MAN AMONG THE DEAD

Yes, just near the Elks' picnic grounds. Remember, Joe? By the lake where we always used to go Fourth of July? Right smart farm.

(*They subside. The group by the grave starts singing "Blessed be the tie that binds."*)

A WOMAN AMONG THE DEAD

I always liked that hymn. I was hopin' they'd sing a hymn.

A MAN AMONG THE DEAD

My wife—my second wife—knows all the verses of about every hymn there is. It just beats the Dutch . . . she can go through them all by heart.

(*Pause. Suddenly* EMILY *appears from among the umbrellas. She is wearing a white dress. Her hair is down her back and tied by a white ribbon like a little girl. She comes slowly, gazing wonderingly at the dead, a little dazed. She stops halfway and smiles faintly.*)

EMILY

Hello.

VOICES AMONG THE DEAD

Hello, Emily. H'lo, M's. Gibbs.

EMILY

Hello, Mother Gibbs.

MRS. GIBBS

Emily.

EMILY

Hello. (*The hymn continues.* EMILY *looks back at the funeral. She says dreamily:*) It's raining.

MRS. GIBBS

Yes. . . . They'll be gone soon, dear. Just rest yourself.

(EMILY *sits down in the empty chair by* MRS. GIBBS.)

EMILY

It seems thousands and thousands of years since I. . . . How stupid they all look. They don't have to look like that!

MRS. GIBBS

Don't look at them now, dear. They'll be gone soon.

EMILY

Oh, I wish I'd been here a long time. I don't like being new here.—How do you do, Mr. Stimson?

SIMON STIMSON

How do you do, Emily.

(EMILY *continues to look about her with a wan and wondering smile; but for a moment her eyes do not return to the funeral group. As though to shut out from her mind the thought of that group she starts speaking to* MRS. GIBBS *with a touch of nervousness.*)

EMILY

Mother Gibbs, George and I have made that farm into just the best place you ever saw. We thought of you all the time. We wanted to show you the new barn and a great long ce-ment drinking fountain for the stock. We bought that out of the money you left us.

MRS. GIBBS

I did?

EMILY

Don't you remember, Mother Gibbs— the legacy you left us? Why, it was over three hundred and fifty dollars.

MRS. GIBBS

Yes, yes, Emily.

EMILY

Well, there's a patent device on this drinking fountain so that it never overflows, Mother Gibbs, and it never sinks below a certain mark they have there. It's fine. (*Her voice trails off and her eyes return to the funeral group.*) It won't be the same to George without me, but it's a lovely farm. (*Suddenly she looks directly at* MRS. GIBBS.) Live people don't understand, do they?

MRS. GIBBS

No, dear—not very much.

EMILY

They're sort of shut up in little boxes, aren't they? I feel as though I knew them last a thousand years ago. . . . My boy is spending the day at Mrs. Carter's. (*She sees* MR. CARTER *among the dead.*) Oh, Mr. Carter, my little boy is spending the day at your house.

MR. CARTER

Is he?

EMILY

Yes, he loves it there.—Mother Gibbs, we have a Ford, too. Never gives any trouble. I don't drive, though. Mother Gibbs, when does this feeling go away?— Of being . . . one of *them?* How long does it . . . ?

MRS. GIBBS

Sh! dear. Just wait and be patient.

EMILY (*With a sigh.*)

I know.—Look, they're finished. They're going.

MRS. GIBBS

Sh—. (*The umbrellas leave the stage.* DR. GIBBS *comes over to his wife's grave and stands before it a moment.* EMILY *looks up at his face.* MRS. GIBBS *does not raise her eyes.*)

EMILY

Look! Father Gibbs is bringing some of my flowers to you. He looks just like George, doesn't he? Oh, Mother Gibbs, I never realized before how troubled and how . . . how in the dark live persons are. From morning till night, that's all they are—troubled.

(DR. GIBBS *goes off.*)

THE DEAD

Little cooler than it was.—Yes, that rain's cooled it off a little. Those North East winds always do the same thing, don't they? If it isn't a rain, it's a three-day blow.—Reckon it may clear up before night; often does.

(*A patient calm falls on the stage. The* STAGE MANAGER *appears at his proscenium pillar, smoking.* EMILY *sits up abruptly with an idea.*)

EMILY

But, Mother Gibbs, one can go back; one can go back there again . . . into living. I feel it. I know it. Why, just then for a moment I was thinking about . . . about the farm . . . and for a minute I *was* there, and my baby was on my lap as plain as day.

MRS. GIBBS

Yes, of course you can.

EMILY

I can go back there and live all those days over again . . . why not?

MRS. GIBBS

All I can say is, Emily, don't.

EMILY (*Takes a few steps toward the* STAGE MANAGER)

But it's true, isn't it? I can go and live . . . back there . . . again.

STAGE MANAGER

Yes, some have tried—but they soon come back here.

MRS. GIBBS

Don't do it, Emily.

MRS. SOAMES

Emily, don't. It's not what you think it'd be.

EMILY

But I won't live over a sad day. I'll choose a happy one—I'll choose the day I first knew that I loved George. Why should that be painful?

(*They are silent. Her question turns to the* STAGE MANAGER.)

STAGE MANAGER

You not only live it; but you watch yourself living it.

EMILY

Yes.

STAGE MANAGER

And as you watch it, you see the thing that they—down there—never know. You see the future. You know what's going to happen afterwards.

EMILY

But is that—painful? Why?

MRS. GIBBS

That's not the only reason why you shouldn't do it, Emily. When you've been here longer you'll see that our life here is our hope that soon we'll forget all that, and think only of what's ahead, and be ready for what's ahead. When you've been here longer you'll understand.

EMILY (*softly*)

But, Mother Gibbs, how can I ever forget that life? It's all I know. It's all I had. (MRS. GIBBS *does not answer.*) Mr. Stimson, did you go back?

SIMON STIMSON (*sharply*)

No.

EMILY

Did you, Mrs. Soames?

MRS. SOAMES

Oh, Emily. It isn't wise. Really, it isn't. All we can do is just warn you. It won't be what you expect.

EMILY (*slowly*)

But it's a thing I must know for myself. I'll choose a happy day, anyway.

MRS. GIBBS

No. At least, choose an unimportant day. Choose the least important day in your life. It will be important enough.

EMILY (*to the* STAGE MANAGER)

Then it can't be since I was married; or since the baby was born. I can choose a birthday at least, can't I?—I choose my twelfth birthday.

STAGE MANAGER

All right. February 11th, 1899. A Tuesday.—Do you want any special time of day?

EMILY

Oh, I want the whole day.

STAGE MANAGER

We'll begin at dawn. You remember it had been snowing for several days; but it had stopped the night before, and they had begun clearing the roads. The sun's coming up.

EMILY (*with a cry*)

There's Main Street . . . why, that's Mr. Morgan's drugstore before he changed it! . . . And there's the livery stable.

(*She walks toward the back of the stage.*)

STAGE MANAGER

Yes, it's 1899. This is fourteen years ago.

EMILY

Oh, that's the town I knew as a little girl. And, look, there's the old white fence that used to be around our house. Oh, I'd forgotten that! Oh, I love it so! Are *they* inside?

STAGE MANAGER

Yes, your mother'll be coming downstairs in a minute to make breakfast.

EMILY (*softly*)

Will she?

STAGE MANAGER

And you remember: your father had been away for several days; he came back on the early morning train.

EMILY

No . . . ?

STAGE MANAGER

He'd been back to his college to make a speech—in Western New York, at Clinton.

EMILY

Look! There's Howie Newsome. There's our policeman. But he's *dead; he died.*

(*The* STAGE MANAGER *retires to his corner. The voices of* HOWIE NEWSOME, CONSTABLE WARREN *and* JOE CROWELL, JR., *are heard at the left of the stage.*)

HOWIE NEWSOME

Whoa, Bessie!—Bessie! Morning, Bill.

BILL

Morning, Howie.

HOWIE NEWSOME

You're up early.

BILL

Been rescuin' a party; darn near froze to death, down by Polish Town thar. Got drunk and lay out in the snowdrifts. Thought he was in bed when I shook'm.

EMILY

Why, there's Joe Crowell. . . .

JOE CROWELL

Good morning, Mr. Warren. 'Morning, Howie.

(MRS. WEBB *has appeared in her kitchen, but* EMILY *does not see her until she calls.*)

MRS. WEBB

Chil-*dren!* Wally! Emily! . . . Time to get up.

EMILY

Mama, here I am! Oh! how young Mama looks! I didn't know Mama was ever that young. Oh!

MRS. WEBB

You can come and dress by the kitchen fire, if you like; but hurry. (HOWIE NEWSOME *has entered along Main Street and brings the milk to* MRS. WEBB'S *door.*) Good morning, Mr. Newsome. Whhhh—it's cold.

HOWIE NEWSOME

Ten below by my barn, Mrs. Webb.

MRS. WEBB

Think of it! Keep yourself wrapped up. (*She takes her bottles in, shuddering.*)

EMILY (*with an effort*)

Mama, I can't find my blue hair ribbon anywhere.

MRS. WEBB

Just open your eyes, dear, that's all. I laid it out for you special—on the dresser, there. If it were a snake it would bite you.

EMILY

Yes, yes. . . .

(*She puts her hand on her heart.* MR. WEBB *comes along Main Street, where he meets* CONSTABLE WARREN.)

MR. WEBB

Good morning, Bill.

BILL

Good morning, Mr. Webb. You're up early.

MR. WEBB

Yes, just been back to my old college in New York State. Been any trouble here?

BILL

Well, I was called up this mornin' to rescue a Polish fella—darn near froze to death he was.

MR. WEBB

We must get it in the paper.

BILL

'Twan't much.

EMILY (*whispers*)

Papa.

(MR. WEBB *shakes the snow off his feet and enters his house.*)

MR. WEBB

Good morning, Mother.

MRS. WEBB

How did it go, Charles?

MR. WEBB

Oh, fine, I guess. I told'm a few things.

MRS. WEBB

Did you sit up on the train all night?

MR. WEBB

Yes. Never could sleep on a Pullman anyway.

MRS. WEBB

Charles, seems to me—we're rich enough so that you could sleep in a train once in a while.

MR. WEBB

Everything all right here?

MRS. WEBB

Yes—can't think of anything that's happened, special. Been right cold. Howie Newsome says it's ten below over to his barn.

MR. WEBB

Yes, well, it's colder than that at Hamilton College. Students' ears are falling off. It ain't Christian.—Paper have any mistakes in it?

MRS. WEBB

None that I noticed. Coffee's ready when you want it. (*He starts upstairs.*) Charles! Don't forget; it's Emily's birthday. Did you remember to get her something?

MR. WEBB (*patting his pocket*)

Yes, I've got something here.

MRS. WEBB

Goodness sakes! I hope she likes what I got for her. I hunted hard enough for it. Children! Hurry up! Hurry up!

MR. WEBB

Where's my girl? Where's my birthday girl?
(*He goes off left.*)

MRS. WEBB

Don't interrupt her now, Charles. You can see her at breakfast. She's slow enough as it is. Hurry up, children! It's seven o'clock. Now, I don't want to call you again.

EMILY (*softly, more in wonder than in grief*)

I can't bear it. They're so young and beautiful. Why did they ever have to get old? Mama, I'm here. I'm grown up. I love you all, everything.—I can't look at everything hard enough. There's the butternut tree. (*She wanders up Main Street.*) There's Mr. Morgan's drugstore. And there's the High School, forever and ever, and ever. And there's the Congregational Church where I got married. Oh, dear. Oh, dear. Oh, dear! (*The* STAGE MANAGER *beckons partially to her. He points to the house. She says a breathless "yes" and goes to the house.*) Good morning, Mama.

MRS. WEBB (*at the foot of the stairs, kissing her in a matter-of-fact way.*)

Well, now, dear, a very happy birthday to my girl and many happy returns. There are some surprises waiting for you on the kitchen table.

EMILY

Oh, Mama, you *shouldn't* have. (*She throws an anguished glance at the* STAGE MANAGER.) I can't—I can't.

MRS. WEBB (*facing the audience, over her stove.*)

But birthday or no birthday, I want you to eat your breakfast good and slow. I want you to grow up and be a good strong girl. (*She goes to the stairs and calls.*) Wally! Wally, wash yourself good. Everything's getting cold down here. (*She returns to the stove with her back to* EMILY. EMILY *opens her parcels.*) That in the blue paper is from your Aunt Carrie and I reckon you can guess who brought the post card album. I found it on the doorstep when I brought in the milk—George Gibbs . . . must have come over in the cold pretty early . . . right nice of him.

EMILY (*to herself.*)

Oh, George! I'd forgotten that. . . .

MRS. WEBB

Chew that bacon slow. It'll help keep you warm on a cold day.

EMILY (*beginning softly but urgently*)

Oh, Mama, just look at me one minute as though you really saw me. Mama, fourteen years have gone by. I'm dead. You're a grandmother, Mama. I married George Gibbs, Mama. Wally's dead, too. Mama, his appendix burst on a camping trip to North Conway. We felt just terrible about it—don't you remember? But, just for a moment now we're all together. Mama, just for a moment we're happy. Let's look at one another.

MRS. WEBB

That in the yellow paper is something I found in the attic among your grandmother's things. You're old enough to wear it now, and I thought you'd like it.

EMILY

And this is from you. Why, Mama, it's just lovely and it's just what I wanted. It's beautiful!

(*She flings her arms around her mother's neck. Her mother goes on with her cooking, but is pleased.*)

MRS. WEBB

Well, I hoped you'd like it. Hunted all over. Your Aunt Norah couldn't find one in Concord, so I had to send all the way to Boston. (*Laughing.*) Wally has something for you, too. He made it at Manual Training class and he's very proud of it. Be sure you make a big fuss about it.—Your father has a surprise for you, too; don't know what it is myself. Sh—here he comes.

MR. WEBB (*off stage*)

Where's my girl? Where's my birthday girl?

EMILY (*in a loud voice to the* STAGE MANAGER)

I can't. I can't go on. Oh! Oh. It goes so fast. We don't have time to look at one another. (*She breaks down sobbing. At a gesture from the* STAGE MANAGER, MRS. WEBB *disappears.*) I didn't realize. So all that was going on and we never noticed. Take me back—up the hill—to my grave. But first: Wait! One more look. Good-by, Good-by, world. Good-by, Grover's Corners . . . Mama and Papa. Good-by to clocks ticking . . . and Mama's sunflowers. And food and coffee. And new-ironed dresses and hot baths . . . and sleeping and waking up. Oh, earth, you're too wonderful for anybody to realize you. (*She looks toward the* STAGE MANAGER *and asks abruptly, through her tears.*) Do any human beings ever realize life while they live it?—every, every minute?

STAGE MANAGER

No. (*Pause.*) The saints and poets, maybe—they do some.

EMILY

I'm ready to go back. (*She returns to her chair beside* MRS. GIBBS.) Mother Gibbs, I should have listened to you. Now I want to be quiet for a while.—Oh, Mother Gibbs, I saw it all. I saw your garden.

MRS. GIBBS

Did you, dear?

EMILY

That's all human beings are!—Just blind people.

MRS. GIBBS

Look, it's clearing up. The stars are coming out.

EMILY

Oh, Mr. Stimson, I should have listened to them.

SIMON STIMSON (*with mounting violence; bitingly*)

Yes, now you know. Now you know! That's what it was to be alive. To move about in a cloud of ignorance; to go up and down trampling on the feelings of those . . . of those about you. To spend and waste time as though you had a million years. To be always at the mercy of one self-centered passion, or another. Now you know—that's the happy existence you wanted to go back and see. Did you shout to 'em? Did you call to 'em?

EMILY

Yes, I did.

SIMON STIMSON

Now you know them as they are: in ignorance and blindness.

MRS. GIBBS (*spiritedly*)

Simon Stimson, that ain't the whole truth and you know it.

(*The dead have begun to stir.*)

THE DEAD

Lemuel, wind's coming up, seems like. —Oh, dear,—I keep remembering things tonight.—It's right cold for June, ain't it?

MRS. GIBBS

Look what you've done, you and your

rebellious spirit stirring us up here.—Emily, look at that star. I forget its name.

THE DEAD

I'm getting to know them all, but I don't know their names.—My boy Joel was a sailor,—knew 'em all. He'd set on the porch evenings and tell 'em all by name. Yes, sir, it was wonderful.—A star's mighty good company.—Yes, yes.—Yes, 'tis.

SIMON STIMSON

Here's one of *them* coming.

THE DEAD

That's funny. 'Taint no time for one of them to be here.—Goodness sakes.

EMILY

Mother Gibbs, it's George.

MRS. GIBBS

Sh, dear. You just rest yourself.

EMILY

It's George.
(GEORGE *enters from the left, and slowly comes toward them.*)

A MAN FROM AMONG THE DEAD

And my boy, Joel, who knew the stars—he used to say it took millions of years for that speck o' light to git to the earth. Don't seem like a body could believe it, but that's what he used to say—millions of years.

ANOTHER

That's what they say.
(GEORGE *flings himself on* EMILY's *grave.*)

THE DEAD

Goodness! That ain't no way to behave!
—He ought to be home.

EMILY

Mother Gibbs?

MRS. GIBBS

Yes, Emily?

EMILY

They don't understand much, do they?

MRS. GIBBS

No, dear, not very much.
(*The* STAGE MANAGER *appears at the right, one hand on a dark curtain which he slowly draws across the scene. In the distance a clock is heard striking the hour very faintly.*)

STAGE MANAGER

Most everybody's asleep in Grover's Corners. There are a few lights on: Shorty Hawkins, down at the depot, has just watched the Albany train go by. And at the livery stable somebody's setting up late and talking.—Yes, it's clearing up. There are the stars—doing their old, old criss-cross journeys in the sky. Scholars haven't settled the matter yet, but they seem to think there are no living beings up there. They're just chalk . . . or fire. Only this one is straining away, straining away all the time to make something of itself. The strain's so bad that every sixteen hours everybody lies down and gets a rest. (*He winds his watch.*) Hm. . . . Eleven o'-clock in Grover's Corners.—You get a good rest, too. Goodnight.

Abe Lincoln in Illinois

BY ROBERT EMMET SHERWOOD

TO MY MOTHER

CHARACTERS

MENTOR GRAHAM
ABE LINCOLN
ANN RUTLEDGE
BEN MATTLING
JUDGE BOWLING GREEN
NINIAN EDWARDS
JOSHUA SPEED
TRUM COGDAL
JACK ARMSTRONG
BAB
FEARGUS
JASP
SETH GALE
NANCY GREEN
WILLIAM HERNDON
ELIZABETH EDWARDS
MARY TODD
THE EDWARDS' MAID
JIMMY GALE
AGGIE GALE
GOBEY
STEPHEN A. DOUGLAS
WILLIE LINCOLN
TAD LINCOLN
ROBERT LINCOLN
THE LINCOLNS' MAID
CRIMMIN
BARRICK
STURVESON
JED
KAVANAGH
MAJOR

Soldiers, Railroad Men, Townspeople

SCENES

ACT ONE: In and about New Salem, Illinois, in the 1830's.

SCENE   I: Mentor Graham's cabin near New Salem, Illinois.

SCENE   II: The Rutledge Tavern, New Salem.

SCENE   III: Bowling Green's house near New Salem.

ACT TWO: In and about Springfield, Illinois, in the 1840's.

SCENE   IV: Law office of Stuart and Lincoln on the second floor of the Court House in Springfield, Illinois.

SCENE   V: Parlor of the Edwards house in Springfield.

SCENE   VI: Again the law office.

SCENE   VII: On the prairie, near New Salem.

SCENE VIII: Again the parlor of the Edwards house.

ACT THREE: In Springfield, 1858-61.

SCENE   IX: A speakers' platform in an Illinois town.

SCENE   X: Parlor of the Lincoln's home.

SCENE   XI: Lincoln campaign headquarters in the Illinois State House.

SCENE   XII: The yards of the railroad station at Springfield.

ABE LINCOLN IN ILLINOIS

ACT ONE

SCENE I

MENTOR GRAHAM's *cabin near New Salem, Illinois. Late at night.*

There is one rude table, piled with books and papers. Over it hangs an oil lamp, the only source of light.

At one side of the table sits MENTOR GRAHAM, *a sharp but patient schoolteacher.*

Across from him is ABE LINCOLN—*young, gaunt, tired but intent, dressed in the ragged clothes of a backwoodsman. He speaks with the drawl of southern Indiana—an accent which is more Kentuckian than middle-western.*

MENTOR *is leaning on the table.* ABE's *chair is tilted back, so that his face is out of the light.* MENTOR *turns a page in a grammar book.*

MENTOR

The Moods. (MENTOR *closes the book and looks at* ABE.) Every one of us has many moods. You yourself have more than your share of them, Abe. They express the various aspects of your character. So it is with the English language—and you must try to consider this language as if it were a living person, who may be awkward and stumbling, or pompous and pretentious, or simple and direct. Name me the five moods.

ABE

The Indicative, Imperative, Potential, Subjunctive and Infinitive.

MENTOR

And what do they signify?

ABE

The Indicative Mood is the easy one. It just indicates a thing—like "He loves," "He is loved"—or, when you put it in the form of a question, "Does he love?" or "Is he loved?" The Imperative Mood is used for commanding, like "Get out and be damned to you."

MENTOR (*smiling*)

Is that the best example you can think of?

ABE

Well—you can put it in the Bible way—"Go thou in peace." But it's still imperative.

MENTOR

The mood derives its name from the implication of command. But you can use it in a very different sense—in the form of the humblest supplication.

ABE

Like "Give us this day our daily bread and forgive us our trespasses."

MENTOR (*reaching for a newspaper in the mess on the table*)

I want you to read this—it's a speech delivered by Mr. Webster before the United States Senate. A fine document, and a perfect usage of the Imperative Mood in its hortatory sense. Here it is. Read this—down here. (*He leans back to listen.*)

ABE (*takes paper, leans forward into the light and reads*)

"Sir," the Senator continued, in the rich deep tones of the historic church bells of his native Boston, "Sir—I have not allowed myself to look beyond the Union, to see what might be hidden in the dark recess behind. While the Union lasts . . ." (ABE *has been reading in a monotone, without inflection.*)

MENTOR (*testily*)

Don't read it off as if it were an inventory of Denton Offut's groceries. Imagine that *you're* making the speech before the Senate, with the fate of your country at stake. Put your own life into it!

ABE

I couldn't use words as long as Dan'l Webster.

MENTOR

That's what you're here for—to learn! Go ahead.

ABE (*reading slowly, gravely*)

"While the Union lasts, we have high prospects spread out before us, for us and our children. Beyond that, I seek not to penetrate the veil. God grant that in my day, at least, the curtain may not rise."

MENTOR

Notice the use of verbs from here on.

ABE (*reads*)

"When my eyes shall be turned to behold for the last time the sun in heaven, may I not see him shining on the broken and dishonored fragments of a once glorious Union; on States dissevered, discordant, belligerent; on a land rent with civil feuds, or drenched, it may be, in fraternal blood! Let their last feeble glance rather behold the glorious ensign of the republic, now known and honored throughout the earth, not a single star of it obscured, bearing for its motto no such miserable interrogatory . . ." (*He stumbles over the pronunciation.*)

MENTOR

Interrogatory.

ABE (*continuing*)

". . . interrogatory as 'What is all this worth?' Nor, those other words of delusion and folly, 'Liberty first and Union afterwards'; but everywhere, spread all over in characters of living light, that other sentiment, dear to every true American heart —Liberty and Union . . .'"

MENTOR

Emphasize the "*and.*"

ABE

"Liberty *and* Union, now and forever, one and inseparable!" (*He puts the paper back on the table.*) He must have had 'em up on their feet cheering with *that,* all right.

MENTOR

Some cheered, and some spat, depending on which section they came from.

ABE

What was he talking about?

MENTOR

It was in the debate over the right of any state to secede from the Union. Hayne had pleaded South Carolina's cause— pleaded it ably. He said that just as we have liberty as individuals—so have we liberty as states—to go as we please. Which means, if we don't like the Union, as expressed by the will of its majority, then we can leave it, and set up a new nation, or many nations—so that this continent might be as divided as Europe. But Webster answered him, all right. He proved that without Union, we'd have precious little liberty left. Now—go on with the Potential Mood.

ABE

That signifies possibility—usually of an unpleasant nature. Like, "If I ever get out of debt, I will probably get right back in again."

MENTOR (*smiles*)

Why did you select that example, Abe?

ABE

Well—it just happens to be the thought that's always heaviest on my mind.

MENTOR

Is the store in trouble again?

ABE (*calmly*)

Yes. Berry's drunk all the whiskey we ought to have sold, and we're going to have to shut up any day now. I guess I'm my father's own son. Give me a steady job, and I'll fail at it.

MENTOR

You haven't been a failure here, Abe. There isn't a manjack in this community that isn't fond of you and anxious to help you get ahead.

ABE (*with some bitterness*)

I know—just like you, Mentor, sitting up late nights, to give me learning, out of the goodness of your heart. And now, Josh Speed and Judge Green and some of the others I owe money to want to get me the job of post-master, thinking that maybe I can handle *that,* since there's only one mail comes in a week. I've got friends, all right—the best friends. But they can't change my luck, or maybe it's just my nature.

MENTOR

What you want to do is get out of New Salem. This poor little forgotten town will never give any one any opportunity.

ABE

Yes—I've thought about moving, think about it all the time. My family have always been movers, shifting about, never knowing what they were looking for, and whatever it was, never finding it. My old father ambled from Virginia, to one place after another in Kentucky, where I was born, and then into Indiana, and then here in Illinois. About all I can remember of when I was a boy was hitching up, and then unhitching, and then hitching up again.

MENTOR

Then get up and go, Abe. Make a new place for yourself in a new world.

ABE

As a matter of fact, Seth Gale and me have been talking a lot about moving—out to Kansas or Nebraska territory. But—wherever I go—it'll be the same story—more friends, more debts.

MENTOR

Well, Abe—just bear in mind that there are always two professions open to people who fail at everything else: there's school-teaching, and there's politics.

ABE

Then I'll choose school-teaching. You go into politics, and you may get elected.

MENTOR

Yes—there's always that possibility.

ABE

And if you get elected, you've got to go to the city. I don't want none of that.

MENTOR

What did I say about two negatives?

ABE

I meant, any of that.

MENTOR

What's your objection to cities, Abe? Have you ever seen one?

ABE

Sure. I've been down river twice to New Orleans. And, do you know, every minute of the time I was there, I was scared?

MENTOR

Scared of what, Abe?

ABE

Well—it sounds kind of foolish—I was scared of people.

MENTOR (*laughs*)

Did you imagine they'd rob you of all your gold and jewels?

ABE (*serious*)

No. I was scared they'd kill me.

MENTOR (*also serious*)

Why? Why should they want to kill you?

ABE

I don't know.

MENTOR (*after a moment*)

You think a lot about death, don't you?

ABE

I've had to, because it has always seemed to be so close to me—always—as far back as I can remember. When I was no higher than this table, we buried my mother. The milksick got her, poor creature. I helped Paw make the coffin—whittled the pegs for it with my own jackknife. We buried her in a timber clearing beside my grandmother, old Betsy Sparrow. I used to go there often and look at the place—used to watch the deer running over her grave with their little feet. I never could kill a deer after that. One time I catched hell from Paw because when he was taking aim I knocked his gun up. And I always compare the looks of those deer with the looks of men—like the men in New Orleans—

that you could see had murder in their hearts.

MENTOR (*after a moment*)

You're a hopeless mess of inconsistency, Abe Lincoln.

ABE

How do you mean, Mentor?

MENTOR

I've never seen any one who is so friendly and at the same time so misanthropic.

ABE

What's that?

MENTOR

A misanthrope is one who distrusts men and avoids their society.

ABE

Well—maybe that's how I am. Oh—I like people, well enough—when you consider 'em one by one. But they seem to look different when they're put into crowds, or mobs, or armies. But I came here to listen to you, and then I do all the talking.

MENTOR

Go right on, Abe. I'll correct you when you say things like "catched hell."

ABE (*grins*)

I know. Whenever I get talking about Paw, I sort of fall back into his language.

But—you've got your own school to teach tomorrow. I'll get along. (*He stands up.*)

MENTOR

Wait a minute. . . . (*He is fishing about among the papers. He takes out a copy of an English magazine.*) There's just one more thing I want to show you. It's a poem. (*He finds the place in the magazine.*) Here it is. You read it, Abe. (*He hands* ABE *the magazine.*)

(ABE *seats himself on the edge of the table, and holds the magazine under the light.*)

ABE (*reads*)

" 'On Death,' written at the age of nineteen by the late John Keats:

'Can death be sleep, when life is but a
   dream,
And scenes of bliss pass as a phantom by?
The transient (*he hesitates on that word*)
   pleasures as a vision seem,
And yet we think the greatest pain's to die.
(*He moves closer to the light.*)
How strange it is that man on earth
   should roam,
And lead a life of woe, but not forsake
His rugged path—nor dare he view alone
His future doom—which is but to
   awake.' "
(*He looks at* MENTOR.) That sure is good, Mentor. It's *fine!* (*He is reading it again, to himself, when the lights fade.*)

End of Scene I

SCENE II

THE RUTLEDGE TAVERN, *New Salem. Noon on the Fourth of July.*

It is a large room, with log walls, but with curtains on the windows and pictures on the walls to give it an air of dressiness. The pictures include likenesses of all the presidents from Washington to Jackson, and there is also a picture (evidently used for campaign purposes) of Henry Clay.

At the left is a door leading to the kitchen. At the back, toward the right, is the main entrance, which is open. The sun is shining brightly.

The furniture of the room consists of two tables, two benches, and various chairs and stools.

BEN MATTLING *is seated on a bench at the rear of the room. He is an ancient, paunchy, watery-eyed veteran of the Revolution, and he wears a cocked hat and the tattered but absurd semblance of a Colonial uniform.* JUDGE BOWLING GREEN *and* NINIAN EDWARDS *come in, followed by* JOSHUA SPEED. BOWLING *is elderly, fat, gentle.* NINIAN *is young, tall, handsome, prosperous.* JOSH *is quiet, mild, solid, thoughtful, well dressed.*

BOWLING (*as they come in*)

This is the Rutledge Tavern, Mr. Edwards. It's not precisely a gilded palace of refreshment.

NINIAN

Make no apologies, Judge Green. As long as the whiskey is wet.
(JOSH *has crossed to the door at the left. He calls off.*)

JOSH

Miss Rutledge.

ANN (*appearing at the door*)

Yes, Mr. Speed?

JOSH

Have you seen Abe Lincoln?

ANN

No. He's probably down at the foot races. (*She goes back into the kitchen.* JOSH *turns to* BOWLING.)

JOSH

I'll find Abe and bring him here.

NINIAN

Remember, Josh, we've got to be back in Springfield before sundown.
(JOSH *has gone out.*)

BOWLING (*to* MATTLING)

Ah, good day, Uncle Ben. Have a seat, Mr. Edwards.
(*They cross to the table at the right.*)

BEN

Good day to you, Bowling.
(ANN *comes in from the kitchen.*)

ANN

Hello, Judge Green.

BOWLING

Good morning, Ann. We'd be grateful for a bottle of your father's best whiskey.

ANN

Yes, Judge. (*She starts to go off.*)

BEN (*stopping her*)

And git me another mug of that Barbadoes rum.

ANN

I'm sorry, Mr. Battling, but I've given you one already and you know my father said you weren't to have any more till you paid for . . .

BEN

Yes, wench—I know what your father said. But if a veteran of the Revolutionary War is to be denied so much as credit, then this country has forgot its gratitude to them that made it.

BOWLING

Bring him the rum, Ann. I'll be happy to pay for it.
(TRUM COGDAL *comes in. He is elderly, persnickety.*)

BEN (*reluctantly*)

I have to say thank you, Judge.

TRUM

Ann, bring me a pot of Sebago tea.

ANN

Yes, Mr. Cogdal. (*She goes out at the left.* TRUM *sits down at the table.*)

BOWLING

Don't say a word, Ben.

TRUM

Well, Mr. Edwards—what's your impression of our great and enterprising metropolis?

NINIAN

Distinctly favorable, Mr. Cogdal. I could not fail to be impressed by the beauty of your location, here on this hilltop, in the midst of the prairie land.

TRUM

Well, we're on the highroad to the West —and when we get the rag, tag and bobtail cleaned out of here, we'll grow. Yes, sir—we'll grow!

NINIAN (*politely*)

I'm sure of it.
(ANN *has returned with the whiskey, rum and tea.*)

BOWLING

Thank you, Ann.

ANN

Has the mud-wagon come in yet?

TRUM

No. I been waiting for it.

BOWLING

Not by any chance expecting a letter, are you, Ann?

ANN

Oh, no—who'd be writing to *me,* I'd like to know?

BOWLING

Well—you never can tell what might happen on the Fourth of July. (*He and* NINIAN *lift their glases.*) But I beg to wish you all happiness, my dear. And let me tell you that Mr. Edwards here is a married man, so you can keep those lively eyes to yourself.

ANN (*giggles*)

Oh, Judge Green—you're just joking me! (*She goes to the kitchen.*)

NINIAN

A mighty pretty girl.

TRUM

Comes of good stock, too.

NINIAN

With the scarcity of females in these parts, it's a wonder some one hasn't snapped her up.

BOWLING

Some one has. The poor girl promised herself to a man who called himself Mc-Niel—it turned out his real name's Mc-Namar. Made some money out here and then left town, saying he'd return soon. She's still waiting for him. But your time is short, Mr. Edwards, so if you tell us just what it is you want in New Salem, we'll do our utmost to . . .

NINIAN

I'm sure you gentlemen know what I want.

TRUM

Naturally, you want votes. Well—you've got mine. Anything to frustrate that tyrant, Andy Jackson. (*He shakes a finger at the picture of* ANDREW JACKSON.)

NINIAN

I assure you that I yield to none in my admiration for the character of our venerable president, but when he goes to the extent of ruining our banking structure, destroying faith in our currency and even driving sovereign states to the point of secession, then, gentlemen, it is time to call a halt.

BOWLING

We got two more years of him—if the old man lives that long. You can't make headway against his popularity.

NINIAN

But we can start now to drive out his minions here in the government of the state of Illinois. We have a great battle cry, "End the reign of Andrew Jackson."

(JACK ARMSTRONG *and three others of the Clary's Grove boys have come in during this speech. The others are named* BAB, FEARGUS *and* JASP. *They are the town bullies—boisterous, good-natured but tough.*)

JACK (*going to the door at the left*)

Miss Rutledge!

ANN (*appearing in the doorway*)

What do *you* want, Jack Armstrong?

JACK

Your humble pardon, Miss Rutledge, and we will trouble you for a keg of liquor.

BAB

And we'll be glad to have it quick, because we're powerful dry.

ANN

You get out of here—you get out of here right now—you low *scum!*

JACK

I believe I said a keg of liquor. Did you hear me say it, boys?

FEARGUS

That's how it sounded to me, Jack.

JASP

Come along with it, Annie——

ANN

If my father were here, he'd take a gun to you, just as he would to a pack of prairie wolves.

JACK

If your Paw was here, he'd be scareder than you. 'Cause he knows we're the wild-cats of Clary's Grove, worse'n any old wolves, and we're a-howlin', and a-spittin' for drink. So get the whiskey, Miss Annie, and save your poor old Paw a lot of ex-penses for damages to his property.
(ANN *goes.*)

TRUM (*in an undertone to* NINIAN)

That's the rag, tag and bobtail I was . . .

JACK

And what are you mumblin' about, old measely-weasely Trum Cogdal—with your cup of tea on the Fourth of July?

BAB

He's a cotton-mouthed traitor and I think we'd better whip him for it.

FEARGUS (*at the same time*)

Squeeze that air tea outen him, Jack.

JASP (*shouting*)

Come on you, Annie, with that liquor!

JACK

And you, too, old fat-pot Judge Bowling Green that sends honest men to prison—and who's the stranger? Looks kind of damn elegant for New Salem.

BOWLING

This is Mr. Ninian Edwards of Spring-field, Jack—and for the Lord's sake, shut up, and sit down, and behave yourselves.

JACK

Ninian Edwards, eh! The Governor's son, I presume. Well—well!

NINIAN (*amiably*)

You've placed me.

JACK

No wonder you've got a New Orleans suit of clothes and a gold fob and a silver-headed cane. I reckon you can buy the best of everything with that steamin old pirate land-grabber for a Paw. I guess them fancy pockets of yourn are pretty well stuffed with the money your Paw stole from us tax-payers—eh, Mr. Edwards?

BAB

Let's take it offen him, Jack.

FEARGUS

Let's give him a lickin', Jack.

JACK (*still to* NINIAN)

What you come here for anyway? Look-in' for a fight? Because if that's what you're a-cravin', I'm your man—wrasslin', clawin', bitin', and tearin'.

ANN (*coming in*)

Jack Armstrong, here's your liquor! Drink it and go away.
(ANN *carries four mugs.*)

JASP

He told you to bring a keg!

JACK (*contemplating the mugs*)

One little noggin apiece? Why—that ain't enough to fill a hollow tooth! Get the keg, Annie.

FEARGUS

Perhaps she can't tote it. I'll get it, Jack.
(*He goes out into the kitchen.*)

ANN (*desperate*)

Aren't there any of you men can do any-thing to protect decent people from these ruffians?

NINIAN

I'll be glad to do whatever I . . . (*He starts to rise.*)

BOWLING (*restraining him*)

I'd be rather careful, Mr. Edwards.

JACK

That's right, Mr. Edwards. You be care-ful. Listen to the old Squire. He's got a round pot but a level head. He's seen the Clary's Grove boys in action, and he can tell you you might get that silver-headed cane rammed down your gullet. Hey, Bab—you tell him what we did to Hank Spears and Gus Hocheimer. Just tell him!

BAB

Jack nailed the two of 'em up in a barr'l and sent 'em rollin' down Salem hill and it jumped the bank and fotched up in the river and when we opened up the barr'l they wasn't inclined to move much.

JACK

Of course, it'd take a bigger barr'l to hold you and your friend here, Squire, but I'd do it for you and I'd do it for any by God rapscallions and sons of thieves that come here a-preachin' treachery and dis-union and pisenin' the name of Old Hickory, the people's friend.
(FEARGUS *returns with the keg.*)

BEN

Kill him, boys! You're the only *real* Americans we got left!

NINIAN (*rising*)

If you gentlemen will step outside, I'll be glad to accommodate you with the fight you seem to be spoiling for.

TRUM

You're committing suicide, Mr. Edwards.

JACK

Oh, no—he ain't. We ain't killers—we're just bone crushers. After a few months, you'll be as good as new, which ain't saying much. You bring that keg, Feargus.
(*They are about to go when* ABE *appears in the door. He now is slightly more respectably dressed, wearing a battered claw-hammer coat and pants that have been "foxed" with buckskin. He carries the mail. Behind him is* JOSH SPEED.)

ABE

The mud-wagon's in! Hello, Jack. Hello, boys. Ain't you fellers drunk yet? Hello, Miss Ann. Got a letter for you. (*There is a marked shyness in his attitude toward* ANN.)

ANN

Thank you, Abe. (*She snatches the letter and runs out with it.*)

BEN

Abe, there's goin' to be a fight!

NINIAN (*to* JACK)

Well—come on, if you're coming.

JACK

All right, boys.

ABE

Fight? Who—and why?

JACK

This is the son of Ninian Edwards, Abe. Come from Springfield lookin' for a little crotch hoist and I'm aimin' to oblige.
(ABE *looks* NINIAN *over.*)

BOWLING

Put a stop to it, Abe. It'd be next door to murder.

JACK

You shut your trap, Pot Green. Murder's too good for any goose-livered enemy of Andy Jackson. Come on, boys!

ABE

Wait a minute, boys. Jack, have you forgotten what day it is?

JACK

No, I ain't! But I reckon the Fourth is as good a day as any to whip a politician!

ABE (*amiably*)

Well, if you've just got to fight, Jack, you shouldn't give preference to strangers. Being post-master of this thriving town, I can rate as a politician, myself, so you'd better try a fall with me—(*He thrusts* JACK *aside and turns to* NINIAN.) And as for you, sir, I haven't the pleasure of your acquaintance; but my name's Lincoln, and I'd like to shake hands with a brave man.

NINIAN (*shaking hands with* ABE)

I'm greatly pleased to know you, Mr. Lincoln.

ABE

You should be. Because I come here just in time to save you quite some embarrassment, not to mention injury. Oh, got a couple of letters for you, Bowling. And here's your *Cincinnati Journal,* Trum.

JACK

Look here, Abe—you're steppin' into something that ain't none of your business.

This is a private matter of patriotic honor.

ABE

Everything in this town is my business, Jack. It's the only kind of business I've got. And besides—I saw Hannah down by the grove and she says to tell you to come on to the picnic and that means *now* or she'll give the cake away to the Straders children and you and the boys'll go hungry. So get moving.

FEARGUS (*to* JACK)

Are you goin' to let Abe talk you out of it?

ABE

Sure he is. (*He turns to* TRUM.) Say, Trum—if you ain't using that *Journal* for a while, would you let me have a read?

TRUM

By all means, Abe. Here you are. (*He tosses the paper to* ABE.)

ABE

Thanks. (*He turns again to* JACK.) You'd better hurry, Jack, or *you'll* get a beating from Hannah.
(*He starts to take the wrapper off, as he goes over to a chair at the left.* JACK *looks at* ABE *for a moment, then laughs.*)

JACK (*to* NINIAN)

All right! Abe Lincoln's saved your hide. I'll consent to callin' off the fight just because he's a friend of mine.

ABE (*as he sits*)

And also because I'm the only one around here you can't lick.

JACK

But I just want to tell you, Mr. Ninian Edwards, Junior, that the next time you come around here a-spreadin' pisen . . .

ABE

Go on, Jack. Hannah's waiting.

JACK (*walking over to* ABE)

I'm going, Abe. But I warn you—you'd better stop this foolishness of readin'—readin'—readin', mornin', noon and night, or you'll be gettin' soft and you won't be the same fightin' man you are now—and

it would break my heart to see you licked by anybody, includin' me! (*He laughs, slaps* ABE *on the back, then turns to go.*) Glad to have met you, Mr. Edwards.
(*He goes out, followed by* BAB *and* JASP. FEARGUS *picks up the keg and starts after them.*)

NINIAN (*to* JACK)

It's been a pleasure.

ABE

Where'd you get that keg, Feargus?

FEARGUS (*nervously*)

Jack told me to take it outen Mis' Rutledge's kitchen and I . . .

ABE

Well—put it down. . . . If you see Seth Gale, tell him I've got a letter for him.

FEARGUS

I'll tell him, Abe.
(FEARGUS *puts down the keg and goes.* JOSH SPEED *laughs and comes up to the table.*)

JOSH

Congratulations, Ninian. I shouldn't have enjoyed taking you home to Mrs. Edwards after those boys had done with you.

NINIAN (*grinning*)

I was aware of the certain consequences, Josh. (*He turns to* ABE.) I'm deeply in your debt, Mr. Lincoln.

ABE

Never mind any thanks, Mr. Edwards. Jack Armstrong talks big but he means well.

NINIAN

Won't you join us in a drink?

ABE

No, thank you.
(*He's reading the paper.* BOWLING *fills the glasses.*)

BOWLING

I'm going to have another! I don't mind telling you, I'm still trembling. (*He hands a glass to* NINIAN, *then drinks himself.*)

TRUM

You see, Mr. Edwards. It's that very kind of lawlessness that's holding our town back.

NINIAN

You'll find the same element in the capital of our nation, and everywhere else, these days. (*He sits down and drinks.*)

ABE

Say, Bowling! It says here that there was a riot in Lyons, France. (*He reads.*) "A mob of men, deprived of employment when textile factories installed the new sewing machines, re-enacted scenes of the Reign of Terror in the streets of this prosperous industrial center. The mobs were suppressed only when the military forces of His French Majesty took a firm hand. The rioters carried banners inscribed with the incendiary words, 'We will live working or die fighting!'" (ABE *looks at the group at the right.*) That's Revolution!

BOWLING

Maybe, but it's a long way off from New Salem.

JOSH

Put the paper down, Abe. We want to talk to you.

ABE

Me? What about? (*He looks curiously at* JOSH, BOWLING *and* NINIAN.)

JOSH

I brought Mr. Edwards here for the sole purpose of meeting you—and with his permission, I shall tell you why.

NINIAN

Go right ahead, Josh.
(*All are looking intently at* ABE.)

JOSH

Abe—how would you like to run for the State Assembly?

ABE

When?

JOSH

Now—for the election in the fall.

ABE

Why?

NINIAN

Mr. Lincoln, I've known you for only a few minutes, but that's long enough to make me agree with Josh Speed that you're precisely the type of man we want. The whole Whig organization will support your candidacy.

ABE

This was all your idea, Josh?

JOSH (*smiling*)

Oh, no, Abe—you're the people's choice!

TRUM

What do *you* think of it, Bowling?

BOWLING (*heartily*)

I think it's as fine a notion as I ever heard. Why, Abe—I can hear you making speeches, right and left, taking your stand on all the issues—secession, Texas, the National Bank crisis, abolitionism—it'll be more fun than we ever had in our lives!

ABE (*rising*)

Isn't anybody going to ask what *I* think?

JOSH (*laughs*)

All right, Abe—*I'll* ask you.

ABE (*after a moment's pause*)

It's a comical notion, all right—and I don't know if I can give you an answer to it, offhand. But my first, hasty impression is that I don't think much of it.

BOWLING

Don't overlook the fact that, if elected, your salary would be three whole dollars a day.

ABE

That's fine money. No doubt of that. And I see what you have in mind, Bowling. I owe you a considerable sum of money; and if I stayed in the legislature for, say, twenty years, I'd be able to pay off—let me see—two dollars and a half a day. . . . (*He is figuring it up on his fingers.*)

BOWLING

I'm not thinking about the debts, Abe.

ABE

I know you ain't, Bowling. But I've got to. And so should you, Mr. Edwards. The Whig party is the party of sound money and God save the National Bank, ain't it?

NINIAN

Why, yes—among other things. . . .

ABE

Well, then—how would it look if you put forward a candidate who has demonstrated no earning power but who has run up the impressive total of fifteen hundred dollars of debts?

BOWLING (*to* NINIAN)

I can tell you something about those debts. Abe started a grocery store in partnership with an unfortunate young man named Berry. Their stock included whiskey, and Berry started tapping the keg until he had consumed all the liquid assets. So the store went bankrupt—and Abe voluntarily assumed all the obligations. That may help to explain to you, Mr. Edwards, why we think pretty highly of him around here.

NINIAN

It's a sentiment with which I concur most heartily.

ABE

I thank you one and all for your kind tributes, but don't overdo them, or I'll begin to think that three dollars a day ain't enough!

JOSH

What's the one thing that you want most, Abe? You want to learn. This will give you your chance to get at a good library, to associate with the finest lawyers in the State.

ABE

I've got a copy of Blackstone, already. Found it in an old junk barrel. And how can I tell that the finest lawyers would welcome association with *me*?

NINIAN

You needn't worry about that. I saw how you dealt with those ruffians. You quite obviously know how to handle men.

ABE

I can handle the Clary's Grove boys because I can outwrassle them—but I can't go around Sangamon County throwing *all* the voters.

BOWLING (*laughing*)

I'll take a chance on that, Abe.

ABE (*to* NINIAN)

Besides—how do you know that my political views would agree with yours? How do you know I wouldn't say the wrong thing?

NINIAN

What *are* your political leanings, Mr. Lincoln?

ABE

They're all toward staying out. . . . What sort of leanings did you want?

NINIAN

We have a need for good conservative men to counteract all the radical firebrands that have swept over this country in the wake of Andrew Jackson. We've got to get this country back to first principles!

ABE

Well—I'm conservative, all right. If I got into the legislature you'd never catch me starting any movements for reform or progress. I'm pretty certain I wouldn't even have the nerve to open my mouth.

JOSH (*laughs*)

I told you, Ninian—he's just the type of candidate you're looking for.
(NINIAN *laughs too, and rises.*)

NINIAN (*crossing toward* ABE)

The fact is, Mr. Lincoln, we want to spike the rumor that ours is the party of the more privileged classes. That is why we seek men of the plain people for candidates. As post-master, you're in an excellent position to establish contacts. While delivering letters, you can also deliver speeches and campaign literature, with which our headquarters will keep you supplied.

ABE

Would you supply me with a suit of

store clothes? A candidate mustn't look
too plain.

NINIAN (*smiling*)

I think even that could be arranged, eh,
Judge?

BOWLING

I think so.

NINIAN (*pompously*)

So—think it over, Mr. Lincoln, and realize that this is opportunity unlimited in
scope. Just consider what it means to be
starting up the ladder in a nation which
is now expanding southward, across the
vast area of Texas; and westward, to the
Empire of the Californias on the Pacific
Ocean. We're becoming a continent, Mr.
Lincoln—and all that we need is men!
(*He looks at his watch.*) And now, gentlemen, if you will excuse me—I must put
in an appearance at the torch-light procession in Springfield this evening, so I
shall have to be moving on. Good-bye, Mr.
Lincoln. This meeting has been a happy
one for me.

ABE (*shaking hands*)

Good-bye, Mr. Edwards. Good luck in
the campaign.

NINIAN

And the same to you.
(*All at the right have risen and are
starting to go, except* BEN MATTLING, *who
is still sitting at the back, drinking.*)

ABE

Here's your paper, Trum.

TRUM

Go ahead and finish it, Abe. I won't be
looking at it yet awhile.

ABE

Thanks, Trum. I'll leave it at your
house.
(TRUM *and* NINIAN *have gone.*)

BOWLING

I'll see you later, Abe. Tell Ann I'll be
back to pay for the liquor.

ABE

I'll tell her, Bowling.

(BOWLING *goes.* JOSH *is looking at* ABE,
who, after a moment, turns to him.)

ABE

I'm surprised at you, Josh. I thought you
were my friend.

JOSH

I know, Abe. But Ninian Edwards asked
me is there anybody in that God-forsaken
town of New Salem that stands a chance
of getting votes, and the only one I could
think of was you. I can see you're embarrassed by this—and you're annoyed. But—
whether you like it or not—you've got to
grow; and here's your chance to get a little
scrap of importance.

ABE

Am I the kind that wants importance?

JOSH

You'll deny it, Abe—but you've got a
funny kind of vanity—which is the same
as saying you've got some pride—and it's
badly in need of nourishment. So, if you'll
agree to this—I don't think you'll be sorry
for it or feel that I've betrayed you.

ABE (*grins*)

Oh—I won't hold it against you, Josh.
(*He walks away and looks out the door.*)
But that Mr. Ninian Edwards—he's rich
and he's prominent and he's got a high-
class education. Politics to him is just a
kind of a game. And maybe I'd like it if I
could play it *his* way. (*He turns to* JOSH.)
But when you get to reading Blackstone,
not to mention the Bible, you can't help
feeling maybe there's some serious responsibility in the giving of laws—and maybe
there's something more important in the
business of government than just getting
the Whig Party back into power.
(SETH GALE *comes in. He is a young,
husky frontiersman, with flashes of the sun
of Western empire in his eyes.*)

SETH

Hey, Abe—Feargus said you've got a letter for me.

ABE (*fishing in his mail pouch*)

Yes.

SETH

Hello, Mr. Speed.

JOSH

How are you, Mr. Gale?

ABE

Here you are, Seth.
(*He hands him a letter.* SETH *takes it to the right, sits down and starts to read.*)

JOSH

I've got to get home to Springfield, Abe, but I'll be down again in a week or so.

ABE

I'll be here, Josh.
(JOSH *goes.* ABE *sits down again at the right, picks up his paper, but doesn't read it.* BEN *stands up and comes down a bit unsteadily.*)

BEN (*angrily*)

Are you going to do it, Abe? Are you goin' to let them make you into a *candidate?*

ABE

I ain't had time to think about it yet.

BEN

Well—I tell you to stop thinkin' before it's too late. Don't let 'em get you. Don't let 'em put you in a store suit that's the uniform of degradation in this miserable country. You're an honest man, Abe Lincoln. You're a good-for-nothin', debt-ridden loafer—but you're an honest man. And you have no place in that den of thieves that's called gov'ment. They'll corrupt you as they've corrupted the whole damn United States. Look at Washington, look at Jefferson, and John Adams—(*He points grandly to the pictures*)—where are they today? Dead! And everything they stood for and fought for and *won*—that's dead too.
(ANN *comes in to collect the mugs from the table at the left.* ABE *looks at her.*) Why —we'd be better off if we was all black niggers held in the bonds of slavery. *They* get fed—*they* get looked after when they're old and sick. (ANN *goes.*) But *you* don't care—you ain't listenin' to me, neither . . .
(*He starts slowly toward the door.*)

ABE

Of course I'm listening, Ben.

BEN

No, you ain't. *I* know. You're goin' to the assembly and join the wolves who're feedin' off the carcass of Liberty. (*He goes out.*)

ABE

You needn't worry. I'm not going.
(ANN *comes in. She crosses to the right to pick up the glasses. She seems extremely subdued.* ABE *looks at her, curiously.*)

ABE

Bowling Green said to tell you he'd be back later, to pay you what he owes.

ANN (*curtly*)

That's all right.
(ANN *puts the glasses and bottle on a tray and picks it up.* ABE *jumps to his feet.*)

ABE

Here, Ann. Let me take that.

ANN (*irritably*)

No—leave it alone! I can carry it! (*She starts across to the left.*)

ABE

Excuse me, Ann. . . .

ANN (*stopping*)

Well?

ABE

Would you come back after you're finished with that? I—I'd like to talk to you.
(SETH *has finished the letter. Its contents seem to have depressed him.*)

ANN

All right. I'll talk to you—if you want.
(*She goes out.* SETH *crosses toward* ABE, *who, during the subsequent dialogue, is continually looking toward the kitchen.*)

SETH

Abe . . . Abe—I got a letter from my folks back in Maryland. It means—I guess I've got to give up the dream we had of moving out into Nebraska territory.

ABE

What's happened, Seth?

SETH (*despondently*)

Well—for one thing, the old man's took sick, and he's pretty feeble.

ABE

I'm sorry to hear that.

SETH

So am I. They've sent for me to come back and work the farm. Measly little thirty-six acres—sandy soil. I tell you, Abe, it's a bitter disappointment to me, when I had my heart all set on going out into the West. And the worst of it is—I'm letting *you* down on it, too.

ABE (*with a glance toward the kitchen*)

Don't think about that, Seth. Maybe I won't be able to move for a while myself. And when your father gets to feeling better, you'll come back . . .

SETH

He won't get to feeling better. Not at his age. I'll be stuck there, just like he was. I'll be pushed in and cramped all the rest of my life, till the malaria gets me, too. . . . Well—there's no use crying about it. If I've got to go back East, I've got to go. (ANN *comes back.*) I'll tell you good-bye, Abe, before I leave.

(*He goes.* ABE *turns and looks at* ANN, *and she at him.*)

ANN

Well—what is it, Abe?

ABE (*rising*)

I just thought—you might like to talk to me.

ANN (*sharply*)

What about?

ABE

That letter you got from New York State.

ANN

What do *you* know about that letter?

ABE

I'm the post-master. I know more than I ought to about people's private affairs. I couldn't help seeing that that was the handwriting of Mr. McNiel. And I couldn't help seeing, from the look on your face, that the bad news you've been afraid of has come.

(ANN *looks at him with surprise. He is a lot more observant than she had thought.*)

ANN

Whatever the letter said, it's no concern of yours, Abe.

ABE

I know that, Ann. But—it appears to me that you've been crying—and it makes me sad to think that something could have hurt you. The thing is—I think quite a lot of you—always have—ever since I first came here, and met you. I wouldn't mention it, only when you're distressed about something it's a comfort sometimes to find a pair of ears to pour your troubles into—and the Lord knows my ears are big enough to hold a lot.

(*Her attitude of hostility softens and she rewards him with a tender smile.*)

ANN

You're a Christian gentleman, Abe Lincoln. (*She sits down.*)

ABE

No, I ain't. I'm a plain, common sucker with a shirt-tail so short I can't sit on it.

ANN (*laughs*)

Well—sit down, anyway, Abe—here, by me.

ABE

Why—it'd be a pleasure. (*He crosses and sits near her.*)

ANN

You can always say something to make a person laugh, can't you?

ABE

Well—I don't even have to *say* anything. A person just has to *look* at me.

ANN

You're right about that letter, Abe. It's the first I've heard from him in months—and now he says he's delayed by family troubles and doesn't know when he'll be able to get to New Salem again. By which he probably means—never.

ABE

I wouldn't say that, Ann.

ANN

I would. (*She looks at him.*) I reckon

you think I'm a silly fool for ever having promised myself to Mr. McNiel.

ABE

I think no such thing. I liked him myself, and still do, and whatever reasons he had for changing his name I'm sure were honorable. He's a smart man, and a handsome one—and I—I wouldn't blame any girl for—loving him.

ANN (*too emphatically*)

I guess I don't love him, Abe. I guess I couldn't love anybody that was as—as faithless as that.

ABE (*trying to appear unconcerned*)

Well, then. There's nothing to fret about. Now—poor Seth Gale—he got some *really* bad news. His father's sick and he has to give up his dream which was to go and settle out west.

ANN (*looks at him*)

I don't believe you know much about females, Abe.

ABE

Probably I don't—although I certainly spend enough time thinking about 'em.

ANN

You're a big man, and you can lick anybody, and you can't understand the feelings of somebody who is weak. But—I'm a female, and I can't help thinking what they'll be saying about me—all the old gossips, all over town. They'll make it out that he deserted me; I'm a rejected woman. They'll give me their sympathy to my face, but they'll snigger at me behind my back. (*She rises and crosses toward the right.*)

ABE

Yes—that's just about what they would do. But—would you let *them* disturb you?

ANN (*rising*)

I told you—it's just weakness—it's just vanity. It's something you couldn't understand, Abe.

(*She has crossed to the window and is staring out.* ABE *twists in his chair to look at her.*)

ABE

Maybe I can understand it, Ann. I've got a kind of vanity myself. Josh Speed said so, and he's right. . . . It's—it's nothing but vanity that's kept me from declaring my inclinations toward you. (*She turns, amazed, and looks at him.*) You see, I don't like to be sniggered at, either. I know what I am—and I know what I look like —and I know that I've got nothing to offer any girl that I'd be in love with.

ANN

Are you saying that you're in love with me, Abe?

ABE (*with deep earnestness*)

Yes—I am saying that. (*He stands up, facing her. She looks intently into his eyes.*) I've been loving you—a long time— with all my heart. You see, Ann—you're a particularly fine girl. You've got sense, and you've got bravery—those are two things that I admire particularly. And you're powerful good to look at, too. So—it's only natural I should have a great regard for you. But—I don't mean to worry you about it, Ann. I only mentioned it because—if you would do me the honor of keeping company with me for a while, it might shut the old gossips' mouths. They'd figure you'd chucked McNiel for—for some one else. Even me.

ANN (*going to him*)

I thought I knew you pretty well, Abe. But I didn't.

ABE (*worried*)

Why do you say that? Do you consider I was too forward, in speaking out as I did?

ANN (*gravely*)

No, Abe. . . . I've always thought a lot of you—the way I thought you were. But —the idea of love between you and me— I can't say how I feel about that, because now you're like some other person, that I'm meeting for the first time.

ABE (*quietly*)

I'm not expecting you to feel anything for me. I'd never dream of expecting such a thing.

ANN

I know that, Abe. You'd be willing to give everything you have and never expect anything in return. Maybe you're different in that way from any man I've ever heard of. And I can tell you this much—now, and truthfully—if I ever do love you, I'll be happy about it—and lucky, to be loving a good, decent man. . . . If you just give me time—to think about it. . . .

ABE (*unable to believe his eyes and ears*)

You mean—if you took time—you might get in your heart something like the feeling I have for you?

ANN (*with great tenderness*)

I don't know, Abe. (*She clutches his lapel.*) But I do know that you're a man who could fill any one's heart—yes, fill it and warm it and make it glad to be living. (ABE *covers her hand with his.*)

ABE

Ann—I've always tried hard to believe what the orators tell us—that this is a land of equal opportunity for all. But I've never been able to credit it, any more than I could agree that God made all men in his own image. But—if I could win you, Ann

—I'd be willing to disbelieve everything I've ever seen with my own eyes, and have faith in everything wonderful that I've ever read in poetry books. (*Both are silent for a moment. Then* ANN *turns away.*) But—I'm not asking you to say anything now. And I won't ask you until the day comes when I know I've got a right to. (*He turns and walks quickly toward the door, picking up his mail pouch.*)

ANN

Abe! Where are you going?

ABE

I'm going to find Bowling Green and tell him a good joke. (*He grins. He is standing in the doorway.*)

ANN

A *joke?* What about?

ABE

I'm going to tell him that I'm a candidate for the assembly of the State of Illinois. (*He goes.*)
(*The light fades.*)

End of Scene II

SCENE III

BOWLING GREEN'S *house near New Salem.*
It is a small room, but the walls are lined with books and family pictures. In the center is a table with a lamp on it. Another light—a candle in a glass globe—is on a bureau at the right. There are comfortable chairs on either side of the table, and a sofa at the left.
At the back, toward the left, is the front door. A rifle is leaning against the wall by the door. There is another door in the right wall. Toward the right, at the back, is a ladder fixed against the wall leading up through an opening to the attic.
It is late in the evening, a year or so after Scene II. A storm is raging outside.
BOWLING *is reading aloud from a sort of pamphlet. His comfortable wife,* NANCY, *is listening and sewing.*

BOWLING

"And how much more interesting did the spectacle become when, starting into full life and animation, as a simultaneous call for 'Pickwick' burst from his follow-ers, that illustrious man slowly mounted into the Windsor chair, on which he had been previously seated, and addressed the club himself had founded."
(BOWLING *chuckles.* NANCY *laughs.*)

NANCY

He sounds precisely like *you*, Bowling. (*There is a knock at the door.*)

NANCY (*nervous*)

That's not Abe's knock. Who can it be?

BOWLING (*rising*)

We don't know yet, my dear.

NANCY

It's a strange hour for any one to be calling. You'd better have that gun ready. (BOWLING *unbolts and opens the door. It is* JOSH SPEED.)

BOWLING

Why—Josh Speed!

JOSH

Good evening, Bowling.

BOWLING

We haven't seen you in a coon's age.

NANCY

Good evening, Mr. Speed.

JOSH

Good evening, Mrs. Green. And I beg you to forgive me for this untimely intrusion.

NANCY

We're delighted to see you. Take your wrap off.

JOSH

Thank you. I've just come down from Springfield. I heard Abe Lincoln was in town and I was told I might find him here.

BOWLING

He's been sleeping here, up in the attic.

NANCY

But he's out now at the Rutledge Farm, tending poor little Ann.

JOSH

Miss Rutledge? What's the matter with her?

NANCY

She's been taken with the brain sickness. It's the most shocking thing. People have been dying from it right and left.

BOWLING

But Ann's young. She'll pull through, all right. Sit down, Josh.

JOSH

Thank you. (*He sits.* BOWLING *places the pamphlet on the top of the bookcase and stands there, filling his pipe.*)

NANCY

I suppose you know that Abe came rushing down from Vandalia the moment he heard she was taken. He's deeply in love with her.

BOWLING

Now, Nancy—don't exaggerate. (JOSH *is listening to all this, intently.*)

JOSH

So Abe is in love. I wondered what has been the matter with him lately.

NANCY

Why, it's written all over his poor, homely face.

JOSH

The last time I saw him, he seemed pretty moody. But when I asked him what was wrong, he said it was his liver.

BOWLING (*laughing*)

That sounds more likely. Has he been getting on well in the Assembly?

JOSH

No. He has just been sitting there—drawing his three dollars a day—and taking no apparent interest in the proceedings. Do you fancy that Miss Rutledge cares anything for him?

NANCY

Indeed she does! She broke her promise to that Mr. McNiel because of her feelings for Abe!

JOSH

Has he any notion of marrying her?

NANCY

It's the only notion of his life right now. And the sooner they are married, the better for both of them.

BOWLING (*seating himself*)

Better for her, perhaps—but the worse for him.

NANCY (*finishing her sewing*)

And why? The Rutledges are fine people, superior in every way to those riffraff Hankses and Lincolns that are Abe's family!

BOWLING

I think you feel as I do, Josh. Abe has his own way to go and—sweet and pretty as Ann undoubtedly is—she'd only be a hindrance to him.

JOSH

I guess it wouldn't matter much if she could give him a little of the happiness he's never had.

NANCY (*rising*)

That's just it! I think as much of Abe as you do, Bowling. But we can't deny that he's a poor man, and he's failed in trade, and he's been in the legislature for a year without accomplishing a blessed thing . . . (*She goes to the bookcase to put her sewing-basket away.*)

BOWLING

He could go to Springfield and set up a law practice and make a good thing of it. Ninian Edwards would help him to get started. And he'd soon forget little Ann. He has just happened to fasten on her his own romantic ideal of what's beautiful and unattainable. Let him ever attain her, and she'd break his heart.

NANCY (*seating herself*)

Do you agree with Bowling on that, Mr. Speed?

JOSH (*sadly*)

I can't say, Mrs. Green. I've abandoned the attempt to predict anything about Abe Lincoln. The first time I ever saw him was when he was piloting that steamboat, the *Talisman*. You remember how she ran into trouble at the dam. I had a valuable load of goods aboard for my father's store, and I was sure that steamboat, goods and all were a total loss. But Abe got her through. It was a great piece of work. I thought, "Here is a reliable man." So I cultivated his acquaintance, believing, in my conceit, that I could help him to fame and fortune. I soon learned differently. I found out that he has plenty of strength and courage in his body—but in his mind he's a hopeless hypochondriac. He can split rails, push a plow, crack jokes, all day—and then sit up all night reading "Hamlet" and brooding over his own fancied resemblance to that melancholy prince. Maybe he's a great philosopher—maybe he's a great fool. I don't know what he is.

BOWLING (*laughs*)

Well—if only Ann had sense enough to see all the things *you* saw, Josh, she'd be so terrified of him she'd run all the way back to York State and find McNiel. At least, *he's* not complicated.

NANCY (*with deeper emotion*)

You're talking about Abe Lincoln as if he were some problem that you found in a book, and it's interesting to try to figure it out. Well—maybe he is a problem —but he's also a man, and a miserable one. And what do you do for his misery? You laugh at his comical jokes and you vote for him on election day and give him board and lodging when he needs it. But all that doesn't give a scrap of satisfaction to Abe's soul—and never will. Because the one thing he needs is a woman with the will to face life for him.

BOWLING

You think he's afraid to face it himself?

NANCY

He is! He listens too much to the whispers, that he heard in the forest where he grew up, and where he always goes now when he wants to be alone. They're the whispers of the women behind him—his dead mother—and *her* mother, who was no better than she should be. He's got that awful fear on him, of not knowing what the whispers mean, or where they're directing him. And none of your backslapping will knock that fear out of him. Only a woman can free him—a woman who loves him truly, and believes in him.

(*There is a knock on the door.*)

BOWLING

That's Abe now. (*He gets up and opens it.*)

(ABE *is there, bareheaded, wet by the storm. He now wears a fairly respectable dark suit of clothes. He looks older and grimmer.*)

BOWLING

Why, hello, Abe! We've been sitting up waiting for you. Come on in out of the wet!

(ABE *comes in.* BOWLING *shuts the door behind him.*)

NANCY

We were reading The Posthumous Papers of the Pickwick Club when Mr. Speed came in.

ABE

Hello, Josh. Glad to see you.

JOSH

Hello, Abe.

(ABE *turns to* NANCY.)

ABE

Nancy . . .

NANCY

Yes, Abe?

ABE

She's dead.

BOWLING

Ann? She's dead?

ABE

Yes. Tonight, the fever suddenly got worse. They couldn't seem to do anything for it.

(NANCY *gives* BOWLING *a swift look, then goes quickly to* ABE *and takes his hand.*)

NANCY

Oh, Abe—I'm so sorry. She was such a dear little girl. Every one who knew her will join in mourning for her.

ABE

I know they will. But it won't do any good. She's dead.

BOWLING

Sit down, Abe, and rest yourself.

ABE

No—I'm not fit company for anybody. I'd better be going. (*He turns toward the door.*)

JOSH (*stopping him*)

No, you don't, Abe. You'll stay right here.

BOWLING

You better do what Josh tells you.

NANCY

Come here, Abe. Please sit down. (ABE *looks from one to the other, then obediently goes to a chair and sits.*) Your bed is ready for you upstairs when you want it.

ABE (*dully*)

You're the best friends I've got in the world, and it seems a pretty poor way to reward you for all that you've given me, to come here now, and inflict you with a corpse.

BOWLING

This is your home, Abe. This is where you're loved.

ABE

Yes, that's right. And I love you, Bowling and Nancy. But I loved her more than everything else that I've ever known.

NANCY

I know you did, Abe. I know it.

ABE

I used to think it was better to be alone. I was always most contented when I was alone. I had queer notions that if you got too close to people, you could see the truth about them, that behind the surface they're all insane, and they could see the same in you. And then—when I saw her, I knew there could be beauty and purity in people—like the purity you sometimes see in the sky at night. When I took hold of her hand, and held it, all fear, all doubt, went out of me. I believed in God. I'd have been glad to work for her until I die, to get for her everything out of life that she wanted. If she thought I could do

it, then I could. That was my belief. . . .
And then I had to stand there, as helpless
as a twig in a whirlpool; I had to stand
there and watch her die. And her father
and mother were there, too, praying to
God for her soul. The Lord giveth, and
the Lord taketh away, blessed be the
name of the Lord! That's what they kept
on saying. But I couldn't pray with them.
I couldn't give any devotion to one who
has the power of death, and uses it. (*He
has stood up, and is speaking with more
passion.*) I'm making a poor exhibition
of myself—and I'm sorry—but—I can't
stand it. I can't live with myself any
longer. I've got to die and be with her
again, or I'll go crazy! (*He goes to the
door and opens it. The storm continues.*)
I can't bear to think of her out there alone!

(NANCY *looks at* BOWLING *with frantic
appeal. He goes to* ABE, *who is standing in
the doorway, looking out.*)

BOWLING (*with great tenderness*)

Abe . . . I want you to go upstairs and
see if you can't get some sleep. . . . Please,
Abe—as a special favor to Nancy and me.

ABE (*after a moment*)

All right, Bowling. (*He turns and goes
to the ladder.*)

NANCY

Here's a light for you, dear Abe. (*She
hands him the candle.*)

ABE

Thank you, Nancy. . . . Good night.
(*He goes up the ladder into the attic.*)
(*They all look up after him.*)

NANCY (*tearful*)

Poor, lonely soul.
(BOWLING *cautions her to be quiet.*)

JOSH

Keep him here with you, Mrs. Green.
Don't let him out of your sight.

BOWLING

We won't, Josh.

JOSH

Good night. (*He picks up his hat and
cloak and goes.*)

BOWLING

Good night, Josh. (*He closes and bolts
the door, then comes down to the table and
picks up the lamp.*)
(NANCY *looks up once more, then goes
out at the right.* BOWLING *follows her out,
carrying the lamp with him. He closes
the door behind him, so that the only light
on the stage is the beam from the attic.*)
Curtain

End of Act One

ACT TWO

SCENE IV

LAW OFFICE *of Stuart and Lincoln on the second floor of the Court House in Springfield, Ill. A sunny summer's afternoon, some five years after the preceding scene.*

*The room is small, with two windows and one door, upstage, which leads to the hall
and staircase.*

*At the right are a table and chair, at the left an old desk, littered with papers. At the
back is a ramshackle bed, with a buffalo robe thrown over it. Below the windows are
some rough shelves, sagging with law books. There is an old wood stove.*

*On the wall above the desk is hung an American flag, with 26 stars. Between the
windows is an election poster, for Harrison and Tyler, with a list of Electors, the last of
whom is Ab'm Lincoln, of Sangamon.*

BILLY HERNDON *is working at the table. He is young, slight, serious-minded, smoldering. He looks up as* ABE *comes in.* ABE *wears a battered plug hat, a light alpaca coat, and*

carries an ancient, threadbare carpet-bag. He is evidently not in a talkative mood. His boots are caked in mud. He is only thirty-one years old, but his youth was buried with Ann Rutledge.

He leaves the office door open, and lettered on it we see the number, 4, and the firm's name—Stuart & Lincoln, Attorneys & Counsellors at Law.

BILLY.

How de do, Mr. Lincoln. Glad to see you back.

ABE

Good day, Billy. (*He sets down the carpet-bag, takes off his hat and puts it on his desk.*)

BILLY

How was it on the circuit, Mr. Lincoln?

ABE

About as usual.

BILLY

Have you been keeping in good health?

ABE

Not particularly. But Doc Henry dosed me enough to keep me going. (*He sits down at the desk and starts looking at letters and papers that have accumulated during his absence. He takes little interest in them, pigeonholing some letters unopened.*)

BILLY

Did you have occasion to make any political speeches?

ABE

Oh—they got me up on the stump a couple of times. Ran into Stephen Douglas —he was out campaigning, of course— and we had some argument in public.

BILLY (*greatly interested*)

That's good! What issues did you and Mr. Douglas discuss?

ABE

Now—don't get excited, Billy. We weren't taking it serious. There was' no blood shed. . . . What's the news here?

BILLY

Judge Stuart wrote that he arrived safely in Washington and the campaign there is getting almost as hot as the weather. Mrs. Fraim stopped in to say she couldn't possibly pay your fee for a while.

ABE

I should hope not. I ought to be paying her, seeing as I defended her poor husband and he hanged.

(BILLY *hands him a letter and watches him intently, while he reads it.*)

BILLY

That was left here by hand, and I promised to call it especially to your attention. It's from the Elijah P. Lovejoy League of Freemen. They want you to speak at an Abolitionist rally next Thursday evening. It'll be a very important affair.

ABE (*reflectively*)

It's funny, Billy—I was thinking about Lovejoy the other day—trying to figure what it is in a man that makes him glad to be a martyr. I was on the boat coming from Quincy to Alton, and there was a gentleman on board with twelve Negroes. He was shipping them down to Vicksburg for sale—had 'em chained six and six together. Each of them had a small iron clevis around his wrist, and this was chained to the main chain, so that those Negroes were strung together precisely like fish on a trot line. I gathered they were being separated forever from their homes—mothers, fathers, wives, children —whatever families the poor creatures had got—going to be whipped into perpetual slavery, and no questions asked. It was quite a shocking sight.

BILLY (*excitedly*)

Then you will give a speech at the Lovejoy rally?

ABE (*wearily*)

I doubt it. That Freemen's League is a pack of hell-roaring fanatics. Talk reason to them and they scorn you for being a mealy-mouth. Let 'em make their own noise. (ABE *has opened a letter. He starts to read it.*)

(BILLY *looks at him with resentful disappointment, but he knows too well that any argument would be futile. He resumes his work. After a moment,* BOWLING GREEN *comes in, followed by* JOSH SPEED.)

BOWLING

Are we interrupting the majesty of the Law?

ABE (*heartily*)

Bowling! (*He jumps up and grasps* BOWLING's *hand.*) How are you, Bowling?

BOWLING

Tolerably well, Abe—and glad to see you.

ABE

This is Billy Herndon—Squire Green, of New Salem. Hello, Josh.

JOSH

Hello, Abe.

BILLY (*shaking hands with* BOWLING)

I'm proud to know you, sir. Mr. Lincoln speaks of you constantly.

BOWLING

Thank you, Mr. Herndon. Are you a lawyer, too?

BILLY (*seriously*)

I hope to be, sir. I'm serving here as a clerk in Judge Stuart's absence.

BOWLING

So now you're teaching others, Abe?

ABE

Just providing a bad example.

BOWLING

I can't believe it. Look at the mess on that desk. Shameful!

ABE

Give me another year of law practice and I'll need a warehouse for the overflow. . . . But—sit yourself down, Bowling, and tell me what brings you to Springfield.

(BOWLING *sits.* JOSH *has sat on the couch, smoking his pipe.* BILLY *is again at the table.*)

BOWLING

I've been up to Lake Michigan—fishing—came in today on the steam-cars—scared me out of a year's growth. But how are you doing, Abe? Josh says you're still broke, but you're a great social success.

ABE

True—on both counts. I'm greatly in demand at all the more elegant functions. You remember Ninian Edwards?

BOWLING

Of course.

ABE

Well, sir—I'm a guest at his mansion regularly. He's got a house so big you could race horses in the parlor. And his wife is one of the Todd family from Kentucky. Very high-grade people. They spell their name with two D's—which is pretty impressive when you consider that one was enough for God.

JOSH

Tell Bowling whom you met over in Rochester.

ABE

The President of the United States!

BOWLING

You don't tell me so!

ABE

Do you see that hand? (*He holds out his right hand, palm upward.*)

BOWLING

Yes—I see it.

ABE

It has shaken the hand of Martin Van Buren!

BOWLING (*laughing*)

Was the President properly respectful to you, Abe?

ABE

Indeed he was! He said to me, "We've been hearing great things of you in Washington." I found out later he'd said the same thing to every other cross-roads politician he'd met. (*He laughs.*) But Billy Herndon there is pretty disgusted with me for associating with the wrong kind of people. Billy's a firebrand—a real, radical abolitionist—and he can't stand anybody who keeps his mouth shut and abides by the Constitution. If he had his way, the whole Union would be set on fire and we'd all be burned to a crisp. Eh, Billy?

BILLY (*grimly*)

Yes, Mr. Lincoln. And if you'll permit me to say so, I think you'd be of more use to your fellow-men if you allowed some of the same incendiary impulses to come out in you.

ABE

You see, Bowling? He wants me to get down into the blood-soaked arena and grapple with all the lions of injustice and oppression.

BOWLING

Mr. Herndon—my profound compliments.

BILLY (*rising and taking his hat*)

Thank you, sir. (*He shakes hands with* BOWLING, *then turns to* ABE:) I have the writ prepared in the Willcox case. I'll take it down to the Clerk of Court to be attested.

ABE

All right, Billy.

BILLY (*to* BOWLING)

Squire Green—Mr. Lincoln regards you and Mr. Speed as the best friends he has on earth, and I should like to beg you, in his presence, for God's sake drag him out of this stagnant pool in which he's rapidly drowning himself. Good day, sir—good day, Mr. Speed.

JOSH

Good day, Billy.
(BILLY *has gone.*)

BOWLING

That's a bright young man, Abe. Seems to have a good grasp of things.

ABE (*looking after* BILLY)

He's going downstairs to the Clerk's office, but he took his hat. Which means that before he comes back to work, he'll have paid a little visit to the Chenery House saloon.

BOWLING

Does the boy drink?

ABE

Yes. He's got great fires in him, but he's putting 'em out fast. . . . Now—tell me about New Salem. (*He leans against the wall near the window.*)

BOWLING

Practically nothing of it left.

ABE

How's that blessed wife of yours?

BOWLING

Nancy's busier than ever, and more than ever concerned about your innermost thoughts and yearnings. In fact, she instructed me expressly to ask what on earth is the matter with you?

ABE (*laughs*)

You can tell her there's nothing the matter. I've been able to pay off my debts to the extent of some seven cents on the dollar, and I'm sound of skin and skeleton.

BOWLING

But why don't we hear more from you and of you?

ABE

Josh can tell you. I've been busy.

BOWLING

What at?

ABE

I'm a candidate.

JOSH (*pointing to the poster*)

Haven't you noticed his name? It's here —at the bottom of the list of Electors on the Whig ticket.

ABE

Yes, sir—if old Tippecanoe wins next fall, I'll be a member of the Electoral College.

BOWLING

The Electoral College! And is that the best you can do?

ABE

Yes—in the limited time at my disposal.
I had a letter from Seth Gale—remember
—he used to live in New Salem and was
always aiming to move West. He's settled down in Maryland now and has a wife
and a son. He says that back East they're
powerful worried about the annexation of
Texas.

BOWLING

They have reason to be. It would probably mean extending slavery through all
the territories, from Kansas and Nebraska
right out to Oregon and California. That
would give the South absolute rule of the
country—and God help the rest of us in
the free states.

JOSH

It's an ugly situation, all right. It's got
the seeds in it of nothing more nor less
than civil war.

ABE

Well, if so, it'll be the abolitionists' own
fault. They know where this trouble might
lead, and yet they go right on agitating.
They ought to be locked up for disturbing
the peace, all of them.

BOWLING

I thought you were opposed to slavery,
Abe. Have you changed your mind about
it?

ABE (*ambles over to the couch and sprawls
on it*)

No. I am opposed to slavery. But I'm
even more opposed to going to war. And,
on top of that, I know what you're getting
at, both of you. (*He speaks to them with
the utmost good nature.*) You're following Billy Herndon's lead—troubling your
kind hearts with concerns about me and
when am I going to amount to something.
Is that it?

BOWLING

Oh, no, Abe. Far be it from me to interfere in your life.

JOSH

Or me, either. If we happen to feel that,
so far, you've been a big disappointment
to us, we'll surely keep it to ourselves.

ABE (*laughs*)

I'm afraid you'll have to do what I've
had to do—which is, learn to accept me
for what I am. I'm no fighting man. I
found that out when I went through the
Black Hawk War, and was terrified that
I might have to fire a shot at an Indian.
Fortunately, the Indians felt the same way,
so I never saw one of them. Now, I know
plenty of men who like to fight; they're
willing to kill, and not scared of being
killed. All right. Let them attend to the
battles that have to be fought.

BOWLING

Peaceable men have sometimes been of
service to their country.

ABE

They may have been peaceable when
they started, but they didn't remain so
long after they'd become mixed in the
great brawl of politics. (*He sits up.*) Suppose I ran for Congress, and got elected.
I'd be right in the thick of that ugly situation you were speaking of. One day I
might have to cast my vote on the terrible
issue of war or peace. It might be war with
Mexico over Texas; or war with England
over Oregon; or even war with our own
people across the Ohio River. What attitude would I take in deciding which way
to vote? "The Liberal attitude," of course.
And what is the Liberal attitude? To go
to war, for a tract of land, or a moral principle? Or to avoid war at all costs? No, sir.
The place for me is in the Electoral College, where all I have to do is vote for the
President whom everybody else elected
four months previous.

BOWLING

Well, Abe—you were always an artful
dodger—and maybe you'll be able to go on
to the end of your days avoiding the clutch
of your own conscience.

(NINIAN EDWARDS *comes in. He is a little
stouter and more prosperous.*)

ABE—JOSH

Hello, Ninian.

NINIAN

Hello. I saw Billy Herndon at the Chenery House and he said you were back from
the circuit. (*He sees* BOWLING.) Why—

it's my good friend Squire Green. How de do, and welcome to Springfield. (*He shakes hands with* BOWLING.)

BOWLING

Thank you, Mr. Edwards.

NINIAN

I just called in, Abe, to tell you you must dine with us. And, Squire, Mrs. Edwards would be honored to receive you, if your engagements will permit—and you, too, Josh.

JOSH

Delighted!

NINIAN

We're proudly exhibiting my sister-in-law, Miss Mary Todd, who has just come from Kentucky to grace our home. She's a very gay young lady—speaks French like a native, recites poetry at the drop of a hat, and knows the names and habits of all the flowers. I've asked Steve Douglas and some of the other eligibles to meet her, so you boys had better get in early.

BOWLING

My compliments to Mrs. Edwards, but my own poor wife awaits me impatiently, I hope.

NINIAN

I appreciate your motives, Squire, and applaud them. You'll be along presently, Abe?

ABE

I wouldn't be surprised.

NINIAN

Good. You'll meet a delightful young lady. And I'd better warn you she's going to survey the whole field of matrimonial prospects and select the one who promises the most. So you'd better be on your guard, Abe, unless you're prepared to lose your standing as a free man.

ABE

I thank you for the warning, Ninian.

NINIAN

Good day to you, Squire. See you later, Josh. (*He goes out.*)

ABE

There, Bowling—you see how things are with me. Hardly a day goes by but what I'm invited to meet some eager young female who has all the graces, including an ability to speak the language of diplomacy.

BOWLING

I'm sorry, Abe, that I shan't be able to hear you carrying on a flirtation in French. (ABE *looks at him, curiously.*)

ABE

I'm not pretending with you, Bowling —or you, Josh. I couldn't fool you any better than I can fool myself. I know what you're thinking about me, and I think so, too. Only I'm not so merciful in considering my own shortcomings, or so ready to forgive them, as you are. But—you talk about civil war—there seems to be one going on inside me all the time. Both sides are right and both are wrong and equal in strength. I'd like to be able to rise superior to the struggle—but—it says in the Bible that a house divided against itself cannot stand, so I reckon there's not much hope. One of these days, I'll just split asunder, and part company with myself—and it'll be a good riddance from both points of view. However—come on. (*He takes his hat.*) You've got to get back to Nancy, and Josh and I have got to make a good impression upon Miss Mary Todd, of Kentucky. (*He waves them to the door. As they go out, the light fades.*)

End of Scene IV

SCENE V

PARLOR *of the Edwards house in Springfield. An evening in November, some six months after the preceding scene.*

There is a fireplace at the right, a heavily curtained bay window at the left, a door at the back leading into the front hall.

At the right, by the fireplace, are a small couch and an easy chair. There is another couch at the left, and a table and chairs at the back. There are family portraits on the walls. It is all moderately elegant.

NINIAN *is standing before the fire, in conversation with* ELIZABETH, *his wife. She is high-bred, ladylike—excessively so. She is, at the moment, in a state of some agitation.*

ELIZABETH

I cannot believe it! It is an outrageous reflection on my sister's good sense.

NINIAN

I'm not so sure of that. Mary has known Abe for several months, and she has had plenty of chance to observe him closely.

ELIZABETH

She has been entertained by him, as we all have. But she has been far more attentive to Edwin Webb and Stephen Douglas and many others who are distinctly eligible.

NINIAN

Isn't it remotely possible that she sees more in Abe than you do?

ELIZABETH

Nonsense! Mr. Lincoln's chief virtue is that he hides no part of his simple soul from any one. He's a most amiable creature, to be sure; but as the husband of a high-bred, high-spirited young lady . . .

NINIAN

Quite so, Elizabeth. Mary *is* high-spirited! That is just why she set her cap for him.
(ELIZABETH *looks at him sharply, then laughs.*)

ELIZABETH

You're making fun of me, Ninian. You're deliberately provoking me into becoming excited about nothing.

NINIAN

No, Elizabeth—I am merely trying to prepare you for a rude shock. You think Abe Lincoln would be overjoyed to capture an elegant, cultivated girl, daughter of the President of the Bank of Kentucky, descendant of a long line of English gentlemen. Well, you are mistaken . . .
(MARY TODD *comes in. She is twenty-two—short, pretty, remarkably sharp. She*

stops short in the doorway, and her suspecting eyes dart from ELIZABETH *to* NINIAN.)

MARY

What were you two talking about?

NINIAN

I was telling your sister about the new song the boys are singing:
"What is the great commotion, motion,
  Our country through?
It is the ball a-rolling on
For Tippecanoe and Tyler, too—for Tippecanoe . . ."

MARY (*with a rather grim smile*)

I compliment you for thinking quickly, Ninian. But you were talking about *me!* (*She looks at* ELIZABETH, *who quails a little before her sister's determination.*) Weren't you?

ELIZABETH

Yes, Mary, we were.

MARY

And quite seriously, I gather.

NINIAN

I'm afraid that our dear Elizabeth has become unduly alarmed . . .

ELIZABETH (*snapping at him*)

Let me say what I have to say! (*She turns to* MARY.) Mary—you must tell me the truth. Are you—have you ever given one moment's serious thought to the possibility of marriage with Abraham Lincoln? (MARY *looks at each of them, her eyes flashing.*) I promise you, Mary, that to me such a notion is too far beyond the bounds of credibility to be . . .

MARY

But Ninian has raised the horrid subject, hasn't he? He has brought the evil scandal out into the open, and we must face it, fearlessly. Let us do so at once, by all means. I shall answer you, Elizabeth: I have given more than one moment's thought to the possibility you mentioned—and I have decided that I shall be Mrs. Lincoln. (*She seats herself on the couch.*) (NINIAN *is about to say, "I told you so," but thinks better of it.* ELIZABETH *can only gasp and gape.*) I have examined, carefully, the qualifications of all the young gentlemen, and some of the old ones, in this neighborhood. Those of Mr. Lincoln seem to me superior to all others, and he is my choice.

ELIZABETH

Do you expect me to congratulate you upon this amazing selection?

MARY

No! I ask for no congratulations, nor condolences, either.

ELIZABETH (*turning away*)

Then I shall offer none.

NINIAN

Forgive me for prying, Mary—but have you as yet communicated your decision to the gentleman himself?

MARY (*with a slight smile at* NINIAN)

Not yet. But he is coming to call this evening, and he will ask humbly for my hand in marriage; and, after I have displayed the proper amount of surprise and confusion, I shall murmur, timidly, "Yes!"

ELIZABETH (*pitiful*)

You make a brave jest of it, Mary. But as for me, I am deeply and painfully shocked. I don't know what to say to you. But I urge you, I beg you, as your elder sister, responsible to our father and our dead mother for your welfare . . .

MARY (*with a certain tenderness*)

I can assure you, Elizabeth—it is useless to beg or command. I have made up my mind.

NINIAN

I admire your courage, Mary, but I should like . . .

ELIZABETH

I think, Ninian, that this is a matter for discussion solely between my sister and myself!

MARY

No! I want to hear what Ninian has to say. (*To* NINIAN.) What is it?

NINIAN

I only wondered if I might ask you another question.

MARY (*calmly*)

You may.

NINIAN

Understand, my dear—I'm not quarreling with you. My affection for Abe is eternal—but—I'm curious to know—what is it about him that makes you choose him for a husband?

MARY (*betraying her first sign of uncertainty*)

I should like to give you a plain, simple answer, Ninian. But I cannot.

ELIZABETH (*jumping at this*)

Of course you cannot! You're rushing blindly into this. You have no conception of what it will mean to your future.

MARY

You're wrong about that, Elizabeth. This is not the result of wild, tempestuous infatuation. I have not been swept off my feet. Mr. Lincoln is a Westerner, but that is his only point of resemblance to Young Lochinvar. I simply feel that of all the men I've ever known, he is the one whose life and destiny I want most to share.

ELIZABETH

Haven't you sense enough to know you could never be happy with him? His breeding—his background—his manner—his whole point of view . . .?

MARY (*gravely*)

I could not be content with a "happy" marriage in the accepted sense of the word. I have no craving for comfort and security.

ELIZABETH

And have you a craving for the kind of life you would lead? A miserable cabin, without a servant, without a stitch of clothing that is fit for exhibition in decent society?

MARY (*raising her voice*)

I have not yet tried poverty, so I cannot say how I should take to it. But I might well prefer it to anything I have previously known—so long as there is forever before me the chance for high adventure—so long as I can know that I am always going forward, with my husband, along a road that leads across the horizon. (*This last is said with a sort of mad intensity.*)

ELIZABETH

And how far do you think you will go with any one like Abe Lincoln, who is lazy and shiftless and prefers to stop constantly along the way to tell jokes?

MARY (*rising; furious*)

He will *not* stop, if I am strong enough to make him go on! And I am strong! I know what *you* expect of me. You want me to do precisely as you have done—and marry a man like Ninian—and I know many, that are *just* like him! But with all due respect to my dear brother-in-law—I don't want that—and I won't have it! Never! You live in a house with a fence around it—presumably to prevent the common herd from gaining access to your sacred precincts—but really to prevent you, yourselves, from escaping from your own narrow lives. In Abraham Lincoln I see a man who has split rails for other men's fences, but who will never build one around himself!

ELIZABETH

What are you *saying,* Mary? You are talking with a degree of irresponsibility that is not far from sheer madness . . .

MARY (*scornfully*)

I imagine it does seem like insanity to you! You married a man who was settled and established in the world, with a comfortable inheritance, and no problems to face. And you've never made a move to change your condition, or improve it. You consider it couldn't be improved. To you, all this represents perfection. But it doesn't to me! I want the chance to *shape* a new life, for myself, and for my husband. Is that irresponsibility?

(*A* MAID *appears.*)

MAID

Mr. Lincoln, ma'am.

ELIZABETH

He's here.

MARY (*firmly*)

I shall see him!

MAID

Will you step in, Mr. Lincoln?
(ABE *comes in, wearing a new suit, his hair nearly neat.*)

ABE

Good evening, Mrs. Edwards. Good evening, Miss Todd. Ninian, good evening.

ELIZABETH

Good evening.

MARY

Good evening, Mr. Lincoln.
(*She sits on the couch at the left.*)

NINIAN

Glad to see you, Abe.
(ABE *sees that there is electricity in the atmosphere of this parlor. He tries hard to be affably casual.*)

ABE

I'm afraid I'm a little late in arriving, but I ran into an old friend of mine, wife of Jack Armstrong, the champion rowdy of New Salem. I believe you have some recollection of him, Ninian.

NINIAN (*smiling*)

I most certainly have. What's he been up to now?

ABE (*stands in front of the fireplace*)

Oh, he's all right, but Hannah, his wife, is in fearful trouble because her son Duff is up for murder and she wants me to defend him. I went over to the jail to interview the boy and he looks pretty tolerably guilty to me. But I used to give him lessons in the game of marbles while his mother foxed my pants for me. (*He turns to* ELIZABETH.) That means, she sewed buckskin around the legs of my pants so I wouldn't tear 'em to shreds going through underbrush when I was surveying. Well—in view of old times, I felt I had to take the case and do what I can to obstruct the orderly processes of justice.

NINIAN (*laughs, with some relief*)

And the boy will be acquitted. I tell you, Abe—this country would be law-abiding and peaceful if it weren't for you lawyers. But—if you will excuse Elizabeth and me, we must hear the children's prayers and see them safely abed.

ABE

Why—I'd be glad to hear their prayers, too.

NINIAN

Oh, no! You'd only keep them up till all hours with your stories. Come along, Elizabeth.
(ELIZABETH *doesn't want to go, but doesn't know what to do to prevent it.*)

ABE (*to* ELIZABETH)

Kiss them good night, for me.

NINIAN

We'd better not tell them you're in the house, or they'll be furious.

ELIZABETH (*making one last attempt*)

Mary! Won't you come with us and say good night to the children?

NINIAN

No, my dear. Leave Mary here—to keep Abe entertained. (*He guides* ELIZABETH *out, following her.*)

MARY (*with a little laugh*)

I don't blame Ninian for keeping you away from those children. They all adore you.

ABE

Well—I always seemed to get along well with children. Probably it's because they never want to take me seriously.

MARY

You understand them—that's the important thing . . . But—do sit down, Mr. Lincoln. (*She indicates that he is to sit next to her.*)

ABE

Thank you—I will. (*He starts to cross to the couch to sit beside* MARY. *She looks at him with melting eyes. The lights fade.*)

End of Scene V

SCENE VI

AGAIN *the Law Office. It is afternoon of New Year's Day, a few weeks after the preceding scene.*
ABE *is sitting, slumped in his chair, staring at his desk. He has his hat and overcoat on. A muffler is hanging about his neck, untied.*
JOSH SPEED *is half-sitting on the table at the right. He is reading a long letter, with most serious attention. At length he finishes it, refolds it very carefully, stares at the floor.*

ABE

Have you finished it, Josh?

JOSH

Yes.

ABE

Well—do you think it's all right?

JOSH

No, Abe—I don't. (ABE *turns slowly and looks at him.*) I think the sending of this

letter would be a most grave mistake—and that is putting it mildly and charitably.

ABE

Have I stated the case too crudely? (ABE *is evidently in a serious state of distress, although he is making a tremendous effort to disguise it by speaking in what he intends to be a coldly impersonal tone. He is struggling mightily to hold himself back from the brink of nervous collapse.*)

JOSH

No—I have no quarrel with your choice of words.. None whatever. If anything, the phraseology is too correct. But your method of doing it, Abe! It's brutal, it's heartless, it's so unworthy of you that I— I'm at a loss to understand how you ever thought you could do it this way.

ABE

I've done the same thing before with a woman to whom I seemed to have become attached. She approved of my action.

JOSH

This is a different woman. (*He walks over to the window, then turns again toward* ABE.) You cannot seem to accept the fact that women are human beings, too, as variable as we are. You act on the assumption that they're all the same one— and that one is a completely unearthly being of your own conception. This letter isn't written to Mary Todd—it's written to yourself. Every line of it is intended to provide salve for your own conscience.

ABE (*rising; coldly*)

Do I understand that you will not deliver it for me?

JOSH

No, Abe—I shall not.

ABE (*angrily*)

Then some one else will!

JOSH (*scornfully*)

Yes. You could give it to the minister, to hand to the bride when he arrives for the ceremony. But—I hope, Abe, you won't send it till you're feeling a little calmer in your mind. . . .

ABE (*vehemently, turning to* JOSH)

How can I ever be calm in my mind until this thing is settled, and out of the way, once and for all? Have you got eyes in your head, Josh? Can't you see that I'm desperate?

JOSH

I can see that plainly, Abe. I think your situation is more desperate even than you imagine, and I believe you should have the benefit of some really intelligent medical advice.

ABE (*seating himself at* BILLY's *table*)

The trouble with me isn't anything that a doctor can cure.

JOSH

There's a good man named Dr. Drake, who makes a specialty of treating people who get into a state of mind like yours, Abe . . .

ABE (*utterly miserable*)

So that's how you've figured it! I've done what I've threatened to do many times before: I've gone crazy. Well—you know me better than most men, Josh— and perhaps you're not far off right. I just feel that I've got to the end of my rope, and I must let go, and drop—and where I'll land, I don't know, and whether I'll survive the fall, I don't know that either. . . . But—this I *do* know: I've got to get out of this thing—I can't go through with it—I've got to have my release!

(JOSH *has turned to the window. Suddenly he turns back, toward* ABE.)

JOSH

Ninian Edwards is coming up. Why not show this letter to him and ask for his opinion. . . .

ABE (*interrupting, with desperation*)

No, no! Don't say a word of any of this to him! Put that letter in your pocket. I can't bear to discuss this business with him, now.

(JOSH *puts the letter in his pocket and crosses to the couch.*)

JOSH

Hello, Ninian.

NINIAN (*heartily, from off*)

Hello, Josh! Happy New Year! (NINIAN *comes in. He wears a handsome, fur-trimmed great-coat, and carries two silver-headed canes, one of them in a baize bag, which he lays down on the table at the right.*)

NINIAN

And Happy New Year, Abe—in fact, the happiest of your whole life!

ABE

Thank you, Ninian. And Happy New Year to you.

NINIAN (*opening his coat*)

That didn't sound much as if you meant it. (*He goes to the stove to warm his hands.*) However, you can be forgiven today, Abe. I suppose you're inclined to be just a wee bit nervous. (*He chuckles and winks at* JOSH.) God—but it's cold in here! Don't you ever light this stove?

ABE

The fire's all laid. Go ahead and light it, if you want.

NINIAN (*striking a match*)

You certainly are in one of your less amiable moods today. (*He lights the stove.*)

JOSH

Abe's been feeling a little under the weather.

NINIAN

So it seems. He looks to me as if he'd been to a funeral.

ABE

That's where I have been.

NINIAN (*disbelieving*)

What? A funeral on your wedding day?

JOSH

They buried Abe's oldest friend, Bowling Green, this morning.

NINIAN (*shocked*)

Oh—I'm mighty sorry to hear that, Abe. And—I hope you'll forgive me for—not having known about it.

ABE

Of course, Ninian.

NINIAN

But I'm glad you were there, Abe, at the funeral. It must have been a great comfort to his family.

ABE

I wasn't any comfort to any one. They asked me to deliver an oration, a eulogy of the deceased—and I tried—and I couldn't say a thing. Why do they expect you to strew a lot of flowery phrases over anything so horrible as a dead body? Do they think that Bowling Green's soul needs quotations to give it peace? All that mattered to me was that he was a good, just man—and I loved him—and he's dead.

NINIAN

Why didn't you say that, Abe?

ABE (*rising*)

I told you—they wanted an oration.

NINIAN

Well, Abe—I think Bowling Green himself would be the first to ask you to put your sadness aside in the prospect of your own happiness, and Mary's—and I'm only sorry that our old friend didn't live to see you two fine people married. (*He is making a gallant attempt to assume a more cheerily nuptial tone.*) I've made all the arrangements with the Reverend Dresser, and Elizabeth is preparing a bang-up dinner—so you can be sure the whole affair will be carried off handsomely *and* painlessly. (BILLY HERNDON *comes in. He carries a bottle in his coat pocket, and is already more than a little drunk and sullen, but abnormally articulate.*) Ah, Billy— Happy New Year!

BILLY

The same to you, Mr. Edwards. (*He puts the bottle down on the table and takes his coat off.*)

NINIAN

I brought you a wedding present. Abe. Thought you'd like to make a brave show when you first walk out with your bride. It came from the same place in Louisville where I bought mine.

(*He picks up one of the canes and hands it proudly to* ABE, *who takes it and inspects it gravely.*)

ABE

It's very fine, Ninian. And I thank you. (*He takes the cane over to his desk and seats himself.*)

NINIAN

Well—I'll frankly confess that in getting it for you, I was influenced somewhat by consideration for Mary and her desire for keeping up appearances. And in that connection—I know you'll forgive me, Josh, and you, too, Billy, if I say something of a somewhat personal nature?

BILLY (*truculent*)

If you want me to leave you, I shall be glad to. . . .

NINIAN

No, please, Billy—I merely want to speak a word or two as another of Abe's friends; it's my last chance before the ceremony. Of course, the fact that the bride is my sister-in-law gives me a little added responsibility in wishing to promote the success of this marriage. (*He crosses to* ABE.) And a success it will be, Abe . . . if only you will bear in mind one thing: you must keep a tight rein on her ambition. My wife tells me that even as a child, she had delusions of grandeur—she predicted to one and all that the man she would marry would be President of the United States. (*He turns to* JOSH.) You know how it is—every boy in the country plans some day to be president, and every little girl plans to marry him. (*Again to* ABE:) But Mary is one who hasn't entirely lost those youthful delusions. So I urge you to beware. Don't let her talk you into any gallant crusades or wild goose chases. Let her learn to be satisfied with the estate to which God hath brought her. With which, I shall conclude my pre-nuptial sermon. (*He buttons his coat.*) I shall see you all at the house at five o'clock, and I want you to make sure that Abe is looking his prettiest.

JOSH

Good-bye, Ninian.

(NINIAN *goes out.* ABE *turns again to the desk and stares at nothing.* BILLY *takes the bottle and a cup from his desk and pours himself a stiff drink. He raises the cup toward* ABE.)

BILLY (*huskily*)

Mr. Lincoln, I beg leave to drink to your health and happiness . . . and to that of the lady who will become your wife. (ABE *makes no response.* BILLY *drinks it down, then puts the cup back on the*

table.) You don't want to accept my toast because you think it wasn't sincere. And I'll admit I've made it plain that I've regretted the step you've taken. I thought that in this marriage, you were lowering yourself—you were trading your honor for some exalted family connections. . . . I wish to apologize for so thinking. . . .

ABE

No apologies required, Billy.

BILLY

I doubt that Miss Todd and I will ever get along well together. But I'm now convinced that our aims are the same—particularly since I've heard the warnings delivered by her brother-in-law. (*A note of scorn colors his allusion to* NINIAN.) If she really is ambitious for you—if she will never stop driving you, goading you—then I say, God bless her, and give her strength! (*He has said all this with* ABE's *back to him.* BILLY *pours himself another drink, nearly emptying the large bottle.* ABE *turns and looks at him.*)

ABE

Have you had all of that bottle today?

BILLY

This bottle? Yes—I have.

JOSH

And why not? It's New Year's Day!

BILLY (*looking at* JOSH)

Thank you, Mr. Speed. Thank you for the defense. And I hope you will permit me to propose one more toast. (*He takes a step toward* ABE.) To the President of the United States, and Mrs. Lincoln! (*He drinks.*)

ABE (*grimly*)

I think we can do without any more toasts, Billy.

BILLY

Very well! That's the last one—until after the wedding. And then, no doubt, the Edwards will serve us with the costliest champagne. And, in case you're apprehensive, I shall be on my best behavior in that distinguished gathering!

ABE

There is not going to be a wedding. (BILLY *stares at him, and then looks at* JOSH, *and then again at* ABE.) I have a letter that I want you to deliver to Miss Todd.

BILLY

What letter? What is it?

ABE

Give it to him, Josh. (JOSH *takes the letter out of his pocket, and puts it in the stove.* ABE *jumps up.*) You have no right to do that!

JOSH

I know I haven't! But it's done. (ABE *is staring at* JOSH.) And don't look at me as if you were planning to break my neck. Of course you could do it, Abe—but you won't. (JOSH *turns to* BILLY.) In that letter, Mr. Lincoln asked Miss Todd for his release. He told her that he had made a mistake in his previous protestations of affection for her, and so he couldn't go through with a marriage which could only lead to endless pain and misery for them both.

ABE (*deeply distressed*)

If that isn't the truth, what is?

JOSH

I'm not disputing the truth of it. I'm only asking you to tell her so, to her face, in the manner of a man.

ABE

It would be a more cruel way. It would hurt her more deeply. For I couldn't help blurting it *all* out—all the terrible things I didn't say in that letter. (*He is speaking with passion.*) I'd have to tell that I have hatred for her infernal ambition—that I don't want to be ridden and driven, upward and onward through life, with her whip lashing me, and her spurs digging into me! If her poor soul craves importance in life, then let her marry Stephen Douglas. He's ambitious, too. . . . I want only to be left alone! (*He sits down again and leans on the table.*)

JOSH (*bitterly*)

Very well, then—tell her all that! It will be more gracious to admit that you're afraid of her, instead of letting her down

flat with the statement that your ardor, such as it was, has cooled.

(BILLY *has been seething with a desire to get into this conversation. Now, with a momentary silence, he plunges.*)

BILLY

May I say something?

ABE

I doubt that you're in much of a condition to contribute. . . .

JOSH

What is it, Billy?

BILLY (*hotly*)

It's just this. Mr. Lincoln, you're not abandoning Miss Mary Todd. No! You're only using her as a living sacrifice, offering her up, in the hope that you will thus gain forgiveness of the gods for your failure to do your own great duty!

ABE (*smoldering*)

Yes! My own great duty. Every one feels called upon to remind me of it, but no one can tell me what it is.

BILLY (*almost tearful*)

I can tell you! I can tell you what is the duty of every man who calls himself an American! It is to perpetuate those truths which were once held to be self-evident: that all men are created equal—that they are endowed with certain inalienable rights—that among these are the right to life, liberty and the pursuit of happiness.

ABE (*angrily*)

And are those rights denied to *me?*

BILLY

Could you ever enjoy them while your mind is full of the awful knowledge that two million of your fellow beings in this country are slaves? Can you take any satisfaction from looking at that flag above your desk, when you know that ten of its stars represent states which are willing to destroy the Union—rather than yield their property rights in the flesh and blood of those slaves? And what of all the States of the future? All the territories of the West—clear out to the Pacific Ocean? Will they be the homes of free men? Are

you answering *that* question to your own
satisfaction? That is your flag, Mr. Lincoln, and you're proud of it. B.......
you doing to save ..
into shreds?

(ABE *jumps to h.*
and speaks with te,
with great passion.)

ABE

I'm minding my own business—that's
what I'm doing! And there'd be no threat
to the Union if others would do the same.
And as to slavery—I'm sick and tired of
this righteous talk about it. When you
know more about law, you'll know that
those property rights you mentioned are
guaranteed by the Constitution. And if the
Union can't stand on the Constitution,
then let it fall!

BILLY

The hell with the Constitution! This is
a matter of the rights of living men to
freedom—and those came before the Constitution! When the Law denies those
rights, then the Law is wrong, and it must
be changed, if not by moral protest, then
by force! There's no course of action that
isn't justified in the defense of freedom!
And don't dare to tell me that any one in
the world knows that better than you do,
Mr. Lincoln. You, who honor the memory of Elijah Lovejoy and every other man
who ever died for that very ideal!

ABE (*turning away from him*)

Yes—I honor them—and envy them—
because they could believe that their ideals
are *worth* dying for. (*He turns to* JOSH
and speaks with infinite weariness.) All
right, Josh—I'll go up now and talk to
Mary—and then I'm going away. . . .

JOSH

BILLY

You're quitting, Mr. Lincoln! As surely
as there's a God in Heaven, He knows
that you're running away from your obligations to Him, and to your fellow-men,
and your own immortal soul!

JOSH (*drawing* BILLY *away from the door*)

Billy—Billy—leave him alone. He's a
sick man.

BILLY (*sitting down at the table*)

What can we do for him, Mr. Speed?
What can we do?

(BILLY *is now actually in tears.*)

JOSH

I don't know, Billy. (*He goes to the window and looks out.*) He'll be in such a
state of emotional upheaval, he'll want to
go away by himself, for a long time. Just
as he did after the death of poor little
Ann Rutledge. He'll go out and wander
on the prairies, trying to grope his way
back into the wilderness from which he
came. There's nothing we can do for him,
Billy. He'll have to do it for himself.

BILLY (*fervently*)

May God be with him!

End of Scene VI

SCENE VII

ON THE PRAIRIE, *near New Salem. It is a clear, cool, moonlit evening, nearly two years
after the preceding scene.*

*In the foreground is a campfire. Around it are packing cases, blanket rolls and one
ancient trunk. In the background is a covered wagon, standing at an angle, so that the
opening at the back of it is visible to the audience.*

SETH GALE *is standing by the fire, holding his seven-year-old son,* JIMMY, *in his arms. The boy is wrapped up in a blanket.*

JIMMY

I don't want to be near the fire, Paw. I'm burning up. Won't you take the blanket offen me, Paw?

SETH

No, son. You're better off if you keep yourself covered.

JIMMY

I want some water, Paw. Can't I have some water?

SETH

Yes! Keep quiet, Jimmy! Gobey's getting the water for you now. (*He looks off to the right, and sees* JACK ARMSTRONG *coming.*) Hello, Jack, I was afraid you'd got lost.

JACK (*coming in*)

I couldn't get lost anywheres around New Salem. How's the boy?

SETH (*with a cautionary look at* JACK)

He—he's a little bit thirsty. Did you find Abe?

JACK

Yes—it took me some time because he'd wandered off—went out to the old cemetery across the river to visit Ann Rutledge's grave.

SETH

Is he coming here?

JACK

He said he'd better go get Doc Chandler who lives on the Winchester Road. He'll be along in a while. (*He comes up to* JIMMY.) How you feelin', Jimmy?

JIMMY

I'm burning . . .
(AGGIE *appears, sees* JACK.)

AGGIE

Oh—I'm glad you're back, Mr. Armstrong.

JACK

There'll be a doctor here soon, Mrs. Gale.

AGGIE

Thank God for that! Bring him into the wagon, Seth. I got a nice, soft bed all ready for him.

SETH

You hear that, Jimmy? Your ma's fixed a place where you can rest comfortable.
(AGGIE *retreats into the wagon.*)

JIMMY

When'll Gobey come back? I'm thirsty. When'll he bring the water?

SETH

Right away, son. You can trust Gobey to get your water. (*He hands* JIMMY *into the wagon.*)

JACK

He's worse, ain't he?

SETH (*in a despairing tone*)

Yes. The fever's been raging something fierce since you left. It'll sure be a relief when Abe gets here. He can always do something to put confidence in you.

JACK

How long since you've seen Abe, Seth?

SETH

Haven't laid eyes on him since I left here —eight—nine years ago. We've corresponded some.

JACK

Well—you may be surprised when you see him. He's changed plenty since he went to Springfield. He climbed up pretty high in the world, but he appears to have slipped down lately. He ain't much like his old comical self.

SETH

Well, I guess we all got to change. (*He starts up, hearing* GOBEY *return.*) Aggie! (GOBEY, *a Negro, comes in from the left, carrying a bucket of water.* AGGIE *appears from the wagon.*) Here's Gobey with the water.

GOBEY

Yes, Miss Aggie. Here you are. (*He hands it up.*)

AGGIE

Thanks, Gobey. (*She goes back into the wagon.*)

GOBEY

How's Jimmy now, Mr. Seth?

SETH

About the same.

GOBEY (*shaking his head*)

I'll get some more water for the cooking. (*He picks up a kettle and a pot and goes.*)

SETH (*to* JACK)

It was a bad thing to have happen, all right—the boy getting sick—when we were on an expedition like this. No doctor —no way of caring for him.

JACK

How long you been on the road, Seth?

SETH

More than three months. Had a terrible time in the Pennsylvania Mountains, fearful rains and every stream flooded. I can tell you, there was more than one occasion when I wanted to turn back and give up the whole idea. But—when you get started —you just can't turn . . . (*He is looking off right.*) Say! Is that Abe coming now?

JACK (*rising*)

Yep. That's him.

SETH (*delighted*)

My God, look at him! Store clothes and a plug hat! Hello—Abe!

ABE

Hello, Seth. (*He comes on and shakes hands, warmly.*) I'm awful glad to see you again, Seth.

SETH

And me, too, Abe.

ABE

It did my heart good when I heard you were on your way West. Where's your boy?

SETH

He's in there—in the wagon. . . . (AGGIE *has appeared from the wagon.*)

AGGIE

Is that the doctor?

SETH

No, Aggie—this is the man I was telling you about I wanted so much to see. This is Mr. Abe Lincoln—my wife, Mrs. Gale.

ABE

Pleased to meet you, Mrs. Gale.

AGGIE

Pleased to meet you, Mr. Lincoln.

ABE

Doc Chandler wasn't home. They said he was expected over at the Boger farm at midnight. I'll go there then and fetch him.

SETH

It'll be a friendly act, Abe.

AGGIE

We'll be in your debt, Mr. Lincoln.

ABE

In the meantime, Mrs. Gale, I'd like to do whatever I can. . . .

SETH

There's nothing to do, Abe. The boy's got the swamp fever, and we're just trying to keep him quiet.

AGGIE (*desperately*)

There's just one thing I would wish—is —is there any kind of a preacher around; this God-forsaken place?

SETH (*worried*)

Preacher?

ABE

Do you know of any, Jack?

JACK

No. There ain't a preacher within twenty miles of New Salem now.

AGGIE

Well—I only thought if there was, we might get him here to say a prayer for Jimmy.

(*She goes back into the wagon.* SETH *looks after her with great alarm.*)

SETH

She wants a preacher. That looks as if she'd given up, don't it?.

JACK

It'd probably just comfort her.

ABE

Is your boy very sick, Seth?

SETH

Yes—he is.

JACK

Why don't *you* speak a prayer, Abe? You could always think of somethin' to say?

ABE

I'm afraid I'm not much of a hand at praying. I couldn't think of a blessed thing that would be of any comfort.

SETH

Never mind. It's just a—a religious idea of Aggie's. Sit down, Abe.

ABE (*looking at the wagon*)

So you've got your dream at last, Seth. You're doing what you and I used to talk about—you're moving.

SETH

Yes, Abe. We got crowded out of Maryland. The city grew up right over our farm. So—we're headed for a place where there's more room. I wrote you—about four months back—to tell you we were starting out, and I'd like to meet up with you here. I thought it was just possible you might consider joining in this trip.

ABE

It took a long time for your letter to catch up with me, Seth. I've just been drifting—down around Indiana and Kentucky where I used to live. (*He sits down on a box.*) Do you aim to settle in Nebraska?

SETH

No, we're not going to stop there. We're going right across the continent—all the way to Oregon.

ABE (*deeply impressed*)

Oregon?

JACK

Sure. That's where they're all headin' for now.

SETH

We're making first for a place called Westport Landing—that's in Kansas right on the frontier—where they outfit the wagon trains for the far West. You join up there with a lot of others who are like-minded, so you've got company when you're crossing the plains and the mountains.

ABE

It's staggering—to think of the distance you're going. And you'll be taking the frontier along with you.

SETH

It may seem like a fool-hardy thing to do—but we heard too many tales of the black earth out there, and the balance of rainfall and sunshine.

JACK

Why don't you go with them, Abe? That country out west is gettin' settled fast. Why—last week alone, I counted more than two hundred wagons went past here—people from all over—Pennsylvania, Connecticut, Vermont—all full of jubilation at the notion of gettin' land. By God, I'm goin' too, soon as I can get me a wagon. They'll need men like me to fight the Indians for 'em—and they'll need men with brains, like you, Abe, to tell 'em how to keep the peace.

ABE (*looking off*)

It's a temptation to go, I can't deny that.

JACK

Then what's stoppin' you from doin' it? You said yourself you've just been driftin'.

ABE

Maybe that's it—maybe I've been drifting too long. . . . (*He changes the subject.*) Is it just the three of you, Seth?

SETH

That's all. The three of us and Gobey, the nigger.

ABE

Is he your slave?

SETH

Gobey? Hell, no! He's a free man! My father freed his father twenty years ago. But we've had to be mighty careful about Gobey. You see, where we come from, folks are pretty uncertain how they feel about the slave question, and lots of good free niggers get snaked over the line into Virginia and then sold down river before you know it. And when you try to go to court and assert their legal rights, you're beaten at every turn by the damned, dirty shyster lawyers. That's why we've been keeping well up in free territory on this trip.

ABE

Do you think it will be free in Oregon?

SETH

Of course it will! It's got to——

ABE (*bitterly*)

Oh no, it hasn't, Seth. Not with the politicians in Washington selling out the whole West piece by piece to the slave traders.

SETH (*vehemently*)

That territory has got to be free! If this country ain't strong enough to protect its citizens from slavery, then we'll cut loose from it and join with Canada. Or, better yet, we'll make a *new* country out there in the far west.

ABE (*gravely*)

A new country?

SETH

Why not?

ABE

I was just thinking—old Mentor Graham once said to me that some day the United States might be divided up into many hostile countries, like Europe.

SETH

Well—let it be! Understand—I love this country and I'd fight for it. And I guess George Washington and the rest of them loved England and fought for it when they were young—but they didn't hesitate to cut loose when the government failed to play fair and square with 'em . . .

JACK

By God, if Andy Jackson was back in the White House, he'd run out them traitors with a horse-whip!

ABE

It'd be a bad day for us Americans, Seth, if we lost you, and your wife, and your son.

SETH (*breaking*)

My son!—Oh—I've been talking big— but it's empty talk. If he dies—there won't be enough spirit left in us to push on any further. What's the use of working for a future when you know there won't be anybody growing up to enjoy it. Excuse me, Abe—but I'm feeling pretty scared.

ABE (*suddenly rises*)

You mustn't be scared, Seth. I know I'm a poor one to be telling you that—because I've been scared all my life. But—seeing you now—and thinking of the big thing you've set out to do—well, it's made me feel pretty small. It's made me feel that I've got to do something, too, to keep you and your kind in the United States of America. You mustn't quit, Seth! Don't let anything beat you—don't you ever give up!

(AGGIE *comes out of the wagon. She is very frightened.*)

AGGIE

Seth!

SETH

What is it, Aggie?

AGGIE

He's worse, Seth! He's moaning in his sleep, and he's grasping for breath. . . .
(*She is crying.* SETH *takes her in his arms.*)

SETH

Never mind, honey. Never mind. When the doctor gets here, he'll fix him up in no time. It's all right, honey. He'll get well.

ABE

If you wish me to, Mrs. Gale—I'll try to speak a prayer.
(*They look at him.*)

JACK

That's the way to talk, Abe!

SETH

We'd be grateful for anything you might say, Abe.
(ABE *takes his hat off. As he starts speaking,* GOBEY *comes in from the left and stops reverently to listen.*)

ABE

Oh God, the father of all living, I ask you to look with gentle mercy upon this little boy who is here, lying sick in this covered wagon. His people are traveling far, to seek a new home in the wilderness, to do your work, God, to make this earth a good place for your children to live in. They can see clearly where they're going, and they're not afraid to face all the perils that lie along the way. I humbly beg you not to take their child from them. Grant him the freedom of life. Do not condemn him to the imprisonment of death. Do not deny him his birthright. Let him know the sight of great plains and high mountains, of green valleys and wide rivers. For this little boy is an American, and these things belong to him, and he to them. Spare him, that he too may strive for the ideal for which his fathers have labored, so faithfully and for so long. Spare him and give him his fathers' strength—give us all strength, O God, to do the work that is before us. I ask you this favor, in the name of *your* son, Jesus Christ, who died upon the Cross to set men free. Amen.

GOBEY (*with fervor*)

Amen!

SETH AND AGGIE (*murmuring*)

Amen!
(ABE *puts his hat on.*)

ABE

It's getting near midnight. I'll go over to the Boger farm and get the doctor. (*He goes out.*)

SETH

Thank you, Abe.

AGGIE

Thank you—thank you, Mr. Lincoln.

GOBEY

God bless you, Mr. Lincoln!
(*The lights fade quickly.*)

End of Scene VII

SCENE VIII

AGAIN *the parlor of the Edwards house. A few days after preceding scene.*
MARY *is seated, reading a book.*
After a moment, the MAID *enters.*

MAID

Miss Mary—Mr. Lincoln is here.

MARY

Mr. Lincoln! (*She sits still a moment in an effort to control her emotions, then sharply closes the book and rises.*)

MAID

Will you see him, Miss Mary?

MARY

Yes—in one moment. (*The* MAID *goes off.* MARY *turns, drops her book on the sofa, then moves over toward the right, strug-*

gling desperately to compose herself. At the fireplace, she stops and turns to face ABE as he enters.) I'm glad to see you again, Mr. Lincoln.

(There is considerable constraint between them. He is grimly determined to come to the point with the fewest possible words; she is making a gallant, wellbred attempt to observe the social amenities.)

ABE

Thank you, Mary. You may well wonder why I have thrust myself on your mercy in this manner.

MARY (quickly)

I'm sure you're always welcome in Ninian's house.

ABE

After my behavior at our last meeting here, I have not been welcome company for myself.

MARY

You've been through a severe illness. Joshua Speed has kept us informed of it. We've been greatly concerned.

ABE

It is most kind of you.

MARY

But you're restored to health now—you'll return to your work, and no doubt you'll be running for the assembly again —or perhaps you have larger plans?

ABE

I have no plans, Mary. (He seems to brace himself.) But I wish to tell you that I am sorry for the things that I said on that unhappy occasion which was to have been our wedding day.

MARY

You need not say anything about that, Mr. Lincoln. Whatever happened then, it was my own fault.

ABE (disturbed by this unforeseen avowal)

Your fault! It was my miserable cowardice——

MARY

I was blinded by my own self-confidence! I—I loved you. (For a moment her firm voice falters, but she immediately masters that tendency toward weakness.) And I believed I could make you love me. I believed we might achieve a real communion of spirit, and the fire of my determination would burn in you. You would become a man and a leader of men! But you didn't wish that. (She turns away.) I knew you had strength—but I did not know you would use it, all of it, to resist your own magnificent destiny.

ABE (deliberately)

It is true, Mary—you once had faith in me which I was far from deserving. But the time has come, at last, when I wish to strive to deserve it. (MARY looks at him, sharply.) When I behaved in that shameful manner toward you, I did so because I thought that our ways were separate and could never be otherwise. I've come to the conclusion that I was wrong. I believe that our destinies are together, for better or for worse, and I again presume to ask you to be my wife. I fully realize, Mary, that taking me back now would involve humiliation for you.

MARY (flaring)

I am not afraid of humiliation, if I know it will be wiped out by ultimate triumph! But there can be no triumph unless you yourself are sure. What was it that brought you to this change of heart and mind?

ABE

On the prairie, I met an old friend of mine who was moving West, with his wife and child, in a covered wagon. He asked me to go with him, and I was strongly tempted to do so. (There is great sadness in his tone—but he seems to collect himself, and turns to her again, speaking with a sort of resignation.) But then I knew that was not my direction. The way I must go is the way you have always wanted me to go.

MARY

And you will promise that never again will you falter, or turn to run away?

ABE

I promise, Mary—if you will have me—
I shall devote myself for the rest of my
days to trying—to do what is right—as
God gives me power to see what is right.

(*She looks at him, trying to search him.
She would like to torment him, for a while,
with artful indecision. But she cannot do
it.*)

MARY

Very well then—I shall be your wife. I
shall fight by your side—till death do us

part. (*She runs to him and clutches him.*)
Abe! I love you—oh, I love you! Whatever becomes of the two of us, I'll die loving you! (*She is sobbing wildly on his
shoulder. Awkwardly, he lifts his hands
and takes hold of her in a loose embrace.
He is staring down at the carpet, over her
shoulder.*)

Curtain

End of Act II

ACT THREE

SCENE IX

A SPEAKERS' PLATFORM *in an Illinois town. It is a summer evening in the year 1858.
A light shines down on the speaker at the front of the platform.
At the back of the platform are three chairs. At the right sits* JUDGE STEPHEN A. DOUG-
LAS—*at the left,* ABE, *who has his plug hat on and makes occasional notes on a piece of
paper on his knee. The chair in the middle is for* NINIAN, *acting as Moderator, who is
now at the front of the platform.*

NINIAN

We have now heard the leading arguments from the two candidates for the high
office of United States Senator from Illinois—Judge Stephen A. Douglas and Mr.
Abraham Lincoln. A series of debates between these two eminent citizens of Illinois
has focused upon our state the attention
of the entire nation, for here are being discussed the vital issues which now affect
the lives of all Americans and the whole
future history of our beloved country. According to the usual custom of debate, each
of the candidates will now speak in rebut-
tal. . . . Judge Douglas.

(NINIAN *retires and sits, as* DOUGLAS
*comes forward. He is a brief but magnetic
man, confident of his powers.*)

DOUGLAS

My fellow citizens: My good friend, Mr.
Lincoln, has addressed you with his usual
artless sincerity, his pure, homely charm,
his perennial native humor. He has even
devoted a generously large portion of his
address to most amiable remarks upon my

fine qualities as a man, if not as a statesman. For which I express deepest gratitude. But—at the same time—I most earnestly beg you not to be deceived by his
seeming innocence, his carefully cultivated
spirit of good will. For in each of his little
homilies lurk concealed weapons. Like
Brutus, in Shakespeare's immortal tragedy,
Mr. Lincoln is an honorable man. But,
also like Brutus, he is an adept at the art
of inserting daggers between an opponent's ribs, just when said opponent least
expects it. Behold me, gentlemen—I am
covered with scars. And yet—somehow or
other—I am still upright. Perhaps because
I am supported by that sturdy prop called
"Truth." Truth—which, crushed to earth
by the assassin's blades, doth rise again!
Mr. Lincoln makes you laugh with his
pungent anecdotes. Then he draws tears
from your eyes with his dramatic pictures
of the plight of the black slave labor in
the South. Always, he guides you skilfully
to the threshold of truth, but then, as you
are about to cross it, diverts your attention
elsewhere. For one thing—he never, by

any mischance, makes reference to the condition of labor here in the North! Oh, no! Perhaps New England is so far beyond the bounds of his parochial ken that he does not know that tens of thousands of working men and women in the textile industry are now on STRIKE! And why are they on strike? Because from early morning to dark of night—fourteen hours a day—those "free" citizens must toil at shattering looms in soulless factories and never see the sun; and then, when their fearful day's work at last comes to its exhausted end, these ill-clad and undernourished laborers must trudge home to their foul abodes in tenements that are not fit habitations for rats! What kind of Liberty is this? And if Mr. Lincoln has not heard of conditions in Massachusetts—how has it escaped his attention that here in our own great state no wheels are now turning on that mighty railroad, the Illinois Central? Because its oppressed workers are also on STRIKE! Because they too demand a living wage! So it is throughout the North. Hungry men, marching through the streets in ragged order, promoting riots, because they are not paid enough to keep the flesh upon the bones of their babies! What kind of Liberty is this? And what kind of equality? Mr. Lincoln harps constantly on this subject of equality. He repeats over and over the argument used by Lovejoy and other abolitionists: to wit, that the Declaration of Independence having declared all men free and equal, by divine law, thus Negro equality is an inalienable right. Contrary to this absurd assumption stands the verdict of the Supreme Court, as it was clearly stated by Chief Justice Taney in the case of Dred Scott. The Negroes are established by this decision as an inferior race of beings, subjugated by the dominant race, enslaved and, therefore, property— like all other property! But Mr. Lincoln is inclined to dispute the constitutional authority of the Supreme Court. He has implied, if he did not say so outright, that the Dred Scott decision was a prejudiced one, which must be over-ruled by the voice of the people. Mr. Lincoln is a lawyer, and I presume, therefore, that he knows that when he seeks to destroy public confidence in the integrity, the inviolability of the Supreme Court, he is preaching *revolution!* He is attempting to stir up odium and rebellion in this country against the constituted authorities; he is stimulating the passions of men to resort to violence and to mobs, instead of to the law. He is setting brother against brother! There can be but one consequence of such inflammatory persuasion—and that is *Civil War!* He asks me to state my opinion of the Dred Scott decision, and I answer him unequivocally by saying, "I take the decisions of the Supreme Court as the law of the land, and I intend to obey them as such!" Nor will I be swayed from that position by all the rantings of all the fanatics who preach "racial equality," who ask us to vote, and eat, and sleep, and marry with Negroes! And I say further—Let each State mind its own business and leave its neighbors alone. If we will stand by that principle, then Mr. Lincoln will find that this great republic can exist forever divided into free and slave states. We can go on as we have done, increasing in wealth, in population, in power, until we shall be the admiration and the terror of the world! (*He glares at the audience, then turns, mopping his brow, and resumes his seat.*)

NINIAN (*rising*)
Mr. Lincoln.
(ABE *glances at his notes, takes his hat off, puts the notes in it, then rises slowly and comes forward. He speaks quietly, reasonably. His words come from an emotion so profound that it needs no advertisement.*)

ABE
Judge Douglas has paid tribute to my skill with the dagger. I thank him for that, but I must also admit that he can do more with that weapon than I can. He can keep ten daggers flashing in the air at one time. Fortunately, he's so good at it that none of the knives ever falls and hurts anybody. The Judge can condone slavery in the South and protest hotly against its extension to the North. He can crowd loyalty to the Union and defense of states' sovereignty into the same breath. Which reminds me—and I hope the Judge will

allow me one more homely little anecdote, because I'd like to tell about a woman down in Kentucky. She came out of her cabin one day and found her husband grappling with a ferocious bear. It was a fight to the death, and the bear was winning. The struggling husband called to his wife, "For heaven's sake, *help* me!" The wife asked what could *she* do? Said the husband, "You could at least *say* something encouraging." But the wife didn't want to seem to be taking sides in this combat, so she just hollered, "Go it husband—go it bear!" Now, you heard the Judge make allusion to those who advocate voting and eating and marrying and sleeping with Negroes. Whether he meant me specifically, I do not know. If he did, I can say that just because I do not want a colored woman for a slave, I don't necessarily want her for a wife. I need not have her for either. I can just leave her alone. In some respects, she certainly is not my equal, any more than I am the Judge's equal, in some respects; but in her natural right to eat the bread she earns with her own hands without asking leave of some one else, she is my equal, and the equal of all others. And as to sleeping with Negroes—the Judge may be interested to know that the slave states have produced more than four hundred thousand mulattoes—and I don't think many of them are the children of abolitionists. That word "abolitionists" brings to mind New England, which also has been mentioned. I assure Judge Douglas that I have been there, and I have seen those cheerless brick prisons called factories, and the workers trudging silently home through the darkness. In those factories, cotton that was picked by black slaves is woven into cloth by white people who are separated from slavery by no more than fifty cents a day. As an American, I cannot be proud that such conditions exist. But— as an American—I can ask: would any of those striking workers in the North elect to change places with the slaves in the South? Will they not rather say, "The remedy is in *our* hands!" And, still as an American, I can say—thank God we live under a system by which men have the *right* to strike! I am not preaching rebel-

lion. I don't have to. This country, with its institutions, belongs to the people who inhabit it. Whenever they shall grow weary of the existing government, they can exercise their constitutional right of amending it, or their revolutionary right to dismember or overthrow it. If the founding fathers gave us anything, they gave us that. And I am not preaching disrespect for the Supreme Court. I am only saying that the decisions of mortal men are often influenced by unjudicial bias— and the Supreme Court is composed of mortal men, most of whom, it so happens, come from the privileged class in the South. There is an old saying that judges are just as honest as other men, and not more so; and in case some of you are wondering who said that, it was Thomas Jefferson. (*He has half turned to* DOUGLAS.) The purpose of the Dred Scott decision is to make property, and nothing but property, of the Negro in all states of the Union. It is the old issue of property rights versus human rights—an issue that will continue in this country when these poor tongues of Judge Douglas and myself shall long have been silent. It is the eternal struggle between two principles. The one is the common right of humanity and the other the divine right of kings. It is the same spirit that says, "You toil and work and earn bread, and I'll eat it." Whether those words come from the mouth of a king who bestrides his people and lives by the fruit of their labor, or from one race of men who seek to enslave another race, it is the same tyrannical principle. As a nation, we began by declaring, "All men are created equal." There was no mention of any exceptions to the rule in the Declaration of Independence. But we now practically read it, "All men are created equal except Negroes." If we accept this doctrine of race or class discrimination, what is to stop us from decreeing in the future that "All men are created equal except Negroes, foreigners, Catholics, Jews, or—just poor people?" That is the conclusion toward which the advocates of slavery are driving us. Many good citizens, North and South, agree with the Judge that we should accept that conclusion— don't stir up trouble—"Let each State mind its own business." That's the safer course, for the time being. But—I advise you to watch out! When you have enslaved any of your fellow beings, dehumanized him, denied him all claim to the dignity of manhood, placed him among the beasts, among the damned, are you quite sure that the demon you have thus created, will not turn and rend *you?* When you begin qualifying freedom, watch out for the consequences to *you!* And I am not preaching civil war. All I am trying to do—now, and as long as I live—is to state and restate the fundamental virtues of our democracy, which have made us great, and which can make us greater. I believe most seriously that the perpetuation of those virtues is now endangered, not only by the honest proponents of slavery, but even more by those who echo Judge Douglas in shouting, "Leave it alone!" This is the complacent policy of indifference to evil, and that policy I cannot but hate. I hate it because of the monstrous injustice of slavery itself. I hate it because it deprives our republic of its just influence in the world; enables the enemies of free institutions everywhere to taunt us as hypocrites; causes the real friends of freedom to doubt our sincerity; and especially because it forces so many good men among ourselves into an open war with the very fundamentals of civil liberty, denying the good faith of the Declaration of Independence, and insisting that there is no right principle of action but *self-interest.* . . . In his final words tonight, the Judge said that we may be "the terror of the world." I don't think we want to be that. I think we would prefer to be the encouragement of the world, the proof that man is at last worthy to be free. But—we shall provide no such encouragement, unless we can establish our ability as a nation to live and grow. And we shall surely do neither if these states fail to remain *united.* There can be no distinction in the definitions of liberty as between one section and another, one race and another, one class and another. "A house divided against itself cannot stand." This government can not endure permanently, half slave and half free!

(*He turns and goes back to his seat.*)
(*The lights fade.*)

End of Scene IX

SCENE X

PARLOR *of the Edwards home, now being used by the Lincolns. Afternoon of a day in the early Spring of 1860.*

ABE *is sitting on the couch at the right, with his seven-year-old son,* TAD, *on his lap. Sitting beside them is another son,* WILLIE, *aged nine. The eldest son,* ROBERT, *a young Harvard student of seventeen, is sitting by the window, importantly smoking a pipe and listening to the story* ABE *has been telling the children.* JOSHUA SPEED *is sitting at the left.*

ABE

You must remember, Tad, the roads weren't much good then—mostly nothing more than trails—and it was hard to find my way in the darkness. . . .

WILLIE

Were you scared?

ABE

Yes—I was scared.

WILLIE

Of Indians?

ABE

No—there weren't any of them left around here. I was afraid I'd get lost, and the boy would die, and it would be all my fault. But, finally, I found the doctor. He was very tired, and wanted to go to bed, and he grumbled a lot, but I made him come along with me then and there.

WILLIE

Was the boy dead?

ABE

No, Willie. He wasn't dead. But he was pretty sick. The doctor gave him a lot of medicine.

TAD

Did it taste bad, Pa?

ABE

I presume it did. But it worked. I never saw those nice people again, but I've heard from them every so often. That little boy was your age, Tad, but now he's a grown man with a son almost as big as you are. He lives on a great big farm, in a valley with a river that runs right down from the tops of the snow mountains. . . .
(MARY *comes in.*)

MARY

Robert! You are smoking in my parlor!

ROBERT (*wearily*)

Yes, Mother. (*He rises.*)

MARY

I have told you that I shall not tolerate tobacco smoke in my parlor or, indeed, in any part of my house, and I mean to . . .

ABE

Come, come, Mary—you must be respectful to a Harvard man. Take it out to the woodshed, Bob.

ROBERT

Yes, Father.

MARY

And this will not happen again!

ROBERT

No, Mother. (*He goes out.*)

ABE

I was telling the boys a story about some pioneers I knew once.

MARY

It's time for you children to make ready for your supper.
(*The* CHILDREN *promptly get up to go.*)

WILLIE

But what happened after that, Pa?

ABE

Nothing. Everybody lived happily ever after. Now run along.
(WILLIE *and* TAD *run out.*)

JOSH

What time *is* it, Mary?

MARY

It's nearly half past four. (*She is shaking the smoke out of the curtains.*)

JOSH

Half past four, Abe. Those men will be here any minute.

ABE (*rising*)

Good Lord!

MARY (*turning sharply to* ABE)

What men?

ABE

Some men from the East. One of them's a political leader named Crimmin—and there's a Mr. Sturveson—he's a manufacturer—and . . .

MARY (*impressed*)

Henry D. Sturveson?

ABE

That's the one—and also the Reverend Dr. Barrick from Boston.

MARY (*sharply*)

What are they coming here for?

ABE

I don't precisely know—but I suspect that it's to see if I'm fit to be a candidate for President of the United States. (MARY *is, for the moment, speechless.*) I suppose they want to find out if we still live in a log cabin and keep pigs under the bed.

MARY (*in a fury*)

And you didn't *tell* me!

ABE

I'm sorry, Mary—the matter just slipped my . . .

MARY

You forgot to tell me that we're having the most important guests who ever crossed the threshold of my house!

ABE

They're not guests. They're only here on business.

MARY (*bitterly*)

Yes! Rather important business, it seems to me. They want to see us as we *are*—crude, sloppy, vulgar Western barbarians, living in a house that reeks of foul tobacco smoke.

ABE

We can explain about having a son at Harvard.

MARY

If I'd only *known!* If you had only given me a little time to prepare for them. Why didn't you put on your best suit? And those filthy old boots!

ABE

Well, Mary, I clean forgot. . . .

MARY

I declare, Abraham Lincoln, I believe you would have treated me with much more consideration if I had been your slave, instead of your wife! You have never, for one moment, stopped to think that perhaps I have some interests, some concerns, in the life we lead together. . . .

ABE

I'll try to clean up my boots a little, Mary.
(*He goes out, glad to escape from this painful scene.* MARY *looks after him. Her lip is quivering. She wants to avoid tears.*)

MARY (*seating herself; bitterly*)

You've seen it all, Joshua Speed. Every bit of it—courtship, if you could call it that, change of heart, change back again, and marriage, eighteen years of it. And you probably think just as all the others do—that I'm a bitter, nagging woman, and I've tried to kill his spirit, and drag him down to my level. . . .
(*JOSH rises and goes over to her.*)

JOSH (*quietly*)

No, Mary. I think no such thing. Remember, I know Abe, too.

MARY

There never could have been another man such as he is! I've read about many that have gone up in the world, and all of them seemed to have to fight to assert themselves every inch of the way, against the opposition of their enemies and the lack of understanding in their own friends. But he's never had any of that. He's never had an enemy, and every one of his friends has always been completely confident in him. Even before I met him, I was told that he had a glorious future, and after I'd known him a day, I was sure of it myself. But he didn't believe it—or, if he did, secretly, he was so afraid of the prospect that he did all in his power to avoid it. He had some poem in his mind, about a life of woe, along a rugged path, that leads to some future doom, and it has been an obsession with him. All these years, I've tried and tried to stir him out of it, but all my efforts have been like so many puny waves, dashing against the Rock of Ages. And now, opportunity, the greatest opportunity, is coming here, to him, right into his own house. And what can I do about it? He *must* take it! He *must* see that this is what he was meant for! But I can't persuade him of it! I'm tired—I'm tired to death! (*The tears now come.*) I thought I could help to shape him, as I knew he should be, and I've succeeded in nothing—but in breaking myself. . . . (*She sobs bitterly.*)
(*JOSH sits down beside her and pats her hand.*)

JOSH (*tenderly*)

I know, Mary. But—there's no reason in heaven and earth for/you to reproach yourself. Whatever becomes of Abe Lincoln is in the hands of a God who controls the destinies of all of us, including lunatics, and saints.
(*ABE comes back.*)

ABE (*looking down at his boots*)

I think they look all right now, Mary.
(*He looks at* MARY, *who is now trying hard to control her emotion.*)

MARY

You can receive the gentlemen in here. I'll try to prepare some refreshment for them in the dining-room.

(*She goes out.* ABE *looks after her, miserably. There are a few moments of silence. At length,* ABE *speaks, in an off-hand manner.*)

ABE

I presume these men *are* pretty influential.

JOSH

They'll have quite a say in the delegations of three states that may swing the nomination away from Seward.

ABE

Suppose, by some miracle, or fluke, they did nominate me; do you think I'd stand a chance of winning the election?

JOSH

An excellent chance, in my opinion. There'll be four candidates in the field, bumping each other, and opening up the track for a dark horse.

ABE

But the dark horse might run in the wrong direction.

JOSH

Yes—you can always do that, Abe. I know *I* wouldn't care to bet two cents on you.

ABE (*grinning*)

It seems funny to be comparing it to a horserace, with an old, spavined hack like me. But I've had some mighty energetic jockeys—Mentor Graham, Bowling Green, Bill Herndon, you, and Mary—most of all, Mary.

JOSH (*looking at* ABE)

They don't count now, Abe. You threw 'em all, long ago. When you finally found yourself running against poor little Douglas, you got the bit between your teeth and went like greased lightning. You'd do the same thing to him again, if you could only decide to get started, which you probably won't . . . (*The doorbell jangles.* JOSH *gets up.*)

ABE

I expect that's them now.

JOSH

I'll go see if I can help Mary. (*He starts for the door but turns and looks at* ABE, *and speaks quietly.*) I'd just like to remind you, Abe—there are pretty nearly thirty million people in this country; most of 'em are common people, like you. They're in serious trouble, and they need somebody who understands 'em, as you do. So—when these gentlemen come in—try to be a *little* bit polite to them. (ABE *grins.* JOSH *looks off.*) However—you won't listen to any advice from me.

(JOSH *goes. The door is opened by a* MAID *and* STURVESON, BARRICK, *and* CRIMMIN *come in.* STURVESON *is elderly, wealthy and bland.* BARRICK *is a soft Episcopalian dignitary.* CRIMMIN *is a shrewd, humorous fixer.*)

ABE

Come right in, gentlemen. Glad to see you again, Mr. Crimmin.
(*They shake hands.*)

CRIMMIN

How de do, Mr. Lincoln. This is Dr. Barrick of Boston, and Mr. Sturveson, of Philadelphia.

DR. BARRICK

Mr. Lincoln.

STURVESON

I'm honored, Mr. Lincoln.

LINCOLN

Thank you, sir. Pray sit down, gentlemen.

STURVESON

Thank you.
(*They sit.*)

CRIMMIN

Will Mrs. Lincoln seriously object if I light a seegar?

LINCOLN

Go right ahead! I regret that Mrs. Lincoln is not here to receive you, but she will join us presently. (*He sits down.*)

BARRICK (*with great benignity*)

I am particularly anxious to meet Mrs. Lincoln, for I believe, with Mr. Longfellow, that 'as unto the bow the cord is, so unto the man is woman.'

STURVESON (*very graciously*)

And we are here dealing with a bow that is stout indeed. (ABE *bows slightly in acknowledgment of the compliment.*) And one with a reputation for shooting straight. So you'll forgive us, Mr. Lincoln, for coming directly to the point.

ABE

Yes, sir. I understand that you wish to inspect the prairie politician in his native lair, and here I am.

STURVESON

It is no secret that we are desperately in need of a candidate—one who is sound, conservative, safe—and clever enough to skate over the thin ice of the forthcoming campaign. Your friends—and there's an increasingly large number of them throughout the country—believe that you are the man.

ABE

Well, Mr. Sturveson, I can tell you that when first I was considered for political office—that was in New Salem, twenty-five years ago—I assured my sponsors of my conservatism. I have subsequently proved it, by never progressing anywhere.

BARRICK (*smiling*)

Then you agree that you are the man we want?

ABE

I'm afraid I can't go quite that far in self-esteem, Dr. Barrick, especially when you have available a statesman and gentleman as eminent as Mr. Seward who, I believe, is both ready and willing.

STURVESON

That's as may be. But please understand that this is not an inquisition. We merely wish to know you better, to gain a clearer idea of your theories on economics, religion and national affairs, in general. To begin with—in one of your memorable debates with Senator Douglas, your opponent indulged in some of his usual demagoguery about industrial conditions in the North, and you replied shrewdly that whereas the slaves in the South . . .

ABE

Yes, I remember the occasion. I replied that I was thankful that laborers in free states have the right to strike. But that wasn't shrewdness, Mr. Sturveson. It was just the truth.

STURVESON

It has gained for you substantial support from the laboring classes, which is all to the good. But it has also caused a certain amount of alarm among business men, like myself.

ABE

I cannot enlarge on the subject. It seems obvious to me that this nation was founded on the supposition that men have the right to protest, violently if need be, against authority that is unjust or oppressive. (*He turns to* BARRICK.) The Boston Tea Party was a kind of strike. So was the Revolution itself. (*Again to* STURVESON.) So was Nicholas Biddle's attempt to organize the banks against the Jackson administration.

STURVESON

Which is all perfectly true—but—the days of anarchy are over. We face an unprecedented era of industrial expansion—mass production of every conceivable kind of goods—railroads and telegraph lines across the continent—all promoted and developed by private enterprise. In this great work, we must have a free hand, and a firm one, Mr. Lincoln. To put it bluntly, would you, if elected, place the interests of labor above those of capital?

ABE

I cannot answer that, bluntly, or any other way; because I cannot tell what I should do, if elected.

STURVESON

But you must have inclinations toward one side or the other. . . .

ABE

I think you know, Mr. Sturveson, that I am opposed to slavery.

BARRICK

And we of New England applaud your sentiments! We deplore the inhumanity of our Southern friends in . . .

ABE (*to* BARRICK)

There are more forms of slavery than that which is inflicted upon the Negroes in the South. I am opposed to all of them. (*He turns again to* STURVESON.) I believe in our democratic system—the just and generous system which opens the way to all—gives hope to all, and consequent energy and progress and improvement of condition to all, including employer and employee alike.

BARRICK

We support your purpose, Mr. Lincoln, in steadfastly proclaiming the rights of men to resist unjust authority. But I am most anxious to know whether you admit One Authority to whom devotion is unquestioned?

ABE

I presume you refer to the Almighty?

BARRICK

I do.

ABE

I think there has never been any doubt of my submission to His will.

BARRICK

I'm afraid there is a great deal of doubt as to your devotion to His church.

ABE

I realize that, Doctor. They say I'm an atheist, because I've always refused to become a church member.

BARRICK

What have been the grounds of your refusal?

ABE

I have found no churches suitable for my own form of worship. I could not give assent without mental reservations to the long, complicated statements of Christian doctrine which characterize their Articles of Belief and Confessions of Faith. But I can promise you, Dr. Barrick—I shall gladly join any church at any time if its sole qualification for membership is obedience to the Saviour's statement of Law and Gospel: 'Thou shalt love the Lord thy God with all thy heart and with all thy soul and with all thy mind, and thou shalt love thy neighbor as thyself.' . . . But— I beg you gentlemen to excuse me for a moment. I believe Mrs. Lincoln is preparing a slight collation, and I must see if I can help with it. . . .

CRIMMIN

Certainly, Mr. Lincoln. (ABE *goes, closing the door behind him.* CRIMMIN *looks at the door, then turns to the others.*) Well?

BARRICK

The man is unquestionably an infidel. An idealist—in his curious, primitive way —but an infidel!

STURVESON

And a radical!

CRIMMIN

A radical? Forgive me, gentlemen, if I enjoy a quiet laugh at that.

STURVESON

Go ahead and enjoy yourself, Crimmin —but I did not like the way he evaded my direct question. I tell you, he's as unscrupulous a demagogue as Douglas. He's a rabble rouser!

CRIMMIN

Of course he is! As a dealer in humbug, he puts Barnum himself to shame.

STURVESON

Quite possibly—but he is not *safe!*

CRIMMIN

Not safe, eh? And what do you mean by that?

STURVESON

Just what I say. A man who devotes himself so whole-heartedly to currying favor with the mob develops the mob mentality. He becomes a preacher of discontent, of mass unrest. . . .

CRIMMIN

And what about Seward? If we put him up, he'll start right in demanding liberation of the slaves—and then there *will* be discontent and unrest! I ask you to believe me when I tell you that this Lincoln *is* safe—in economics and theology and everything else. After all—what is the essential qualification that we demand of the candidate of our party? It is simply this: that he be able to get himself elected! And there is the man who can do that. (*He points off-stage.*)

STURVESON (*smiling*)

I should like to believe you!

BARRICK

So say we all of us!

CRIMMIN

Then just keep faith in the eternal stupidity of the voters, which is what *he* will appeal to. In that uncouth rail splitter you may observe one of the smoothest, slickest politicians that ever hoodwinked a yokel mob! You complain that he evaded your questions. Of course he did, and did it perfectly! Ask him about the labor problem, and he replies, "I believe in democracy." Ask his views on religion, and he says, "Love thy neighbor as thyself." Now—you know you couldn't argue with that, either of you. I tell you, gentlemen, he's a vote-getter if I ever saw one. His very name is right—Abraham Lincoln! Honest Old Abe! He'll play the game

with us now, and he'll go right on playing it when we get him into the White House. He'll do just what we tell him. . . .

DR. BARRICK (*cautioning him*)

Careful, Mr. Crimmin. . . .
(ABE *returns.*)

ABE

If you gentlemen will step into the dining-room, Mrs. Lincoln would be pleased to serve you with a cup of tea.

BARRICK

Thank you.

STURVESON

This is most gracious.
(*He and* BARRICK *move off toward the door.*)

ABE

Or perhaps something stronger for those who prefer it.
(STURVESON *and* BARRICK *go.* CRIMMIN *is looking for a place to throw his cigar.*)

ABE (*heartily*)

Bring your seegar with you, Mr. Crimmin!

CRIMMIN

Thank you—thank you!
(*He smiles at* ABE, *gives him a slap on the arm, and goes out,* ABE *following. The lights fade.*)

End of Scene X

SCENE XI

LINCOLN *campaign headquarters in the Illinois State House. The evening of Election Day, November 6th, 1860.*

It is a large room with a tall window opening out on to a wide balcony. There are doors upper right and upper left. At the left is a table littered with newspapers and clippings. There are many chairs about, and a liberal supply of spittoons.

At the back is a huge chart of the thirty-three states, with their electoral votes, and a space opposite each side for the posting of bulletins. A short ladder gives access to Alabama and Arkansas at the top of the list.

On the wall at the left is an American flag. At the right is a map of the United States, on which each state is marked with a red, white or blue flag.

ABE *is sitting at the table, with his back to the audience, reading newspaper clippings. He wears his hat and has spectacles on.* MRS. LINCOLN *is sitting at the right of the table, her eyes darting nervously from* ABE, *to the chart, to the map. She wears her bonnet, tippet and muff.*

ROBERT LINCOLN *is standing near her, studying the map.* NINIAN EDWARDS *is sitting at the left of the table and* JOSH SPEED *is standing near the chart. They are both smoking cigars and watching the chart.*

The door at the left is open, and through it the clatter of telegraph instruments can be heard. The window is partly open, and we can hear band music from the square below, and frequent cheers from the assembled mob, who are watching the election returns flashed from a magic lantern on the State House balcony.

Every now and then, a telegraph operator named JED *comes in from the left and tacks a new bulletin up on the chart. Another man named* PHIL *is out on the balcony taking bulletins from* JED.

ROBERT

What do those little flags mean, stuck into the map?

JOSH

Red means the state is sure for us. White means doubtful. Blue means hopeless.

(ABE *tosses the clipping he has been reading on the table and picks up another.*)

(JED *comes in and goes up to pin bulletins opposite Illinois, Maryland and New York.*)

NINIAN (*rising to look*)

Lincoln and Douglas neck and neck in Illinois.

(JOSH *and* ROBERT *crowd around the chart.*)

JOSH

Maryland is going all for Breckenridge and Bell. Abe—you're nowhere in Maryland.

MARY (*with intense anxiety*)

What of New York?

JED (*crossing to the window*)

Say, Phil—when you're not getting bulletins, keep that window closed. We can't hear ourselves think.

PHIL

All right. Only have to open 'er up again. (*He closes the window.*)

MARY

What does it say about New York?

(JED *goes.*)

NINIAN

Douglas a hundred and seventeen thousand—Lincoln a hundred and six thousand.

MARY (*desperately, to* ABE)

He's winning from you in New York, Abe!

JOSH

Not yet, Mary. These returns so far are mostly from the city where Douglas is bound to run the strongest.

ABE (*interested in a clipping*)

I see the New York *Herald* says I've got the soul of a Uriah Heep encased in the body of a baboon. (*He puts the clipping aside and starts to read another.*)

NINIAN (*who has resumed his seat*)

You'd better change that flag on Rhode Island from red to white, Bob. It looks doubtful to me.

(ROBERT, *glad of something to do, changes the flag as directed.*)

MARY

What does it look like in Pennsylvania, Ninian?

NINIAN

There's nothing to worry about there, Mary. It's safe for Abe. In fact, you needn't worry at all.

MARY (*very tense*)

Yes. You've been saying that over and over again all evening. There's no need to worry. But how can we help worrying when every new bulletin shows Douglas ahead.

JOSH

But every one of them shows Abe gaining.

NINIAN (*mollifying*)

Just give them time to count all the votes in New York and then you'll be on your way to the White House.

MARY

Oh, why don't they hurry with it? Why don't those returns come in?

ABE (*preoccupied*)

They'll come in—soon enough.

(BILLY HERNDON *comes in from the right. He has been doing a lot of drinking but has hold of himself.*)

BILLY

That mob down there is sickening! They cheer every bulletin that's flashed on the wall, whether the news is good or bad. And they cheer every picture of every candidate, including George Washington, with the same, fine, ignorant enthusiasm.

JOSH

That's logical. They can't tell 'em apart.

BILLY (*to* ABE)

There are a whole lot of reporters down there. They want to know what will be your first official action after you're elected.

NINIAN

What do you want us to tell 'em, Abe?

ABE (*still reading*)

Tell 'em I'm thinking of growing a beard.

JOSH

A beard?

NINIAN (*amused*)

Whatever put that idea into your mind?

ABE (*picking up another clipping*)

I had a letter the other day from some little girl. She said I ought to have whiskers, to give me more dignity. And I'll need it—if elected.

(JED *arrives with new bulletins.* BILLY, NINIAN, JOSH *and* ROBERT *huddle around* JED, *watching him post the bulletins.*)

MARY

What do they say now?

(*Jed goes to the window and gives some bulletins to* PHIL.)

MARY

Is there anything new from New York?

NINIAN

Connecticut—Abe far in the lead. That's eleven safe electoral votes anyway. Missouri—Douglas thirty-five thousand—Bell thirty-three—Breckenridge sixteen—Lincoln, eight. . . .

(*Cheers from the crowd outside until* PHIL *closes the window.* JED *returns to the office at the left.*)

MARY

What are they cheering for?

BILLY

They don't know!

ABE (*with another clipping*)

The Chicago *Times* says, "Lincoln breaks down! Lincoln's heart fails him! His tongue fails him! His legs fail him! He fails all over! The people refuse to support him! They laugh at him! Douglas is champion of the people! Douglas skins the living dog!"

(*He tosses the clipping aside.* MARY *stands up.*)

MARY (*her voice is trembling*)

I can't stand it any longer!'

ABE

Yes, my dear—I think you'd better go home. I'll be back before long.

MARY (*hysterical*)

I won't go home! You only want to be rid of me. That's what you've wanted ever since the day we were married—and before that. Anything to get me out of your sight, because you hate me! (*Turning to* JOSH, NINIAN *and* BILLY.) And it's the same with all of you—all of his friends —you hate me—you wish I'd never come into his life.

JOSH

No, Mary.

(ABE *has stood up, quickly, at the first storm signal. He himself is in a fearful state of nervous tension—in no mood to treat* MARY *with patient indulgence. He looks sharply at* NINIAN *and at the others.*)

ABE

Will you please step out for a moment?

NINIAN

Certainly, Abe.

(*He and the others go into the telegraph office.* JOSH *gestures to* ROBERT *to go with them.* ROBERT *casts a black look at his mother and goes. . . .* ABE *turns on* MARY *with strange savagery.*)

ABE

Damn you! Damn you for taking every opportunity you can to make a public fool of me—and yourself! It's bad enough, God knows, when you act like that in the privacy of our own home. But here—in front of people! You're not to do that again. Do you hear me? You're never to do that again!

(MARY *is so aghast at this outburst that her hysterical temper vanishes, giving way to blank terror.*)

MARY (*in a faint, strained voice*)

Abe! You cursed at me. Do you realize what you did? You cursed at me.

(ABE *has the impulse to curse at her again, but with considerable effort, he controls it.*)

ABE (*in a strained voice*)

I lost my temper, Mary. And I'm sorry for it. But I still think you should go home rather than endure the strain of this—this Death Watch.

(*She stares at him, uncomprehendingly, then turns and goes to the door.*)

MARY (*at the door*)

This is the night I dreamed about, when I was a child, when I was an excited young girl, and all the gay young gentlemen of Springfield were courting me, and I fell in love with the least likely of them. This is the night when I'm waiting to hear that my husband has become President of the United States. And even if he does—it's ruined, for me. It's too late. . . .

(*She opens the door and goes out.* ABE *looks after her, anguished, then turns quickly, crosses to the door at the left and opens it.*)

ABE (*calling off*)

Bob! (ROBERT *comes in.*) Go with your Mother.

ROBERT

Do I have to?

ABE

Yes! Hurry! Keep right with her till I get home.

(ROBERT *has gone.* ABE *turns to the window.* PHIL *opens it.*)

PHIL

Do you think you're going to make it, Mr. Lincoln?

ABE

Oh—there's nothing to worry about.

CROWD OUTSIDE (*singing*)

Old Abe Lincoln came out of the wilderness
  Out of the wilderness
  Out of the wilderness
Old Abe Lincoln came out of the wilderness
  Down in Illinois!

(NINIAN, JOSH, BILLY, *and* JED *come in, the latter to post new bulletins. After* JED *has communicated these,* PHIL *again closes the window.* JED *goes.*)

NINIAN

It looks like seventy-four electoral votes sure for you. Twenty-seven more probable. New York's will give you the election.

(ABE *walks around the room.* JOSH *has been looking at* ABE.)

JOSH

Abe, could I get you a cup of coffee?

ABE

No, thanks, Josh.

NINIAN

Getting nervous, Abe?

ABE

No. I'm just thinking what a blow it would be to Mrs. Lincoln if I should lose.

NINIAN

And what about me? I have ten thousand dollars bet on you.

BILLY (*scornfully*)

I'm afraid that the loss to the nation would be somewhat more serious than that.

JOSH

How would you feel, Abe?

ABE (*sitting on the chair near the window*)

I guess I'd feel the greatest sense of relief of my life.

(JED *comes in with a news despatch.*)

JED

Here's a news despatch. (*He hands it over and goes.*)

NINIAN (*reads*)

"Shortly after nine o'clock this evening, Mr. August Belmont stated that Stephen A. Douglas has piled up a majority of fifty thousand votes in New York City and carried the state."

BILLY

Mr. Belmont be damned!

(CRIMMIN *comes in, smoking a cigar, looking contented.*)

CRIMMIN

Good evening, Mr. Lincoln. Good evening, gentlemen—and how are you all feeling *now*?

(*They all greet him.*)

NINIAN

Look at this, Crimmin. (*He hands the despatch to* CRIMMIN.)

CRIMMIN (*smiles*)

Well—Belmont is going to fight to the last ditch, which is just what he's lying in now. I've been in Chicago and the outlook there is cloudless. In fact, Mr. Lincoln, I came down tonight to protect you from the office-seekers. They're lining up downstairs already. On the way in I counted four Ministers to Great Britain and eleven Secretaries of State.

(JED *has come in with more bulletins to put on the chart and then goes to the window to give* PHIL *the bulletins.*)

BILLY (*at the chart*)

There's a bulletin from New York! Douglas a hundred and eighty-three thousand—Lincoln a hundred and eighty-*one* thousand!

(JED *goes.*)

JOSH

Look out, Abe. You're catching up!

CRIMMIN

The next bulletin from New York will show you winning. Mark my words, Mr. Lincoln, this election is all wrapped up tightly in a neat bundle, ready for delivery on your doorstep tonight. We've fought the good fight, and we've won!

ABE (*pacing up and down the room*)

Yes—we've fought the good fight—in the dirtiest campaign in the history of corrupt politics. And if I have won, then I must cheerfully pay my political debts. All those who helped to nominate and elect me must be paid off. I have been gambled all around, bought and sold a hundred times. And now I must fill all the dishonest pledges made in my name.

NINIAN

We realize all that, Abe—but the fact remains that you're winning. Why, you're even beating the coalition in Rhode Island!

ABE

I've got to step out for a moment. (*He goes out at the right.*)

NINIAN (*cheerfully*)

Poor Abe.

CRIMMIN

You gentlemen have all been close friends of our Candidate for a long time so perhaps you could answer a question that's been puzzling me considerably. Can I possibly be correct in supposing that he doesn't want to win?

JOSH

The answer is—yes.

CRIMMIN (*looking toward the right*)

Well—I can only say that, for me, this is all a refreshingly new experience.

BILLY (*belligerently*)

Would *you* want to become President of the United States at this time? Haven't you been reading the newspapers lately?

CRIMMIN

Why, yes—I try to follow the events of the day.

BILLY (*in a rage*)

Don't you realize that they've raised ten thousand volunteers in South Carolina? They're arming them! The Governor has issued a proclamation saying that if Mr. Lincoln is elected, the State will secede to-morrow, and every other state south of the Dixon line will go with it. Can you see what that means? War! Civil War! And *he'll* have the whole terrible responsibility for it—a man who has never wanted anything in his life but to be let alone, in peace!

NINIAN

Calm down, Billy. Go get yourself another drink.

(JED *rushes in.*)

JED

Mr. Edwards, here it is! (*He hands a news despatch to* NINIAN, *then rushes to the window to attract* PHIL's *attention and communicate the big news.*)

NINIAN (*reads*)

"At 10:30 tonight the New York *Herald* conceded that Mr. Lincoln has carried the state by a majority of at least twenty-five thousand and has won the election!" (*He tosses the despatch in the air.*) He's won! He's won! Hurrah!

(*All on the stage shout, cheer, embrace and slap each other.*)

BILLY

God be praised! God be praised!

CRIMMIN

I knew it! I never had a doubt of it! (JED *is on the balcony, shouting through a megaphone.*)

JED

Lincoln is elected! Honest Old Abe is our next President!

(*A terrific cheer ascends from the crowd below.* ABE *returns. They rush at him.* BILLY *shakes hands with him, too deeply moved to speak.*)

NINIAN

You've carried New York, Abe! You've won! Congratulations!

CRIMMIN

My congratulations, Mr. President. This is a mighty achievement for all of us! (JED *comes in and goes to* ABE.)

JED

My very best, Mr. Lincoln!

ABE (*solemnly*)

Thank you—thank you all very much. (*He comes to the left.* JOSH *is the last to shake his hand.*)

JOSH

I congratulate you, Abe.

ABE

Thanks, Josh.

NINIAN

Listen to them, Abe. Listen to that crazy, howling mob down there.

CRIMMIN

It's all for you, Mr. Lincoln.

NINIAN

Abe, get out there and let 'em see you!

ABE

No. I don't want to go out there. I—I guess I'll be going on home, to tell Mary. (*He starts toward the door.*)

(*A short, stocky officer named* KAVANAGH *comes in from the right. He is followed by two soldiers.*)

CRIMMIN

This is Captain Kavanagh, Mr. President.

KAVANAGH (*salutes*)

I've been detailed to accompany you, Mr. Lincoln, in the event of your election.

ABE

I'm grateful, Captain. But I don't need you.

KAVANAGH

I'm afraid you've got to have us, Mr. Lincoln. I don't like to be alarming, but I guess you know as well as I do what threats have been made.

ABE (*wearily*)

I see . . . Well—Good night, Josh—

Ninian—Mr. Crimmin—Billy. Thank you for your good wishes.

(*He starts for the door. The others bid him good night, quietly.*)

KAVANAGH

One moment, sir. With your permission, I'll go first.

(*He goes out,* ABE *after him, the two other soldiers follow. The light fades.*)

End of Scene XI

SCENE XII

THE YARDS *of the railroad station at Springfield. The date is February 11, 1861.*

At the right, at an angle toward the audience, is the back of a railroad car. From behind this, off to the upper left, runs a ramp. Flags and bunting are draped above.

In a row downstage are soldiers, with rifles and bayonets fixed, and packs on their backs, standing at ease. Off to the left is a large crowd, whose excited murmuring can be heard.

KAVANAGH *is in the foreground. A* BRAKEMAN *with a lantern is inspecting the wheels of the car, at the left. A* WORKMAN *is at the right, polishing the rails of the car.* KAVANAGH *is pacing up and down, chewing a dead cigar. He looks at his watch. A swaggering* MAJOR *of militia comes down the ramp from the left.*

MAJOR

I want you men to form up against this ramp. (*To* KAVANAGH; *with a trace of scorn.*) You seem nervous, Mr. Kavanagh.

KAVANAGH

Well—I am nervous. For three months I've been guarding the life of a man who doesn't give a damn what happens to him. I heard today that they're betting two to one in Richmond that he won't be alive to take the oath of office on March the 4th.

MAJOR

I'd like to take some of that money. The State Militia is competent to protect the person of our Commander-in-Chief.

KAVANAGH

I hope the United States Army is competent to help. But those Southerners are mighty good shots. And I strongly suggest that your men be commanded to keep watch through every window of every

car, especially whenever the train stops— at a town, or a tank, or anywhere. And if any alarm is sounded, at any point along the line . . .

MAJOR (*a trifle haughty*)

There's no need to command my men to show courage in an emergency.

KAVANAGH

No slur was intended, Major—but we must be prepared in advance for everything.

(*A brass band off to the left strikes up the campaign song, "Old Abe Lincoln came out of the wilderness." The crowd starts to sing it, more and more voices taking it up. A* CONDUCTOR *comes out of the car and looks at his watch. There is a commotion at the left as* NINIAN *and* ELIZABETH EDWARDS, *and* JOSH, BILLY *and* CRIMMIN *come in and are stopped by the soldiers. The* MAJOR *goes forward, bristling with importance.*)

MAJOR

Stand back, there! Keep the crowd back there, you men!

NINIAN

I'm Mr. Lincoln's brother-in-law.

MAJOR

What's your name?

KAVANAGH

I know him, Major. That's Mr. and Mrs. Edwards, and Mr. Speed and Mr. Herndon with them. I know them all. You can let them through.

MAJOR

Very well. You can pass.

(*They come down to the right. The* MAJOR *goes off at the left.*)

CRIMMIN

How is the President feeling today? Happy?

NINIAN

Just as gloomy as ever.

BILLY (*emotionally*)

He came down to the office, and when I asked him what I should do about the sign, "Lincoln and Herndon," he said, "Let it hang there. Let our clients understand that this election makes no difference to the firm. If I live, I'll be back some time, and then we'll go right on practising just as if nothing had happened."

ELIZABETH

He's always saying that—"If I live" . . .
(*A tremendous cheer starts and swells off-stage at the left. The* MAJOR *comes on, briskly.*)

MAJOR (*to* KAVANAGH)

The President has arrived! (*To his men*) Attention! (*The* MAJOR *strides down the platform and takes his position by the car, looking off to the left.*)

KAVANAGH (*to* NINIAN *and the others*)

Would you mind stepping back there? We want to keep this space clear for the President's party.

(*They move upstage, at the right. The cheering is now very loud.*)

MAJOR

Present—Arms!
(*The soldiers come to the Present. The* MAJOR *salutes. Preceded by soldiers who are looking sharply to the right and left,* ABE *comes in from the left, along the platform. He will be fifty-two years old tomorrow. He wears a beard. Over his shoulders is his plaid shawl. In his right hand he carries his carpet-bag; his left hand is leading* TAD. *Behind him are* MARY, ROBERT *and* WILLIE, *and the* MAID. *All, except* MARY, *are also carrying bags. She carries a bunch of flowers. When they come to the car,* ABE *hands his bag up to the* CONDUCTOR, *then lifts* TAD *up.* MARY, ROBERT, WILLIE *and the* MAID *get on board, while* ABE *steps over to talk to* NINIAN *and the others. During this, there is considerable commotion at the left, as the crowd tries to surge forward.*)

MAJOR (*rushing forward*)

Keep 'em back! Keep 'em back, men!
(*The* SOLDIERS *have broken their file on the platform and are in line, facing the crowd.* KAVANAGH *and his men are close to* ABE. *Each of them has his hand on his revolver, and is keeping a sharp lookout.*)

KAVANAGH

Better get on board, Mr. President.
(ABE *climbs up on to the car's back platform. There is a great increase in the cheering when the crowd sees him. They shout: "Speech! Speech! Give us a speech, Abe! Speech, Mr. President! Hurray for Old Abe!" Etc. . . .* ABE *turns to the crowd, takes his hat off and waves it with a half-hearted gesture. The cheering dies down.*)

NINIAN

They want you to say something, Abe.
(*For a moment,* ABE *stands still, looking off to the left.*)

ABE

My dear friends—I have to say good-bye to you. I am going now to Washington, with my new whiskers—of which I hope you approve.

(The crowd roars with laughter at that. More shouts of "Good Old Abe!" In its exuberant enthusiasm, the crowd again surges forward, at and around the SOLDIERS, *who shout, "Get back, there! Stand back, you!")*

ABE *(to the* MAJOR*)*

It's all right—let them come on. They're all old friends of mine.

(The MAJOR *allows his men to retreat so that they form a ring about the back of the car.* KAVANAGH *and his men are on the car's steps, watching. The crowd—an assortment of townspeople, including some Negroes—fills the stage.)*

ABE

No one, not in my situation, can appreciate my feelings of sadness at this parting. To this place, and the kindness of you people, I owe everything. I have lived here a quarter of a century, and passed from a young to an old man. Here my children have been born and one is buried. I now leave, not knowing when or whether ever I may return. I am called upon to assume the Presidency at a time when eleven of our sovereign states have announced their intention to secede from the Union, when threats of war increase in fierceness from day to day. It is a grave duty which I now face. In preparing for it, I have tried to enquire: what great principle or ideal is it that has kept this Union so long together? And I believe that it was not the mere matter of separation of the colonies from the motherland, but that sentiment in the Declaration of Independence which gave liberty to the people of this country and hope to all the world. This sentiment was the fulfillment of an ancient dream, which men have held through all time, that they might one day shake off their chains and find freedom in the brotherhood of life. We gained democracy, and now there is the question whether it is fit to survive. Perhaps we have come to the dreadful day of awakening, and the dream is ended. If so, I am afraid it must be ended forever. I cannot believe that ever again will men have the opportunity we have had. Perhaps we should admit that, and concede that our ideals of liberty and equality are decadent and doomed. I have heard of an eastern monarch who once charged his wise men to invent him a sentence which would be true and appropriate in all times and situations. They presented him the words, "And this too shall pass away." That is a comforting thought in time of affliction—"And this too shall pass away." And yet— *(Suddenly he speaks with quiet but urgent authority.)*—let us believe that it is not true! Let us live to prove that we can cultivate the natural world that is about us, and the intellectual and moral world that is within us, so that we may secure an individual, social and political prosperity, whose course shall be forward, and which, while the earth endures, shall not pass away. . . . I commend you to the care of the Almighty, as I hope that in your prayers you will remember me. . . . Good-bye, my friends and neighbors.

(He leans over the railing of the car platform to say good-bye to NINIAN, ELIZABETH, JOSH, BILLY *and* CRIMMIN, *shaking each by the hand. The band off-stage strikes up "John Brown's Body." The cheering swells. The* CONDUCTOR *looks at his watch and speaks to the* MAJOR, *who gets on board the train. The crowd on stage is shouting "Good-bye, Abe," "Good-bye, Mr. Lincoln," "Good luck, Abe," "We trust you, Mr. Lincoln.")*

(As the band swings into the refrain, "Glory, Glory Hallelujah," the crowd starts to sing, the number of voices increasing with each word.)

*(*KAVANAGH *tries to speak to* ABE *but can't be heard. He touches* ABE'S *arm, and* ABE *turns on him, quickly.)*

KAVANAGH

Time to pull out, Mr. President. Better get inside the car.

(These words cannot be heard by the audience in the general uproar of singing. NINIAN, ELIZABETH, JOSH *and* BILLY *are up on the station platform. The* SOLDIERS *are starting to climb up on to the train.* ABE *gives one last wistful wave of his hat to the crowd, then turns and goes into the car, followed by* KAVANAGH, *the* MAJOR *and the* SOLDIERS. *The band reaches the last line of the song.)*

ALL *(singing)*

His soul goes marching on.

(The BRAKEMAN, *downstage, is waving his lantern. The* CONDUCTOR *swings aboard. The crowd is cheering, waving hats and handkerchiefs. The shrill screech of the engine whistle sounds from the right.)*

Curtain